FROM BEOWULF TO THOMAS HARDY

TEXTS SELECTED AND EDITED
BY

ROBERT SHAFER, PH.D.

PROFESSOR OF LITERATURE AND FELLOW
OF THE GRADUATE SCHOOL,
UNIVERSITY OF CINCINNATI

REVISED EDITION

VOLUME I

GARDEN CITY NEW YORK
DOUBLEDAY, DORAN & COMPANY, INC.

PRINTED IN THE UNITED STATES
AT
THE COUNTRY LIFE PRESS, GARDEN CITY, N. Y.

THIRD PRINTING OF REVISED EDITION

Mollie Burling '36.
Gibbons 28.

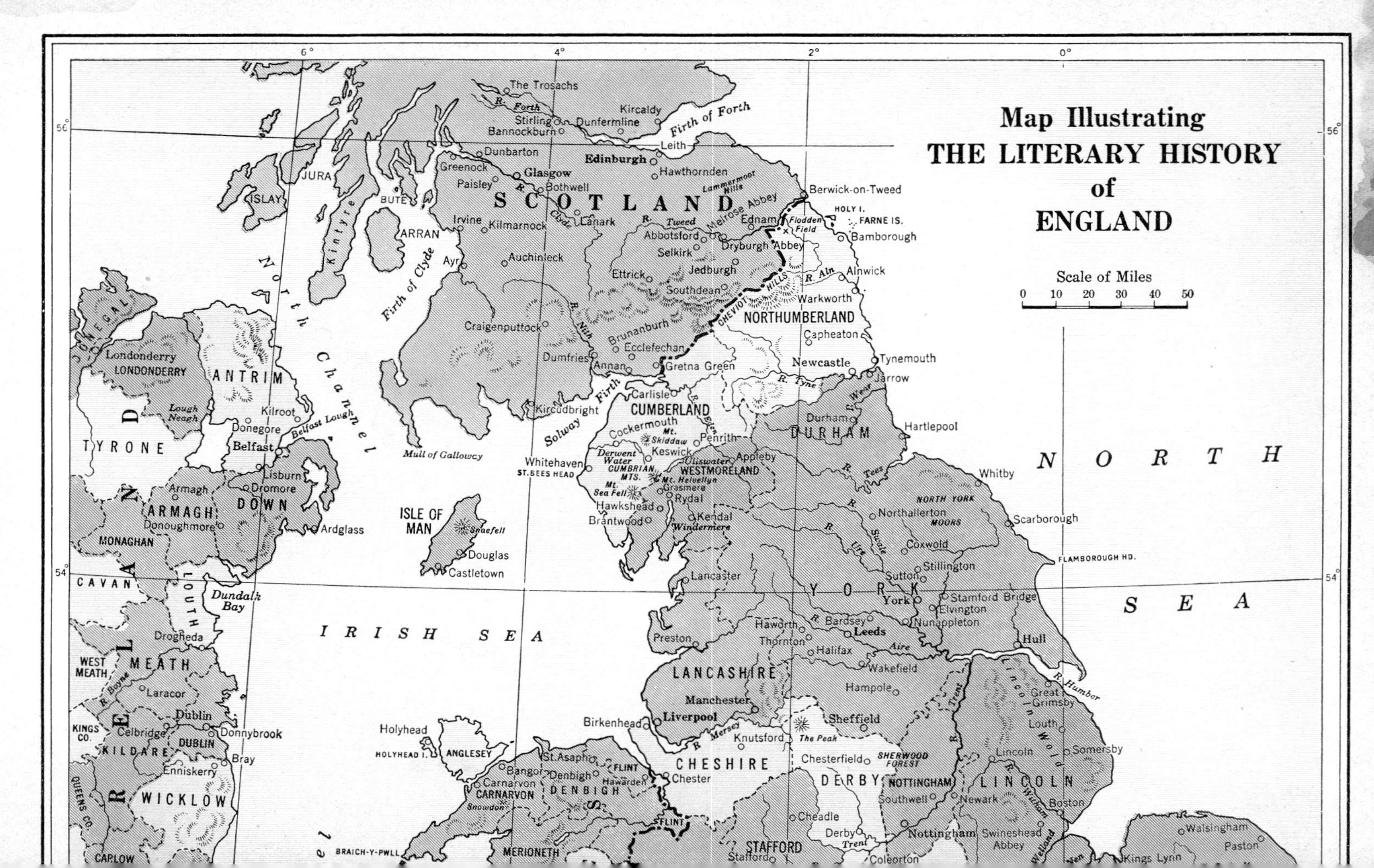
Map Illustrating
THE LITERARY HISTORY
of
ENGLAND
Scale of Miles
0 10 20 30 40 50
N O R T H S E A
I R I S H S E A
North Channel
S C O T L A N D
NORTHUMBERLAND
CUMBERLAND
WESTMORELAND
DURHAM
Y O R K
LANCASHIRE
CHESHIRE
DERBY
NOTTINGHAM
LINCOLN
STAFFORD
FLINT
DENBIGH
CARNARVON
MERIONETH
ANGLESEY
ISLE OF MAN
ANTRIM
LONDONDERRY
TYRONE
ARMAGH
DOWN
MONAGHAN
CAVAN
LOUTH
MEATH
WEST MEATH
DUBLIN
KILDARE
WICKLOW
KINGS CO.
QUEENS CO.
CARLOW
JURA
ISLAY
BUTE
ARRAN
Kintyre
Firth of Forth
Firth of Clyde
Solway Firth
Mull of Galloway
Dundalk Bay
Belfast Lough
Lough Neagh
The Trosachs
Stirling
Bannockburn
Dunfermline
Kircaldy
Leith
Edinburgh
Hawthornden
Dunbarton
Greenock
Glasgow
Paisley
Bothwell
Irvine
Kilmarnock
Lanark
Ayr
Auchinleck
Craigenputtock
Dumfries
Annan
Ecclefechan
Brunanburh
Gretna Green
Kircudbright
Abbotsford
Selkirk
Ettrick
Jedburgh
Southdean
Melrose Abbey
Dryburgh Abbey
Ednam
Flodden Field
Lammermoor Hills
Cheviot Hills
Berwick-on-Tweed
HOLY I.
FARNE IS.
Bamborough
Alnwick
Warkworth
Capheaton
Newcastle
Tynemouth
Jarrow
Durham
Hartlepool
Carlisle
Cockermouth
Mt. Skiddaw
Penrith
Keswick
Derwent Water
Ullswater
Appleby
Whitehaven
ST. BEES HEAD
CUMBRIAN MTS.
Mt. Helvellyn
Grasmere
Rydal
Mt. Sea Fell
Hawkshead
Brantwood
Kendal
Windermere
Lancaster
Preston
Whitby
Scarborough
FLAMBOROUGH HD.
North York Moors
Northallerton
Coxwold
Stillington
Sutton
York
Stamford Bridge
Elvington
Nunappleton
Bardsey
Leeds
Haworth
Thornton
Halifax
Wakefield
Hampole
Hull
Manchester
Liverpool
Birkenhead
Knutsford
Chester
Hawarden
Sheffield
The Peak
Chesterfield
Sherwood Forest
Southwell
Nottingham
Cheadle
Derby
Coleorton
Stafford
Newark
Lincoln
Swineshead Abbey
Boston
Louth
Great Grimsby
Somersby
Lincoln Wold
Walsingham
Paston
Kings Lynn
R. Humber
R. Forth
R. Clyde
R. Tweed
R. Nith
R. Aln
R. Tyne
R. Wear
R. Tees
R. Eden
R. Swale
R. Ure
R. Aire
R. Mersey
R. Trent
R. Witham
R. Welland
R. Boyne
Snaefell
Douglas
Castletown
Holyhead
HOLYHEAD I.
BRAICH-Y-PWLL
Bangor
Carnarvon
Snowdon
St. Asaph
Denbigh
Londonderry
Kilroot
Donegore
Belfast
Lisburn
Dromore
Armagh
Donoughmore
Ardglass
Drogheda
Laracor
Dublin
Celbridge
Donnybrook
Bray
Enniskerry
56°
54°
6°
4°
2°
0°

CARDIGAN BAY
St. George's Channel
Wexford
CARDIGAN
PEMBROKE
CARMARTHEN
RADNOR
BRECKNOCK
GLAMORGAN
MONMOUTH
HEREFORD
WORCESTER
WARWICK
NORTHAMPTON
HUNTINGDON
CAMBRIDGE
SUFFOLK
ESSEX
HERTFORD
BEDFORD
BUCKINGHAM
OXFORD
GLOUCESTER
BERKSHIRE
MIDDLESEX
WILTSHIRE
SURREY
KENT
SUSSEX
HAMPSHIRE
SOMERSET
DORSET
DEVON
CORNWALL
Birmingham
London
Bristol
Cardiff
Southampton
Portsmouth
Plymouth
Brighton
R. Thames
Bristol Channel
Barnstaple Bay
LUNDY I.
HARTLAND PT.
ST. DAVIDS HD.
Milford Haven
LANDS END
LIZARD HEAD
SCILLY IS.
Eddystone L.H.
START PT.
PORTLAND BILL
SELSEY BILL
BEACHY HEAD
NORTH FORELAND
ISLE OF WIGHT
The Solent
Strait of Dover
ENGLISH CHANNEL
ALDERNEY
GUERNSEY
SARK
JERSEY
CHANNEL ISLANDS
Cherbourg
Havre
Dieppe
Boulogne
Calais
FRANCE
GENERAL DRAFTING CO., INC., N.Y.

FROM BEOWULF TO THOMAS HARDY

VOLUME I

Conventions of the Lyrics. } Paper I
× Influence of Wyatt + Surrey. } second term

"With varying vanities, from every part,
They shift the moving Toyshop of their heart"
"Rape of the Lock". Pope.

"Charms strike the sight, but merit wins
the soul" — Pope.

"Fools rush in where angels fear to tread"

"True Wit is Nature to Advantage dressed"

"To err is human, to forgive divine"

"A perfect judge will read each work of Wit
With the same spirit its author writ"

"A little learning is a dangerous thing"

"True ease in writing comes from art, not chance
as those move easiest who have learned to
dance".

"One Truth is clear, Whatever is, is Right".

TO THE MEMORY OF

JOHN KESTER BONNELL

SCHOLAR, TEACHER, FRIEND

PREFACE

These volumes are designed primarily for the introductory course in the general history of English literature given in many colleges and universities. The plan they follow is based on the conviction, gained from my own experience and that of many other teachers, that anthologies and collections of extracts are more useful to those who know literature than to those who are just learning to know it. It is of little permanent use for the learner to read a few pages of fragments from the work of an important writer; it may even do him harm rather than good. These volumes represent an effort to consult the learner's actual needs; and to this end not only have writers of minor importance, and works which can profitably be studied only by the mature student, been excluded, but the writers who are represented are, I hope, adequately represented. As far as possible, only pieces complete in themselves have been chosen for inclusion, and the texts selected are printed without omissions. The amount of material included in the volumes is more than can be studied and discussed in the average course running through a single academic year. This may enable teachers to avoid the almost prohibitive expense of using a number of different textbooks for the work of one course, and yet at the same time enable them in large measure to enjoy the advantage of a considerable range of possible selection. Some of the texts, too, may be found useful for the purpose of supplementary reading. Such reading is very desirable, and most teachers wish to encourage it, but not all college and university libraries can supply the necessary books when the number of students enrolled in a course is large.

The annotation is, I believe, sufficient for accurate though fairly rapid reading. I have endeavored to provide explanations wherever they are really needed, but have aimed to take up as little space as possible with such matter. The purpose of these volumes is best served by the inclusion within them of the maximum amount of literature, and there has been in recent years a wholesome reaction from excessive annotation. In the first volume a glossary is provided for the selections from Chaucer, *Piers Plowman*, the Popular Ballads, and Spenser.

In general, modern usage has been followed in the matters of spelling and punctuation, though the selections from Chaucer and *Piers Plowman*, some of the ballads, and the first book of Spenser's *Faerie Queene* have been printed in their original form—the symbols ð and ȝ, however, being replaced by their modern equivalents, and modern usage being followed with respect to i, j, u, and v.

Any one who undertakes a work of this sort incurs at every turn obligations to previous editors. Not only am I deeply indebted to them, but also to many friends and colleagues who have given me advice or assistance in the course of the four or five years during which these volumes have been preparing. It would be impossible for me here to name all those who have thus aided me, and I must be content with one compendious and general acknowledgment. I am, however, particularly indebted to the Macmillan

Company for making it possible for me to use the late Professor Gummere's translation of *Beowulf;* to my friend and former colleague Professor Joseph M. Beatty, Jr., of Goucher College, for assistance with the glossary in the present volume; to Professor Morris W. Croll, of Princeton University, for reading some of the proofs and making several valuable suggestions; and to Miss Hilda Buttenwieser, Miss Estelle Hunt, and Miss Dorothy Sisson, all of the University of Cincinnati, for help in the preparation of the manuscript.

In so large and complex a work as this, involving almost countless details, it is practically inevitable that mistakes should occur. I have taken all possible pains to secure accuracy both in text and in notes, but I can hardly hope to be more fortunate in this than others have been, and I shall be grateful to any who use these volumes for pointing out to me any errors they may find, of whatever sort, so that they may be promptly corrected.

ROBERT SHAFER.

1 March, 1924.

The necessity of making new plates for the next impression of this work has given me a welcome opportunity to revise it. From time to time suggestions have come to hand for which I have felt grateful, but upon which no action could be taken until a new edition should be needed. The two volumes have now been carefully revised, and new texts, which fill about three hundred and seventy-five pages, have been added. To make room for this large amount of new matter, some texts formerly included have had to be sacrificed; but nothing, I hope, has been discarded which the great majority of those teaching the introductory course now regard as essential for that purpose. Considerations of space have forced me to abridge several of the new texts, but in the present edition, as in the former one, there is no expurgated piece. All editorial omissions are indicated by asterisks (*).

I cannot conclude this note without giving thanks to my wife, whose aid in the revision has been constant and invaluable.

R. S.

15 December, 1930.

CONTENTS

CONTENTS

Rearranged according to Types

Those who conduct the introductory course in literature by means of a survey of typical forms may find the following list useful. In it the contents of the two volumes of this work are arranged according to types, with references to volumes and pages.

From Beowulf to Thomas Hardy contains texts—in nearly all cases complete pieces—designed to illustrate the course of English literature from its beginning to the present day. To carry out this design, the texts are arranged chronologically, with historical and critical introductions. Both the amount of material and the kind of material included were determined by the belief that students should form a sound conception of English literature as a whole and in its historical development.

Whether English literature is being studied historically or by types, the chronological arrangement is, we believe, the most satisfactory. In itself it insures something of the historical perspective essential in any study of literature. And, besides, the classification of literature by types is always and of necessity a fluid and approximate matter. Many methods are equally possible, and for various purposes different methods are best. No classification by types is likely to suit two teachers equally well; for, even when there is agreement as to the best or most useful method for a specific purpose, there is still room for many differences of opinion as to the place within a system of classification where a given piece of literature is to be put. Probably no one has ever looked through a classified list without at once seeing what he considered serious mistakes of judgment. *From Beowulf to Thomas Hardy* enables teachers to make their own classifications in accordance with their own judgment and in accordance with the needs of their own students.

The following arrangement by types is intended as a suggestion for this purpose. We hope that it may be practically useful, and to this end strict consistency has been sacrificed for what we venture to call common sense. Some types of literature are important and significant for their form, others for their method, and others for their content. We have tried to distinguish important types, regardless of the system of classification which any one taken by itself might suggest as appropriate for the whole body of literature.

I. EPIC

II. NARRATIVE IN VERSE

III. BALLAD

IV. DRAMA

V. REFLECTIVE POEMS (Other than Lyrics)

VI. LYRIC

VII. EPIGRAM

VIII. DIDACTIC VERSE

IX. ALLEGORY

X. SATIRE

XI. ESSAY

XII. DIALOGUE

XIII. BIOGRAPHY AND AUTOBIOGRAPHY

XIV. HISTORY

XV. PROSE FICTION

FROM BEOWULF TO THOMAS HARDY

VOLUME I

THE GEATS.

SWERTING

HRETHEL

HEREBEALD, HAETHCYN, HYGELAC, D. mar. ECGTHEOW.

(Beowulf)

The Danes.

SCYLD

BEOWULF

HEALFDANE

HEOROGAR, HROTHGAR, HALGA, D. mar. ONELA.

FROM BEOWULF TO THOMAS HARDY

BEOWULF

There is only one extant manuscript of *Beowulf*. It is bound with some other Anglo-Saxon texts in a volume belonging to the collection of Sir Robert Cotton (1571–1631), which is now in the British Museum. This manuscript was written by two scribes about A. D. 1000. The poem was probably composed in the first half of the eighth century. Of its author nothing is directly known, though the internal evidence of the poem enables us to picture him to ourselves "as a man connected in some way with an Anglian court, a royal chaplain or abbot of noble birth or, it may be, a monk friend of his, who possessed an actual knowledge of court life and addressed himself to an aristocratic, in fact a royal audience. A man well versed in Germanic and Scandinavian heroic lore, familiar with secular Anglo-Saxon poems of the type exemplified by *Widsith*, *Finnsburg*, *Deor*, and *Waldere*, and a student of Biblical poems of the Cædmonian cycle, a man of notable taste and culture and informed with a spirit of broad-minded Christianity" (Fr. Klaeber, *Beowulf*, p. cxxii). The poem consists of two parts, joined to each other only by the person of the hero. The first part has three divisions. Beowulf's fight with Grendel, his fight with Grendel's mother, and his return to his own land. In the second part is narrated Beowulf's fight, after the passage of many years, with a dragon. The events of the poem take place entirely in Denmark and southern Sweden, and England is nowhere mentioned in it. It is considered practically certain that the stories of the conflict with the Grendel race and of the slaying of the dragon are of direct Scandinavian origin. The Anglian author, however, fuses with these many other elements from other sources—notably the pervasive Christian coloring, which deeply affects the character of the poem. But notwithstanding the latter, *Beowulf* gives us a faithful picture of many phases of ancient Germanic life, moral as well as material, and particularly of Germanic military ideals. Practically the only direct historical data of the poem are the several allusions to the raid of Hygelac which took place between A. D. 512 and 520. It has been conjectured that a person named Beowulf actually accompanied Hygelac on this raid and so distinguished himself by exceptional bravery that he gradually became a center of heroic legend. Whether this be so or not the Beowulf of the poem is obviously an idealized, heroic figure, not an historical character.

The translation here printed reproduces the meter of the original as far as that is possible in modern English. Each verse contains four accented syllables together with a freely varying number of unaccented ones, and each verse contains a marked pause between the second and third accented syllables. The accented syllables are, with the exceptions presently to be noted, distinguished by alliteration—that is, they begin with the same sound. They occur at the beginning of a word, save that prefixes are disregarded. Like consonant sounds alliterate with each other, whether they are indicated by the same letter or not; thus *card* and *kitchen* alliterate with each other, as also *noon* and *knight*, and be*deck* and *indict*. Any vowel sound alliterates with any other vowel sound. The fourth accented syllable never alliterates with the third in Anglo-Saxon verse of the best period; but the third always alliterates with the first or second, and in the majority of cases with both. Occasionally the fourth accented syllable alliterates with the second, and more rarely with the first, when either of these is not in alliteration with the third.

The first eleven lines of *Beowulf* are subjoined in their original form:

Hwæt, we Gar-Dena　　in geardagum,
þeodcyninga　　þrym gefrunon,
hu þa æþelingas　　ellen fremedon!
Oft Scyld Scefing　　sceaþena þreatum,
monegum mægþum　　meodo-setla ofteah,
egsode eorl[as],　　syððan ærest wearð
feasceaft funden;　　he þæs frofre gebad,
weox under wolcnum,　　weorðmyndum þah,
oðþæt him æghwylc　　þara ymbsittendra
ofer hron-rade　　hyran scolde,
gomban gyldan;　　þæt wæs god cyning!

PRELUDE OF THE FOUNDER OF THE DANISH HOUSE[1]

Lo, praise of the prowess of people-kings
of spear-armed Danes, in days long sped,
we have heard, and what honor the athelings won!
Oft Scyld the Scefing from squadroned foes,
from many a tribe, the mead-bench tore,
awing the earls. Since erst he lay
friendless, a foundling, fate repaid him:
for he waxed under welkin, in wealth he throve,
till before him the folk, both far and near,
who house by the whale-path,[2] heard his mandate,
gave him gifts: a good king he!
To him an heir was afterward born,
a son in his halls, whom heaven sent
to favor the folk, feeling their woe
that erst they had lacked an earl for leader
so long a while; the Lord endowed him,
the Wielder of Wonder, with world's renown.
Famed was this Beowulf:[3] far flew the boast of him,
son of Scyld, in the Scandian lands.
So becomes it a youth to quit him well
with his father's friends, by fee and gift,
that to aid him, agéd, in after days,
come warriors willing, should war draw nigh,
liegemen loyal: by lauded deeds
shall an earl have honor in every clan.
Forth he fared at the fated moment,
sturdy Scyld to the shelter of God.
Then they bore him over to ocean's billow,
loving clansmen, as late he charged them,
while wielded words the winsome Scyld,
the leader belovéd who long had ruled. . . .
In the roadstead rocked a ring-dight vessel,
ice-flecked, outbound, atheling's barge:
there laid they down their darling lord
on the breast of the boat, the breaker-of-rings,
by the mast the mighty one. Many a treasure
fetched from far was freighted with him.
No ship have I known so nobly dight
with weapons of war and weeds of battle,
with breastplate and blade: on his bosom lay
a heapéd hoard that hence should go
far o'er the flood with him floating away.
No less these loaded the lordly gifts,
thanes' huge treasure, than those had done
who in former time forth had sent him
sole on the seas, a suckling child.
High o'er his head they hoist the standard,
a gold-wove banner; let billows take him,
gave him to ocean. Grave were their spirits,
mournful their mood. No man is able
to say in sooth, no son of the halls,
no hero 'neath heaven,—who harbored that freight!

I

Now Beowulf bode in the burg of the Scyldings,
leader belovéd, and long he ruled
in fame with all folk, since his father had gone
away from the world, till awoke an heir,
haughty Healfdene, who held through life,
sage and sturdy, the Scyldings glad.
Then, one after one, there woke to him,
to the chieftain of clansmen, children four:
Heorogar, then Hrothgar, then Halga brave;
and I heard that —— was ——'s queen,[4]
the Heathoscylfing's helpmate dear.
To Hrothgar was given such glory of war,
such honor of combat, that all his kin
obeyed him gladly till great grew his band
of youthful comrades. It came in his mind
to bid his henchmen a hall uprear,
a master mead-house, mightier far
than ever was seen by the sons of earth,
and within it, then, to old and young
he would all allot that the Lord had sent him,
save only the land and the lives of his men.
Wide, I heard, was the work commanded,
for many a tribe this mid-earth round,
to fashion the folkstead. It fell, as he ordered,
in rapid achievement that ready it stood there,
of halls the noblest: Heorot[5] he named it
whose message had might in many a land.
Not reckless of promise, the rings he dealt,
treasure at banquet: there towered the hall,
high, gabled wide, the hot surge waiting
of furious flame.[6] Nor far was that day
when father and son-in-law stood in feud
for warfare and hatred that woke again.
With envy and anger an evil spirit
endured the dole in his dark abode,
that he heard each day the din of revel
high in the hall: there harps rang out,
clear song of the singer. He sang who knew
tales of the early time of man,
how the Almighty made the earth,
fairest fields enfolded by water,
set, triumphant, sun and moon
for a light to lighten the land-dwellers,

[1]This translation is from *The Oldest English Epic*, by Francis B. Gummere, copyrighted by the Macmillan Company. Reprinted by permission.

[2]The sea.

[3]Not Beowulf the Geat, hero of the poem.

[4]The first of the missing names is lost and the second imperfect in the original.

[5]The word means stag (hart). The hall was so named because of decorations in the gables resembling the antlers of a deer.

[6]Sooner or later these halls burned down.

and braided bright the breast of earth
with limbs and leaves, made life for all
of mortal beings that breathe and move.
So lived the clansmen in cheer and revel
a winsome life, till one began
to fashion evils, that fiend of hell.
Grendel this monster grim was called,
march-riever[1] mighty, in moorland living,
in fen and fastness; fief of the giants
the hapless wight a while had kept
since the Creator his exile doomed.
On kin of Cain was the killing avenged
by sovran God for slaughtered Abel.
Ill fared his feud, and far was he driven,
for the slaughter's sake, from sight of men.
Of Cain awoke all that woful breed,
Etins[2] and elves and evil-spirits,
as well as the giants that warred with God
weary while: but their wage was paid them!

II

Went he forth to find at fall of night
that haughty house, and heed wherever
the Ring-Danes, outreveled, to rest had gone.
Found within it the atheling band
asleep after feasting and fearless of sorrow,
of human hardship. Unhallowed wight,
grim and greedy, he grasped betimes,
wrathful, reckless, from resting-places,
thirty of the thanes, and thence he rushed
fain of his fell spoil, faring homeward,
laden with slaughter, his lair to seek.
Then at the dawning, as day was breaking,
the might of Grendel to men was known;
then after wassail was wail uplifted,
loud moan in the morn. The mighty chief,
atheling excellent, unblithe sat,
labored in woe for the loss of his thanes,
when once had been traced the trail of the fiend,
spirit accurst: too cruel that sorrow,
too long, too loathsome. Not late the respite;
with night returning, anew began
ruthless murder; he recked no whit,
firm in his guilt, of the feud and crime.
They were easy to find who elsewhere sought
in room remote their rest at night,
bed in the bowers,[3] when that bale was shown,
was seen in sooth, with surest token,—
the hall-thane's[4] hate. Such held themselves
far and fast who the fiend outran!
Thus ruled unrighteous and raged his fill
one against all; until empty stood
that lordly building, and long it bode so.
Twelve years' tide the trouble he bore,
sovran of Scyldings, sorrows in plenty,
boundless cares. There came unhidden
tidings true to the tribes of men,
in sorrowful songs, how ceaselessly Grendel
harassed Hrothgar, what hate he bore him,
what murder and massacre, many a year,
feud unfading,—refused consent
to deal with any of Daneland's earls,
make pact of peace, or compound for gold:
still less did the wise men ween to get
great fee for the feud from his fiendish hands.
But the evil one ambushed old and young,
death-shadow dark, and dogged them still,
lured, and lurked in the livelong night
of misty moorlands: men may say not
where the haunts of these Hell-Runes[5] be.
Such heaping of horrors the hater of men,
lonely roamer, wrought unceasing,
harassings heavy. O'er Heorot he lorded,
gold-bright hall, in gloomy nights;
and ne'er could the prince approach his throne,
—'twas judgment of God,—or have joy in his hall.
Sore was the sorrow to Scyldings'-friend,
heart-rending misery. Many nobles
sat assembled, and searched out counsel
how it were best for bold-hearted men
against harassing terror to try their hand.
Whiles they vowed in their heathen fanes
altar-offerings, asked with words
that the slayer-of-souls would succor give them
for the pain of their people. Their practice this,
their heathen hope; 'twas Hell they thought of
in mood of their mind. Almighty they knew not,
Doomsman of Deeds and dreadful Lord,
nor Heaven's-Helmet heeded they ever,
Wielder-of-Wonder.—Woe for that man
who in harm and hatred hales his soul
to fiery embraces;—nor favor nor change
awaits he ever. But well for him
that after death-day may draw to his Lord,
and friendship find in the Father's arms!

III

Thus seethed unceasing the son of Healfdene
with the woe of these days; not wisest men
assuaged his sorrow; too sore the anguish,
loathly and long, that lay on his folk,
most baneful of burdens and bales of the night.

This heard in his home Hygelac's thane,
great among Geats, of Grendel's doings.

---

[1]Border-raider. [2]Giants.

[3]Smaller buildings near the hall.

[4]Grendel's. He is so described because he has made himself master of the hall.

[5]Witches of hell.

He was the mightiest man of valor
in that same day of this our life,
stalwart and stately. A stout wave-walker
he bade make ready. Yon battle-king, said he,
far o'er the swan-road he fain would seek,
the noble monarch who needed men!
The prince's journey by prudent folk
was little blamed, though they loved him dear;
they whetted the hero, and hailed good omens.
And now the bold one from bands of Geats
comrades chose, the keenest of warriors
e'er he could find; with fourteen men
the sea-wood[1] he sought, and, sailor proved,
led them on to the land's confines.
Time had now flown; afloat was the ship,
boat under bluff. On board they climbed,
warriors ready; waves were churning
sea with sand; the sailors bore
on the breast of the bark their bright array,
their mail and weapons: the men pushed off,
on its willing way, the well-braced craft.
Then moved o'er the waters by might of the wind
the bark like a bird with breast of foam,
till in season due, on the second day,
the curvéd prow such course had run
that sailors now could see the land,
sea-cliffs shining, steep high hills,
headlands broad. Their haven was found,
their journey ended. Up then quickly
the Weders'[2] clansmen climbed ashore,
anchored their sea-wood, with armor clashing
and gear of battle: God they thanked
for passing in peace o'er the paths of the sea.
Now saw from the cliff a Scylding clansman,
a warden that watched the water-side,
how they bore o'er the gangway glittering shields,
war-gear in readiness; wonder seized him
to know what manner of men they were.
Straight to the strand his steed he rode,
Hrothgar's henchman; with hand of might
he shook his spear, and spake in parley.
"Who are ye, then, ye arméd men,
mailéd folk, that yon mighty vessel
have urged thus over the ocean ways,
here o'er the waters? A warden I,
sentinel set o'er the sea-march here,
lest any foe to the folk of Danes
with harrying fleet should harm the land.
No aliens ever at ease thus bore them,
linden-wielders: yet word-of-leave
clearly ye lack from clansmen here,
my folk's agreement.—A greater ne'er saw I
of warriors in world than is one of you,—
yon hero in harness! No henchman he
worthied by weapons, if witness his features,
his peerless presence! I pray you, though, tell
your folk and home, lest hence ye fare
suspect to wander your way as spies
in Danish land. Now, dwellers afar,
ocean-travelers, take from me
simple advice: the sooner the better
I hear of the country whence ye came."

IV

To him the stateliest spake in answer;
the warriors' leader his word-hoard unlocked:—
"We are by kin of the clan of Geats,
and Hygelac's own hearth-fellows we.
To folk afar was my father known,
noble atheling, Ecgtheow named.
Full of winters, he fared away
agéd from earth; he is honored still
through width of the world by wise men all.
To thy lord and liege in loyal mood
we hasten hither, to Healfdene's son,
people-protector: be pleased to advise us!
To that mighty-one come we on mickle errand,
to the lord of the Danes; nor deem I right
that aught be hidden. We hear—thou knowest
if sooth it is—the saying of men,
that amid the Scyldings a scathing monster,
dark ill-doer, in dusky nights
shows terrific his rage unmatched,
hatred and murder. To Hrothgar I
in greatness of soul would succor bring,
so the Wise-and-Brave may worst his foes,—
if ever the end of ills is fated,
of cruel contest, if cure shall follow,
and the boiling care-waves cooler grow;
else ever afterward anguish-days
he shall suffer in sorrow while stands in place
high on its hill that house unpeered!"
Astride his steed, the strand-ward answered,
clansman unquailing: "The keen-souled thane
must be skilled to sever and sunder duly
words and works, if he well intends.
I gather, this band is graciously bent
to the Scyldings' master. March, then, bearing
weapons and weeds the way I show you.
I will bid my men your boat meanwhile
to guard for fear lest foemen come,—
your new-tarred ship by shore of ocean
faithfully watching till once again
it waft o'er the waters those well-loved thanes,
—winding-necked wood,—to Weders' bounds,

[1]A ship. [2]Another name for the Geats.

heroes such as the hest of fate
shall succor and save from the shock of war."
They bent them to march,—the boat lay still,
fettered by cable and fast at anchor,
broad-bosomed ship.—Then shone the boars[1]
over the cheek-guard; chased with gold,
keen and gleaming, guard it kept
o'er the man of war, as marched along
heroes in haste, till the hall they saw,
broad of gable and bright with gold:
that was the fairest, 'mid folk of earth,
of houses 'neath heaven, where Hrothgar lived,
and the gleam of it lightened o'er lands afar.
The sturdy shieldsman showed that bright
burg-of-the-boldest; bade them go
straightway thither; his steed then turned,
hardy hero, and hailed them thus:—
"'Tis time that I fare from you. Father Almighty
in grace and mercy guard you well,
safe in your seekings. Seaward I go,
'gainst hostile warriors hold my watch."

V

Stone-bright the street: it showed the way
to the crowd of clansmen. Corselets glistened
hand-forged, hard; on their harness bright
the steel ring sang, as they strode along
in mail of battle, and marched to the hall.
There, weary of ocean, the wall along
they set their bucklers, their broad shields, down,
and bowed them to bench: the breastplates clanged,
war-gear of men; their weapons stacked,
spears of the seafarers stood together,
gray-tipped ash: that iron band
was worthily weaponed!—A warrior proud
asked of the heroes their home and kin.
"Whence, now, bear ye burnished shields,
harness gray and helmets grim,
spears in multitude? Messenger, I,
Hrothgar's herald! Heroes so many
ne'er met I as strangers of mood so strong.
'Tis plain that for prowess, not plunged into exile,
for high-hearted valor, Hrothgar ye seek!"
Him the sturdy-in-war bespake with words,
proud earl of the Weders answer made,
hardy 'neath helmet:—"Hygelac's, we,
fellows at board; I am Beowulf named.
I am seeking to say to the son of Healfdene
this mission of mine, to thy master-lord,
the doughty prince, if he deign at all
grace that we greet him, the good one, now."
Wulfgar spake, the Wendles' chieftain,
whose might of mind to many was known,
his courage and counsel: "The king of Danes,
the Scyldings' friend, I fain will tell,
the Breaker-of-Rings, as the boon thou askest,
the faméd prince, of thy faring hither,
and, swiftly after, such answer bring
as the doughty monarch may deign to give."
Hied then in haste to where Hrothgar sat
white-haired and old, his earls about him,
till the stout thane stood at the shoulder there
of the Danish king: good courtier he!
Wulfgar spake to his winsome lord:—
"Hither have fared to thee far-come men
o'er the paths of ocean, people of Geatland;
and the stateliest there by his sturdy band
is Beowulf named. This boon they seek,
that they, my master, may with thee
have speech at will: nor spurn their prayer
to give them hearing, gracious Hrothgar!
In weeds of the warrior worthy they,
methinks, of our liking; their leader most surely,
a hero that hither his henchmen has led."

VI

Hrothgar answered, helmet of Scyldings:—
"I knew him of yore in his youthful days;
his agéd father was Ecgtheow named,
to whom, at home, gave Hrethel the Geat
his only daughter. Their offspring bold
fares hither to seek the steadfast friend.
And seamen, too, have said me this,—
who carried my gifts to the Geatish court,
thither for thanks,—he has thirty men's
heft of grasp in the gripe of his hand,
the bold-in-battle. Blesséd God
out of his mercy this man hath sent
to Danes of the West, as I ween indeed,
against horror of Grendel. I hope to give
the good youth gold for his gallant thought.
Be thou in haste, and bid them hither,
clan of kinsmen, to come before me;
and add this word,—they are welcome guests
to folk of the Danes."
[To the door of the hall
Wulfgar went] and the word declared:—
"To you this message my master sends,
East-Danes' king, that your kin he knows,
hardy heroes, and hails you all
welcome hither o'er waves of the sea!
Ye may wend your way in war-attire,
and under helmets Hrothgar greet;
but let here the battle-shields bide your parley,
and wooden war-shafts wait its end."
Uprose the mighty one, ringed with his men,
brave band of thanes: some bode without,
battle-gear guarding, as bade the chief.
Then hied that troop where the herald led them,
under Heorot's roof: [the hero strode,]

[1] Images of boars on Beowulf's helmet.

hardy 'neath helm, till the hearth he neared.
Beowulf spake,—his breastplate gleamed,
war-net woven by wit of the smith:—
"Thou Hrothgar, hail! Hygelac's I,
kinsman and follower. Fame a plenty
have I gained in youth! These Grendel-deeds
I heard in my home-land heralded clear.
Seafarers say how stands this hall,
of buildings best, for your band of thanes
empty and idle, when evening sun
in the harbor of heaven is hidden away.
So my vassals advised me well,—
brave and wise, the best of men,—
O sovran Hrothgar, to seek thee here,
for my nerve and my might they knew full well.
Themselves had seen me from slaughter come
blood-flecked from foes, where five I bound,
and that wild brood worsted. I' the waves I slew
nicors[1] by night, in need and peril
avenging the Weders, whose woe they sought,—
crushing the grim ones. Grendel now,
monster cruel, be mine to quell
in single battle! So, from thee,
thou sovran of the Shining-Danes,
Scyldings'-bulwark, a boon I seek,—
and, Friend-of-the-folk, refuse it not,
O Warriors'-shield, now I've wandered far,—
that I alone with my liegemen here,
this hardy band, may Heorot purge!
More I hear, that the monster dire,
in his wanton mood, of weapons recks not;
hence shall I scorn—so Hygelac stay,
king of my kindred, kind to me!—
brand or buckler to bear in the fight,
gold-colored targe: but with gripe alone
must I front the fiend and fight for life,
foe against foe. Then faith be his
in the doom of the Lord whom death shall take.
Fain, I ween, if the fight he win,
in this hall of gold my Geatish band
will he fearless eat,—as oft before,—
my noblest thanes. Nor need'st thou then
to hide my head;[2] for his shall I be,
dyed in gore, if death must take me;
and my blood-covered body he'll bear as prey,
ruthless devour it, the roamer-lonely,
with my life-blood redden his lair in the fen:
no further for me need'st food prepare!
To Hygelac send, if Hild[3] should take me,
best of war-weeds, warding my breast,
armor excellent, heirloom of Hrethel
and work of Wayland.[4] Fares Wyrd[5] as she must."

VII

Hrothgar spake, the Scyldings'-helmet:—
"For fight defensive, Friend my Beowulf,
to succor and save, thou hast sought us here.
Thy father's combat a feud enkindled
when Heatholaf with hand he slew
among the Wylfings; his Weder kin
for horror of fighting feared to hold him.
Fleeing, he sought our South-Dane folk,
over surge of ocean the Honor-Scyldings,
when first I was ruling the folk of Danes,
wielded, youthful, this widespread realm,
this hoard-hold of heroes. Heorogar was dead,
my elder brother, had breathed his last,
Healfdene's bairn: he was better than I!
Straightway the feud with fee I settled,
to the Wylfings sent, o'er watery ridges,
treasures olden: oaths he swore me.
Sore is my soul to say to any
of the race of man what ruth for me
in Heorot Grendel with hate hath wrought,
what sudden harryings. Hall-folk fail me,
my warriors wane; for Wyrd hath swept them
into Grendel's grasp. But God is able
this deadly foe from his deeds to turn!
Boasted full oft, as my beer they drank,
earls o'er the ale-cup, armèd men,
that they would bide in the beer-hall here,
Grendel's attack with terror of blades.
Then was this mead-house at morning tide
dyed with gore, when the daylight broke,
all the boards of the benches blood-besprinkled,
gory the hall: I had heroes the less,
doughty dear-ones that death had reft.
—But sit to the banquet, unbind thy words,
hardy hero, as heart shall prompt thee."

Gathered together, the Geatish men
in the banquet-hall on bench assigned,
sturdy-spirited, sat them down,
hardy-hearted. A henchman attended,
carried the carven cup in hand,
served the clear mead. Oft minstrels sang
blithe in Heorot. Heroes reveled,
no dearth of warriors, Weder and Dane.

VIII

Unferth spake, the son of Ecglaf,
who sat at the feet of the Scyldings' lord,
unbound the battle-runes.[6]—Beowulf's quest,

[1] Sea monsters.
[2] The reference is either to interment or to the custom of covering the head of the dead with a cloth.
[3] War. Gummere supposes that war is here personified.
[4] The Germanic Vulcan.
[5] Destiny.
[6] Began the battle or word-combat which follows.

sturdy seafarer's, sorely galled him;
ever he envied that other men
should more achieve in middle-earth
of fame under heaven than he himself.—
"Art thou that Beowulf, Breca's rival,
who emulous swam on the open sea,
when for pride the pair of you proved the floods,
and wantonly dared in waters deep
to risk your lives? No living man,
or lief or loath, from your labor dire
could you dissuade, from swimming the main.
Ocean-tides with your arms ye covered,
with strenuous hands the sea-streets measured,
swam o'er the waters. Winter's storm
rolled the rough waves. In realm of sea
a sennight strove ye. In swimming he topped thee,
had more of main! Him at morning-tide
billows bore to the Battling Reamas,
whence he hied to his home so dear,
beloved of his liegemen, to land of Brondings,
fastness fair, where his folk he ruled,
town and treasure. In triumph o'er thee
Beanstan's bairn[1] his boast achieved.
So ween I for thee a worse adventure,
—though in buffet of battle thou brave hast been,
in struggle grim,—if Grendel's approach
thou dar'st await through the watch of night!"

Beowulf spake, bairn of Ecgtheow:—
"What a deal hast uttered, dear my Unferth,
drunken with beer, of Breca now,
told of his triumph! Truth I claim it,
that I had more of might in the sea
than any man else, more ocean-endurance.
We twain had talked, in time of youth,
and made our boast,—we were merely boys,
striplings still,—to stake our lives
far at sea: and so we performed it.
Naked swords, as we swam along,
we held in hand, with hope to guard us
against the whales. Not a whit from me
could he float afar o'er the flood of waves,
haste o'er the billows; nor him I abandoned.
Together we twain on the tides abode
five nights full till the flood divided us,
churning waves and chillest weather,
darkling night, and the northern wind
ruthless rushed on us: rough was the surge.
Now the wrath of the sea-fish rose apace;
yet me 'gainst the monsters my mailéd coat,
hard and hand-linked, help afforded,—
battle-sark braided my breast to ward,
garnished with gold. There grasped me firm
and haled me to bottom the hated foe,
with grimmest gripe. 'Twas granted me, though,
to pierce the monster with point of sword,
with blade of battle: huge beast of the sea
was whelmed by the hurly through hand of mine.

IX

"Me thus often the evil monsters
thronging threatened. With thrust of my sword,
the darling, I dealt them due return!
Nowise had they bliss from their booty then
to devour their victim, vengeful creatures,
seated to banquet at bottom of sea;
but at break of day, by my brand sore hurt,
on the edge of ocean up they lay,
put to sleep by the sword. And since, by them
on the fathomless sea-ways sailor-folk
are never molested.—Light from east,
came bright God's beacon; the billows sank,
so that I saw the sea-cliffs high,
windy walls. For Wyrd oft saveth
earl undoomed if he doughty be!
And so it came that I killed with my sword
nine of the nicors. Of night-fought battles
ne'er heard I a harder 'neath heaven's dome,
nor adrift on the deep a more desolate man!
Yet I came unharmed from that hostile clutch,
though spent with swimming. The sea upbore me,
flood of the tide, on Finnish land,
the welling waters. No wise of thee
have I heard men tell such terror of falchions,
bitter battle. Breca ne'er yet,
not one of you pair, in the play of war
such daring deed has done at all
with bloody brand,—I boast not of it!—
though thou wast the bane[2] of thy brethren dear,
thy closest kin, whence curse of hell
awaits thee, well as thy wit may serve!
For I say in sooth, thou son of Ecglaf,
never had Grendel these grim deeds wrought,
monster dire, on thy master dear,
in Heorot such havoc, if heart of thine
were as battle-bold as thy boast is loud!
But he has found no feud will happen;
from sword-clash dread of your Danish clan
he vaunts him safe, from the Victor-Scyldings.
He forces pledges, favors none
of the land of Danes, but lustily murders,
fights and feasts, nor feud he dreads
from Spear-Dane men. But speedily now
shall I prove him the prowess and pride of the Geats,

[1]Breca.

[2]Murderer.

shall bid him battle. Blithe to mead
go he that listeth, when light of dawn
this morrow morning o'er men of earth,
ether-robed sun from the south shall beam!"
Joyous then was the Jewel-giver,
hoar-haired, war-brave; help awaited
the Bright-Danes' prince, from Beowulf hearing,
folk's good shepherd, such firm resolve.
Then was laughter of liegemen loud resounding
with winsome words. Came Wealhtheow forth,
queen of Hrothgar, heedful of courtesy,
gold-decked, greeting the guests in hall;
and the high-born lady handed the cup
first to the East-Danes' heir and warden,
bade him be blithe at the beer-carouse,
the land's beloved one. Lustily took he
banquet and beaker, battle-famed king.
Through the hall then went the Helmings' Lady,
to younger and older everywhere
carried the cup, till came the moment
when the ring-graced queen, the royal-hearted,
to Beowulf bore the beaker of mead.
She greeted the Geats' lord, God she thanked
in wisdom's words, that her will was granted,
that at last on a hero her hope could lean
for comfort in terrors. The cup he took,
hardy-in-war, from Wealhtheow's hand,
and answer uttered the eager-for-combat.
Beowulf spake, bairn of Ecgtheow:—
"This was my thought, when my thanes and I
bent to the ocean and entered our boat,
that I would work the will of your people
fully, or fighting fall in death,
in fiend's gripe fast. I am firm to do
an earl's brave deed, or end the days
of this life of mine in the mead-hall here."
Well these words to the woman seemed,
Beowulf's battle-boast.—Bright with gold
the stately dame by her spouse sat down.
Again, as erst, began in hall
warriors' wassail and words of power,
the proud-band's revel, till presently
the son of Healfdene hastened to seek
rest for the night; he knew there waited
fight for the fiend in that festal hall,
when the sheen of the sun they saw no more,
and dusk of night sank darkling nigh,
and shadowy shapes came striding on,
wan under welkin. The warriors rose.
Man to man, he made harangue,
Hrothgar to Beowulf, bade him hail,
let him wield the wine hall: a word he added:—
"Never to any man erst I trusted,
since I could heave up hand and shield,
this noble Dane-Hall, till now to thee.
Have now and hold this house unpeered;
remember thy glory; thy might declare;
watch for the foe! No wish shall fail thee
if thou bidest the battle with bold-won life."

X

Then Hrothgar went with his hero-train,
defense-of-Scyldings, forth from hall;
fain would the war-lord Wealhtheow seek,
couch of his queen. The King-of-Glory
against this Grendel a guard had set,
so heroes heard, a hall-defender,
who warded the monarch and watched for the monster.
In truth, the Geats' prince gladly trusted
his mettle, his might, the mercy of God!
Cast off then his corselet of iron,
helmet from head; to his henchman gave,—
choicest of weapons,—the well-chased sword,
bidding him guard the gear of battle.
Spake then his Vaunt the valiant man,
Beowulf Geat, ere the bed he sought:—
"Of force in fight no feebler I count me,
in grim war-deeds, than Grendel deems him.
Not with the sword, then, to sleep of death
his life will I give, though it lie in my power.
No skill is his to strike against me,
my shield to hew though he hardy be,
bold in battle; we both, this night
shall spurn the sword, if he seek me here,
unweaponed, for war. Let wisest God,
sacred Lord, on which side soever
doom decree as he deemeth right."
Reclined then the chieftain, and cheek-pillows held
the head of the earl, while all about him
seamen hardy on hall-beds sank.
None of them thought that thence their steps
to the folk and fastness that fostered them,
to the land they loved, would lead them back!
Full well they wist that on warriors many
battle-death seized, in the banquet-hall,
of Danish clan. But comfort and help,
war-weal weaving, to Weder folk
the Master gave, that, by might of one,
over their enemy all prevailed,
by single strength. In sooth 'tis told
that highest God o'er human kind
hath wielded ever!—Thro' wan night striding,
came the walker-in-shadow. Warriors slept
whose hest was to guard the gabled hall,—
all save one. 'Twas widely known
that against God's will the ghostly ravager
him could not hurl to haunts of darkness;
wakeful, ready, with warrior's wrath,
bold he bided the battle's issue.

XI

Then from the moorland, by misty crags,
with God's wrath laden, Grendel came.

The monster was minded of mankind now
sundry to seize in the stately house.
Under welkin he walked, till the wine-palace there,
gold-hall of men, he gladly discerned,
flashing with fretwork. Not first time, this,
that he the home of Hrothgar sought,—
yet ne'er in his life-day, late or early,
such hardy heroes, such hall-thanes, found!
To the house the warrior walked apace,
parted from peace;[1] the portal opened,
though with forged bolts fast, when his fists had struck it,
and baleful he burst in his blatant rage,
the house's mouth. All hastily, then,
o'er fair-paved floor the fiend trod on,
ireful he strode; there streamed from his eyes
fearful flashes, like flame to see.
He spied in hall the hero-band,
kin and clansmen clustered asleep,
hardy liegemen. Then laughed his heart;
for the monster was minded, ere morn should dawn,
savage, to sever the soul of each,
life from body, since lusty banquet
waited his will! But Wyrd forbade him
to seize any more of men on earth
after that evening. Eagerly watched
Hygelac's kinsman his curséd foe,
how he would fare in fell attack.
Not that the monster was minded to pause!
Straightway he seized a sleeping warrior
for the first, and tore him fiercely asunder,
the bone-frame bit, drank blood in streams,
swallowed him piecemeal: swiftly thus
the lifeless corse was clear devoured,
e'en feet and hands. Then farther he hied;
for the hardy hero with hand he grasped,
felt for the foe with fiendish claw,
for the hero reclining,—who clutched it boldly,
prompt to answer, propped on his arm.
Soon then saw that shepherd-of-evils
that never he met in this middle-world,
in the ways of earth, another wight
with heavier hand-gripe; at heart he feared,
sorrowed in soul,—none the sooner escaped!
Fain would he flee, his fastness seek,
the den of devils: no doings now
such as oft he had done in days of old!
Then bethought him the hardy Hygelac-thane
of his boast at evening: up he bounded,
grasped firm his foe, whose fingers cracked.
The fiend made off, but the earl close followed.
The monster meant—if he might at all—
to fling himself free, and far away
fly to the fens,—knew his fingers' power
in the gripe of the grim one. Gruesome march
to Heorot this monster of harm had made!
Din filled the room; the Danes were bereft,
castle-dwellers and clansmen all,
earls, of their ale. Angry were both
those savage hall-guards: the house resounded.
Wonder it was the wine-hall firm
in the strain of their struggle stood, to earth
the fair house fell not; too fast it was
within and without by its iron bands
craftily clamped; though there crashed from sill
many a mead-bench—men have told me—
gay with gold, where the grim foes wrestled.
So well had weened the wisest Scyldings
that not ever at all might any man
that bone-decked, brave house break asunder,
crush by craft,—unless clasp of fire
in smoke engulfed it.—Again uprose
din redoubled. Danes of the North
with fear and frenzy were filled, each one,
who from the wall that wailing heard,
God's foe sounding his grisly song,
cry of the conquered, clamorous pain
from captive of hell. Too closely held him
he who of men in might was strongest
in that same day of this our life.

XII

Not in any wise would the earls'-defense
suffer that slaughterous stranger to live,
useless deeming his days and years
to men on earth. Now many an earl
of Beowulf brandished blade ancestral,
fain the life of their lord to shield,
their praiséd prince, if power were theirs;
never they knew,—as they neared the foe,
hardy-hearted heroes of war,
aiming their swords on every side
the accursed to kill,—no keenest blade,
no fairest of falchions fashioned on earth,
could harm or hurt that hideous fiend!
He was safe, by his spells, from sword of battle,
from edge of iron. Yet his end and parting
on that same day of this our life
woful should be, and his wandering soul
far off flit to the fiends' domain.
Soon he found, who in former days,
harmful in heart and hated of God,
on many a man such murder wrought,
that the frame of his body failed him now.
For him the keen-souled kinsman of Hygelac
held in hand; hateful alive
was each to other. The outlaw dire
took mortal hurt; a mighty wound
showed on his shoulder, and sinews cracked,
and the bone-frame burst. To Beowulf now
the glory was given, and Grendel thence
death-sick his den in the dark moor sought,
noisome abode: he knew too well

[1] *I. e.*, doomed to hell.

that here was the last of life, an end
of his days on earth.—To all the Danes
by that bloody battle the boon had come.
From ravage had rescued the roving stranger
Hrothgar's hall; the hardy and wise one
had purged it anew. His night-work pleased him,
his deed and its honor. To Eastern Danes
had the valiant Geat his vaunt made good,
all their sorrow and ills assuaged,
their bale of battle borne so long,
and all the dole they erst endured,
pain a-plenty.—'Twas proof of this,
when the hardy-in-fight a hand laid down,
arm and shoulder,—all, indeed,
of Grendel's gripe,—'neath the gabled roof.

XIII

Many at morning, as men have told me,
warriors gathered the gift-hall round,
folk-leaders faring from far and near,
o'er wide-stretched ways, the wonder to view,
trace of the traitor. Not troublous seemed
the enemy's end to any man
who saw by the gait of the graceless foe
how the weary-hearted, away from thence,
baffled in battle and banned, his steps
death-marked dragged to the devils' mere.[1]
Bloody the billows were boiling there,
turbid the tide of tumbling waves
horribly seething, with sword-blood hot,
by that doomed one dyed, who in den of the moor
laid forlorn his life adown,
his heathen soul,—and hell received it.
Home then rode the hoary clansmen
from that merry journey, and many a youth,
on horses white, the hardy warriors,
back from the mere. Then Beowulf's glory
eager they echoed, and all averred
that from sea to sea, or south or north,
there was no other in earth's domain,
under vault of heaven, more valiant found,
of warriors none more worthy to rule!
(On their lord beloved they laid no slight,
gracious Hrothgar: a good king he!)
From time to time, the tried-in-battle
their gray steeds set to gallop amain,
and ran a race when the road seemed fair.
From time to time, a thane of the king,
who had made many vaunts, and was mindful of verses,
stored with sagas and songs of old,
bound word to word in well-knit rime,
welded his lay; this warrior soon
of Beowulf's quest right cleverly sang,
and artfully added an excellent tale,
in well-ranged words, of the warlike deeds
he had heard in saga of Sigemund.
Strange the story: he said it all,—
the Wælsing's wanderings wide, his struggles,
which never were told to tribes of men,
the feuds and the frauds, save to Fitela only,
when of these doings he deigned to speak,
uncle to nephew; as ever the twain
stood side by side in stress of war,
and multitude of the monster kind
they had felled with their swords. Of Sigemund grew,
when he passed from life, no little praise;
for the doughty-in-combat a dragon killed
that herded the hoard: under hoary rock
the atheling dared the deed alone,
fearful quest, nor was Fitela there.
Yet so it befell, his falchion pierced
that wondrous worm;[2]—on the wall it struck,
best blade; the dragon died in its blood.
Thus had the dread-one by daring achieved
over the ring-hoard to rule at will,
himself to pleasure; a sea-boat he loaded,
and bore on its bosom the beaming gold,
son of Wæls; the worm was consumed.
He had of all heroes the highest renown
among races of men, this refuge-of-warriors,
for deeds of daring that decked his name
since the hand and heart of Heremod
grew slack in battle. He, swiftly banished
to mingle with monsters at mercy of foes,
to death was betrayed; for torrents of sorrow
had lamed him too long; a load of care
to earls and athelings all he proved.
Oft indeed, in earlier days,
for the warrior's wayfaring wise men mourned,
who had hoped of him help from harm and bale,
and had thought their sovran's son would thrive,
follow his father, his folk protect,
the hoard and the stronghold, heroes' land,
home of Scyldings.—But here, thanes said,
the kinsman of Hygelac kinder seemed
to all: the other was urged to crime!
And afresh to the race, the fallow roads
by swift steeds measured! The morning sun
was climbing higher. Clansmen hastened
to the high-built hall, those hardy-minded,
the wonder to witness. Warden of treasure,
crowned with glory, the king himself,
with stately band from the bride-bower strode;
and with him the queen and her crowd of maidens
measured the path to the mead-house fair.

XIV

Hrothgar spake,—to the hall he went,
stood by the steps, the steep roof saw,

[1]Sea or lake of the water monsters.

[2]Dragon.

garnished with gold, and Grendel's hand:—
"For the sight I see to the Sovran Ruler
be speedy thanks! A throng of sorrows
I have borne from Grendel; but God still works
wonder on wonder, the Warden-of-Glory.
It was but now that I never more
for woes that weighed on me waited help
long as I lived, when, laved in blood,
stood sword-gore-stained this stateliest house,—
widespread woe for wise men all,
who had no hope to hinder ever
foes infernal and fiendish sprites
from havoc in hall. This hero now,
by the Wielder's might, a work has done
that not all of us erst could ever do
by wile and wisdom. Lo, well can she say
whoso of women this warrior bore
among sons of men, if still she liveth,
that the God of the ages was good to her
in the birth of her bairn. Now, Beowulf, thee,
of heroes best, I shall heartily love
as mine own, my son; preserve thou ever
this kinship new: thou shalt never lack
wealth of the world that I wield as mine!
Full oft for less have I largess showered,
my precious hoard, on a punier man,
less stout in struggle. Thyself hast now
fulfilled such deeds, that thy fame shall endure
through all the ages. As ever he did,
well may the Wielder reward thee still!"
Beowulf spake, bairn of Ecgtheow:—
"This work of war most willingly
we have fought, this fight, and fearlessly dared
force of the foe. Fain, too, were I
hadst thou but seen himself, what time
the fiend in his trappings tottered to fall!
Swiftly, I thought, in strongest gripe
on his bed of death to bind him down,
that he in the hent of this hand of mine
should breathe his last: but he broke away.
Him I might not—the Maker willed not—
hinder from flight, and firm enough hold
the life-destroyer: too sturdy was he,
the ruthless, in running! For rescue, however,
he left behind him his hand in pledge,
arm and shoulder; nor aught of help
could the curséd one thus procure at all.
None the longer liveth he, loathsome fiend,
sunk in his sins, but sorrow holds him
tightly grasped in gripe of anguish,
in baleful bonds, where bide he must,
evil outlaw, such awful doom
as the Mighty Maker shall mete him out."

More silent seemed the son of Ecglaf[1]
in boastful speech of his battle-deeds,
since athelings all, through the earl's great prowess,
beheld that hand, on the high roof gazing,[2]
foeman's fingers,—the forepart of each
of the sturdy nails to steel was likest,—
heathen's "hand-spear," hostile warrior's
claw uncanny. 'Twas clear, they said,
that him no blade of the brave could touch,
how keen soever, or cut away
that battle-hand bloody from baneful foe.

XV

There was hurry and hest in Heorot now
for hands to bedeck it, and dense was the throng
of men and women the wine-hall to cleanse,
the guest-room to garnish. Gold-gay shone the hangings
that were wove on the wall, and wonders many
to delight each mortal that looks upon them.
Though braced within by iron bands,
that building bright was broken sorely;
rent were its hinges; the roof alone
held safe and sound, when, seared with crime,
the fiendish foe his flight essayed,
of life despairing.—No light thing that,
the flight for safety,—essay it who will!
Forced of fate, he shall find his way
to the refuge ready for race of man,
for soul-possessors, and sons of earth;
and there his body on bed of death
shall rest after revel.
Arrived was the hour
when to hall proceeded Healfdene's son:
the king himself would sit to banquet.
Ne'er heard I of host in haughtier throng
more graciously gathered round giver-of-rings!
Bowed then to bench those bearers-of-glory,
fain of the feasting. Featly received
many a mead-cup the mighty-in-spirit,
kinsmen who sat in the sumptuous hall,
Hrothgar and Hrothulf.[3] Heorot now
was filled with friends; the folk of Scyldings
ne'er yet had tried the traitor's deed.

To Beowulf gave the bairn of Healfdene
a gold-wove banner, guerdon of triumph,
broidered battle-flag, breastplate and helmet;
and a splendid sword was seen of many
borne to the brave one. Beowulf took
cup in hall: for such costly gifts
he suffered no shame in that soldier throng.
For I heard of few heroes, in heartier mood,
with four such gifts, so fashioned with gold,
on the ale-bench honoring others thus!

[1]Unferth, Beowulf's opponent in the word-combat.

[2]*I. e.*, Beowulf had placed Grendel's arm as high as he could reach over the door on the outside of the hall.

[3]Hrothgar's nephew.

O'er the roof of the helmet high, a ridge,
wound with wires, kept ward o'er the head,
lest the relict-of-files[1] should fierce invade,
sharp in the strife, when that shielded hero
should go to grapple against his foes.
Then the earls'-defense[2] on the floor bade lead
coursers eight, with carven head-gear,
adown the hall: one horse was decked
with a saddle all shining and set in jewels;
'twas the battle-seat of the best of kings,
when to play of swords the son of Healfdene
was fain to fare. Ne'er failed his valor
in the crush of combat when corpses fell.
To Beowulf over them both then gave
the refuge-of-Ingwines right and power,
o'er war-steeds and weapons: wished him joy of them.
Manfully thus the mighty prince,
hoard-guard for heroes, that hard fight repaid
with steeds and treasures contemned by none
who is willing to say the sooth aright.

XVI

And the lord of earls, to each that came
with Beowulf over the briny ways,
an heirloom there at the ale-bench gave,
precious gift; and the price bade pay
in gold for him whom Grendel erst
murdered,—and fain of them more had killed,
had not wisest God their Wyrd averted,
and the man's brave mood. The Maker then
ruled human kind, as here and now.
Therefore is insight always best,
and forethought of mind. How much awaits him
of lief and of loath, who long time here,
through days of warfare this world endures!

Then song and music mingled sounds
in the presence of Healfdene's head-of-armies
and harping was heard with the hero-lay
as Hrothgar's singer the hall-joy woke
along the mead-seats, making his song
of that sudden raid on the sons of Finn.[3]

Healfdene's hero, Hnæf the Scylding,
was fated to fall in the Frisian slaughter.
Hildeburh needed not hold in value
her enemies' honor! Innocent both
were the loved ones she lost at the linden-play,
bairn and brother; they bowed to fate,
stricken by spears; 'twas a sorrowful woman!
None doubted why the daughter of Hoc
bewailed her doom when dawning came,
and under the sky she saw them lying,
kinsmen murdered, where most she had kenned
of the sweets of the world! By war were swept, too,
Finn's own liegemen, and few were left;
in the parleying-place he could ply no longer
weapon, nor war could he wage on Hengest,
and rescue his remnant by right of arms
from the prince's thane. A pact he offered:
another dwelling the Danes should have,
hall and high-seat, and half the power
should fall to them in Frisian land;
and at the fee-gifts, Folcwald's son
day by day the Danes should honor,
the folk of Hengest favor with rings,
even as truly, with treasure and jewels,
with fretted gold, as his Frisian kin
he meant to honor in ale-hall there.
Pact of peace they plighted further
on both sides firmly. Finn to Hengest
with oath, upon honor, openly promised
that woful remnant, with wise-men's aid,
nobly to govern, so none of the guests
by word or work should warp the treaty,
or with malice of mind bemoan themselves
as forced to follow their fee-giver's slayer,
lordless men, as their lot ordained.
Should Frisian, moreover, with foeman's taunt,
that murderous hatred to mind recall,
then edge of the sword must seal his doom.
Oaths were given, and ancient gold
heaped from hoard.—The hardy Scylding,
battle-thane best,[4] on his balefire lay.
All on the pyre were plain to see
the gory sark, the gilded swine-crest,
boar of hard iron, and athelings many
slain by the sword: at the slaughter they fell.
It was Hildeburh's hest, at Hnæf's own pyre
the bairn of her body on brands to lay,
his bones to burn, on the balefire placed,
at his uncle's side. In sorrowful dirges
bewept them the woman: great wailing ascended.
Then wound up to welkin the wildest of death-fires,

[1]Sword. [2]Hrothgar.

[3]As with the story of Sigemund and Heremod above, the poet assumes that his readers know the tale of Finn and his feud, and so merely gives a summary. Gummere gives the following explanation: Finn, a Frisian chieftain, who nevertheless has a "castle" outside the Frisian border, marries Hildeburh, a Danish princess; and her brother, Hnæf, with many other Danes, pays Finn a visit. Relations between the two peoples have been strained before. Something starts the old feud anew; and the visitors are attacked in their quarters. Hnæf is killed; so is a son of Hildeburh. Many fall on both sides. Peace is patched up; a stately funeral is held; and the surviving visitors become in a way vassals or liegemen of Finn, going back with him to Frisia. So matters rest a while. Hengest is now leader of the Danes; but he is set upon revenge for his former lord, Hnæf. Probably he is killed in feud; but his clansmen, Guthlaf and Oslaf, gather at their home a force of sturdy Danes, come back to Frisia, storm Finn's stronghold, kill him, and carry back their kinswoman Hildeburh.

[4]Hnæf.

roared o'er the hillock: heads all were melted,
gashes burst, and blood gushed out
from bites[1] of the body. Balefire devoured,
greediest spirit, those spared not by war
out of either folk: their flower was gone.

XVII

Then hastened those heroes their home to see,
friendless, to find the Frisian land,
houses and high burg. Hengest still
through the death-dyed winter dwelt with Finn,
holding pact, yet of home he minded,
though powerless his ring-decked prow to drive
over the waters, now waves rolled fierce
lashed by the winds, or winter locked them
in icy fetters. Then fared another
year to men's dwellings, as yet they do,
the sunbright skies, that their season ever
duly await. Far off winter was driven;
fair lay earth's breast; and fain was the rover,
the guest, to depart, though more gladly he pondered
on wreaking his vengeance than roaming the deep,
and how to hasten the hot encounter
where sons of the Frisians were sure to be.
So he escaped not the common doom,
when Hun with "Lafing," the light-of-battle,
best of blades, his bosom pierced:
its edge was famed with the Frisian earls.
On fierce-heart Finn there fell likewise,
on himself at home, the horrid sword-death;
for Guthlaf and Oslaf of grim attack
had sorrowing told, from sea-ways landed,
mourning their woes. Finn's wavering spirit
bode not in breast. The burg was reddened
with blood of foemen, and Finn was slain,
king amid clansmen; the queen was taken.
To their ship the Scylding warriors bore
all the chattels the chieftain owned,
whatever they found in Finn's domain
of gems and jewels. The gentle wife
o'er paths of the deep to the Danes they bore,
led to her land.
The lay was finished,
the gleeman's song. Then glad rose the revel;
bench-joy brightened. Bearers draw
from their "wonder-vats" wine. Comes Wealhtheow forth,
under gold-crown goes where the good pair sit,
uncle and nephew, true each to the other one,
kindred in amity. Unferth the spokesman
at the Scylding lord's feet sat: men had faith in his spirit,
his keenness of courage, though kinsmen had found him
unsure at the sword-play. The Scylding queen spoke:
"Quaff of this cup, my king and lord,
breaker of rings, and blithe be thou,
gold-friend of men; to the Geats here speak
such words of mildness as man should use.
Be glad with thy Geats; of those gifts be mindful,
or near or far, which now thou hast.
Men say to me, as son thou wishest
yon hero to hold. Thy Heorot purged,
jewel-hall brightest, enjoy while thou canst,
with many a largess; and leave to thy kin
folk and realm when forth thou goest
to greet thy doom. For gracious I deem
my Hrothulf, willing to hold and rule
nobly our youths, if thou yield up first,
prince of Scyldings, thy part in the world.
I ween with good he will well requite
offspring of ours, when all he minds
that for him we did in his helpless days
of gift and grace to gain him honor!"
Then she turned to the seat where her sons were placed,
Hrethric and Hrothmund, with heroes' bairns,
young men together: the Geat, too, sat there,
Beowulf brave, the brothers between.

XVIII

A cup she gave him, with kindly greeting
and winsome words. Of wounden gold,
she offered, to honor him, arm-jewels twain,
corselet and rings, and of collars the noblest
that ever I knew the earth around.
Ne'er heard I so mighty, 'neath heaven's dome,
a hoard-gem of heroes, since Hama bore
to his bright-built burg the Brisings' necklace,
jewel and gem casket.—Jealousy fled he,
Eormenric's hate: chose help eternal.
Hygelac Geat, grandson of Swerting,
on the last of his raids this ring bore with him,
under his banner the booty defending,
the war-spoil warding; but Wyrd o'erwhelmed him
what time, in his daring, dangers he sought,
feud with Frisians. Fairest of gems
he bore with him over the beaker-of-waves,
sovran strong: under shield he died.
Fell the corpse of the king into keeping of Franks,
gear of the breast, and that gorgeous ring;
weaker warriors won the spoil,
after gripe of battle, from Geatland's lord,
and held the death-field.
Din rose in hall.
Wealhtheow spake amid warriors, and said:—
"This jewel enjoy in thy jocund youth,
Beowulf loved, these battle-weeds wear,

[1]From wounds.

a royal treasure, and richly thrive!
Preserve thy strength, and these striplings here
counsel in kindness: requital be mine.
Hast done such deeds, that for days to come
thou art famed among folk both far and near,
so wide as washeth the wave of Ocean
his windy walls. Through the ways of life
prosper, O prince! I pray for thee
rich possessions. To son of mine
be helpful in deed and uphold his joys!
Here every earl to the other is true,
mild of mood, to the master loyal!
Thanes are friendly, the throng obedient,
liegemen are reveling: list and obey!"
Went then to her place.—That was proudest of feasts;
flowed wine for the warriors. Wyrd they knew not,
destiny dire, and the doom to be seen
by many an earl when eve should come,
and Hrothgar homeward hasten away,
royal, to rest. The room was guarded
by an army of earls, as erst was done.
They bared the bench-boards; abroad they spread
beds and bolsters.—One beer-carouser
in danger of doom lay down in the hall.—
At their heads they set their shields of war,
bucklers bright; on the bench were there
over each atheling, easy to see,
the high battle-helmet, the haughty spear,
the corselet of rings. 'Twas their custom so
ever to be for battle prepared,
at home, or harrying, which it were,
even as oft as evil threatened
their sovran king.—They were clansmen good.

XIX

Then sank they to sleep. With sorrow one bought
his rest of the evening,—as ofttime had happened
when Grendel guarded that golden hall,
evil wrought, till his end drew nigh,
slaughter for sins. 'Twas seen and told
how an avenger survived the fiend,
as was learned afar. The livelong time
after that grim fight, Grendel's mother,
monster of women, mourned her woe.
She was doomed to dwell in the dreary waters,
cold sea-courses, since Cain cut down
with edge of the sword his only brother,
his father's offspring: outlawed he fled,
marked with murder, from men's delights,
warded the wilds.—There woke from him
such fate-sent ghosts as Grendel, who,
war-wolf horrid, at Heorot found
a warrior watching and waiting the fray,
with whom the grisly one grappled amain.
But the man remembered his mighty power
the glorious gift that God had sent him,
in his Maker's mercy put his trust
for comfort and help: so he conquered the foe,
felled the fiend, who fled abject,
reft of joy, to the realms of death,
mankind's foe. And his mother now,
gloomy and grim, would go that quest
of sorrow, the death of her son to avenge.
To Heorot came she, where helmeted Danes
slept in the hall. Too soon came back
old ills of the earls, when in she burst,
the mother of Grendel. Less grim, though, that terror,
e'en as terror of woman in war is less,
might of maid, than of men in arms
when, hammer-forgéd, the falchion hard,
sword gore-stained, through swine of the helm,
crested, with keen blade carves amain.
Then was in hall the hard-edge drawn,
the swords on the settles, and shields a-many
firm held in hand: nor helmet minded
nor harness of mail, whom that horror seized.
Haste was hers; she would hie afar
and save her life when the liegemen saw her.
Yet a single atheling up she seized
fast and firm, as she fled to the moor.
He was for Hrothgar of heroes the dearest,
of trusty vassals betwixt the seas,
whom she killed on his couch, a clansman famous,
in battle brave.—Nor was Beowulf there,
another house had been held apart,
after giving of gold, for the Geat renowned.—
Uproar filled Heorot; the hand all had viewed
blood-flecked, she bore with her; bale was returned,
dole in the dwellings: 'twas dire exchange
where Dane and Geat were doomed to give
the lives of loved ones. Long-tried king,
the hoary hero, at heart was sad
when he knew his noble no more lived,
and dead indeed was his dearest thane.
To his bower was Beowulf brought in haste,
dauntless victor. As daylight broke,
along with his earls the atheling lord,
with his clansmen, came, where the king abode
waiting to see if the Wielder-of-All
would turn this tale of trouble and woe.
Strode o'er floor the famed-in-strife,
with his hand-companions,—the hall resounded,—
wishing to greet the wise old king,
Ingwines' lord; he asked if the night
had passed in peace to the prince's mind.

XX

Hrothgar spake, helmet-of-Scyldings:—
"Ask not of pleasure! Pain is renewed

to Danish folk. Dead is Æschere,
of Yrmenlaf the elder brother,
my sage adviser and stay in council,
shoulder-comrade in stress of fight
when warriors clashed and we warded our heads,
hewed the helm-boars: hero famed
should be every earl as Æschere was!
But here in Heorot a hand hath slain him
of wandering death-sprite. I wot not whither,
proud of the prey, her path she took,
fain of her fill. The feud she avenged
that yesternight, unyieldingly,
Grendel in grimmest grasp thou killedst,—
seeing how long these liegemen mine
he ruined and ravaged. Reft of life,
in arms he fell. Now another comes,
keen and cruel, her kin to avenge,
faring far in feud of blood:
so that many a thane shall think, who e'er
sorrows in soul for that sharer of rings,
this is hardest of heart-bales. The hand lies low
that once was willing each wish to please.
Land-dwellers here and liegemen mine,
who house by those parts, I have heard relate
that such a pair they have sometimes seen,
march-stalkers mighty the moorland haunting,
wandering spirits: one of them seemed,
so far as my folk could fairly judge,
of womankind; and one, accursed,
in man's guise trod the misery-track
of exile, though huger than human bulk.
Grendel in days long gone they named him,
folk of the land; his father they knew not,
nor any brood that was born to him
of treacherous spirits. Untrod is their home;
by wolf-cliffs haunt they and windy headlands,
fenways fearful, where flows the stream
from mountains gliding to gloom of the rocks,
underground flood. Not far is it hence
in measure of miles that the mere expands,
and o'er it the frost-bound forest hanging,
sturdily rooted, shadows the wave.
By night is a wonder weird to see,
fire on the waters. So wise lived none
of the sons of men, to search those depths!
Nay, though the heath-rover, harried by dogs,
the horn-proud hart, this holt should seek,
long distance driven, his dear life first
on the brink he yields ere he brave the plunge
to hide his head: 'tis no happy place!
Thence the welter of waters washes up
wan to welkin when winds bestir
evil storms, and air grows dusk,
and the heavens weep. Now is help once more
with thee alone! The land thou knowst not,
place of fear, where thou findest out
that sin-flecked being. Seek if thou dare!
I will reward thee, for waging this fight,
with ancient treasure, as erst I did,
with winding gold, if thou winnest back."

XXI

Beowulf spake, bairn of Ecgtheow:
"Sorrow not, sage! It beseems us better
friends to avenge than fruitlessly mourn them.
Each of us all must his end abide
in the ways of the world; so win who may
glory ere death! When his days are told,
that is the warrior's worthiest doom.
Rise, O realm-warder! Ride we anon.
and mark the trail of the mother of Grendel.
No harbor shall hide her—heed my promise!—
enfolding of field or forested mountain
or floor of the flood, let her flee where she will!
But thou this day endure in patience,
as I ween thou wilt, thy woes each one."
Leaped up the graybeard: God he thanked,
mighty Lord, for the man's brave words.
For Hrothgar soon a horse was saddled
wave-maned steed. The sovran wise
stately rode on; his shield-armed men
followed in force. The footprints led
along the woodland, widely seen,
a path o'er the plain, where she passed, and trod
the murky moor; of men-at-arms
she bore the bravest and best one, dead,
him who with Hrothgar the homestead ruled.
On then went the atheling-born
o'er stone-cliffs steep and strait defiles,
narrow passes and unknown ways,
headlands sheer, and the haunts of the nicors.
Foremost he[1] fared, a few at his side
of the wiser men, the ways to scan,
till he found in a flash the forested hill
hanging over the hoary rock,
a woful wood: the waves below
were dyed in blood. The Danish men
had sorrow of soul, and for Scyldings all,
for many a hero, 'twas hard to bear,
ill for earls, when Æschere's head
they found by the flood on the foreland there.
Waves were welling, the warriors saw,
hot with blood; but the horn sang oft
battle-song bold. The band sat down,
and watched on the water worm-like things,
sea-dragons strange that sounded the deep,
and nicors that lay on the ledge of the ness[2]
—such as oft essay at hour of morn
on the road-of-sails their ruthless quest—
and sea-snakes and monsters. These started away,
swollen and savage that song to hear,
that war-horn's blast. The warden of Geats,

---

[1]Probably Hrothgar. [2]Cliff.

with bolt from bow, then balked of life,
of wave-work, one monster; amid its heart
went the keen war-shaft; in water it seemed
less doughty in swimming whom death had seized.
Swift on the billows, with boar-spears well
hooked and barbed, it was hard beset,
done to death and dragged on the headland,
wave-roamer wondrous. Warriors viewed the
grisly guest.
Then girt him Beowulf
in martial mail, nor mourned for his life.
His breastplate broad and bright of hues,
woven by hand, should the waters try;
well could it ward the warrior's body
that battle should break on his breast in vain
nor harm his heart by the hand of a foe.
And the helmet white that his head protected
was destined to dare the deeps of the flood,
through wave-whirl win: 'twas wound with chains,
decked with gold, as in days of yore
the weapon-smith worked it wondrously,
with swine-forms set it, that swords nowise,
brandished in battle, could bite that helm.
Nor was that the meanest of mighty helps
which Hrothgar's orator[1] offered at need:
"Hrunting" they named the hilted sword,
of old-time heirlooms easily first;
iron was its edge, all etched with poison,
with battle-blood hardened, nor blenched it at fight
in hero's hand who held it ever,
on paths of peril prepared to go
to folkstead[2] of foes. Not first time this
it was destined to do a daring task.
For he bore not in mind, the bairn of Ecglaf
sturdy and strong, that speech he had made,
drunk with wine, now this weapon he lent
to a stouter swordsman. Himself, though, durst not
under welter of waters wager his life
as loyal liegeman. So lost he his glory,
honor of earls. With the other not so,
who girded him now for the grim encounter.

XXII

Beowulf spake, bairn of Ecgtheow:—
"Have mind, thou honored offspring of Healfdene,
gold-friend of men, now I go on this quest,
sovran wise, what once was said:
if in thy cause it came that I
should lose my life, thou wouldst loyal bide
to me, though fallen, in father's place!
Be guardian, thou, to this group of my thanes,
my warrior-friends, if War should seize me;

[1]Unferth. [2]Battle-place.

and the goodly gifts thou gavest me,
Hrothgar beloved, to Hygelac send!
Geatland's king may ken by the gold,
Hrethel's son see, when he stares at the treasure,
that I got me a friend for goodness famed,
and joyed while I could in my jewel-bestower.
And let Unferth wield this wondrous sword,
earl far-honored, this heirloom precious,
hard of edge: with Hrunting I
seek doom of glory, or Death shall take me."

After these words the Weder-Geat lord
boldly hastened, biding never
answer at all: and ocean floods
closed o'er the hero. Long while of the day
fled ere he felt the floor of the sea.
Soon found the fiend who the flood-domain
sword-hungry held these hundred winters,
greedy and grim, that some guest from above,
some man, was raiding her monster-realm.
She grasped out for him with grisly claws,
and the warrior seized; yet scathed she not
his body hale; the breastplate hindered,
as she strove to shatter the sark of war,
the linkéd harness, with loathsome hand.
Then bore this brine-wolf, when bottom she touched,
the lord of rings to the lair she haunted,
whiles vainly he strove, though his valor held,
weapon to wield against wondrous monsters
that sore beset him; sea-beasts many
tried with fierce tusks to tear his mail,
and swarmed on the stranger. But soon he marked
he was now in some hall, he knew not which,
where water never could work him harm,
nor through the roof could reach him ever
fangs of the flood. Firelight he saw,
beams of a blaze that brightly shone.
Then the warrior was ware of that wolf-of-the-deep,
mere-wife monstrous. For mighty stroke
he swung his blade, and the blow withheld not.
Then sang on her head that seemly blade
its war-song wild. But the warrior found
the light-of-battle[3] was loath to bite,
to harm the heart: its hard edge failed
the noble at need, yet had known of old
strife hand to hand, and had helmets cloven,
doomed men's fighting-gear. First time, this,
for the gleaming blade that its glory fell.
Firm still stood, nor failed in valor,
heedful of high deeds, Hygelac's kinsman;
flung away fretted sword, featly jeweled,
the angry earl; on earth it lay
steel-edged and stiff. His strength he trusted,

[3]The sword, Hrunting.

hand-gripe of might. So man shall do
whenever in war he weens to earn him
lasting fame, nor fears for his life!
Seized then by shoulder, shrank not from combat,
the Geatish war-prince Grendel's mother.
Flung then the fierce one, filled with wrath,
his deadly foe, that she fell to ground.
Swift on her part she paid him back
with grisly grasp, and grappled with him.
Spent with struggle, stumbled the warrior,
fiercest of fighting-men, fell adown.
On the hall-guest she hurled herself, hent her short sword,
broad and brown-edged, the bairn to avenge,
The sole-born son.—On his shoulder lay
braided breast-mail, barring death,
withstanding entrance of edge or blade.
Life would have ended for Ecgtheow's son,
under wide earth for that earl of Geats,
had his armor of war not aided him,
battle-net hard, and holy God
wielded the victory, wisest Maker.
The Lord of Heaven allowed his cause;
and easily rose the earl erect.

XXIII

'Mid the battle-gear saw he a blade triumphant,
old-sword of Eotens,[1] with edge of proof,
warriors' heirloom, weapon unmatched,
—save only 'twas more than other men
to bandy-of-battle could bear at all—
as the giants had wrought it, ready and keen.
Seized then its chain-hilt the Scyldings' chieftain,
bold and battle-grim, brandished the sword,
reckless of life, and so wrathfully smote
that it gripped her neck and grasped her hard,
her bone-rings breaking; the blade pierced through
that fated-one's flesh: to floor she sank.
Bloody the blade: he was blithe of his deed.
Then blazed forth light. 'Twas bright within
as when from the sky there shines unclouded
heaven's candle. The hall he scanned.
By the wall then went he; his weapon raised
high by its hilts the Hygelac-thane,
angry and eager. That edge was not useless
to the warrior now. He wished with speed
Grendel to guerdon for grim raids many,
for the war he waged on Western-Danes
oftener far than an only time,
when of Hrothgar's hearth-companions
he slew in slumber, in sleep devoured,
fifteen men of the folk of Danes,
and as many others outward bore,
his horrible prey. Well paid for that
the wrathful prince! For now prone he saw
Grendel stretched there, spent with war,
spoiled of life, so scathed had left him
Heorot's battle. The body sprang far
when after death it endured the blow,
sword-stroke savage, that severed its head.

Soon, then, saw the sage companions
who waited with Hrothgar, watching the flood,
that the tossing waters turbid grew,
blood-stained the mere. Old men together,
hoary-haired, of the hero spake;
the warrior would not, they weened, again,
proud of conquest, come to seek
their mighty master. To many it seemed
the wolf-of-the-waves had won his life.
The ninth hour came. The noble Scyldings
left the headland; homeward went
the gold-friend of men.[2] But the guests sat on,
stared at the surges, sick in heart,
and wished, yet weened not, their winsome
lord again to see.

Now that sword began,
from blood of the fight, in battle-droppings,
war-blade, to wane: 'Twas a wondrous thing
that all of it melted as ice is wont
when frosty fetters the Father loosens,
unwinds the wave-bonds, wielding all
seasons and times: the true God he!

Nor took from that dwelling the duke of the Geats
precious things, though a plenty he saw,
save only the head and that hilt withal
blazoned with jewels: the blade had melted,
burned was the bright sword, her blood was so hot,
so poisoned the hell-sprite who perished within there.
Soon he was swimming who safe saw in combat
downfall of demons; up-dove through the flood.
The clashing waters were cleansèd now,
waste of waves, where the wandering fiend
her life-days left and this lapsing world.
Swam then to strand the sailors'-refuge,
sturdy-in-spirit, of sea-booty glad,
of burden brave he bore with him.
Went then to greet him, and God they thanked,
the thane-band choice of their chieftain blithe,
that safe and sound they could see him again.
Soon from the hardy one helmet and armor
deftly they doffed: now drowsed the mere,
water 'neath welkin, with war-blood stained.

Forth they fared by the footpaths thence,
merry at heart the highways measured,
well-known roads. Courageous men
carried the head from the cliff by the sea,

[1]Giants.

[2]Hrothgar.

an arduous task for all the band,
the firm in fight, since four were needed
on the shaft-of-slaughter[1] strenuously
to bear to the gold-hall Grendel's head.
So presently to the palace there
foemen fearless, fourteen Geats,
marching came. Their master-of-clan
mighty amid them the meadow-ways trod.
Strode then within the sovran thane
fearless in fight, of fame renowned,
hardy hero, Hrothgar to greet.
And next by the hair into hall was borne
Grendel's head, where the henchmen were drinking,
an awe to clan and queen alike,
a monster of marvel: the men looked on.

XXIV

Beowulf spake, bairn of Ecgtheow:—
"Lo, now, this sea-booty, son of Healfdene,
Lord of Scyldings, we've lustily brought thee,
sign of glory; thou seest it here.
Not lightly did I with my life escape!
In war under water this work I essayed
with endless effort; and even so
my strength had been lost had the Lord not shielded me.
Not a whit could I with Hrunting do
in work of war, though the weapon is good;
yet a sword the Sovran of Men vouchsafed me
to spy on the wall there, in splendor hanging,
old, gigantic,—how oft He guides
the friendless wight!—and I fought with that brand,
felling in fight, since fate was with me,
the house's wardens. That war-sword then
all burned, bright blade, when the blood gushed o'er it,
battle-sweat hot; but the hilt I brought back
from my foes. So avenged I their fiendish deeds,
death-fall of Danes, as was due and right.
And this is my hest, that in Heorot now
safe thou canst sleep with thy soldier band,
and every thane of all thy folk
both old and young; no evil fear,
Scyldings' lord, from that side again,
aught ill for thy earls, as erst thou must!"
Then the golden hilt, for that gray-haired leader,
hoary hero, in hand was laid,
giant-wrought, old. So owned and enjoyed it
after downfall of devils, the Danish lord,
wonder-smiths' work, since the world was rid
of that grim-souled fiend, the foe of God,
murder-marked, and his mother as well.
Now it passed into power of the people's king,
best of all that the oceans bound
who have scattered their gold o'er Scandia's isle.
Hrothgar spake—the hilt he viewed,
heirloom old, where was etched the rise
of that far-off fight when the floods o'erwhelmed,
raging waves, the race of giants
(fearful their fate!), a folk estranged
from God Eternal: whence guerdon due
in that waste of waters the Wielder paid them.
So on the guard of shining gold
in runic staves it was rightly said
for whom the serpent-traced sword was wrought,
best of blades, in bygone days,
and the hilt well wound.—The wise-one spake,
son of Healfdene; silent were all:—
"Lo, so may he say who sooth and right
follows 'mid folk, of far times mindful,
a land-warden old, that this earl belongs
to the better breed! So, borne aloft,
thy fame must fly, O friend my Beowulf,
far and wide o'er folksteads many. Firmly thou shalt all maintain,
mighty strength with mood of wisdom. Love of mine will I assure thee,
as, awhile ago, I promised: thou shalt prove a stay in future,
in far-off years, to folk of thine,
to the heroes a help. Was not Heremod thus
to offspring of Ecgwela, Honor-Scyldings,
nor grew for their grace, but for grisly slaughter,
for doom of death to the Danishmen.
He slew, wrath-swollen, his shoulder-comrades,
companions at board! So he passed alone,
chieftain haughty, from human cheer.
Though him the Maker with might endowed,
delights of power, and uplifted high
above all men, yet blood-fierce his mind,
his breast-hoard, grew; no bracelets gave he
to Danes as was due; he endured all joyless
strain of struggle and stress of woe,
long feud with his folk. Here find thy lesson!
Of virtue advise thee! This verse I have said for thee,
wise from lapsed winters. Wondrous seems
how to sons of men Almighty God
in the strength of His spirit sendeth wisdom,
estate, high station: He swayeth all things.
Whiles He letteth right lustily fare
the heart of the hero of high-born race,—
in seat ancestral assigns him bliss,
his folk's sure fortress in fee to hold,
puts in his power great parts of the earth,
empire so ample, that end of it
this wanter-of-wisdom weeneth none.
So he waxes in wealth; nowise can harm him
illness or age; no evil cares

[1] Spear.

shadow his spirit; no sword-hate threatens
from ever an enemy: all the world
wends at his will; no worse he knoweth,
till all within him obstinate pride
waxes and wakes while the warden slumbers,
the spirit's sentry; sleep is too fast
which masters his might, and the murderer nears,
stealthily shooting the shafts from his bow!

XXV

"Under harness his heart then is hit indeed
by sharpest shafts; and no shelter avails
from foul behest of the hellish fiend.
Him seems too little what long he possessed.
Greedy and grim, no golden rings
he gives for his pride; the promised future
forgets he and spurns, with all God has sent him,
Wonder-Wielder, of wealth and fame.
Yet in the end it ever comes
that the frame of the body fragile yields,
fated falls; and there follows another
who joyously the jewels divides,
the royal riches, nor recks of his forebear.
Ban, then, such baleful thoughts, Beowulf dearest,
best of men, and the better part choose,
profit eternal; and temper thy pride,
warrior famous! The flower of thy might
lasts now a while: but erelong it shall be
that sickness or sword thy strength shall minish,
or fang of fire, or flooding billow,
or bite of blade, or brandished spear,
or odious age; or the eyes' clear beam
wax dull and darken: Death even thee
in haste shall o'erwhelm, thou hero of war!
So the Ring-Danes these half-years a hundred I ruled,
wielded 'neath welkin, and warded them bravely
from mighty-ones many o'er middle-earth,
from spear and sword, till it seemed for me
no foe could be found under fold of the sky.
Lo, sudden the shift! To me seated secure
came grief for joy when Grendel began
to harry my home, the hellish foe;
for those ruthless raids, unresting I suffered
heart-sorrow heavy. Heaven be thanked,
Lord Eternal, for life extended
that I on this head all hewn and bloody,
after long evil, with eyes may gaze!
—Go to the bench now! Be glad at banquet,
warrior worthy! A wealth of treasure
at dawn of day, be dealt between us!"
Glad was the Geats' lord, going betimes
to seek his seat, as the Sage commanded.
Afresh, as before, for the famed-in-battle,
for the band of the hall, was a banquet dight
nobly anew. The Night-Helm darkened
dusk o'er the drinkers.
The doughty ones rose:
for the hoary-headed would hasten to rest,
agéd Scylding; and eager the Geat,
shield-fighter sturdy, for sleeping yearned.
Him wander-weary, warrior-guest
from far, a hall-thane heralded forth,
who by custom courtly cared for all
needs of a thane as in those old days
warrior-wanderers wont to have.
So slumbered the stout-heart. Stately the hall
rose gabled and gilt where the guest slept on
till a raven black the rapture-of-heaven[1]
blithe-heart boded. Bright came flying
shine after shadow. The swordsmen hastened,
athelings all were eager homeward
forth to fare; and far from thence
the great-hearted guest would guide his keel.
Bade then the hardy-one Hrunting be brought
to the son of Ecglaf, the sword bade him take,
excellent iron, and uttered his thanks for it,
quoth that he counted it keen in battle,
"war-friend" winsome: with words he slandered not
edge of the blade: 'twas a big-hearted man!
Now eager for parting and armed at point
warriors waited, while went to his host
that Darling of Danes. The doughty atheling
to high-seat hastened and Hrothgar greeted.

XXVI

Beowulf spake, bairn of Ecgtheow:—
"Lo, we seafarers say our will,
far-come men, that we fain would seek
Hygelac now. We here have found
hosts to our heart: thou hast harbored us well.
If ever on earth I am able to win me
more of thy love, O lord of men,
aught anew, than I now have done,
for work of war I am willing still!
If it come to me ever across the seas
that neighbor foemen annoy and fright thee,—
as they that hate thee erewhile have used,—
thousands then of thanes I shall bring,
heroes to help thee. Of Hygelac I know,
ward of his folk, that, though few his years,
the lord of the Geats will give me aid
by word and by work, that well I may serve thee,
wielding the war-wood to win thy triumph
and lending thee might when thou lackest men.
If thy Hrethric should come to court of Geats,

[1]The sun.

a sovran's son, he will surely there
find his friends. A far-off land
each man should visit who vaunts him brave."
Him then answering, Hrothgar spake:—
"These words of thine the wisest God
sent to thy soul! No sager counsel
from so young in years e'er yet have I heard.
Thou art strong of main and in mind art wary,
art wise in words! I ween indeed
if ever it hap that Hrethel's heir[1]
by spear be seized, by sword-grim battle,
by illness or iron, thine elder and lord,
people's leader,—and life be thine,—
no seemlier man will the Sea-Geats find
at all to choose for their chief and king,
for hoard-guard of heroes, if hold thou wilt
thy kinsman's kingdom! Thy keen mind pleases me
the longer the better, Beowulf loved!
Thou hast brought it about that both our peoples,
sons of the Geat and Spear-Dane folk,
shall have mutual peace, and from murderous strife,
such as once they waged, from war refrain.
Long as I rule this realm so wide,
let our hoards be common, let heroes with gold
each other greet o'er the gannet's-bath,[2]
and the ringed-prow bear o'er rolling waves
tokens of love. I trow my landfolk
towards friend and foe are firmly joined,
and honor they keep in the olden way."
To him in the hall, then, Healfdene's son
gave treasures twelve, and the trust-of-earls
bade him fare with the gifts to his folk beloved,
hale to his home, and in haste return.
Then kissed the king of kin renowned,
Scylding's chieftain, that choicest thane,
and fell on his neck. Fast flowed the tears
of the hoary-headed. Heavy with winters,
he had chances twain,[3] but he clung to this,—
that each should look on the other again,
and hear him in hall. Was this hero so dear to him,
his breast's wild billows he banned in vain;
safe in his soul a secret longing,
locked in his mind, for that lovéd man
burned in his blood. Then Beowulf strode,
glad of his gold-gifts, the grass-plot o'er,
warrior blithe. The wave-roamer bode
riding at anchor, its owner awaiting.
As they hastened onward, Hrothgar's gift
they lauded at length.—'Twas a lord unpeered,
every way blameless, till age had broken
—it spareth no mortal—his splendid might.

[1]Hygelac. [2]The sea.
[3]*I. e.*, he might or might not see Beowulf again.

XXVII

Came now to ocean the ever-courageous
hardy henchmen, their harness bearing,
woven war-sarks. The warden marked,
trusty as ever, the earl's return.
From the height of the hill no hostile words
reached the guests as he rode to greet them;
but "Welcome!" he called to that Weder clan
as the sheen-mailed spoilers to ship marched on.
Then on the strand, with steeds and treasure
and armor their roomy and ring-dight ship
was heavily laden: high its mast
rose over Hrothgar's hoarded gems.
A sword to the boat-guard Beowulf gave,
mounted with gold; on the mead-bench since
he was better esteemed, that blade possessing,
heirloom old.—Their ocean-keel boarding,
they drove through the deep, and Daneland left.
A sea-cloth was set, a sail with ropes,
firm to the mast; the flood-timbers moaned;[4]
nor did wind over billows that wave-swimmer blow
across from her course. The craft sped on,
foam-necked it floated forth o'er the waves,
keel firm-bound over briny currents,
till they got them sight of the Geatish cliffs,
home-known headlands. High the boat,
stirred by winds, on the strand updrove.
Helpful at haven the harbor-guard stood,
who long already for loved companions
by the water had waited and watched afar.
He bound to the beach the broad-bosomed ship
with anchor-bands, lest ocean-billows
that trusty timber should tear away.
Then Beowulf bade them bear the treasure,
gold and jewels; no journey far
was it thence to go to the giver of rings,
Hygelac Hrethling: at home he dwelt
by the sea-wall close, himself and clan.
Haughty that house, a hero the king,
high the hall, and Hygd[5] right young,
wise and wary, though winters few
in those fortress walls she had found a home,
Hæreth's daughter. Nor humble her ways,
nor grudged she gifts to the Geatish men,
of precious treasure. Not Thryth's pride showed she,
folk-queen famed, or that fell deceit.
Was none so daring that durst make bold
(save her lord alone) of the liegemen dear
that lady full in the face to look,
but forgéd fetters he found his lot,
bonds of death! And brief the respite;

[4]From the boat's speed. [5]Hygelac's queen.

soon as they seized him, his sword-doom was spoken,
and the burnished blade a baleful murder
proclaimed and closed. No queenly way
for woman to practice, though peerless she,
that the weaver-of-peace[1] from warrior dear
by wrath and lying his life should reave!
But. Hemming's kinsman hindered this.—
For over their ale men also told
that of these folk-horrors fewer she wrought,
onslaughts of evil, after she went,
gold-decked bride, to the brave young prince,
atheling haughty, and Offa's hall
o'er the fallow flood at her father's bidding
safely sought, where since she prospered,
royal, thronéd, rich in goods,
fain of the fair life fate had sent her,
and leal in love to the lord of warriors.
He, of all heroes I heard of ever
from sea to sea, of the sons of earth,
most excellent seemed. Hence Offa was praised
for his fighting and feeing by far-off men,
the spear-bold warrior; wisely he ruled
over his empire. Eomer woke to him,
help of heroes, Hemming's kinsman,
grandson of Garmund, grim in war.

XXVIII

Hastened the hardy one, henchmen with him,
sandy strand of the sea to tread
and widespread ways. The world's great candle,
sun shone from south. They strode along
with sturdy steps to the spot they knew
where the battle-king young, his burg within,
slayer of Ongentheow, shared the rings,
shelter-of-heroes. To Hygelac
Beowulf's coming was quickly told,—
that there in the court the clansmen's refuge,
the shield-companion sound and alive,
hale from the hero-play homeward strode.
With haste in the hall, by highest order,
room for the rovers was readily made.
By his sovran he sat, come safe from battle,
kinsman by kinsman. His kindly lord
he first had greeted in gracious form,
with manly words. The mead dispensing,
came through the high hall Hæreth's daughter,
winsome to warriors, wine-cup bore
to the hands of the heroes. Hygelac then
his comrade fairly with question plied
in the lofty hall, sore longing to know
what manner of sojourn the Sea-Geats made.
"What came of thy quest, my kinsman Beowulf,
when thy yearnings suddenly swept thee yonder

[1]Wife.

battle to seek o'er the briny sea,
combat in Heorot? Hrothgar couldst thou
aid at all, the honored chief,
in his wide-known woes? With waves of care
my sad heart seethed; I sore mistrusted
my loved one's venture: long I begged thee
by no means to seek that slaughtering monster,
but suffer the South-Danes to settle their feud
themselves with Grendel. Now God be thanked
that safe and sound I can see thee now!"
Beowulf spake, the bairn of Ecgtheow:—
"'Tis known and unhidden, Hygelac Lord,
to many men, that meeting of ours,
struggle grim between Grendel and me,
which we fought on the field where full too many
sorrows he wrought for the Scylding-Victors,
evils unending. These all I avenged.
No boast can be from breed of Grendel,
any on earth, for that uproar at dawn,
from the longest-lived of the loathsome race
in fleshly fold!—But first I went
Hrothgar to greet in the hall of gifts,
where Healfdene's kinsman high-renowned,
soon as my purpose was plain to him,
assigned me a seat by his son and heir.
The liegemen were lusty; my life-days never
such merry men over mead in hall
have I heard under heaven! The high-born queen,
people's peace-bringer, passed through the hall,
cheered the young clansmen, clasps of gold,
ere she sought her seat, to sundry gave.
Oft to the heroes Hrothgar's daughter,
to earls in turn, the ale-cup tendered,—
she whom I heard these hall-companions
Freawaru name, when fretted gold
she proffered the warriors. Promised is she,
gold-decked maid, to the glad son of Froda.
Sage this seems to the Scyldings'-friend,
kingdom's-keeper: he counts it wise
the woman to wed so and ward off feud,
store of slaughter. But seldom ever
when men are slain, does the murder-spear sink
but briefest while, though the bride be fair!
"Nor haply will like it the Heathobard lord,
and as little each of his liegemen all,
when a thane of the Danes, in that doughty throng,
goes with the lady along their hall,
and on him the old-time heirlooms glisten
hard and ring-decked, Heathobard's treasure,
weapons that once they wielded fair
until they lost at the linden-play[2]

[2]Battle.

liegeman leal and their lives as well.
Then, over the ale, on this heirloom gazing,
some ash-wielder old who has all in mind
that spear-death of men,—he is stern of mood,
heavy at heart,—in the hero young
tests the temper and tries the soul
and war-hate wakens, with words like these:—
Canst thou not, comrade, ken that sword
which to the fray thy father carried
in his final feud, 'neath the fighting-mask,
dearest of blades, when the Danish slew him
and wielded the war-place on Withergild's fall,
after havoc of heroes, those hardy Scyldings?
Now, the son of a certain slaughtering Dane,
proud of his treasure, paces this hall,
joys in the killing, and carries the jewel[1]
that rightfully ought to be owned by thee!
Thus he urges and eggs him all the time
with keenest words, till occasion offers
that Freawaru's thane, for his father's deed,
after bite of brand in his blood must slumber,
losing his life; but that liegeman flies
living away, for the land he kens.
And thus be broken on both their sides
oaths of the earls, when Ingeld's breast
wells with war-hate, and wife-love now
after the care-billows cooler grows.
"So I hold not high the Heathobards' faith
due to the Danes, or their during love
and pact of peace.—But I pass from that,
turning to Grendel, O giver-of-treasure,
and saying in full how the fight resulted,
hand-fray of heroes. When heaven's jewel
had fled o'er far fields, that fierce sprite came,
night-foe savage, to seek us out
where safe and sound we sentried the hall.
To Hondscio then was that harassing deadly,
his fall there was fated. He first was slain,
girded warrior. Grendel on him
turned murderous mouth, on our mighty kinsman,
and all of the brave man's body devoured.
Yet none the earlier, empty-handed,
would the bloody-toothed murderer, mindful of bale,
outward go from the gold-decked hall:
but me he attacked in his terror of might,
with greedy hand grasped me. A glove[2] hung by him
wide and wondrous, wound with bands;
and in artful wise it all was wrought,
by devilish craft, of dragon-skins.
Me therein, an innocent man,
the fiendish foe was fain to thrust
with many another. He might not so,
when I all angrily upright stood.
'Twere long to relate how that land-destroyer
I paid in kind for his cruel deeds;
yet there, my prince, this people of thine
got fame by my fighting. He fled away,
and a little space his life preserved;
but there stayed behind him his stronger hand
left in Heorot; heartsick thence
on the floor of the ocean that outcast fell.
Me for this struggle the Scyldings'-friend
paid in plenty with plates of gold,
with many a treasure, when morn had come
and we all at the banquet-board sat down.
Then was song and glee. The gray-haired Scylding
much tested, told of the times of yore.
Whiles the hero his harp bestirred,
wood-of-delight; now lays he chanted
of sooth and sadness, or said aright
legends of wonder, the wide-hearted king;
or for years of his youth he would yearn at times,
for strength of old struggles, now stricken with age,
hoary hero: his heart surged full
when, wise with winters, he wailed their flight.
Thus in the hall the whole of that day
at ease we feasted, till fell o'er earth
another night. Anon full ready
in greed of vengeance, Grendel's mother
set forth all doleful. Dead was her son
through war-hate of Weders; now, woman monstrous,
with fury fell a foeman she slew,
avenged her offspring. From Æschere old,
loyal councilor, life was gone;
nor might they e'en when morning broke,
those Danish people, their death-done comrade
burn with brands, on balefire lay
the man they mourned. Under mountain stream
she had carried the corpse with cruel hands.
For Hrothgar that was the heaviest sorrow
of all that had laden the lord of his folk.
The leader then, by thy life, besought me
(sad was his soul) in the sea-waves' coil
to play the hero and hazard my being
for glory of prowess: my guerdon he pledged.
I then in the waters—'tis widely known—
that sea-floor-guardian savage found.
Hand-to-hand there a while we struggled;
billows welled blood; in the briny hall
her head I hewed with a hardy blade
from Grendel's mother,—and gained my life,
though not without danger. My doom was not yet.
Then the haven-of-heroes, Healfdene's son,
gave me in guerdon great gifts of price.

[1] Sword. [2] *I. e.*, a kind of sack.

XXXI[1]

"So held this king to the customs old,
that I wanted for nought in the wage I gained,
the meed of my might; he made me gifts,
Healfdene's heir, for my own disposal.
Now to thee, my prince, I proffer them all,
gladly give them. Thy grace alone
can find me favor. Few indeed
have I of kinsmen, save, Hygelac, thee!"
Then he bade them bear him the boar-head standard,
the battle-helm high, and breastplate gray,
the splendid sword; then spake in form:—
"Me this war-gear the wise old prince,
Hrothgar, gave, and his hest he added,
that its story be straightway said to thee.—
A while it was held by Heorogar king,
for long time lord of the land of Scyldings;
yet not to his son the sovran left it,
to daring Heoroweard,—dear as he was to him,
his harness of battle.—Well hold thou it all!"
And I heard that soon passed o'er the path of this treasure,
all apple-fallow, four good steeds,
each like the others; arms and horses
he gave to the king. So should kinsmen be,
not weave one another the net of wiles,
or with deep-hid treachery death contrive
for neighbor and comrade. His nephew was ever
by hardy Hygelac held full dear,
and each kept watch o'er the other's weal.
I heard, too, the necklace to Hygd he presented,
wonder-wrought treasure, which Wealhtheow gave him,
sovran's daughter: three steeds he added,
slender and saddle-gay. Since such gift
the gem gleamed bright on the breast of the queen.
Thus showed his strain the son of Ecgtheow
as a man remarked for mighty deeds
and acts of honor. At ale he slew not
comrade or kin; nor cruel his mood,
though of sons of earth his strength was greatest,
a glorious gift that God had sent
the splendid leader. Long was he spurned,
and worthless by Geatish warriors held;
him at mead the master-of-clans
failed full oft to favor at all.
Slack and shiftless the strong men deemed him,
profitless prince; but payment came,
to the warrior honored, for all his woes.—
Then the bulwark-of-earls bade bring within,
hardy chieftain, Hrethel's heirloom
garnished with gold: no Geat e'er knew
in shape of a sword a statelier prize.
The brand he laid in Beowulf's lap;
and of hides assigned him seven thousand,
with house and high-seat. They held in common
land alike by their line of birth,
inheritance, home: but higher the king
because of his rule o'er the realm itself.

Now further it fell with the flight of years,
with harryings horrid, that Hygelac perished,
and Heardred, too, by hewing of swords
under the shield-wall slaughtered lay,
when him at the van of his victor-folk
sought hardy heroes, Heatho-Scilfings,
in arms o'erwhelming Hereric's nephew.
Then Beowulf came as king this broad
realm to wield; and he ruled it well
fifty winters,[2] a wise old prince,
warding his land, until One began
in the dark of night, a Dragon, to rage.
In the grave on the hill a hoard it guarded,
in the stone-barrow steep. A strait path reached it,
unknown to mortals. Some man, however,
came by chance that cave within
to the heathen hoard. In hand he took
a golden goblet, nor gave he it back,
stole with it away, while the watcher slept,
by thievish wiles: for the warden's wrath
prince and people must pay betimes!

XXXII

That way he went with no will of his own,
in danger of life, to the dragon's hoard,
but for pressure of peril, some prince's thane.
He fled in fear the fatal scourge,
seeking shelter, a sinful man,
and entered in. At the awful sight
tottered that guest, and terror seized him;
yet the wretched fugitive rallied anon
from fright and fear ere he fled away,
and took the cup from that treasure-hoard.
Of such besides there was store enough,
heirlooms old, the earth below,
which some earl forgotten, in ancient years,
left the last of his lofty race,
heedfully there had hidden away,
dearest treasure. For death of yore
had hurried all hence; and he alone
left to live, the last of the clan,
weeping his friends, yet wished to bide
warding the treasure, his one delight,
though brief his respite. The barrow, new-ready,
to strand and sea-waves stood anear,

[1]Sections XXIX and XXX are not indicated in the original.

[2]Not to be taken literally. What is really meant is, "for a long time."

hard by the headland, hidden and closed;
there laid within it his lordly heirlooms
and heapéd hoard of heavy gold
that warden of rings. Few words he spake:—
"Now hold thou, earth, since heroes may not,
what earls have owned! Lo, erst from thee
brave men brought it! But battle-death seized
and cruel killing my clansmen all,
robbed them of life and a liegeman's joys.
None have I left to lift the sword,
or to cleanse the carven cup of price,
beaker bright. My brave are gone.
And the helmet hard, all haughty with gold,
shall part from its plating. Polishers sleep
who could brighten and burnish the battle-mask;
and those weeds of war that were wont to brave
over bicker of shields the bite of steel
rust with their bearer. The ringéd mail
fares not far with famous chieftain,
at side of hero! No harp's delight,
no glee-wood's gladness! No good hawk now
flies through the hall! Nor horses fleet
stamp in the burgstead! Battle and death
the flower of my race have reft away."
Mournful of mood, thus he moaned his woe,
alone, for them all, and unblithe wept
by day and by night, till death's fell wave
o'erwhelmed his heart. His hoard-of-bliss
that old ill-doer open found,
who, blazing at twilight the barrows haunteth,
naked foe-dragon flying by night
folded in fire: the folk of earth
dread him sore. 'Tis his doom to seek
hoard in the graves, and heathen gold
to watch, many-wintered: nor wins he thereby!
Powerful this plague-of-the-people thus
held the house of the hoard in earth
three hundred winters; till One aroused
wrath in his breast, to the ruler bearing
that costly cup and the king implored
for bond of peace. So the barrow was plundered,
borne off was booty. His boon was granted
that wretched man; and his ruler saw
first time what was fashioned in far-off days.
When the dragon awoke, new woe was kindled.
O'er the stone he snuffed. The stark-heart found
footprint of foe who so far had gone
in his hidden craft by the creature's head.—
So may the undoomed easily flee
evils and exile, if only he gain
the grace of The Wielder!—That warden of gold
o'er the ground went seeking, greedy to find
the man who wrought him such wrong in sleep.
Savage and burning, the barrow he circled
all without; nor was any there,
none in the waste. . . . Yet war he desired,
was eager for battle. The barrow he entered,
sought the cup, and discovered soon
that some one of mortals had searched his treasure,
his lordly gold. The guardian waited
ill-enduring till evening came;
boiling with wrath was the barrow's keeper,
and fain with flame the foe to pay
for the dear cup's loss.—Now day was fled
as the worm had wished. By its wall no more
was it glad to bide, but burning flew
folded in flame: a fearful beginning
for sons of the soil; and soon it came,
in the doom of their lord, to a dreadful end.

XXXIII

Then the baleful fiend its fire belched out,
and bright homes burned. The blaze stood high
all landsfolk frighting. No living thing
would that loathly one leave as aloft it flew.
Wide was the dragon's warring seen,
its fiendish fury far and near,
as the grim destroyer those Geatish people
hated and hounded. To hidden lair,
to its hoard it hastened at hint of dawn.
Folk of the land it had lapped in flame,
with bale and brand. In its barrow it trusted,
its battling and bulwarks: that boast was vain!

To Beowulf then the bale was told
quickly and truly: the king's own home,
of buildings the best, in brand-waves melted,
that gift-throne of Geats. To the good old man
sad in heart, 'twas heaviest sorrow.
The sage assumed that his sovran God
he had angered, breaking ancient law,
and embittered the Lord. His breast within
with black thoughts welled, as his wont was never.
The folk's own fastness that fiery dragon
with flame had destroyed, and the stronghold all
washed by waves; but the warlike king,
prince of the Weders, plotted vengeance.
Warriors'-bulwark, he bade them work
all of iron—the earl's commander—
a war-shield wondrous: well he knew
that forest-wood against fire were worthless,
linden could aid not.—Atheling brave,
he was fated to finish this fleeting life,
his days on earth, and the dragon with him,

though long it had watched o'er the wealth of the hoard!—
Shame he reckoned it, sharer-of-rings,
to follow the flyer-afar with a host,
a broad-flung band; nor the battle feared he,
nor deemed he dreadful the dragon's warring,
its vigor and valor: ventures desperate
he had passed a-plenty, and perils of war,
contest-crash, since, conqueror proud,
Hrothgar's hall he had wholly purged,
and in grapple had killed the kin of Grendel,
loathsome breed! Not least was that
of hand-to-hand fights where Hygelac fell,
when the ruler of Geats in rush of battle,
lord of his folk, in the Frisian land,
son of Hrethel, by sword-draughts died,
by brands down-beaten. Thence Beowulf fled
through strength of himself and his swimming power,
though alone, and his arms were laden with thirty
coats of mail, when he came to the sea!
Nor yet might Hetwaras haughtily boast
their craft of contest, who carried against him
shields to the fight: but few escaped
from strife with the hero to seek their homes!
Then swam over ocean Ecgtheow's son
lonely and sorrowful, seeking his land,
where Hygd made him offer of hoard and realm,
rings and royal-seat, reckoning naught
the strength of her son to save their kingdom
from hostile hordes, after Hygelac's death.
No sooner for this could the stricken ones
in any wise move that atheling's mind
over young Heardred's head as lord
and ruler of all the realm to be:
yet the hero upheld him with helpful words,
aided in honor, till, older grown,
he wielded the Weder-Geats.—Wandering exiles
sought him o'er seas, the sons of Ohtere,
who had spurned the sway of the Scylfings'-helmet,
the bravest and best that broke the rings,
in Swedish land, of the sea-king's line,
haughty hero. Hence Heardred's end.
For shelter he gave them, sword-death came,
the blade's fell blow, to bairn of Hygelac;
but the son of Ongentheow sought again
house and home when Heardred fell,
leaving Beowulf lord of Geats
and gift-seat's master.—A good king he!

XXXIV

The fall of his lord he was fain to requite
in after days; and to Eadgils he proved
friend to the friendless, and forces sent
over the sea to the son of Ohtere,
weapons and warriors: well repaid he
those care-paths cold when the king he slew.
Thus safe through struggles the son of Ecgtheow
had passed a plenty, through perils dire,
with daring deeds, till this day was come
that doomed him now with the dragon to strive.
With comrades eleven the lord of Geats
swollen in rage went seeking the dragon.
He had heard whence all the harm arose
and the killing of clansmen; that cup of price
on the lap of the lord had been laid by the finder.
In the throng was this one thirteenth man,
starter of all the strife and ill,
care-laden captive; cringing thence
forced and reluctant, he led them on
till he came in ken of that cavern-hall,
the barrow delved near billowy surges,
flood of ocean. Within 'twas full
of wire-gold and jewels; a jealous warden,
warrior trusty, the treasures held,
lurked in his lair. Not light the task
of entrance for any of earth-born men!
Sat on the headland the hero king,
spake words of hail to his hearth-companions,
gold-friend of Geats. All gloomy his soul,
wavering, death-bound. Wyrd full nigh
stood ready to greet the gray-haired man,
to seize his soul-hoard, sunder apart
life and body. Not long would be
the warrior's spirit enwound with flesh.
Beowulf spake, the bairn of Ecgtheow:—
"Through store of struggles I strove in youth,
mighty feuds; I mind them all.
I was seven years old when the sovran of rings,
friend-of-his-folk, from my father took me,
had me, and held me, Hrethel the king,
with food and fee, faithful in kinship.
Ne'er, while I lived there, he loathlier found me,
bairn in the burg, than his birthright sons,
Herebeald and Hæthcyn and Hygelac mine.
For the eldest of these, by unmeet chance,
by kinsman's deed, was the death-bed strewn,
when Hæthcyn killed him with horny bow,
his own dear liege laid low with an arrow,
missed the mark and his mate shot down,
one brother the other, with bloody shaft.
A feeless fight and a fearful sin,
horror to Hrethel; yet, hard as it was,
unavenged must the atheling die!
Too awful it is for an agéd man
to bide and bear, that his bairn so young
rides on the gallows. A rime he makes,
sorrow-song for his son there hanging
as rapture of ravens; no rescue now
can come from the old, disabled man!
Still is he minded, as morning breaks,

of the heir gone elsewhere; another he hopes not
he will bide to see his burg within
as ward for his wealth, now the one has found
doom of death that the deed incurred.
Forlorn he looks on the lodge of his son,
wine-hall waste and wind-swept chambers
reft of revel. The rider sleepeth,
the hero, far-hidden; no harp resounds,
in the courts no wassail, as once was heard.

XXXV

"Then he goes to his chamber, a grief-song chants
alone for his lost. Too large all seems,
homestead and house. So the helmet-of-Weders
hid in his heart for Herebeald
waves of woe. No way could he take
to avenge on the slayer slaughter so foul;
nor e'en could he harass that hero at all
with loathing deed, though he loved him not.
And so for the sorrow his soul endured,
men's gladness he gave up and God's light chose.
Lands and cities he left his sons
(as the wealthy do) when he went from earth.
There was strife and struggle 'twixt Swede and Geat
o'er the width of waters; war arose,
hard battle-horror, when Hrethel died,
and Ongentheow's offspring grew
strife-keen, bold, nor brooked o'er the seas
pact of peace, but pushed their hosts
to harass in hatred by Hreosnabeorh.
Men of my folk for that feud had vengeance,
for woful war ('tis widely known),
though one of them bought it with blood of his heart,
a bargain hard: for Hæthcyn proved
fatal that fray, for the first-of-Geats.
At morn, I heard, was the murderer killed
by kinsman for kinsman, with clash of sword,
when Ongentheow met Eofor there.
Wide split the war-helm: wan he fell,
hoary Scylfing; the hand that smote him
of feud was mindful, nor flinched from the death-blow.

—"For all that he[1] gave me, my gleaming sword
repaid him at war,—such power I wielded,—
for lordly treasure: with land he entrusted me,
homestead and house. He had no need
from Swedish realm, or from Spear-Dane folk,
or from men of the Gifths, to get him help,—
some warrior worse for wage to buy!
Ever I fought in the front of all,
sole to the fore; and so shall I fight
while I bide in life and this blade shall last
that early and late hath loyal proved
since for my doughtiness Dæghrefn fell,
slain by my hand, the Hugas' champion.
Nor fared he thence to the Frisian king
with the booty back, and breast-adornments;
but, slain in struggle, that standard-bearer
fell, atheling brave. Not with blade was he slain,
but his bones were broken by brawny gripe,
his heart-waves stilled.—The sword-edge now,
hard blade and my hand, for the hoard shall strive."
Beowulf spake, and a battle-vow made,
his last of all: "I have lived through many
wars in my youth; now once again,
old folk-defender, feud will I seek,
do doughty deeds, if the dark destroyer
forth from his cavern come to fight me!"
Then hailed he the helmeted heroes all,
for the last time greeting his liegemen dear,
comrades of war: "I should carry no weapon,
no sword to the serpent, if sure I knew
how, with such enemy, else my vows
I could gain as I did in Grendel's day.
But fire in this fight I must fear me now,
and poisonous breath; so I bring with me
breastplate and board.[2] From the barrow's keeper
no footbreadth flee I. One fight shall end
our war by the wall, as Wyrd allots,
all mankind's master. My mood is bold
but forbears to boast o'er this battling-flyer.
—Now abide by the barrow, ye breastplate-mailed,
ye heroes in harness, which of us twain
better from battle-rush bear his wounds.
Wait ye the finish. The fight is not yours,
nor meet for any but me alone
to measure might with this monster here
and play the hero. Hardily I
shall win that wealth, or war shall seize,
cruel killing, your king and lord!"
Up stood then with shield the sturdy champion,
stayed by the strength of his single manhood,
and hardy 'neath helmet his harness bore
under cleft of the cliffs: no coward's path!
Soon spied by the wall that warrior chief,
survivor of many a victory-field
where foemen fought with furious clashings,
an arch of stone; and within, a stream
that broke from the barrow. The brooklet's wave
was hot with fire. The hoard that way
he never could hope unharmed to near,

[1] Hygelac.

[2] Shield.

or endure those deeps, for the dragon's flame.
Then let from his breast, for he burst with rage,
the Weder-Geat prince a word outgo;
stormed the stark-heart; stern went ringing
and clear his cry 'neath the cliff-rocks gray.
The hoard-guard heard a human voice;
his rage was enkindled. No respite now
for pact of peace! The poison-breath
of that foul worm first came forth from the cave,
hot reek-of-fight: the rocks resounded.
Stout by the stone-way his shield he raised,
lord of the Geats, against the loathed-one;
while with courage keen that coiléd foe
came seeking strife. The sturdy king
had drawn his sword, not dull of edge,
heirloom old; and each of the two
felt fear of his foe, though fierce their mood.
Stoutly stood with his shield high-raised
the warrior king, as the worm now coiled
together amain: the mailed-one waited.
Now, spire by spire, fast sped and glided
that blazing serpent. The shield protected
soul and body a shorter while
for the hero-king than his heart desired,
could his will have wielded the welcome respite
but once in his life! But Wyrd denied it,
and victory's honors.—His arm he lifted,
lord of the Geats, the grim foe smote
with atheling's heirloom. Its edge was turned,
brown-blade, on the bone, and bit more feebly
than its noble master had need of then
in his baleful stress.—Then the barrows' keeper
waxed full wild for that weighty blow,
cast deadly flames; wide drove and far
those vicious fires. No victor's glory
the Geats' lord boasted; his brand had failed,
naked in battle, as never it should,
excellent iron!—'Twas no easy path
that Ecgtheow's honored heir must tread
over the plain to the place of the foe;
for against his will he must win a home
elsewhere far, as must all men, leaving
this lapsing life!—Not long it was
ere those champions grimly closed again.
The hoard-guard was heartened; high heaved his breast
once more; and by peril was pressed again,
enfolded in flames, the folk-commander!
Nor yet about him his band of comrades,
sons of athelings, arméd stood
with warlike front: to the woods they bent them
their lives to save. But the soul of one
with care was cumbered. Kinship true
can never be marred in a noble mind!

XXXVI

Wiglaf his name was, Weohstan's son,
linden-thane loved, the lord of Scylfings,
Ælfhere's kinsman. His king he now saw
with heat under helmet hard oppressed.
He minded the prizes his prince had given him,
wealthy seat of the Wægmunding line,
and folk-rights that his father owned.
Not long he lingered. The linden yellow,
his shield, he seized; the old sword he drew:—
as heirloom of Eanmund earth-dwellers knew it,
who was slain by the sword-edge, son of Ohtere,
friendless exile, erst in fray
killed by Weohstan, who won for his kin
brown-bright helmet, breastplate ringed,
old sword of Eotens, Onela's gift,
weeds of war of the warrior-thane,
battle-gear brave: though a brother's child
had been felled, the feud was unfelt by Onela.
For winters this war-gear Weohstan kept,
breastplate and board, till his bairn had grown
earlship to earn as the old sire did:
then he gave him, mid Geats, the gear of battle,
portion huge, when he passed from life,
fared agéd forth. For the first time now
with his leader-lord the liegeman young
was bidden to share the shock of battle.
Neither softened his soul, nor the sire's bequest
weakened in war. So the worm found out
when once in fight the foes had met!
Wiglaf spake,—and his words were sage;
sad in spirit, he said to his comrades:—
"I remember the time, when mead we took,
what promise we made to this prince of ours,
in the banquet-hall, to our breaker-of-rings,
for gear of combat to give him requital,
for hard-sword and helmet, if hap should bring
stress of this sort! Himself who chose us
from all his army to aid him now,
urged us to glory, and gave these treasures,
because he counted us keen with the spear
and hardy 'neath helm, though this hero-work
our leader hoped unhelped and alone
to finish for us,—folk-defender
who hath got him glory greater than all men
for daring deeds! Now the day is come
that our noble master has need of the might
of warriors stout. Let us stride along
the hero to help while the heat is about him
glowing and grim! For God is my witness
I am far more fain the fire should seize
along with my lord these limbs of mine!
Unsuiting it seems our shields to bear
homeward hence, save here we essay
to fell the foe and defend the life
of the Weders' lord. I wot 'twere shame

on the law of our land if alone the king
out of Geatish warriors woe endured
and sank in the struggle! My sword and helmet,
breastplate and board, for us both shall serve!"
Through slaughter-reek strode he to succor his chieftain,
his battle-helm bore, and brief words spake:—
"Beowulf dearest, do all bravely,
as in youthful days of yore thou vowedst
that while life should last thou wouldst let no wise
thy glory droop! Now, great in deeds,
atheling steadfast, with all thy strength
shield thy life! I will stand to help thee."
At the words the worm came once again,
murderous monster mad with rage,
with fire-billows flaming, its foes to seek,
the hated men. In heat-waves burned
that board[1] to the boss, and the breastplate failed
to shelter at all the spear-thane young.
Yet quickly under his kinsman's shield
went eager the earl, since his own was now
all burned by the blaze. The bold king again
had mind of his glory: with might his glaive
was driven into the dragon's head,—
blow nerved by hate. But Nægling was shivered,
broken in battle was Beowulf's sword,
old and gray. 'Twas granted him not
that ever the edge of iron at all
could help him at strife: too strong was his hand,
so the tale is told, and he tried too far
with strength of stroke all swords he wielded,
though sturdy their steel: they steaded him nought.
Then for the third time thought on its feud
that folk-destroyer, fire-dread dragon,
and rushed on the hero, where room allowed,
battle-grim, burning; its bitter teeth
closed on his neck, and covered him
with waves of blood from his breast that welled.

XXXVII

'Twas now, men say, in his sovran's need
that the earl made known his noble strain,
craft and keenness and courage enduring.
Heedless of harm, though his hand was burned,
hardy-hearted, he helped his kinsman.
A little lower the loathsome beast
he smote with sword; his steel drove in
bright and burnished; that blaze began
to lose and lessen. At last the king
wielded his wits again, war-knife drew,
a biting blade by his breastplate hanging,
and the Weders'-helm smote that worm asunder,
felled the foe, flung forth its life.
So had they killed it, kinsmen both,
athelings twain: thus an earl should be
in danger's day!—Of deeds of valor
this conqueror's-hour of the king was last,
of his work in the world. The wound began,
which that dragon-of-earth had erst inflicted,
to swell and smart; and soon he found
in his breast was boiling, baleful and deep,
pain of poison. The prince walked on,
wise in his thought, to the wall of rock;
then sat, and stared at the structure of giants,
where arch of stone and steadfast column
upheld forever that hall in earth.
Yet here must the hand of the henchman peerless
lave with water his winsome lord,
the king and conqueror covered with blood,
with struggle spent, and unspan his helmet.
Beowulf spake in spite of his hurt,
his mortal wound; full well he knew
his portion now was past and gone
of earthly bliss, and all had fled
of his file of days, and death was near:
"I would fain bestow on son of mine
this gear of war, were given me now
that any heir should after me come
of my proper blood. This people I ruled
fifty winters. No folk-king was there,
none at all, of the neighboring clans
who war would wage me with 'warriors'-friends'[2]
and threat me with horrors. At home I bided
what fate might come, and I cared for mine own;
feuds I sought not, nor falsely swore
ever on oath. For all these things,
though fatally wounded, fain am I!
From the Ruler-of-Man no wrath shall seize me,
when life from my frame must flee away,
for killing of kinsmen! Now quickly go
and gaze on that hoard 'neath the hoary rock,
Wiglaf loved, now the worm lies low,
sleeps, heart-sore, of his spoil bereaved.
And fare in haste. I would fain behold
the gorgeous heirlooms, golden store,
have joy in the jewels and gems, lay down
softlier for sight of this splendid hoard
my life and the lordship I long have held."

XXXVIII

I have heard that swiftly the son of Weohstan

[1] Wiglaf's shield.

[2] Swords.

at wish and word of his wounded king,—
war-sick warrior,—woven mail-coat,
battle-sark, bore 'neath the barrow's roof.
Then the clansman keen, of conquest proud,
passing the seat, saw store of jewels
and glistening gold the ground along;
by the wall were marvels, and many a vessel
in the den of the dragon, the dawn-flier old:
unburnished bowls of bygone men
reft of richness; rusty helms
of the olden age; and arm-rings many
wondrously woven.—Such wealth of gold,
booty from barrow, can burden with pride
each human wight: let him hide it who will!—
His glance too fell on a gold-wove banner
high o'er the hoard, of handiwork noblest,
brilliantly broidered; so bright its gleam,
all the earth-floor he easily saw
and viewed all these vessels. No vestige now
was seen of the serpent: the sword had ta'en him.
Then, I heard, the hill of its hoard was reft,
old work of giants, by one alone;
he burdened his bosom with beakers and plate
at his own good will, and the ensign took,
brightest of beacons.—The blade of his lord
—its edge was iron—had injured deep
one that guarded the golden hoard
many a year and its murder-fire
spread hot round the barrow in horror-billows
at midnight hour, till it met its doom.
Hasted the herald, the hoard so spurred him
his track to retrace; he was troubled by doubt,
high-souled hero, if haply he'd find
alive, where he left him, the lord of Weders,
weakening fast by the wall of the cave.
So he carried the load. His lord and king
he found all bleeding, famous chief,
at the lapse of life. The liegeman again
plashed him with water, till point of word
broke through the breast-hoard. Beowulf spake,
sage and sad, as he stared at the gold:—
"For the gold and treasure, to God my thanks,
to the Wielder-of-Wonders, with words I say,
for what I behold, to Heaven's Lord,
for the grace that I give such gifts to my folk
or ever the day of my death be run!
Now I've bartered here for booty of treasure
the last of my life, so look ye well
to the needs of my land! No longer I tarry.
A barrow bid ye the battle-famed raise
for my ashes. 'Twill shine by the shore of the flood,
to folk of mine memorial fair
on Hronës Headland high uplifted,
that ocean-wanderers oft may hail
Beowulf's Barrow, as back from far
they drive their keels o'er the darkling wave."
From his neck he unclasped the collar of gold,
valorous king, to his vassal gave it
with bright-gold helmet, breastplate, and ring,
to the youthful thane: bade him use them in joy.
"Thou art end and remnant of all our race,
the Wægmunding name. For Wyrd hath swept them,
all my line, to the land of doom,
earls in their glory: I after them go."
This word was the last which the wise old man
harbored in heart ere hot death-waves
of balefire he chose. From his bosom fled
his soul to seek the saints' reward.

XXXIX

It was heavy hap for that hero young
on his lord beloved to look and find him
lying on earth with life at end,
sorrowful sight. But the slayer too,
awful earth-dragon, empty of breath,
lay felled in fight, nor, fain of its treasure,
could the writhing monster rule it more.
For edges of iron had ended its days,
hard and battle-sharp, hammers' leaving;[1]
and that flier-afar had fallen to ground
hushed by its hurt, its hoard all near,
no longer lusty aloft to whirl
at midnight, making its merriment seen,
proud of its prizes: prone it sank
by the handiwork of the hero-king.
Forsooth among folk but few achieve,
—though sturdy and strong, as stories tell me,
and never so daring in deed of valor,—
the perilous breath of a poison-foe
to brave, and to rush on the ring-hoard hall,
whenever his watch the warden keeps
bold in the barrow. Beowulf paid
the price of death for that precious hoard;
and each of the foes had found the end
of this fleeting life.
Befell erelong
that the laggards in war the wood had left,
trothbreakers, cowards, ten together,
fearing before to flourish a spear
in the sore distress of their sovran lord.
Now in their shame their shields they carried,
armor of fight, where the old man lay;
and they gazed on Wiglaf. Wearied he sat
at his sovran's shoulder, shieldsman good,
to wake him with water. Nowise it availed.
Though well he wished it, in world no more
could he barrier life for that leader-of-battles
nor baffle the will of all-wielding God.
Doom of the Lord was law o'er the deeds
of every man, as it is to-day.

[1] Well forged.

Grim was the answer, easy to get,
from the youth for those that had yielded to fear!
Wiglaf spake, the son of Weohstan,—
mournful he looked on those men unloved:—
"Who sooth will speak, can say indeed
that the ruler who gave you golden rings
and the harness of war in which ye stand
—for he at ale-bench often-times
bestowed on hall-folk helm and breastplate,
lord to liegemen, the likeliest gear
which near or far he could find to give,—
threw away and wasted these weeds of battle,
on men who failed when the foemen came!
Not at all could the king of his comrades-in-arms
venture to vaunt, though the Victory-Wielder,
God, gave him grace that he got revenge
sole with his sword in stress and need.
To rescue his life, 'twas little that I
could serve him in struggle; yet shift I made
(hopeless it seemed) to help my kinsman.
Its strength ever waned, when with weapon I struck
that fatal foe, and the fire less strongly
flowed from its head.—Too few the heroes
in throe of contest that thronged to our king!
Now gift of treasure and girding of sword,
joy of the house and home-delight
shall fail your folk; his freehold-land
every clansman within your kin
shall lose and leave, when lords highborn
hear afar of that flight of yours,
a fameless deed. Yea, death is better
for liegemen all than a life of shame!"

XL

That battle-toil bade he at burg to announce,
at the fort on the cliff, where, full of sorrow,
all the morning earls had sat,
daring shieldsmen, in doubt of twain:
would they wail as dead, or welcome home,
their lord belovéd? Little kept back
of the tidings new, but told them all,
the herald that up the headland rode.—
"Now the willing-giver to Weder folk
in death-bed lies, the Lord of Geats
on the slaughter-bed sleeps by the serpent's deed!
And beside him is stretched that slayer-of-men
with knife-wounds sick: no sword availed
on the awesome thing in any wise
to work a wound. There Wiglaf sitteth,
Weohstan's bairn, by Beowulf's side,
the living earl by the other dead,
and heavy of heart a head-watch keeps
o'er friend and foe.—Now our folk may look
for waging of war when once unhidden
to Frisian and Frank the fall of the king
is spread afar.—The strife began
when hot on the Hugas Hygelac fell
and fared with his fleet to the Frisian land.
Him there the Hetwaras humbled in war,
plied with such prowess their power o'erwhelming
that the bold-in-battle bowed beneath it
and fell in fight. To his friends no wise
could that earl give treasure! And ever since
the Merowings' favor has failed us wholly.
Nor aught expect I of peace and faith
from Swedish folk. 'Twas spread afar
how Ongentheow reft at Ravenswood
Hæthcyn Hrethling of hope and life,
when the folk of Geats for the first time sought
in wanton pride the Warlike-Scylfings.
Soon the sage old sire of Ohtere,
ancient and awful, gave answering blow;
the sea-king he slew, and his spouse redeemed,
his good wife rescued, though robbed of her gold,
mother of Ohtere and Onela.
Then he followed his foes, who fled before him
sore beset and stole their way,
bereft of a ruler, to Ravenswood.
With his host he besieged there what swords had left,
the weary and wounded; woes he threatened
the whole night through to that hard-pressed throng:
some with the morrow his sword should kill,
some should go to the gallows-tree
for rapture of ravens. But rescue came
with dawn of day for those desperate men
when they heard the horn of Hygelac sound,
tones of his trumpet; the trusty king
had followed their trail with faithful band.

XLI

"The bloody swath of Swedes and Geats
and the storm of their strife, were seen afar,
how folk against folk the fight had wakened.
The ancient king with his atheling band
sought his citadel, sorrowing much:
Ongentheow earl went up to his burg.
He had tested Hygelac's hardihood,
the proud one's prowess, would prove it no longer,
defied no more those fighting-wanderers
nor hoped from the seamen to save his hoard,
his bairn and his bride: so he bent him again,
old, to his earth-walls. Yet after him came
with slaughter for Swedes the standards of Hygelac
o'er peaceful plains in pride advancing,
till Hrethelings fought in the fencéd town.
Then Ongentheow with edge of sword,
the hoary-bearded, was held at bay,
and the folk-king there was forced to suffer

Eofor's anger. In ire, at the king
Wulf Wonreding with weapon struck;
and the chieftain's blood, for that blow, in streams
flowed 'neath his hair. No fear felt he,
stout old Scylfing, but straightway repaid
in better bargain that bitter stroke
and faced his foe with fell intent.
Nor swift enough was the son of Wonred
answer to render the agéd chief;
too soon on his head the helm was cloven;
blood-bedecked he bowed to earth,
and fell adown: not doomed was he yet,
and well he waxed, though the wound was sore.
Then the hardy Hygelac-thane,
when his brother fell, with broad brand smote,
giants'-sword crashing through giants'-helm
across the shield-wall: sank the king,
his folk's old herdsman, fatally hurt.
There were many to bind the brother's wounds
and lift him, fast as fate allowed
his people to wield the place-of-war.
But Eofor took from Ongentheow,
earl from other, the iron-breastplate,
hard sword hilted, and helmet too,
and the hoar-chief's harness to Hygelac carried,
who took the trappings, and truly promised
rich fee 'mid folk,—and fulfilled it so.
For that grim strife gave the Geatish lord,
Hrethel's offspring, when home he came,
to Eofor and Wulf a wealth of treasure.
Each of them had a hundred thousand
in land and linked rings; nor at less price reckoned
mid-earth men such mighty deeds!
And to Eofor he gave his only daughter
in pledge of grace, the pride of his home.

"Such is the feud, the foeman's rage,
death-hate of men: so I deem it sure
that the Swedish folk will seek us home
for this fall of their friends, the fighting-Scylfings,
when once they learn that our warrior leader
lifeless lies, who land and hoard
ever defended from all his foes,
furthered his folk's weal, finished his course
a hardy hero.—Now haste is best,
that we go to gaze on our Geatish lord,
and bear the bountiful breaker-of-rings
to the funeral pyre. No fragments merely
shall burn with the warrior. Wealth of jewels,
gold untold and gained in terror,
treasure at last with his life obtained,
all of that booty the brands shall take,
fire shall eat it. No earl must carry
memorial jewel. No maiden fair
shall wreathe her neck with noble ring:
nay, sad in spirit and shorn of her gold,
oft shall she pass o'er paths of exile
now our lord all laughter has laid aside,
all mirth and revel. Many a spear
morning-cold shall be clasped amain,
lifted aloft; nor shall lilt of harp
those warriors wake; but the wan-hued raven,
fain o'er the fallen, his feast shall praise
and boast to the eagle how bravely he ate
when he and the wolf were wasting the slain."

So he told his sorrowful tidings,
and little he lied, the loyal man
of word or of work. The warriors rose;
sad, they climbed to the Cliff-of-Eagles,
went, welling with tears, the wonder to view.
Found on the sand there, stretched at rest,
their lifeless lord, who had lavished rings
of old upon them. Ending-day
had dawned on the doughty-one; death had seized
in woful slaughter the Weders' king.
There saw they, besides, the strangest being,
loathsome, lying their leader near,
prone on the field. The fiery dragon,
fearful fiend, with flame was scorched.
Reckoned by feet, it was fifty measures
in length as it lay. Aloft erewhile
it had reveled by night, and anon come back,
seeking its den; now in death's sure clutch
it had come to the end of its earth-hall joys.
By it there stood the stoups and jars;
dishes lay there, and dear-decked swords
eaten with rust, as, on earth's lap resting,
a thousand winters they waited there.
For all that heritage huge, that gold
of bygone men, was bound by a spell,
so the treasure-hall could be touched by none
of human kind,—save that Heaven's King,
God himself, might give whom he would,
Helper of Heroes, the hoard to open,—
even such a man as seemed to him meet.

XLII

A perilous path, it proved, he trod
who heinously hid, that hall within,
wealth under wall! Its watcher had killed
one of a few, and the feud was avenged
in woful fashion. Wondrous seems it,
what manner a man of might and valor
oft ends his life, when the earl no longer
in mead-hall may live with loving friends.
So Beowulf, when that barrow's warden
he sought, and the struggle; himself knew not
in what wise he should wend from the world at last.
For princes potent, who placed the gold,
with a curse to doomsday covered it deep,
so that marked with sin the man should be,
hedged with horrors, in hell-bonds fast,

racked with plagues, who should rob their hoard.
Yet no greed for gold, but the grace of heaven,
ever the king had kept in view.
  Wiglaf spake, the son of Weohstan:—
"At the mandate of one, oft warriors many
sorrow must suffer; and so must we.
The people's-shepherd showed not aught
of care for our counsel, king belovéd!
That guardian of gold he should grapple not, urged we,
but let him lie where he long had been
in his earth-hall waiting the end of the world,
the hest of heaven.—This hoard is ours,
but grievously gotten; too grim the fate
which thither carried our king and lord.
I was within there, and all I viewed,
the chambered treasure, when chance allowed me
(and my path was made in no pleasant wise)
under the earth-wall. Eager, I seized
such heap from the hoard as hands could bear
and hurriedly carried it hither back
to my liege and lord. Alive was he still,
still wielding his wits. The wise old man
spake much in his sorrow, and sent you greetings
and bade that ye build, when he breathed no more,
on the place of his balefire a barrow high,
memorial mighty. Of men was he
worthiest warrior wide earth o'er
the while he had joy of his jewels and burg.
Let us set out in haste now, the second time
to see and search this store of treasure,
these wall-hid wonders,—the way I show you,—
where, gathered near, ye may gaze your fill
at broad-gold and rings. Let the bier, soon made,
be all in order when out we come,
our king and captain to carry thither
—man beloved—where long he shall bide
safe in the shelter of sovran God."
Then the bairn of Weohstan bade command,
hardy chief, to heroes many
that owned their homesteads, hither to bring
firewood from far—o'er the folk they ruled—
for the famed-one's funeral. "Fire shall devour
and wan flames feed on the fearless warrior
who oft stood stout in the iron-shower,
when, sped from the string, a storm of arrows
shot o'er the shield-wall: the shaft held firm,
featly feathered, followed the barb."[1]
And now the sage young son of Weohstan
seven chose of the chieftain's thanes,
the best he found that band within,
and went with these warriors, one of eight,
under hostile roof. In hand one bore
a lighted torch and led the way.
No lots they cast for keeping the hoard
when once the warriors saw it in hall,
altogether without a guardian,
lying there lost. And little they mourned
when they had hastily haled it out,
dear-bought treasure! The dragon they cast,
the worm, o'er the wall for the wave to take,
and surges swallowed that shepherd of gems.
Then the woven gold on a wain was laden—
countless quite!—and the king was borne,
hoary hero, to Hronës-Ness.

XLIII

Then fashioned for him the folk of Geats
firm on the earth a funeral-pile,
and hung it with helmets and harness of war
and breastplates bright, as the boon he asked;
and they laid amid it the mighty chieftain,
heroes mourning their master dear.
Then on the hill that hugest of balefires
the warriors wakened. Wood-smoke rose
black over blaze, and blent was the roar
of flame with weeping (the wind was still),
till the fire had broken the frame of bones,
hot at the heart. In heavy mood
their misery moaned they, their master's death.
Wailing her woe, the widow[2] old,
her hair unbound, for Beowulf's death
sung in her sorrow, and said full oft
she dreaded the doleful days to come,
deaths enow, and doom of battle,
and shame.—The smoke by the sky was devoured.
  The folk of the Weders fashioned there
on the headland a barrow broad and high,
by ocean-farers far descried:
in ten days' time their toil had raised it,
the battle-brave's beacon. Round brands of the pyre
a wall they built, the worthiest ever
that wit could prompt in their wisest men.
They placed in the barrow that precious booty,
the rounds and the rings they had reft erewhile,
hardy heroes, from hoard in cave,—
trusting the ground with treasure of earls,
gold in the earth, where ever it lies
useless to men as of yore it was.
  Then about that barrow the battle-keen rode,
atheling-born, a band of twelve,
lament to make, to mourn their king,

[1]Professor Garnett's translation (Gummere's note).

[2]Nothing has been said of Beowulf's wife in the poem. It has been conjectured that he may have married Hygd.

chant their dirge, and their chieftain honor.
They praised his earlship, his acts of prowess
worthily witnessed: and well it is
that men their master-friend mightily laud,
heartily love, when hence he goes
from life in the body forlorn away.

Thus made their mourning the men of Geatland,
for their hero's passing his hearth-companions:
quoth that of all the kings of earth,
of men he was mildest and most belovéd,
to his kin the kindest, keenest for praise.

THE WANDERER[1]

This poem is preserved in the Exeter Book, a manuscript volume left with other books to his church by Leofric (first bishop of Exeter, died A. D. 1071). The volume is still in the cathedral library at Exeter. The author of the poem is unknown, as well as the date of its composition, though it has been conjectured that this elegiac lyric was written probably in the first quarter of the eighth century. "Over the body of the poem lie the shadows of fatalism, and a profound sense of the instability of the earth and its joys" (J. Duncan Spaeth, *Old English Poetry*, p. 247). This theme is a characteristic one in Anglo-Saxon literature.

"STILL the lone one and desolate waits for his Maker's ruth—
God's good mercy, albeit so long it tarry, in sooth.
Careworn and sad of heart, on the watery ways must he
Plow with the hand-grasped oar—how long?—the rime-cold sea,
Tread thy paths of exile, O Fate, who art cruelty."
  Thus did a wanderer speak, being heart-full of woe, and all
Thoughts of the cruel slayings, and pleasant comrades' fall:
"Morn by morn I, alone, am fain to utter my woe;
Now is there none of the living to whom I dare to show
Plainly the thought of my heart; in very sooth I know
Excellent is it in man that his breast he straightly bind,
Shut fast his thinkings in silence, whatever he have in his mind.
The man that is weary in heart, he never can fate withstand;
The man that grieves in his spirit, he finds not the helper's hand.
Therefore the glory-grasper full heavy of soul may be.
So, far from my fatherland, and mine own good kinsmen free,
I must bind my heart in fetters, for long, ah! long ago,
The earth's cold darkness covered my giver of gold brought low;
And I, sore stricken and humbled, and winter-saddened, went
Far over the frost-bound waves to seek for the dear content
Of the hall of the giver of rings; but far nor near could I find
Who felt the love of the mead-hall, or who with comforts kind
Would comfort me, the friendless. 'T is he alone will know,
Who knows, being desolate too, how evil a fere is woe;
For him the path of the exile, and not the twisted gold;
For him the frost in his bosom, and not earth-riches old.
  "O, well he remembers the hall-men, the treasure bestowed in the hall;
The feast that his gold-giver made him, the joy at its highth, at its fall;
He knows who must be forlorn for his dear lord's counsels gone,
Where sleep and sorrow together are binding the lonely one;
When himthinks he clasps and kisses his leader of men, and lays
His hands and head on his knee, as when, in the good yore-days,
He sat on the throne of his might, in the strength that wins and saves.
But the friendless man awakes, and he sees the yellow waves,
And the sea-birds dip to the sea, and broaden their wings to the gale,
And he sees the dreary rime, and the snow commingled with hail.
O, then are the wounds of his heart the sorer much for this,
The grief for the loved and lost made new by the dream of old bliss.
His kinsmen's memory comes to him as he lies asleep,
And he greets it with joy, with joy, and the heart in his breast doth leap;

---

[1]The translation is by Emily H. Hickey. It is reprinted here with the permission of the editors and publishers from *Select Translations from Old English Poetry*, edited by A. S. Cook and C. B. Tinker, and published by Messrs. Ginn and Company.

But out of his ken the shapes of his warrior-comrades swim
To the land whence seafarers bring no dear old saws for him;
Then fresh grows sorrow and new to him whose bitter part
Is to send o'er the frost-bound waves full often his weary heart.
For this do I look around this world, and cannot see
Wherefore or why my heart should not grow dark in me.
When I think of the lives of the leaders, the clansmen mighty in mood;
When I think how sudden and swift they yielded the place where they stood.
So droops this mid-earth and falls, and never a man is found
Wise ere a many winters have girt his life around.
Full patient the sage must be, and he that would counsel teach—
Not over-hot in his heart, nor over-swift in his speech;
Nor faint of soul nor secure, nor fain for the fight nor afraid;
Nor ready to boast before he know himself well arrayed.
The proud-souled man must bide when he utters his vaunt, until
He know of the thoughts of the heart, and whitherward turn they will.
The prudent must understand how terror and awe shall be,
When the glory and weal of the world lie waste, as now men see
On our mid-earth, many a where, the wind-swept walls arise,
And the ruined dwellings and void, and the rime that on them lies.
The wine-halls crumble, bereft of joy the warriors lie,
The flower of the doughty fallen, the proud ones fair to the eye.
War took off some in death, and one did a strong bird bear
Over the deep; and one—his bones did the gray wolf share;
And one was hid in a cave by a comrade sorrowful-faced.
O, thus the Shaper of men hath laid the earth all waste,
Till the works of the city-dwellers, the works of the giants of earth,
Stood empty and lorn of the burst of the mighty revelers' mirth.
"Who wisely hath mused on this wallstead, and ponders this dark life well,
In his heart he hath often bethought him of slayings many and fell,
And these be the words he taketh, the thoughts of his heart to tell:
'Where is the horse and the rider? Where is the giver of gold?
Where be the seats at the banquet? Where be the hall-joys of old?
Alas for the burnished cup, for the byrnied chief to-day!
Alas for the strength of the prince! for the time hath passed away—
Is hid 'neath the shadow of night, as it never had been at all.
Behind the dear and doughty there standeth now a wall,
A wall that is wondrous high, and with wondrous snake-work wrought.
The strength of the spears hath fordone the earls and hath made them naught,
The weapons greedy of slaughter, and she, the mighty Wyrd;
And the tempests beat on the rocks, and the storm-wind that maketh afeard—
The terrible storm that fetters the earth, the winter-bale,
When the shadow of night falls wan, and wild is the rush of the hail,
The cruel rush from the north, which maketh men to quail.
Hardship-full is the earth, o'erturned when the stark Wyrds say:
Here is the passing of riches, here friends are passing away;
And men and kinsfolk pass, and nothing and none may stay;
And all this earth-stead here shall be empty and void one day.' . ."

THE SEAFARER[1]

This poem is, like *The Wanderer*, preserved in the Exeter Book. Its author and date of composition are unknown, though it was probably written in the eighth century. The first part has been thought by some scholars to be a dialogue between an old mariner who knows the sea from bitter experience and a young man eager to go to sea. This is only conjecture, though it is plain that two opposed moods are realized by the poet and expressed. It has also been supposed that the second part is by a different and later hand, but this too is only conjecture.

PART I

I CAN sing of myself a true song, of my voyages telling,
How oft through laborious days, through the wearisome hours
I have suffered; have borne tribulations; explored in my ship,
Mid the terrible rolling of waves, habitations of sorrow.
Benumbed by the cold, oft the comfortless night-watch hath held me
At the prow of my craft as it tossed about under the cliffs.
My feet were imprisoned with frost, were fettered with ice-chains,
Yet hotly were wailing the querulous sighs round my heart;
And hunger within me, sea-wearied, made havoc of courage.
This he, whose lot happily chances on land, doth not know;
Nor how I on the ice-cold sea passed the winter in exile,
In wretchedness, robbed of my kinsmen, with icicles hung.
The hail flew in showers about me; and there I heard only
The roar of the sea, ice-cold waves, and the song of the swan;
For pastime the gannets' cry served me; the kittiwakes' chatter
For laughter of men; and for mead-drink the call of the sea-mews.
When storms on the rocky cliffs beat, then the terns, icy-feathered,
Made answer; full oft the sea-eagle forebodingly screamed,
The eagle with pinions wave-wet. There none of my kinsmen
Might gladden my desolate soul; of this little he knows
Who possesses the pleasures of life, who has felt in the city
Some hardship, some trifling adversity, proud and wine-flushed.
How weary I oft had to tarry upon the sea-way!
The shadows of night became darker, it snowed from the north;
The world was enchained by the frost; hail fell upon earth;
'Twas the coldest of grain. Yet the thoughts of my heart now are throbbing
To test the high streams, the salt waves in tumultuous play.
Desire in my heart ever urges my spirit to wander,
To seek out the home of the stranger in lands afar off.
There is no one that dwells upon earth, so exalted in mind,
So large in his bounty, nor yet of such vigorous youth,
Nor so daring in deeds, nor to whom his liege lord is so kind,
But that he has always a longing, a seafaring passion
For what the Lord God shall bestow, be it honor or death.
No heart for the harp has he, nor for acceptance of treasure,
No pleasure has he in a wife, no delight in the world,
Nor in aught save the roll of the billows; but always a longing,
A yearning uneasiness, hastens him on to the sea.
The woodlands are captured by blossoms, the hamlets grow fair,
Broad meadows are beautiful, earth again bursts into life,
And all stir the heart of the wanderer eager to journey,

[1]The translation is by LaMotte Iddings. It is reprinted here with the permission of the editors and publishers from *Select Translations from Old English Poetry*, edited by A. S. Cook and C. B. Tinker, and published by Messrs. Ginn and Company.

So he meditates going afar on the pathway of tides.
The cuckoo, moreover, gives warning with sorrowful note,
Summer's harbinger sings, and forebodes to the heart bitter sorrow.
The nobleman comprehends not, the luxurious man,
What some must endure, who travel the farthest in exile.

Now my spirit uneasily turns in the heart's narrow chamber,
Now wanders forth over the tide, o'er the home of the whale,
To the ends of the earth—and comes back to me. Eager and greedy,
The lone wanderer screams, and resistlessly drives my soul onward,
Over the whale-path, over the tracts of the sea.

PART II

The delights of the Lord are far dearer to me than this dead,
Fleeting life upon earth, for I cannot believe that earth's riches
For ever endure. Each one of three things, ere its time comes,
Is always uncertain: violence, age, and disease
Wrench the soul away, doomed to depart. This is praise from the living,
From those who speak afterwards, this the best fame after death—
That ere he departed he labored, and wrought daring deeds
'Gainst the malice of fiends, and the devil; so men shall extol him,
His praise among angels shall live, ever, world without end,
His the blessing of life everlasting, and joy mid the hosts.

The days have departed, all pomps of earth's kingdom have vanished;
There now are no kings, no emperors now, no gold-givers
As of yore, when they wrought in their midst the most glorious deeds,
And lived in the lordliest power. This glory has fallen,
Delights have all vanished away; the weak ones remain,
And these govern the world, obtaining their pleasure with effort.
Power has declined, earth's glory grows aged and sear,
Like every man now in the world; old age overtakes him,
His countenance loses its color, gray-haired he laments;
He has seen his old friends, sons of princes, consigned to the earth.

This garment of flesh has no power, when the spirit escapes,
To drink in the sweet nor to taste of the bitter; it then
Has no power to stretch forth the hands or to think with the mind.
Though the grave should be covered with gold by the nearest of kin,
Be buried along with the dead in masses of treasure,
Still that will not go with them. Gold can no substitute be
For the fear of the Lord, to the soul which is laden with sin,
Which aforetime, so long as it lived, kept that treasure concealed.

Great is the fear of the Lord; the earth trembles before it;
He established the unmovable earth, the world and the heavens.
Foolish is he who stands not in awe of the Lord—
Unexpectedly death comes upon him; but happy is he
Who lives humble in mind, to him cometh honor from heaven;
God doth establish the soul that believes in His might.

One should check a strong will, and should govern it firmly,
Be true unto men, and be clean in his manner of life. . . .
Fate, God the Creator, is stronger than any man's will.

Come, let us reflect where our home is, consider the way
By which we go thither; then let us each strive to press forward
To joy everlasting, where life has its source in God's love,
Where is heavenly hope. Then to Him who is holy be thanks,
Because He hath honored us; thanks to the Ruler of Heaven,
The Lord everlasting, throughout all the ages! Amen.

THE BATTLE OF BRUNANBURH[1]

This poem is preserved in four of the six extant manuscripts of the Saxon Chronicle—in the Parker MS. in the library of Corpus Christi College, Cambridge, and in three Cotton MSS. in the British Museum. Its author is unknown, but the date under which it is entered in the Chronicle is A. D. 937. The poem describes an historical event. Tennyson, whose translation is printed here, prefixed to it the following note: "Constantinus, King of the Scots, after having sworn allegiance to Æthelstan, allied himself with the Danes of Ireland under Anlaf, and invading England, was defeated by Æthelstan and his brother Edmund with great slaughter at Brunanburh in the year 937." Æthelstan reigned over the West-Saxons and Mercians from A. D. 925 to 940, and extended his influence throughout England. The site of Brunanburh is unknown. The most likely conjecture hitherto advanced is apparently that it is Bramber, near Preston in Lancashire.

I

ATHELSTAN King,
Lord among Earls,
Bracelet-bestower and
Baron of Barons,
He with his brother,
Edmund Atheling,
Gaining a lifelong
Glory in battle,
Slew with the sword-edge
There by Brunanburh,
Brake the shield-wall,
Hewed the linden-wood,
Hacked the battle-shield,
Sons of Edward with hammered brands.

II

Theirs was a greatness
Got from their grandsires—
Theirs that so often in
Strife with their enemies
Struck for their hoards and their hearths and their homes.

III

Bowed the spoiler,
Bent the Scotsman,
Fell the ship-crews
Doomed to the death.
All the field with blood of the fighters
Flowed, from when first the great
Sun-star of morning-tide,
Lamp of the Lord God
Lord everlasting,
Glode over earth till the glorious creature
Sank to his setting.

IV

There lay many a man
Marred by the javelin,
Men of the Northland
Shot over shield.
There was the Scotsman
Weary of war.

V

We the West-Saxons,
Long as the daylight
Lasted, in companies
Troubled the track of the host that we hated.
Grimly with swords that were sharp from the grind-stone,
Fiercely we hacked at the flyers before us.

VI

Mighty the Mercian,
Hard was his hand-play,
Sparing not any of
Those that with Anlaf,
Warriors over the
Weltering waters
Borne in the bark's-bosom,
Drew to this island—
Doomed to the death.

VII

Five young kings put asleep by the sword stroke,
Seven strong Earls of the army of Anlaf
Fell on the war-field, numberless numbers,
Shipmen and Scotsmen.

[1]This translation is by Alfred Tennyson. Tennyson stated that he more or less availed himself of his son's prose translation of the poem published in the *Contemporary Review*, November, 1876.

VIII

Then the Norse leader,
Dire was his need of it,
Few were his following,
Fled to his war-ship;
Fleeted his vessel to sea with the king in it,
Saving his life on the fallow flood.

IX

Also the crafty one,
Constantinus,
Crept to his North again,
Hoar-headed hero!

X

Slender warrant had
He to be proud of
The welcome of war-knives—
He that was reft of his
Folk and his friends that had
Fallen in conflict,
Leaving his son too
Lost in the carnage,
Mangled to morsels,
A youngster in war!

XI

Slender reason had
He to be glad of
The clash of the war-glaive—
Traitor and trickster
And spurner of treaties—
He nor had Anlaf
With armies so broken
A reason for bragging
That they had the better
In perils of battle
On places of slaughter—
The struggle of standards,
The rush of the javelins,
The crash of the charges,
The wielding of weapons—
The play that they played with
The children of Edward.

XII

Then with their nailed prows
Parted the Norsemen, a
Blood-reddened relic of
Javelins over
The jarring breaker, the deap-sea billow,
Shaping their way toward Dyflen[1] again,
Shamed in their souls.

XIII

Also the brethren,
King and Atheling,
Each in his glory,
Went to his own in his own West-Saxonland,
Glad of the war.

XIV

Many a carcase they left to be carrion,
Many a livid one, many a sallow-skin—
Left for the white-tailed eagle to tear it, and
Left for the horny-nibbed raven to rend it, and
Gave to the garbagin war-hawk to gorge it, and
That gray beast, the wolf of the weald.

XV

Never had huger
Slaughter of heroes
Slain by the sword-edge—
Such as old writers
Have writ of in histories—
Hapt in this isle, since
Up from the East hither
Saxon and Angle from
Over the broad billow
Broke into Britain with
Haughty war-workers who
Harried the Welshman, when
Earls that were lured by the
Hunger of glory gat
Hold of the land.

[1] Dublin.

THE BATTLE OF MALDON[1]

The unique manuscript in the Cotton collection in which *The Battle of Maldon* was preserved, was destroyed by fire in 1731. Fortunately this manuscript had been printed at Oxford five years before, by Thomas Hearne in his history of Glastonbury. Hearne's transcript has thus become our only source for the text of the poem. The author is unknown; he may have been one of the monks of Ely. The date of the poem is determined by the date of the battle described, for *The Battle of Maldon*, like *The Battle of Brunanburh*, describes an historical event. In the Saxon Chronicle under the year 991 there occurs the following entry: "In this year came Unlaf with ninety-three ships to Stan [Folkstone], and laid waste the country round about, and from there he went to Sandwich and so on to Ipswich and harried all the country. And then he came to Maldon where the ealdorman Byrhtnoth with his force came to meet him and fought against him. And they slew the ealdorman there and were masters of the field of battle, and afterwards peace was made with them and the King received him at the bishop's hands." This Unlaf was the famous Olaf Trygvasson, the favorite hero of Norse history. The site of the battle has been thus described by Freeman (*Norman Conquest*, I, 268): "The battle took place near the town of Maldon [in Essex], on the banks of the tidal river Panta, now called the Blackwater. The town lies on a hill; immediately at its base flows one branch of the river while another, still crossed by a medieval bridge, flows at a little distance to the north. The Danish ships seem to have lain in the branch nearest to the town and their crews must have occupied the space between the two streams, while Byrhtnoth came to the rescue from the north. He seems to have halted on the spot now occupied by the church of Heybridge, having both streams between him and the town."

He bade each youth turn loose his horse and drive it far away,
And onward go with steadfast heart to mingle in the fray.
  When Offa's kinsman saw the Earl no cowardice would brook,
Off from his wrist to woodland wide his falcon dear he shook;
He joined the ranks, and straightway then might all men clearly know
Never the knight would shrink from fight when armed against the foe.
  Beside his liege lord Eadric, too, in battle sought to be;
Forth to the war he bore his spear—a dauntless heart had he—
The while he with his hands could grasp the buckler and broad sword;
Right well he kept the vow he pledged to fight before his lord.
  There Byrhtnoth then arrayed his men and taught them how to stand,
To keep their ranks, and fearless grasp the buckler in the hand.
And when they were in order set, he lighted from his steed
Among his own loved household-men whom he knew good at need.
  The herald of the Vikings stood beside the river shore,
And the sea-rover's haughty words before the Earl he bore:
"From seamen bold I come: they bid that thou shalt straightway send
Treasure for ransom; better 'twill be for you in the end
To buy with gifts our onslaught off than with us war to hold.
No need to fight if ye agree—we'll make a peace for gold:
If so thou orderest it, who here among the rest art chief,
That thou wilt set thy people free, then bid for their relief,
That they shall to the seamen give as seamen shall decree
Treasure for peace; then take ye peace, and we will put to sea
With booty-laden ships, and peace henceforth between us be!"
  Then Byrhtnoth lifted up his voice—his shield he brandished high,
And shook his slender ashen shaft—and thus he made reply.

[1]The translation is by H. W. Lumsden. It was first published in *Macmillan's Magazine* (Vol. 55). It is here reprinted from *Select Translations from Old English Poetry* with the permission of the editors, A. S. Cook and C. B. Tinker, and of the publishers, Messrs. Ginn and Company. A few lines are missing from both the beginning and the end of the poem.

Wrathful and resolute he spake: "O thou sea-robber, hear
What saith this folk! To you they give no tribute but the spear,
The venomed point, the old keen edge, and all the battle-gear
That works no good for you in fight! Go, seamen's herald, say
This message of yet deeper hate: that here, an Earl, I stay
Undaunted with my men to guard the kingdom, folk, and land
Of Æthelred my lord. In war the heathen shall not stand!
That ye should with our spoil go hence unfought, since thus ye came
So far into this land of ours, too great meseems the shame!
Nor think ye to win gold with ease—rather shall grim war-play
And sword and spear our compact make ere we will tribute pay!"
With that he bade his men go forth; their bucklers then they bore
Till at the landing-place they stood beside the river-shore.
Neither could reach the other there—between them flowed the tide;
For after ebb the flood rolled up, it filled the channel wide.
And till their spears together clashed too long the time did seem
To Vikings and East-Saxon ranks arrayed by Panta's stream,
For neither could the other hurt save by the arrows' flight
Till ebb of tide. Then ready there and burning for the fight
The Vikings stood, the seamen host. But Wulfstan—warrior old,
The son of Ceola—with his kin by Byrhtnoth sent to hold
The bridge against them, with the lance the foremost Viking slew
Who stepped, foolhardy, on the bridge. With Wulfstan heroes two,
Ælfhere and Maccus, firmly stood, no passage would they yield,
But bravely fought against the foe while they could weapons wield.
Now when the hated strangers saw the bridge-wards there so stout,
They changed their ground, and to the ford they led their forces out.
Then for the heathen host the Earl made way, and overbold
Men heard the son of Byrhthelm shout across the waters cold:
"Lo! here is room for you! Come on, come warriors to the fray!
God only knows which of us twain shall hold the field to-day."
Then onward came the wolves of war, they recked not of the flood;
Westward o'er Panta's gleaming waves they bore their shields and stood
Upon the bank. There 'gainst their foes were Byrhtnoth's men arrayed,
And at his word they held their ground and buckler-war they made.
Now drew the time of glorious deeds, the tide of battle nigh;
And now the fatal hour was come when death-doomed men must die!
Now loud uprose the battle-cry, and, greedy for their prey,
The ravens wheeled, the eagles screamed. On earth was noise of fray!
From hand was hurled the sharp-filed spear, the whetted arrow flew,
The bow was busy, shield met spear, and fierce the combat grew;
On either side brave soldiers fell. There Byrhtnoth's kinsman died,
Wulfmær, his sister's son, all hewn with sword-wounds deep and wide.
But to the Vikings recompense was fully paid; I know
That Eadward smote one with his sword, nor did the stroke forego
Till at his feet the doomed foe lay. For this his lord gave thanks
To his bower-thane in season due. Thus stoutly in the ranks
The warriors fought with weapons sharp, and each one strove to be
The first whose spear might reach the life of death-doomed enemy.
On earth was slaughter! Firm they stood; and Byrhtnoth's words of flame
Stirred every heart to bide the brunt and win a glorious name.
Forth went the hero old in war, he raised his sheltering shield
And shook his spear, and onward went into the battlefield.
Thus of one mind went earl to churl—alike their fell intent.
A southern lance the warrior's lord now pierced, by Viking sent;
But with his shield he thrust at it, the shaft to splinters broke,
And bent the head till out it sprang; then fierce his wrath awoke,
And at the foe who dealt the wound he hurled his deadly spear.
Skilled was the leader of the host—he sent the javelin sheer
Through the youth's neck; his guiding hand that Viking sought to slay;

And then another swift he shot, through corslet it made way,
And in the heart through rings of mail the venomed lance-head stood.
The blither was the Earl for that—he laughed, the bold of mood,
And for the day's work rendered thanks that God to him had given.
But from a warrior's clenchéd hand a dart was fiercely driven,
Too sure it went, and pierced the noble thane of Æthelred.
Besides him stood a beardless youth—a boy in battle dread—
Young Wulfmær, son of Wulfstan; he swift from the hero drew
The bloody dart and hurled it back; the hardened spear-head flew,
And on the earth the Viking lay who thus had reached his lord.
Then rushed a warrior armed to seize the goodly graven sword,
Bracelets, and corslet of the Earl, but Byrhtnoth drew his blade,
Brown-edged and broad, and fierce the strokes he on his corslet laid.
Too soon another smote his arm and hindered him. Then rolled
On earth the yellow-hilted sword, nor longer could he hold
Keen blade, nor weapon wield; but still the gray-haired leader bade
His men keep heart and onward press, good comrades undismayed.
No longer could he stand upright, his eyes to heaven he bent:
"Ruler of nations! I give thanks for all that Thou hast lent
Of joys in this world. Now have I, O gracious Lord! most need
That Thou show favor to my soul, that it to Thee may speed,
And to Thy Kingdom, Lord of angels! pass in peace. I pray
That hell-foes do me no despite."
They hewed him as he lay—
The heathen dogs!—and two with him, Ælfnoth and Wulfmær; there
Beside their lord they gave their lives. Then those who did not dare
To bide the battle turned away, and foremost in the flight
Were Odda's sons: Godric forsook his leader and the fight;
On his lord's horse he basely leaped—he who from that kind man
Had many a horse received—and with him both his brothers ran.
Godrinc and Godwy turned and fled, they cared not for the strife,
But sought the fastness of the wood and saved their coward life!
And many more ran with them than beseemed if they had thought
Of all the good in happier times the Earl for them had wrought,
So in the mead-hall at the moot had Offa said one day,
That many there spoke boldly who at need would fall away.
Thus fell the leader of the host, the Earl of Æthelred,
And all his hearth-companions saw that there their lord lay dead.
But hotly thither came proud thanes and dauntless men drew nigh;
One thing alone they all desired—to take revenge or die!
Young Ælfwine, Ælfric's son was he, thus boldly spake to all
And cheered them on: "O think how oft we've sat—brave men in hall!—
And on the benches o'er the mead made boast of deeds in fight!
Now let the truly brave be seen! I will in all men's sight
Uphold my ancestry; I come of noble Mercian race,
Ealhelm my grandsire was—a ruler wise and high in place;
And never shall my people's thanes reproach me that I fled
To seek my native land, and left my leader lying dead—
To me the worst of ills, for he my kinsman was and lord!"
Then forward burning for revenge he rushed, and with his sword
He smote a seaman 'mong the foe (on earth the heathen lay
Hewn with the weapon) and he cheered his comrades to the fray.
"Ælfwine, well said!" cried Offa then, and shook his ashen spear,
"Full surely it behoves us all, when slain our lord lies here,
To cheer each other on to fight while we can weapons wield,
Good sword, hard brand, or lance! Nigh lost to us hath been the field
Through Godric, Odda's dastard son; when on the noble steed
He rode away, too many deemed it was our lord indeed,
And thus the folk were all dismayed—broken the buckler-wall;
On his foul deed that wrought such flight my curses ever fall!"
Leofsunu to the warriors spake and raised his linden shield:

"A vow I've made that one foot's length here will I never yield,
But to revenge my dear loved lord right onward will I fare!
Round Stourmere never shall they say—the sturdy fighters there—
The scornful words that, now my lord is fallen, I turned from fray
And went home lordless! No! me rather spear and sword shall slay!"
Wrathful he rushed, he scorned to flee, but fought with steadfast heart.
Dunhere (an aged churl was he) then spoke and shook his dart;
Each warrior to revenge the earl he bade, and loud o'er all,
"Let him," he cried, "who on the foe would wreak his leader's fall
Brook no delay, nor care for life!" And onward went they then—
Regardless of their lives they went. Fiercely the household men,
The grim spear-bearers fought; to God they prayed that they might take
Full vengeance on their enemies for their loved leader's sake.
The hostage Æscferth, Ecglaf's son, now helped them readily,
(Of stout Northumbrian race he came); never at all paused he
In war-play, but continually he let his arrows go;
Sometimes with them he struck a shield, and sometimes pierced a foe;
With every shot he dealt a wound while he could weapons wield.
Eager and fierce tall Eadward stood, the foremost in the field,
Never a foot length would he flee, thus haughtily he spoke,
Nor turn his back on his dead lord! The buckler-wall he broke,
And fought the foe till, ere he died, full vengeance he had wrought,
For his wealth-giver, on the Danes. And fiercely likewise fought
His noble comrade Sigbyrht's brother Ætheric, brave and true,
And many more; the keeléd shields they clove, they sternly slew.
All broken was the buckler's edge—dreadful the corslets' song!
Now Offa struck and felled to earth a seaman 'mid the throng,
But there Gadd's kinsman bit the dust—too soon was Offa slain!
Yet he fulfilled the vow he pledged his lord that both again
Should ride safe homeward to the burgh, or wounded in the fray
Die on the battle-field. Thane-like, beside his lord, he lay!
Loud clashed the shields! Oft went the spear through doomed man's house of life!
The Vikings, burning for the war, came on. Then to the strife
Wigstan the son of Thurstan rushed, and in the crowd slew three
Ere he lay dead. 'Twas fiercest moot! The warriors steadfastly
In battle stood and wounded fell. On earth was slaughter dire!
Oswald and Ealdwold all the while still kept the ranks entire,
And both the brothers with fit words besought their kinsmen dear
Unflinchingly to bide the brunt and wield the sword and spear.
Then Byrhtwold the old comràde spoke; he shook his ashen dart
And grasped his shield and proudly cried: "The bolder be each heart,
Each spirit sterner, valor more, now that our strength is less!
Here our good leader lies on earth; may he who now from stress
Of war-play turns, for ever rue! Full old of years am I—
Hence will I never, but beside my lord I hope to lie,
The man beloved!"
So Godric, too, the son of Æthelgar,
Cheered on the warriors to the fight. Oft flew his spear afar—
His deadly spear—and Vikings smote: then rushing on the foe
Foremost of all he cut and hewed till battle laid him low.
Not that same Godric he who turned from fight. . .

SIR GAWAIN AND THE GREEN KNIGHT[1]

This poem is preserved in a manuscript of the Cotton collection in the British Museum. The manuscript dates from the end of the fourteenth century or early in the fifteenth, but the poem was probably written about 1370. Of the author nothing is known save what can be gathered from this poem—or from this poem and from the *Pearl*, *Purity*, and *Patience* (three other poems found in the same manuscript) if, as some scholars think on the basis of internal evidence, all four poems are by the same author. In either case we can say that the author was probably a native of Lancashire, as he uses the West Midland dialect; he was also a highly educated and cultivated gentleman, familiar with the best society of his day. "He had a keen eye, a vivid imagination, and a love for external phenomena, that gave him a power for description unequaled in Middle English literature. He was a lover of details; but he handled the details with a constructive power and a picturesqueness that create vivid impressions or realistic scenes. His observation of dress, of color, of position, of relative location, of deportment, enabled him at the opening of the piece to make of a conventional situation an intense, rich, dramatic scene with a splendid background. . . . He caught, and makes us feel, the very spirit of nature in varied moods, spring, summer, autumn —but especially nature in her wilder aspects, the biting winter, the icy rain, the dreary forest, the rugged rocks, the snow-covered country, and the cold hills lost in mist" (J. E. Wells, *Manual of the Writings in Middle English*, pp. 56–57). It should be added that this author had, too, real feeling for the higher spirit of chivalry and an uncommon fineness of nature. It is believed that he drew the materials for his story from a Norman-French romance now lost—which, in turn, was based on Celtic legend—but that their perfection of treatment is all his own. *Sir Gawain and the Green Knight* is by general consent the best of the English romances. It is also interesting for the picture it gives of the earlier Gawain; for in the beginning Gawain was without peer for courage and courtesy among the knights of the Round Table. It was only later that he came to be depreciated for the sake of others, and it is unfortunate that both Malory and Tennyson have contributed to make him best known as an "empty-headed, empty-hearted worldling."

I

After the siege and the assault of Troy, when that burg was destroyed and burnt to ashes, and the traitor tried for his treason, the noble Æneas and his kin sailed forth to become princes and patrons of well-nigh all the Western Isles. Thus Romulus built Rome (and gave to the city his own name, which it bears even to this day); and Ticius turned him to Tuscany; and Langobard raised him up dwellings in Lombardy; and Felix Brutus sailed far over the French flood, and founded the kingdom of Britain, wherein have been war and waste and wonder, and bliss and bale, ofttimes since.

And in that kingdom of Britain have been wrought more gallant deeds than in any other; but of all British kings Arthur was the most valiant, as I have heard tell; therefore will I set forth a wondrous adventure that fell out in his time. And if ye will listen to me, but for a little while, I will tell it even as it stands in story stiff and strong, fixed in the letter, as it hath long been known in the land.

King Arthur lay at Camelot upon a Christmas-tide, with many a gallant lord and lovely lady, and all the noble brotherhood of the Round Table. There they held rich revels with gay talk and jest; one while they would ride forth to joust and tourney, and again back to the court to make carols;[2] for there was the feast holden fifteen days with all the mirth that men could devise, song and glee, glorious to hear, in the daytime, and dancing at night. Halls and chambers were crowded with noble guests, the bravest of knights and the loveliest of ladies, and Arthur himself was the comeliest king that ever held a court. For all this fair folk were in their youth, the fairest and most fortunate

[1]This translation is by Miss Jessie L. Weston. It forms the first volume in the series of "Arthurian Romances unrepresented in Malory's *Morte d' Arthur*" published by David Nutt.

[2]Dances accompanied by song.

under heaven, and the king himself of such fame that it were hard now to name so valiant a hero.

Now the New Year had but newly come in, and on that day a double portion was served on the high table to all the noble guests, and thither came the king with all his knights, when the service in the chapel had been sung to an end. And they greeted each other for the New Year, and gave rich gifts, the one to the other (and they that received them were not wroth, that may ye well believe!), and the maidens laughed and made mirth till it was time to get them to meat. Then they washed and sat them down to the feasting in fitting rank and order, and Guinevere the queen, gaily clad, sat on the high daïs. Silken was her seat, with a fair canopy over her head, of rich tapestries of Tars, embroidered, and studded with costly gems; fair she was to look upon, with her shining gray eyes, a fairer woman might no man boast himself of having seen.

But Arthur would not eat till all were served, so full of joy and gladness was he, even as a child; he liked not either to lie long, or to sit long at meat, so worked upon him his young blood and his wild brain. And another custom he had also, that came of his nobility, that he would never eat upon an high day till he had been advised of some knightly deed, or some strange and marvelous tale, of his ancestors, or of arms, or of other ventures. Or till some stranger knight should seek of him leave to joust with one of the Round Table, that they might set their lives in jeopardy, one against another, as fortune might favor them. Such was the king's custom when he sat in hall at each high feast with his noble knights; therefore on that New Year tide, he abode, fair of face, on the throne, and made much mirth withal.

Thus the king sat before the high tables, and spake of many things; and there good Sir Gawain was seated by Guinevere the queen, and on her other side sat Agravain, *à la dure main;*[1] both were the king's sister's sons and full gallant knights. And at the end of the table was Bishop Bawdewyn, and Ywain, King Urien's son, sat at the other side alone. These were worthily served on the daïs, and at the lower tables sat many valiant knights. Then they bare the first course with the blast of trumpets and waving of banners, with the sound of drums and pipes, of song and lute, that many a heart was uplifted at the melody. Many were the dainties, and rare the meats; so great was the plenty they might scarce find room on the board to set on the dishes. Each helped himself as he liked best, and to each two were twelve dishes, with great plenty of beer and wine.

Now I will say no more of the service, but that ye may know there was no lack, for there drew near a venture that the folk might well have left their labor to gaze upon. As the sound of the music ceased, and the first course had been fitly served, there came in at the hall door one terrible to behold, of stature greater than any on earth; from neck to loin so strong and thickly made, and with limbs so long and so great that he seemed even as a giant. And yet he was but a man, only the mightiest that might mount a steed; broad of chest and shoulders and slender of waist, and all his features of like fashion; but men marveled much at his color, for he rode even as a knight, yet was green all over.

For he was clad all in green, with a straight coat, and a mantle above; all decked and lined with fur was the cloth and the hood that was thrown back from his locks and lay on his shoulders. Hose had he of the same green, and spurs of bright gold with silken fastenings richly worked; and all his vesture was verily green. Around his waist and his saddle were bands with fair stones set upon silken work, 't were too long to tell of all the trifles that were embroidered thereon—birds and insects in gay gauds of green and gold. All the trappings of his steed were of metal of like enamel, even the stirrups that he stood in stained of the same, and stirrups and saddle-bow alike gleamed and shone with green stones. Even the steed on which he rode was of the same hue, a green horse, great and strong, and hard to hold, with broidered bridle, meet for the rider.

The knight was thus gaily dressed in green, his hair falling around his shoulders; on his breast hung a beard, as thick and green as a bush, and the beard and the hair of his head were clipped all round above his elbows. The lower part of his sleeves was fastened with clasps in the same wise as a king's mantle. The horse's mane was crisp and plaited with

[1] Of the hard hand.

many a knot folded in with gold thread about the fair green, here a twist of the hair, here another of gold. The tail was twined in like manner, and both were bound about with a band of bright green set with many a precious stone; then they were tied aloft in a cunning knot, whereon rang many bells of burnished gold. Such a steed might no other ride, nor had such ever been looked upon in that hall ere that time; and all who saw that knight spake and said that a man might scarce abide his stroke.

The knight bore no helm nor hauberk, neither gorget nor breast-plate, neither shaft nor buckler to smite nor to shield, but in one hand he had a holly-bough, that is greenest when the groves are bare, and in his other an ax, huge and uncomely, a cruel weapon in fashion, if one would picture it. The head was an ell-yard long, the metal all of green steel and gold, the blade burnished bright, with a broad edge, as well shapen to shear as a sharp razor. The steel was set into a strong staff, all bound round with iron, even to the end, and engraved with green in cunning work. A lace was twined about it, that looped at the head, and all adown the handle it was clasped with tassels on buttons of bright green richly broidered.

The knight rideth through the entrance of the hall, driving straight to the high daïs, and greeted no man, but looked ever upwards; and the first words he spake were, "Where is the ruler of this folk? I would gladly look upon that hero, and have speech with him." He cast his eyes on the knights, and mustered[1] them up and down, striving ever to see who of them was of most renown.

Then was there great gazing to behold that chief, for each man marveled what it might mean that a knight and his steed should have even such a hue as the green grass; and that seemed even greener than green enamel on bright gold. All looked on him as he stood, and drew near unto him, wondering greatly what he might be; for many marvels had they seen, but none such as this, and phantasm and faërie did the folk deem it. Therefore were the gallant knights slow to answer, and gazed astounded, and sat stone still in a deep silence through that goodly hall, as if a slumber were fallen upon them. I deem it was not all for doubt, but some for courtesy that they might give ear unto his errand.

Then Arthur beheld this adventurer before his high daïs, and knightly he greeted him, for fearful was he never. "Sir," he said, "thou art welcome to this place—lord of this hall am I, and men call me Arthur. Light thee down, and tarry awhile, and what thy will is, that shall we learn after."

"Nay," quoth the stranger, "so help me he that sitteth on high, 't was not mine errand to tarry any while in this dwelling; but the praise of this thy folk and thy city is lifted up on high, and thy warriors are holden for the best and most valiant of those who ride mail-clad to the fight. The wisest and the worthiest of this world are they, and well proven in all knightly sports. And here, as I have heard tell, is fairest courtesy; therefore have I come hither as at this time. Ye may be sure by the branch that I bear here that I come in peace, seeking no strife. For had I willed to journey in warlike guise I have at home both hauberk and helm, shield and shining spear, and other weapons to mine hand, but since I seek no war, my raiment is that of peace. But if thou be as bold as all men tell, thou wilt freely grant me the boon I ask."

And Arthur answered, "Sir Knight, if thou cravest battle here thou shalt not fail for lack of a foe."

And the knight answered, "Nay, I ask no fight; in faith here on the benches are but beardless children; were I clad in armor on my steed there is no man here might match me. Therefore I ask in this court but a Christmas jest, for that it is Yule-tide and New Year, and there are here many fain for sport. If any one in this hall holds himself so hardy, so bold both of blood and brain, as to dare strike me one stroke for another, I will give him as a gift this ax, which is heavy enough, in sooth, to handle as he may list, and I will abide the first blow, unarmed as I sit. If any knight be so bold as to prove my words, let him come swiftly to me here, and take this weapon; I quit claim to it, he may keep it as his own, and I will abide his stroke, firm on the floor. Then shalt thou give me the right to deal him another, the respite of a year and a day shall he have. Now haste, and let see whether any here dare say aught."

Now if the knights had been astounded at the first, yet stiller were they all, high and

[1] Surveyed.

low, when they had heard his words. The knight on his steed straightened himself in the saddle, and rolled his eyes fiercely round the hall; red they gleamed under his green and bushy brows. He frowned and twisted his beard, waiting to see who should rise, and when none answered he cried aloud in mockery, "What, is this Arthur's hall, and these the knights whose renown hath run through many realms? Where are now your pride and your conquests, your wrath, and anger, and mighty words? Now are the praise and the renown of the Round Table overthrown by one man's speech, since all keep silence for dread ere ever they have seen a blow!"

With that he laughed so loudly that the blood rushed to the king's fair face for very shame; he waxed wroth, as did all his knights, and sprang to his feet, and drew near to the stranger and said, "Now by heaven, foolish is thy asking, and thy folly shall find its fitting answer. I know no man aghast at thy great words. Give me here thine ax and I shall grant thee the boon thou hast asked." Lightly he sprang to him and caught at his hand, and the knight, fierce of aspect, lighted down from his charger.

Then Arthur took the ax and gripped the haft, and swung it round, ready to strike. And the knight stood before him, taller by the head than any in the hall; he stood, and stroked his beard, and drew down his coat, no more dismayed for the king's threats than if one had brought him a drink of wine.

Then Gawain, who sat by the queen, leaned forward to the king and spake, "I beseech ye, my lord, let this venture be mine. Would ye but bid me rise from this seat, and stand by your side, so that my liege lady thought it not ill, then would I come to your counsel before this goodly court. For I think it not seemly when such challenges be made in your hall that ye yourself should undertake it, while there are many bold knights who sit beside ye, none are there, methinks, of readier will under heaven, or more valiant in open field. I am the weakest, I wot, and the feeblest of wit, and it will be the less loss of my life if ye seek sooth. For save that ye are mine uncle, naught is there in me to praise, no virtue is there in my body save your blood, and since this challenge is such folly that it beseems ye not to take it, and I have asked it from ye first, let it fall to me, and if I bear myself ungallantly, then let all this court blame me."

Then they all spake with one voice that the king should leave this venture and grant it to Gawain.

Then Arthur commanded the knight to rise, and he rose up quickly and knelt down before the king, and caught hold of the weapon; and the king loosed his hold of it, and lifted up his hand, and gave him his blessing, and bade him be strong both of heart and hand. "Keep thee well, nephew," quoth Arthur, "that thou give him but the one blow, and if thou redest[1] him rightly I trow thou shalt well abide the stroke he may give thee after."

Gawain stepped to the stranger, ax in hand, and he, never fearing, awaited his coming. Then the Green Knight spake to Sir Gawain, "Make we our covenant ere we go further. First, I ask thee, knight, what is thy name? Tell me truly, that I may know thee."

"In faith," quoth the good knight, "Gawain am I, who give thee this buffet, let what may come of it; and at this time twelvemonth will I take another at thine hand with whatsoever weapon thou wilt, and none other."

Then the other answered again, "Sir Gawain, so may I thrive as I am fain to take this buffet at thine hand," and he quoth further, "Sir Gawain, it liketh me well that I shall take at thy fist that which I have asked here, and thou hast readily and truly rehearsed all the covenant that I asked of the king, save that thou shalt swear me, by thy troth, to seek me thyself wherever thou hopest that I may be found, and win thee such reward as thou dealest me to-day, before this folk."

"Where shall I seek thee?" quoth Gawain. "Where is thy place? By him that made me, I wot never where thou dwellest, nor know I thee, knight, thy court, nor thy name. But teach me truly all that pertaineth thereto, and tell me thy name, and I shall use all my wit to win my way thither, and that I swear thee for sooth, and by my sure troth."

"That is enough in the New Year, it needs no more," quoth the Green Knight to the gallant Gawain, "if I tell thee truly when I have taken the blow, and thou hast smitten

[1]Handlest.

me; then will I teach thee of my house and home, and mine own name, then mayest thou ask thy road and keep covenant. And if I waste no words then farest thou the better, for thou canst dwell in thy land, and seek no further. But take now thy toll, and let see how thou strikest."

"Gladly will I," quoth Gawain, handling his ax.

Then the Green Knight swiftly made him ready, he bowed down his head, and laid his long locks on the crown that his bare neck might be seen. Gawain gripped his ax and raised it on high, the left foot he set forward on the floor, and let the blow fall lightly on the bare neck. The sharp edge of the blade sundered the bones, smote through the neck, and clave it in two, so that the edge of the steel bit on the ground, and the fair head fell to the earth that many struck it with their feet as it rolled forth. The blood spurted forth, and glistened on the green raiment, but the knight neither faltered nor fell; he started forward with out-stretched hand, and caught the head, and lifted it up; then he turned to his steed, and took hold of the bridle, set his foot in the stirrup, and mounted. His head he held by the hair, in his hand. Then he seated himself in his saddle as if naught ailed him, and he were not headless. He turned his steed about, the grim corpse bleeding freely the while, and they who looked upon him doubted them much for the covenant.

For he held up the head in his hand, and turned the face towards them that sat on the high daïs, and it lifted up the eyelids and looked upon them and spake as ye shall hear. "Look, Gawain, that thou art ready to go as thou hast promised, and seek loyally till thou find me, even as thou hast sworn in this hall in the hearing of these knights. Come thou, I charge thee, to the Green Chapel; such a stroke as thou hast dealt thou hast deserved, and it shall be promptly paid thee on New Year's morn. Many men know me as the Knight of the Green Chapel, and if thou askest, thou shalt not fail to find me. Therefore it behooves thee to come, or to yield thee as recreant."

With that he turned his bridle, and galloped out at the hall door, his head in his hands, so that the sparks flew from beneath his horse's hoofs. Whither he went none knew, no more than they wist whence he had come; and the king and Gawain they gazed and laughed, for in sooth this had proved a greater marvel than any they had known aforetime.

Though Arthur the king was astonished at his heart, yet he let no sign of it be seen, but spake in courteous wise to the fair queen: "Dear lady, be not dismayed, such craft is well suited to Christmas-tide when we seek jesting, laughter, and song, and fair carols of knights and ladies. But now I may well get me to meat, for I have seen a marvel I may not forget." Then he looked on Sir Gawain, and said gaily, "Now, fair nephew, hang up thine ax, since it has hewn enough," and they hung it on the dossal[1] above the daïs, where all men might look on it for a marvel, and by its true token tell of the wonder. Then the twain sat them down together, the king and the good knight, and men served them with a double portion, as was the share of the noblest, with all manner of meat and of minstrelsy. And they spent that day in gladness, but Sir Gawain must well bethink him of the heavy venture to which he had set his hand.

II

This beginning of adventures had Arthur at the New Year; for he yearned to hear gallant tales, though his words were few when he sat at the feast. But now had they stern work on hand. Gawain was glad to begin the jest in the hall, but ye need have no marvel if the end be heavy. For though a man be merry in mind when he has well drunk, yet a year runs full swiftly, and the beginning but rarely matches the end.

For Yule was now over-past, and the year after, each season in its turn following the other. For after Christmas comes crabbed Lent, that will have fish for flesh and simpler cheer. But then the weather of the world chides with winter; the cold withdraws itself, the clouds uplift, and the rain falls in warm showers on the fair plains. Then the flowers come forth, meadows and grove are clad in green, the birds make ready to build, and sing sweetly for solace of the soft summer that follows thereafter. The blossoms bud and blow in the hedgerows rich and rank,

[1]Tapestry.

and noble notes enough are heard in the fair woods.

After the season of summer, with the soft winds, when zephyr breathes lightly on seeds and herbs, joyous indeed is the growth that waxes thereout when the dew drips from the leaves beneath the blissful glance of the bright sun. But then comes harvest and hardens the grain, warning it to wax ripe ere the winter. The drought drives the dust on high, flying over the face of the land; the angry wind of the welkin wrestles with the sun; the leaves fall from the trees and light upon the ground, and all brown are the groves that but now were green, and ripe is the fruit that once was flower. So the year passes into many yesterdays, and winter comes again, as it needs no sage to tell us.

When the Michaelmas moon was come in with warnings of winter, Sir Gawain bethought him full oft of his perilous journey. Yet till All Hallows Day he lingered with Arthur, and on that day they made a great feast for the hero's sake, with much revel and richness of the Round Table. Courteous knights and comely ladies, all were in sorrow for the love of that knight, and though they spake no word of it, many were joyless for his sake.

And after meat, sadly Sir Gawain turned to his uncle, and spake of his journey, and said, "Liege lord of my life, leave from you I crave. Ye know well how the matter stands without more words; to-morrow am I bound to set forth in search of the Green Knight." Then came together all the noblest knights, Ywain and Erec, and many another. Sir Dodinel le Sauvage, the Duke of Clarence, Launcelot and Lionel, and Lucan the Good, Sir Bors and Bedivere, valiant knights both, and many another hero, with Sir Mador de la Porte, and they all drew near, heavy at heart, to take counsel with Sir Gawain. Much sorrow and weeping was there in the hall to think that so worthy a knight as Gawain should wend his way to seek a deadly blow, and should no more wield his sword in fight. But the knight made ever good cheer, and said, "Nay, wherefore should I shrink? What may a man do but prove his fate?"

He dwelt there all that day, and on the morn he arose and asked betimes for his armor; and they brought it unto him on this wise: first, a rich carpet was stretched on the floor (and brightly did the gold gear glitter upon it), then the knight stepped upon it, and handled the steel; clad he was in a doublet of silk, with a close hood, lined fairly throughout. Then they set the steel shoes upon his feet, and wrapped his legs with greaves, with polished knee-caps, fastened with knots of gold. Then they cased his thighs in cuisses closed with thongs, and brought him the byrnie of bright steel rings sewn upon a fair stuff. Well burnished braces they set on each arm with good elbow-pieces, and gloves of mail, and all the goodly gear that should shield him in his need. And they cast over all a rich surcoat, and set the golden spurs on his heels, and girt him with a trusty sword fastened with a silken bawdrick. When he was thus clad his harness was costly, for the least loop or latchet gleamed with gold. So armed as he was he hearkened Mass and made his offering at the high altar. Then he came to the king, and the knights of his court, and courteously took leave of lords and ladies, and they kissed him, and commended him to Christ.

With that was Gringalet ready, girt with a saddle that gleamed gaily with many golden fringes, enriched and decked anew for the venture. The bridle was all barred about with bright gold buttons, and all the covertures and trappings of the steed, the crupper and the rich skirts, accorded with the saddle; spread fair with the rich red gold that glittered and gleamed in the rays of the sun.

Then the knight called for his helmet, which was well lined throughout, and set it high on his head, and hasped it behind. He wore a light kerchief over the ventail, that was broidered and studded with fair gems on a broad silken ribbon, with birds of gay color, and many a turtle[1] and true-lover's knot interlaced thickly, even as many a maiden had wrought diligently for seven winters long. But the circlet which crowned his helmet was yet more precious, being adorned with a device in diamonds. Then they brought him his shield, which was of bright red, with the pentangle painted thereon in gleaming gold. And why that noble prince bare the pentangle I am minded to tell you, though my tale tarry thereby. It is a sign that Solomon set erewhile, as betokening truth; for it is a figure with

[1]Turtle-dove.

five points and each line overlaps the other, and nowhere hath it beginning or end, so that in English it is called "the endless knot." And therefore was it well suiting to this knight and to his arms, since Gawain was faithful in five and five-fold, for pure was he as gold, void of all villainy and endowed with all virtues. Therefore he bare the pentangle on shield and surcoat as truest of heroes and gentlest of knights.

For first he was faultless in his five senses; and his five fingers never failed him; and all his trust upon earth was in the five wounds that Christ bare on the cross, as the Creed tells. And wherever this knight found himself in stress of battle he deemed well that he drew his strength from the five joys which the Queen of Heaven had of her Child. And for this cause did he bear an image of Our Lady on the one half of his shield, that whenever he looked upon it he might not lack for aid. And the fifth five that the hero used were frankness and fellowship above all, purity and courtesy that never failed him, and compassion that surpasses all; and in these five virtues was that hero wrapped and clothed. And all these, fivefold, were linked one in the other, so that they had no end, and were fixed on five points that never failed, neither at any side were they joined or sundered, nor could ye find beginning or end. And therefore on his shield was the knot shapen, red-gold upon red, which is the pure pentangle. Now was Sir Gawain ready, and he took his lance in hand, and bade them all farewell, he deemed it had been for ever.

Then he smote the steed with his spurs, and sprang on his way, so that sparks flew from the stones after him. All that saw him were grieved at heart, and said one to the other, "By Christ, 't is great pity that one of such noble life should be lost! I' faith, 't were not easy to find his equal upon earth. The king had done better to have wrought more warily. Yonder knight should have been made a duke; a gallant leader of men is he, and such a fate had beseemed him better than to be hewn in pieces at the will of an elfish man, for mere pride. Who ever knew a king to take such counsel as to risk his knights on a Christmas jest?" Many were the tears that flowed from their eyes when that goodly knight rode from the hall. He made no delaying, but went his way swiftly, and rode many a wild road, as I heard say in the book.

So rode Sir Gawain through the realm of Logres,[1] on an errand that he held for no jest. Often he lay companionless at night, and must lack the fare that he liked. No comrade had he save his steed, and none save God with whom to take counsel. At length he drew nigh to North Wales, and left the isles of Anglesey on his left hand, crossing over the fords by the foreland over at Holyhead, till he came into the wilderness of Wirral,[2] where but few dwell who love God and man of true heart. And ever he asked, as he fared, of all whom he met, if they had heard any tidings of a Green Knight in the country thereabout, or of a Green Chapel? And all answered him, "Nay," never in their lives had they seen any man of such a hue. And the knight wended his way by many a strange road and many a rugged path, and the fashion of his countenance changed full often ere he saw the Green Chapel.

Many a cliff did he climb in that unknown land, where afar from his friends he rode as a stranger. Never did he come to a stream or a ford but he found a foe before him, and that one so marvelous, so foul and fell, that it behooved him to fight. So many wonders did that knight behold, that it were too long to tell the tenth part of them. Sometimes he fought with dragons and wolves; sometimes with wild men that dwelt in the rocks; another while with bulls, and bears, and wild boars, or with giants of the high moorland that drew near to him. Had he not been a doughty knight, enduring, and of well-proved valor, and a servant of God, doubtless he had been slain, for he was oft in danger of death. Yet he cared not so much for the strife; what he deemed worse was when the cold clear water was shed from the clouds, and froze ere it fell on the fallow ground. More nights than enough he slept in his harness on the bare rocks, near slain with the sleet, while the stream leapt bubbling from the crest of the hills, and hung in hard icicles over his head.

Thus in peril and pain, and many a hardship, the knight rode alone till Christmas Eve, and in that tide he made his prayer to the Blessed Virgin that she would guide his

---

[1] England. [2] In Cheshire.

steps and lead him to some dwelling. On that morning he rode by a hill, and came into a thick forest, wild and drear; on each side were high hills, and thick woods below them of great hoar oaks, a hundred together, of hazel and hawthorn with their trailing boughs intertwined, and rough ragged moss spreading everywhere. On the bare twigs the birds chirped piteously, for pain of the cold. The knight upon Gringalet rode lonely beneath them, through marsh and mire, much troubled at heart lest he should fail to see the service of the Lord, who on that self-same night was born of a maiden for the cure of our grief; and therefore he said, sighing, "I beseech thee, Lord, and Mary thy gentle Mother, for some shelter where I may hear Mass, and thy matins at morn. This I ask meekly, and thereto I pray my Paternoster, Ave, and Credo." Thus he rode praying, and lamenting his misdeeds, and he crossed himself, and said, "May the Cross of Christ speed me."

Now that knight had crossed himself but thrice ere he was aware in the wood of a dwelling within a moat, above a lawn, on a mound surrounded by many mighty trees that stood round the moat. 'Twas the fairest castle that ever a knight owned; built in a meadow with a park all about it, and a spiked palisade, closely driven, that enclosed the trees for more than two miles. The knight was ware of the hold from the side, as it shone through the oaks. Then he lifted off his helmet, and thanked Christ and Saint Julian that they had courteously granted his prayer, and hearkened to his cry. "Now," quoth the knight, "I beseech ye, grant me fair hostel." Then he pricked Gringalet with his golden spurs, and rode gaily towards the great gate, and came swiftly to the bridge end.

The bridge was drawn up and the gates close shut; the walls were strong and thick, so that they might fear no tempest. The knight on his charger abode on the bank of the deep double ditch that surrounded the castle. The walls were set deep in the water, and rose aloft to a wondrous height; they were of hard hewn stone up to the corbels, which were adorned beneath the battlements with fair carvings, and turrets set in between with many a loophole; a better barbican Sir Gawain had never looked upon. And within he beheld the high hall, with its tower and many windows with carven cornices, and chalk-white chimneys on the turreted roofs that shone fair in the sun. And everywhere, thickly scattered on the castle battlements, were pinnacles, so many that it seemed as if it were all wrought out of paper, so white was it.

The knight on his steed deemed it fair enough, if he might come to be sheltered within it to lodge there while that the holyday lasted. He called aloud, and soon there came a porter of kindly countenance, who stood on the wall and greeted this knight and asked his errand.

"Good sir," quoth Gawain, "wilt thou go mine errand to the high lord of the castle, and crave for me lodging?"

"Yea, by Saint Peter," quoth the porter. "In sooth I trow that ye be welcome to dwell here so long as it may like ye."

Then he went, and came again swiftly, and many folk with him to receive the knight. They let down the great drawbridge, and came forth and knelt on their knees on the cold earth to give him worthy welcome. They held wide open the great gates, and courteously he bade them rise, and rode over the bridge. Then men came to him and held his stirrup while he dismounted, and took and stabled his steed. There came down knights and squires to bring the guest with joy to the hall. When he raised his helmet there were many to take it from his hand, fain to serve him, and they took from him sword and shield.

Sir Gawain gave good greeting to the noble and the mighty men who came to do him honor. Clad in his shining armor they led him to the hall, where a great fire burned brightly on the floor; and the lord of the household came forth from his chamber to meet the hero fitly. He spake to the knight, and said: "Ye are welcome to do here as it likes ye. All that is here is your own to have at your will and disposal."

"Gramercy!" quoth Gawain, "may Christ requite ye."

As friends that were fain each embraced the other; and Gawain looked on the knight who greeted him so kindly, and thought 't was a bold warrior that owned that burg.

Of mighty stature he was, and of high age; broad and flowing was his beard, and of a bright hue. He was stalwart of limb, and strong in his stride, his face fiery red, and his speech free: in sooth he seemed one well fitted to be a leader of valiant men.

Then the lord led Sir Gawain to a chamber, and commanded folk to wait upon him, and at his bidding there came men enough who brought the guest to a fair bower. The bedding was noble, with curtains of pure silk wrought with gold, and wondrous coverings of fair cloth all embroidered. The curtains ran on ropes with rings of red gold, and the walls were hung with carpets of Orient, and the same spread on the floor. There with mirthful speeches they took from the guest his byrnie and all his shining armor, and brought him rich robes of the choicest in its stead. They were long and flowing, and became him well, and when he was clad in them all who looked on the hero thought that surely God had never made a fairer knight: he seemed as if he might be a prince without peer in the field where men strive in battle.

Then before the hearth-place, whereon the fire burned, they made ready a chair for Gawain, hung about with cloth and fair cushions; and there they cast around him a mantle of brown samite, richly embroidered and furred within with costly skins of ermine, with a hood of the same, and he seated himself in that rich seat, and warmed himself at the fire, and was cheered at heart. And while he sat thus, the serving men set up a table on trestles, and covered it with a fair white cloth, and set thereon salt-cellar, and napkin, and silver spoons; and the knight washed at his will, and set him down to meat.

The folk served him courteously with many dishes seasoned of the best, a double portion. All kinds of fish were there, some baked in bread, some broiled on the embers, some sodden,[1] some stewed and savored with spices, with all sorts of cunning devices to his taste. And often he called it a feast, when they spake gaily to him all together, and said, "Now take ye this penance, and it shall be for your amendment." Much mirth thereof did Sir Gawain make.

Then they questioned that prince courteously of whence he came; and he told them that he was of the court of Arthur, who is the rich royal king of the Round Table, and that it was Gawain himself who was within their walls, and would keep Christmas with them, as the chance had fallen out. And when the lord of the castle heard those tidings he laughed aloud for gladness, and all men in that keep were joyful that they should be in the company of him to whom belonged all fame, and valor, and courtesy, and whose honor was praised above that of all men on earth. Each said softly to his fellow, "Now shall we see courteous bearing, and the manner of speech befitting courts. What charm lieth in gentle speech shall we learn without asking, since here we have welcomed the fine father of courtesy. God has surely shown us his grace since he sends us such a guest as Gawain! When men shall sit and sing, blithe for Christ's birth, this knight shall bring us to the knowledge of fair manners, and it may be that hearing him we may learn the cunning speech of love."

By the time the knight had risen from dinner it was near nightfall. Then chaplains took their way to the chapel, and rang loudly, even as they should, for the solemn evensong of the high feast. Thither went the lord, and the lady also, and entered with her maidens into a comely closet, and thither also went Gawain. Then the lord took him by the sleeve and led him to a seat, and called him by his name, and told him he was of all men in the world the most welcome. And Sir Gawain thanked him truly, and each kissed the other, and they sat gravely together throughout the service.

Then was the lady fain to look upon that knight; and she came forth from her closet with many fair maidens. The fairest of ladies was she in face, and figure, and coloring, fairer even than Guinevere, so the knight thought. She came through the chancel to greet the hero; another lady held her by the left hand, older than she, and seemingly of high estate, with many nobles about her. But unlike to look upon were those ladies, for if the younger were fair, the elder was yellow. Rich red were the cheeks of the one, rough and wrinkled those of the other; the kerchiefs of the one were broidered with many glistening pearls, her throat and neck bare, and whiter than the snow that lies on the hills; the neck of the other was swathed in a gorget, with a white wimple over her black chin.

[1]Boiled.

Her forehead was wrapped in silk with many folds, worked with knots, so that naught of her was seen save her black brows, her eyes, her nose, and her lips, and those were bleared, and ill to look upon. A worshipful lady in sooth one might call her! In figure was she short and broad, and thickly made—far fairer to behold was she whom she led by the hand.

When Gawain beheld that fair lady, who looked at him graciously, with leave of the lord he went towards them, and, bowing low, he greeted the elder, but the younger and fairer he took lightly in his arms, and kissed her courteously, and greeted her in knightly wise. Then she hailed him as friend, and he quickly prayed to be counted as her servant, if she so willed. Then they took him between them, and talking, led him to the chamber, to the hearth, and bade them bring spices, and they brought them in plenty with the good wine that was wont to be drunk at such seasons. Then the lord sprang to his feet and bade them make merry, and took off his hood, and hung it on a spear, and bade him win the worship thereof who should make most mirth that Christmas-tide. "And I shall try, by my faith, to fool it with the best, by the help of my friends, ere I lose my raiment." Thus with gay words the lord made trial to gladden Gawain with jests that night, till it was time to bid them light the tapers, and Sir Gawain took leave of them and gat him to rest.

In the morn when all men call to mind how Christ our Lord was born on earth to die for us, there is joy, for his sake, in all dwellings of the world; and so was there here on that day. For high feast was held, with many dainties and cunningly cooked messes. On the daïs sat gallant men, clad in their best. The ancient dame sat on the high seat with the lord of the castle beside her. Gawain and the fair lady sat together, even in the midst of the board when the feast was served; and so throughout all the hall each sat in his degree, and was served in order. There was meat, there was mirth, there was much joy, so that to tell thereof would take me too long, though peradventure I might strive to declare it. But Gawain and that fair lady had much joy of each other's company through her sweet words and courteous converse. And there was music made before each prince, trumpets and drums, and merry pipings; each man hearkened his minstrel, and they too hearkened theirs.

So they held high feast that day and the next, and the third day thereafter, and the joy on Saint John's Day was fair to hearken, for 't was the last of the feast and the guests would depart in the gray of the morning. Therefore they awoke early, and drank wine, and danced fair carols, and at last, when it was late, each man took his leave to wend early on his way. Gawain would bid his host farewell, but the lord took him by the hand, and led him to his own chamber beside the hearth, and there he thanked him for the favor he had shown him in honoring his dwelling at that high season, and gladdening his castle with his fair countenance. "I wis, sir, that while I live I shall be held the worthier that Gawain has been my guest at God's own feast."

"Gramercy, sir," quoth Gawain, "in good faith, all the honor is yours, may the High King give it you, and I am but at your will to work your behest, inasmuch as I am beholden to you in great and small by rights."

Then the lord did his best to persuade the knight to tarry with him, but Gawain answered that he might in no wise do so. Then the host asked him courteously what stern behest had driven him at the holy season from the king's court, to fare all alone, ere yet the feast was ended?

"Forsooth," quoth the knight, "ye say but the truth: 't is a high quest and a pressing that hath brought me afield, for I am summoned myself to a certain place, and I know not whither in the world I may wend to find it; so help me Christ, I would give all the kingdom of Logres an I might find it by New Year's morn. Therefore, sir, I make request of you that ye tell me truly if ye ever heard word of the Green Chapel, where it may be found, and the Green Knight that keeps it. For I am pledged by solemn compact sworn between us to meet that knight at the New Year if so I were on life; and of that same New Year it wants but little—I' faith, I would look on that hero more joyfully than on any other fair sight! Therefore, by your will, it behooves me to leave you, for I have but barely three days, and I would as fain fall dead as fail of mine errand."

Then the lord quoth, laughing, "Now must ye needs stay, for I will show you your goal, the Green Chapel, ere your term be at an end, have ye no fear! But ye can take your ease, friend, in your bed, till the fourth day, and go forth on the first of the year and come to that place at mid-morn to do as ye will. Dwell here till New Year's Day, and then rise and set forth, and ye shall be set in the way; 't is not two miles hence."

Then was Gawain glad, and he laughed gaily. "Now I thank you for this above all else. Now my quest is achieved I will dwell here at your will, and otherwise do as ye shall ask."

Then the lord took him, and set him beside him, and bade the ladies be fetched for their greater pleasure, tho' between themselves they had solace. The lord, for gladness, made merry jest, even as one who wist not what to do for joy; and he cried aloud to the knight, "Ye have promised to do the thing I bid ye: will ye hold to this behest, here, at once?"

"Yea, forsooth," said that true knight, "while I abide in your burg I am bound by your behest."

"Ye have traveled from far," said the host, "and since then ye have waked with me, ye are not well refreshed by rest and sleep, as I know. Ye shall therefore abide in your chamber, and lie at your ease to-morrow at Mass-tide, and go to meat when ye will with my wife, who shall sit with you, and comfort you with her company till I return; and I shall rise early and go forth to the chase." And Gawain agreed to all this courteously.

"Sir knight," quoth the host, "we will make a covenant. Whatsoever I win in the wood shall be yours, and whatever may fall to your share, that shall ye exchange for it. Let us swear, friend, to make this exchange, however our hap may be, for worse or for better."

"I grant ye your will," quoth Gawain the good; "if ye list so to do, it liketh me well."

"Bring hither the wine-cup, the bargain is made," so said the lord of that castle. They laughed each one, and drank of the wine, and made merry, these lords and ladies, as it pleased them. Then with gay talk and merry jest they rose, and stood, and spoke softly, and kissed courteously, and took leave of each other. With burning torches, and many a serving-man, was each led to his couch; yet ere they gat them to bed the old lord oft repeated their covenant, for he knew well how to make sport.

III

Full early, ere daylight, the folk rose up; the guests who would depart called their grooms, and they made them ready, and saddled the steeds, tightened up the girths, and trussed up their mails. The knights, all arrayed for riding, leapt up lightly, and took their bridles, and each rode his way as pleased him best.

The lord of the land was not the last. Ready for the chase, with many of his men, he ate a sop hastily when he had heard Mass, and then with blast of the bugle fared forth to the field. He and his nobles were to horse ere daylight glimmered upon the earth.

Then the huntsmen coupled their hounds, unclosed the kennel door, and called them out. They blew three blasts gaily on the bugles, the hounds bayed fiercely, and they that would go a-hunting checked and chastised them. A hundred hunters there were of the best, so I have heard tell. Then the trackers gat them to the trysting-place and uncoupled the hounds, and the forest rang again with their gay blasts.

At the first sound of the hunt the game quaked for fear, and fled, trembling, along the vale. They betook them to the heights, but the liers in wait turned them back with loud cries; the harts they let pass them, and the stags with their spreading antlers, for the lord had forbidden that they should be slain, but the hinds and the does they turned back, and drave down into the valleys. Then might ye see much shooting of arrows. As the deer fled under the boughs a broad whistling shaft smote and wounded each sorely, so that, wounded and bleeding, they fell dying on the banks. The hounds followed swiftly on their tracks, and hunters, blowing the horn, sped after them with ringing shouts as if the cliffs burst asunder. What game escaped those that shot was run down at the outer ring. Thus were they driven on the hills, and harassed at the waters, so well did the men know their work, and the greyhounds were so great and swift that they ran them down as fast as the hunters could slay them. Thus the lord passed the day in mirth and joyfulness, even to nightfall.

So the lord roamed the woods, and Gawain, that good knight, lay ever a-bed, curtained about, under the costly coverlet, while the daylight gleamed on the walls. And as he lay half slumbering, he heard a little sound at the door, and he raised his head, and caught back a corner of the curtain, and waited to see what it might be. It was the lovely lady, the lord's wife; she shut the door softly behind her, and turned towards the bed; and Gawain was shamed, laid him down softly and made as if he slept. And she came lightly to the bedside, within the curtain, and sat herself down beside him, to wait till he wakened. The knight lay there awhile, and marveled within himself what her coming might betoken; and he said to himself, "'T were more seemly if I asked her what hath brought her hither." Then he made feint to waken, and turned towards her, and opened his eyes as one astonished, and crossed himself; and she looked on him laughing, with her cheeks red and white, lovely to behold, and small smiling lips.

"Good morrow, Sir Gawain," said that fair lady; "ye are but a careless sleeper, since one can enter thus. Now are ye taken unawares, and lest ye escape me I shall bind you in your bed; of that be ye assured!" Laughing, she spake these words.

"Good morrow, fair lady," quoth Gawain blithely. "I will do your will, as it likes me well. For I yield me readily, and pray your grace, and that is best, by my faith, since I needs must do so." Thus he jested again, laughing. "But an ye would, fair lady, grant me this grace that ye pray your prisoner to rise. I would get me from bed, and array me better, then could I talk with ye in more comfort."

"Nay, forsooth, fair sir," quoth the lady, "ye shall not rise, I will rede[1] ye better. I shall keep ye here, since ye can do no other, and talk with my knight whom I have captured. For I know well that ye are Sir Gawain, whom all the world worships, wheresoever ye may ride. Your honor and your courtesy are praised by lords and ladies, by all who live. Now ye are here and we are alone, my lord and his men are afield; the serving men in their beds, and my maidens also, and the door shut upon us. And since in this hour I have him that all men love I shall use my time well with speech, while it lasts. Ye are welcome to my company, for it behooves me in sooth to be your servant."

"In good faith," quoth Gawain, "I think me that I am not him of whom ye speak, for unworthy am I of such service as ye here proffer. In sooth, I were glad if I might set myself by word or service to your pleasure; a pure joy would it be to me!"

"In good faith, Sir Gawain," quoth the gay lady, "the praise and the prowess that pleases all ladies I lack them not, nor hold them light; yet are there ladies enough who would liever now have the knight in their hold, as I have ye here, to dally with your courteous words, to bring them comfort and to ease their cares, than much of the treasure and the gold that are theirs. And now, through the grace of Him who upholds the heavens, I have wholly in my power that which they all desire!"

Thus the lady, fair to look upon, made him great cheer, and Sir Gawain, with modest words, answered her again: "Madam," he quoth, "may Mary requite ye, for in good faith I have found in ye a noble frankness. Much courtesy have other folk shown me, but the honor they have done me is naught to the worship of yourself, who knoweth but good."

"By Mary," quoth the lady, "I think otherwise; for were I worth all the women alive, and had I the wealth of the world in my hand, and might choose me a lord to my liking, then, for all that I have seen in ye, Sir Knight, of beauty and courtesy and blithe semblance, and for all that I have hearkened and hold for true, there should be no knight on earth to be chosen before ye."

"Well, I wot," quoth Sir Gawain, "that ye have chosen a better; but I am proud that ye should so prize me, and as your servant do I hold ye my sovereign, and your knight am I, and may Christ reward ye."

So they talked of many matters till midmorn was past, and ever the lady made as though she loved him, and the knight turned her speech aside. For though she were the brightest of maidens, yet had he forborne to show her love for the danger that awaited him, and the blow that must be given without delay.

[1] Manage.

Then the lady prayed her leave from him, and he granted it readily. And she gave him good-day, with laughing glance, but he must needs marvel at her words:

"Now He that speeds fair speech reward ye this disport; but that ye be Gawain my mind misdoubts me greatly."

"Wherefore?" quoth the knight quickly, fearing lest he had lacked in some courtesy.

And the lady spake: "So true a knight as Gawain is holden, and one so perfect in courtesy, would never have tarried so long with a lady but he would of his courtesy have craved a kiss at parting."

Then quoth Gawain, "I wot I will do even as it may please ye, and kiss at your commandment, as a true knight should who forbears to ask for fear of displeasure."

At that she came near and bent down and kissed the knight, and each commended the other to Christ, and she went forth from the chamber softly.

Then Sir Gawain rose and called his chamberlain and chose his garments, and when he was ready he gat him forth to Mass, and then went to meat, and made merry all day till the rising of the moon, and never had a knight fairer lodging than had he with those two noble ladies, the elder and the younger.

And ever the lord of the land chased the hinds through holt and heath till eventide, and then with much blowing of bugles and baying of hounds they bore the game homeward; and by the time daylight was done all the folk had returned to that fair castle. And when the lord and Sir Gawain met together, then were they both well pleased. The lord commanded them all to assemble in the great hall, and the ladies to descend with their maidens, and there, before them all, he bade the men fetch in the spoil of the day's hunting, and he called unto Gawain, and counted the tale of the beasts, and showed them unto him, and said, "What think ye of this game, Sir Knight? Have I deserved of ye thanks for my woodcraft?"

"Yea, I wis," quoth the other, "here is the fairest spoil I have seen this seven year in the winter season."

"And all this do I give ye, Gawain," quoth the host, "for by accord of covenant ye may claim it as your own."

"That in sooth," quoth the other, "I grant you that same; and I have fairly won this within walls, and with as good will do I yield it to you." With that he clasped his hands round the lord's neck and kissed him as courteously as he might. "Take ye here my spoils, no more have I won; ye should have it freely, though it were greater than this."

"'T is good," said the host, "gramercy thereof. Yet were I fain to know where ye won this same favor, and if it were by your own wit?"

"Nay," answered Gawain, "that was not in the bond. Ask me no more: ye have taken what was yours by right, be content with that."

They laughed and jested together, and sat them down to supper, where they were served with many dainties; and after supper they sat by the hearth, and wine was served out to them; and oft in their jesting they promised to observe on the morrow the same covenant that they had made before, and whatever chance might betide, to exchange their spoil, be it much or little, when they met at night. Thus they renewed their bargain before the whole court, and then the night-drink was served, and each courteously took leave of the other and gat him to bed.

By the time the cock had crowed thrice the lord of the castle had left his bed; Mass was sung and meat fitly served. The folk were forth to the wood ere the day broke, with hound and horn they rode over the plain, and uncoupled their dogs among the thorns. Soon they struck on the scent, and the hunt cheered on the hounds who were first to seize it, urging them with shouts. The others hastened to the cry, forty at once, and there rose such a clamor from the pack that the rocks rang again. The huntsmen spurred them on with shouting and blasts of the horn; and the hounds drew together to a thicket betwixt the water and a high crag in the cliff beneath the hillside. There where the rough rock fell ruggedly they, the huntsmen, fared to the finding, and cast about round the hill and the thicket behind them. The knights wist well what beast was within, and would drive him forth with the bloodhounds. And as they beat the bushes, suddenly over the beaters there rushed forth a wondrous great and fierce boar, long since had he left the herd to roam by himself. Grunting, he cast many to the ground, and fled forth at his best speed, without more mischief. The men hallooed loudly and cried, "Hay! Hay!" and blew the horns to urge on the hounds, and rode swiftly after the boar. Many a time did he turn to bay and tare the hounds, and they yelped, and howled shrilly. Then the men made ready their arrows and shot at him, but the points were turned on his thick hide, and the barbs would not bite upon him, for the shafts shivered in pieces, and the head but leapt again wherever it hit.

But when the boar felt the stroke of the arrows he waxed mad with rage, and turned on the hunters and tare many, so that, affrighted, they fled before him. But the lord on a swift steed pursued him, blowing his bugle; as a gallant knight he rode through the woodland chasing the boar till the sun grew low.

So did the hunters this day, while Sir Gawain lay in his bed lapped in rich gear; and the lady forgat not to salute him, for early was she at his side, to cheer his mood.

She came to the bedside and looked on the knight, and Gawain gave her fit greeting, and she greeted him again with ready words, and sat her by his side and laughed, and with a sweet look she spoke to him:

"Sir, if ye be Gawain, I think it a wonder that ye be so stern and cold, and care not for the courtesies of friendship, but if one teach ye to know them ye cast the lesson out of your mind. Ye have soon forgotten what I taught ye yesterday, by all the truest tokens that I knew!"

"What is that?" quoth the knight. "I trow I know not. If it be sooth that ye say, then is the blame mine own."

"But I taught ye of kissing," quoth the fair lady. "Wherever a fair countenance is shown him, it behooves a courteous knight quickly to claim a kiss."

"Nay, my dear," said Sir Gawain, "cease that speech; that durst I not do lest I were denied, for if I were forbidden I wot I were wrong did I further entreat."

"I' faith," quoth the lady merrily, "ye may not be forbid, ye are strong enough to constrain by strength an ye will, were any so discourteous as to give ye denial."

"Yea, by heaven," said Gawain, "ye speak well; but threats profit little in the land where I dwell, and so with a gift that is given not of good will! I am at your commandment to kiss when ye like, to take or to leave as ye list."

Then the lady bent her down and kissed him courteously.

And as they spake together she said, "I would learn somewhat from ye, an ye would not be wroth, for young ye are and fair, and so courteous and knightly as ye are known to be, the head of all chivalry, and versed in all wisdom of love and war—'t is ever told of true knights how they adventured their lives for their true love, and endured hardships for her favors, and avenged her with valor, and eased her sorrows, and brought joy to her bower; and ye are the fairest knight of your time, and your fame and your honor are everywhere, yet I have sat by ye here twice, and never a word have I heard of love! Ye who are so courteous and skilled in such love ought surely to teach one so young and unskilled some little craft of true love! Why are ye so unlearned who art otherwise so famous? Or is it that ye deemed me unworthy to hearken to your teaching? For shame, Sir Knight! I come hither alone and sit at your side to learn of ye some skill; teach me of your wit, while my lord is from home."

"In good faith," quoth Gawain, "great is my joy and my profit that so fair a lady as ye are should deign to come hither, and trouble ye with so poor a man, and make sport with your knight with kindly countenance, it pleaseth me much. But that I, in my turn, should take it upon me to tell of love and such like matters to ye who know more by half, or a hundred fold, of such craft than I do, or ever shall in all my lifetime, by my troth 't were folly indeed! I will work your will to the best of my might as I am bounden, and evermore will I be your servant, so help me Christ!"

Then often with guile she questioned that knight that she might win him to woo her, but he defended himself so fairly that none might in any wise blame him, and naught but bliss and harmless jesting was there between them. They laughed and talked together till at last she kissed him, and craved her leave of him, and went her way.

Then the knight rose and went forth to Mass, and afterward dinner was served and he sat and spake with the ladies all day. But the lord of the castle rode ever over the land chasing the wild boar, that fled through the thickets, slaying the best of his hounds and breaking their backs in sunder; till at last he was so weary he might run no longer, but made for a hole in a mound by a rock. He got the mound at his back and faced the hounds, whetting his white tusks and foaming at the mouth. The huntsmen stood aloof, fearing to draw nigh him; so many of them had been already wounded that they were loath to be torn with his tusks, so fierce he was and mad with rage. At length the lord himself came up, and saw the beast at bay, and the men standing aloof. Then quickly he sprang to the ground and drew out a bright blade, and waded through the stream to the boar.

When the beast was aware of the knight with weapon in hand, he set up his bristles and snorted loudly, and many feared for their lord lest he should be slain. Then the boar leapt upon the knight so that beast and man were one atop of the other in the water; but the boar had the worst of it, for the man had marked, even as he sprang, and set the point of his brand to the beast's chest, and drove it up to the hilt, so that the heart was split in twain, and the boar fell snarling, and was swept down by the water to where a hundred hounds seized on him, and the men drew him to shore for the dogs to slay.

Then was there loud blowing of horns and baying of hounds, the huntsmen smote off the boar's head, and hung the carcass by the four feet to a stout pole, and so went on their way homewards. The head they bore before the lord himself, who had slain the beast at the ford by force of his strong hand.

It seemed him o'er long ere he saw Sir Gawain in the hall, and he called, and the guest came to take that which fell to his share. And when he saw Gawain the lord laughed aloud, and bade them call the ladies and the household together, and he showed them the game, and told them the tale, how they hunted the wild boar through the woods, and of his length and breadth and height; and Sir Gawain commended his deeds and praised him for his valor, well proven, for so mighty a beast had he never seen before.

Then they handled the huge head, and the lord said aloud, "Now, Gawain, this game is your own by sure covenant, as ye right well know."

"'T is sooth," quoth the knight, "and as truly will I give ye all I have gained." He took the host round the neck, and kissed him courteously twice. "Now are we quits," he said, "this eventide, of all the covenants that we made since I came hither."

And the lord answered, "By Saint Giles, ye are the best I know; ye will be rich in a short space if ye drive such bargains!"

Then they set up the tables on trestles, and covered them with fair cloths, and lit waxen tapers on the walls. The knights sat and were served in the hall, and much game and glee was there round the hearth, with many songs, both at supper and after; song of Christmas, and new carols, with all the mirth one may think of. And ever that lovely lady sat by the knight, and with still stolen looks made such feint of pleasing him, that Gawain marveled much, and was wroth with himself, but he could not for his courtesy return her fair glances, but dealt with her cunningly, however she might strive to wrest the thing.

When they had tarried in the hall so long as it seemed them good, they turned to the inner chamber and the wide hearth-place, and there they drank wine, and the host proffered to renew the covenant for New Year's Eve; but the knight craved leave to depart on the morrow, for it was nigh to the term when he must fulfil his pledge. But the lord would withhold him from so doing, and prayed him to tarry, and said:

"As I am a true knight I swear my troth that ye shall come to the Green Chapel to achieve your task on New Year's morn, long before prime.[1] Therefore abide ye in your bed, and I will hunt in this wood, and hold ye to the covenant to exchange with me against all the spoil I may bring hither. For twice have I tried ye, and found ye true, and the morrow shall be the third time and the best. Make we merry now while we may, and think on joy, for misfortune may take a man whensoever it wills."

Then Gawain granted his request, and they brought them drink, and they gat them with lights to bed.

Sir Gawain lay and slept softly, but the lord, who was keen on woodcraft, was afoot early. After Mass he and his men ate a morsel, and he asked for his steed; all the

[1] Probably nine o'clock.

knights who should ride with him were already mounted before the hall gates.

'T was a fair frosty morning, for the sun rose red in ruddy vapor, and the welkin was clear of clouds. The hunters scattered them by a forest side, and the rocks rang again with the blast of their horns. Some came on the scent of a fox, and a hound gave tongue; the huntsmen shouted, and the pack followed in a crowd on the trail. The fox ran before them, and when they saw him they pursued him with noise and much shouting, and he wound and turned through many a thick grove, often cowering and hearkening in a hedge. At last by a little ditch he leapt out of a spinney, stole away slily by a copse path, and so out of the wood and away from the hounds. But he went, ere he wist, to a chosen tryst, and three started forth on him at once, so he must needs double back, and betake him to the wood again.

Then was it joyful to hearken to the hounds; when all the pack had met together and had sight of their game they made as loud a din as if all the lofty cliffs had fallen clattering together. The huntsmen shouted and threatened, and followed close upon him so that he might scarce escape, but Reynard was wily, and he turned and doubled upon them and led the lord and his men over the hills, now on the slopes, now in the vales, while the knight at home slept through the cold morning beneath his costly curtains.

But the fair lady of the castle rose betimes, and clad herself in a rich mantle that reached even to the ground, left her throat and her fair neck bare, and was bordered and lined with costly furs. On her head she wore no golden circlet, but a network of precious stones, that gleamed and shone through her tresses in clusters of twenty together. Thus she came into the chamber, closed the door after her, and set open a window, and called to him gaily, "Sir Knight, how may ye sleep? The morning is so fair."

Sir Gawain was deep in slumber, and in his dream he vexed him much for the destiny that should befall him on the morrow, when he should meet the knight at the Green Chapel, and abide his blow; but when the lady spake he heard her, and came to himself, and roused from his dream and answered swiftly. The lady came laughing, and kissed him courteously, and he welcomed her fittingly with a cheerful countenance. He saw her so glorious and gaily dressed, so faultless of features and complexion, that it warmed his heart to look upon her.

They spake to each other smiling, and all was bliss and good cheer between them. They exchanged fair words, and much happiness was therein, yet was there a gulf between them, and she might win no more of her knight, for that gallant prince watched well his words—he would neither take her love, nor frankly refuse it. He cared for his courtesy, lest he be deemed churlish, and yet more for his honor lest he be traitor to his host. "God forbid," quoth he to himself, "that it should so befall." Thus with courteous words did he set aside all the special speeches that came from her lips.

Then spake the lady to the knight, "Ye deserve blame if ye hold not that lady who sits beside ye above all else in the world, if ye have not already a love whom ye hold dearer, and like better, and have sworn such firm faith to that lady that ye care not to loose it—and that am I now fain to believe. And now I pray ye straitly that ye tell me that in truth, and hide it not."

And the knight answered, "By Saint John" (and he smiled as he spake) "no such love have I, nor do I think to have yet awhile."

"That is the worst word I may hear," quoth the lady, "but in sooth I have mine answer; kiss me now courteously, and I will go hence; I can but mourn as a maiden that loves much."

Sighing, she stooped down and kissed him, and then she rose up and spake as she stood, "Now, dear, at our parting do me this grace, give me some gift, if it were but thy glove, that I may bethink me of my knight, and lessen my mourning."

"Now, I wis," quoth the knight, "I would that I had here the most precious thing that I possess on earth that I might leave ye as love-token, great or small, for ye have deserved forsooth more reward than I might give ye. But it is not to your honor to have at this time a glove for reward as gift from Gawain, and I am here on a strange errand, and have no man with me, nor mails with goodly things—that mislikes me much, lady, at this time; but each man must fare as he is taken, if for sorrow and ill."

"Nay, knight highly honored," quoth that lovesome lady, "though I have naught of yours, yet shall ye have somewhat of mine." With that she reached him a ring of red gold with a sparkling stone therein, that shone even as the sun (wit ye well, it was worth many marks); but the knight refused it, and spake readily.

"I will take no gift, lady, at this time. I have none to give, and none will I take."

She prayed him to take it, but he refused her prayer, and sware in sooth that he would not have it.

The lady was sorely vexed, and said, "If ye refuse my ring as too costly, that ye will not be so highly beholden to me, I will give you my girdle as a lesser gift." With that she loosened a lace that was fastened at her side, knit upon her kirtle under her mantle. It was wrought of green silk, and gold, only braided by the fingers, and that she offered to the knight, and besought him though it were of little worth that he would take it, and he said nay, he would touch neither gold nor gear ere God give him grace to achieve the adventure for which he had come hither. "And therefore, I pray ye, displease ye not, and ask me no longer, for I may not grant it. I am dearly beholden to ye for the favor ye have shown me, and ever, in heat and cold, will I be your true servant."

"Now," said the lady, "ye refuse this silk, for it is simple in itself, and so it seems, indeed; lo, it is small to look upon and less in cost, but whoso knew the virtue that is knit therein he would, peradventure, value it more highly. For whatever knight is girded with this green lace, while he bears it knotted about him there is no man under heaven can overcome him, for he may not be slain for any magic on earth."

Then Gawain bethought him, and it came into his heart that this were a jewel for the jeopardy that awaited him when he came to the Green Chapel to seek the return blow—could he so order it that he should escape unslain, 't were a craft worth trying. Then he bare with her chiding, and let her say her say, and she pressed the girdle on him and prayed him to take it, and he granted her prayer, and she gave it him with good will, and besought him for her sake never to reveal it but to hide it loyally from her lord, and the knight agreed that never should any man know it, save they two alone. He thanked her often and heartily, and she kissed him for the third time.

Then she took her leave of him, and when she was gone Sir Gawain rose, and clad him in rich attire, and took the girdle, and knotted it round him, and hid it beneath his robes. Then he took his way to the chapel, and sought out a priest privily and prayed him to teach him better how his soul might be saved when he should go hence; and there he shrived him, and showed his misdeeds, both great and small, and besought mercy and craved absolution; and the priest assoiled[1] him, and set him as clean as if doomsday had been on the morrow. And afterwards Sir Gawain made him merry with the ladies, with carols, and all kinds of joy, as never he did but that one day, even to nightfall; and all the men marveled at him, and said that never since he came thither had he been so merry.

Meanwhile the lord of the castle was abroad chasing the fox; awhile he lost him, and as he rode through a spinney he heard the hounds near at hand, and Reynard came creeping through a thick grove, with all the pack at his heels. Then the lord drew out his shining brand, and cast it at the beast, and the fox swerved aside for the sharp edge, and would have doubled back, but a hound was on him ere he might turn, and right before the horse's feet they all fell on him, and worried him fiercely, snarling the while.

Then the lord leapt from his saddle, and caught the fox from the jaws, and held it aloft over his head, and hallooed loudly, and many brave hounds bayed as they beheld it; and the hunters hied them thither, blowing their horns; all that bare bugles blew them at once, and all the others shouted. 'T was the merriest meeting that ever men heard, the clamor that was raised at the death of the fox. They rewarded the hounds, stroking them and rubbing their heads, and took Reynard and stripped him of his coat; then blowing their horns, they turned them homewards, for it was nigh nightfall.

The lord was gladsome at his return, and found a bright fire on the hearth, and the knight beside it, the good Sir Gawain, who was in joyous mood for the pleasure he had had with the ladies. He wore a robe of blue,

[1] Absolved.

that reached even to the ground, and a surcoat richly furred, that became him well. A hood like to the surcoat fell on his shoulders, and all alike were done about with fur. He met the host in the midst of the floor, and jesting, he greeted him, and said, "Now shall I be first to fulfil our covenant which we made together when there was no lack of wine." Then he embraced the knight, and kissed him thrice, as solemnly as he might.

"Of a sooth," quoth the other, "ye have good luck in the matter of this covenant, if ye made a good exchange!"

"Yet, it matters naught of the exchange," quoth Gawain, "since what I owe is swiftly paid."

"Marry," said the other, "mine is behind, for I have hunted all this day, and naught have I got but this foul fox-skin, and that is but poor payment for three such kisses as ye have here given me."

"Enough," quoth Sir Gawain, "I thank ye, by the Rood."

Then the lord told them of his hunting, and how the fox had been slain.

With mirth and minstrelsy, and dainties at their will, they made them as merry as a folk well might till 't was time for them to sever, for at last they must needs betake them to their beds. Then the knight took his leave of the lord, and thanked him fairly.

"For the fair sojourn that I have had here at this high feast may the High King give ye honor. I give ye myself, as one of your servants, if ye so like; for I must needs, as you know, go hence with the morn, and ye will give me, as ye promised, a guide to show me the way to the Green Chapel, an God will suffer me on New Year's Day to deal the doom of my weird."[1]

"By my faith," quoth the host, "all that ever I promised, that shall I keep with good will." Then he gave him a servant to set him in the way, and lead him by the downs, that he should have no need to ford the stream, and should fare by the shortest road through the groves; and Gawain thanked the lord for the honor done him. Then he would take leave of the ladies, and courteously he kissed them, and spake, praying them to receive his thanks, and they made like reply; then with many sighs they commended him to Christ, and he departed courteously from that fold. Each man that he met he thanked him for his service and his solace, and the pains he had been at to do his will; and each found it as hard to part from the knight as if he had ever dwelt with him.

Then they led him with torches to his chamber, and brought him to his bed to rest. That he slept soundly I may not say, for the morrow gave him much to think on. Let him rest awhile, for he was near that which he sought, and if ye will but listen to me I will tell ye how it fared with him thereafter.

IV

Now the New Year drew nigh, and the night passed, and the day chased the darkness, as is God's will; but wild weather wakened therewith. The clouds cast the cold to the earth, with enough of the north to slay them that lacked clothing. The snow drave smartly, and the whistling wind blew from the heights, and made great drifts in the valleys. The knight, lying in his bed, listened, for though his eyes were shut, he might sleep but little, and hearkened every cock that crew.

He arose ere the day broke, by the light of a lamp that burned in his chamber, and called to his chamberlain, bidding him bring his armor and saddle his steed. The other gat him up, and fetched his garments, and robed Sir Gawain.

First he clad him in his clothes to keep off the cold, and then in his harness, which was well and fairly kept. Both hauberk and plates were well burnished, the rings of the rich byrnie freed from rust, and all as fresh as at first, so that the knight was fain to thank them. Then he did on each piece, and bade them bring his steed, while he put the fairest raiment on himself; his coat with its fair cognizance, adorned with precious stones upon velvet, with broidered seams, and all furred within with costly skins. And he left not the lace, the lady's gift, that Gawain forgot not, for his own good. When he had girded on his sword he wrapped the gift twice about him, swathed around his waist. The girdle of green silk set gaily and well upon the royal red cloth, rich to behold, but the knight ware it not for pride of the pendants, polished though they were with fair gold that gleamed

[1] To take the judgment of my fate.

brightly on the ends, but to save himself from sword and knife, when it behooved him to abide his hurt without question. With that the hero went forth, and thanked that kindly folk full often.

Then was Gringalet ready, that was great and strong, and had been well cared for and tended in every wise; in fair condition was that proud steed, and fit for a journey. Then Gawain went to him, and looked on his coat, and said by his sooth, "There is a folk in this place that thinketh on honor; much joy may they have, and the lord who maintains them, and may all good betide that lovely lady all her life long. Since they for charity cherish a guest, and hold honor in their hands, may he who holds the heaven on high requite them, and also ye all. And if I might live anywhile on earth, I would give ye full reward, readily, if so I might." Then he set foot in the stirrup and bestrode his steed, and his squire gave him his shield, which he laid on his shoulder. Then he smote Gringalet with his golden spurs, and the steed pranced on the stones and would stand no longer.

By that his man was mounted, who bare his spear and lance, and Gawain quoth, "I commend this castle to Christ, may he give it ever good fortune." Then the drawbridge was let down, and the broad gates unbarred and opened on both sides; the knight crossed himself, and passed through the gateway, and praised the porter, who knelt before the prince, and gave him good-day, and commended him to God. Thus the knight went on his way, with the one man who should guide him to that dread place where he should receive rueful payment.

The two went by hedges where the boughs were bare, and climbed the cliffs where the cold clings. Naught fell from the heavens, but 't was ill beneath them; mist brooded over the moor and hung on the mountains; each hill had a cap, a great cloak, of mist. The streams foamed and bubbled between their banks, dashing sparkling on the shores where they shelved downwards. Rugged and dangerous was the way through the woods, till it was time for the sun-rising. Then were they on a high hill; the snow lay white beside them, and the man who rode with Gawain drew rein by his master.

"Sir," he said, "I have brought ye hither, and now ye are not far from the place that ye have sought so specially. But I will tell ye for sooth, since I know ye well, and ye are such a knight as I well love, would ye follow my counsel ye would fare the better. The place whither ye go is accounted full perilous, for he who liveth in that waste is the worst on earth, for he is strong and fierce; and loveth to deal mighty blows; taller he is than any man on earth, and greater of frame than any four in Arthur's court, or in any other. And this is his custom at the Green Chapel; there may no man pass by that place, however proud his arms, but he does him to death by force of his hand, for he is a discourteous knight, and shows no mercy. Be he churl or chaplain who rides by that chapel, monk or mass-priest, or any man else, he thinks it as pleasant to slay them as to pass alive himself. Therefore, I tell ye, as sooth as ye sit in saddle, if ye come there and that knight know it, ye shall be slain, though ye had twenty lives; trow me that truly! He has dwelt here full long and seen many a combat; ye may not defend ye against his blows. Therefore, good Sir Gawain, let the man be, and get ye away some other road; for God's sake seek ye another land, and there may Christ speed ye! And I will hie me home again, and I promise ye further that I will swear by God and the saints, or any other oath ye please, that I will keep counsel faithfully, and never let any wit the tale that ye fled for fear of any man."

"Gramercy," quoth Gawain, but ill-pleased. "Good fortune be his who wishes me good, and that thou wouldst keep faith with me I will believe; but didst thou keep it never so truly, an I passed here and fled for fear as thou sayest, then were I a coward knight, and might not be held guiltless. So I will to the chapel let chance what may, and talk with that man, even as I may list, whether for weal or for woe as fate may have it. Fierce though he may be in fight, yet God knoweth well how to save his servants."

"Well," quoth the other, "now that ye have said so much that ye will take your own harm on yourself, and ye be pleased to lose your life, I will neither let[1] nor keep ye. Have here your helm and the spear in your hand, and ride down this same road beside the rock till ye come to the bottom of the

[1]Hinder.

valley, and there look a little to the left hand, and ye shall see in that vale the chapel, and the grim man who keeps it. Now fare ye well, noble Gawain; for all the gold on earth I would not go with ye nor bear ye fellowship one step further. With that the man turned his bridle into the wood, smote the horse with his spurs as hard as he could, and galloped off, leaving the knight alone.

Quoth Gawain, "I will neither greet nor moan, but commend myself to God, and yield me to his will."

Then the knight spurred Gringalet, and rode adown the path close in by a bank beside a grove. So he rode through the rough thicket, right into the dale, and there he halted, for it seemed him wild enough. No sign of a chapel could he see, but high and burnt banks on either side and rough rugged crags with great stones above. An ill-looking place he thought it.

Then he drew in his horse and looked round to seek the chapel, but he saw none and thought it strange. Then he saw as it were a mound on a level space of land by a bank beside the stream where it ran swiftly; the water bubbled within as if boiling. The knight turned his steed to the mound, and lighted down and tied the rein to the branch of a linden; and he turned to the mound and walked round it, questioning with himself what it might be. It had a hole at the end and at either side, and was overgrown with clumps of grass, and it was hollow within as an old cave or the crevice of a crag; he knew not what it might be.

"Ah," quoth Gawain, "can this be the Green Chapel? Here might the devil say his matins at midnight! Now I wis there is wizardry here. 'T is an ugly oratory, all overgrown with grass, and 't would well beseem that fellow in green to say his devotions on devil's wise. Now feel I in five wits, 't is the foul fiend himself who hath set me this tryst, to destroy me here! This is a chapel of mischance: ill-luck betide it, 't is the cursedest kirk that ever I came in!"

Helmet on head and lance in hand, he came up to the rough dwelling, when he heard over the high hill beyond the brook, as it were in a bank, a wondrous fierce noise, that rang in the cliff as if it would cleave asunder. 'Twas as if one ground a scythe on a grindstone, it whirred and whetted like water on a mill-wheel and rushed and rang, terrible to hear.

"By God," quoth Gawain, "I trow that gear is preparing for the knight who will meet me here. Alas! naught may help me, yet should my life be forfeit, I fear not a jot!" With that he called aloud. "Who waiteth in this place to give me tryst. Now is Gawain come hither: if any man will aught of him let him hasten hither now or never."

"Stay," quoth one on the bank above his head, "and ye shall speedily have that which I promised ye." Yet for a while the noise of whetting went on ere he appeared, and then he came forth from a cave in the crag with a fell weapon, a Danish ax newly dight, wherewith to deal the blow. An evil head it had, four feet large, no less, sharply ground, and bound to the handle by the lace that gleamed brightly. And the knight himself was all green as before, face and foot, locks and beard, but now he was afoot. When he came to the water he would not wade it, but sprang over with the pole of his ax, and strode boldly over the bent that was white with snow.

Sir Gawain went to meet him, but he made no low bow. The other said, "Now, fair sir, one may trust thee to keep tryst. Thou art welcome, Gawain, to my place. Thou hast timed thy coming as befits a true man. Thou knowest the covenant set between us: at this time twelve months agone thou didst take that which fell to thee, and I at this New Year will readily requite thee. We are in this valley, verily alone, here are no knights to sever us, do what we will. Have off thy helm from thine head, and have here thy pay; make me no more talking than I did then when thou didst strike off my head with one blow."

"Nay," quoth Gawain, "by God that gave me life, I shall make no moan whatever befall me, but make thou ready for the blow and I shall stand still and say never a word to thee, do as thou wilt."

With that he bent his head and showed his neck all bare, and made as if he had no fear, for he would not be thought a-dread.

Then the Green Knight made him ready and grasped his grim weapon to smite Gawain. With all his force he bore it aloft with a mighty feint of slaying him: had it fallen as straight as he aimed he who was ever doughty of deed had been slain by the blow. But Gawain swerved aside as the ax came gliding down to slay him as he stood, and shrank a little with the shoulders, for the sharp iron. The other heaved up the blade and rebuked the prince with many proud words:

"Thou art not Gawain," he said, "who is held so valiant, that never feared he man by hill or vale, but thou shrinkest for fear ere thou feelest hurt. Such cowardice did I never hear of Gawain! Neither did *I* flinch from thy blow, or make strife in King Arthur's hall. My head fell to my feet, and yet I fled not; but thou didst wax faint of heart ere any harm befell. Wherefore must I be deemed the braver knight."

Quoth Gawain, "I shrank once, but so will I no more; though an my head fall on the stones I cannot replace it. But haste, Sir Knight, by thy faith, and bring me to the point, deal me my destiny, and do it out of hand, for I will stand thee a stroke and move no more till thine ax have hit me—my troth on it."

"Have at thee, then," quoth the other, and heaved aloft the ax with fierce mien, as if he were mad. He struck at him fiercely but wounded him not, withholding his hand ere it might strike him.

Gawain abode the stroke, and flinched in no limb, but stood still as a stone or the stump of a tree that is fast rooted in the rocky ground with a hundred roots.

Then spake gaily the man in green, "So now thou hast thine heart whole it behooves me to smite. Hold aside thy hood that Arthur gave thee, and keep thy neck thus bent lest it cover it again."

Then Gawain said angrily, "Why talk on thus? Thou dost threaten too long. I hope thy heart misgives thee."

"For sooth," quoth the other, "so fiercely thou speakest I will no longer let thine errand wait its reward." Then he braced himself to strike, frowning with lips and brow, 't was no marvel that it pleased but ill him who hoped for no rescue. He lifted the ax lightly and let it fall with the edge of the blade on the bare neck. Though he struck swiftly, it hurt him no more than on the one side where it severed the skin. The sharp blade cut into the flesh so that the blood ran over his shoulder to the ground. And when the knight saw the blood staining the snow, he sprang forth, swift-foot, more than a spear's length, seized his helmet and set it on his head, cast his shield over his shoulder, drew out his bright sword, and spake boldly (never since he was born was he half so blithe), "Stop, Sir Knight, bid me no more blows, I have stood a stroke here without flinching, and if thou give me another, I shall requite thee, and give thee as good again. By the covenant made betwixt us in Arthur's hall but one blow falls to me here. Halt, therefore."

Then the Green Knight drew off from him and leaned on his ax, setting the shaft on the ground, and looked on Gawain as he stood all armed and faced him fearlessly—at heart it pleased him well. Then he spake merrily in a loud voice, and said to the knight, "Bold sir, be not so fierce; no man here hath done thee wrong, nor will do, save by covenant, as we made at Arthur's court. I promised thee a blow and thou hast it—hold thyself well paid! I release thee of all other claims. If I had been so minded I might perchance have given thee a rougher buffet. First I menaced thee with a feigned one, and hurt thee not for the covenant that we made in the first night, and which thou didst hold truly. All the gain didst thou give me as a true man should. The other feint I proffered thee for the morrow: my fair wife kissed thee, and thou didst give me her kisses—for both those days I gave thee two blows without scathe—true man, true return. But the third time thou didst fail, and therefore hadst thou that blow. For 't is *my* weed thou wearest, that same woven girdle, my own wife wrought it, that do I wot for sooth. Now know I well thy kisses, and thy conversation, and the wooing of my wife, for 't was mine own doing. I sent her to try thee, and in sooth I think thou art the most faultless knight that ever trod earth. As a pearl among white peas is of more worth than they, so is Gawain, i' faith, by other knights. But thou didst lack a little, Sir Knight, and wast wanting in loyalty, yet that was for no evil work, nor for wooing neither, but because thou lovedst thy life—therefore I blame thee the less."

Then the other stood a great while, still sorely angered and vexed within himself; all the blood flew to his face, and he shrank for shame as the Green Knight spake; and the first words he said were, "Cursed be ye, cowardice and covetousness, for in ye is the destruction of virtue." Then he loosed the girdle, and gave it to the knight. "Lo, take there the falsity, may foul befall it! For fear of thy blow cowardice bade me make friends with covetousness and forsake the customs of largess and loyalty, which befit all knights. Now am I faulty and false and have been afeared: from treachery and untruth come sorrow and care. I avow to thee, Sir Knight, that I have ill done; do then thy will. I shall be more wary hereafter."

Then the other laughed and said gaily, "I wot I am whole of the hurt I had, and thou hast made such free confession of thy misdeeds, and hast so borne the penance of mine ax edge, that I hold thee absolved from that sin, and purged as clean as if thou hadst never sinned since thou wast born. And this girdle that is wrought with gold and green, like my raiment, do I give thee, Sir Gawain, that thou mayest think upon this chance when thou goest forth among princes of renown, and keep this for a token of the adventure of the Green Chapel, as it chanced between chivalrous knights. And thou shalt come again with me to my dwelling and pass the rest of this feast in gladness." Then the lord laid hold of him, and said, "I wot we shall soon make peace with my wife, who was thy bitter enemy."

"Nay, forsooth," said Sir Gawain, and seized his helmet and took it off swiftly, and thanked the knight: "I have fared ill, may bliss betide thee, and may he who rules all things reward thee swiftly. Commend me to that courteous lady, thy fair wife, and to the other my honored ladies, who have beguiled their knight with skilful craft. But 't is no marvel if one be made a fool and brought to sorrow by women's wiles, for so was Adam beguiled by one, and Solomon by many, and Samson all too soon, for Delilah dealt him his doom; and David thereafter was wedded with Bathsheba, which brought him much sorrow—if one might love a woman and believe her not, 't were great gain! And since all they were beguiled by women, methinks 't is the less blame to me that I was misled! But as for thy girdle, that will I take with good will, not for gain of the gold, nor for samite, nor silk, nor the costly pendants, neither for weal nor for worship, but in sign of my frailty. I shall look upon it when I ride in renown and remind myself of the fault and faintness of the flesh; and so when pride uplifts me for prowess of arms, the sight of this lace shall humble my heart. But one thing would I pray, if it displease thee not: since thou art lord of yonder land wherein I have dwelt, tell me what thy rightful name may be, and I will ask no more."

"That will I truly," quoth the other. "Bernlak de Hautdesert am I called in this land. Morgain le Fay dwelleth in mine house, and through knowledge of clerkly craft hath she taken many. For long time was she the mistress of Merlin, who knew well all you knights of the court. Morgain the goddess is she called therefore, and there is none so haughty but she can bring him low. She sent me in this guise to yon fair hall to test the truth of the renown that is spread abroad of the valor of the Round Table. She taught me this marvel to betray your wits, to vex Guinevere and fright her to death by the man who spake with his head in his hand at the high table. That is she who is at home, that ancient lady, she is even thine aunt, Arthur's half-sister, the daughter of the Duchess of Tintagel, who afterward married King Uther. Therefore I bid thee, knight, come to thine aunt, and make merry in thine house; my folk love thee, and I wish thee as well as any man on earth, by my faith, for thy true dealing."

But Sir Gawain said nay, he would in no wise do so; so they embraced and kissed, and commended each other to the Prince of Paradise, and parted right there, on the cold ground. Gawain on his steed rode swiftly to the king's hall, and the Green Knight got him whithersoever he would.

Sir Gawain, who had thus won grace of his life, rode through wild ways on Gringalet; oft he lodged in a house, and oft without, and many adventures did he have and came off victor full often, as at this time I cannot relate in tale. The hurt that he had in his neck was healed, he bare the shining girdle as a baldric bound by his side, and made fast with a knot 'neath his left arm, in token that he was taken in a fault—and thus he came in safety again to the court.

Then joy awakened in that dwelling when the king knew that the good Sir Gawain was come, for he deemed it gain. King Arthur kissed the knight, and the queen also, and many valiant knights sought to embrace him.

They asked him how he had fared, and he told them all that had chanced to him—the adventure of the chapel, the fashion of the knight, the love of the lady—at last of the lace. He showed them the wound in the neck which he won for his disloyalty at the hand of the knight; the blood flew to his face for shame as he told the tale.

"Lo, lady," he quoth, and handled the lace, "this is the bond of the blame that I bear in my neck, this is the harm and the loss I have suffered, the cowardice and covetousness in which I was caught, the token of my covenant in which I was taken. And I must needs wear it so long as I live, for none may hide his harm, but undone it may not be, for if it hath clung to thee once, it may never be severed."

Then the king comforted the knight, and the court laughed loudly at the tale, and all made accord that the lords and the ladies who belonged to the Round Table, each hero among them, should wear bound about him a baldric of bright green for the sake of Sir Gawain. And to this was agreed all the honor of the Round Table, and he who ware it was honored the more thereafter, as it is testified in the book of romance. That in Arthur's days this adventure befell, the book of Brutus bears witness. For since that bold knight came hither first, and the siege and the assault were ceased at Troy, I wis

Many a venture herebefore
Hath fallen such as this:
May He that bare the crown of thorn
Bring us unto His bliss.

Amen.

WILLIAM LANGLAND(?)

The Vision of William concerning Piers the Plowman has been traditionally attributed to one William Langland, to whom Skeat assigned, for convenience' sake, the conjectural dates c. 1332–c. 1400. On the basis of the author's supposed references to himself within the poem a biography has also been made up. The author's name, however, has been disputed, and likewise the identification with him of the "Will" of the poem, and as a matter of fact nothing is certainly known about the poem's authorship. *Piers the Plowman* exists in three versions, known as the A-, B-, and C-texts. The A-text was written in 1362 or shortly thereafter. It is 2567 lines in length. The B-text was written probably in 1376 or 1377; for this the A-text was taken as a basis, was thoroughly made over, and was considerably enlarged, the number of lines in this text being 7242. The C-text was written probably some time between 1393 and 1399; it is a revision of the B-text with many comparatively small changes, and contains 7357 lines. Until recent years these versions have been accepted as the work of one writer. In 1906, however, Professor J. M. Manly asserted that the A-text was the work of three writers, and that the B- and C-texts were by two different authors, each other than the writers of the A-text. Proof of these assertions has not yet appeared, and the published work of other scholars since 1906 has on the whole gone to show that their proof would be more difficult than may have been at first supposed. Consequently, although the question of single or multiple authorship remains an open one and can perhaps never be settled, it seems justifiable to retain, at least provisionally, the traditional name William Langland.

Piers the Plowman was in its own age and in the fifteenth century one of the most popular and valued pieces of literature in the English language, as is evinced by the fact that no less than forty-seven manuscripts of it are still extant. This popularity was deserved. The poem is, after the *Canterbury Tales* of Chaucer, "the greatest piece of Middle English literature; it is one of the greatest of the medieval vision poems, and, as a vision poem, in many respects second only to the *Divine Comedy;* it is one of the foremost of the writings in English in which allegory is used" (J. E. Wells, *Manual of the Writings in Middle English*, p. 264). Moreover, to any student of the fourteenth century the poem is a necessary complement to the work of Chaucer, picturing as it does the life of the lower classes, and reflecting as it does the convictions and aspirations of simple-hearted men of deep feeling. *Piers the Plowman* has little of conscious art, its language is rough and broken, and it is written in the old alliterative meter, but its author felt intensely, saw deeply, and dealt greatly with the great issues of life.

Only the Prologue of the B-text is here printed. It may be well to give Skeat's summary of it, which is as follows: "The author describes how, weary of wandering, he sits down to rest upon Malvern Hills, and there falls asleep and dreams. In his vision, the world and its people are represented to him by a field full of folk, busily engaged in their avocations. The field was situate between the tower of Truth, who is God the Father, and the dungeon which is the abode of evil spirits. In it there were plowmen and spendthrifts, anchorites, merchants, jesters, beggars, pilgrims, hermits, friars, a pardoner with his bulls, and priests who deserted their cures. There was also a king, to whom an angel speaks words of advice. Then was seen suddenly a rout of rats and mice, conspiring to bell the cat, from doing which they were dissuaded by a wise mouse. There were also lawsergeants, burgesses, tradesmen, laborers, and taverners touting for custom."

THE VISION OF WILLIAM CONCERNING PIERS THE PLOWMAN

PROLOGUE

IN A somer seson · whan soft was the sonne,
I shope me in shroudes · as I a shepe were,
In habite as an heremite · unholy of workes,
Went wyde in this world · wondres to here.
Ac on a May mornynge · on Malverne hulles,
Me byfel a ferly · of fairy, me thougte;
I was wery forwandred · and went me to reste
Under a brode banke · bi a bornes side,
And as I lay and lened · and loked in the wateres,
I slombred in a slepyng · it sweyved so merye.
Thanne gan I to meten · a merveilouse swevene,

That I was in a wildernesse · wist I never where;
As I bihelde in-to the est · an hiegh to the sonne,
I seigh a toure on a toft · trielich ymaked;
A depe dale binethe · a dongeon there-Inne,
With depe dyches & derke · and dredful of sight.
A faire felde ful of folke · fonde I there by-twene,
Of alle maner of men · the mene and the riche,
Worchyng and wandryng · as the worlde asketh.
Some putten hem to the plow · pleyed ful selde,
In settyng and in sowyng · swonken ful harde,
And wonnen that wastours · with glotonye destruyeth.
 And some putten hem to pruyde · apparailed hem thereafter,
In contenaunce of clothyng · comen disgised.
 In prayers and in penance · putten hem manye,
Al for love of owre lorde · lyveden ful streyte,
In hope forto have · heveneriche blisse;
As ancres and heremites · that holden hem in here selles,
And coveiten nought in contre · to kairen aboute,
For no likerous liflode · her lykam to plese.
 And somme chosen chaffare · they cheven the bettere,
As it semeth to owre sygt · that suche men thryveth;
And somme murthes to make · as mynstralles conneth,
And geten gold with here glee · giltles, I leve.
Ac japers & jangelers · Judas chylderen,
Feynen hem fantasies · and foles hem maketh,
And han here witte at wille · to worche, gif thei sholde;
That Poule precheth of hem · I nel nought preve it here;
Qui turpiloquium loquitur[1] · is luciferes hyne.
 Bidders and beggeres · fast aboute gede,
With her belies and her bagges · of bred ful ycrammed;
Fayteden for here fode · fougten atte ale;
In glotonye, god it wote · gon hij to bedde,
And risen with ribaudye · tho roberdes knaves;
Slepe and sori sleuthe · seweth hem evre.
 Pilgrymes and palmers · pligted hem togidere
To seke seynt James · and seyntes in Rome.
Thei went forth in here wey · with many wise tales,
And hadden leve to lye · al here lyf after.
I seigh somme that seiden · thei had ysougt seyntes:
To eche a tale that thei tolde · here tonge was tempred to lye,
More than to sey soth · it semed bi here speche.
 Heremites on an heep · with hoked staves,
Wenten to Walsyngham · and here wenches after;
Grete lobyes and longe · that loth were to swynke,
Clotheden hem in copis · to ben knowen fram othere;
And shopen hem heremites · here ese to have.
 I fonde there Freris · alle the foure ordres,
Preched the peple · for profit of hem-selven,
Glosed the gospel · as hem good lyked,
For coveitise of copis · construed it as thei wolde.
Many of this maistres Freris · mowe clothen hem at lykyng,
For here money and marchandise · marchen togideres.
For sith charite hath be chapman · and chief to shryve lordes,
Many ferlis han fallen · in a fewe yeris.
But holychirche and hij · holde better togideres,
The most myschief on molde · is mountyng wel faste.
 There preched a Pardonere · as he a prest were,
Brougte forth a bulle · with bishopes seles,
And seide that hym-self mygte · assoilen hem alle
Of falshed of fastyng · of vowes ybroken.
 Lewed men leved hym wel · and lyked his wordes,
Comen up knelyng · to kissen his bulles;
He bonched hem with his brevet · & blered here eyes,
And raugte with his ragman · rynges and broches;
Thus they geven here golde · glotones to kepe
And leveth such loseles · that lecherye haunten.
Were the bischop yblissed · and worth bothe his eres,
His seel shulde nougt be sent · to deceyve the peple.
Ac it is naugt by the bischop · that the boy precheth,
For the parisch prest and the pardonere · parten the silver,
That the poraille of the parisch · sholde have, gif thei nere.
 Persones and parisch prestes · pleyned hem to the bischop,
That here parisshes were pore · sith the pestilence tyme,
To have a lycence and a leve · at London to dwelle,

[1] He who uses vile language.

And syngen there for symonye · for silver is swete.
Bischopes and bachelers · bothe maistres and doctours,
That han cure under criste · and crounyng in tokne
And signe that thei sholden · shryven here paroschienes,
Prechen and prey for hem · and the pore fede,
Liggen in London · in lenten, an elles.
Somme serven the kyng · and his silver tellen,
In cheker and in chancerye · chalengen his dettes
Of wardes and wardmotes · weyves and streyves.
And some serven as servantz · lordes and ladyes,
And in stede of stuwardes · sytten and demen.
Here messe and here matynes · and many of here oures
Arn don undevoutlych; · drede is at the laste
Lest crist in consistorie · acorse ful manye.
I parceyved of the power · that Peter had to kepe,
To bynde and to unbynde · as the boke telleth,
How he it left with love · as owre lorde hight,
Amonges foure vertues · the best of all vertues,
That cardinales ben called · & closyng gatis,
There crist is in kyngdome · to close and to shutte,
And to opne it to hem · and hevene blisse shewe.
Ac of the cardinales atte Courte · that caugt of that name,
And power presumed in hem · a Pope to make,
To han that power that Peter hadde · inpugnen I nelle;
For in love and letterure · the eleccioun bilongeth,
For-thi I can and can naugte · of courte speke more.
 Thanne come there a kyng · knygthod hym ladde,
Migt of the comunes · made hym to regne,
And thanne cam kynde wytte · and clerkes he made,
For to conseille the kyng · and the comune save.
 The kyng and knygthode · and clergye bothe
Casten that the comune · shulde hem-self fynde.
 The comune contreved · of kynde witte craftes,
And for profit of alle the poeple · plowmen ordeygned,
To tilie and travaile · as trewe lyf asketh.
The kynge and the comune · and kynde witte the thridde
Shope lawe & lewte · eche man to knowe his owne.
 Thanne loked up a lunatik · a lene thing with-alle,
And knelyng to the kyng · clergealy he seyde;
"Crist kepe the, sire kyng · and thi kyngriche,
And leve the lede thi londe · so leute the lovye,
And for thi rigtful rewlyng · be rewarded in hevene!"
 And sithen in the eyre an hiegh · an angel of hevene
Lowed to speke in latyn— · for lewed men ne coude
Jangle ne jugge · that justifie hem shulde,
But suffren & serven— · for-thi seyde the angel,
"*Sum Rex, sum Princeps · neutrum fortasse deinceps;—*
O qui iura regis · Christi specialia regis,
Hoc quod agas melius · iustus es, esto pius!
Nudum ius a te · vestiri vult pietate;
Qualia vis metere · talia grana sere.
Si ius nudatur · nudo de iure metatur;
Si seritur pietas · de pietate metas!"[1]
Thanne greved hym a Goliardeys · a glotoun of wordes,
And to the angel an heig · answered after,
"*Dum rex a regere · dicatur nomen habere,*
Nomen habet sine re · nisi studet iura tenere."[2]
 And thanne gan alle the comune · crye in vers of latin,
To the kynges conseille · construe ho-so wolde—
"*Precepta Regis · sunt nobis vincula legis.*"[3]
 With that ran there a route · of ratones at ones,
And smale mys myd hem · mo then a thousande,
And comen to a conseille · for here comune profit;
For a cat of a courte · cam whan hym lyked,
And overlepe hem lygtlich · and laugte hem at his wille,
And pleyde with hem perilouslych · and possed hem aboute.
"For doute of dyverse dredes · we dar nougte wel loke;
And gif we grucche of his gamen · he wil greve us alle,
Cracche us, or clowe us · and in his cloches holde,

---

[1][You say] "I am a king, I am a prince," [but you will be] neither perhaps hereafter. O you who administer the special laws of Christ the King, that you may do this the better, as you are just, be also merciful! Naked justice you must clothe with mercy; as you would reap you must sow the seeds. If justice is stripped bare, from bare justice may [your] harvest be reaped; if mercy is sown, may you reap a harvest of mercy!

[2]While the ruler is said to take his name from ruling, he has the name without the thing unless he strives to maintain the laws.

[3]The commands of the king to us are the bonds of the law.

That us lotheth the lyf · or he lete us passe.
Mygte we with any witte · his wille withstonde,
We mygte be lordes aloft · and lyven at owre ese."
  A raton of renon · most renable of tonge,
Seide for a sovereygne · help to hym-selve;—
"I have ysein segges," quod he · "in the cite of London
Beren biges ful brigte · abouten here nekkes,
And some colers of crafty werk; · uncoupled thei wenden
Bothe in wareine & in waste · where hem leve lyketh;
And otherwhile thei aren elles-where · as I here telle.
Were there a belle on here beig · bi Jesu, as me thynketh,
Men mygte wite where thei went · and awei renne!
And rigt so," quod that ratoun · "reson me sheweth,
To bugge a belle of brasse · or of brigte sylver,
And knitten on a colere · for owre comune profit,
And hangen it up-on the cattes hals · thanne here we mowen
Where he ritt or rest · or renneth to playe.
And gif him list for to laike · thenne loke we mowen,
And peren in his presence · ther-while hym plaie liketh,
And gif him wrattheth, be ywar · and his weye shonye."
  Alle this route of ratones · to this reson thei assented.
Ac tho the belle was ybougt · and on the beige hanged,
There ne was ratoun in alle the route · for alle the rewme of Fraunce,
That dorst have ybounden the belle · aboute the cattis nekke,
Ne hangen it aboute the cattes hals · al Engelonde to wynne;
And helden hem unhardy · and here conseille feble,
And leten here laboure lost · & alle here longe studye.
  A mous that moche good · couthe, as me thougte,
Stroke forth sternly · and stode biforn hem alle,
And to the route of ratones · reherced these wordes;
"Thoug we culled the catte · yut sholde ther come another,
To cracchy us and al owre kynde · thoug we crope under benches.
For-thi I conseille alle the comune · to lat the catte worthe,
And be we never so bolde · the belle hym to shewe;
For I herde my sire seyn · is sevene yere ypassed,
There the catte is a kitoun · the courte is ful elyng;
That witnisseth holiwrite · who-so wil it rede,
  Ve terre ubi puer rex est, &c.[1]
For may no renke there rest have · for ratones bi nygte;
The while he caccheth conynges · he coveiteth nougt owre caroyne,
But fet hym al with venesoun · defame we hym nevere.
For better is a litel losse · than a longe sorwe,
The mase amonge us alle · thoug we mysse a schrewe.
For many mannus malt · we mys wolde destruye,
And also ye route of ratones · rende mennes clothes,
Nere that cat of that courte · that can yow overlepe;
For had ye rattes yowre wille · ye couthe nougt reule yowre-selve.
I sey for me," quod the mous · "I se so mykel after,
Shal never the cat ne the kitoun · bi my conseille be greved,
Ne carpyng of this coler · that costed me neure.
And thoug it had coste me catel · biknowen it I nolde,
But suffre as hym-self wolde · to do as hym liketh,
Coupled & uncoupled · to cacche what thei mowe.
For-thi uche a wise wigte I warne · wite wel his owne."—
  What this meteles bemeneth · ye men that be merye,
Devine ye, for I ne dar · bi dere god in hevene!
  Yit hoved there an hondreth · in houves of selke,
Seriauntz it semed · that serveden atte barre,
Plededen for penyes · and poundes the lawe,
And nougt for love of owre lorde · unlese here lippes onis.
Thou mygtest better mete the myste · on malverne hulles,
Than gete a momme of here mouthe · but money were shewed.
  Barones an burgeis · and bonde-men als
I seig in this assemble · as ye shul here after.
Baxsteres & brewesteres · and bocheres manye,
Wollewebsteres · and weveres of lynnen,
Taillours and tynkeres · & tolleres in marketes,
Masons and mynours · and many other craftes.

[1]Alas for the land whose king is a child (Ecclesiastes x, 16).

Of alkin libbyng laboreres · lopen forth somme,
As dykers & delveres · that doth here dedes ille,
And dryven forth the longe day · with "*Dieu vous save, Dame Emme!*"[1]
Cokes and here knaves · crieden, "hote pies, hote!
Gode gris and gees · gowe dyne, gowe!"
Taverners un-til hem · tolde the same,
"White wyn of Oseye · and red wyn of Gascoigne,
Of the Ryne and of the Rochel · the roste to defye."—
Al this seig I slepyng · and sevene sythes more.

[1]God save you, Lady Emma! (Evidently the refrain of some popular song.)

GEOFFREY CHAUCER (c. 1340–1400)

Chaucer was born in London, the son of a wine-merchant who was in some way connected with the court of Edward III. He is the earliest English writer about whose life and works we have reasonably full knowledge. Though our knowledge of his life is confined almost exclusively to its external course, still, what we do know is definite and dependable. The reason is that Chaucer from an early age was connected with the English court or government, so that the outlines of his public career can be traced from documentary evidence. We first hear of him as attached to the household of the wife of Prince Lionel, the third son of Edward III, in 1357. The only known evidence concerning the date of Chaucer's birth is contained in testimony he gave in a suit in 1386, when he stated that he was forty years or more of age and had borne arms for twenty-seven years. This statement agrees with the record of his service with the English army in France in 1359 (when he was taken prisoner by the French), and suggests 1340 as a probable date for his birth. In 1367 he was granted a pension for his services as valet in the king's household. Probably about this time Chaucer married Philippa, a lady who is thought to have been a sister-in-law of John of Gaunt. In 1372–1373 he was sent on a diplomatic mission to Italy. In 1374 he was given a post in the customs. In 1377 he was in Flanders and France on diplomatic service, and in 1378 went again to Italy. In 1382 he was given an additional post in the customs and three years later was allowed to exercise his office through a deputy. In 1386 he sat as a member of Parliament for Kent; in the same year he was for some reason deprived of his offices in the customs. Later he again held public offices, being appointed clerk of the king's works at Westminster in 1389 and holding the same office at Windsor in 1390, while he received a pension which was increased in 1394 and again in 1399; but despite this help Chaucer seems to have been in some financial difficulty from the time of his reverses in 1386 until shortly before his death. He died in 1400 and was buried in Westminster Abbey.

Chaucer's literary career has been divided into three periods: the French and Latin period (to 1373), the Italian period (1373–1385), and the English period (1385–1400). This division is convenient and is roughly in accordance with the facts. It should be kept in mind, however, that it is only approximate and that the so-called periods are not mutually exclusive. As a young man Chaucer made himself familiar with what was closest to hand—the Latin literature that was known to everyone of any education, and French poetry of his own time or shortly before. His acquaintance with the work of Dante, Petrarch, and Boccaccio probably dates from his first Italian journey in 1373. All that he learned from these varied sources was of use to him throughout his life, and what is meant in terming his last fifteen years an "English" period is that his apprenticeship was definitely over, and that he then wrote with a free command of his material which enabled him, more clearly than before, to exhibit himself in his work. In his first period Chaucer translated at least parts of the French *Romance of the Rose*, an allegorical poem of the thirteenth century, and wrote the *Book of the Duchess*, which shows the influence of French allegorical love poetry. In his second period he began, but did not finish, *The House of Fame*, he wrote *The Parliament of Fowls*, he translated Boethius' *Consolation of Philosophy*, and he wrote *Troilus and Criseyda*, a long and highly finished narrative poem based upon, and in part translated from, Boccaccio's *Filostrato*. In his third period he wrote *The Legend of Good Women* and *The Canterbury Tales*, leaving both unfinished. Chaucer won for himself immediately a foremost place in literature, and his works were an important influence in determining the dominance of London English. He was a deft craftsman, and his verse is remarkable for its smoothness, ease, grace, and variety. He was not a man of profound insight or deep seriousness, and this has cost him a place among the greatest poets; but he was a keen observer of the appearances of things and of the less profound traits of human character, which, with his mastery of a precise and finished style, enabled him to tell a story supremely well. His poetry might show us, even if we knew nothing of his public career, that he was a successful man of the world. He took men and things as he found them and was content to describe, as he so well could, and not to judge. He had, to be sure, his standards, and they were not low, but neither were they deeply felt. His nature was catholic and he viewed the human scene with whimsical detachment;—with a constant enjoyment, too which he still communicates to all his readers.

THE CANTERBURY TALES

THE PROLOGUE[1]

WHAN that Aprille with his shoures sote
The droghte of Marche hath perced to the rote,
And bathed every veyne in swich licour,
Of which vertu engendred is the flour;
Whan Zephirus eek with his swete breeth
Inspired hath in every holt and heeth
The tendre croppes, and the yonge sonne
Hath in the Ram[2] his halfe cours y-ronne,
And smale fowles maken melodye,
That slepen al the night with open yë,
(So priketh hem nature in hir corages):
Than longen folk to goon on pilgrimages
(And palmers for to seken straunge strondes)
To ferne halwes, couthe in sondry londes;
And specially, from every shires ende
Of Engelond, to Caunterbury they wende,
The holy blisful martir[3] for to seke,
That hem hath holpen, whan that they were seke.
 Bifel that, in that seson on a day,[4]
In Southwerk at the Tabard as I lay
Redy to wenden on my pilgrimage
To Caunterbury with ful devout corage,
At night was come in-to that hostelrye
Wel nyne and twenty in a companye,
Of sondry folk, by aventure y-falle
In felawshipe, and pilgrims were they alle,
That toward Caunterbury wolden ryde;
The chambres and the stables weren wyde,
And wel we weren esed atte beste.
And shortly, whan the sonne was to reste,
So hadde I spoken with hem everichon,
That I was of hir felawshipe anon,
And made forward erly for to ryse,
To take our wey, ther as I yow devyse.
 But natheles, whyl I have tyme and space,
Er that I ferther in this tale pace,
Me thinketh it acordaunt to resoun,
To telle yow al the condicioun
Of ech of hem, so as it semed me,
And whiche they weren, and of what degree;
And eek in what array that they were inne:
And at a knight than wol I first biginne.
 A KNIGHT ther was, and that a worthy man,
That fro the tyme that he first bigan
To ryden out, he loved chivalrye,
Trouthe and honour, fredom and curteisye.
Ful worthy was he in his lordes werre,
And therto hadde he riden (no man ferre)
As wel in Cristendom as hethenesse,
And ever honoured for his worthinesse.
 At Alisaundre he was, whan it was wonne;
Ful ofte tyme he hadde the bord bigonne
Aboven alle naciouns in Pruce.
In Lettow hadde he reysed and in Ruce,
No Cristen man so ofte of his degree.
In Gernade at the sege eek hadde he be
Of Algezir, and riden in Belmarye.
At Lyeys was he, and at Satalye,
Whan they were wonne; and in the Grete See
At many a noble aryve hadde he be.
At mortal batailles hadde he been fiftene,
And foughten for our feith at Tramissene
In listes thryes, and ay slayn his fo.
This ilke worthy knight had been also
Somtyme with the lord of Palatye,
Ageyn another hethen in Turkye:
And evermore he hadde a sovereyn prys.
And though that he were worthy, he was wys,
And of his port as meke as is a mayde.
He never yet no vileinye ne sayde
In al his lyf, un-to no maner wight.
He was a verray parfit gentil knight.
But for to tellen yow of his array,
His hors were gode, but he was nat gay.
Of fustian he wered a gipoun
Al bismotered with his habergeoun;
For he was late y-come from his viage,
And wente for to doon his pilgrimage.
 With him ther was his sone, a yong SQUYER,
A lovyere, and a lusty bacheler,
With lokkes crulle, as they were leyd in presse.
Of twenty yeer of age he was, I gesse.
Of his stature he was of evene lengthe,
And wonderly deliver, and greet of strengthe.
And he had been somtyme in chivachye,
In Flaundres, in Artoys, and Picardye,
And born him wel, as of so litel space,
In hope to stonden in his lady grace.
Embrouded was he, as it were a mede
Al ful of fresshe floures, whyte and rede.
Singinge he was, or floytinge, al the day;
He was as fresh as is the month of May.
Short was his goune, with sleves longe and wyde.
Wel coude he sitte on hors, and faire ryde.
He coude songes make and wel endyte,
Juste and eek daunce, and wel purtreye and wryte.
So hote he lovede, that by nightertale
He sleep namore than dooth a nightingale.
Curteys he was, lowly, and servisable,
And carf biforn his fader at the table.
 A YEMAN hadde he, and servaunts namo

[1]The *Prologue*, besides describing the pilgrims, outlines Chaucer's general design. This calls for about 120 stories, two told by each pilgrim on the way to Canterbury, and two on the way back. Chaucer seems later to have modified this plan, reducing the number of tales by one-half. But even so he left the work far from completed. We have only 24 tales, several of them unfinished.

[2]Sign of the zodiac, Aries.

[3]Thomas à Becket.

[4]The day was 16 April, and the year may be supposed to be 1387 (Skeat).

At that tyme, for him liste ryde so;
And he was clad in cote and hood of grene;
A sheef of pecok-arwes brighte and kene
Under his belt he bar ful thriftily;
(Wel coude he dresse his takel yemanly:
His arwes drouped noght with fetheres lowe),
And in his hand he bar a mighty bowe.
A not-heed hadde he, with a broun visage.
Of wode-craft wel coude he all the usage.
Upon his arm he bar a gay bracer,
And by his syde a swerd and a bokeler,
And on that other syde a gay daggere,
Harneised wel, and sharp as point of spere;
A Cristofre on his brest of silver shene.
An horn he bar, the bawdrik was of grene;
A forster was he, soothly, as I gesse.
Ther was also a Nonne, a PRIORESSE,
That of hir smyling was ful simple and coy;
Hir gretteste ooth was but by sëynt Loy;
And she was cleped madame Eglentyne.
Ful wel she song the service divyne,
Entuned in hir nose ful semely;
And Frensh she spak ful faire and fetisly,
After the scole of Stratford atte Bowe,[1]
For Frensh of Paris was to hir unknowe.
At mete wel y-taught was she with-alle;
She leet no morsel from hir lippes falle,
Ne wette hir fingres in hir sauce depe.
Wel coude she carie a morsel, and wel kepe,
That no drope ne fille up-on hir brest.
In curteisye was set ful muche hir lest.
Hir over lippe wyped she so clene,
That in hir coppe was no ferthing sene
Of grece, whan she dronken hadde hir draughte.
Ful semely after hir mete she raughte,
And sikerly she was of greet disport,
And ful plesaunt, and amiable of port,
And peyned hir to countrefete chere
Of court, and been estatlich of manere,
And to ben holden digne of reverence.
But, for to speken of hir conscience,
She was so charitable and so pitous,
She wolde wepe, if that she sawe a mous
Caught in a trappe, if it were deed or bledde.
Of smale houndes had she, that she fedde
With rosted flesh, or milk and wastel-breed.
But sore weep she if oon of hem were deed,
Or if men smoot it with a yerde smerte:
And al was conscience and tendre herte.
Ful semely hir wimpel pinched was;
Hir nose tretys; hir eyen greye as glas;
Hir mouth ful smal, and ther-to softe and reed;
But sikerly she hadde a fair forheed;
It was almost a spanne brood, I trowe;
For, hardily, she was nat undergrowe.
Ful fetis was hir cloke, as I was war.

[1]A convent near London.

Of smal coral aboute hir arm she bar
A peire of bedes, gauded al with grene;
And ther-on heng a broche of gold ful shene,
On which there was first write a crowned A,
And after, *Amor vincit omnia.*[2]
Another NONNE with hir hadde she,
That was hir chapeleyne, and PREESTES THREE.
A MONK ther was, a fair for the maistrye,
An out-rydere, that lovede venerye;
A manly man, to been an abbot able.
Ful many a deyntee hors hadde he in stable:
And, whan he rood, men mighte his brydel here
Ginglen in a whistling wind as clere,
And eek as loude as dooth the chapel-belle
Ther as this lord was keper of the celle.
The reule of seint Maure or of seint Beneit,
By-cause that it was old and som-del streit,
This ilke monk leet olde thinges pace,
And held after the newe world the space.
He yaf nat of that text a pulled hen,
That seith, that hunters been nat holy men;
Ne that a monk, whan he is cloisterlees,
Is lykned til a fish that is waterlees;
This is to seyn, a monk out of his cloistre.
But thilke text held he nat worth an oistre;
And I seyde, his opinioun was good.
What sholde he studie, and make him-selven wood,
Upon a book in cloistre alwey to poure,
Or swinken with his handes, and laboure,
As Austin bit? How shal the world be served?
Lat Austin have his swink to him reserved.
Therfore he was a pricasour aright;
Grehoundes he hadde, as swifte as fowel in flight;
Of priking and of hunting for the hare
Was al his lust, for no cost wolde he spare.
I seigh his sleves purfiled at the hond
With grys, and that the fyneste of a lond;
And, for to festne his hood under his chin,
He hadde of gold y-wroght a curious pin:
A love-knotte in the gretter ende ther was.
His heed was balled, that shoon as any glas,
And eek his face, as he had been anoint.
He was a lord ful fat and in good point;
His eyen stepe, and rollinge in his heed,
That stemed as a forneys of a leed;
His botes souple, his hors in greet estat.
Now certeinly he was a fair prelat;
He was nat pale as a for-pyned goost.
A fat swan loved he best of any roost.
His palfrey was as broun as is a berye.
A FRERE ther was, a wantown and a merye,
A limitour, a ful solempne man.
In alle the ordres foure[3] is noon that can
So muche of daliaunce and fair langage.

[2]Love conquers all things.

[3]Dominicans, Franciscans, Carmelites, and Austin Friars.

He hadde maad ful many a mariage
Of yonge wommen, at his owne cost.
Un-to his ordre he was a noble post.
Ful wel biloved and famulier was he
With frankeleyns over-al in his contree,
And eek with worthy wommen of the toun:
For he had power of confessioun,
As seyde him-self, more than a curat,
For of his ordre he was licentiat.
Ful swetely herde he confessioun,
And plesaunt was his absolucioun;
He was an esy man to yeve penaunce
Ther as he wiste to han a good pitaunce;
For unto a povre ordre for to yive
Is signe that a man is wel y-shrive.
For if he yaf, he dorste make avaunt,
He wiste that a man was repentaunt.
For many a man so hard is of his herte,
He may nat wepe al-thogh him sore smerte.
Therfore, in stede of weping and preyeres,
Men moot yeve silver to the povre freres.
His tipet was ay farsed ful of knyves
And pinnes, for to yeven faire wyves.
And certeinly he hadde a mery note;
Wel coude he singe and pleyen on a rote.
Of yeddinges he bar utterly the prys.
His nekke whyt was as the flour-de-lys;
Ther-to he strong was as a champioun.
He knew the tavernes wel in every toun,
And everich hostiler and tappestere
Bet than a lazar or a beggestere;
For un-to swich a worthy man as he
Acorded nat, as by his facultee,
To have with seke lazars aqueyntaunce.
It is nat honest, it may nat avaunce
For to delen with no swich poraille,
But al with riche and sellers of vitaille.
And over-al, ther as profit sholde aryse,
Curteys he was, and lowly of servyse.
Ther nas no man no-wher so vertuous.
He was the beste beggere in his hous;
And yaf a certeyn ferme for the graunt;
Noon of his bretheren cam ther in his haunt;
For thogh a widwe hadde noght a sho,
So plesaunt was his "*In principio*,"[1]
Yet wolde he have a ferthing, er he wente.
His purchas was wel bettre than his rente.
And rage he coude, as it were right a whelpe.
In love-dayes ther coude he muchel helpe.
For there he was nat lyk a cloisterer,
With a thredbar cope, as is a povre scoler,
But he was lyk a maister or a pope.
Of double worsted was his semi-cope,
That rounded as a belle out of the presse.
Somwhat he lipsed, for his wantownesse,
To make his English swete up-on his tonge;
And in his harping, whan that he had songe,
His eyen twinkled in his heed aright,

[1]In the beginning. (Opening words of the Gospel of St. John, a text much qu ted by the friars.)

As doon the sterres in the frosty night.
This worthy limitour was cleped Huberd.
A Marchant was ther with a forked berd,
In mottelee, and hye on horse he sat,
Up-on his heed a Flaundrish bever hat;
His botes clasped faire and fetisly.
His resons he spak ful solempnely,
Souninge alway th'encrees of his winning.
He wolde the see were kept for any thing
Bitwixe Middelburgh and Orewelle.[2]
Wel coude he in eschaunge sheeldes selle.
This worthy man ful wel his wit bisette;
Ther wiste no wight that he was in dette,
So estatly was he of his governaunce,
With his bargaynes, and with his chevisaunce.
For sothe he was a worthy man with-alle,
But sooth to seyn, I noot how men him calle.
A Clerk ther was of Oxenford also,
That un-to logik hadde longe y-go.
As lene was his hors as is a rake,
And he nas nat right fat, I undertake;
But loked holwe, and ther-to soberly.
Ful thredbar was his overest courtepy;
For he had geten him yet no benefyce,
Ne was so worldly for to have offyce.
For him was lever have at his beddes heed
Twenty bokes, clad in blak or reed,
Of Aristotle and his philosophye,
Than robes riche, or fithele, or gay sautrye.
But al be that he was a philosophre,
Yet hadde he but litel gold in cofre;[3]
But al that he mighte of his freendes hente,
On bokes and on lerninge he it spente,
And bisily gan for the soules preye
Of hem that yaf him wher-with to scoleye.
Of studie took he most cure and most hede.
Noght o word spak he more than was nede,
And that was seyd in forme and reverence,
And short and quik, and ful of hy sentence.
Souninge in moral vertu was his speche,
And gladly wolde he lerne, and gladly teche.
A Sergeant of the Lawe, war and wys,
That often hadde been at the parvys,
Ther was also, ful riche of excellence.
Discreet he was, and of greet reverence:
He semed swich, his wordes weren so wyse.
Justyce he was ful often in assyse,
By patente, and by pleyn commissioun;
For his science, and for his heigh renoun
Of fees and robes hadde he many oon.
So greet a purchasour was no-wher noon.
Al was fee simple to him in effect,[4]

[2]The former a port on an island off the coast of the Netherlands, the latter an English port at the mouth of the Orwell river. He wanted the sea-route between the two kept open at any expense.

[3]The reference is to the alchemists, who were also termed philosophers. It was commonly believed that they could turn base metals into gold.

[4]The meaning is that he could untie any entail, or restriction on land.

His purchasing mighte nat been infect.
No-wher so bisy a man as he ther nas,
And yet he semed bisier than he was.
In termes hadde he caas and domes alle,
That from the tyme of king William were falle.
Therto he coude endyte, and make a thing,
Ther coude no wight pinche at his wryting;
And every statut coude he pleyn by rote.
He rood but hoomly in a medlee cote
Girt with a ceint of silk, with barres smale;
Of his array telle I no lenger tale.

A Frankeleyn was in his companye;
Whyt was his berd, as is the dayesye.
Of his complexioun he was sangwyn.
Wel loved he by the morwe a sop in wyn.
To liven in delyt was ever his wone,
For he was Epicurus owne sone,
That heeld opinioun, that pleyn delyt
Was verraily felicitee parfyt.
An housholdere, and that a greet, was he;
Seint Julian[1] he was in his contree.
His breed, his ale, was alwey after oon;
A bettre envyned man was no-wher noon.
With-oute bake mete was never his hous,
Of fish and flesh, and that so plentevous,
It snewed in his hous of mete and drinke,
Of alle deyntees that men coude thinke.
After the sondry sesons of the yeer,
So chaunged he his mete and his soper.
Ful many a fat partrich hadde he in mewe,
And many a breem and many a luce in stewe.
Wo was his cook, but-if his sauce were
Poynaunt and sharp, and redy al his gere.
His table dormant in his halle alway
Stood redy covered al the longe day.
At sessiouns ther was he lord and sire;
Ful ofte tyme he was knight of the shire.
An anlas and a gipser al of silk
Heng at his girdel, whyt as morne milk.
A shirreve hadde he been, and a countour;
Was no-wher such a worthy vavasour.

An Haberdassher and a Carpenter,
A Webbe, a Dyere, and a Tapicer,
Were with us eek, clothed in o liveree,
Of a solempne and greet fraternitee.
Ful fresh and newe hir gere apyked was;
Hir knyves were y-chaped noght with bras,
But al with silver, wroght ful clene and weel,
Hir girdles and hir pouches every-deel.
Wel semed ech of hem a fair burgeys,
To sitten in a yeldhalle on a deys.
Everich, for the wisdom that he can,
Was shaply for to been an alderman.
For catel hadde they y-nogh and rente,
And eek hir wyves wolde it wel assente;
And elles certein were they to blame.
It is ful fair to been y-clept "*ma dame*,"
And goon to vigilyës al bifore,
And have a mantel royalliche y-bore.

A Cook they hadde with hem for the nones,
To boille the chiknes with the mary-bones,
And poudre-marchant tart, and galingale.
Wel coude he knowe a draughte of London ale.
He coude roste, and sethe, and broille, and frye,
Maken mortreux, and wel bake a pye.
But greet harm was it, as it thoughte me,
That on his shine a mormal hadde he;
For blankmanger, that made he with the beste.

A Shipman was ther, woning fer by weste:
For aught I woot, he was of Dertemouthe.
He rood up-on a rouncy, as he couthe,
In a gowne of falding to the knee.
A daggere hanging on a laas hadde he
Aboute his nekke under his arm adoun.
The hote somer had maad his hewe al broun;
And, certeinly, he was a good felawe.
Ful many a draughte of wyn had he y-drawe
From Burdeux-ward, whyl that the chapman sleep.[2]
Of nyce conscience took he no keep.
If that he faught, and hadde the hyer hond,
By water he sente hem hoom to every lond.[3]
But of his craft to rekene wel his tydes,
His stremes and his daungers him bisydes,
His herberwe and his mone, his lodemenage,
Ther nas noon swich from Hulle to Cartage.
Hardy he was, and wys to undertake;
With many a tempest hadde his berd been shake.
He knew wel alle the havenes, as they were,
From Gootlond to the cape of Finistere,
And every cryke in Britayne and in Spayne;
His barge y-cleped was the Maudelayne.

With us ther was a Doctour of Phisyk,
In al this world ne was ther noon him lyk
To speke of phisik and of surgerye;
For he was grounded in astronomye.[4]
He kepte his pacient a ful greet del
In houres, by his magik naturel.
Wel coude he fortunen the ascendent
Of his images for his pacient.
He knew the cause of everich maladye,
Were it of hoot or cold, or moiste, or drye,
And where engendred, and of what humour;
He was a verrey parfit practisour.
The cause y-knowe, and of his harm the rote,
Anon he yaf the seke man his bote.
Ful redy hadde he his apothecaries,
To sende him drogges and his letuaries,
For ech of hem made other for to winne;

---

[1]The patron saint of hospitality.

[2]He had stolen wine from the casks he was carrying from Bordeaux.

[3]Threw them overboard.

[4]"Astronomye." This is really astrology. The physician knew well how to watch for a favorable astrological hour for the making of images to be used as charms in the treatment of his patient.

Hir frendschipe nas nat newe to biginne.
Wel knew he th'olde Esculapius,
And Deiscorides, and eek Rufus,
Old Ypocras, Haly, and Galien;
Serapion, Razis, and Avicen;
Averrois, Damascien, and Constantyn;
Bernard, and Gatesden, and Gilbertyn.[1]
Of his diete mesurable was he,
For it was of nc superfluitee,
But of greet norissing and digestible.
His studie was but litel on the bible.
In sangwin and in pers he clad was al,
Lyned with taffata and with sendal;
And yet he was but esy of dispence;
He kepte that he wan in pestilence.
For gold in phisik is a cordial,
Therfore he lovede gold in special.

A good WYF was ther of bisyde BATHE,
But she was som-del deef, and that was scathe.
Of clooth-making she hadde swiche an haunt,
She passed hem of Ypres and of Gaunt.
In all the parisshe wyf ne was ther noon
That to th'offring bifore hir sholde goon;
And if ther dide, certeyn, so wrooth was she,
That she was out of alle charitee.
Hir coverchiefs ful fyne were of ground;
I dorste swere they weyeden ten pound
That on a Sonday were upon hir heed.
Hir hosen weren of fyn scarlet reed,
Ful streite y-teyd, and shoos ful moiste and newe.
Bold was hir face, and fair, and reed of hewe.
She was a worthy womman al hir lyve,
Housbondes at chirche-dore she hadde fyve,
Withouten other companye in youthe;
But therof nedeth nat to speke as nouthe.
And thryes hadde she been at Jerusalem;
She hadde passed many a straunge streem;
At Rome she hadde been, and at Boloigne,
In Galice at seint Jame,[2] and at Cologne.
She coude muche of wandring by the weye:
Gat-tothed was she, soothly for to seye.
Up-on an amblere esily she sat,
Y-wimpled wel, and on hir heed an hat
As brood as is a bokeler or a targe;
A foot-mantel aboute hir hipes large,
And on hir feet a paire of spores sharpe.
In felawschip wel coude she laughe and carpe.
Of remedyes of love she knew per-chaunce,
For she coude of that art the olde daunce.

A good man was ther of religioun,
And was a povre PERSOUN of a toun;
But riche he was of holy thoght and werk.
He was also a lerned man, a clerk,
That Cristes gospel trewely wolde preche;
His parisshens devoutly wolde he teche.
Benigne he was, and wonder diligent,

[1]All great medical authorities.

[2]Compostella in Spain.

And in adversitee ful pacient;
And swich he was y-preved ofte sythes.
Ful looth were him to cursen for his tythes,
But rather wolde he yeven, out of doute,
Un-to his povre parisshens aboute
Of his offring, and eek of his substaunce.
He coude in litel thing han suffisaunce.
Wyd was his parisshe, and houses fer a-sonder,
But he ne lafte nat, for reyn ne thonder,
In siknes nor in meschief, to visyte
The ferreste in his parisshe, muche and lyte,
Up-on his feet, and in his hand a staf.
This noble ensample to his sheep he yaf,
That first he wroghte, and afterward he taughte;
Out of the gospel he tho wordes caughte;[3]
And this figure he added eek ther-to,
That if gold ruste, what shal iren do?
For if a preest be foul, on whom we truste,
No wonder is a lewed man to ruste;
And shame it is, if a preest take keep,
A shiten shepherde and a clene sheep.
Wel oghte a preest ensample for to yive,
By his clennesse, how that his sheep shold live.
He sette nat his benefice to hyre,
And leet his sheep encombred in the myre,
And ran to London, un-to sëynt Poules,
To seken him a chaunterie for soules,[4]
Or with a bretherhed to been withholde;[5]
But dwelte at hoom, and kepte wel his folde,
So that the wolf ne made it nat miscarie;
He was a shepherde and no mercenarie.
And though he holy were, and vertuous,
He was to sinful man nat despitous,
Ne of his speche daungerous ne digne,
But in his teching discreet and benigne.
To drawen folk to heven by fairnesse
By good ensample, was his bisinesse:
But it were any persone obstinat,
What-so he were, of heigh or lowe estat,
Him wolde he snibben sharply for the nones.
A bettre preest, I trowe that nowher noon is.
He wayted after no pompe and reverence,
Ne maked him a spyced conscience,
But Cristes lore, and his apostles twelve,
He taughte, and first he folwed it him-selve.

With him ther was a PLOWMAN, was his brother,
That hadde y-lad of dong ful many a fother,
A trewe swinker and a good was he,
Livinge in pees and parfit charitee.
God loved he best with al his hole herte
At alle tymes, thogh him gamed or smerte,
And thanne his neighebour right as him-selve.
He wolde thresshe, and ther-to dyke and delve,
For Cristes sake, for every povre wight,

[3]St. Matthew, v, 19.

[4]There were 35 chantries at St. Paul's, served by 54 priests who said masses for the dead.

[5]"Or to remain in retirement with some fraternity."

Withouten hyre, if it lay in his might.
His tythes payed he ful faire and wel,
Bothe of his propre swink and his catel.
In a tabard he rood upon a mere.
Ther was also a Reve and a Millere,
A Somnour and a Pardoner also,
A Maunciple, and my-self; ther were namo.
The MILLER was a stout carl, for the nones,
Ful big he was of braun, and eek of bones;
That proved wel, for over-al ther he cam,
At wrastling he wolde have alwey the ram.[1]
He was short-sholdred, brood, a thikke knarre,
Ther nas no dore that he nolde heve of harre,
Or breke it, at a renning, with his heed.
His berd as any sowe or fox was reed,
And ther-to brood, as though it were a spade.
Up-on the cop right of his nose he hade
A werte, and ther-on stood a tuft of heres,
Reed as the bristles of a sowes eres;
His nose-thirles blake were and wyde.
A swerd and bokeler bar he by his syde;
His mouth as greet was as a greet forneys.
He was a janglere and a goliardeys,
And that was most of sinne and harlotryes.
Wel coude he stelen corn, and tollen thryes;
And yet he hadde a thombe of gold, pardee.
A whyt cote and a blew hood wered he.
A baggepype wel coude he blowe and sowne,
And ther-with-al he broghte us out of towne.
A gentil MAUNCIPLE was ther of a temple,
Of which achatours mighte take exemple
For to be wyse in bying of vitaille.
For whether that he payde, or took by taille,
Algate he wayted so in his achat,
That he was ay biforn and in good stat.
Now is nat that of God a ful fair grace,
That swich a lewed mannes wit shal pace
The wisdom of an heep of lerned men?
Of maistres hadde he mo than thryes ten,
That were of lawe expert and curious;
Of which ther were a doseyn in that hous
Worthy to been stiwardes of rente and lond
Of any lord that is in Engelond,
To make him live by his propre good,
In honour dettelees, but he were wood,
Or live as scarsly as him list desire;
And able for to helpen al a shire
In any cas that mighte falle or happe;
And yit this maunciple sette hir aller cappe.
The REVE was a sclendre colerik man,
His berd was shave as ny as ever he can.
His heer was by his eres round y-shorn.
His top was dokked lyk a preest biforn.
Ful longe were his legges, and ful lene,
Y-lyk a staf, ther was no calf y-sene.
Wel coude he kepe a gerner and a binne;
Ther was noon auditour coude on him winne.
Wel wiste he, by the droghte, and by the reyn,
The yelding of his seed, and of his greyn.
His lordes sheep, his neet, his dayerye,
His swyn, his hors, his stoor, and his pultrye,
Was hoolly in this reves governing,
And by his covenaunt yaf the rekening,
Sin that his lord was twenty yeer of age;
Ther coude no man bringe him in arrerage.[2]
Ther nas baillif, ne herde, ne other hyne,
That he ne knew his sleighte and his covyne;
They were adrad of him, as of the deeth.
His woning was ful fair up-on an heeth,
With grene treës shadwed was his place.
He coude bettre than his lord purchace.
Ful riche he was astored prively,
His lord wel coude he plesen subtilly,
To yeve and lene him of his owne good,
And have a thank, and yet a cote and hood.
In youthe he lerned hadde a good mister;
He was a wel good wrighte, a carpenter.
This reve sat up-on a ful good stot,
That was al pomely grey, and highte Scot.
A long surcote of pers up-on he hade,
And by his syde he bar a rusty blade.
Of Northfolk was this reve, of which I telle,
Bisyde a toun men clepen Baldeswelle,
Tukked he was, as is a frere, aboute,
And ever he rood the hindreste of our route.
A SOMNOUR was ther with us in that place,
That hadde a fyr-reed cherubinnes face,
For sawcefleem he was, with eyen narwe.
As hoot he was, and lecherous, as a sparwe;
With scalled browes blake, and piled berd;
Of his visage children were aferd.
Ther nas quik-silver, litarge, ne brimstoon,
Boras, ceruce, ne oille of tartre noon,
Ne oynement that wolde clense and byte,
That him mighte helpen of his whelkes whyte,
Nor of the knobbes sittinge on his chekes.
Wel loved he garleek, oynons, and eek lekes,
And for to drinken strong wyn, reed as blood.
Than wolde he speke, and crye as he were wood.
And whan that he wel dronken hadde the wyn,
Than wolde he speke no word but Latyn.
A fewe termes hadde he, two or three,
That he had lerned out of som decree;
No wonder is, he herde it al the day;
And eek ye knowen wel, how that a jay
Can clepen "Watte," as well as can the pope.
But who-so coude in other thing him grope,
Thanne hadde he spent al his philosophye;
Ay "*Questio quid iuris*"[3] wolde he crye.
He was a gentil harlot and a kinde;
A bettre felawe sholde men noght finde.
He wolde suffre, for a quart of wyn,
A good felawe to have his concubyn
A twelf-month, and excuse him atte fulle:

[1]The prize.

[2]Catch him in arrears.

[3]What is the law on this point?

Full prively a finch eek coude he pulle.
And if he fond o-wher a good felawe,
He wolde techen him to have non awe,
In swich cas, of the erchedeknes curs,
But-if a mannes soule were in his purs;
For in his purs he sholde y-punisshed be.
"Purs is the erchedeknes helle," seyde he.
But well I woot he lyed right in dede;
Of cursing oghte ech gilty man him drede—
For curs wol slee, right as assoilling saveth—
And also war him of a *significavit*.[1]
In daunger hadde he at his owne gyse
The yonge girles of the diocyse,
And knew hir counseil, and was al hir reed.
A gerland hadde he set up-on his heed,
As greet as it were for an ale-stake;
A bokeler hadde he maad him of a cake.
With him ther rood a gentil PARDONER
Of Rouncival,[2] his freend and his compeer,
That streight was comen fro the court of Rome.
Ful loude he song, "Com hider, love, to me."
This somnour bar to him a stif burdoun,
Was never trompe of half so greet a soun.
This pardoner hadde heer as yelow as wex,
But smothe it heng, as dooth a strike of flex;
By ounces henge his lokkes that he hadde,
And ther-with he his shuldres overspradde;
But thinne it lay, by colpons oon and oon;
But hood, for jolitee, ne wered he noon,
For it was trussed up in his walet.
Him thoughte, he rood al of the newe jet;
Dischevele, save his cappe, he rood al bare.
Swiche glaringe eyen hadde he as an hare.
A vernicle hadde he sowed on his cappe.
His walet lay biforn him in his lappe,
Bret-ful of pardoun come from Rome al hoot.
A voys he hadde as smal as hath a goot.
No berd hadde he, ne never sholde have,
As smothe it was as it were late y-shave;
I trowe he were a gelding or a mare.
But of his craft, fro Berwik into Ware,
Ne was ther swich another pardoner.
For in his male he hadde a pilwe-beer,
Which that, he seyde, was our lady veyl:
He seyde, he hadde a gobet of the seyl
That sëynt Peter hadde, whan that he wente
Up-on the see, til Jesu Crist him hente.
He hadde a croys of latoun, ful of stones,
And in a glas he hadde pigges bones.
But with thise relikes, whan that he fond
A povre person dwelling up-on lond,
Up-on a day he gat him more moneye
Than that the person gat in monthes tweye.
And thus, with feyned flaterye and japes,
He made the person and the peple his apes.
But trewely to tellen, atte laste,
He was in chirche a noble ecclesiaste.
Wel coude he rede a lessoun or a storie,
But alderbest he song an offertorie;
For wel he wiste, whan that song was songe,
He moste preche, and wel affyle his tonge,
To winne silver, as he ful wel coude;
Therefore he song so meriely and loude.
Now have I told you shortly, in a clause,
Th'estat, th'array, the nombre, and eek the cause
Why that assembled was this companye
In Southwerk, at this gentil hostelrye,
That highte the Tabard, faste by the Belle.
But now is tyme to yow for to telle
How that we baren us that ilke night,
Whan we were in that hostelrye alight.
And after wol I telle of our viage,
And al the remenaunt of our pilgrimage.
But first I pray yow, of your curteisye,
That ye n'arette it nat my vileinye,
Thogh that I pleynly speke in this matere,
To telle yow hir wordes and hir chere;
Ne thogh I speke hir wordes properly.
For this ye knowen al-so wel as I,
Who-so shal telle a tale after a man,
He moot reherce, as ny as ever he can,
Everich a word, if it be in his charge,
Al speke he never so rudeliche and large;
Or elles he moot telle his tale untrewe,
Or feyne thing, or finde wordes newe.
He may nat spare, al-thogh he were his brother;
He moot as wel seye o word as another.
Crist spak him-self ful brode in holy writ,
And wel ye woot, no vileinye is it.
Eek Plato seith, who-so that can him rede,
The wordes mote be cosin to the dede.[3]
Also I prey yow to foryeve it me,
Al have I nat set folk in hir degree
Here in this tale, as that they sholde stonde;
My wit is short, ye may wel understonde.
Greet chere made our hoste us everichon,
And to the soper sette us anon;
And served us with vitaille at the beste.
Strong was the wyn, and wel to drinke us leste.
A semely man our hoste was with-alle
For to han been a marshal in an halle;
A large man he was with eyen stepe,
A fairer burgeys is ther noon in Chepe:[4]
Bold of his speche, and wys, and wel y-taught,
And of manhod him lakkede right naught.
Eek therto he was right a mery man,
And after soper pleyen he bigan,
And spak of mirthe amonges othere thinges,
Whan that we hadde maad our rekeninges;
And seyde thus: "Now, lordinges, trewely,
Ye been to me right welcome hertely:

[1] A writ of excommunication, which usually began with this word.

[2] An hospital near Charing Cross, London.

[3] Chaucer took this from Boethius, *De Consolatione*, bk. III, pr. 12. *Cf.* Plato, *Timaeus*, 29B.

[4] Cheapside.

For by my trouthe, if that I shal nat lye,
I ne saugh this yeer so mery a companye
At ones in this herberwe as is now.
Fayn wolde I doon yow mirthe, wiste I how.
And of a mirthe I am right now bithoght,
To doon yow ese, and it shal coste noght.
Ye goon to Caunterbury; God yow spede,
The blisful martir quyte yow your mede.
And wel I woot, as ye goon by the weye,
Ye shapen yow to talen and to pleye;
For trewely, confort ne mirthe is noon
To ryde by the weye doumb as a stoon;
And therfore wol I maken yow disport,
As I seyde erst, and doon yow som confort.
And if yow lyketh alle, by oon assent,
Now for to stonden at my jugement,
And for to werken as I shal yow seye,
To-morwe, whan ye ryden by the weye,
Now, by my fader soule, that is deed,
But ye be merye, I wol yeve yow myn heed.
Hold up your hond, withouten more speche."
Our counseil was nat longe for to seche;
Us thoughte it was noght worth to make it wys,
And graunted him withouten more avys,
And bad him seye his verdit, as him leste.
"Lordinges," quod he, "now herkneth for the beste;
But tak it not, I prey yow, in desdeyn;
This is the poynt, to speken short and pleyn,
That ech of yow, to shorte with your weye,
In this viage, shal telle tales tweye,
To Caunterbury-ward, I mene it so,
And hom-ward he shal tellen othere two,
Of aventures that whylom han bifalle,
And which of yow that bereth him best of alle,
That is to seyn, that telleth in this cas
Tales of best sentence and most solas,
Shal have a soper at our aller cost
Here in this place, sitting by this post,
Whan that we come agayn fro Caunterbury.
And for to make yow the more mery,
I wol my-selven gladly with yow ryde,
Right at myn owne cost, and be your gyde.
And who-so wol my jugement withseye
Shal paye al that we spenden by the weye.
And if ye vouche-sauf that it be so,
Tel me anon, with-outen wordes mo,
And I wol erly shape me therfore."
This thing was graunted, and our othes swore
With ful glad herte, and preyden him also
That he wold vouche-sauf for to do so,
And that he wolde been our governour,
And of our tales juge and reportour,
And sette a soper at a certeyn prys;
And we wold reuled been at his devys,
In heigh and lowe; and thus, by oon assent,
We been acorded to his jugement.
And ther-up-on the wyn was fet anon;
We dronken, and to reste wente echon,
With-outen any lenger taryinge.
A-morwe, whan that day bigan to springe,
Up roos our host, and was our aller cok,
And gadrede us togidre, alle in a flok,
And forth we riden, a litel more than pas,
Un-to the watering of seint Thomas.
And there our host bigan his hors areste,
And seyde; "Lordinges, herkneth, if yow leste.
Ye woot your forward, and I it yow recorde.
If even-song and morwe-song acorde,
Lat see now who shal telle the firste tale.
As ever mote I drinke wyn or ale,
Who-so be rebel to my jugement
Shal paye for al that by the weye is spent.
Now draweth cut, er that we ferrer twinne;
He which that hath the shortest shal biginne.
Sire knight," quod he, "my maister and my lord,
Now draweth cut, for that is myn acord.
Cometh neer," quod he, "my lady prioresse;
And ye, sir clerk, lat be your shamfastnesse,
Ne studieth noght; ley hond to, every man."
Anon to drawen every wight bigan,
And shortly for to tellen, as it was,
Were it by aventure, or sort, or cas,
The sothe is this, the cut fil to the knight,
Of which ful blythe and glad was every wight;
And telle he moste his tale, as was resoun,
By forward and by composicioun,
As ye han herd; what nedeth wordes mo?
And whan this gode man saugh it was so,
As he that wys was and obedient
To kepe his forward by his free assent,
He seyde: "Sin I shal beginne the game,
What, welcome be the cut, a Goddes name!
Now lat us ryde, and herkneth what I seye."
And with that word we riden forth our weye;
And he bigan with right a mery chere
His tale anon, and seyde in this manere.[1]

THE PRIORESSES PROLOGUE

"Wel seyd, by *corpus dominus*,"[2] quod our hoste,
"Now longe moot thou sayle by the coste,
Sir gentil maister, gentil marineer!
God yeve this monk a thousand last quad yeer!
A ha! felawes! beth ware of swiche a jape!
The monk putte in the mannes hood an ape,
And in his wyves eek, by seint Austin!
Draweth no monkes more un-to your in.
But now passe over, and lat us seke aboute,
Who shal now telle first, of all this route,
Another tale"; and with that word he sayde,

[1]Here follow the tales of the Knight, the Miller, the Reeve, and the Cook, the last unfinished. On the morning of the second day the Man of Law tells the first tale, then the Shipman tells one, and then the Host turns to the Prioress.

[2]By the body of our Lord.

As curteisly as it had been a mayde,
"My lady Prioresse, by your leve,
So that I wiste I sholde yow nat greve,
I wolde demen that ye tellen sholde
A tale next, if so were that ye wolde.
Now wol ye vouche-sauf, my lady dere?"
"Gladly," quod she, and seyde as ye shal here.

THE PRIORESSES TALE

Domine, dominus noster.[1]

O Lord our lord, thy name how merveillous
Is in this large worlde y-sprad—quod she:—
For noght only thy laude precious
Parfourned is by men of dignitee,
But by the mouth of children thy bountee
Parfourned is, for on the brest soukinge
Som tyme shewen they thyn heryinge.

Wherfor in laude, as I best can or may,
Of thee, and of the whyte lily flour
Which that thee bar, and is a mayde alway,
To telle a storie I wol do my labour;
Not that I may encresen hir honour;
For she hir-self is honour, and the rote
Of bountee, next hir sone, and soules bote.—

O moder mayde! o mayde moder free!
O bush unbrent, brenninge in Moyses sighte,
That ravisedest doun fro the deitee,
Thurgh thyn humblesse, the goost that in th'alighte,
Of whos vertu, whan he thyn herte lighte,
Conceived was the fadres sapience,
Help me to telle it in thy reverence!

Lady! thy bountee, thy magnificence,
Thy vertu, and thy grete humilitee
Ther may no tonge expresse in no science;
For som-tyme, lady, er men praye to thee,
Thou goost biforn of thy benignitee,
And getest us the light, thurgh thy preyere,
To gyden us un-to thy sone so dere.

My conning is so wayk, o blisful quene,
For to declare thy grete worthinesse,
That I ne may the weighte nat sustene,
But as a child of twelf monthe old, or lesse,
That can unnethes any word expresse,
Right so fare I, and therfor I yow preye,
Gydeth my song that I shal of yow seye.

Here Biginneth the Prioresses Tale[2]

Ther was in Asie, in a greet citee,
Amonges Cristen folk, a Jewerye,
Sustened by a lord of that contree
For foule usure and lucre of vilanye,
Hateful to Crist and to his companye;
And thurgh the strete men mighte ryde or wende,
For it was free, and open at either ende.

A litel scole of Cristen folk ther stood
Doun at the ferther ende, in which ther were
Children an heep, y-comen of Cristen blood,
That lerned in that scole yeer by yere
Swich maner doctrine as men used there,
This is to seyn, to singen and to rede,
As smale children doon in hir childhede.

Among thise children was a widwes sone,
A litel clergeon, seven yeer of age,
That day by day to scole was his wone,
And eek also, wher-as he saugh th'image
Of Cristes moder, hadde he in usage,
As him was taught, to knele adoun and seye
His *Ave Marie*,[3] as he goth by the weye.

Thus hath this widwe hir litel sone y-taught
Our blisful lady, Cristes moder dere,
To worshipe ay, and he forgat it naught,
For sely child wol alday sone lere;
But ay, whan I remembre on this matere,
Seint Nicholas stant ever in my presence,
For he so yong to Crist did reverence.

This litel child, his litel book lerninge,
As he sat in the scole at his prymer,
He *Alma redemptoris*[4] herde singe,
As children lerned hir antiphoner;
And, as he dorste, he drough him ner and ner,
And herkned ay the wordes and the note,
Til he the firste vers coude al by rote.

Noght wiste he what this Latin was to seye,
For he so yong and tendre was of age;
But on a day his felaw gan he preye
T'expounden him this song in his langage,
Or telle him why this song was in usage;
This preyde he him to construe and declare
Ful ofte tyme upon his knowes bare.

His felaw, which that elder was than he,
Answerde him thus: "this song, I have herd seye,
Was maked of our blisful lady free,
Hir to salue, and eek hir for to preye
To been our help and socour whan we deye.
I can no more expounde in this matere;
I lerne song, I can but smal grammere."

[1] O Lord, our Lord.

[2] Chaucer probably based this tale on some Latin prose legend current in his day. The theme, the murder of a Christian child by Jews, was a popular one in the Middle Ages, and at least 29 versions of it are known.

[3] Hail Mary—the first two words of a short prayer made up from St. Luke, i, 28 and 42.

[4] Gracious Mother of the Redeemer. There is more than one medieval hymn with this beginning.

"And is this song maked in reverence
Of Cristes moder?" seyde this innocent;
"Now certes, I wol do my diligence
To conne it al, er Cristemasse is went;
Though that I for my prymer shal be shent,
And shal be beten thryës in an houre,
I wol it conne, our lady for to honoure."

His felaw taughte him homward prively,
Fro day to day, til he coude it by rote,
And than he song it wel and boldely
Fro word to word, acording with the note;
Twyës a day it passed thurgh his throte,
To scoleward and homward whan he wente;
On Cristes moder set was his entente.

As I have seyd, thurgh-out the Jewerye
This litel child, as he cam to and fro,
Ful merily than wolde he singe, and crye
O Alma redemptoris ever-mo.
The swetnes hath his herte perced so
Of Cristes moder, that, to hir to preye,
He can nat stinte of singing by the weye.

Our firste fo, the serpent Sathanas,
That hath in Jewes herte his waspes nest,
Up swal, and seide, "O Hebraik peple, allas!
Is this to yow a thing that is honest,
That swich a boy shal walken as him lest
In your despyt, and singe of swich sentence,
Which is agayn your lawes reverence?"

Fro thennes forth the Jewes han conspyred
This innocent out of this world to chace;
An homicyde ther-to han they hyred,
That in an aley hadde a privee place;
And as the child gan for-by for to pace,
This cursed Jew him hente and heeld him faste,
And kitte his throte, and in a pit him caste.

I seye that in a wardrobe they him threwe
Wher-as these Jewes purgen hir entraille.
O cursed folk of Herodes al newe,
What may your yvel entente yow availle?
Mordre wol out, certein, it wol nat faille,
And namely ther th'onour of god shal sprede,
The blood out creyth on your cursed dede.

"O martir, souded to virginitee,
Now maystou singen, folwing ever in oon
The whyte lamb celestial," quod she,
"Of which the grete evangelist, seint John,
In Pathmos wroot, which seith that they that goon
Biforn this lamb, and singe a song al newe,
That never, fleshly, wommen they ne knewe."

This povre widwe awaiteth al that night
After hir litel child, but he cam noght;
For which, as sone as it was dayes light,
With face pale of drede and bisy thoght,
She hath at scole and elles-wher him soght,
Til finally she gan so fer espye
That he last seyn was in the Jewerye.

With modres pitee in hir brest enclosed,
She gooth, as she were half out of hir minde,
To every place wher she hath supposed
By lyklihede hir litel child to finde;
And ever on Cristes moder meke and kinde
She cryde, and atte laste thus she wroghte,
Among the cursed Jewes she him soghte.

She frayneth and she preyeth pitously
To every Jew that dwelte in thilke place,
To telle hir, if hir child wente oght for-by.
They seyde, "nay"; but Jesu, of his grace,
Yaf in hir thought, inwith a litel space,
That in that place after hir sone she cryde,
Wher he was casten in a pit bisyde.

O grete god, that parfournest thy laude
By mouth of innocents, lo heer thy might!
This gemme of chastitee, this emeraude,
And eek of martirdom the ruby bright,
Ther he with throte y-corven lay upright,
He "*Alma redemptoris*" gan to singe
So loude, that al the place gan to ringe.

The Cristen folk, that thurgh the strete wente,
In coomen, for to wondre up-on this thing,
And hastily they for the provost sente;
He cam anon with-outen tarying,
And herieth Crist that is of heven king,
And eek his moder, honour of mankinde,
And after that, the Jewes leet he binde.

This child with pitous lamentacioun
Up-taken was, singing his song alway;
And with honour of greet processioun
They carien him un-to the nexte abbay.
His moder swowning by the bere lay;
Unnethe might the peple that was there
This newe Rachel bringe fro his bere.

With torment and with shamful deth echon
This provost dooth thise Jewes for to sterve,
That of this mordre wiste, and that anon;
He nolde no swich cursednesse observe.
Yvel shal have, that yvel wol deserve.
Therfor with wilde hors he dide hem drawe,[1]
And after that he heng hem by the lawe.

Up-on his bere ay lyth this innocent
Biforn the chief auter, whyl masse laste,
And after that, the abbot with his covent
Han sped hem for to burien him ful faste;
And whan they holy water on him caste,

[1] *Sc.* to the gallows.

Yet spak this child, whan spreynd was holy water,
And song—"*O Alma redemptoris mater!*"

This abbot, which that was an holy man
As monkes been, or elles oghten be,
This yonge child to conjure he bigan,
And seyde, "o dere child, I halse thee,
In vertu of the holy Trinitee,
Tel me what is thy cause for to singe,
Sith that thy throte is cut, to my seminge?"

"My throte is cut un-to my nekke-boon,"
Seyde this child, "and, as by wey of kinde,
I sholde have deyed, ye, longe tyme agoon,
But Jesu Crist, as ye in bokes finde,
Wil that his glorie laste and be in minde;
And, for the worship of his moder dere,
Yet may I singe '*O Alma*' loude and clere.

This welle of mercy, Cristes moder swete,
I lovede alwey, as after my conninge;
And whan that I my lyf sholde forlete,
To me she cam, and bad me for to singe
This antem verraily in my deyinge,
As ye han herd, and, whan that I had songe,
Me thoughte, she leyde a greyn up-on my tonge.

Wherfor I singe, and singe I moot certeyn
In honour of that blisful mayden free,
Til fro my tonge of-taken is the greyn;
And afterward thus seyde she to me,
'My litel child, now wol I fecche thee
Whan that the greyn is fro thy tonge y-take;
Be nat agast, I wol thee nat forsake.'"

This holy monk, this abbot, him mene I,
His tonge out-caughte, and took a-wey the greyn,
And he yaf up the goost ful softely.
And whan this abbot had this wonder seyn,
His salte teres trikled doun as reyn,
And gruf he fil al plat up-on the grounde,
And stille he lay as he had been y-bounde.

The covent eek lay on the pavement
Weping, and herien Cristes moder dere,
And after that they ryse, and forth ben went,
And toke awey this martir fro his bere,
And in a tombe of marbul-stones clere
Enclosen they his litel body swete;
Ther he is now, god leve us for to mete.

O yonge Hugh of Lincoln, slayn also
With cursed Jewes, as it is notable,
For it nis but a litel whyle ago;
Preye eek for us, we sinful folk unstable,
That, of his mercy, god so merciable
On us his grete mercy multiplye,
For reverence of his moder Marye. Amen.

THE NONNE PREESTES TALE[1]

A POVRE widwe, somdel stape in age,
Was whylom dwelling in a narwe cotage,
Bisyde a grove, stonding in a dale.
This widwe, of which I telle yow my tale,
Sin thilke day that she was last a wyf,
In pacience ladde a ful simple lyf,
For litel was hir catel and hir rente;
By housbondrye, of such as God hir sente,
She fond hir-self, and eek hir doghtren two.
Three large sowes hadde she, and namo,
Three kyn, and eek a sheep that highte Malle.
Ful sooty was hir bour, and eek hir halle,
In which she eet ful many a sclendre meel.
Of poynaunt sauce hir neded never a deel.
No deyntee morsel passed thurgh hir throte;
Hir dyete was accordant to hir cote.
Repleccioun ne made hir never syk;
Attempree dyete was al hir phisyk,
And exercyse, and hertes suffisaunce.
The goute lette hir no-thing for to daunce,
N'apoplexye shente nat hir heed;
No wyn ne drank she, neither whyt ne reed;
Hir bord was served most with whyt and blak,
Milk and broun breed, in which she fond no lak,
Seynd bacoun, and somtyme an ey or tweye,
For she was as it were a maner deye.
  A yerd she hadde, enclosed al aboute
With stikkes, and a drye dich with-oute,
In which she hadde a cok, hight Chauntecleer,
In al the land of crowing nas his peer.
His vois was merier than the mery orgon
On messe-dayes that in the chirche gon;
Wel sikerer was his crowing in his logge,
Than is a clokke, or an abbey orlogge.
By nature knew he ech ascencioun
Of equinoxial in thilke toun;
For whan degrees fiftene were ascended,
Thanne crew he, that it mighte nat been amended.
His comb was redder than the fyn coral,
And batailed, as it were a castel-wal.
His bile was blak, and as the jeet it shoon;
Lyk asur were his legges, and his toon;
His nayles whytter than the lilie flour,
And lyk the burned gold was his colour.
This gentil cok hadde in his governaunce
Sevene hennes, for to doon al his plesaunce,
Whiche were his sustres and his paramours,

[1] Following the Prioress's tale the Host asks Chaucer for a story. He begins *Sir Thopas*, a burlesque of the popular romances of the day, but is soon interrupted by the Host, who is bored. Thereupon Chaucer begins anew, and tells the edifying prose *Tale of Melibeus*. The Monk's tale follows (also interrupted, by the Knight), and then the Host turns to the Nun's Priest. The immediate source of this story is not known, but there were popular cycles dealing with Reynard the Fox.

And wonder lyk to him, as of colours.
Of whiche the faireste hewed on hir throte
Was cleped faire damoysele Pertelote.
Curteys she was, discreet, and debonaire,
And compaignable, and bar hir-self so faire,
Sin thilke day that she was seven night old,
That trewely she hath the herte in hold
Of Chauntecleer loken in every lith;
He loved hir so, that wel was him therwith.
But such a joye was it to here hem singe,
Whan that the brighte sonne gan to springe,
In swete accord, "my lief is faren in londe."
For thilke tyme, as I have understonde,
Bestes and briddes coude speke and singe.
  And so bifel, that in a daweninge,
As Chauntecleer among his wyves alle
Sat on his perche, that was in the halle,
And next him sat this faire Pertelote,
This Chauntecleer gan gronen in his throte,
As man that in his dreem is drecched sore.
And whan that Pertelote thus herde him rore,
She was agast, and seyde, "O herte dere,
What eyleth yow, to grone in this manere?
Ye been a verray sleper, fy for shame!"
And he answerde and seyde thus, "madame,
I pray yow, that ye take it nat a-grief:
By god, me mette I was in swich meschief
Right now, that yet myn herte is sore afright.
Now god," quod he, "my swevene recche aright,
And keep my body out of foul prisoun!
Me mette, how that I romed up and doun
Withinne our yerde, wher-as I saugh a beste,
Was lyk an hound, and wolde han maad areste
Upon my body, and wolde han had me deed.
His colour was bitwixe yelwe and reed;
And tipped was his tail, and bothe his eres,
With blak, unlyk the remenant of his heres;
His snowte smal, with glowinge eyen tweye.
Yet of his look for fere almost I deye;
This caused me my groning, doutelees."
  "Avoy!" quod she, "fy on yow, hertelees!
Allas!" quod she, "for, by that god above,
Now han ye lost myn herte and al my love;
I can nat love a coward, by my feith.
For certes, what so any womman seith,
We alle desyren, if it mighte be,
To han housbondes hardy, wyse, and free,
And secree, and no nigard, ne no fool,
Ne him that is agast of every tool,
Ne noon avauntour, by that god above!
How dorste ye seyn for shame unto your love,
That any thing mighte make yow aferd?
Have ye no mannes herte, and han a berd?
Allas! and conne ye been agast of swevenis?
No-thing, god wot, but vanitee, in sweven is.
Swevenes engendren of replecciouns,
And ofte of fume, and of complecciouns,
Whan humours been to habundant in a wight.
Certes this dreem, which ye han met to-night,
Cometh of the grete superfluitee
Of youre rede *colera*, pardee,
Which causeth folk to dreden in here dremes
Of arwes, and of fyr with rede lemes,
Of grete bestes, that they wol hem byte,
Of contek, and of whelpes grete and lyte;
Right as the humour of malencolye
Causeth ful many a man, in sleep, to crye,
For fere of blake beres, or boles blake,
Or elles, blake develes wole hem take.
Of othere humours coude I telle also,
That werken many a man in sleep ful wo;
But I wol passe as lightly as I can.
  Lo Catoun,[1] which that was so wys a man,
Seyde he nat thus, ne do no fors of dremes?
Now, sire," quod she, "whan we flee fro the bemes,
For Goddes love, as tak som laxatyf;
Up peril of my soule, and of my lyf,
I counseille yow the beste, I wol nat lye,
That bothe of colere and of malencolye
Ye purge yow; and for ye shul nat tarie,
Though in this toun is noon apotecarie,
I shal my-self to herbes techen yow,
That shul ben for your hele, and for your prow;
And in our yerd tho herbes shal I finde,
The whiche han of hir propretee, by kinde,
To purgen yow binethe, and eek above.
Forget not this, for goddes owene love!
Ye been ful colerik of compleccioun.
Ware the sonne in his ascencioun
Ne fynde yow nat repleet of humours hote;
And if it do, I dar wel leye a grote,
That ye shul have a fevere terciane,
Or an agu, that may be youre bane.
A day or two ye shul have digestyves
Of wormes, er ye take your laxatyves,
Of lauriol, centaure, and fumetere,
Or elles of ellebor, that groweth there,
Of catapuce, or of gaytres beryis,
Of erbe yve, growing in our yerd, that mery is;
Pekke hem up right as they growe, and ete hem in.
Be mery, housbond, for your fader kin!
Dredeth no dreem; I can say yow namore."
  "Madame," quod he, "*graunt mercy* of[2] your lore.
But nathelees, as touching daun Catoun,
That hath of wisdom such a greet renoun,
Though that he bad no dremes for to drede,
By god, men may in olde bokes rede
Of many a man, more of auctoritee
Than ever Catoun was, so mote I thee,

[1] Dionysius Cato, a medieval writer.
[2] Many thanks for.

That al the revers seyn of his sentence,
And han wel founden by experience,
That dremes ben significaciouns,
As wel of joye as tribulaciouns
That folk enduren in this lyf present.
Ther nedeth make of this noon argument;
The verray preve sheweth it in dede.
  Oon of the gretteste auctours that men rede
Seith, thus, that whylom two felawes wente
On pilgrimage, in a ful good entente;
And happed so, thay come into a toun,
Wher-as ther was swich congregacioun
Of peple, and eek so streit of herbergage,
That they ne founde as muche as o cotage
In which they bothe mighte y-logged be.
Wherfor thay mosten, of necessitee,
As for that night, departen compaignye;
And ech of hem goth to his hostelrye,
And took his logging as it wolde falle.
That oon of hem was logged in a stalle,
Fer in a yerd, with oxen of the plough;
That other man was logged wel y-nough,
As was his aventure, or his fortune,
That us governeth alle as in commune.
  And so bifel, that, longe er it were day,
This man mette in his bed, ther-as he lay,
How that his felawe gan up-on him calle,
And seyde, 'allas! for in an oxes stalle
This night I shal be mordred ther I lye.
Now help me, dere brother, er I dye;
In alle haste com to me,' he sayde.
This man out of his sleep for fere abrayde;
But whan that he was wakned of his sleep,
He turned him, and took of this no keep;
Him thoughte his dreem nas but a vanitee.
Thus twyës in his sleping dremed he.
And atte thridde tyme yet his felawe
Cam, as him thoughte, and seide, 'I am now slawe;
Bihold my blody woundes, depe and wyde!
Arys up erly in the morwe-tyde,
And at the west gate of the toun,' quod he,
'A carte ful of dong ther shaltow see,
In which my body is hid ful prively;
Do thilke carte aresten boldely.
My gold caused my mordre, sooth to sayn';
And tolde him every poynt how he was slayn,
With a ful pitous face, pale of hewe.
And truste wel, his dreem he fond ful trewe;
For on the morwe, as sone as it was day,
To his felawes in he took the way;
And whan that he cam to this oxes stalle,
After his felawe he bigan to calle.
  The hostiler answered him anon,
And seyde, 'sire, your felawe is agon,
As sone as day he wente out of the toun.'
This man gan fallen in suspecioun,
Remembring on his dremes that he mette,
And forth he goth, no lenger wolde he lette,
Unto the west gate of the toun, and fond
A dong-carte, as it were to donge lond,
That was arrayed in the same wyse
As ye han herd the dede man devyse;
And with an hardy herte he gan to crye
Vengeaunce and justice of this felonye:—
'My felawe mordred is this same night,
And in this carte he lyth gapinge upright.
I crye out on the ministres,' quod he,
'That sholden kepe and reulen this citee;
Harrow! allas! her lyth my felawe slayn!'
What sholde I more un-to this tale sayn?
The peple out-sterte, and caste the cart to grounde,
And in the middel of the dong they founde
The dede man, that mordred was al newe.
  O blisful god, that art so just and trewe!
Lo, how that thou biwreyest mordre alway!
Mordre wol out, that see we day by day.
Mordre is so wlatsom and abhominable
To God, that is so just and resonable,
That he ne wol nat suffre it heled be;
Though it abyde a yeer, or two, or three,
Mordre wol out, this my conclusioun.
And right anoon, ministres of that toun
Han hent the carter, and so sore him pyned,
And eek the hostiler so sore engyned,
That they biknewe hir wikkednesse anoon,
And were an-hanged by the nekke-boon.
  Here may men seen that dremes been to drede,
And certes, in the same book I rede,
Right in the nexte chapitre after this
(I gabbe nat, so have I joye or blis),
Two men that wolde han passed over see,
For certeyn cause, in-to a fer contree,
If that the wind ne hadde been contrarie,
That made hem in a citee for to tarie,
That stood ful mery upon an haven-syde.
But on a day, agayn the even-tyde,
The wind gan chaunge, and blew right as hem leste.
Jolif and glad they wente un-to hir reste,
And casten hem ful erly for to saille;
But to that oo man fil a greet mervaille.
That oon of hem, in sleping as he lay,
Him mette a wonder dreem, agayn the day;
Him thoughte a man stood by his beddes syde,
And him comaunded, that he sholde abyde,
And seyde him thus, 'if thou to-morwe wende,
Thou shalt be dreynt; my tale is at an ende.'
He wook, and tolde his felawe what he mette,
And preyde him his viage for to lette;
As for that day, he preyde him to abyde.
His felawe, that lay by his beddes syde,
Gan for to laughe, and scorned him ful faste.
'No dreem,' quod he, 'may so myn herte agaste,
That I wol lette for to do my thinges.
I sette not a straw by thy dreminges,

For swevenes been but vanitees and japes.
Men dreme al-day of owles or of apes,
And eke of many a mase therwithal;
Men dreme of thing that never was ne shal.
But sith I see that thou wolt heer abyde,
And thus for-sleuthen wilfully thy tyde,
God wot it reweth me; and have good day.'
And thus he took his leve, and wente his way.
But er that he hadde halfe his cours y-seyled,
Noot I nat why, ne what mischaunce it eyled,
But casuelly the shippes botme rente,
And ship and man under the water wente
In sighte of othere shippes it byside,
That with hem seyled at the same tyde.
And therfor, faire Pertelote so dere,
By swiche ensamples olde maistow lere,
That no man sholde been to recchelees
Of dremes, for I sey thee, doutelees,
That many a dreem ful sore is for to drede.
  Lo, in the lyf of seint Kenelm, I rede,
That was Kenulphus sone, the noble king
Of Mercenrike,[1] how Kenelm mette a thing;
A lyte er he was mordred, on a day,
His mordre in his avisioun he say.
His norice him expouned every del
His sweven, and bad him for to kepe him wel
For traisoun; but he nas but seven yeer old,
And therfore litel tale hath he told
Of any dreem, so holy was his herte.
By god, I hadde lever than my sherte
That ye had rad his legende, as have I.
Dame Pertelote, I sey yow trewely,
Macrobeus, that writ th'avisioun
In Affrike of the worthy Cipioun,
Affermeth dremes, and seith that they been
Warning of thinges that men after seen.
  And forther-more, I pray yow loketh wel
In th'olde testament, of Daniel,
If he held dremes any vanitee.
Reed eek of Joseph, and ther shul ye see
Wher dremes ben somtyme (I sey nat alle)
Warning of thinges that shul after falle.
Loke of Egipt the king, daun Pharao,
His bakere and his boteler also,
Wher they ne felte noon effect in dremes.
Who-so wol seken actes of sondry remes,
May rede of dremes many a wonder thing.
  Lo Cresus, which that was of Lyde king,
Mette he nat that he sat upon a tree,
Which signified he sholde anhanged be?
Lo heer Andromacha, Ectores wyf,
That day that Ector sholde lese his lyf,
She dremed on the same night biforn,
How that the lyf of Ector sholde be lorn,
If thilke day he wente in-to bataille;
She warned him, but it mighte nat availle;
He wente for to fighte nathelees,
But he was slayn anoon of Achilles.

[1]Mercia.

But thilke tale is al to long to telle,
And eek it is ny day, I may nat dwelle.
Shortly I seye, as for conclusioun,
That I shal han of this avisioun
Adversitee; and I seye forther-more,
That I ne telle of laxatyves no store,
For they ben venimous, I woot it wel;
I hem defye, I love hem never a del.
  Now let us speke of mirthe, and stinte al this;
Madame Pertelote, so have I blis,
Of o thing god hath sent me large grace;
For whan I see the beautee of your face,
Ye ben so scarlet-reed about your yën,
It maketh al my drede for to dyen;
For, also siker as *In principio,*
Mulier est hominis confusio;[2]
Madame, the sentence of this Latin is—
Womman is mannes joye and al his blis.
For whan I fele a-night your softe syde,
Al-be-it that I may nat on you ryde,
For that our perche is maad so narwe, alas!
I am so ful of joye and of solas
That I defye bothe sweven and dreem."
And with that word he fley doun fro the beem,
For it was day, and eek his hennes alle;
And with a chuk he gan hem for to calle,
For he had founde a corn, lay in the yerd.
Royal he was, he was namore aferd;
He fethered Pertelote twenty tyme,
And trad as ofte, er that it was pryme.
He loketh as it were a grim leoun;
And on his toos he rometh up and doun,
Him deyned not to sette his foot to grounde.
He chukketh, whan he hath a corn y-founde,
And to him rennen thanne his wyves alle.
Thus royal, as a prince is in his halle,
Leve I this Chauntecleer in his pasture;
And after wol I telle his aventure.
  Whan that the month in which the world bigan,
That highte March, whan god first maked man,
Was complet, and [y]-passed were also,
Sin March bigan, thritty dayes and two,
Bifel that Chauntecleer, in all his pryde,
His seven wyves walking by his syde,
Caste up his eyen to the brighte sonne,
That in the signe of Taurus hadde y-ronne
Twenty degrees and oon, and somwhat more;
And knew by kynde, and by noon other lore,
That it was pryme, and crew with blisful stevene.
"The sonne," he sayde, "is clomben up on hevene
Fourty degrees and oon, and more, y-wis.
Madame Pertelote, my worldes blis,
Herkneth thise blisful briddes how they singe,

[2]In the beginning woman is man's undoing.

And see the fresshe floures how they springe;
Ful is myn herte of revel and solas."
But sodeinly him fil a sorweful cas;
For ever the latter ende of joye is wo.
God woot that worldly joye is sone ago;
And if a rethor coude faire endyte,
He in a cronique saufly mighte it wryte,
As for a sovereyn notabilitee.
Now every wys man, lat him herkne me;
This storie is al-so trewe, I undertake,
As is the book of Launcelot de Lake,[1]
That wommen holde in ful gret reverence.
Now wol I torne agayn to my sentence.
  A col-fox, ful of sly iniquitee,
That in the grove hadde woned yeres three,
By heigh imaginacioun forn-cast,
The same night thurgh-out the hegges brast
Into the yerd, ther Chauntecleer the faire
Was wont, and eek his wyves, to repaire;
And in a bed of wortes stille he lay,
Til it was passed undern of the day,
Wayting his tyme on Chauntecleer to falle,
As gladly doon thise homicydes alle,
That in awayt liggen to mordre men.
O false mordrer, lurking in thy den!
O newe Scariot, newe Genilon![2]
False dissimilour, O Greek Sinon,
That broghtest Troye al outrely to sorwe!
O Chauntecleer, acursed be that morwe,
That thou into that yerd flough fro the bemes!
Thou were ful wel y-warned by thy dremes,
That thilke day was perilous to thee.
But what that god forwoot mot nedes be,
After the opinioun of certeyn clerkis.
Witnesse on him, that any perfit clerk is,
That in scole is gret altercacioun
In this matere, and greet disputisoun,
And hath ben of an hundred thousand men.
But I ne can not bulte it to the bren,
As can the holy doctour Augustyn,
Or Boëce, or the bishop Bradwardyn,
Whether that goddes worthy forwiting
Streyneth me nedely for to doon a thing,
(Nedely clepe I simple necessitee);
Or elles, if free choys be graunted me
To do that same thing, or do it noght,
Though god forwoot it, er that it was wroght;
Or if his witing streyneth nevere a del
But by necessitee condicionel.
I wol not han to do of swich matere;
My tale is of a cok, as ye may here,
That took his counseil of his wyf, with sorwe,
To walken in the yerd upon that morwe
That he had met the dreem, that I yow tolde.
Wommennes counseils been ful ofte colde;
Wommannes counseil broghte us first to wo,
And made Adam fro paradys to go,
Ther-as he was ful mery, and wel at ese.—
But for I noot, to whom it mighte displese,
If I counseil of wommen wolde blame,
Passe over, for I seyde it in my game.
Rede auctours, wher they trete of swich matere,
And what thay seyn of wommen ye may here.
Thise been the cokkes wordes, and nat myne;
I can noon harm of no womman divyne.—
  Faire in the sond, to bathe hir merily,
Lyth Pertelote, and alle hir sustres by,
Agayn the sonne; and Chauntecleer so free
Song merier than the mermayde in the see;
For Phisiologus[3] seith sikerly,
How that they singen wel and merily.
And so bifel that, as he caste his yë,
Among the wortes, on a boterflye,
He was war of this fox that lay ful lowe.
No-thing ne liste him thanne for to crowe,
But cryde anon, "cok, cok," and up he sterte,
As man that was affrayed in his herte.
For naturelly a beest desyreth flee
Fro his contrarie, if he may it see,
Though he never erst had seyn it with his yë.
  This Chauntecleer, whan he gan him espye,
He wolde han fled, but that the fox anon
Seyde, "Gentil sire, allas! wher wol ye gon?
Be ye affrayed of me that am your freend?
Now certes, I were worse than a feend,
If I to yow wolde harm or vileinye.
I am nat come your counseil for t'espye;
But trewely, the cause of my cominge
Was only for to herkne how that ye singe.
For trewely ye have as mery a stevene
As eny aungel hath, that is in hevene;
Therwith ye han in musik more felinge
Than hadde Boëce, or any that can singe.
My lord your fader (god his soule blesse!)
And eek your moder, of hir gentilesse,
Han in myn hous y-been, to my gret ese;
And certes, sire, ful fayn wolde I yow plese.
But for men speke of singing, I wol saye,
So mote I brouke wel myn eyen tweye,
Save yow, I herde never man so singe,
As dide your fader in the morweninge;
Certes, it was of herte, al that he song.
And for to make his voys the more strong,
He wolde so peyne him, that with bothe his yën
He moste winke, so loude he wolde cryen,
And stonden on his tiptoon ther-with-al,
And strecche forth his nekke long and smal.
And eek he was of swich discrecioun,
That ther nas no man in no regioun
That him in song or wisdom mighte passe.
I have wel rad in daun Burnel the Asse,[4]

[1]A prose romance.

[2]The betrayer of Roland.

[3]The Bestiary, a popular collection containing moralized descriptions of animals.

[4]A Latin poem by Nigellus Wireker entitled *Burnellus or the Mirror of Fools* (written towards the close of the twelfth century).

Among his vers, how that ther was a cok,
For that a preestes sone yaf him a knok
Upon his leg, whyl he was yong and nyce,
He made him for to lese his benefyce.
But certeyn, ther nis no comparisoun
Bitwix the wisdom and discrecioun
Of youre fader, and of his subtiltee.
Now singeth, sire, for seinte Charitee,
Let see, conne ye your fader countrefete?"
This Chauntecleer his winges gan to bete,
As man that coude his tresoun nat espye,
So was he ravisshed with his flaterye.
Allas! ye lordes, many a fals flatour
Is in your courtes, and many a losengeour,
That plesen yow wel more, by my feith,
Than he that soothfastnesse unto yow seith.
Redeth Ecclesiaste of flaterye;[1]
Beth war, ye lordes, of hir trecherye.
This Chauntecleer stood hye up-on his toos,
Strecching his nekke, and heeld his eyen cloos,
And gan to crowe loude for the nones;
And daun Russel the fox sterte up at ones,
And by the gargat hente Chauntecleer,
And on his bak toward the wode him beer,
For yet ne was ther no man that him sewed.
O destinee, that mayst nat been eschewed!
Allas, that Chauntecleer fleigh fro the bemes!
Allas, his wyf ne roghte nat of dremes!
And on a Friday fil al this meschaunce.
O Venus, that art goddesse of plesaunce,
Sin that thy servant was this Chauntecleer,
And in thy service dide al his poweer,
More for delyt, than world to multiplye,
Why woldestow suffre him on thy day to dye?
O Gaufred, dere mayster soverayn,
That, whan thy worthy king Richard was slayn
With shot, compleynedest his deth so sore,
Why ne hadde I now thy sentence and thy lore,
The Friday for to chyde, as diden ye?
(For on a Friday soothly slayn was he.)
Than wolde I shewe yow how that I coude pleyne
For Chauntecleres drede, and for his peyne.
Certes, swich cry ne lamentacioun
Was never of ladies maad, whan Ilioun
Was wonne, and Pirrus with his streite swerd,
Whan he hadde hent king Priam by the berd,
And slayn him (as saith us *Eneydos*),[2]
As maden alle the hennes in the clos,
Whan they had seyn of Chauntecleer the sighte.
But sovereynly dame Pertelote shrighte,
Ful louder than dide Hasdrubales wyf,
Whan that hir housbond hadde lost his lyf,
And that the Romayns hadde brend Cartage;

[1]Ecclesiasticus (in *Apocrypha*), xii, 10, 11, 16.
[2]*Æneid*, II, 544.

She was so ful of torment and of rage,
That wilfully into the fyr she sterte,
And brende hir-selven with a stedfast herte.
O woful hennes, right so cryden ye,
As, whan that Nero brende the citee
Of Rome, cryden senatoures wyves,
For that hir housbondes losten alle hir lyves;
Withouten gilt this Nero hath hem slayn.
Now wol I torne to my tale agayn:—
This sely widwe, and eek hir doghtres two,
Herden thise hennes crye and maken wo,
And out at dores sterten they anoon,
And syen the fox toward the grove goon,
And bar upon his bak the cok away;
And cryden, "Out! harrow! and weylaway!
Ha, ha, the fox!" and after him they ran,
And eek with staves many another man;
Ran Colle our dogge, and Talbot, and Gerland,
And Malkin, with a distaf in hir hand;
Ran cow and calf, and eek the verray hogges
So were they fered for berking of the dogges
And shouting of the men and wimmen eke,
They ronne so, hem thoughte hir herte breke.
They yelleden as feendes doon in helle;
The dokes cryden as men wolde hem quelle;
The gees for fere flowen over the trees;
Out of the hyve cam the swarm of bees;
So hidous was the noyse, a! *benedicite!*[3]
Certes, he Jakke Straw,[4] and his meynee,
Ne made never shoutes half so shrille,
Whan that they wolden any Fleming kille,
As thilke day was maad upon the fox.
Of bras thay broghten bemes, and of box,
Of horn, of boon, in whiche they blewe and pouped,
And therwithal thay shryked and they houped;
It semed as that heven sholde falle.
Now, gode men, I pray yow herkneth alle!
Lo, how fortune turneth sodeinly
The hope and pryde eek of hir enemy!
This cok, that lay upon the foxes bak,
In al his drede, un-to the fox he spak,
And seyde, "sire, if that I were as ye,
Yet sholde I seyn (as wis god helpe me),
Turneth agayn, ye proude cherles alle!
A verray pestilence up-on yow falle!
Now am I come un-to this wodes syde,
Maugree your heed, the cok shal heer abyde;
I wol him ete in feith, and that anon."—
The fox answerde, "in feith, it shal be don,"—
And as he spak that word, al sodeinly
This cok brak from his mouth deliverly,
And heighe up-on a tree he fleigh anon.
And whan the fox saugh that he was y-gon,

[3]Literally, "Blessings on you."
[4]Leader of an insurrection in 1381. Walsingham states that when he and his men killed Flemings they raised a "most horrible clamor."

"Allas!" quod he, "O Chauntecleer, allas!
I have to yow," quod he, "y-doon trespas,
In-as-muche as I maked yow aferd,
Whan I yow hente, and broghte out of the yerd;
But, sire, I dide it in no wikke entente;
Com doun, and I shal telle yow what I mente.
I shal seye sooth to yow, god help me so."
"Nay than," quod he, "I shrewe us bothe two,
And first I shrewe my-self, bothe blood and bones,
If thou bigyle me ofter than ones.
Thou shalt na-more, thurgh thy flaterye,
Do me to singe and winke with myn yë.
For he that winketh, whan he sholde see,
Al wilfully, god lat him never thee!"
"Nay," quod the fox, "but god yeve him meschaunce,
That is so undiscreet of governaunce,
That jangleth whan he sholde holde his pees."
Lo, swich it is for to be recchelees,
And necligent, and truste on flaterye.
But ye that holden this tale a folye,
As of a fox, or of a cok and hen,
Taketh the moralitee, good men.
For seint Paul seith, that al that writen is,
To our doctryne it is y-write, y-wis.[1]
Taketh the fruyt, and lat the chaf be stille.
Now, gode god, if that it be thy wille,
As seith my lord,[2] so make us alle good men;
And bringe us to his heighe blisse. Amen.

WORDS OF THE HOST[3]

OUR Hoste gan to swere as he were wood,
"Harrow!" quod he, "by nayles and by blood!
This was a fals cherl and a fals justyse!
As shamful deeth as herte may devyse
Come to thise juges and hir advocats!
Algate this sely mayde is slayn, allas!
Allas! to dere boghte she beautee!
Wherfore I seye al day, as men may see,
That yiftes of fortune or of nature
Ben cause of deeth to many a creature.
Hir beautee was hir deeth, I dar wel sayn;
Allas! so pitously as she was slayn!
Of bothe yiftes that I speke of now
Men han ful ofte more harm than prow.
But trewely, myn owene mayster dere,
This is a pitous tale for to here.
But natheles, passe over, is no fors;
I prey to god, so save thy gentil cors,
And eek thyne urinals and thy jordanes,
Thyn Ypocras, and eek thy Galianes,
And every boist ful of thy letuarie;
God blesse hem, and our lady seinte Marie!
So mot I theen, thou art a propre man,
And lyk a prelat, by seint Ronyan![4]
Seyde I nat wel? I can nat speke in terme;
But wel I woot, thou doost my herte to erme,
That I almost have caught a cardiacle.
By corpus bones! but I have triacle,
Or elles a draught of moyste and corny ale,
Or but I here anon a mery tale,
Myn herte is lost for pitee of this mayde.
Thou bel amy, thou Pardoner," he seyde,
"Tel us som mirthe or japes right anon."
"It shall be doon," quod he, "by seint Ronyon!
But first," quod he, "heer at this ale-stake
I wol both drinke, and eten of a cake."
But right anon thise gentils gonne to crye,
"Nay! lat him telle us of no ribaudye;
Tel us som moral thing, that we may lere
Som wit, and thanne wol we gladly here."
"I graunte, y-wis," quod he, "but I mot thinke
Up-on som honest thing, whyl that I drinke."

THE PROLOGUE OF THE PARDONERS TALE

Radix malorum est Cupiditas: Ad Thimotheum, sexto.[5]

"LORDINGS," quod he, "in chirches whan I preche,
I peyne me to han an hauteyn speche,
And ringe it out as round as gooth a belle,
For I can al by rote that I telle.
My theme is alwey oon, and ever was—
'*Radix malorum est Cupiditas.*'
First I pronounce whennes that I come,
And than my bulles shewe I, alle and somme.
Our lige lordes seel on my patente,
That shewe I first, my body to warente,
That no man be so bold, ne preest ne clerk,
Me to destourbe of Cristes holy werk;
And after that than telle I forth my tales,
Bulles of popes and of cardinales,
Of patriarkes, and bishoppes I shewe;
And in Latyn I speke a wordes fewe,
To saffron with my predicacioun,
And for to stire men to devocioun.
Than shewe I forth my longe cristal stones,

[1] Second Timothy, iii, 16.

[2] A note in one of the manuscripts explains this as referring to the Archbishop of Canterbury.

[3] Following the Nun's Priest's Tale there is an evident break, after which, in the now accepted arrangement of the tales, come the Physician's Tale (immediately preceding the above "words of the Host") and the Pardoner's Tale. The Physician's Tale, to which the Host refers, was one of afflicted innocence, the story of Appius and Virginia, in which the latter's father slays her as the only means of protecting her from shame at the hands of Appius.

[4] St. Ronan, whose name will be familiar to readers of Scott Little besides his name is known of him.

[5] Greed is the root of all evil. First Timothy, vi, 10.

Y-crammed ful of cloutes and of bones;
Reliks been they, as wenen they echoon.
Than have I in latoun a sholder-boon
Which that was of an holy Jewes shepe.
'Good men,' seye I, 'tak of my wordes kepe;
If that this boon be wasshe in any welle,
If cow, or calf, or sheep, or oxe swelle
That any worm hath ete, or worm y-stonge,
Tak water of that welle, and wash his tonge,
And it is hool anon; and forthermore,
Of pokkes and of scabbe, and every sore
Shal every sheep be hool, that of this welle
Drinketh a draughte; tak kepe eek what I telle.
If that the good-man, that the bestes oweth,
Wol every wike, er that the cok him croweth,
Fastinge, drinken of this welle a draughte,
As thilke holy Jewe our eldres taughte,
His bestes and his stoor shal multiplye.
And, sirs, also it heleth jalousye;
For, though a man be falle in jalous rage,
Let maken with this water his potage,
And never shal he more his wyf mistriste,
Though he the sooth of hir defaute wiste;
Al had she taken preestes two or three.
  Heer is a miteyn eek, that ye may see.
He that his hond wol putte in this miteyn,
He shal have multiplying of his greyn,
Whan he hath sowen, be it whete or otes,
So that he offre pens, or elles grotes.
  Good men and wommen, o thing warne I yow,
If any wight be in this chirche now,
That hath doon sinne horrible, that he
Dar nat, for shame, of it y-shriven be,
Or any womman, be she yong or old,
That hath y-maad hir housbond cokewold,
Swich folk shul have no power ne no grace
To offren to my reliks in this place.
And who-so findeth him out of swich blame,
He wol com up and offre in goddes name,
And I assoille him by the auctoritee
Which that by bulle y-graunted was to me.'
  By this gaude have I wonne, yeer by yeer,
An hundred mark sith I was Pardoner.
I stonde lyk a clerk in my pulpet,
And whan the lewed peple is doun y-set,
I preche, so as ye han herd bifore,
And telle an hundred false japes more.
Than peyne I me to strecche forth the nekke,
And est and west upon the peple I bekke,
As doth a dowve sitting on a berne.
Myn hondes and my tonge goon so yerne,
That it is joye to see my bisinesse.
Of avaryce and of swich cursednesse
Is al my preching, for to make hem free
To yeve her pens, and namely un-to me.
For my entente is nat but for to winne,
And no-thing for correccioun of sinne.
I rekke never, whan that they ben beried,
Though that her soules goon a-blakeberied!
For certes, many a predicacioun
Comth ofte tyme of yvel entencioun;
Som for plesaunce of folk and flaterye,
To been avaunced by ipocrisye,
And som for veyne glorie, and som for hate.
For, whan I dar non other weyes debate,
Than wol I stinge him with my tonge smerte
In preching, so that he shal nat asterte
To been defamed falsly, if that he
Hath trespased to my brethren or to me.
For, though I telle noght his propre name,
Men shal wel knowe that it is the same
By signes and by othere circumstances.
Thus quyte I folk that doon us displesances;
Thus spitte I out my venim under hewe
Of holynesse, to seme holy and trewe.
  But shortly myn entente I wol devyse;
I preche of no-thing but for coveityse.
Therfor my theme is yet, and ever was—
'*Radix malorum est cupiditas*.'
Thus can I preche agayn that same vyce
Which that I use, and that is avaryce.
But, though my-self be gilty in that sinne,
Yet can I maken other folk to twinne
From avaryce, and sore to repente.
But that is nat my principal entente.
I preche no-thing but for coveityse;
Of this matere it oughte y-nogh suffyse.
  Than telle I hem ensamples many oon
Of olde stories, longe tyme agoon:
For lewed peple loven tales olde;
Swich thinges can they wel reporte and holde.
What? trowe ye, the whyles I may preche,
And winne gold and silver for I teche,
That I wol live in povert wilfully?
Nay, nay, I thoghte it never trewely!
For I wol preche and begge in sondry londes;
I wol not do no labour with myn hondes,
Ne make baskettes, and live therby,
Because I wol nat beggen ydelly.
I wol non of the apostles counterfete;
I wol have money, wolle, chese, and whete,
Al were it yeven of the povrest page,
Or of the povrest widwe in a village,
Al sholde hir children sterve for famyne.
Nay! I wol drinke licour of the vyne,
And have a joly wenche in every toun.
But herkneth, lordings, in conclusioun;
Your lyking is that I shal telle a tale.
Now, have I dronke a draughte of corny ale,
By god, I hope I shal yow telle a thing
That shal, by resoun, been at your lyking.
For, though myself be a ful vicious man,
A moral tale yet I yow telle can,
Which I am wont to preche, for to winne.
Now holde your pees, my tale I wol be-ginne."

THE PARDONERS TALE[1]

IN FLAUNDRES whylom was a companye
Of yonge folk, that haunteden folye,
As ryot, hasard, stewes, and tavernes,
Wher-as, with harpes, lutes, and g釘ternes,
They daunce and pleye at dees bothe day and night,
And ete also and drinken over hir might,
Thurgh which they doon the devel sacrifyse
With-in that develes temple, in cursed wyse,
By superfluitee abhominable;
Hir othes been so grete and so dampnable,
That it is grisly for to here hem swere;
Our blissed lordes body they to-tere;
Hem thoughte Jewes rente him noght y-nough;
And ech of hem at otheres sinne lough.
And right anon than comen tombesteres
Fetys and smale, and yonge fruytesteres,
Singers with harpes, baudes, wafereres,
Whiche been the verray develes officeres
To kindle and blowe the fyr of lecherye,
That is annexed un-to glotonye;
The holy writ take I to my witnesse,
That luxurie is in wyn and dronkenesse.
Lo, how that dronken Loth, unkindely,
Lay by his doghtres two, unwitingly;
So dronke he was, he niste what he wroghte.
Herodes, (who-so wel the stories soghte),
Whan he of wyn was replet at his feste,
Right at his owene table he yaf his heste
To sleen the Baptist John ful giltelees.
Senek seith eek a good word doutelees;
He seith, he can no difference finde
Bitwix a man that is out of his minde
And a man which that is dronkelewe,
But that woodnesse, y-fallen in a shrewe,
Persevereth lenger than doth dronkenesse.
O glotonye, ful of cursednesse,
O cause first of our confusioun,
O original of our dampnacioun,
Til Crist had boght us with his blood agayn!
Lo, how dere, shortly for to sayn,
Aboght was thilke cursed vileinye;
Corrupt was al this world for glotonye!
Adam our fader, and his wyf also,
Fro Paradys to labour and to wo
Were driven for that vyce, it is no drede;
For whyl that Adam fasted, as I rede,
He was in Paradys; and whan that he
Eet of the fruyt defended on the tree,
Anon he was out-cast to wo and peyne.
O glotonye, on thee wel oghte us pleyne!
O, wiste a man how many maladyes
Folwen of excesse and of glotonyes,
He wolde been the more mesurable
Of his diete, sittinge at his table.
Allas! the shorte throte, the tendre mouth,
Maketh that, Est and West, and North and South,
In erthe, in eir, in water men to-swinke
To gete a glotoun deyntee mete and drinke!
Of this matere, o Paul, wel canstow trete,
"Mete un-to wombe, and wombe eek un-to mete,
Shal god destroyen bothe," as Paulus seith.[2]
Allas! a foul thing is it, by my feith,
To seye this word, and fouler is the dede,
Whan man so drinketh of the whyte and rede,
That of his throte he maketh his privee,
Thurgh thilke cursed superfluitee.
The apostel weping seith ful pitously,
"Ther walken many of whiche yow told have I,
I seye it now weping with pitous voys,
[That] they been enemys of Cristes croys,
Of whiche the ende is deeth, wombe is her god."[3]
O wombe! O bely! O stinking cod,
Fulfild of donge and of corrupcioun!
At either ende of thee foul is the soun.
How greet labour and cost is thee to finde!
Thise cokes, how they stampe, and streyne, and grinde,
And turnen substaunce in-to accident,[4]
To fulfille al thy likerous talent!
Out of the harde bones knokke they
The mary, for they caste noght a-wey
That may go thurgh the golet softe and swote;
Of spicerye, of leef, and bark, and rote
Shal been his sauce y-maked by delyt,
To make him yet a newer appetyt.
But certes, he that haunteth swich delyces
Is deed, whyl that he liveth in tho vyces.
A lecherous thing is wyn, and dronkenesse
Is ful of stryving and of wrecchednesse.
O dronke man, disfigured is thy face,
Sour is thy breeth, foul artow to embrace,
And thurgh thy dronke nose semeth the soun
As though thou seydest ay "Sampsoun, Sampsoun";
And yet, god wot, Sampsoun drank never no wyn.
Thou fallest, as it were a stiked swyn;
Thy tonge is lost, and al thyn honest cure;
For dronkenesse is verray sepulture
Of mannes wit and his discrecioun.
In whom that drinke hath dominacioun,

[1]This story is of Eastern origin, and its theme has been often used from early times to the present day—for example by Boccaccio, *Decameron*, 6th Day, 10th Tale (apparently not Chaucer's source, which is unknown) and by Kipling, *The King's Ankus*. The Pardoner's final comment makes the tale a sort of sermon or *exemplum* of avarice.

[2]First Corinthians, vi, 13.

[3]Philippians, iii, 18–19.

[4]An allusion to disputes between the realists and the nominalists among medieval philosophers. The meaning is that cooks so changed the very nature of the things they prepared that those who ate them could not tell what they originally were.

He can no conseil kepe, it is no drede.
Now kepe yow fro the whyte and fro the rede,
And namely fro the whyte wyn of Lepe,[1]
That is to selle in Fish-strete or in Chepe.[2]
This wyn of Spayne crepeth subtilly
In othere wynes, growing faste by,[3]
Of which ther ryseth swich fumositee,
That whan a man hath dronken draughtes three,
And weneth that he be at hoom in Chepe,
He is in Spayne, right at the toune of Lepe,
Nat at the Rochel, ne at Burdeux toun;
And thanne wol he seye, "Sampsoun, Sampsoun."
But herkneth, lordings, o word, I yow preye,
That alle the sovereyn actes, dar I seye,
Of victories in th'olde testament,
Thurgh verray god, that is omnipotent,
Were doon in abstinence and in preyere;
Loketh the Bible, and ther ye may it lere.
  Loke, Attila, the grete conquerour,
Deyde in his sleep, with shame and dishonour,
Bledinge ay at his nose in dronkenesse;
A capitayn shoulde live in sobrenesse.
And over al this, avyseth yow right wel
What was comaunded un-to Lamuel—[4]
Nat Samuel, but Lamuel, seye I—
Redeth the Bible, and finde it expresly
Of wyn-yeving to hem that han justyse.
Na-more of this, for it may wel suffyse.
  And now that I have spoke of glotonye,
Now wol I yow defenden hasardrye.
Hasard is verray moder of lesinges,
And of deceite, and cursed forsweringes,
Blaspheme of Crist, manslaughtre, and wast also
Of catel and of tyme; and forthermo,
It is repreve and contrarie of honour
For to ben holde a commune hasardour.
And ever the hyër he is of estaat,
The more is he holden desolaat.
If that a prince useth hasardrye,
In alle governaunce and policye
He is, as by commune opinioun,
Y-holde the lasse in reputacioun.
  Stilbon,[5] that was a wys embassadour,
Was sent to Corinthe, in ful greet honour,
Fro Lacidomie, to make hir alliaunce.
And when he cam, him happede, par chaunce,
That alle the grettest that were of that lond,
Pleyinge atte hasard he hem fond.
For which, as sone as it mighte be,
He stal him hoom agayn to his contree,
And seyde, "ther wol I nat lese my name;
N'I wol nat take on me so greet defame,
Yow for to allye un-to none hasardours.
Sendeth othere wyse embassadours;
For, by my trouthe, me were lever dye,
Than I yow sholde to hasardours allye.
For ye that been so glorious in honours
Shul nat allyen yow with hasardours
As by my wil, ne as by my tretee."
This wyse philosophre thus seyde he.
  Loke eek that, to the king Demetrius
The king of Parthes, as the book seith us,[6]
Sente him a paire of dees of gold in scorn,
For he hadde used hasard ther-biforn;
For which he heeld his glorie or his renoun
At no value or reputacioun.
Lordes may finden other maner pley
Honeste y-nough to dryve the day awey.
  Now wol I speke of othes false and grete
A word or two, as olde bokes trete.
Gret swering is a thing abhominable,
And false swering is yet more reprevable.
The heighe god forbad swering at al,
Witnesse on Mathew;[7] but in special
Of swering seith the holy Jeremye,[8]
"Thou shalt seye sooth thyn othes, and nat lye,
And swere in dome, and eek in rightwisnesse";
But ydel swering is a cursednesse.
Bihold and see, that in the firste table
Of heighe goddes hestes honurable,
How that the seconde heste of him is this—
"Tak nat my name in ydel or amis."[9]
Lo, rather[10] he forbedeth swich swering
Than homicyde or many a cursed thing;
I seye that, as by ordre, thus it stondeth;
This knowen, that his hestes understondeth,
How that the second heste of god is that.
And forther over, I wol thee telle al plat,
That vengeance shal nat parten from his hous,
That of his othes is to outrageous.
"By goddes precious herte, and by his nayles,
And by the blode of Crist, that it is in Hayles,[11]
Seven is my chaunce, and thyn is cink and treye;
By goddes armes, if thou falsly pleye,
This dagger shal thurgh-out thyn herte go"—
This fruyt cometh of the bicched bones two,

[1]It was near Cadiz.

[2]Cheapside, London.

[3]The Pardoner says that the mixture must come from the closeness of the vineyards to each other, but means that it comes from the closeness of the casks in the vintners' cellars. The wines of La Rochelle and Bordeaux were milder than the Spanish wines.

[4]Lemuel. Proverbs, xxxi, 1, 4, 5.

[5]Should be Chilon. The story is in John of Salisbury's *Policraticus*, bk. I, ch. 5.

[6]*Policraticus*, bk. I, ch. 5.

[7]St. Matthew, v, 34.

[8]Jeremiah, iv, 2.

[9]Formerly the first and second commandments were considered as one, the tenth being divided into two to make up the number; hence the Pardoner refers to the third commandment as the second. It is in the first table, *i. e.*, the group teaching man's duty to God; those in the second table teaching his duty to his neighbor.

[10]*I. e.*, earlier in the list of commandments.

[11]The Abbey of Hailes, or Hales, in Gloucestershire.

Forswering, ire, falsnesse, homicyde.
Now, for the love of Crist that for us dyde,
Leveth your othes, bothe grete and smale;
But, sirs, now wol I telle forth my tale.

THISE ryotoures three, of whiche I telle,
Longe erst er pryme rong of any belle,
Were set hem in a taverne for to drinke;
And as they satte, they herde a belle clinke
Biforn a cors, was caried to his grave;
That oon of hem gan callen to his knave,
"Go bet," quod he, "and axe redily,
What cors is this that passeth heer forby;
And look that thou reporte his name wel."
"Sir," quod this boy, "it nedeth never-a-del.
It was me told, er ye cam heer, two houres;
He was, pardee, an old felawe of youres;
And sodeynly he was y-slayn to-night,
For-dronke, as he sat on his bench upright;
Ther cam a privee theef, men clepeth Deeth,
That in this contree al the peple sleeth,
And with his spere he smoot his herte a-two,
And wente his wey with-outen wordes mo.
He hath a thousand slayn this pestilence:
And, maister, er ye come in his presence,
Me thinketh that it were necessarie
For to be war of swich an adversarie:
Beth redy for to mete him evermore.
Thus taughte me my dame, I sey na-more."
"By seinte Marie," seyde this taverner,
"The child seith sooth, for he hath slayn this yeer,
Henne over a myle, with-in a greet village,
Both man and womman, child and hyne, and page.
I trowe his habitacioun be there;
To been avysed greet wisdom it were,
Er that he dide a man a dishonour."
"Ye, goddes armes," quod this ryotour,
"Is it swich peril with him for to mete?
I shal him seke by wey and eek by strete,
I make avow to goddes digne bones!
Herkneth, felawes, we three been al ones;
Lat ech of us holde up his hond til other,
And ech of us bicomen otheres brother,
And we wol sleen this false traytour Deeth;
He shal be slayn, which that so many sleeth,
By goddes dignitee, er it be night."
Togidres han thise three her trouthes plight,
To live and dyen ech of hem for other,
As though he were his owene y-boren brother.
And up they sterte al dronken, in this rage,
And forth they goon towardes that village,
Of which the taverner had spoke biforn,
And many a grisly ooth than han they sworn,
And Cristes blessed body they to-rente—
"Deeth shal be deed, if that they may him hente."

Whan they han goon nat fully half a myle,
Right as they wolde han troden over a style,
An old man and a povre with hem mette.
This olde man ful mekely hem grette,
And seyde thus, "now, lordes, god yow see!"
The proudest of thise ryotoures three
Answerde agayn, "what? carl, with sory grace,
Why artow al forwrapped save thy face?
Why livestow so longe in so greet age?"
This olde man gan loke in his visage,
And seyde thus, "for I ne can nat finde
A man, though that I walked in-to Inde,
Neither in citee nor in no village,
That wolde chaunge his youthe for myn age;
And therfore moot I han myn age stille,
As longe time as it is goddes wille.
Ne deeth, allas! ne wol nat han my lyf;
Thus walke I, lyk a restelees caityf,
And on the ground, which is my modres gate,
I knokke with my staf, bothe erly and late,
And seye, 'leve moder, leet me in!
Lo, how I vanish, flesh, and blood, and skin!
Allas! whan shul my bones been at reste?
Moder, with yow wolde I chaunge my cheste,
That in my chambre longe tyme hath be,
Ye! for an heyre clout to wrappe me!'
But yet to me she wol nat do that grace,
For which ful pale and welked is my face.
But, sirs, to yow it is no curteisye
To speken to an old man vileinye,
But he trespasse in worde, or elles in dede.
In holy writ ye may your-self wel rede,
'Agayns an old man, hoor upon his heed,
Ye sholde aryse';[1] wherfor I yeve yow reed,
Ne dooth un-to an old man noon harm now,
Na-more than ye wolde men dide to yow
In age, if that ye so longe abyde;
And god be with yow, wher ye go or ryde.
I moot go thider as I have to go."
"Nay, olde cherl, by god, thou shalt nat so,"
Seyde this other hasardour anon;
"Thou partest nat so lightly, by seint John!
Thou spak right now of thilke traitour Deeth,
That in this contree alle our frendes sleeth.
Have heer my trouthe, as thou art his aspye,
Tel wher he is, or thou shalt it abye,
By god, and by the holy sacrament!
For soothly thou art oon of his assent,
To sleen us yonge folk, thou false theef!"
"Now, sirs," quod he, "if that yow be so leef
To finde Deeth, turne up this croked wey,
For in that grove I lafte him, by my fey,
Under a tree, and ther he wol abyde;
Nat for your boost he wol him no-thing hyde.
See ye that ook? right ther ye shul him finde.
God save yow, that boghte agayn mankinde,

[1] Leviticus, xix, 32.

And yow amende!"—thus seyde this olde man.
And everich of thise ryotoures ran,
Til he cam to that tree, and ther they founde
Of florins fyne of golde y-coyned rounde
Wel ny an eighte busshels, as hem thoughte.
No lenger thanne after Deeth they soughte,
But ech of hem so glad was of that sighte,
For that the florins been so faire and brighte,
That doun they sette hem by this precious hord.
The worste of hem he spake the firste word.
"Brethren," quod he, "tak kepe what I seye;
My wit is greet, though that I bourde and pleye.
This tresor hath fortune un-to us yiven,
In mirthe and jolitee our lyf to liven,
And lightly as it comth, so wol we spende.
Ey! goddes precious dignitee! who wende
To-day, that we sholde han so fair a grace?
But mighte this gold be caried fro this place
Hoom to myn hous, or elles un-to youres—
For wel ye woot that al this gold is oures—
Than were we in heigh felicitee.
But trewely, by daye it may nat be;
Men wolde seyn that we were theves stronge,
And for our owene tresor doon us honge.
This tresor moste y-caried be by nighte
As wysly and as slyly as it mighte.
Wherfore I rede that cut among us alle
Be drawe, and lat see wher the cut wol falle;
And he that hath the cut with herte blythe
Shal renne to the toune, and that ful swythe,
And bringe us breed and wyn ful prively.
And two of us shul kepen subtilly
This tresor wel; and, if he wol nat tarie,
Whan it is night, we wol this tresor carie
By oon assent, wher-as us thinketh best."
That oon of hem the cut broughte in his fest,
And bad hem drawe, and loke wher it wol falle;
And it fil on the yongeste of hem alle;
And forth toward the toun he wente anon.
And al-so sone as that he was gon,
That oon of hem spak thus un-to that other,
"Thou knowest wel thou art my sworne brother,
Thy profit wol I telle thee anon.
Thou woost wel that our felawe is agon;
And heer is gold, and that ful greet plentee,
That shal departed been among us three.
But natheles, if I can shape it so
That it departed were among us two,
Hadde I nat doon a freendes torn to thee?"
That other answerde, "I noot how that may be;
He woot how that the gold is with us tweye,
What shal we doon, what shal we to him seye?"
"Shal it be conseil?" seyde the firste shrewe,
"And I shal tellen thee, in wordes fewe,
What we shal doon, and bringe it wel aboute."
"I graunte," quod that other, "out of doute,
That, by my trouthe, I wol thee nat biwreye."
"Now," quod the firste, "thou woost wel we be tweye,
And two of us shul strenger be than oon.
Look whan that he is set, and right anoon
Arys, as though thou woldest with him pleye;
And I shal ryve him thurgh the sydes tweye
Whyl that thou strogelest with him as in game,
And with thy dagger look thou do the same;
And than shal al this gold departed be,
My dere freend, bitwixen me and thee;
Than may we bothe our lustes al fulfille,
And pleye at dees right at our owene wille."
And thus acorded been thise shrewes tweye
To sleen the thridde, as ye han herd me seye.
This yongest, which that wente un-to the toun,
Ful ofte in herte he rolleth up and doun
The beautee of thise florins newe and brighte.
"O lord!" quod he, "if so were that I mighte
Have al this tresor to my-self allone,
Ther is no man that liveth under the trone
Of god, that sholde live so mery as I!"
And atte laste the feend, our enemy,
Putte in his thought that he shold poyson beye,
With which he mighte sleen his felawes tweye;
For-why the feend fond him in swich lyvinge,
That he had leve him to sorwe bringe,
For this was outrely his fulle entente
To sleen hem bothe, and never to repente.
And forth he gooth, no lenger wolde he tarie,
Into the toun, un-to a pothecarie,
And preyed him, that he him wolde selle
Som poyson, that he mighte his rattes quelle;
And eek ther was a polcat in his hawe,
That, as he seyde, his capouns hadde y-slawe,
And fayn he wolde wreke him, if he mighte,
On vermin, that destroyed him by nighte.
The pothecarie answerde, "and thou shalt have
A thing that, al-so god my soule save,
In al this world ther nis no creature,
That ete or dronke hath of this confiture
Noght but the mountance of a corn of whete,
That he ne shal his lyf anon forlete;
Ye, sterve he shal, and that in lasse whyle
Than thou wolt goon a paas nat but a myle;
This poyson is so strong and violent."
This cursed man hath in his hond y-hent
This poyson in a box, and sith he ran
In-to the nexte strete, un-to a man,
And borwed [of] him large botels three;
And in the two his poyson poured he;
The thridde he kepte clene for his drinke.
For al the night he shoop him for to swinke
In caryinge of the gold out of that place.

And whan this ryotour, with sory grace,
Had filled with wyn his grete botels three,
To his felawes agayn repaireth he.
What nedeth it to sermone of it more?
For right as they had cast his deeth bifore,
Right so they han him slayn, and that anon.
And whan that this was doon, thus spak that oon,
"Now lat us sitte and drinke, and make us merie,
And afterward we wol his body berie."
And with that word it happed him, par cas,
To take the botel ther the poyson was,
And drank, and yaf his felawe drinke also,
For which anon they storven bothe two.
But, certes, I suppose that Avicen[1]
Wroot never in no canon, ne in no fen,
Mo wonder signes of empoisoning
Than hadde thise wrecches two, er hir ending.
Thus ended been thise homicydes two,
And eek the false empoysoner also.

O cursed sinne, ful of cursednesse!
O traytours homicyde, o wikkednesse!
O glotonye, luxurie, and hasardrye!
Thou blasphemour of Crist with vileinye
And othes grete, of usage and of pryde!
Allas! mankinde, how may it bityde,
That to thy creatour which that thee wroghte,
And with his precious herte-blood thee boghte,
Thou art so fals and so unkinde, allas!
Now, goode men, god forgeve yow your trespas,
And ware yow fro the sinne of avaryce.
Myn holy pardoun may yow alle waryce,
So that ye offre nobles or sterlinges,
Or elles silver broches, spones, ringes.
Boweth your heed under this holy bulle!
Cometh up, ye wyves, offreth of your wolle!
Your name I entre heer in my rolle anon;
In-to the blisse of hevene shul ye gon;
I yow assoile, by myn heigh power,
Yow that wol offre, as clene and eek as cleer
As ye were born; and, lo, sirs, thus I preche.
And Jesu Crist, that is our soules leche,
So graunte yow his pardon to receyve;
For that is best; I wol yow nat deceyve.
But sirs, o word forgat I in my tale,
I have relikes and pardon in my male,
As faire as any man in Engelond,
Whiche were me yeven by the popes hond.
If any of yow wol, of devocioun,
Offren, and han myn absolucioun,
Cometh forth anon, and kneleth heer adoun,
And mekely receyveth my pardoun:
Or elles, taketh pardon as ye wende,
Al newe and fresh, at every tounes ende,
So that ye offren alwey newe and newe
Nobles and pens, which that be gode and trewe.
It is an honour to everich that is heer,
That ye mowe have a suffisant pardoneer
T'assoille yow, in contree as ye ryde,
For aventures which that may bityde.
Peraventure ther may falle oon or two
Doun of his hors, and breke his nekke atwo.
Look which a seuretee is it to yow alle
That I am in your felaweship y-falle,
That may assoille yow, bothe more and lasse,
Whan that the soule shal fro the body passe.
I rede that our hoste heer shal biginne,
For he is most envoluped in sinne.
Com forth, sir hoste, and offre first anon,
And thou shalt kisse the reliks everichon,
Ye, for a grote! unbokel anon thy purs.
"Nay, nay," quod he, "than have I Cristes curs!
Lat be," quod he, "it shal nat be, so thee'ch!
Thou woldest make me kisse thyn old breech,
And swere it were a relik of a seint,
Thogh it were with thy fundement depeint!
But by the croys which that seint Eleyne fond,
I wolde I hadde thy coillons in myn hond
In stede of relikes or of seintuarie;
Lat cutte hem of, I wol thee helpe hem carie;
They shul be shryned in an hogges tord."
This pardoner answerde nat a word;
So wrooth he was, no word ne wolde he seye.
"Now," quod our host, "I wol no lenger pleye
With thee, ne with noon other angry man."
But right anon the worthy Knight bigan,
Whan that he saugh that al the peple lough,
"Na-more of this, for it is right y-nough;
Sir Pardoner, be glad and mery of chere;
And ye, sir host, that been to me so dere,
I prey yow that ye kisse the Pardoner.
And Pardoner, I prey thee, drawe thee neer,
And, as we diden, lat us laughe and pleye."
Anon they kiste, and riden forth hir weye.[2]

CHAUCERS WORDES UNTO ADAM, HIS OWNE SCRIVEYN

ADAM scriveyn, if ever it thee bifalle
Boece or Troilus to wryten newe,
Under thy lokkes thou most have the scalle,
But after my making thou wryte trewe.
So ofte a daye I mot thy werk renewe,
Hit to correcte and eek to rubbe and scrape;
And al is through thy negligence and rape.

[1]Avicenna (A. D. 980–1037), celebrated Arabian physician and philosopher. As Chaucer (or the Pardoner) perhaps did not understand, "Canon" is the general title of Avicenna's treatise on medicine.

[2]The Pardoner's tale concludes what, in the present arrangement of the *Canterbury Tales*, is the third group. There follow six more groups, in which eleven stories are told.

TRUTH

BALADE DE BON CONSEYL

FLEE fro the prees, and dwelle with soth-
fastnesse,
Suffyce unto thy good,[1] though hit be smal;
For hord hath hate, and climbing tikelnesse,
Prees hath envye, and wele blent overal;
Savour no more than thee bihove shal;
Werk wel thy-self, that other folk canst rede;
And trouthe shal delivere, hit is no drede.

Tempest thee noght al croked to redresse,
In trust of hir that turneth as a bal:
Gret reste stant in litel besinesse;
And eek be war to sporne ageyn an al;
Stryve noght, as doth the crokke with the wal.
Daunte thy-self, that dauntest otheres dede;
And trouthe shal delivere, hit is no drede.

That thee is sent, receyve in buxumnesse,
The wrastling for this worlde axeth a fal.
Her nis non hoom, her nis but wildernesse:
Forth, pilgrim, forth! Forth, beste, out of
thy stal!
Know thy contree, look up, thank God of al;
Hold the hye wey, and lat thy gost thee lede:
And trouthe shal delivere, hit is no drede.

ENVOY

Therfore, thou vache,[2] leve thyn old wrecched-
nesse
Unto the worlde; leve now to be thral;
Crye him mercy, that of his hy goodnesse
Made thee of noght, and in especial
Draw unto him, and pray in general
For thee, and eek for other, hevenlich mede;
And trouthe shal delivere, hit is no drede.

LAK OF STEDFASTNESSE

BALADE

SOM tyme this world was so stedfast and
stable,
That mannes word was obligacioun,
And now hit is so fals and deceivable,
That word and deed, as in conclusioun,
Ben no-thing lyk, for turned up so doun
Is al this world for mede and wilfulnesse,
That al is lost for lak of stedfastnesse.

What maketh this world to be so variable,
But lust that folk have in dissensioun?
Among us now a man is holde unable,
But-if he can, by som collusioun,
Don his neighbour wrong or oppressioun.
What causeth this, but wilful wrecchednesse,
That al is lost, for lak of stedfastnesse?

Trouthe is put doun, resoun is holden fable;
Vertu hath now no dominacioun,
Pitee exyled, no man is merciable.
Through covetyse is blent discrecioun;
The world hath mad a permutacioun
Fro right to wrong, fro trouthe to fikelnesse,
That al is lost, for lak of stedfastnesse.

LENVOY TO KING RICHARD

O prince, desyre to be honourable,
Cherish thy folk and hate extorcioun!
Suffre no thing, that may be reprevable
To thyn estat, don in thy regioun.
Shew forth thy swerd of castigacioun,
Dred God, do law, love trouthe and worthi-
nesse,
And wed thy folk agein to stedfastnesse.

THE COMPLEINT OF CHAUCER TO HIS EMPTY PURSE[3]

TO YOU, my purse, and to non other wight
Compleyne I, for ye be my lady dere!
I am so sory, now that ye be light;
For certes, but ye make me hevy chere,
Me were as leef be leyd up-on my bere;
For whiche un-to your mercy thus I crye:
Beth hevy ageyn, or elles mot I dye!

Now voucheth sauf this day, or hit be night,
That I of you the blisful soun may here,
Or see your colour lyk the sonne bright,
That of yelownesse hadde never pere.
Ye be my lyf, ye be myn hertes stere,
Quene of comfort and of good companye:
Beth hevy ageyn, or elles mot I dye!

Now purs, that be to me my lyves light,
And saveour, as doun in this worlde here,
Out of this toune help me through your might,
Sin that ye wole nat been my tresorere;
For I am shave as nye as any frere.
But yit I pray un-to your curtesye:
Beth hevy ageyn, or elles mot I dye!

LENVOY DE CHAUCER

O conquerour of Brutes Albioun!
Which that by lyne and free eleccioun
Ben verray king, this song to you I sende;
And ye, that mowen al our harm amende,
Have minde up-on my supplicacioun!

[1] Be content with your property.

[2] It is now known that this poem was addressed to one of Chaucer's friends, Sir Philip la Vache; "vache" (beast) is therefore used with double meaning.

[3] This is probably one of the last poems Chaucer wrote, inasmuch as the envoy, at least, cannot have been written before 30 September, 1399, when Parliament formally acknowledged Henry IV's right to the English throne. The appeal, it may be added, was successful.

POPULAR BALLADS

A popular ballad is "a song that tells a story," and that has come out of the past through oral tradition. We do not know the authors of any true ballads; on the contrary, it has been contended that no true ballad was composed by an individual. Ballads are thought to have originated at a very early stage of culture when communities were still largely undifferentiated, when they acted spontaneously as groups, and when the individual had scarcely become conscious of himself. "Persons," in other words, had not yet appeared, although communities had, and the homogeneous members of these communities lived one collective life. So, it is thought, they danced and sang, and what they sang were ballads. Yet no one had composed a ballad, but around some refrain, perhaps beginning in a mere inarticulate cry, here a member of the group and there a member of the group had thrown a line or two which simply "came" on the spur of the moment, with the ultimate result that a song telling a connected story sprang into existence. It was thus unpremeditated, spontaneous, the composition not of a person but of a community. All this, however, evidently relates to a stage of life about which we know very little and may accordingly theorize with considerable freedom. The account just given has been widely accepted, but it has, too, been acutely challenged on the ground that while we know little enough about primitive life, what we do know hardly bears out these claims for the possibilities of spontaneous collective action. Consequently it is urged that ballads, like other and later kinds of literature, must have had individual authors. But, while the question of ballad-origins remains unsettled, it is of course true that, as long as a poem is handed from one generation to another orally, it is subject to change and thus does become in a real sense the product as well as the possession of a community; and so much we can safely say of the English and Scottish popular ballads. As we have them, they show no obvious signs of individual authorship, they are objective, impersonal, unreflective, and in many cases evidently had a long period of life before they attained a fixed form through being written down. More than three hundred popular ballads are extant. Of these only eleven come from manuscripts older than the seventeenth century, but the time when a ballad reached its final form through writing or printing is not significant of its real age. The oldest of the English and Scottish ballads probably had their origin in the thirteenth century, and others which are founded on historical events can be definitely assigned to the fourteenth and fifteenth centuries. There was no very serious interest in ballads among cultivated people until the middle of the eighteenth century. It was then that Bishop Percy discovered a folio manuscript, written about 1650, which remains still the most important collection of ballads. Percy printed his famous *Reliques of Ancient English Poetry* in 1765. The book was at once a sign of growing interest in ballad-literature and a stimulant to further search for additional ballads. A little later Sir Walter Scott became a notable collector of ballads from the mouths of people in whose families they had been handed down orally; and in the nineteenth century a definitive collection of the extant ballads was published by Professor F. J. Child (*The English and Scottish Popular Ballads*, 1882–1898).

Simplicity is the outstanding characteristic of the ballads. Their language is direct and unfigurative. Conventional epithets and standing phrases abound. Stanzas consist generally either of a couplet of verses of four accents with alternating refrain, or of four lines rhyming *abcb*, of which the first and third have four accents and the second and fourth three. The usual themes fall into a few broadly popular types—domestic tragedy, supernatural occurrences, the life of outlaws, riddles, historical events, and humorous incidents.

RIDDLES WISELY EXPOUNDED

THERE was a lady of the North Country,
  Lay the bent to the bonny broom
And she had lovely daughters three.
  Fa la la la, fa la la la ra re.

There was a knight of noble worth
Which also livéd in the North.

The knight, of courage stout and brave,
A wife he did desire to have.

He knockéd at the ladie's gate
One evening when it was late.

The eldest sister let him in,
And pinned the door with a silver pin.

The second sister she made his bed,
And laid soft pillows under his head.

The youngest daughter that same night,
She went to bed to this young knight.

And in the morning, when it was day,
These words unto him she did say:

"Now you have had your will," quoth she,
"I pray, sir knight, will you marry me?"

The young brave knight to her replied,
"Thy suit, fair maid, shall not be denied.

"If thou canst answer me questions three,
This very day will I marry thee."

"Kind sir, in love, O then," quoth she,
"Tell me what your [three] questions be."

"O what is longer than the way,
Or what is deeper than the sea?

"Or what is louder than the horn,
Or what is sharper than a thorn?

"Or what is greener than the grass,
Or what is worse then a woman was?"

"O love is longer than the way,
And hell is deeper than the sea.

"And thunder is louder than the horn,
And hunger is sharper than a thorn.

"And poyson is greener than the grass,
And the Devil is worse than woman was."

When she these questions answered had,
The knight became exceeding glad.

And having [truly] tried her wit,
He much commended her for it.

And after, as it is verified,
He made of her his lovely bride.

So now, fair maidens all, adieu,
This song I dedicate to you.

I wish that you may constant prove
Unto the man that you do love.

THE DOUGLAS TRAGEDY

"Rise up, rise up, now Lord Douglas," she says,
"And put on your armour so bright;
Let it never be said that a daughter of thine
Was married to a lord under night.

"Rise up, rise up, my seven bold sons,
And put on your armour so bright,
And take better care of your youngest sister,
For your eldest's awa the last night."

He's mounted her on a milk-white steed,
And himself on a dapple gray,
With a bugelet horn hung down his side;
And lightly they rode away.

Lord William look'd o'er his left shoulder,
To see what he could see,
And there he spy'd her seven brethren bold
Come riding over the lea.

"Light down, light down, Lady Margret," he said,
"And hold my steed in your hand,
Until that against your seven brethren bold,
And your father, I mak' a stand."

O, there she stood, and bitter she stood,
And never did shed one tear,
Until that she saw her seven brethren fa',
And her father, who lov'd her so dear. 24

"O hold your hand, Lord William!" she said,
"For your strokes they are wondrous sair;
True lovers I can get many an ane,
But a father I can never get mair."

O she's ta'en out her handkerchief,
It was o' the holland sae fine,
And aye she dighted her father's wounds,
That were redder than the wine.

"O chuse, O chuse, Lady Margret," he said,
"O whether will ye gang or bide?"
"I'll gang, I'll gang, Lord William," she said,
"For ye've left me no other guide." 36

He's lifted her on a milk-white steed,
And himself on a dapple gray,
With a bugelet horn hung down by his side;
And slowly they baith rade away.

O they rade on, and on they rade,
And a' by the light of the moon,
Until they came to yon wan water,
And there they lighted doun.

They lighted doun to tak' a drink
Of the spring that ran sae clear,
And doun the stream ran his gude heart's blood,
And sair she gan to fear.

"Hold up, hold up, Lord William," she says,
"For I fear that you are slain."—
"'Tis naething but the shadow of my scarlet cloak,
That shines in the water sae plain."

O they rade on, and on they rade,
And a' by the light of the moon,
Until they cam' to his mother's ha' door,
And there they lighted doun.

"Get up, get up, lady mother," he says,
"Get up, and let me in!
Get up, get up, lady mother," he says,
"For this night my fair lady I've win.

"O mak my bed, lady mother," he says,
"O mak it braid and deep,
And lay Lady Margret close at my back,
And the sounder I will sleep."

Lord William was dead lang ere midnight,
Lady Margret lang ere day,
And all true lovers that go thegither,
May they have mair luck than they!

Lord William was buried in St. Mary's kirk,
Lady Margret in Mary's quire;
Out o' the lady's grave grew a bonny red rose,
And out o' the knight's a brier.

And they twa met, and they twa plat,
And fain they wad be near;
And a' the warld might ken right weel
They were twa lovers dear.

But bye and rade the Black Douglas,
And wow but he was rough!
For he pulled up the bonny brier,
And flang 't in St. Mary's Lough.

ROBIN HOOD AND GUY OF GISBORNE[1]

When shawes beene sheene, and shradds full fayre,
And leeves both large and longe,
Itt is merry, walking in the fayre fforrest,
To heare the small birds songe.

The woodweele sang, and wold not cease,
Amongst the leaves a lyne:
And it is by two wight yeomen,
By deare God, that I meane.

. . . . .

"Me thought they did mee beate and binde,
And tooke my bow mee froe;
If I bee Robin a-live in this lande,
I 'le be wrocken on both them towe."

"Sweavens are swift, master," quoth John,
"As the wind that blowes ore a hill;
Ffor if itt be never soe lowde this night,
To-morrow it may be still."

"Buske yee, bowne yee, my merry men all,
Ffor John shall goe with mee;
For I 'le goe seeke yond wight yeomen
In greenwood where the bee."

They cast on their gowne of greene,
A shooting gone are they,
Untill they came to the merry greenwood,
Where they had gladdest bee;
There were the ware of [a] wight yeoman,
His body leaned to a tree.

A sword and a dagger he wore by his side,
Had beene many a mans bane,
And he was cladd in his capull-hyde,
Topp, and tayle, and mayne.

"Stand you still, master," quoth Litle John,
"Under this trusty tree,
And I will goe to yond wight yeoman,
To know his meaning trulye."

"A, John, by me thou setts noe store,
And that's a ffarley thinge;
How offt send I my men beffore,
And tarry my-selfe behinde?

"It is noe cunning a knave to ken,
And a man but heare him speake;
And itt were not for bursting of my bowe,
John, I wold thy head breake."

But often words they breeden bale,
That parted Robin and John;
John is gone to Barn[e]sdale,
The gates he knowes eche one.

And when hee came to Barnesdale,
Great heavinesse there hee hadd;
He ffound two of his fellowes
Were slaine both in a slade,

And Scarlett a ffoote flyinge was,
Over stockes and stone,
For the sheriffe with seven score men
Fast after him is gone.

[1] Tradition has it that Robin Hood was an historical character, an outlaw of the early fourteenth century. This is, to say the least, extremely improbable. As he is portrayed in the ballads, at any rate, he is a typical figure, an idealized outlaw, the champion of common folk against oppression. As such he was extremely popular, there being some 40 ballads about him. We know from a reference in the B-text of *Piers Plowman* that he was a familiar character at least as early as 1377.

A few verses are lost between stanzas 2 and 3, and the story itself has suffered some derangement. Robin dreams that two yeomen beat and bind him, and goes to seek them. One is Sir Guy, the other the sheriff of Nottingham; but we are not told how Robin knew that the sheriff was out against him, had attacked his camp, and had taken John prisoner.

"Yett one shoote I 'le shoote," sayes Litle John,
"With Crist his might and mayne;
I 'le make yond fellow that flyes soe fast
To be both glad and ffaine."

John bent up a good veiwe bow,
And ffetteled him to shoote;
The bow was made of a tender boughe,
And fell downe to his foote.

"Woe worth thee, wicked wood," sayd Litle John,
"That ere thou grew on a tree!
Ffor this day thou art my bale,
My boote when thou shold bee!"

This shoote it was but looselye shott,
The arrowe flew in vaine,
And it mett one of the sheriffes men;
Good William a Trent was slaine.

It had beene better for William a Trent
To hange upon a gallowe
Then for to lye in the greenwoode,
There slaine with an arrowe.

And it is sayd, when men be mett,
Six can doe more then three:
And they have tane Litle John,
And bound him ffast to a tree.

"Thou shalt be drawen by dale and downe," quoth the sheriffe,
"And hanged hye on a hill:"
"But thou may ffayle," quoth Litle John,
"If itt be Christs owne will."

Let us leave talking of Litle John,
For hee is bound fast to a tree,
And talke of Guy and Robin Hood,
In the green woode where they bee.

How these two yeomen together they mett,
Under the leaves of lyne,
To see what marchandise they made
Even at that same time.

"Good morrow, good fellow," quoth Sir Guy;
"Good morrow, good ffellow," quoth hee;
"Methinkes by this bow thou beares in thy hand,
A good archer thou seems to bee."

"I am wilfull of my way," quoth Sir Guye,
"And of my morning tyde:"
"I 'le lead thee through the wood," quoth Robin,
"Good ffellow, I 'le be thy guide."

"I seeke an outlaw," quoth Sir Guye
"Men call him Robin Hood;
I had rather meet with him upon a day
Then forty pound of golde."

"If you tow mett, itt wold be seene whether were better
Afore yee did part awaye;
Let us some other pastime find,
Good ffellow, I thee pray.

"Let us some other masteryes make,
And wee will walke in the woods even;
Wee may chance mee[t] with Robin Hoode
Att some unsett steven."

They cutt them downe the summer shroggs
Which grew both under a bryar,
And sett them three score rood in twinn,
To shoote the prickes full neare.

"Leade on, good ffellow," sayd Sir Guye,
"Lead on, I doe bidd thee:"
"Nay, by my faith," quoth Robin Hood,
"The leader thou shalt bee."

The first good shoot that Robin ledd
Did not shoote an inch the pricke ffroe;
Guy was an archer good enoughe,
But he cold neere shoote soe.

The second shoote Sir Guy shott,
He shott within the garlande;
But Robin Hoode shott it better then hee,
For he clove the good pricke-wande.

"Gods blessing on thy heart!" sayes Guye,
"Goode ffellow, thy shooting is goode;
For an thy hart be as good as thy hands,
Thou were better then Robin Hood.

"Tell me thy name, good ffellow," quoth Guy,
"Under the leaves of lyne:"
"Nay, by my faith," quoth good Robin,
"Till thou have told me thine."

"I dwell by dale and downe," quoth Guye,
"And I have done many a curst turne;
And he that calles me by my right name
Calles me Guye of good Gysborne."

"My dwelling is in the wood," sayes Robin;
"By thee I set right nought;
My name is Robin Hood of Barnesdale,
A ffellow thou has long sought."

He that had neither beene a kithe nor kin
Might have seene a full fayre sight,
To see how together these yeomen went,
With blades both browne and bright.

To have seene how these yeomen together foug[ht],
  Two howers of a summers day;
Itt was neither Guy nor Robin Hood
  That ffettled them to flye away.

Robin was reacheles on a roote,
  And stumbled at that tyde,
And Guy was quicke and nimble withall,
  And hitt him ore the left side.

"Ah, deere Lady!" sayd Robin Hoode,
  "Thou art both mother and may!
I thinke it was never mans destinye
  To dyė before his day."

Robin thought on Our Lady deere,
  And soone leapt up againe,
And thus he came with an awkwarde stroke;
  Good Sir Guy hee has slayne.

He tooke Sir Guys head by the hayre,
  And sticked itt on his bowes end:
"Thou hast beene traytor all thy liffe,
  Which thing must have an ende."

Robin pulled forth an Irish kniffe,
  And nicked Sir Guy in the fface,
That hee was never on a woman borne
  Cold tell who Sir Guye was.

Saies, Lye there, lye there, good Sir Guye,
  And with me be not wrothe;
If thou have had the worse stroakes at my hand,
  Thou shalt have the better cloathe.

Robin did off his gowne of greene,
  Sir Guye hee did it throwe;
And hee put on that capull-hyde,
  That cladd him topp to toe.

"The bowe, the arrowes, and litle horne,
  And with me now I 'le beare;
Ffor now I will goe to Barn[e]sdale,
  To see how my men doe ffare."

Robin sett Guyes horne to his mouth,
  A lowd blast in it he did blow;
That beheard the sheriffe of Nottingham,
  As he leaned under a lowe.

"Hearken! hearken!" sayd the sheriffe,
  "I heard noe tydings but good;
For yonder I heare Sir Guyes horne blowe,
  For he hath slaine Robin Hoode.

"For yonder I heare Sir Guyes horne blow,
  Itt blowes soe well in tyde,
For yonder comes that wighty yeoman,
  Cladd in his capull-hyde.

"Come hither, thou good Sir Guy,
  Aske of mee what thou wilt have:"
"I 'le none of thy gold," sayes Robin Hood,
  "Nor I 'le none of itt have.

"But now I have slaine the master," he sayd,
  "Let me goe strike the knave;
This is all the reward I aske,
  Nor noe other will I have."

"Thou art a madman," said the shiriffe,
  "Thou sholdest have had a knights ffee;
Seeing thy asking [hath] beene soe badd,
  Well granted it shall be."

But Litle John heard his master speake,
  Well he knew that was his steven;
"Now shall I be loset," quoth Litle John,
  "With Christs might in heaven."

But Robin hee hyed him towards Litle John,
  Hee thought hee wold loose him belive;
The sheriffe and all his companye
  Fast after him did drive.

"Stand abacke! stand abacke!" sayd Robin;
  "Why draw you mee soe neere?
Itt was never the use in our countrye
  One's shrift another shold heere."

But Robin pulled forth an Irysh kniffe,
  And losed John hand and ffoote,
And gave him Sir Guyes bow in his hand,
  And bade it be his boote.

But John tooke Guyes bow in his hand—
  His arrowes were rawstye by the roote;
The sherriffe saw Litle John draw a bow
  And ffettle him to shoote.

Towards his house in Nottingam
  He ffled full fast away,
And soe did all his companye,
  Not one behind did stay.

But he cold neither soe fast goe,
  Nor away soe fast runn,
But Litle John, with an arrow broade,
  Did cleave his heart in twinn.

ROBIN HOOD AND THE MONK[1]

In somer, when the shawes be sheyne,
  And leves be large and long,
Hit is full mery in feyre foreste
  To here the foulys song:

[1] This is the oldest of the extant Robin Hood ballads. It comes from a manuscript of about 1450 which is now in the Cambridge University Library.

To se the dere draw to the dale,
And leve the hilles hee,
And shadow hem in the levés grene,
Under the grene-wode tre.

Hit befel on Whitsontide,
Erly in a May mornyng,
The son up feyre can shyne,
And the briddis mery can syng.

"This is a mery mornyng," said Litull John,
"Be hym that dyed on tre;
A more mery man then I am one
Lyves not in Cristianté.

"Pluk up thi hert, my dere mayster,"
Litull John can sey,
"And thynk hit is a full fayre tyme
In a mornyng of May."

"Ye, on thyng greves me," seid Robyn,
"And does my hert mych woo;
That I may not no solem day
To mas nor matyns goo.

"Hit is a fourtnet and more," seid he,
"Syn I my savyour see;
To day wil I to Notyngham," seid Robyn,
"With the myght of mylde Marye."

Than spake Moche, the mylner sun,
Ever more wel hym betyde!
"Take twelve of thi wyght yemen,
Well weppynd, be thi side.
Such on wolde thi selfe slon,
That twelve dar not abyde."

"Of all my mery men," seid Robyn,
"Be my feith I wil non have,
But Litull John shall beyre my bow,
Till that me list to drawe."

"Thou shall beyre thin own," seid Litull Jon,
"Maister, and I wyl beyre myne,
And we well shete a peny," seid Litull Jon,
"Under the grene-wode lyne."

"I will not shete a peny," seyd Robyn Hode,
"In feith, Litull John, with the,
But ever for on as thou shetis," seide Robyn,
"In feith I holde the thre."

Thus shet thei forth, these yemen too
Bothe at buske and brome,
Til Litull John wan of his maister
Five shillings to hose and shone.

A ferly strife fel them betwene,
As they went bi the wey;
Litull John seid he had won five shillings,
And Robyn Hode seid schortly nay.

With that Robyn Hode lyed Litul Jon,
And smote hym with his hande;
Litul Jon waxed wroth therwith,
And pulled out his bright bronde.

"Were thou not my maister," seid Litull John,
"Thou shuldis by hit ful sore;
Get the a man wher thou w[ilt],
For thou getis me no more."

Then Robyn goes to Notyngham,
Hym selfe mornyng allone,
And Litull John to mery Scherwode,
The pathes he knew ilkone.

Whan Robyn came to Notyngham,
Sertenly withouten layn,
He prayed to God and myld Mary
To bryng hym out save agayn.

He gos in to Seynt Mary chirch,
And kneled down before the rode;
Alle that ever were the church within
Beheld wel Robyn Hode.

Beside hym stod a gret-hedid munke,
I pray to God woo he be!
Fful sone he knew gode Robyn,
As sone as he hym se.

Out at the durre he ran,
Fful sone and anon;
Alle the gatis of Notyngham
He made to be sparred everychon.

"Rise up," he seid, "thou prowde schereff,
Buske the and make the bowne;
I have spyed the kynggis felon,
Ffor sothe he is in this town.

"I have spyed the false felon,
As he stondis at his masse;
Hit is long of the," seide the munke,
"And ever he fro us passe.

"This traytur name is Robyn Hode,
Under the grene-wode lynde;
He robbyt me onys of a hundred pound,
Hit shalle never out of my mynde."

Up then rose this prowde shereff,
And radly made hym gare;
Many was the moder son
To the kyrk with hym can fare.

In at the durres thei throly thrast,
With staves full gode wone;
"Alas, alas!" seid Robyn Hode,
"Now mysse I Litull John."

But Robyn toke out a too-hond sworde,
That hangit down be his kne;
Ther `as the schereff and his men stode thyckust,
The thurwarde wolde he.

Thryes thorowout them he ran then,
For sothe as I yow sey,
And woundyt mony a moder son,
And twelve he slew that day.

His sworde upon the schireff hed
Sertanly he brake in too;
"The smyth that the made," seid Robyn,
"I pray to God wyrke hym woo!

"Ffor now am I weppynlesse," said Robyn,
"Alasse! agayn my wylle;
But if I may fle these traytors fro,
I wot thei wil me kyll."

Robyn in to the churché ran,
Throout hem everilkon,

. . . . .

Sum fel in swonyng as thei were dede,
And lay stil as any stone;
Non of theym were in her mynde
But only Litull Jon.

"Let be your rule," seid Litull Jon,
"Ffor his luf that dyed on tre,
Ye that shulde be dugty men;
Het is gret shame to se.

"Oure maister has been hard bystode
And yet scapyd away;
Pluk up your hertis, and leve this mone,
And harkyn what I shal say.

"He has servyd Oure Lady many a day,
And yet wil, securly;
Therfor I trust in hir specialy
No wyckud deth shal he dye.

"Therfor be glad," seid Litul John,
"And let this mournyng be;
And I shal be the munkis gyde,
With the myght of mylde Mary.

. . . .

"We will go but we too;
And I mete hym," seid Litul John,

. . .

"Loke that ye kepe wel owre tristil-tre,
Under the levys smale,
And spare non of this venyson,
That gose in thys vale."

Fforthe then went these yemen too,
Litul John and Moche on fere,
And lokid on Moch emys hows,
The hye way lay full nere.

Litul John stode at a wyndow in the mornyng,
And lokid forth at a stage;
He was war wher the munke came ridyng,
And with hym a litul page.

"Be my feith," seid Litul John to Moch,
"I can the tel tithyngus gode;
I see wher the munke cumys rydyng,
I know hym be his wyde hode."

They went in to the way, these yemen bothe,
As curtes men and hende;
Thei spyrred tithyngus at the munke,
As they hade bene his frende.

"Ffro whens come ye?" seid Litull Jon,
"Tel us tithyngus, I yow pray,
Off a false owtlay, [callid Robyn Hode,]
Was takyn yisterday.

"He robbyt me and my felowes bothe
Of twenti marke in serten;
If that false owtlay be takyn,
Ffor sothe we wolde be fayn."

"So did he me," seid the munke,
"Of a hundred pound and more;
I layde furst hande hym apon,
Ye may thonke me therfore."

"I pray God thanke you," seid Litull John,
"And we will when we may;
We wil go with you, with your leve,
And bryng yow on your way.

"Ffor Robyn Hode hase many a wilde felow,
I tell you in certen;
If thei wist ye rode this way,
In feith ye shulde be slayn."

As thei went talking be the way,
The munke and Litull John,
John toke the munkis horse be the hede,
Fful sone and anon.

Johne toke the munkis horse be the hed,
Ffor sothe as I yow say;
So did Much the litull page,
Ffor he shulde not scape away.

Be the golett of the hode
John pulled the munke down;
John was nothyng of hym agast,
He lete hym falle on his crown.

Litull John was so[re] agrevyd,
And drew owt his swerde in hye;
This munke saw he shulde be ded,
Lowd mercy can he crye.

"He was my maister," seid Litull John,
"That thou hase browgt in bale;
Shalle thou never cum at our kyng,
Ffor to telle hym tale."

John smote of the munkis hed,
No longer wolde he dwell;
So did Moch the litull page,
Ffor ferd lest he wolde tell.

Ther thei beryed hem bothe,
In nouther mosse nor lyng,
And Litull John and Much infere
Bare the letturs to oure kyng.

. . . . .

He knelid down upon his kne:
"God yow save, my lege lorde,
Ihesus yow save and se!

"God yow save, my lege kyng!"
To speke John was full bolde;
He gaf hym the letturs in his hond,
The kyng did hit unfold.

The kyng red the letturs anon,
And seid, "So mot I the,
Ther was never yoman in mery Inglond
I longut so sore to se.

"Wher is the munke that these shuld have brougt?"
Oure kyng can say:
"Be my trouth," seid Litull John,
"He dyed after the way."

The kyng gaf Moch and Litul Jon
Twenti pound in sertan,
And made theim yemen of the crown,
And bade theim go agayn.

He gaf John the seel in hand,
The sheref for to bere,
To bryng Robyn hym to,
And no man do hym dere.

John toke his leve at oure kyng,
The sothe as I yow say;
The next way to Notyngham
To take, he gede the way.

Whan John came to Notyngham
The gatis were sparred ychon;
John callid up the porter,
He answerid sone anon.

"What is the cause," seid Litul Jon,
"Thou sparris the gates so fast?"
"Because of Robyn Hode," seid [the] porter,
"In depe prison is cast.

"John and Moch and Wyll Scathlok,
Ffor sothe as I yow say,
Thei slew oure men upon our wallis,
And sawten us every day."

Litull John spyrred after the schereff,
And sone he hym fonde;
He oppyned the kyngus prive seell,
And gaf hym in his honde.

Whan the scheref saw the kyngus seell,
He did of his hode anon:
"Wher is the munke that bare the letturs?"
He seid to Litull John.

"He is so fayn of hym," seid Litul John,
"Ffor sothe as I yow say,
He has made hym abot of Westmynster,
A lorde of that abbay."

The scheref made John gode chere,
And gaf hym wyne of the best;
At nygt thei went to her bedde,
And every man to his rest.

When the scheref was on slepe,
Dronken of wyne and ale,
Litul John and Moch for sothe
Toke the way unto the jale.

Litul John callid up the jayler,
And bade hym rise anon:
He seyd Robyn Hode had brokyn prison,
And out of hit was gon.

The porter rose anon sertan,
As sone as he herd John calle;
Litul John was redy with a swerd,
And bare hym to the walle.

"Now wil I be porter," seid Litul John,
"And take the keyes in honde:"
He toke the way to Robyn Hode,
And sone he hym unbonde.

He gaf hym a gode swerd in his hond,
His hed [ther] with for to kepe,
And ther as the walle was lowyst
Anon down can thei lepe.

Be that the cok began to crow,
The day began to spryng;
The scheref fond the jaylier ded,
The comyn bell made he ryng.

He made a crye thoroout al the tow[n],
Wheder he be yoman or knave,
That cowthe bryng hym Robyn Hode,
His warison he shuld have.

"Ffor I dar never," said the scheref,
"Cum before oure kyng;
Ffor if I do, I wot serten
Ffor sothe he wil me heng."

The scheref made to seke Notyngham,
Bothe be strete and stye,
And Robyn was in mery Scherwode,
As ligt as lef on lynde.

Then bespake gode Litull John,
To Robyn Hode can he say,
I have done the a gode turne for an evyll,
Quyte the whan thou may.

"I have done the a gode turne," seid Litull John,
"Ffor sothe as I yow say;
I have brougt the under grene-wode lyne;
Ffare wel, and have gode day."

"Nay, be my trouth," seid Robyn Hode,
"So shall hit never be;
I make the maister," seid Robyn Hode,
"Off alle my men and me."

"Nay, be my trouth," seid Litull John,
"So shalle hit never be;
But lat me be a felow," seid Litull John,
"No noder kepe I be."

Thus John gate Robyn Hod out of prison,
Sertan withoutyn layn;
Whan his men saw hym hol and sounde,
Ffor sothe they were full fayne.

They filled in wyne, and made hem glad,
Under the levys smale,
And gete pastes of venyson,
That gode was with ale.

Than worde came to oure kyng
How Robyn Hode was gon,
And how the scheref of Notyngham
Durst never loke hym upon.

Then bespake oure cumly kyng,
In an angur hye:
"Litull John hase begyled the schereff,
In faith so hase he me.

"Litul John has begyled us bothe,
And that full wel I se;
Or ellis the schereff of Notyngham
Hye hongut shulde he be.

"I made hem yemen of the crowne,
And gaf hem fee with my hond;
I gaf hem grith," seid oure kyng,
"Thorowout all mery Inglond.

"I gaf theym grith," then seid oure kyng;
"I say, so mot I the,
Ffor sothe soch a yeman as he is on
In all Inglond ar not thre.

"He is trew to his maister," seid our kyng;
"I sey, be swete Seynt John,
He lovys better Robyn Hode
Then he dose us ychon.

"Robyn Hode is ever bond to hym,
Bothe in strete and stalle;
Speke no more of this mater," seid oure kyng,
"But John has begyled us alle."

Thus endys the talkyng of the munke
And Robyn Hode i-wysse;
God, that is ever a crowned kyng,
Bryng us all to his blisse!

ROBIN HOOD'S DEATH

When Robin Hood and Little John,
Down a down a down a down,
Went oer yon bank of broom,
Said Robin Hood bold to Little John,
We have shot for many a pound.
Hey, *etc.*

But I am not able to shoot one shot more,
My broad arrows will not flee;
But I have a cousin lives down below,
Please God, she will bleed me.

Now Robin he is to fair Kirkly gone,
As fast as he can win;
But before he came there, as we do hear,
He was taken very ill.

And when he came to fair Kirkly-hall,
He nockd all at the ring,
But none was so ready as his cousin herself
For to let bold Robin in.

"Will you please to sit down, cousin Robin," she said,
"And drink some beer with me?"
"No, I will neither eat nor drink,
Till I am blooded by thee."

"Well, I have a room, cousin Robin," she said,
"Which you did never see,
And if you please to walk therein,
You blooded by me shall be."

She took him by the lily-white hand,
And led him to a private room,
And there she blooded bold Robin Hood,
While one drop of blood would run down.

She blooded him in a vein of the arm,
And locked him up in the room;
Then did he bleed all the live-long day,
Until the next day at noon.

He then bethought him of a casement there,
Thinking for to get down;
But was so weak he could not leap,
He could not get him down.

He then bethought him of his buglehorn,
Which hung low down to his knee;
He set his horn unto his mouth,
And blew out weak blasts three.

Then Little John, when hearing him,
As he sat under a tree,
"I fear my master is now near dead,
He blows so wearily."

Then Little John to fair Kirkly is gone,
As fast as he can dree;
But when he came to Kirkly-hall,
He broke locks two or three:

Until he came bold Robin to see,
Then he fell on his knee;
"A boon, a boon," cries Little John,
"Master, I beg of thee."

"What is that boon," said Robin Hood,
"Little John, [thou] begs of me?"
"It is to burn fair Kirkly-hall,
And all their nunnery."

"Now nay, now nay," quoth Robin Hood,
"That boon I'll not grant thee;
I never hurt woman in all my life,
Nor men in woman's company.

"I never hurt fair maid in all my time,
Nor at mine end shall it be;
But give me my bent bow in my hand,
And a broad arrow I'll let flee
And where this arrow is taken up,
There shall my grave digged be.

"Lay me a green sod under my head,
And another at my feet;
And lay my bent bow by my side,
Which was my music sweet;
And make my grave of gravel and green,
Which is most right and meet.

"Let me have length and breadth enough,
With a green sod under my head;
That they may say, when I am dead,
Here lies bold Robin Hood."

These words they readily granted him,
Which did bold Robin please:
And there they buried bold Robin Hood,
Within the fair Kirkleys.

THE HUNTING OF THE CHEVIOT[1]

The Persë owt off Northombarlonde,
and avowe to God mayd he
That he wold hunte in the mowntayns
off Chyviat within days thre,
In the magger of doughtë Dogles,
and all that ever with him be.

The fattiste hartes in all Cheviat
he sayd he wold kyll, and cary them away;
"Be my feth," sayd the dougheti Doglas agayn,
"I wyll let that hontyng yf that I may."

The[n] the Persë owt off Banborowe cam,
with him a myghtee meany,
With fifteen hondrith archares bold off blood and bone;
the wear chosen owt of shyars thre.

This begane on a Monday at morn,
in Cheviat the hillys so he;
The chylde may rue that ys un-born,
it wos the mor pittë.

The dryvars thorowe the woodës went,
for to reas the dear;
Bomen byckarte uppone the bent
with ther browd aros cleare.

Then the wyld thorowe the woodës went,
on every sydë shear;
Greahondes thorowe the grevis glent,
for to kyll thear dear.

This begane in Chyviat the hyls abone,
yerly on a Monnyn-day;
Be that it drewe to the oware off none,
a hondrith fat hartës ded ther lay.

The blewe a mort uppone the bent,
the semblyde on sydis shear;
To the quyrry then the Persë went,
to se the bryttlynge off the deare.

[1]This is probably a later and confused account of the fight dealt with in the ballad called *The Battle of Otterburn.* The battle took place in 1388. Sir Philip Sidney's famous praise is generally referred to this ballad, though it would fit *Otterburn* almost as well: "Certainly I must confess my own barbarousness. I never heard the old song of Percy and Douglas that I found not my heart moved more than with a trumpet," *etc.* (*Defence of Poesie*). Addison criticized with high praise a younger and more corrupted version (*Chevy Chase*) of *The Hunting of the Cheviot*, in Nos. 70 and 74 of the *Spectator*.

He sayd, It was the Duglas promys
  this day to met me hear;
But I wyste he wolde faylle, verament;
  a great oth the Persë swear.

At the laste a squyar off Northomberlonde
  lokyde at his hand full ny;
He was war a the doughetie Doglas commynge,
  with him a myghttë meany.

Both with spear, bylle, and brande,
  yt was a myghtti sight to se;
Hardyar men, both off hart nor hande,
  wear not in Cristiantë.

The wear twenti hondrith spear-men good,
  withoute any feale;
The wear borne along be the watter a Twyde,
  yth bowndës of Tividale.

"Leave of the brytlyng of the dear," he sayd,
  "and to your boÿs lock ye tayk good hede;
For never sithe ye wear on your mothars borne
  had ye never so mickle nede."

The dougheti Dogglas on a stede,
  he rode alle his men beforne;
His armor glytteryde as dyd a glede;
  a boldar barne was never born.

"Tell me whos men ye ar," he says,
  "Or whos men that ye be:
Who gave youe leave to hunte in this Chyviat chays,
  in the spyt of myn and of me."

The first mane that ever him an answear mayd,
  yt was the good lord Persë:
"We wyll not tell the whoys men we ar," he says,
  "nor whos men that we be;
But we wyll hounte hear in this chays,
  in the spyt of thyne and of the.

"The fattiste hartës in all Chyviat
  we have kyld, and cast to carry them away:"
"Be my troth," sayd the doughetë Dogglas agay[n],
  "therfor the ton of us shall de this day."

Then sayd the doughtë Doglas
  unto the lord Persë:
"To kyll alle these giltles men.
  alas, it wear great pittë!

"But, Persë, thowe art a lord of lande,
  I am a yerle callyd within my contrë;
Let all our men uppone a parti stande,
  and do the battell off the and of me."

"Nowe Cristes cors on his crowne," sayd the lorde Persë,
  "who-so-ever ther-to says nay!
Be my troth, doughttë Doglas," he says,
  "thou shalt never se that day.

"Nethar in Ynglonde, Skottlonde, nar France,
  nor for no man of a woman born,
But, and fortune be my chance,
  I dar met him, on man for on."

Then bespayke a squyar off Northombarlonde,
  Richard Wytharyngton was his nam;
"It shall never be told in Sothe-Ynglonde," he says,
  "To Kyng Herry the Fourth for sham.

"I wat youe byn great lordës twaw,
  I am a poor squyar of lande;
I wylle never se my captayne fyght on a fylde,
  and stande my selffe and loocke on,
But whylle I may my weppone welde,
  I wylle not [fayle] both hart and hande."

That day, that day, that dredfull day!
  the first fit here I fynde;
And youe wyll here any mor a the hountynge a the Chyviat,
  yet ys ther mor behynde.

The Ynglyshe men hade ther bowys yebent,
  ther hartes wer good yenoughe;
The first off arros that the shote off,
  seven skore spear-men the sloughe.

Yet byddys the yerle Doglas uppon the bent,
  a captayne good yenoughe,
And that was sene verament,
  for he wrought hom both woo and wouche.

The Dogglas partyd his ost in thre,
  lyk a cheffe cheften off pryde;
With suar spears off myghttë tre,
  the cum in on every syde;

Thrughe our Ynglyshe archery
  gave many a wounde fulle wyde;
Many a doughetë the garde to dy,
  which ganyde them no pryde.

The Ynglyshe men let ther boÿs be,
  and pulde owt brandes that wer brighte;
It was a hevy syght to se
  bryght swordes on basnites lyght.

Thorowe ryche male and myneyeple,
many sterne the strocke done streght;
Many a freyke that was fulle fre,
ther undar foot dyd lyght.

At last the Duglas and the Persë met,
lyk to captayns of myght and of mayne;
The swapte togethar tylle the both swat,
with swordes that wear of fyn myllan.

Thes worthë freckys for to fyght,
ther-to the wear fulle fayne,
Tylle the bloode owte off thear basnetes sprente,
as ever dyd heal or ra[y]n.

"Yelde the, Persë," sayde the Doglas,
"and i feth I shalle the brynge
Wher thowe shalte have a yerls wagis
of Jamy our Skottish kynge.

"Thoue shalte have thy ransom fre,
I hight the hear this thinge;
For the manfullyste man yet art thowe
that ever I conqueryd in filde fighttynge."

"Nay," sayd the lord Persë,
"I tolde it the beforne,
That I wolde never yeldyde be
to no man of a woman born."

With that ther cam an arrowe hastely,
forthe off a myghttë wane;
Hit hathe strekene the yerle Duglas
in at the brest-bane.

Thorowe lyvar and longës bathe
the sharpe arrowe ys gane,
That never after in all his lyffe-days
he spayke mo wordës but ane:
That was, "Fyghte ye, my myrry men, whyllys ye may,
for my lyff-days ben gan."

The Persë leanyde on his brande,
and sawe the Duglas de;
He tooke the dede mane by the hande,
and sayd, "Wo ys me for the!

"To have savyde thy lyffe, I wolde have partyde with
my landes for years thre,
For a better man, of hart nare of hande,
was nat in all the north contrë."

Off all that se a Skottishe knyght,
was callyd Ser Hewe the Monggombyrry;
He sawe the Duglas to the deth was dyght,
he spendyd a spear, a trusti tre.

He rod uppone a corsiare
throughe a hondrith archery:
He never stynttyde, nar never blane,
tylle he came to the good lord Persë.

He set uppone the lorde Persë
a dynte that was full soare;
With a suar spear of a myghttë tre
clean thorow the body he the Persë ber,

A the tothar syde that a man myght se
a large cloth-yard and mare:
Towe bettar captayns wear nat in Cristiantë
then that day slan wear ther.

An archar off Northomberlonde
say slean was the lord Persë;
He bar a bende bowe in his hand,
was made off trusti tre.

An arow that a cloth-yarde was lang
to the harde stele halyde he;
A dynt that was both sad and soar
he sat on Ser Hewe the Monggombyrry.

The dynt yt was both sad and sar
that he of Monggomberry sete;
The swane-fethars that his arrowe bar
with his hart-blood the wear wete.

Ther was never a freake wone foot wolde fle,
but still in stour dyd stand,
Heawyng on yche othar, whylle the myghte dre,
with many a balfull brande.

This battell begane in Chyviat
an owar before the none,
And when even-songe bell was rang,
the battell was nat half done.

The tocke . . . on ethar hande[1]
be the lyght off the mone;
Many hade no strength for to stande,
in Chyviat the hillys abon.

Of fifteen hondrith archars of Ynglonde
went away but seventi and thre;
Of twenti hondrith spear-men of Skotlonde,
but even five and fifti.

But all wear slayne Cheviat within;
the hade no streng[th]e to stand on by;
The chylde may rue that ys unborne,
it was the mor pittë.

[1]Words are missing in the manuscript. "Rest" has been suggested to fill the gap; and also "them off"—*i.e.*, "they took themselves off."

Thear was slayne, withe the lord Persë,
 Ser Johan of Agerstone,
Ser Rogar, the hinde Hartly,
 Ser Wyllyam, the bolde Hearone.

Ser Jorg, the worthë Loumle,
 a knyghte of great renowen,
Ser Raff, the ryche Rugbe,
 with dyntes wear beaten dowene.

For Wetharryngton my harte was wo,
 that ever he slayne shulde be;
For when both his leggis wear hewyne in to,
 yet he knyled and fought on hys kny.

Ther was slayne, with the dougheti Duglas,
 Ser Hewe the Monggombyrry,
Ser Davy Lwdale, that worthë was,
 his sistars son was he.

Ser Charls a Murrë in that place,
 that never a foot wolde fle;
Ser Hewe Maxwelle, a lorde he was,
 with the Doglas dyd he dey.

So on the morrowe the mayde them byears
 off birch and hasell so g[r]ay;
Many wedous, with wepyng tears,
 cam to fache ther makys away.

Tivydale may carpe off care,
 Northombarlond may mayk great mon,
For towe such captayns as slayne wear thear
 on the March-parti shall never be non.

Word ys commen to Eddenburrowe,
 to Jamy the Skottishe kynge,[1]
That dougheti Duglas, lyff-tenant of the Marches,
 he lay slean Chyviot within.

His handdës dyd he weal and wryng,
 he sayd, Alas, and woe ys me!
Such an othar captayn Skotland within,
 he sayd, ye-feth shuld never be.

Worde ys commyn to lovly Londone,
 till the fourth Harry our kynge,
That lord Persë, leyff-tenante of the Marchis,
 he lay slayne Chyviat within.

"God have merci on his solle," sayde Kyng Harry,
 "good lord, yf thy will it be!
I have a hondrith captayns in Ynglonde," he sayd,
 "as good as ever was he:
But, Persë, and I brook my lyffe,
 thy deth well quyte shall be."

As our noble kynge mayd his avowe,
 lyke a noble prince of renowen,
For the deth of the lord Persë
 he dyde the battell of Hombylldown;

Wher syx and thrittë Skottishe knyghtes
 on a day wear beaten down;
Glendale glytteryde on ther armor bryght,
 over castille, towar, and town.

This was the hontynge off the Cheviat,
 that tear begane this spurn;
Old men that knowen the grownde well yenoughe
 call it the battell of Otterburn.

At Otterburn begane this spurne,
 uppone a Monnynday;
Ther was the doughtë Doglas slean,
 the Persë never went away.

Ther was never a tym on the Marche-partës
 sen the Doglas and the Persë met,
But yt ys mervele and the rede blude ronne not,
 as the reane doys in the stret.

Ihesue Crist our balys bete,
 and to the blys us brynge!
Thus was the hountynge of the Chivyat:
 God send us alle good endyng!

SIR PATRICK SPENS

THE king sits in Dunfermlin town,
 Sae merrily drinkin the wine:
"Whare will I get a mariner,
 Will sail this ship o mine?"

Then up bespak a bonny boy,
 Sat just at the king's knee:
"Sir Patrick Spence is the best seaman,
 That eer set foot on sea."

The king has written a braid letter,
 Seald it wi his ain hand;
He has sent word to Sir Patrick,
 To come at his command.

"O wha is this, or wha is that,
 Has tald the king o me?
For I was never a good seaman,
 Nor ever intend to be."

They mounted sail on Munenday morn,
 Wi a' the haste they may,
And they hae landed in Norraway,
 Upon the Wednesday.

[1] James I.

They hadna been a month, a month
  In Norraway but three,
Till lads o Norraway began to say,
  Ye spend a' our white monie.

"Ye spend a' our good kingis goud,
  But and our queenis fee:"
"Ye lie, ye lie, ye liars loud,
  Sae weel's I hear you lie.

"For I brought as much white money
  As will gain my men and me;
I brought half a fou o good red goud
  Out oer the sea with me.

"Be 't wind or weet, be 't snaw or sleet,
  Our ships maun sail the morn:"
"O ever alack! my master dear,
  I fear a deadly storm.

"I saw the new moon late yestreen,
  Wi the auld moon in her arm;
And if we gang to sea, master,
  I fear we'll suffer harm."

They hadna sailed a league on sea,
  A league but barely ane,
Till anchors brak, and tap-masts lap;
  There came a deadly storm.

"Whare will I get a bonny boy
  Will tak thir sails in hand,
That will gang up to the tap-mast,
  See an he ken dry land?"

Laith, laith were our good Scots lords
  To weet their leathern shoon;
But or the morn at fair day-light,
  Their hats were wat aboon.

Mony was the feather bed,
  That flottered on the faem,
And mony was the good Scots lord
  Gaed awa that neer cam hame,
And mony was the fatherless bairn
  That lay at hame greetin.

It's forty miles to Aberdeen,
  And fifty fathoms deep;
And there lyes a' our good Scots lords,
  Wi Sir Patrick at their feet.

The ladies crackt their fingers white,
  The maidens tore their hair,
A' for the sake o their true loves,
  For them they neer saw mair.

Lang, lang may our ladies stand,
  Wi their fans in their hand,
Ere they see Sir Patrick and his men
  Come sailing to the land.

THE THREE RAVENS

There were three ravens sat on a tree,
  Downe a downe, hay down, hay downe,
There were three ravens sat on a tree,
  With a downe,
There were three ravens sat on a tree,
They were as blacke as they might be.
  With a downe, derrie, derrie, derrie, downe,
    downe.

The one of them said to his mate,
"Where shall we our breakefast take?"

"Downe in yonder greene field,
There lies a knight slain under his shield.

"His hounds they lie downe at his feete,
So well they can their master keepe.

"His haukes they flie so eagerly,
There's no fowle dare him come nie."

Downe there comes a fallow doe,
As great with yong as she might goe.

She lift up his bloudy hed,
And kist his wounds that were so red.

She got him up upon her backe,
And carried him to earthen lake.

She buried him before the prime,
She was dead herselfe ere even-song time.

God send every gentleman,
Such haukes, such hounds, and such a leman.

EDWARD

"Why dois your brand sae drap wi bluid,
        Edward, Edward,
Why dois your brand sae drap wi bluid,
  And why sae sad gang yee O?"
"O I hae killed my hauke sae guid,
        Mither, mither,
O I hae killed my hauke sae guid,
  And I had nae mair bot hee O."

"Your haukis bluid was nevir sae reid,
        Edward, Edward,
Your haukis bluid was nevir sae reid,
  My deir son I tell thee O."
"O I hae killed my reid-roan steid,
        Mither, mither,
O I hae killed my reid-roan steid,
  That erst was sae fair and frie O."

"Your steid was auld, and ye hae gat mair,
Edward, Edward,
Your steid was auld, and ye hae gat mair,
Sum other dule ye drie O."
"O I hae killed my fadir deir,
Mither, mither,
O I hae killed my fadir deir,
Alas, and wae is mee O!"

"And whatten penance wul ye drie for that,
Edward, Edward?
And whatten penance will ye drie for that?
My deir son, now tell me O."
"Ile set my feit in yonder boat,
Mither, mither,
Ile set my feit in yonder boat,
And Ile fare ovir the sea O."

"And what wul ye doe wi your towirs and your ha,
Edward, Edward?
And what wul ye doe wi your towirs and your ha,
That were sae fair to see O?"
"Ile let thame stand tul they doun fa,
Mither, mither,
Ile let thame stand tul they doun fa,
For here nevir mair maun I bee O."

"And what wul ye leive to your bairns and your wife,
Edward, Edward?
And what wul ye leive to your bairns and your wife,
Whan ye gang ovir the sea O?"
"The warldis room, late them beg thrae life,
Mither, mither,
The warldis room, late them beg thrae life,
For thame nevir mair wul I see O."

"And what wul ye leive to your ain mither deir,
Edward, Edward?
And what wul ye leive to your ain mither deir?
My deir son, now tell me O."
"The curse of hell frae me sall ye beir,
Mither, mither,
The curse of hell frae me sall ye beir,
Sic counseils ye gave to me O."

THE TWA SISTERS

THERE was twa sisters in a bowr,
Edinburgh, Edinburgh,
There was twa sisters in a bowr,
Stirling for ay.
There was twa sisters in a bowr,
There came a knight to be their wooer;
Bonny Saint Johnston stands upon Tay.

He courted the eldest wi glove an ring,
But he lovd the youngest above a' thing.

He courted the eldest wi brotch an knife,
But lovd the youngest as his life.

The eldest she was vexéd sair,
An much envi'd her sister fair.

Into her bowr she could not rest,
Wi grief an spite she almos brast.

Upon a morning fair an clear,
She cried upon her sister dear:

"O sister, come to yon sea stran,
And see our father's ships come to lan."

She 's taen her by the milk-white han,
And led her down to yon sea stran.

The younges[t] stood upon a stane,
The eldest came an threw her in

She tooke her by the middle sma,
An dashd her bonny back to the jaw.

"O sister, sister, tak my han,
An Ise mack you heir to a' my lan.

"O sister, sister, tak my middle,
An yes get my goud and my gouden girdle.

"O sister, sister, save my life,
An I swear Ise never be nae man's wife."

"Foul fa the han that I should tacke,
It twin'd me an my wardles make.

"Your cherry cheeks an yallow hair
Gars me gae maiden for evermair."

Sometimes she sank, an sometimes she swam,
Till she came down yon bonny mill-dam.

O out it came the miller's son,
An saw the fair maid swimmin in.

"O father, father, draw your dam,
Here's either a mermaid or a swan."

The miller quickly drew the dam,
An there he found a drownd woman.

You coudna see her yallow hair
For gold and pearle that were so rare.

You coudna see her middle sma
For gouden girdle that was sae braw.

You coudna see her fingers white,
For gouden rings that was sae gryte.

An by there came a harper fine,
That harpéd to the king at dine.

When he did look that lady upon,
He sighd and made a heavy moan.

He's taen three locks o her yallow hair,
An wi them strung his harp sae fair.

The first tune he did play and sing,
Was, "Farewell to my father the king."

The nextin tune that he playd syne,
Was, "Farewell to my mother the queen."

The lasten tune that he playd then,
Was, "Wae to my sister, fair Ellen."

THE TWA BROTHERS

THERE were twa brethren in the north,
They went to school thegithar;
The one unto the other said,
Will you try a warsle afore?

They wrestled up, they wrestled down,
Till Sir John fell to the ground,
And there was a knife in Sir Willie's pouch,
Gied him a deadlie wound.

"Oh brither dear, take me on your back,
Carry me to yon burn clear,
And wash the blood from off my wound,
And it will bleed nae mair."

He took him up upon his back,
Carried him to yon burn clear,
And washd the blood from off his wound,
And aye it bled the mair.

"Oh brother dear, take me on your back,
Carry me to yon kirk-yard,
And dig a grave baith wide and deep,
And lay my body there."

He's taen him up upon his back,
Carried him to yon kirk-yard,
And dug a grave both deep and wide,
And laid his body there.

"But what will I say to my father dear,
Should he chance to say, Willie, whar's John?"
"Oh say that he's to England gone,
To buy him a cask of wine."

"And what shall I say to my mother dear,
Should she chance to say, Willie, whar's John?"
"Oh say that he's to England gone,
To buy her a new silk gown."

"And what will I say to my sister dear,
Should she chance to say, Willie, whar's John?"
"Oh say that he's to England gone,
To buy her a wedding ring."

"What will I say to her you loe dear,
Should she cry, Why tarries my John?"
"Oh tell her I lie in fair Kirk-land,
And home will never come."

THE CRUEL BROTHER

THERE was three ladies playd at the ba,
With a hey ho and a lillie gay,
There came a knight and played oer them a'.
As the primrose spreads so sweetly.

The eldest was baith tall and fair,
But the youngest was beyond compare.

The midmost had a graceful mien,
But the youngest lookd like beautie's queen.

The knight bowd low to a' the three,
But to the youngest he bent his knee.

The ladie turned her head aside,
The knight he woo'd her to be his bride.

The ladie blushd a rosy red,
And sayd, "Sir knight, I'm too young to wed."

"O ladie fair, give me your hand,
And I'll make you ladie of a' my land."

"Sir knight, ere ye my favor win,
You maun get consent frae a' my kin."

He's got consent frae her parents dear,
And likewise frae her sisters fair.

He's got consent frae her kin each one,
But forgot to spiek to her brother John.

Now, when the wedding day was come,
The knight would take his bonny bride home.

And many a lord and many a knight
Came to behold that ladie bright.

And there was nae man that did her see,
But wishd himself bridegroom to be.

Her father dear led her down the stair,
And her sisters twain they kissd her there.

Her mother dear led her thro the closs,
And her brother John set her on her horse.

She leand her oer the saddle-bow,
To give him a kiss ere she did go.

He has taen a knife, baith lang and sharp,
And stabbd that bonny bride to the heart.

She hadno ridden half thro the town,
Until her heart's blude staind her gown.

"Ride softly on," says the best young man,
"For I think our bonny bride looks pale and
wan."

"O lead me gently up yon hill,
And I'll there sit down, and make my will."

"O what will you leave to your father dear?"
"The silver-shode steed that brought me
here."

"What will you leave to your mother dear?"
"My velvet pall and my silken gear."

"What will you leave to your sister Anne?"
"My silken scarf and my gowden fan."

"What will you leave to your sister Grace?"
"My bloody cloaths to wash and dress."

"What will you leave to your brother John?"
"The gallows-tree to hang him on."

"What will you leave to your brother John's
wife?"
"The wilderness to end her life."

This ladie fair in her grave was laid,
And many a mass was oer her said.

But it would have made your heart right sair,
To see the bridegroom rive his haire.

THE WIFE OF USHER'S WELL

THERE lived a wife at Usher's Well,
And a wealthy wife was she;
She had three stout and stalwart sons,
And sent them oer the sea.

They hadna been a week from her,
A week but barely ane,
Whan word came to the carline wife
That her three sons were gane.

They hadna been a week from her,
A week but barely three,
Whan word came to the carlin wife
That her sons she'd never see.

"I wish the wind may never cease,
Nor fashes in the flood,
Till my three sons come hame to me,
In earthly flesh and blood."

It fell about the Martinmass,
When nights are lang and mirk,
The carlin wife's three sons came hame,
And their hats were o the birk.

It neither grew in syke nor ditch,
Nor yet in only sheugh;
But at the gates o Paradise,
That birk grew fair eneugh.

. . . . .

"Blow up the fire, my maidens,
Bring water from the well;
For a' my house shall feast this night,
Since my three sons are well."

And she has made to them a bed,
She's made it large and wide,
And she's taen her mantle her about,
Sat down at the bed-side.

. . . . .

Up then crew the red, red cock,
And up and crew the gray;
The eldest to the youngest said,
'Tis time we were away.

The cock he hadna crawd but once,
And clappd his wings at a',
When the youngest to the eldest said,
Brother, we must awa.

"The cock doth craw, the day doth daw,
The channerin worm doth chide;
Gin we be mist out o our place,
A sair pain we maun bide.

"Fare ye weel, my mother dear!
Fareweel to barn and byre!
And fare ye weel, the bonny lass
That kindles my mother's fire!"

KEMP OWYNE[1]

HER mother died when she was young,
Which gave her cause to make great moan;
Her father married the warst woman
That ever lived in Christendom.

[1]Owyne is Owain or Ywain, one of King Arthur's knights. Disenchantment by a kiss is common in romance, but none is known in which Ywain has this adventure.

She servéd her with foot and hand,
  In every thing that she could dee,
Till once, in an unlucky time,
  She threw her in ower Craigy's sea.

Says, "Lie you there, dove Isabel,
  And all my sorrows lie with thee;
Till Kemp Owyne come ower the sea,
  And borrow you with kisses three,
Let all the warld do what they will,
  Oh borrowed shall you never be!"

Her breath grew strang, her hair grew lang,
  And twisted thrice about the tree,
And all the people, far and near,
  Thought that a savage beast was she.

These news did come to Kemp Owyne,
  Where he lived, far beyond the sea;
He hasted him to Craigy's sea,
  And on the savage beast lookd he.

Her breath was strang, her hair was lang,
  And twisted was about the tree,
And with a swing she came about:
  "Come to Craigy's sea, and kiss with me.

"Here is a royal belt," she cried,
  "That I have found in the green sea;
And while your body it is on,
  Drawn shall your blood never be;
But if you touch me, tail or fin,
  I vow my belt your death shall be."

He steppéd in, gave her a kiss,
  The royal belt he brought him wi;
Her breath was strang, her hair was lang,
  And twisted twice about the tree,
And with a swing she came about:
  "Come to Craigy's sea, and kiss with me.

"Here is a royal ring," she said,
  "That I have found in the green sea;
And while your finger it is on,
  Drawn shall your blood never be;
But if you touch me, tail or fin,
  I swear my ring your death shall be."

He steppéd in, gave her a kiss,
  The royal ring he brought him wi;
Her breath was strang, her hair was lang,
  And twisted ance about the tree,
And with a swing she came about:
  "Come to Craigy's sea, and kiss with me.

"Here is a royal brand," she said,
  "That I have found in the green sea;
And while your body it is on,
  Drawn shall your blood never be;
But if you touch me, tail or fin,
  I swear my brand your death shall be."

He steppéd in, gave her a kiss,
  The royal brand he brought him wi;
Her breath was sweet, her hair grew short,
  And twisted nane about the tree,
And smilingly she came about,
  As fair a woman as fair could be.

THOMAS RYMER[1]

True Thomas lay oer yond grassy bank,
  And he beheld a ladie gay,
A ladie that was brisk and bold,
  Come riding oer the fernie brae.

Her skirt was of the grass-green silk,
  Her mantel of the velvet fine,
At ilka tett of her horse's mane
  Hung fifty silver bells and nine.

True Thomas he took off his hat,
  And bowed him low down till his knee:
"All hail, thou mighty Queen of Heaven!
  For your peer on earth I never did see."

"O no, O no, True Thomas," she says,
  "That name does not belong to me;
I am but the queen of fair Elfland,
  And I'm come here for to visit thee.

. . . .

"But ye maun go wi me now, Thomas,
  True Thomas, ye maun go wi me,
For ye maun serve me seven years,
  Thro weel or wae as may chance to be."

She turned about her milk-white steed,
  And took True Thomas up behind,
And aye wheneer her bridle rang,
  The steed flew swifter than the wind.

For forty days and forty nights
  He wade thro red blude to the knee,
And he saw neither sun nor moon,
  But heard the roaring of the sea.

O they rade on, and further on,
  Until they came to a garden green:
"Light down, light down, ye ladie free,
  Some of that fruit let me pull to thee."

"O no, O no, True Thomas," she says,
  "That fruit maun not be touched by thee,
For a' the plagues that are in hell
  Light on the fruit of this countrie.

[1]This story is told in fuller detail in the poem called *Thomas of Erceldoune*, a fifteenth-century romance and probably the source of the ballad. Thomas of Erceldoune is an historical character; he lived in southern Scotland in the thirteenth century.

"But I have a loaf here in my lap,
  Likewise a bottle of claret wine,
And now ere we go farther on,
  We'll rest a while, and ye may dine."

When he had eaten and drunk his fill,
  "Lay down your head upon my knee,"
The lady sayd, "ere we climb yon hill,
  And I will show you fairlies three.

"O see not ye yon narrow road,
  So thick beset wi thorns and briers?
That is the path of righteousness,
  Tho after it but few enquires.

"And see not ye that braid braid road,
  That lies across yon lillie leven?
That is the path of wickedness,
  Tho some call it the road to heaven.

"And see not ye that bonny road,
  Which winds about the fernie brae?
That is the road to fair Elfland,
  Whe[re] you and I this night maun gae.

"But Thomas, ye maun hold your tongue,
  Whatever you may hear or see,
For gin ae word you should chance to speak,
  You will neer get back to your ain countrie."

He has gotten a coat of the even cloth,
  And a pair of shoes of velvet green,
And till seven years were past and gone
  True Thomas on earth was never seen.

SIR HUGH, OR, THE JEW'S DAUGHTER[1]

Four and twenty bonny boys
  Were playing at the ba,
And by it came him sweet Sir Hugh,
  And he playd oer them a'.

He kicked the ba with his right foot,
  And catchd it wi his knee,
And throuch-and-thro the Jew's window
  He gard the bonny ba flee.

He's doen him to the Jew's castell,
  And walkd it round about;
And there he saw the Jew's daughter,
  At the window looking out.

"Throw down the ba, ye Jew's daughter,
  Throw down the ba to me!"

"Never a bit," says the Jew's daughter,
  "Till up to me come ye."

"How will I come up? How can I come up?
  How can I come to thee?
For as ye did to my auld father,
  The same ye'll do to me."

She's gane till her father's garden,
  And pu'd an apple red and green;
'T was a' to wyle him sweet Sir Hugh,
  And to entice him in.

She's led him in through ae dark door,
  And sae has she thro nine;
She's laid him on a dressing-table,
  And stickit him like a swine.

And first came out the thick, thick blood,
  And syne came out the thin,
And syne came out the bonny heart's blood;
  There was nae mair within.

She's rowd him in a cake o lead,
  Bade him lie still and sleep;
She's thrown him in Our Lady's draw-well,
  Was fifty fathom deep.

When bells were rung, and mass was sung,
  And a' the bairns came hame,
When every lady gat hame her son,
  The Lady Maisry gat nane.

She's taen her mantle her about,
  Her coffer by the hand,
And she's gane out to seek her son,
  And wanderd oer the land.

She's doen her to the Jew's castell,
  Where a' were fast asleep:
"Gin ye be there, my sweet Sir Hugh,
  I pray you to me speak."

She's doen her to the Jew's garden,
  Thought he had been gathering fruit:
"Gin ye be there, my sweet Sir Hugh,
  I pray you to me speak."

She neard Our Lady's deep draw-well,
  Was fifty fathom deep:
"Whareer ye be, my sweet Sir Hugh,
  I pray you to me speak."

"Gae hame, gae hame, my mither dear,
  Prepare my winding sheet,
And at the back o merry Lincoln
  The morn I will you meet."

Now Lady Maisry is gane hame,
  Made him a winding sheet,

[1]This is based on an alleged murder which took place in 1255. The popularity of such stories in the Middle Ages has been mentioned in the note to Chaucer's Prioress's Tale, which has the same theme. As has been said, these stories are as credible as the miracles asserted to have been worked by the relics of the young saints.

And at the back o merry Lincoln
The dead corpse did her meet.

And a' the bells o merry Lincoln
Without men's hands were rung,
And a' the books o merry Lincoln
Were read without man's tongue,
And neer was such a burial
Sin Adam's days begun.

GET UP AND BAR THE DOOR

It fell about the Martinmas time,
And a gay time it was then,
When our goodwife got puddings to make,
And she's boild them in the pan.

The wind sae cauld blew south and north,
And blew into the floor;
Quoth our goodman to our goodwife,
"Gae out and bar the door."

"My hand is in my hussyfskap,
Goodman, as ye may see;
An it should nae be barrd this hundred year,
It's no be barrd for me."

They made a paction tween them twa,
They made it firm and sure,
That the first word whaeer shoud speak,
Shoud rise and bar the door.

Then by there came two gentlemen,
At twelve o clock at night,
And they could neither see house nor hall,
Nor coal nor candle-light.

"Now whether is this a rich man's house,
Or whether is it a poor?"
But neer a word wad ane o them speak,
For barring of the door.

And first they ate the white puddings,
And then they ate the black;
Tho muckle thought the goodwife to hersel,
Yet neer a word she spake.

Then said the one unto the other,
"Here, man, tak ye my knife;
Do ye tak aff the auld man's beard,
And I'll kiss the goodwife."

"But there's nae water in the house,
And what shall we do than?"
"What ails ye at the pudding-broo,
That boils into the pan?"

O up then started our good man,
An angry man was he:
"Will ye kiss my wife before my een,
And scad me wi pudding-bree?"

Then up and started our goodwife,
Gied three skips on the floor:
"Goodman, you've spoken the foremost word,
Get up and bar the door."

EVERYMAN

The authorship of *Everyman* is not known. The play made its appearance some time during the fifteenth century. Its text is preserved in four early editions, none of which is dated, though all must have appeared between 1493 and 1537—dates which mark the limits of the period during which the two printers of the editions, Pynson and Skot, did their work. It is considered probable by many scholars that *Everyman* is a translation of a Dutch play, *Elckerlijk* (ascribed to Dorlandus), which was in print before the earliest edition of *Everyman*. This, however, is by no means certain, as *Everyman* may be really the earlier of the two, or both may go back to some common source now unknown. The importance of this unsettled question, moreover, may easily be exaggerated, inasmuch as *Everyman* as it now stands is a thoroughly English play, with none of the earmarks of a mere translation, and has its inherent right to the place it has won in English literature.

Everyman is a morality;—that is, it is a dramatized moral allegory, a form of play which was one of the results of the one-time great popularity of allegory. In allegory inanimate things or abstract qualities—generally the latter—are personified in order to give them greater reality and interest. The English moralities were in the beginning vehicles of religious and moral instruction; later the type was made the instrument of religious controversy and was also used in exhibiting the value of learning. The great theme of the earlier moralities was the life of man conceived as a conflict between good and evil, a conflict which begins with birth and ends only with death. In its entirety this is a practically endless subject and the writers of moralities tended to narrow its scope, with proportionate gain in simplicity of plan, directness, and power. Thus some moralities exhibit a crucial conflict between two groups, virtues and vices, for possession of the soul of man. Another plan was to picture the coming of death, and this is done in *Everyman*. The play shows the measure of dramatic quality and power which the morality was capable of attaining when it was at its best.

CHARACTERS

EVERYMAN	STRENGTH
GOD: ADONAI	DISCRETION
DEATH	FIVE-WITS
MESSENGER	BEAUTY
FELLOWSHIP	KNOWLEDGE
COUSIN	CONFESSION
KINDRED	ANGEL
GOODS	DOCTOR
GOOD-DEEDS	

Here beginneth a treatise how the High Father of Heaven sendeth death to summon every creature to come and give account of their lives in this world and is in manner of a moral play.

MESSENGER. I pray you all give your audience,
And hear this matter with reverence,
By figure a moral play—
The *Summoning of Everyman* called it is,
That of our lives and ending shows
How transitory we be all day.
This matter is wondrous precious,
But the intent of it is more gracious,
And sweet to bear away.
The story saith,—Man, in the beginning,
Look well, and take good heed to the ending,
Be you never so gay!
Ye think sin in the beginning full sweet,
Which in the end causeth thy soul to weep,
When the body lieth in clay.
Here shall you see how *Fellowship* and *Jollity*,
Both *Strength*, *Pleasure*, and *Beauty*,
Will fade from thee as flower in May.
For ye shall hear, how our Heaven-King
Calleth *Everyman* to a general reckoning:
Give audience, and hear what he doth say.

GOD. I perceive here in my majesty,
How that all creatures be to me unkind,
Living without dread in worldly prosperity:
Of ghostly sight the people be so blind,
Drowned in sin, they know me not for their God;
In worldly riches is all their mind,
They fear not my rightwiseness, the sharp rod;
My law that I showed, when I for them died,
They forget clean, and shedding of my blood red;
I hanged between two, it cannot be denied;
To get them life I suffered to be dead;

I healed their feet, with thorns hurt was my head:
I could do no more than I did truly,
And now I see the people do clean forsake me.
They use the seven deadly sins damnable;
As pride, covetise, wrath, and lechery,
Now in the world be made commendable;
And thus they leave of angels the heavenly company;
Everyman liveth so after his own pleasure,
And yet of their life they be nothing sure:
I see the more that I them forbear
The worse they be from year to year;
All that liveth appaireth[1] fast,
Therefore I will in all the haste
Have a reckoning of Everyman's person;
For and I leave the people thus alone
In their life and wicked tempests,
Verily they will become much worse than beasts;
For now one would by envy another up eat;
Charity they all do clean forget.
I hoped well that Everyman
In my glory should make his mansion,
And thereto I had them all elect;
But now I see, like traitors deject,
They thank me not for the pleasure that I to them meant,
Nor yet for their being that I them have lent;
I proffered the people great multitude of mercy,
And few there be that asketh it heartily;
They be so cumbered with worldly riches,
That needs on them I must do justice,
On Everyman living without fear.
Where art thou, *Death*, thou mighty messenger?

DEATH. Almighty God, I am here at your will,
Your commandment to fulfil.

GOD. Go thou to *Everyman*,
And show him in my name
A pilgrimage he must on him take,
Which he in no wise may escape;
And that he bring with him a sure reckoning
Without delay or any tarrying.

DEATH. Lord, I will in the world go run over all,
And cruelly outsearch both great and small;
Every man will I beset that liveth beastly
Out of God's laws, and dreadeth not folly:
He that loveth riches I will strike with my dart,
His sight to blind, and from heaven to depart,
Except that alms be his good friend,
In hell for to dwell, world without end.
Lo, yonder I see *Everyman* walking;
Full little he thinketh on my coming;
His mind is on fleshly lusts and his treasure,
And great pain it shall cause him to endure
Before the Lord Heaven King.
Everyman, stand still; whither art thou going
Thus gaily? Hast thou thy Maker forget?

EVERYMAN. Why askst thou?
Wouldest thou wete?[2]

DEATH. Yea, sir, I will show you;
In great haste I am sent to thee
From God out of his majesty.

EVERYMAN. What, sent to me?

DEATH. Yea, certainly.
Though thou have forgot him here,
He thinketh on thee in the heavenly sphere,
As, or we depart, thou shalt know.

EVERYMAN. What desireth God of me?

DEATH. That shall I show thee;
A reckoning he will needs have
Without any longer respite.

EVERYMAN. To give a reckoning longer leisure I crave;
This blind matter troubleth my wit.

DEATH. On thee thou must take a long journey:
Therefore thy book of count with thee thou bring;
For turn again thou cannot by no way,
And look thou be sure of thy reckoning:
For before God thou shalt answer, and show
Thy many bad deeds and good but a few;
How thou hast spent thy life, and in what wise,
Before the chief lord of paradise.
Have ado that we were in that way,
For, wete thou well, thou shalt make none attournay.[3]

EVERYMAN. Full unready I am such reckoning to give.
I know thee not: what messenger art thou?

DEATH. I am *Death*, that no man dreadeth.
For every man I rest and no man spareth;
For it is God's commandment
That all to me should be obedient.

EVERYMAN. O *Death*, thou comest when I had thee least in mind;
In thy power it lieth me to save,
Yet of my good will I give thee, if ye will be kind,
Yea, a thousand pound shalt thou have,
And defer this matter till another day.

DEATH. *Everyman*, it may not be by no way;
I set not by gold, silver, nor riches,
Nor by pope, emperor, king, duke, nor princes.
For and I would receive gifts great,

[1] Is impaired.

[2] Know. [3] Mediator.

All the world I might get;
But my custom is clean contrary.
I give thee no respite: come hence, and not tarry.

EVERYMAN. Alas, shall I have no longer respite?
I may say *Death* giveth no warning:
To think on thee, it maketh my heart sick,
For all unready is my book of reckoning.
But twelve year and I might have abiding,
My counting book I would make so clear,
That my reckoning I should not need to fear.
Wherefore, *Death*, I pray thee, for God's mercy,
Spare me till I be provided of remedy.

DEATH. Thee availeth not to cry, weep, and pray:
But haste thee lightly that you were gone the journey,
And prove thy friends if thou can.
For, wete thou well, the tide abideth no man,
And in the world each living creature
For *Adam's* sin must die of nature.

EVERYMAN. *Death*, if I should this pilgrimage take,
And my reckoning surely make,
Show me, for saint *charity*,
Should I not come again shortly?

DEATH. No, *Everyman;* and thou be once there,
Thou mayst never more come here,
Trust me verily.

EVERYMAN. O gracious God, in the high seat celestial,
Have mercy on me in this most need;
Shall I have no company from this vale terrestrial
Of mine acquaintance that way me to lead?

DEATH. Yea, if any be so hardy,
That would go with thee and bear thee company.
Hie thee that you were gone to God's magnificence,
Thy reckoning to give before his presence.
What, weenest thou thy life is given thee,
And thy worldly goods also?

EVERYMAN. I had wend so, verily.

DEATH. Nay, nay; it was but lent thee;
For as soon as thou art go,
Another awhile shall have it, and then go therefro
Even as thou hast done.
Everyman, thou art mad; thou hast thy wits five,
And here on earth will not amend thy life,
For suddenly I do come.

EVERYMAN. O wretched caitiff, whither shall I flee,
That I might scape this endless sorrow!
Now, gentle *Death*, spare me till to-morrow,
That I may amend me
With good advisement.

DEATH. Nay, thereto I will not consent,
Nor no man will I respite,
But to the heart suddenly I shall smite
Without any advisement.
And now out of thy sight I will me hie;
See thou make thee ready shortly,
For thou mayst say this is the day
That no man living may scape away.

EVERYMAN. Alas, I may well weep with sighs deep;
Now have I no manner of company
To help me in my journey, and me to keep;
And also my writing is full unready.
How shall I do now for to excuse me?
I would to God I had never be gete![1]
To my soul a full great profit it had be;
For now I fear pains huge and great.
The time passeth; Lord, help that all wrought;
For though I mourn it availeth nought.
The day passeth, and is almost a-go;
I wot not well what for to do.
To whom were I best my complaint to make?
What, and I to *Fellowship* thereof spake,
And showed him of this sudden chance?
For in him is all mine affiance;
We have in the world so many a day
Be on good friends in sport and play.
I see him yonder, certainly;
I trust that he will bear me company;
Therefore to him will I speak to ease my sorrow.
Well met, good *Fellowship*, and good morrow!

FELLOWSHIP *speaketh. Everyman*, good morrow by this day.
Sir, why lookest thou so piteously?
If any thing be amiss, I pray thee, me say,
That I may help to remedy.

EVERYMAN. Yea, good *Fellowship*, yea,
I am in great jeopardy.

FELLOWSHIP. My true friend, show to me your mind;
I will not forsake thee, unto my life's end,
In the way of good company.

EVERYMAN. That was well spoken, and lovingly.

FELLOWSHIP. Sir, I must needs know your heaviness;
I have pity to see you in any distress;
If any have you wronged ye shall revenged be,
Though I on the ground be slain for thee,—
Though that I know before that I should die.

[1]Been born.

EVERYMAN. Verily, *Fellowship*, gramercy.
FELLOWSHIP. Tush! by thy thanks I set not a straw.
Show me your grief, and say no more.
EVERYMAN. If I my heart should to you break,
And then you to turn your mind from me,
And would not me comfort, when you hear me speak,
Then should I ten times sorrier be.
FELLOWSHIP. Sir, I say as I will do in deed.
EVERYMAN. Then be you a good friend at need:
I have found you true here before.
FELLOWSHIP. And so ye shall evermore;
For, in faith, and thou go to Hell,
I will not forsake thee by the way!
EVERYMAN. Ye speak like a good friend; I believe you well;
I shall deserve it, and I may.
FELLOWSHIP. I speak of no deserving, by this day.
For he that will say and nothing do
Is not worthy with good company to go;
Therefore show me the grief of your mind,
As to your friend most loving and kind.
EVERYMAN. I shall show you how it is;
Commanded I am to go a journey,
A long way, hard and dangerous,
And give a strait count without delay
Before the high judge Adonai.[1]
Wherefore I pray you, bear me company,
As ye have promised, in this journey.
FELLOWSHIP. That is matter indeed! Promise is duty,
But, and I should take such a voyage on me,
I know it well, it should be to my pain:
Also it make me afeard, certain.
But let us take counsel here as well as we can,
For your words would fear a strong man.
EVERYMAN. Why, ye said, If I had need,
Ye would me never forsake, quick nor dead,
Though it were to hell truly.
FELLOWSHIP. So I said, certainly,
But such pleasures be set aside, thee sooth to say:
And also, if we took such a journey,
When should we come again?
EVERYMAN. Nay, never again till the day of doom.
FELLOWSHIP. In faith, then will not I come there!
Who hath you these tidings brought?
EVERYMAN. Indeed, *Death* was with me here.
FELLOWSHIP. Now, by God that all hath bought,
If *Death* were the messenger,
For no man that is living to-day
I will not go that loath journey—
Not for the father that begat me!
EVERYMAN. Ye promised other wise, pardie.
FELLOWSHIP. I wot well I say so truly;
And yet if thou wilt eat, and drink, and make good cheer,
Or haunt to women, the lusty company,
I would not forsake you, while the day is clear,
Trust me verily!
EVERYMAN. Yea, thereto ye would be ready;
To go to mirth, solace, and play,
Your mind will sooner apply
Than to bear me company in my long journey.
FELLOWSHIP. Now, in good faith, I will not that way.
But and thou wilt murder, or any man kill,
In that I will help thee with a good will!
EVERYMAN. O that is a simple advice indeed!
Gentle *fellow*, help me in my necessity;
We have loved long, and now I need,
And now, gentle *Fellowship*, remember me.
FELLOWSHIP. Whether ye have loved me or no,
By Saint John, I will not with thee go.
EVERYMAN. Yet I pray thee, take the labor, and do so much for me
To bring me forward, for saint charity,
And comfort me till I come without the town.
FELLOWSHIP. Nay, and thou would give me a new gown,
I will not a foot with thee go;
But and you had tarried I would not have left thee so.
And as now, God speed thee in thy journey,
For from thee I will depart as fast as I may.
EVERYMAN. Whither away, *Fellowship?* will you forsake me?
FELLOWSHIP. Yea, by my fay, to God I betake thee.
EVERYMAN. Farewell, good *Fellowship;* for this my heart is sore;
Adieu for ever, I shall see thee no more.
FELLOWSHIP. In faith, *Everyman*, farewell now at the end;
For you I will remember that parting is mourning.
EVERYMAN. Alack! shall we thus depart indeed?
Our Lady, help, without any more comfort,
Lo, *Fellowship* forsaketh me in my most need:
For help in this world whither shall I resort?
Fellowship herebefore with me would merry make;
And now little sorrow for me doth he take.
It is said, in prosperity men friends may find,
Which in adversity be full unkind.

[1] God.

Now whither for succor shall I flee,
Since that *Fellowship* hath forsaken me?
To my kinsmen I will truly,
Praying them to help me in my necessity;
I believe that they will do so,
For kind will creep where it may not go.
I will go say, for yonder I see them go.
Where be ye now, my friends and kinsmen?

KINDRED. Here be we now at your commandment.
Cousin, I pray you show us your intent
In any wise, and not spare.

COUSIN. Yea, *Everyman*, and to us declare
If ye be disposed to go any whither,
For wete you well, we will live and die together.

KINDRED. In wealth and woe we will with you hold,
For over his kin a man may be bold.

EVERYMAN. Gramercy, my friends and kinsmen kind.
Now shall I show you the grief of my mind:
I was commanded by a messenger,
That is an high king's chief officer;
He bade me go a pilgrimage to my pain,
And I know well I shall never come again;
Also I must give a reckoning straight,
For I have a great enemy, that hath me in wait,
Which intendeth me for to hinder.

KINDRED. What account is that which ye must render?
That would I know.

EVERYMAN. Of all my works I must show
How I have lived and my days spent;
Also of ill deeds, that I have used
In my time, since life was me lent;
And of all virtues that I have refused.
Therefore I pray you go thither with me,
To help to make mine account, for saint *charity*.

COUSIN. What, to go thither? Is that the matter?
Nay, *Everyman*, I had liefer fast bread and water
All this five year and more.

EVERYMAN. Alas, that ever I was bore![1]
For now shall I never be merry
If that you forsake me.

KINDRED. Ah, sir; what, ye be a merry man!
Take good heart to you, and make no moan.
But one thing I warn you, by Saint Anne,
As for me, ye shall go alone.

EVERYMAN. My *Cousin*, will you not with me go?

COUSIN. No, by our Lady; I have the cramp in my toe.
Trust not to me, for, so God me speed,
I will deceive you in your most need.

KINDRED. It availeth not us to tice.
Ye shall have my maid with all my heart;
She loveth to go to feasts, there to be nice,
And to dance, and abroad to start:
I will give her leave to help you in that journey,
If that you and she may agree.

EVERYMAN. Now show me the very effect of your mind.
Will you go with me, or abide behind?

KINDRED. Abide behind? yea, that I will and I may!
Therefore farewell until another day.

EVERYMAN. How should I be merry or glad?
For fair promises to me make,
But when I have most need, they me forsake.
I am deceived; that maketh me sad.

COUSIN. Cousin *Everyman*, farewell now,
For verily I will not go with you;
Also of mine own an unready reckoning
I have to account; therefore I make tarrying.
Now, God keep thee, for now I go.

EVERYMAN. Ah, *Jesus*, is all come hereto?
Lo, fair words maketh fools feign;
They promise and nothing will do certain.
My kinsmen promised me faithfully
For to abide with me steadfastly,
And now fast away do they flee:
Even so *Fellowship* promised me.
What friend were best me of to provide?
I lose my time here longer to abide.
Yet in my mind a thing there is;—
All my life I have loved riches;
If that my good now help me might,
He would make my heart full light.
I will speak to him in this distress.—
Where art thou, my *Goods* and riches?

GOODS. Who calleth me? *Everyman?* what haste thou hast.
I lie here in corners, trussed and piled so high,
And in chests I am locked so fast,
Also sacked in bags, thou mayst see with thine eye,
I cannot stir; in packs low I lie.
What would ye have, lightly me say.

EVERYMAN. Come hither, *Good*, in all the haste thou may,
For of counsel I must desire thee.

GOODS. Sir, and ye in the world have trouble or adversity,
That can I help you to remedy shortly.

EVERYMAN. It is another disease that grieveth me;
In this world it is not, I tell thee so.
I am sent for another way to go,
To give a straight account general
Before the highest *Jupiter* of all;

[1]Born.

And all my life I have had joy and pleasure in thee.
Therefore I pray thee go with me,
For, peradventure, thou mayst before God Almighty
My reckoning help to clean and purify;
For it is said ever among,
That money maketh all right that is wrong.

GOODS. Nay, *Everyman*, I sing another song,
I follow no man in such voyages;
For and I went with thee
Thou shouldst fare much the worse for me;
For because on me thou did set thy mind,
Thy reckoning I have made blotted and blind,
That thine account thou cannot make truly;
And that hast thou for the love of me.

EVERYMAN. That would grieve me full sore,
When I should come to that fearful answer.
Up, let us go thither together.

GOODS. Nay, not so, I am too brittle, I may not endure;
I will follow no man one foot, be ye sure.

EVERYMAN. Alas, I have thee loved, and had great pleasure
All my life-days on good and treasure.

GOODS. That is to thy damnation without lesing,
For my love is contrary to the love everlasting.
But if thou had me loved moderately during,
As, to the poor give part of me,
Then shouldst thou not in this dolor be,
Nor in this great sorrow and care.

EVERYMAN. Lo, now was I deceived or I was ware,
And all I may wyte[1] my spending of time.

GOODS. What, weenest thou that I am thine?

EVERYMAN. I had wend so.

GOODS. Nay, *Everyman*, I say no;
As for a while I was lent thee,
A season thou hast had me in prosperity;
My condition is man's soul to kill;
If I save one, a thousand I do spill;
Weenest thou that I will follow thee?
Nay, from this world, not verily.

EVERYMAN. I had wend otherwise.

GOODS. Therefore to thy soul *Good* is a thief;
For when thou art dead, this is my guise
Another to deceive in the same wise
As I have done thee, and all to his soul's reprief.

EVERYMAN. O false *Good*, cursed thou be!
Thou traitor to God, that hast deceived me,
And caught me in thy snare.

GOODS. Marry, thou brought thyself in care,
Whereof I am glad,
I must needs laugh, I cannot be sad.

EVERYMAN. Ah, *Good*, thou hast had long my hearty love;
I gave thee that which should be the Lord's above.
But wilt thou not go with me in deed?
I pray thee truth to say.

GOODS. No, so God me speed,
Therefore farewell, and have good day.

EVERYMAN. Oh, to whom shall I make my moan
For to go with me in that heavy journey?
First *Fellowship* said he would with me gone;
His words were very pleasant and gay,
But afterward he left me alone.
Then spake I to my kinsmen all in despair,
And also they gave me words fair,
They lacked no fair speaking,
But all forsake me in the ending.
Then went I to my *Goods* that I loved best,
In hope to have comfort, but there had I least;
For my *Goods* sharply did me tell
That he bringeth many into hell.
Then of myself I was ashamed,
And so I am worthy to be blamed;
Thus may I well myself hate.
Of whom shall I now counsel take?
I think that I shall never speed
Till that I go to my *Good-Deed*,
But alas, she is so weak,
That she can neither go nor speak;
Yet will I venture on her now.—
My *Good-Deeds*, where be you?

GOOD-DEEDS. Here I lie cold in the ground;
Thy sins hath me sore bound,
That I cannot stir.

EVERYMAN. O, *Good-Deeds*, I stand in fear;
I must you pray of counsel,
For help now should come right well.

GOOD-DEEDS. *Everyman*, I have understanding
That ye be summoned account to make
Before *Messias*, of Jerusalem King;
And you do by me[2] that journey with you will I take.

EVERYMAN. Therefore I come to you, my moan to make;
I pray you, that ye will go with me.

GOOD-DEEDS. I would full fain, but I cannot stand verily.

EVERYMAN. Why, is there anything on you fall?

GOOD-DEEDS. Yea, sir, I may thank you of all;
If ye had perfectly cheered me,
Your book of account now full ready had be.
Look, the books of your works and deeds eke;

[1]Blame.

[2]If you take my counsel.

Oh, see how they lie under the feet,
To your soul's heaviness.

EVERYMAN. Our Lord *Jesus*, help me!
For one letter here I cannot see.

GOOD-DEEDS. There is a blind reckoning in time of distress!

EVERYMAN. *Good-Deeds*, I pray you, help me in this need,
Or else I am for ever damned indeed;
Therefore help me to make reckoning
Before the redeemer of all things,
That king is, and was, and ever shall.

GOOD-DEEDS. *Everyman*, I am sorry of your fall,
And fain would I help you, and I were able.

EVERYMAN. *Good-Deeds*, your counsel I pray you give me.

GOOD-DEEDS. That shall I do verily;
Though that on my feet I may not go.
I have a sister, that shall with you also,
Called *Knowledge*, which shall with you abide,
To help you to make that dreadful reckoning.

KNOWLEDGE. *Everyman*, I will go with thee, and be thy guide,
In thy most need to go by thy side.

EVERYMAN. In good condition I am now in every thing,
And am wholly content with this good thing;
Thanked be God my Creator.

GOOD-DEEDS. And when he hath brought thee there,
Where thou shalt heal thee of thy smart,
Then go you with your reckoning and your *Good-Deeds* together
For to make you joyful at heart
Before the blessed Trinity.

EVERYMAN. My *Good-Deeds*, gramercy;
I am well content, certainly,
With your words sweet.

KNOWLEDGE. Now go we together lovingly,
To *Confession*, that cleansing river.

EVERYMAN. For joy I weep; I would we were there;
But, I pray you, give me cognition
Where dwelleth that holy man, *Confession*.

KNOWLEDGE. In the house of salvation:
We shall find him in that place.
That shall us comfort by God's grace.
Lo, this is *Confession*; kneel down and ask mercy,
For he is in good conceit with God Almighty.

EVERYMAN. O glorious fountain that all uncleanness doth clarify,
Wash from me the spots of vices unclean,
That on me no sin may be seen;
I come with *Knowledge* for my redemption,
Repent with hearty and full contrition;
For I am commanded a pilgrimage to take,
And great accounts before God to make.
Now, I pray you, *Shrift*, mother of salvation,
Help my good deeds for my piteous exclamation.

CONFESSION. I know your sorrow well, *Everyman;*
Because with *Knowledge* ye come to me,
I will you comfort as well as I can,
And a precious jewel I will give thee,
Called penance, wise voider of adversity;
Therewith shall your body chastised be,
With abstinence and perseverance in God's service:
Here shall you receive that scourge of me
Which is penance strong, that ye must endure,
To remember thy Savior was scourged for thee
With sharp scourges, and suffered it patiently;
So must thou, or thou scape that painful pilgrimage;
Knowledge, keep him in this voyage,
And by that time *Good-Deeds* will be with thee.
But in any wise, be sure of mercy,
For your time draweth fast, and ye will saved be;
Ask God mercy, and He will grant truly,
When with the scourge of penance man doth him bind,
The oil of forgiveness then shall he find.

EVERYMAN. Thanked be God for his gracious work!
For now I will my penance begin;
This hath rejoiced and lighted my heart,
Though the knots be painful and hard within.

KNOWLEDGE. *Everyman*, look your penance that ye fulfil,
What pain that ever it to you be,
And *Knowledge* shall give you counsel at will,
How your accounts ye shall make clearly.

EVERYMAN. O eternal God, O heavenly figure,
O way of rightwiseness, O goodly vision,
Which descended down in a virgin pure
Because he would *Everyman* redeem,
Which *Adam* forfeited by his disobedience;
O blessed Godhead, elect and high-divine,
Forgive my grievous offense;
Here I cry thee mercy in this presence.
O ghostly treasure, O ransomer and redeemer
Of all the world, hope and conductor,
Mirror of joy, and founder of mercy,
Which illumineth heaven and earth thereby,
Hear my clamorous complaint, though it late be;

Receive my prayers; unworthy in this heavy life,
Though I be, a sinner most abominable,
Yet let my name be written in *Moses'* table;
O *Mary*, pray to the Maker of all thing,
Me for to help at my ending,
And save me from the power of my enemy,
For *Death* assaileth me strongly;
And, Lady, that I may by means of thy prayer
Of your Son's glory to be partaker,
By the means of his passion I it crave,
I beseech you, help my soul to save.—
Knowledge, give me the scourge of penance;
My flesh therewith shall give a quittance:
I will now begin, if God give me grace.

KNOWLEDGE. *Everyman*, God give you time and space:
Thus I bequeath you in the hands of our Savior,
Thus may you make your reckoning sure.

EVERYMAN. In the name of the Holy Trinity,
My body sore punished shall be:
Take this body for the sin of the flesh;
Also thou delightest to go gay and fresh,
And in the way of damnation thou did me bring;
Therefore suffer now strokes and punishing.
Now of penance I will wade the water clear
To save me from purgatory, that sharp fire.

GOOD-DEEDS. I thank God, now I can walk and go;
And am delivered of my sickness and woe.
Therefore with *Everyman* I will go, and not spare;
His good works I will help him to declare.

KNOWLEDGE. Now, *Everyman*, be merry and glad;
Your *Good-Deeds* cometh now; ye may not be sad;
Now is your *Good-Deeds* whole and sound,
Going upright upon the ground.

EVERYMAN. My heart is light, and shall be evermore;
Now will I smite faster than I did before.

GOOD-DEEDS. *Everyman*, pilgrim, my special friend,
Blessed be thou without end;
For thee is prepared the eternal glory.
Ye have me made whole and sound,
Therefore I will bide by thee in every stound.[1]

EVERYMAN. Welcome, my *Good-Deeds;* now I hear thy voice,
I weep for very sweetness of love.

KNOWLEDGE. Be no more sad, but ever rejoice,
God seeth thy living in his throne above;
Put on this garment to thy behove,
Which is wet with your tears,
Or else before God you may it miss,
When you to your journey's end come shall.

EVERYMAN. Gentle *Knowledge*, what do you it call?

KNOWLEDGE. It is a garment of sorrow:
From pain it will you borrow;
Contrition it is,
That getteth forgiveness;
It pleaseth God passing well.

GOOD-DEEDS. *Everyman*, will you wear it for your heal?

EVERYMAN. Now blessed be *Jesu, Mary's* Son!
For now have I on true contrition.
And let us go now without tarrying;
Good-Deeds, have we clear our reckoning?

GOOD-DEEDS. Yea, indeed I have it here.

EVERYMAN. Then I trust we need not fear;
Now, friends, let us not part in twain.

KNOWLEDGE. Nay, *Everyman*, that will we not, certain.

GOOD-DEEDS. Yet must thou lead with thee
Three persons of great might.

EVERYMAN. Who should they be?

GOOD-DEEDS. *Discretion* and *Strength* they hight,[2]
And thy *Beauty* may not abide behind.

KNOWLEDGE. Also ye must call to mind
Your *Five-Wits* as for your counselors.

GOOD-DEEDS. You must have them ready at all hours.

EVERYMAN. How shall I get them hither?

KNOWLEDGE. You must call them all together,
And they will hear you incontinent.

EVERYMAN. My friends, come hither and be present
Discretion, *Strength*, my *Five-Wits*, and *Beauty*.

BEAUTY. Here at your will we be all ready.
What will ye that we should do?

GOOD-DEEDS. That ye would with *Everyman* go,
And help him in his pilgrimage,
Advise you, will ye with him or not in that voyage?

STRENGTH. We will bring him all thither,
To his help and comfort, ye may believe me.

DISCRETION. So will we go with him all together.

EVERYMAN. Almighty God, loved thou be,
I give thee laud that I have hither brought
Strength, *Discretion*, *Beauty*, and *Five-Wits;* lack I nought;
And my *Good-Deeds*, with *Knowledge* clear,
All be in my company at my will here;
I desire no more to my business.

STRENGTH. And I, *Strength*, will by you stand in distress,

[1] Season.

[2] Are called.

Though thou would in battle fight on the ground.
FIVE-WITS. And though it were through the world round,
We will not depart for sweet nor sour.
BEAUTY. No more will I unto death's hour,
Whatsoever thereof befall.
DISCRETION. *Everyman*, advise you first of all;
Go with a good advisement and deliberation;
We all give you virtuous monition
That all shall be well.
EVERYMAN. My friends, hearken what I will tell:
I pray God reward you in his heavenly sphere.
Now hearken, all that be here,
For I will make my testament
Here before you all present.
In alms half my good I will give with my hands twain
In the way of charity, with good intent,
And the other half still shall remain
In quiet to be returned there it ought to be.
This I do in despite of the fiend of hell
To go quite out of his peril
Ever after and this day.
KNOWLEDGE. *Everyman*, hearken what I say;
Go to priesthood, I you advise,
And receive of him in any wise
The holy sacrament and ointment together;
Then shortly see ye turn again hither;
We will all abide you here.
FIVE-WITS. Yea, *Everyman*, hie you that ye ready were,
There is no emperor, king, duke, nor baron,
That of God hath commission,
As hath the least priest in the world being;
For of the blessed sacraments pure and benign,
He beareth the keys and thereof hath the cure
For man's redemption, it is ever sure;
Which God for our soul's medicine
Gave us out of his heart with great pine;
Here in this transitory life, for thee and me
The blessed sacraments seven there be,
Baptism, confirmation, with priesthood good,
And the sacrament of God's precious flesh and blood,
Marriage, the holy extreme unction, and penance;
These seven be good to have in remembrance,
Gracious sacraments of high divinity.
EVERYMAN. Fain would I receive that holy body
And meekly to my ghostly father I will go.
FIVE-WITS. *Everyman*, that is the best that ye can do:
God will you to salvation bring,
For priesthood exceedeth all other thing;
To us Holy Scripture they do teach,
And converteth man from sin heaven to reach;
God hath to them more power given,
Than to any angel that is in heaven;
With five words he may consecrate
God's body in flesh and blood to make,
And handleth his maker between his hands;
The priest bindeth and unbindeth all bands,
Both in earth and in heaven;
Thou ministers all the sacraments seven;
Though we kissed thy feet thou were worthy;
Thou art surgeon that cureth sin deadly:
No remedy we find under God
But all only priesthood.
Everyman, God gave priests that dignity,
And setteth them in his stead among us to be;
Thus be they above angels in degree.
KNOWLEDGE. If priests be good it is so surely;
But when Jesus hanged on the cross with great smart
There he gave, out of his blessed heart,
The same sacrament in great torment:
He sold them not to us, that Lord Omnipotent.
Therefore Saint Peter the apostle doth say
That Jesu's curse hath all they
Which God their Savior do buy or sell,
Or they for any money do take or tell.
Sinful priests giveth the sinners example bad;
Their children sitteth by other men's fires, I have heard;
And some haunteth women's company,
With unclean life, as lusts of lechery:
These be with sin made blind.
FIVE-WITS. I trust to God no such may we find;
Therefore let us priesthood honor,
And follow their doctrine for our souls' succor;
We be their sheep, and they shepherds be
By whom we all be kept in surety.
Peace, for yonder I see *Everyman* come,
Which hath made true satisfaction.
GOOD-DEEDS. Methinketh it is he indeed.
EVERYMAN. Now Jesu be our alder speed.[1]
I have received the sacrament for my redemption,
And then mine extreme unction:
Blessed be all they that counseled me to take it!

[1]Help in all things.

And now, friends, let us go without longer respite;
I thank God that ye have tarried so long.
Now set each of you on this rod your hand,
And shortly follow me:
I go before, there I would be; God be our guide.
STRENGTH. *Everyman*, we will not from you go
Till ye have gone this voyage long.
DISCRETION. I, *Discretion*, will bide by you also.
KNOWLEDGE. And though this pilgrimage be never so strong,
I will never part you fro:
Everyman, I will be as sure by thee
As ever I did by Judas Maccabee.
EVERYMAN. Alas, I am so faint I may not stand,
My limbs under me do fold;
Friends, let us not turn again to this land,
Not for all the world's gold.
For into this cave must I creep
And turn to the earth and there to sleep.
BEAUTY. What, into this grave? alas!
EVERYMAN. Yea, there shall you consume more and less.
BEAUTY. And what, should I smother here?
EVERYMAN. Yea, by my faith, and never more appear.
In this world live no more we shall,
But in heaven before the highest Lord of all.
BEAUTY. I cross out all this; adieu by Saint *John;*
I take my tap in my lap and am gone.[1]
EVERYMAN. What, *Beauty*, whither will ye?
BEAUTY. Peace, I am deaf; I look not behind me,
Not and thou would give me all the gold in thy chest.
EVERYMAN. Alas, whereto may I trust?
Beauty goeth fast away hie;
She promised with me to live and die.
STRENGTH. *Everyman*, I will thee also forsake and deny;
Thy game liketh me not at all.
EVERYMAN. Why, then ye will forsake me all.
Sweet *Strength*, tarry a little space.
STRENGTH. Nay, sir, by the rood of grace
I will hie me from thee fast,
Though thou weep till thy heart brast.[2]
EVERYMAN. Ye would ever bide by me, ye said.
STRENGTH. Yea, I have you far enough conveyed;
Ye be old enough, I understand,
Your pilgrimage to take on hand;
I repent me that I hither came.
EVERYMAN. *Strength*, you to displease I am to blame;
Will you break promise that is debt?
STRENGTH. In faith, I care not;
Thou art but a fool to complain,
You spend your speech and waste your brain;
Go thrust thee into the ground.
EVERYMAN. I had wend surer I should you have found.
He that trusteth in his *Strength*
She him deceiveth at the length.
Both *Strength* and *Beauty* forsaketh me,
Yet they promised me fair and lovingly.
DISCRETION. *Everyman*, I will after *Strength* be gone,
As for me I will leave you alone.
EVERYMAN. Why, *Discretion*, will ye forsake me?
DISCRETION. Yea, in faith, I will go from thee,
For when *Strength* goeth before
I follow after evermore.
EVERYMAN. Yet, I pray thee, for the love of the Trinity,
Look in my grave once piteously.
DISCRETION. Nay, so nigh will I not come.
Farewell, every one!
EVERYMAN. O all thing faileth, save God alone;
Beauty, Strength, and *Discretion;*
For when *Death* bloweth his blast,
They all run from me full fast.
FIVE-WITS. *Everyman*, my leave now of thee I take;
I will follow the other, for here I thee forsake.
EVERYMAN. Alas! then may I wail and weep,
For I took you for my best friend.
FIVE-WITS. I will no longer thee keep;
Now farewell, and there an end.
EVERYMAN. O Jesu, help, all hath forsaken me!
GOOD-DEEDS. Nay, *Everyman*, I will bide with thee,
I will not forsake thee indeed;
Thou shalt find me a good friend at need.
EVERYMAN. Gramercy, *Good-Deeds;* now may I true friends see;
They have forsaken me every one;
I loved them better than my *Good-Deeds* alone.
Knowledge, will ye forsake me also?
KNOWLEDGE. Yea, *Everyman*, when ye to death do go:
But not yet for no manner of danger.
EVERYMAN. Gramercy, *Knowledge*, with all my heart,

[1]A proverbial expression used to describe a hasty departure. In the beginning it was used literally of a woman taking her tap—a quantity of flax for spinning—and distaff in her lap or apron, in going to or from a friend's house.

[2]Burst.

KNOWLEDGE. Nay, yet I will not from hence depart,
Till I see where ye shall be come.
EVERYMAN. Methinketh, alas, that I must be gone,
To make my reckoning and my debts pay,
For I see my time is nigh spent away.
Take example, all ye that this do hear or see,
How they that I loved best do forsake me,
Except my *Good-Deeds* that bideth truly.
GOOD-DEEDS. All earthly things is but vanity:
Beauty, *Strength*, and *Discretion*, do man forsake,
Foolish friends and kinsmen, that fair spake,
All fleeth save *Good-Deeds*, and that am I.
EVERYMAN. Have mercy on me, God most mighty;
And stand by me, thou Mother and Maid, holy *Mary*.
GOOD-DEEDS. Fear not, I will speak for thee.
EVERYMAN. Here I cry God mercy.
GOOD-DEEDS. Short our end, and minish our pain;
Let us go and never come again.
EVERYMAN. Into thy hands, Lord, my soul I commend;
Receive it, Lord, that it be not lost;
As thou me boughtest, so me defend,
And save me from the fiend's boast,
That I may appear with that blessed host
That shall be saved at the day of doom.
In manus tuas—of might's most
For ever—*commendo spiritum meum*.[1]
KNOWLEDGE. Now hath he suffered that we all shall endure;
The *Good-Deeds* shall make all sure.
Now hath he made ending;
Methinketh that I hear angels sing
And make great joy and melody,
Where *Everyman's* soul received shall be.
ANGEL. Come, excellent elect spouse to Jesu:
Hereabove thou shalt go
Because of thy singular virtue:
Now the soul is taken the body fro;
Thy reckoning is crystal-clear.
Now shalt thou into the heavenly sphere,
Unto the which all ye shall come
That liveth well before the day of doom.
DOCTOR. This moral men may have in mind;
Ye hearers, take it of worth, old and young,
And forsake pride, for he deceiveth you in the end,
And remember *Beauty*, *Five-Wits*, *Strength*, and *Discretion*,
They all at the last do *Everyman* forsake,
Save his *Good-Deeds*, there doth he take.
But beware, and they be small
Before God, he hath no help at all.
None excuse may be there for *Everyman;*
Alas, how shall he do then?
For after death amends may no man make,
For then mercy and pity do him forsake.
If his reckoning be not clear when he do come,
God will say—*ite maledicti in ignem æternum*.[2]
And he that hath his account whole and sound,
High in heaven he shall be crowned;
Unto which place God bring us all thither
That we may live body and soul together.
Thereto help the Trinity,
Amen, say ye, for saint *charity*.

[1]To thy hands I commend my soul.

[2]Hence, accursed one, into eternal fire.

SIR THOMAS MALORY (c. 1400–1471)

Very little is known about the life of Malory. The year generally given as that of his birth is approximate only. He lived at Newbold Revell, in Warwickshire. He served in the French wars with Richard Beauchamp, Earl of Warwick, a renowned representative of the chivalric ideal. Malory was also conspicuous on the Lancastrian side in the wars of the Roses. In 1445, he was a member of Parliament for Warwickshire. He was "a gentleman of an ancient house, and a soldier"—a man whose career, as far as we know anything about it, seems eminently appropriate to the compiler of the *Morte d'Arthur.* This book Malory finished in 1469, and it was first printed in 1485, by William Caxton (c. 1421–1491), the earliest English printer. Caxton issued the first book printed in English from his press at Bruges about 1475—the *Recuyell of the Histories of Troy.* In 1476 he returned to England, set up a press near Westminster, and in 1477 printed there the *Dictes and Seyings of the Philosophers.* Caxton deserves a place in the history of English literature not only because he was the earliest English printer, but also because he himself translated many of the books he printed (for example, the *Recuyell of the Histories of Troy* just mentioned and *The Golden Legend*) and carefully edited the books not written by himself and supplied them with prefaces.

Caxton tells us in his Preface printed below that Malory took the *Morte d'Arthur* "out of certain books of French, and reduced it into English." This is so; Malory translated from a number of French romances, whose volume is said to be about ten times as great as that of the *Morte d'Arthur* itself. These French romances told no connected story; on the contrary, they were frequently inconsistent with each other, and this, together with their number, probably accounts sufficiently for the incongruities in Malory's book. Malory seems to have chosen the stories that pleased him best, with the general design of giving an account of Arthur's life from birth to death. This is done only in the loosest fashion, but it is a mark of originality on Malory's part, inasmuch as Arthur is thus given an importance which he does not have in the French romances.

LE MORTE D'ARTHUR

CAXTON'S PREFACE

After that I had accomplished and finished divers histories, as well of contemplation as of other historical and worldly acts of great conquerors and princes, and also certain books of ensamples and doctrine, many noble and divers gentlemen of this realm of England came and demanded me, many and ofttimes, wherefore that I have not do made[1] and imprinted the noble history of the Sangreal, and of the most renowned Christian king, first and chief of the three best Christian and worthy, King Arthur, which ought most to be remembered among us English men tofore all other Christian kings. For it is notoriously known through the universal world that there be nine worthy and the best that ever were. That is to wit three paynims, three Jews, and three Christian men. As for the paynims they were tofore the Incarnation of Christ, which were named, the first Hector of Troy, of whom the history is come both in ballad and in prose; the second Alexander the Great; and the third Julius Cæsar, Emperor of Rome, of whom the histories be well-known and had. And as for the three Jews which also were tofore the Incarnation of our Lord, of whom the first was Duke Joshua which brought the children of Israel into the land of behest; the second David, King of Jerusalem; and the third Judas Maccabæus: of these three the Bible rehearseth all their noble histories and acts. And sith the said Incarnation have been three noble Christian men stalled[2] and admitted through the universal world into the number of the nine best and worthy, of whom was first the noble Arthur, whose noble acts I purpose to write in this present book here following. The second was Charlemagne or Charles the Great, of whom the history is had in many places both in French and English; and the third and last was Godfrey of Bouillon, of whose acts and life I made a book unto the excellent prince and king of

[1]Had made.

[2]Installed.

noble memory, King Edward the Fourth. The said noble gentlemen instantly required me to imprint the history of the said noble king and conqueror, King Arthur, and of his knights, with the history of the Sangreal, and of the death and ending of the said Arthur; affirming that I ought rather to imprint his acts and noble feats, than of Godfrey of Bouillon, or any of the other eight, considering that he was a man born within this realm, and king and emperor of the same; and that there be in French divers and many noble volumes of his acts, and also of his knights. To whom I answered, that divers men hold opinion that there was no such Arthur, and that all such books as be made of him be but feigned and fables, by cause that some chronicles make of him no mention nor remember him no thing, nor of his knights. Whereto they answered and one in special said, that in him that should say or think that there was never such a king called Arthur, might well be credited great folly and blindness; for he said that there were many evidences of the contrary: first ye may see his sepulture in the Monastery of Glastonbury. And also in Polichronicon,[1] in the fifth book the sixth chapter, and in the seventh book the twenty-third chapter, where his body was buried and after found and translated into the said monastery. Ye shall see also in the history of Bochas,[2] in his book *De Casu Principum*, part of his noble acts, and also of his fall. Also Galfridus[3] in his British book recounteth his life; and in divers places of England many remembrances be yet of him and shall remain perpetually, and also of his knights. First in the Abbey of Westminster, at Saint Edward's shrine, remaineth the print of his seal in red wax closed in beryl, in which is written *Patricius Arthurus, Britannie, Gallie, Germanie, Dacie, Imperator.*[4] Item in the castle of Dover ye may see Gawaine's skull and Craddock's mantle: at Winchester the Round Table: at other places Launcelot's sword and many other things. Then all these things considered, there can no man reasonably gainsay but there was a king of this land named Arthur. For in all places, Christian and heathen, he is reputed and taken for one of the nine worthy, and the first of the three Christian men. And also he is more spoken of beyond the sea, more books made of his noble acts than there be in England, as well in Dutch, Italian, Spanish, and Greek, as in French. And yet of record remain in witness of him in Wales, in the town of Camelot,[5] the great stones and marvelous works of iron, lying under the ground, and royal vaults, which divers now living hath seen. Wherefore it is a marvel why he is no more renowned in his own country, save only it accordeth to the Word of God, which saith that no man is accept for a prophet in his own country. Then all these things foresaid alleged, I could not well deny but that there was such a noble king named Arthur, and reputed one of the nine worthy, and first and chief of the Christian men; and many noble volumes be made of him and of his noble knights in French, which I have seen and read beyond the sea, which be not had in our maternal tongue, but in Welsh be many and also in French, and some in English, but no where nigh all. Wherefore, such as have late been drawn out briefly into English I have after the simple conning that God hath sent to me, under the favor and correction of all noble lords and gentlemen, emprised[6] to imprint a book of the noble histories of the said King Arthur, and of certain of his knights, after a copy unto me delivered, which copy Sir Thomas Malory did take out of certain books of French, and reduced it into English. And I, according to my copy, have done set it in imprint, to the intent that noble men may see and learn the noble acts of chivalry, the gentle and virtuous deeds that some knights used in those days, by which they came to honor; and how they that were vicious were punished and oft put to shame and rebuke; humbly beseeching all noble lords and ladies, with all other estates, of what estate or degree they be of, that shall see and read in this said book and work that they take the good and honest acts in their remembrance, and to follow the same. Wherein they shall find many joyous and pleasant histories, and noble and renowned acts of humanity, gentleness, and

[1]A history of the world, written in Latin by Ranulph Higden (died c. 1364).

[2]Boccaccio. The book (*On the Fall of Princes*) tells of the misfortunes of illustrious men.

[3]Geoffrey of Monmouth, whose *History of the Kings of Britain* (written in Latin, probably about 1140) contains much fabulous matter.

[4]Noble Arthur, Emperor of Britain, Gaul, Germany, and Dacia.

[5]A legendary town, where Arthur held his court.

[6]Undertaken.

chivalries. For herein may be seen noble chivalry, courtesy, humanity, friendliness, hardiness, love, friendship, cowardice, murder, hate, virtue, and sin. Do after the good and leave the evil, and it shall bring you to good fame and renown. And for to pass the time this book shall be pleasant to read in; but for to give faith and believe that all is true that is contained herein, ye be at your liberty; but all is written for our doctrine, and for to beware that we fall not to vice nor sin; but to exercise and follow virtue; by which we may come and attain to good fame and renown in this life, and after this short and transitory life, to come unto everlasting bliss in heaven, the which he grant us that reigneth in heaven, the blessed Trinity. Amen.

Then to proceed forth in this said book, which I direct unto all noble princes, lords and ladies, gentlemen or gentlewomen, that desire to read or hear read of the noble and joyous history of the great conqueror and excellent king, King Arthur, sometime king of this noble realm, then called Britain. I, William Caxton, simple person, present this book following, which I have emprised to imprint; and treateth of the noble acts, feats of arms of chivalry, prowess, hardiness, humanity, love, courtesy and very gentleness, with many wonderful histories and adventures. And for to understand briefly the content of this volume, I have divided it into twenty-one books, and every book chaptered as hereafter shall by God's grace follow. The first book shall treat how Uther Pendragon gat the noble conqueror King Arthur, and containeth twenty-eight chapters. The second book treateth of Balin the noble knight, and containeth nineteen chapters. The third book treateth of the marriage of King Arthur to Queen Guenever, with other matters, and containeth fifteen chapters. The fourth book, how Merlin was assotted,[1] and of war made to King Arthur, and containeth twenty-nine chapters. The fifth book treateth of the conquest of Lucius the emperor, and containeth twelve chapters. The sixth book treateth of Sir Launcelot and Sir Lionel, and marvelous adventures, and containeth eighteen chapters. The seventh book treateth of a noble knight called Sir Gareth, and named by Sir Kay, Beaumains, and containeth thirty-six chapters. The eighth book treateth of the birth of Sir Tristram the noble knight, and of his acts, and containeth forty-one chapters. The ninth book treateth of a knight named by Sir Kay, La Cote Male Taile, and also of Sir Tristram, and containeth forty-four chapters. The tenth book treateth of Sir Tristram and other marvelous adventures, and containeth eighty-eight chapters. The eleventh book treateth of Sir Launcelot and Sir Galahad, and containeth fourteen chapters. The twelfth book treateth of Sir Launcelot and his madness, and containeth fourteen chapters. The thirteenth book treateth how Galahad came first to King Arthur's court, and the quest how the Sangreal was begun, and containeth twenty chapters. The fourteenth book treateth of the quest of the Sangreal, and containeth ten chapters. The fifteenth book treateth of Sir Launcelot, and containeth six chapters. The sixteenth book treateth of Sir Bors and Sir Lionel his brother, and containeth seventeen chapters. The seventeenth book treateth of the Sangreal, and containeth twenty-three chapters. The eighteenth book treateth of Sir Launcelot and the queen, and containeth twenty-five chapters. The nineteenth book treateth of Queen Guenever and Launcelot, and containeth thirteen chapters. The twentieth book treateth of the piteous death of Arthur, and containeth twenty-two chapters. The twenty-first book treateth of his last departing, and how Sir Launcelot came to revenge his death, and containeth thirteen chapters. The sum is twenty-one books, which contain the sum of five hundred and seven chapters, as more plainly shall follow hereafter.

BOOK XXI

CHAPTER I

HOW SIR MORDRED PRESUMED AND TOOK ON HIM TO BE KING OF ENGLAND, AND WOULD HAVE MARRIED THE QUEEN, HIS UNCLE'S WIFE

As Sir Mordred was ruler of all England, he did do make[2] letters as though that they came from beyond the sea, and the letters specified that King Arthur was slain in battle

[1]Besotted.

[2]Have made.

with Sir Launcelot. Wherefore Sir Mordred made a parliament, and called the lords together, and there he made them to choose him king; and so was he crowned at Canterbury, and held a feast there fifteen days; and afterward he drew him unto Winchester, and there he took the Queen Guenever, and said plainly that he would wed her which was his uncle's wife and his father's wife. And so he made ready for the feast, and a day prefixed that they should be wedded; wherefore Queen Guenever was passing heavy. But she durst not discover her heart, but spake fair, and agreed to Sir Mordred's will. Then she desired of Sir Mordred for to go to London, to buy all manner of things that longed unto the wedding. And by cause of her fair speech Sir Mordred trusted her well enough, and gave her leave to go. And so when she came to London she took the Tower of London, and suddenly in all haste possible she stuffed it with all manner of victual, and well garnished it with men, and so kept it. Then when Sir Mordred wist[1] and understood how he was beguiled, he was passing wroth out of measure. And a short tale for to make, he went and laid a mighty siege about the Tower of London, and made many great assaults thereat, and threw many great engines unto them, and shot great guns. But all might not prevail[2] Sir Mordred, for Queen Guenever would never for fair speech nor for foul, would never trust to come in his hands again. Then came the Bishop of Canterbury, the which was a noble clerk and an holy man, and thus he said to Sir Mordred: Sir, what will ye do? will ye first displease God and sithen[3] shame yourself and all knighthood? Is not King Arthur your uncle, no farther but your mother's brother, and on her himself King Arthur begat you upon his own sister, therefore how may you wed your father's wife? Sir, said the noble clerk, leave this opinion or I shall curse you with book and bell and candle. Do thou thy worst, said Sir Mordred, wit thou well I shall defy thee. Sir, said the Bishop, and wit you well I shall not fear me to do that me ought to do. Also where ye noise where my lord Arthur is slain, and that is not so, and therefore ye will make a foul work in this land. Peace, thou false priest, said Sir Mordred, for an thou chafe me any more I shall make strike off thy head. So the Bishop departed and did the cursing in the most orgulist[4] wise that might be done, and then Sir Mordred sought the Bishop of Canterbury, for to have slain him. Then the Bishop fled, and took part of his goods with him, and went nigh unto Glastonbury; and there he was as priest hermit in a chapel, and lived in poverty and in holy prayers, for well he understood that mischievous war was at hand. Then Sir Mordred sought on Queen Guenever by letters and sondes,[5] and by fair means and foul means, for to have her to come out of the Tower of London; but all this availed not, for she answered him shortly, openly and privily, that she had lever slay herself than to be married with him. Then came word to Sir Mordred that King Arthur had araised the siege for Sir Launcelot, and he was coming homeward with a great host, to be avenged upon Sir Mordred; wherefore Sir Mordred made write[6] writs to all the barony of this land, and much people drew to him. For then was the common voice among them that with Arthur was none other life but war and strife, and with Sir Mordred was great joy and bliss. Thus was Sir Arthur depraved,[7] and evil said of. And many there were that King Arthur had made up of nought, and given them lands, might not then say him a good word. Lo ye all Englishmen, see ye not what a mischief here was! for he that was the most king and knight of the world, and most loved the fellowship of noble knights, and by him they were all upholden, now might not these Englishmen hold them content with him. Lo thus was the old custom and usage of this land; and also men say that we of this land have not yet lost nor forgotten that custom and usage. Alas, this is a great default of us Englishmen, for there may no thing please us no term. And so fared the people at that time, they were better pleased with Sir Mordred than they were with King Arthur; and much people drew unto Sir Mordred, and said they would abide with him for better and for worse. And so Sir Mordred drew with a great host to Dover, for there he heard say that Sir Arthur would arrive, and so he thought to beat his own father from his lands; and the most part of all England held with Sir Mordred, the people were so new fangle.

[1]Heard. [2]Avail. [3]Afterwards.

[4]Insolent. [5]Messages. [6]Had written. [7]Slandered.

CHAPTER II

HOW AFTER THAT KING ARTHUR HAD TIDINGS, HE RETURNED AND CAME TO DOVER, WHERE SIR MORDRED MET HIM TO LET[1] HIS LANDING; AND OF THE DEATH OF SIR GAWAINE

AND so as Sir Mordred was at Dover with his host, there came King Arthur with a great navy of ships, and galleys, and carracks. And there was Sir Mordred ready awaiting upon his landing, to let[1] his own father to land upon the land that he was king over. Then there was launching of great boats and small, and full of noble men of arms; and there was much slaughter of gentle knights, and many a full bold baron was laid full low, on both parties. But King Arthur was so courageous that there might no manner of knights let him to land, and his knights fiercely followed him; and so they landed maugre[2] Sir Mordred and all his power, and put Sir Mordred aback, that he fled and all his people. So when this battle was done, King Arthur let bury his people that were dead. And then was noble Sir Gawaine found in a great boat, lying more than half dead. When Sir Arthur wist that Sir Gawaine was laid so low, he went unto him; and there the king made sorrow out of measure, and took Sir Gawaine in his arms, and thrice he there swooned. And then when he awaked, he said: Alas, Sir Gawaine, my sister's son, here now thou liest, the man in the world that I loved most; and now is my joy gone, for now, my nephew Sir Gawaine, I will discover me unto your person: in Sir Launcelot and you I most had my joy, and mine affiance,[3] and now have I lost my joy of you both; wherefore all mine earthly joy is gone from me. Mine uncle King Arthur, said Sir Gawaine, wit you well my death day is come, and all is through mine own hastiness and willfulness; for I am smitten upon the old wound the which Sir Launcelot gave me, on the which I feel well I must die; and had Sir Launcelot been with you as he was, this unhappy war had never begun; and of all this am I causer, for Sir Launcelot and his blood, through their prowess, held all your cankered enemies in subjection and danger. And now, said Sir Gawaine, ye shall miss Sir Launcelot. But alas, I would not accord with him, and therefore, said Sir Gawaine, I pray you, fair uncle, that I may have paper, pen, and ink, that I may write to Sir Launcelot a cedle[4] with mine own hands. And then when paper and ink was brought, then Gawaine was set up weakly by King Arthur, for he was shriven a little tofore; and then he wrote thus, as the French book maketh mention: Unto Sir Launcelot, flower of all noble knights that ever I heard of or saw by my days, I, Sir Gawaine, King Lot's son of Orkney, sister's son unto the noble King Arthur, send thee greeting, and let thee have knowledge that the tenth day of May I was smitten upon the old wound that thou gavest me afore the city of Benwick, and through the same wound that thou gavest me I am come to my death day. And I will that all the world wit, that I, Sir Gawaine, knight of the Table Round, sought my death, and not through thy deserving, but it was mine own seeking; wherefore I beseech thee, Sir Launcelot, to return again unto this realm, and see my tomb, and pray some prayer more or less for my soul. And this same day that I wrote this cedle, I was hurt to the death in the same wound, the which I had of thy hand, Sir Launcelot; for of a more nobler man might I not be slain. Also Sir Launcelot, for all the love that ever was betwixt us, make no tarrying, but come over the sea in all haste, that thou mayst with thy noble knights rescue that noble king that made thee knight, that is my lord Arthur; for he is full straitly bestad[5] with a false traitor, that is my half-brother, Sir Mordred; and he hath let crown him king, and would have wedded my lady Queen Guenever, and so had he done had she not put herself in the Tower of London. And so the tenth day of May last past, my lord Arthur and we all landed upon them at Dover; and there we put that false traitor, Sir Mordred, to flight, and there it misfortuned me to be stricken upon thy stroke. And at the date of this letter was written, but two hours and a half afore my death, written with mine own hand, and so subscribed with part of my heart's blood. And I require thee, most famous knight of the world, that thou wilt see my tomb. And then Sir Gawaine wept, and King Arthur wept; and then they swooned both. And when they awaked both, the king made Sir Gawaine

[1] Prevent. [2] Despite. [3] Trust.

[4] Note. [5] Hard pressed.

to receive his Savior. And then Sir Gawaine prayed the king for to send for Sir Launcelot, and to cherish him above all other knights. And so at the hour of noon Sir Gawaine yielded up the spirit; and then the king let inter him in a chapel within Dover Castle; and there yet all men may see the skull of him, and the same wound is seen that Sir Launcelot gave him in battle. Then was it told the king that Sir Mordred had pyghte a new field[1] upon Barham Down. And upon the morn the king rode thither to him, and there was a great battle betwixt them, and much people was slain on both parties; but at the last Sir Arthur's party stood best, and Sir Mordred and his party fled into Canterbury.

CHAPTER III

HOW AFTER, SIR GAWAINE'S GHOST APPEARED TO KING ARTHUR, AND WARNED HIM THAT HE SHOULD NOT FIGHT THAT DAY

AND then the king let search all the towns for his knights that were slain, and interred them; and salved them with soft salves that so sore were wounded. Then much people drew unto King Arthur. And then they said that Sir Mordred warred upon King Arthur with wrong. And then King Arthur drew him with his host down by the seaside westward toward Salisbury; and there was a day assigned betwixt King Arthur and Sir Mordred, that they should meet upon a down beside Salisbury, and not far from the seaside; and this day was assigned on a Monday after Trinity Sunday, whereof King Arthur was passing glad, that he might be avenged upon Sir Mordred. Then Sir Mordred araised much people about London, for they of Kent, Southsex, and Surrey, Estsex, and of Southfolk, and of Northfolk, held the most part with Sir Mordred; and many a full noble knight drew unto Sir Mordred and to the king: but they that loved Sir Launcelot drew unto Sir Mordred. So upon Trinity Sunday at night, King Arthur dreamed a wonderful dream, and that was this: that him seemed he sat upon a chaflet[2] in a chair, and the chair was fast to a wheel, and thereupon sat King Arthur in the richest cloth of gold that might be made; and the king thought there was under him, far from him, an hideous deep black water, and therein were all manner of serpents, and worms, and wild beasts foul and horrible; and suddenly the king thought the wheel turned up so down, and he fell among the serpents, and every beast took him by a limb; and then the king cried as he lay in his bed and slept: Help. And then knights, squires, and yeomen awaked the king; and then he was so amazed that he wist not where he was; and then he fell on slumbering again, not sleeping nor thoroughly waking. So the king seemed verily that there came Sir Gawaine unto him with a number of fair ladies with him. And when King Arthur saw him, then he said: Welcome, my sister's son; I weened thou hadst been dead, and now I see thee on live, much am I beholding unto almighty Jesu. O fair nephew and my sister's son, what be these ladies that hither be come with you? Sir, said Sir Gawaine, all these be ladies for whom I have foughten when I was man living, and all these are those that I did battle for in righteous quarrel; and God hath given them that grace at their great prayer, by cause I did battle for them, that they should bring me hither unto you: thus much hath God given me leave, for to warn you of your death; for an ye fight as tomorn with Sir Mordred, as ye both have assigned, doubt ye not ye must be slain, and the most part of your people on both parties. And for the great grace and goodness that almighty Jesu hath unto you, and for pity of you, and many more other good men there shall be slain, God hath sent me to you of his special grace, to give you warning that in no wise ye do battle as tomorn, but that ye take a treaty for a month day; and proffer you largely,[3] so as tomorn to be put in a delay. For within a month shall come Sir Launcelot with all his noble knights, and rescue you worshipfully, and slay Sir Mordred, and all that ever will hold with him. Then Sir Gawaine and all the ladies vanished. And anon the king called upon his knights, squires, and yeomen, and charged them wightly[4] to fetch his noble lords and wise bishops unto him. And when they were come, the king told them his avision, what Sir Gawaine had told him, and warned him that if he fought on the morn he should be slain. Then the king commanded Sir Lucan

[1] Taken up a new position. [2] Platform.

[3] Make generous proposals. [4] Quickly.

the Butler, and his brother Sir Bedivere, with two bishops with them, and charged them in any wise, an they might, Take a treaty for a month day with Sir Mordred, and spare not, proffer him lands and goods as much as ye think best. So then they departed, and came to Sir Mordred, where he had a grim host of an hundred thousand men. And there they entreated Sir Mordred long time; and at the last Sir Mordred was agreed for to have Cornwall and Kent, by Arthur's days: after, all England, after the days of King Arthur.

CHAPTER IV

HOW BY MISADVENTURE OF AN ADDER THE BATTLE BEGAN, WHERE MORDRED WAS SLAIN, AND ARTHUR HURT TO THE DEATH

THEN were they condescended that King Arthur and Sir Mordred should meet betwixt both their hosts, and every each of them should bring fourteen persons; and they came with this word unto Arthur. Then said he: I am glad that this is done: and so he went into the field. And when Arthur should depart, he warned all his host that an they see any sword drawn: Look ye come on fiercely, and slay that traitor, Sir Mordred, for I in no wise trust him. In likewise Sir Mordred warned his host that: An ye see any sword drawn, look that ye come on fiercely, and so slay all that ever before you standeth; for in no wise I will not trust for this treaty, for I know well my father will be avenged on me. And so they met as their appointment was, and so they were agreed and accorded thoroughly; and wine was fetched, and they drank. Right soon came an adder out of a little heath bush, and it stung a knight on the foot. And when the knight felt him stung, he looked down and saw the adder, and then he drew his sword to slay the adder, and thought of none other harm. And when the host on both parties saw that sword drawn, then they blew beamous,[1] trumpets, and horns, and shouted grimly. And so both hosts dressed them together. And King Arthur took his horse, and said: Alas, this unhappy day! and so rode to his party. And Sir Mordred in likewise. And never was there seen a more dolefuller battle in no Christian land; for there was but rushing and riding, foining[2] and striking, and many a grim word was there spoken either to other, and many a deadly stroke. But ever King Arthur rode throughout the battle of Sir Mordred many times, and did full nobly as a noble king should, and at all times he fainted never; and Sir Mordred that day put him in devoir,[3] and in great peril. And thus they fought all the long day, and never stinted till the noble knights were laid to the cold earth; and ever they fought still till it was near night, and by that time was there an hundred thousand laid dead upon the down. Then was Arthur wood[4] wroth out of measure, when he saw his people so slain from him. Then the king looked about him, and then was he ware, of all his host and of all his good knights, were left no more on live but two knights; that one was Sir Lucan the Butler, and his brother Sir Bedivere, and they were full sore wounded. Jesu mercy, said the king, where are all my noble knights become? Alas that ever I should see this doleful day, for now, said Arthur, I am come to mine end. But would to God that I wist where were that traitor Sir Mordred, that hath caused all this mischief. Then was King Arthur ware where Sir Mordred leaned upon his sword among a great heap of dead men. Now give me my spear, said Arthur unto Sir Lucan, for yonder I have espied the traitor that all this woe hath wrought. Sir, let him be, said Sir Lucan, for he is unhappy; and if ye pass this unhappy day ye shall be right well revenged upon him. Good lord, remember ye of your night's dream, and what the spirit of Sir Gawaine told you this night, yet God of his great goodness hath preserved you hitherto. Therefore for God's sake, my lord, leave off by this, for blessed be God ye have won the field, for here we be three on live, and with Sir Mordred is none on live; and if ye leave off now this wicked day of destiny is past. Tide me death, betide me life, saith the king, now I see him yonder alone he shall never escape mine hands, for at a better avail shall I never have him. God speed you well, said Sir Bedivere. Then the king gat his spear in both his hands, and ran toward Sir Mordred, crying: Traitor, now is thy death day come. And when Sir Mordred heard Sir Arthur, he ran until him with his sword drawn in his hand. And there King

[1] Horns.

[2] Thrusting. [3] Duty. [4] Mad.

Arthur smote Sir Mordred under the shield, with a foin of his spear, throughout the body, more than a fathom. And when Sir Mordred felt that he had his death wound he thrust himself with the might that he had up to the bur of King Arthur's spear. And right so he smote his father Arthur, with his sword holden in both his hands, on the side of the head, that the sword pierced the helmet and the brain pan, and therewithal Sir Mordred fell stark dead to the earth; and the noble Arthur fell in a swoon to the earth, and there he swooned ofttimes. And Sir Lucan the Butler and Sir Bedivere ofttimes heaved him up. And so weakly they led him betwixt them both, to a little chapel not far from the seaside. And when the king was there he thought him well eased. Then heard they people cry in the field. Now go thou, Sir Lucan, said the king, and do me to wit what betokens that noise in the field. So Sir Lucan departed, for he was grievously wounded in many places. And so as he yede,[1] he saw and hearkened by the moonlight, how that pillers,[2] and robbers were come into the field, to pill and to rob many a full noble knight of brooches, and beads, of many a good ring, and of many a rich jewel; and who that were not dead all out, there they slew them for their harness and their riches. When Sir Lucan understood this work, he came to the king as soon as he might, and told him all what he had heard and seen. Therefore by my rede,[3] said Sir Lucan, it is best that we bring you to some town. I would it were so, said the king.

CHAPTER V

HOW KING ARTHUR COMMANDED TO CAST HIS SWORD EXCALIBUR INTO THE WATER, AND HOW HE WAS DELIVERED TO LADIES IN A BARGE

But I may not stand, mine head works so. Ah Sir Launcelot, said King Arthur, this day have I sore missed thee; alas, that ever I was against thee, for now have I my death, whereof Sir Gawaine me warned in my dream. Then Sir Lucan took up the king the one part, and Sir Bedivere the other part, and in the lifting the king swooned; and Sir Lucan fell in a swoon with the lift, that the part of his guts fell out of his body, and therewith the noble knight's heart brast.[4] And when the king awoke, he beheld Sir Lucan, how he lay foaming at the mouth, and part of his guts lay at his feet. Alas, said the king, this is to me a full heavy sight, to see this noble duke so die for my sake, for he would have holpen me, that had more need of help than I. Alas, he would not complain him, his heart was so set to help me: now Jesu have mercy upon his soul! Then Sir Bedivere wept for the death of his brother. Leave this mourning and weeping, said the king, for all this will not avail me, for wit thou well an I might live myself, the death of Sir Lucan would grieve me evermore; but my time hieth fast, said the king. Therefore, said Arthur unto Sir Bedivere, take thou Excalibur, my good sword, and go with it to yonder water side, and when thou comest there I charge thee throw my sword in that water, and come again and tell me what thou there seest. My lord, said Bedivere, your commandment shall be done, and lightly[5] bring you word again. So Sir Bedivere departed, and by the way he beheld that noble sword, that the pommel and the haft was all of precious stones; and then he said to himself: If I throw this rich sword in the water, thereof shall never come good, but harm and loss. And then Sir Bedivere hid Excalibur under a tree. And so, as soon as he might, he came again unto the king, and said he had been at the water, and had thrown the sword in the water. What saw thou there? said the king. Sir, he said, I saw nothing but waves and winds. That is untruly said of thee, said the king, therefore go thou lightly again, and do my commandment; as thou art to me lief and dear, spare not, but throw it in. Then Sir Bedivere returned again, and took the sword in his hand; and then him thought sin and shame to throw away that noble sword, and so efte[6] he hid the sword, and returned again, and told to the king that he had been at the water, and done his commandment. What saw thou there? said the king. Sir, he said, I saw nothing but the waters wappe[7] and waves wanne.[8] Ah, traitor untrue, said King Arthur, now hast thou betrayed me twice. Who would

[1]Went. [2]Pillagers. [3]Counsel.

[4]Burst. [5]Swiftly. [6]Afterwards. [7]Ripple. [8]Grow dark.

have weened that, thou hast been to me so lief and dear? and thou art named a noble knight, and would betray me for the richness of the sword. But now go again lightly, for thy long tarrying putteth me in great jeopardy of my life, for I have taken cold. And but if thou do now as I bid thee, if ever I may see thee, I shall slay thee with mine own hands; for thou wouldst for my rich sword see me dead. Then Sir Bedivere departed, and went to the sword, and lightly took it up, and went to the water side; and there he bound the girdle about the hilts, and then he threw the sword as far into the water as he might; and there came an arm and an hand above the water and met it, and caught it, and so shook it thrice and brandished, and then vanished away the hand with the sword in the water. So Sir Bedivere came again to the king, and told him what he saw. Alas, said the king, help me hence, for I dread me I have tarried over long. Then Sir Bedivere took the king upon his back, and so went with him to that water side. And when they were at the water side, even fast by the bank hoved a little barge with many fair ladies in it, and among them all was a queen, and all they had black hoods, and all they wept and shrieked when they saw King Arthur. Now put me into the barge, said the king. And so he did softly; and there received him three queens with great mourning; and so they set them down, and in one of their laps King Arthur laid his head. And then that queen said: Ah, dear brother, why have ye tarried so long from me? alas, this wound on your head hath caught over-much cold. And so then they rowed from the land, and Sir Bedivere beheld all those ladies go from him. Then Sir Bedivere cried: Ah my lord Arthur, what shall become of me, now ye go from me and leave me here alone among mine enemies? Comfort thyself, said the king, and do as well as thou mayest, for in me is no trust for to trust in; for I will into the vale of Avilion[1] to heal me of my grievous wound: and if thou hear never more of me, pray for my soul. But ever the queens and ladies wept and shrieked, that it was pity to hear. And as soon as Sir Bedivere had lost the sight of the barge, he wept and wailed, and so took the forest; and so he went all that night, and in the morning he was ware betwixt two holts hoar, of a chapel and an hermitage.

CHAPTER VI

HOW SIR BEDIVERE FOUND HIM ON THE MORROW DEAD IN AN HERMITAGE, AND HOW HE ABODE THERE WITH THE HERMIT

THEN was Sir Bedivere glad, and thither he went; and when he came into the chapel, he saw where lay an hermit groveling on all four, there fast by a tomb was new graven.[2] When the hermit saw Sir Bedivere he knew him well, for he was but little tofore Bishop of Canterbury, that Sir Mordred flemed.[3] Sir, said Bedivere, what man is there interred that ye pray so fast for? Fair son, said the hermit, I wot not verily, but by deeming. But this night, at midnight, here came a number of ladies, and brought hither a dead corpse, and prayed me to bury him; and here they offered an hundred tapers, and they gave me an hundred besants.[4] Alas, said Sir Bedivere, that was my lord King Arthur, that here lieth buried in this chapel. Then Sir Bedivere swooned; and when he awoke he prayed the hermit he might abide with him still there, to live with fasting and prayers. For from hence will I never go, said Sir Bedivere, by my will, but all the days of my life here to pray for my lord Arthur. Ye are welcome to me, said the hermit, for I know ye better than ye ween that I do. Ye are the bold Bedivere, and the full noble duke, Sir Lucan the Butler, was your brother. Then Sir Bedivere told the hermit all as ye have heard tofore. So there bode Sir Bedivere with the hermit that was tofore Bishop of Canterbury, and there Sir Bedivere put upon him poor clothes, and served the hermit full lowly in fasting and in prayers. Thus of Arthur I find never more written in books that be authorized nor more of the very certainty of his death heard I never read, but thus was he led away in a ship wherein were three queens; that one was King Arthur's sister, Queen Morgan le Fay; the other was the Queen of Northgalis; the third was the Queen of the Waste Lands. Also there was Nimue, the

[1] Avalon, home of spirits of the departed.

[2] Dug. [3] Put to flight.

[4] Coin first made at Byzantium (Constantinople).

chief lady of the lake, that had wedded Pelleas the good knight; and this lady had done much for King Arthur, for she would never suffer Sir Pelleas to be in no place where he should be in danger of his life; and so he lived to the uttermost of his days with her in great rest. More of the death of King Arthur could I never find, but that ladies brought him to his burials; and such one was buried there, that the hermit bare witness that sometime was Bishop of Canterbury, but yet the hermit knew not in certain that he was verily the body of King Arthur: for this tale Sir Bedivere, knight of the Table Round, made it to be written.

CHAPTER VII

OF THE OPINION OF SOME MEN OF THE DEATH OF KING ARTHUR; AND HOW QUEEN GUENEVER MADE HER A NUN IN ALMESBURY

YET some men say in many parts of England that King Arthur is not dead, but had by the will of our Lord Jesu into another place; and men say that he shall come again, and he shall win the holy cross. I will not say it shall be so, but rather I will say, here in this world he changed his life. But many men say that there is written upon his tomb this verse: *Hic jacet Arthurus Rex, quondam Rex que futurus.*[1] Thus leave I here Sir Bedivere with the hermit, that dwelled that time in a chapel beside Glastonbury, and there was his hermitage. And so they lived in their prayers, and fastings, and great abstinence. And when Queen Guenever understood that King Arthur was slain, and all the noble knights, Sir Mordred and all the remnant, then the queen stole away, and five ladies with her, and so she went to Almesbury; and there she let make herself a nun, and ware white clothes and black, and great penance she took, as ever did sinful lady in this land, and never creature could make her merry; but lived in fasting, prayers, and alms-deeds, that all manner of people marveled how virtuously she was changed. Now leave we Queen Guenever in Almesbury, a nun in white clothes and black, and there she was abbess and ruler as reason would; and turn we from her, and speak we of Sir Launcelot du Lake.

[1]Here lies King Arthur, King formerly and so to be in the future.

CHAPTER VIII

HOW WHEN SIR LAUNCELOT HEARD OF THE DEATH OF KING ARTHUR, AND OF SIR GAWAINE, AND OTHER MATTERS, HE CAME INTO ENGLAND

AND when he heard in his country that Sir Mordred was crowned king in England, and made war against King Arthur, his own father, and would let him to land in his own land; also it was told Sir Launcelot how that Sir Mordred had laid siege about the Tower of London, by cause the queen would not wed him; then was Sir Launcelot wroth out of measure, and said to his kinsmen: Alas, that double traitor Sir Mordred, now me repenteth that ever he escaped my hands, for much shame hath he done unto my lord Arthur; for all I feel by the doleful letter that my lord Sir Gawaine sent me, on whose soul Jesu have mercy, that my lord Arthur is full hard bestad. Alas, said Sir Launcelot, that ever I should live to hear that most noble king that made me knight thus to be overset with his subject in his own realm. And this doleful letter that my lord, Sir Gawaine, hath sent me afore his death, praying me to see his tomb, wit you well his doleful words shall never go from mine heart, for he was a full noble knight as ever was born; and in an unhappy hour was I born that ever I should have that unhap to slay first Sir Gawaine, Sir Gaheris the good knight, and mine own friend Sir Gareth, that full noble knight. Alas, I may say I am unhappy, said Sir Launcelot, that ever I should do thus unhappily, and, alas, yet might I never have hap to slay that traitor, Sir Mordred. Leave your complaints, said Sir Bors, and first revenge you of the death of Sir Gawaine; and it will be well done that ye see Sir Gawaine's tomb, and secondly that ye revenge my lord Arthur, and my lady, Queen Guenever. I thank you, said Sir Launcelot, for ever ye will my worship. Then they made them ready in all the haste that might be, with ships and galleys, with Sir Launcelot and his host to pass into England. And so he passed over the sea till he came to Dover, and there he landed with seven kings, and the number was hideous to behold. Then Sir Launcelot spered[1] of men of Dover where was King Arthur become. Then the people told him how that he was slain, and Sir Mordred and an hundred thousand died on a day; and how Sir Mordred gave King Arthur there the first battle at his landing, and there was good Sir Gawaine slain; and on the morn Sir Mordred fought with the king upon Barham Down, and there the king put Sir Mordred to the worse. Alas, said Sir Launcelot, this is the heaviest tidings that ever came to me. Now, fair sirs, said Sir Launcelot, show me the tomb of Sir Gawaine. And then certain people of the town brought him into the Castle of Dover, and showed him the tomb. Then Sir Launcelot kneeled down and wept, and prayed heartily for his soul. And that night he made a dole, and all they that would come had as much flesh, fish, wine and ale, and every man and woman had twelve pence, come who would. Thus with his own hand dealt he this money, in a mourning gown; and ever he wept, and prayed them to pray for the soul of Sir Gawaine. And on the morn all the priests and clerks that might be gotten in the country were there, and sang mass of *requiem*;[2] and there offered first Sir Launcelot, and he offered an hundred pound; and then the seven kings offered forty pound apiece; and also there was a thousand knights, and each of them offered a pound; and the offering dured from morn till night, and Sir Launcelot lay two nights on his tomb in prayers and weeping. Then on the third day Sir Launcelot called the kings, dukes, earls, barons, and knights, and said thus: My fair lords, I thank you all of your coming into this country with me, but we came too late, and that shall repent me while I live, but against death may no man rebel. But sithen[3] it is so, said Sir Launcelot, I will myself ride and seek my lady, Queen Guenever, for as I hear say she hath had great pain and much disease; and I heard say that she is fled into the west. Therefore ye all shall abide me here, and but if I come again within fifteen days, then take your ships and your fellowship, and depart into your country, for I will do as I say to you.

CHAPTER IX

HOW SIR LAUNCELOT DEPARTED TO SEEK THE QUEEN GUENEVER, AND HOW HE FOUND HER AT ALMESBURY

Then came Sir Bors de Ganis, and said: My lord Sir Launcelot, what think ye for to do, now to ride in this realm? wit ye well ye shall find few friends. Be as be may, said Sir Launcelot, keep you still here, for I will forth on my journey, and no man nor child shall go with me. So it was no boot to strive, but he departed and rode westerly, and there he sought a seven or eight days; and at the last he came to a nunnery, and then was Queen Guenever ware of Sir Launcelot as he walked in the cloister. And when she saw him there she swooned thrice, that all the ladies and gentlewomen had work enough to hold the queen up. So when she might speak, she called ladies and gentlewomen to her, and said: Ye marvel, fair ladies, why I make this fare. Truly, she said, it is for the sight of yonder knight that yonder standeth; wherefore I pray you all call him to me. When Sir Launcelot was brought to her, then she said to all the ladies: Through this man and me hath all this war been wrought, and the death of the most noblest knights of the world; for through our love that we have loved together is my most noble lord slain. Therefore, Sir Launcelot, wit thou well I am set in such a plight to get my soul heal; and yet I trust through God's grace that after my death to have a sight of the blessed face of Christ, and at domesday to sit on his right side, for as sinful as ever I was are saints in heaven. Therefore, Sir Launcelot, I require thee and beseech thee heartily, for all the love that ever was betwixt us, that thou never see me more in the visage; and I command thee, on God's behalf, that thou forsake my company, and to thy kingdom thou turn again, and keep well thy realm from war and wrake;[4] for as well as I have loved thee, mine heart will not serve me to see thee, for through thee and me is the flower of kings and knights destroyed; therefore, Sir Launcelot, go to thy realm, and there take thee a wife, and live with her with joy and bliss; and I pray thee heartily, pray for me to our Lord that I may amend my misliving. Now, sweet madam, said Sir

[1]Asked. [2]Mass for the dead. [3]Since.

[4]Ruin.

Launcelot, would ye that I should now return again unto my country, and there to wed a lady? Nay, madam, wit you well that shall I never do, for I shall never be so false to you of that I have promised; but the same destiny that ye have taken you to, I will take me unto, for to please Jesu, and ever for you I cast me specially to pray. If thou wilt do so, said the queen, hold thy promise, but I may never believe but that thou wilt turn to the world again. Well, madam, said he, ye say as pleaseth you, yet wist you me never false of my promise, and God defend but I should forsake the world as ye have done. For in the quest of the Sangreal I had forsaken the vanities of the world had not your lord been. And if I had done so at that time, with my heart, will, and thought, I had passed all the knights that were in the Sangreal except Sir Galahad, my son. And therefore, lady, sithen ye have taken you to perfection, I must needs take me to perfection, of right. For I take record of God, in you I have had mine earthly joy; and if I had found you now so disposed, I had cast to have you into mine own realm.

CHAPTER X

HOW SIR LAUNCELOT CAME TO THE HERMITAGE WHERE THE ARCHBISHOP OF CANTERBURY WAS, AND HOW HE TOOK THE HABIT ON HIM

But sithen I find you thus disposed, I ensure you faithfully, I will ever take me to penance, and pray while my life lasteth, if I may find any hermit, either gray or white, that will receive me. Wherefore, madam, I pray you kiss me and never no more. Nay, said the queen, that shall I never do, but abstain you from such works: and they departed. But there was never so hard an hearted man but he would have wept to see the dolor that they made; for there was lamentation as they had been stung with spears; and many times they swooned, and the ladies bare the queen to her chamber. And Sir Launcelot awoke and went and took his horse, and rode all that day and all night in a forest, weeping. And at the last he was ware of an hermitage and a chapel stood betwixt two cliffs; and then he heard a little bell ring to mass, and thither he rode and alit, and tied his horse to the gate, and heard mass. And he that sang mass was the Bishop of Canterbury. Both the Bishop and Sir Bedivere knew Sir Launcelot, and they spake together after mass. But when Sir Bedivere had told his tale all whole, Sir Launcelot's heart almost brast for sorrow, and Sir Launcelot threw his arms abroad, and said: Alas, who may trust this world. And then he kneeled down on his knee, and prayed the Bishop to shrive him and assoil[1] him. And then he besought the Bishop that he might be his brother. Then the Bishop said: I will gladly; and there he put an habit upon Sir Launcelot, and there he served God day and night with prayers and fastings. Thus the great host abode at Dover. And then Sir Lionel took fifteen lords with him, and rode to London to seek Sir Launcelot; and there Sir Lionel was slain and many of his lords. Then Sir Bors de Ganis made the great host for to go home again; and Sir Bors, Sir Ector de Maris, Sir Blamore, Sir Bleoberis, with more other of Sir Launcelot's kin, took on them to ride all England over-thwart and endlong, to seek Sir Launcelot. So Sir Bors by fortune rode so long till he came to the same chapel where Sir Launcelot was; and so Sir Bors heard a little bell knell, that rang to mass; and there he alit and heard mass. And when mass was done, the Bishop, Sir Launcelot, and Sir Bedivere, came to Sir Bors. And when Sir Bors saw Sir Launcelot in that manner clothing, then he prayed the Bishop that he might be in the same suit. And so there was an habit put upon him, and there he lived in prayers and fasting. And within half a year, there was come Sir Galihud, Sir Galihodin, Sir Blamore, Sir Bleoberis, Sir Villiars, Sir Clarras, and Sir Gahalantine. So all these seven noble knights there abode still. And when they saw Sir Launcelot had taken him to such perfection, they had no list to depart, but took such an habit as he had. Thus they endured in great penance six year; and then Sir Launcelot took the habit of priesthood of the Bishop, and a twelvemonth he sang mass. And there was none of these other knights but they read in books, and holp for to sing mass, and rang bells, and did bodily all manner of service. And so their horses went where they would, for they took no regard of no worldly riches. For when

[1]Absolve.

they saw Sir Launcelot endure such penance, in prayers, and fastings, they took no force[1] what pain they endured, for to see the noblest knight of the world take such abstinence that he waxed full lean. And thus upon a night, there came a vision to Sir Launcelot, and charged him, in remission of his sins, to haste him unto Almesbury: And by then thou come there, thou shalt find Queen Guenever dead. And therefore take thy fellows with thee, and purvey them of an horse bier, and fetch thou the corpse of her, and bury her by her husband, the noble King Arthur. So this advision came to Sir Launcelot thrice in one night.

CHAPTER XI

HOW SIR LAUNCELOT WENT WITH HIS SEVEN FELLOWS TO ALMESBURY, AND FOUND THERE QUEEN GUENEVER DEAD, WHOM THEY BROUGHT TO GLASTONBURY

THEN Sir Launcelot rose up or[2] day, and told the hermit. It were well done, said the hermit, that ye made you ready, and that you disobey not the advision. Then Sir Launcelot took his seven fellows with him, and on foot they yede[3] from Glastonbury to Almesbury, the which is little more than thirty mile. And thither they came within two days, for they were weak and feeble to go. And when Sir Launcelot was come to Almesbury within the nunnery, Queen Guenever died but half an hour afore. And the ladies told Sir Launcelot that Queen Guenever told them all or she passed, that Sir Launcelot had been priest near a twelvemonth, And hither he cometh as fast as he may to fetch my corpse; and beside my lord, King Arthur, he shall bury me. Wherefore the queen said in hearing of them all: I beseech Almighty God that I may never have power to see Sir Launcelot with my worldly eyen; and thus, said all the ladies, was ever her prayer these two days, till she was dead. Then Sir Launcelot saw her visage, but he wept not greatly, but sighed. And so he did all the observance of the service himself, both the dirge at night, and on the morn he sang mass. And there was ordained an horse bier; and so with an hundred torches ever burning about the corpse of the queen, and ever Sir Launcelot with his seven fellows went about the horse bier, singing and reading many an holy orison, and frankincense upon the corpse incensed. Thus Sir Launcelot and his seven fellows went on foot from Almesbury unto Glastonbury. And when they were come to the chapel and the hermitage, there she had a dirge, with great devotion. And on the morn the hermit that sometime was Bishop of Canterbury sang the mass of *requiem* with great devotion. And Sir Launcelot was the first that offered, and then also his seven fellows. And then she was wrapped in cered cloth of Raines,[4] from the top to the toe, in thirtyfold; and after she was put in a web of lead, and then in a coffin of marble. And when she was put in the earth Sir Launcelot swooned, and lay long still, while the hermit came and awaked him, and said: Ye be to blame, for ye displease God with such manner of sorrow making. Truly, said Sir Launcelot, I trust I do not displease God, for He knoweth mine intent. For my sorrow was not, nor is not, for any rejoicing of sin, but my sorrow may never have end. For when I remember of her beauty, and of her noblesse that was both with her king and with her, so when I saw his corpse and her corpse so lie together, truly mine heart would not serve to sustain my careful[5] body. Also when I remember me how by my default, mine orgulity[6] and my pride, that they were both laid full low, that were peerless that ever was living of Christian people, wit you well, said Sir Launcelot, this remembered, of their kindness and mine unkindness, sank so to mine heart, that I might not sustain myself. So the French book maketh mention.

CHAPTER XII

HOW SIR LAUNCELOT BEGAN TO SICKEN, AND AFTER DIED, WHOSE BODY WAS BORNE TO JOYOUS GARD FOR TO BE BURIED

THEN Sir Launcelot never after ate but little meat, ne drank, till he was dead. For then he sickened more and more, and dried, and dwined[7] away. For the Bishop nor none of his fellows might not make him to eat, and little he drank, that he was waxen by a cubit shorter than he was, that the people could

[1]Account. [2]Before. [3]Went.

[4]Waxed cloth from Rennes, in Brittany.
[5]Distressed. [6]Arrogance. [7]Dwindled.

not know him. For evermore, day and night, he prayed, but sometime he slumbered a broken sleep; ever he was lying groveling on the tomb of King Arthur and Queen Guenever. And there was no comfort that the Bishop, nor Sir Bors, nor none of his fellows, could make him, it availed not. So within six weeks after, Sir Launcelot fell sick, and lay in his bed; and then he sent for the Bishop that there was hermit, and all his true fellows. Then Sir Launcelot said with dreary steven:[1] Sir Bishop, I pray you give to me all my rites that longeth to a Christian man. It shall not need you, said the hermit and all his fellows, it is but heaviness of your blood, ye shall be well mended by the grace of God tomorn. My fair lords, said Sir Launcelot, wit you well my careful body will into the earth, I have warning more than now I will say; therefore give me my rites. So when he was houseled and enelid,[2] and had all that a Christian man ought to have, he prayed the Bishop that his fellows might bear his body to Joyous Gard. Some men say it was Alnwick, and some men say it was Bamborough. Howbeit, said Sir Launcelot, me repenteth sore, but I made mine avow sometime, that in Joyous Gard I would be buried. And by cause of breaking of mine avow, I pray you all, lead me thither. Then there was weeping and wringing of hands among his fellows. So at a season of the night they all went to their beds, for they all lay in one chamber. And so after midnight, against day, the Bishop that was hermit, as he lay in his bed asleep, he fell upon a great laughter. And therewithal the fellowship awoke, and came to the Bishop, and asked him what he ailed. Ah Jesu mercy, said the Bishop, why did ye awake me? I was never in all my life so merry and so well at ease. Wherefore? said Sir Bors. Truly, said the Bishop, here was Sir Launcelot with me with more angels than ever I saw men in one day. And I saw the angels heave up Sir Launcelot unto heaven, and the gates of heaven opened against him. It is but dretching of swevens,[3] said Sir Bors, for I doubt not Sir Launcelot aileth nothing but good. It may well be, said the Bishop; go ye to his bed, and then shall ye prove the sooth. So when Sir Bors and his fellows came to his bed they found him stark dead, and he lay as he had smiled, and the sweetest savor about him that ever they felt. Then was there weeping and wringing of hands, and the greatest dole they made that ever made men. And on the morn the Bishop did his mass of *requiem;* and after, the Bishop and all the nine knights put Sir Launcelot in the same horse bier that Queen Guenever was laid in tofore that she was buried. And so the Bishop and they all together went with the body of Sir Launcelot daily, till they came to Joyous Gard; and ever they had an hundred torches burning about him. And so within fifteen days they came to Joyous Gard. And there they laid his corpse in the body of the quire, and sang and read many psalters and prayers over him and about him. And ever his visage was laid open and naked, that all folks might behold him. For such was the custom in those days, that all men of worship should so lie with open visage till that they were buried. And right thus as they were at their service, there came Sir Ector de Maris, that had seven years sought all England, Scotland, and Wales, seeking his brother, Sir Launcelot.

CHAPTER XIII

HOW SIR ECTOR FOUND SIR LAUNCELOT HIS BROTHER DEAD, AND HOW CONSTANTINE REIGNED NEXT AFTER ARTHUR; AND OF THE END OF THIS BOOK

AND when Sir Ector heard such noise and light in the quire of Joyous Gard, he alit and put his horse from him, and came into the quire, and there he saw men sing and weep. And all they knew Sir Ector, but he knew not them. Then went Sir Bors unto Sir Ector, and told him how there lay his brother, Sir Launcelot, dead; and then Sir Ector threw his shield, sword, and helm from him. And when he beheld Sir Launcelot's visage, he fell down in a swoon. And when he waked it were hard any tongue to tell the doleful complaints that he made for his brother. Ah Launcelot, he said, thou were head of all Christian knights, and now I dare say, said Sir Ector, thou Sir Launcelot, there thou liest, that thou were never matched of earthly knight's hand. And thou were the courteoust knight that ever bare shield. And thou were the truest friend to thy lover that ever bestrad

[1]Voice.

[2]Given the Holy Sacrament and anointed.

[3]The troubling of dreams.

horse. And thou were the truest lover of a sinful man that ever loved woman. And thou were the kindest man that ever struck with sword. And thou were the goodliest person that ever came among press of knights. And thou were the meekest man and the gentlest that ever ate in hall among ladies. And thou were the sternest knight to thy mortal foe that ever put spear in the rest. Then there was weeping and dolor out of measure. Thus they kept Sir Launcelot's corpse on loft fifteen days, and then they buried it with great devotion. And then at leisure they went all with the Bishop of Canterbury to his hermitage, and there they were together more than a month. Then Sir Constantine, that was Sir Cador's son of Cornwall, was chosen king of England. And he was a full noble knight, and worshipfully he ruled this realm. And then this King Constantine sent for the Bishop of Canterbury, for he heard say where he was. And so he was restored unto his Bishopric, and left that hermitage. And Sir Bedivere was there ever still hermit to his life's end. Then Sir Bors de Ganis, Sir Ector de Maris, Sir Gahalantine, Sir Galihud, Sir Galihodin, Sir Blamore, Sir Bleoberis, Sir Villiars le Valiant, Sir Clarrus of Clermont, all these knights drew them to their countries. Howbeit King Constantine would have had them with him, but they would not abide in this realm. And there they all lived in their countries as holy men. And some English books make mention that they went never out of England after the death of Sir Launcelot, but that was but favor of makers.[1] For the French book maketh mention, and is authorized, that Sir Bors, Sir Ector, Sir Blamore, and Sir Beloberis, went into the Holy Land thereas Jesu Christ was quick and dead, and anon as they had stablished their lands. For the book saith, so Sir Launcelot commanded them for to do, or ever he passed out of this world. And these four knights did many battles upon the miscreants or Turks. And there they died upon a Good Friday for God's sake.

Here is the end of the book of King Arthur, and of his noble knights of the Round Table, that when they were whole together there was ever an hundred and forty. And here is the end of the death of Arthur. I pray you all, gentlemen and gentlewomen that readeth this book of Arthur and his knights, from the beginning to the ending, pray for me while I am on live, that God send me good deliverance, and when I am dead, I pray you all pray for my soul. For this book was ended the ninth year of the reign of King Edward the Fourth, by Sir Thomas Maleore, knight, as Jesu help him for his great might, as he is the servant of Jesu both day and night.

Thus endeth this noble and joyous book entitled Le Morte Darthur. Notwithstanding it treateth of the birth, life, and acts of the said King Arthur, of his noble knights of the Round Table, their marvelous enquests and adventures, the achieving of the Sangreal, and in the end the dolorous death and departing out of this world of them all. Which book was reduced into English by Sir Thomas Malory, knight, as afore is said, and by me divided into twenty-one books, chaptered and imprinted, and finished in the abbey Westminster the last day of July the year of our Lord MCCCCLXXXV.

Caxton me fieri fecit.[2]

[1]The fiction of poets.

[2]Caxton caused me to be made.

JOHN LYLY (1554?–1606)

Of Lyly's life not much is known. He was born in either 1553 or 1554. In the spring of 1569 he entered Magdalen College, Oxford, taking his bachelor's degree in 1573 and his master's degree in 1575. In the following year he was perhaps at Cambridge; he became a master of arts of Cambridge in 1579. In 1578 he published the book for which he is still most widely known, *Euphues, the Anatomy of Wit*, the immediate success of which led to the publication of a second part, *Euphues and his England*, in 1580. Lyly was in point of time the first of a group of men known, from their education, as "university wits," who attempted to make their way in London by what they could earn from their pens. With the exception of *Euphues* their best remembered work lies in the field of the drama. In the decade from 1580 to 1590 they managed practically to effect the transition from medieval to Elizabethan playwriting, and so cleared the way for Shakespeare and his contemporaries and successors. Lyly's comedies, though now perhaps not very frequently read, are from this point of view of great importance, the chief ones being *Endimion*, *Sapho and Phao*, *Campaspe*, and *Gallathea*. As these titles serve to indicate, Lyly drew his subject-matter from pastoral tradition or classical myth; though this, in many of his plays, he used to veil political or social allegory bearing on current events. In 1588 Lyly obtained a minor post in the Revels Office which he held until 1604. He made repeated attempts to gain the Mastership of the Revels, but failed to do so and was apparently embittered by his failure. He sat in Parliament four times between 1589 and 1601.

To the modern reader the style of *Euphues* seems frigid, as indeed it is, and one concedes that its interest is chiefly historical. Yet the book will hardly be read except because of its style. It is a tale, and it has been called "the earliest English novel," but this unduly stretches the meaning of "novel," for the story is slight and of secondary importance, serving really as a framework to hold together a collection of letters and moral discussions. Moreover, the content of the book as a whole is primarily a means to an end. That is to say, it was meant as a vehicle for a certain kind of style, which had indeed been known for several centuries in Latin prose, but was more artistic and elaborate than anything yet attempted in English. Lyly's book gave a new life to this old fashion, but only a temporary one, and Euphuism, as the style was called, soon became a proper subject for jokes. But Euphuism is misunderstood if it is thought of as a mere affectation in speech. The truth is that Lyly was a pioneer. He was in effect the discoverer of English literary prose, and we owe it to him probably more than to any other one man that prose came to be regarded equally with verse as an artistic medium. If his style now seems merely quaint and curious, it should be remembered that Lyly was one who showed the way, and that our better standards have been made possible by the fact that later writers were able to take advantage of his successes as well as of his failures.

EUPHUES, THE ANATOMY OF WIT

VERY PLEASANT FOR ALL GENTLEMEN TO READ, AND MOST NECESSARY TO REMEMBER: WHEREIN ARE CONTAINED THE DELIGHTS THAT WIT FOLLOWETH IN HIS YOUTH BY THE PLEASANTNESS OF LOVE, AND THE HAPPINESS HE REAPETH IN AGE BY THE PERFECTNESS OF WISDOM

A COOLING CARD FOR PHILAUTUS AND ALL FOND LOVERS.[1]

MUSING with myself, being idle, how I might be well employed, friend Philautus, I could find nothing either more fit to continue our friendship, or of greater force to dissolve our folly, than to write a remedy for that which many judge past cure; for love, Philautus, with the which I have been so tormented that I have lost my time, thou so troubled that thou hast forgot reason, both so mangled with repulse, inveigled by deceit, and almost murdered by disdain, that I can neither remember our miseries without grief, nor redress our mishaps without groans. How wantonly, yea, and how willingly have we abused our golden time and misspent our gotten treasure! How curious were we to please our lady, how careless to displease our Lord! How devout in serving our goddess, how desperate in forgetting our God! Ah,

[1]A "pamphlet" written by Euphues to "bridle the overlashing affections" of his friend Philautus, "yet generally to be applied to all lovers."

my Philautus, if the wasting of our money might not dehort us, yet the wounding of our minds should deter us; if reason might nothing persuade us to wisdom, yet shame should provoke us to wit. If Lucilla[1] read this trifle, she will straight proclaim Euphues for a traitor, and, seeing me turn my tippet,[2] will either shut me out for a wrangler, or cast me off for a wiredrawer;[3] either convince me of malice in bewraying their sleights, or condemn me of mischief in arming young men against fleeting minions. And what then? Though Curio be as hot as a toast, yet Euphues is as cold as a clock; though he be a cock of the game, yet Euphues is content to be craven and cry creek;[4] though Curio be old huddle, and twang "*ipse*, he,"[5] yet Euphues had rather shrink in the wetting than waste in the wearing. I know Curio to be steel to the back, standard-bearer in Venus's camp, sworn to the crew, true to the crown, knight marshal to Cupid, and heir apparent to his kingdom. But by that time that he hath eaten but one bushel of salt with Lucilla, he shall taste ten quarters[6] of sorrow in his love; then shall he find for every pint of honey a gallon of gall, for every dram of pleasure an ounce of pain, for every inch of mirth an ell of moan. And yet, Philautus, if there be any man in despair to obtain his purpose, or so obstinate in his opinion that, having lost his freedom by folly, would also lose his life for love, let him repair hither, and he shall reap such profit as will either quench his flames or assuage his fury; either cause him to renounce his lady as most pernicious, or redeem his liberty as most precious. Come, therefore, to me, all ye lovers that have been deceived by fancy, the glass of pestilence, or deluded by women, the gate to perdition; be as earnest to seek a medicine as you were eager to run into a mischief; the earth bringeth forth as well endive to delight the people as hemlock to endanger the patient; as well the rose to distill as the nettle to sting; as well the bee to give honey as the spider to yield poison.

If my lewd life, gentlemen, have given you offense, let my good counsel make amends; if by my folly any be allured to lust, let them by my repentance be drawn to continency. Achilles's spear could as well heal as hurt; the Scorpion, though he sting, yet he stints the pain; though the herb Nerius poison the sheep, yet is it a remedy to man against poison; though I have infected some by example, yet I hope I shall comfort many by repentance. Whatsoever I speak to men, the same also I speak to women; I mean not to run with the hare and hold with the hound, to carry fire in the one hand and water in the other; neither to flatter men as altogether faultless, neither to fall out with women as altogether guilty; for, as I am not minded to pick a thank with the one, so am I not determined to pick a quarrel with the other; if women be not perverse, they shall reap profit by remedy of pleasure. If Phyllis were now to take counsel, she would not be so foolish to hang herself, neither Dido so fond to die for Æneas, neither Pasiphaë so monstrous to love a bull, nor Phedra so unnatural to be enamored of her son.

This is, therefore, to admonish all young imps and novices in love not to blow the coals of fancy with desire, but to quench them with disdain. When love tickleth thee, decline it, lest it stifle thee; rather fast than surfeit; rather starve than strive to exceed. Though the beginning of love bring delight, the end bringeth destruction. For, as the first draught of wine doth comfort the stomach, the second inflame the liver, the third fume into the head, so the first sip of love is pleasant, the second perilous, the third pestilent. If thou perceive thyself to be enticed with their wanton glances or allured with their wicked guiles, either enchanted with their beauty or enamored with their bravery, enter with thyself into this meditation: What shall I gain if I obtain my purpose? nay, rather, what shall I lose in winning my pleasure? If my lady yield to be my lover, is it not likely she will be another's leman? and if she be a modest matron, my labor is lost. This, therefore, remaineth; that either I must pine in cares or perish with curses.

If she be chaste, then is she coy; if light, then is she impudent; if a grave matron, who can woo her? if a lewd minion, who would

[1] Lucilla was betrothed to Philautus, but, when she saw Euphues, fell in love with him, he returning her love. This broke the friendship of Euphues and Philautus; but a little later Lucilla fell in love anew with one Curio and married him, whereupon Euphues and Philautus renewed their friendship.

[2] Proverbial expression meaning to change sides

[3] Precisian.

[4] Confess himself beaten.

[5] Though Curio be embraced as her loved one and sing "I am the man."

[6] There are 8 bushels to the quarter.

wed her? if one of the Vestal Virgins, they have vowed virginity; if one of Venus's court, they have vowed dishonesty. If I love one that is fair, it will kindle jealousy; if one that is foul, it will convert me into frenzy. If fertile to bear children, my care is increased; if barren, my curse is augmented; if honest, I shall fear her death; if immodest, I shall be weary of her life.

To what end, then, shall I live in love, seeing always it is life more to be feared than death? for all my time wasted in sighs and worn in sobs, for all my treasure spent on jewels and spilled in jollity, what recompense shall I reap besides repentance? What other reward shall I have than reproach? What other solace than endless shame? But haply thou wilt say, "If I refuse their courtesy I shall be accounted a mecock,[1] a milksop, taunted and retaunted with check and checkmate, flouted and reflouted with intolerable glee."

Alas, fond fool, art thou so pinned to their sleeves that thou regardest more their babble than thine own bliss, more their frumps than thine own welfare? Wilt thou resemble the kind spaniel,[2] which, the more he is beaten the fonder he is, or the foolish eyas,[3] which will never away? Dost thou not know that women deem none valiant unless he be too venturous?—that they account one a dastard if he be not desperate, a pinch-penny if he be not prodigal; if silent, a sot, if full of words, a fool? Perversely do they always think of their lovers and talk of them scornfully, judging all to be clowns which be no courtiers, and all to be pinglers,[4] that be not coursers.

Seeing therefore the very blossom of love is sour, the bud cannot be sweet. In time prevent danger, lest untimely thou run into a thousand perils. Search the wound while it is green; too late cometh the salve when the sore festereth, and the medicine bringeth double care when the malady is past cure.

Beware of delays. What less than the grain of mustard seed?—in time, almost what thing is greater than the stalk thereof? The slender twig groweth to a stately tree, and that which with the hand might easily have been pulled up will hardly with the ax be hewn down. The least spark, if it be not quenched, will burst into a flame; the least moth in time eateth the thickest cloth; and I have read that, in a short space, there was a town in Spain undermined with conies, in Thessaly with moles, with frogs in France, in Africa with flies. If these silly worms in tract of time overthrow so stately towns, how much more will love, which creepeth secretly into the mind (as the rust doth into the iron and is not perceived), consume the body, yea, and confound the soul. Defer not from hour to day, from day to month, from month to year, and always remain in misery.

He that to-day is not willing will to-morrow be more willful. But, alas, it is no less common than lamentable to behold the tottering estate of lovers, who think by delays to prevent dangers, with oil to quench fire, with smoke to clear the eyesight. They flatter themselves with a feinting farewell, deferring ever until to-morrow, when as their morrow doth always increase their sorrow. Let neither their amiable countenances, neither their painted protestations, neither their deceitful promises, allure thee to delays. Think this with thyself, that the sweet songs of Calypso were subtle snares to entice Ulysses; that the crab then catcheth the oyster when the sun shineth; that hyena, when she speaketh like a man, deviseth most mischief; that women when they be most pleasant pretend most treachery.

Follow Alexander, which, hearing the commendation and singular comeliness of the wife of Darius, so courageously withstood the assaults of fancy that he would not so much as take a view of her beauty. Imitate Cyrus, a king endued with such continency that he loathed to look on the heavenly hue of Panthea; and, when Araspus told him that she excelled all mortal wights in amiable show, "By so much the more," said Cyrus, "I ought to abstain from her sight; for if I follow thy counsel in going to her, it may be I shall desire to continue with her, and by my light affection neglect my serious affairs." Learn of Romulus to refrain from wine, be it never so delicate; of Agesilaus to despise costly apparel, be it never so curious; of Diogenes to detest women, be they never so comely. He that toucheth pitch shall be defiled; the sore eye infecteth the sound; the society with women breedeth security in the soul, and maketh all the senses senseless. Moreover, take this counsel as an article of

[1]A tame-spirited man. [2]True-bred spaniel.
[3]Nestling or unfledged bird. [4]Loiterers.

thy creed, which I mean to follow as the chief argument of my faith, that idleness is the only nurse and nourisher of sensual appetite, the sole maintenance of youthful affection, the first shaft that Cupid shooteth into the hot liver of a heedless lover. I would to God I were not able to find this for a truth by mine own trial, and I would the example of others' idleness had caused me rather to avoid that fault than experience of mine own folly. How dissolute have I been in striving against good counsel, how resolute in standing in mine own conceit, how forward to wickedness, how wanton with too much cockering,[1] how wayward in hearing correction! Neither was I much unlike these abbey lubbers in my life (though far unlike them in belief) which labored till they were cold, ate till they sweat, and lay in bed till their bones ached. Hereof cometh it, gentlemen, that love creepeth into the mind of privy craft, and keepeth this hold by main courage.

The man being idle, the mind is apt to all uncleanness; the mind being void of exercise, the man is void of honesty. Doth not the rust fret the hardest iron if it be not used? Doth not the moth eat the finest garment if it be not worn? Doth not moss grow on the smoothest stone if it be not stirred? Doth not impiety infect the wisest wit if it be given to idleness? Is not the standing water sooner frozen than the running stream? Is not he that sitteth more subject to sleep than he that walketh? Doth not common experience make this common unto us, that the fattest ground bringeth forth nothing but weeds if it be not well tilled, that the sharpest wit inclineth only to wickedness if it be not exercised? Is it not true which Seneca reporteth, that as too much bending breaketh the bow, so too much remission spoileth the mind? Besides this, immoderate sleep, immodest play, unsatiable swilling of wine doth so weaken the senses and bewitch the soul that, before we feel the motion of love, we are resolved into lust. Eschew idleness, my Philautus, so shalt thou easily unbend the bow and quench the brands of Cupid. Love gives place to labor; labor, and thou shalt never love. Cupid is a crafty child, following those at an inch that study pleasure, and flying those swiftly that take pains. Bend thy mind to the law, whereby thou mayest have understanding of old and ancient customs; defend thy clients; enrich thy coffers; and carry credit in thy country. If law seem loathsome unto thee, search the secrets of physic, whereby thou mayest know the hidden natures of herbs; whereby thou mayest gather profit to thy purse and pleasure to thy mind. What can be more exquisite in human affairs than for every fever, be it never so hot, for every palsy, be it never so cold, for every infection, be it never so strange, to give a remedy? The old verse standeth as yet in his old virtue: That Galen giveth goods, Justinian honors. If thou be so nice that thou canst no way brook the practice of physic, or so unwise that thou wilt not beat thy brains about the institutes of the law, confer all thy study, all thy time, all thy treasure to the attaining of the sacred and sincere knowledge of divinity; by this mayest thou bridle thine incontinency, rein thine affections, restrain thy lust. Here shalt thou behold, as it were in a glass, that all the glory of man is as the grass; that all things under heaven are but vain; that our life is but a shadow, a warfare, a pilgrimage, a vapor, a bubble, a blast; of such shortness that David saith it is but a span long; of such sharpness that Job noteth it replenished with all miseries; of such uncertainty that we are no sooner born but we are subject to death; the one foot no sooner on the ground but the other ready to slip into the grave. Here shalt thou find ease for thy burden of sin, comfort for the conscience pined with vanity, mercy for thine offenses by the martyrdom of thy sweet Savior. By this thou shalt be able to instruct those that be weak, to confute those that be obstinate, to confound those that be erroneous, to confirm the faithful, to comfort the desperate, to cut off the presumptuous, to save thine own soul by thy sure faith, and edify the hearts of many by thy sound doctrine. If this seem too strait a diet for thy straining disease, or too holy a profession for so hollow a person, then employ thyself to martial feats, to jousts, to tourneys, yea, to all torments, rather than to loiter in love and spend thy life in the laps of ladies; what more monstrous can there be than to see a young man abuse those gifts to his own shame which God hath given him for his own preferment? What greater infamy than to confer the sharp wit to the making of lewd sonnets, to the idola-

[1] Coddling.

trous worshiping of their ladies, to the vain delights of fancy, to all kind of vice, as it were against kind and course of nature? Is it not folly to show wit to women, which are neither able nor willing to receive fruit thereof? Dost thou not know that the tree Silvacenda beareth no fruit in Pharos?[1] That the Persian trees in Rhodes do only wax green but never bring forth apple?[2]

That amomus and nardus will only grow in India, balsamum only in Syria; that in Rhodes no eagle will build her nest, no owl live in Crete, no wit spring in the will of women? Mortify, therefore, thy affections, and force not nature against nature to strive in vain. Go into the country, look to thy grounds, yoke thine oxen, follow thy plow, graft thy trees, behold thy cattle, and devise with thyself how the increase of them may increase thy profit. In autumn pull thine apples, in summer ply thy harvest, in the spring trim thy gardens, in the winter, thy woods, and thus, beginning to delight to be a good husband, thou shalt begin to detest to be in love with an idle housewife; when profit shall begin to fill thy purse with gold, then pleasure shall have no force to defile thy mind with love. For honest recreation after thy toil, use hunting or hawking; either rouse the deer, or unperch the pheasant; so shalt thou root out the remembrance of thy former love, and repent thee of thy foolish lust. And, although thy sweetheart bind thee by oath always to hold a candle at her shrine, and to offer thy devotion to thine own destruction, yet go, run, fly into the country; neither water thou thy plants, in that thou departest from thy pigsny,[3] neither stand in a mammering[4] whether it be best to depart or not; but by how much the more thou art unwilling to go, by so much the more hasten thy steps, neither feign for thyself any sleeveless excuse whereby thou mayest tarry. Neither let rain nor thunder, neither lightning nor tempest, stay thy journey; and reckon not with thyself how many miles thou hast gone—that showeth weariness; but how many thou hast to go—that proveth manliness. But foolish and frantic lovers will deem my precepts hard, and esteem my persuasions haggard;[5] I must of force confess that it is a corrosive to the stomach of a lover, but a comfort to a godly liver to run through a thousand pikes to escape ten thousand perils. Sour potions bring sound health; sharp purgations make short diseases; and the medicine, the more bitter it is, the more better it is in working. To heal the body we try physic, search cunning, prove sorcery, venture through fire and water, leaving nothing unsought that may be gotten for money, be it never so much or procured by any means, be they never so unlawful. How much more ought we to hazard all things for the safeguard of mind, and quiet of conscience! And, certes, easier will the remedy be when the reason is espied; do you not know the nature of women, which is grounded only upon extremities?

Do they think any man to delight in them unless he dote on them? Any to be zealous except they be jealous? Any to be fervent in case he be not furious? If he be cleanly, then term they him proud; if mean in apparel, a sloven; if tall, a longis; if short, a dwarf; if bold, blunt; if shamefaced, a coward; insomuch as they have neither mean in their frumps, nor measure in their folly. But at the first the ox wieldeth not the yoke, nor the colt the snaffle, nor the lover good counsel; yet time causeth the one to bend his neck, the other to open his mouth, and should enforce the third to yield his right to reason. Lay before thine eyes the slights and deceits of thy lady, her snatching in jest and keeping in earnest, her perjury, her impiety, the countenance she showeth to thee of course, the love she beareth to others of zeal, her open malice, her dissembled mischief.

O, I would in repeating their vices thou couldst be as eloquent as in remembering them thou oughtst to be penitent! Be she never so comely, call her counterfeit; be she never so straight, think her crooked. And wrest all parts of her body to the worst, be she never so worthy. If she be well set, then call her a boss; if slender, a hazel twig; if nutbrown, as black as a coal; if well colored, a painted wall; if she be pleasant, then is she a wanton; if sullen, a clown; if honest, then is she coy; if impudent, a harlot.

Search every vein and sinew of their dis-

[1] The island near Alexandria on which Ptolemy I built a lighthouse.

[2] Lyly has in mind Pliny's statement (*Natural History*, xvi, 58) that in general trees do not bear except where they are indigenous.

[3] Thy loved one.

[4] Hesitation.

[5] Wild? A haggard is a wild hawk.

position; if she have no sight in descant, desire her to chant it; if no cunning to dance, request her to trip it; if no skill in music, proffer her the lute; if an ill gait, then walk with her; if rude in speech, talk with her; if she be jag-toothed, tell her some merry jest to make her laugh; if pink-eyed, some doleful history to cause her weep: in the one her grinning will show her deformed; in the other her whining, like a pig half roasted.

It is a world to see how commonly we are blinded with the collusions of women, and more enticed by their ornaments being artificial than their proportion being natural. I loathe almost to think on their ointments and apothecary drugs, the sleeking of their faces, and all their slibber[1] sauces which bring queasiness to the stomach and disquiet to the mind.

Take from them their periwigs, their paintings, their jewels, their rolls, their bolsterings, and thou shalt soon perceive that a woman is the least part of herself. When they be once robbed of their robes, then will they appear so odious, so ugly, so monstrous, that thou wilt rather think them serpents than saints; and so like hags that thou wilt fear rather to be enchanted than enamored. Look in their closets, and there shalt thou find an apothecary's shop of sweet confections, a surgeon's box of sundry salves, a pedlar's pack of new fangles. Besides all this, their shadows,[2] their spots,[3] their lawns, their lyfkies,[4] their ruffs, their rings, show them rather cardinals' courtesans than modest matrons, and more carnally affected than moved in conscience. If every one of these things severally be not of force to move thee, yet all of them jointly shall mortify thee.

Moreover, to make thee the more stronger to strive against these sirens, and more subtle to deceive these tame serpents, my counsel is that thou have more strings to thy bow than one; it is safe riding at two anchors; a fire divided in twain burneth slower; a fountain running into many rivers is of less force; the mind enamored on two women is less affected with desire and less infected with despair: one love expelleth another, and the remembrance of the latter quencheth the concupiscence of the first.

Yet, if thou be so weak, being bewitched with their wiles that thou hast neither will to eschew nor wit to avoid their company, if thou be either so wicked that thou wilt not, or so wedded that thou canst not abstain from their glances, yet at the least dissemble thy grief. If thou be as hot as the mount Etna, feign thyself as cold as the hill Caucasus; carry two faces in one hood; cover thy flaming fancy with feigned ashes; show thyself sound when thou art rotten; let thy hue be merry when thy heart is melancholy; bear a pleasant countenance with a pined[5] conscience, a painted sheath with a leaden dagger.[6] Thus, dissembling thy grief, thou mayest recure thy disease. Love creepeth in by stealth, and by stealth slideth away.

If she break promise with thee in the night, or absent herself in the day, seem thou careless, and then will she be careful; if thou languish, then will she be lavish of her honor, yea, and of the other strange beast, her honesty. Stand thou on thy pantofles,[7] and she will veil bonnet. Lie thou aloof, and she will seize on the lure; if thou pass by her door and be called back, either seem deaf and not to hear, or desperate, and not to care. Fly the places, the parlors, the portals wherein thou hast been conversant with thy lady; yea, Philautus, shun the street where Lucilla doth dwell, lest the sight of her window renew the sum of thy sorrow.

Yet, although I would have thee precise in keeping these precepts, yet would I have thee to avoid solitariness—that breeds melancholy; melancholy, madness; madness, mischief and utter desolation. Have ever some faithful fere[8] with whom thou mayest communicate thy counsels: some Pylades to encourage Orestes, some Damon to release Pythias, some Scipio to recure[9] Lælius. Phyllis in wandering the woods hanged herself; Asiarchus, forsaking company, spoiled himself with his own bodkin;[10] Biarus, a Roman, more wise than fortunate, being alone, destroyed himself with a potsherd. Beware solitariness. But, although I would have thee use company for thy recreation, yet would I have thee always to leave the company of those that accompany thy lady;

[1]Dirty.
[2]Borders attached to bonnets to shield complexion.
[3]Patches. [4]Bodices.

[5]Tortured.
[6]A proverbial expression for false appearances.
[7]A proverbial expression for pride.
[8]Comrade. [9]Recover. [10]Small dagger.

yea, if she have any jewel of thine in her custody, rather lose it than go for it, lest in seeking to recover a trifle thou renew thine old trouble. Be not curious to curl thy hair, nor careful to be neat in thine apparel; be not prodigal of thy gold nor precise in thy going; be not like the Englishman, which preferreth every strange fashion before the use of his country; be thou dissolute,[1] lest thy lady think thee foolish in framing thyself to every fashion for her sake. Believe not their oaths and solemn protestations, their exorcisms and conjurations, their tears which they have at commandment, their alluring looks, their treading on the toe, their unsavory toys.

Let every one loathe his lady and be ashamed to be her servant. It is riches and ease that nourisheth affection; it is play, wine, and wantonness that feedeth a lover as fat as a fool; refrain from all such meats as shall provoke thine appetite to lust, and all such means as may allure thy mind to folly. Take clear water for strong wine, brown bread for fine manchet,[2] beef and brewis[3] for quails and partridge; for ease, labor; for pleasure, pain; for surfeiting, hunger; for sleep, watching; for the fellowship of ladies, the company of philosophers. If thou say to me, "Physician, heal thyself," I answer that I am meetly well purged of that disease; and yet was I never more willing to cure myself than to comfort my friend. And, seeing the cause that made in me so cold a devotion should make in thee also as frozen a desire, I hope thou wilt be as ready to provide a salve as thou wast hasty in seeking a sore. And yet, Philautus, I would not that all women should take pepper in the nose,[4] in that I have disclosed the legerdemains of a few, for well I know none will wince unless she be galled, neither any be offended unless she be guilty. Therefore I earnestly desire thee that thou show this cooling card to none except thou show also this my defense to them all. For, although I weigh nothing the ill will of light housewives, yet would I be loath to lose the good will of honest matrons. Thus, being ready to go to Athens, and ready there to entertain thee whensoever thou shalt repair thither, I bid thee farewell, and fly women.

Thine ever,

EUPHUES.

[1] Disheveled.

[2] The finest white bread.

[3] Broth obtained from boiling salted beef.

[4] Take offense.

CHRISTOPHER MARLOWE (1564-1593)

Marlowe was born at Canterbury on 6 February, 1564. His father belonged to the shoemakers' and tanners' guild of the town. In 1579 the boy entered the King's School at Canterbury, and two years later passed thence to Corpus Christi College, Cambridge. He was graduated B. A. in 1584, M. A. in 1587. While at the King's School he had held a scholarship, and during his Cambridge years he held another—one created in 1575 by the will of Archbishop Matthew Parker. After 1584 his periods of residence at the University were much broken, and in the spring of 1587 his absence apparently gave opportunity for the spread of damaging rumors concerning him, which threatened to prevent his receiving his higher degree. It seems nearly certain that he was in reality engaged in some secret governmental service, and that he obtained his degree as a consequence of the intervention of the Privy Council. His retention of his scholarship for six years implied the intention of taking orders in the Anglican Church. It has been inferred that his failure to do so was the result of "the growth of his speculative views." (F. S. Boas, *Marlowe and his Circle.*) At all events, he went from Cambridge to London, and at once began writing for the theaters, chiefly for the Lord Admiral's Company. In the autumn of 1589 he was involved in some trouble which necessitated his securing bond to avoid imprisonment. In May, 1593, he was summoned before the Privy Council, but before the month was out he lay murdered in a Deptford tavern. He had gone thither on 30 May with three companions, Ingram Frizer, Nicholas Skeres, and Robert Poley. The four had spent most of the day in the tavern of Eleanor Bull, and in the evening Frizer and Marlowe had begun to quarrel over the payment of the reckoning. Marlowe, in sudden anger, had seized Frizer's dagger and inflicted two wounds on his head; whereupon the latter, struggling with Marlowe, had managed to get back his dagger and had given Marlowe a mortal wound over his right eye, causing instant death. This is the account returned by the coroner's jury of 16 men (discovered in the Public Record Office, London, in 1925, by Professor J. Leslie Hotson), and there is no good reason to doubt its substantial accuracy. Frizer was soon pardoned on the ground that he had acted in self-defense, and he survived—a churchwarden during his last 22 years—until August, 1627.

Immediately after his death Marlowe was charged with atheism, by an informer, Richard Baines, and by his one-time friend Thomas Kyd, author of *The Spanish Tragedy*. Later, others joined in the accusation, and it seems evident that wild utterances of the poet's gave a more than plausible basis for it, though what was meant was not atheism in the present sense of the word. Marlowe was associated more or less closely with a small group of men who were interested in the new birth of science which was one phase of the Renaissance, and interested in religious problems turned up by the revolt of philosophy and science against scholasticism; and there can be no doubt that he held opinions definitely heterodox in character. But there is no evidence that he embraced an anti-theistic philosophy. The extant evidence suggests simply that he was encouraged by the new skepticism to indulge in ribald speech concerning the miraculous element in Christianity.

Marlowe's *Tamburlaine*, Part I, was performed in 1587, *Doctor Faustus* probably in 1588, and *The Jew of Malta* in 1589. In these three plays and in *Tamburlaine*, Part II, and *Edward II* he wrote such poetry as England had not before known. To a lofty and intense imagination he united a command of language and a skill in versification which put him easily above the other dramatists who preceded Shakespeare. He wrote his plays in blank verse, and with such mastery that he established it as the verse of Elizabethan tragedy. And in the pictures he drew, in *Tamburlaine* of the craving for universal political power, in *Doctor Faustus* of the craving for unlimited power got through knowledge, and in *The Jew of Malta* of the craving for boundless wealth, he exhibited an important—if not indeed the central—aspect of the Renaissance, with its sudden accession of unbounded confidence in human capacity and its corresponding expansion of desires. In so doing he seems, it is true, in contrast with Shakespeare, for example, curiously remote from the ways and life of his time—but this is a mere deceptive appearance. "The Elizabethan world is never photographed or portrayed in his works; but its ideas and aspirations find nowhere a truer revelation; none of his contemporaries reflect its spirit, its desires and efforts better than he. A simple instance of such transmutation comes to mind. To us, looking back over 300 years, one of the most significant series of events in that age is the vast enterprise which inspired and organized the voyages of discovery. . . . The wonders and highly-colored fantasies reported by the voyagers appealed to the credulity of poets and public alike; Shakespeare clothes with concrete forms the marvels of the Bermudas. But if we turn back to the year 1593 when much of this was already current, Marlowe has little to tell us of the wonders and marvels, of dog-headed men and the sun coming up like thunder out of the far East. . . . Yet this is not the whole truth." For "deep in Marlowe's mind lay certain memories, the impressions left by those Westward voyages." Witness the dying words of Mortimer in *Edward II:*

"Weep not for Mortimer
That scorns the world, and as a traveler
Goes to discover countries yet unknown."

"The lives and deaths of the voyagers had made no emotional—far less any sentimental—appeal to him. But they had remained an image of eternal forth-faring." And in fact "Marlowe is, of all Elizabethans, the truest explorer. His career is a long voyage of discovery; his America is always just beyond the horizon. He endeavors, blindly and passionately at first, later with more sureness and clarity, to map new territory; new thought, and truths ascertained by thought; new dreams, visions and ecstasies created by the imagination." (U. M. Ellis-Fermor, *Marlowe.*)

THE TRAGICAL HISTORY OF DOCTOR FAUSTUS[1]

DRAMATIS PERSONÆ

THE POPE.	SCHOLARS, FRIARS, *and* ATTENDANTS.
CARDINAL OF LORRAIN.	DUCHESS OF VANHOLT.
THE EMPEROR OF GERMANY.	
DUKE OF VANHOLT.	
FAUSTUS.	LUCIFER.
VALDES *and*	BELZEBUB.
CORNELIUS, *friends to Faustus.*	MEPHISTOPHILIS.
	GOOD ANGEL.
WAGNER, *servant to Faustus.*	EVIL ANGEL.
	THE SEVEN DEADLY SINS.
CLOWN.	
ROBIN.	DEVILS.
RALPH.	SPIRITS *in the shapes of Alexander the Great, of his Paramour, and of Helen.*
VINTNER.	
HORSE-COURSER.	
A KNIGHT.	
AN OLD MAN.	CHORUS.

Enter Chorus

CHORUS. Not marching now in fields of Thrasymene,
Where Mars did mate[2] the Carthaginians;
Nor sporting in the dalliance of love,
In courts of kings where state is overturned;
Nor in the pomp of proud audacious deeds,
Intends our Muse to vaunt her heavenly verse:
Only this, gentlemen,—we must perform
The form of Faustus' fortunes, good or bad:
To patient judgments we appeal our plaud,
And speak for Faustus in his infancy.
Now is he born, his parents base of stock,
In Germany, within a town called Rhodes:[3]
Of riper years, to Wertenberg he went,
Whereas his kinsmen chiefly brought him up.
So soon he profits in divinity,
The fruitful plot of scholarism graced,[4]
That shortly he was graced with doctor's name,
Excelling all whose sweet delight disputes
In heavenly matters of theology;
Till swol'n with cunning, of a self-conceit,
His waxen wings did mount above his reach,
And, melting, heavens conspired his overthrow;
For, falling to a devilish exercise,
And glutted [now] with learning's golden gifts,
He surfeits upon curséd necromancy;
Nothing so sweet as magic is to him,
Which he prefers before his chiefest bliss:
And this the man that in his study sits.
[*Exit.*

FAUSTUS *discovered in his study.*

FAUST. Settle thy studies, Faustus, and begin
To sound the depth of that thou wilt profess:[5]

[1]The earliest edition of *Doctor Faustus* extant is the quarto of 1604, on which the present reprint is based. In 1616 and in 1663 appeared versions which differ widely from the text of 1604, but the generally accepted opinion is that the earliest version of the play is the one nearest to what Marlowe wrote. The German *Faustbuch,* as it is usually called, in which the legend of Faustus first appeared in print, was published at Frankfurt in 1587. It instantly attained wide popularity, and from it Marlowe drew the material for his play. There is difficulty in the question whether he used the German book or had access to a manuscript translation (the English translation was apparently not printed before 1590 at the earliest); the latter supposition, however, is the more probable one.

[2]Pit himself against.

[3]Roda, not far from Jena.

[4]*I. e.,* gracing.

[5]Teach.

Having commenced, be a divine in show,
Yet level at the end of every art,
And live and die in Aristotle's works.
Sweet Analytics,[1] 'tis thou hast ravished me!
Bene disserere est finis logices.[2]
Is to dispute well logic's chiefest end?
Affords this art no greater miracle?
Then read no more; thou hast attained that end:
A greater subject fitteth Faustus' wit:
Bid ὄν και μὴ ὄν[3] farewell; Galen come,
Seeing, *Ubi desinit philosophus, ibi incipit medicus:*[4]
Be a physician, Faustus; heap up gold,
And be eternized for some wondrous cure:
Summum bonum medicinæ sanitas,[5]
The end of physic is our body's health.
Why, Faustus, hast thou not attained that end?
Is not thy common talk sound aphorisms?
Are not thy bills[6] hung up as monuments,
Whereby whole cities have escaped the plague,
And thousand desperate maladies been eased?
Yet art thou still but Faustus, and a man.
Couldst thou make men to live eternally,
Or, being dead, raise them to life again,
Then this profession were to be esteemed.
Physic, farewell! Where is Justinian? [*Reads.*
Si una eademque res legatur duobus, alter rem, alter valorem rei, etc.[7]
A pretty case of paltry legacies! [*Reads.*
Exhæreditare filium non potest pater, nisi, etc.[8]
Such is the subject of the institute,
And universal body of the law:
This study fits a mercenary drudge,
Who aims at nothing but external trash;
Too servile and illiberal for me.
When all is done, divinity is best:
Jerome's Bible, Faustus, view it well. [*Reads.*
Stipendium peccati mors est. Ha! *Stipendium, etc.*
The reward of sin is death: that's hard. [*Reads.*
Si peccasse negamus, fallimur, et nulla est in nobis veritas;
If we say that we have no sin, we deceive ourselves, and there's no truth in us.
Why, then, belike we must sin, and so consequently die:
Ay, we must die an everlasting death.
What doctrine call you this, *Che sera, sera,*
What will be, shall be? Divinity, adieu!
These metaphysics of magicians,
And necromantic books are heavenly;
Lines, circles, scenes, letters, and characters;
Ay, these are those that Faustus most desires.
O, what a world of profit and delight,
Of power, of honor, of omnipotence,
Is promised to the studious artisan!
All things that move between the quiet poles
Shall be at my command: emperors and kings
Are but obeyed in their several provinces,
Nor can they raise the wind, or rend the clouds;
But his dominion that exceeds in this,
Stretcheth as far as doth the mind of man;
A sound magician is a mighty god:
Here, Faustus, try thy brains to gain a deity.

Enter WAGNER.

Wagner, commend me to my dearest friends,
The German Valdes and Cornelius;
Request them earnestly to visit me.

WAG. I will, sir. [*Exit.*

FAUST. Their conference will be a greater help to me
Than all my labors, plod I ne'er so fast.

Enter GOOD ANGEL *and* EVIL ANGEL.

G. ANG. O, Faustus, lay thy damnéd book aside,
And gaze not on it, lest it tempt thy soul,
And heap God's heavy wrath upon thy head!
Read, read the Scriptures:—that is blasphemy.

E. ANG. Go forward, Faustus, in that famous art
Wherein all Nature's treasure is contained:
Be thou on earth as Jove is in the sky,
Lord and commander of these elements. [*Exeunt Angels.*

FAUST. How am I glutted with conceit of this!
Shall I make spirits fetch me what I please,
Resolve me of all ambiguities,
Perform what desperate enterprise I will?
I'll have them fly to India for gold,
Ransack the ocean for orient pearl,
And search all corners of the new-found world

[1]Logic. [2]To argue well is the end of logic.
[3]Being and not being (an Aristotelian phrase).
[4]Where the philosopher leaves off the physician begins.
[5]Translated in the following line. Other passages in Latin translated in the text are left without note.
[6]Pronouncements.
[7]If one and the same thing is willed to two persons, one receives the thing, the other the value of the thing, *etc.*
[8]A father cannot disinherit his son, unless, *etc.*

For pleasant fruits and princely delicates;
I'll have them read me strange philosophy,
And tell the secrets of all foreign kings;
I'll have them wall all Germany with brass,
And make swift Rhine circle fair Wertenberg;
I'll have them fill the public schools with silk,
Wherewith the students shall be bravely clad;
I'll levy soldiers with the coin they bring,
And chase the Prince of Parma from our land,
And reign sole king of all the provinces;
Yea, stranger engines for the brunt of war,
Than was the fiery keel at Antwerp's bridge,
I'll make my servile spirits to invent.

Enter VALDES *and* CORNELIUS

Come, German Valdes and Cornelius,
And make me blest with your sage conference.
Valdes, sweet Valdes, and Cornelius,
Know that your words have won me at the last
To practice magic and concealéd arts:
Yet not your words only, but mine own fantasy,
That will receive no object; for my head
But ruminates on necromantic skill.
Philosophy is odious and obscure;
Both law and physic are for petty wits;
Divinity is basest of the three,
Unpleasant, harsh, contemptible, and vile:
'Tis magic, magic, that hath ravished me.
Then, gentle friends, aid me in this attempt;
And I, that have with concise syllogisms
Graveled the pastors of the German church,
And made the flowering pride of Wertenberg
Swarm to my problems, as the infernal spirits
On sweet Musæus when he came to hell,
Will be as cunning as Agrippa was,
Whose shadow made all Europe honor him.

VALD. Faustus, these books, thy wit, and our experience,
Shall make all nations to canonize us.
As Indian Moors[1] obey their Spanish lords,
So shall the subjects of every element
Be always serviceable to us three;
Like lions shall they guard us when we please;
Like Almain rutters[2] with their horsemen's staves.
Or Lapland giants, trotting by our sides;
Sometimes like women, or unwedded maids,
Shadowing more beauty in their airy brows
Than have the white breasts of the queen of love:
From Venice shall they drag huge argosies,
And from America the golden fleece
That yearly stuffs old Philip's treasury;
If learnéd Faustus will be resolute.

FAUST. Valdes, as resolute am I in this
As thou to live: therefore object it not.

CORN. The miracles that magic will perform
Will make thee vow to study nothing else.
He that is grounded in astrology,
Enriched with tongues, well seen in minerals,
Hath all the principles magic doth require:
Then doubt not, Faustus, but to be renowned,
And more frequented for this mystery
Than heretofore the Delphian oracle.
The spirits tell me they can dry the sea,
And fetch the treasure of all foreign wrecks,
Ay, all the wealth that our forefathers hid
Within the massy entrails of the earth:
Then tell me, Faustus, what shall we three want?

FAUST. Nothing, Cornelius. O, this cheers my soul!
Come, show me some demonstrations magical,
That I may conjure in some lusty grove,
And have these joys in full possession.

VALD. Then haste thee to some solitary grove,
And bear wise Bacon's[3] and Albertus' works,
The Hebrew Psalter, and New Testament;
And whatsoever else is requisite
We will inform thee ere our conference cease.

CORN. Valdes, first let him know the words of art;
And then, all other ceremonies learned,
Faustus may try his cunning by himself.

VALD. First I'll instruct thee in the rudiments,
And then wilt thou be perfecter than I.

FAUST. Then come and dine with me, and, after meat,
We'll canvass every quiddity thereof;
For, ere I sleep, I'll try what I can do:
This night I'll conjure, though I die therefore.

[*Exeunt.*

Enter two SCHOLARS.

FIRST SCHOL. I wonder what's become of Faustus, that was wont to make our schools ring with *sic probo*.[4]

SEC. SCHOL. That shall we know, for see, here comes his boy.

---

[1] American Indians. [2] Troopers.

[3] Roger Bacon. [4] Thus I demonstrate.

Enter WAGNER.

FIRST SCHOL. How now, sirrah! where's thy master?

WAG. God in heaven knows.

SEC. SCHOL. Why, dost not thou know?

WAG. Yes, I know; but that follows not.

FIRST SCHOL. Go to, sirrah! leave your jesting, and tell us where he is.

WAG. That follows not necessary by force of argument, that you, being licentiates, should stand upon; therefore acknowledge your error, and be attentive.

SEC. SCHOL. Why, didst thou not say thou knewest?

WAG. Have you any witness on't?

FIRST SCHOL. Yes, sirrah, I heard you.

WAG. Ask my fellow if I be a thief.

SEC. SCHOL. Well, you will not tell us?

WAG. Yes, sir, I will tell you; yet, if you were not dunces, you would never ask me such a question, for is not he *corpus naturale?*[1] and is not that *mobile?*[2] then wherefore should you ask me such a question? But that I am by nature phlegmatic, slow to wrath, and prone to lechery (to love, I would say), it were not for you to come within forty foot of the place of execution, although I do not doubt to see you both hanged the next sessions. Thus having triumphed over you, I will set my countenance like a precisian,[3] and begin to speak thus:—Truly, my dear brethren, my master is within at dinner, with Valdes and Cornelius, as this wine, if it could speak, would inform your worships: and so, the Lord bless you, preserve you, and keep you, my dear brethren, my dear brethren! [*Exit.*

FIRST SCHOL. Nay, then, I fear he has fallen into that damned art for which they two are infamous through the world.

SEC. SCHOL. Were he a stranger, and not allied to me, yet should I grieve for him. But, come, let us go and inform the Rector, and see if he by his grave counsel can reclaim him.

FIRST SCHOL. O, but I fear me nothing can reclaim him!

SEC. SCHOL. Yet let us try what we can do. [*Exeunt.*

Enter FAUSTUS *to conjure.*

FAUST. Now that the gloomy shadow of the earth,
Longing to view Orion's drizzling look,
Leaps from th' antarctic world unto the sky,
And dims the welkin with her pitchy breath,
Faustus, begin thine incantations,
And try if devils will obey thy hest,
Seeing thou hast prayed and sacrificed to them.
Within this circle is Jehovah's name,
Forward and backward anagrammatized,
Th' abbreviated names of holy saints,
Figures of every adjunct to the heavens,
And characters of signs and erring stars,
By which the spirits are enforced to rise:
Then fear not, Faustus, but be resolute,
And try the uttermost magic can perform.—
Sint mihi dei Acherontis propitii! Valeat numen triplex Jehovæ! Ignei, aërii, aquatani spiritus, salvete! Orientis princeps Belzebub, inferni ardentis monarcha, et Demogorgon, propitiamus vos, ut appareat et surgat Mephistophilis; quid tu moraris? Per Jehovam, Gehennam, et consecratam aquam quam nunc spargo, signumque crucis quod nunc facio, et per vota nostra, ipse nunc surgat nobis dicatus Mephistophilis![4]

Enter MEPHISTOPHILIS.

I charge thee to return, and change thy shape;
Thou art too ugly to attend on me:
Go, and return an old Franciscan friar;
That holy shape becomes a devil best.
[*Exit Mephistophilis.*
I see there's virtue in my heavenly words:
Who would not be proficient in this art?
How pliant is this Mephistophilis,
Full of obedience and humility!
Such is the force of magic and my spells:
Now, Faustus, thou art conjurer laureate,
That canst command great Mephistophilis:
Quin regis Mephistophilis fratris imagine.[5]

Re-enter MEPHISTOPHILIS *like a Franciscan friar.*

MEPH. Now, Faustus, what wouldst thou have me do?

FAUST. I charge thee wait upon me whilst I live,
To do whatever Faustus shall command,
Be it to make the moon drop from her sphere,
Or the ocean to overwhelm the world.

[1]Natural body. [2]Movable. [3]*I.e.*, a puritan.

[4]Gods of Acheron, grant me your aid! The triple deity of Jehovah assist me! Spirits of fire, air, water, all hail! Belzebub, Prince of the East, ruler of the fiery realms, and Demogorgon, I supplicate you, that Mephistophilis may rise and appear; why do you delay? By Jehovah, Gehenna, and the holy water I now sprinkle, and the sign of the cross I now make, and by my prayer, may Mephistophilis now called by me arise!

[5]Verily you have power in the image of your brother Mephistophilis.

MEPH. I am a servant to great Lucifer,
And may not follow thee without his leave:
No more than he commands must we perform.
FAUST. Did not he charge thee to appear to me?
MEPH. No, I came hither of mine own accord.
FAUST. Did not my conjuring speeches raise thee? speak.
MEPH. That was the cause, but yet *per accidens;*[1]
For, when we hear one rack the name of God,
Abjure the Scriptures and his Savior Christ,
We fly, in hope, to get his glorious soul;
Nor will we come, unless he use such means
Whereby he is in danger to be damned.
Therefore the shortest cut for conjuring
Is stoutly to abjure the Trinity,
And pray devoutly to the prince of hell.
FAUST. So Faustus hath
Already done; and holds this principle,
There is no chief but only Belzebub;
To whom Faustus doth dedicate himself.
This word "damnation" terrifies not him,
For he confounds hell in Elysium:
His ghost be with the old philosophers!
But, leaving these vain trifles of men's souls,
Tell me what is that Lucifer thy lord?
MEPH. Arch-regent and commander of all spirits.
FAUST. Was not that Lucifer an angel once?
MEPH. Yes, Faustus, and most dearly loved of God.
FAUST. How comes it, then, that he is prince of devils?
MEPH. O, by aspiring pride and insolence;
For which God threw him from the face of heaven.
FAUST. And what are you that live with Lucifer?
MEPH. Unhappy spirits that fell with Lucifer,
Conspired against our God with Lucifer,
And are for ever damned with Lucifer.
FAUST. Where are you damned?
MEPH. In hell.
FAUST. How comes it, then, that thou art out of hell?
MEPH. Why, this is hell, nor am I out of it.
Think'st thou that I, who saw the face of God,
And tasted the eternal joys of heaven,
Am not tormented with ten thousand hells,
In being deprived of everlasting bliss?
O, Faustus, leave these frivolous demands,
Which strike a terror to my fainting soul!
FAUST. What, is great Mephistophilis so passionate
For being deprivéd of the joys of heaven?
Learn thou of Faustus manly fortitude,
And scorn those joys thou never shalt possess.
Go bear these tidings to great Lucifer:
Seeing Faustus hath incurred eternal death
By desperate thoughts against Jove's deity,
Say, he surrenders up to him his soul,
So he will spare him four-and-twenty years,
Letting him live in all voluptuousness;
Having thee ever to attend on me,
To give me whatsoever I shall ask,
To tell me whatsoever I demand,
To slay mine enemies, and aid my friends,
And always be obedient to my will.
Go and return to mighty Lucifer,
And meet me in my study at midnight,
And then resolve me of thy master's mind.
MEPH. I will, Faustus. [*Exit.*
FAUST. Had I as many souls as there be stars,
I'd give them all for Mephistophilis.
By him I'll be great emperor of the world,
And make a bridge thorough the moving air,
To pass the ocean with a band of men;
I'll join the hills that bind the Afric shore,
And make that country continent to Spain,
And both contributory to my crown:
The Emperor shall not live but by my leave,
Nor any potentate of Germany.
Now that I have obtained what I desired,
I'll live in speculation[2] of this art,
Till Mephistophilis return again. [*Exit.*

Enter WAGNER *and* CLOWN.

WAG. Sirrah boy, come hither.

CLOWN. How, boy! swowns, boy! I hope you have seen many boys with such pickadevaunts[3] as I have: boy, quotha!

WAG. Tell me, sirrah, hast thou any comings in?

CLOWN. Ay, and goings out too; you may see else.

WAG. Alas, poor slave! see how poverty jesteth in his nakedness! the villain is bare and out of service, and so hungry that I know he would give his soul to the devil for a shoulder of mutton, though it were blood-raw.

CLOWN. How! my soul to the devil for a shoulder of mutton, though 'twere blood-raw! not so, good friend: by'r lady, I had need have it well roasted, and good sauce to it, if I pay so dear.

WAG. Well, wilt thou serve me, and I'll make thee go like *Qui mihi discipulus?*[4]

---

[1]By accident.

[2]Study. [3]Beards trimmed to a sharp point.

[4]Who will be my pupil?

CLOWN. How, in verse?

WAG. No, sirrah; in beaten silk and staves-acre.[1]

CLOWN. How, how, knaves-acre![2] ay, I thought that was all the land his father left him. Do you hear? I would be sorry to rob you of your living.

WAG. Sirrah, I say in staves-acre.

CLOWN. Oho, oho, staves-acre! why, then, belike, if I were your man I should be full of vermin.

WAG. So thou shalt, whether thou beest with me or no. But, sirrah, leave your jesting, and bind yourself presently unto me for seven years, or I'll turn all the lice about thee into familiars, and they shall tear thee in pieces.

CLOWN. Do you hear, sir? you may save that labor; they are too familiar with me already: swowns, they are as bold with my flesh as if they had paid for their meat and drink.

WAG. Well, do you hear, sirrah? hold, take these guilders. [*Gives money.*

CLOWN. Gridirons! what be they?

WAG. Why, French crowns.

CLOWN. Mass, but for the name of French crowns, a man were as good have as many English counters. And what should I do with these?

WAG. Why, now, sirrah, thou art at an hour's warning, whensoever and wheresoever the devil shall fetch thee.

CLOWN. No, no; here, take your gridirons again.

WAG. Truly, I'll none of them.

CLOWN. Truly, but you shall.

WAG. Bear witness I gave them him.

CLOWN. Bear witness I give them you again.

WAG. Well, I will cause two devils presently to fetch thee away—Baliol and Belcher!

CLOWN. Let your Baliol and your Belcher come here, and I'll knock them, they were never so knocked since they were devils: say I should kill one of them, what would folks say? "Do ye see yonder tall fellow in the round slop?[3] he has killed the devil." So I should be called Kill-devil all the parish over.

Enter two DEVILS; *and the* CLOWN *runs up and down crying.*

WAG. Baliol and Belcher,—spirits, away! [*Exeunt Devils.*

CLOWN. What, are they gone? a vengeance on them! they have vile long nails. There was a he-devil and a she-devil: I'll tell you how you shall know them; all he-devils has horns, and all she-devils has clifts and cloven feet.

WAG. Well, sirrah, follow me.

CLOWN. But, do you hear? if I should serve you, would you teach me to raise up Banios and Belcheos?

WAG. I will teach thee to turn thyself to anything, to a dog, or a cat, or a mouse, or a rat, or anything.

CLOWN. How! a Christian fellow to a dog, or a cat, a mouse, or a rat! no, no, sir; if you turn me into anything, let it be in the likeness of a little pretty frisking flea, that I may be here and there and everywhere: O, I'll tickle the pretty wenches' plackets! I'll be amongst them, i'faith.

WAG. Well, sirrah, come.

CLOWN. But, do you hear, Wagner?

WAG. How!—Baliol and Belcher!

CLOWN. O Lord! I pray, sir, let Baliol and Belcher go sleep.

WAG. Villain, call me Master Wagner, and let thy left eye be diametarily[4] fixed upon my right heel, with *quasi vestigiis nostris insistere.*[5] [*Exit.*

CLOWN. God forgive me, he speaks Dutch fustian.
Well, I'll follow him; I'll serve him, that's flat. [*Exit.*

FAUSTUS *discovered in his study.*

FAUST. Now, Faustus, must
Thou needs be damned, and canst thou not be saved:
What boots it, then, to think of God or heaven?
Away with such vain fancies, and despair;
Despair in God, and trust in Belzebub:
Now go not backward; no, Faustus, be resolute:
Why waver'st thou? O, something soundeth in mine ears,
"Abjure this magic, turn to God again!"
Ay, and Faustus will turn to God again.
To God? he loves thee not;
The god thou serv'st is thine own appetite,
Wherein is fixed the love of Belzebub:
To him I'll build an altar and a church,
And offer lukewarm blood of new-born babes.

Enter GOOD ANGEL *and* EVIL ANGEL.

G. ANG. Sweet Faustus, leave that execrable art.

[1]Species of larkspur, used for destroying vermin.
[2]Name given to Poultney Street, London.
[3]Wide knickerbockers.
[4]Diametrically.
[5]As if to follow in my footsteps.

FAUST. Contrition, prayer, repentance—what of them?
G. ANG. O, they are means to bring thee unto heaven!
E. ANG. Rather illusions, fruits of lunacy,
That make men foolish that do trust them most.
G. ANG. Sweet Faustus, think of heaven and heavenly things.
E. ANG. No, Faustus; think of honor and of wealth. [*Exeunt Angels.*
FAUST. Of Wealth!
Why, the signiory of Emden shall be mine.
When Mephistophilis shall stand by me,
What god can hurt thee, Faustus? thou art safe:
Cast no more doubts.—Come, Mephistophilis,
And bring glad tidings from great Lucifer;—
Is't not midnight?—come, Mephistophilis,
Veni, veni Mephistophile![1]

Enter MEPHISTOPHILIS.

Now tell me what says Lucifer, thy lord?
MEPH. That I shall wait on Faustus whilst he lives,
So he will buy my service with his soul.
FAUST. Already Faustus hath hazarded that for thee.
MEPH. But, Faustus, thou must bequeath it solemnly,
And write a deed of gift with thine own blood;
For that security craves great Lucifer.
If thou deny it, I will back to hell.
FAUST. Stay, Mephistophilis, and tell me, what good will my soul do thy lord?
MEPH. Enlarge his kingdom.
FAUST. Is that the reason why he tempts us thus?
MEPH. *Solamen miseris socios habuisse doloris.*[2]
FAUST. Why, have you any pain, that torture others?
MEPH. As great as have the human souls of men.
But, tell me, Faustus, shall I have thy soul?
And I will be thy slave, and wait on thee,
And give thee more than thou hast wit to ask.
FAUST. Ay, Mephistophilis, I give it thee.
MEPH. Then, Faustus, stab thy arm courageously,
And bind thy soul, that at some certain day
Great Lucifer may claim it as his own;
And then be thou as great as Lucifer.

[1]Come, come Mephistophilis!
[2]Misery loves company.

FAUST. [*Stabbing his arm*] Lo, Mephistophilis, for love of thee,
I cut mine arm, and with my proper blood
Assure my soul to be great Lucifer's,
Chief lord and regent of perpetual night!
View here the blood that trickles from mine arm,
And let it be propitious for my wish.
MEPH. But, Faustus, thou must
Write it in manner of a deed of gift.
FAUST. Ay, so I will [*Writes*]. But, Mephistophilis,
My blood congeals, and I can write no more.
MEPH. I'll fetch thee fire to dissolve it straight. [*Exit.*
FAUST. What might the staying of my blood portend?
Is it unwilling I should write this bill?
Why streams it not, that I may write afresh?
Faustus gives to thee his soul: ah, there it stayed!
Why shouldst thou not? is not thy soul thine own?
Then write again, *Faustus gives to thee his soul.*

Re-enter MEPHISTOPHILIS *with a chafer of coals.*

MEPH. Here's fire; come, Faustus, set it on.
FAUST. So, now the blood begins to clear again;
Now will I make an end immediately. [*Writes.*
MEPH. O, what will not I do to obtain his soul! [*Aside.*
FAUST. *Consummatum est;*[3] this bill is ended,
And Faustus hath bequeathed his soul to Lucifer.
But what is this inscription on mine arm?
Homo, fuge;[4] whither should I fly?
If unto God, he'll throw me down to hell.
My senses are deceived; here's nothing writ:—
I see it plain; here in this place is writ,
Homo, fuge; yet shall not Faustus fly.
MEPH. I'll fetch him somewhat to delight his mind. [*Aside, and then exit.*

Re-enter MEPHISTOPHILIS *with* DEVILS, *who give crowns and rich apparel to* FAUSTUS, *dance, and then depart.*

FAUST. Speak, Mephistophilis, what means this show?
MEPH. Nothing, Faustus, but to delight thy mind withal,
And to show thee what magic can perform.

[3]It is finished. [4]O man, flee!

FAUST. But may I raise up spirits when I please?

MEPH. Ay, Faustus, and do greater things than these.

FAUST. Then there's enough for a thousand souls.
Here, Mephistophilis, receive this scroll,
A deed of gift of body and of soul:
But yet conditionally that thou perform
All articles prescribed between us both.

MEPH. Faustus, I swear by hell and Lucifer
To effect all promises between us made!

FAUST. Then hear me read them. [*Reads.*] *On these conditions following. First that Faustus may be a spirit in form and substance. Secondly, that Mephistophilis shall be his servant, and at his command. Thirdly, that Mephistophilis shall do for him, and bring him whatsoever he desires. Fourthly, that he shall be in his chamber or house invisible. Lastly, that he shall appear to the said John Faustus, at all times, in what form or shape soever he please. I, John Faustus, of Wertenberg, Doctor, by these presents, do give both body and soul to Lucifer, prince of the East, and his minister Mephistophilis; and furthermore grant unto them, that, twenty-four years being expired, the articles above-written inviolate, full power to fetch or carry the said John Faustus, body and soul, flesh, blood, or goods, into their habitation wheresoever. By me, John Faustus.*

MEPH. Speak, Faustus, do you deliver this as your deed?

FAUST. Ay, take it, and the devil give thee good on't!

MEPH. Now, Faustus, ask what thou wilt.

FAUST. First will I question with thee about hell.
Tell me, where is the place that men call hell?

MEPH. Under the heavens.

FAUST. Ay, but whereabout?

MEPH. Within the bowels of these elements,
Where we are tortured and remain for ever:
Hell hath no limits, nor is circumscribed
In one self place; for where we are is hell,
And where hell is, there must we ever be:
And, to conclude, when all the world dissolves,
And every creature shall be purified,
All places shall be hell that are not heaven.

FAUST. Come, I think hell's a fable.

MEPH. Ay, think so still, till experience change thy mind.

FAUST. Why, think'st thou, then, that Faustus shall be damned?

MEPH. Ay, of necessity, for here's the scroll
Wherein thou hast given thy soul to Lucifer.

FAUST. Ay, and body too: but what of that?
Think'st thou that Faustus is so fond[1] to imagine
That, after this life, there is any pain?
Tush, these are trifles and mere old wives' tales.

MEPH. But, Faustus, I am an instance to prove the contrary,
For I am damned, and am now in hell.

FAUST. How! now in hell!
Nay, an this be hell, I'll willingly be damned here:
What! walking, disputing, *etc.*
But, leaving off this, let me have a wife,
The fairest maid in Germany;
For I am wanton and lascivious,
And cannot live without a wife.

MEPH. How! a wife!
I prithee, Faustus, talk not of a wife.

FAUST. Nay, sweet Mephistophilis, fetch me one, for I will have one.

MEPH. Well, thou wilt have one? Sit there till I come: I'll fetch thee a wife in the devil's name. [*Exit.*

Re-enter MEPHISTOPHILIS *with a* DEVIL *dressed like a* WOMAN, *with fireworks.*

MEPH. Tell me, Faustus, how dost thou like thy wife?

FAUST. A plague on her for a hot whore!

MEPH. Tut, Faustus,
Marriage is but a ceremonial toy;
If thou lovest me, think no more of it.
I'll cull thee out the fairest courtesans,
And bring them every morning to thy bed:
She whom thine eye shall like, thy heart shall have,
Be she as chaste as was Penelope,
As wise as Saba,[2] or as beautiful
As was bright Lucifer before his fall.
Hold, take this book, peruse it thoroughly: [*Gives book.*
The iterating of these lines brings gold;
The framing of this circle on the ground
Brings whirlwinds, tempests, thunder, and lightning;
Pronounce this thrice devoutly to thyself,
And men in armor shall appear to thee,
Ready to execute what thou desir'st.

FAUST. Thanks, Mephistophilis: yet fain would I have a book wherein I might behold all spells and incantations, that I might raise up spirits when I please.

MEPH. Here they are in this book. [*Turns to them.*

---

[1]Foolish. [2]Queen of Sheba.

FAUST. Now would I have a book where I might see all characters and planets of the heavens, that I might know their motions and dispositions.

MEPH. Here they are too. [*Turns to them.*

FAUST. Nay, let me have one book more,—and then I have done,—wherein I might see all plants, herbs, and trees, that grow upon the earth.

MEPH. Here they be.

FAUST. O, thou art deceived.

MEPH. Tut, I warrant thee. [*Turns to them.*

FAUST. When I behold the heavens, then I repent,
And curse thee, wicked Mephistophilis,
Because thou hast deprived me of those joys.

MEPH. Why, Faustus,
Thinkest thou heaven is such a glorious thing?
I tell thee, 'tis not half so fair as thou,
Or any man that breathes on earth.

FAUST. How prov'st thou that?

MEPH. 'Twas made for man, therefore is man more excellent.

FAUST. If it were made for man, 'twas made for me:
I will renounce this magic and repent.

Enter GOOD ANGEL *and* EVIL ANGEL.

G. ANG. Faustus, repent; yet God will pity thee.

E. ANG. Thou art a spirit; God cannot pity thee.

FAUST. Who buzzeth in mine ears I am a spirit?
Be I a devil, yet God may pity me;
Ay, God will pity me, if I repent.

E. ANG. Ay, but Faustus never shall repent.
[*Exeunt Angels.*

FAUST. My heart's so hardened, I cannot repent:
Scarce can I name salvation, faith, or heaven,
But fearful echoes thunder in mine ears,
"Faustus, thou art damned!" then swords, and knives,
Poison, guns, halters, and envenomed steel
Are laid before me to dispatch myself;
And long ere this I should have slain myself,
Had not sweet pleasure conquered deep despair.
Have not I made blind Homer sing to me
Of Alexander's love and Œnon's death?
And hath not he, that built the walls of Thebes
With ravishing sound of his melodious harp,
Made music with my Mephistophilis?
Why should I die, then, or basely despair!
I am resolved; Faustus shall ne'er repent.—
Come, Mephistophilis, let us dispute again,
And argue of divine astrology.
Tell me, are there many heavens above the moon?
Are all celestial bodies but one globe,
As is the substance of this centric earth?

MEPH. As are the elements, such are the spheres,
Mutually folded in each other's orb,
And, Faustus,
All jointly move upon one axletree,
Whose terminus is termed the world's wide pole;
Nor are the names of Saturn, Mars, or Jupiter
Feigned, but are erring stars.

FAUST. But, tell me, have they all one motion, both *situ et tempore?*[1]

MEPH. All jointly move from east to west in twenty-four hours upon the poles of the world; but differ in their motion upon the poles of the zodiac.

FAUST. Tush,
These slender trifles Wagner can decide:
Hath Mephistophilis no greater skill?
Who knows not the double motion of the planets?
The first is finished in a natural day;
The second thus; as Saturn in thirty years; Jupiter in twelve; Mars in four; the Sun, Venus, and Mercury in a year; the Moon in twenty-eight days. Tush, these are freshmen's suppositions. But, tell me, hath every sphere a dominion or *intelligentia?*

MEPH. Ay.

FAUST. How many heavens or spheres are there?

MEPH. Nine; the seven planets, the firmament, and the empyreal heaven.

FAUST. Well, resolve me in this question; why have we not conjunctions, oppositions, aspects, eclipses, all at one time, but in some years we have more, in some less?

MEPH. *Per inæqualem motum respectu totius.*[2]

FAUST. Well, I am answered. Tell me, who made the world?

MEPH. I will not.

FAUST. Sweet Mephistophilis, tell me.

MEPH. Move me not, for I will not tell thee.

FAUST. Villain, have I not bound thee to tell me anything?

MEPH. Ay, that is not against our kingdom; but this is.
Think thou on hell, Faustus, for thou art damned.

---

[1]In direction and time.

[2]On account of their unequal motion in relation to the whole.

FAUST. Think, Faustus, upon God that made the world.
MEPH. Remember this. [*Exit.*
FAUST. Ay, go, accurséd spirit, to ugly hell!
'Tis thou hast damned distresséd Faustus' soul.
Is't not too late?

Re-enter GOOD ANGEL *and* EVIL ANGEL.

E. ANG. Too late.
G. ANG. Never too late, if Faustus can repent.
E. ANG. If thou repent, devils shall tear thee in pieces.
G. ANG. Repent, and they shall never raze thy skin. [*Exeunt Angels.*
FAUST. Ah, Christ, my Savior,
Seek to save distresséd Faustus' soul!

Enter LUCIFER, BELZEBUB, *and* MEPHISTOPHILIS.

LUC. Christ cannot save thy soul, for he is just:
There's none but I have interest in the same.
FAUST. O, who art thou that look'st so terrible?
LUC. I am Lucifer,
And this is my companion-prince in hell.
FAUST. O, Faustus, they are come to fetch away thy soul!
LUC. We come to tell thee thou dost injure us;
Thou talk'st of Christ, contrary to thy promise:
Thou shouldst not think of God: think of the devil,
And of his dam too.
FAUST. Nor will I henceforth: pardon me in this,
And Faustus vows never to look to heaven,
Never to name God, or to pray to Him,
To burn his Scriptures, slay his ministers,
And make my spirits pull his churches down.
LUC. Do so, and we will highly gratify thee. Faustus, we are come from hell to show thee some pastime: sit down, and thou shalt see all the Seven Deadly Sins appear in their proper shapes.
FAUST. That sight will be as pleasing unto me,
As Paradise was to Adam, the first day
Of his creation.
LUC. Talk not of Paradise nor creation; but mark this show: talk of the devil, and nothing else.—Come away!

Enter the SEVEN DEADLY SINS.

Now, Faustus, examine them of their several names and dispositions.

FAUST. What art thou, the first?
PRIDE. I am Pride. I disdain to have any parents. I am like to Ovid's flea; I can creep into every corner of a wench; sometimes, like a periwig, I sit upon her brow; or, like a fan of feathers, I kiss her lips; indeed, I do—what do I not? But, fie, what a scent is here! I'll not speak another word, except the ground were perfumed, and covered with cloth of arras.
FAUST. What art thou, the second?
COVET. I am Covetousness, begotten of an old churl, in an old leathern bag: and, might I have my wish, I would desire that this house and all the people in it were turned to gold, that I might lock you up in my good chest: O, my sweet gold!
FAUST. What art thou, the third?
WRATH. I am Wrath. I had neither father nor mother: I leaped out of a lion's mouth when I was scarce half an hour old; and ever since I have run up and down the world with this case of rapiers, wounding myself when I had nobody to fight withal. I was born in hell; and look to it, for some of you shall be my father.[1]
FAUST. What art thou, the fourth?
ENVY. I am Envy, begotten of a chimney-sweeper and an oyster-wife. I cannot read, and therefore wish all books were burned. I am lean with seeing others eat. O, that there would come a famine through all the world, that all might die, and I live alone! then thou shouldst see how fat I would be. But must thou sit, and I stand? come down, with a vengeance!
FAUST. Away, envious rascal!—What art thou, the fifth?
GLUT. Who I, sir? I am Gluttony. My parents are all dead, and the devil a penny they have left me, but a bare pension, and that is thirty meals a day, and ten bevers,[2]—a small trifle to suffice nature. O, I come of a royal parentage! my grandfather was a Gammon of Bacon, my grandmother a Hogshead of Claret-wine; my godfathers were these, Peter Pickle-herring and Martin Martlemas-beef; O, but my godmother, she was a jolly gentlewoman, and well-beloved in every good town and city; her name was Mistress Margery March-beer. Now, Faustus, thou hast heard all my progeny; wilt thou bid me to supper?

[1] *I. e.*, one of the devils must be my father.
[2] Refreshments between breakfast and dinner.

FAUST. No, I'll see thee hanged: thou wilt eat up all my victuals.

GLUT. Then the devil choke thee!

FAUST. Choke thyself, glutton!—What art thou, the sixth?

SLOTH. I am Sloth. I was begotten on a sunny bank, where I have lain ever since; and you have done me great injury to bring me from thence: let me be carried thither again by Gluttony and Lechery. I'll not speak another word for a king's ransom.

FAUST. What are you, Mistress Minx, the seventh and last?

LECHERY. Who I, sir? I am one that loves an inch of raw mutton better than an ell of fried stock-fish; and the first letter of my name begins with L.

FAUST. Away, to hell, to hell!

[*Exeunt the Sins.*

LUC. Now, Faustus, how dost thou like this?

FAUST. O, this feeds my soul!

LUC. Tut, Faustus, in hell is all manner of delight.

FAUST. O, might I see hell, and return again,
How happy were I then!

LUC. Thou shalt; I will send for thee at midnight.
In meantime take this book; peruse it thoroughly,
And thou shalt turn thyself into what shape thou wilt.

FAUST. Great thanks, mighty Lucifer!
This will I keep as chary as my life.

LUC. Farewell, Faustus, and think on the devil.

FAUST. Farewell, great Lucifer.

[*Exeunt Lucifer and Belzebub.*

Come, Mephistophilis. [*Exeunt.*

Enter CHORUS.

CHOR. Learnéd Faustus,
To know the secrets of astronomy
Graven in the book of Jove's high firmament,
Did mount himself to scale Olympus' top,
Being seated in a chariot burning bright,
Drawn by the strength of yoky dragons' necks.
He now is gone to prove cosmography,
And, as I guess, will first arrive in Rome,
To see the Pope and manner of his court,
And take some part of holy Peter's feast,
That to this day is highly solemnized.

[*Exit.*

Enter FAUSTUS *and* MEPHISTOPHILIS.

FAUST. Having now, my good Mephistophilis,
Passed with delight the stately town of Trier,[1]
Environed round with airy mountain-tops,
With walls of flint, and deep-entrenchéd lakes,
Not to be won by any conquering prince;
From Paris next, coasting the realm of France,
We saw the river Maine fall into Rhine,
Whose banks are set with groves of fruitful vines;
Then up to Naples, rich Campania,
Whose buildings fair and gorgeous to the eye,
The streets straight forth, and paved with finest brick,
Quarter the town in four equivalents:
There saw we learnéd Maro's[2] golden tomb,
The way he cut, an English mile in length,
Thorough a rock of stone, in one night's space;
From thence to Venice, Padua, and the rest,
In one of which a sumptuous temple stands,
That threats the stars with her aspiring top.
Thus hitherto hath Faustus spent his time:
But tell me now what resting-place is this?
Hast thou, as erst I did command,
Conducted me within the walls of Rome?

MEPH. Faustus, I have; and, because we will not be unprovided, I have taken up his Holiness' privy-chamber for our use.

FAUST. I hope his Holiness will bid us welcome.

MEPH. Tut, 'tis no matter, man; we'll be bold with his good cheer.
And now, my Faustus, that thou mayst perceive
What Rome containeth to delight thee with,
Know that this city stands upon seven hills
That underprop the groundwork of the same:
[Just through the midst runs flowing Tiber's stream
With winding banks that cut it in two parts;]
Over the which four stately bridges lean,
That make safe passage to each part of Rome:
Upon the bridge called Ponte Angelo
Erected is a castle passing strong,
Within whose walls such store of ordnance are,
And double cannons framed of carvéd brass,
As match the days within one complete year;

[1]Treves.

[2]Virgil, who in the Middle Ages was thought to have been a magician.

Besides the gates, and high pyramidés,
Which Julius Cæsar brought from Africa.
FAUST. Now, by the kingdoms of infernal rule,
Of Styx, of Acheron, and the fiery lake
Of ever-burning Phlegethon, I swear
That I do long to see the monuments
And situation of bright-splendent Rome:
Come, therefore, let's away.
MEPH. Nay, Faustus, stay: I know you'd fain see the Pope
And take some part of holy Peter's feast,
Where thou shalt see a troop of bald-pate friars,
Whose *summum bonum*[1] is in belly-cheer.
FAUST. Well, I'm content to compass then some sport,
And by their folly make us merriment.
Then charm me, that I
May be invisible, to do what I please,
Unseen of any whilst I stay in Rome.
[*Mephistophilis charms him.*
MEPH. So, Faustus; now
Do what thou wilt, thou shalt not be discerned.

Sound a Sennet.[2] *Enter the* POPE *and the* CARDINAL OF LORRAIN *to the banquet, with* FRIARS *attending.*

POPE. My lord of Lorrain, will't please you draw near?
FAUST. Fall to, and the devil choke you, an you spare!
POPE. How now! who's that which spake?—Friars, look about.
FIRST FRIAR. Here's nobody, if it like your Holiness.
POPE. My lord, here is a dainty dish was sent me from the Bishop of Milan.
FAUST. I thank you, sir. [*Snatches the dish.*
POPE. How now! who's that which snatched the meat from me? will no man look?—My lord, this dish was sent me from the Cardinal of Florence.
FAUST. You say true; I'll ha't.
[*Snatches the dish.*
POPE. What, again!—My lord, I'll drink to your grace.
FAUST. I'll pledge your grace.
[*Snatches the cup.*
C. OF LOR. My lord, it may be some ghost, newly crept out of purgatory, come to beg a pardon of your Holiness.
POPE. It may be so.—Friars, prepare a dirge to lay the fury of this ghost.—Once again, my lord, fall to.
[*The Pope crosses himself.*

[1]Highest good.
[2]Set of notes on trumpet or cornet.

FAUST. What, are you crossing of yourself?
Well, use that trick no more, I would advise you.
[*The Pope crosses himself again.*
Well, there's the second time. Aware the third;
I give you fair warning.
[*The Pope crosses himself again, and Faustus hits him a box of the ear; and they all run away.*
Come on, Mephistophilis; what shall we do?
MEPH. Nay, I know not: we shall be cursed with bell, book, and candle.
FAUST. How! bell, book, and candle,—candle, book, and bell,—
Forward and backward, to curse Faustus to hell!
Anon you shall hear a hog grunt, a calf bleat, and an ass bray,
Because it is Saint Peter's holiday.

Re-enter all the FRIARS *to sing the Dirge.*

FIRST FRIAR. Come, brethren, let's about our business with good devotion.

They sing:
Cursed be he that stole away his Holiness' meat from the table!
maledicat Dominus![3]
Cursed be he that struck his Holiness a blow on the face!
maledicat Dominus!
Cursed be he that took Friar Sandelo a blow on the pate!
maledicat Dominus!
Cursed be he that disturbeth our holy dirge!
maledicat Dominus!
Cursed be he that took away his Holiness' wine!
maledicat Dominus! Et omnes Sancti![4]
Amen!
[*Mephistophilis and Faustus beat the Friars, and fling fireworks among them; and so exeunt.*

Enter CHORUS.

CHOR. When Faustus had with pleasure ta'en the view
Of rarest things, and royal courts of kings,
He stayed his course, and so returnéd home;
Where such as bear his absence but with grief,
I mean his friends and near'st companions,
Did gratulate his safety with kind words,

[3]May the Lord curse him.
[4]And all the saints.

And in their conference of what befell,
Touching his journey through the world and air,
They put forth questions of astrology,
Which Faustus answered with such learnéd skill
As they admired and wondered at his wit.
Now is his fame spread forth in every land:
Amongst the rest the Emperor is one,
Carolus the Fifth, at whose palace now
Faustus is feasted 'mongst his noblemen.
What there he did, in trial of his art,
I leave untold; your eyes shall see ['t] performed. [*Exit.*

Enter ROBIN THE OSTLER, *with a book in his hand.*

ROBIN. O, this is admirable! here I ha' stolen one of Doctor Faustus' conjuring books, and, i'faith, I mean to search some circles for my own use. Now will I make all the maidens in our parish dance at my pleasure, stark naked, before me; and so by that means I shall see more than e'er I felt or saw yet.

Enter RALPH, *calling* ROBIN.

RALPH. Robin, prithee, come away; there's a gentleman tarries to have his horse, and he would have his things rubbed and made clean: he keeps such a chafing with my mistress about it; and she has set me to look thee out; prithee, come away.

ROBIN. Keep out, keep out, or else you are blown up, you are dismembered, Ralph: keep out, for I am about a roaring piece of work.

RALPH. Come, what dost thou with that same book? thou canst not read?

ROBIN. Yes, my master and mistress shall find that I can read, he for his forehead, she for her private study; she's born to bear with me, or else my art fails.

RALPH. Why, Robin, what book is that?

ROBIN. What book! why, the most intolerable book for conjuring that e'er was invented by any brimstone devil.

RALPH. Canst thou conjure with it?

ROBIN. I can do all these things easily with it; first, I can make thee drunk with ippocras[1] at any tavern in Europe for nothing; that's one of my conjuring works.

RALPH. Our Master Parson says that's nothing.

ROBIN. True, Ralph: and more, Ralph, if thou hast any mind to Nan Spit, our kitchen-maid, then turn her and wind her to thy own use, as often as thou wilt, and at midnight.

RALPH. O, brave, Robin! shall I have Nan Spit, and to mine own use? On that condition I'll feed thy devil with horse-bread as long as he lives, of free cost.

ROBIN. No more, sweet Ralph: let's go and make clean our boots, which lie foul upon our hands, and then to our conjuring in the devil's name. [*Exeunt.*

Enter ROBIN *and* RALPH *with a silver goblet.*

ROBIN. Come, Ralph: did not I tell thee, we were for ever made by this Doctor Faustus' book? *ecce, signum!*[2] here's a simple purchase[3] for horse-keepers: our horses shall eat no hay as long as this lasts.

RALPH. But, Robin, here comes the Vintner.

ROBIN. Hush! I'll gull him supernaturally.

Enter VINTNER.

Drawer, I hope all is paid; God be with you!—Come, Ralph.

VINT. Soft, sir; a word with you. I must yet have a goblet paid from you, ere you go.

ROBIN. I a goblet, Ralph, I a goblet!—I scorn you; and you are but a, *etc.*[4] I a goblet! search me.

VINT. I mean so, sir, with your favor. [*Searches Robin.*

ROBIN. How say you now?

VINT. I must say somewhat to your fellow.—You, sir!

RALPH. Me, sir! me, sir! search your fill. [*Vintner searches him.*] Now, sir, you may be ashamed to burden honest men with a matter of truth.

VINT. Well, one of you hath this goblet about you.

ROBIN. You lie, drawer, 'tis afore me [*Aside*].—Sirrah you, I'll teach you to impeach honest men;—stand by;—I'll scour you for a goblet;—stand aside you had best, I charge you in the name of Belzebub.—Look to the goblet, Ralph [*Aside to Ralph*].

VINT. What mean you, sirrah?

ROBIN. I'll tell you what I mean. [*Reads from a book*] *Sanctobulorum Periphrasticon*—nay, I'll tickle you, Vintner.—Look to the goblet, Ralph [*Aside to Ralph*]. [*Reads*] *Polypragmos Belseborams fra-*

[1]Wine sweetened and spiced.

[2]Behold, the proof! [3]A clear gain.

[4]The actor was expected to speak the abuse extemporaneously.

manto pacostiphos tostu, Mephistophilis, etc.

Enter MEPHISTOPHILIS, *sets squibs at their backs, and then exit. They run about.*

VINT. *O, nomine Domini!*[1] what meanest thou, Robin? thou hast no goblet.

RALPH. *Peccatum peccatorum!*[2]—Here's thy goblet, good Vintner.

[*Gives the goblet to Vintner, who exit.*

ROBIN. *Misericordia pro nobis!*[3] what shall I do? Good devil, forgive me now, and I'll never rob thy library more.

Re-enter MEPHISTOPHILIS.

MEPH. Monarch of hell, under whose black survey
Great potentates do kneel with awful fear,
Upon whose altars thousand souls do lie,
How am I vexéd with these villains' charms?
From Constantinople am I hither come,
Only for pleasure of these damnéd slaves.

ROBIN. How, from Constantinople! you have had a great journey: will you take sixpence in your purse to pay for your supper and be gone?

MEPH. Well, villains, for your presumption, I transform thee into an ape, and thee into a dog; and so be gone! [*Exit.*

ROBIN. How, into an ape! that's brave: I'll have fine sport with the boys; I'll get nuts and apples enow.

RALPH. And I must be a dog.

ROBIN. I'faith, thy head will never be out of the pottage-pot.

[*Exeunt.*

Enter EMPEROR, FAUSTUS, *and a* KNIGHT, *with* ATTENDANTS.

EMP. Master Doctor Faustus, I have heard strange report of thy knowledge in the black art, how that none in my empire nor in the whole world can compare with thee for the rare effects of magic: they say thou hast a familiar spirit, by whom thou canst accomplish what thou list. This, therefore, is my request, that thou let me see some proof of thy skill, that mine eyes may be witnesses to confirm what mine ears have heard reported: and here I swear to thee, by the honor of mine imperial crown, that, whatever thou doest, thou shalt be no ways prejudiced or endamaged.

KNIGHT. I'faith, he looks much like a conjurer. [*Aside.*

[1]In the name of the Lord.
[2]Sin of sins. [3]Mercy upon us.

FAUST. My gracious sovereign, though I must confess myself far inferior to the report men have published, and nothing answerable to the honor of your imperial majesty, yet, for that love and duty binds me thereunto, I am content to do whatsoever your majesty shalt command me.

EMP. Then, Doctor Faustus, mark what I shall say.
As I was sometime solitary set
Within my closet, sundry thoughts arose
About the honor of mine ancestors,
How they had won by prowess such exploits,
Got such riches, subdued so many kingdoms,
As we that do succeed, or they that shall
Hereafter possess our throne, shall
(I fear me) ne'er attain to that degree
Of high renown and great authority:
Amongst which kings is Alexander the Great,
Chief spectacle of the world's pre-eminence,
The bright shining of whose glorious acts
Lightens the world with his reflecting beams,
As when I hear but motion[4] made of him,
It grieves my soul I never saw the man:
If, therefore, thou, by cunning of thine art,
Canst raise this man from hollow vaults below,
Where lies entombed this famous conqueror,
And bring with him his beauteous paramour,
Both in their right shapes, gesture, and attire
They used to wear during their time of life,
Thou shalt both satisfy my just desire,
And give me cause to praise thee whilst I live.

FAUST. My gracious lord, I am ready to accomplish your request, so far forth as by art and power of my spirit I am able to perform.

KNIGHT. I'faith, that's just nothing at all. [*Aside.*

FAUST. But, if it like your grace, it is not in my ability to present before your eyes the true substantial bodies of those two deceased princes, which long since are consumed to dust.

KNIGHT. Ay, marry, Master Doctor, now there's a sign of grace in you, when you will confess the truth. [*Aside.*

FAUST. But such spirits as can lively resemble Alexander and his paramour shall ap-

[4]Mention.

pear before your grace, in that manner that they both lived in, in their most flourishing estate; which I doubt not shall sufficiently content your imperial majesty.

EMP. Go to, Master Doctor; let me see them presently.

KNIGHT. Do you hear, Master Doctor? you bring Alexander and his paramour before the Emperor!

FAUST. How then, sir?

KNIGHT. I'faith, that's as true as Diana turned me to a stag.

FAUST. No, sir; but, when Actæon died, he left the horns for you.—Mephistophilis, be gone. [*Exit Mephistophilis.*

KNIGHT. Nay, an you go to conjuring, I'll be gone. [*Exit.*

FAUST. I'll meet with you anon for interrupting me so.—
Here they are, my gracious lord.

Re-enter MEPHISTOPHILIS *with* SPIRITS *in the shapes of* ALEXANDER *and his* PARAMOUR.

EMP. Master Doctor, I heard this lady, while she lived, had a wart or mole in her neck: how shall I know whether it be so or no?

FAUST. Your highness may boldly go and see.

EMP. Sure, these are no spirits, but the true substantial bodies of those two deceased princes. [*Exeunt Spirits.*

FAUST. Wilt please your highness now to send for the knight that was so pleasant with me here of late?

EMP. One of you call him forth.
[*Exit Attendant.*

Re-enter the KNIGHT *with a pair of horns on his head.*

How now, sir knight! why, I had thought thou hadst been a bachelor, but now I see thou hast a wife, that not only gives thee horns, but makes thee wear them. Feel on thy head.

KNIGHT. Thou damnéd wretch and execrable dog,
Bred in the concave of some monstrous rock,
How dar'st thou thus abuse a gentleman?
Villain, I say, undo what thou hast done!

FAUST. O, not so fast, sir! there's no haste: but, good, are you remembered how you crossed me in my conference with the Emperor? I think I have met with you for it.

EMP. Good Master Doctor, at my entreaty release him: he hath done penance sufficient.

FAUST. My gracious lord, not so much for the injury he offered me here in your presence, as to delight you with some mirth, hath Faustus worthily requited this injurious knight; which being all I desire, I am content to release him of his horns:—and, sir knight, hereafter speak well of scholars.—Mephistophilis, transform him straight. [*Mephistophilis removes the horns.*]—Now, my good lord, having done my duty, I humbly take my leave.

EMP. Farewell, Master Doctor: yet, ere you go,
Expect from me a bounteous reward.
[*Exeunt Emperor, Knight, and attendants.*

FAUST. Now, Mephistophilis, the restless course
That time doth run with calm and silent foot,
Shortening my days and thread of vital life,
Calls for the payment of my latest years:
Therefore, sweet Mephistophilis, let us
Make haste to Wertenberg.

MEPH. What, will you go on horse-back or on foot?

FAUST. Nay, till I'm past this fair and pleasant green, I'll walk on foot.

Enter a HORSE-COURSER.

HORSE-C. I have been all this day seeking one Master Fustian: mass, see where he is!—God save you Master Doctor!

FAUST. What, horse-courser! you are well met.

HORSE-C. Do you hear, sir? I have brought you forty dollars for your horse.

FAUST. I cannot sell him so: if thou likest him for fifty, take him.

HORSE-C. Alas, sir, I have no more!—I pray you, speak for me.

MEPH. I pray you, let him have him: he is an honest fellow, and he has a great charge, neither wife nor child.

FAUST. Well, come, give me your money [*Horse-Courser gives Faustus the money*]: my boy will deliver him to you. But I must tell you one thing before you have him; ride him not into the water, at any hand.

HORSE-C. Why, sir, will he not drink of all waters?

FAUST. O, yes, he will drink of all waters; but ride him not into the water; ride him over hedge or ditch, or where thou wilt, but not into the water.

HORSE-C. Well, sir.—Now am I made man for ever: I'll not leave my horse for forty: if he had but the quality of hey-ding-ding, hey-ding-ding, I'd make a brave living on him: he has a buttock as slick as an eel [*Aside.*]—Well, God b'wi'ye, sir: your boy will deliver him me: but, hark you, sir; if my horse be sick or ill at ease, if I bring his water to you, you'll tell me what it is?

FAUST. Away, you villain! what, dost think I am a horse-doctor? 1298

[*Exit Horse-Courser.*

What art thou, Faustus, but a man condemned to die?
Thy fatal time doth draw to final end;
Despair doth drive distrust into my thoughts:
Confound these passions with a quiet sleep:
Tush, Christ did call the thief upon the Cross; 1303
Then rest thee, Faustus, quiet in conceit.

[*Sleeps in his chair.*

Re-enter HORSE-COURSER, *all wet, crying.*

HORSE-C. Alas, alas! Doctor Fustian, quotha? mass, Doctor Lopus[1] was never such a doctor: has given me a purgation, has purged me of forty dollars; I shall never see them more. But yet, like an ass as I was, I would not be ruled by him, for he bade me I should ride him into no water; now I, thinking my horse had had some rare quality that he would not have had me known of, I, like a venturous youth, rid him into the deep pond at the town's end. I was no sooner in the middle of the pond, but my horse vanished away, and I sat upon a bottle[2] of hay, never so near drowning in my life. But I'll seek out my doctor, and have my forty dollars again, or I'll make it the dearest horse!—O, yonder is his snipper-snapper. Do you hear? you hey-pass,[3] where's your master? 1324

MEPH. Why, sir, what would you? you cannot speak with him.

HORSE-C. But I will speak with him.

MEPH. Why, he's fast asleep: come some other time. 1328

HORSE-C. I'll speak with him now, or I'll break his glass-windows about his ears.

MEPH. I tell thee, he has not slept this eight nights.

HORSE-C. An he have not slept this eight weeks, I'll speak with him. 1334

MEPH. See, where he is, fast asleep.

HORSE-C. Ay, this is he.—God save you, Master Doctor, Master Doctor, Master Doctor Fustian! forty dollars, forty dollars for a bottle of hay! 1339

MEPH. Why, thou seest he hears thee not.

HORSE-C. So-ho, ho! so-ho, ho! [*Hollows in his ear.*] No, will you not wake? I'll make you wake ere I go. [*Pulls Faustus by the leg, and pulls it away.*] Alas, I am undone! what shall I do? 1345

FAUST. O, my leg, my leg!—Help, Mephistophilis! call the officers.—My leg, my leg!

MEPH. Come, villain, to the constable.

HORSE-C. O, Lord, sir, let me go, and I'll give you forty dollars more! 1350

MEPH. Where be they?

HORSE-C. I have none about me: come to my ostry[4] and I'll give them you.

MEPH. Be gone quickly.

[*Horse-Courser runs away.*

FAUST. What, is he gone? farewell he! Faustus has his leg again, and the Horse-Courser, I take it, a bottle of hay for his labor: well, this trick shall cost him forty dollars more. 1359

Enter WAGNER.

How now, Wagner! what's the news with thee?

WAG. Sir, the Duke of Vanholt doth earnestly entreat your company.

FAUST. The Duke of Vanholt! an honorable gentleman, to whom I must be no niggard of my cunning.—Come, Mephistophilis, let's away to him. [*Exeunt.* 1367

Enter the DUKE OF VANHOLT, *the* DUCHESS, *and* FAUSTUS.

DUKE. Believe me, Master Doctor, this merriment hath much pleased me.

FAUST. My gracious lord, I am glad it contents you so well.—But it may be, madam, you take no delight in this. I have heard that great-bellied women do long for some dainties or other: what is it, madam? tell me, and you shall have it. 1376

DUCHESS. Thanks, good Master Doctor: and, for I see your courteous intent to pleasure me, I will not hide from you the thing my heart desires; and, were it now summer, as it is January and the dead time of the winter, I would desire no better meat than a dish of ripe grapes. 1383

FAUST. Alas, madam, that's nothing!—Mephistophilis, be gone. [*Exit Mephistophilis.*] Were it a greater thing than this, so it would content you, you should have it. 1388

[1]Roderigo Lopez, private physician to Queen Elizabeth, hanged in 1594 for conspiring to poison her.

[2]Bundle. [3]Juggler.

[4]Inn.

Re-enter MEPHISTOPHILIS *with grapes.*

Here they be, madam: wilt please you taste on them?

DUKE. Believe me, Master Doctor, this makes me wonder above the rest, that being in the dead time of winter and in the month of January, how you should come by these grapes.

FAUST. If it like your grace, the year is divided into two circles over the whole world, that, when it is here winter with us, in the contrary circle it is summer with them, as in India, Saba, and farther countries in the east; and by means of a swift spirit that I have, I had them brought hither, as you see.—How do you like them, madam? be they good?

DUCHESS. Believe me, Master Doctor, they be the best grapes that e'er I tasted in my life before.

FAUST. I am glad they content you so, madam.

DUKE. Come, madam, let us in, where you must well reward this learned man for the great kindness he hath showed to you.

DUCHESS. And so I will, my lord; and, whilst I live, rest beholding for this courtesy.

FAUST. I humbly thank your grace.

DUKE. Come, Master Doctor, follow us, and receive your reward. [*Exeunt.*

Enter WAGNER.

WAG. I think my master means to die shortly,
For he hath given to me all his goods:
And yet, methinks, if that death were near,
He would not banquet, and carouse, and swill
Amongst the students, as even now he doth,
Who are at supper with such belly-cheer
As Wagner ne'er beheld in all his life.
See, where they come! belike the feast is ended. [*Exit.*

Enter FAUSTUS *with two or three* SCHOLARS, *and* MEPHISTOPHILIS.

FIRST SCHOL. Master Doctor Faustus, since our conference about fair ladies, which was the beautifulest in all the world, we have determined with ourselves that Helen of Greece was the admirablest lady that ever lived: therefore, Master Doctor, if you will do us that favor, as to let us see that peerless dame of Greece, whom all the world admires for majesty, we should think ourselves much beholding unto you.

FAUST. Gentlemen,
For that I know your friendship is unfeigned,
And Faustus' custom is not to deny
The just requests of those that wish him well
You shall behold that peerless dame of Greece,
No otherways for pomp and majesty
Than when Sir Paris crossed the seas with her,
And brought the spoils to rich Dardania.
Be silent, then, for danger is in words.

[*Music sounds, and Helen passeth over the stage.*

SEC. SCHOL. Too simple is my wit to tell her praise,
Whom all the world admires for majesty.

THIRD SCHOL. No marvel though the angry Greeks pursued
With ten years' war the rape of such a queen,
Whose heavenly beauty passeth all compare.

FIRST SCHOL. Since we have seen the pride of Nature's works,
And only paragon of excellence,
Let us depart; and for this glorious deed
Happy and blest be Faustus evermore!

FAUST. Gentlemen, farewell: the same I wish to you. [*Exeunt Scholars.*

Enter an OLD MAN.

OLD MAN. Ah, Doctor Faustus, that I might prevail
To guide thy steps unto the way of life,
By which sweet path thou mayst attain the goal
That shall conduct thee to celestial rest!
Break heart, drop blood, and mingle it with tears,
Tears falling from repentant heaviness
Of thy most vile and loathsome filthiness,
The stench whereof corrupts the inward soul
With such flagitious crimes of heinous sin
As no commiseration may expel,
But mercy, Faustus, of thy Savior sweet,
Whose blood alone must wash away thy guilt.

FAUST. Where art thou, Faustus? wretch, what hast thou done?
Damned art thou, Faustus, damned; despair and die!
Hell calls for right, and with a roaring voice
Says, "Faustus, come; thine hour is almost come;"
And Faustus now will come to do thee right.

[*Mephistophilis gives him a dagger.*

OLD MAN. Ah, stay, good Faustus, stay thy desperate steps!
I see an angel hovers o'er thy head,
And, with a vial full of precious grace,

Offers to pour the same into thy soul:
Then call for mercy, and avoid despair.

FAUST. Ah, my sweet friend, I feel
Thy words to comfort my distresséd soul!
Leave me a while to ponder on my sins.

OLD MAN. I go, sweet Faustus; but with heavy cheer,
Fearing the ruin of thy hopeless soul. [*Exit.*

FAUST. Accurséd Faustus, where is mercy now?
I do repent; and yet I do despair:
Hell strives with grace for conquest in my breast:
What shall I do to shun the snares of death?

MEPH. Thou traitor, Faustus, I arrest thy soul
For disobedience to my sovereign lord:
Revolt, or I'll in piece-meal tear thy flesh.

FAUST. Sweet Mephistophilis, entreat thy lord
To pardon my unjust presumption,
And with my blood again I will confirm
My former vow I made to Lucifer.

MEPH. Do it, then, quickly, with unfeignéd heart,
Lest greater danger do attend thy drift.

FAUST. Torment, sweet friend, that base and crooked age,[1]
That durst dissuade me from thy Lucifer,
With greatest torments that our hell affords.

MEPH. His faith is great; I cannot touch his soul;
But what I may afflict his body with
I will attempt, which is but little worth.

FAUST. One thing, good servant, let me crave of thee,
To glut the longing of my heart's desire,—
That I might have unto my paramour
That heavenly Helen which I saw of late,
Whose sweet embracings may extinguish clean
Those thoughts that do dissuade me from my vow,
And keep mine oath I made to Lucifer.

MEPH. Faustus, this, or what else thou shalt desire,
Shall be performed in twinkling of an eye.

Re-enter HELEN.

FAUST. Was this the face that launched a thousand ships,
And burnt the topless towers of Ilium?—
Sweet Helen, make me immortal with a kiss.— [*Kisses her.*
Her lips suck forth my soul: see, where it flies!
Come, Helen, come, give me my soul again.
Here will I dwell, for heaven is in these lips,
And all is dross that is not Helena.
I will be Paris, and for love of thee,
Instead of Troy, shall Wertenberg be sacked;
And I will combat with weak Menelaus,
And wear thy colors on my pluméd crest;
Yes, I will wound Achilles in the heel,
And then return to Helen for a kiss.
O, thou art fairer than the evening air
Clad in the beauty of a thousand stars;
Brighter art thou than flaming Jupiter
When he appeared to hapless Semele;
More lovely than the monarch of the sky
In wanton Arethusa's azured arms;
And none but thou shalt be my paramour! [*Exeunt.*

Enter the OLD MAN.

OLD MAN. Accurséd Faustus, miserable man,
That from thy soul exclud'st the grace of heaven,
And fly'st the throne of his tribunal-seat!

Enter DEVILS.

Satan begins to sift me with his pride:
As in this furnace God shall try my faith,
My faith, vile hell, shall triumph over thee,
Ambitious fiends, see how the heavens smile
At your repulse, and laugh your state to scorn!
Hence, hell! for hence I fly unto my God.
[*Exeunt—on one side, Devils, on the other, Old Man.*

Enter FAUSTUS, *with* SCHOLARS.

FAUST. Ah, gentlemen!

FIRST SCHOL. What ails Faustus?

FAUST. Ah, my sweet chamber-fellow, had I lived with thee, then had I lived still! but now I die eternally. Look, comes he not? comes he not?

SEC. SCHOL. What means Faustus?

THIRD SCHOL. Belike he is grown into some sickness by being over-solitary.

FIRST SCHOL. If it be so, we'll have physicians to cure him.—'Tis but a surfeit; never fear, man.

FAUST. A surfeit of deadly sin, that hath damned both body and soul.

SEC. SCHOL. Yet, Faustus, look up to heaven; remember God's mercies are infinite.

FAUST. But Faustus' offense can ne'er be pardoned: the serpent that tempted Eve may be saved, but not Faustus. Ah, gentlemen, hear me with patience, and

[1]The Old Man.

tremble not at my speeches! Though my heart pants and quivers to remember that I have been a student here these thirty years, O, would I had never seen Wertenberg, never read book! and what wonders I have done, all Germany can witness, yea, all the world; for which Faustus hath lost both Germany and the world, yea, heaven itself, heaven, the seat of God, the throne of the blessed, the kingdom of joy; and must remain in hell for ever, hell, ah, hell, for ever! Sweet friends, what shall become of Faustus, being in hell for ever? 1573

THIRD SCHOL. Yet, Faustus, call on God.

FAUST. On God, whom Faustus hath abjured! on God, whom Faustus hath blasphemed! Ah, my God, I would weep! but the devil draws in my tears. Gush forth blood, instead of tears! yea, life and soul! O, he stays my tongue! I would lift up my hands; but see, they hold them, they hold them! 1582

ALL. Who, Faustus?

FAUST. Lucifer and Mephistophilis. Ah, gentlemen, I gave them my soul for my cunning! 1586

ALL. God forbid!

FAUST. God forbade it, indeed; but Faustus hath done it: for vain pleasure of twenty-four years hath Faustus lost eternal joy and felicity. I writ them a bill with mine own blood: the date is expired; the time will come, and he will fetch me. 1593

FIRST SCHOL. Why did not Faustus tell us of this before, that divines might have prayed for thee?

FAUST. Oft have I thought to have done so; but the devil threatened to tear me in pieces, if I named God, to fetch both body and soul, if I once gave ear to divinity: and now 'tis too late. Gentlemen, away, lest you perish with me. 1602

SEC. SCHOL. O, what shall we do to save Faustus?

FAUST. Talk not of me, but save yourselves, and depart. 1606

THIRD SCHOL. God will strengthen me; I will stay with Faustus.

FIRST SCHOL. Tempt not God, sweet friend; but let us into the next room, and there pray for him. 1611

FAUST. Ay, pray for me, pray for me; and what noise soever ye hear, come not unto me, for nothing can rescue me.

SEC. SCHOL. Pray thou, and we will pray that God may have mercy upon thee. 1616

FAUST. Gentlemen, farewell: if I live till morning, I'll visit you; if not, Faustus is gone to hell.

ALL. Faustus, farewell.

[*Exeunt Scholars.—The clock strikes eleven.*

FAUST. Ah, Faustus, 1621
Now hast thou but one bare hour to live,
And then thou must be damned perpetually!
Stand still, you ever-moving spheres of heaven,
That time may cease, and midnight never come;
Fair Nature's eye, rise, rise again, and make
Perpetual day; or let this hour be but 1627
A year, a month, a week, a natural day,
That Faustus may repent and save his soul!
O lente, lente currite, noctis equi![1]
The stars move still, time runs, the clock will strike,
The devil will come, and Faustus must be damned. 1632
O, I'll leap up to my God!—Who pulls me down?—
See, see, where Christ's blood streams in the firmament!
One drop would save my soul, half a drop: ah, my Christ!—
Ah, rend not my heart for naming of my Christ! 1636
Yet will I call on him: O, spare me, Lucifer!—
Where is it now? 'tis gone: and see, where God
Stretcheth out his arm, and bends his ireful brows!
Mountains and hills, come, come, and fall on me, 1640
And hide me from the heavy wrath of God!
No, no!
Then will I headlong run into the earth:
Earth, gape! O, no, it will not harbor me!
You stars that reigned at my nativity,
Whose influence hath allotted death and hell, 1645
Now draw up Faustus, like a foggy mist,
Into the entrails of yon laboring clouds,
That, when you vomit forth into the air,
My limbs may issue from your smoky mouths,
So that my soul may but ascend to heaven!

[*The clock strikes the half-hour.*

Ah, half the hour is past! 'twill all be past anon. 1651
O God,
If thou wilt not have mercy on my soul,
Yet for Christ's sake, whose blood hath ransomed me,
Impose some end to my incessant pain;

[1]Run slowly, slowly, horses of night (Ovid, *Amores*, i, 13).

Let Faustus live in hell a thousand years,
A hundred thousand, and at last be saved;
O, no end is limited to damnéd souls!
Why wert thou not a creature wanting soul?
Or why is this immortal that thou hast?
Ah, Pythagoras' metempsychosis, were that true,
This soul should fly from me, and I be changed
Unto some brutish beast! all beasts are happy,
For, when they die,
Their souls are soon dissolved in elements;
But mine must live still to be plagued in hell.
Curst be the parents that engendered me!
No, Faustus, curse thyself, curse Lucifer
That hath deprived thee of the joys of heaven.

[The clock strikes twelve.

O, it strikes, it strikes! Now, body, turn to air,
Or Lucifer will bear thee quick to hell!

[Thunder and lightning.

O soul, be changed into little water-drops,
And fall into the ocean—ne'er be found!

Enter Devils.

My God, my God, look not so fierce on me!
Adders and serpents, let me breathe a while!
Ugly hell, gape not! come not, Lucifer!
I'll burn my books!—Ah, Mephistophilis!

[Exeunt Devils with Faustus.

Enter CHORUS.

CHOR. Cut is the branch that might have grown full straight,
And burnéd is Apollo's laurel-bough,
That sometime grew within this learnéd man.
Faustus is gone: regard his hellish fall,
Whose fiendful fortune may exhort the wise,
Only to wonder at unlawful things,
Whose deepness doth entice such forward wits
To practice more than heavenly power permits.

[Exit.

SIR PHILIP SIDNEY (1554–1586)

Sidney came of a distinguished family and was born at Penshurst on 30 November, 1554. King Philip of Spain, then in England, was one of his godfathers (whence the boy's name). In 1564 he entered Shrewsbury School. Fulke Greville, later the first Baron Brooke, of Warwick Castle, and Sidney's constant and admiring friend, entered the same school on the same day. Many years after the death of his friend, Greville, in dedicating his own works to Sidney's memory, wrote: Of his youth "I will report no other wonder but this, that though I lived with him, and knew him from a child, yet I never knew him other than a man; with such staidness of mind, lovely and familiar gravity, as carried grace and reverence above greater years. His talk ever of knowledge, and his very play tending to enrich his mind, so as even his teachers found something in him to observe and learn, above that which they had usually read or taught." From Shrewsbury Sidney proceeded to Christ Church, Oxford, in 1567 or 1568, where he found in the University —if we are to believe a contemporary writer— some 1700 fit companions, all "distinguished for their modesty, taciturnity, obedience, and devotion to their studies." Notwithstanding, it seems highly probable that he left Oxford to study, for at least a short time, at Cambridge. In May, 1572, he went to the Continent, traveling first to Paris (where he witnessed the massacre of St. Bartholomew), and thence to Frankfort, where he spent about nine months with the humanist and diplomatist Hubert Languet. He went next (with Languet) to Vienna, penetrated Hungary, and then spent some months in Italy, returning to stay through a winter in Vienna, and then to journey on through the Low Countries to England in May, 1575. In July he was at Kenilworth when the Earl of Leicester received Queen Elizabeth there; and later in the summer, it is said, he first saw Stella (Penelope Devereux, daughter of the Earl of Essex, then aged about 13). The sonnets, *Astrophel and Stella*, were mostly written by 1581 (first published 1591, 1598). In 1577 Sidney was sent as an ambassador to the Continent. In 1580 he was virtually banished from Elizabeth's Court because of his protest against her project of marriage with the Duke of Anjou, and at this time he wrote the *Arcadia* (published 1590, 1593). In the following year he sat in Parliament, and in 1583 Elizabeth knighted him. In the same year he married Frances, daughter of Sir Francis Walsingham, who bore him a daughter in 1585.

In 1579 one Stephen Gosson published an attack upon stage-plays and upon "poets and pipers and such peevish cattle," entitled *The School of Abuse.* This he dedicated to Sidney without having obtained leave to do so, and was —as Edmund Spenser wrote—"for his labor scorned, if at least it be in the goodness of that nature to scorn." It is frequently said, though with little reason, that Sidney wrote his *Defense of Poesy* in reply to Gosson. He does, of course, unmistakably refer to Gosson's pamphlet, but also to other recent attacks; and, in any case, the *Defense* is far more than a reply to ignorant zealots who thought they were serving the causes of religion and decency in attacking drama and poetry. The *Defense* was probably begun in 1580, and finished in 1583 or 1584 (first published in 1595). It marks the real beginning, and remains to this day one of the fairest monuments, of English literary criticism. "In its mingling of gravity and gayety, of colloquialism and dignified, elevated speech, it is a true reflection of Sidney's character. His mind plays easily over the field which he is treating, and the enthusiasm of his personality fuses the seemingly incongruous elements. More than history or philosophy or any of the sciences, he maintains, poetry tends to elevate the whole man. Its delightful teaching leads us to virtuous action, the rational object of all learning. Sidney's love of beauty includes the beauty of a well-ordered life; all other beauty reaches but to dust. It is because, like Arnold, he believes that as time passes our race will find a surer and surer stay in poetry that he urges its claims in such unqualified terms. . . . His criticisms of contemporary literature missed the mark in some instances, but his book endures because in essence it is profoundly true, and because it is a true reflex of the author's versatile, high-minded, gracious personality." (M. W. Wallace, *Life of Sidney*, p. 240.)

During the winter of 1584–1585 Sidney sat again in Parliament, and in the latter year he was appointed Governor of Flushing, assuming the office on 21 November. He thus went to play his part in the unwilling assistance which Elizabeth gave to the Dutch against Spain. Ten months later occurred the battle at Zutphen in which Sidney received a mortal wound. Instantly weakened, he was forced to retire, though still able to ride his horse. "In which sad progress," wrote Fulke Greville, "passing along by the rest of the army, where his uncle the general was, and being thirsty with excess of bleeding, he called for drink which was presently brought him; but as he was putting the bottle to his mouth, he saw a poor soldier carried along, who had eaten his last at the same feast, ghastly casting up his eyes at the bottle. Which Sir Philip perceiving, took it from his head before he drank, and delivered it to the poor man with these words, 'Thy necessity is yet greater than mine.' And when he had pledged this poor soldier, he was presently carried to Arnheim." There he awaited death 26 days, until the end came on 17 October. Amidst universal mourning his body was conveyed to London and given, in old St. Paul's Cathedral, magnificent burial, fitly typifying the hold he had come to have upon the hearts and imaginations of the English as the ideal embodiment of the virtues of the Renaissance gentleman and courtier.

THE DEFENSE OF POESY[1] (1595)

When the right virtuous Edward Wotton[2] and I were at the Emperor's[3] court together, we gave ourselves to learn horsemanship of John Pietro Pugliano, one that with great commendation had the place of an esquire in his stable; and he, according to the fertileness of the Italian wit, did not only afford us the demonstration of his practice, but sought to enrich our minds with the contemplations therein which he thought most precious. But with none I remember mine ears were at any time more loaden, than when—either angered with slow payment, or moved with our learner-like admiration—he exercised his speech in the praise of his faculty. He said soldiers were the noblest estate of mankind, and horsemen the noblest of soldiers. He said they were the masters of war and ornaments of peace, speedy goers and strong abiders, triumphers both in camps and courts. Nay, to so unbelieved a point he proceeded, as that no earthly thing bred such wonder to a prince as to be a good horseman; skill of government was but a *pedanteria*[4] in comparison. Then would he add certain praises, by telling what a peerless beast the horse was, the only serviceable courtier without flattery, the beast of most beauty, faithfulness, courage, and such more, that if I had not been a piece of a logician before I came to him, I think he would have persuaded me to have wished myself a horse. But thus much at least with his no few words he drave into me, that self-love is better than any gilding to make that seem gorgeous wherein ourselves be parties.

Wherein if Pugliano's strong affection and weak arguments will not satisfy you, I will give you a nearer example of myself, who, I know not by what mischance, in these my not old years and idlest times, having slipped into the title of a poet, am provoked to say something unto you in the defense of that my unelected vocation, which if I handle with more good will than good reasons, bear with me, since the scholar is to be pardoned that followeth the steps of his master. And yet I must say that, as I have just cause to make a pitiful defense of poor poetry, which from almost the highest estimation of learning is fallen to be the laughing-stock of children, so have I need to bring some more available proofs, since the former is by no man barred of his deserved credit, the silly latter hath had even the names of philosophers used to the defacing of it, with great danger of civil war among the Muses.

And first, truly, to all them that, professing learning, inveigh against poetry, may justly be objected that they go very near to ungratefulness, to seek to deface that which, in the noblest nations and languages that are known, hath been the first light-giver to ignorance, and first nurse, whose milk by little and little enabled them to feed afterwards of tougher knowledges. And will they now play the hedgehog, that, being received into the den, drave out his host? Or rather the vipers, that with their birth kill their parents? Let learned Greece in any of her manifold sciences be able to show me one book before Musæus, Homer, and Hesiod, all three nothing else but poets. Nay, let any history be brought that can say any writers were there before them, if they were not men of the same skill, as Orpheus, Linus, and some other are named, who, having been the first of that country that

---

[1]In preparation of the text, A. S. Cook's modernization, based on both of the editions of 1595, was found useful.

[2]1548–1626, later first Baron Wotton, half-brother to Sir Henry Wotton. One of the pall-bearers at Sidney's funeral.

[3]Maximilian II (1527–1576).

[4]Species of pedantry.

made pens deliverers of their knowledge to their posterity, may justly challenge to be called their fathers in learning. For not only in time they had this priority—although in itself antiquity be venerable—but went before them as causes, to draw with their charming sweetness the wild untamed wits to an admiration of knowledge. So as Amphion was said to move stones with his poetry to build Thebes, and Orpheus to be listened to by beasts,—indeed stony and beastly people. So among the Romans were Livius Andronicus and Ennius; so in the Italian language the first that made it aspire to be a treasure-house of science were the poets Dante, Boccaccio, and Petrarch; so in our English were Gower and Chaucer, after whom, encouraged and delighted with their excellent foregoing, others have followed to beautify our mother-tongue, as well in the same kind as in other arts.

This did so notably show itself, that the philosophers of Greece durst not a long time appear to the world but under the masks of poets. So Thales, Empedocles, and Parmenides sang their natural philosophy in verses; so did Pythagoras and Phocylides their moral counsels; so did Tyrtæus in war matters, and Solon in matters of policy; or rather they, being poets, did exercise their delightful vein in those points of highest knowledge which before them lay hidden to the world. For that wise Solon was directly a poet it is manifest, having written in verse the notable fable of the Atlantic Island which was continued by Plato. And truly even Plato whosoever well considereth, shall find that in the body of his work though the inside and strength were philosophy, the skin as it were and beauty depended most of poetry. For all standeth upon dialogues; wherein he feigneth many honest burgesses of Athens to speak of such matters that, if they had been set on the rack, they would never have confessed them; besides his poetical describing the circumstances of their meetings, as the well-ordering of a banquet, the delicacy of a walk,[1] with interlacing mere tales, as Gyges' Ring[2] and others, which who knoweth not to be flowers of poetry did never walk into Apollo's garden.

And even historiographers, although their lips sound of things done, and verity be written in their foreheads, have been glad to borrow both fashion and perchance weight of the poets. So Herodotus entitled his history by the name of the nine Muses; and both he and all the rest that followed him either stole or usurped of poetry their passionate describing of passions, the many particularities of battles which no man could affirm, or, if that be denied me, long orations put in the mouths of great kings and captains, which it is certain they never pronounced.

So that truly neither philosopher nor historiographer could at the first have entered into the gates of popular judgments, if they had not taken a great passport of poetry, which in all nations at this day, where learning flourisheth not, is plain to be seen; in all which they have some feeling of poetry. In Turkey, besides their lawgiving divines they have no other writers but poets. In our neighbor country Ireland, where truly learning goeth very bare, yet are their poets held in a devout reverence. Even among the most barbarous and simple Indians, where no writing is, yet have they their poets, who make and sing songs (which they call *areytos*[3]), both of their ancestors' deeds and praises of their gods,—a sufficient probability that, if ever learning come among them, it must be by having their hard dull wits softened and sharpened with the sweet delights of poetry; for until they find a pleasure in the exercise of the mind, great promises of much knowledge will little persuade them that know not the fruits of knowledge. In Wales, the true remnant of the ancient Britons, as there are good authorities to show the long time they had poets which they called bards, so through all the conquests of Romans, Saxons, Danes, and Normans, some of whom did seek to ruin all memory of learning from among them, yet do their poets even to this day last; so as it is not more notable in soon beginning, than in long continuing.

But since the authors of most of our sciences were the Romans, and before them the Greeks, let us a little stand upon their authorities, but even so far as to see what names they have given unto this now scorned skill. Among the Romans a poet was called *vates*, which is as much as a diviner, foreseer, or prophet, as by his conjoined words, *vaticinium* and *vaticinari*, is manifest; so heavenly a title did that ex-

[1]*Symposium; Phaedrus.*

[2]*Republic*, Bk. II (359–360).

[3]The native word was picked up by the Spaniards in the West Indies.

cellent people bestow upon this heart-ravishing knowledge. And so far were they carried into the admiration thereof, that they thought in the chanceable hitting upon any such verses great foretokens of their following fortunes were placed; whereupon grew the word of *Sortes Virgilianæ*, when by sudden opening Virgil's book they lighted upon some verse of his making. Whereof the *Histories of the Emperors' Lives*[1] are full: as of Albinus, the governor of our island, who in his childhood met with this verse,

Arma amens capio, nec sat rationis in armis,[2]

and in his age performed it. Although it were a very vain and godless superstition, as also it was to think that spirits were commanded by such verses—whereupon this word charms, derived of *carmina*, cometh—so yet serveth it to show the great reverence those wits were held in, and altogether not[3] without ground, since both the oracles of Delphos and Sibylla's prophecies were wholly delivered in verses; for that same exquisite observing of number and measure in words, and that high-flying liberty of conceit[4] proper to the poet, did seem to have some divine force in it.

And may not I presume a little further to show the reasonableness of this word *vates*, and say that the holy David's Psalms are a divine poem? If I do, I shall not do it without the testimony of great learned men, both ancient and modern. But even the name of Psalms will speak for me, which, being interpreted, is nothing but Songs; then, that it is fully written in meter, as all learned Hebricians agree, although the rules be not yet fully found; lastly and principally, his handling his prophecy, which is merely poetical. For what else is the awaking his musical instruments, the often and free changing of persons, his notable prosopopœias,[5] when he maketh you, as it were, see God coming in His majesty, his telling of the beasts' joyfulness and hills' leaping, but a heavenly poesy, wherein almost he showeth himself a passionate lover of that unspeakable and everlasting beauty to be seen by the eyes of the mind, only cleared by faith? But truly now having named him, I fear I seem to profane that holy name, applying it to poetry, which is among us thrown down to so ridiculous an estimation. But they that with quiet judgments will look a little deeper into it, shall find the end and working of it such as, being rightly applied, deserveth not to be scourged out of the church of God.

But now let us see how the Greeks named it and how they deemed of it. The Greeks called him ποιητήν, which name hath, as the most excellent, gone through other languages. It cometh of this word ποιεῖν, which is "to make"; wherein I know not whether by luck or wisdom we Englishmen have met with the Greeks in calling him a maker.[6] Which name how high and incomparable a title it is, I had rather were known by marking the scope of other sciences than by any partial allegation. There is no art delivered unto mankind that hath not the works of nature for his principal object, without which they could not consist, and on which they so depend as they become actors and players, as it were, of what nature will have set forth. So doth the astronomer look upon the stars, and, by that he seeth, set down what order nature hath taken therein. So do the geometrician and arithmetician in their divers sorts of quantities. So doth the musician in times tell you which by nature agree, which not. The natural philosopher thereon hath his name, and the moral philosopher standeth upon the natural virtues, vices, and passions of man; and "follow nature," saith he, "therein, and thou shalt not err." The lawyer saith what men have determined, the historian what men have done. The grammarian speaketh only of the rules of speech, and the rhetorician and logician, considering what in nature will soonest prove and persuade, thereon give artificial rules, which still are compassed within the circle of a question, according to the proposed matter. The physician weigheth the nature of man's body, and the nature of things helpful or hurtful unto it. And the metaphysic, though it be in the second and abstract notions, and therefore be counted supernatural, yet doth he, indeed, build upon the depth of nature.

Only the poet, disdaining to be tied to any such subjection, lifted up with the vigor of his own invention, doth grow, in effect, into an-

[1] The *Augustan Histories*.

[2] To arms I rush in frenzy,—not that good cause is shown for arms. (*Æneid*, II, 314.)

[3] Not altogether.

[4] Imaginative invention.

[5] Personifications.

[6] The word was used to signify a poet particularly in Scotland and by the Scottish Chaucerians.

other nature, in making things either better than nature bringeth forth, or, quite anew, forms such as never were in nature, as the heroes, demi-gods, cyclops, chimeras, furies, and such like; so as he goeth hand in hand with nature, not enclosed within the narrow warrant of her gifts, but freely ranging within the zodiac of his own wit. Nature never set forth the earth in so rich tapestry as divers poets have done; neither with pleasant rivers, fruitful trees, sweet-smelling flowers, nor whatsoever else may make the too-much-loved earth more lovely; her world is brazen, the poets only deliver a golden.

But let those things alone, and go to man—for whom as the other things are, so it seemeth in him her uttermost cunning is employed—and know whether she have brought forth so true a lover as Theagenes;[1] so constant a friend as Pylades; so valiant a man as Orlando;[2] so right a prince as Xenophon's Cyrus; so excellent a man every way as Virgil's Æneas? Neither let this be jestingly conceived, because the works of the one be essential, the other in imitation or fiction; for any understanding knoweth the skill of each artificer standeth in that idea, or fore-conceit of the work, and not in the work itself. And that the poet hath that idea is manifest, by delivering them forth in such excellency as he hath imagined them. Which delivering forth, also, is not wholly imaginative, as we are wont to say by[3] them that build castles in the air; but so far substantially it worketh, not only to make a Cyrus, which had been but a particular excellency, as nature might have done, but to bestow a Cyrus upon the world to make many Cyruses, if they will learn aright why and how that maker made him. Neither let it be deemed too saucy a comparison to balance the highest point of man's wit with the efficacy of nature; but rather give right honor to the Heavenly Maker of that maker, who, having made man to His own likeness, set him beyond and over all the works of that second nature. Which in nothing he showeth so much as in poetry, when with the force of a divine breath he bringeth things forth far surpassing her doings, with no small argument to the incredulous of that first accursed fall of Adam,—since our erected wit maketh us know what perfection is, and yet our infected will keepeth us from reaching unto it. But these arguments will by few be understood, and by fewer granted; thus much I hope will be given me, that the Greeks with some probability of reason gave him the name above all names of learning.

Now let us go to a more ordinary opening of him, that the truth may be the more palpable; and so, I hope, though we get not so unmatched a praise as the etymology of his names will grant, yet his very description, which no man will deny, shall not justly be barred from a principal commendation.

Poesy, therefore, is an art of imitation, for so Aristotle termeth it in his word *μίμησις*, that is to say, a representing, counterfeiting, or figuring forth; to speak metaphorically, a speaking picture, with this end,—to teach and delight.

Of this have been three general kinds. The chief, both in antiquity and excellency, were they that did imitate the inconceivable excellencies of God. Such were David in his Psalms; Solomon in his Song of Songs, in his Ecclesiastes and Proverbs; Moses and Deborah in their Hymns; and the writer of Job; which, beside other, the learned Emanuel Tremellius[4] and Franciscus Junius[5] do entitle the poetical part of the Scripture. Against these none will speak that hath the Holy Ghost in due holy reverence. In this kind, though in a full wrong divinity, were Orpheus, Amphion, Homer in his *Hymns*, and many other, both Greeks and Romans. And this poesy must be used by whosoever will follow St. James's counsel in singing psalms when they are merry;[6] and I know is used with the fruit of comfort by some, when, in sorrowful pangs of their death-bringing sins, they find the consolation of the never-leaving goodness.

The second kind is of them that deal with matters philosophical: either moral, as Tyrtæus, Phocylides, and Cato;[7] or natural, as Lucretius and Virgil's *Georgics;* or astro-

[1] In the romance, *Ethiopic History*, by Heliodorus.

[2] Hero of Ariosto's *Orlando Furioso*.

[3] Of.

[4] 1510–1580, Biblical scholar. A Jew of Ferrara, he was converted to Catholic Christianity, later became a Protestant, and lived for a time at Oxford.

[5] 1545–1602, French Protestant; taught theology at Neustadt, Heidelberg, and Leyden.

[6] See James, v, 13.

[7] A certain Dionysius Cato who lived, perhaps, in the third century A.D. His moral distichs were widely popular in the Middle Age, and were still used in Elizabethan schools.

nomical, as Manilius and Pontanus;[1] or historical, as Lucan; which who mislike, the fault is in their judgment quite out of taste, and not in the sweet food of sweetly uttered knowledge.

But because this second sort is wrapped within the fold of the proposed subject, and takes not the free course of his own invention, whether they properly be poets or no let grammarians dispute, and go to the third, indeed right poets, of whom chiefly this question ariseth. Betwixt whom and these second is such a kind of difference as betwixt the meaner sort of painters, who counterfeit only such faces as are set before them, and the more excellent, who having no law but wit, bestow that in colors upon you which is fittest for the eye to see,—as the constant though lamenting look of Lucretia,[2] when she punished in herself another's fault; wherein he painteth not Lucretia, whom he never saw, but painteth the outward beauty of such a virtue. For these third be they which most properly do imitate to teach and delight; and to imitate borrow nothing of what is, hath been, or shall be; but range, only reined with learned discretion, into the divine consideration of what may be and should be. These be they that, as the first and most noble sort may justly be termed *vates*, so these are waited on in the excellentest languages and best understandings with the foredescribed name of poets. For these, indeed, do merely make to imitate, and imitate both to delight and teach, and delight to move men to take that goodness in hand, which without delight they would fly as from a stranger; and teach to make them know that goodness whereunto they are moved:—which being the noblest scope to which ever any learning was directed, yet want there not idle tongues to bark at them.

These be subdivided into sundry more special denominations. The most notable be the heroic, lyric, tragic, comic, satiric, iambic, elegiac, pastoral, and certain others, some of these being termed according to the matter they deal with, some by the sort of verse they liked best to write in,—for indeed the greatest part of poets have appareled their poetical inventions in that numberous kind of writing which is called verse. Indeed but appareled, verse being but an ornament and no cause to poetry, since there have been many most excellent poets that never versified, and now swarm many versifiers that need never answer to the name of poets. For Xenophon, who did imitate so excellently as to give us *effigiem justi imperii*—the portraiture of a just empire under the name of Cyrus (as Cicero saith of him)—made therein an absolute heroical poem; so did Heliodorus in his sugared invention of that picture of love in Theagenes and Chariclea;[3] and yet both these wrote in prose. Which I speak to show that it is not riming and versing that maketh a poet—no more than a long gown maketh an advocate, who, though he pleaded in armor, should be an advocate and no soldier—but it is that feigning notable images of virtues, vices, or what else, with that delightful teaching, which must be the right describing note to know a poet by. Although indeed the senate of poets hath chosen verse as their fittest raiment, meaning, as in matter they passed all in all, so in manner to go beyond them; not speaking, table-talk fashion, or like men in a dream, words as they chanceably fall from the mouth, but peizing[4] each syllable of each word by just proportion, according to the dignity of the subject.

Now therefore it shall not be amiss, first to weigh this latter sort of poetry by his works, and then by his parts; and if in neither of these anatomies he be condemnable, I hope we shall obtain a more favorable sentence. This purifying of wit, this enriching of memory, enabling of judgment, and enlarging of conceit, which commonly we call learning, under what name soever it come forth or to what immediate end soever it be directed, the final end is to lead and draw us to as high a perfection as our degenerate souls, made worse by their clay lodgings, can be capable of. This, according to the inclination of man, bred many-formed impressions. For some that thought this felicity principally to be gotten by knowledge, and no knowledge to be so high or heavenly as acquaintance with the stars, gave themselves to astronomy; others, persuading themselves to be demi-gods if they knew the causes of things, became natural and supernatural philosophers. Some an admirable delight drew to music, and some the certainty of demonstration to the mathe-

[1] 1426–1503, Italian scholar of the Renaissance. Sidney refers to his *Urania*, an astronomical poem in 5 books.

[2] See Livy, i. 58.

[3] The *Ethiopic History*, referred to above.

[4] Poising, weighing.

matics; but all, one and other, having this scope:—to know, and by knowledge to lift up the mind from the dungeon of the body to the enjoying his own divine essence. But when by the balance of experience it was found that the astronomer, looking to the stars, might fall into a ditch, that the inquiring philosopher might be blind in himself, and the mathematician might draw forth a straight line with a crooked heart; then lo! did proof, the overruler of opinions, make manifest, that all these are but serving sciences, which, as they have each a private end in themselves, so yet are they all directed to the highest end of the mistress-knowledge, by the Greeks called *ἀρχιτεκτονική*,[1] which stands, as I think, in the knowledge of a man's self, in the ethic and politic consideration, with the end of well-doing, and not of well-knowing only:—even as the saddler's next end is to make a good saddle, but his further end to serve a nobler faculty, which is horsemanship; so the horseman's to soldiery; and the soldier not only to have the skill, but to perform the practice of a soldier. So that the ending end of all earthly learning being virtuous action, those skills that most serve to bring forth that have a most just title to be princes over all the rest; wherein, if we can show, the poet is worthy to have it before any other competitors.

Among whom as principal challengers step forth the moral philosophers; whom, me thinketh, I see coming towards me with a sullen gravity, as though they could not abide vice by daylight; rudely clothed, for to witness outwardly their contempt of outward things; with books in their hands against glory, whereto they set their names; sophistically speaking against subtility; and angry with any man in whom they see the foul fault of anger. These men, casting largess as they go of definitions, divisions, and distinctions, with a scornful interrogative do soberly ask whether it be possible to find any path so ready to lead a man to virtue, as that which teacheth what virtue is, and teacheth it not only by delivering forth his very being, his causes and effects, but also by making known his enemy, vice, which must be destroyed, and his cumbersome servant, passion, which must be mastered; by showing the generalities that contain it, and the specialities that are derived from it; lastly, by plain setting down how it extendeth itself out of the limits of a man's own little world, to the government of families, and maintaining of public societies?

The historian scarcely giveth leisure to the moralist to say so much, but that he, loaden with old mouse-eaten records, authorizing himself for the most part upon other histories, whose greatest authorities are built upon the notable foundation of hearsay; having much ado to accord differing writers, and to pick truth out of partiality; better acquainted with a thousand years ago than with the present age, and yet better knowing how this world goeth than how his own wit runneth; curious for antiquities and inquisitive of novelties, a wonder to young folks and a tyrant in table-talk; denieth, in a great chafe, that any man for teaching of virtue and virtuous actions is comparable to him. "I am *testis temporum, lux veritatis, vita memoriæ, magistra vitæ, nuntia vetustatis*.[2] The philosopher," saith he, "teacheth a disputative virtue, but I do an active. His virtue is excellent in the dangerless Academy of Plato, but mine showeth forth her honorable face in the battles of Marathon, Pharsalia, Poitiers, and Agincourt. He teacheth virtue by certain abstract considerations, but I only bid you follow the footing of them that have gone before you. Old-aged experience goeth beyond the fine-witted philosopher; but I give the experience of many ages. Lastly, if he make the song-book, I put the learner's hand to the lute; and if he be the guide, I am the light." Then would he allege you innumerable examples, confirming story by story, how much the wisest senators and princes have been directed by the credit of history, as Brutus, Alphonsus of Aragon[3]—and who not, if need be? At length the long line of their disputation maketh a point in this,—that the one giveth the precept, and the other the example.

Now whom shall we find, since the question standeth for the highest form in the school of learning, to be moderator? Truly, as me seemeth, the poet; and if not a moderator, even the man that ought to carry the title from them both, and much more from all

[1]Fulke Greville calls this the "architectonical art."

[2]History, the evidence of time, the light of truth, the life of memory, the directress of life, the herald of antiquity (Cicero, *De Oratore*, II, ix, 36.)

[3]Alphonso V of Aragon and I of Sicily (1416–1458).

other serving sciences. Therefore compare we the poet with the historian and with the moral philosopher; and if he go beyond them both, no other human skill can match him. For as for the divine, with all reverence it is ever to be excepted, not only for having his scope as far beyond any of these as eternity exceedeth a moment, but even for passing each of these in themselves. And for the lawyer, though *Jus* be the daughter of Justice, and Justice the chief of virtues, yet because he seeketh to make men good rather *formidine pœnæ* than *virtutis amore;*[1] or, to say righter, doth not endeavor to make men good, but that their evil hurt not others; having no care, so he be a good citizen, how bad a man he be; therefore, as our wickedness maketh him necessary, and necessity maketh him honorable, so is he not in the deepest truth to stand in rank with these, who all endeavor to take naughtiness away, and plant goodness even in the secretest cabinet of our souls. And these four are all that any way deal in that consideration of men's manners, which being the supreme knowledge, they that best breed it deserve the best commendation.

The philosopher therefore and the historian are they which would win the goal, the one by precept, the other by example; but both not having both, do both halt. For the philosopher, setting down with thorny arguments the bare rule, is so hard of utterance and so misty to be conceived, that one that hath no other guide but him shall wade in him till he be old, before he shall find sufficient cause to be honest. For his knowledge standeth so upon the abstract and general that happy is that man who may understand him, and more happy that can apply what he doth understand. On the other side, the historian, wanting the precept, is so tied, not to what should be but to what is, to the particular truth of things and not to the general reason of things, that his example draweth no necessary consequence, and therefore a less fruitful doctrine.

Now doth the peerless poet perform both; for whatsoever the philosopher saith should be done, he giveth a perfect picture of it in some one by whom he presupposeth it was done, so as he coupleth the general notion with the particular example. A perfect picture, I say; for he yieldeth to the powers of the mind an image of that whereof the philosopher bestoweth but a wordish description, which doth neither strike, pierce, nor possess the sight of the soul so much as that other doth. For as, in outward things, to a man that had never seen an elephant or a rhinoceros, who should tell him most exquisitely all their shapes, color, bigness, and particular marks; or of a gorgeous palace, an architector,[2] with declaring the full beauties, might well make the hearer able to repeat, as it were by rote, all he had heard, yet should never satisfy his inward conceit with being witness to itself of a true lively knowledge; but the same man, as soon as he might see those beasts well painted, or that house well in model, should straightways grow, without need of any description, to a judicial comprehending of them: so no doubt the philosopher, with his learned definitions, be it of virtues or vices, matters of public policy or private government, replenisheth the memory with many infallible grounds of wisdom, which notwithstanding lie dark before the imaginative and judging power, if they be not illuminated or figured forth by the speaking picture of poesy.

Tully[3] taketh much pains, and many times not without poetical helps, to make us know the force love of our country hath in us. Let us but hear old Anchises speaking in the midst of Troy's flames,[4] or see Ulysses, in the fullness of all Calypso's delights, bewail his absence from barren and beggarly Ithaca.[5] Anger, the Stoics said, was a short madness.[6] Let but Sophocles bring you Ajax on a stage, killing and whipping sheep and oxen, thinking them the army of Greeks, with their chieftains Agamemnon and Menelaus, and tell me if you have not a more familiar insight into anger, than finding in the schoolmen his genus and difference. See whether wisdom and temperance in Ulysses and Diomedes, valor in Achilles, friendship in Nisus and Euryalus,[7] even to an ignorant man carry not an apparent shining. And, contrarily, the remorse of conscience in Œdipus;[8] the soon-repenting pride of Agamemnon;[8] the self-devouring cruelty in his father Atreus;[9] the violence of ambition in the

---

[1]Rather from the fear of punishment than from the love of virtue. (Horace, *Epistles*, I, xvi, 52–53.)

[2]Architect. [3]M. Tullius Cicero. [4]*Æneid*, II, 634–650.

[5]*Odyssey*, V, 149–158.

[6]Horace, *Epistles*, I, ii, 62; Seneca, *De Ira*, I, 1.

[7]*Æneid*, IX, 176–182, 433–445.

[8]In Æschylus's *Agamemnon*.

[9]*Ibid.*, ll. 1555–1580.

two Theban brothers;[1] the sour sweetness of revenge in Medea;[2] and, to fall lower, the Terentian Gnatho[3] and our Chaucer's Pandar[4] so expressed that we now use their names to signify their trades; and finally, all virtues, vices, and passions so in their own natural states laid to the view, that we seem not to hear of them, but clearly to see through them.

But even in the most excellent determination of goodness, what philosopher's counsel can so readily direct a prince, as the feigned Cyrus in Xenophon? Or a virtuous man in all fortunes, as Æneas in Virgil? Or a whole commonwealth, as the way of Sir Thomas More's *Utopia?* I say the way, because where Sir Thomas More erred, it was the fault of the man, and not of the poet; for that way of patterning a commonwealth was most absolute, though he, perchance, hath not so absolutely performed it. For the question is, whether the feigned image of poesy, or the regular instruction of philosophy, hath the more force in teaching. Wherein if the philosophers have more rightly showed themselves philosophers than the poets have attained to the high top of their profession,—as in truth,

Mediocribus esse poetis
Non Dii, non homines, non concessere columnæ,—[5]

it is, I say again, not the fault of the art, but that by few men that art can be accomplished.

Certainly, even our Savior Christ could as well have given the moral commonplaces of uncharitableness and humbleness as the divine narration of Dives and Lazarus; or of disobedience and mercy, as that heavenly discourse of the lost child and the gracious father; but that his through-searching wisdom knew the estate of Dives burning in hell, and of Lazarus in Abraham's bosom, would more constantly, as it were, inhabit both the memory and judgment. Truly, for myself, me seems I see before mine eyes the lost child's disdainful prodigality, turned to envy a swine's dinner; which by the learned divines are thought not historical acts, but instructing parables.

[1]Eteocles and Polynices, Æschylus's *Seven against Thebes.*

[2]Euripides' *Medea.*

[3]In Terence's *Eunuch.*

[4]In Chaucer's *Troilus and Cressida.*

[5]Mediocrity in poets is condemned by gods and men, and by booksellers too. (Horace, *De Arte Poetica,* 372–373.)

For conclusion, I say the philosopher teacheth, but he teacheth obscurely, so as the learned only can understand him; that is to say, he teacheth them that are already taught. But the poet is the food for the tenderest stomachs; the poet is indeed the right popular philosopher. Whereof Æsop's tales give good proof; whose pretty allegories, stealing under the formal tales of beasts, make many, more beastly than beasts, begin to hear the sound of virtue from those dumb speakers.

But now may it be alleged that if this imagining of matters be so fit for the imagination, then must the historian needs surpass, who bringeth you images of true matters, such as indeed were done, and not such as fantastically or falsely may be suggested to have been done. Truly, Aristotle himself, in his *Discourse of Poesy,* plainly determineth this question, saying that poetry is *φιλοσοφώτερον* and *σπουδαιότερον,* that is to say, it is more philosophical and more studiously serious than history. His reason is, because poesy dealeth with *καθόλου,* that is to say with the universal consideration, and the history with *καθ' ἕκαστον,* the particular. "Now," saith he, "the universal weighs what is fit to be said or done, either in likelihood or necessity—which the poesy considereth in his imposed names; and the particular only marketh whether Alcibiades did, or suffered, this or that": thus far Aristotle. Which reason of his, as all his, is most full of reason.

For, indeed, if the question were whether it were better to have a particular act truly or falsely set down, there is no doubt which is to be chosen, no more than whether you had rather have Vespasian's picture right as he was, or, at the painter's pleasure, nothing resembling. But if the question be for your own use and learning, whether it be better to have it set down as it should be or as it was, then certainly is more doctrinable the feigned Cyrus in Xenophon than the true Cyrus in Justin;[6] and the feigned Æneas in Virgil than the right Æneas in Dares Phrygius;[7] as to a lady that desired to fashion her countenance to the best grace, a painter should more benefit

[6]Second century A.D. His history is an abridgment of an older one. His account of Cyrus (I, 4–8) probably comes ultimately from Heroditus.

[7]"An apocryphal history of the Trojan war passed current in the Middle Age under this name, and was regarded as the authentic account of an eye-witness and participant." (Cook.) Sidney followed contemporaries in still assuming it to be authentic.

her to portrait a most sweet face, writing Canidia upon it, than to paint Canidia as she was, who, Horace sweareth, was foul and ill-favored.[1]

If the poet do his part aright, he will show you in Tantalus, Atreus, and such like, nothing that is not to be shunned; in Cyrus, Æneas, Ulysses, each thing to be followed. Where[2] the historian, bound to tell things as things were, cannot be liberal—without he will be poetical—of a perfect pattern; but, as in Alexander, or Scipio himself, show doings, some to be liked, some to be misliked; and then how will you discern what to follow but by your own discretion, which you had without reading Quintus Curtius? And whereas a man may say, though in universal consideration of doctrine the poet prevaileth, yet that the history, in his saying such a thing was done, doth warrant a man more in that he shall follow,—the answer is manifest: that if he stand upon that *was*, as if he should argue, because it rained yesterday therefore it should rain to-day, then indeed it hath some advantage to a gross conceit. But if he know an example only informs a conjectured likelihood, and so go by reason, the poet doth so far exceed him as he is to frame his example to that which is most reasonable, be it in warlike, politic, or private matters; where the historian in his bare *was* hath many times that which we call fortune to overrule the best wisdom. Many times he must tell events whereof he can yield no cause; or if he do, it must be poetically.

For, that a feigned example hath as much force to teach as a true example—for as for to move, it is clear, since the feigned may be tuned to the highest key of passion—let us take one example wherein a poet and a historian do concur. Herodotus and Justin do both testify that Zopyrus, king Darius's faithful servant, seeing his master long resisted by the rebellious Babylonians, feigned himself in extreme disgrace of his king; for verifying of which he caused his own nose and ears to be cut off, and so flying to the Babylonians, was received, and for his known valor so far credited, that he did find means to deliver them over to Darius. Much-like matter doth Livy record of Tarquinius and his son. Xenophon excellently feigneth such another stratagem, performed by Abradatas in Cyrus's behalf. Now would I fain know, if occasion be presented unto you to serve your prince by such an honest dissimulation, why do you not as well learn it of Xenophon's fiction as of the other's verity? and, truly, so much the better, as you shall save your nose by the bargain; for Abradatas did not counterfeit so far.

So, then, the best of the historian is subject to the poet; for whatsoever action or faction, whatsoever counsel, policy, or war-stratagem the historian is bound to recite, that may the poet, if he list, with his imitation make his own, beautifying it both for further teaching and more delighting, as it pleaseth him; having all, from Dante's Heaven to his Hell, under the authority of his pen. Which if I be asked what poets have done? so as I might well name some, yet say I, and say again, I speak of the art, and not of the artificer.

Now, to that which commonly is attributed to the praise of history, in respect of the notable learning is gotten by marking the success, as though therein a man should see virtue exalted and vice punished,—truly that commendation is peculiar to poetry and far off from history. For, indeed, poetry ever setteth virtue so out in her best colors, making Fortune her well-waiting handmaid, that one must needs be enamored of her. Well may you see Ulysses in a storm, and in other hard plights; but they are but exercises of patience and magnanimity, to make them shine the more in the near following prosperity. And, of the contrary part, if evil men come to the stage, they ever go out—as the tragedy writer answered to one that misliked the show of such persons—so manacled as they little animate folks to follow them. But the historian, being captived to the truth of a foolish world, is many times a terror from well-doing, and an encouragement to unbridled wickedness. For see we not valiant Miltiades[3] rot in his fetters? The just Phocion[4] and the accomplished Socrates put to death like traitors? The cruel Severus[5] live prosperously? The excellent Severus[6] miserably murdered? Sylla and Marius dying in their beds? Pompey and Cicero slain then, when they would have

[1]See his *Epodes*, V, and *Satires*, I, viii.

[2]Whereas.

[3]The victor at Marathon. (See Cicero, *Republic*, I, iii, 5.)

[4]See Plutarch's life of him.

[5]Septimius Severus (A.D. 193–211).

[6]Alexander Severus (A.D. 222–235).

thought exile a happiness? See we not virtuous Cato[1] driven to kill himself, and rebel Cæsar so advanced that his name yet, after sixteen hundred years, lasteth in the highest honor? And mark but even Cæsar's own words of the forenamed Sylla—who in that only did honestly, to put down his dishonest tyranny—*literas nescivit*:[2] as if want of learning caused him to do well. He meant it not by poetry, which, not content with earthly plagues, deviseth new punishments in hell for tyrants; nor yet by philosophy, which teacheth *occidendos esse*;[3] but, no doubt, by skill in history, for that indeed can afford you Cypselus, Periander,[4] Phalaris,[5] Dionysius,[6] and I know not how many more of the same kennel, that speed well enough in their abominable injustice or usurpation.

I conclude, therefore, that he excelleth history, not only in furnishing the mind with knowledge, but in setting it forward to that which deserveth to be called and accounted good; which setting forward, and moving to well-doing, indeed setteth the laurel crown upon the poet as victorious, not only of the historian, but over the philosopher, howsoever in teaching it may be questionable. For suppose it be granted—that which I suppose with great reason may be denied—that the philosopher, in respect of his methodical proceeding, teach more perfectly than the poet, yet do I think that no man is so much φιλοφιλόσοφος[7] as to compare the philosopher in moving with the poet. And that moving is of a higher degree than teaching, it may by this appear, that it is well nigh both the cause and the effect of teaching; for who will be taught, if he be not moved with desire to be taught? And what so much good doth that teaching bring forth—I speak still of moral doctrine—as that it moveth one to do that which it doth teach? For, as Aristotle saith, it is not γνῶσις but πρᾶξις[8] must be the fruit; and how πρᾶξις cannot be, without being moved to practice, it is no hard matter to consider. The philosopher showeth you the way, he informeth you of the particularities, as well of the tediousness of the way, as of the pleasant lodging you shall have when your journey is ended, as of the many by-turnings that may divert you from your way; but this is to no man but to him that will read him, and read him with attentive, studious painfulness; which constant desire whosoever hath in him, hath already passed half the hardness of the way, and therefore is beholding to the philosopher but for the other half. Nay, truly, learned men have learnedly thought, that where once reason hath so much overmastered passion as that the mind hath a free desire to do well, the inward light each mind hath in itself is as good as a philosopher's book; since in nature we know it is well to do well, and what is well and what is evil, although not in the words of art which philosophers bestow upon us; for out of natural conceit the philosophers drew it. But to be moved to do that which we know, or to be moved with desire to know, *hoc opus, hic labor est*.[9]

Now therein of all sciences—I speak still of human, and according to the human conceit—is our poet the monarch. For he doth not only show the way, but giveth so sweet a prospect into the way as will entice any man to enter into it. Nay, he doth, as if your journey should lie through a fair vineyard, at the very first give you a cluster of grapes, that full of that taste you may long to pass further. He beginneth not with obscure definitions, which must blur the margent with interpretations, and load the memory with doubtfulness. But he cometh to you with words set in delightful proportion, either accompanied with, or prepared for, the well-enchanting skill of music; and with a tale, forsooth, he cometh unto you, with a tale which holdeth children from play, and old men from the chimney-corner, and, pretending no more, doth intend the winning of the mind from wickedness to virtue; even as the child is often brought to take most wholesome things, by hiding them in such other as have a pleasant taste,—which, if one should begin to tell them the nature of the aloes or rhubarb they should receive, would sooner take their physic at their ears than at their mouth. So is it in men, most of which are childish in the best things, till they be cradled in their graves,—glad they will be to

[1]Cato of Utica.

[2]Was an ignorant fellow.

[3]That they are to be slain.

[4]Concerning both see Herodotus, V, 92.

[5]Tyrant of Agrigentum. (*Cf.* Cicero, *De Officiis*, II, vii, 26.)

[6]Tyrant of Syracuse. (*Cf.* Cicero, *Tusc. Disp.*, V, 20.)

[7]A friend to the philosopher.

[8]Not knowledge but practice.

[9]This is the task, this is the struggle. (*Æneid*, VI, 129.)

hear the tales of Hercules, Achilles, Cyrus, Æneas; and, hearing them, must needs hear the right description of wisdom, valor, and justice; which, if they had been barely, that is to say philosophically, set out, they would swear they be brought to school again.

That imitation whereof poetry is, hath the most conveniency to nature of all other; insomuch that, as Aristotle saith, those things which in themselves are horrible, as cruel battles, unnatural monsters, are made in poetical imitation delightful. Truly, I have known men, that even with reading *Amadis de Gaule*, which, God knoweth, wanteth much of a perfect poesy, have found their hearts moved to the exercise of courtesy, liberality, and especially courage. Who readeth Æneas carrying old Anchises on his back, that wisheth not it were his fortune to perform so excellent an act? Whom do not those words of Turnus move, the tale of Turnus having planted his image in the imagination?

Fugientem hæc terra videbit?
Usque adeone mori miserum est?[1]

Where the philosophers, as they scorn to delight, so must they be content little to move—saving wrangling whether virtue be the chief or the only good, whether the contemplative or the active life do excel—which Plato and Boethius well knew, and therefore made Mistress Philosophy very often borrow the masking raiment of Poesy. For even those hard-hearted evil men who think virtue a school-name, and know no other good but *indulgere genio*,[2] and therefore despise the austere admonitions of the philosopher, and feel not the inward reason they stand upon, yet will be content to be delighted, which is all the good-fellow poet seemeth to promise; and so steal to see the form of goodness—which seen, they cannot but love—ere themselves be aware, as if they took a medicine of cherries.

Infinite proofs of the strange effects of this poetical invention might be alleged; only two shall serve, which are so often remembered as I think all men know them. The one of Menenius Agrippa,[3] who, when the whole people of Rome had resolutely divided themselves from the senate, with apparent show of utter ruin, though he were, for that time, an excellent orator, came not among them upon trust either of figurative speeches or cunning insinuations, and much less with far-fet[4] maxims of philosophy, which, especially if they were Platonic, they must have learned geometry before they could well have conceived; but, forsooth, he behaves himself like a homely and familiar poet. He telleth them a tale, that there was a time when all the parts of the body made a mutinous conspiracy against the belly, which they thought devoured the fruits of each other's labor; they concluded they would let so unprofitable a spender starve. In the end, to be short—for the tale is notorious, and as notorious that it was a tale—with punishing the belly they plagued themselves. This, applied by him, wrought such effect in the people, as I never read that ever words brought forth but then so sudden and so good an alteration; for upon reasonable conditions a perfect reconcilement ensued.

The other is of Nathan the prophet,[5] who, when the holy David had so far forsaken God as to confirm adultery with murder, when he was to do the tenderest office of a friend, in laying his own shame before his eyes,—sent by God to call again so chosen a servant, how doth he it but by telling of a man whose beloved lamb was ungratefully taken from his bosom? The application most divinely true, but the discourse itself feigned; which made David (I speak of the second and instrumental cause) as in a glass to see his own filthiness, as that heavenly Psalm of Mercy well testifieth.

By these, therefore, examples and reasons, I think it may be manifest that the poet, with that same hand of delight, doth draw the mind more effectually than any other art doth. And so a conclusion not unfitly ensueth: that as virtue is the most excellent resting-place for all worldly learning to make his end of, so poetry, being the most familiar to teach it, and most princely to move towards it, in the most excellent work is the most excellent workman.

But I am content not only to decipher him by his works—although works in commendation or dispraise must ever hold a high authority—but more narrowly will examine his parts; so that, as in a man, though all

[1]Shall this land see Turnus a fugitive? Is it so passing hard to die? (*Æneid*, XII, 645–646.)

[2]To give their genius free play. (Persius, *Satires*, V, 151.)

[3]See Livy, II, 32.

[4]Far-fetched.

[5]See 2 Samuel, xii.

together may carry a presence full of majesty and beauty, perchance in some one defectious piece we may find a blemish.

Now in his parts, kinds, or species, as you list to term them, it is to be noted that some poesies have coupled together two or three kinds,—as tragical and comical, whereupon is risen the tragi-comical; some, in the like manner, have mingled prose and verse, as Sannazzaro[1] and Boethius;[2] some have mingled matters heroical and pastoral; but that cometh all to one in this question, for, if severed they be good, the conjunction cannot be hurtful. Therefore, perchance forgetting some, and leaving some as needless to be remembered, it shall not be amiss in a word to cite the special kinds, to see what faults may be found in the right use of them.

Is it then the pastoral poem which is misliked?—for perchance where the hedge is lowest they will soonest leap over. Is the poor pipe disdained, which sometimes out of Melibœus' mouth can show the misery of people under hard lords and ravening soldiers, and again, by Tityrus, what blessedness is derived to them that lie lowest from the goodness of them that sit highest? sometimes, under the pretty tales of wolves and sheep, can include the whole considerations of wrong-doing and patience; sometimes show that contention for trifles can get but a trifling victory; where perchance a man may see that even Alexander and Darius, when they strave who should be cock of this world's dunghill, the benefit they got was that the after-livers may say:

Hæc memini et victum frustra contendere Thyrsim;
Ex illo Corydon, Corydon est tempore nobis.[3]

Or is it the lamenting elegiac, which in a kind heart would move rather pity than blame; who bewaileth, with the great philosopher Heraclitus, the weakness of mankind and the wretchedness of the world; who surely is to be praised, either for compassionate accompanying just causes of lamentation, or for rightly painting out how weak be the passions of woefulness?

Is it the bitter but wholesome iambic, who rubs the galled mind, in making shame the trumpet of villainy with bold and open crying out against naughtiness?

Or the satiric? who

Omne vafer vitium ridenti tangit amico;[4]

who sportingly never leaveth till he make a man laugh at folly, and at length ashamed to laugh at himself, which he cannot avoid without avoiding the folly; who, while *circum præcordia ludit,*[5] giveth us to feel how many headaches a passionate life bringeth us to,—how, when all is done,

Est Ulubris, animus si nos non deficit æquus.[6]

No, perchance it is the comic; whom naughty play-makers and stage-keepers have justly made odious. To the argument of abuse I will answer after. Only thus much now is to be said, that the comedy is an imitation of the common errors of our life, which he representeth in the most ridiculous and scornful sort that may be, so as it is impossible that any beholder can be content to be such a one. Now, as in geometry the oblique must be known as well as the right, and in arithmetic the odd as well as the even; so in the actions of our life who seeth not the filthiness of evil, wanteth a great foil to perceive the beauty of virtue. This doth the comedy handle so, in our private and domestical matters, as with hearing it we get, as it were, an experience what is to be looked for of a niggardly Demea, of a crafty Davus, of a flattering Gnatho, of a vain-glorious Thraso;[7] and not only to know what effects are to be expected, but to know who be such, by the signifying badge given them by the comedian. And little reason hath any man to say that men learn evil by seeing it so set out; since, as I said before, there is no man living, but by the force truth hath in nature, no sooner seeth these men play their parts, but wisheth them *in pistrinum,*[8] although perchance the sack of his own faults lie so behind his back, that he seeth not himself to dance the same measure,—whereto yet nothing can more open his eyes

[1] 1458–1530, Neapolitan scholar and poet. Sidney refers to his *Arcadia.*

[2] In his *Consolation of Philosophy.*

[3] These verses I remember, and how the vanquished Thyrsis vainly strove. From that day it has been with us Corydon, none but Corydon. (Virgil, *Eclogues*, VII, 69–70.)

[4] Cunningly probes every fault while making his friend laugh. (Persius, *Sat.*, I, 116.)

[5] He plays about the heart-strings. (*Ibid.*, 117.)

[6] Even Ulubrae may be a happy place of abode, if we preserve a balanced mind. (The line cannot be translated without expanding it. Horace, *Epistles*, I, xi, 30.)

[7] All characters in the plays of Terence.

[8] In the mill. (The place of punishment, as one learns from Plautus and Terence, for troublesome slaves.)

than to find his own actions contemptibly set forth.

So that the right use of comedy will, I think, by nobody be blamed, and much less of the high and excellent tragedy, that openeth the greatest wounds, and showeth forth the ulcers that are covered with tissue; that maketh kings fear to be tyrants, and tyrants manifest their tyrannical humors; that with stirring the effects of admiration and commiseration teacheth the uncertainty of this world, and upon how weak foundations gilden roofs are builded; that maketh us know:

Qui sceptra sævus duro imperio regit,
Timet timentes, metus in auctorem redit.[1]

But how much it can move, Plutarch yieldeth a notable testimony of the abominable tyrant Alexander Pheræus;[2] from whose eyes a tragedy, well made and represented, drew abundance of tears, who without all pity had murdered infinite numbers, and some of his own blood; so as he that was not ashamed to make matters for tragedies, yet could not resist the sweet violence of a tragedy. And if it wrought no further good in him, it was that he, in despite of himself, withdrew himself from hearkening to that which might mollify his hardened heart. But it is not the tragedy they do mislike, for it were too absurd to cast out so excellent a representation of whatsoever is most worthy to be learned.

Is it the lyric that most displeaseth, who with his tuned lyre and well-accorded voice, giveth praise, the reward of virtue, to virtuous acts; who giveth moral precepts and natural problems; who sometimes raiseth up his voice to the height of the heavens, in singing the lauds of the immortal God? Certainly I must confess mine own barbarousness; I never heard the old song of Percy and Douglas that I found not my heart moved more than with a trumpet; and yet it is sung but by some blind crowder,[3] with no rougher voice than rude style; which being so evil appareled in the dust and cobwebs of that uncivil age, what would it work, trimmed in the gorgeous eloquence of Pindar? In Hungary I have seen it the manner at all feasts, and other such meetings, to have songs of their ancestors' valor, which that right soldier-like nation think the chiefest kindlers of brave courage. The incomparable Lacedæmonians did not only carry that kind of music ever with them to the field, but even at home, as such songs were made, so were they all content to be singers of them; when the lusty men were to tell what they did, the old men what they had done, and the young men what they would do. And where a man may say that Pindar many times praiseth highly victories of small moment, matters rather of sport than virtue; as it may be answered, it was the fault of the poet, and not of the poetry, so indeed the chief fault was in the time and custom of the Greeks, who set those toys at so high a price that Philip of Macedon reckoned a horse-race won at Olympus[4] among his three fearful felicities. But as the unimitable Pindar often did, so is that kind most capable and most fit to awake the thoughts from the sleep of idleness, to embrace honorable enterprises.

There rests the heroical, whose very name, I think, should daunt all backbiters. For by what conceit can a tongue be directed to speak evil of that which draweth with it no less champions than Achilles, Cyrus, Æneas, Turnus, Tydeus,[5] Rinaldo?[6] who doth not only teach and move to a truth, but teacheth and moveth to the most high and excellent truth; who maketh magnanimity and justice shine through all misty fearfulness and foggy desires; who, if the saying of Plato and Tully be true, that who could see virtue would be wonderfully ravished with the love of her beauty, this man setteth her out to make her more lovely, in her holiday apparel, to the eye of any that will deign not to disdain until they understand. But if anything be already said in the defense of sweet poetry, all concurreth to the maintaining the heroical, which is not only a kind, but the best and most accomplished kind of poetry. For, as the image of each action stirreth and instructeth the mind, so the lofty image of such worthies most inflameth the mind with desire to be worthy, and informs with counsel how to be worthy. Only let Æneas be worn in the tablet of your memory, how he governeth himself in the ruin of his country; in the preserving his old father, and carrying away his religious ceremonies; in obeying the god's commandment

[1]The savage tyrant who governs his peoples harshly fears those who fear him, and thus fear recoils upon the author of fear. (Seneca, *Œdipus*, 705–706.)

[2]In his *Life of Pelopidas*, 29.

[3]Fiddler.

[4]*I.e.*, Olympia.

[5]See *Iliad*, IV.

[6]See Ariosto's *Orlando Furioso*.

to leave Dido, though not only all passionate kindness, but even the human consideration of virtuous gratefulness, would have craved other of him; how in storms, how in sports, how in war, how in peace, how a fugitive, how victorious, how besieged, how besieging, how to strangers, how to allies, how to enemies, how to his own; lastly, how in his inward self, and how in his outward government; and I think, in a mind most prejudiced with a prejudicating humor, he will be found in excellency fruitful,—yea, even as Horace saith, *melius Chrysippo et Crantore*.[1] But truly I imagine it falleth out with these poet-whippers as with some good women who often are sick, but in faith they cannot tell where. So the name of poetry is odious to them, but neither his cause nor effects, neither the sum that contains him nor the particularities descending from him, give any fast handle to their carping dispraise.

Since, then, poetry is of all human learnings the most ancient and of most fatherly antiquity, as from whence other learnings have taken their beginnings; since it is so universal that no learned nation doth despise it, nor barbarous nation is without it; since both Roman and Greek gave divine names unto it, the one of "prophesying," the other of "making," and that indeed that name of "making" is fit for him, considering that whereas other arts retain themselves within their subject, and receive, as it were, their being from it, the poet only bringeth his own stuff, and doth not learn a conceit out of a matter, but maketh matter for a conceit; since neither his description nor his end containeth any evil, the thing described cannot be evil; since his effects be so good as to teach goodness, and delight the learners of it; since therein—namely in moral doctrine, the chief of all knowledges—he doth not only far pass the historian, but for instructing is well nigh comparable to the philosopher, and for moving leaveth him behind him; since the Holy Scripture, wherein there is no uncleanness, hath whole parts in it poetical, and that even our Savior Christ vouchsafed to use the flowers of it; since all his kinds are not only in their united forms, but in their several dissections fully commendable; I think, and think I think rightly, the laurel crown appointed for triumphant captains doth worthily, of all other learnings, honor the poet's triumph.

But because we have ears as well as tongues, and that the lightest reasons that may be will seem to weigh greatly, if nothing be put in the counter-balance, let us hear, and, as well as we can, ponder, what objections be made against this art, which may be worthy either of yielding or answering.

First, truly, I no tenot only in these *μισομούσοι*, poet-haters, but in all that kind of people who seek a praise by dispraising others, that they do prodigally spend a great many wandering words in quips and scoffs, carping and taunting at each thing which, by stirring the spleen, may stay the brain from a through-beholding the worthiness of the subject. Those kind of objections, as they are full of a very idle easiness—since there is nothing of so sacred a majesty but that an itching tongue may rub itself upon it—so deserve they no other answer, but, instead of laughing at the jest, to laugh at the jester. We know a playing wit can praise the discretion of an ass, the comfortableness of being in debt, and the jolly commodity of being sick of the plague. So of the contrary side, if we will turn Ovid's verse,[2]

Ut lateat virtus proximitate mali,

"that good lie hid in nearness of the evil," Agrippa[3] will be as merry in showing the vanity of science, as Erasmus[4] was in commending of folly; neither shall any man or matter escape some touch of these smiling railers. But for Erasmus and Agrippa, they had another foundation than the superficial part would promise. Marry, these other pleasant fault-finders, who will correct the verb before they understand the noun, and confute others' knowledge before they confirm their own, I would have them only remember that scoffing cometh not of wisdom; so as the best title in true English they get with their merriments is to be called good fools,—for so have our grave forefathers ever termed that humorous kind of jesters.

But that which giveth greatest scope to their scorning humor is riming and versing. It is already said, and as I think truly said, it is

[1]Better than Chrysippus and Crantor. (*Epistles*, I, ii, 4.)

[2]*Art of Love*, II, 662.

[3]Henry Cornelius Agrippa (1486–1535), German scholar, whose treatise *On the Vanity of Arts and Sciences* (written in Latin) was published in 1527.

[4]His *Praise of Folly* was written in 1509.

not riming and versing that maketh poesy. One may be a poet without versing, and a versifier without poetry. But yet presuppose it were inseparable—as indeed it seemeth Scaliger[1] judgeth—truly it were an inseparable commendation. For if *oratio* next to *ratio*, speech next to reason, be the greatest gift bestowed upon mortality, that cannot be praiseless which doth most polish that blessing of speech; which considereth each word, not only as a man may say by his forcible quality, but by his best-measured quantity; carrying even in themselves a harmony,—without, perchance, number, measure, order, proportion be in our time grown odious.

But lay aside the just praise it hath by being the only fit speech for music—music, I say, the most divine striker of the senses—thus much is undoubtedly true, that if reading be foolish without remembering, memory being the only treasurer of knowledge, those words which are fittest for memory are likewise most convenient for knowledge. Now that verse far exceedeth prose in the knitting up of the memory, the reason is manifest; the words, besides their delight, which hath a great affinity to memory, being so set, as one cannot be lost but the whole work fails; which, accusing itself, calleth the remembrance back to itself, and so most strongly confirmeth it. Besides, one word so, as it were, begetting another, as, be it in rime or measured verse, by the former a man shall have a near guess to the follower. Lastly, even they that have taught the art of memory have showed nothing so apt for it as a certain room divided into many places, well and throughly known; now that hath the verse in effect perfectly, every word having his natural seat, which seat must needs make the word remembered. But what needeth more in a thing so known to all men? Who is it that ever was a scholar that doth not carry away some verses of Virgil, Horace, or Cato, which in his youth he learned, and even to his old age serve him for hourly lessons? as:

Percontatorem fugito, nam garrulus idem est.
Dum sibi quisque placet, credula turba sumus.[2]

But the fitness it hath for memory is notably proved by all delivery of arts, wherein, for the most part, from grammar to logic, mathematic, physic, and the rest, the rules chiefly necessary to be borne away are compiled in verses. So that verse being in itself sweet and orderly, and being best for memory, the only handle of knowledge, it must be in jest that any man can speak against it.

Now then go we to the most important imputations laid to the poor poets; for aught I can yet learn they are these:

First, that there being many other more fruitful knowledges, a man might better spend his time in them than in this.

Secondly, that it is the mother of lies.

Thirdly, that it is the nurse of abuse, infecting us with many pestilent desires, with a siren's sweetness drawing the mind to the serpent's tail of sinful fancies,—and herein especially comedies give the largest field to ear,[3] as Chaucer saith; how, both in other nations and in ours, before poets did soften us, we were full of courage, given to martial exercises, the pillars of manlike liberty, and not lulled asleep in shady idleness with poets' pastimes.

And, lastly and chiefly, they cry out with an open mouth, as if they had overshot Robin Hood, that Plato banished them out of his Commonwealth. Truly this is much, if there be much truth in it.

First, to the first, that a man might better spend his time is a reason indeed; but it doth, as they say, but *petere principium*.[4] For if it be, as I affirm, that no learning is so good as that which teacheth and moveth to virtue, and that none can both teach and move thereto so much as poesy, then is the conclusion manifest that ink and paper cannot be to a more profitable purpose employed. And certainly, though a man should grant their first assumption, it should follow, me thinks, very unwillingly, that good is not good because better is better. But I still and utterly deny that there is sprung out of earth a more fruitful knowledge.

To the second, therefore, that they should be the principal liars, I answer paradoxically, but truly, I think truly, that of all writers under the sun the poet is the least liar; and though he would, as a poet can scarcely be a liar. The astronomer, with his cousin the

[1]Julius Caesar Scaliger (1484–1558), Italian humanist. His *Poetics*, one of the important sources of Sidney's *Defense*, was published in 1561.

[2]Avoid a curious man; he is sure to be a gossip. (Horace, *Epistles*, I, xviii, 69.) And: While each one is satisfying himself, we are ever a credulous set. (Ovid, *Rem. Love*, 686.)

[3]To plow. [4]Beg the question.

geometrician, can hardly escape when they take upon them to measure the height of the stars. How often, think you, do the physicians lie, when they aver things good for sicknesses, which afterwards send Charon a great number of souls drowned in a potion before they come to his ferry? And no less of the rest which take upon them to affirm. Now for the poet, he nothing affirmeth, and therefore never lieth. For, as I take it, to lie is to affirm that to be true which is false; so as the other artists, and especially the historian, affirming many things, can, in the cloudy knowledge of mankind, hardly escape from many lies. But the poet, as I said before, never affirmeth. The poet never maketh any circles about your imagination, to conjure you to believe for true what he writeth. He citeth not authorities of other histories, but even for his entry calleth the sweet Muses to inspire into him a good invention; in troth, not laboring to tell you what is or is not, but what should or should not be. And therefore though he recount things not true, yet because he telleth them not for true he lieth not; without we will say that Nathan lied in his speech, before alleged, to David; which, as a wicked man durst scarce say, so think I none so simple would say that Æsop lied in the tales of his beasts; for who thinketh that Æsop wrote it for actually true, were well worthy to have his name chronicled among the beasts he writeth of. What child is there that, coming to a play, and seeing Thebes written in great letters upon an old door, doth believe that it is Thebes? If then a man can arrive at that child's-age, to know that the poet's persons and doings are but pictures what should be, and not stories what have been, they will never give the lie to things not affirmatively but allegorically and figuratively written. And therefore, as in history looking for truth, they may go away full-fraught with falsehood, so in poesy looking but for fiction, they shall use the narration but as an imaginative ground-plot of a profitable invention. But hereto is replied that the poets give names to men they write of, which argueth a conceit of an actual truth, and so, not being true, proveth a falsehood. And doth the lawyer lie then, when, under the names of John of the Stile, and John of the Nokes, he putteth his case?[1] But that is easily answered: their naming of men is but to make their picture the more lively, and not to build any history. Painting men, they cannot leave men nameless. We see we cannot play at chess but that we must give names to our chess-men; and yet, me thinks, he were a very partial champion of truth that would say we lied for giving a piece of wood the reverend title of a bishop. The poet nameth Cyrus and Æneas no other way than to show what men of their fames, fortunes, and estates should do.

Their third is, how much it abuseth men's wit, training it to wanton sinfulness and lustful love. For indeed that is the principal, if not the only, abuse I can hear alleged. They say the comedies rather teach than reprehend amorous conceits. They say the lyric is larded with passionate sonnets, the elegiac weeps the want of his mistress, and that even to the heroical Cupid hath ambitiously climbed. Alas! Love, I would thou couldst as well defend thyself as thou canst offend others! I would those on whom thou dost attend could either put thee away, or yield good reason why they keep thee! But grant love of beauty to be a beastly fault, although it be very hard, since only man, and no beast, hath that gift to discern beauty; grant that lovely name of Love to deserve all hateful reproaches, although even some of my masters the philosophers spent a good deal of their lamp-oil in setting forth the excellency of it; grant, I say, whatsoever they will have granted,—that not only love, but lust, but vanity, but, if they list, scurrility, possesseth many leaves of the poets' books; yet think I when this is granted, they will find their sentence may with good manners put the last words foremost, and not say that poetry abuseth man's wit, but that man's wit abuseth poetry. For I will not deny, but that man's wit may make poesy, which should be εἰκαστική, which some learned have defined, figuring forth good things, to be φανταστική, which doth contrariwise infect the fancy with unworthy objects;[2] as the painter that should give to the eye either some excellent perspective, or some fine picture fit for building or fortification, or containing in it some notable example, as Abraham sacrificing his son Isaac, Judith killing Holofernes, David fighting with Goliath, may leave those, and please an ill-pleased eye with wanton shows of better-

[1]Analogous to our "John Doe" legal actions.

[2]This distinction is derived from Plato's *Sophist*, 235–236.

hidden matters. But what! shall the abuse of a thing make the right use odious? Nay, truly, though I yield that poesy may not only be abused, but that being abused, by the reason of his sweet charming force, it can do more hurt than any other army of words, yet shall it be so far from concluding that the abuse should give reproach to the abused, that contrariwise it is a good reason, that whatsoever, being abused, doth most harm, being rightly used—and upon the right use each thing receiveth his title—doth most good. Do we not see the skill of physic, the best rampire[1] to our often-assaulted bodies, being abused, teach poison, the most violent destroyer? Doth not knowledge of law, whose end is to even and right all things, being abused, grow the crooked fosterer of horrible injuries? Doth not, to go in the highest, God's word abused breed heresy, and His name abused become blasphemy? Truly a needle cannot do much hurt, and as truly—with leave of ladies be it spoken—it cannot do much good. With a sword thou mayst kill thy father, and with a sword thou mayst defend thy prince and country. So that, as in their calling poets the fathers of lies they say nothing, so in this their argument of abuse they prove the commendation.

They allege herewith, that before poets began to be in price our nation hath set their hearts' delight upon action, and not upon imagination; rather doing things worthy to be written, than writing things fit to be done. What that before-time was, I think scarcely Sphinx can tell; since no memory is so ancient that hath the precedence of poetry. And certain it is that, in our plainest homeliness, yet never was the Albion nation without poetry. Marry, this argument, though it be leveled against poetry, yet is it indeed a chain-shot against all learning,—or bookishness, as they commonly term it. Of such mind were certain Goths, of whom it is written that, having in the spoil of a famous city taken a fair library, one hangman—belike fit to execute the fruits of their wits—who had murdered a great number of bodies, would have set fire in it. "No," said another very gravely, "take heed what you do; for while they are busy about these toys, we shall with more leisure conquer their countries." This, indeed, is the ordinary doctrine of ignorance, and many words sometimes I have heard spent in it; but because this reason is generally against all learning, as well as poetry, or rather all learning but poetry; because it were too large a digression to handle, or at least too superfluous, since it is manifest that all government of action is to be gotten by knowledge, and knowledge best by gathering many knowledges, which is reading; I only, with Horace, to him that is of that opinion

Jubeo stultum esse libenter;[2]

for as for poetry itself, it is the freest from this objection, for poetry is the companion of the camps. I dare undertake, Orlando Furioso or honest King Arthur will never displease a soldier; but the quiddity of *ens*, and *prima materia*,[3] will hardly agree with a corselet. And therefore, as I said in the beginning, even Turks and Tartars are delighted with poets. Homer, a Greek, flourished before Greece flourished; and if to a slight conjecture a conjecture may be opposed, truly it may seem, that as by him their learned men took almost their first light of knowledge, so their active men received their first motions of courage. Only Alexander's example may serve, who by Plutarch is accounted of such virtue, that Fortune was not his guide but his footstool; whose acts speak for him, though Plutarch did not; indeed the phœnix of warlike princes. This Alexander left his schoolmaster, living Aristotle, behind him, but took dead Homer with him. He put the philosopher Callisthenes to death, for his seeming philosophical, indeed mutinous, stubbornness; but the chief thing he was ever heard to wish for was that Homer had been alive. He well found he received more bravery of mind by the pattern of Achilles, than by hearing the definition of fortitude. And therefore if Cato misliked Fulvius for carrying Ennius with him to the field, it may be answered that if Cato misliked it, the noble Fulvius liked it, or else he had not done it. For it was not the excellent Cato Uticensis, whose authority I would much more have reverenced; but it was the former,[4] in truth a bitter punisher of faults, but else a man that had never sacrificed to the Graces. He misliked and cried out upon all Greek

[1]Rampart, defense.

[2]Cheerfully bid him be a fool. (This is Sidney's meaning The words are altered from Horace, *Satires*, I, i, 63.)

[3]Metaphysical terms.

[4]*I. e.*, Cato the Censor. Cato of Utica was his great grandson.

learning; and yet, being fourscore years old, began to learn it, belike fearing that Pluto understood not Latin. Indeed, the Roman laws allowed no person to be carried to the wars but he that was in the soldiers' roll. And therefore though Cato misliked his unmustered person, he misliked not his work. And if he had, Scipio Nasica,[1] judged by common consent the best Roman, loved him. Both the other Scipio brothers, who had by their virtues no less surnames than of Asia and Afric, so loved him that they caused his body to be buried in their sepulcher. So as Cato's authority being but against his person, and that answered with so far greater than himself, is herein of no validity.

But now, indeed, my burthen is great, that Plato's name is laid upon me, whom, I must confess, of all philosophers I have ever esteemed most worthy of reverence; and with great reason, since of all philosophers he is the most poetical; yet if he will defile the fountain out of which his flowing streams have proceeded, let us boldly examine with what reasons he did it.

First, truly, a man might maliciously object that Plato, being a philosopher, was a natural enemy of poets. For, indeed, after the philosophers had picked out of the sweet mysteries of poetry the right discerning true points of knowledge, they forthwith, putting it in method, and making a school-art of that which the poets did only teach by a divine delightfulness, beginning to spurn at their guides, like ungrateful prentices were not content to set up shops for themselves, but sought by all means to discredit their masters; which by the force of delight being barred them, the less they could overthrow them the more they hated them. For, indeed, they found for Homer seven cities strave who should have him for their citizen; where many cities banished philosophers, as not fit members to live among them. For only repeating certain of Euripides' verses, many Athenians had their lives saved of the Syracusans, where the Athenians themselves thought many philosophers unworthy to live. Certain poets as Simonides and Pindar, had so prevailed with Hiero the First, that of a tyrant they made him a just king; where Plato could do so little with Dionysius, that he himself of a philosopher was made a slave.

[1]See Livy, XXIX, 14.

But who should do thus, I confess, should requite the objections made against poets with like cavilations against philosophers; as likewise one should do that should bid one read *Phædrus* or *Symposium* in Plato, or the *Discourse of Love* in Plutarch, and see whether any poet do authorize abominable filthiness, as they do.

Again, a man might ask out of what commonwealth Plato doth banish them. In sooth, thence where he himself alloweth community of women.[2] So as belike this banishment grew not for effeminate wantonness, since little should poetical sonnets be hurtful when a man might have what woman he listed. But I honor philosophical instructions, and bless the wits which bred them, so as they be not abused, which is likewise stretched to poetry. Saint Paul himself, who yet, for the credit of poets, allegeth twice two poets, and one of them by the name of a prophet,[3] setteth a watchword upon philosophy,[4]—indeed upon the abuse. So doth Plato upon the abuse, not upon poetry. Plato found fault that the poets of his time filled the world with wrong opinions of the gods, making light tales of that unspotted essence, and therefore would not have the youth depraved with such opinions. Herein may much be said; let this suffice: the poets did not induce such opinions, but did imitate those opinions already induced. For all the Greek stories can well testify that the very religion of that time stood upon many and many-fashioned gods; not taught so by the poets, but followed according to their nature of imitation. Who list may read in Plutarch the discourses of Isis and Osiris, of the cause why Oracles ceased, of the Divine Providence, and see whether the theology of that nation stood not upon such dreams,—which the poets indeed superstitiously observed; and truly, since they had not the light of Christ, did much better in it than the philosophers, who, shaking off superstition, brought in atheism.

Plato therefore, whose authority I had much rather justly construe than unjustly resist, meant not in general of poets, in those words of which Julius Scaliger saith, *Qua authoritate*

[2]This statement and that which follows are very misleading.

[3]In Acts, xvii, 28 (Aratus, Cleanthes); Titus, i, 12 (Epimenides); 1 Corinthians, xv, 33 (Menander). St. Paul does not name these poets, but quotes from them. The passage in Acts is found in both Aratus and Cleanthes.

[4]See Colossians, ii, 8.

barbari quidam atque hispidi abuti velint ad poetas e republica exigendos;[1] but only meant to drive out those wrong opinions of the Deity, whereof now, without further law, Christianity hath taken away all the hurtful belief, perchance, as he thought, nourished by the then esteemed poets. And a man need go no further than to Plato himself to know his meaning; who, in his dialogue called *Ion*, giveth high and rightly divine commendation unto poetry. So as Plato, banishing the abuse, not the thing, not banishing it, but giving due honor unto it, shall be our patron and not our adversary. For, indeed, I had much rather, since truly I may do it, show their mistaking of Plato, under whose lion's skin they would make an ass-like braying against poesy, than go about to overthrow his authority; whom, the wiser a man is, the more just cause he shall find to have in admiration; especially since he attributeth unto poesy more than myself do, namely to be a very inspiring of a divine force, far above man's wit, as in the forenamed dialogue is apparent.

Of the other side, who would show the honors have been by the best sort of judgments granted them, a whole sea of examples would present themselves: Alexanders, Cæsars, Scipios, all favorers of poets; Lælius, called the Roman Socrates, himself a poet, so as part of *Heautontimoroumenos* in Terence was supposed to be made by him. And even the Greek Socrates, whom Apollo confirmed to be the only wise man, is said to have spent part of his old time in putting Æsop's *Fables* into verses; and therefore full evil should it become his scholar, Plato, to put such words in his master's mouth against poets. But what needs more? Aristotle writes the *Art of Poesy;* and why, if it should not be written? Plutarch teacheth the use to be gathered of them; and how, if they should not be read? And who reads Plutarch's either history or philosophy, shall find he trimmeth both their garments with guards of poesy. But I list not to defend poesy with the help of his underling historiography. Let it suffice that it is a fit soil for praise to dwell upon; and what dispraise may set upon it, is either easily overcome, or transformed into just commendation.

So that since the excellencies of it may be so easily and so justly confirmed, and the low-creeping objections so soon trodden down: it not being an art of lies, but of true doctrine; not of effeminateness, but of notable stirring of courage; not of abusing man's wit, but of strengthening man's wit; not banished, but honored by Plato; let us rather plant more laurels for to engarland our poets' heads—which honor of being laureate, as besides them only triumphant captains were, is a sufficient authority to show the price they ought to be held in—than suffer the ill-savored breath of such wrong speakers once to blow upon the clear springs of poesy.

But since I have run so long a career in this matter, me thinks, before I give my pen a full stop, it shall be but a little more lost time to inquire why England, the mother of excellent minds, should be grown so hard a stepmother to poets; who certainly in wit ought to pass all others, since all only proceedeth from their wit, being indeed makers of themselves, not takers of others. How can I but exclaim,

Musa, mihi causas memora, quo numine læso?[2]

Sweet poesy! that hath anciently had kings, emperors, senators, great captains, such as, besides a thousand others, David, Adrian,[3] Sophocles, Germanicus,[4] not only to favor poets, but to be poets; and of our nearer times can present for her patrons a Robert, King of Sicily;[5] the great King Francis of France;[6] King James of Scotland;[7] such cardinals as Bembus and Bibbiena;[8] such famous preachers and teachers as Beza and Melancthon;[9] so learned philosophers as Fracastorius[10] and Scaliger; so great orators as Pontanus and Muretus;[11] so piercing wits as George Buchanan;[12] so grave counselors as—besides many, but before all—that Hospital of France,[13] than whom, I think, that realm never brought

[1]Which authority [Plato's] certain rude and barbarous persons desire to abuse, in order to banish poets out of the commonwealth. (*Poetics*, i, 2.)

[2]O Muse, relate to me the causes, tell me in what had her will been offended? (*Æneid*, I, 12.)

[3]Hadrian, Roman emperor (A.D. 76–138).

[4]Nephew and adopted son of the emperor Tiberius. (15 B.C.–A.D. 19.)

[5]Robert II of Anjou (1275–1343).

[6]Francis I (1494–1547).

[7]Probably James I (1394–1437).

[8]Bembus (1470–1547); Bibbiena (1470–1520).

[9]Beza (1519–1605); Melancthon (1497–1560).

[10]1483–1553; lived chiefly at Verona.

[11]French humanist (1526–1585).

[12]Scottish humanist (1506–1582).

[13]Michel de l'Hôpital (1504–1573), Chancellor of France.

forth a more accomplished judgment more firmly builded upon virtue; I say these, with numbers of others, not only to read others' poesies but to poetize for others' reading. That poesy, thus embraced in all other places, should only find in our time a hard welcome in England, I think the very earth lamenteth it, and therefore decketh our soil with fewer laurels than it was accustomed. For heretofore poets have in England also flourished; and, which is to be noted, even in those times when the trumpet of Mars did sound loudest. And now that an over-faint quietness should seem to strew the house for poets, they are almost in as good reputation as the mountebanks at Venice. Truly even that, as of the one side it giveth great praise to poesy, which, like Venus—but to better purpose—hath rather be troubled in the net with Mars, than enjoy the homely quiet of Vulcan; so serves it for a piece of a reason why they are less grateful to idle England, which now can scarce endure the pain of a pen. Upon this necessarily followeth, that base men with servile wits undertake it, who think it enough if they can be rewarded of the printer. And so as Epaminondas is said, with the honor of his virtue to have made an office, by his exercising it, which before was contemptible, to become highly respected; so these men, no more but setting their names to it, by their own disgracefulness disgrace the most graceful poesy. For now, as if all the Muses were got with child to bring forth bastard poets, without any commission they do post over the banks of Helicon, till they make their readers more weary than post-horses; while, in the mean time, they,

Queis meliore luto finxit præcordia Titan,[1]

are better content to suppress the outflowings of their wit, than by publishing them to be accounted knights of the same order.

But I that, before ever I durst aspire unto the dignity, am admitted into the company of the paper-blurrers, do find the very true cause of our wanting estimation is want of desert, taking upon us to be poets in despite of Pallas. Now wherein we want desert were a thankworthy labor to express; but if I knew, I should have mended myself. But as I never desired the title, so have I neglected the means to come by it; only, overmastered by some thoughts, I yielded an inky tribute unto them. Marry, they that delight in poesy itself should seek to know what they do and how they do; and especially look themselves in an unflattering glass of reason, if they be inclinable unto it. For poesy must not be drawn by the ears, it must be gently led, or rather it must lead; which was partly the cause that made the ancient learned affirm it was a divine gift, and no human skill, since all other knowledges lie ready for any that hath strength of wit, a poet no industry can make if his own genius be not carried into it. And therefore is it an old proverb: *Orator fit, poeta nascitur*.[2] Yet confess I always that, as the fertilest ground must be manured, so must the highest-flying wit have a Dædalus to guide him. That Dædalus, they say, both in this and in other, hath three wings to bear itself up into the air of due commendation: that is, art, imitation, and exercise. But these neither artificial rules nor imitative patterns, we much cumber ourselves withal. Exercise indeed we do, but that very fore-backwardly, for where we should exercise to know, we exercise as having known; and so is our brain delivered of much matter which never was begotten by knowledge. For there being two principal parts, matter to be expressed by words, and words to express the matter, in neither we use art or imitation rightly. Our matter is *quodlibet*[3] indeed, though wrongly performing Ovid's verse,

Quicquid conabar dicere, versus erat,[4]

never marshaling it into any assured rank, that almost the readers cannot tell where to find themselves.

Chaucer, undoubtedly, did excellently in his *Troilus and Cressida;* of whom, truly, I know not whether to marvel more, either that he in that misty time could see so clearly, or that we in this clear age walk so stumblingly after him. Yet had he great wants, fit to be forgiven in so reverend antiquity. I account the *Mirror of Magistrates*[5] meetly furnished of beautiful parts; and in the Earl of Surrey's lyrics many things tasting of a noble birth,

---

[1]Whose hearts the Titan [Prometheus] has molded out of better clay. (Altered from Juvenal, *Satires*, XIV, 34–35.)

[2]The orator is made, the poet is born.

[3]Indifferent.

[4]Whatever I tried to express turned out to be poetry. (*Tristia*, IV, x, 26. Quoted inexactly.)

[5]First published in 1559.

and worthy of a noble mind. The *Shepherd's Calendar*[1] hath much poetry in his eclogues, indeed worthy the reading, if I be not deceived. That same framing of his style to an old rustic language I dare not allow, since neither Theocritus in Greek, Virgil in Latin, nor Sannazzaro in Italian did affect it. Besides these, I do not remember to have seen but few (to speak boldly) printed, that have poetical sinews in them. For proof whereof, let but most of the verses be put in prose, and then ask the meaning, and it will be found that one verse did but beget another, without ordering at the first what should be at the last; which becomes a confused mass of words, with a tinkling sound of rime, barely accompanied with reason.

Our tragedies and comedies not without cause cried out against, observing rules neither of honest civility nor of skilful poetry, excepting *Gorboduc*,[2]—again I say of those that I have seen. Which notwithstanding as it is full of stately speeches and well-sounding phrases, climbing to the height of Seneca's style, and as full of notable morality, which it doth most delightfully teach, and so obtain the very end of poesy; yet in truth it is very defectious in the circumstances, which grieveth me, because it might not remain as an exact model of all tragedies. For it is faulty both in place and time, the two necessary companions of all corporal actions. For where the stage should always represent but one place, and the uttermost time presupposed in it should be, both by Aristotle's precept and common reason, but one day; there is both many days and many places inartificially imagined.

But if it be so in *Gorboduc*, how much more in all the rest? where you shall have Asia of the one side, and Afric of the other, and so many other under-kingdoms, that the player, when he cometh in, must ever begin with telling where he is, or else the tale will not be conceived. Now ye shall have three ladies walk to gather flowers, and then we must believe the stage to be a garden. By and by we hear news of shipwreck in the same place, and then we are to blame if we accept it not for a rock. Upon the back of that comes out a hideous monster with fire and smoke, and then the miserable beholders are bound to take it for a cave. While in the mean time two armies fly in, represented with four swords and bucklers, and then what hard heart will not receive it for a pitched field?

Now of time they are much more liberal. For ordinary it is that two young princes fall in love; after many traverses she is got with child, delivered of a fair boy, he is lost, groweth a man, falleth in love, and is ready to get another child,—and all this in two hours' space; which how absurd it is in sense even sense may imagine, and art hath taught, and all ancient examples justified, and at this day the ordinary players in Italy will not err in. Yet will some bring in an example of *Eunuchus*[3] in Terence, that containeth matter of two days, yet far short of twenty years. True it is, and so was it to be played in two days, and so fitted to the time it set forth. And though Plautus have in one place done amiss, let us hit with him, and not miss with him. But they will say, How then shall we set forth a story which containeth both many places and many times? And do they not know that a tragedy is tied to the laws of poesy, and not of history; not bound to follow the story, but having liberty either to feign a quite new matter, or to frame the history to the most tragical conveniency? Again, many things may be told which cannot be showed,—if they know the difference betwixt reporting and representing. As for example I may speak, though I am here, of Peru, and in speech digress from that to the description of Calicut;[4] but in action I cannot represent it without Pacolet's horse.[5] And so was the manner the ancients took, by some *Nuntius*[6] to recount things done in former time or other place.

Lastly, if they will represent a history, they must not, as Horace saith, begin *ab ovo*,[7] but they must come to the principal point of that one action which they will represent. By example this will be best expressed. I have a story of young Polydorus,[8] delivered for safety's sake, with great riches, by his

[1]By Edmund Spenser. It was dedicated to Sidney.

[2]By Thomas Sackville (Lord Buckhurst, 1536–1608) and Thomas Norton (1532–1584). First published in 1565.

[3]A slip. Sidney meant to refer to the *Heautontimorumenos* of Terence.

[4]In India.

[5]In the romance of *Valentine and Orson*.

[6]Messenger.

[7]From the very beginning. (*Satires*, I, iii, 6. Also *De Arte Poetica*, 147.)

[8]Euripides, *Hecuba*.

father Priamus to Polymnestor, King of Thrace, in the Trojan war time. He, after some years, hearing the overthrow of Priamus, for to make the treasure his own murdereth the child; the body of the child is taken up by Hecuba; she, the same day, findeth a sleight to be revenged most cruelly of the tyrant. Where now would one of our tragedy-writers begin, but with the delivery of the child? Then should he sail over into Thrace, and so spend I know not how many years, and travel numbers of places. But where doth Euripides? Even with the finding of the body, leaving the rest to be told by the spirit of Polydorus. This needs no further to be enlarged; the dullest wit may conceive it.

But, besides these gross absurdities, how all their plays be neither right tragedies nor right comedies, mingling kings and clowns, not because the matter so carrieth it, but thrust in the clown by head and shoulders to play a part in majestical matters, with neither decency nor discretion; so as neither the admiration and commiseration, nor the right sportfulness, is by their mongrel tragi-comedy obtained. I know Apuleius did somewhat so,[1] but that is a thing recounted with space of time, not represented in one moment; and I know the ancients have one or two examples of tragi-comedies, as Plautus hath *Amphytrio*. But, if we mark them well, we shall find that they never, or very daintily, match hornpipes and funerals. So falleth it out that, having indeed no right comedy in that comical part of our tragedy, we have nothing but scurrility, unworthy of any chaste ears, or some extreme show of doltishness, indeed fit to lift up a loud laughter, and nothing else; where the whole tract of a comedy should be full of delight, as the tragedy should be still maintained in a well-raised admiration.

But our comedians think there is no delight without laughter, which is very wrong; for though laughter may come with delight, yet cometh it not of delight, as though delight should be the cause of laughter; but well may one thing breed both together. Nay, rather in themselves they have, as it were, a kind of contrariety. For delight we scarcely do, but in things that have a conveniency to ourselves, or to the general nature; laughter almost ever cometh of things most disproportioned to ourselves and nature. Delight hath a joy in it either permanent or present; laughter hath only a scornful tickling. For example, we are ravished with delight to see a fair woman, and yet are far from being moved to laughter. We laugh at deformed creatures, wherein certainly we cannot delight. We delight in good chances, we laugh at mischances. We delight to hear the happiness of our friends and country, at which he were worthy to be laughed at that would laugh. We shall, contrarily, laugh sometimes to find a matter quite mistaken and go down the hill against the bias, in the mouth of some such men, as for the respect of them one shall be heartily sorry he cannot choose but laugh, and so is rather pained than delighted with laughter. Yet deny I not but that they may go well together. For as in Alexander's picture well set out we delight without laughter, and in twenty mad antics we laugh without delight; so in Hercules, painted, with his great beard and furious countenance, in woman's attire, spinning at Omphale's commandment, it breedeth both delight and laughter; for the representing of so strange a power in love, procureth delight, and the scornfulness of the action stirreth laughter.

But I speak to this purpose, that all the end of the comical part be not upon such scornful matters as stir laughter only, but mixed with it that delightful teaching which is the end of poesy. And the great fault, even in that point of laughter, and forbidden plainly by Aristotle, is that they stir laughter in sinful things, which are rather execrable than ridiculous; or in miserable, which are rather to be pitied than scorned. For what is it to make folks gape at a wretched beggar or a beggarly clown, or, against law of hospitality, to jest at strangers because they speak not English so well as we do? what do we learn? since it is certain:

Nil habet infelix paupertas durius in se,
Quam quod ridiculos homines facit.[2]

But rather a busy loving courtier; a heartless threatening Thraso; a self-wise-seeming schoolmaster; a wry-transformed traveler: these if we saw walk in stage-names, which we play naturally, therein were delightful laugh-

[1]In his *Metamorphoses*.

[2]Poverty, bitter though it be, has no sharper pang than this, that it makes men ridiculous. (Juvenal, *Satires*, III, 152–153.)

ter and teaching delightfulness,—as in the other, the tragedies of Buchanan do justly bring forth a divine admiration.

But I have lavished out too many words of this play-matter. I do it, because as they are excelling parts of poesy, so is there none so much used in England, and none can be more pitifully abused; which, like an unmannerly daughter, showing a bad education, causeth her mother Poesy's honesty to be called in question.

Other sorts of poetry almost have we none, but that lyrical kind of songs and sonnets, which, Lord if he gave us so good minds, how well it might be employed, and with how heavenly fruits both private and public, in singing the praises of the immortal beauty, the immortal goodness of that God who giveth us hands to write, and wits to conceive!—of which we might well want words, but never matter; of which we could turn our eyes to nothing, but we should ever have new-budding occasions.

But truly, many of such writings as come under the banner of unresistible love, if I were a mistress would never persuade me they were in love; so coldly they apply fiery speeches, as men that had rather read lovers' writings, and so caught up certain swelling phrases—which hang together like a man which once told me the wind was at north-west and by south, because he would be sure to name winds enough—than that in truth they feel those passions, which easily, as I think, may be bewrayed by that same forcibleness, or *energia* (as the Greeks call it) of the writer. But let this be a sufficient, though short note, that we miss the right use of the material point of poesy.

Now for the outside of it, which is words, or (as I may term it) diction, it is even well worse, so is that honey-flowing matron eloquence appareled, or rather disguised, in a courtesan-like painted affectation: one time with so far-fet words, that many seem monsters—but must seem strangers—to any poor Englishman; another time with coursing of a letter, as if they were bound to follow the method of a dictionary; another time with figures and flowers extremely winter-starved.

But I would this fault were only peculiar to versifiers, and had not as large possession among prose-printers, and, which is to be marveled, among many scholars, and, which is to be pitied, among some preachers. Truly I could wish—if at least I might be so bold to wish in a thing beyond the reach of my capacity—the diligent imitators of Tully and Demosthenes (most worthy to be imitated) did not so much keep Nizolian[1] paper-books of their figures and phrases, as by attentive translation, as it were devour them whole, and make them wholly theirs. For now they cast sugar and spice upon every dish that is served to the table; like those Indians, not content to wear ear-rings at the fit and natural place of the ears, but they will thrust jewels through their nose and lips, because they will be sure to be fine. Tully, when he was to drive out Catiline as it were with a thunder-bolt of eloquence, often used that figure of repetition, as *Vivit. Vivit? Immo vero etiam in senatum venit*,[2] *etc.* Indeed, inflamed with a well-grounded rage, he would have his words, as it were, double out of his mouth; and so do that artificially, which we see men in choler do naturally. And we, having noted the grace of those words, hale them in sometime to a familiar epistle, when it were too much choler to be choleric. How well store of *similiter*[3] *cadences* doth sound with the gravity of the pulpit, I would but invoke Demosthenes' soul to tell, who with a rare daintiness useth them. Truly they have made me think of the sophister that with too much subtility would prove two eggs three, and though he might be counted a sophister, had none for his labor. So these men bringing in such a kind of eloquence, well may they obtain an opinion of a seeming fineness, but persuade few,—which should be the end of their fineness.

Now for similitudes in certain printed discourses, I think all herbarists, all stories of beasts, fowls, and fishes are rifled up, that they may come in multitudes to wait upon any of our conceits, which certainly is as absurd a surfeit to the ears as is possible. For the force of a similitude not being to prove any thing to a contrary disputer, but only to explain to a willing hearer; when that is done, the rest is a most tedious prattling, rather overswaying the memory from the purpose

---

[1]The Italian Marius Nizolius (1498–1566) compiled a Ciceronian lexicon.

[2]He lives. He lives? Yes, he comes even into the senate. (Cicero, *Catiline*, I, 2.)

[3]Similar.

whereto they were applied, than any whit informing the judgment, already either satisfied or by similitudes not to be satisfied.

For my part, I do not doubt, when Antonius and Crassus, the great forefathers of Cicero in eloquence, the one (as Cicero testifieth of them) pretended not to know art, the other not to set by it, because with a plain sensibleness they might win credit of popular ears, which credit is the nearest step to persuasion, which persuasion is the chief mark of oratory,—I do not doubt, I say, but that they used these knacks very sparingly; which who doth generally use any man may see doth dance to his own music, and so be noted by the audience more careful to speak curiously than truly. Undoubtedly (at least to my opinion undoubtedly) I have found in divers small-learned courtiers a more sound style than in some professors of learning; of which I can guess no other cause, but that the courtier following that which by practice he findeth fittest to nature, therein, though he know it not, doth according to art, though not by art; where the other, using art to show art and not to hide art—as in these cases he should do—flieth from nature, and indeed abuseth art.

But what! me thinks I deserve to be pounded for straying from poetry to oratory. But both have such an affinity in the wordish consideration, that I think this digression will make my meaning receive the fuller understanding:—which is not to take upon me to teach poets how they should do, but only, finding myself sick among the rest, to show some one or two spots of the common infection grown among the most part of writers; that, acknowledging ourselves somewhat awry, we may bend to the right use both of matter and manner: whereto our language giveth us great occasion, being, indeed, capable of any excellent exercising of it.

I know some will say it is a mingled language. And why not so much the better, taking the best of both the other? Another will say it wanteth grammar. Nay, truly, it hath that praise that it wanteth not grammar. For grammar it might have, but it needs it not; being so easy in itself, and so void of those cumbersome differences of cases, genders, moods, and tenses, which, I think, was a piece of the Tower of Babylon's curse, that a man should be put to school to learn his mother-tongue. But for the uttering sweetly and properly the conceits of the mind, which is the end of speech, that hath it equally with any other tongue in the world; and is particularly happy in compositions of two or three words together, near the Greek, far beyond the Latin,—which is one of the greatest beauties can be in a language.

Now of versifying there are two sorts, the one ancient, the other modern. The ancient marked the quantity of each syllable, and according to that framed his verse; the modern observing only number, with some regard of the accent, the chief life of it standeth in that like sounding of the words, which we call rime. Whether of these be the more excellent would bear many speeches; the ancient no doubt more fit for music, both words and tune observing quantity; and more fit lively to express divers passions, by the low or lofty sound of the well-weighed syllable. The latter likewise with his rime striketh a certain music to the ear; and, in fine, since it doth delight, though by another way, it obtaineth the same purpose; there being in either, sweetness, and wanting in neither, majesty. Truly the English, before any other vulgar language I know, is fit for both sorts. For, for the ancient, the Italian is so full of vowels that it must ever be cumbered with elisions; the Dutch so, of the other side, with consonants, that they cannot yield the sweet sliding fit for a verse. The French in his whole language hath not one word that hath his accent in the last syllable saving two, called antepenultima, and little more hath the Spanish; and therefore very gracelessly may they use dactyls. The English is subject to none of these defects. Now for rime, though we do not observe quantity, yet we observe the accent very precisely, which other languages either cannot do, or will not do so absolutely. That cæsura, or breathing-place in the midst of the verse, neither Italian nor Spanish have, the French and we never almost fail of.

Lastly, even the very rime itself the Italian cannot put in the last syllable, by the French named the masculine rime, but still in the next to the last, which the French call the female, or the next before that, which the Italians term *sdrucciola*. The example of the former is *buono: suono;* of the *sdrucciola* is *femina: semina*. The French, of the other side, hath both the male, as *bon: son*, and the female, as *plaise: taise;* but the *sdrucciola* he hath not. Where the English hath all three, as *due: true*, *father: rather*, *motion: potion;* with much more which might be said, but that already I find the triflingness of this discourse is much too much enlarged.

So that since the ever praiseworthy poesy is full of virtue-breeding delightfulness, and void of no gift that ought to be in the noble name of learning; since the blames laid against it are either false or feeble; since the cause why it is not esteemed in England is the fault of poet-apes, not poets; since, lastly, our tongue is most fit to honor poesy, and to be honored by poesy; I conjure you all that have had the evil luck to read this ink-wasting toy of mine, even in the name of the Nine Muses, no more to scorn the sacred mysteries of poesy; no more to laugh at the name of poets, as though they were next inheritors to fools; no more to jest at the reverend title of "a rimer"; but to believe, with Aristotle, that they were the ancient treasurers of the Grecians' divinity; to believe, with Bembus, that they were first bringers-in of all civility; to believe, with Scaliger, that no philosopher's precepts can sooner make you an honest man than the reading of Virgil; to believe, with Clauserus, the translator of Cornutus, that it pleased the Heavenly Deity by Hesiod and Homer, under the veil of fables, to give us all knowledge, logic, rhetoric, philosophy natural and moral, and *quid non?*[1] to believe, with me, that there are many mysteries contained in poetry which of purpose were written darkly, lest by profane wits it should be abused; to believe, with Landino,[2] that they are so beloved of the gods, that whatsoever they write proceeds of a divine fury; lastly, to believe themselves, when they tell you they will make you immortal by their verses.

Thus doing, your name shall flourish in the printers' shops. Thus doing, you shall be of kin to many a poetical preface. Thus doing, you shall be most fair, most rich, most wise, most all; you shall dwell upon superlatives. Thus doing, though you be *libertino patre natus*,[3] you shall suddenly grow *Herculea proles*,[4]

Si quid mea carmina possunt.[5]

Thus doing, your soul shall be placed with Dante's Beatrice or Virgil's Anchises.

But if—fie of such a but!—you be born so near the dull-making cataract of Nilus, that you cannot hear the planet-like music of poetry; if you have so earth-creeping a mind that it cannot lift itself up to look to the sky of poetry, or rather, by a certain rustical disdain, will become such a mome[6] as to be a Momus of poetry; then, though I will not wish unto you the ass's ears of Midas, nor to be driven by a poet's verses, as Bubonax[7] was, to hang himself; nor to be rimed to death, as is said to be done in Ireland; yet thus much curse I must send you in the behalf of all poets:—that while you live you live in love, and never get favor for lacking skill of a sonnet; and when you die, your memory die from the earth for want of an epitaph.

[1]What not?

[2]Florentine humanist (1424–1504).

[3]The son of a freedman. (Horace, *Satires*, I, vi, 6.)

[4]Herculean offspring.

[5]If my song can ought avail. (*Æneid*, IX, 446.)

[6]Fool.

[7]"Sidney is referring to the tale of *Hipponax*, . . . of whom one story was that he satirized the statuary *Bupalus* so bitterly that he hanged himself. By some confusion . . . he has combined the two names." (Shuckburgh.)

EDMUND SPENSER (1552?–1599)

The year of Spenser's birth is known only by inference from a sonnet which he wrote in 1593. His father came of a northern family and was a gentleman by birth; he was, however, a man in humble circumstances and followed the trade of cloth-making in London. Spenser was sent to the Merchant Tailors' School then newly founded, where he was fortunate in being trained by Richard Mulcaster. Thence he proceeded in 1569 to Pembroke Hall, Cambridge. He took his B. A. in 1573 and his M. A. in 1576. At Cambridge Spenser formed a lasting friendship with Gabriel Harvey, a Fellow of Pembroke and one of the notable figures of the University; there too, of course, he came under strong puritan influences which also were lasting in their effects. When he left Cambridge Spenser went for a time among his kinsmen in the north of England. In 1578 he was a secretary in the household of John Young, Bishop of Rochester. In 1579 he was back in London, in the household of Robert Dudley, Earl of Leicester, where he became acquainted with Sir Philip Sidney who, there is reason to believe, inspired in Spenser the same admiration which all others who came in contact with him felt for him. These new attachments were made possible through Spenser's friendship with Gabriel Harvey. In 1579, too, Spenser published *The Shepherd's Calendar*, a series of twelve pastoral eclogues, in which he clearly announced himself as a significant new force in English poetry. But poetry, of course, as Ben Jonson complained, brought in no money, and Spenser was perforce at this time seeking public office. In 1580 he was successful in a manner which, it has generally been thought, was little to his taste. He went to Ireland as secretary to Lord Grey of Wilton, then Lord Deputy of Ireland. And in Ireland Spenser stayed, save for two lengthy visits to London, until within a few months of his death. In 1589 he came to London with Sir Walter Raleigh, who had been in Ireland, to publish the first three books of the *Faerie Queene* in 1590. Again in 1595 Spenser came back to London and published, in 1596, a new edition of the *Faerie Queene* containing three additional books, and his *Four Hymns*, and *Prothalamion*. In publishing the *Faerie Queene* Spenser sought, if not a more substantial recognition than the pension which Elizabeth gave him, at any rate a more important one—and he was disappointed. What he wanted was a place at Court and the end of his exile in Ireland. It is probable, however, that Spenser's disappointment has been exaggerated. His eyes were open to the corruption which surrounded life at Court, and at the same time his career in Ireland was at once honorable and successful. He filled several offices there, and in 1588 was granted an estate of some 3000 acres in the County of Cork. He found congenial friends in Ireland, and there he met and married Elizabeth Boyle (1594). Certainly also his virtual retirement from the larger world was conducive to that soberly meditative life which was his true life, and which found great expression in the *Faerie Queene* and in such shorter poems as the *Four Hymns*. And to this, one thinks, Spenser himself can hardly have been blind, however much at times he may have yearned for a life which would have made his achievement as a poet immeasurably more difficult, if not impossible. In 1598 there occurred an insurrection in Ireland in the course of which Spenser's castle of Kilcolman was pillaged and burned, he and his family escaping to Cork. In December he was sent thence to London with dispatches, and there he fell ill, and died on 16 January, 1599. He was buried in Westminster Abbey. According to tradition Spenser died not only broken-hearted over the loss of a child in the burning of Kilcolman, but also in the direst poverty, unable to buy necessary food. Contemporaries, among them Ben Jonson and Camden, gave countenance to the story, and it may well be that Spenser was suffering a temporary lack of ready money. No definite evidence, however, supports this legend, and it is extremely difficult to reconcile it with known facts concerning Spenser's general circumstances.

Spenser is in his poetry what Sidney was in his life, the English embodiment of the Renaissance ideal. He aimed in the *Faerie Queene* to write an heroic poem, in emulation of Ariosto and Tasso, thought in his day to be the legitimate inheritors of Homer and Virgil; and as an Englishman he aimed to write an English poem which should follow national tradition both in language and in content. Hence he modeled himself upon Chaucer and drew on Arthurian legend, while at the same time he attempted to connect his country's heroic past with the great figures of his own day. The poem he wrote was, to be sure, an allegory, in this as in the life it pictured different enough from the *Iliad* and the *Æneid*, but it should be remembered that in the sixteenth century—and, indeed, until much later—practically everybody still supposed that the classical epics were allegories. The plan Spenser formed for his poem, typical of the Renaissance in its ambitious largeness and left uncompleted, he explains himself in the letter to Sir Walter Raleigh which is printed below.

Spenser is, as has been well said, "among the very greatest of our poets, but the significance of his poetry in the history of our literature is even greater than its intrinsic value. He recreated English prosody, giving back to our verse the fluidity and the grace that it had lost since the days of Chaucer, and extending the range of its achievement; he created English poetic diction, lifting it from anarchy and stiffness, daring greatly, but triumphing whether in the simple or the ornate, widening its scope, but at the same time never failing to give it ease and flexibility, so that language became to him a willing servant, and could voice the subtlest shades of mood or fancy. By means of this rich and varied style, fully expressive of his high seriousness, his spirituality, his inexhaustible sense of beauty, he has exercised a spell that has been potent for three centuries, and none has called so many poets to their vocation" (E. de Sélincourt, Introduction to Spenser's *Poetical Works*, pp. xxxix-xl).

THE FAERIE QUEENE

A LETTER OF THE AUTHOR'S,

EXPOUNDING HIS WHOLE INTENTION IN THE COURSE OF THIS WORKE: WHICH, FOR THAT IT GIVETH GREAT LIGHT TO THE READER, FOR THE BETTER UNDERSTANDING IS HEREUNTO ANNEXED.

To the Right Noble and Valorous SIR WALTER RALEIGH, KNIGHT; Lord Wardein of the Stanneryes, and Her Majesties Liefetenaunt of the County of Cornewayll.

SIR, knowing how doubtfully all allegories may be construed, and this booke of mine, which I have entituled the *Faery Queene*, being a continued allegory, or darke conceit, I have thought good, as well for avoyding of gealous opinions and misconstructions, as also for your better light in reading thereof (being so by you commanded), to discover unto you the general intention and meaning, which in the whole course thereof I have fashioned, without expressing of any particular purposes, or by-accidents therein occasioned. The generall end therefore of all the booke is to fashion a gentleman or noble person in vertuous and gentle discipline: which for that I conceived shoulde be most plausible and pleasing, being coloured with an historicall fiction, the which the most part of men delight to read, rather for variety of matter than for profite of the ensample, I chose the historye of King Arthure, as most fitte for the excellency of his person, being made famous by many men's former workes, and also furthest from the daunger of envy, and suspition of present time. In which I have followed all the antique Poets historicall: first Homere, who in the Persons of Agamemnon and Ulysses hath ensampled a good governour and a vertuous man, the one in his Ilias, the other in his Odysseis; then Virgil, whose like intention was to doe in the person of Aeneas; after him Ariosto comprised them both in his Orlando: and lately Tasso dissevered them againe, and formed both parts in two persons, namely that part which they in Philosophy call Ethice, or vertues of a private man, coloured in his Rinaldo; the other named Politice in his Godfredo. By ensample of which excellente poets, I labour to pourtraict in Arthure, before he was king, the image of a brave knight, perfected in the twelve private morall vertues, as Aristotle hath devised; the which is the purpose of these first twelve bookes:[1] which if I finde to be well accepted, I may be perhaps encoraged to frame the other part of pollititicke vertues in his person, after that hee came to be king.

To some, I know, this methode will seeme displeasaunt, which had rather have good discipline delivered plainly in way of precepts, or sermoned at large, as they use, than thus clowdily enwrapped in Allegoricall devises. But such, me seeme, should be satisfide with the use of these dayes, seeing all things accounted by their showes, and nothing esteemed of, that is not delightfull and pleasing to commune sence.[2] For this cause is Xenophon preferred before Plato, for that the one, in the exquisite depth of his judgement, formed a commune welth, such as it should be; but the other in the person of Cyrus, and the Persians, fashioned a governement, such as might best be: so much more profitable and gratious is doctrine by

---

[1] Of these Spenser completed only six, and a fragment probably designed for the seventh.

[2] *I.e.*, the senses, in opposition to the reason.

ensample, than by rule. So have I laboured to doe in the person of Arthure: whome I conceive, after his long education by Timon, to whom he was by Merlin delivered to be brought up, so soone as he was borne of the Lady Igrayne, to have seene in a dream or vision the Faery Queen, with whose excellent beauty ravished, he awaking resolved to seeke her out; and so being by Merlin armed, and by Timon throughly instructed, he went to seeke her forth in Faerye Land. In that Faery Queene I meane glory in my generall intention, but in my particular I conceive the most excellent and glorious person of our soveraine the Queene, and her kingdome in Faery Land. And yet, in some places els, I doe otherwise shadow her. For considering she beareth two persons, the one of a most royall queene or empresse, the other of a most vertuous and beautifull Lady, this latter part in some places I doe expresse in Belphœbe, fashioning her name according to your owne excellent conceipt of Cynthia (Phœbe and Cynthia being both names of Diana). So in the person of Prince Arthure I sette forth magnificence in particular, which vertue, for that (according to Aristotle and the rest) it is the perfection of all the rest, and conteineth in it them all, therefore in the whole course I mention the deedes of Arthure applyable to that vertue which I write of in that booke. But of the xii. other vertues, I make xii. other knights the patrones, for the more variety of the history: of which these three bookes contayn three.[1] The first of the Knight of the Redcrosse, in whome I expresse Holynes: The seconde of Sir Guyon, in whome I sette forth Temperaunce: The third of Britomartis, a lady knight, in whome I picture Chastity. But, because the beginning of the whole worke seemeth abrupte, and as depending upon other antecedents, it needs that ye know the occasion of these three knights severall adventures. For the methode of a poet historical is not such as of an historiographer. For an historiographer discourseth of affayres orderly as they were donne, accounting as well the times as the actions; but a poet thrusteth into the middest, even where it most concerneth him, and there recoursing to the thinges forepaste, and divining of thinges to come, maketh a pleasing analysis of all.

[1]This letter was first published in the edition of 1590, which contained only the first three books.

The beginning therefore of my history, if it were to be told by an historiographer, should be the twelfth booke, which is the last; where I devise that the Faery Queene kept her annuall feaste xii. dayes; upon which xii. severall dayes, the occasions of the xii. severall advantures happed, which, being undertaken by xii. severall knights, are in these xii. books severally handled and discoursed. The first was this. In the beginning of the feast, there presented himselfe a tall clownishe younge man, who, falling before the Queene of Faries, desired a boone (as the manner then was) which during that feast she might not refuse: which was that hee might have the atchievement of any adventure, which during that feaste should happen: that being graunted, he rested him on the floore, unfitte through his rusticity for a better place. Soone after entred a faire ladye in mourning weedes, riding on a white asse, with a dwarfe behind her leading a warlike steed, that bore the armes of a knight, and his speare in the dwarfes hand. Shee, falling before the Queene of Faeries, complayned that her father and mother, an ancient king and queene, had bene by an huge dragon many years shut up in a brasen castle, who thence suffred them not to yssew; and therefore besought the Faery Queene to assygne her some one of her knights to take on him that exployt. Presently that clownish person, upstarting, desired that adventure: whereat the Queene much wondering, and the lady much gaine-saying, yet he earnestly importuned his desire. In the end the lady told him, that unlesse that armour which she brought, would serve him (that is, the armour of a Christian man specified by Saint Paul, vi. Ephes.), that he could not succeed in that enterprise: which being forthwith put upon him with dewe furnitures thereunto, he seemed the goodliest man in al that company, and was well liked of the lady. And eftesoones taking on him knighthood, and mounting on that straunge courser, he went forth with her on that adventure: where beginneth the first booke, *viz.*,

A gentle knight was pricking on the playne, *etc.*

The second day there came in a palmer, bearing an infant with bloody hands, whose parents he complained to have bene slayn by an enchaunteresse called Acrasia; and therefore craved of the Faery Queene, to appoint him some knight to performe that adventure; which being assigned to Sir Guyon, he presently went forth with that same palmer: which is the beginning of the second booke and the whole subject thereof. The third day there came in a groome, who complained before the Faery Queene, that a vile enchaunter, called Busirane, had in hand a most faire lady, called Amoretta, whom he kept in most grievous torment, because she would not yield him the pleasure of her body. Whereupon Sir Scudamour, the lover of that lady, presently tooke on him that adventure. But being unable to performe it by reason of the hard enchauntments, after long sorrow, in the end met with Britomartis, who succoured him, and reskewed his love.

But by occasion hereof many other adventures are intermedled, but rather as accidents then intendments: as the love of Britomart, the overthrow of Marinell, the misery of Florimell, the vertuousness of Belphœbe, the lasciviousnes of Hellenora, and many the like.

Thus much, Sir, I have briefly overronne, to direct your understanding to the welhead of the history, that from thence gathering the whole intention of the conceit ye may, as in a handfull, gripe al the discourse, which otherwise may happily seeme tedious and confused. So, humbly craving the continuance of your honourable favour towards me, and th'eternall establishment of your happines, I humbly take leave.

23 January, 1589.

Yours most humbly affectionate,

ED. SPENSER.

THE FIRST BOOKE OF THE FAERIE QUEENE

CONTAYNING

THE LEGENDE OF THE KNIGHT OF THE RED CROSSE, OR OF HOLINESSE

1

Lo I the man, whose Muse whilome did maske,
As time her taught, in lowly Shepheards weeds,[1]
Am now enforst a far unfitter taske,
For trumpets sterne to chaunge mine Oaten reeds,
And sing of Knights and Ladies gentle deeds;
Whose prayses having slept in silence long,
Me, all too meane, the sacred Muse areeds
To blazon broad emongst her learnéd throng:
Fierce warres and faithfull loves shall moralize my song.

2

Helpe then, O holy Virgin chiefe of nine,[2]
Thy weaker Novice to performe thy will,
Lay forth out of thine everlasting scryne
The antique rolles, which there lye hidden still,
Of Faerie knights and fairest *Tanaquill*,[3]
Whom that most noble Briton Prince[4] so long
Sought through the world, and suffered so much ill,
That I must rue his undeservéd wrong:
O helpe thou my weake wit, and sharpen my dull tong.

[1] In the *Shepherd's Calendar* (1579).

[2] Calliope, muse of heroic poetry; though according to some Spenser means Clio, the muse of history.

[3] A British princess, representing Queen Elizabeth.

[4] Prince Arthur.

3

And thou most dreaded impe of highest *Jove*,
Faire *Venus* sonne, that with thy cruell dart
At that good knight so cunningly didst rove,
That glorious fire it kindled in his hart,
Lay now thy deadly Heben bow apart,
And with thy mother milde come to mine ayde:
Come both, and with you bring triumphant *Mart*,[5]
In loves and gentle jollities arrayd,
After his murdrous spoiles and bloudy rage allayd.

4

And with them eke, O Goddesse heavenly bright,[6]
Mirrour of grace and Majestie divine,
Great Lady of the greatest Isle, whose light
Like *Phœbus* lampe throughout the world doth shine,
Shed thy faire beames into my feeble eyne,
And raise my thoughts too humble and too vile,
To thinke of that true glorious type of thine,
The argument of mine afflicted stile:
The which to heare, vouchsafe, O dearest dred a-while.

CANTO I

The Patron of true Holinesse,
Foule Errour doth defeate:
Hypocrisie him to entrape,
Doth to his home entreate.

1

A GENTLE KNIGHT was pricking on the plaine,
Y-cladd in mightie armes and silver shielde,

[5] Mars. [6] Queen Elizabeth.

Wherein old dints of deepe wounds did remaine,
The cruell markes of many' a bloudy fielde;
Yet armes till that time did he never wield:
His angry steede did chide his foming bitt,
As much disdayning to the curbe to yield:
Full jolly knight he seemd, and faire did sitt,
As one for knightly giusts and fierce encounters fitt.

2

But on his brest a bloudie Crosse he bore,
The deare remembrance of his dying Lord,
For whose sweete sake that glorious badge he wore,
And dead as living ever him ador'd:
Upon his shield the like was also scor'd,
For soveraine hope, which in his helpe he had:
Right faithfull true he was in deede and word,
But of his cheere did seeme too solemne sad;
Yet nothing did he dread, but ever was ydrad.

3

Upon a great adventure he was bond,
That greatest *Gloriana*[1] to him gave,
That greatest Glorious Queene of *Faerie* lond,
To winne him worship, and her grace to have,
Which of all earthly things he most did crave;
And ever as he rode, his hart did earne
To prove his puissance in battell brave
Upon his foe, and his new force to learne;
Upon his foe, a Dragon horrible and stearne.[2]

4

A lovely Ladie[3] rode him faire beside,
Upon a lowly Asse more white then snow,
Yet she much whiter, but the same did hide
Under a vele, that wimpled was full low,
And over all a blacke stole she did throw,
As one that inly mournd: so was she sad,
And heavie sat upon her palfrey slow;
Seeméd in heart some hidden care she had,
And by her in a line[4] a milke white lambe she lad.

5

So pure and innocent, as that same lambe,
She was in life and every vertuous lore,
And by descent from Royall lynage came
Of ancient Kings and Queenes, that had of yore
Their scepters stretcht from East to Westerne shore,
And all the world in their subjection held;
Till that infernall feend with foule uprore
Forwasted all their land, and them expeld:
Whom to avenge, she had this Knight from far compeld.

[1]Queen Elizabeth. [2]The dragon typifies sin.
[3]Una, who typifies truth. [4]By a cord.

6

Behind her farre away a Dwarfe[5] did lag,
That lasie seemd in being ever last,
Or wearièd with bearing of her bag
Of needments at his backe. Thus as they past,
The day with cloudes was suddeine overcast,
And angry *Jove* an hideous storme of raine
Did poure into his Lemans lap so fast,
That every wight to shrowd it did constrain,
And this fair couple eke to shroud themselves were fain.

7

Enforst to seeke some covert nigh at hand,
A shadie grove not far away they spide,
That promist ayde the tempest to withstand:
Whose loftie trees yclad with sommers pride,
Did spred so broad, that heavens light did hide,
Not perceable with power of any starre:
And all within were pathes and alleies wide,
With footing worne, and leading inward farre:
Faire harbour that them seemes; so in they entred arre.

8

And foorth they passe, with pleasure forward led,
Joying to heare the birdes sweete harmony,
Which therein shrouded from the tempest dred,
Seemd in their song to scorne the cruell sky.
Much can they prayse the trees so straight and hy,
The sayling Pine,[6] the Cedar proud and tall,
The vine-prop Elme, the Poplar never dry,[7]
The builder Oake, sole king of forrests all,
The Aspine good for staves, the Cypresse funerall.[8]

9

The Laurell, meed of mightie Conquerours
And Poets sage, the Firre that weepeth still,[9]
The Willow worne of forlorne Paramours,
The Eugh obedient to the benders will,
The Birch for shaftes, the Sallow for the mill,
The Mirrhe sweete bleeding in the bitter wound,[10]
The warlike Beech,[11] the Ash for nothing ill,
The fruitful Olive, and the Platane round,
The carver Holme, the Maple seeldom inward sound.

[5]Typifying prudence.
[6]Used for the masts of ships.
[7]Because it grows best in moist soil.
[8]Symbolic of death.
[9]It exudes resin.
[10]Myrrh is fragrant though bitter.
[11]"There is a tradition that the war chariots of the ancients were made of beech" (Winstanley).

10

Led with delight, they thus beguile the way,
Untill the blustring storme is overblowne;
When weening to returne, whence they did stray,
They cannot finde that path, which first was showne,
But wander too and fro in wayes unknowne,
Furthest from end then, when they neerest weene,
That makes them doubt, their wits be not their owne:
So many pathes, so many turnings seene,
That which of them to take, in diverse doubt they been.

11

At last resolving forward still to fare,
Till that some end they finde or in or out,
That path they take, that beaten seemd most bare,
And like to lead the labyrinth about;[1]
Which when by tract they hunted had throughout,
At length it brought them to a hollow cave,
Amid the thickest woods. The Champion stout
Eftsoones dismounted from his courser brave,
And to the Dwarfe awhile his needlesse spere he gave.

12

Be well aware, quoth then that Ladie milde,
Least suddaine mischiefe ye too rash provoke:
The danger hid, the place unknowne and wilde,
Breedes dreadfull doubts: Oft fire is without smoke,
And perill without show: therefore your stroke
Sir knight with-hold, till further triall made.
Ah Ladie (said he) shame were to revoke
The forward footing for an hidden shade:[2]
Vertue gives her selfe light, through darkenesse for to wade.

13

Yea but (quoth she) the perill of this place
I better wot then you, though now too late,
To wish you backe returne with foule disgrace,
Yet wisedome warnes, whilest foot is in the gate,
To stay the steppe, ere forcéd to retrate.
This is the wandring wood, this *Errours den*,
A monster vile, whom God and man does hate:
Therefore I read beware. Fly fly (quoth then
The fearefull Dwarfe:) this is no place for living men.

[1]Out of.

[2]It were a shame to turn back because of an imagined danger.

14

But full of fire and greedy hardiment,
The youthfull knight could not for ought be staide,
But forth unto the darksome hole he went,
And lookéd in: his glistring armor made
A little glooming light, much like a shade,
By which he saw the ugly monster plaine,
Halfe like a serpent horribly displaide,
But th'other halfe did womans shape retaine,
Most lothsom, filthie, foule, and full of vile disdaine.

15

And as she lay upon the durtie ground,
Her huge long taile her den all overspred,
Yet was in knots and many boughtes upwound,
Pointed with mortall sting. Of her there bred[3]
A thousand yong ones, which she dayly fed,
Sucking upon her poisonous dugs, each one
Of sundry shapes, yet all ill favoréd:
Soone as that uncouth light upon them shone,
Into her mouth they crept, and suddain all were gone.

16

Their dam upstart, out of her den effraide,
And rushéd forth, hurling her hideous taile
About her curséd head, whose folds displaid
Were stretcht now forth at length without entraile.
She lookt about, and seeing one in mayle
Arméd to point, sought backe to turne againe;
For light she hated as the deadly bale,
Ay wont in desert darknesse to remaine,
Where plaine none might her see, nor she see any plaine.

17

Which when the valiant Elfe[4] perceiv'd, he lept
As Lyon fierce upon the flying pray,
And with his trenchand blade her boldly kept
From turning backe, and forcéd her to stay:
Therewith enrag'd she loudly gan to bray,
And turning fierce, her speckled taile advaunst,
Threatning her angry sting, him to dismay:
Who nought aghast, his mightie hand enhaunst:
The stroke down from her head unto her shoulder glaunst.

18

Much daunted with that dint, her sence was dazd,

[3]There were born.

[4]The Knight is so called because he is a fairy knight.

Yet kindling rage, her selfe she gathered round,
And all attonce her beastly body raizd
With doubled forces high above the ground:
Tho wrapping up her wrethed sterne arownd,
Lept fierce upon his shield, and her huge traine
All suddenly about his body wound,
That hand or foot to stirre he strove in vaine;
God helpe the man so wrapt in *Errours* endlesse traine.

19

His Lady sad to see his sore constraint,
Cride out, Now now Sir Knight, shew what ye bee,
Add faith unto your force, and be not faint:
Strangle her, else she sure will strangle thee.
That when he heard, in great perplexitie,
His gall did grate for griefe and high disdaine,[1]
And knitting all his force got one hand free,
Wherewith he grypt her gorge with so great paine,
That soone to loose her wicked bands did her constraine.

20

Therewith she spewd out of her filthy maw
A floud of poyson horrible and blacke,
Full of great lumpes of flesh and gobbets raw,
Which stunck so vildly, that it forst him slacke
His grasping hold, and from her turne him backe:
Her vomit full of bookes and papers was,[2]
With loathly frogs and toades, which eyes did lacke,
And creeping sought way in the weedy gras:
Her filthy parbreake all the place defiléd has.

21

As when old father *Nilus* gins to swell
With timely pride above the *Ægyptian* vale,
His fattie waves do fertile slime outwell,
And overflow each plaine and lowly dale:
But when his later spring gins to avale,
Huge heapes of mudd he leaves, wherein there breed
Ten thousand kindes of creatures, partly male
And partly female of his fruitfull seed;
Such ugly monstrous shapes elswhere may no man reed.

22

The same so sore annoyéd has the knight,
That welnigh chokéd with the deadly stinke,
His forces faile, ne can no longer fight.
Whose corage when the feend perceiv'd to shrinke,
She pouréd forth out of her hellish sinke
Her fruitfull curséd spawne of serpents small,
Deforméd monsters, fowle, and blacke as inke,
Which swarming all about his legs did crall,
And him encombred sore, but could not hurt at all.

23

As gentle Shepheard in sweete even-tide,
When ruddy *Phœbus* gins to welke in west,
High on an hill, his flocke to vewen wide,
Markes which do byte their hasty supper best;
A cloud of combrous gnattes do him molest,
All striving to infixe their feeble stings,
That from their noyance he no where can rest,
But with his clownish hands their tender wings
He brusheth oft, and oft doth mar their murmurings.

24

Thus ill bestedd, and fearefull more of shame,
Then of the certaine perill he stood in,
Halfe furious unto his foe he came,
Resolv'd in minde all suddenly to win,
Or soone to lose, before he once would lin;
And strooke at her with more then manly force,
That from her body full of filthie sin
He raft her hatefull head without remorse;
A streame of cole black bloud forth gushéd from her corse.

25

Her scattred brood, soone as their Parent deare
They saw so rudely falling to the ground,
Groning full deadly, all with troublous feare,
Gathred themselves about her body round,
Weening their wonted entrance to have found
At her wide mouth: but being there withstood
They flockéd all about her bleeding wound,
And suckéd up their dying mothers blood,
Making her death their life, and eke her hurt their good.

26

That detestable sight him much amazde,
To see th'unkindly Impes of heaven accurst,
Devoure their dam; on whom while so he gazd,
Having all satisfide their bloudy thurst,
Their bellies swolne he saw with fulnesse burst,
And bowels gushing forth: well worthy end
Of such as drunke her life, the which them nurst;

[1]His anger was kindled by his pain and great disgust.

[2]The allusion is to pamphlets written by Catholics against protestantism.

Now needeth him no lenger labour spend,
His foes have slaine themselves, with whom he should contend.

27

His Ladie seeing all, that chaunst, from farre
Approcht in hast to greet his victorie,
And said, Faire knight, borne under happy starre,
Who see your vanquisht foes before you lye:
Well worthy be you of that Armorie,[1]
Wherein ye have great glory wonne this day,
And proov'd your strength on a strong enimie,
Your first adventure: many such I pray,
And henceforth ever wish, that like succeed it may.

28

Then mounted he upon his Steede againe,
And with the Lady backward sought to wend;
That path he kept, which beaten was most plaine.
Ne ever would to any by-way bend,
But still did follow one unto the end,
The which at last out of the wood them brought.
So forward on his way (with God to frend)
He passeth forth, and new adventure sought;
Long way he travelléd, before he heard of ought.

29

At length they chaunst to meet upon the way
An agéd Sire,[2] in long blacke weedes yclad,
His feete all bare, his beard all hoarie gray,
And by his belt his booke he hanging had;
Sober he seemde, and very sagely sad,
And to the ground his eyes were lowly bent,
Simple in shew, and voyde of malice bad,
And all the way he prayéd, as he went,
And often knockt his brest, as one that did repent.

30

He faire the knight saluted, louting low,
Who faire him quited, as that courteous was:
And after askéd him, if he did know
Of straunge adventures, which abroad did pas.
Ah my deare Sonne (quoth he) how should, alas,
Silly old man, that lives in hidden cell,
Bidding his beades all day for his trespas,
Tydings of warre and worldly trouble tell?
With holy father fits not with such things to mell.

31

But if of daunger which hereby doth dwell,
And homebred evill ye desire to heare,
Of a straunge man I can you tidings tell,
That wasteth all this countrey farre and neare.
Of such (said he) I chiefly do inquere,
And shall you well reward to shew the place,
In which that wicked wight his dayes doth weare
For to all knighthood it is foule disgrace,
That such a curséd creature lives so long a space.

32

Far hence (quoth he) in wastfull wildernesse
His dwelling is, by which no living wight
May ever passe, but thorough great distresse.
Now (sayd the Lady) draweth toward night,
And well I wote, that of your later fight
Ye all forwearied be: for what so strong,
But wanting rest will also want of might?
The Sunne that measures heaven all day long,
At night doth baite his steedes the *Ocean* waves emong.

33

Then with the Sunne take Sir, your timely rest,
And with new day new worke at once begin:
Untroubled night they say gives counsell best.
Right well Sir knight ye have adviséd bin,
(Quoth then that aged man;) the way to win
Is wisely to advise: now day is spent;
Therefore with me ye may take up your In[3]
For this same night. The knight was well content:
So with that godly father to his home they went.

34

A little lowly Hermitage it was,
Downe in a dale, hard by a forests side,
Far from resort of people, that did pas
In travell to and froe: a little wyde[4]
There was an holy Chappell edifyde,
Wherein the Hermite dewly wont to say
His holy things each morne and eventyde:
Thereby a Christall streame did gently play,
Which from a sacred fountaine welléd forth alway.

35

Arrivéd there, the little house they fill,
Ne looke for entertainement, where none was:
Rest is their feast, and all things at their will;
The noblest mind the best contentment has.
With faire discourse the evening so they pas:
For that old man of pleasing wordes had store,
And well could file his tongue as smooth as glas;
He told of Saintes and Popes, and evermore
He strowd an *Ave-Mary*[5] after and before.

[1]The armor of a Christian man.

[2]Archimago, a disguised enchanter, who typifies hypocrisy.

[3]Your resting-place. [4]A short distance away.

[5]A prayer to the Virgin Mary.

36

The drouping Night thus creepeth on them fast,
And the sad humour loading their eye liddes,
As messenger of *Morpheus* on them cast
Sweet slombring deaw, the which to sleepe them biddes.
Unto their lodgings then his guestes he riddes:
Where when all drownd in deadly sleepe he findes,
He to his study goes, and there amiddes
His Magick bookes and artes of sundry kindes,
He seekes out mighty charmes, to trouble sleepy mindes.

37

Then choosing out few wordes most horrible,
(Let none them read) thereof did verses frame,
With which and other spelles like terrible,
He bad awake blacke *Plutoes* griesly Dame,[1]
And curséd heaven, and spake reprochfull shame
Of highest God, the Lord of life and light;
A bold bad man, that dar'd to call by name
Great *Gorgon*, Prince of darknesse and dead night,
At which *Cocytus* quakes, and *Styx* is put to flight.[2]

38

And forth he cald out of deepe darknesse dred
Legions of Sprights, the which like little flyes
Fluttring about his ever damnéd hed,
A-waite whereto their service he applyes,
To aide his friends, or fray his enimies:
Of those he chose out two, the falsest twoo,
And fittest for to forge true-seeming lyes;
The one of them he gave a message too,
The other by him selfe staide other worke to doo.

39

He making speedy way through sperséd ayre,
And through the world of waters wide and deepe,
To *Morpheus* house doth hastily repaire.
Amid the bowels of the earth full steepe,
And low, where dawning day doth never peepe,
His dwelling is; there *Tethys*[3] his wet bed
Doth ever wash, and *Cynthia*[4] still doth steepe
In silver deaw his ever-drouping hed,
Whiles sad Night over him her mantle black doth spred.

40

Whose double gates he findeth lockéd fast,
The one faire fram'd of burnisht Yvory,
The other all with silver overcast;
And wakefull dogges before them farre do lye,
Watching to banish Care their enimy,
Who oft is wont to trouble gentle sleepe.
By them the Sprite doth passe in quietly,
And unto *Morpheus* comes, whom drownéd deepe
In drowsie fit he findes: of nothing he takes keepe.

41

And more, to lulle him in his slumber soft,
A trickling streame from high rocke tumbling downe
And ever-drizling raine upon the loft,
Mixt with a murmuring winde, much like the sowne
Of swarming Bees, did cast him in a swowne:
No other noyse, nor peoples troublous cryes,
As still are wont t'annoy the walléd towne,
Might there be heard: but carelesse Quiet lyes,
Wrapt in eternall silence farre from enemyes.

42

The messenger approching to him spake,
But his wast wordes returnd to him in vaine:
So sound he slept, that nought mought him awake.
Then rudely he him thrust, and pusht with paine,
Whereat he gan to stretch: but he againe
Shooke him so hard, that forcéd him to speake.
As one then in a dreame, whose dryer braine[5]
Is tost with troubled sights and fancies weake,
He mumbled soft, but would not all his silence breake.

43

The Sprite then gan more boldly him to wake,
And threatned unto him the dreaded name
Of *Hecate*:[6] whereat he gan to quake,
And lifting up his lumpish head, with blame
Halfe angry askéd him, for what he came.
Hither (quoth he) me *Archimago* sent,
He that the stubborne Sprites can wisely tame,
He bids thee to him send for his intent
A fit false dreame, that can delude the sleepers sent.

44

The God obayde, and calling forth straight way
A diverse dreame out of his prison darke,
Delivered it to him, and downe did lay
His heavie head, devoide of carefull carke,

[1]Proserpine. [2]Two rivers in Hades.
[3]The ocean. [4]The moon.

[5]It was once supposed that the brain, when too dry, gave rise to troubled dreams.
[6]Goddess of Hades, the patroness of witches.

Whose sences all were straight benumbd and starke.
He backe returning by the Yvorie dore,
Remounted up as light as chearefull Larke,
And on his litle winges the dreame he bore
In hast unto his Lord, where he him left afore.

45

Who all this while with charmes and hidden artes,
Had made a Lady of that other Spright,
And fram'd of liquid ayre her tender partes
So lively, and so like in all mens sight,
That weaker sence it could have ravisht quight:
The maker selfe for all his wondrous witt,
Was nigh beguiléd with so goodly sight:
Her all in white he clad, and over it
Cast a blacke stole, most like to seeme for *Una* fit.

46

Now when that ydle dreame was to him brought,
Unto that Elfin knight he bad him fly,
Where he slept soundly void of evill thought,
And with false shewes abuse his fantasy,
In sort as he him schooléd privily:
And that new creature borne without her dew,[1]
Full of the makers guile, with usage sly
He taught to imitate that Lady trew,
Whose semblance she did carrie under feignéd hew.

47

Thus well instructed, to their worke they hast,
And comming where the knight in slomber lay,
The one upon his hardy head him plast,
And made him dreame of loves and lustfull play,
That nigh his manly hart did melt away,
Bathéd in wanton blis and wicked joy:
Then seeméd him his Lady by him lay,
And to him playnd, how that false wingéd boy,[2]
Her chast hart had subdewd, to learne Dame pleasures toy.

48

And she her selfe of beautie soveraigne Queene,
Faire Venus seemde unto his bed to bring
Her, whom he waking evermore did weene,
To be the chastest flowre, that ay did spring
On earthly braunch, the daughter of a king,
Now a loose Leman to vile service bound:
And eke the *Graces* seeméd all to sing,

[1]Born unnaturally. [2]Cupid.

Hymen Iö Hymen,[3] dauncing all around,
Whilst freshest *Flora*[4] her with Yvie girlond crownd.

49

In this great passion of unwonted lust,
Or wonted feare of doing ought amis,
He started up, as seeming to mistrust,
Some secret ill, or hidden foe of his:
Lo there before his face his Lady is,
Under blake stole hyding her bayted hooke,
And as halfe blushing offred him to kis,
With gentle blandishment and lovely looke,
Most like that virgin true, which for her knight him took.

50

All cleane dismayd to see so uncouth sight,
And halfe enragéd at her shamelesse guise,
He thought have slaine her in his fierce despight:
But hasty heat tempring with sufferance wise,
He stayde his hand, and gan himselfe advise
To prove his sense, and tempt her faignéd truth.
Wringing her hands in wemens pitteous wise,
Tho can she weepe, to stirre up gentle ruth,
Both for her noble bloud, and for her tender youth.

51

And said, Ah Sir, my liege Lord and my love,
Shall I accuse the hidden cruell fate,
And mightie causes wrought in heaven above,
Or the blind God, that doth me thus amate,
For hopéd love to winne me certaine hate?
Yet thus perforce he bids me do, or die.
Die is my dew: yet rew my wretched state
You, whom my hard avenging destinie
Hath made judge of my life or death indifferently.

52

Your owne deare sake forst me at first to leave
My Fathers kingdome, There she stopt with teares;
Her swollen hart her speach seemd to bereave,
And then againe begun, My weaker yeares
Captiv'd to fortune and frayle worldly feares,
Fly to your faith for succour and sure ayde:
Let me not dye in languor and long teares.
Why Dame (quoth he) what hath ye thus dismayd?
What frayes ye, that were wont to comfort me affrayd?

[3]Hymen was the god of marriage.
[4]Goddess of flowers.

53

Love of your selfe, she said, and deare constraint
Lets me not sleepe, but wast the wearie night
In secret anguish and unpittied plaint,
Whiles you in carelesse sleepe are drownéd quight.
Her doubtfull words made that redoubted knight
Suspect her truth: yet since no'untruth he knew,
Her fawning love with foule disdainefull spight
He would not shend, but said, Deare dame I rew,
That for my sake unknowne such griefe unto you grew.

54

Assure your selfe, it fell not all to ground;
For all so deare as life is to my hart,
I deeme your love, and hold me to you bound;
Ne let vaine feares procure your needlesse smart,
Where cause is none, but to your rest depart.
Not all content, yet seemd she to appease
Her mournefull plaintes, beguiléd of her art,[1]
And fed with words, that could not chuse but please,
So slyding softly forth, she turnd as to her ease.

55

Long after lay he musing at her mood,
Much griev'd to thinke that gentle Dame so light,
For whose defence he was to shed his blood.
At last dull wearinesse of former fight
Having yrockt asleepe his irkesome spright,
That troublous dreame gan freshly tosse his braine,
With bowres, and beds, and Ladies deare delight:
But when he saw his labour all was vaine,
With that misforméd spright he backe returnd againe.

CANTO II

The guilefull great Enchaunter parts
The Redcrosse Knight from Truth:
Into whose stead faire falshood steps,
And workes him wofull ruth.

1

By this the Northerne wagoner[2] had set
His sevenfold teme[3] behind the stedfast starre,[4]
That was in Ocean waves yet never wet,
But firme is fixt, and sendeth light from farre
To all, that in the wide deepe wandring arre:
And chearefull Chaunticlere with his note shrill
Had warnéd once, that *Phœbus* fiery carre[5]
In hast was climbing up the Easterne hill,
Full envious that night so long his roome did fill.

2

When those accurséd messengers of hell,
That feigning dreame, and that faire-forgéd Spright
Came to their wicked maister, and gan tell
Their bootelesse paines, and ill succeeding night:
Who all in rage to see his skilfull might
Deluded so, gan threaten hellish paine
And sad *Proserpines* wrath, them to affright.
But when he saw his threatning was but vaine,
He cast about, and searcht his balefull bookes againe.

3

Eftsoones he tooke that miscreated faire,
And that false other Spright, on whom he spred
A seeming body of the subtile aire,
Like a young Squire, in loves and lusty-hed
His wanton dayes that ever loosely led,
Without regard of armes and dreaded fight:
Those two he tooke, and in a secret bed,
Covered with darknesse and misdeeming night,
Them both together laid, to joy in vaine delight.

4

Forthwith he runnes with feignéd faithfull hast
Unto his guest, who after troublous sights
And dreames, gan now to take more sound repast,
Whom suddenly he wakes with fearefull frights,
As one aghast with feends or damnéd sprights,
And to him cals, Rise rise unhappy Swaine,
That here wex old in sleepe, whiles wicked wights
Have knit themselves in *Venus* shamefull chaine;
Come see, where your false Lady doth her honour staine.

5

All in amaze he suddenly up start
With sword in hand, and with the old man went;
Who soone him brought into a secret part,
Where that false couple were full closely ment

[1]Disappointed in her art. [2]Boötes.
[3]Charles's Wain, or the Great Bear. [4]The pole star.

[5]The sun.

In wanton lust and lewd embracément:
Which when he saw, he burnt with gealous fire,
The eye of reason was with rage yblent,
And would have slaine them in his furious ire,
But hardly was restreinéd of that agéd sire.

6

Returning to his bed in torment great,
And bitter anguish of his guiltie sight,
He could not rest, but did his stout heart eat,
And wast his inward gall with deepe despight,
Yrkesome of life, and too long lingring night.
At last faire *Hesperus* in highest skie
Had spent his lampe,[1] and brought forth dawning light,
Then up he rose, and clad him hastily;
The Dwarfe him brought his steed: so both away do fly.

7

Now when the rosy-fingred Morning faire,
Weary of agéd *Tithones* saffron bed,
Had spred her purple robe through deawy aire,
And the high hils *Titan*[2] discoveréd,
The royall virgin shooke off drowsy-hed,
And rising forth out of her baser bowre,
Lookt for her knight, who far away was fled,
And for her Dwarfe, that wont to wait each houre;
Then gan she waile and weepe, to see that woefull stowre.

8

And after him she rode with so much speede
As her slow beast could make, but all in vaine;
For him so far had borne his light-foot steede,
Prickéd with wrath and fiery fierce disdaine,
That him to follow was but fruitlesse paine;
Yet she her weary limbes would never rest,
But every hill and dale, each wood and plaine
Did search, sore grievéd in her gentle brest,
He so ungently left her, whom she lovéd best.

9

But subtill *Archimago*, when his guests
He saw divided into double parts,
And *Una* wandring in woods and forrests,
Th'end of his drift,[3] he praisd his divelish arts,
That had such might over true meaning harts;
Yet rests not so, but other meanes doth make,
How he may worke unto her further smarts:
For her he hated as the hissing snake,
And in her many troubles did most pleasure take.

10

He then devisde himselfe how to disguise;
For by his mightie science[4] he could take
As many formes and shapes in seeming wise,
As ever *Proteus*[5] to himselfe could make:
Sometime a fowle, sometime a fish in lake,
Now like a foxe, now like a dragon fell,
That of himselfe he oft for feare would quake,
And oft would flie away. O who can tell
The hidden power of herbes, and might of Magicke spell?

11

But now seemde best, the person to put on
Of that good knight, his late beguiléd guest:
In mighty armes he was yclad anon:
And silver shield: upon his coward brest
A bloudy crosse, and on his craven crest
A bounch of haires discolourd diversly:
Full jolly knight he seemde, and well addrest,
And when he sate upon his courser free,
Saint George himself ye would have deeméd him to be.

12

But he the knight, whose semblaunt he did beare,
The true *Saint George* was wandred far away,
Still flying from his thoughts and gealous feare;
Will was his guide, and griefe led him astray.
At last him chaunst to meete upon the way
A faithlesse Sarazin[6] all arm'd to point,
In whose great shield was writ with letters gay
Sans foy:[7] full large of limbe and every joint
He was, and caréd not for God or man a point.

13

He had a faire companion of his way,
A goodly Lady[8] clad in scarlot red,
Purfled with gold and pearle of rich assay,
And like a *Persian* mitre[9] on her hed.
She wore, with crownes and owches garnishéd,
The which her lavish lovers to her gave;
Her wanton palfrey all was overspred
With tinsell trappings, woven like a wave,
Whose bridle rung with golden bels and bosses brave.

[1]The morning star had yielded place to dawn.
[2]The sun. [3]The end he aimed at.
[4]His magic. [5]A sea-god.
[6]Used as a generic term for pagans.
[7]Faithless.
[8]Duessa, typifying falsehood, who calls herself Fidessa. She probably represents Mary, Queen of Scots—though it has also been suggested that she represents Mary Tudor—and the Roman Catholic Church.
[9]The papal crown is meant.

14

With faire disport and courting dalliaunce
She intertainde her lover all the way:
But when she saw the knight his speare advaunce,
She soone left off her mirth and wanton play,
And bad her knight addresse him to the fray:
His foe was nigh at hand. He, prickt with pride
And hope to winne his Ladies heart that day,
Forth spurréd fast: adowne his coursers side
The red bloud trickling staind the way, as he did ride.

15

The knight of the *Redcrosse* when him he spide,
Spurring so hote with rage dispiteous,
Gan fairely couch his speare, and towards ride:
Soone meete they both, both fell and furious,
That daunted with their forces hideous,
Their steeds do stagger, and amazéd stand,
And eke themselves too rudely rigorous,
Astonied with the stroke of their owne hand,
Do backe rebut, and each to other yeeldeth land.

16

As when two rams stird with ambitious pride,
Fight for the rule of the rich fleecéd flocke,
Their hornéd fronts so fierce on either side
Do meete, that with the terrour of the shocke
Astonied both, stand sencelesse as a blocke,
Forgetfull of the hanging victory:
So stood these twaine, unmovéd as a rocke,
Both staring fierce, and holding idely,
The broken reliques[1] of their former cruelty.

17

The *Sarazin* sore daunted with the buffe
Snatcheth his sword, and fiercely to him flies;
Who well it wards, and quyteth cuff with cuff:
Each others equall puissaunce envies,
And through their iron sides with cruelties
Does seeke to perce: repining courage yields
No foote to foe. The flashing fier flies
As from a forge out of their burning shields,
And streames of purple bloud new dies the verdant fields.

18

Curse on that Crosse (quoth then the *Sarazin*)
That keepes thy body from the bitter fit;[2]
Dead long ygoe I wote thou haddest bin,
Had not that charme from thee forwarnéd it:
But yet I warne thee now assuréd sitt,
And hide thy head. Therewith upon his crest
With rigour so outrageous he smitt,
That a large share it hewd out of the rest,
And glauncing downe his shield, from blame him fairely blest.[3]

19

Who thereat wondrous wroth, the sleeping spark
Of native vertue gan eftsoones revive,
And at his haughtie helmet making mark,
So hugely stroke, that it the steele did rive,
And cleft his head. He tumbling downe alive,
With bloudy mouth his mother earth did kis,
Greeting his grave: his grudging ghost did strive
With the fraile flesh; at last it flitted is,
Whither the soules do fly of men, that live amis.

20

The Lady when she saw her champion fall,
Like the old ruines of a broken towre,
Staid not to waile his woefull funerall,
But from him fled away with all her powre;
Who after her as hastily gan scowre,
Bidding the Dwarfe with him to bring away
The *Sarazins* shield, signe of the conqueroure.
Her soone he overtooke, and bad to stay,
For present cause was none of dread her to dismay.

21

She turning backe with ruefull countenaunce,
Cride, Mercy mercy Sir vouchsafe to show
On silly Dame, subject to hard mischaunce,
And to your mighty will. Her humblesse low
In so ritch weedes and seeming glorious show,
Did much emmove his stout heroïcke heart,
And said, Deare dame, your suddein overthrow
Much rueth me; but now put feare apart,
And tell, both who ye be, and who that tooke your part.

22

Melting in teares, then gan she thus lament;
The wretched woman, whom unhappy howre
Hath now made thrall to your commandement,
Before that angry heavens list to lowre,
And fortune false betraide me to your powre,
Was (O what now availeth that I was!)
Borne the sole daughter of an Emperour,
He that the wide West under his rule has,
And high hath set his throne, where *Tiberis* doth pas.[4]

[1]The broken shafts of their lances.

[2]Death.

[3]Delivered him from harm.

[4]The Pope, at Rome, where the river Tiber passes.

23

He in the first flowre of my freshest age,
Betrothéd me unto the onely haire
Of a most mighty king, most rich and sage;
Was never Prince so faithfull and so faire,
Was never Prince so meeke and debonaire;
But ere my hopéd day of spousall shone,
My dearest Lord fell from high honours staire,
Into the hands of his accurséd fone,
And cruelly was slaine, that shall I ever mone.

24

His blesséd body spoild of lively breath,
Was afterward, I know not how, convaid
And from me hid: of whose most innocent death
When tidings came to me unhappy maid,
O how great sorrow my sad soule assaid.
Then forth I went his woefull corse to find,
And many yeares throughout the world I straid,
A virgin widow, whose deepe wounded mind
With love, long time did languish as the striken hind.

25

At last it chauncéd this proud *Sarazin*,
To meete me wandring, who perforce me led
With him away, but yet could never win
The Fort, that Ladies hold in soveraigne dread.
There lies he now with foule dishonour dead,
Who whiles he liv'de, was calléd proud *Sans foy*,
The eldest of three brethren, all three bred
Of one bad sire, whose youngest is *Sans joy*,[1]
And twixt them both was borne the bloudy bold *Sans loy*.[2]

26

In this sad plight, friendlesse, unfortunate,
Now miserable I *Fidessa* dwell,
Craving of you in pitty of my state,
To do none ill, if please ye not do well.
He in great passion all this while did dwell,
More busying his quicke eyes, her face to view,
Then his dull eares, to heare what she did tell;
And said, faire Lady hart of flint would rew
The undeservéd woes and sorrowes, which ye shew.

27

Henceforth in safe assuraunce may ye rest,
Having both found a new friend you to aid,
And lost an old foe, that did you molest:
Better new friend then an old foe is said.
With chaunge of cheare the seeming simple maid
Let fall her eyen, as shamefast to the earth,
And yeelding soft, in that she nought gainsaid,
So forth they rode, he feining seemely merth,
And she coy lookes: so dainty they say maketh derth.[3]

28

Long time they thus together traveiléd,
Till weary of their way, they came at last,
Where grew two goodly trees, that faire did spred
Their armes abroad, with gray mosse overcast,
And their greene leaves trembling with every blast,
Made a calme shadow far in compasse round:
The fearefull Shepheard often there aghast
Under them never sat, ne wont there sound
His mery oaten pipe, but shund th'unlucky ground.

29

But this good knight soone as he them can spie,
For the coole shade him thither hastly got:
For golden *Phœbus* now ymounted hie,
From fiery wheeles of his faire chariot
Hurléd his beame so scorching cruell hot,
That living creature mote it not abide;
And his new Lady it enduréd not.
There they alight, in hope themselves to hide
From the fierce heat, and rest their weary limbs a tide.

30

Faire seemely pleasaunce each to other makes,
With goodly purposes there as they sit:
And in his falséd fancy he her takes
To be the fairest wight, that livéd yit;
Which to expresse, he bends his gentle wit,
And thinking of those braunches greene to frame
A girlond for her dainty forehead fit,
He pluckt a bough: out of whose rift there came
Small drops of gory bloud, that trickled downe the same.

31

Therewith a piteous yelling voyce was heard,
Crying, O spare with guilty hands to teare
My tender sides in this rough rynd embard,
But fly, ah fly far hence away, for feare
Least to you hap, that happened to me heare,
And to this wretched Lady, my deare love,
O too deare love, love bought with death too deare.

[1]Without happiness. [2]Lawless.

[3]Coyness causes desire.

Astond he stood, and up his haire did hove,
And with that suddein horror could no member move.

32

At last whenas the dreadfull passion
Was overpast, and manhood well awake,
Yet musing at the straunge occasion,
And doubting much his sence, he thus bespake;
What voyce of damnéd Ghost from *Limbo* lake,[1]
Or guilefull spright wandring in empty aire,
Both which fraile men do oftentimes mistake,
Sends to my doubtfull eares these speaches rare,[2]
And ruefull plaints, me bidding guiltlesse bloud to spare?

33

Then groning deepe, Nor damnéd Ghost (quoth he),
Nor guilefull sprite to thee these wordes doth speake,
But once a man *Fradubio*,[3] now a tree,
Wretched man, wretched tree; whose nature weake,
A cruell witch her curséd will to wreake,
Hath thus transformd, and plast in open plaines,
Where *Boreas*[4] doth blow full bitter bleake,
And scorching Sunne does dry my secret vaines:
For though a tree I seeme, yet cold and heat me paines.

34

Say on *Fradubio* then, or man, or tree,
Quoth then the knight, by whose mischievous arts
Art thou misshapéd thus, as now I see?
He oft finds med'cine, who his griefe imparts;
But double griefs afflict concealing harts,
As raging flames who striveth to suppresse.
The author then (said he) of all my smarts,
Is one *Duessa* a false sorceresse,
That many errant knights hath brought to wretchednesse.

35

In prime of youthly yeares, when corage hot
The fire of love and joy of chevalree
First kindled in my brest, it was my lot
To love this gentle Lady, whom ye see,
Now not a Lady, but a seeming tree;
With whom as once I rode accompanyde,
Me chauncéd of a knight encountred bee,
That had a like faire Lady by his syde,
Like a faire Lady, but did fowle *Duessa* hyde.

36

Whose forgéd beauty he did take in hand,[5]
All other Dames to have exceeded farre;
I in defence of mine did likewise stand,
Mine, that did then shine as the Morning starre:
So both to battell fierce arraungéd arre,
In which his harder fortune was to fall
Under my speare: such is the dye of warre:
His Lady left as a prise martiall,
Did yield her comely person, to be at my call.

37

So doubly lov'd of Ladies unlike faire,
Th'one seeming such, the other such indeede,
One day in doubt I cast for to compare,
Whether in beauties glorie did exceede;[6]
A Rosy girlond was the victors meede:
Both seemde to win, and both seemde won to bee,
So hard the discord was to be agreede.
Frælissa[7] was as faire, as faire mote bee,
And ever false *Duessa* seemde as faire as shee.

38

The wicked witch now seeing all this while
The doubtfull ballaunce equally to sway,
What not by right, she cast to win by guile,
And by her hellish science raisd streightway
A foggy mist, that overcast the day,
And a dull blast, that breathing on her face,
Dimméd her former beauties shining ray,
And with foule ugly forme did her disgrace:
Then was she faire alone, when none was faire in place.

39

Then cride she out, Fye, fye, deforméd wight,
Whose borrowed beautie now appeareth plaine
To have before bewitchéd all mens sight;
O leave her soone, or let her soone be slaine.
Her loathly visage viewing with disdaine,
Eftsoones I thought her such, as she me told,
And would have kild her; but with faignéd paine,
The false witch did my wrathfull hand withhold;
So left her, where she now is turnd to treen mould.[8]

40

Thenceforth I tooke *Duessa* for my Dame,
And in the witch unweening joyd long time,

[1] Hades. [2] Speech thin and faint.
[3] One of doubtful faith. [4] The north wind.

[5] Did maintain. [6] Which of the two excelled.
[7] Typifies such faith as is possible to a doubter.
[8] To the shape of a tree.

Ne ever wist, but that she was the same,
Till on a day (that day is every Prime,
When Witches wont do penance for their crime)
I chaunst to see her in her proper hew,
Bathing her selfe in origane and thyme:
A filthy foule old woman I did vew,
That ever to have toucht her, I did deadly rew.

41

Her neather partes misshapen, monstruous,
Were hidd in water, that I could not see,
But they did seeme more foule and hideous,
Then womans shape man would beleeve to bee.
Thenceforth from her most beastly companie
I gan refraine, in minde to slip away,
Soone as appeard safe opportunitie:
For danger great, if not assur'd decay
I saw before mine eyes, if I were knowne to stray.

42

The divelish hag by chaunges of my cheare[1]
Perceiv'd my thought, and drownd in sleepie night,
With wicked herbes and ointments did besmeare
My bodie all, through charmes and magicke might,
That all my senses were bereavéd quight:
Then brought she me into this desert waste,
And by my wretched lovers side me pight,
Where now enclosd in wooden wals full faste,
Banisht from living wights, our wearie dayes we waste.

43

But how long time, said then the Elfin knight,
Are you in this misformėd house to dwell?
We may not chaunge (quoth he) this evil plight,
Till we be bathéd in a living well;
That is the terme prescribéd by the spell.
O how, said he, mote I that well out find,
That may restore you to your wonted well?[2]
Time and suffiséd fates to former kynd
Shall us restore,[3] none else from hence may us unbynd.

44

The false *Duessa*, now *Fidessa* hight,
Heard how in vaine *Fradubio* did lament,
And knew well all was true. But the good knight
Full of sad feare and ghastly dreriment,
When all this speech the living tree had spent,
The bleeding bough did thrust into the ground,
That from the bloud he might be innocent,
And with fresh clay did close the wooden wound:
Then turning to his Lady, dead with feare her found.

45

Her seeming dead he found with feignéd feare,
As all unweeting of that well she knew,
And paynd himselfe with busie care to reare
Her out of carelesse swowne. Her eylids blew
And dimméd sight with pale and deadly hew
At last she up gan lift: with trembling cheare
Her up he tooke, too simple and too trew,
And oft her kist. At length all passéd feare,
He set her on her steede, and forward forth did beare.

[1]By the change in my countenance.

[2]Accustomed well-being.

[3]Time and the fitting hour shall restore us to our former nature.

CANTO III

Forsaken Truth long seekes her love,
And makes the Lyon mylde,
Marres blind Devotions mart, and fals
In hand of leachour vylde.

1

NOUGHT is there under heav'ns wide hollownesse,
That moves more deare compassion of mind,
Then beautie brought t'unworthy wretchednesse
Through envies snares or fortunes freakes unkind:
I, whether lately through her brightnesse blind,
Or through alleageance and fast fealtie,
Which I do owe unto all woman kind,
Feele my heart perst with so great agonie,
When such I see, that all for pittie I could die.

2

And now it is empassionéd so deepe,
For fairest *Unaes* sake, of whom I sing,
That my fraile eyes these lines with teares do steepe,
To thinke how she through guilefull handeling,
Though true as touch,[4] though daughter of a king,
Though faire as ever living wight was faire,
Though nor in word nor deede ill meriting,
Is from her knight divorcéd in despaire
And her due loves deriv'd to that vile witches share.

[4]Touchstone, used to test gold.

3

Yet she most faithfull Ladie all this while
Forsaken, wofull, solitarie mayd
Farre from all peoples prease, as in exile,
In wildernesse and wastfull deserts strayd,
To seeke her knight; who subtilly betrayd
Through that late vision, which th'Enchaunter wrought,
Had her abandond. She of nought affrayd,
Through woods and wastnesse wide him daily sought;
Yet wishéd tydings none of him unto her brought.

4

One day nigh wearie of the yrkesome way,
From her unhastie beast she did alight,
And on the grasse her daintie limbes did lay
In secret shadow, farre from all mens sight:
From her faire head her fillet she undight,
And laid her stole aside. Her angels face
As the great eye of heaven shynéd bright,
And made a sunshine in the shadie place;
Did never mortall eye behold such heavenly grace.

5

It fortunéd out of the thickest wood
A ramping Lyon[1] rushéd suddainly,
Hunting full greedie after salvage blood;
Soone as the royall virgin he did spy,
With gaping mouth at her ran greedily,
To have attonce devour'd her tender corse:
But to the pray when as he drew more ny,
His bloudie rage asswagéd with remorse,
And with the sight amazd, forgat his furious forse.

6

In stead thereof he kist her wearie feet,
And lickt her lilly hands with fawning tong,
As he her wrongéd innocence did weet.
O how can beautie maister the most strong,
And simple truth subdue avenging wrong?
Whose yeelded pride and proud submission,
Still dreading death, when she had markéd long,
Her hart gan melt in great compassion,
And drizling teares did shed for pure affection.

7

The Lyon Lord of every beast in field
Quoth she, his princely puissance doth abate,
And mightie proud to humble weake does yield,
Forgetfull of the hungry rage, which late
Him prickt, in pittie of my sad estate:
But he my Lyon, and my noble Lord
How does he find in cruell hart to hate
Her that him lov'd, and ever most adord,
As the God of my life? why hath he me abhord?

8

Redounding teares did choke th'end of her plaint,
Which softly ecchoed from the neighbour wood;
And sad to see her sorrowfull constraint
The kingly beast upon her gazing stood;
With pittie calmd, downe fell his angry mood.
At last in close hart shutting up her paine,
Arose the virgin borne of heavenly brood,
And to her snowy Palfrey got againe,
To seeke her strayéd Champion, if she might attaine.

9

The Lyon would not leave her desolate,
But with her went along, as a strong gard
Of her chast person, and a faithfull mate
Of her sad troubles and misfortunes hard:
Still when she slept, he kept both watch and ward,
And when she wakt, he waited diligent,
With humble service to her will prepard:
From her faire eyes he tooke commaundement,
And ever by her lookes conceivéd her intent.

10

Long she thus traveiléd through deserts wyde,
By which she thought her wandring knight shold pas,
Yet never shew of living wight espyde;
Till that at length she found the troden gras,
In which the tract of peoples footing was,
Under the steepe foot of a mountaine hore;
The same she followes, till at last she has
A damzell spyde[2] slow footing her before,
That on her shoulders sad a pot of water bore.

11

To whom approching she to her gan call,
To weet, if dwelling place were nigh at hand;
But the rude wench her answer'd nought at all,
She could not heare, nor speake, nor understand;
Till seeing by her side the Lyon stand,
With suddaine feare her pitcher downe she threw,
And fled away: for never in that land

[1]Probably typifying reason.

[2]Abessa, representing superstition.

Face of faire Ladie she before did vew,[1]
And that dread Lyons looke her cast in deadly hew.[2]

12

Full fast she fled, ne ever lookt behynd,
As if her life upon the wager lay,
And home she came, whereas her mother blynd[3]
Sate in eternall night: nought could she say,
But suddaine catching hold, did her dismay
With quaking hands, and other signes of feare:
Who full of ghastly fright and cold affray,
Gan shut the dore. By this arrivéd there
Dame *Una*, wearie Dame, and entrance did requere.

13

Which when none yeelded, her unruly Page
With his rude clawes the wicket open rent,
And let her in; where of his cruell rage
Nigh dead with feare, and faint astonishment,
She found them both in darkesome corner pent;
Where that old woman day and night did pray
Upon her beades devoutly penitent;
Nine hundred *Pater nosters*[4] every day,
And thrise nine hundred *Aves*[5] she was wont to say.

14

And to augment her painefull pennance more,
Thrise every weeke in ashes she did sit,
And next her wrinkled skin rough sackcloth wore,
And thrise three times did fast from any bit:[6]
But now for feare her beads she did forget.
Whose needlesse dread for to remove away,
Faire *Una* framéd words and count'nance fit:
Which hardly doen, at length she gan them pray,
That in their cotage small, that night she rest her may.

15

The day is spent, and commeth drowsie night,
When every creature shrowded is in sleepe;
Sad *Una* downe her laies in wearie plight,
And at her feet the Lyon watch doth keepe:
In stead of rest, she does lament, and weepe
For the late losse of her deare lovéd knight,
And sighes, and grones, and evermore does steepe
Her tender brest in bitter teares all night,
All night she thinks too long, and often lookes for light.

16

Now when *Aldeboran*[7] was mounted hie
Above the shynie *Cassiopeias* chaire,[8]
And all in deadly sleepe did drownéd lie,
One[9] knockéd at the dore, and in would fare;
He knockéd fast, and often curst, and sware,
That readie entrance was not at his call:
For on his backe a heavy load he bare
Of nightly stelths and pillage severall,[10]
Which he had got abroad by purchase criminall.[11]

17

He was to weet a stout and sturdie thiefe,
Wont to robbe Churches of their ornaments,
And poore mens boxes of their due reliefe,
Which given was to them for good intents;
The holy Saints of their rich vestiments
He did disrobe, when all men carelesse slept,
And spoild the Priests of their habiliments,
Whiles none the holy things in safety kept;
Then he by cunning sleights in at the window crept.

18

And all that he by right or wrong could find,
Unto this house he brought, and did bestow
Upon the daughter of this woman blind,
Abessa daughter of *Corceca* slow,
With whom he whoredome used, that few did know,
And fed her fat with feast of offerings,
And plentie, which in all the land did grow;
Ne sparéd he to give her gold and rings:
And now he to her brought part of his stolen things.

19

Thus long the dore with rage and threats he bet,
Yet of those fearefull women none durst rize,
The Lyon frayéd them, him in to let:
He would no longer stay him to advize,
But open breakes the dore in furious wize,
And entring is; when that disdainfull beast
Encountring fierce, him suddaine doth surprize,
And seizing cruell clawes on trembling brest,
Under his Lordly foot him proudly hath supprest.

---

[1]Abessa has never beheld Truth, whose very appearance now terrifies her.

[2]Made her as pale as death.

[3]Corceca, representing blind devotion.

[4]Our Father; the Lord's Prayer.

[5]Prayer to the Virgin.

[6]She fasted three whole days of each week.

[7]A star of the constellation of Taurus.

[8]The constellation called by this name.

[9]Kirkrapine, or Church-Robber.

[10]Thefts by night and pillage in various places.

[11]By criminal means.

20

Him booteth not resist, nor succour call,
His bleeding hart is in the vengers hand,
Who streight him rent in thousand peeces
small,
And quite dismembred hath: the thirstie land
Drunke up his life; his corse left on the strand.
His fearefull friends weare out the wofull night,
Ne dare to weepe, nor seeme to understand
The heavie hap, which on them is alight,
Affraid, least to themselves the like mishappen
might.

21

Now when broad day the world discoveréd has,
Up *Una* rose, up rose the Lyon eke,
And on their former journey forward pas,
In wayes unknowne, her wandring knight to
seeke,
With paines farre passing that long wandring
Greeke,[1]
That for his love refuséd deitie;
Such were the labours of this Lady meeke,
Still seeking him, that from her still did flie,
Then furthest from her hope, when most she
weenéd nie.

22

Soone as she parted thence, the fearefull
twaine,
That blind old woman and her daughter deare
Came forth, and finding *Kirkrapine* there
slaine,
For anguish great they gan to rend their heare,
And beat their brests, and naked flesh to teare.
And when they both had wept and wayld their
fill,
Then forth they ranne like two amazéd deare,
Halfe mad through malice, and revenging will,
To follow her, that was the causer of their ill.

23

Whom overtaking, they gan loudly bray,
With hollow howling, and lamenting cry,
Shamefully at her rayling all the way,
And her accusing of dishonesty,
That was the flowre of faith and chastity;
And still amidst her rayling, she did pray,
That plagues, and mischiefs, and long misery
Might fall on her, and follow all the way,
And that in endlesse error she might ever
stray.

24

But when she saw her prayers nought prevaile,
She backe returnéd with some labour lost;
And in the way as she did weepe and waile,
A knight her met in mighty armes embost,
Yet knight was not for all his bragging bost,

[1]Ulysses.

But subtill *Archimag*, that *Una* sought
By traynes[2] into new troubles to have tost:
Of that old woman tydings he besought,
If that of such a Ladie she could tellen ought.

25

Therewith she gan her passion to renew,
And cry, and curse, and raile, and rend her
heare,
Saying, that harlot she too lately knew,
That causd her shed so many a bitter teare,
And so forth told the story of her feare:
Much seeméd he to mone her haplesse chaunce,
And after for that Ladie did inquere;
Which being taught, he forward gan advaunce
His faire enchaunted steed, and eke his
charméd launce.

26

Ere long he came, where *Una* traveild slow,
And that wilde Champion wayting her besyde:
Whom seeing such, for dread he durst not
show
Himselfe too nigh at hand, but turnéd wyde[3]
Unto an hill; from whence when she him spyde,
By his like seeming shield, her knight by name
She weend it was, and towards him gan ryde:
Approching nigh, she wist it was the same,
And with faire fearefull humblesse towards
him shee came.

27

And weeping said, Ah my long lackéd Lord,
Where have ye bene thus long out of my sight?
Much fearèd I to have bene quite abhord,
Or ought have done,[4] that ye displeasen might,
That should as death unto my deare hart light:
For since mine eye your joyous sight did mis,
My chearefull day is turnd to chearelesse
night,
And eke my night of death the shadow is;
But welcome now my light, and shining lampe
of blis.

28

He thereto meeting said, My dearest Dame,
Farre be it from your thought, and fro my will,
To thinke that knighthood I so much should
shame,
As you to leave, that have me lovéd still,
And chose in Faery court of meere goodwill,
Where noblest knights were to be found on
earth:
The earth shall sooner leave her kindly skill
To bring forth fruit, and make eternall derth.
Then I leave you, my liefe, yborne of heavenly
berth.

[2]By tricks. [3]Turned aside.
[4]Or to have done something.

29

And sooth to say, why I left you so long,
Was for to seeke adventure in strange place,
Where *Archimago* said a felon strong
To many knights did daily worke disgrace;
But knight he now shall never more deface:
Good cause of mine excuse; that mote ye please
Well to accept, and evermore embrace
My faithfull service, that by land and seas
Have vowd you to defend, now then your plaint appease.

30

His lovely words her seemd due recompence
Of all her passéd paines: one loving howre
For many yeares of sorrow can dispence:
A dram of sweet is worth a pound of sowre:
She has forgot, how many a wofull stowre
For him she late endur'd; she speakes no more
Of past: true is, that true love hath no powre
To looken backe; his eyes be fixt before.
Before her stands her knight, for whom she toyld so sore.

31

Much like, as when the beaten marinere,
That long hath wandred in the *Ocean* wide.
Oft soust in swelling *Tethys*[1] saltish teare,
And long time having tand his tawney hide
With blustring breath of heaven, that none can bide,
And scorching flames of fierce *Orions* hound,[2]
Soone as the port from farre he has espide,
His chearefull whistle merrily doth sound,
And *Nereus*[3] crownes with cups;[4] his mates him pledg around.

32

Such joy made *Una*, when her knight she found;
And eke th'enchaunter joyous seemd no lesse,
Then the glad marchant, that does vew from ground
His ship farre come from watrie wildernesse,
He hurles out vowes, and *Neptune* oft doth blesse:
So forth they past, and all the way they spent
Discoursing of her dreadfull late distresse,
In which he askt her, what the Lyon ment:
Who told her all that fell in journey as she went.[5]

33

They had not ridden farre, when they might see
One pricking towards them with hastie heat,
Full strongly armd, and on a courser free,
That through his fiercenesse foméd all with sweat,
And the sharpe yron did for anger eat,
When his hot ryder spurd his chaufféd side;
His looke was sterne, and seeméd still to threat
Cruell revenge, which he in hart did hyde,
And on his shield *Sans loy* in bloudie lines was dyde.

34

When nigh he drew unto this gentle payre
And saw the Red-crosse, which the knight did beare,
He burnt in fire, and gan eftsoones prepare
Himselfe to battell with his couchéd speare.
Loth was that other, and did faint through feare,
To taste th'untryéd dint of deadly steele;
But yet his Lady did so well him cheare,
That hope of new goodhap he gan to feele;
So bent his speare, and spurnd his horse with yron heele.

35

But that proud Paynim forward came so fierce,
And full of wrath, that with his sharp-head speare
Through vainely crosséd shield he quite did pierce,
And had his staggering steede not shrunke for feare,
Through shield and bodie eke he should him beare:
Yet so great was the puissance of his push,
That from his saddle quite he did him beare:
He tombling rudely downe to ground did rush,
And from his goréd wound a well of bloud did gush.

36

Dismounting lightly from his loftie steed,
He to him lept, in mind to reave his life,
And proudly said, Lo there the worthie meed
Of him, that slew *Sansfoy* with bloudie knife;
Henceforth his ghost freed from repining strife,
In peace may passen over *Lethe* lake,[6]
When morning altars purgd with enemies life,
The blacke infernall *Furies* doen aslake:
Life from *Sansfoy* thou tookst, *Sansloy* shall from thee take.

[1] Sea-goddess, wife of Oceanus.

[2] Sirius, the dog star.

[3] The sea-god.

[4] Salutes with cups full of wine.

[5] *I.e.*, who told all that befell her, *etc.* Possibly the line should be emended to read, "Who told all that her fell," *etc.*

[6] Lethe: river of forgetfulness in Hades. The lines mean that Sansfoy's soul had been kept from entering Hades because of his desire that he be revenged, and that now he may enter because the Furies, who demand vengeance for the slain, will be appeased by the death of the (supposed) Red Cross Knight.

37

Therewith in haste his helmet gan unlace,
Till *Una* cride, O hold that heavie hand,
Deare Sir, what ever that thou be in place:
Enough is, that thy foe doth vanquisht stand
Now at thy mercy: Mercie not withstand:
For he is one the truest knight alive,
Though conquered now he lie on lowly land,
And whilest him fortune favourd, faire did thrive
In bloudie field: therefore of life him not deprive.

38

Her piteous words might not abate his rage,
But rudely rending up his helmet, would
Have slaine him straight: but when he sees his age,
And hoarie head of *Archimago* old,
His hastie hand he doth amazéd hold,
And halfe ashaméd, wondred at the sight:
For the old man well knew he, though untold,
In charmes and magicke to have wondrous might,
Ne ever wont in field, ne in round lists[1] to fight.

39

And said, Why *Archimago*, lucklesse syre,
What doe I see? what hard mishap is this,
That hath thee hither brought to taste mine yre?
Or thine the fault, or mine the error is,
In stead of foe to wound my friend amis?
He answered nought, but in a traunce still lay,
And on those guilefull dazéd eyes of his
The cloud of death did sit. Which doen away,
He left him lying so, ne would no lenger stay.

40

But to the virgin comes, who all this while
Amaséd stands, her selfe so mockt to see
By him, who has the guerdon of his guile,
For so misfeigning her true knight to bee:
Yet is she now in more perplexitie,
Left in the hand of that same Paynim bold,
From whom her booteth not at all to flie;
Who by her cleanly garment catching hold,
Her from her Palfrey pluckt, her visage to behold.

41

But her fierce servant full of kingly awe
And high disdaine, when as his soveraine Dame
So rudely handled by her foe he sawe,
With gaping jawes full greedy at him came,
And ramping on his shield, did weene the same
Have reft away with his sharpe rending clawes:
But he was stout, and lust did now inflame
His corage more, that from his griping pawes
He hath his shield redeem'd, and foorth his swerd he drawes.

42

O then too weake and feeble was the forse
Of salvage beast, his puissance to withstand:
For he was strong, and of so mightie corse,
As ever wielded speare in warlike hand,
And feates of armes did wisely understand.
Eftsoones he percéd through his chauféd chest
With thrilling point of deadly yron brand,
And launcht his Lordly hart: with death opprest
He roar'd aloud, whiles life forsooke his stubborne brest.

43

Who now is left to keepe the forlorne maid
From raging spoile of lawlesse victors will?
Her faithfull gard remov'd, her hope dismaid,
Her selfe a yeelded pray to save or spill.
He now Lord of the field, his pride to fill,
With foule reproches, and disdainfull spight
Her vildly entertaines, and will or nill,[2]
Beares her away upon his courser light:
Her prayers nought prevaile, his rage is more of might.

44

And all the way, with great lamenting paine,
And piteous plaints she filleth his dull eares,
That stony hart could riven have in twaine,
And all the way she wets with flowing teares:
But he enrag'd with rancor, nothing heares.
Her servile beast yet would not leave her so,
But followes her farre off, ne ought he feares,
To be partaker of her wandring woe,
More mild in beastly kind,[3] then that her beastly foe.

CANTO IV

To sinfull house of Pride, Duessa
guides the faithfull knight,
Where brothers death to wreak Sansjoy
doth chalenge him to fight.

1

YOUNG KNIGHT, what ever that dost armes professe,
And through long labours huntest after fame,
Beware of fraud, beware of ficklenesse,
In choice, and change of thy deare lovéd Dame,

[1]In tournaments.

[2]Whether she will or not.

[3]In his nature as a beast.

Least thou of her beleeve too lightly blame,
And rash misweening doe thy hart remove:
For unto knight there is no greater shame,
Then lightnesse and inconstancie in love;
That doth this *Redcrosse* knights ensample plainly prove.

2

Who after that he had faire *Una* lorne,
Through light misdeeming of her loialtie,
And false *Duessa* in her sted had borne,
Callèd *Fidess'*, and so supposed to bee;
Long with her traveild, till at last they see
A goodly building,[1] bravely garnishèd,
The house of mightie Prince it seemd to bee:
And towards it a broad high way that led,
All bare through peoples feet, which thither traveilèd.

3

Great troupes of people traveild thitherward
Both day and night, of each degree and place,[2]
But few returnèd, having scapèd hard,
With balefull beggerie, or foule disgrace,
Which ever after in most wretched case,
Like loathsome lazars, by the hedges lay.
Thither *Duessa* bad him bend his pace:
For she is wearie of the toilesome way,
And also nigh consumèd is the lingring day.

4

A stately Pallace built of squarèd bricke,
Which cunningly was without morter laid,
Whose wals were high, but nothing strong, nor thick,
And golden foile all over them displaid,
That purest skye with brightnesse they dismaid:
High lifted up were many loftie towres,
And goodly galleries farre over laid,
Full of faire windowes, and delightfull bowres;
And on the top a Diall told the timely howres.

5

It was a goodly heape for to behould,
And spake the praises of the workmans wit;
But full great pittie, that so faire a mould
Did on so weake foundation ever sit:
For on a sandie hill, that still did flit,
And fall away, it mounted was full hie,
That every breath of heaven shakèd it:
And all the hinder parts, that few could spie,
Were ruinous and old, but painted cunningly.

6

Arrivèd there they passèd in forth right;[3]
For still to all the gates stood open wide,
Yet charge of them was to a Porter hight
Cald *Malvenù*,[4] who entrance none denide:
Thence to the hall, which was on every side
With rich array and costly arras dight:
Infinite sorts of people did abide
There waiting long, to win the wishèd sight
Of her, that was the Lady of that Pallace bright.

7

By them they passe, all gazing on them round,
And to the Presence mount; whose glorious vew
Their frayle amazèd senses did confound:
In living Princes court none ever knew
Such endlesse richesse, and so sumptuous shew;
Ne *Persia* selfe, the nourse of pompous pride
Like ever saw. And there a noble crew
Of Lordes and Ladies stood on every side,
Which with their presence faire, the place much beautifide.

8

High above all a cloth of State was spred,
And a rich throne, as bright as sunny day,
On which there sate most brave embellishèd
With royall robes and gorgeous array,
A mayden Queene, that shone as *Titans* ray,[5]
In glistring gold, and peerelesse pretious stone:
Yet her bright blazing beautie did assay
To dim the brightnesse of her glorious throne,
As envying her selfe, that too exceeding shone.

9

Exceeding shone, like *Phœbus* fairest childe,[6]
That did presume his fathers firie wayne,
And flaming mouthes of steedes unwonted wilde
Through highest heaven with weaker hand to rayne;
Proud of such glory and advancement vaine,
While flashing beames do daze his feeble eyen,
He leaves the welkin way most beaten plaine,
And rapt with whirling wheeles, inflames the skyen,
With fire not made to burne, but fairely for to shyne.

10

So proud she shynèd in her Princely state,
Looking to heaven, for earth she did disdayne;
And sitting high, for lowly she did hate:
Lo underneath her scornefull feete, was layne
A dreadfull Dragon with an hideous trayne,
And in her hand she held a mirrhour bright,
Wherein her face she often vewèd fayne,

[1]The House of Pride. [2]Of every rank and fortune.
[3]Passed straight in.

[4]Ill-come. [5]As the sun's rays.
[6]Phaethon, Apollo's son.

And in her selfe-lov'd semblance tooke delight;
For she was wondrous faire, as any living wight.

11

Of griesly *Pluto* she the daughter was,
And sad *Proserpina* the Queene of hell;
Yet did she thinke her pearelesse worth to pas
That parentage, with pride so did she swell,
And thundring *Jove*, that high in heaven doth dwell,
And wield the world, she claymèd for her syre,
Or if that any else did *Jove* excell:
For to the highest she did still aspyre,
Or if ought higher were then that, did it desyre.

12

And proud *Lucifera* men did her call,
That made her selfe a Queene, and crowned to be,
Yet rightfull kingdome she had none at all,
Ne heritage of native soveraintie,
But did usurpe with wrong and tyrannie
Upon the scepter, which she now did hold:
Ne ruld her Realmes with lawes, but pollicie,[1]
And strong advizement of six wizards old,[2]
That with their counsels bad her kingdome did uphold.

13

Soone as the Elfin knight in presence came,
And false *Duessa* seeming Lady faire,
A gentle Husher, *Vanitie* by name
Made rowme, and passage for them did prepaire:
So goodly brought them to the lowest staire
Of her high throne, where they on humble knee
Making obeysaunce, did the cause declare,
Why they were come, her royall state to see,
To prove the wide report of her great Majestee.

14

With loftie eyes, halfe loth to looke so low,
She thankèd them in her disdainefull wise,
Ne other grace vouchsafèd them to show
Of Princesse worthy, scarse them bad arise.
Her Lordes and Ladies all this while devise
Themselves to setten forth to straungers sight:
Some frounce their curlèd haire in courtly guise,
Some prancke their ruffes, and others trimly dight
Their gay attire: each others greater pride does spight.

[1]Tricks, Machiavellian tactics.

[2]The rest of the Seven Deadly Sins, of which Pride (Lucifera) is the chief.

15

Goodly they all that knight do entertaine,
Right glad with him to have increast their crew:
But to *Duess'* each one himselfe did paine
All kindnesse and faire courtesie to shew;
For in that court whylome her well they knew:
Yet the stout Faerie mongst the middest crowd
Thought all their glorie vaine in knightly vew,
And that great Princesse too exceeding prowd,
That to strange knight no better countenance allowd.

16

Suddein upriseth from her stately place
The royall Dame, and for her coche doth call:
All hurtlen forth,[3] and she with Princely pace,
As faire *Aurora* in her purple pall,
Out of the East the dawning day doth call:
So forth she comes: her brightnesse brode doth blaze;
The heapes of people thronging in the hall,
Do ride each other, upon her to gaze:
Her glorious glitterand light doth all mens eyes amaze.

17

So forth she comes, and to her coche does clyme,
Adornèd all with gold, and girlonds gay,
That seemd as fresh as *Flora* in her prime,
And strove to match, in royall rich array,
Great *Junoes* golden chaire, the which they say
The Gods stand gazing on, when she does ride
To *Joves* high house through heavens braspavèd way
Drawne of fair Pecocks, that excell in pride,
And full of *Argus* eyes[4] their tailes dispredden wide.

18

But this was drawne of six unequall beasts,
On which her six sage Counsellours did ryde,
Taught to obay their bestiall beheasts,
With like conditions to their kinds applyde:[5]
Of which the first, that all the rest did guyde,
Was sluggish *Idlenesse* the nourse of sin;
Upon a slouthfull Asse he chose to ryde,
Arayd in habit blacke, and amis thin,
Like to an holy Monck, the service to begin.

19

And in his hand his Portesse still he bare,
That much was worne, but therein little red,

[3]Rush forth jostling each other.

[4]Argus, who had a hundred eyes, perished in Juno's service. She placed his eyes in the tail of her peacock as a memorial to him.

[5]The animals are of like nature with their riders.

For of devotion he had little care,
Still drownd in sleepe, and most of his dayes ded;
Scarse could he once uphold his heavie hed,
To looken, whether it were night or day:
May seeme the wayne was very evill led,
When such an one had guiding of the way,
That knew not, whether right he went, or else astray.

20

From worldly cares himselfe he did esloyne,
And greatly shunnéd manly exercise,
From every worke he chalengéd essoyne,
For contemplation sake: yet otherwise,
His life he led in lawlesse riotise;
By which he grew to grievous malady;
For in his lustlesse limbs through evill guise
A shaking fever raignd continually:
Such one was *Idlenesse*, first of this company.

21

And by his side rode loathsome *Gluttony*,
Deforméd creature, on a filthie swyne,
His belly was up-blowne with luxury,
And eke with fatnesse swollen were his eyne,
And like a Crane his necke was long and fyne,
With which he swallowd up excessive feast,
For want whereof poore people oft did pyne;
And all the way, most like a brutish beast,
He spuéd up his gorge, that all did him deteast.

22

In greene vine leaves he was right fitly clad;
For other clothes he could not weare for heat,
And on his head an yvie girland had,
From under which fast trickled downe the sweat:
Still as he rode, he somewhat still did eat,
And in his hand did beare a bouzing can,
Of which he supt so oft, that on his seat
His dronken corse he scarse upholden can,
In shape and life more like a monster, then a man.

23

Unfit he was for any worldly thing,
And eke unhable once to stirre or go,
Not meet to be of counsell to a king,
Whose mind in meat and drinke was drownéd so,
That from his friend he seldome knew his fo:
Full of diseases was his carcas blew,
And a dry dropsie[1] through his flesh did flow:
Which by misdiet daily greater grew:
Such one was *Gluttony*, the second of that crew.

[1] Perhaps Spenser means a dropsy causing thirst.

24

And next to him rode lustfull *Lechery*,
Upon a bearded Goat, whose rugged haire,
And whally eyes (the signe of gelosy)
Was like the person selfe, whom he did beare:
Who rough, and blacke, and filthy did appeare,
Unseemely man to please faire Ladies eye;
Yet he of Ladies oft was lovéd deare,
When fairer faces were bid standen by:
O who does know the bent of womens fantasy?

25

In a greene gowne he clothéd was full faire,
Which underneath did hide his filthinesse,
And in his hand a burning hart he bare,
Full of vaine follies, and new fanglenesse:
For he was false, and fraught with ficklenesse,
And learnéd had to love with secret lookes,
And well could daunce, and sing with ruefulnesse,
And fortunes tell, and read in loving bookes,
And thousand other wayes, to bait his fleshly hookes.

26

Inconstant man, that lovéd all he saw,
And lusted after all, that he did love,
Ne would his looser life be tide to law,
But joyd weake wemens hearts to tempt and prove
If from their loyall loves he might them move;
Which lewdnesse fild him with reprochfull paine
Of that fowle evill, which all men reprove,
That rots the marrow, and consumes the braine:
Such one was *Lecherie*, the third of all this traine.

27

And greedy *Avarice* by him did ride,
Upon a Camell loaden all with gold;
Two iron coffers hong on either side,
With precious mettall full, as they might hold,
And in his lap an heape of coine he told;
For of his wicked pelfe his God he made,
And unto hell him selfe for money sold;
Accurséd usurie was all his trade,
And right and wrong ylike in equall ballaunce waide.

28

His life was nigh unto deaths doore yplast,
And thred-bare cote, and cobled shoes he ware,
Ne scarse good morsell all his life did tast,
But both from backe and belly still did spare,
To fill his bags, and richesse to compare;[2]
Yet chylde ne kinsman living had he none
To leave them to; but thorough daily care

[2] To gather riches.

To get, and nightly feare to lose his owne,
He led a wretched life unto him selfe unknowne.

29

Most wretched wight, whom nothing might suffise,
Whose greedy lust did lacke in greatest store,[1]
Whose need had end, but no end covetise,
Whose wealth was want, whose plenty made him pore,
Who had enough, yet wishéd ever more;
A vile disease, and eke in foote and hand
A grievous gout tormented him full sore,
That well he could not touch, nor go, nor stand:
Such was one *Avarice*, the fourth of this faire band.

30

And next to him malicious *Envie* rode,
Upon a ravenous wolfe, and still did chaw
Betweene his cankred teeth a venemous tode,
That all the poison ran about his chaw;
But inwardly he chawéd his owne maw
At neighbours wealth, that made him ever sad;
For death it was, when any good he saw,
And wept, that cause of weeping none he had,
But when he heard of harme, he wexéd wondrous glad.

31

All in a kirtle of discolourd say
He clothéd was, ypainted full of eyes;
And in his bosome secretly there lay
An hatefull Snake, the which his taile uptyes
In many folds, and mortall sting implyes.
Still as he rode, he gnasht his teeth, to see
Those heapes of gold with griple Covetyse,
And grudgéd at the great felicitie
Of proud *Lucifera*, and his owne companie.

32

He hated all good workes and vertuous deeds,
And him no lesse, that any like did use,[2]
And who with gracious bread the hungry feeds,
His almes for want of faith he doth accuse;
So every good to bad he doth abuse:
And eke the verse of famous Poets witt
He does backebite, and spightfull poison spues
From leprous mouth on all, that ever writt:
Such one vile *Envie* was, that fifte in row did sitt.

33

And him beside rides fierce revenging *Wrath*,
Upon a Lion, loth for to be led;
And in his hand a burning brond he hath,
The which he brandisheth about his hed;
His eyes did hurle forth sparkles fiery red,
And staréd sterne on all, that him beheld,
As ashes pale of hew and seeming ded;
And on his dagger still his hand he held,
Trembling through hasty rage, when choler in him sweld.

34

His ruffin raiment all was staind with blood,
Which he had spilt, and all to rags yrent,
Through unadvizéd rashnesse woxen wood;
For of his hands he had no governement,
Ne car'd for[3] bloud in his avengement:
But when the furious fit was overpast,
His cruell facts he often would repent;
Yet wilfull man he never would forecast,[4]
How many mischieves should ensue his heedlesse hast.

35

Full many mischiefes follow cruell *Wrath:*
Abhorréd bloudshed, and tumultuous strife,
Unmanly murder, and unthrifty scath,[5]
Bitter despight, with rancours rusty knife,
And fretting griefe the enemy of life;
All these, and many evils moe haunt ire,
The swelling Splene,[6] and Frenzy raging rife,
The shaking Palsey, and Saint *Fraunces* fire:[7]
Such one was *Wrath*, the last of this ungodly tire.

36

And after all, upon the wagon beame
Rode *Satan*, with a smarting whip in hand,
With which he forward lasht the laesie teme,
So oft as *Slowth* still in the mire did stand.
Huge routs of people did about them band,
Showting for joy, and still before their way
A foggy mist had covered all the land;
And underneath their feet, all scattered lay
Dead sculs and bones of men, whose life had gone astray.

37

So forth they marchen in this goodly sort,
To take the solace of the open aire,
And in fresh flowring fields themselves to sport;
Emongst the rest rode that false Lady faire,
The fowle *Duessa*, next unto the chaire
Of proud *Lucifera*, as one of the traine:
But that good knight would not so nigh repaire,

[1]He was greedy, yet amidst wealth denied his desires.

[2]He hated not only good deeds but also any who performed them.

[3]Shrank from.

[4]He never would pause to reflect.

[5]Destructive damage.

[6]The spleen was thought to be the seat of anger.

[7]Probably erysipelas.

Him selfe estraunging from their joyaunce vaine,
Whose fellowship seemd far unfit for warlike swaine.

38

So having solacéd themselves a space
With pleasaunce of the breathing fields yfed,
They backe returnéd to the Princely Place;
Whereas an errant knight in armes ycled,
And heathnish shield, wherein with letters red
Was writ *Sans joy*, they new arrivéd find:
Enflam'd with fury and fiers hardy-hed,
He seemd in hart to harbour thoughts unkind,
And nourish bloudy vengeaunce in his bitter mind.

39

Who when the shaméd shield of slaine *Sans foy*
He spide with that same Faery champions page,
Bewraying him, that did of late destroy
His eldest brother, burning all with rage
He to him leapt, and that same envious[1] gage
Of victors glory from him snatcht away:
But th'Elfin knight, which ought[2] that warlike wage,
Disdaind to loose the meed he wonne in fray,
And him rencountring fierce, reskewd the noble pray.

40

Therewith they gan to hurtlen greedily,
Redoubted battaile ready to darrayne,
And clash their shields, and shake their swords on hy,
That with their sturre they troubled all the traine;
Till that great Queene upon eternall paine
Of high displeasure, that ensewen might,
Commaunded them their fury to refraine,
And if that either to that shield had right,
In equall lists they should the morrow next it fight.

41

Ah dearest Dame (quoth then the Paynim bold),
Pardon the errour of enragéd wight,
Whom great griefe made forget the raines to hold
Of reasons rule, to see this recreant knight,
No knight, but treachour full of false despight
And shamefull treason, who through guile hath slayn
The prowest knight, that ever field did fight,
Even stout *Sans foy* (O who can then refrayn?)
Whose shield he beares renverst, the more to heape disdayn.

42

And to augment the glorie of his guile,
His dearest love the faire *Fidessa* loe
Is there possesséd of the traytour vile,
Who reapes the harvest sowen by his foe,
Sowen in bloudy field, and bought with woe:
That brothers hand shall dearely well requight
So be, O Queene, you equall favour showe.
Him litle answerd th'angry Elfin knight;
He never meant with words, but swords to plead his right.

43

But threw his gauntlet as a sacred pledge,
His cause in combat the next day to try:
So been they parted both, with harts on edge,[3]
To be aveng'd each on his enimy.
That night they pas in joy and jollity,
Feasting and courting both in bowre and hall;
For Steward was excessive *Gluttonie*,
That of his plenty pouréd forth to all;
Which doen, the Chamberlain *Slowth* did to rest them call.

44

Now whenas darkesome night had all displayd
Her coleblacke curtein over brightest skye,
The warlike youthes on dayntie couches layd,
Did chace away sweet sleepe from sluggish eye,
To muse on meanes of hopéd victory.
But whenas *Morpheus*[4] had with leaden mace
Arrested all that courtly company,
Up-rose *Duessa* from her resting place,
And to the Paynims lodging comes with silent pace.

45

Whom broad awake she finds, in troublous fit,
Forecasting, how his foe he might annoy,
And him amoves with speaches seeming fit:
Ah deare *Sans joy*, next dearest to *Sans foy*,
Cause of my new griefe, cause of my new joy,
Joyous, to see his ymage in mine eye,
And greev'd, to thinke how foe did him destroy,
That was the flowre of grace and chevalrye;
Lo his *Fidessa* to thy secret faith I flye.

46

With gentle wordes he can her fairely greet,
And bad say on the secret of her hart.
Then sighing soft, I learne that litle sweet
Oft tempred is (quoth she) with muchell smart:
For since my brest was launcht with lovely dart
Of deare *Sansfoy*, I never joyéd howre,
But in eternall woes my weaker hart

[1] *I.e.*, envied. [2] Owned.

[3] In furious anger. [4] God of sleep.

Have wasted, loving him with all my powre,
And for his sake have felt full many an heavie
 stowre.

47

At last when perils all I weenéd past,
And hop'd to reape the crop of all my care,[1]
Into new woes unweeting I was cast,
By this false faytor, who unworthy ware
His worthy shield, whom he with guilefull
 snare
Entrappéd slew, and brought to shamefull
 grave.
Me silly maid away with him he bare,
And ever since hath kept in darksome cave,
For that I would not yeeld, that to *Sans-foy*
 I gave.

48

But since faire Sunne hath sperst that lowring
 clowd,
And to my loathéd life now shewes some light,
Under your beames I will me safely shrowd,
From dreaded storme of his disdainfull spight:
To you th'inheritance belongs by right
Of brothers prayse, to you eke longs his love.
Let not his love, let not his restlesse spright
Be unreveng'd, that calles to you above
From wandring *Stygian* shores,[2] where it doth
 endlesse move.

49

Thereto said he, faire Dame be nought dismaid
For sorrowes past; their griefe is with them
 gone:
Ne yet of present perill be affraid;
For needlesse feare did never vantage none,
And helplesse hap it booteth not to mone,[3]
Dead is *Sans-foy*, his vitall paines are past,
Though greevéd ghost for vengeance deepe
 do grone:
He lives, that shall him pay his dewties last,[4]
And guiltie Elfin bloud shall sacrifice in hast.

50

O but I feare the fickle freakes (quoth shee)
Of fortune false, and oddes of armes in field.
Why dame (quoth he) what oddes can ever bee,
Where both do fight alike, to win or yield?
Yea but (quoth she) he beares a charméd
 shield,
And eke enchaunted armes, that none can
 perce,
Ne none can wound the man, that does them
 wield.
Charmd or enchaunted (answerd he then
 ferce)
I no whit reck, ne you the like need to reherce.

51

But faire *Fidessa*, sithens fortunes guile,
Or enimies powre hath now captivéd you,
Returne from whence ye came, and rest a while
Till morrow next, that I the Elfe subdew,
And with *Sans-foyes* dead dowry you endew.
Ay me, that is a double death (she said)
With proud foes sight my sorrow to renew:
Where ever yet I be, my secret aid
Shall follow you, So passing forth she him
 obaid.

CANTO V

The faithfull knight in equall field
subdewes his faithlesse foe.
Whom false Duessa saves, and for
his cure to hell does goe.

1

THE noble hart, that harbours vertuous
 thought,
And is with child of glorious great intent,
Can never rest, untill it forth have brought
Th'eternall brood of glorie excellent:
Such restlesse passion did all night torment
The flaming corage of that Faery knight,
Devizing, how that doughtie turnament
With greatest honour he atchieven might;
Still did he wake, and still did watch for
 dawning light.

2

At last the golden Orientall gate,
Of greatest heaven gan to open faire,
And *Phœbus* fresh, as bridegrome to his mate,
Came dauncing forth, shaking his deawie
 haire:
And hurld his glistring beames through gloomy
 aire.
Which when the wakeful Elfe perceiv'd,
 streight way
He started up, and did him selfe prepaire,
In sun-bright armes, and battailous array:
For with that Pagan proud he combat will that
 day.

3

And forth he comes into the commune hall,
Where earely waite him many a gazing eye,
To weet what end to straunger knights may
 fall.
There many Minstrales maken melody,
To drive away the dull melancholy,
And many Bardes, that to the trembling chord
Can tune their timely voyces cunningly,

[1]The reward for all my trouble.

[2]Shores of the Styx where ghosts wander till they are carried across that river.

[3]It is of no use to lament what cannot be helped.

[4]Pay him his last dues.

And many Chroniclers, that can record
Old loves, and warres for Ladies doen by many
a Lord.

4

Soone after comes the cruell Sarazin,
In woven maile all arméd warily,
And sternly lookes at him, who not a pin
Does care for looke of living creatures eye.
They bring them wines of *Greece* and *Araby*,
And daintie spices fetcht from furthest *Ynd*,
To kindle heat of corage privily:
And in the wine a solemne oth they bynd
T'observe the sacred lawes of armes, that are
assynd.

5

At last forth comes that far renowméd Queene,
With royall pomp and Princely majestie;
She is ybrought unto a paléd greene,[1]
And placéd under stately canapee,
The warlike feates of both those knights to see.
On th'other side in all mens open vew
Duessa placéd is, and on a tree
Sans-foy his shield is hangd with bloudy hew:
Both those the lawrell girlonds[2] to the victor
dew.

6

A shrilling trompet sownded from on hye,
And unto battaill bad them selves addresse:
Their shining shieldes about their wrestes they
tye,
And burning blades about their heads do
blesse,
The instruments of wrath and heavinesse:
With greedy force each other doth assayle,
And strike so fiercely, that they do impresse
Deepe dinted furrowes in the battred mayle;
The yron walles to ward their blowes are
weake and fraile.

7

The Sarazin was stout, and wondrous strong,
And heapéd blowes like yron hammers great:
For after bloud and vengeance he did long.
The knight was fiers, and full of youthly heat:
And doubled strokes, like dreaded thunders
threat:
For all for prayse and honour he did fight.
Both stricken strike, and beaten both do beat,
That from their shields forth flyeth firie light,
And helmets hewen deepe, shew marks of
eithers might.

8

So th'one for wrong, the other strives for right:
As when a Gryfon seizéd of his pray,
A Dragon fiers encountreth in his flight,
Through widest ayre making his ydle way,
That would his rightfull ravine rend away:
With hideous horrour both together smight,
And souce so sore, that they the heavens
affray:
The wise Southsayer seeing so sad sight,
Th'amazéd vulgar tels of warres and mortall
fight.

9

So th'one for wrong, the other strives for right,
And each to deadly shame would drive his foe:
The cruell steele so greedily doth bight
In tender flesh, that streames of bloud down
flow,
With which the armes, that earst so bright did
show
Into a pure vermillion now are dyde:
Great ruth in all the gazers harts did grow,
Seeing the goréd woundes to gape so wyde,
That victory they dare not wish to either side.

10

At last the Paynim chaunst to cast his eye,
His suddein eye, flaming with wrathfull fyre,
Upon his brothers shield, which hong thereby:
Therewith redoubled was his raging yre,
And said, Ah wretched sonne of wofull syre,
Doest thou sit wayling by black *Stygian* lake,
Whilest here thy shield is hangd for victors
hyre,
And sluggish german doest thy forces slake,
To after-send his foe, that him may overtake?

11

Goe caytive Elfe, him quickly overtake,
And soone redeeme from his long wandring
woe;
Goe guiltie ghost, to him my message make,
That I his shield have quit from dying foe.
Therewith upon his crest he stroke him so,
That twise he reeléd, readie twise to fall;
End of the doubtfull battell deeméd tho
The lookers on, and lowd to him gan call
The false *Duessa*, Thine the shield, and I, and
all.

12

Soone as the Faerie heard his Ladie speake,
Out of his swowning dreame he gan awake,
And quickning faith, that earst was woxen
weake,
The creeping deadly cold away did shake:
Tho mov'd with wrath, and shame, and Ladies
sake,
Of all attonce he cast avengd to bee,
And with so'exceeding furie at him strake,
That forcéd him to stoupe upon his knee;
Had he not stoupéd so, he should have cloven
bee.

[1] A grassed plot enclosed by palings.

[2] *I.e.*, both Duessa and the shield are to be the victor's rewards.

13

And to him said, Goe now proud Miscreant,
Thy selfe thy message doe to german deare,
Alone he wandring thee too long doth want:
Goe say, his foe thy shield with his doth beare.
Therewith his heavie hand he high gan reare,
Him to have slaine; when loe a darkesome clowd
Upon him fell: he no where doth appeare,
But vanisht is. The Elfe him cals alowd,
But answer none receives: the darknes him does shrowd.

14

In haste *Duessa* from her place arose,
And to him running said, O prowest knight,
That ever Ladie to her love did chose,
Let now abate the terror of your might,
And quench the flame of furious despight,
And bloudie vengeance; lo th'infernall powres
Covering your foe with cloud of deadly night,
Have borne him hence to *Plutoes* balefull bowres.
The conquest yours, I yours, the shield, and glory yours.

15

Not all so satisfide, with greedie eye
He sought all round about his thirstie blade
To bath in bloud of faithlesse enemy;
Who all that while lay hid in secret shade:
He standes amazéd, how he thence should fade.
At last the trumpets, Triumph sound on hie,
And running Heralds humble homage made,
Greeting him goodly with new victorie,
And to him brought the shield, the cause of enmitie.

16

Wherewith he goeth to that soveraine Queene,
And falling her before on lowly knee,
To her makes present of his service seene:
Which she accepts, with thankes, and goodly gree,
Greatly advauncing[1] his gay chevalree.
So marcheth home, and by her takes the knight,
Whom all the people follow with great glee,
Shouting, and clapping all their hands on hight,
That all the aire it fils, and flyes to heaven bright.

17

Home is he brought, and laid in sumptuous bed:
Where many skilfull leaches him abide,
To salve his hurts, that yet still freshly bled.
In wine and oyle they wash his woundés wide,
And softly can embalme[2] on every side.
And all the while, most heavenly melody
About the bed sweet musicke did divide,[3]
Him to beguile of griefe and agony:
And all the while *Duessa* wept full bitterly.

18

As when a wearie traveller that strayes
By muddy shore of broad seven-mouthéd *Nile*,
Unweeting of the perillous wandring wayes,
Doth meet a cruell craftie Crocodile,
Which in false griefe hyding his harmefull guile,
Doth weepe full sore, and sheddeth tender teares:
The foolish man, that pitties all this while
His mournefull plight, is swallowd up unwares,
Forgetfull of his owne, that mindes anothers cares.

19

So wept *Duessa* untill eventide,
That shyning lampes in *Joves* high house were light:
Then forth she rose, ne lenger would abide,
But comes unto the place, where th'Hethen knight
In slombring swownd nigh voyd of vitall spright,
Lay cover'd with inchaunted cloud all day:
Whom when she found, as she him left in plight,[4]
To wayle his woefull case she would not stay,
But to the easterne coast of heaven makes speedy way.

20

Where griesly *Night*, with visage deadly sad,
That *Phœbus* chearefull face durst never vew,
And in a foule blacke pitchie mantle clad,
She findes forth comming from her darkesome mew,
Where she all day did hide her hated hew.
Before the dore her yron charet stood,
Alreadie harnesséd for journey new;
And coleblacke steedes yborne of hellish brood,
That on their rustie bits did champ, as they were wood.

21

Who when she saw *Duessa* sunny bright,
Adornd with gold and jewels shining cleare,
She greatly grew amazéd at the sight,
And th'unacquainted light[5] began to feare:

[1]Courteously praising.

[2]And gently they anointed him.

[3]Did play elaborately.

[4]She found him in the same condition as when she had left him.

[5]The unaccustomed light.

For never did such brightnesse there appeare,
And would have backe retyréd to her cave,
Untill the witches speech she gan to heare,
Saying, Yet O thou dreaded Dame, I crave
Abide, till I have told the message, which I have.

22

She stayd, and foorth *Duessa* gan proceede,
O thou most auncient Grandmother of all,[1]
More old then *Jove*, whom thou at first didst breede,
Or that great house of Gods cælestiall,
Which wast begot in *Dæmogorgons* hall,
And sawst the secrets of the world unmade,[2]
Why suffredst thou thy Nephewes deare to fall
With Elfin sword, most shamefully betrade?
Lo where the stout *Sansjoy* doth sleepe in deadly shade.

23

And him before,[3] I saw with bitter eyes
The bold *Sansfoy* shrinke underneath his speare;
And now the pray of fowles in field he lyes,
Nor wayld of friends, nor laid on groning beare,
That whylome was to me too dearely deare.
O what of Gods then boots it to be borne,
If old *Aveugles*[4] sonnes so evill heare?[5]
Or who shall not great *Nightês* children scorne,
When two of three her Nephews are so fowle forlorne?

24

Up then, up dreary Dame, of darknesse Queene,
Go gather up the reliques of thy race,
Or else goe them avenge, and let be seene,
That dreaded *Night* in brightest day hath place,
And can the children of faire light deface.
Her feeling speeches some compassion moved
In hart, and chaunge in that great mothers face:
Yet pittie in her hart was never proved
Till then: for evermore she hated, never loved.

25

And said, Deare daughter rightly may I rew
The fall of famous children borne of mee,
And good successes, which their foes ensew:[6]
But who can turne the streame of destinee,

[1]Night and Earth were daughters of Chaos and older than the Olympian gods.

[2]The secrets of Chaos, existing when the world was yet unmade.

[3]And before this happened to him.

[4]Spiritual Blindness.

[5]Are brought to such disgrace.

[6]Which befall their foes.

Or breake the chayne of strong necessitee,
Which fast is tyde to *Joves* eternall seat?
The sonnes of Day he favoureth, I see,
And by my ruines thinkes to make them great:
To make one great by others losse, is bad excheat.

26

Yet shall they not escape so freely all;
For some shall pay the price of others guilt:
And he the man that made *Sansfoy* to fall,
Shall with his owne bloud price that he hath spilt.
But what art thou, that telst of Nephews kilt?
I that do seeme not I, *Duessa* am,
(Quoth she) how ever now in garments gilt,
And gorgeous gold arayd I to thee came;
Duessa I, the daughter of Deceipt and Shame.

27

Then bowing downe her agéd backe, she kist
The wicked witch, saying; In that faire face
The false resemblance of Deceipt, I wist
Did closely lurke; yet so true-seeming grace
It carried, that I scarse in darkesome place
Could it discerne, though I the mother bee
Of falshood, and root of *Duessaes* race.
O welcome child, whom I have longd to see,
And now have seene unwares. Lo now I go with thee.

28

Then to her yron wagon she betakes,
And with her beares the fowle welfavourd witch:
Through mirkesome aire her readie way she makes.
Her twyfold Teme, of which two blacke as pitch,
And two were browne, yet each to each unlich,
Did softly swim away, ne ever stampe,
Unlesse she chaunst their stubborne mouths to twitch;
Then foming tarre, their bridles they would champe,
And trampling the fine element,[7] would fiercely rampe.

29

So well they sped, that they be come at length
Unto the place, whereas the Paynim lay,
Devoid of outward sense,[8] and native strength,
Coverd with charméd cloud from vew of day,
And sight of men, since his late luckelesse fray.
His cruell wounds with cruddy bloud congealéd,
They binden up so wisely, as they may,

[7]The air. [8]Unconscious.

And handle softly, till they can be healéd:
So lay him in her charet, close in night concealéd.

30

And all the while she stood upon the ground,
The wakefull dogs did never cease to bay,
As giving warning of th'unwonted sound,
With which her yron wheeles did them affray,
And her darke griesly looke them much dismay;
The messenger of death, the ghastly Owle
With drearie shriekes did also her bewray;
And hungry Wolves continually did howle,
At her abhorréd face, so filthy and so fowle.

31

Thence turning backe in silence soft they stole,
And brought the heavie corse with easie pace
To yawning gulfe of deepe *Avernus* hole.
By that same hole an entrance darke and bace
With smoake and sulphure hiding all the place,
Descends to hell: there creature never past,
That backe returnéd without heavenly grace;
But dreadfull *Furies*, which their chaines have brast,
And damnéd sprights sent forth to make ill men aghast.

32

By that same way the direfull dames doe drive
Their mournefull charet, fild with rusty blood,
And downe to *Plutoes* house are come bilive:
Which passing through, on every side them stood
The trembling ghosts with sad amazéd mood,
Chattring their yron teeth, and staring wide
With stonie eyes; and all the hellish brood
Of feends infernall flockt on every side,
To gaze on earthly wight, that with the Night durst ride.

33

They pas the bitter waves of *Acheron*,[1]
Where many soules sit wailing woefully,
And come to fiery flood of *Phlegeton*,[1]
Whereas the damnéd ghosts in torments fry,
And with sharpe shrilling shriekes doe bootlesse cry,
Cursing high *Jove*, the which them thither sent.
The house of endlesse paine is built thereby,
In which ten thousand sorts of punishment
The curséd creatures doe eternally torment.

34

Before the threshold dreadfull *Cerberus*[2]
His three deforméd heads did lay along,
Curléd with thousand adders venemous,
And lilléd forth his bloudie flaming tong:
At them he gan to reare his bristles strong,
And felly gnarre, untill dayes enemy
Did him appease; then downe his taile he hong
And suffered them to passen quietly:
For she in hell and heaven had power equally.

35

There was *Ixion* turnéd on a wheele,
For daring tempt the Queene of heaven[3] to sin;
And *Sisyphus* an huge round stone did reele
Against an hill, ne might from labour lin;
There thirstie *Tantalus* hong by the chin;[4]
And *Tityus* fed a vulture on his maw;
Typhœus joynts were stretchéd on a gin,
Theseus condemned to endlesse slouth by law,
And fifty sisters[5] water in leake vessels draw.

36

They all beholding worldly wights in place,[6]
Leave off their worke, unmindfull of their smart,
To gaze on them; who forth by them doe pace,
Till they be come unto the furthest part:
Where was a Cave ywrought by wondrous art,
Deepe, darke, uneasie, dolefull, comfortlesse,
In which sad *Æsculapius* farre apart
Emprisond was in chaines remedilesse,
For that *Hippolytus* rent corse he did redresse.[7]

37

Hippolytus a jolly huntsman was,
That wont in charet chace the foming Bore;
He all his Peeres in beautie did surpas,
But Ladies love as losse of time forbore:
His wanton stepdame[8] lovéd him the more,
But when she saw her offred sweets refused
Her love she turnd to hate, and him before
His father fierce of treason false accused,
And with her gealous termes his open eares abused.

38

Who all in rage his Sea-god syre besought,
Some curséd vengeance on his sonne to cast:
From surging gulf two monsters straight were brought,
With dread whereof his chasing steedes aghast,
Both charet swift and huntsman overcast.
His goodly corps on ragged cliffs yrent,
Was quite dismembred, and his members chast

[1]River of Hades. [2]The dog who guarded Hades.

[3]Hera.

[4]Tantalus was punished with the sight of food and water which he could never reach.

[5]The Danaides, who slew their husbands.

[6]Beholding living creatures there.

[7]Did heal. [8]Phaedra.

Scattered on every mountaine, as he went,
That of *Hippolytus* was left no moniment.

39

His cruell stepdame seeing what was donne,
Her wicked dayes with wretched knife did end,
In death avowing th'innocence of her sonne.
Which hearing, his rash Syre began to rend
His haire, and hastie tongue, that did offend:
Tho gathering up the relicks of his smart[1]
By *Dianes* meanes, who was *Hippolyts* frend,
Them brought to *Æsculape*, that by his art
Did heale them all againe, and joynéd every part.

40

Such wondrous science in mans wit to raine
When *Jove* avizd, that could the dead revive,
And fates expiréd could renew againe,
Of endlesse life he might him not deprive,
But unto hell did thrust him downe alive,
With flashing thunderbolt ywounded sore:
Where long remaining, he did alwaies strive
Himselfe with salves to health for to restore,
And slake the heavenly fire, that ragéd evermore.

41

There auncient Night arriving, did alight
From her nigh wearie waine, and in her armes
To *Æsculapius* brought the wounded knight:
Whom having softly disarayd of armes,
Tho gan to him discover all his harmes,
Beseeching him with prayer, and with praise,
If either salves, or oyles, or herbes, or charmes
A fordonne wight from dore of death mote raise,
He would at her request prolong her nephews daies.

42

Ah Dame (quoth he) thou temptest me in vaine,
To dare the thing, which daily yet I rew,
And the old cause of my continued paine
With like attempt to like end to renew.
Is not enough, that thrust from heaven dew
Here endlesse penance for one fault I pay,
But that redoubled crime with vengeance new
Thou biddest me to eeke? Can Night defray
The wrath of thundring *Jove*, that rules both night and day?

43

Not so (quoth she) but sith that heavens king
From hope of heaven hath thee excluded quight,
Why fearest thou, that canst not hope for thing,
And fearest not, that more thee hurten might,
Now in the powre of everlasting Night?
Goe to then, O thou farre renowméd sonne
Of great *Apollo*, shew thy famous might
In medicine, that else hath to thee wonne
Great paines, and greater praise, both never to be donne.[2]

44

Her words prevaild: And then the learnéd leach
His cunning hand gan to his wounds to lay,
And all things else, the which his art did teach:
Which having seene, from thence arose away
The mother of dread darknesse, and let stay
Aveugles sonne there in the leaches cure,
And backe returning tooke her wonted way,
To runne her timely race, whilst *Phœbus* pure
In westerne waves his wearie wagon did recure.

45

The false *Duessa* leaving noyous Night,
Returnd to stately pallace of dame Pride;
Where when she came, she found the Faery knight
Departed thence, albe his woundés wide
Not throughly heald, unreadie were to ride.[3]
Good cause he had to hasten thence away;
For on a day his wary Dwarfe had spide,
Where in a dongeon deepe huge numbers lay
Of caytive wretched thrals, that wayléd night and day.

46

A ruefull sight, as could be seene with eie;
Of whom he learnéd had in secret wise
The hidden cause of their captivitie,
How mortgaging their lives to *Covetise*,
Through wastfull Pride, and wanton Riotise,
They were by law of that proud Tyrannesse
Provokt with *Wrath*, and *Envies* false surmise,
Condemnéd to that Dongeon mercilesse,
Where they should live in woe, and die in wretchednesse.

47

There was that great proud king of *Babylon*,[4]
That would compell all nations to adore,
And him as onely God to call upon,
Till through celestiall doome throwne out of dore,
Into an Oxe he was transform'd of yore:

[1]The fragments of Hippolytus's body.

[2]Never to be ended. [3]For riding.

[4]Nebuchadnezzar.

There also was king *Crœsus*, that enhaunst
His heart too high through his great riches store;
And proud *Antiochus*, the which advaunst
His curséd hand gainst God, and on his altars daunst.

48

And them long time before, great *Nimrod* was,
That first the world with sword and fire warrayd;
And after him old *Ninus*[1] farre did pas
In princely pompe, of all the world obayd;
There also was that mightie Monarch[2] layd
Low under all, yet above all in pride,
That name of native syre did fowle upbrayd,
And would as *Ammons* sonne be magnifide,
Till scornd of God and man a shamefull death he dide.[3]

49

All these together in one heape were throwne,
Like carkases of beasts in butchers stall.
And in another corner wide were strowne
The antique ruines of the *Romaines* fall:
Great *Romulus*[4] the Grandsyre of them all,
Proud *Tarquin*, and too lordly *Lentulus*,
Stout *Scipio*, and stubborne *Hanniball*,
Ambitious *Sylla*, and sterne *Marius*,
High *Cæsar*, great *Pompey*, and fierce *Antonius*.[5]

50

Amongst these mighty men were wemen mixt,
Proud wemen, vaine, forgetfull of their yoke:[6]
The bold *Semiramis*,[7] whose sides transfixt
With sonnes owne blade, her fowle reproches spoke;
Faire *Sthenobœa*,[8] that her selfe did choke
With wilfull cord, for wanting of her will;
High minded *Cleopatra*, that with stroke
Of Aspés sting her selfe did stoutly kill:
And thousands moe the like, that did that dongeon fill.

51

Besides the endlesse routs of wretched thralles,
Which thither were assembled day by day,
From all the world after their wofull falles,
Through wicked pride, and wasted wealthes decay.
But most of all, which in that Dongeon lay
Fell from high Princes courts, or Ladies bowres,
Where they in idle pompe, or wanton play,
Consuméd had their goods, and thriftlesse howres,
And lastly throwne themselves into these heavy stowres.

52

Whose case when as the carefull Dwarfe had tould,
And made ensample of their mournefull sight
Unto his maister, he no lenger would
There dwell in perill of like painefull plight,
But early rose, and ere that dawning light
Discovered had the world to heaven wyde,
He by a privie Posterne tooke his flight,
That of no envious eyes he mote be spyde:
For doubtlesse death ensewd, if any him descryde.

53

Scarce could he footing find in that fowle way,
For many corses, like a great Lay-stall
Of murdred men which therein strowéd lay,
Without remorse, or decent funerall:
Which all through that great Princesse pride did fall
And came to shamefull end. And them beside
Forth ryding underneath the castell wall,
A donghill of dead carkases he spide,
The dreadfull spectacle of that sad house of *Pride*.

CANTO VI

From lawlesse lust by wondrous grace
fayre Una is releast:
Whom salvage nation does adore,
and learnes her wise beheast.

1

As WHEN a ship, that flyes faire under saile,
An hidden rocke escapéd hath unwares,
That lay in waite her wrack for to bewaile,[9]
The Marriner yet halfe amazéd stares
At perill past, and yet in doubt ne dares
To joy at his foole-happie oversight:[10]
So doubly is distrest twixt joy and cares
The dreadlesse courage of this Elfin knight,
Having escapt so sad ensamples in his sight.

[1]According to legend the founder of Nineveh.

[2]Alexander the Great, who dishonored the name of his father Philip, in allowing himself to be called the son of Jupiter Ammon.

[3]It was believed that Alexander died of drunkenness.

[4]Legendary founder of Rome.

[5]Mark Antony.

[6]Forgetful of the subordination proper to their sex.

[7]According to legend the wife of Ninus.

[8]Slew herself because of love for Bellerophon.

[9]To cause her wreck to be bewailed.

[10]At his blindly lucky escape.

2

Yet sad he was that his too hastie speed
The faire *Duess'* had forst him leave behind;
And yet more sad, that *Una* his deare dreed
Her truth had staind with treason so unkind;
Yet crime in her could never creature find,
But for his love, and for her owne selfe sake,
She wandred had from one to other *Ynd*,[1]
Him for to seeke, ne ever would forsake,
Till her unwares the fierce *Sansloy* did overtake.

3

Who after *Archimagoes* fowle defeat,
Led her away into a forrest wilde,
And turning wrathfull fire to lustfull heat,
With beastly sin thought her to have defilde,
And made the vassall of his pleasures vilde.
Yet first he cast by treatie, and by traynes,
Her to perswade, that stubborne fort to yilde:
For greater conquest of hard love he gaynes,
That workes it to his will, then he that it constraines.

4

With fawning wordes he courted her a while,
And looking lovely, and oft sighing sore,
Her constant hart did tempt with diverse guile:
But wordes and lookes, and sighes she did abhore,
As rocke of Diamond stedfast evermore.
Yet for to feed his fyrie lustfull eye,
He snatcht the vele, that hong her face before;
Then gan her beautie shine, as brightest skye,
And burnt his beastly hart t'efforce her chastitye.

5

So when he saw his flatt'ring arts to fayle,
And subtile engines bat from batteree,
With greedy force he gan the fort assayle,
Whereof he weend possessèd soone to bee,
And win rich spoile of ransackt chastetee.
Ah heavens, that do this hideous act behold,
And heavenly virgin thus outragèd see,
How can ye vengeance just so long withhold,
And hurle not flashing flames upon that Paynim bold?

6

The pitteous maiden carefull comfortlesse,
Does throw out thrilling shriekes, and shrieking cryes,
The last vaine helpe of womens great distresse,
And with loud plaints importuneth the skyes,
That molten starres do drop like weeping eyes;
And *Phœbus* flying so most shamefull sight,
His blushing face in foggy cloud implyes,
And hides for shame. What wit of mortall wight
Can now devise to quit a thrall from such a plight?

7

Eternall providence exceeding thought,
Where none appeares can make her selfe a way:
A wondrous way it for this Lady wrought,
From Lyons clawes to pluck the gripèd pray.
Her shrill outcryes and shriekes so loud did bray,
That all the woodes and forestes did resownd;
A troupe of *Faunes* and *Satyres*[2] far away
Within the wood were dauncing in a rownd,
Whiles old *Sylvanus*[3] slept in shady arber sownd.

8

Who when they heard that pitteous strainèd voice,
In hast forsooke their rurall meriment,
And ran towards the far rebownded noyce,
To weet, what wight so loudly did lament.
Unto the place they come incontinent:
Whom when the raging Sarazin espide,
A rude, mishapen, monstrous rablement,
Whose like he never saw, he durst not bide,
But got his ready steed, and fast away gan ride.

9

The wyld woodgods arrivèd in the place,
There find the virgin dolefull desolate,
With ruffled rayments, and faire blubbred face,
As her outrageous foe had left her late,
And trembling yet through feare of former hate;
All stand amazèd at so uncouth sight,
And gin to pittie her unhappie state;
All stand astonied at her beautie bright,
In their rude eyes unworthie of so wofull plight.

10

She more amaz'd, in double dread doth dwell;
And every tender part for feare does shake:
As when a greedie Wolfe through hunger fell
A seely Lambe farre from the flocke does take,

[1]From the East to the West Indies, figurative expression for a great distance.

[2]The Latin and Greek wood-gods. Here, however, they represent unenlightened mankind, "common people."

[3]Roman woodland deity, here simply the chief figure among the fauns and satyrs.

Of whom he meanes his bloudie feast to make,
A Lyon spyes fast running towards him,
The innocent pray in hast he does forsake,
Which quit from death yet quakes in every lim
With chaunge of feare, to see the Lyon looke so grim.

11

Such fearefull fit assaid her trembling hart,
Ne word to speake, ne joynt to move she had:
The salvage nation feele her secret smart,
And read her sorrow in her count'nance sad;
Their frowning forheads with rough hornes yclad,
And rusticke horror[1] all aside doe lay,
And gently grenning, shew a semblance glad
To comfort her, and feare to put away,
Their backward bent knees teach her humbly to obay.[2]

12

The doubtfull Damzell dare not yet commit
Her single person to their barbarous truth,
But still twixt feare and hope amazd does sit,
Late learnd what harme to hastie trust ensu'th,
They in compassion of her tender youth,
And wonder of her beautie soveraine,
Are wonne with pitty and unwonted ruth,
And all prostrate upon the lowly plaine,
Do kisse her feete, and fawne on her with count'nance faine.

13

Their harts she ghesseth by their humble guise,
And yieldes her to extremitie of time;[3]
So from the ground she fearelesse doth arise,
And walketh forth without suspect of crime:[4]
They all as glad, as birdes of joyous Prime,
Thence lead her forth, about her dauncing round,
Shouting, and singing all a shepheards ryme
And with greene braunches strowing all the ground,
Do worship her, as Queene, with olive girlond cround.

14

And all the way their merry pipes they sound,
That all the woods with doubled Eccho ring,
And with their hornéd feet[5] do weare the ground,
Leaping like wanton kids in pleasant Spring.
So towards old *Sylvanus* they her bring;
Who with the noyse awakéd, commeth out,
To weet the cause, his weake steps governing,
And agéd limbs on Cypresse stadle stout,
And with an yvie twyne his wast is girt about.

15

Far off he wonders, what them makes so glad,
Or *Bacchus* merry fruit they did invent,
Or *Cybeles* franticke rites have made them mad;
They drawing nigh, unto their God present
That flowre of faith and beautie excellent.
The God himselfe vewing that mirrhour rare,[6]
Stood long amazd, and burnt in his intent;[7]
His owne faire *Dryope* now he thinkes not faire,
And *Pholoe* fowle, when her to this he doth compaire.

16

The woodborne people fall before her flat,
And worship her as Goddesse of the wood:
And old *Sylvanus* selfe bethinkes not, what
To thinke of wight so faire, but gazing stood,
In doubt to deeme her borne of earthly brood;
Sometimes Dame *Venus* selfe he seemes to see,
But *Venus* never had so sober mood;
Sometimes *Diana* he her takes to bee,
But misseth bow, and shaftes, and buskins to her knee.

17

By vew of her he ginneth to revive
His ancient love, and dearest *Cyparisse*,
And calles to mind his pourtraiture alive,
How faire he was, and yet not faire to this,[8]
And how he slew with glauncing dart amisse
A gentle Hynd, the which the lovely boy
Did love as life, above all worldly blisse;
For griefe whereof the lad n'ould after joy,[9]
But pynd away in anguish and selfe-wild annoy.[10]

18

The wooddy Nymphes, faire *Hamadryades*[11]
Her to behold do thither runne apace,
And all the troupe of light-foot *Naiades*,[12]
Flocke all about to see her lovely face:

[1]Country roughness.
[2]They teach their knees (backward-bent like those of a goat) to obey her humbly—*i.e.*, they kneel or bow low to her.
[3]Accommodates herself to the extremity she is in.
[4]Without fear of the satyrs.
[5]Horny feet.
[6]Una is a mirror in the sense that in her appearance she reflects the heavenly beauty.
[7]In his gaze.
[8]In comparison with Una.
[9]Would not thereafter be joyous.
[10]Self-willed distress.
[11]Spirits of the trees.
[12]Water-nymphs.

But when they vewéd have her heavenly grace,
They envie her in their malitious mind,
And fly away for feare of fowle disgrace:
But all the *Satyres* scorne their woody kind,
And henceforth nothing faire, but her on earth they find.

19

Glad of such lucke, the luckelesse lucky maid,[1]
Did her content to please their feeble eyes,[2]
And long time with that salvage people staid,
To gather breath in many miseries.
During which time her gentle wit she plyes,
To teach them truth, which worshipt her in vaine,
And made her th'Image of Idolatryes;
But when their bootlesse zeale she did restraine
From her own worship, they her Asse would worship fayn.

20

It fortunéd a noble warlike knight,[3]
By just occasion to that forrest came,
To seeke his kindred, and the lignage right,
From whence he tooke his well deservéd name:
He had in armes abroad wonne muchell fame,
And fild far landes with glorie of his might,
Plaine, faithfull, true, and enimy of shame,
And ever lov'd to fight for Ladies right,
But in vaine glorious frayes he litle did delight.

21

A Satyres sonne yborne in forrest wyld,
By straunge adventure as it did betyde,
And there begotten of a Lady myld,
Faire *Thyamis* the daughter of *Labryde*,
That was in sacred bands of wedlocke tyde
To *Therion*, a loose unruly swayne;
Who had more joy to raunge the forrest wyde,
And chase the salvage beast with busie payne,
Then serve his Ladies love, and wast in pleasures vayne.

22

The forlorne mayd did with loves longing burne,
And could not lacke her lovers company,
But to the wood she goes, to serve her turne,
And seeke her spouse, that from her still does fly,
And followes other game and venery:
A Satyre chaunst her wandring for to find,
And kindling coles of lust in brutish eye,
The loyall links of wedlocke did unbind,
And made her person thrall unto his beastly kind.

23

So long in secret cabin there he held
Her captive to his sensuall desire,
Till that with timely fruit her belly sweld,
And bore a boy unto that salvage sire:
Then home he suffred her for to retire,
For ransome leaving him the late borne childe;
Whom till to ryper yeares he gan aspire,
He noursled up in life and manners wilde,
Emongst wild beasts and woods, from lawes of men exilde.

24

For all he taught the tender ymp, was but
To banish cowardize and bastard feare;
His trembling hand he would him force to put
Upon the Lyon and the rugged Beare,
And from the she Beares teats her whelps to teare;
And eke wyld roring Buls he would him make
To tame, and ryde their backes not made to beare;
And the Robuckes in flight to overtake,
That every beast for feare of him did fly and quake.

25

Thereby so fearelesse, and so fell he grew,
That his owne sire and maister of his guise
Did often tremble at his horrid vew,
And oft for dread of hurt would him advise,
The angry beasts not rashly to despise,
Not too much to provoke; for he would learne
The Lyon stoup to him in lowly wise,
(A lesson hard) and make the Libbard sterne
Leave roaring, when in rage he for revenge did earne.

26

And for to make his powre approvéd more,
Wyld beasts in yron yokes he would compell;
The spotted Panther, and the tuskéd Bore,
The Pardale swift, and the Tigre cruell;
The Antelope, and Wolfe both fierce and fell;
And them constraine in equall teme to draw.
Such joy he had, their stubborne harts to quell,
And sturdie courage tame with dreadfull aw,
That his beheast they fearéd, as a tyrans law.

[1]Both unlucky, in her wanderings, and lucky, in her new-found friends.

[2]Feeble to discern spiritual things. As immediately appears, they cannot distinguish between truth and its symbols.

[3]Sir Satyrane, who typifies natural morality, not enlightened by revealed truth.

27

His loving mother came upon a day
Unto the woods, to see her little sonne;
And chaunst unwares to meet him in the way,
After his sportes, and cruell pastime donne,
When after him a Lyonesse did runne,
That roaring all with rage, did lowd requere
Her children deare, whom he away had
wonne:
The Lyon whelpes she saw how he did beare,
And lull in rugged armes, withouten childish
feare.

28

The fearefull Dame all quakéd at the sight,
And turning backe, gan fast to fly away,
Untill with love revokt from vaine affright
She hardly yet perswaded was to stay,
And then to him these womanish words gan
say;
Ah *Satyrane*, my dearling, and my joy,
For love of me leave off this dreadfull play,
To dally thus with death, is no fit toy,
Go find some other play-fellowes, mine own
sweet boy.

29

In these and like delights of bloudy game
He traynéd was, till ryper yeares he raught,
And there abode, whilst any beast of name
Walkt in that forest, whom he had not taught
To feare his force: and then his courage haught
Desird of forreine foemen to be knowne,
And far abroad for straunge adventures
sought:
In which his might was never overthrowne,
But through all Faery lond his famous worth
was blown.

30

Yet evermore it was his manner faire,
After long labours and adventures spent,
Unto those native woods for to repaire,
To see his sire and ofspring auncient.[1]
And now he thither came for like intent;
Where he unwares the fairest *Una* found,
Straunge Lady, in so straunge habiliment,
Teaching the Satyres, which her sat around,
Trew sacred lore,[2] which from her sweet lips
did redound.

31

He wondred at her wisedome heavenly rare,
Whose like in womens wit he never knew;
And when her curteous deeds he did compare,[3]
Gan her admire, and her sad sorrowes rew,
Blaming of Fortune, which such troubles
threw,
And joyd to make proofe of her crueltie
On gentle Dame, so hurtlesse, and so trew:
Thenceforth he kept her goodly company,
And learnd her discipline of faith and veritie.

32

But she all vowd unto the *Redcrosse* knight,
His wandring perill closely did lament,
Ne in this new acquaintaunce could delight,
But her deare heart with anguish did torment,
And all her wit in secret counsels spent,
How to escape. At last in privie wise
To *Satyrane* she shewéd her intent;
Who glad to gain such favour, gan devise,
How with that pensive Maid he best might
thence arise.[4]

33

So on a day when Satyres all were gone,
To do their service to *Sylvanus* old,
The gentle virgin left behind alone
He led away with courage stout and bold.
Too late it was, to Satyres to be told,[5]
Or ever hope recover her againe:
In vaine he seekes that having cannot hold.
So fast he carried her with carefull paine,
That they the woods are past, and come now
to the plaine.

34

The better part now of the lingring day,
They traveild had, when as they farre espide
A wearie wight forwandring by the way,
And towards him they gan in hast to ride,
To weet of newes, that did abroad betide,
Or tydings of her knight of the *Redcrosse*.
But he them spying, gan to turne aside,
For feare as seemd, or for some feignéd losse;
More greedy they of newes, fast towards him
do crosse.

35

A silly man, in simple weedes forworne,
And soild with dust of the long driéd way;
His sandales were with toilesome travell torne,
And face all tand with scorching sunny ray,
As he had traveild many a sommers day,
Through boyling sands of *Arabie* and *Ynde;*
And in his hand a *Jacobs* staffe,[6] to stay
His wearie limbes upon: and eke behind,
His scrip did hang, in which his needments he
did bind.

[1] And his ancient lineage—the satyrs.

[2] The Gospel as interpreted by the protestant reformers.

[3] Compare with her present surroundings?

[4] Depart thence.

[5] It was too late now for the satyrs to hear of it.

[6] A pilgrim's staff.

36

The knight approching nigh, of him inquerd
Tydings of warre, and of adventures new;
But warres, nor new adventures none he herd.
Then *Una* gan to aske, if ought he knew,
Or heard abroad of that her champion trew,
That in his armour bare a croslet red.
Aye me, Deare dame (quoth he) well may I rew
To tell the sad sight, which mine eies have red:
These eyes did see that knight both living and eke ded.

37

That cruell word her tender hart so thrild,
That suddein cold did runne through every vaine,
And stony horrour all her sences fild
With dying fit, that downe she fell for paine.
The knight her lightly rearéd up againe,
And comforted with curteous kind reliefe:
Then wonne from death, she bad him tellen plaine
The further processe of her hidden griefe;[1]
The lesser pangs can beare, who hath endur'd the chiefe.

38

Then gan the Pilgrim thus, I chaunst this day,
This fatall day, that shall I ever rew,
To see two knights in travell on my way
(A sory sight) arraung'd in battell new,
Both breathing vengeaunce, both of wrathfull hew;
My fearefull flesh did tremble at their strife,
To see their blades so greedily imbrew,
That drunke with bloud, yet thristed after life:
What more? the *Redcrosse* knight was slaine with Paynim knife.

39

Ah dearest Lord (quoth she) how might that bee,
And he the stoutest knight, that ever wonne?
Ah dearest dame (quoth he) how might I see
The thing, that might not be, and yet was donne?
Where is (said *Satyrane*) that Paynims sonne,
That him of life, and us of joy hath reft?
Not far away (quoth he) he hence doth wonne
Foreby a fountaine, where I late him left
Washing his bloudy wounds, that through the steele were cleft.

40

Therewith the knight thence marchéd forth in hast,
Whiles *Una* with huge heavinesse opprest,
Could not for sorrow follow him so fast;
And soone he came, as he the place had ghest,
Whereas that *Pagan* proud him selfe did rest,
In secret shadow by a fountaine side:
Even he it was, that earst would have supprest
Faire *Una:* whom when *Satyrane* espide,
With fowle reprochfull words he boldly him defide.

41

And said, Arise thou curséd Miscreaunt,
That hast with knightlesse guile and trecherous train
Faire knighthood fowly shamed, and doest vaunt
That good knight of the *Redcrosse* to have slain:
Arise, and with like treason now maintain
Thy guilty wrong, or else thee guilty yield.
The Sarazin this hearing, rose amain,
And catching up in hast his three square shield,[2]
And shining helmet, soone him buckled to the field.

42

And drawing nigh him said, Ah misborne Elfe,
In evill houre thy foes thee hither sent,
Anothers wrongs to wreake upon thy selfe:
Yet ill thou blamest me, for having blent
My name with guile and traiterous intent;
That *Redcrosse* knight, perdie, I never slew,
But had he beene, where earst his armes were lent,
Th'enchaunter vaine his errour should not rew:
But thou his errour shalt, I hope now proven trew.

43

Therewith they gan, both furious and fell,
To thunder blowes, and fiersly to assaile
Each other bent his enimy to quell,
That with their force they perst both plate and maile,
And made wide furrowes in their fleshes fraile,
That it would pitty any living eie.
Large floods of bloud adowne their sides did raile;
But floods of bloud could not them satisfie:
Both hungred after death: both chose to win, or die.

44

So long they fight, and fell revenge pursue,
That fainting each, themselves to breathen let,
And oft refreshéd, battell oft renue:
As when two Bores with rancling malice met,

[1]The details as yet unknown to her.

[2]Shield with three equal sides.

Their gory sides fresh bleeding fiercely fret,
Till breathlesse both them selves aside retire,
Where foming wrath, their cruell tuskes they whet,
And trample th'earth, the whiles they may respire;
Then backe to fight againe, new breathéd and entire.

45

So fiersly, when these knights had breathéd once,
They gan to fight returne, increasing more
Their puissant force, and cruell rage attonce,
With heapéd strokes more hugely, then before,
That with their drerie wounds and bloudy gore
They both deforméd, scarsely could be known.
By this sad *Una* fraught with anguish sore,
Led with their noise, which through the aire was thrown,
Arriv'd, where they in erth their fruitles bloud had sown.

46

Whom all so soone as that proud Sarazin
Espide, he gan revive the memory
Of his lewd lusts, and late attempted sin,
And left the doubtfull battell hastily,
To catch her, newly offred to his eie:
But *Satyrane* with strokes him turning, staid,
And sternely bad him other businesse plie,
Then hunt the steps of pure unspotted Maid:
Wherewith he all enrag'd, these bitter speaches said.

47

O foolish faeries sonne, what furie mad
Hath thee incenst, to hast thy dolefull fate?
Were it not better, I that Lady had,
Then that thou hadst repented it too late?
Most sencelesse man he, that himselfe doth hate,
To love another. Lo then for thine ayd
Here take thy lovers token on thy pate.
So they two fight; the whiles the royall Mayd
Fled farre away, of that proud Paynim sore afrayd.

48

But that false *Pilgrim*, which that leasing told,
Being in deed old *Archimage*, did stay
In secret shadow, all this to behold,
And much rejoycéd in their bloudy fray:
But when he saw the Damsell passe away
He left his stond, and her pursewd apace,
In hope to bring her to her last decay.
But for to tell her lamentable cace,
And eke this battels end, will need another place.[1]

[1]But Spenser never told the outcome of this battle.

CANTO VII

The Redcrosse knight is captive made
by Gyaunt proud opprest,
Prince Arthur meets with Una greatly
with those newes distrest.

1

WHAT man so wise, what earthly wit so ware,
As to descry the crafty cunning traine,
By which deceipt doth maske in visour faire,
And cast her colours dyéd deepe in graine,
To seeme like Truth, whose shape she well can faine,
And fitting gestures to her purpose frame;
The guiltlesse man with guile to entertaine?
Great maistresse of her art was that false Dame,
The false *Duessa*, clokéd with *Fidessaes* name.

2

Who when returning from the drery *Night*,
She fownd not in that perilous house of *Pryde*,
Where she had left, the noble *Redcrosse* knight,
Her hopéd pray, she would no lenger bide,
But forth she went, to seeke him far and wide.
Ere long she fownd, whereas he wearie sate,
To rest him selfe, foreby a fountaine side,
Disarméd all of yron-coted Plate,
And by his side his steed the grassy forage ate.

3

He feedes upon the cooling shade, and bayes
His sweatie forehead in the breathing wind,
Which through the trembling leaves full gently playes
Wherein the cherefull birds of sundry kind
Do chaunt sweet musick, to delight his mind:
The Witch approching gan him fairely greet,
And with reproch of carelesnesse unkind
Upbrayd, for leaving her in place unmeet,
With fowle words tempring faire, soure gall with hony sweet.

4

Unkindnesse past, they gan of solace treat,
And bathe in pleasaunce of the joyous shade,
Which shielded them against the boyling heat,
And with greene boughes decking a gloomy glade,
About the fountaine like a girlond made;
Whose bubbling wave did ever freshly well,
Ne ever would through fervent sommer fade:
The sacred Nymph, which therein wont to dwell,
Was out of *Dianes* favour, as it then befell.

5

The cause was this: one day when *Phœbe*[1] fayre
With all her band was following the chace,
This Nymph, quite tyr'd with heat of scorching ayre,
Sat downe to rest in middest of the race:
The goddesse wroth gan fowly her disgrace,
And bad the waters, which from her did flow,
Be such as she her selfe was then in place.
Thence forth her waters waxéd dull and slow,
And all that drunke thereof, did faint and feeble grow.

6

Hereof this gentle knight unweeting was,
And lying downe upon the sandie graile,
Drunke of the streame, as cleare as cristall glas;
Eftsoones his manly forces gan to faile,
And mightie strong was turnd to feeble fraile.
His chaungéd powres at first them selves not felt,
Till crudled cold his corage gan assaile,
And chearefull bloud in faintnesse chill did melt,
Which like a fever fit through all his body swelt.

7

Yet goodly court he made still to his Dame,
Pourd out in loosnesse on the grassy grownd,
Both carelesse of his health, and of his fame:
Till at the last he heard a dreadful sownd,
Which through the wood loud bellowing, did rebownd,
That all the earth for terrour seemd to shake,
And trees did tremble. Th'Elfe therewith astownd,
Upstarted lightly from his looser make,
And his unready weapons gan in hand to take.

8

But ere he could his armour on him dight,
Or get his shield, his monstrous enimy
With sturdie steps came stalking in his sight,
An hideous Geant[2] horrible and hye,
That with his talnesse seemd to threat the skye,
The ground eke gronéd under him for dreed;
His living like saw never living eye,
Ne durst behold: his stature did exceed
The hight of three the tallest sonnes of mortall seed.

9

The greatest Earth his uncouth mother was,
And blustring *Æolus* his boasted sire,
Who with his breath, which through the world doth pas,
Her hollow womb did secretly inspire,
And fild her hidden caves with stormie yre,
That she conceiv'd; and trebling the dew time,
In which the wombes of women do expire,
Brought forth this monstrous masse of earthly slime,
Puft up with emptie wind, and fild with sinfull crime.

10

So growen great through arrogant delight
Of th'high descent, whereof he was yborne,
And through presumption of his matchlesse might,
All other powres and knighthood he did scorne.
Such now he marcheth to this man forlorne,
And left to losse: his stalking steps are stayde
Upon a snaggy Oke, which he had torne
Out of his mothers bowelles, and it made
His mortall mace, wherewith his foemen he dismayde.

11

That when the knight he spide, he gan advance
With huge force and insupportable mayne,
And towardes him with dreadfull fury praunce;
Who haplesse, and eke hopelesse, all in vaine
Did to him pace, sad battaile to darrayne,
Disarmd, disgrast, and inwardly dismayde,
And eke so faint in every joynt and vaine,
Through that fraile fountaine, which him feeble made,
That scarsely could he weeld his bootlesse single blade.

12

The Geaunt strooke so maynly mercilesse,
That could have overthrowne a stony towre.
And were not heavenly grace, that him did blesse,
He had beene pouldred all, as thin as flowre:
But he was wary of that deadly stowre,
And lightly lept from underneath the blow:
Yet so exceeding was the villeins powre,
That with the wind it did him overthrow,
And all his sences stound, that still he lay full low.

13

As when that divelish yron Engin wrought
In deepest Hell, and framd by *Furies* skill,
With windy Nitre and quick Sulphur fraught
And ramd with bullet round, ordaind to kill,

---

[1] Artemis.

[2] Orgoglio, typifying pride; not the pride of life typified by Lucifera, but the pride of a corrupt church immersed in temporal affairs—the Roman Catholic Church as Spenser saw it

Conceiveth fire, the heavens it doth fill
With thundring noyse, and all the ayre doth choke,
That none can breath, nor see, nor heare at will,
Through smouldry cloud of duskish stincking smoke,
That th'onely breath him daunts, who hath escapt the stroke.

14

So daunted when the Geaunt saw the knight
His heavie hand he heavéd up on hye,
And him to dust thought to have battred quight,
Untill *Duessa* loud to him gan crye;
O great *Orgoglio*, greatest under skye,
O hold thy mortall hand for Ladies sake,
Hold for my sake, and do him not to dye,
But vanquisht thine eternall bondslave make,
And me thy worthy meed unto thy Leman take.

15

He hearkned, and did stay from further harmes,
To gayne so goodly guerdon, as she spake:
So willingly she came into his armes,
Who her as willingly to grace did take,
And was possesséd of his new found make,
Then up he tooke the slombred sencelesse corse,
And ere he could out of his swowne awake,
Him to his castle brought with hastie forse,
And in a Dongeon deepe him threw without remorse.

16

From that day forth *Duessa* was his deare,
And highly honourd in his haughtie eye,
He gave her gold and purple pall to weare,
And triple crowne set on her head full hye,
And her endowd with royall majestye:
Then for to make her dreaded more of men,
And peoples harts with awfull terrour tye,
A monstrous beast[1] ybred in filthy fen
He chose, which he had kept long time in darksome den.

17

Such one it was, as that renowméd Snake[2]
Which great *Alcides* in *Stremona* slew,
Long fostred in the filth of *Lerna* lake,
Whose many heads out budding ever new,
Did breed him endlesse labour to subdew:
But this same Monster much more ugly was;
For seven great heads out of his body grew,
And yron brest, and backe of scaly bras,
And all embrewd in bloud, his eyes did shine as glas.

18

His tayle was stretchéd out in wondrous length,
That to the house of heavenly gods it raught,
And with extorted powre, and borrow'd strength,
The ever-burning lamps from thence it brought,
And prowdly threw to ground, as things of nought;
And underneath his filthy feet did tread
The sacred things, and holy heasts foretaught.
Upon this dreadful Beast with sevenfold head
He set the false *Duessa*, for more aw and dread.

19

The wofull Dwarfe, which saw his maisters fall,
Whiles he had keeping of his grasing steed,
And valiant knight become a caytive thrall,
When all was past, tooke up his forlorne weed,
His mightie armour, missing most at need;
His silver shield, now idle maisterlesse;
His poynant speare, that many made to bleed,
The ruefull moniments of heavinesse,
And with them all departes, to tell his great distresse.

20

He had not travaild long, when on the way
He wofull Ladie, wofúll *Una* met,
Fast flying from the Paynims greedy pray,
Whilest *Satyrane* him from pursuit did let:
Who when her eyes she on the Dwarfe had set,
And saw the signes, that deadly tydings spake,
She fell to ground for sorrowfull regret,
And lively breath her sad brest did forsake,
Yet might her pitteous hart be seene to pant and quake.

21

The messenger of so unhappie newes,
Would faine have dyde: dead was his hart within,
Yet outwardly some little comfort shewes:
At last recovering hart, he does begin
To rub her temples, and to chaufe her chin,
And every tender part does tosse and turne:
So hardly he the flitted life does win,
Unto her native prison to retourne:
Then gins her grievéd ghost thus to lament and mourne.

[1] *Cf.* Revelation, xvii, 3.
[2] The Lernean Hydra, slain by Hercules.

22

Ye dreary instruments of dolefull sight,
That doe this deadly spectacle behold,
Why do ye lenger feed on loathéd light,
Or liking find to gaze on earthly mould,
Sith cruell fates the carefull threeds unfould,
The which my life and love together tyde?
Now let the stony dart of senselesse cold
Perce to my hart, and pas through every side,
And let eternall night so sad sight fro me hide.

23

O lightsome day, the lampe of highest *Jove*,
First made by him, mens wandring wayes to
guyde,
When darkenesse he in deepest dongeon drove,
Henceforth thy hated face for ever hyde,
And shut up heavens windowes shyning wyde:
For earthly sight can nought but sorrow breed,
And late repentance, which shall long abyde.
Mine eyes no more on vanitie shall feed,
But seeléd up with death, shall have their
deadly meed.

24

Then downe againe she fell unto the ground;
But he her quickly rearéd up againe:
Thrise did she sinke adowne in deadly
swownd,
And thrise he her reviv'd with busie paine:
At last when life recover'd had the raine,
And over-wrestled his strong enemie,
With foltring tong, and trembling every vaine,
Tell on (quoth she) the wofull Tragedie,
The which these reliques sad present unto
mine eie.

25

Tempestuous fortune hath spent all her spight,
And thrilling sorrow throwne his utmost dart;
Thy sad tongue cannot tell more heavy
plight,
Then that I feele, and harbour in mine hart:
Who hath endur'd the whole, can beare each
part.
If death it be, it is not the first wound,
That launchéd hath my brest with bleeding
smart.
Begin, and end the bitter balefull stound;
If lesse, then that I feare, more favour I have
found.

26

Then gan the Dwarfe the whole discourse
declare,
The subtill traines of *Archimago* old;
The wanton loves of false *Fidessa* faire,
Bought with the bloud of vanquisht Paynim
bold:
The wretched payre transform'd to treen
mould;
The house of Pride, and perils round about;
The combat, which he with *Sansjoy* did hould;
The lucklesse conflict with the Gyant stout,
Wherein captiv'd, of life or death he stood in
doubt.[1]

27

She heard with patience all unto the end,
And strove to maister sorrowfull assay,[2]
Which greater grew, the more she did contend,
And almost rent her tender hart in tway;
And love fresh coles unto her fire did lay:
For greater love, the greater is the losse.
Was never Ladie lovéd dearer day,
Then she did love the knight of the *Redcrosse*,[3]
For whose deare sake so many troubles her
did tosse.

28

At last when fervent sorrow slakéd was,
She up arose, resolving him to find
Alive or dead: and forward forth doth pas,
All as the Dwarfe the way to her assynd:
And evermore in constant carefull mind
She fed her wound with fresh renewéd bale;
Long tost with stormes, and bet with bitter
wind.
High over hils, and low adowne the dale,
She wandred many a wood, and measurd
many a vale.

29

At last she chauncéd by good hap to meet
A goodly knight,[4] faire marching by the way
Together with his Squire, arayéd meet:
His glitterand armour shinéd farre away,
Like glauncing light of *Phœbus* brightest ray;
From top to toe no place appearéd bare,
That deadly dint of steele endanger may:
Athwart his brest a bauldrick brave he ware,
That shynd, like twinkling stars, with stons
most pretious rare.

30

And in the midst thereof one pretious stone
Of wondrous worth, and eke of wondrous
mights,
Shapt like a Ladies head, exceeding shone,
Like *Hesperus* emongst the lesser lights,

[1]Since the knight had been carried off a captive, the dwarf did not know whether he was still alive or dead.

[2]The attack of sorrow.

[3]Lady never loved daylight more than she loved the Red Cross Knight.

[4]Prince Arthur, typifying that virtue which comprehends all the rest, magnanimity, and, in this book of the *Faerie Queene*, Heavenly Grace.

And strove for to amaze the weaker sights;
Thereby his mortall blade full comely hong
In yvory sheath, ycarv'd with curious slights;
Whose hilts were burnisht gold, and handle strong
Of mother pearle, and buckled with a golden tong.

31

His haughtie helmet, horrid all with gold,
Both glorious brightnesse, and great terrour bred;
For all the crest a Dragon did enfold
With greedie pawes, and over all did spred
His golden wings: his dreadfull hideous hed
Close couchéd on the bever, seem'd to throw
From flaming mouth bright sparkles fierie red,
That suddeine horror to faint harts did show;
And scaly tayle was stretcht adowne his backe full low.

32

Upon the top of all his loftie crest,
A bunch of haires discolourd diversly,
With sprincled pearle, and gold full richly drest,
Did shake, and seem'd to daunce for jollity,
Like to an Almond tree ymounted hye
On top of greene Selinis all alone,
With blossomes brave bedeckéd daintily;
Whose tender locks do tremble every one
At every little breath, that under heaven is blowne.

33

His warlike shield all closely cover'd was,
Ne might of mortall eye be ever seene;
Not made of steele, nor of enduring bras,
Such earthly mettals soone consuméd bene:
But all of Diamond perfect pure and cleene
It framéd was, one massie entire mould,
Hewen out of Adamant rocke with engines keene,
That point of speare it never percen could,
Ne dint of direfull sword divide the substance would.

34

The same to wight he never wont disclose,
But when as monsters huge he would dismay,
Or daunt unequall armies of his foes,
Or when the flying heavens he would affray;
For so exceeding shone his glistring ray,
That *Phœbus* golden face it did attaint,[1]
As when a cloud his beames doth over-lay;
And silver *Cynthia* wexéd pale and faint,
As when her face is staynd with magicke arts constraint.[2]

35

No magicke arts hereof had any might,
Nor bloudie wordes of bold Enchaunters call,
But all that was not such, as seemd in sight,
Before that shield did fade, and suddeine fall:
And when him list the raskall routes appall,
Men into stones therewith he could transmew,
And stones to dust, and dust to nought at all;
And when him list the prouder lookes subdew,
He would them gazing blind, or turne to other hew.

36

Ne let it seeme, that credence this exceedes,
For he that made the same, was knowne right well
To have done much more admirable deedes.
It *Merlin* was, which whylome did excell
All living wightes in might of magicke spell:
Both shield, and sword, and armour all he wrought
For this young Prince, when first to armes he fell;
But when he dyde, the Faerie Queene it brought
To Faerie lond, where yet it may be seene, if sought.

37

A gentle youth, his dearely lovéd Squire
His speare of heben wood behind him bare,
Whose harmefull head, thrice heated in the fire,
Had riven many a brest with pikehead square;
A goodly person, and could menage faire,
His stubborne steed with curbéd canon bit,
Who under him did trample as the aire,
And chauft, that any on his backe should sit;
The yron rowels into frothy fome he bit.

38

When as this knight nigh to the Ladie drew,
With lovely court he gan her entertaine;
But when he heard her answeres loth, he knew
Some secret sorrow did her heart distraine:
Which to allay, and calme her storming paine,
Faire feeling words he wisely gan display,
And for her humour fitting purpose faine,
To tempt the cause it selfe for to bewray;
Wherewith emmov'd, these bleeding words she gan to say.

39

What worlds delight, or joy of living speach
Can heart, so plung'd in sea of sorrowes deepe,
And heapéd with so huge misfortunes, reach?
The carefull cold[3] beginneth for to creepe,

[1]It was more brilliant than the sun. The light of truth outshines all others.

[2]It was believed that witches caused eclipses of the moon.

[3]The chill of grief.

And in my heart his yron arrow steepe,
Soone as I thinke upon my bitter bale:
Such helplesse harmes yts better hidden keepe,[1]
Then rip up griefe, where it may not availe,
My last left comfort is, my woes to weepe and waile.

40

Ah Ladie deare, quoth then the gentle knight,
Well may I weene, your griefe is wondrous great;
For wondrous great griefe groneth in my spright,
Whiles thus I heare you of your sorrowes treat.
But wofull Ladie let me you intrete,
For to unfold the anguish of your hart:
Mishaps are maistred by advice discrete,
And counsell mittigates the greatest smart;
Found never helpe, who never would his hurts impart.

41

O but (quoth she) great griefe will not be tould,
And can more easily be thought, then said.
Right so; (quoth he) but he, that never would,
Could never: will to might gives greatest aid.
But griefe (quoth she) does greater grow displaid,
If then it find not helpe, and breedes despaire.
Despaire breedes not (quoth he) where faith is staid.
No faith so fast (quoth she) but flesh does paire.
Flesh may empaire (quoth he) but reason can repaire.

42

His goodly reason, and well guided speach
So deepe did settle in her gratious thought,
That her perswaded to disclose the breach,
Which love and fortune in her heart had wrought,
And said; Faire Sir, I hope good hap hath brought
You to inquire the secrets of my griefe,
Or that your wisedome will direct my thought,
Or that your prowesse can me yield reliefe:
Then heare the storie sad, which I shall tell you briefe.

43

The forlorne Maiden, whom your eyes have seene
The laughing stocke of fortunes mockeries,
Am th'only daughter of a King and Queene,
Whose parents deare, whilest equall destinies
Did runne about,[2] and their felicities
The favourable heavens did not envy,
Did spread their rule through all the territories,
Which *Phison* and *Euphrates* floweth by,
And *Gehons*[3] golden waves doe wash continually.

44

Till that their cruell curséd enemy,
An huge great Dragon horrible in sight,
Bred in the loathly lakes of *Tartary*,[4]
With murdrous ravine, and devouring might
Their kingdome spoild, and countrey wasted quight:
Themselves, for feare into his jawes to fall,
He forst to castle strong to take their flight,
Where fast embard in mightie brasen wall,
He has them now foure yeres besiegd to make them thrall.

45

Full many knights adventurous and stout
Have enterprizd that Monster to subdew;
From every coast that heaven walks about,[5]
Have thither come the noble Martiall crew,
That famous hard atchievements still pursew,
Yet never any could that girlond win,
But all still shronke, and still he greater grew:
All they for want of faith, or guilt of sin,
The pitteous pray of his fierce crueltie have bin.

46

At last yledd with farre reported praise,
Which flying fame throughout the world had spred,
Of doughtie knights, whom Faery land did raise,
That noble order high of Maidenhed,
Forthwith to court of *Gloriane* I sped,
Of *Gloriane* great Queene of glory bright,
Whose kingdomes seat *Cleopolis*[6] is red,
There to obtaine some such redoubted knight,
That Parents deare from tyrants powre deliver might.

47

It was my chance (my chance was faire and good)
There for to find a fresh unprovéd knight,
Whose manly hands imbrew'd in guiltie blood
Had never bene, ne ever by his might

[1]Misfortunes which cannot be helped it is better to keep hidden.

[2]While the destinies moved equably.

[3]The three rivers of the Garden of Eden. Una's parents represent mankind, and were dispossessed of their territory by the dragon of sin.

[4]Tartarus, or hell.

[5]Spenser speaks in terms of the Ptolemaic astronomy, according to which the heavens revolve about the earth.

[6]The city of glory.

Had throwne to ground the unregarded right:
Yet of his prowesse proofe he since hath made
(I witnesse am) in many a cruell fight;
The groning ghosts of many one dismaide
Have felt the bitter dint of his avenging blade.

48

And ye the forlorne reliques of his powre,
His byting sword, and his devouring speare,
Which have enduréd many a dreadful stowre,
Can speake his prowesse, that did earst you beare,
And well could rule: now he hath left you heare,
To be the record of his ruefull losse,
And of my dolefull disaventurous deare:[1]
O heavie record of the good *Redcrosse*,
Where have you left your Lord, that could so well you tosse?

49

Well hopéd I, and faire beginnings had,
That he my captive langour should redeeme,
Till all unweeting, an Enchaunter bad
His sence abusd, and made him to misdeeme
My loyalty, not such as it did seeme;
That rather death desire, then such despight.
Be judge ye heavens, that all things right esteeme,
How I him lov'd, and love with all my might,
So thought I eke of him, and thinke I thought aright.

50

Thenceforth me desolate he quite forsooke,
To wander, where wilde fortune would me lead,
And other bywaies he himselfe betooke,
Where never foot of living wight did tread,
That brought not backe the balefull body dead;
In which him chauncéd false *Duessa* meete,
Mine onely foe, mine onely deadly dread,
Who with her witchcraft and misseeming sweete,
Inveigled him to follow her desires unmeete.

51

At last by subtill sleights she him betraid
Unto his foe, a Gyant huge and tall,
Who him disarméd, dissolute, dismaid,
Unwares surprised, and with mightie mall
The monster mercilesse him made to fall,
Whose fall did never foe before behold;
And now in darkesome dungeon, wretched thrall,
Remedilesse, for aie he doth him hold;
This is my cause of griefe, more great, then may be told.

52

Ere she had ended all, she gan to faint:
But he her comforted and faire bespake,
Certes, Madame, ye have great cause of plaint,
That stoutest heart, I weene, could cause to quake.
But be of cheare, and comfort to you take:
For till I have acquit your captive knight,
Assure your selfe, I will you not forsake.
His chearefull words reviv'd her chearelesse spright,
So forth they went, the Dwarfe them guiding ever right.

[1]My grievous unfortunate injury.

CANTO VIII

Faire virgin to redeeme her deare
brings Arthur to the fight:
Who slayes that Gyant, wounds and beast,
and strips Duessa quight.

1

AY ME, how many perils doe enfold
The righteous man, to make him daily fall?
Were not, that heavenly grace doth him uphold,
And stedfast truth acquite him out of all.
Her love is firme, her care continuall,
So oft as he through his owne foolish pride,
Or weaknesse is to sinfull bands made thrall:
Else should this *Redcrosse* knight in bands have dyde,
For whose deliverance she this Prince doth thither guide.

2

They sadly traveild thus, untill they came
Nigh to a castle builded strong and hie:
Then cryde the Dwarfe, lo yonder is the same,
In which my Lord my liege doth lucklesse lie,
Thrall to that Gyants hatefull tyrannie:
Therefore, deare Sir, your mightie powres assay.
The noble knight alighted by and by
From loftie steede, and bad the Ladie stay,
To see what end of fight should him befall that day.

3

So with the Squire, th'admirer of his might,
He marchéd forth towards that castle wall;
Whose gates he found fast shut, ne living wight
To ward the same, nor answere commers call.

Then tooke that Squire an horne of bugle small,
Which hong adowne his side in twisted gold,
And tassels gay. Wyde wonders over all
Of that same hornes great vertues weren told,
Which had approvéd bene in uses manifold.

4

Was never wight, that heard that shrilling sound,
But trembling feare did feele in every vaine;
Three miles it might be easie heard around,
And Ecchoes three answerd it selfe againe:
No false enchauntment, nor deceiptfull traine
Might once abide the terror of that blast,
But presently was voide and wholly vaine:
No gate so strong, no locke so firme and fast,
But with that percing noise flew open quite, or brast.

5

The same before the Geants gate he blew,
That all the castle quakéd from the ground,
And every dore of freewill open flew.
The Gyant selfe dismaiéd with that sownd,
Where he with his *Duessa* dalliance fownd,
In hast came rushing forth from inner bowre,
With staring countenance sterne, as one astownd,
And staggering steps, to weet, what suddein stowre,
Had wrought that horror strange, and dar'd his dreaded powre.

6

And after him the proud *Duessa* came,
High mounted on her manyheaded beast,
And every head with fyrie tongue did flame,
And every head was crownéd on his creast,
And bloudie mouthéd with late cruell feast.
That when the knight beheld, his mightie shild
Upon his manly arme he soone addrest,
And at him fiercely flew, with courage fild,
And eger greedinesse through every member thrild.

7

Therewith the Gyant buckled him to fight,
Inflam'd with scornefull wrath and high disdaine,
And lifting up his dreadfull club on hight,
All arm'd with ragged snubbes and knottie graine,
Him thought at first encounter to have slaine.
But wise and warie was that noble Pere,
And lightly leaping from so monstrous maine,
Did faire avoide the violence him nere;
It booted nought, to thinke, such thunderbolts to beare.

8

Ne shame he thought to shunne so hideous might:
The idle stroke, enforcing furious way,
Missing the marke of his misaymêd sight
Did fall to ground, and with his heavie sway
So deepely dinted in the driven clay,
That three yardes deepe a furrow up did throw:
The sad earth wounded with so sore assay,
Did grone full grievous underneath the blow,
And trembling with strange feare, did like an earthquake show.

9

As when almightie *Jove* in wrathfull mood,
To wreake the guilt of mortall sins is bent,
Hurles forth his thundring dart with deadly food,
Enrold in flames, and smouldring dreriment,
Through riven cloudes and molten firmament;
The fierce threeforkéd engin making way,
Both loftie towres and highest trees hath rent,
And all that might his angrie passage stay,
And shooting in the earth, casts up a mount of clay.

10

His boystrous club, so buried in the ground,
He could not rearen up againe so light,[1]
But that the knight him at avantage found,
And whiles he strove his combred clubbe to quight
Out of the earth, with blade all burning bright
He smote off his left arme, which like a blocke
Did fall to ground, depriv'd of native might;
Large streames of bloud out of the trunckéd stocke
Forth gushéd, like fresh water streame from riven rocke.

11

Dismaiéd with so desperate deadly wound,
And eke impatient of unwonted paine,
He loudly brayd with beastly yelling sound,
That all the fields rebellowéd againe;
As great a noyse, as when in Cymbrian plaine[2]
An heard of Bulles, whom kindly rage doth sting,
Do for the milkie mothers want complaine,
And fill the fields with troublous bellowing,
The neighbour woods around with hollow murmur ring.

---

[1]So quickly.

[2]Possibly the modern Crimea.

12

That when his deare *Duessa* heard, and saw
The evill stownd, that daungerd her estate,
Unto his aide she hastily did draw
Her dreadfull beast, who swolne with bloud of late
Came ramping forth with proud presumpteous gate,
And threatned all his heads like flaming brands.
But him the Squire made quickly to retrate,
Encountring fierce with single sword in hand,
And twixt him and his Lord did like a bulwarke stand.

13

The proud *Duessa* full of wrathfull spight,
And fierce disdaine, to be affronted so,
Enforst her purple beast with all her might
That stop out of the way to overthroe,
Scorning the let of so unequall foe:
But nathemore would that courageous swayne
To her yeeld passage, gainst his Lord to goe,
But with outrageous strokes did him restraine,
And with his bodie bard the way atwixt them twaine.

14

Then tooke the angrie witch her golden cup,[1]
Which still she bore, replete with magick artes;
Death and despeyre did many thereof sup,
And secret poyson through their inner parts,
Th'eternall bale of heavie wounded harts;
Which after charmes and some enchauntments said,
She lightly sprinkled on his weaker parts;
Therewith his sturdie courage soone was quayd,
And all his senses were with suddeine dread dismayd.

15

So downe he fell before the cruell beast,
Who on his necke his bloudie clawes did seize,
That life nigh crusht out of his panting brest:
No powre he had to stirre, nor will to rize.
That when the carefull knight gan well avise,
He lightly left the foe, with whom he fought,
And to the beast gan turne his enterprise:
For wondrous anguish in his hart it wrought,
To see his lovéd Squire into such thraldome brought.

16

And high advauncing his bloud-thirstie blade,
Stroke one of those deforméd heads so sore,
That of his puissance proud ensample made;
His monstrous scalpe downe to his teeth it tore,
And that misforméd shape mis-shapéd more:
A sea of bloud gusht from the gaping wound,
That her gay garments staynd with filthy gore,
And overflowéd all the field around;
That over shoes in bloud he waded on the ground.

17

Thereat he roaréd for exceeding paine,
That to have heard, great horror would have bred,
And scourging th'emptie ayre with his long traine,
Through great impatience of his grievéd hed
His gorgeous ryder from her loftie sted
Would have cast downe, and trod in durtie myre,
Had not the Gyant soone her succouréd;
Who all enrag'd with smart and franticke yre,
Came hurtling in full fierce, and forst the knight retyre.

18

The force, which wont in two to be disperst,
In one alone left hand he now unites,
Which is through rage more strong then both were erst;
With which his hideous club aloft he dites,
And at his foe with furious rigour smites,
That strongest Oake might seeme to overthrow:
The stroke upon his shield so heavie lites,
That to the ground it doubleth him full low
What mortall wight could ever beare so monstrous blow?

19

And in his fall his shield, that covered was,
Did loose his vele by chaunce, and open flew:
The light whereof, that heavens light did pas,
Such blazing brightnesse through the aier threw,
That eye mote not the same endure to vew.
Which when the Gyaunt spyde with staring eye,
He downe let fall his arme, and soft withdrew
His weapon huge, that heavéd was on hye
For to have slaine the man, that on the ground did lye.

20

And eke the fruitfull-headed beast, amaz'd
At flashing beames of that sunshiny shield,
Became starke blind, and all his senses daz'd,
That downe he tumbled on the durtie field,

[1] *Cf.* Revelation, xvii, 4.

And seem'd himselfe as conqueréd to yield.
Whom when his maistresse proud perceiv'd to fall,
Whiles yet his feeble feet for faintnesse reeld,
Unto the Gyant loudly she gan call,
O helpe *Orgoglio*, helpe, or else we perish all.

21

At her so pitteous cry was much amoov'd
Her champion stout, and for to ayde his frend,
Againe his wonted angry weapon proov'd:
But all in vaine: for he has read his end
In that bright shield, and all their forces[1] spend
Themselves in vaine: for since that glauncing sight,
He hath no powre to hurt, nor to defend;
As where th'Almighties lightning brond does light,
It dimmes the dazéd eyen, and daunts the senses quight.

22

Whom when the Prince, to battell new addrest,
And threatning high his dreadfull stroke did see,
His sparkling blade about his head he blest,
And smote off quite his right leg by the knee,
That downe he tombled; as an agéd tree,
High growing on the top of rocky clift,
Whose hartstrings with keene steele nigh hewen be,
The mightie trunck halfe rent, with ragged rift
Doth roll adowne the rocks, and fall with fearefull drift.

23

Or as a Castle rearéd high and round,
By subtile engins and malitious slight
Is underminéd from the lowest ground,
And her foundation forst, and feebled quight,
At last downe falles, and with her heapéd hight
Her hastie ruine does more heavie make,
And yields it selfe unto the victours might;
Such was this Gyaunts fall, that seemd to shake
The stedfast globe of earth, as it for feare did quake.

24

The knight then lightly leaping to the pray,
With mortall steele him smot againe so sore,
That headlesse his unweldy bodie lay,
All wallowd in his owne fowle bloudy gore,
Which flowéd from his wounds in wondrous store,
But soone as breath out of his breast did pas,
That huge great body, which the Gyaunt bore,
Was vanisht quite, and of that monstrous mas
Was nothing left, but like an emptie bladder was.

25

Whose grievous fall, when false *Duessa* spide,
Her golden cup she cast unto the ground,
And crownéd mitre rudely threw aside;
Such percing griefe her stubborne hart did wound,
That she could not endure that dolefull stound,
But leaving all behind her, fled away:
The light-foot Squire her quickly turnd around,
And by hard meanes enforcing her to stay,
So brought unto his Lord, as his deservéd pray.

26

The royall Virgin, which beheld from farre,
In pensive plight, and sad perplexitie,
The whole atchievement of this doubtfull warre,
Came running fast to greet his victorie,
With sober gladnesse, and myld modestie,
And with sweet joyous cheare him thus bespake;
Faire braunch of noblesse, flowre of chevalrie.
That with your worth the world amazéd make.
How shall I quite the paines, ye suffer for my sake?

27

And you fresh bud of vertue springing fast,[2]
Whom these sad eyes saw nigh unto deaths dore,
What hath poore Virgin for such perill past,
Wherewith you to reward? Accept therefore
My simple selfe, and service evermore;
And he that high does sit, and all things see
With equall eyes,[3] their merites to restore,
Behold what ye this day have done for mee,
And what I cannot quite, requite with usuree.

28

But sith the heavens, and your faire handeling
Have made you maister of the field this day,
Your fortune maister eke with governing,
And well begun end all so well, I pray,
Ne let that wicked woman scape away;
For she it is, that did my Lord bethrall,
My dearest Lord, and deepe in dongeon lay,
Where he his better dayes hath wasted all.
O heare, how piteous he to you for ayd does call.

[1]Referring to Duessa as well as Orgoglio?

[2]The Squire. [3]With impartial eyes.

29

Forthwith he gave in charge unto his Squire,
That scarlot whore to keepen carefully;
Whiles he himselfe with greedie great desire
Into the Castle entred forcibly.
Where living creature none he did espye;
Then gan he lowdly through the house to call:
But no man car'd[1] to answere to his crye.
There raignd a solemne silence over all,
Nor voice was heard, nor wight was seene in bowre or hall.

30

At last with creeping crooked pace forth came
An old old man, with beard as white as snow,
That on a staffe his feeble steps did frame,
And guide his wearie gate both too and fro:
For his eye sight him failéd long ygo,
And on his arme a bounch of keyes he bore,
The which unuséd rust did overgrow:
Those were the keyes of every inner dore,
But he could not them use, but kept them still in store.

31

But very uncouth sight was to behold,
How he did fashion his untoward pace,
For as he forward moov'd his footing old,
So backward still was turned his wrincled face,
Unlike to men, who ever as they trace,
Both feet and face one way are wont to lead.
This was the auncient keeper of that place,
And foster father of the Gyant dead;
His name *Ignaro*[2] did his nature right aread.

32

His reverend haires and holy gravitie
The knight much honord, as beseeméd well,
And gently askt, where all the people bee,
Which in that stately building wont to dwell.
Who answerd him full soft, he could not tell.
Againe he askt, where that same knight was layd,
Whom great *Orgoglio* with his puissaunce fell
Had made his caytive thrall, againe he sayde,
He could not tell: ne ever other answere made.

33

Then askéd he, which way he in might pas:
He could not tell, againe he answeréd.
Thereat the curteous knight displeaséd was,
And said, Old sire, it seemes thou hast not red
How ill it fits with that same silver hed
In vaine to mocke, or mockt in vaine to bee:
But if thou be, as thou art pourtrahéd
With natures pen, in ages grave degree,
Aread in graver wise,[3] what I demaund of thee.

34

His answere likewise was, he could not tell.
Whose sencelesse speach, and doted ignorance
When as the noble Prince had markéd well,
He ghest his nature by his countenance,
And calmd his wrath with goodly temperance.
Then to him stepping, from his arme did reach
Those keyes, and made himselfe free enterance.
Each dore he opened without any breach;
There was no barre to stop, nor foe him to empeach.

35

There all within full rich arayd he found,
With royall arras and resplendent gold.
And did with store of every thing abound,
That greatest Princes presence might behold.
But all the floore (too filthy to be told)
With bloud of guiltlesse babes, and innocents trew,
Which there were slaine, as sheepe out of the fold,
Defiléd was, that dreadfull was to vew,
And sacred ashes over it was strowéd new.

36

And there beside of marble stone was built
An Altare, carv'd with cunning imagery,
On which true Christians bloud was often spilt,
And holy Martyrs often doen to dye,
With cruell malice and strong tyranny:
Whose blesséd sprites from underneath the stone
To God for vengeance cryde continually,
And with great griefe were often heard to grone,
That hardest heart would bleede, to heare their piteous mone.

37

Through every rowme he sought, and every bowr,
But no where could he find that wofull thrall:
At last he came unto an yron doore,
That fast was lockt, but key found not at all
Emongst that bounch, to open it withall;
But in the same a little grate was pight,
Through which he sent his voyce, and lowd did call
With all his powre to weet, if living wight
Were houséd there within, whom he enlargen might.

38

Therewith an hollow, dreary, murmuring voyce
These piteous plaints and dolours did resound:
O who is that, which brings me happy choyce
Of death, that here lye dying every stound,

[1]Took the trouble. [2]Ignorance.
[3]Answer more seriously.

Yet live perforce in balefull darkenesse bound?
For now three Moones have changéd thrice their hew,
And have beene thrice hid underneath the ground,
Since I the heavens chearefull face did vew,
O welcome thou, that doest of death bring tydings trew.

39

Which when that Champion heard, with percing point
Of pitty deare his hart was thrilléd sore,
And trembling horrour ran through every joynt,
For ruth of gentle knight so fowle forlore:
Which shaking off, he rent that yron dore,
With furious force, and indignation fell;
Where entred in, his foot could find no flore,
But all a deepe descent, as darke as hell,
That breathéd ever forth a filthie banefull smell.

40

But neither darkenesse fowle, nor filthy bands,
Nor noyous smell his purpose could withhold,
(Entire affection hateth nicer hands[1])
But that with constant zeale, and courage bold,
After long paines and labours manifold,
He found the meanes that Prisoner up to reare;
Whose feeble thighes, unhable to uphold
His pinéd corse, him scarce to light could beare.
A ruefull spectacle of death and ghastly drere.

41

His sad dull eyes deepe sunck in hollow pits,
Could not endure th'unwonted sunne to view;
His bare thin cheekes for want of better bits,[2]
And empty sides deceivéd of their dew,[3]
Could make a stony hart his hap to rew;
His rawbone armes, whose mighty brawnéd bowrs
Were wont to rive steele plates, helmets hew,
Were cleane consum'd, and all his vitall powres
Decayd, and all his flesh shronk up like withered flowres.

42

Whom when his Lady saw, to him she ran
With hasty joy: to see him made her glad,
And sad to view his visage pale and wan,
Who earst in flowres of freshest youth was clad.
Tho when her well of teares she wasted had,
She said, Ah dearest Lord, what evill starre
On you hath fround, and pourd his influence bad,
That of your selfe ye thus berobbéd arre,
And this misseeming hew your manly looks doth marre?

43

But welcome now my Lord, in wele or woe,
Whose presence I have lackt too long a day;
And fie on Fortune mine avowéd foe,
Whose wrathfull wreakes them selves do now alay.
And for these wrongs shall treble penaunce pay
Of treble good; good growes of evils priefe.
The chearelesse man, whom sorrow did dismay,
Had no delight to treaten of his griefe;
His long enduréd famine needed more reliefe.

44

Faire Lady, then said that victorious knight,
The things, that grievous were to do, or beare,
Them to renew, I wote, breeds no delight;
Best musicke breeds delight in loathing eare:
But th'onely good, that growes of passéd feare,
Is to be wise, and ware of like agein.
This dayes ensample hath this lesson deare
Deepe written in my heart with yron pen,
That blisse may not abide in state of mortall men.

45

Henceforth sir knight, take to you wonted strength,
And maister these mishaps with patient might;
Loe where your foe lyes stretcht in monstrous length,
And loe that wicked woman in your sight,
The roote of all your care, and wretched plight,
Now in your powre, to let her live, or dye.
To do her dye (quoth *Una*) were despight,
And shame t'avenge[4] so weake an enimy;
But spoile her of her scarlot robe, and let her fly.

46

So as she bad, that witch they disaraid,
And robd of royall robes, and purple pall,
And ornaments that richly were displaid;
Ne sparéd they to strip her naked all.
Then when they had despoild her tire and call,
Such as she was, their eyes might her behold,
That her mishapéd parts did them appall,
A loathly, wrinckled hag, ill favoured, old,
Whose secret filth good manners biddeth not be told.

47

Her craftie head was altogether bald,
And as in hate of honorable eld,

[1]Hands too dainty. [2]Better food.
[3]Cheated of their due.
[4]To take vengeance on.

Was overgrowne with scurfe and filthy scald;
Her teeth out of her rotten gummes were feld,
And her sowre breath abhominably smeld;
Her driéd dugs, like bladders lacking wind,
Hong downe, and filthy matter from them weld;
Her wrizled skin as rough, as maple rind,
So scabby was, that would have loathd all womankind.

48

Her neather parts, the shame of all her kind,
My chaster Muse for shame doth blush to write;
But at her rompe she growing had behind
A foxes taile, with dong all fowly dight;
And eke her feete most monstrous were in sight;
For one of them was like an Eagles claw,
With griping talaunts armd to greedy fight,
The other like a Beares uneven paw:
More ugly shape yet never living creature saw.

49

Which when the knights beheld, amazd they were,
And wondred at so fowle deforméd wight.
Such then (said *Una*) as she seemeth here,
Such is the face of falshood, such the sight
Of fowle *Duessa*, when her borrowed light
Is laid away, and counterfesaunce knowne.
Thus when they had the witch disrobéd quight,
And all her filthy feature open showne,
They let her goe at will, and wander wayes unknowne.

50

She flying fast from heavens hated face,
And from the world that her discovered wide,
Fled to the wastfull wildernesse apace,
From living eyes her open shame to hide,
And lurkt in rocks and caves long unespide.
But that faire crew of knights, and *Una* faire
Did in that castle afterwards abide,
To rest them selves, and weary powres repaire,
Where store they found of all, that dainty was and rare.

CANTO IX

His loves and lignage Arthur tells,
The knights knit friendly bands:
Sir Trevisan flies from Despayre,
Whom Redcrosse knight withstands.

1

O GOODLY golden chaine,[1] wherewith yfere
The vertues linkéd are in lovely wize:
And noble minds of yore allyéd were,
In brave poursuit of chevalrous emprize,
That none did others saféty despize,
Nor aid envy to him, in need that stands,
But friendly each did others prayse devize,
How to advaunce with favourable hands,
As this good Prince redeemd the *Redcrosse* knight from bands.

2

Who when their powres, empaird through labour long,
With dew repast they had recuréd well,
And that weake captive wight now wexéd strong,
Them list no lenger there at leasure dwell,
But forward fare, as their adventures fell,
But ere they parted, *Una* faire besought
That straunger knight his name and nation tell;
Least so great good, as he for her had wrought,
Should die unknown, and buried be in thankelesse thought.

3

Faire virgin (said the Prince) ye me require
A thing without the compas of my wit:
For both the lignage and the certain Sire,
From which I sprong, from me are hidden yit.
For all so soone as life did me admit
Into this world, and shewéd heavens light,
From mothers pap I taken was unfit:
And streight delivered to a Faery knight,
To be upbrought in gentle thewes and martiall might.

4

Unto old *Timon* he me brought bylive,
Old *Timon*, who in youthly yeares hath beene
In warlike feates th'expertest man alive,
And is the wisest now on earth I weene;
His dwelling is low in a valley greene,
Under the foot of *Rauran* mossy hore,
From whence the river *Dee* as silver cleene
His tombling billowes rolls with gentle rore:
There all my dayes he traind me up in vertuous lore.

5

Thither the great Magicien *Merlin* came,
As was his use, ofttimes to visit me:
For he had charge my discipline to frame,
And Tutours nouriture to oversee.[2]
Him oft and oft I askt in privitie,
Of what loines and what lignage I did spring:
Whose aunswere bad me still assuréd bee,
That I was sonne and heire unto a king,
As time in her just terme the truth to light should bring.

[1]The quality typified by Arthur, "magnificence," or magnanimity, in which all other virtues meet.

[2]And to supervise the training imposed by my tutor.

6

Well worthy impe, said then the Lady gent,
And Pupill fit for such a Tutours hand.
But what adventure, or what high intent
Hath brought you hither into Faery land,
Aread Prince *Arthur*, crowne of Martiall band?
Full hard it is (quoth he) to read aright
The course of heavenly cause, or understand
The secret meaning of th'eternall might,
That rules mens wayes, and rules the thoughts of living wight.

7

For whither he through fatal deepe foresight[1]
Me hither sent, for cause to me unghest,
Or that fresh bleeding wound, which day and night
Whilome doth rancle in my riven brest,
With forcéd fury following his[2] behest,
Me hither brought by wayes yet never found,
You to have helpt I hold my selfe yet blest.
Ah curteous knight (quoth she) what secret wound
Could ever find,[3] to grieve the gentlest hart on ground?

8

Deare Dame (quoth he) you sleeping sparkes awake,
Which troubled once, into huge flames will grow,
Ne ever will their fervent fury slake,
Till living moysture into smoke do flow,
And wasted life do lye in ashes low.
Yet sithens silence lesseneth not my fire,
But told it flames, and hidden it does glow,
I will revele, what ye so much desire:
Ah Love, lay downe thy bow, the whiles I may respire.

9

It was in freshest flowre of youthly yeares,
When courage first does creepe in manly chest,
Then first the coale of kindly heat appeares
To kindle love in every living brest;
But me had warnd old *Timons* wise behest,
Those creeping flames by reason to subdew,
Before their rage grew to so great unrest,
As miserable lovers use to rew,
Which still wex old in woe, whiles woe still wexeth new.

10

That idle name of love, and lovers life,
As losse of time, and vertues enimy
I ever scornd, and joyd to stirre up strife,
In middest of their mournfull Tragedy,
Ay wont to laugh, when them I heard to cry,
And blow the fire, which them to ashes brent:
Their God himselfe, griev'd at my libertie,
Shot many a dart at me with fiers intent,
But I them warded all with wary government.[4]

11

But all in vaine: no fort can be so strong,
Ne fleshly brest can armèd be so sound,
But will at last be wonne with battrie long,
Or unawares at disavantage found;
Nothing is sure, that growes on earthly ground:
And who most trustes in arme of fleshly might,
And boasts, in beauties chaine not to be bound,
Doth soonest fall in disaventrous fight,
And yeeldes his caytive neck to victours most despight.

12

Ensample make of him your haplesse joy,[5]
And of my selfe now mated, as ye see;
Whose prouder[6] vaunt that proud avenging boy
Did soone pluck downe, and curbd my libertie.
For on a day prickt forth with jollitie
Of looser life, and heat of hardiment,
Raunging the forest wide on courser free,
The fields, the floods, the heavens with one consent
Did seeme to laugh on me, and favour mine intent.[7]

13

For-wearied with my sports, I did alight
From loftie steed, and downe to sleepe me layd;
The verdant gras my couch did goodly dight,
And pillow was my helmet faire displayd:
Whiles every sence the humour sweet embayd,
And slombring soft my hart did steale away,
Me seemèd, by my side a royall Mayd
Her daintie limbes full softly down did lay:
So faire a creature yet saw never sunny day.

14

Most goodly glee and lovely blandishment
She to me made, and bad me love her deare,
For dearely sure her love was to me bent,
As when just time expired[8] should appeare.
But whether dreames delude, or true it were,
Was never hart so ravisht with delight,
Ne living man like words did ever heare,
As she to me delivered all that night;
And at her parting said, She Queene of Faeries hight.

[1] Deep prophetic foresight.
[2] Its. [3] Choose.

[4] Self-control. [5] The Red Cross Knight.
[6] Too proud. [7] Join in my pleasure.
[8] As in due course of time.

15

When I awoke, and found her place devoyd,
And nought but presséd gras, where she had lyen,
I sorrowed all so much, as earst I joyd,
And washéd all her place with watry eyen.
From that day forth I lov'd that face divine;
From that day forth I cast in carefull mind,
To seeke her out with labour, and long tyne,
And never vow to rest,[1] till her I find,
Nine monethes I seeke in vaine yet ni'll that vow unbind.

16

Thus as he spake, his visage wexéd pale,
And chaunge of hew great passion did bewray;
Yet still he strove to cloke his inward bale,
And hide the smoke, that did his fire display,
Till gentle *Una* thus to him gan say;
O happy Queene of Faeries, that hast found
Mongst many, one that with his prowesse may
Defend thine honour, and thy foes confound:
True Loves are often sown, but seldom grow on ground.[2]

17

Thine, O then, said the gentle *Redcrosse* knight,
Next to that Ladies love, shalbe the place,
O fairest virgin, full of heavenly light,
Whose wondrous faith, exceeding earthly race,
Was firmest fixt in mine extremest case.
And you, my Lord, the Patrone[3] of my life,
Of that great Queene may well gaine worthy Grace:
For onely worthy you through prowes priefe
Yf living man mote worthy be, to be her liefe.

18

So diversly discoursing of their loves,
The golden Sunne his glistring head gan shew,
And sad remembraunce now the Prince amoves,
With fresh desire his voyage to pursew:
Als *Una* earnd her traveill to renew.
Then those two knights, fast friendship for to bynd,
And love establish each to other trew,
Gave goodly gifts, the signes of gratefull mynd,
And eke the pledges firme, right hands together joynd.

19

Prince *Arthur* gave a boxe of Diamond sure,
Embowd with gold and gorgeous ornament,

[1]And vow never to rest.
[2]On earth. [3]Preserver.

Wherein were closd few drops of liquor pure,
Of wondrous worth, and vertue excellent,
That any wound could heale incontinent:
Which to requite, the *Redcrosse* knight him gave
A booke, wherein his Saveours testament
Was writ with golden letters rich and brave;
A worke of wondrous grace, and able soules to save.

20

Thus beene they parted, *Arthur* on his way
To seeke his love, and th'other for to fight
With *Unaes* foe, that all her realme did pray.[4]
But she now weighing the decayéd plight,
And shrunken synewes of her chosen knight,
Would not a while her forward course pursew,
Ne bring him forth in face of dreadfull fight,
Till he recovered had his former hew:
For him to be yet weake and wearie well she knew.

21

So as they traveild, lo they gan espy
An arméd knight towards them gallop fast,
That seeméd from some fearéd foe to fly,
Or other griesly thing, that him agast.
Still as he fled, his eye was backward cast,
As if his feare[5] still followed him behind;
Als flew his steed, as he his bands had brast,
And with his wingéd heeles did tread the wind,
As he had beene a fole of *Pegasus* his kind.[6]

22

Nigh as he drew, they might perceive his head
To be unarmd, and curld uncombéd heares
Upstaring stiffe, dismayd with uncouth dread;
Nor drop of bloud in all his face appeares
Nor life in limbe: and to increase his feares,
In fowle reproch of knighthoods faire degree,
About his neck an hempen rope he weares,
That with his glistring armes does ill agree;[7]
But he of rope or armes has now no memoree.

23

The *Redcrosse* knight toward him crosséd fast,
To weet, what mister wight was so dismayd:
There him he finds all sencelesse and aghast,
That of him selfe he seemd to be afrayd;
Whom hardly he from flying forward stayd,
Till he these wordes to him deliver might;
Sir knight, aread who hath ye thus arayd,

[4]Did ravage. [5]The object of his fear.
[6]Of the race of Pegasus.
[7]Hanging was a punishment reserved for common criminals. A knight if executed would be beheaded.

And eke from whom make ye this hasty flight:
For never knight I saw in such misseeming plight.

24

He answerd nought at all, but adding new
Feare to his first amazment, staring wide
With stony eyes, and hartlesse hollow hew,
Astonisht stood, as one that had aspide
Infernall furies, with their chaines untide.
Him yet againe, and yet againe bespake
The gentle knight; who nought to him replide,
But trembling every joynt did inly quake,
And foltring tongue at last these words seemd forth to shake.

25

For Gods deare love, Sir knight, do me not stay;
For loe he comes, he comes fast after mee.
Eft looking backe would faine have runne away;
But he him forst to stay, and tellen free
The secret cause of his perplexitie:
Yet nathemore by his bold hartie speach,
Could his bloud-frosen hart emboldned bee,
But through his boldnesse rather feare did reach,
Yet forst, at last he made through silence suddein breach.

26

And am I now in safetie sure (quoth he)
From him, that would have forcéd me to dye?
And is the point of death now turnd fro mee,
That I may tell this haplesse history?
Feare nought (quoth he), no daunger now is nye.
Then shall I you recount a ruefull cace
(Said he), the which with this unlucky eye
I late beheld, and had not greater grace
Me reft from it, had bene partaker of the place.

27

I lately chaunst (Would I had never chaunst)
With a faire knight to keepen companee,
Sir *Terwin* hight, that well himselfe advaunst
In all affaires, and was both bold and free,
But not so happie as mote happie bee:
He lov'd, as was his lot, a Ladie gent,
That him againe lov'd in the least degree:[1]
For she was proud, and of too high intent,
And joyd to see her lover languish and lament.

28

From whom returning sad and comfortlesse,
As on the way together we did fare,
We met that villen (God from him me blesse)
That curséd wight, from whom I scapt whyleare,
A man of hell, that cals himselfe *Despaire:*
Who first us greets, and after faire areedes
Of tydings strange, and of adventures rare:
So creeping close, as Snake in hidden weedes,
Inquireth of our states, and of our knightly deedes.

29

Which when he knew, and felt our feeble harts
Embost with bale, and bitter byting griefe,
Which love had launchéd with his deadly darts,
With wounding words and termes of foule repriefe,
He pluckt from us all hope of due reliefe,
That earst us held in love of lingring life;
Then hopelesse hartlesse, gan the cunning thiefe
Perswade us die, to stint all further strife:
To me he lent this rope, to him a rustie knife.

30

With which sad instrument of hastie death,
That wofull lover, loathing lenger light,
A wide way made to let forth living breath.
But I more fearefull, or more luckie wight,
Dismayd with that deforméd dismall sight,
Fled fast away, halfe dead with dying feare:
Ne yet assur'd of life by you, Sir knight,
Whose like infirmitie like chaunce may beare:
But God you never let his charméd speeches heare.

31

How may a man (said he) with idle speach
Be wonne, to spoyle the Castle of his health?
I wote (quoth he) whom triall late did teach,
That like would not for all this worldés wealth:
His subtill tongue, like dropping honny, mealt'th[2]
Into the hart, and searcheth every vaine,
That ere one be aware, by secret stealth
His powre is reft, and weaknesse doth remaine.
O never Sir desire to try his guilefull traine.

32

Certes (said he) hence shall I never rest,
Till I that treachours art have heard and tride;
And you Sir knight, whose name mote I request,
Of grace do me unto his cabin guide.
I that hight *Trevisan* (quoth he) will ride
Against my liking backe, to doe you grace:
But not for gold nor glee will I abide
By you, when ye arrive in that same place;
For lever had I die, then see his deadly face.

[1]Not at all.

[2]Melteth.

33

Ere long they come, where that same wicked wight
His dwelling has, low in an hollow cave,
Farre underneath a craggie clift ypight,
Darke, dolefull, drearie, like a greedie grave,
That still for carrion carcases doth crave:
On top whereof aye dwelt the ghastly Owle,
Shrieking his balefull note, which ever drave
Farre from that haunt all other chearefull fowle;
And all about it wandring ghostes did waile and howle.

34

And all about old stockes and stubs of trees,
Whereon nor fruit, nor leafe was ever seene,
Did hang upon the ragged rocky knees;[1]
On which had many wretches hangéd beene,
Whose carcases were scattered on the greene,
And throwne about the cliffs. Arrivéd there,
That bare-head knight for dread and dolefull teene,
Would faine have fled, ne durst approchen neare,
But th'other forst him stay, and comforted in feare.

35

That darkesome cave they enter, where they find
That curséd man, low sitting on the ground,
Musing full sadly in his sullein mind;
His griesie lockes, long growén, and unbound,
Disordred hong about his shoulders round,
And hid his face; through which his hollow eyne
Lookt deadly dull, and staréd as astound;
His raw-bone cheekes through penurie and pine,
Were shronke into his jawes as he did never dine.

36

His garment nought but many ragged clouts,
With thornes together pind and patchéd was,
The which his naked sides he wrapt abouts;
And him beside there lay upon the gras
A drearie corse, whose life away did pas,
All wallowd in his owne yet luke-warme blood,
That from his wound yet welléd fresh alas;
In which a rustie knife fast fixéd stood,
And made an open passage for the gushing flood.

37

Which piteous spectacle, approving trew
The wofull tale that *Trevisan* had told,
When as the gentle *Redcrosse* knight did vew,
With firie zeale he burnt in courage bold,
Him to avenge, before his bloud were cold,
And to the villein said, Thou damnéd wight,
The author of this fact, we here behold,
What justice can but judge against thee right,
With thine owne bloud to price his bloud, here shed in sight?

38

What franticke fit (quoth he) hath thus distraught
Thee, foolish man, so rash a doome to give?
What justice ever other judgement taught,
But he should die, who merites not to live?
None else to death this man despayring drive,
But his owne guiltie mind deserving death.
Is then unjust to each his due to give?
Or let him die, that loatheth living breath?
Or let him die at ease, that liveth here uneath?

39

Who travels by the wearie wandring way,
To come unto his wishéd home in haste,
And meetes a flood, that doth his passage stay,
Is not great grace to helpe him over past,
Or free his feet, that in the myre sticke fast?
Most envious man, that grieves at neighbours good,
And fond, that joyest in the woe thou hast,
Why wilt not let him passe, that long hath stood
Upon the banke, yet wilt thy selfe not[2] passe the flood?

40

He there does now enjoy eternall rest
And happie ease, which thou doest want and crave,
And further from it daily wanderest:
What if some litle paine the passage have,
That makes fraile flesh to feare the bitter wave?
Is not short paine well borne, that brings long ease,
And layes the soule to sleepe in quiet grave?
Sleepe after toyle, port after stormie seas,
Ease after warre, death after life does greatly please.

41

The knight much wondred at his suddeine wit,
And said, The terme of life is limited,
Ne may a man prolong, nor shorten it;
The souldier may not move from watchfull sted,

[1]Jagged projections of the rock.

[2]Even if you yourself will not.

Nor leave his stand, untill his Captaine bed.
Who life did limit by almightie doome,
(Quoth he) knowes best the termes establishéd;
And he, that points the Centonell[1] his roome,
Doth license him depart at sound of morning droome.

42

Is not his deed, what ever thing is donne,
In heaven and earth? did not he all create
To die againe? all ends that was begonne.
Their times in his eternall booke of fate
Are written sure, and have their certaine date.
Who then can strive with strong necessitie,
That holds the world in his still chaunging state,
Or shunne the death ordaynd by destinie?
When houre of death is come, let none aske whence, nor why.

43

The lenger life, I wote the greater sin,
The greater sin, the greater punishment:
All those great battels, which thou boasts to win,
Through strife, and bloud-shed, and avengément,
Now praysd, hereafter deare thou shalt repent:
For life must life, and bloud must bloud repay.
Is not enough thy evill life forespent?[2]
For he, that once hath misséd the right way,
The further he doth goe, the further he doth stray.

44

Then do no further goe, no further stray,
But here lie downe, and to thy rest betake,
Th'ill to prevent, that life ensewen may.
For what hath life, that may it lovéd make,
And gives not rather cause it to forsake?
Feare, sicknesse, age, losse, labour, sorrow, strife,
Paine, hunger, cold, that makes the hart to quake;
And ever fickle fortune rageth rife,
All which, and thousands mo do make a loathsome life.

45

Thou wretched man, of death hast greatest need,
If in true ballance thou wilt weigh thy state:
For never knight, that daréd warlike deede,
More lucklesse disaventures did amate:
Witnesse the dongeon deepe, wherein of late
Thy life shut up, for death so oft did call;
And though good lucke prolongéd hath thy date,
Yet death then, would the like mishaps forestall,
Into the which hereafter thou maiest happen fall.

46

Why then doest thou, O man of sin, desire
To draw thy dayes forth to their last degree?
Is not the measure of thy sinfull hire[3]
High heapéd up with huge iniquitie,
Against the day of wrath, to burden thee?
Is not enough, that to this Ladie milde
Thou falséd hast thy faith with perjurie,
And sold thy selfe to serve *Duessa* vilde,
With whom in all abuse thou hast thy selfe defilde?

47

Is not he just, that all this doth behold
From highest heaven, and beares an equall eye?
Shall he thy sins up in his knowledge fold,
And guiltie be of thine impietie?
Is not his law, Let every sinner die:
Die shall all flesh? what then must needs be donne,
Is it not better to doe willinglie,
Then linger, till the glasse be all out ronne?
Death is the end of woes: die soone, O faeries sonne.

48

The knight was much enmovéd with his speach,
That as a swords point through his hart did perse,
And in his conscience made a secret breach,
Well knowing true all, that he did reherse,
And to his fresh remembrance did reverse
The ugly vew of his deforméd crimes,
That all his manly powres it did disperse,
As he were charméd with inchaunted rimes,
That oftentimes he quakt, and fainted oftentimes.

49

In which amazement, when the Miscreant
Perceivéd him to waver weake and fraile,
Whiles trembling horror did his conscience dant,
And hellish anguish did his soule assaile,
To drive him to despaire, and quite to quaile,
He shew'd him painted in a table[4] plaine,
The damnéd ghosts, that doe in torments waile,

[1]Sentinel.
[2]Is not enough of your life spent in evil-doing?
[3]Service to sin.
[4]Picture.

And thousand feends that doe them endlesse paine
With fire and brimstone, which for ever shall remaine.

50

The sight whereof so throughly him dismaid,
That nought but death before his eyes he saw,
And ever burning wrath before him laid,
By righteous sentence of th'Almighties law:
Then gan the villein him to overcraw,
And brought unto him swords, ropes, poison, fire,
And all that might him to perdition draw;
And bad him choose, what death he would desire:
For death was due to him, that had provokt Gods ire.

51

But when as none of them he saw him take,
He to him raught a dagger sharpe and keene,
And gave it him in hand: his hand did quake,
And tremble like a leafe of Aspin greene,
And troubled bloud through his pale face was seene
To come, and goe with tydings from the hart,
As it a running messenger had beene.
At last resolv'd to worke his finall smart,
He lifted up his hand, that backe againe did start.

52

Which when as *Una* saw, through every vaine
The crudled cold ran to her well of life,
As in a swowne: but soone reliv'd againe;
Out of his hand she snatcht the cursèd knife,
And threw it to the ground, enragèd rife,
And to him said, Fie, fie, faint harted knight,
What meanest thou by this reprochfull strife?
Is this the battell, which thou vauntst to fight
With that fire-mouthèd Dragon, horrible and bright?

53

Come, come away, fraile, feeble, fleshly wight,
Ne let vaine words bewitch thy manly hart,
Ne divelish thoughts dismay thy constant spright.
In heavenly mercies hast thou not a part?
Why shouldst thou then despeire, that chosen art?
Where justice growes, there grows eke greater grace,
The which doth quench the brond of hellish smart,
And that accurst hand-writing doth deface;
Arise, Sir knight arise, and leave this cursèd place.

54

So up he rose, and thence amounted streight.
Which when the carle beheld, and saw his guest
Would safe depart, for all his subtill sleight,
He chose an halter from among the rest,
And with it hung himselfe, unbid unblest.[1]
But death he could not worke himselfe thereby;
For thousand times he so himselfe had drest,
Yet nathelesse it could not doe him die,
Till he should die his last, that is eternally.

CANTO X

Her faithfull knight faire Una brings
to house of Holinesse,
Where he is taught repentance, and
the way to heavenly blesse.

1

WHAT man is he, that boasts of fleshly might,
And vaine assurance of mortality,
Which all so soone, as it doth come to fight,
Against spirituall foes, yeelds by and by,
Or from the field most cowardly doth fly?
Ne let the man ascribe it to his skill,
That thorough grace hath gainèd victory.
If any strength we have, it is to ill,
But all the good is Gods, both power and eke will.

2

By that, which lately hapned, *Una* saw,
That this her knight was feeble, and too faint;
And all his sinews woxen weake and raw,
Through long enprisonment, and hard constraint,
Which he endurèd in his late restraint,
That yet he was unfit for bloudie fight:
Therefore to cherish him with diets daint,
She cast to bring him, where he chearen might,
Till he recovered had his late decayèd plight.

3

There was an auntient house not farre away,
Renowmd throughout the world for sacred lore,
And pure unspotted life: so well they say
It governd was, and guided evermore,
Through wisedome of a matrone grave and hore;
Whose onely joy was to relieve the needes
Of wretched soules, and helpe the helpelesse pore:
All night she spent in bidding of her bedes,
And all the day in doing good and godly deedes.

[1]Without prayer or blessing.

4

Dame *Cælia*[1] men did her call, as thought
From heaven to come, or thither to arise,
The mother of three daughters, well upbrought
In goodly thewes, and godly exercise:
The eldest two most sober, chast, and wise,
Fidelia and *Speranza*[2] virgins were
Though spousd, yet wanting wedlocks solemnize;
But faire *Charissa*[3] to a lovely fere
Was linckéd, and by him had many pledges dere.

5

Arrivéd there, the dore they find fast lockt;
For it was warely watchéd night and day,
For feare of many foes: but when they knockt,
The Porter opened unto them streight way:
He was an agéd syre, all hory gray,
With lookes full lowly cast, and gate full slow,
Wont on a staffe his feeble steps to stay,
Hight *Humiltá*.[4] They passe in stouping low;
For streight and narrow was the way, which he did show.

6

Each goodly thing is hardest to begin,
But entred in a spacious court they see,
Both plaine, and pleasant to be walkéd in,
Where them does meete a francklin faire and free,
And entertaines with comely courteous glee,
His name was *Zele*, that him right well became,
For in his speeches and behaviour hee
Did labour lively to expresse the same,
And gladly did them guide, till to the Hall they came.

7

There fairely them receives a gentle Squire,
Of milde demeanure, and rare courtesie,
Right cleanly clad in comely sad attire;
In word and deede that shew'd great modestie,
And knew his good to all of each degree,[5]
Hight *Reverence*. He them with speeches meet
Does faire entreat; no courting nicetie,
But simple true, and eke unfainéd sweet,
As might become a Squire so great persons to greet.

8

And afterwards them to his Dame he leades,
That agéd Dame, the Ladie of the place:
Who all this while was busie at her beades:
Which doen, she up arose with seemely grace,
And toward them full matronely did pace.
Where when that fairest *Una* she beheld,
Whom well she knew to spring from heavenly race,
Her hart with joy unwonted inly sweld,
As feeling wondrous comfort in her weaker eld.

9

And her embracing said, O happie earth,
Whereon thy innocent feet doe ever tread,
Most vertuous virgin borne of heavenly berth,
That to redeeme thy woefull parents head,
From tyrans rage, and ever-dying dread,[6]
Hast wandred through the world now long a day;
Yet ceasest not thy wearie soles to lead,
What grace hath thee now hither brought this way?
Or doen thy feeble feet unweeting hither stray?

10

Strange thing it is an errant knight to see
Here in this place, or any other wight,
That hither turnes his steps. So few there bee,
That chose the narrow path, or seeke the right:
All keepe the broad high way, and take delight
With many rather for to go astray,
And be partakers of their evill-plight,
Then with a few to walke the rightest way;
O foolish men, why haste ye to your owne decay?

11

Thy selfe to see, and tyréd limbs to rest,
O matrone sage (quoth she) I hither came,
And this good knight his way with me addrest,
Led with thy prayses and broad-blazéd fame,
That up to heaven is blowne. The auncient Dame
Him goodly greeted in her modest guise,
And entertaynd them both, as best became,
With all the court'sies, that she could devise,
Ne wanted ought, to shew her bounteous or wise.

12

Thus as they gan of sundry things devise,
Loe two most goodly virgins came in place,
Ylinkéd arme in arme in lovely wise,
With countenance demure, and modest grace,
They numbred even steps and equall pace:
Of which the eldest, that *Fidelia* hight,
Like sunny beames threw from her Christall face,
That could have dazd the rash beholders sight,
And round about her head did shine like heavens light.

[1]Knowledge of heavenly things. [2]Faith and Hope.
[3]Charity. [4]Humility.
[5]Knew how to bear himself towards men of every rank.

[6]Constant fear of death.

13

She was araiéd all in lilly white,
And in her right hand bore a cup of gold,
With wine and water fild up to the hight,
In which a Serpent did himselfe enfold,[1]
That horrour made to all, that did behold;
But she no whit did chaunge her constant mood:
And in her other hand she fast did hold
A booke,[2] that was both signd and seald with blood,
Wherein darke things were writ, hard to be understood.

14

Her younger sister, that *Speranza* hight,
Was clad in blew,[3] that her beseeméd well;
Not all so chearefull seeméd she of sight,[4]
As was her sister; whether dread did dwell,
Or anguish in her hart, is hard to tell:
Upon her arme a silver anchor lay,[5]
Whereon she leanéd ever, as befell:
And ever up to heaven, as she did pray,
Her stedfast eyes were bent, ne swarvéd other way.

15

They seeing *Una*, towards her gan wend,
Who them encounters with like courtesie;
Many kind speeches they betwene them spend,
And greatly joy each other well to see:
Then to the knight with shamefast modestie
They turne themselves, at *Unaes* meeke request,
And him salute with well beseeming glee;
Who faire them quites, as him beseeméd best,
And goodly gan discourse of many a noble gest.

16

Then *Una* thus: But she your sister deare,
The deare *Charissa* where is she become?
Or wants she health, or busie is elsewhere?
Ah no, said they, but forth she may not come:
For she of late is lightned of her wombe,
And hath encreast the world with one sonne more,
That her to see should be but troublesome.
Indeede (quoth she) that should be trouble sore,
But thankt be God, and her encrease so evermore.

[1]The serpent, because it casts off its skin, has sometimes been taken as a type of immortality.
[2]The New Testament, signed and sealed with Christ's blood.
[3]The color of constancy.
[4]In appearance.
[5]Another symbol of constancy.

17

Then said the agéd *Cœlia*, Deare dame,
And you good Sir, I wote that of your toyle,
And labours long, through which ye hither came,
Ye both forwearied be: therefore a whyle
I read you rest, and to your bowres recoyle.
Then calléd she a Groome, that forth him led
Into a goodly lodge, and gan despoile
Of puissant armes, and laid in easie bed;
His name was meeke *Obedience* rightfully ared.

18

Now when their wearie limbes with kindly rest,
And bodies were refresht with due repast,
Faire *Una* gan *Fidelia* faire request,
To have her knight into her schoolehouse plaste,
That of her heavenly learning he might taste,
And heare the wisedome of her words divine.
She graunted, and that knight so much agraste,
That she him taught celestiall discipline,
And opened his dull eyes, that light mote in them shine.

19

And that her sacred Booke, with bloud ywrit,
That none could read, except she did them teach,
She unto him discloséd every whit,
And heavenly documents[6] thereout did preach,
That weaker wit of man could never reach,
Of God, of grace, of justice, of free will,
That wonder was to heare her goodly speach:
For she was able, with her words to kill,
And raise againe to life the hart, that she did thrill.

20

And when she list poure out her larger spright,
She would commaund the hastie Sunne to stay,
Or backward turne his course from heavens hight;
Sometimes great hostes of men she could dismay,
Dry-shod to passe, she parts the flouds in tway;
And eke huge mountaines from their native seat
She would commaund, themselves to beare away,
And throw in raging sea with roaring threat.
Almightie God her gave such powre, and puissance great.

[6]Instructions.

21

The faithfull knight, now grew in litle space,
By hearing her, and by her sisters lore,
To such perfection of all heavenly grace,
That wretched world he gan for to abhore,
And mortall life gan loath, as thing forlore,
Greev'd with remembrance of his wicked wayes,
And prickt with anguish of his sinnes so sore,
That he desirde, to end his wretched dayes:
So much the dart of sinfull guilt the soule dismayes.

22

But wise *Speranza* gave him comfort sweet,
And taught him how to take assuréd hold
Upon her silver anchor, as was meet;
Else had his sinnes so great, and manifold
Made him forget all that *Fidelia* told.
In this distresséd doubtfull agonie,
When him his dearest *Una* did behold,
Disdeining life, desiring leave to die,
She found her selfe assayld with great perplexitie.

23

And came to *Cælia* to declare her smart,
Who well acquainted with that commune plight,
Which sinfull horror workes in wounded hart,
Her wisely comforted all that she might,
With goodly counsell and advisement right;
And streightway sent with carefull diligence,
To fetch a Leach, the which had great insight
In that disease of grievéd conscience,
And well could cure the same; His name was *Patience.*

24

Who comming to that soule-diseaséd knight,
Could hardly him intreat, to tell his griefe:
Which knowne, and all that noyd his heavie spright,
Well searcht, eftsoones he gan apply reliefe
Of salves and med'cines, which had passing priefe,
And thereto added words of wondrous might:
By which to ease he him recuréd briefe,
And much asswag'd the passion of his plight,
That he his paine endur'd, as seeming now more light.

25

But yet the cause and root of all his ill,
Inward corruption, and infected sin,
Not purg'd nor heald, behind remainéd still,
And festring sore did rankle yet within,
Close creeping twixt the marrow and the skin.
Which to extirpe, he laid him privily
Downe in a darkesome lowly place farre in,
Whereas he meant his corrosives to apply,
And with streight diet tame his stubborne malady.

26

In ashes and sackcloth he did array
His daintie corse, proud humors to abate,
And dieted with fasting every day,
The swelling of his wounds to mitigate,
And made him pray both earely and eke late:
And ever as superfluous flesh did rot
Amendment readie still at hand did wayt,
To pluck it out with pincers firie whot,
That soone in him was left no one corrupted jot.

27

And bitter *Penance* with an yron whip,
Was wont him once to disple every day:
And sharpe *Remorse* his hart did pricke and nip,
That drops of bloud thence like a well did play;
And sad *Repentance* uséd to embay,
His bodie in salt water smarting sore,
The filthy blots of sinne to wash away.
So in short space they did to health restore
The man that would not live, but earst lay at deathes dore.

28

In which his torment often was so great,
That like a Lyon he would cry and rore,
And rend his flesh, and his owne synewes eat.
His owne deare *Una* hearing evermore
His ruefull shriekes and gronings, often tore
Her guiltlesse garments, and her golden heare,
For pitty of his paine and anguish sore;
Yet all with patience wisely she did beare;
For well she wist, his crime could else be never cleare.

29

Whom thus recover'd by wise Patience,
And trew *Repentance* they to *Una* brought:
Who joyous of his curéd conscience,
Him dearely kist, and fairely eke besought
Himselfe to chearish, and consuming thought
To put away out of his carefull brest.
By this *Charissa*, late in child-bed brought,
Was woxen strong, and left her fruitfull nest:
To her faire *Una* brought this unacquainted guest.

30

She was a woman in her freshest age,
Of wondrous beauty, and of bountie rare,
With goodly grace, and comely personage,
That was on earth not easie to compare;

Full of great love, but *Cupids* wanton snare
As hell she hated, chast in worke and will;
Her necke and breasts were ever open bare,
That ay thereof her babes might sucke their fill;
The rest was all in yellow robes[1] arayéd still.

31

A multitude of babes about her hong,
Playing their sports, that joyd her to behold,
Whom still she fed, whiles they were weake and young,
But thrust them forth still, as they wexéd old:
And on her head she wore a tyre of gold,
Adornd with gemmes and owches wondrous faire,
Whose passing price uneath was to be told;
And by her side there sate a gentle paire
Of turtle doves, she sitting in an yvorie chaire.

32

The knight and *Una* entring, faire her greet,
And bid her joy of that her happie brood;
Who them requites with court'sies seeming meet,[2]
And entertaines with friendly chearefull mood.
Then *Una* her besought, to be so good,
As in her vertuous rules to schoole her knight,
Now after all his torment well withstood,
In that sad house of *Penaunce*, where his spright
Had past the paines of hell, and long enduring night.

33

She was right joyous of her just request,
And taking by the hand that Faeries sonne,
Gan him instruct in every good behest,
Of love, and righteousnesse, and well to donne,[3]
And wrath, and hatred warély to shonne,
That drew on men Gods hatred, and his wrath,
And many soules in dolours had fordonne:
In which when him she well instructed hath,
From thence to heaven she teacheth him the ready path.

34

Wherein his weaker wandring steps to guide,
An auncient matrone she to her does call,
Whose sober lookes her wisedome well descride:[4]
Her name was *Mercie*, well knowne over all,
To be both gratious, and eke liberall:
To whom the carefull charge of him she gave,
To lead aright, that he should never fall
In all his wayes through this wide worldés wave,
That Mercy in the end his righteous soule might save.

35

The godly Matrone by the hand him beares
Forth from her presence, by a narrow way,
Scattred with bushy thornes, and ragged breares,
Which still before him she remov'd away,
That nothing might his ready passage stay:
And ever when his feet encombred were,
Or gan to shrinke, or from the right to stray,
She held him fast, and firmely did upbeare,
As carefull Nourse her child from falling oft does reare.

36

Eftsoones unto an holy Hospitall,
That was fore by the way, she did him bring,
In which seven Bead-men[5] that had vowéd all
Their life to service of high heavens king
Did spend their dayes in doing godly thing:
There gates to all were open evermore,
That by the wearie way were traveiling,
And one sate wayting ever them before,
To call in commers-by, that needy were and pore.

37

The first of them that eldest was, and best,
Of all the house had charge and governement,
As Guardian and Steward of the rest:
His office was to give entertainement
And lodging, unto all that came, and went:
Not unto such, as could him feast againe,
And double quite, for that he on them spent
But such, as want of harbour did constraine:
Those for Gods sake his dewty was to entertaine.

38

The second was as Almner of the place,
His office was, the hungry for to feed,
And thirsty give to drinke, a worke of grace:
He feard not once him selfe to be in need,
Ne car'd to hoord for those, whom he did breede:
The grace of God he layd up still in store,
Which as a stocke he left unto his seede:
He had enough, what need him care for more?
And had he lesse, yet some he would give to the pore.

39

The third had of their wardrobe custodie,
In which were not rich tyres, nor garments gay,

[1]Symbolic of maternity.
[2]With proper courtesy.
[3]Well-doing. [4]Revealed.

[5]Men of prayer.

The plumes of pride, and wings of vanitie,
But clothes meet to keepe keene could away,
And naked nature seemely to aray;
With which bare wretched wights he dayly clad,
The images of God in earthly clay;
And if that no spare cloths to give he had,
His owne coate he would cut, and it distribute glad.

40

The fourth appointed by his office was,
Poore prisoners to relieve with gratious ayd,
And captives to redeeme with price of bras,
From Turkes and Sarazins, which them had stayd;
And though they faultie were, yet well he wayd,
That God to us forgiveth every howre
Much more then that, why they in bands were layd,
And he[1] that harrowd hell with heavie stowre,
The faultie soules from thence brought to his heavenly bowre.

41

The fift had charge sicke persons to attend,
And comfort those, in point of death which lay;
For them most needeth comfort in the end,
When sin, and hell, and death do most dismay
The feeble soule departing hence away.
All is but lost, that living we bestow,
If not well ended at our dying day.
O man have mind of that last bitter throw;
For as the tree does fall, so lyes it ever low.

42

The sixt had charge of them now being dead,
In seemely sort their corses to engrave,[2]
And deck with dainty flowres their bridall bed,
That to their heavenly spouse both sweet and brave
They might appeare, when he their soules shall save.
The wondrous workemanship of Gods owne mould,
Whose face he made, all beasts to feare, and gave
All in his hand, even dead we honour should.
Ah dearest God me graunt, I dead be not defould.

43

The seventh now after death and buriall done,
Had charge the tender Orphans of the dead
And widowes ayd,[3] least they should be undone:
In face of judgement he their right would plead,
Ne ought the powre of mighty men did dread
In their defence, nor would for gold or fee
Be wonne their rightfull causes downe to tread:
And when they stood in most necessitee,
He did supply their want, and gave them ever free.

44

There when the Elfin knight arrivéd was,
The first and chiefest of the seven, whose care
Was guests to welcome, towardes him did pas:
Where seeing *Mercie*, that his steps up bare,
And alwayes led, to her with reverence rare
He humbly louted in meeke lowlinesse,
And seemely welcome for her did prepare:
For of their order she was Patronesse,
Albe *Charissa* were their chiefest founderesse.

45

There she awhile him stayes, him selfe to rest,
That to the rest more able he might bee:
During which time, in every good behest
And godly worke of Almes and charitee
She him instructed with great industree;
Shortly therein so perfect he became,
That from the first unto the last degree,
His mortall life he learnéd had to frame
In holy righteousnesse, without rebuke or blame.

46

Thence forward by that painfull way they pas,
Forth to an hill, that was both steepe and hy;
On top whereof a sacred chappell was,
And eke a litle Hermitage thereby,
Wherein an aged holy man did lye,
That day and night said his devotion,
Ne other worldly busines did apply;
His name was heavenly *Contemplation;*
Of God and goodnesse was his meditation.

47

Great grace that old man to him given had;
For God he often saw from heavens hight,
All were his earthly eyen both blunt and bad,
And through great age had lost their kindly sight,
Yet wondrous quick and persant was his spright,
As Eagles eye, that can behold the Sunne:
That hill they scale with all their powre and might,

[1]Christ who, when he descended into hell, redeemed the souls of the patriarchs and of others.

[2]To bury

[3]And widows to aid.

That his frayle thighes nigh wearie and fordonne
Gan faile, but by her helpe the top at last he wonne.

48

There they do finde that godly agéd Sire,
With snowy lockes adowne his shoulders shed,
As hoarie frost with spangles doth attire
The mossy braunches of an Oke halfe ded.
Each bone might through his body well be red,
And every sinew seene through his long fast:
For nought he car'd[1] his carcas long unfed;
His mind was full of spirituall repast,
And pyn'd his flesh, to keepe his body low and chast.

49

Who when these two approching he aspide,
At their first presence grew agrievéd sore,
That forst him lay his heavenly thoughts aside;
And had he not that Dame respected more,
Whom highly he did reverence and adore,
He would not once have movéd for the knight.
They him saluted standing far afore;
Who well them greeting, humbly did requight,
And askéd, to what end they clomb that tedious height.

50

What end (quoth she) should cause us take such paine,
But that same end, which every living wight
Should make his marke, high heaven to attaine?
Is not from hence the way, that leadeth right
To that most glorious house, that glistreth bright
With burning starres, and everliving fire,
Whereof the keyes are to thy hand behight
By wise *Fidelia?* she doth thee require,
To shew it to this knight, according his desire.

51

Thrise happy man, said then the father grave,
Whose staggering steps thy steady hand doth lead,
And shewes the way, his sinfull soule to save.
Who better can the way to heaven aread,
Then thou thy selfe, that was both borne and bred
In heavenly throne, where thousand Angels shine?
Thou doest the prayers of the righteous sead
Present before the majestie divine,
And his avenging wrath to clemencie incline.

[1]Cared for.

52

Yet since thou bidst, thy pleasure shalbe donne.
Then come thou man of earth, and see the way,
That never yet was seene of Faeries sonne,
That never leads the traveiler astray,
But after labours long, and sad delay,
Brings them to joyous rest and endlesse blis.
But first thou must a season fast and pray,
Till from her bands the spright assoiléd is,
And have her strength recur'd from fraile infirmitis.

53

That done, he leads him to the highest Mount;
Such one, as that same mighty man of God,[2]
That bloud-red billowes like a walléd front
On either side disparted with his rod,
Till that his army dry-foot through them yod,
Dwelt fortie dayes upon; where writ in stone
With bloudy letters by the hand of God,
The bitter doome of death and balefull mone
He did receive, while flashing fire about him shone.

54

Or like that sacred hill,[3] whose head full hie,
Adornd with fruitfull Olives all arownd,
Is, as it were for endlesse memory
Of that deare Lord, who oft thereon was fownd,
For ever with a flowring girlond crownd:
Or like that pleasaunt Mount,[4] that is for ay
Through famous Poets verse each where renownd,
On which the thrise three learnéd Ladies[5] play
Their heavenly notes, and make full many a lovely lay.

55

From thence, far off he unto him did shew
A litle path, that was both steepe and long,
Which to a goodly Citie led his vew;
Whose wals and towres were builded high and strong
Of perle and precious stone, that earthly tong
Cannot describe, nor wit of man can tell;
Too high a ditty for my simple song;
The Citie of the great king hight it well,
Wherein eternall peace and happinesse doth dwell.

56

As he thereon stood gazing, he might see
The blesséd Angels to and fro descend
From highest heaven, in gladsome companee,
And with great joy into that Citie wend,

[2]Moses. [3]The Mount of Olives.
[4]Parnassus. [5]The nine muses.

As commonly[1] as friend does with his frend.
Whereat he wondred much, and gan enquere,
What stately building durst so high extend
Her loftie towres unto the starry sphere,
And what unknowen nation there empeopled were.

57

Faire knight (quoth he) *Hierusalem* that is,
The new *Hierusalem*, that God has built
For those to dwell in, that are chosen his,
His chosen people purg'd from sinfull guilt,
With piteous bloud, which cruelly was spilt
On curséd tree, of that unspotted lam,
That for the sinnes of all the world was kilt:
Now are they Saints all in that Citie sam,
More deare unto their God, then younglings to their dam.

58

Till now, said then the knight, I weenéd well,
That great *Cleopolis*, where I have beene,
In which that fairest *Faerie Queene* doth dwell
The fairest Citie was, that might be seene;
And that bright towre all built of christall cleene,
Panthea, seemd the brightest thing, that was:
But now by proofe all otherwise I weene;
For this great Citie that does far surpas,
And this bright Angels towre quite dims that towre of glas.

59

Most trew, then said the holy agéd man;
Yet is *Cleopolis* for earthly fame,
The fairest peece, that eye beholden can:
And well beseemes all knights of noble name,
That covet in th'immortall booke of fame
To be eternizéd, that same to haunt,
And doen their service to that soveraigne Dame,
That glorie does to them for guerdon graunt:
For she is heavenly borne, and heaven may justly vaunt.

60

And thou faire ymp, sprong out from English race,
How ever now accompted Elfins sonne,
Well worthy doest thy service for her grace,
To aide a virgin desolate foredonne.
But when thou famous victorie hast wonne,
And high emongst all knights hast hong thy shield,
Thenceforth the suit of earthly conquest shonne,
And wash thy hands from guilt of bloudy field:
For bloud can nought but sin, and wars but sorrowes yield.

[1]Sociably.

61

Then seeke this path, that I to thee presage,[2]
Which after all to heaven shall thee send;
Then peaceably thy painefull pilgrimage
To yonder same *Hierusalem* do bend,
Where is for thee ordaind a blesséd end:
For thou emongst those Saints, whom thou doest see,
Shalt be a Saint, and thine owne nations frend
And Patrone: thou Saint *George* shalt calléd bee,
Saint *George* of mery England, the signe of victoree.

62

Unworthy wretch (quoth he) of so great grace,
How dare I thinke such glory to attaine?
These that have it attaind, were in like cace
(Quoth he) as wretched, and liv'd in like paine.
But deeds of armes must I at last be faine,
And Ladies love to leave so dearely bought?
What need of armes, where peace doth ay remaine,
(Said he) and battailes none are to be fought?
As for loose loves are vaine, and vanish into nought.

63

O let me not (quoth he) then turne againe
Backe to the world, whose joyes so fruitlesse are;
But let me here for aye in peace remaine,
Or streight way on that last long voyage fare,
That nothing may my present hope empare.
That may not be (said he) ne maist thou yit
Forgo that royall maides bequeathéd care,
Who did her cause into thy hand commit,
Till from her curséd foe thou have her freely quit.

64

Then shall I soone, (quoth he) so God me grace,
Abet that virgins cause disconsolate,
And shortly backe returne unto this place,
To walke this way in Pilgrims poore estate.
But now aread, old father, why of late
Didst thou behight me borne of English blood,
Whom all a Faeries sonne doen nominate?
That word shall I (said he) avouchen good,
Sith to thee is unknowne the cradle of thy brood.

65

For well I wote, thou springst from ancient race
Of *Saxon* kings, that have with mightie hand
And many bloudie battailes fought in place
High reard their royall throne in *Britane* land,

[2]Point out.

And vanquisht them, unable to withstand:
From thence a Faerie thee unweeting reft,
There as thou slepst in tender swadling band,
And her base Elfin brood there for thee left.
Such men do Chaungelings call, so chaunged by Faeries theft.

66

Thence she thee brought into this Faerie lond,
And in an heapéd furrow did thee hyde,
Where thee a Ploughman all unweeting fond,
As he his toylesome teme that way did guyde,
And brought thee up in ploughmans state to byde,
Whereof *Georgos*[1] he thee gave to name;
Till prickt with courage, and thy forces pryde,
To Faery court thou cam'st to seeke for fame,
And prove thy puissaunt armes, as seemes thee best became.

67

O holy Sire (quoth he) how shall I quight
The many favours I with thee have found,
That hast my name and nation red aright,
And taught the way that does to heaven bound?
This said, adowne he lookéd to the ground,
To have returnd, but dazéd were his eyne,
Through passing brightnesse, which did quite confound
His feeble sence, and too exceeding shyne.
So darke are earthly things compard to things divine.

68

At last whenas himselfe he gan to find,
To *Una* back he cast him to retire;
Who him awaited still with pensive mind.
Great thankes and goodly meed to that good syre,
He thence departing gave for his paines hyre.[2]
So came to *Una*, who him joyd to see,
And after little rest, gan him desire,
Of her adventure mindfull for to bee.
So leave they take of *Cœlia*, and her daughters three.

CANTO XI

The knight with that old Dragon fights
two dayes incessantly:
The third him overthrowes, and gayns
most glorious victory.

1

High time now gan it wex for *Una faire*,
To thinke of those her captive Parents deare,
And their forwasted kingdome to repaire:
Whereto whenas they now approchéd neare,
With hartie words her knight she gan to cheare,
And in her modest manner thus bespake;
Deare knight, as deare, as ever knight was deare,
That all these sorrowes suffer for my sake,
High heaven behold the tedious toyle, ye for me take.

2

Now are we come unto my native soyle,
And to the place, where all our perils dwell;
Here haunts that feend, and does his dayly spoyle,
Therefore henceforth be at your keeping well,[3]
And ever ready for your foeman fell.
The sparke of noble courage now awake,
And strive your excellent selfe to excell;
That shall ye evermore renowméd make,
Above all knights on earth, that batteill undertake.

3

And pointing forth, lo yonder is (said she)
The brasen towre in which my parents deare
For dread of that huge feend emprisond be,
Whom I from far see on the walls appeare,
Whose sight my feeble soule doth greatly cheare:
And on the top of all I do espye
The watchman wayting tydings glad to heare,
That O my parents might I happily
Unto you bring, to ease you of your misery.

4

With that they heard a roaring hideous sound,
That all the ayre with terrour filléd wide,
And seemd uneath[4] to shake the stedfast ground.
Eftsoones that dreadfull Dragon they espide,
Where stretcht he lay upon the sunny side,
Of a great hill, himselfe like a great hill.
But all so soone, as he from far descride
Those glistring armes, that heaven with light did fill,
He rousd himselfe full blith, and hastned them untill.

5

Then bad the knight his Lady yede aloofe,
And to an hill her selfe withdraw aside,
From whence she might behold that battailles proof
And eke be safe from daunger far descryde:

[1] Greek γεωργός, meaning husbandman.
[2] As a reward for his trouble.
[3] Be carefully on your guard.
[4] Almost.

She him obayd, and turnd a little wyde.
Now O thou sacred Muse,[1] most learnéd Dame,
Faire ympe of *Phœbus*, and his agéd bride,[2]
The Nourse of time, and everlasting fame,
That warlike hands ennoblest with immortall name;

6

O gently come into my feeble brest,
Come gently, but not with that mighty rage,
Wherewith the martiall troupes thou doest infest,
And harts of great Heroës doest enrage,
That nought their kindled courage may aswage,
Soone as thy dreadfull trompe begins to sownd;
The God of warre with his fiers equipage
Thou doest awake, sleepe never he so sownd,
And fearéd nations doest with horrour sterne astownd.

7

Faire Goddesse lay that furious fit aside,
Till I of warres and bloudy *Mars* do sing,
And Briton fields with Sarazin bloud bedyde,
Twixt that great faery Queene and Paynim king,[3]
That with their horrour heaven and earth did ring,
A worke of labour long, and endlesse prayse:
But now a while let downe that haughtie string,
And to my tunes thy second tenor rayse,
That I this man of God his godly armes may blaze.

8

By this the dreadfull Beast drew nigh to hand,
Halfe flying, and halfe footing in his hast,
That with his largenesse measuréd much land,
And made wide shadow under his huge wast;
As mountaine doth the valley overcast.
Approching nigh, he rearéd high afore
His body monstrous, horrible, and vast,
Which to increase his wondrous greatnesse more,
Was swolne with wrath, and poyson, and with bloudy gore.

9

And over, all with brasen scales was armd,
Like plated coate of steele, so couchéd neare,[4]
That nought mote perce, ne might his corse be harmd
With dint of sword, nor push of pointed speare;
Which as an Eagle, seeing pray appeare,
His aery plumes doth rouze, full rudely dight,
So shakéd he, that horrour was to heare,
For as the clashing of an Armour bright,
Such noyse his rouzéd scales did send unto the knight.

10

His flaggy wings when forth he did display,
Were like two sayles, in which the hollow wynd
Is gathered full, and worketh speedy way:
And eke the pennes, that did his pineons bynd,
Were like mayne-yards, with flying canvas lynd,
With which whenas him list the ayre to beat,
And there by force unwonted passage find,
The cloudes before him fled for terrour great,
And all the heavens stood still amazéd with his threat.

11

His huge long tayle wound up in hundred foldes,
Does overspred his long bras-scaly backe,
Whose wreathéd boughts when ever he unfoldes,
And thicke entangled knots adown does slacke,
Bespotted all with shields of red and blacke,
It sweepeth all the land behind him farre,
And of three furlongs does but litle lacke;
And at the point two stings in-fixéd arre,
Both deadly sharpe, that sharpest steele exceeden farre.

12

But stings and sharpest steele did far exceed
The sharpnesse of his cruell rending clawes;
Dead was it sure, as sure as death in deed,
What ever thing does touch his ravenous pawes,
Or what within his reach he ever drawes.
But his most hideous head my toung to tell,
Does tremble: for his deepe devouring jawes
Wide gapéd, like the griesly mouth of hell,
Through which into his darke abisse all ravin fell.

13

And that more wondrous was, in either jaw
Three ranckes of yron teeth enraungéd were,
In which yet trickling bloud and gobbets raw
Of late devouréd bodies did appeare,
That sight thereof bred cold congealéd feare:
Which to increase, and all atonce to kill,
A cloud of smoothering smoke and sulphur seare

[1] Calliope (but see note above, Introd. Stanzas, 2).

[2] The muses were the children of Apollo and Mnemosyne, or Memory.

[3] Spenser here refers to a later part of the *Faerie Queene* which was never written.

[4] So closely placed.

Out of his stinking gorge forth steemé d still,
That all the ayre about with smoke and stench
did fill.

14

His blazing eyes, like two bright shining
shields,
Did burne with wrath, and sparkled living
fyre;
As two broad Beacons, set in open fields,
Send forth their flames farre off to every shyre,
And warning give, that enemies conspyre,
With fire and sword the region to invade;
So flam'd his eyne with rage and rancorous
yre:
But farre within, as in a hollow glade,
Those glaring lampes were set, that made a
dreadfull shade.

15

So dreadfully he towards him did pas,
Forelifting up aloft his speckled brest,
And often bounding on the brusé d gras,
As for great joyance of his newcome guest.
Eftsoones he gan advance his haughtie crest,
As chauffé d Bore his bristles doth upreare,
And shoke his scales to battell readie drest;
That made the *Redcrosse* knight nigh quake
for feare,
As bidding bold defiance to his foeman neare.

16

The knight gan fairely couch his steadie
speare,
And fiercely ran at him with rigorous might:
The pointed steele arriving rudely theare,
His harder hide would neither perce, nor bight,
But glauncing by forth passé d forward right;
Yet sore amové d with so puissant push,
The wrathfull beast about him turné d light,
And him so rudely passing by, did brush
With his long tayle, that horse and man to
ground did rush.

17

Both horse and man up lightly rose againe,
And fresh encounter towards him addrest:
But th'idle stroke yet backe recoyld in vaine,
And found no place his deadly point to rest.
Exceeding rage enflam'd the furious beast,
To be avengé d of so great despight;
For never felt his imperceable brest
So wondrous force, from hand of living wight;
Yet had he prov'd the powre of many a
puissant knight.

18

Then with his waving wings displayé d wyde,
Himselfe up high he lifted from the ground,
And with strong flight did forcibly divide
The yielding aire, which nigh too feeble found
Her flitting partes, and element unsound,
To beare so great a weight: he cutting way
With his broad sayles, about him soaré d
round:
At last low stouping with unweldie sway,
Snatcht up both horse and man, to beare
them quite away.

19

Long he them bore above the subject plaine,[1]
So farre as Ewghen bow a shaft may send,
Till struggling strong did him at last con-
straine,
To let them downe before his flighté s end:
As hagard hauke presuming to contend
With hardie fowle, above his hable might,[2]
His wearie pounces all in vaine doth spend,
To trusse the pray too heavie for his flight;
Which comming downe to ground, does free
it selfe by fight.

20

He so disseizé d of his gryping grosse,[3]
The knight his thrillant speare againe assayd
In his bras-plated body to embosse,
And three mens strength unto the stroke he
layd;
Wherewith the stiffe beame quaké d, as af-
frayd,
And glauncing from his scaly necke, did glyde
Close under his left wing, then broad displayd.
The percing steele there wrought a wound full
wyde,
That with the uncouth smart the Monster
lowdly cryde.

21

He cryde, as raging seas are wont to rore,
When wintry storme his wrathfull wreck does
threat,
The rolling billowes beat the ragged shore,
As they the earth would shoulder from her
seat,
And greedie gulfe does gape, as he would eat
His neighbour element in his revenge:
Then gin the blustring brethren boldly threat,
To move the world from off his stedfast henge,
And boystrous battell make, each other to
avenge.[4]

22

The steely head stucke fast still in his flesh,
Till with his cruell clawes he snatcht the wood,
And quite asunder broke. Forth flowé d fresh
A gushing river of blacke goarie blood,

[1] *I.e.*, the plain lying below.
[2] Above the capacity of his ability.
[3] So dispossessed of his awkward handful
[4] To take vengeance on each other.

That drownéd all the land, whereon he stood;
The streame thereof would drive a watermill.
Trebly augmented was his furious mood
With bitter sense of his deepe rooted ill,
That flames of fire he threw forth from his
large nosethrill.

23

His hideous tayle then hurléd he about,
And therewith all enwrapt the nimble thyes
Of his froth-fomy steed, whose courage stout
Striving to loose the knot, that fast him tyes,
Himselfe in streighter bandes too rash im-
plyes,
That to the ground he is perforce constraynd
To throw his rider: who can quickly ryse
From off the earth, with durty bloud distaynd,
For that reprochfull fall right fowly he dis-
daynd.

24

And fiercely tooke his trenchand blade in
hand,
With which he stroke so furious and so fell,
That nothing seemd the puissance could with-
stand:
Upon his crest the hardned yron fell,
But his more hardned crest was armd so well,
That deeper dint therein it would not make;
Yet so extremely did the buffe him quell,
That from thenceforth he shund the like to
take,
But when he saw them come, he did them still
forsake.

25

The knight was wrath to see his stroke be-
guyld,
And smote againe with more outrageous
might;
But backe againe the sparckling steele recoyld,
And left not any marke, where it did light;
As if in Adamant rocke it had bene pight.
The beast impatient of his smarting wound,
And of so fierce and forcible despight,
Thought with his wings to stye above the
ground;
But his late wounded wing unserviceable
found.

26

Then full of griefe and anguish vehement,
He lowdly brayd, that like was never heard,
And from his wide devouring oven sent
A flake of fire, that flashing in his beard,
Him all amazd, and almost made affeard:
The scorching flame sore swingéd all his face,
And through his armour all his bodie seard,
That he could not endure so cruell cace,
But thought his armes to leave, and helmet
to unlace.

27

Now that great Champion of the antique
world,[1]
Whom famous Poetes verse so much doth
daunt,
And hath for twelve huge labours high extold,
So many furies and sharpe fits did haunt,
When him the poysoned garment did enchaunt
With *Centaures* bloud, and bloudie verses
charm'd,
As did this knight twelve thousand dolours
daunt,
Whom fyrie steele now burnt, that earst him
arm'd,
That erst him goodly arm'd, now most of all
him harm'd.

28

Faint, wearie, sore, emboyléd, grievéd, brent
With heat, toyle, wounds, armes, smart, and
inward fire
That never man such mischiefes did torment;
Death better were, death did he oft desire,
But death will never come, when needes re-
quire.
Whom so dismayd when that his foe beheld,
He cast to suffer him no more respire,
But gan his sturdie sterne about to weld,
And him so strongly stroke, that to the
ground him feld.

29

It fortunéd (as faire it then befell)
Behind his backe unweeting, where he stood,
Of auncient time there was a springing well,
From which fast trickled forth a silver flood,
Full of great vertues, and for med'cine good.
Whylome, before that curséd Dragon got
That happie land, and all with innocent blood
Defyld those sacred waves, it rightly hot
The well of life,[2] ne yet his vertues had forgot.

30

For unto life the dead it could restore,
And guilt of sinfull crimes cleane wash away;
Those that with sicknesse were infected sore,
It could recure, and agéd long decay
Renew, as one were borne that very day.
Both *Silo*[3] this, and *Jordan*[4] did excell,
And th'English *Bath*, and eke the german
Spau,
Ne can *Cephise*,[5] nor *Hebrus*[6] match this well:
Into the same the knight backe overthrowen,
fell.

---

[1]Hercules.

[2]*Cf.* Revelation, xxii, 1. The well represents divine grace.

[3]The pool of Siloam (St. John, ix, 7).

[4]Naaman was healed in the Jordan (2 Kings, v, 14).

[5]The river Cephisus, near Athens.

[6]A river in Thrace.

31

Now gan the golden *Phœbus* for to steepe
His fierie face in billowes of the west,
And his faint steedes watred in Ocean deepe,
Whiles from their journall labours they did rest,
When that infernall Monster, having kest
His wearie foe into that living well,
Can high advance his broad discoloured brest,
Above his wonted pitch, with countenance fell,
And clapt his yron wings, as victor he did dwell.

32

Which when his pensive Ladie saw from farre,
Great woe and sorrow did her soule assay,
As weening that the sad end of the warre,
And gan to highest God entirely pray,
That fearéd chance from her to turne away;
With folded hands and knees full lowly bent
All night she watcht, ne once adowne would lay
Her daintie limbs in her sad dreriment,
But praying still did wake, and waking did lament.

33

The morrow next gan early to appeare,
That Titan rose to runne his daily race;
But early ere the morrow next gan reare
Out of the sea faire *Titans* deawy face,
Up rose the gentle virgin from her place,
And lookéd all about, if she might spy
Her lovéd knight to move his manly pace:
For she had great doubt of his saféty,
Since late she saw him fall before his enemy.

34

At last she saw, where he upstarted brave
Out of the well, wherein he drenchéd lay;
As Eagle fresh out of the Ocean wave,
Where he hath left his plumes all hoary gray,
And deckt himselfe with feathers youthly gay,[1]
Like Eyas hauke up mounts unto the skies,
His newly budded pineons to assay,
And marveiles at himselfe, still as he flies:
So new this new-borne knight to battell new did rise.

35

Whom when the damnéd feend so fresh did spy,
No wonder if he wondred at the sight,
And doubted, whether his late enemy
It were, or other new supplied knight.
He, now to prove his late renewéd might,
High brandishing his bright deaw-burning[2] blade,
Upon his crested scalpe so sore did smite,
That to the scull a yawning wound it made:
The deadly dint his dulléd senses all dismaid.

36

I wote not, whether the revenging steele
Were hardned with that holy water dew,
Wherein he fell, or sharper edge did feele,
Or his baptizéd hands now greater grew;
Or other secret vertue did ensew;
Else never could the force of fleshly arme,
Ne molten mettall[3] in his bloud embrew:
For till that stownd could never wight him harme,
By subtilty, nor slight, nor might, nor mighty charme.

37

The cruell wound enragéd him so sore,
That loud he yelléd for exceeding paine;
As hundred ramping Lyons seem'd to rore,
Whom ravenous hunger did thereto constraine:
Then gan he tosse aloft his stretchéd traine,
And therewith scourge the buxome aire so sore,
That to his force to yeelden it was faine;
Ne ought his sturdie strokes might stand afore,
That high trees overthrew, and rocks in peeces tore.

38

The same advauncing high above his head,
With sharpe intended sting so rude him smot,
That to the earth him drove, as stricken dead,
Ne living wight would have him life behot:
The mortall sting his angry needle shot
Quite through his shield, and in his shoulder seasd,
Where fast it stucke, ne would there out be got:
The griefe thereof him wondrous sore diseasd,
Ne might his rankling paine with patience be appeasd.

39

But yet more mindfull of his honour deare,
Then of the grievous smart, which him did wring,
From loathéd soile he can him lightly reare,
And strove to loose the farre infixéd sting:
Which when in vaine he tryde with struggeling,
Inflam'd with wrath, his raging blade he heft,
And stroke so strongly, that the knotty string
Of his huge taile he quite asunder cleft,
Five joynts thereof he hewd, and but the stump him left.

[1]The tradition that the eagle could renew its youth is an old one. *Cf.* Psalms, ciii, 5.

[2]Shining with the dew of the well.

[3]Nor any metal that ever was melted.

40

Hart cannot thinke, what outrage, and what cryes,
With foule enfouldred smoake and flashing fire,
The hell-bred beast threw forth unto the skyes,
That all was coveréd with darknesse dire:
Then fraught with rancour, and engorgéd ire,
He cast at once him to avenge for all,
And gathering up himselfe out of the mire,
With his uneven wings did fiercely fall,
Upon his sunne-bright shield, and gript it fast withall.

41

Much was the man encombred with his hold,
In feare to lose his weapon in his paw,
Ne wist yet, how his talants to unfold;
Nor harder was from *Cerberus* greedie jaw
To plucke a bone, then from his cruell claw
To reave by strength the gripéd gage away:
Thrise he assayd it from his foot to draw,
And thrise in vaine to draw it did assay,
It booted nought to thinke, to robbe him of his pray.

42

Tho when he saw no power might prevaile,
His trustie sword he cald to his last aid,
Wherewith he fiercely did his foe assaile,
And double blowes about him stoutly laid,
That glauncing fire out of the yron plaid;
As sparckles from the Andvile use to fly,
When heavie hammers on the wedge are swaid;
Therewith at last he forst him to unty[1]
One of his grasping feete, him to defend thereby.

43

The other foot, fast fixéd on his shield
Whenas no strength, nor stroks mote him constraine
To loose, ne yet the warlike pledge to yield,
He smot thereat with all his might and maine,
That nought so wondrous puissance might sustaine;
Upon the joynt the lucky steele did light,
And made such way, that hewd it quite in twaine;
The paw yet misséd not his minisht might,
But hong still on the shield, as it at first was pight.

44

For griefe thereof, and divelish despight,
From his infernall fournace forth he threw
Huge flames, that dimméd all the heavens light,
Enrold in duskish smoke and brimstone blew;
As burning *Aetna* from his boyling stew
Doth belch out flames, and rockes in peeces broke,
And ragged ribs of mountaines molten new,
Enwrapt in coleblacke clouds and filthy smoke,
That all the land with stench, and heaven with horror choke.

45

The heate whereof, and harmefull pestilence
So sore him noyd, that forst him to retire
A little backward for his best defence,
To save his bodie from the scorching fire,
Which he from hellish entrailes did expire.
It chaunst (eternall God that chaunce did guide)
As he recoyléd backward, in the mire
His nigh forwearied feeble feet did slide,
And downe he fell, with dread of shame sore terrifide.

46

There grew a goodly tree him faire beside,
Loaden with fruit and apples rosie red,
As they in pure vermilion had beene dide,
Whereof great vertues over all were red:
For happie life to all, which thereon fed,
And life eke everlasting did befall:
Great God it planted in that blesséd sted
With his almightie hand, and did it call
The tree of life, the crime of our first fathers fall.[2]

47

In all the world like was not to be found,
Save in that soile, where all good things did grow,
And freely sprong out of the fruitfull ground,
As incorrupted Nature did them sow,
Till that dread Dragon all did overthrow.
Another like faire tree eke grew thereby,
Whereof who so did eat, eftsoones did know
Both good and ill:[3] O mornefull memory:
That tree through one mans fault hath doen us all to dy.

48

From that first tree forth flowd, as from a well,
A trickling streame of Balme,[4] most soveraine
And daintie deare,[5] which on the ground still fell,
And overflowéd all the fertill plaine,

[1]To loosen.

[2]The cause of reproach to Adam. *Cf.* Genesis, iii, 22–23.

[3]*Cf.* Genesis, ii, 9.

[4]Suggested by Revelation, xxii, 2.

[5]Very precious.

As it had deawéd bene with timely raine:
Life and long health that gratious ointment gave,
And deadly woundes could heale and reare againe
The senselesse corse appointed for the grave.
Into that same he fell: which did from death him save.

49

For nigh thereto the ever damnéd beast
Durst not approch, for he was deadly made,
And all that life preservéd, did detest:
Yet he it oft adventur'd to invade.
By this the drooping day-light gan to fade,
And yeeld his roome to sad succeeding night,
Who with her sable mantle gan to shade
The face of earth, and wayes of living wight,
And high her burning torch[1] set up in heaven bright.

50

When gentle *Una* saw the second fall
Of her deare knight, who wearie of long fight,
And faint through losse of bloud, mov'd not at all,
But lay as in a dreame of deepe delight,
Besmeard with pretious Balme, whose vertuous might
Did heale his wounds, and scorching heat alay,
Againe she stricken was with sore affright,
And for his safetie gan devoutly pray;
And watch the noyous night, and wait for joyous day.

51

The joyous day gan early to appeare,
And faire *Aurora* from the deawy bed
Of aged *Tithone* gan herselfe to reare,
With rosie cheekes, for shame as blushing red;
Her golden lockes for haste were loosely shed
About her eares, when *Una* her did marke
Clymbe to her charet, all with flowers spred;
From heaven high to chase the chearelesse darke,
With merry note her loud salutes the mounting larke.

52

Then freshly up arose the doughtie knight,
All healéd of his hurts and woundés wide,
And did himselfe to battell readie dight;
Whose early foe awaiting him beside
To have devourd, so soone as day he spyde,
When now he saw himselfe so freshly reare,
As if late fight had nought him damnifyde,
He woxe dismayd, and gan his fate to feare;
Nathlesse with wonted rage he him advauncéd neare.

[1]The moon.

53

And in his first encounter, gaping wide,
He thought attonce him to have swallowd quight,
And rusht upon him with outragious pride;
Who him r'encountring fierce, as hauke in flight,
Perforce rebutted backe. The weapon bright
Taking advantage of his open jaw,
Ran through his mouth with so importune might,
That deepe emperst his darksome hollow maw,
And back retyrd,[2] his life bloud forth with all did draw.

54

So downe he fell, and forth his life did breath,
That vanisht into smoke and cloudés swift;
So downe he fell, that th'earth him underneath
Did grone, as feeble so great load to lift;
So downe he fell, as an huge rockie clift,
Whose false foundation waves have washt away,
With dreadfull poyse is from the mayneland rift,
And rolling downe, great *Neptune* doth dismay;
So downe he fell, and like an heapéd mountaine lay.

55

The knight himselfe even trembled at his fall,
So huge and horrible a masse it seem'd;
And his deare Ladie, that beheld it all,
Durst not approch for dread, which she misdeem'd,[3]
But yet at last, when as the direfull feend
She saw not stirre, off-shaking vaine affright,
She nigher drew, and saw that joyous end:
Then God she praysd, and thankt her faithfull knight,
That had atchiev'd so great a conquest by his might.

CANTO XII

Faire Una to the Redcrosse knight
betrouthéd is with joy:
Though false Duessa it to barre
her false sleights doe imploy.

1

BEHOLD I see the haven nigh at hand,
To which I meane my wearie course to bend;
Vere the maine shete, and beare up with the land,
The which afore is fairely to be kend,

[2]When it was withdrawn.
[3]In which she was mistaken.

And seemeth safe from stormes, that may
offend;
There this faire virgin wearie of her way
Must landed be, now at her journeyes end:
There eke my feeble barke a while may stay,
Till merry wind and weather call her thence
away.

2

Scarsely had *Phœbus* in the glooming East
Yet harnesséd his firie-footed teeme,
Ne reard above the earth his flaming creast,
When the last deadly smoke aloft did steeme,
That signe of last outbreathéd life did seeme,
Unto the watchman on the castle wall;
Who thereby dead that balefull Beast did
deeme,
And to his Lord and Ladie lowd can call,
To tell, how he had seene the Dragons fatall
fall.

3

Uprose with hastie joy, and feeble speed
That agéd Sire, the Lord of all that land,
And lookéd forth, to weet, if true indeede
Those tydings were, as he did understand,
Which whenas true by tryall he out fond,
He bad to open wyde his brazen gate,
Which long time had bene shut, and out of
hond
Proclayméd joy and peace through all his
state;
For dead now was their foe, which them for-
rayéd late.

4

Then gan triumphant Trompets sound on hie,
That sent to heaven the ecchoéd report
Of their new joy, and happie victorie
Gainst him, that had them long opprest with
tort,
And fast imprisonéd in siegéd fort.
Then all the people, as in solemne feast,
To him assembled with one full consort,
Rejoycing at the fall of that great beast,
From whose eternall bondage now they were
releast.

5

Forth came that auncient Lord and agéd
Queene,
Arayd in antique robes downe to the ground,
And sad habiliments right well beseene;[1]
A noble crew about them waited round
Of sage and sober Peres, all gravely gownd;
Whom farre before did march a goodly band
Of tall young men, all hable armes to sownd,[2]

[1]Sober garments which well became them.

[2]Able to bear arms.

But now they laurell braunches bore in hand;
Glad signe of victorie and peace in all their
land.

6

Unto that doughtie Conquerour they came,
And him before themselves prostrating low,
Their Lord and Patrone loud did him pro-
clame,
And at his feet their laurell boughes did throw.
Soone after them all dauncing on a row
The comely virgins came, with girlands dight,
As fresh as flowres in medow greene do grow,
When morning deaw upon their leaves doth
light:
And in their hands sweet Timbrels all upheld
on hight.

7

And them before, the fry of children young
Their wanton sports and childish mirth did
play,
And to the Maydens sounding tymbrels sung
In well attunéd notes, a joyous lay,
And made delightfull musicke all the way,
Untill they came, where that faire virgin stood;
As faire *Diana* in fresh sommers day,
Beholds her Nymphes, enraung'd in shadie
wood,
Some wrestle, some do run, some bathe in
christall flood.

8

So she beheld those maydens meriment
With chearefull vew; who when to her they
came,
Themselves to ground with gratious hum-
blesse bent,
And her ador'd by honorable name,
Lifting to heaven her everlasting fame:
Then on her head they set a girland greene,
And crownéd her twixt earnest and twixt
game;
Who in her selfe-resemblance well beseene,[3]
Did seeme such, as she was, a goodly maiden
Queene.

9

And after, all the raskall many ran,
Heapéd together in rude rablement,
To see the face of that victorious man:
Whom all admiréd, as from heaven sent,
And gazd upon with gaping wonderment.
But when they came, where that dead Dragon
lay,
Stretcht on the ground in monstrous large
extent,
The sight with idle feare did them dismay,
Ne durst approch him nigh, to touch, or once
assay.

[3]*I.e.*, she now looked like her real self.

10

Some feard, and fled; some feard and well it faynd;
One that would wiser seeme, then all the rest,
Warnd him not touch, for yet perhaps remaynd
Some lingring life within his hollow brest,
Or in his wombe might lurke some hidden nest
Of many Dragonets, his fruitfull seed;
Another said, that in his eyes did rest
Yet sparckling fire, and bad thereof take heed;
Another said, he saw him move his eyes indeed.

11

One mother, when as her foolehardie chyld
Did come too neare, and with his talants play,
Halfe dead through feare, her litle babe revyld,
And to her gossips gan in counsell say;
How can I tell, but that his talants may
Yet scratch my sonne, or rend his tender hand?
So diversly themselves in vaine they fray;
Whiles some more bold, to measure him nigh stand,
To prove how many acres he did spread of land.

12

Thus flockéd all the folke him round about,
The whiles that hoarie king, with all his traine,
Being arrivéd, where that champion stout
After his foes defeasance did remaine,
Him goodly greetes, and faire does entertaine,
With princely gifts of yvorie and gold,
And thousand thankes him yeelds for all his paine.
Then when his daughter deare he does behold,
Her dearely doth imbrace, and kisseth manifold.

13

And after to his Pallace he them brings,
With shaumes, and trompets, and with Clarions sweet;
And all the way the joyous people sings,
And with their garments strowes the pavéd street:
Whence mounting up, they find purveyance meet
Of all, that royall Princes court became,
And all the floore was underneath their feet
Bespred with costly scarlot of great name,[1]
On which they lowly sit, and fitting purpose frame.

14

What needs me tell their feast and goodly guize,
In which was nothing riotous nor vaine?
What needs of daintie dishes to devize,
Of comely services, or courtly trayne?
My narrow leaves cannot in them containe
The large discourse of royall Princes state.
Yet was their manner then but bare and plaine:
For th'antique world excesse and pride did hate;
Such proud luxurious pompe is swollen up but late.

15

Then when with meates and drinkes of every kinde
Their fervent appetites they quenchéd had,
That auncient Lord gan fit occasion finde,
Of straunge adventures, and of perils sad,
Which in his travell him befallen had,
For to demaund of his renowméd guest:
Who then with utt'rance grave, and count'nance sad,
From point to point, as is before exprest,
Discourst his voyage long, according his request.

16

Great pleasure mixt with pittifull regard,
That godly King and Queene did passionate,
Whiles they his pittifull adventures heard,
That oft they did lament his lucklesse state,
And often blame the too importune fate,
That heapd on him so many wrathfull wreakes:
For never gentle knight, as he of late,
So tosséd was in fortunes cruell freakes;
And all the while salt teares bedeawd the hearers cheaks.

17

Then said the royall Pere in sober wise;
Deare Sonne, great beene the evils, which ye bore
From first to last in your late enterprise,
That I note, whether prayse, or pitty more:
For never living man, I weene, so sore
In sea of deadly daungers was distrest;
But since now safe ye seiséd have the shore,
And well arrivéd are (high God be blest),
Let us devize of ease and everlasting rest.

18

Ah dearest Lord, said then that doughty knight,
Of ease or rest I may not yet devize;
For by the faith, which I to armes have plight,
I bounden am streight after this emprize,
As that your daughter can ye well advize,
Backe to returne to that great Faerie Queene,
And her to serve six yeares in warlike wize,

[1] Of great value.

Gainst that proud Paynim king, that workes her teene:
Therefore I ought crave pardon, till I there have beene.

19

Unhappie falles that hard necessitie,
(Quoth he) the troubler of my happie peace,
And vowéd foe of my felicitie;
Ne I against the same can justly preace:
But since that band ye cannot now release,
Nor doen undo (for vowes may not be vaine);
Soone as the terme of those six yeares shall cease,
Ye then shall hither backe returne againe,
The marriage to accomplish vowd betwixt you twain.

20

Which for my part I covet to performe,
In sort as through the world I did proclame,
That who so kild that monster most deforme,
And him in hardy battaile overcame,
Should have mine onely daughter to his Dame,
And of my kingdome heire apparaunt bee:
Therefore since now to thee perteines the same,
By dew desert of noble chevalree,
Both daughter and eke kingdome, lo I yield to thee.

21

Then forth he calléd that his daughter faire,
The fairest *Un'* his onely daughter deare,
His onely daughter, and his onely heyre;
Who forth proceeding with sad sober cheare,
As bright as doth the morning starre appeare
Out of the East, with flaming lockes bedight,
To tell that dawning day is drawing neare,
And to the world does bring long wishéd light;
So faire and fresh that Lady shewd her selfe in sight.

22

So faire and fresh, as freshest flowre in May;
For she had layd her mournefull stole aside,
And widow-like sad wimple throwne away,
Wherewith her heavenly beautie she did hide,
Whiles on her wearie journey she did ride;
And on her now a garment she did weare,
All lilly white, withoutten spot, or pride,
That seemd like silke and silver woven neare,
But neither silke nor silver therein did appeare.

23

The blazing brightnesse of her beauties beame,
And glorious light of her sunshyny face
To tell, were as to strive against the streame.
My ragged rimes are all too rude and bace,
Her heavenly lineaments for to enchace.
Ne wonder; for her owne deare lovéd knight,
All were she dayly with himselfe in place,
Did wonder much at her celestiall sight:
Oft had he seene her faire, but never so faire dight.

24

So fairely dight, when she in presence came,
She to her Sire made humble reverence,
And bowéd low, that her right well became,
And added grace unto her excellence:
Who with great wisedome, and grave eloquence
Thus gan to say. But eare he thus had said,
With flying speede, and seeming great pretence,
Came running in, much like a man dismaid,
A Messenger with letters, which his message said.

25

All in the open hall amazéd stood,
At suddeinnesse of that unwarie[1] sight,
And wondred at his breathlesse hastie mood.
But he for nought would stay his passage right,[2]
Till fast[3] before the king he did alight;
Where falling flat, great humblesse he did make,
And kist the ground, whereon his foot was pight;
Then to his hands that writ he did betake,
Which he disclosing, red thus, as the paper spake.

26

To thee, most mighty king of *Eden* faire,
Her greeting sends in these sad lines addrest,
The wofull daughter, and forsaken heire
Of that great Emperour of all the West;[4]
And bids thee be advizéd for the best,
Ere thou thy daughter linck in holy band
Of wedlocke to that new unknowen guest:
For he already plighted his right hand
Unto another love, and to another land.

27

To me sad mayd, or rather widow sad,
He was affiauncéd long time before,
And sacred pledges he both gave, and had,
False erraunt knight, infamous, and forswore:
Witnesse the burning Altars, which he swore,
And guiltie heavens of[5] his bold perjury,
Which though he hath polluted oft of yore,
Yet I to them for judgement just do fly,
And them conjure t'avenge this shamefull injury.

[1]Unexpected. [2]His passage straight ahead.
[3]Close. [4]The pope. [5]Heavens infected by.

28

Therefore since mine he is, or free or bond,
Or false or trew, or living or else dead,
Withhold, O soveraine Prince, your hasty hond
From knitting league with him, I you aread;
Ne weene my right with strength adowne to tread,
Through weakenesse of my widowhed, or woe:
For truth is strong, her rightfull cause to plead,
And shall find friends, if need requireth soe,
So bids thee well to fare, Thy neither friend, nor foe, *Fidessa.*

29

When he these bitter byting words had red,
The tydings straunge did him abashéd make,
That still he sate long time astonishéd
As in great muse, ne word to creature spake.
At last his solemne silence thus he brake,
With doubtfull eyes fast fixéd on his guest;
Redoubted knight, that for mine onely sake
Thy life and honour late adventurest,
Let nought be hid from me, that ought to be exprest.

30

What meane these bloudy vowes, and idle threats,
Throwne out from womanish impatient mind?
What heavens? what altars? what enragéd heates
Here heapéd up with termes of love unkind,
My conscience cleare with guilty bands would bind?
High God be witnesse, that I guiltlesse ame.
But if your selfe, Sir knight, ye faultie find,
Or wrappéd be in loves of former Dame,
With crime do not it cover, but disclose the same.

31

To whom the *Redcrosse* knight this answere sent,
My Lord, my King, be nought hereat dismayd,
Till well ye wote by grave intendiment,
What woman, and wherefore doth me upbrayd
With breach of love, and loyalty betrayd.
It was in my mishaps, as hitherward
I lately traveild, that unwares I strayd
Out of my way, through perils straunge and hard;
That day should faile me, ere I had them all declard.

32

There did I find, or rather I was found
Of this false woman, that *Fidessa* hight,
Fidessa hight the falsest Dame on ground,
Most false *Duessa*, royall richly dight,
That easie was to invegle weaker sight:
Who by her wicked arts, and wylie skill,
Too false and strong for earthly skill or might,
Unwares me wrought unto her wicked will,
And to my foe betrayd, when least I fearéd ill.

33

Then steppéd forth the goodly royall Mayd,
And on the ground her selfe prostrating low,
With sober countenaunce thus to him sayd;
O pardon me, my soveraigne Lord, to show
The secret treasons, which of late I know
To have bene wroght by that false sorceresse.
She onely she it is, that earst did throw
This gentle knight into so great distresse,
That death him did awaite in dayly wretchednesse.

34

And now it seemes, that she subornéd hath
This craftie messenger with letters vaine,
To worke new woe and improvided scath,[1]
By breaking of the band betwixt us twaine;
Wherein she uséd hath the practicke paine[2]
Of this false footman, clokt with simplenesse,
Whom if ye please for to discover plaine,
Ye shall him *Archimago* find, I ghesse,
The falsest man alive; who tries shall find no lesse.

35

The king was greatly movéd at her speach,
And all with suddein indignation fraight,
Bad on that Messenger rude hands to reach.
Eftsoones the Gard, which on his state did wait,
Attacht that faitor false, and bound him strait:
Who seeming sorely chauffféd at his band,
As chainéd Beare, whom cruell dogs do bait,
With idle force did faine them to withstand,
And often semblaunce made to scape out of their hand.

36

But they him layd full low in dungeon deepe,
And bound him hand and foote with yron chains.
And with continuall watch did warely keepe;
Who then would thinke, that by his subtile trains
He could escape fowle death or deadly paines?
Thus when that Princes wrath was pacifide,
He gan renew the late forbidden banes,
And to the knight his daughter deare he tyde,
With sacred rites and vowes for ever to abyde.

[1]Unforeseen harm. [2]Artful pains.

37

His owne two hands the holy knots did knit,
That none but death for ever can devide;
His owne two hands, for such a turne most fit,
The housling fire did kindle and provide,
And holy water thereon sprinckled wide;
At which the bushy Teade a groome did light,
And sacred lampe in secret chamber hide,
Where it should not be quenchéd day nor night,
For feare of evill fates, but burnen ever bright.

38

Then gan they sprinckle all the posts with wine,
And made great feast to solemnize that day;
They all perfumde with frankencense divine,
And precious odours fetcht from far away,
That all the house did sweat with great aray:
And all the while sweete Musicke did apply
Her curious skill, the warbling notes to play,
To drive away the dull Melancholy;
The whiles one sung a song of love and jollity.

39

During the which there was an heavenly noise
Heard sound through all the Pallace pleasantly,
Like as it had bene many an Angels voice,
Singing before th'eternall majesty,
In their trinall triplicities[1] on hye;
Yet wist no creature, whence that heavenly sweet
Proceeded, yet each one felt secretly
Himselfe thereby reft of his sences meet,
And ravishéd with rare impression in his sprite.

40

Great joy was made that day of young and old,
And solemne feast proclaimd throughout the land,
That their exceeding merth may not be told:
Suffice it heare by signes to understand
The usuall joyes at knitting of loves band.
Thrise happy man the knight himselfe did hold,
Possesséd of his Ladies hart and hand,
And ever, when his eye did her behold,
His heart did seeme to melt in pleasures manifold.

41

Her joyous presence and sweet company
In full content he there did long enjoy,
Ne wicked envie, ne vile gealosy
His deare delights were able to annoy:
Yet swimming in that sea of blisfull joy,
He nought forgot, how he whilome had sworne,
In case he could that monstrous beast destroy,
Unto his Farie Queene backe to returne:
The which he shortly did, and *Una* left to mourne.

42

Now strike your sailes ye jolly Mariners,
For we be come unto a quiet rode,
Where we must land some of our passengers,
And light this wearie vessell of her lode.
Here she a while may make her safe abode,
Till she repairéd have her tackles spent,[2]
And wants supplide. And then againe abroad
On the long voyage whereto she is bent:
Well may she speede and fairely finish her intent.

[1]It was believed that there were nine orders of angels, grouped in three ranks of three each.

EPITHALAMION[3]

Ye learnéd sisters,[4] which have oftentimes
Beene to me ayding, others to adorne,
Whom ye thought worthy of your gracefull rymes,
That even the greatest did not greatly scorne
To heare theyr names sung in your simple layes,
But joyéd in theyr prayse;
And when ye list your owne mishaps to mourne,
Which death, or love, or fortunes wreck did rayse,
Your string could soone to sadder tenor turne,
And teach the woods and waters to lament
Your dolefull dreriment:
Now lay those sorrowfull complaints aside,
And having all your heads with girland crownd,
Helpe me mine owne loves prayses to resound;
Ne let the same of any be envide:
So Orpheus did for his owne bride:
So I unto my selfe alone will sing;
The woods shall to me answer, and my Eccho ring.

Early, before the worlds light-giving lampe
His golden beame upon the hils doth spred,
Having disperst the nights unchearefull dampe,
Doe ye awake, and, with fresh lustyhed
Go to the bowre of my belovéd love,
My truest turtle dove:

[2]Her worn-out tackle.

[3]Written, as Spenser tells in the poem, for his own marriage in 1594.

[4]The muses.

Bid her awake; for Hymen[1] is awake,
And long since ready forth his maske to move,
With his bright Tead[2] that flames with many a flake,
And many a bachelor to waite on him,
In theyr fresh garments trim.
Bid her awake therefore, and soone her dight,
For lo! the wishéd day is come at last,
That shall, for al the paynes and sorrowes past,
Pay to her usury of long delight:
And whylest she doth her dight,
Doe ye to her of joy and solace sing,
That all the woods may answer, and your eccho ring.

Bring with you all the Nymphes that you can heare,
Both of the rivers and the forrests greene,
And of the sea that neighbours to her neare,
Al with gay girlands goodly wel beseene.[3]
And let them also with them bring in hand
Another gay girland,
For my fayre love, of lillyes and of roses,
Bound truelove wize with a blew silke riband.
And let them make great store of bridale poses,
And let them eeke bring store of other flowers,
To deck the bridale bowers.
And let the ground whereas her foot shall tread,
For feare the stones her tender foot should wrong,
Be strewed with fragrant flowers all along,
And diapred[4] lyke the discolored mead.
Which done, doe at her chamber dore awayt,
For she will waken strayt;
The whiles doe ye this song unto her sing,
The woods shall to you answer, and your Eccho ring.

Ye nymphes of Mulla,[5] which with carefull heed
The silver scaly trouts doe tend full well,
And greedy pikes which use therein to feed,
(Those trouts and pikes all others doo excell)
And ye likewise which keepe the rushy lake,[6]
Where none doo fishes take,
Bynd up the locks the which hang scatterd light,
And in his waters, which your mirror make,
Behold your faces as the christall bright,
That when you come whereas my love doth lie,
No blemish she may spie.
And eke ye lightfoot mayds which keepe the deere
That on the hoary mountayne use to towre,
And the wylde wolves, which seeke them to devoure,
With your steele darts doo chace from comming neer,
Be also present heere,
To helpe to decke her, and to help to sing,
That all the woods may answer, and your eccho ring.

Wake now, my love, awake! for it is time:
The Rosy Morne long since left Tithones bed,
All ready to her silver coche to clyme,
And Phœbus gins to shew his glorious hed.
Hark how the cheerefull birds do chaunt theyr laies,
And carroll of loves praise!
The merry Larke hir mattins sings aloft,
The thrush replyes, the Mavis[7] descant playes,
The Ouzell[8] shrills, the Ruddock[9] warbles soft,
So goodly all agree, with sweet consent,[10]
To this dayes merriment.
Ah! my deere love, why doe ye sleepe thus long,
When meeter were that ye should now awake,
T'awayt the comming of your joyous make,[11]
And hearken to the birds love-learnéd song,
The deawy leaves among?
For they of joy and pleasance to you sing,
That all the woods them answer, and theyr eccho ring.

My love is now awake out of her dreame,
And her fayre eyes, like stars that dimméd were
With darksome cloud, now shew theyr goodly beams
More bright then Hesperus[12] his head doth rere.
Come now, ye damzels, daughters of delight,
Helpe quickly her to dight.
But first come ye, fayre houres, which were begot
In Joves sweet paradice, of Day and Night,
Which doe the seasons of the yeare allot,
And al that ever in this world is fayre
Do make and still repayre.
And ye three handmayds[13] of the Cyprian Queene,
The which doe still adorne her beauties pride,
Helpe to addorne my beautifullest bride:
And as ye her array, still throw betweene
Some graces to be seene:
And as ye use to Venus, to her sing,
The whiles the woods shal answer, and your eccho ring.

[1]God of marriage. [2]Torch.
[3]Well arrayed. [4]Variegated.
[5]The river Awbeg, south of Kilcolman.
[6]Kilcolman was beside a lake.

[7]Song-thrush. [8]Blackbird. [9]Robin.
[10]Harmony. [11]Mate. [12]The morning star.
[13]The Graces.

Now is my love all ready forth to come:
Let all the virgins therefore well awayt,
And ye fresh boyes, that tend upon her groome,
Prepare your selves, for he is comming strayt.
Set all your things in seemely good aray,
Fit for so joyfull day,
The joyfulst day that ever sunne did see.
Faire Sun, shew forth thy favourable ray,
And let thy lifull heat not fervent be,
For feare of burning her sunshyny face,
Her beauty to disgrace.
O fayrest Phœbus, father of the Muse,
If ever I did honour thee aright,
Or sing the thing that mote[1] thy mind delight,
Doe not thy servants simple boone refuse,
But let this day, let this one day be myne,
Let all the rest be thine.
Then I thy soverayne prayses loud wil sing,
That all the woods shal answer, and theyr
eccho ring.

Harke how the Minstrels gin to shrill aloud
Their merry Musick that resounds from
far,
The pipe, the tabor,[2] and the trembling Croud,[3]
That well agree withouten breach or jar.
But most of all the Damzels doe delite,
When they their tymbrels smyte,
And thereunto doe daunce and carrol sweet,
That all the sences they doe ravish quite,
The whyles the boyes run up and downe the
street,
Crying aloud with strong confuséd noyce,
As if it were one voyce.
Hymen, Iö Hymen, Hymen,[4] they do shout,
That even to the heavens theyr shouting shrill
Doth reach, and all the firmament doth fill;
To which the people, standing all about,
As in approvance doe thereto to applaud,
And loud advaunce her laud,
And evermore they Hymen, Hymen sing,
That al the woods them answer, and theyr
eccho ring.

Loe! where she comes along with portly pace,
Lyke Phœbe, from her chamber of the East,
Arysing forth to run her mighty race,
Clad all in white, that seemes a virgin best.
So well it her beseemes, that ye would weene
Some angell she had beene.
Her long loose yellow locks lyke golden wyre,
Sprinckled with perle, and perling flowres
atweene,
Doe lyke a golden mantle her attyre,
And being crownéd with a girland greene,
Seeme lyke some mayden Queene.

[1]Might. [2]Drum. [3]Fiddle.

[4]Refrain of Roman nuptial song. Spenser in this poem follows in a general way the Latin tradition exemplified in Catullus LXI and LXII.

Her modest eyes, abashéd to behold
So many gazers as on her do stare,
Upon the lowly ground affixéd are;
Ne dare lift up her countenance too bold,
But blush to heare her prayses sung so loud,
So farre from being proud.
Nathlesse doe ye still loud her prayses sing,
That all the woods may answer, and your
eccho ring.

Tell me, ye merchants daughters, did ye see
So fayre a creature in your towne before,
So sweet, so lovely, and so mild as she,
Adornd with beautyes grace and vertues
store?
Her goodly eyes lyke Saphyres shining bright,
Her forehead yvory white,
Her cheekes lyke apples which the sun hath
rudded,
Her lips lyke cherryes charming men to byte,
Her brest like to a bowle of creame uncrudded,[5]
Her paps lyke lyllies budded,
Her snowie necke lyke to a marble towre,
And all her body like a pallace fayre,
Ascending uppe, with many a stately stayre,
To honors seat and chastities sweet bowre.
Why stand ye still, ye virgins, in amaze,
Upon her so to gaze,
Whiles ye forget your former lay to sing,
To which the woods did answer, and your
eccho ring.

But if ye saw that which no eyes can see,
The inward beauty of her lively spright,[6]
Garnisht with heavenly guifts of high degree,
Much more then would ye wonder at that
sight,
And stand astonisht, lyke to those which red[7]
Medusaes mazeful hed.[8]
There dwels sweet love and constant chas-
tity,
Unspotted fayth, and comely womanhood,
Regard of honour, and mild modesty;
There vertue raynes as Queene in royal throne,
And giveth lawes alone,
The which the base affections doe obay,
And yeeld theyr services unto her will;
Ne thought of thing uncomely ever may
Thereto approch to tempt her mind to ill.
Had ye once seene these her celestial threa-
sures,
And unrevealéd pleasures,
Then would ye wonder, and her prayses sing,
That al the woods should answer, and your
echo ring.

Open the temple gates unto my love,
Open them wide that she may enter in,

[5]Uncurdled. [6]Spirit. [7]Saw.

[8]Medusa's hair was turned into serpents.

And all the postes adorne as doth behove,
And all the pillours deck with girlands trim,
For to recyve this Saynt with honour dew,
That commeth in to you.
With trembling steps and humble reverence,
She commeth in before th' almighties vew:
Of her, ye virgins, learne obedience,
When so ye come into those holy places,
To humble your proud faces.
Bring her up to th' high altar, that she may
The sacred ceremonies there partake,
The which do endlesse matrimony make;
And let the roring Organs loudly play
The praises of the Lord in lively notes,
The whiles with hollow throates
The Choristers the joyous Antheme sing,
That al the woods may answere, and their eccho ring.

Behold, whiles she before the altar stands,
Hearing the holy priest that to her speakes,
And blesseth her with his two happy hands,
How the red roses flush up in her cheekes,
And the pure snow with goodly vermill stayne,
Like crimsin dyde in grayne:[1]
That even th' Angels, which continually
About the sacred Altare doe remaine,
Forget their service and about her fly,
Ofte peeping in her face, that seemes more fayre,
The more they on it stare.
But her sad[2] eyes, still fastened on the ground,
Are governéd with goodly modesty,
That suffers not one looke to glaunce awry,
Which may let in a little thought unsownd.
Why blush ye, love, to give to me your hand,
The pledge of all our band?[3]
Sing, ye sweet Angels, Alleluya sing,
That all the woods may answere, and your eccho ring.

Now al is done; bring home the bride againe,
Bring home the triumph of our victory,
Bring home with you the glory of her gaine,
With joyance bring her and with jollity.
Never had man more joyfull day then this,
Whom heaven would heape with blis.
Make feast therefore now all this live long day;
This day for ever to me holy is;
Poure out the wine without restraint or stay,
Poure not by cups, but by the belly full,
Poure out to all that wull,
And sprinkle all the postes and wals with wine,
That they may sweat, and drunken be withall.
Crowne ye God Bacchus with a coronall,

[1]In scarlet dye. [2]Sober. [3]Tie.

And Hymen also crowne with wreathes of vine;
And let the Graces daunce unto the rest,
For they can doo it best:
The whiles the maydens doe theyr carroll sing,
The which the woods shal answer, and theyr eccho ring.

Ring ye the bels, ye yong men of the towne,
And leave your wonted labors for this day:
This day is holy; doe ye write it downe,
That ye for ever it remember may.
This day[4] the sunne is in his chiefest hight,
With Barnaby the bright,
From whence declining daily by degrees,
He somewhat loseth of his heat and light,
When once the Crab[5] behind his back he sees.
But for this time it ill ordainéd was,
To chose the longest day in all the yeare,
And shortest night, when longest fitter weare:
Yet never day so long, but late would passe.
Ring ye the bels, to make it weare away,
And bonefiers make all day,
And daunce about them, and about them sing:
That all the woods may answer, and your eccho ring.

Ah! when will this long weary day have end,
And lende me leave to come unto my love?
How slowly do the houres theyr numbers spend!
How slowly does sad Time his feathers move!
Haste thee, O fayrest Planet,[6] to thy home
Within the Westerne fome:
Thy tyréd steedes long since have need of rest.
Long though it be, at last I see it gloome,
And the bright evening star with golden creast
Appeare out of the East.
Fayre childe of beauty, glorious lampe of love,
That all the host of heaven in rankes doost lead,
And guydest lovers through the nightés dread,
How chearefully thou lookest from above,
And seemst to laugh atweene thy twinkling light,
As joying in the sight
Of these glad many, which for joy doe sing,
That all the woods them answer, and their echo ring!

Now ceasse, ye damsels, your delights forepast;
Enough is it that all the day was youres:
Now day is doen, and night is nighing fast:
Now bring the Bryde into the brydall boures.

[4]St. Barnabas's day is 11 June. The old calendar being ten days out, it was also the longest day.
[5]One of the signs of the zodiac.
[6]The sun.

Now night is come, now soone her disaray,
And in her bed her lay;
Lay her in lillies and in violets,
And silken courteins over her display,
And odourd sheetes, and Arras[1] coverlets.
Behold how goodly my faire love does ly
In proud humility!
Like unto Maia, when as Jove her tooke
In Tempe, lying on the flowry gras,
Twixt sleepe and wake, after she weary was
With bathing in the Acidalian brooke.
Now it is night, ye damsels may be gon,
And leave my love alone,
And leave likewise your former lay to sing:
The woods no more shal answere, nor your echo ring.

Now welcome, night! thou night so long expected,
That long daies labour doest at last defray,
And all my cares, which cruell love collected,
Hast sumd in one, and cancellèd for aye:
Spread thy broad wing over my love and me,
That no man may us see,
And in thy sable mantle us enwrap,
From feare of perrill and foule horror free.
Let no false treason seeke us to entrap,
Nor any dread disquiet once annoy
The safety of our joy:
But let the night be calme and quietsome,
Without tempestuous storms or sad afray:
Lyke as when Jove with fayre Alcmena lay,
When he begot the great Tirynthian groome:[2]
Or lyke as when he with thy selfe did lie,
And begot Majesty.
And let the mayds and yongmen cease to sing:
Ne let the woods them answer, nor theyr eccho ring.

Let no lamenting cryes, nor dolefull teares,
Be heard all night within, nor yet without:
Ne let false whispers, breeding hidden feares,
Breake gentle sleepe with misconceivèd dout.
Let no deluding dreames, nor dreadful sights,
Make sudden sad affrights;
Ne let house-fyres, nor lightnings helplesse[3] harmes,
Ne let the Pouke,[4] nor other evill sprights,
Ne let mischivous witches with theyr charmes,
Ne let hob Goblins, names whose sence we see not,
Fray us with things that be not.
Let not the shriech Oule, nor the Storke be heard,
Nor the night Raven that still deadly yels,
Nor damnèd ghosts cald up with mighty spels,
Nor griesly vultures make us once affeard:
Ne let th' unpleasant Quyre of Frogs still croking
Make us to wish theyr choking.
Let none of these theyr drery accents sing;
Ne let the woods them answer, nor theyr eccho ring.

But let stil Silence trew night watches keepe,
That sacred peace may in assurance rayne,
And tymely sleep, when it is tyme to sleepe,
May poure his limbs forth on your pleasant playne,
The whiles an hundred little wingèd loves,
Like divers fethered doves,
Shall fly and flutter round about your bed,
And in the secret darke that none reproves,
Their prety stealthes shall worke, and snares shal spread
To filch away sweet snatches of delight,
Conceald through covert night.
Ye sonnes of Venus, play your sports at will:
For greedy pleasure, careless of your toyes,
Thinks more upon her paradise of joyes,
Then what ye do, albe it good or ill.
All night therefore attend your merry play,
For it will soone be day:
Now none doth hinder you, that say or sing,
Ne will the woods now answer, nor your Eccho ring.

Who is the same which at my window peepes?
Or whose is that faire face that shines so bright?
Is it not Cinthia,[5] she that never sleepes,
But walkes about high heaven al the night?
O fayrest goddesse, do thou not envy
My love with me to spy:
For thou likewise didst love, though now unthought,
And for a fleece of woll, which privily
The Latmian shephard[6] once unto thee brought,
His pleasures with thee wrought.
Therefore to us be favorable now;
And sith of wemens labours thou hast charge,
And generation goodly dost enlarge,
Encline thy will t' effect our wishfull vow,
And the chast wombe informe with timely seed,
That may our comfort breed:
Till which we cease our hopefull hap[7] to sing,
Ne let the woods us answere, nor our Eccho ring.

And thou, great Juno, which with awful might
The lawes of wedlock still dost patronize,
And the religion of the faith first plight

[1] Coverlets from Arras. [2] Hercules.
[3] Irreparable. [4] Puck, Robin Goodfellow.

[5] The moon. [6] Endymion. [7] Fortune.

With sacred rites hast taught to solemnize,
And eeke for comfort often callėd art
Of women in their smart,
Eternally bind thou this lovely band,
And all thy blessings unto us impart.
And thou, glad Genius, in whose gentle hand
The bridale bowre and geniall bed remaine,
Without blemish or staine,
And the sweet pleasures of theyr loves delight
With secret ayde doest succour and supply,
Till they bring forth the fruitfull progeny,
Send us the timely fruit of this same night.
And thou, fayre Hebe,[1] and thou, Hymen free,
Grant that it may so be.
Til which we cease your further prayse to
sing,
Ne any woods shal answer, nor your Eccho
ring.

And ye high heavens, the temple of the gods,
In which a thousand torches flaming bright
Doe burne, that to us wretched earthly
clods
In dreadful darknesse lend desirėd light,
And all ye powers which in the same remayne,
More then we men can fayne,[2]
Poure out your blessing on us plentiously,
And happy influence upon us raine,
That we may raise a large posterity,
Which from the earth, which they may long
possesse
With lasting happinesse,
Up to your haughty pallaces may mount,
And for the guerdon[3] of theyr glorious merit,
May heavenly tabernacles there inherit,
Of blessėd Saints for to increase the count.
So let us rest, sweet love, in hope of this,
And cease till then our tymely joyes to sing:
The woods no more us answer, nor our eccho
ring.

Song, made in lieu of many ornaments
With which my love should duly have bene
dect,
Which cutting off through hasty accidents,[4]
Ye would not stay your dew time to expect,[5]
But promist both to recompens,
Be unto her a goodly ornament,
And for[6] short time an endlesse moniment.

[1]Cup-bearer to the gods.

[2]Imagine.
[3]Reward.
[4]Accidents of haste.
[5]Await.
[6]Instead of.

FRANCIS BACON (1561-1626)

Francis Bacon was the son of Sir Nicholas Bacon, lord keeper of the great seal under Queen Elizabeth. His mother was the sister-in-law of Lord Burghley, long Elizabeth's trusted adviser, so that it may fairly be said that Bacon was born a member of the governing class of England; and as one destined for public service he was brought up. In 1573 he went to Trinity College, Cambridge, staying there until the end of 1575. In 1576 he entered Gray's Inn to study the law, leaving, however, in 1577 for two years' residence in France in the household of the English ambassador. The death of his father left him to shift largely for himself, and he turned immediately to the law. He was admitted an utter barrister in 1582. In 1584 he entered Parliament and thus actively began his long political career. He persistently sought advancement through the friendship of the great—through Lord Burghley, then through the Earl of Essex, and then through Sir Robert Cecil, Burghley's son—and he sought to deserve friendship by his statesmanlike advice. His abilities were striking and his advice was good, yet the opening he wanted to a great career was long denied him. He was knighted in 1603, at the accession of James; in 1607 he was made solicitor-general, in 1613 attorney-general, in 1616 privy councillor, in 1617 lord keeper of the great seal, and in 1618 lord chancellor. In the same year he was created Baron Verulam, and in 1621 Viscount St. Alban. Later in 1621, however, came his sudden and complete downfall. He was impeached on the charge of bribery, confessed his guilt, and was sentenced by the House of Lords to a fine of £40,000 and to imprisonment in the Tower during the king's pleasure, while he was disabled from sitting in Parliament and from coming within the verge of the Court, *i. e.*, within twelve miles of the Court. The fine was immediately converted into a trust fund for Bacon's use and his imprisonment lasted only a few days; within a year, too, he was allowed again to present himself at Court, but his exclusion from Parliament was not relaxed and Bacon was politically a broken man. The remaining years of his life were devoted to study and writing. Born on 22 January, 1561, he died on 9 April, 1626.

Pope called Bacon "the wisest, brightest, meanest of mankind," and the line has stuck. Yet, while no one would for a moment contend that Bacon had either the elevation of character or the detachment of a saint, it is no less certain that he has suffered from grave misunderstanding. While not condoning his moral obtuseness, one should in justice remember that he simply suffered from the defects, as he enjoyed the advantages, of the clearly marked type of mind to which we owe the achievements of modern science. Morality is concerned with imperfectly realized ideals, it seeks to bend men to the commands of an invisible kingdom. Bacon, on the other hand, saw things and men as they are, and viewed his world as a field for the realization of human purposes. In politics he was simply consistent in following out the point of view which, as enunciated in the *Novum Organum*, has caused him to be heralded —not as the founder, as some mistakenly have said, but—as the great prophet of modern science. In politics Bacon undoubtedly wished to find a place for himself, and in this took, not a mean, but a common-sense view of his situation. Not less clearly, however, he wanted to use his power when he obtained it for public ends, for furthering the greatness of his country and bettering the condition of its members. And for the achievement of his personal and public purposes he followed what, as things were in his day, was the only practicable method—the method of rising through favor of the great. If he was blind to the loss of dignity involved in seeking such favor, this was because his mind was centered on his end and because he judged means simply in relation to their probable efficacy. Again, in accepting gifts as a judge, Bacon merely followed the common custom of his day, and he was more scrupulous than other judges in that he appears not to have allowed the gifts to bias his judgments. If we may smile at the naïveté which blinded him to the enmities this was bound to arouse, still, we cannot avoid agreement with his own statement. "I was," he said, "the justest judge that was in England these fifty years, but it was the justest sentence in Parliament that was these two hundred years."

When he was a young man Bacon wrote, "I have as vast contemplative ends as I have moderate civil ends; for I have taken all knowledge to be my province." This was the second of the two related purposes of his life. A child of the Renaissance both in the vastness of his outlook and in his confidence in human powers, he saw the importance of knowledge in life as he understood it. And as he sought in public life an opportunity for the application of knowledge to the betterment of the condition of his country and its inhabitants, so he sought also to map out the field of knowledge and to elaborate a right method for its discovery. The former he attempted to achieve in *The Advancement of Learning* (1605) and, more fully, in the amplified Latin version of that book published in 1623. His imperfect formulation of scientific method is contained in his *Novum Organum* (1620). His fragmentary *New Atlantis* is a literary picture of the advantages to man which he saw in the pursuit of science. His *History of Henry VII*, one of the fruits of his retirement after 1621, is a masterly historical work which deservedly also occupies a high place in literature. But to most readers Bacon will always be known chiefly through his *Essays*, those "dispersed meditations," "set down rather significantly than curiously," on which, in all probability, he never supposed that his fame would largely depend. Ten essays were published in 1597; in the second edition of 1612 they had grown to thirty-eight, and in the third edition of 1625 there were fifty-eight, while many of the earlier essays were amplified. They probably take their title from Montaigne's *Essais* (1580), though the two books have little in common save that both consist of dispersed notes on life set down by a man of the world. Bacon's *Essays* introduced a new form into English literature, and they represent the man as he was, shrewd, incisive, somewhat hard, and yet on occasion finely imaginative.

ESSAYS OR COUNSELS CIVIL AND MORAL

1.—OF TRUTH

"What is truth?" said jesting Pilate,[1] and would not stay for an answer. Certainly there be that delight in giddiness, and count it a bondage to fix a belief; affecting free-will in thinking, as well as in acting. And though the sects of philosophers of that kind be gone, yet there remain certain discoursing wits which are of the same veins, though there be not so much blood in them as was in those of the ancients. But it is not only the difficulty and labor which men take in finding out of truth, nor again that when it is found it imposeth upon men's thoughts, that doth bring lies in favor; but a natural though corrupt love of the lie itself. One of the later school of the Grecians examineth the matter, and is at a stand to think what should be in it, that men should love lies; where neither they make for pleasure, as with poets; nor for advantage, as with the merchant; but for the lie's sake. But I cannot tell: this same truth is a naked and open day-light, that doth not show the masques and mummeries and triumphs of the world, half so stately and daintily as candle-lights. Truth may perhaps come to the price of a pearl, that showeth best by day; but it will not rise to the price of a diamond or carbuncle, that showeth best in varied lights. A mixture of a lie doth ever add pleasure. Doth any man doubt, that if there were taken out of men's minds vain opinions, flattering hopes, false valuations, imaginations as one would, and the like, but it would leave the minds of a number of men poor shrunken things, full of melancholy and indisposition, and unpleasing to themselves? One of the fathers, in great severity, called poesy *vinum dæmonum*,[2] because it filleth the imagination, and yet it is but with the shadow of a lie. But it is not the lie that passeth through the mind, but the lie that sinketh in and settleth in it, that doth the hurt, such as we spake of before. But howsoever these things are thus in men's depraved judgments and affections, yet truth, which only doth judge itself, teacheth that the inquiry of truth, which is the love-making or wooing of it, the knowledge of truth, which is the presence of it, and the belief of truth, which is the enjoying of it, is the sovereign good of human nature. The first creature of God, in the works of the days, was the light of the sense; the last was the light of reason; and his sabbath work, ever since, is the illumination of his Spirit. First he breathed light upon the face of the matter or chaos; then he breathed light into the face of man; and still he breatheth and inspireth light into the face of his chosen. The poet[3] that beautified the sect[4] that was otherwise inferior to the rest, saith yet excellently well: "It is a pleasure to stand upon the shore, and to see ships tossed upon the sea: a pleasure to stand in the window of a castle, and to see a battle and the adventures thereof below: but no pleasure is comparable to the standing upon the vantage

[1]*Cf.* St. John, xviii, 38.

[2]Wine of devils. A phrase of similar meaning is used by Augustine (*Confessions*, I, xvi, 26).

[3]Lucretius. Bacon paraphrases a passage at the beginning of Bk. II of Lucretius's poem *On the Nature of Things*.

[4]The Epicureans.

ground of truth" (a hill not to be commanded, and where the air is always clear and serene), "and to see the errors, and wanderings, and mists, and tempests, in the vale below": so always that this prospect be with pity, and not with swelling or pride. Certainly, it is heaven upon earth, to have a man's mind move in charity, rest in providence, and turn upon the poles of truth.

To pass from theological and philosophical truth, to the truth of civil business: it will be acknowledged, even by those that practice it not, that clear and round[1] dealing is the honor of man's nature; and that mixture of falsehood is like alloy in coin of gold and silver; which may make the metal work the better, but it embaseth it. For these winding and crooked courses are the goings of the serpent; which goeth basely upon the belly, and not upon the feet. There is no vice that doth so cover a man with shame as to be found false and perfidious. And therefore Montaigne saith prettily, when he inquired the reason, why the word of the lie should be such a disgrace and such an odious charge? saith he: "If it be well weighed, to say that a man lieth, is as much to say as that he is brave towards God and a coward towards men."[2] For a lie faces God, and shrinks from man. Surely the wickedness of falsehood and breach of faith cannot possibly be so highly expressed, as in that it shall be the last peal to call the judgments of God upon the generations of men; it being foretold, that when Christ cometh, "he shall not find faith upon the earth."[3]

5.—OF ADVERSITY

It was an high speech of Seneca (after the manner of the Stoics), "That the good things which belong to prosperity are to be wished; but the good things that belong to adversity are to be admired." *Bona rerum secundarum optabilia, adversarum mirabilia.* Certainly, if miracles be the command over nature, they appear most in adversity. It is yet a higher speech of his than the other (much too high for a heathen), "It is true greatness to have in one the frailty of a man, and the security of a god." *Vere magnum, habere fragilitatem hominis, securitatem dei.*[4] This would have done better in poesy, where transcendences are more allowed. And the poets indeed have been busy with it; for it is in effect the thing which is figured in that strange fiction of the ancient poets, which seemeth not to be without mystery; nay, and to have some approach to the state of a Christian: that "Hercules, when he went to unbind Prometheus (by whom human nature is represented), sailed the length of the great ocean in an earthen pot or pitcher": lively describing Christian resolution, that saileth in the frail bark of the flesh through the waves of the world. But to speak in a mean.[5] The virtue of prosperity is temperance; the virtue of adversity is fortitude; which in morals is the more heroical virtue. Prosperity is the blessing of the Old Testament; adversity is the blessing of the New; which carrieth the greater benediction, and the clearer revelation of God's favor. Yet even in the Old Testament, if you listen to David's harp, you shall hear as many hearse-like airs as carols; and the pencil of the Holy Ghost hath labored more in describing the afflictions of Job than the felicities of Solomon. Prosperity is not without many fears and distastes; and adversity is not without comforts and hopes. We see in needleworks and embroideries, it is more pleasing to have a lively work upon a sad and solemn ground, than to have a dark and melancholy work upon a lightsome ground: judge therefore of the pleasure of the heart by the pleasure of the eye. Certainly virtue is like precious odors, most fragrant when they are incensed or crushed: for prosperity doth best discover vice; but adversity doth best discover virtue.

6.—OF SIMULATION AND DISSIMULATION

Dissimulation is but a faint kind of policy or wisdom; for it asketh a strong wit and a strong heart to know when to tell truth, and to do it. Therefore it is the weaker sort of politics that are the great dissemblers.

Tacitus saith: "Livia sorted well with the arts of her husband and dissimulation of her son";[6] attributing arts or policy to Augustus, and dissimulation to Tiberius. And again, when Mucianus encourageth Vespasian to take arms against Vitellius, he saith: "We rise not against the piercing judgment of

[1]Straightforward. [2]*Essays*, II, 18. [3]St. Luke, xviii, 8.
[4]Both passages are inexactly quoted from Seneca's *Epistles*.

[5]To speak temperately. [6]*Annals*, V, 1.

Augustus, nor the extreme caution or closeness of Tiberius."[1] These properties, of arts or policy, and dissimulation or closeness, are indeed habits and faculties several and to be distinguished. For if a man have that penetration of judgment as he can discern what things are to be laid open, and what to be secreted, and what to be showed at half lights, and to whom, and when (which indeed are arts of state and arts of life, as Tacitus well calleth them), to him a habit of dissimulation is a hindrance and a poorness. But if a man cannot obtain to that judgment, then it is left to him, generally, to be close, and a dissembler. For where a man cannot choose or vary in particulars, there it is good to take the safest and wariest way in general; like the going softly by one that cannot well see. Certainly the ablest men that ever were have had all an openness and frankness of dealing, and a name of certainty and veracity; but then they were like horses well managed; for they could tell passing well when to stop or turn; and at such times when they thought the case indeed required dissimulation, if then they used it, it came to pass that the former opinion spread abroad of their good faith and clearness of dealing made them almost invisible.

There be three degrees of this hiding and veiling of a man's self. The first, closeness, reservation, and secrecy; when a man leaveth himself without observation, or without hold to be taken, what he is. The second, dissimulation, in the negative; when a man lets fall signs and arguments, that he is not that he is. And the third, simulation, in the affirmative; when a man industriously and expressly feigns and pretends to be that he is not.

For the first of these, secrecy: it is indeed the virtue of a confessor; and assuredly the secret man heareth many confessions; for who will open himself to a blab or a babbler? But if a man be thought secret, it inviteth discovery; as the more close air sucketh in the more open: and as in confession the revealing is not for worldly use, but for the ease of a man's heart, so secret men come to the knowledge of many things in that kind; while men rather discharge their minds than impart their minds. In few words, mysteries are due to secrecy. Besides (to say truth) nakedness is uncomely, as well in mind as body; and it addeth no small reverence to men's manners and actions, if they be not altogether open. As for talkers and futile persons, they are commonly vain and credulous withal. For he that talketh what he knoweth, will also talk what he knoweth not. Therefore set it down, *that an habit of secrecy is both politic and moral.* And in this part, it is good that a man's face give his tongue leave to speak. For the discovery of a man's self by the tracts[2] of his countenance is a great weakness and betraying; by how much it is many times more marked and believed than a man's words.

For the second, which is dissimulation: it followeth many times upon secrecy by a necessity; so that he that will be secret must be a dissembler in some degree. For men are too cunning to suffer a man to keep an indifferent[3] carriage between both, and to be secret, without swaying the balance on either side. They will so beset a man with questions, and draw him on, and pick it out of him, that, without an absurd silence, he must show an inclination one way; or if he do not, they will gather as much by his silence as by his speech. As for equivocations, or oraculous speeches, they cannot hold out long. So that no man can be secret, except he give himself a little scope of dissimulation; which is, as it were, but the skirts or train of secrecy.

But for the third degree, which is simulation and false profession: that I hold more culpable, and less politic; except it be in great and rare matters. And therefore a general custom of simulation (which is this last degree) is a vice, rising either of a natural falseness or fearfulness, or of a mind that hath some main faults, which because a man must needs disguise, it maketh him practice simulation in other things, lest his hand should be out of use.

The great advantages of simulation and dissimulation are three. First, to lay asleep opposition, and to surprise. For where a man's intentions are published, it is an alarm to call up all that are against them. The second is, to reserve to a man's self a fair retreat. For if a man engage himself by a manifest declaration, he must go through, or take a fall. The third is, the better to discover the mind of another. For to him that opens himself men will hardly show themselves adverse; but will (fair)[4] let him go on, and turn their

[1] *Hist.*, II, 76.

[2] Features. [3] Impartial. [4] Rather.

peech to freedom of thought. it is a good shrewd proverb of ...aniard, "Tell a lie and find a truth"; as if there were no way of discovery but by simulation. There be also three disadvantages, to set it even. The first, that simulation and dissimulation commonly carry with them a show of fearfulness, which in any business doth spoil the feathers of round[1] flying up to the mark. The second, that it puzzleth and perplexeth the conceits[2] of many that perhaps would otherwise co-operate with him, and makes a man walk almost alone to his own ends. The third and greatest is, that it depriveth a man of one of the most principal instruments for action, which is trust and belief. The best composition and temperature[3] is to have openness in fame and opinion; secrecy in habit; dissimulation in seasonable use; and a power to feign, if there be no remedy.

7.—OF PARENTS AND CHILDREN

THE joys of parents are secret, and so are their griefs and fears: they cannot utter the one, nor they will not utter[4] the other. Children sweeten labors, but they make misfortunes more bitter: they increase the cares of life, but they mitigate the remembrance of death. The perpetuity by generation is common to beasts; but memory, merit, and noble works are proper to men: and surely a man shall see the noblest works and foundations have proceeded from childless men, which have sought to express the images of their minds, where those of their bodies have failed: so the care of posterity is most in them that have no posterity. They that are the first raisers of their houses are most indulgent towards their children; beholding them as the continuance not only of their kind but of their work; and so both children and creatures.

The difference in affection of parents towards their several children is many times unequal, and sometimes unworthy, especially in the mother; as Solomon saith: "A wise son rejoiceth the father, but an ungracious son shames the mother."[5] A man shall see, where there is a house full of children, one or two of the eldest respected, and the youngest made wantons; but in the midst some that are as it were forgotten, who many times nevertheless prove the best. The illiberality of parents in allowance towards their children is an harmful error; makes them base; acquaints them with shifts;[6] makes them sort with mean company; and makes them surfeit more when they come to plenty: and therefore the proof is best, when men keep their authority towards their children, but not their purse. Men have a foolish manner (both parents and schoolmasters and servants) in creating and breeding an emulation between brothers during childhood, which many times sorteth to discord when they are men, and disturbeth families. The Italians make little difference between children and nephews or near kinsfolks; but so they be of the lump, they care not though they pass not through their own body. And, to say truth, in nature it is much a like matter; insomuch that we see a nephew sometimes resembleth an uncle or a kinsman more than his own parents, as the blood happens. Let parents choose betimes the vocations and courses they mean their children should take; for then they are most flexible; and let them not too much apply themselves to the disposition of their children, as thinking they will take best to that which they have most mind to. It is true, that if the affection or aptness of the children be extraordinary, then it is good not to cross it; but generally the precept is good, *Optimum elige, suave et facile illud faciet consuetudo.*[7] Younger brothers are commonly fortunate, but seldom or never where the elder are disinherited.

8.—OF MARRIAGE AND SINGLE LIFE

HE THAT hath wife and children hath given hostages to fortune; for they are impediments to great enterprises, either of virtue or mischief. Certainly, the best works, and of greatest merit for the public, have proceeded from the unmarried or childless men, which both in affection and means have married and endowed the public. Yet it were great reason that those that have children should have greatest care of future times; unto which they know they must transmit their dearest pledges. Some there are, who though they lead a single

[1] *I.e.*, swiftly. [2] Thoughts. [3] Temperament. [4] Nor will they utter. [5] Proverbs, x, 1.

[6] Deceptions.

[7] Choose the best; habit will make it pleasant and easy. (Plutarch attributes this saying to Pythagoras.)

life, yet their thoughts do end with themselves, and account future times impertinences. Nay, there are some other that account wife and children but as bills of charges. Nay more, there are some foolish rich covetous men that take a pride in having no children, because they may be thought so much the richer. For perhaps they have heard some talk: "Such an one is a great rich man," and another except to it: "Yea, but he hath a great charge of children"; as if it were an abatement to his riches. But the most ordinary cause of a single life is liberty; especially in certain self-pleasing and humorous[1] minds, which are so sensible of every restraint, as they will go near to think their girdles and garters to be bonds and shackles. Unmarried men are best friends, best masters, best servants; but not always best subjects; for they are light to run away; and almost all fugitives are of that condition. A single life doth well with churchmen; for charity will hardly water the ground where it must first fill a pool. It is indifferent for judges and magistrates; for if they be facile and corrupt, you shall have a servant five times worse than a wife. For soldiers, I find the generals commonly in their hortatives put men in mind of their wives and children; and I think the despising of marriage amongst the Turks maketh the vulgar soldier more base. Certainly wife and children are a kind of discipline of humanity; and single men, though they be many times more charitable, because their means are less exhaust,[2] yet, on the other side, they are more cruel and hard-hearted (good to make severe inquisitors), because their tenderness is not so oft called upon. Grave natures, led by custom, and therefore constant, are commonly loving husbands; as was said of Ulysses, *Vetulam suam prætulit immortalitati*.[3] Chaste women are often proud and froward, as presuming upon the merit of their chastity. It is one of the best bonds both of chastity and obedience in the wife, if she think her husband wise; which she will never do if she find him jealous. Wives are young men's mistresses; companions for middle age; and old men's nurses. So as a man may have a quarrel[4] to marry when he will. But yet he was reputed one of the wise men, that made answer to the question, when a man should marry? "A young man not yet, an elder man not at all."[5] It is often seen that bad husbands have very good wives; whether it be that it raiseth the price of their husband's kindness when it comes; or that the wives take a pride in their patience. But this never fails, if the bad husbands were of their own choosing, against their friends' consent; for then they will be sure to make good their own folly.

10.—OF LOVE

THE stage is more beholding to love than the life of man. For as to the stage, love is ever matter of comedies, and now and then of tragedies: but in life it doth much mischief; sometimes like a siren, sometimes like a fury. You may observe, that amongst all the great and worthy persons (whereof the memory remaineth, either ancient or recent), there is not one that hath been transported to the mad degree of love; which shows that great spirits and great business do keep out this weak passion. You must except, nevertheless, Marcus Antonius,[6] the half partner of the empire of Rome, and Appius Claudius,[7] the decemvir and lawgiver: whereof the former was indeed a voluptuous man, and inordinate; but the latter was an austere and wise man: and therefore it seems (though rarely) that love can find entrance not only into an open heart, but also into a heart well fortified, if watch be not well kept. It is a poor saying of Epicurus, *Satis magnum alter alteri theatrum sumus:*[8] as if man, made for the contemplation of heaven and all noble objects, should do nothing but kneel before a little idol, and make himself subject, though not of the mouth (as beasts are), yet of the eye, which was given them for higher purposes. It is a strange thing to note the excess of this passion, and how it braves the nature and value of things, by this, that the speaking in a perpetual hyperbole is comely in nothing but in love. Neither is it merely in the phrase; for whereas it hath been well said[9] that the arch-flatterer, with whom all the petty flatterers have in-

---

[1] Whimsical. [2] Exhausted.

[3] He preferred his aged wife to immortality (which had been offered him by Calypso).

[4] An excuse.

[5] The saying is ascribed by Plutarch to Thales, one of the "seven wise men" of Greece.

[6] Cleopatra's lover. [7] The lover of Virginia.

[8] We are to one another an ample spectacle (quoted by Seneca, *Epistles*, I, vii, 11).

[9] By Plutarch.

telligence, is a man's self, certainly the lover is more. For there was never proud man thought so absurdly well of himself as the lover doth of the person loved: and therefore it was well said: "That it is impossible to love and to be wise."[1] Neither doth this weakness appear to others only, and not to the party loved, but to the loved most of all, except the love be reciprocal. For it is a true rule, that love is ever rewarded either with the reciproque[2] or with an inward and secret contempt. By how much the more men ought to beware of this passion, which loseth not only other things, but itself. As for the other losses, the poet's relation doth well figure them: That he[3] that preferred Helena, quitted the gifts of Juno and Pallas. For whosoever esteemeth too much of amorous affection, quitteth both riches and wisdom. This passion hath his floods in the very times of weakness; which are great prosperity and great adversity (though this latter hath been less observed): both which times kindle love, and make it more fervent, and therefore show it to be the child of folly. They do best, who, if they cannot but admit love, yet make it keep quarter,[4] and sever it wholly from their serious affairs and actions of life; for if it check[5] once with business, it troubleth men's fortunes, and maketh men that they can no ways be true to their own ends. I know not how, but martial men are given to love: I think it is but as they are given to wine; for perils commonly ask to be paid in pleasures. There is in man's nature a secret inclination and motion towards love of others, which, if it be not spent upon some one or a few, doth naturally spread itself towards many, and maketh men become humane and charitable; as it is seen sometime in friars. Nuptial love maketh mankind; friendly love perfecteth it; but wanton love corrupteth and embaseth it.

11.—OF GREAT PLACE

MEN in great places are thrice servants: servants of the sovereign or state; servants of fame; and servants of business. So as they have no freedom, neither in their persons, nor in their actions, nor in their times. It is a strange desire, to seek power and to lose liberty; or to seek power over others and to lose power over a man's self. The rising unto place is laborious, and by pains men come to greater pains; and it is sometimes base, and by indignities men come to dignities. The standing is slippery; and the regress is either a downfall, or at least an eclipse, which is a melancholy thing. *Cum non sis qui fueris, non esse cur velis vivere.*[6] Nay, retire men cannot when they would; neither will they when it were reason; but are impatient of privateness, even in age and sickness, which require the shadow:[7] like old townsmen, that will be still sitting at their street door, though thereby they offer age to scorn. Certainly, great persons had need to borrow other men's opinions, to think themselves happy; for if they judge by their own feeling, they cannot find it: but if they think with themselves what other men think of them, and that other men would fain be as they are, then they are happy as it were by report, when perhaps they find the contrary within. For they are the first that find their own griefs, though they be the last that find their own faults. Certainly, men in great fortunes are strangers to themselves, and while they are in the puzzle of business they have no time to tend their health, either of body or mind. *Illi mors gravis incubat, qui notus nimis omnibus, ignotus moritur sibi.*[8] In place there is license to do good and evil; whereof the latter is a curse: for in evil the best condition is not to will, the second not to can.[9] But power to do good is the true and lawful end of aspiring. For good thoughts (though God accept them) yet towards men are little better than good dreams, except they be put in act; and that cannot be without power and place, as the vantage and commanding ground. Merit and good works is the end of man's motion; and conscience[10] of the same is the accomplishment of man's rest. For if a man can be partaker of God's theater, he shall likewise be partaker of God's rest. *Et conversus Deus ut aspiceret opera quæ fecerunt manus suæ, vidit quod omnia essent bona nimis;*[11] and then the Sabbath. In

---

[1]Publius Syrus. [2]Returned affection. [3]Paris.
[4]Keep within bounds. [5]Interfere.

[6]When you are no longer what you were, there is no reason why you should wish to keep on living (Cicero).
[7]Retirement.
[8]Sad is the fate of him who ends his days all too well known to others, but a stranger to himself (Seneca, *Thyestes*).
[9]To know. [10]Consciousness.
[11]And God, turning back to look upon the works which his hands had made, saw that all were very good (Genesis, I, 31, quoted inexactly from the Vulgate).

the discharge of thy place, set before thee the best examples; for imitation is a globe of precepts. And after a time set before thee thine own example; and examine thyself strictly, whether thou didst not best at first. Neglect not also the examples of those that have carried themselves ill in the same place; not to set off thyself by taxing their memory, but to direct thyself what to avoid. Reform, therefore, without bravery or scandal of former times and persons; but yet set it down to thyself as well to create good precedents as to follow them. Reduce things to the first institution, and observe wherein and how they have degenerate; but yet ask counsel of both times; of the ancient time, what is best; and of the latter time, what is fittest. Seek to make thy course regular, that men may know beforehand what they may expect; but be not too positive and peremptory; and express thyself well when thou digressest from thy rule. Preserve the right of thy place, but stir not questions of jurisdiction: and rather assume thy right in silence and *de facto*,[1] than voice it with claims and challenges. Preserve likewise the rights of inferior places; and think it more honor to direct in chief than to be busy in all. Embrace and invite helps and advices touching the execution of thy place; and do not drive away such as bring thee information as meddlers, but accept of them in good part. The vices of authority are chiefly four: delays, corruption, roughness, and facility.[2] For delays; give easy access; keep times appointed; go through with that which is in hand; and interlace not business but of necessity. For corruption; do not only bind thine own hands or thy servants' hands from taking, but bind the hands of suitors also from offering. For integrity used doth the one; but integrity professed, and with a manifest detestation of bribery, doth the other. And avoid not only the fault, but the suspicion. Whosoever is found variable, and changeth manifestly without manifest cause, giveth suspicion of corruption. Therefore always when thou changest thine opinion or course, profess it plainly and declare it, together with the reasons that move thee to change; and do not think to steal[3] it. A servant or a favorite, if he be inward,[4] and no other apparent cause of esteem, is commonly thought but a by-way to close corruption. For roughness, it is a needless cause of discontent: severity breedeth fear, but roughness breedeth hate. Even reproofs from authority ought to be grave, and not taunting. As for facility, it is worse than bribery. For bribes come but now and then; but if importunity or idle respects[5] lead a man, he shall never be without. As Solomon saith: "To respect persons is not good; for such a man will transgress for a piece of bread."[6] It is most true that was anciently spoken, "A place showeth the man": and it showeth some to the better, and some to the worse. *Omnium consensu capax imperii, nisi imperasset*,[7] saith Tacitus of Galba; but of Vespasian he saith, *Solus imperantium Vespasianus mutatus in melius*:[8] though the one was meant of sufficiency,[9] the other of manners and affection. It is an assured sign of a worthy and generous spirit, whom honor amends. For honor is, or should be, the place of virtue; and as in nature things move violently to their place, and calmly in their place; so virtue in ambition is violent, in authority settled and calm. All rising to great place is by a winding stair; and if there be factions, it is good to side a man's self whilst he is in the rising, and to balance himself when he is placed. Use the memory of thy predecessor fairly and tenderly; for if thou dost not, it is a debt will sure be paid when thou art gone. If thou have colleagues, respect them, and rather call them when they look not for it, than exclude them when they have reason to look to be called. Be not too sensible or too remembering of thy place in conversation and private answers to suitors; but let it rather be said, "When he sits in place he is another man."

12.—OF BOLDNESS

It is a trivial grammar-school text, but yet worthy a wise man's consideration. Question was asked of Demosthenes, "What was the chief part of an orator?" he answered "Action": what next? "Action": what next again? "Action." He said it that knew it

[1]As a matter of fact. [2]Lack of firmness.
[3]Hide. [4]Intimate.

[5]Considerations. [6]Proverbs, xxviii, 21.
[7]All men would have thought him competent to rule if they had not seen him as a ruler.
[8]Of all the emperors Vespasian alone changed for the better.
[9]Ability.

best, and had by nature himself no advantage in that he commended. A strange thing, that that part of an orator which is but superficial, and rather the virtue of a player, should be placed so high above those other noble parts of invention, elocution, and the rest; nay, almost alone, as if it were all in all. But the reason is plain. There is in human nature generally more of the fool than of the wise; and therefore those faculties by which the foolish part of men's minds is taken are most potent. Wonderful like is the case of boldness in civil business: what first? "Boldness": what second and third? "Boldness." And yet boldness is a child of ignorance and baseness, far inferior to other parts. But nevertheless it doth fascinate and bind hand and foot those that are either shallow in judgment or weak in courage, which are the greatest part; yea, and prevaileth with wise men at weak times. Therefore we see it hath done wonders in popular[1] states, but with senates and princes less; and more ever upon the first entrance of bold persons into action than soon after; for boldness is an ill keeper of promise. Surely, as there are mountebanks for the natural body, so are there mountebanks for the politic body; men that undertake great cures, and perhaps have been lucky in two or three experiments, but want the grounds[2] of science, and therefore cannot hold out. Nay, you shall see a bold fellow many times do Mahomet's miracle. Mahomet made the people believe that he would call an hill to him, and from the top of it offer up his prayers for the observers of his law. The people assembled; Mahomet called the hill to come to him, again and again; and when the hill stood still, he was never a whit abashed, but said: "If the hill will not come to Mahomet, Mahomet will go to the hill." So these men, when they have promised great matters and failed most shamefully, yet (if they have the perfection of boldness) they will but slight it over, and make a turn, and no more ado. Certainly, to men of great judgment, bold persons are a sport to behold; nay, and to the vulgar also, boldness hath somewhat of the ridiculous. For if absurdity be the subject of laughter, doubt you not but great boldness is seldom without some absurdity. Especially it is a sport to see, when a bold fellow is out of countenance; for that puts his face into a most shrunken and wooden posture; as needs it must; for in bashfulness the spirits do a little go and come; but with bold men, upon like occasion, they stand at a stay; like a stale[3] at chess, where it is no mate, but yet the game cannot stir. But this last were fitter for a satire than for a serious observation. This is well to be weighed, that boldness is ever blind; for it seeth not dangers and inconveniences. Therefore it is ill in counsel, good in execution; so that the right use of bold persons is, that they never command in chief, but be seconds, and under the direction of others. For in counsel it is good to see dangers; and in execution not to see them, except they be very great.

[1]Democratic. [2]Foundations.

16.—OF ATHEISM

I HAD rather believe all the fables in the Legend, and the Talmud, and the Alcoran,[4] than that this universal frame is without a mind. And therefore God never wrought miracle to convince[5] atheism, because his ordinary works convince it. It is true, that a little philosophy[6] inclineth man's mind to atheism; but depth in philosophy bringeth men's minds about to religion: for while the mind of man looketh upon second causes scattered, it may sometimes rest in them, and go no further; but when it beholdeth the chain of them, confederate and linked together, it must needs fly to Providence and Deity. Nay, even that school which is most accused of atheism doth most demonstrate religion; that is, the school of Leucippus and Democritus and Epicurus. For it is a thousand times more credible, that four mutable elements and one immutable fifth essence, duly and eternally placed, need no God, than that an army of infinite small portions or seeds unplaced should have produced this order and beauty without a divine marshal. The Scripture saith: "The fool hath said in his heart, there is no God":[7] it is not said, "The fool hath thought in his heart": so as he rather saith it by rote to himself, as that he would have, than that he can thoroughly believe it, or be persuaded of it. For none

[3]Stale-mate, where the king cannot move, save into check.
[4]Or Koran. [5]Confute.
[6]Natural philosophy, or science.
[7]Psalms, xiv, 1, and liii, 1.

deny there is a God but those for whom it maketh that there were no God. It appeareth in nothing more, that atheism is rather in the lip than in the heart of man, than by this; that atheists will ever be talking of that their opinion, as if they fainted in it within themselves, and would be glad to be strengthened by the consent of others: nay more, you shall have atheists strive to get disciples, as it fareth with other sects: and, which is most of all, you shall have of them that will suffer for atheism, and not recant; whereas, if they did truly think that there were no such thing as God, why should they trouble themselves? Epicurus is charged that he did but dissemble for his credit's sake, when he affirmed there were blessed natures, but such as enjoyed themselves without having respect to the government of the world. Wherein they say he did temporize, though in secret he thought there was no God. But certainly he is traduced; for his words are noble and divine: *Non deos vulgi negare profanum, sed vulgi opiniones diis applicare profanum.*[1] Plato could have said no more. And although he had the confidence to deny the administration, he had not the power to deny the nature. The Indians of the West have names for their particular gods, though they have no name for God: as if the heathens should have had the names Jupiter, Apollo, Mars, *etc.*, but not the word *Deus;* which shows that even those barbarous people have the notion, though they have not the latitude and extent of it. So that against atheists the very savages take part with the very subtlest philosophers. The contemplative atheist is rare; a Diagoras, a Bion, a Lucian perhaps, and some others; and yet they seem to be more than they are; for that all that impugn a received religion, or superstition, are, by the adverse part, branded with the name of atheists. But the great atheists indeed are hypocrites; which are ever handling holy things, but without feeling; so as they must needs be cauterized in the end. The causes of atheism are: divisions in religion, if they be many; for any one main division addeth zeal to both sides, but many divisions introduce atheism. Another is, scandal of priests; when it is come to that which S. Bernard saith: *Non est jam dicere, ut populus, sic sacerdos; quia nec sic populus, ut sacerdos.*[2] A third is, custom of profane scoffing in holy matters, which doth by little and little deface the reverence of religion. And lastly, learned times, specially with peace and prosperity; for troubles and adversities do more bow men's minds to religion. They that deny a God destroy man's nobility; for certainly man is of kin to the beasts by his body; and if he be not of kin to God by his spirit, he is a base and ignoble creature. It destroys likewise magnanimity, and the raising of human nature; for take an example of a dog, and mark what a generosity and courage he will put on when he finds himself maintained by a man, who to him is in stead of a god, or *melior natura;*[3] which courage is manifestly such as that creature, without that confidence of a better nature than his own, could never attain. So man, when he resteth and assureth himself upon divine protection and favor, gathereth a force and faith which human nature in itself could not obtain. Therefore, as atheism is in all respects hateful, so in this, that it depriveth human nature of the means to exalt itself above human frailty. As it is in particular persons, so it is in nations: never was there such a state for magnanimity as Rome: of this state hear what Cicero saith: *Quam volumus licet, patres conscripti, nos amemus, tamen nec numero Hispanos, nec robore Gallos, nec calliditate Pœnos, nec artibus Græcos, nec denique hoc ipso hujus gentis et terræ domestico nativoque sensu Italos ipsos et Latinos; sed pietate, ac religione, atque hâc unâ sapientiâ, quod Deorum immortalium numine omnia regi gubernarique perspeximus, omnes gentes nationesque superavimus.*[4]

17.—OF SUPERSTITION

IT WERE better to have no opinion of God at all, than such an opinion as is unworthy of him: for the one is unbelief, the other is

[1]It is not impious to say that the gods of men do not exist; it is impious rather to apply to the gods the foolish notions of men (Diogenes Laertius).

[2]It can no longer be said, "As the people are so is the priest," because the people are not now like the priest (*i.e.*, the priest is worse).

[3]Better nature.

[4]We may plume ourselves as we will, O senators, yet we have not conquered the Spaniards by force of numbers, nor the Gauls by superior might, nor the Carthaginians by strategy, nor the Greeks by our culture, nor lastly the Italians and Latins by the power of internal organization which is peculiar to this people and this land; but it is because of our devotion and our piety and, above all, our realization that human events are ruled and guided by the power of the immortal gods that we have conquered all nations and all peoples.

contumely: and certainly superstition is the reproach of the Deity. Plutarch saith well to that purpose: "Surely (saith he) I had rather a great deal men should say there was no such man at all as Plutarch, than that they should say that there was one Plutarch that would eat his children as soon as they were born"; as the poets speak of Saturn. And as the contumely is greater towards God, so the danger is greater towards men. Atheism leaves a man to sense, to philosophy, to natural piety, to laws, to reputation; all which may be guides to an outward moral virtue, though religion were not; but superstition dismounts all these, and erecteth an absolute monarchy in the minds of men. Therefore atheism did never perturb states; for it makes men wary of themselves, as looking no further: and we see the times inclined to atheism (as the time of Augustus Cæsar) were civil[1] times. But superstition hath been the confusion of many states, and bringeth in a new *primum mobile*,[2] that ravisheth all the spheres of government. The master of superstition is the people; and in all superstition wise men follow fools; and arguments are fitted to practice, in a reversed order. It was gravely said by some of the prelates in the Council of Trent,[3] where the doctrine of the schoolmen[4] bare great sway, "that the schoolmen were like astronomers, which did feign eccentrics and epicycles, and such engines of orbs, to save the phenomena, though they knew there were no such things"; and in like manner, that the schoolmen had framed a number of subtle and intricate axioms and theorems, to save the practice of the church. The causes of superstition are: pleasing and sensual rites and ceremonies; excess of outward and pharisaical holiness; over-great reverence of traditions, which cannot but load the church; the stratagems of prelates for their own ambition and lucre; the favoring too much of good intentions, which openeth the gate to conceits and novelties; the taking an aim at divine matters by human, which cannot but breed mixture of imaginations; and lastly, barbarous times, especially joined with calamities and disasters. Superstition, without a veil, is a deformed thing; for, as it addeth deformity to an ape to be so like a man, so the similitude of superstition to religion makes it the more deformed. And as wholesome meat corrupteth to little worms, so good forms and orders corrupt into a number of petty observances. There is a superstition in avoiding superstition, when men think to do best if they go furthest from the superstition formerly received: therefore care would be had that (as it fareth in ill purgings) the good be not taken away with the bad; which commonly is done, when the people is the reformer.

23.—OF WISDOM FOR A MAN'S SELF

AN ANT is a wise creature for itself, but it is a shrewd[5] thing in an orchard or garden. And certainly men that are great lovers of themselves waste the public. Divide with reason between self-love and society; and be so true to thyself, as thou be not false to others, specially to thy king and country. It is a poor center of a man's actions, himself. It is right earth. For that only stands fast upon his own center; whereas all things that have affinity with the heavens move upon the center of another, which they benefit.[6] The referring of all to a man's self is more tolerable in a sovereign prince; because themselves are not only themselves, but their good and evil is at the peril of the public fortune. But it is a desperate evil in a servant to a prince, or a citizen in a republic. For whatsoever affairs pass such a man's hands, he crooketh them to his own ends; which must needs be often eccentric to[7] the ends of his master or state. Therefore let princes, or states, choose such servants as have not this mark; except they mean their service should be made but the accessory. That which maketh the effect more pernicious is that all proportion is lost. It were disproportion enough for the servant's good to be preferred before the master's; but yet it is a greater extreme, when a little good of the servant shall carry things against a great good of the master's. And yet that is

[1]Tranquil.

[2]First-moved; in the Ptolemaic astronomy, the outermost of the spheres surrounding the earth, which was first moved and which carried along by its momentum the spheres within.

[3]Council of the Roman Catholic Church whose meetings began in 1545.

[4]Medieval philosophers.

[5]Mischievous.

[6]Bacon writes in terms of the Ptolemaic astronomy which he accepted, and according to which the earth is the center of the universe.

[7]Different from.

the case of bad officers, treasurers, ambassadors, generals, and other false and corrupt servants; which set a bias upon their bowl,[1] of their own petty ends and envies, to the overthrow of their master's great and important affairs. And for the most part, the good such servants receive is after the model of their own fortune; but the hurt they sell for that good is after the model of their master's fortune. And certainly it is the nature of extreme self-lovers, as they will set an house on fire, and it were but to roast their eggs; and yet these men many times hold credit with their masters, because their study is but to please them and profit themselves; and for either respect[2] they will abandon the good of their affairs.

Wisdom for a man's self is, in many branches thereof, a depraved thing. It is the wisdom of rats, that will be sure to leave a house somewhat before it fall. It is the wisdom of the fox, that thrusts out the badger, who digged and made room for him. It is the wisdom of crocodiles, that shed tears when they would devour. But that which is specially to be noted is, that those which (as Cicero says of Pompey) are *sui amantes sine rivali*,[3] are many times unfortunate. And whereas they have all their time sacrificed to themselves, they become in the end themselves sacrifices to the inconstancy of fortune, whose wings they thought by their self-wisdom to have pinioned.

27.—OF FRIENDSHIP

IT HAD been hard for him that spake it to have put more truth and untruth together in a few words, than in that speech: "Whosoever is delighted in solitude is either a wild beast or a god."[4] For it is most true that a natural and secret hatred and aversation[5] towards society, in any man, hath somewhat of the savage beast; but it is most untrue that it should have any character at all of the divine nature; except it proceed, not out of a pleasure in solitude, but out of a love and desire to sequester a man's self for a higher conversation:[6] such as is found to have been falsely and feignedly in some of the heathen; as Epimenides the Candian, Numa the Roman, Empedocles the Sicilian, and Apollonius of Tyana; and truly and really in divers of the ancient hermits and holy fathers of the church. But little do men perceive what solitude is, and how far it extendeth. For a crowd is not company, and faces are but a gallery of pictures, and talk but a tinkling cymbal, where there is no love. The Latin adage meeteth with it a little, *Magna civitas, magna solitudo;*[7] because in a great town friends are scattered; so that there is not that fellowship, for the most part, which is in less neighborhoods. But we may go further and affirm most truly, that it is a mere and miserable solitude to want true friends, without which the world is but a wilderness; and even in this sense also of solitude, whosoever in the frame of his nature and affections is unfit for friendship, he taketh it of the beast, and not from humanity.

A principal fruit of friendship is the ease and discharge of the fullness and swellings of the heart, which passions of all kinds do cause and induce. We know diseases of stoppings and suffocations are the most dangerous in the body; and it is not much otherwise in the mind: you may take sarza[8] to open the liver, steel to open the spleen, flower of sulphur for the lungs, castoreum[9] for the brain; but no receipt openeth the heart, but a true friend, to whom you may impart griefs, joys, fears, hopes, suspicions, counsels, and whatsoever lieth upon the heart to oppress it, in a kind of civil shrift or confession.

It is a strange thing to observe how high a rate great kings and monarchs do set upon this fruit of friendship whereof we speak: so great, as they purchase it many times at the hazard of their own safety and greatness. For princes, in regard of the distance of their fortune from that of their subjects and servants, cannot gather this fruit, except (to make themselves capable thereof) they raise some persons to be as it were companions and almost equals to themselves, which many times sorteth to inconvenience. The modern languages give unto such persons the name of favorites, or *privadoes;* as if it were matter of grace, or conversation. But the

[1]Place a weight in one side of their ball.
[2]Consideration.
[3]Lovers of themselves without a rival.
[4]Aristotle, in his *Politics*.
[5]Aversion. [6]Mode of life.

[7]A great city is a great solitude.
[8]Sarsaparilla. [9]A secretion of the beaver.

Roman name attaineth the true use and cause thereof, naming them *participes curarum;*[1] for it is that which tieth the knot. And we see plainly that this hath been done, not by weak and passionate princes only, but by the wisest and most politic that ever reigned; who have oftentimes joined to themselves some of their servants, whom both themselves have called friends, and allowed others likewise to call them in the same manner, using the word which is received between private men.

L. Sylla, when he commanded Rome, raised Pompey (after surnamed the Great) to that height, that Pompey vaunted himself for Sylla's overmatch. For when he had carried the consulship for a friend of his, against the pursuit of Sylla, and that Sylla did a little resent thereat, and began to speak great, Pompey turned upon him again, and in effect bade him be quiet, "for that more men adored the sun rising than the sun setting."[2] With Julius Cæsar, Decimus Brutus had obtained that interest, as he set him down in his testament for heir in remainder after his nephew. And this was the man that had power with him to draw him forth to his death. For when Cæsar would have discharged the senate, in regard of some ill presages, and specially a dream of Calpurnia, this man lifted him gently by the arm out of his chair telling him he hoped he would not dismiss the senate till his wife had dreamed a better dream.[3] And it seemeth his favor was so great, as Antonius, in a letter which is recited *verbatim* in one of Cicero's *Philippics,* calleth him *venefica,* "witch"; as if he had enchanted Cæsar. Augustus raised Agrippa (though of mean birth) to that height, as, when he consulted with Mæcenas about the marriage of his daughter Julia, Mæcenas took the liberty to tell him, "that he must either marry his daughter to Agrippa, or take away his life; there was no third way, he had made him so great."[4] With Tiberius Cæsar, Sejanus had ascended to that height, as they two were termed and reckoned as a pair of friends. Tiberius in a letter to him saith, *Hæc pro amicitiâ nostrâ non occultavi;*[5] and the whole senate dedicated an altar to Friendship, as to a goddess, in respect of the great dearness of friendship between them two. The like or more was between Septimius Severus and Plautianus. For he forced his eldest son to marry the daughter of Plautianus; and would often maintain Plautianus in doing affronts to his son; and did write also in a letter to the senate by these words: "I love the man so well, as I wish he may over-live me."[6] Now if these princes had been as a Trajan, or a Marcus Aurelius, a man might have thought that this had proceeded of an abundant goodness of nature; but being men so wise, for such strength and severity of mind, and so extreme lovers of themselves, as all these were, it proveth most plainly that they found their own felicity (though as great as ever happened to mortal men) but as an half piece, except they might have a friend to make it entire: and yet, which is more, they were princes that had wives, sons, nephews; and yet all these could not supply the comfort of friendship.

It is not to be forgotten, what Commineus observeth of his first master, Duke Charles the Hardy; namely, that he would communicate his secrets with none; and least of all, those secrets which troubled him most. Whereupon he goeth on and saith, that towards his latter time "that closeness did impair and a little perish his understanding." Surely Commineus might have made the same judgment also, if it had pleased him, of his second master, Lewis the Eleventh, whose closeness was indeed his tormentor. The parable of Pythagoras is dark, but true; *Cor ne edito,* "Eat not the heart." Certainly, if a man would give it a hard phrase, those that want friends to open themselves unto are cannibals of their own hearts. But one thing is most admirable (wherewith I will conclude this first fruit of friendship), which is, that this communicating of a man's self to his friend works two contrary effects; for it redoubleth joys, and cutteth griefs in halfs. For there is no man that imparteth his joys to his friend, but he joyeth the more; and no man that imparteth his griefs to his friend, but he grieveth the less. So that it is in truth of operation upon a man's mind, of like virtue as the alchemists

[1]Partners of their sorrows. [2]Plutarch, *Life of Pompey.*
[3]Plutarch, *Life of Cæsar.* [4]Dion Cassius, LVI, 6.
[5]Such is our friendship that even this I have not kept from you (Tacitus, *Annals,* IV, 40).

[6]Dion Cassius, LXXV, 15.

use to attribute to their stone for man's body; that it worketh all contrary effects, but still to the good and benefit of nature. But yet, without praying in aid[1] of alchemists, there is a manifest image of this in the ordinary course of nature. For in bodies, union strengtheneth and cherisheth any natural action; and, on the other side, weakeneth and dulleth any violent impression: and even so is it of minds.

The second fruit of friendship is healthful and sovereign for the understanding, as the first is for the affections. For friendship maketh indeed a fair day in the affections, from storm and tempests; but it maketh daylight in the understanding, out of darkness and confusion of thoughts. Neither is this to be understood only of faithful counsel, which a man receiveth from his friend; but before you come to that, certain it is that whosoever hath his mind fraught with many thoughts, his wits and understanding do clarify and break up, in the communicating and discoursing with another: he tosseth his thoughts more easily; he marshaleth them more orderly; he seeth how they look when they are turned into words; finally, he waxeth wiser than himself; and that more by an hour's discourse than by a day's meditation. It was well said by Themistocles to the king of Persia, "that speech was like cloth of Arras, opened and put abroad; whereby the imagery doth appear in figure; whereas in thoughts they lie but as in packs."[2] Neither is this second fruit of friendship, in opening the understanding, restrained only to such friends as are able to give a man counsel: (they indeed are best); but even without that, a man learneth of himself, and bringeth his own thoughts to light, and whetteth his wits as against a stone, which itself cuts not. In a word, a man were better relate himself to a statue or picture, than to suffer his thoughts to pass in smother.

Add now, to make this second fruit of friendship complete, that other point, which lieth more open, and falleth within vulgar observation; which is faithful counsel from a friend. Heraclitus saith well in one of his enigmas: "Dry light is ever the best." And certain it is that the light that a man receiveth by counsel from another is drier and purer than that which cometh from his own understanding and judgment; which is ever infused and drenched in his affections and customs. So as there is as much difference between the counsel that a friend giveth, and that a man giveth himself, as there is between the counsel of a friend and of a flatterer. For there is no such flatterer as is a man's self; and there is no such remedy against flattery of a man's self as the liberty of a friend. Counsel is of two sorts; the one concerning manners, the other concerning business. For the first; the best preservative to keep the mind in health is the faithful admonition of a friend. The calling of a man's self to a strict account is a medicine, sometime, too piercing and corrosive. Reading good books of morality is a little flat and dead. Observing our faults in others is sometimes unproper for our case. But the best receipt (best, I say, to work, and best to take) is the admonition of a friend. It is a strange thing to behold what gross errors and extreme absurdities many (especially of the greater sort) do commit, for want of a friend to tell them of them, to the great damage both of their fame and fortune. For as S. James saith, they are as men, "that look sometimes into a glass, and presently forget their own shape and favor."[3] As for business, a man may think, if he will, that two eyes see no more than one; or that a gamester seeth always more than a looker-on; or that a man in anger is as wise as he that hath said over the four and twenty letters; or that a musket may be shot off as well upon the arm as upon a rest; and such other fond and high imaginations, to think himself all in all. But when all is done, the help of good counsel is that which setteth business straight. And if any man think that he will take counsel, but it shall be by pieces; asking counsel in one business of one man, and in another business of another man; it is well (that is to say, better perhaps than if he asked none at all); but he runneth two dangers. One, that he shall not be faithfully counseled; for it is a rare thing except it be from a perfect and entire friend to have counsel given, but such as shall be bowed and crooked to some ends which he hath that giveth it. The other, that he

[1] Calling in the aid.

[2] Plutarch, *Life of Themistocles*.

[3] St. James, i, 23–24.

shall have counsel given, hurtful and unsafe (though with good meaning), and mixed partly of mischief and partly of remedy: even as if you would call a physician, that is thought good for the cure of the disease you complain of, but is unacquainted with your body; and therefore may put you in way for a present cure, but overthroweth your health in some other kind; and so cure the disease and kill the patient. But a friend that is wholly acquainted with a man's estate will beware, by furthering any present business, how he dasheth upon other inconvenience. And therefore rest not upon scattered counsels; they will rather distract and mislead than settle and direct.

After these two noble fruits of friendship (peace in the affections, and support of the judgment) followeth the last fruit, which is like the pomegranate, full of many kernels; I mean aid and bearing a part in all actions and occasions. Here the best way to represent to life the manifold use of friendship is to cast and see how many things there are which a man cannot do himself; and then it will appear that it was a sparing speech of the ancients, to say, "that a friend is another himself": for that a friend is far more than himself. Men have their time, and die many times in desire of some things which they principally take to heart; the bestowing of a child, the finishing of a work, or the like. If a man have a true friend, he may rest almost secure that the care of those things will continue after him. So that a man hath as it were two lives in his desires. A man hath a body, and that body is confined to a place; but where friendship is, all offices of life are as it were granted to him and his deputy. For he may exercise them by his friend. How many things are there which a man cannot, with any face or comeliness, say or do himself! A man can scarce allege his own merits with modesty, much less extol them; a man cannot sometimes brook to supplicate or beg; and a number of the like. But all these things are graceful in a friend's mouth, which are blushing in a man's own. So again, a man's person hath many proper relations which he cannot put off. A man cannot speak to his son but as a father; to his wife but as a husband; to his enemy but upon terms: whereas a friend may speak as the case requires, and not as it sorteth with the person. But to enumerate these things were endless: I have given the rule, where a man cannot fitly play his own part: if he have not a friend, he may quit the stage.

28.—OF EXPENSE

Riches are for spending, and spending for honor and good actions. Therefore extraordinary expense must be limited by the worth of the occasion; for voluntary undoing may be as well for a man's country as for the kingdom of heaven. But ordinary expense ought to be limited by a man's estate; and governed with such regard, as it be within his compass; and not subject to deceit and abuse of servants; and ordered to the best show, that the bills may be less than the estimation abroad. Certainly, if a man will keep but of even hand,[1] his ordinary expenses ought to be but to the half of his receipts; and if he think to wax rich, but to the third part. It is no baseness for the greatest to descend and look into their own estate. Some forbear it, not upon negligence alone, but doubting to bring themselves into melancholy, in respect they shall find it broken. But wounds cannot be cured without searching.[2] He that cannot look into his own estate at all, had need both choose well those whom he employeth, and change them often; for new are more timorous and less subtle. He that can look into his estate but seldom, it behoveth him to turn all to certainties. A man had need, if he be plentiful in some kind of expense, to be as saving again in some other. As, if he be plentiful in diet, to be saving in apparel; if he be plentiful in the hall, to be saving in the stable; and the like. For he that is plentiful in expenses of all kinds will hardly be preserved from decay. In clearing of a man's estate, he may as well hurt himself in being too sudden, as in letting it run on too long. For hasty selling is commonly as disadvantageable as interest. Besides, he that clears at once will relapse; for finding himself out of straits, he will revert to his customs: but he that cleareth by degrees induceth a habit of frugality, and gaineth as well upon his mind as upon his estate. Certainly, who hath a state to repair may not despise small things: and commonly it is less dishonorable to abridge petty

[1]Will manage prudently. [2]Probing.

charges, than to stoop to petty gettings. A man ought warily to begin charges which once begun will continue: but in matters that return not he may be more magnificent.

32.—OF DISCOURSE

SOME in their discourse desire rather commendation of wit, in being able to hold all arguments, than of judgment, in discerning what is true; as if it were a praise to know what might be said, and not what should be thought. Some have certain commonplaces and themes wherein they are good, and want variety; which kind of poverty is for the most part tedious, and, when it is once perceived, ridiculous. The honorablest part of talk is to give the occasion; and again to moderate and pass to somewhat else; for then a man leads the dance. It is good, in discourse, and speech of conversation, to vary and intermingle speech of the present occasion with arguments; tales with reasons; asking of questions with telling of opinions; and jest with earnest: for it is a dull thing to tire, and, as we say now, to jade[1] anything too far. As for jest, there be certain things which ought to be privileged from it; namely, religion, matters of state, great persons, any man's present business of importance, and any case that deserveth pity. Yet there be some that think their wits have been asleep, except they dart out somewhat that is piquant and to the quick: that is a vein which would be bridled:

Parce, puer, stimulis, et fortius utere loris.[2]

And generally, men ought to find the difference between saltness[3] and bitterness. Certainly, he that hath a satirical vein, as he maketh others afraid of his wit, so he had need be afraid of others' memory. He that questioneth much, shall learn much, and content much; but especially if he apply his questions to the skill of the persons whom he asketh: for he shall give them occasion to please themselves in speaking, and himself shall continually gather knowledge. But let his questions not be troublesome; for that is fit for a poser.[4] And let him be sure to leave other men their turns to speak. Nay, if there be any that would reign and take up all the time, let him find means to take them off and to bring others on; as musicians use to do with those that dance too long galliards. If you dissemble sometimes your knowledge of that you are thought to know, you shall be thought another time to know that you know not. Speech of a man's self ought to be seldom, and well chosen. I knew one was wont to say in scorn: "He must needs be a wise man, he speaks so much of himself": and there is but one case wherein a man may commend himself with good grace, and that is in commending virtue in another, especially if it be such a virtue whereunto himself pretendeth. Speech of touch[5] towards others should be sparingly used; for discourse ought to be as a field, without coming home to any man. I knew two noblemen, of the west part of England, whereof the one was given to scoff, but kept ever royal cheer in his house: the other would ask of those that had been at the other's table: "Tell truly, was there never a flout or dry blow[6] given?" to which the guest would answer: "Such and such a thing passed": the lord would say: "I thought he would mar a good dinner." Discretion of speech is more than eloquence; and to speak agreeably to him with whom we deal, is more than to speak in good words or in good order. A good continued speech, without a good speech of interlocution, shows slowness; and a good reply or second speech, without a good settled speech, showeth shallowness and weakness. As we see in beasts, that those that are weakest in the course, are yet nimblest in the turn; as it is betwixt the greyhound and the hare. To use too many circumstances, ere one come to the matter, is wearisome; to use none at all, is blunt.

34.—OF RICHES

I CANNOT call riches better than the baggage of virtue. The Roman word is better, *impedimenta*.[7] For as the baggage is to an army, so is riches to virtue. It cannot be spared nor left behind, but it hindereth the march; yea, and the care of it sometimes loseth or disturbeth the victory. Of great riches there is no real use, except it be in the

[1]Overdrive.
[2]Use the whip lightly, lad, and pull hard on the reins (Ovid, *Metamorphoses*, II, 126).
[3]Wit. [4]Examiner.

[5]Speech wounding others.
[6]Jeer or hard knock. [7]Hindrances.

distribution; the rest is but conceit. So saith Solomon: "Where much is, there are many to consume it; and what hath the owner but the sight of it with his eyes?"[1] The personal fruition in any man cannot reach to feel great riches: there is a custody of them; or a power of dole and donative of them; or a fame of them; but no solid use to the owner. Do you not see what feigned prices are set upon little stones and rarities? and what works of ostentation are undertaken, because there might seem to be some use of great riches? But then you will say, they may be of use to buy men out of dangers or trouble. As Solomon saith: "Riches are as a stronghold, in the imagination of the rich man."[2] But this is excellently expressed, that it is in imagination, and not always in fact. For certainly great riches have sold[3] more men than they have brought out. Seek not proud riches, but such as thou mayest get justly, use soberly, distribute cheerfully, and leave contentedly. Yet have no abstract nor friarly contempt of them. But distinguish, as Cicero saith well of Rabirius Posthumus: *In studio rei amplificandæ apparebat non avaritiæ prædam sed instrumentum bonitati quæri.*[4] Hearken also to Solomon, and beware of hasty gathering of riches: *Qui festinat ad divitias non erit insons.*[5] The poets feign that when Plutus (which is Riches) is sent from Jupiter, he limps and goes slowly; but when he is sent from Pluto, he runs and is swift of foot: meaning, that riches gotten by good means and just labor pace slowly; but when they come by the death of others (as by the course of inheritance, testaments, and the like), they come tumbling upon a man. But it might be applied likewise to Pluto, taking him for the devil. For when riches come from the devil (as by fraud and oppression and unjust means), they come upon speed. The ways to enrich are many, and most of them foul. Parsimony is one of the best, and yet is not innocent; for it withholdeth men from works of liberality and charity. The improvement of the ground is the most natural obtaining of riches; for it is our great mother's blessing, the earth's; but it is slow. And yet, where men of great wealth do stoop to husbandry, it multiplieth riches exceedingly. I knew a nobleman in England, that had the greatest audits[6] of any man in my time: a great grazier, a great sheep-master, a great timber man, a great collier, a great corn-master, a great lead-man, and so of iron, and a number of the like points of husbandry: so as the earth seemed a sea to him, in respect of the perpetual importation. It was truly observed by one, that himself came very hardly to a little riches, and very easily to great riches. For when a man's stock is come to that, that he can expect the prime of markets,[7] and overcome[8] those bargains which for their greatness are few men's money, and be partner in the industries of younger men, he cannot but increase mainly.[9] The gains of ordinary trades and vocations are honest, and furthered by two things chiefly: by diligence, and by a good name for good and fair dealing. But the gains of bargains are of a more doubtful nature; when men shall wait upon others' necessity, broke[10] by servants and instruments to draw them on, put off others cunningly that would be better chapmen,[11] and the like practices, which are crafty and naught. As for the chopping of bargains, when a man buys, not to hold, but to sell over again, that commonly grindeth double, both upon the seller and upon the buyer. Sharings do greatly enrich, if the hands be well chosen that are trusted. Usury is the certainest means of gain, though one of the worst; as that whereby a man doth eat his bread *in sudore vultûs alieni,*[12] and besides, doth plow upon Sundays. But yet, certain though it be, it hath flaws; for that the scriveners and brokers do value unsound men, to serve their own turn. The fortune in being the first in an invention, or in a privilege, doth cause sometimes a wonderful overgrowth in riches; as it was with the first sugar man in the Canaries: therefore if a man can play the true logician, to have as well judgment as invention, he may do great matters; especially if the times be fit. He that resteth upon gains certain, shall hardly grow to great riches: and he that puts all

[1]Ecclesiastes, v, 11.

[2]Proverbs, xviii, 11.

[3]Betrayed.

[4]In desiring to increase his wealth he seemed to be seeking not so much the spoils of greed as the means for generosity.

[5]He who grows rich quickly will not be free from sin (Proverbs, xxviii, 20).

[6]Accounts.

[7]Wait until the market is most favorable.

[8]Take advantage of.

[9]Greatly.

[10]Negotiate.

[11]Traders.

[12]By the sweat of another's brow.

upon adventures, doth oftentimes break and come to poverty: it is good therefore to guard adventures with certainties that may uphold losses. Monopolies, and coemption[1] of wares for re-sale, where they are not restrained, are great means to enrich; especially if the party have intelligence what things are like to come into request, and so store himself beforehand. Riches gotten by service, though it be of the best rise, yet when they are gotten by flattery, feeding humors, and other servile conditions, they may be placed amongst the worst. As for fishing for testaments and executorships (as Tacitus saith of Seneca, *testamenta et orbos tanquam indagine capi*[2]) it is yet worse; by how much men submit themselves to meaner persons than in service. Believe not much them that seem to despise riches; for they despise them that despair of them; and none worse, when they come to them. Be not penny-wise; riches have wings, and sometimes they fly away of themselves, sometimes they must be set flying to bring in more. Men leave their riches either to their kindred, or to the public; and moderate portions prosper best in both. A great state left to an heir, is as a lure to all the birds of prey round about to seize on him, if he be not the better stablished in years and judgment. Likewise glorious gifts and foundations are like sacrifices without salt; and but the painted sepulchers of alms, which soon will putrefy and corrupt inwardly. Therefore measure not thine advancements[3] by quantity, but frame them by measure: and defer not charities till death; for certainly, if a man weigh it rightly, he that doth so is rather liberal of another man's than of his own.

38.—OF NATURE IN MEN

Nature is often hidden, sometimes overcome, seldom extinguished. Force maketh nature more violent in the return; doctrine and discourse maketh nature less importune;[4] but custom only doth alter and subdue nature. He that seeketh victory over his nature, let him not set himself too great nor too small tasks: for the first will make him dejected by often failings; and the second will make him a small proceeder, though by often prevailings. And at the first let him practice with helps, as swimmers do with bladders or rushes; but after a time let him practice with disadvantages, as dancers do with thick shoes. For it breeds great perfection, if the practice be harder than the use. Where nature is mighty, and therefore the victory hard, the degrees had need be: first, to stay and arrest nature in time, like to him that would say over the four and twenty letters when he was angry; then, to go less in quantity, as if one should, in forbearing wine, come from drinking healths to a draught at a meal; and lastly, to discontinue altogether. But if a man have the fortitude and resolution to enfranchise himself at once, that is the best:

Optimus ille animi vindex lædentia pectus
Vincula qui rupit, dedoluitque semel.[5]

Neither is the ancient rule amiss, to bend nature as a wand to a contrary extreme, whereby to set it right; understanding it, where the contrary extreme is no vice. Let not a man force a habit upon himself with a perpetual continuance, but with some intermission. For both the pause reinforceth the new onset; and if a man that is not perfect be ever in practice, he shall as well practice his errors as his abilities, and induce one habit of both; and there is no means to help this but by seasonable intermissions. But let not a man trust his victory over his nature too far; for nature will lay buried a great time, and yet revive upon the occasion or temptation;—like as it was with Æsop's damsel, turned from a cat to a woman, who sat very demurely at the board's end till a mouse ran before her. Therefore let a man either avoid the occasion altogether, or put himself often to it that he may be little moved with it. A man's nature is best perceived in privateness, for there is no affectation; in passion, for that putteth a man out of his precepts; and in a new case or experiment, for there custom leaveth him. They are happy men whose natures sort with their vocations; otherwise they may say, *Multum incola fuit anima mea*,[6] when they converse in those things they do not affect. In studies, whatsoever a man commandeth upon himself, let him set hours for it; but

[1]Purchasing all there is of a commodity.

[2]Taking in bequests and wardships as with a net.

[3]Gifts. [4]Troublesome.

[5]He frees his spirit best who, bursting the chains that bruise his breast, ends his sufferings once for all (Ovid, *Remedy of Love*, 293–294).

[6]My soul dwelt in a strange land (Psalms, cxx, 6).

whatsoever is agreeable to his nature, let him take no care for any set times; for his thoughts will fly to it of themselves, so as the spaces of other business or studies will suffice. A man's nature runs either to herbs or weeds; therefore let him seasonably water the one and destroy the other.

42.—OF YOUTH AND AGE

A MAN that is young in years may be old in hours, if he have lost no time. But that happeneth rarely. Generally, youth is like the first cogitations, not so wise as the second. For there is a youth in thoughts as well as in ages. And yet the invention of young men is more lively than that of the old; and imaginations stream into their minds better, and, as it were, more divinely. Natures that have much heat, and great and violent desires and perturbations, are not ripe for action till they have passed the meridian of their years: as it was with Julius Cæsar, and Septimius Severus. Of the latter of whom it is said, *Juventutem egit erroribus, imo furoribus, plenam.*[1] And yet he was the ablest emperor, almost, of all the list. But reposed natures may do well in youth. As it is seen in Augustus Cæsar, Cosmus,[2] Duke of Florence, Gaston de Foix, and others. On the other side, heat and vivacity in age is an excellent composition for business. Young men are fitter to invent than to judge; fitter for execution than for counsel; and fitter for new projects than for settled business. For the experience of age, in things that fall within the compass of it, directeth them; but in new things, abuseth them. The errors of young men are the ruin of business; but the errors of aged men amount but to this, that more might have been done, or sooner. Young men, in the conduct and manage[3] of actions, embrace more than they can hold; stir more than they can quiet; fly to the end, without consideration of the means and degrees; pursue some few principles which they have chanced upon absurdly; care[4] not to innovate, which draws unknown inconveniences; use extreme remedies at first; and, that which doubleth all errors, will not acknowledge or retract them; like an unready horse, that will neither stop nor turn. Men of age object too much, consult too long, adventure too little, repent too soon, and seldom drive business home to the full period, but content themselves with a mediocrity of success. Certainly, it is good to compound employments of both; for that will be good for the present, because the virtues of either age may correct the defects of both; and good for succession, that young men may be learners, while men in age are actors; and, lastly, good for extern[5] accidents, because authority followeth old men, and favor and popularity youth. But for the moral part, perhaps youth will have the pre-eminence, as age hath for the politic. A certain rabbin, upon the text, "Your young men shall see visions, and your old men shall dream dreams,"[6] inferreth that young men are admitted nearer to God than old, because vision is a clearer revelation than a dream. And certainly, the more a man drinketh of the world, the more it intoxicateth; and age doth profit rather in the powers of understanding, than in the virtues of the will and affections. There be some have an over-early ripeness in their years, which fadeth betimes. These are, first, such as have brittle wits, the edge whereof is soon turned; such as was Hermogenes the rhetorician, whose books are exceeding subtle, who afterwards waxed stupid. A second sort is of those that have some natural dispositions which have better grace in youth than in age; such as is a fluent and luxuriant speech, which becomes youth well, but not age: so Tully saith of Hortensius, *Idem manebat, neque idem decebat.*[7] The third is of such as take too high a strain at the first, and are magnanimous more than tract of years can uphold. As was Scipio Africanus, of whom Livy saith in effect, *Ultima primis cedebant.*[8]

47.—OF NEGOTIATING

IT IS generally better to deal by speech than by letter; and by the mediation of a third than by a man's self. Letters are good, when a man would draw an answer by letter back again; or when it may serve for a man's justification afterwards to produce his own

[1]He spent his youth in folly, nay, in madness (Spartianus).
[2]*I.e.*, Cosimo de' Medici. [3]Management. [4]Hesitate.

[5]External. [6]Joel, ii, 28.
[7]He remained the same, but it was no longer becoming (Cicero).
[8]His latter days fell short of the first.

letter; or where it may be danger to be interrupted, or heard by pieces. To deal in person is good, when a man's face breedeth regard, as commonly with inferiors; or in tender cases, where a man's eye upon the countenance of him with whom he speaketh may give him a direction how far to go; and generally, where a man will reserve to himself liberty either to disavow or to expound. In choice of instruments, it is better to choose men of a plainer sort, that are like to do that that is committed to them, and to report back again faithfully the success, than those that are cunning to contrive out of other men's business somewhat to grace themselves, and will help the matter in report for satisfaction sake. Use also such persons as affect[1] the business wherein they are employed; for that quickeneth much; and such as are fit for the matter; as bold men for expostulation, fair-spoken men for persuasion, crafty men for inquiry and observation, froward and absurd men for business that doth not well bear out itself. Use also such as have been lucky and prevailed before in things wherein you have employed them; for that breeds confidence, and they will strive to maintain their prescription.[2] It is better to sound a person, with whom one deals, afar off, than to fall upon the point at first; except you mean to surprise him by some short question. It is better dealing with men in appetite,[3] than with those that are where they would be. If a man deal with another upon conditions, the start or first performance is all; which a man cannot reasonably demand, except either the nature of the thing be such which must go before; or else a man can persuade the other party that he shall still need him in some other thing; or else that he be counted the honester man. All practice[4] is to discover, or to work. Men discover themselves in trust; in passion; at unawares; and of necessity, when they would have somewhat done and cannot find an apt pretext. If you would work any man, you must either know his nature and fashions, and so lead him; or his ends, and so persuade him; or his weakness and disadvantages, and so awe him; or those that have interest in him, and so govern him. In dealing with cunning persons, we must ever consider their ends, to interpret their speeches; and it is good to say little to them, and that which they least look for. In all negotiations of difficulty, a man may not look to sow and reap at once; but must prepare business, and so ripen it by degrees.

50.—OF STUDIES

STUDIES serve for delight, for ornament, and for ability. Their chief use for delight is in privateness and retiring; for ornament, is in discourse; and for ability, is in the judgment and disposition of business. For expert men can execute, and perhaps judge of particulars, one by one; but the general counsels, and the plots and marshaling of affairs, come best from those that are learned. To spend too much time in studies is sloth; to use them too much for ornament is affectation; to make judgment wholly by their rules is the humor of a scholar. They perfect nature, and are perfected by experience; for natural abilities are like natural plants, that need pruning by study; and studies themselves do give forth directions too much at large, except they be bounded in by experience. Crafty men contemn studies; simple men admire them; and wise men use them: for they teach not their own use; but that is a wisdom without them and above them, won by observation. Read not to contradict and confute; nor to believe and take for granted; nor to find talk and discourse; but to weigh and consider. Some books are to be tasted, others to be swallowed, and some few to be chewed and digested: that is, some books are to be read only in parts; others to be read, but not curiously;[5] and some few to be read wholly, and with diligence and attention. Some books also may be read by deputy, and extracts made of them by others; but that would be only in the less important arguments, and the meaner sort of books; else distilled books are like common distilled waters, flashy[6] things. Reading maketh a full man; conference a ready man; and writing an exact man. And therefore, if a man write little, he had need have a great memory; if he confer little, he had need have a present wit; and if he read little, he had need have much cunning, to seem to know that he doth not. Histories make men wise; poets witty; the mathematics subtle; natural

[1]Are inclined to. [2]Reputation.
[3]Anxious to advance. [4]Negotiation.

[5]Not with great care. [6]Insipid.

philosophy deep; moral grave; logic and rhetoric able to contend. *Abeunt studia in mores.*[1] Nay, there is no stond[2] or impediment in the wit, but may be wrought out by fit studies: like as diseases of the body may have appropriate exercises. Bowling is good for the stone and reins;[3] shooting for the lungs and breast; gentle walking for the stomach; riding for the head; and the like. So if a man's wit be wandering, let him study the mathematics; for in demonstrations, if his wit be called away never so little, he must begin again: if his wit be not apt to distinguish or find differences, let him study the schoolmen; for they are *cymini sectores:*[4] if he be not apt to beat over matters, and to call one thing to prove and illustrate another, let him study the lawyers' cases: so every defect of the mind may have a special receipt.

53.—OF PRAISE

Praise is the reflection of virtue. But it is as the glass or body which giveth the reflection. If it be from the common people, it is commonly false and naught; and rather followeth vain persons than virtuous. For the common people understand not many excellent virtues. The lowest virtues draw praise from them; the middle virtues work in them astonishment or admiration; but of the highest virtues they have no sense or perceiving at all. But shows, and *species virtutibus similes,*[5] serve best with them. Certainly, fame is like a river, that beareth up things light and swollen, and drowns things weighty and solid. But if persons of quality and judgment concur, then it is as the Scripture saith, *Nomen bonum instar unguenti fragrantis:*[6] it filleth all round about, and will not easily away: for the odors of ointments are more durable than those of flowers. There be so many false points of praise, that a man may justly hold it a suspect. Some praises proceed merely of flattery: and if he be an ordinary flatterer, he will have certain common attributes, which may serve every man: if he be a cunning flatterer, he will follow the arch-flatterer, which is a man's self; and wherein a man thinketh best of himself, therein the flatterer will uphold him most: but if he be an impudent flatterer, look wherein a man is conscious to himself that he is most defective and is most out of countenance in himself, that will the flatterer entitle him to perforce, *spretâ conscientiâ.*[7] Some praises come of good wishes and respects, which is a form due in civility to kings and great persons, *laudando præcipere;*[8] when by telling men what they are, they represent to them what they should be. Some men are praised maliciously to their hurt, thereby to stir envy and jealousy towards them; *pessimum genus inimicorum laudantium;*[9] insomuch as it was a proverb amongst the Grecians, that "he that was praised to his hurt should have a push[10] rise upon his nose:" as we say, "that a blister will rise upon one's tongue that tells a lie." Certainly moderate praise, used with opportunity, and not vulgar, is that which doth the good. Solomon saith: "He that praiseth his friend aloud, rising early, it shall be to him no better than a curse."[11] Too much magnifying of man or matter doth irritate contradiction, and procure envy and scorn. To praise a man's self cannot be decent, except it be in rare cases; but to praise a man's office or profession, he may do it with good grace, and with a kind of magnanimity. The cardinals of Rome, which are theologues,[12] and friars, and schoolmen, have a phrase of notable contempt and scorn towards civil business: for they call all temporal business, of wars, embassages, judicature, and other employments, *sbirrerie,* which is under-sheriffries, as if they were but matters for under-sheriffs and catchpoles;[13] though many times those under-sheriffries do more good than their high speculations. St. Paul when he boasts of himself, he doth oft interlace, "I speak like a fool";[14] but speaking of his calling, he saith, *Magnificabo apostolatum meum.*[15]

56.—OF JUDICATURE

Judges ought to remember that their office is *jus dicere,* and not *jus dare;* to interpret

[1] Studies develop into manners (Ovid, *Heroides,* XV, 83).
[2] Hindrance. [3] Kidneys.
[4] Splitters of cumin, *i. e.,* hair-splitters.
[5] Virtue's counterfeits.
[6] A good name is like a fragrant ointment (Ecclesiastes, vii, 1, inexactly quoted).

[7] Silencing his better judgment.
[8] To admonish by means of praise.
[9] Invidious flatterers are the worst class (Tacitus).
[10] Pimple. [11] Proverbs, xxvii, 14.
[12] Theologians. [13] Bailiffs' assistants.
[14] II Corinthians, xi, 23.
[15] I shall magnify my office (Romans, xi, 13).

law, and not to make law, or give law. Else will it be like the authority claimed by the church of Rome; which, under pretext of exposition of Scripture, doth not stick[1] to add and alter, and to pronounce that which they do not find, and by show of antiquity to introduce novelty. Judges ought to be more learned than witty, more reverend than plausible, and more advised than confident. Above all things, integrity is their portion and proper virtue. "Cursed" (saith the law) "is he that removeth the land-mark."[2] The mislayer of a mere stone is to blame. But it is the unjust judge that is the capital remover of land-marks, when he defineth amiss of lands and property. One foul sentence doth more hurt than many foul examples. For these do but corrupt the stream; the other corrupteth the fountain. So saith Solomon: *Fons turbatus, et vena corrupta, est justus cadens in causâ suâ coram adversario.*[3] The office of judges may have reference unto the parties that sue; unto the advocates that plead; unto the clerks and ministers of justice underneath them; and to the sovereign or state above them.

First, for the causes or parties that sue. "There be" (saith the Scripture) "that turn judgment into wormwood";[4] and surely there be also that turn it into vinegar; for injustice maketh it bitter, and delays make it sour. The principal duty of a judge is to suppress force and fraud; whereof force is the more pernicious when it is open, and fraud when it is close and disguised. Add thereto contentious suits, which ought to be spewed out, as the surfeit of courts. A judge ought to prepare his way to a just sentence, as God useth to prepare his way, by raising valleys and taking down hills: so when there appeareth on either side an high hand, violent prosecution, cunning advantages taken, combination, power, great counsel, then is the virtue of a judge seen, to make inequality equal; that he may plant his judgment as upon an even ground. *Qui fortiter emungit, elicit sanguinem;*[5] and where the wine-press is hard wrought, it yields a harsh wine, that tastes of the grapestone. Judges must beware of hard constructions and strained inferences; for there is no worse torture than the torture of laws. Specially in case of laws penal, they ought to have care that that which was meant for terror be not turned into rigor; and that they bring not upon the people that shower whereof the Scripture speaketh, *Pluet super eos laqueos:*[6] for penal laws pressed are a *shower of snares* upon the people. Therefore let penal laws, if they have been sleepers of long, or if they be grown unfit for the present time, be by wise judges confined in the execution:

Judicis officium est, ut res, ita tempora rerum, etc.[7]

In causes of life and death, judges ought (as far as the law permitteth) in justice to remember mercy; and to cast a severe eye upon the example, but a merciful eye upon the person.

Secondly, for the advocates and counsel that plead. Patience and gravity of hearing is an essential part of justice; and an overspeaking judge is no well tuned cymbal. It is no grace to a judge first to find that which he might have heard in due time from the bar; or to show quickness of conceit in cutting off evidence or counsel too short; or to prevent information by questions, though pertinent. The parts of a judge in hearing are four: to direct the evidence; to moderate length, repetition, or impertinency of speech; to recapitulate, select, and collate the material points of that which hath been said; and to give the rule or sentence. Whatsoever is above these is too much; and proceedeth either of glory and willingness to speak or of impatience to hear, or of shortness of memory, or of want of a staid and equal attention. It is a strange thing to see that the boldness of advocates should prevail with judges; whereas they should imitate God, in whose seat they sit; who "represseth the presumptuous," and "giveth grace to the modest."[8] But it is more strange, that judges should have noted favorites; which cannot but cause multiplication of fees, and suspicion of by-ways. There is due from the judge to the advocate some commendation and gracing, where causes are well handled and fair pleaded; especially towards the side which obtaineth not; for that

[1] Hesitate. [2] Deuteronomy, xxvii, 17.

[3] As a troubled fountain and corrupted spring, so is the righteous man that must give way before his opponent (Proverbs, xxv, 26).

[4] Amos, v, 7.

[5] Hard pressure draws blood (Proverbs, xxx, 33).

[6] He will rain down snares upon them (Psalms, xi, 6).

[7] The judge must consider the times as well as the circumstances of things (Ovid).

[8] St. James, iv, 6.

upholds in the client the reputation of his counsel, and beats down in him the conceit[1] of his cause. There is likewise due to the public a civil reprehension of advocates, where there appeareth cunning counsel, gross neglect, slight information, indiscreet pressing, or an over-bold defense. And let not the counsel at the bar chop[2] with the judge, nor wind himself into the handling of the cause anew after the judge hath declared his sentence: but on the other side, let not the judge meet the cause half way, nor give occasion to the party to say, his counsel or proofs were not heard.

Thirdly, for that that concerns clerks and ministers. The place of justice is an hallowed place; and therefore not only the bench, but the foot-pace and precincts and purprise[3] thereof, ought to be preserved without scandal and corruption. For certainly, "Grapes" (as the Scripture saith) "will not be gathered of thorns or thistles";[4] neither can justice yield her fruit with sweetness amongst the briars and brambles of catching and polling[5] clerks and ministers. The attendance of courts is subject to four bad instruments. First, certain persons that are sowers of suits; which make the court swell, and the country pine. The second sort is of those that engage courts in quarrels of jurisdiction, and are not truly *amici curiæ*, but *parasiti curiæ*,[6] in puffing a court up beyond her bounds, for their own scraps and advantage. The third sort is of those that may be accounted the left hands of courts; persons that are full of nimble and sinister tricks and shifts, whereby they pervert the plain and direct courses of courts, and bring justice into oblique lines and labyrinths. And the fourth is the poller[7] and exacter of fees; which justifies the common resemblance of the courts of justice to the bush, whereunto while the sheep flies for defense in weather, he is sure to lose part of his fleece. On the other side, an ancient clerk, skillful in precedents, wary in proceeding, and understanding in the business of the court, is an excellent finger of a court, and doth many times point the way to the judge himself.

Fourthly, for that which may concern the sovereign and estate. Judges ought above all to remember the conclusion of the Roman Twelve Tables, *Salus populi suprema lex;*[8] and to know that laws, except they be in order to that end, are but things captious, and oracles not well inspired. Therefore it is an happy thing in a state when kings and states do often consult with judges; and again, when judges do often consult with the king and state: the one, when there is matter of law intervenient in business of state; the other, when there is some consideration of state intervenient in matter of law. For many times the things deduced to judgment may be *meum* and *tuum*,[9] when the reason and consequence thereof may trench to point of estate:[10] I call matter of estate, not only the parts of sovereignty, but whatsoever introduceth any great alteration or dangerous precedent, or concerneth manifestly any great portion of people. And let no man weakly conceive that just laws and true policy have any antipathy: for they are like the spirits and sinews, that one moves with the other. Let judges also remember that Solomon's throne was supported by lions on both sides: let them be lions, but yet lions under the throne; being circumspect that they do not check or oppose any points of sovereignty. Let not judges also be so ignorant of their own right, as to think there is not left to them, as a principal part of their office, a wise use and application of laws. For they may remember what the Apostle saith of a greater law than theirs: *Nos scimus quia lex bona est, modo quis eâ utatur legitime.*[11]

57.—OF ANGER

To seek to extinguish anger utterly is but a bravery[12] of the Stoics. We have better oracles: "Be angry, but sin not. Let not the sun go down upon your anger."[13] Anger must be limited and confined, both in race and in time. We will first speak, how the natural inclination and habit *to be angry* may be attempered and calmed. Secondly, how the particular motions of anger may be

---

1Opinion. 2Have words.
3Enclosure. 4St. Matthew, vii, 16. 5Plundering.
6Friends of the court, but parasites of the court.
7Plunderer.

8The people's safety is the supreme law (Cicero, *Of Laws*, III, 3).
9Mine and thine.
10May extend to concern the state.
11We know that the law is good if a man use it lawfully (1 Timothy, i, 8).
12Boast. 13Ephesians, iv, 26.

repressed, or at least refrained from doing mischief. Thirdly, how to raise anger, or appease anger, in another.

For the first; there is no other way but to meditate and ruminate well upon the effects of anger, how it troubles man's life. And the best time to do this is to look back upon anger when the fit is thoroughly over. Seneca saith well, "that anger is like ruin, which breaks itself upon that it falls." The Scripture exhorteth us "to possess our souls in patience."[1] Whosoever is out of patience, is out of possession of his soul. Men must not turn bees;

—*animasque in vulnere ponunt.*[2]

Anger is certainly a kind of baseness; as it appears well in the weakness of those subjects in whom it reigns; children, women, old folks, sick folks. Only men must beware that they carry their anger rather with scorn than with fear; so that they may seem rather to be above the injury than below it: which is a thing easily done, if a man will give law to himself in it.

For the second point; the causes and motives of anger are chiefly three. First, to be too sensible of hurt: for no man is angry that feels not himself hurt: and therefore tender and delicate persons must needs be oft angry; they have so many things to trouble them, which more robust natures have little sense of. The next is, the apprehension and construction of the injury offered to be, in the circumstances thereof, full of contempt. For contempt is that which putteth an edge upon anger, as much or more than the hurt itself. And therefore, when men are ingenious in picking out circumstances of contempt, they do kindle their anger much. Lastly, opinion of the touch[3] of a man's reputation, doth multiply and sharpen anger. Wherein the remedy is, that a man should have, as Consalvo was wont to say, *telam honoris crassiorem*.[4] But in all refrainings of anger, it is the best remedy to win time; and to make a man's self believe, that the opportunity of his revenge is not yet come, but that he foresees a time for it; and so to still himself in the mean time, and reserve it.

To contain[5] anger from mischief, though it take hold of a man, there be two things whereof you must have special caution. The one, of extreme bitterness of words; especially if they be aculeate[6] and proper; for *communia maledicta*[7] are nothing so much: and again, that in anger a man reveal no secrets; for that makes him not fit for society. The other, that you do not peremptorily break off, in any business, in a fit of anger; but howsoever you show bitterness, do not act anything that is not revocable.

For raising and appeasing anger in another; it is done chiefly by choosing of times, when men are frowardest and worst disposed, to incense them. Again, by gathering (as was touched before) all that you can find out, to aggravate the contempt. And the two remedies are by the contraries. The former, to take good times, when first to relate to a man an angry business; for the first impression is much. And the other is, to sever, as much as may be, the construction of the injury from the point of contempt; imputing it to misunderstanding, fear, passion, or what you will.

[1] St. Luke, xxi, 19.

[2] And spend their lives in stinging (Virgil, *Georgics*, IV, 238).

[3] Censure.

[4] A stout web of honor.

[5] Restrain.

[6] Stinging.

[7] General abuses.

LYRIC POETRY OF THE SIXTEENTH AND SEVENTEENTH CENTURIES

English lyric poetry of the sixteenth century is a new beginning, and has its sources not in older native literature, but in Italy. Late in the century Spenser went back to Chaucer, and to some extent in language, even more in the modulation and melody of his verse, continued and developed a national tradition, which he in turn handed on to Milton. The evidence for this is to be found, however, chiefly in Spenser's longer poems, *The Shepherd's Calendar* and *The Faerie Queene*, while much earlier in the century the course which the Elizabethan lyric was to take had been pretty clearly marked out by members of the Renaissance court of Henry VIII. The two chief poets of this earlier period were Sir Thomas Wyatt and Henry Howard, Earl of Surrey. The immediate source of their inspiration is clearly in Italy, in Petrarch and his followers, and their manner is, except at rare moments, tentative and experimental. That a new thing, however, had come into English poetry was made unmistakable when many of the poems written by Wyatt and Surrey, together with others by Grimald and by "uncertain authors," were collected and printed by Richard Tottel in 1557. This, *Tottel's Miscellany* as it is commonly called, was the first of a series of collections of lyrics by various writers which appeared during the latter half of the sixteenth century. The poems which Tottel printed are in large part imitative—the groping efforts of cultivated men to transplant into their own country the style, the subject-matter, and the forms of the Petrarchian lyric. Full mastery of the new kind of poetry and freedom of expression hardly came before 1580, but when they did come they seemed to come suddenly, and for some fifteen or twenty years there was a veritable outburst of lyric song, gay, easy, rich, and musical, as remarkable for its spontaneity and abandon as for its frequent intensity, and perhaps even more remarkable for the great numbers who not only felt the lyrical impulse but proved themselves able to give it well-nigh perfect expression. The more notable of the miscellanies into which many, though by no means all, of the lyrics of the period were collected were *A Handful of Pleasant Delights* (1584), *The Phoenix' Nest* (1593), *England's Helicon* (1600), and Davison's *Poetical Rhapsody* (1602).

Of the various forms which the lyric took only one can be specifically mentioned here—the sonnet. Petrarch had not only written some of his greatest poetry in sonnet-form but had connected his sonnets in a sequence, so that in effect they told the story of his moods and feelings, above all of the course of his love, and of other things as they related themselves to that central theme. The sonnet-sequence made its way to England along with the rest, and particularly in the decade from 1590 to 1600 became extraordinarily popular, it being estimated that several thousand sonnets were then written. The most notable of the sequences were Sir Philip Sidney's *Astrophel and Stella*, Samuel Daniel's *Delia*, Michael Drayton's *Idea*, Spenser's *Amoretti*, and Shakespeare's *Sonnets*.

On the whole, the Elizabethan burst of song was as brief as it was splendid. Violent passions are short-lived, action gives way to reflection, spontaneous expression develops into more deliberate art, and so it was with the lyric in the closing years of the sixteenth century. Its exuberance became distasteful, its sweetness cloying, and Ben Jonson, lifting the same chastening voice of good sense in the lyric as in the drama, set the example of restraint, of greater attention to form, and of practice enlightened by study of the best models of classical Greek and Roman poetry. At the same time John Donne reacted harshly and powerfully from the sweetness and the veneer of conventional Platonism of the Petrarchians in their love-poetry. Probably literary historians have tended to make too much of the personal influence of Jonson and Donne. Probably they were not so much actually leaders of new movements in poetry as the earliest men to feel strongly, each in his own way, a pronounced change in the whole intellectual and emotional life of England which gathered force in the early years of the seventeenth century. One way of putting it is that a period of expansive, youthful feeling was succeeded by a period of doubt mixed with disillusionment. Certainly something like this took place, and the change made itself felt throughout literature, and not merely within the little field of the lyric; yet it still remains useful within that field to remember that Jonson and Donne were the prophets of the new age. It should also be remembered, however, that some continued, as in every generation, to live in the past and to express the influences which for them were still potent, the most notable instance of this being the so-called school of Spenserians who continued to echo their master until well into the troubled years of the middle of the seventeenth century.

SIR THOMAS WYATT
(1503–1542)

THE LOVER FOR SHAME-FASTNESS HIDETH HIS DESIRE WITHIN HIS FAITHFUL HEART

THE long love that in my thought doth harbor,
And in my heart doth keep his residence,
Into my face presseth with bold pretense,
And therein campeth spreading his banner.
She that me learns to love and suffer,
And wills that in my trust, and lust's negligence,[1]
Be reined by reason, shame, and reverence,
With his hardiness takes displeasure.
Wherewithal[2] unto the heart's forest he fleeth,
Leaving his enterprise with pain and cry,
And there him hideth, and not appeareth.
What may I do, when my master feareth?
But in the field with him to live and die?
For good is the life ending faithfully.

THE WAVERING LOVER WILLETH, AND DREADETH, TO MOVE HIS DESIRE

SUCH vain thought as wonted to mislead me
In desert hope, by well assuréd moan,
Makes me from company to live alone,
In following her whom reason bids me flee.
She flyeth as fast by gentle cruelty;
And after her my heart would fain be gone,
But arméd sighs my way do stop anon,
'Twixt hope and dread locking my liberty.
Yet as I guess, under disdainful brow
One beam of pity is in her cloudy look,
Which comforteth the mind, that erst for fear shook;
And therewithal bolded, I seek the way how
To utter the smart that I suffer within;
But such it is, I not[3] how to begin.

THE LOVER HAVING DREAMED OF ENJOYING OF HIS LOVE, COMPLAINETH THAT THE DREAM IS NOT EITHER LONGER OR TRUER

UNSTABLE dream, according to the place,
Be steadfast once, or else at least be true.
By tasted sweetness make me not to rue
The sudden loss of thy false feignéd grace.
By good respect in such a dangerous case
Thou broughtst not her into this tossing mew,[4]
But madest my sprite[5] live, my care to renew.
My body in tempest her succor to embrace.
The body dead, the sprite had his desire;
Painless was th' one, the other in delight.
Why then, alas! did it not keep it right,
Returning to leap into the fire,
And where it was at wish, it could not remain?
Such mocks of dreams they turn to deadly pain!

[1]Careless confidence. [2]Whereupon.
[3]Know not. [4]Cage. [5]Spirit.

DESCRIPTION OF THE CONTRARIOUS PASSIONS IN A LOVER

I FIND no peace, and all my war is done;
I fear and hope, I burn, and freeze like ice;
I fly above the wind, yet can I not arise;
And nought I have, and all the world I seize on,
That loseth nor locketh, holdeth me in prison,
And holdeth me not, yet can I scape no wise;
Nor letteth me live, nor die, at my devise,[6]
And yet of death it giveth me occasion.
Without eye I see; and without tongue I plain:[7]
I desire to perish, and yet I ask health;
I love another, and thus I hate myself;
I feed me in sorrow, and laugh in all my pain.
Likewise displeaseth me both death and life,
And my delight is causer of this strife.

THE LOVER COMPARETH HIS STATE TO A SHIP IN PERILOUS STORM TOSSED ON THE SEA

MY GALLEY chargéd with forgetfulness
Thorough sharp seas, in winter nights doth pass,
'Tween rock and rock; and eke mine enemy, alas,
That is my lord, steereth with cruelness,
And every hour, a thought in readiness,
As though that death were light in such a case.
An endless wind doth tear the sail apace
Of forcéd sighs, and trusty fearfulness.
A rain of tears, a cloud of dark disdain
Hath done the wearied cords great hinderance,
Wreathed with error, and eke with ignorance.
The stars be hid that led me to this pain;
Drownéd is reason that should me comfort,
And I remain despairing of the port.

[6]Desire. [7]Lament.

A RENOUNCING OF LOVE

Farewell, Love, and all thy laws for ever!
Thy baited hooks shall tangle me no more:
Senec[1] and Plato call me from thy lore
To perfect wealth my wit for to endeavor.
In blind error when I did persévever,
Thy sharp repulse, that pricketh aye so sore,
Hath taught me to set in trifles no store;
And 'scape forth, since liberty is lever.[2]
Therefore, farewell! go trouble younger
    hearts,
And in me claim no more authority.
With idle youth go use thy property,
And thereon spend thy many brittle darts;
For hitherto though I have lost my time,
Me list no longer rotten boughs to climb.

THE LOVER SENDETH SIGHS TO MOVE HIS SUIT

Go, burning sighs, unto the frozen heart
Go, break the ice which pity's painful dart
Might never pierce: and if mortal prayer
In heaven may be heard, at least I desire
That death or mercy be end of smart.
Take with thee pain, whereof I have my part,
And eke the flame from which I cannot start,
And leave me then in rest, I you require.
Go, burning sighs, fulfill that I desire,
I must go work, I see, by craft and art,
For truth and faith in her is laid apart:
Alas, I cannot therefore assail her,
With pitiful complaint and scalding fire,
That from my breast deceivably doth start.

THE LOVER COMPLAINETH THE UNKINDNESS OF HIS LOVE

My lute, awake, perform the last
Labor that thou and I shall waste,
And end that I have now begun.
And when this song is sung and past,
My lute, be still, for I have done.

As to be heard where ear is none,
As lead to grave[3] in marble stone,
My song may pierce her heart as soon.
Should we then sigh, or sing, or moan?
No, no, my lute, for I have done.

The rocks do not so cruelly
Repulse the waves continually,
As she my suit and affection;
So that I am past remedy,
Whereby my lute and I have done.

Proud of the spoil that thou hast got
Of simple hearts through Lovës shot,
By whom unkind thou hast them won,
Think not he hath his bow forgot,
Although my lute and I have done.

Vengeance shall fall on thy disdain
That makest but game on earnest pain.
Think not alone under the sun
Unquit to cause thy lovers plain,[4]
Although my lute and I have done.

Perchance thee lie withered and old,
The winter nights that are so cold,
Plaining in vain unto the moon;
Thy wishes then dare not be told.
Care then who list, for I have done.

And then may chance thee to repent
The time that thou hast lost and spent
To cause thy lovers sigh and swoon;
Then shalt thou know beauty but lent,
And wish and want, as I have done.

Now cease, my lute, this is the last
Labor that thou and I shall waste,
And ended is that we begun.
Now is the song both sung and past,
My lute, be still, for I have done.

AN EARNEST SUIT TO HIS UNKIND MISTRESS NOT TO FORSAKE HIM

And wilt thou leave me thus?
Say nay, say nay, for shame!
To save thee from the blame
Of all my grief and grame.[5]
And wilt thou leave me thus?
Say nay! say nay!

And wilt thou leave me thus,
That hath loved thee so long
In wealth and woe among:
And is thy heart so strong
As for to leave me thus?
Say nay! say nay!

And wilt thou leave me thus,
That hath given thee my heart
Never for to depart
Neither for pain nor smart:
And wilt thou leave me thus?
Say nay! say nay!

And wilt thou leave me thus,
And have no more pity
Of him that loveth thee?
Alas, thy cruelty!
And wilt thou leave me thus?
Say nay! say nay!

[1]Seneca. [2]Preferable. [3]Engrave.

[4]To lament. [5]Sorrow.

THE LOVER BESEECHETH HIS MISTRESS NOT TO FORGET HIS STEADFAST FAITH AND TRUE INTENT

Forget not yet the tried intent
Of such a truth as I have meant;
My great travail so gladly spent,
Forget not yet!

Forget not yet when first began
The weary life ye know, since whan
The suit, the service none tell can;
Forget not yet!

Forget not yet the great assays,
The cruel wrong, the scornful ways,
The painful patience in delays,
Forget not yet!

Forget not yet, forget not this,
How long ago hath been, and is,
The mind that never meant amiss—
Forget not yet!

Forget not then thine own approved,
The which so long hath thee so loved,
Whose steadfast faith yet never moved:
Forget not this!

OF THE MEAN AND SURE ESTATE[1]

WRITTEN TO JOHN POINS

My mother's maids, when they did sew and spin,
They sung sometime a song of the field mouse
That, for because her livelihood was but thin,
Would needs go seek her townish sister's house.
She thought herself enduréd too much pain;
The stormy blasts her cave so sore did souse
That when the furrows swimméd with the rain,
She must lie cold and wet in sorry plight;
And worse than that, bare meat there did remain
To comfort her when she her house had dight;[2]
Sometime a barley corn; sometime a bean,
For which she labored hard both day and night
In harvest time whilst she might go and glean;
And when her store was stroyéd[3] with the flood,
Then welaway! for she undone was clean.
Then was she fain to take, instead of food,
Sleep, if she might, her hunger to beguile.
"My sister," quoth she, "hath a living good,
And hence from me she dwelleth not a mile,
In cold and storm she lieth warm and dry
In bed of down, the dirt doth not defile
Her tender foot, she laboreth not as I.
Richly she feedeth, and at the rich man's cost,
And for her meat she needs not crave nor cry.
By sea, by land, of the delicates, the most
Her cater[4] seeks and spareth for no peril,
She feedeth on boiled bacon, meat, and roast,
And hath thereof neither charge nor travail;
And, when she list, the liquor of the grape
Doth glad her heart till that her belly swell."
And at this journey she maketh but a jape;[5]
So forth she goeth, trusting of all this wealth
With her sister her part so for to shape,
That if she might keep herself in health,
To live a lady while her life doth last.
And to the door now is she come by stealth,
And with her foot anon she scrapeth full fast.
Th' other, for fear, durst not well scarce appear,
Of every noise so was the wretch aghast.
At last she askéd softly who was there,
And in her language as well as she could.
"Peep!" quoth the other sister, "I am here."
"Peace," quoth the town mouse, "why speakest thou so loud?"
And by the hand she took her fair and well.
"Welcome," quoth she, "my sister, by the Rood!"
She feasted her, that joy it was to tell
The fare they had; they drank the wine so clear,
And, as to purpose now and then it fell,
She cheeréd her with "How, sister, what cheer!"
Amid this joy befell a sorry chance,
That, welaway! the stranger bought full dear
The fare she had, for, as she looked askance,
Under a stool she spied two steaming[6] eyes
In a round head with sharp ears. In France
Was never mouse so feared, for, though unwise
Had not y-seen such a beast before,
Yet had nature taught her after her guise
To know her foe and dread him evermore.
The towny mouse fled, she knew whither to go;
Th'other had no shift, but wonders sore
Feared of her life. At home she wished her tho,[7]
And to the door, alas! as she did skip,
The heaven it would, lo! and eke her chance was so,

[1]This poem is based upon Horace, *Satires* II, 6. It is not, of course, a lyric, but deserves inclusion here to indicate the range of Wyatt's experiments.
[2]Ordered. [3]Destroyed.

[4]Caterer. [5]Jest. [6]Gleaming. [7]Then.

At the threshold her silly foot did trip;
And ere she might recover it again,
The traitor cat had caught her by the hip,
And made her there against her will remain,
That had forgot her poor surety and rest
For seeming wealth wherein she thought to reign.
Alas, my Poins, how men do seek the best
And find the worst by error as they stray!
And no marvel; when sight is so opprest,
And blinds the guide, anon out of the way
Goeth guide and all in seeking quiet life.
O wretched minds, there is no gold that may
Grant that you seek; no war, no peace, no strife.
No, no, although thy head were hooped with gold,
Sergeant with mace, halberd, sword, nor knife,
Cannot repulse the care that follow should.
Each kind of life hath with him his disease.
Live in delight even as thy lust would,
And thou shalt find, when lust doth most thee please,
It irketh straight, and by itself doth fade.
A small thing is it that may thy mind appease.
None of ye all there is that is so mad
To seek for grapes on brambles or on briars;
Nor none, I trow, that hath his wit so bad
To set his hay[1] for conies over rivers,
Nor ye set not a drag-net for an hare;
And yet the thing that most is your desire
Ye do mis-seek with more travail and care.
Make plain thine heart, that it be not knotted
With hope or dread, and see thy will be bare
From all effects whom vice hath ever spotted.
Thyself content with that is thee assigned,
And use it well that is to thee allotted.
Then seek no more out of thyself to find
The thing that thou hast sought so long before,
For thou shalt feel it sticking in thy mind.
Mad, if ye list to continue your sore,
Let present pass and gape on time to come,
And deep yourself in travail more and more.
Henceforth, my Poins, this shall be all and some,
These wretched fools shall have naught else of me;
But to the great God and to his high dome,[2]
None other pain pray I for them to be,
But, when the rage doth lead them from the right,
That, looking backward, virtue they may see,
Even as she is so goodly fair and bright,
And whilst they clasp their lusts in arms across,
Grant them, good Lord, as thou mayst of thy might,
To fret inward for losing such a loss.

HENRY HOWARD, EARL OF SURREY

(1517?–1547)

DESCRIPTION OF SPRING WHEREIN EACH THING RENEWS, SAVE ONLY THE LOVER

The soote[3] season that bud and bloom forth brings,
With green hath clad the hill and eke the vale;
The nightingale with feathers new she sings;
The turtle[4] to her mate hath told her tale:
Summer is come, for every spray now springs;
The hart hath hung his old head on the pale;
The buck in brake his winter coat he flings;
The fishes float with new repairéd scale;
The adder all her slough away she slings;
The swift swallow pursueth the flies smale;
The busy bee her honey now she mings.[5]
Winter is worn, that was the flowers' bale:
And thus I see among these pleasant things
Each care decays, and yet my sorrow springs!

COMPLAINT OF A LOVER REBUKED

Love, that doth reign and live within my thought,
And build his seat within my captive breast,
Clad in the arms wherein with me he fought,
Oft in my face he doth his banner rest.
But she that taught me love, and suffer pain,
My doubtful hope and eke my hot desire
With shamefast look to shadow and refrain,
Her smiling grace converteth straight to ire.
And coward Love then to the heart apace
Taketh his flight, where he doth lurk and plain
His purpose lost, and dare not show his face.
For my lord's guilt thus faultless bide I pain.
Yet from my lord shall not my foot remove;
Sweet is the death that taketh end by love.

VOW TO LOVE FAITHFULLY HOWSOEVER HE BE REWARDED

Set me whereas the sun doth parch the green,
Or where his beams may not dissolve the ice;
In temperate heat, where he is felt and seen;
In presence prest of people, mad or wise;
Set me in high, or yet in low degree;
In longest night, or in the longest day;
In clearest sky, or where clouds thickest be;
In lusty youth, or when my hairs are gray:

[1]Snare. [2]Judgment. [3]Sweet. [4]Turtle-dove. [5]Mixes.

Set me in heaven, in earth, or else in hell;
In hill, or dale, or in the foaming flood;
Thrall, or at large, alive whereso I dwell;
Sick or in health, in evil fame or good;
Hers will I be, and only with this thought
Content myself, although my chance be naught.

COMPLAINT OF THE ABSENCE OF HER LOVER BEING UPON THE SEA

O HAPPY dames! that may embrace
The fruit of your delight;
Help to bewail the woeful case,
And eke the heavy plight,
Of me, that wonted to rejoice
The fortune of my pleasant choice:
Good ladies, help to fill my mourning voice.

In ship freight with rememberance
Of thoughts and pleasures past,
He sails that hath in governance
My life, while it will last;
With scalding sighs, for lack of gale,
Furthering his hope, that is his sail,
Toward me, the sweet port of his avail.[1]

Alas, how oft in dreams I see
Those eyes that were my food;
Which sometime so delighted me,
That yet they do me good;
Wherewith I wake with his return,
Whose absent flame did make me burn:
But when I find the lack, Lord, how I mourn!

When other lovers in arms across,
Rejoice their chief delight,
Drownéd in tears to mourn my loss,
I stand the bitter night
In my window, where I may see
Before the winds how the clouds flee:
Lo, what a mariner love hath made me!

And in green waves when the salt flood
Doth rise by rage of wind,
A thousand fancies in that mood,
Assail my restless mind.
Alas, now drencheth[2] my sweet foe,
That with the spoil of my heart did go,
And left me; but, alas, why did he so?

And when the seas wax calm again,
To chase from me annoy,
My doubtful hope doth cause me pain;
So dread cuts off my joy.
Thus is my wealth mingled with woe,
And of each thought a doubt doth grow;
Now he comes! Will he come? Alas, no, no!

[1]Advantage. [2]Drowneth.

A PRAISE OF HIS LOVE WHEREIN HE REPROVETH THEM THAT COMPARE THEIR LADIES WITH HIS

GIVE place, ye lovers, here before
That spent your boasts and brags in vain;
My lady's beauty passeth more
The best of yours, I dare well sayn,[3]
Than doth the sun the candle light,
Or brightest day the darkest night.

And thereto hath a troth[4] as just
As had Penelope the fair;
For what she saith, ye may it trust
As it by writing sealéd were:
And virtues hath she many mo[5]
Than I with pen have skill to show.

I could rehearse, if that I would,
The whole effect of Nature's plaint,
When she had lost the perfect mold,
The like to whom she could not paint:
With wringing hands, how she did cry,
And what she said, I know it, I.

I know she swore with raging mind,
Her kingdom only set apart,
There was no loss by law of kind[6]
That could have gone so near her heart.
And this was chiefly all her pain:
She could not make the like again.

Sith Nature thus gave her the praise,
To be the chiefest work she wrought;
In faith, methink, some better ways
On your behalf might well be sought,
Than to compare, as ye have done,
To match the candle with the sun.

THE MEANS TO ATTAIN HAPPY LIFE

MARTIAL,[7] the things that do attain
The happy life be these, I find:
The riches left, not got with pain;
The fruitful ground; the quiet mind;
The equal friend; no grudge, no strife;
No charge of rule, no governance;
Without disease, the healthful life;
The household of continuance;
The mean[8] diet, no delicate fare;
True wisdom joined with simpleness;
The night dischargéd of all care,
Where wine the wit may not oppress;

[3]Say. [4]Faithfulness. [5]More. [6]Nature.

[7]The Latin epigrammatist. This poem is a translation of his epigram *To Himself*.

[8]Moderate.

The faithful wife, without debate;
Such sleeps as may beguile the night:
Contented with thine own estate,
Ne wish for death, ne fear his might.

OF THE DEATH OF SIR T[HOMAS] W[YATT]

W. RESTETH here, that quick could never rest;
Whose heavenly gifts, encreaséd by disdain,
And virtue sank the deeper in his breast;
Such profit he by envy could obtain.
A head where wisdom mysteries did frame;
Whose hammers beat still in that lively brain
As on a stithe[1] where that some work of fame
Was daily wrought to turn to Britain's gain.
A visage stern and mild, where both did grow,
Vice to condemn, in virtue to rejoice;
Amid great storms, whom grace assuréd so
To live upright and smile at fortune's choice.
A hand that taught what might be said in rime;
That reft[2] Chaucer the glory of his wit:
A mark, the which (unperfected, for time)
Some may approach, but never none shall hit.
A tongue that served in foreign realms his king;
Whose courteous talk to virtue did enflame
Each noble heart; a worthy guide to bring
Our English youth by travail unto fame.
An eye whose judgment none affect[3] could blind,
Friends to allure, and foes to reconcile;
Whose piercing look did represent a mind
With virtue fraught, reposéd, void of guile.
A heart where dread was never so imprest,
To hide the thought that might the truth advance;
In neither fortune lost, nor yet represt,
To swell in wealth, or yield unto mischance.
A valiant corse,[4] where force and beauty met;
Happy, alas, too happy, but for foes!
Lived, and ran the race that Nature set:
Of manhood's shape, where she the mold did lose.
But to the heavens that simple[5] soul is fled,
Which left with such as covet Christ to know
Witness of faith that never shall be dead,
Sent for our health, but not receivéd so.
Thus for our guilt, this jewel have we lost;
The earth his bones, the heavens possess his ghost!

ANONYMOUS

A STUDENT AT HIS BOOK[6]

A STUDENT at his book, so placed
That wealth he might have won,
From book to wife did fleet in haste,
From wealth to woe did run.
Now, who hath played a feater cast,[7]
Since juggling first begun?
In knitting of himself so fast,
Himself he hath undone.

BACK AND SIDE GO BARE[8]

Chorus

BACK and side go bare, go bare,
Both foot and hand go cold;
But, belly, God send thee good ale enough,
Whether it be new or old.

I cannot eat but little meat,
My stomach is not good;
But sure I think that I can drink
With him that wears a hood.
Though I go bare, take ye no care,
I am nothing a-cold;
I stuff my skin so full within
Of jolly good ale and old.

I love no roast but a nutbrown toast,
And a crab[9] laid in the fire;
A little bread shall do me stead,[10]
Much bread I not desire.
No frost nor snow, no wind, I trow,
Can hurt me if I would,
I am so wrapped and thoroughly lapped
Of jolly good ale and old.

And Tib my wife, that as her life
Loveth well good ale to seek,
Full oft drinks she, till ye may see
The tears run down her cheek.
Then doth she trowl[11] to me the bowl,
Even as a maltworm should,
And saith "Sweetheart, I have take my part
Of this jolly good ale and old."

Now let them drink till they nod and wink,
Even as good fellows should do;
They shall not miss to have the bliss
Good ale doth bring men to.
And all poor souls that have scoured bowls,
Or have them lustily trowled,
God save the lives of them and their wives,
Whether they be young or old.

[1]Anvil. [2]Took from. [3]No affections. [4]Body.
[5]*I.e.*, incorruptible.
[6]One of the poems by "uncertain authors" in Tottel's *Miscellany* (1557).
[7]A neater trick.
[8]From *Gammer Gurton's Needle* (written c. 1562).

[9]Apple. [10]Be sufficient. [11]Pass.

JOHN LYLY
(1553–1606)

APELLES' SONG[1]

Cupid and my Campaspe played
At cards for kisses; Cupid paid.
He stakes his quiver, bows and arrows,
His mother's doves and team of sparrows;
Loses them too; then down he throws
The coral of his lip, the rose
Growing on's cheek (but none knows how);
With these, the crystal of his brow,
And then the dimple of his chin;
All these did my Campaspe win.
At last he set[2] her both his eyes;
She won, and Cupid blind did rise.
O Love, has she done this to thee?
What shall, alas! become of me?

SPRING'S WELCOME

What bird so sings, yet so does wail?
O 'tis the ravished nightingale.
"Jug, jug, jug, jug, tereu," she cries,
And still her woes at midnight rise.
Brave prick-song! who is 't now we hear?
None but the lark so shrill and clear;
Now at heaven's gates she claps her wings,
The morn not waking till she sings.
Hark, hark, with what a pretty throat
Poor robin redbreast tunes his note!
Hark how the jolly cuckoos sing,
"Cuckoo," to welcome in the spring!
"Cuckoo," to welcome in the spring!

SIR PHILIP SIDNEY
(1554–1586)

ASTROPHEL AND STELLA

I

Loving in truth, and fain in verse my love to show,
That she, dear she, might take some pleasure of my pain,—
Pleasure might cause her read, reading might make her know,
Knowledge might pity win, and pity grace obtain,—
I sought fit words to paint the blackest face of woe,
Studying inventions fine, her wits to entertain,
Oft turning others' leaves, to see if thence would flow
Some fresh and fruitful showers upon my sunburnt brain.
But words came halting forth, wanting Invention's stay;
Invention, Nature's child, fled step-dame Study's blows;
And others' feet still seemed but strangers' in my way.
Thus, great with child to speak, and helpless in my throes,
Biting my truant pen, beating myself for spite;
"Fool," said my Muse to me, "look in thy heart, and write."

[1]This and the following song are both from *Campaspe* (1584). It is possible that the songs in Lyly's plays are by another hand.

[2]Wagered.

15

You that do search for every purling spring
Which from the ribs of old Parnassus[3] flows,
And every flower, not sweet perhaps, which grows
Near thereabouts, into your poesy wring;
You that do dictionary's method bring
Into your rimes, running in rattling rows;
You that poor Petrarch's long deceaséd woes
With new-born sighs and denizened[4] wit do sing;
You take wrong ways; those far-fet[5] helps be such
As do bewray a want of inward touch,
And sure, at length stolen goods do come to light:
But if, both for your love and skill, your name
You seek to nurse at fullest breasts of Fame,
Stella behold, and then begin to indite.

31

With how sad steps, O Moon, thou climb'st the skies!
How silently, and with how wan a face!
What, may it be that even in heavenly place
That busy archer his sharp arrows tries!
Sure, if that long-with-love-acquainted eyes
Can judge of love, thou feel'st a lover's case,
I read it in thy looks; thy languished grace,
To me, that feel the like, thy state descries,

[3]Abode of Apollo and the muses.

[4]Adopted, *i. e.*, borrowed.

[5]Far-fetched.

Then, even of fellowship, O Moon, tell me,
Is constant love deemed there but want of wit?
Are beauties there as proud as here they be?
Do they above love to be loved, and yet
Those lovers scorn whom that love doth possess?
Do they call virtue there ungratefulness?

39

Come, Sleep! O Sleep, the certain knot of peace,
The baiting-place of wit, the balm of woe,
The poor man's wealth, the prisoner's release,
Th' indifferent judge between the high and low;
With shield of proof shield me from out the press
Of those fierce darts Despair at me doth throw:
O make in me those civil wars to cease;
I will good tribute pay, if thou do so.
Take thou of me smooth pillows, sweetest bed,
A chamber deaf of noise and blind of light,
A rosy garland and a weary head:
And if these things, as being thine by right,
Move not thy heavy grace, thou shalt in me,
Livelier than elsewhere, Stella's image see.

41

Having this day my horse, my hand, my lance
Guided so well that I obtained the prize,
Both by the judgment of the English eyes
And of some sent from that sweet enemy, France;
Horsemen my skill in horsemanship advance,
Town folks my strength; a daintier judge applies
His praise to sleight which from good use doth rise;
Some lucky wits impute it but to chance;
Others, because of both sides I do take
My blood from them who did excel in this,
Think Nature me a man-at-arms did make.
How far they shot awry! the true cause is,
Stella looked on, and from her heavenly face
Sent forth the beams which made so fair my race.

64

No more! My Dear, no more these counsels try!
O give my passions leave to run their race!
Let Fortune lay on me her worst disgrace!
Let folk o'ercharged with brain, against me cry!
Let clouds bedim my face, break in mine eye!
Let me no steps but of lost labor trace!
Let all the earth in scorn recount my case;
But do not will me from my love to fly!
I do not envy Aristotle's wit;
Nor do aspire to Cæsar's bleeding fame;
Nor ought do care, though some above me sit;
Nor hope, nor wish another course to frame:
But that which once may win thy cruel heart.
Thou art my wit, and thou my virtue art.

95

Leave me, O Love, which reachest but to dust,
And thou, my mind, aspire to higher things!
Grow rich in that which never taketh rust:
Whatever fades, but fading pleasure brings.
Draw in thy beams, and humble all thy might
To that sweet yoke where lasting freedoms be;
Which breaks the clouds and opens forth the light
That doth both shine and give us sight to see.
O take fast hold! let that light be thy guide
In this small course which birth draws out to death,
And think how evil becometh him to slide
Who seeketh Heaven, and comes of heavenly breath.
Then farewell, world! thy uttermost I see:
Eternal Love, maintain thy life in me!

ELEVENTH SONG

"Who is it that this dark night
Underneath my window plaineth?"
It is one who from thy sight
Being, ah! exiled, disdaineth
Every other vulgar light.

"Why, alas! and are you he?
Be not yet those fancies changed?"
Dear, when you find change in me,
Though from me you be estranged,
Let my change to ruin be.

"Well, in absence this will die;
Leave to see, and leave to wonder."
Absence sure will help, if I
Can learn how myself to sunder
From what in my heart doth lie.

"But time will these thoughts remove;
Time doth work what no man knoweth."
Time doth as the subject prove;
With time still the affection groweth
In the faithful turtle-dove.

"What if we new beauties see?
Will not they stir new affection?"
I will think they pictures be,
(Image-like, of saint's perfection)
Poorly counterfeiting thee.

"But your reason's purest light
Bids you leave such minds to nourish."

Dear, do reason no such spite;
Never doth thy beauty flourish
More than in my reason's sight.

"But the wrongs Love bears will make
Love at length leave undertaking."
No, the more fools it do shake,
In the ground of so firm making,
Deeper still they drive the stake.

"Peace, I think that some give ear!
Come no more, lest I get anger!"
Bliss, I will my bliss forbear;
Fearing, sweet, you to endanger;
But my soul shall harbor there.

"Well, be gone! be gone, I say,
Lest that Argus'[1] eyes perceive you!"
O unjust is Fortune's sway,
Which can make me thus to leave you;
And from louts to run away.

MY TRUE—LOVE HATH MY HEART

My true-love hath my heart and I have his,
By just exchange one for the other given:
I hold his dear, and mine he cannot miss,
There never was a better bargain driven:
My true-love hath my heart, and I have his.

His heart in me keeps him and me in one.
My heart in him his thoughts and senses guides:
He loves my heart, for once it was his own,
I cherish his because in me it bides:
My true-love hath my heart, and I have his.

MY SHEEP ARE THOUGHTS[2]

My sheep are thoughts, which I both guide and serve;
Their pasture is fair hills of fruitless love,
On barren sweets they feed, and feeding sterve.[3]
I wail their lot, but will not other prove;
My sheep-hook is wan hope, which all upholds;
My weeds,[4] desire, cut out in endless folds;
What wool my sheep shall bear, whilst thus they live,
In you it is, you must the judgment give.

SIR EDWARD DYER

(1550?–1607)

MY MIND TO ME A KINGDOM IS

My mind to me a kingdom is;
Such present joys therein I find
That it excels all other bliss
That earth affords or grows by kind:[5]
Though much I want which most would have,
Yet still my mind forbids to crave.

No princely pomp, no wealthy store,
No force to win the victory,
No wily wit to salve a sore,
No shape to feed a loving eye;
To none of these I yield as thrall:
For why? My mind doth serve for all.

I see how plenty surfeits oft,
And hasty climbers soon do fall;
I see that those which are aloft
Mishap doth threaten most of all;
They get with toil, they keep with fear:
Such cares my mind could never bear.

Content to live, this is my stay;
I seek no more than may suffice;
I press to bear no haughty sway;
Look, what I lack my mind supplies:
Lo, thus I triumph like a king,
Content with that my mind doth bring.

Some have too much, yet still do crave;
I little have, and seek no more.
They are but poor, though much they have,
And I am rich with little store:
They poor, I rich; they beg, I give;
They lack, I leave; they pine, I live.

I laugh not at another's loss;
I grudge not at another's pain;
No worldly waves my mind can toss;
My state at one doth still remain:
I fear no foe, I fawn no friend;
I loathe not life, nor dread my end.

Some weigh their pleasure by their lust,
Their wisdom by their rage of will;
Their treasure is their only trust;
A cloakéd craft their store of skill:
But all the pleasure that I find
Is to maintain a quiet mind.

My wealth is health and perfect ease;
My conscience clear my chief defense;
I neither seek by bribes to please,
Nor by deceit to breed offense:
Thus do I live; thus will I die;
Would all did so as well as I!

---

[1]Argus had one hundred eyes.
[2]From Sidney's *Arcadia*.
[3]Starve. [4]Clothes. [5]Natu

SIR WALTER RALEIGH

(1552?–1618)

HIS PILGRIMAGE

GIVE me my scallop-shell[1] of quiet,
  My staff of faith to walk upon,
My scrip[2] of joy, immortal diet,
  My bottle of salvation,
My gown of glory, hope's true gage;[3]
And thus I'll take my pilgrimage.

Blood must be my body's balmer;
  No other balm will there be given;
Whilst my soul, like a quiet palmer,
  Traveleth towards the land of heaven,
Over the silver mountains,
Where spring the nectar fountains.
    There will I kiss
    The bowl of bliss;
And drink mine everlasting fill
Upon every milken hill.
My soul will be a-dry before;
But, after, it will thirst no more.

Then by that happy blissful day
  More peaceful pilgrims I shall see,
That have cast off their rags of clay,
  And walk appareled fresh like me.
    I'll take them first,
    To quench their thirst
  And taste of nectar suckets,[4]
    At those clear wells
    Where sweetness dwells,
Drawn up by saints in crystal buckets.

  And when our bottles and all we
Are filled with immortality,
Then the blesséd paths we'll travel,
Strowed with rubies thick as gravel;
Ceilings of diamonds, sapphire floors,
High walls of coral, and pearly bowers.

  From thence to heaven's bribeless hall,
Where no corrupted voices brawl;
No conscience molten into gold;
No forged accuser bought or sold;
No cause deferred, no vain-spent journey,
For there Christ is the King's attorney,
Who pleads for all, without degrees,
And he hath angels[5] but no fees.

  And when the grand twelve million jury
Of our sins, with direful fury,
Against our souls black verdicts give,
Christ pleads his death; and then we live.
  Be Thou my speaker, taintless pleader!
Unblotted lawyer! true proceeder!
Thou giv'st salvation, even for alms,
Not with a bribéd lawyer's palms.

  And this is mine eternal plea
To him that made heaven and earth and sea:
That, since my flesh must die so soon,
And want a head to dine next noon,
Just at the stroke, when my veins start and
    spread,
Set on my soul an everlasting head!

Then am I ready, like a palmer fit,
To tread those blest paths; which before I writ.

[1]One of the badges of a pilgrim.
[2]Wallet. [3]Pledge. [4]Sweetmeats.
[5]Used with double meaning; it was also the name of a coin.

GEORGE PEELE

(1558?–1597?)

CUPID'S CURSE[6]

ŒNONE. FAIR and fair, and twice so fair,
    As fair as any may be;
  The fairest shepherd on our green,
    A love for any lady.
PARIS. Fair and fair, and twice so fair,
    As fair as any may be;
  Thy love is fair for thee alone,
    And for no other lady.
ŒN. My love is fair, my love is gay,
    As fresh as bin the flowers in May,
  And of my love my roundelay,
    My merry, merry roundelay,
  Concludes with Cupid's curse,—
    "They that do change old love for new,
  Pray gods they change for worse!"
AMBO SIMUL.[7] They that do change, *etc.*
ŒN. Fair and fair, *etc.*
PAR. Fair and fair, *etc.*
  Thy love is fair, *etc.*
ŒN. My love can pipe, my love can sing,
  My love can many a pretty thing,
  And of his lovely praises ring
  My merry, merry roundelays,
    Amen to Cupid's curse,—
  "They that do change," *etc.*
PAR. They that do change, *etc.*
AMBO. Fair and fair, *etc.*

[6]From the *Arraignment of Paris* (1584).

[7]Both together.

HARVESTMEN A-SINGING[1]

All ye that lovely lovers be,
Pray you for me:
Lo, here we come a-sowing, a-sowing,
And so sweet fruits of love;
In your sweet hearts well may it prove!
Lo, here we come a-reaping, a-reaping,
To reap our harvest-fruit!
And thus we pass the year so long,
And never be we mute.

ROBERT GREENE
(1560?–1592)

SWEET ARE THE THOUGHTS THAT SAVOR OF CONTENT[2]

Sweet are the thoughts that savor of content;
The quiet mind is richer than a crown;
Sweet are the nights in careless slumber spent;
The poor estate scorns fortune's angry frown:
Such sweet content, such minds, such sleep, such bliss,
Beggars enjoy, when princes oft do miss.

The homely house that harbors quiet rest;
The cottage that affords no pride nor care;
The mean that 'grees with country music best;
The sweet consort of mirth and music's fare;
Obscuréd life sets down a type of bliss:
A mind content both crown and kingdom is.

WEEP NOT, MY WANTON[3]

Weep not, my wanton, smile upon my knee,
When thou art old there's grief enough for thee.
Mother's wag, pretty boy,
Father's sorrow, father's joy;
When thy father first did see
Such a boy by him and me,
He was glad, I was woe,
Fortune changéd made him so,
When he left his pretty boy
Last his sorrow, first his joy.

Weep not, my wanton, smile upon my knee,
When thou art old there's grief enough for thee.
Streaming tears that never stint,
Like pearl-drops from a flint,
Fell by course from his eyes,
That one another's place supplies;
Thus he grieved in every part,
Tears of blood fell from his heart,
When he left his pretty boy,
Father's sorrow, father's joy.

Weep not, my wanton, smile upon my knee,
When thou art old there's grief enough for thee.
The wanton smiled, father wept,
Mother cried, baby leapt;
More he crowed, more we cried,
Nature could not sorrow hide:
He must go, he must kiss
Child and mother, baby bless,
For he left his pretty boy,
Father's sorrow, father's joy.
Weep not, my wanton, smile upon my knee,
When thou art old there's grief enough for thee.

MICHAEL DRAYTON
(1563–1631)

TO HIS COY LOVE

I pray thee, leave, love me no more,
Call home the heart you gave me!
I but in vain that saint adore
That can but will not save me.
These poor half-kisses kill me quite—
Was ever man thus servéd?
Amidst an ocean of delight
For pleasure to be stervéd?[4]
Show me no more those snowy breasts
With azure riverets branchéd,
Where, whilst mine eye with plenty feasts,
Yet is my thirst not stanchéd;
O Tantalus, thy pains ne'er tell!
By me thou art prevented:[5]
'Tis nothing to be plagued in hell,
But thus in heaven tormented!

Clip[6] me no more in those dear arms,
Nor thy life's comfort call me,
O these are but too powerful charms,
And do but more enthral me!

[1] From *The Old Wives' Tale* (c. 1590).
[2] From *The Farewell to Folly* (1591).
[3] From *Menaphon* (1589).
[4] Killed.
[5] Anticipated.
[6] Embrace.

But see how patient I am grown
  In all this coil[1] about thee:
Come, nice thing, let my heart alone,
  I cannot live without thee!

IDEA

TO THE READER OF THESE SONNETS

INTO these loves, who but for passion looks,
At this first sight, here let him lay them by,
And seek elsewhere in turning other books,
Which better may his labor satisfy.
No far-fetched sigh shall ever wound my breast;
Love from mine eye a tear shall never wring;
Nor in "Ah me's!" my whining sonnets drest!
A libertine! fantasticly I sing!
My verse is the true image of my mind,
Ever in motion, still desiring change;
And as thus, to variety inclined,
So in all humors sportively I range!
My Muse is rightly of the English strain,
That cannot long one fashion entertain.

61

SINCE there's no help, come, let us kiss and part!
Nay, I have done; you get no more of me!
And I am glad, yea, glad, with all my heart,
That thus so cleanly I myself can free.
Shake hands for ever! Cancel all our vows!
And when we meet at any time again,
Be it not seen in either of our brows,
That we one jot of former love retain!
Now at the last gasp of Love's latest breath,
When, his pulse failing, Passion speechless lies;
When Faith is kneeling by his bed of death,
And Innocence is closing up his eyes—
Now, if thou wouldst, when all have given him over,
From death to life thou might'st him yet recover!

ODE XI

TO THE VIRGINIAN VOYAGE

You brave heroic minds,
Worthy your country's name,
  That honor still pursue;
  Go and subdue!
Whilst loitering hinds
Lurk here at home with shame.

Britons, you stay too long;
Quickly aboard bestow you!
  And with a merry gale
  Swell your stretched sail,
With vows as strong
As the winds that blow you!

Your course securely steer,
West-and-by-south forth keep!
  Rocks, lee-shores, nor shoals,
  When Eolus[2] scowls,
You need not fear,
So absolute the deep.

And cheerfully at sea,
Success you still entice,
  To get the pearl and gold;
  And ours to hold,
Virginia,
Earth's only Paradise.

Where Nature hath in store
Fowl, venison, and fish;
  And the fruitful'st soil,—
  Without your toil,
Three harvests more,
All greater than your wish.

And the ambitious vine
Crowns with his purple mass
  The cedar reaching high
  To kiss the sky,
The cypress, pine,
And useful sassafras.

To whom, the Golden Age[3]
Still Nature's laws doth give:
  Nor other cares attend,
  But them to defend
From winter's rage,
That long there doth not live.

When as the luscious smell
Of that delicious land,
  Above the seas that flows,
  The clear wind throws,
Your hearts to swell,
Approaching the dear strand.

In kenning[4] of the shore
(Thanks to God first given!)
  O you, the happiest men,
  Be frolic then!
Let cannons roar,
Frightening the wide heaven!

And in regions far,
Such heroes bring ye forth
  As those from whom we came!
  And plant our name
Under that star
Not known unto our North!

[1]Disturbance.

[2]God of winds.
[3]A fabled period of peace and plenty.
[4]Recognition.

And as there plenty grows
The laurel everywhere,
Apollo's sacred tree,
You may it see
A poet's brows
To crown, that may sing there.

Thy Voyages attend,
Industrious Hakluyt![1]
Whose reading shall inflame
Men to seek fame;
And much commend
To after times thy wit.

ODE XII

TO THE CAMBRO-BRITONS AND THEIR HARP HIS BALLAD OF AGINCOURT

Fair stood the wind for France,
When we our sails advance;
Nor now to prove our chance
Longer will tarry;
But putting to the main,
At Caux, the mouth of Seine,
With all his martial train
Landed King Harry.[2]

And taking many a fort,
Furnished in warlike sort,
Marcheth towards Agincourt[3]
In happy hour;
Skirmishing day by day,
With those that stopped his way,
Where the French general lay
With all his power.

Which, in his height of pride,
King Henry to deride,
His ransom to provide,
To the King sending;
Which he neglects the while,
As from a nation vile,
Yet, with an angry smile,
Their fall portending.

And turning to his men,
Quoth our brave Henry then:
"Though they to one be ten
Be not amazéd!
Yet have we well begun:
Battles so bravely won
Have ever to the sun
By Fame been raiséd!

"And for myself," quoth he,
"This my full rest shall be:
England ne'er mourn for me,
Nor more esteem me!
Victor I will remain.
Or on this earth lie slain;
Never shall she sustain
Loss to redeem me!

"Poitiers and Cressy[4] tell,
When most their pride did swell,
Under our swords they fell.
No less our skill is,
Than when our Grandsire great,
Claiming the regal seat,
By many a warlike feat
Lopped the French lilies."

The Duke of York so dread
The eager vanward led;
With the main, Henry sped
Amongst his henchmen;
Exeter had the rear,
A braver man not there!
O Lord, how hot they were
On the false Frenchmen!

They now to fight are gone;
Armor on armor shone;
Drum now to drum did groan:
To hear, was wonder;
That, with the cries they make,
The very earth did shake;
Trumpet to trumpet spake;
Thunder to thunder.

Well it thine age became,
O noble Erpingham,
Which didst the signal aim
To our hid forces!
When, from a meadow by,
Like a storm suddenly,
The English archery
Stuck the French horses.

With Spanish yew so strong;
Arrows a cloth-yard long,
That like to serpents stung,
Piercing the weather.
None from his fellow starts;
But, playing manly parts,
And like true English hearts,
Stuck close together.

[1]Richard Hakluyt (1553–1616), compiler of a famous collection of narratives of Elizabethan voyages, first published in 1589.

[2]Henry V.

[3]The battle of Agincourt was fought on 25 October, 1415.

[4]Victories of the English in France during the Hundred Years' War. The battle of Crécy took place on 26 August, 1346; that of Poitiers on 19 September, 1356.

When down their bows they threw,
And forth their bilboes[1] drew,
And on the French they flew:
Not one was tardy.
Arms were from shoulders sent,
Scalps to the teeth were rent,
Down the French peasants went:
Our men were hardy.

This while our noble King,
His broad sword brandishing,
Down the French host did ding,[2]
As to o'erwhelm it.
And many a deep wound lent;
His arms with blood besprent,
And many a cruel dent
Bruiséd his helmet.

Gloucester, that duke so good,
Next of the royal blood,
For famous England stood
With his brave brother.
Clarence, in steel so bright,
Though but a maiden knight,
Yet in that furious fight
Scarce such another!

Warwick in blood did wade;
Oxford, the foe invade,
And cruel slaughter made,
Still as they ran up.
Suffolk his ax did ply;
Beaumont and Willoughby
Bare them right doughtily;
Ferrers, and Fanhope.

Upon Saint Crispin's Day
Fought was this noble fray;
Which Fame did not delay
To England to carry.
O, when shall English men
With such acts fill a pen?
Or England breed again
Such a King Harry?

WILLIAM SHAKESPEARE
(1564–1616)

SONNETS

15

When I consider everything that grows
Holds in perfection but a little moment,
That this huge stage presenteth nought but shows
Whereon the stars in secret influence comment;
When I perceive that men as plants increase,
Cheered and checked even by the self-same sky;
Vaunt in their youthful sap, at height decrease,
And wear their brave state out of memory;
Then the conceit[3] of this inconstant stay
Sets you most rich in youth before my sight,
Where wasteful Time debateth[4] with Decay,
To change your day of youth to sullied night;
And all in war with Time for love of you,
As he takes from you, I engraft you new.

18

Shall I compare thee to a summer's day?
Thou art more lovely and more temperate:
Rough winds do shake the darling buds of May,
And summer's lease hath all too short a date;
Sometime too hot the eye of heaven shines,
And often is his gold complexion dimmed;
And every fair from fair sometime declines,
By chance or nature's changing course untrimmed:
But thy eternal summer shall not fade
Nor lose possession of that fair thou ow'st;
Nor shall Death brag thou wand'rest in his shade,
When in eternal lines to time thou grow'st;
So long as men can breathe or eyes can see,
So long lives this and this gives life to thee.

25

Let those who are in favor with their stars
Of public honor and proud titles boast,
Whilst I, whom fortune of such triumph bars,
Unlooked for[5] joy in that I honor most.
Great princes' favorites their fair leaves spread
But as the marigold at the sun's eye,
And in themselves their pride lies buriéd,
For at a frown they in their glory die.
The painful warrior famouséd for fight,
After a thousand victories once foiled,
Is from the book of honor razéd quite,
And all the rest forgot for which he toiled.
Then happy I, that love and am beloved
Where I may not remove nor be removed.

29

When, in disgrace with Fortune and men's eyes,

[1] Swords. [2] Strike. [3] Thought. [4] Contends.

[5] Unnoticed.

I all alone beweep my outcast state,
And trouble deaf heaven with my bootless cries,
And look upon myself and curse my fate,
Wishing me like to one more rich in hope,
Featured like him, like him with friends possessed,
Desiring this man's art, and that man's scope,
With what I most enjoy contented least;
Yet in these thoughts myself almost despising,
Haply I think on thee; and then my state,
Like to the lark at break of day arising
From sullen earth, sings hymns at heaven's gate;
For thy sweet love remembered such wealth brings
That then I scorn to change my state with kings.

30

WHEN to the sessions of sweet silent thought
I summon up remembrance of things past,
I sigh the lack of many a thing I sought,
And with old woes new wail my dear time's waste;
Then can I drown an eye, unused to flow,
For precious friends hid in death's dateless night,
And weep afresh love's long since canceled woe,
And moan the expense of many a vanished sight:
Then can I grieve at grievances foregone,
And heavily from woe to woe tell[1] o'er,
The sad account of fore-bemoanéd moan,
Which I new pay as if not paid before.
But if the while I think on thee, dear friend,
All losses are restored and sorrows end.

31

THY bosom is endearéd with all hearts
Which I by lacking have supposéd dead;
And there reigns love and all love's loving parts,
And all those friends which I thought buriéd.
How many a holy and obsequious tear
Hath dear religious love stolen from mine eye
As interest of the dead, which now appear
But things removed that hidden in thee lie!
Thou art the grave where buried love doth live,
Hung with the trophies of my lovers gone,
Who all their parts of me to thee did give,
That due of many[2] now is thine alone.
Their images I loved I view in thee,
And thou, all they, hast all the all of me.

[1]Count.
[2]So that what belonged to many.

55

NOT marble, nor the gilded monuments
Of princes, shall outlive this powerful rime;
But you shall shine more bright in these contents[3]
Than unswept stone besmeared with sluttish time.
When wasteful war shall statues overturn,
And broils root out the work of masonry,
Nor Mars his sword nor war's quick fire shall burn
The living record of your memory.
'Gainst death and all-oblivious enmity
Shall you pace forth; your praise shall still find room
Even in the eyes of all posterity
That wear this world out to the ending doom.
So, till the judgment that[4] yourself arise,
You live in this, and dwell in lovers' eyes.

57

BEING your slave, what should I do but tend
Upon the hours and times of your desire?
I have no precious time at all to spend,
Nor services to do, till you require.
Nor dare I chide the world-without-end hour
Whilst I, my sovereign, watch the clock for you,
Nor think the bitterness of absence sour
When you have bid your servant once adieu;
Nor dare I question with my jealous thought
Where you may be, or your affairs suppose,
But, like a sad slave, stay and think of nought
Save, where you are how happy you make those.
So true a fool is love that in your will
Though you do anything, he thinks no ill.

60

LIKE as the waves make towards the pebbled shore,
So do our minutes hasten to their end;
Each changing place with that which goes before,
In sequent toil all forwards do contend.
Nativity, once in the main of light,
Crawls to maturity, wherewith being crowned,
Crooked[5] eclipses 'gainst his glory fight,
And Time that gave doth now his gift confound.
Time doth transfix the flourish[6] set on youth
And delves the parallels in beauty's brow,
Feeds on the rarities of nature's truth,
And nothing stands but for his scythe to mow;
And yet to times in hope[7] my verse shall stand,
Praising thy worth, despite his cruel hand.

[3]In these verses. [4]When. [5]Malignant.
[6]Ornamentation. [7]Future times.

64

When I have seen by Time's fell hand defaced
The rich proud cost of outworn buried age;
When sometime lofty towers I see down-razed
And brass eternal slave to mortal rage;
When I have seen the hungry ocean gain
Advantage on the kingdom of the shore,
And the firm soil win of the watery main,
Increasing store with loss and loss with store;
When I have seen such interchange of state,
Or state[1] itself confounded to decay
Ruin hath taught me thus to ruminate,
That Time will come and take my love away.
  This thought is as a death, which cannot choose
  But weep to have that which it fears to lose.

71

No longer mourn for me when I am dead
Than you shall hear the surly sullen bell
Give warning to the world that I am fled
From this vile world, with vilest worms to dwell.
Nay, if you read this line, remember not
The hand that writ it; for I love you so
That I in your sweet thoughts would be forgot
If thinking on me then should make you woe.
O, if, I say, you look upon this verse
When I perhaps compounded am with clay,
Do not so much as my poor name rehearse,
But let your love even with my life decay,
  Lest the wise world should look into your moan
  And mock you with me after I am gone.

73

That time of year thou mayst in me behold
When yellow leaves, or none, or few, do hang
Upon those boughs which shake against the cold,
Bare ruined choirs where late the sweet birds sang.
In me thou see'st the twilight of such day
As after sunset fadeth in the west,
Which by and by black night doth take away,
Death's second self, that seals up all in rest.
In me thou see'st the glowing of such fire
That on the ashes of his youth doth lie,
As the death-bed whereon it must expire,
Consumed with that which it was nourished by.
  This thou perceiv'st, which makes thy love more strong,
  To love that well which thou must leave ere long.

[1]Greatness.

90

Then hate me when thou wilt; if ever, now;
Now, while the world is bent my deeds to cross,
Join with the spite of fortune, make me bow,
And do not drop in for an after-loss:
Ah, do not, when my heart hath scaped this sorrow,
Come in the rearward of a conquered woe;
Give not a windy night a rainy morrow,
To linger out a purposed overthrow.
If thou wilt leave me, do not leave me last,
When other petty griefs have done their spite,
But in the onset come; so shall I taste
At first the very worst of fortune's might,
  And other strains of woe, which now seem woe,
  Compared with loss of thee will not seem so.

94

They that have power to hurt and will do none,
That do not do the thing they most do show,
Who, moving others, are themselves as stone,
Unmovéd, cold, and to temptation slow,
They rightly do inherit heaven's graces
And husband nature's riches from expense;
They are the lords and owners of their faces,
Others but stewards of their excellence.[2]
The summer's flower is to the summer sweet,
Though to itself it only live and die,
But if that flower with base infection meet,
The basest weed outbraves his dignity:
  For sweetest things turn sourest by their deeds;
  Lilies that fester smell far worse than weeds.

97

How like a winter hath my absence been
From thee, the pleasure of the fleeting year!
What freezings have I felt, what dark days seen!
What old December's bareness everywhere!
And yet this time removed[3] was summer's time,
The teeming autumn, big with rich increase,
Bearing the wanton burden of the prime,[4]
Like widowed wombs after their lords' decease.
Yet this abundant issue seemed to me
But hope of orphans[5] and unfathered fruit;
For summer and his pleasures wait on thee,
And, thou away, the very birds are mute;
  Or, if they sing, 'tis with so dull a cheer
  That leaves look pale, dreading the winter's near.

[2]Beautiful persons who are commanded by their passions hold their beauty as stewards for the commanders, their passions, which are the real owners.

[3]Time of my absence. [4]Spring.

[5]Hope such as orphans bring.

98

From you have I been absent in the spring,
When proud-pied[1] April, dressed in all his trim,
Hath put a spirit of youth in everything,
That heavy Saturn[2] laughed and leaped with him.
Yet nor the lays of birds nor the sweet smell
Of different flowers in[3] odor and in hue
Could make me any summer's story[4] tell,
Or from their proud lap pluck them where they grew;
Nor did I wonder at the lily's white,
Nor praise the deep vermilion in the rose;
They were but sweet, but figures of delight
Drawn after you, you pattern of all those.
Yet seemed it winter still, and, you away,
As with your shadow I with these did play.

106

When in the chronicle of wasted time
I see descriptions of the fairest wights,[5]
And beauty making beautiful old rime
In praise of ladies dead and lovely knights;
Then, in the blazon of sweet beauty's best,
Of hand, of foot, of lip, of eye, of brow,
I see their antique pen would have expressed
Even such a beauty as you master[6] now.
So all their praises are but prophecies
Of this our time, all you prefiguring;
And, for they looked but with divining eyes,
They had not skill enough your worth to sing:
For we, which now behold these present days,
Have eyes to wonder, but lack tongues to praise.

109

O, never say that I was false of heart,
Though absence seemed my flame to qualify.[7]
As easy might I from myself depart
As from my soul, which in thy breast doth lie.
That is my home of love; if I have ranged,
Like him that travels I return again,
Just to the time, not with the time exchanged,[8]
So that myself bring water for my stain.
Never believe, though in my nature reigned
All frailties that besiege all kinds of blood,
That it could so preposterously be stained,
To leave for nothing all thy sum of good;
For nothing this wide universe I call,
Save thou, my rose; in it thou art my all.

[1]Gaily colored.
[2]Planet credited in astrology with producing a sluggish and gloomy temperament in those born under its influence.
[3]Flowers different in.
[4]Probably means, any cheerful story.
[5]People. [6]Have. [7]Moderate.
[8]Punctual, not altered by the time.

110

Alas, 'tis true I have gone here and there
And made myself a motley[9] to the view,
Gored[10] mine own thoughts, sold cheap what is most dear,
Made old offenses of affections new;
Most true it is that I have looked on truth
Askance and strangely: but, by all above,
These blenches[11] gave my heart another youth,
And worse essays proved thee my best of love.
Now all is done, have what shall have no end:
Mine appetite I never more will grind[12]
On newer proof, to try an older friend,
A god in love, to whom I am confined.
Then give me welcome, next my heaven the best,
Even to thy pure and most most loving breast.

111

O, for my sake do you with Fortune chide,
The guilty goddess of my harmful deeds,
That did not better for my life provide
Than public means which public manners breeds.
Thence comes it that my name receives a brand,
And almost thence my nature is subdued
To what it works in, like the dyer's hand.
Pity me, then, and wish I were renewed;
Whilst, like a willing patient, I will drink
Potions of eisel[13] 'gainst my strong infection;
No bitterness that I will bitter think,
Nor double penance, to correct correction.
Pity me then, dear friend, and I assure ye
Even that your pity is enough to cure me.

116

Let me not to the marriage of true minds
Admit impediments. Love is not love
Which alters when it alteration finds,
Or bends with the remover to remove.
O, no! it is an ever-fixéd mark
That looks on tempests and is never shaken;
It is the star to every wand'ring bark,
Whose worth's unknown, although his height be taken.
Love's not Time's fool,[14] though rosy lips and cheeks
Within his bending sickle's compass come;
Love alters not with his brief hours and weeks,
But bears it out even to the edge of doom.
If this be error and upon me proved,
I never writ, nor no man ever loved.

[9]Jester. [10]Injured. [11]Aberrations.
[12]Whet. [13]Vinegar. [14]The sport of time.

129

THE expense of spirit in a waste of shame
Is lust in action; and till action, lust
Is perjured, murd'rous, bloody, full of blame,
Savage, extreme, rude, cruel, not to trust,
Enjoyed no sooner but despiséd straight,
Past reason hunted, and no sooner had
Past reason hated, as a swallowed bait
On purpose laid to make the taker mad;
Mad in pursuit and in possession so;
Had, having, and in quest to have, extreme;
A bliss in proof,[1] and proved, a very woe;
Before, a joy proposed; behind, a dream.
All this the world well knows; yet none knows well
To shun the heaven that leads men to this hell.

130

MY MISTRESS' eyes are nothing like the sun;
Coral is far more red than her lips' red;
If snow be white, why then her breasts are dun;
If hairs be wires, black wires grow on her head.
I have seen roses damasked, red and white,
But no such roses see I in her cheeks;
And in some perfumes is there more delight
Than in the breath that from my mistress reeks.
I love to hear her speak, yet well I know
That music hath a far more pleasing sound;
I grant I never saw a goddess go;
My mistress, when she walks, treads on the ground:
And yet, by heaven, I think my love as rare
As any she belied with false compare.

146

POOR soul, the center of my sinful earth,[2]
[Thrall to] these rebel powers that thee array,
Why dost thou pine within and suffer dearth,
Painting thy outward walls so costly gay?
Why so large cost, having so short a lease,
Dost thou upon thy fading mansion spend?
Shall worms, inheritors of this excess,
Eat up thy charge? Is this thy body's end?
Then, soul, live thou upon thy servant's loss,
And let that pine to aggravate[3] thy store;
Buy terms divine[4] in selling hours of dross;
Within be fed, without be rich no more;
So shalt thou feed on Death, that feeds on men,
And Death once dead, there's no more dying then.

[1]In experience. [2]My body.
[3]Increase. [4]Eternity.

SONGS FROM THE PLAYS

WHEN DAISIES PIED[5]

WHEN daisies pied and violets blue,
And lady-smocks all silver-white,
And cuckoo-buds of yellow hue
Do paint the meadows with delight,
The cuckoo then, on every tree,
Mocks married men; for thus sings he,
Cuckoo!
Cuckoo, cuckoo!—O word of fear,
Unpleasing to a married ear!

When shepherds pipe on oaten straws,
And merry larks are plowmen's clocks,
When turtles[6] tread, and rooks, and daws,
And maidens bleach their summer smocks
The cuckoo then, on every tree,
Mocks married men; for thus sings he,
Cuckoo!
Cuckoo, cuckoo!—O word of fear,
Unpleasing to a married ear!

WHEN ICICLES HANG BY THE WALL

WHEN icicles hang by the wall,
And Dick the shepherd blows his nail,
And Tom bears logs into the hall,
And milk comes frozen home in pail,
When blood is nipped and ways be foul,
Then nightly sings the staring owl,
"Tu-whit, tu-who!" a merry note,
While greasy Joan doth keel[7] the pot.

When all aloud the wind doth blow,
And coughing drowns the parson's saw,
And birds sit brooding in the snow,
And Marian's nose looks red and raw,
When roasted crabs[8] hiss in the bowl,
Then nightly sings the staring owl,
"Tu-whit, tu-who!" a merry note,
While greasy Joan doth keel the pot.

WHO IS SYLVIA?[9]

WHO is Sylvia? what is she,
That all our swains commend her?
Holy, fair, and wise is she;
The heaven such grace did lend her,
That she might admiréd be.

Is she kind as she is fair?
For beauty lives with kindness.
Love doth to her eyes repair
To help him of his blindness,
And, being helped, inhabits there.

[5]This and the following song are from *Love's Labor's Lost.*
[6]Turtle-doves. [7]Skim. [8]Apples.
[9]From *Two Gentlemen of Verona.*

Then to Sylvia let us sing,
That Sylvia is excelling;
She excels each mortal thing
Upon the dull earth dwelling:
To her let us garlands bring.

TELL ME, WHERE IS FANCY BRED[1]

Tell me, where is fancy bred,
Or in the heart, or in the head?
How begot, how nourishéd?
Reply, reply.
It is engendered in the eyes,
With gazing fed; and fancy dies
In the cradle where it lies:
Let us all ring fancy's knell;
I'll begin it,—Ding-dong, bell.
Ding, dong, bell.

UNDER THE GREENWOOD TREE[2]

Under the greenwood tree
Who loves to lie with me,
And turn his merry note
Unto the sweet bird's throat,
Come hither! come hither! come hither!
Here shall he see
No enemy
But winter and rough weather.

Who doth ambition shun
And loves to live i' the sun,
Seeking the food he eats
And pleased with what he gets,
Come hither! come hither! come hither!
Here shall he see
No enemy
But winter and rough weather.

BLOW, BLOW, THOU WINTER WIND

Blow, blow, thou winter wind!
Thou art not so unkind
As man's ingratitude;
Thy tooth is not so keen,
Because thou art not seen,
Although thy breath be rude.

Heigh ho! sing, heigh ho! unto the green holly:
Most friendship is feigning, most loving mere folly:
Then, heigh ho, the holly!
This life is most jolly.

Freeze, freeze, thou bitter sky!
That dost not bite so nigh
As benefits forgot;
Though thou the waters warp,
Thy sting is not so sharp
As friend remembered not.

Heigh ho! sing, heigh ho! *etc.*

SIGH NO MORE[3]

Sigh no more, ladies, sigh no more!
Men were deceivers ever,
One foot in sea and one on shore,
To one thing constant never:
Then sigh not so, but let them go,
And be you blithe and bonny,
Converting all your sounds of woe
Into Hey nonny, nonny!

Sing no more ditties, sing no moe[4]
Of dumps so dull and heavy!
The fraud of men was ever so,
Since summer first was leafy:
Then sigh not so, but let them go,
And be you blithe and bonny,
Converting all your sounds of woe
Into Hey nonny, nonny!

O MISTRESS MINE[5]

O Mistress mine, where are you roaming?
O, stay and hear; your true love's coming,
That can sing both high and low:
Trip no further, pretty sweeting,
Journeys end in lovers meeting,
Every wise man's son doth know.

What is love? 't is not hereafter;
Present mirth hath present laughter;
What's to come is still unsure:
In delay there lies no plenty;
Then come kiss me, sweet and twenty,
Youth's a stuff will not endure.

TAKE, O, TAKE THOSE LIPS AWAY[6]

Take, O, take those lips away,
That so sweetly were forsworn;
And those eyes, the break of day,
Lights that do mislead the morn:
But my kisses bring again,
Bring again;
Seals of love, but sealed in vain,
Sealed in vain!

COME, THOU MONARCH OF THE VINE[7]

Come, thou monarch of the vine,
Plumpy Bacchus with pink eyne![8]

[1]From *The Merchant of Venice.*
[2]This and the following song are from *As You Like It.*
[3]From *Much Ado about Nothing.*
[4]More.
[5]From *Twelfth Night.*
[6]From *Measure for Measure.*
[7]From *Antony and Cleopatra.*
[8]Eyes.

In thy vats our cares be drowned,
With thy grapes our hairs be crowned!
Cup us, till the world go round,
Cup us, till the world go round!

HARK, HARK! THE LARK[1]

HARK, hark! the lark at heaven's gate sings,
And Phœbus 'gins arise,
His steeds to water at those springs
On chaliced flowers that lies;
And winking Mary-buds begin
To ope their golden eyes:
With everything that pretty is,
My lady sweet, arise!
Arise, arise!

FEAR NO MORE THE HEAT O' THE SUN

FEAR no more the heat o' th' sun,
Nor the furious winter's rages;
Thou thy worldly task hast done,
Home art gone, and ta'en thy wages:
Golden lads and girls all must,
As chimney-sweepers, come to dust.

Fear no more the frown o' th' great;
Thou art past the tyrant's stroke;
Care no more to clothe and eat;
To thee the reed is as the oak:
The Scepter, Learning, Physic, must
All follow this, and come to dust.

Fear no more the lightning-flash,
Nor th' all-dreaded thunder-stone;
Fear not slander, censure rash;
Thou hast finished joy and moan:
All lovers young, all lovers must
Consign to thee, and come to dust.

No exorciser harm thee!
Nor no witchcraft charm thee!
Ghost unlaid forbear thee!
Nothing ill come near thee!
Quiet consummation have;
And renownéd be thy grave!

FULL FATHOM FIVE THY FATHER LIES[2]

FULL fathom five thy father lies:
Of his bones are coral made;
Those are pearls that were his eyes;
Nothing of him that doth fade
But doth suffer a sea-change
Into something rich and strange.
Sea-nymphs hourly ring his knell;
Ding-dong!
Hark! now I hear them,—Ding-dong, bell!

THOMAS CAMPION

(1567–1619)

FOLLOW THY FAIR SUN

FOLLOW thy fair sun, unhappy shadow,
Though thou be black as night,
And she made all of light,
Yet follow thy fair sun, unhappy shadow.

Follow her whose light thy light depriveth,
Though here thou liest disgraced,
And she in heaven is placed,
Yet follow her whose light the world reviveth.

Follow those pure beams whose beauty burneth,
That so have scorchéd thee,
As thou still black must be,
Till her kind beams thy black to brightness turneth.

Follow her while yet her glory shineth:
There comes a luckless night,
That will dim all her light;
And this the black unhappy shade divineth.

Follow still, since so thy fates ordainéd;
The Sun must have his shade,
Till both at once do fade,
The Sun still proud, the shadow still disdainéd.

FOLLOW YOUR SAINT

FOLLOW your Saint, follow with accents sweet;
Haste you, sad notes, fall at her flying feet;
There, wrapt in cloud of sorrow, pity move,
And tell the ravisher of my soul I perish for her love:
But if she scorns my never-ceasing pain,
Then burst with sighing in her sight and ne'er return again.

All that I sung still to her praise did tend,
Still she was first; still she my songs did end.
Yet she my love and music both doth fly,
The music that her echo is and beauty's sympathy;
Then let my notes pursue her scornful flight:
It shall suffice that they were breathed and died for her delight.

[1]This and the following song are from *Cymbeline*.

[2]From *The Tempest*.

THERE IS A GARDEN IN HER FACE

There is a garden in her face
Where roses and white lilies grow;
A heavenly paradise is that place,
Wherein all pleasant fruits do flow:
There cherries grow, which none may buy
Till "Cherry-ripe" themselves do cry.

Those cherries fairly do enclose
Of orient pearl a double row,
Which when her lovely laughter shows,
They look like rosebuds filled with snow;
Yet them nor peer nor prince can buy
Till "Cherry-ripe" themselves do cry.

Her eyes like angels watch them still;
Her brows like bended bows do stand,
Threatening with piercing frowns to kill
All that attempt, with eye or hand,
Those sacred cherries to come nigh
Till "Cherry-ripe" themselves do cry.

WHEN THOU MUST HOME

When thou must home to shades of underground,
And there arrived, a new admiréd guest,
The beauteous spirits do engirt thee round,
White Iope, blithe Helen, and the rest,
To hear the stories of thy finished love
From that smooth tongue whose music hell can move;

Then wilt thou speak of banqueting delights,
Of masques and revels which sweet youth did make,
Of tourneys and great challenges of knights,
And all these triumphs for thy beauty's sake:
When thou hast told these honors done to thee,
Then tell, O tell, how thou didst murder me.

NOW WINTER NIGHTS ENLARGE

Now winter nights enlarge
The number of their hours;
And clouds their storms discharge
Upon the airy towers.
Let now the chimneys blaze,
And cups o'erflow with wine,
Let well-tuned words amaze
With harmony divine.
Now yellow waxen lights
Shall wait on honey love;
While youthful revels, masques, and courtly sights,
Sleep's leaden spells remove.

This time doth well dispense
With lovers' long discourse;
Much speech hath some defense,
Though beauty no remorse.
All do not all things well:
Some measures comely tread,
Some knotted riddles tell,
Some poems smoothly read.
The summer hath his joys
And winter his delights;
Though love and all his pleasures are but toys,
They shorten tedious nights.

ROSE–CHEEKED LAURA

Rose-cheeked Laura, come,
Sing thou smoothly with thy beauty's
Silent music, either other
Sweetly gracing.

Lovely forms do flow
From consent[1] divinely framéd;
Heav'n is music, and thy beauty's
Birth is heavenly.

These dull notes we sing
Discords need for helps to grace them;
Only beauty purely loving
Knows no discord,

But still moves delight,
Like clear springs renewed by flowing,
Ever perfect, ever in them-
selves eternal.

NEVER LOVE

Never love, unless you can
Bear with all the faults of man:
Men sometimes will jealous be,
Though but little cause they see,
And hang the head, as discontent,
And speak what straight they will repent.

Men that but one Saint adore,
Make a show of love to more:
Beauty must be scorned in none,
Though but truly served in one:
For what is courtship, but disguise?
True hearts may have dissembling eyes.

Men when their affairs require,
Must awhile themselves retire;
Sometimes hunt, and sometimes hawk,
And not ever sit and talk.
If these, and such like you can bear,
Then like, and love, and never fear.

[1]Harmony.

BEAUTY IS BUT A PAINTED HELL

Beauty is but a painted hell:
Aye me, aye me,
She wounds them that admire it,
She kills them that desire it;
Give her pride but fuel,
No fire is more cruel.

Pity from ev'ry heart is fled:
Aye me, aye me,
Since false desire could borrow
Tears of dissembled sorrow,
Constant vows turn truthless,
Love cruel, Beauty ruthless.

Sorrow can laugh, and Fury sing:
Aye me, aye me,
My raving griefs discover
I lived too true a lover;
The first step to madness
Is the excess of sadness.

THE MAN OF LIFE UPRIGHT

The man of life upright,
Whose guiltless heart is free
From all dishonest deeds,
Or thought of vanity;

The man whose silent days
In harmless joys are spent,
Whom hopes cannot delude,
Nor sorrow discontent;

That man needs neither towers
Nor armor for defense,
Nor secret vaults to fly
From thunder's violence.

He only can behold
With unaffrighted eyes
The horrors of the deep
And terrors of the skies.

Thus, scorning all the cares
That fate or fortune brings,
He makes the heav'n his book,
His wisdom heav'nly things,

Good thoughts his only friends,
His wealth a well-spent age,
The earth his sober inn
And quiet pilgrimage.

BEN JONSON
(1573?-1637)

HYMN TO DIANA

Queen and Huntress, chaste and fair,
Now the sun is laid to sleep,
Seated in thy silver chair
State in wonted manner keep:
Hesperus entreats thy light,
Goddess excellently bright.

Earth, let not thy envious shade
Dare itself to interpose;
Cynthia's shining orb was made
Heaven to clear when day did close:
Bless us then with wishéd sight,
Goddess excellently bright.

Lay thy bow of pearl apart
And thy crystal-shining quiver;
Give unto the flying hart
Space to breathe, how short soever:
Thou that mak'st a day of night,
Goddess excellently bright.

SONG: TO CELIA

Come, my Celia, let us prove,
While we can, the sports of love.
Time will not be ours for ever;
He, at length, our good will sever;
Spend not then his gifts in vain.
Suns that set may rise again;
But if once we lose this light,
'T is with us perpetual night.
Why should we defer our joys?
Fame and rumor are but toys.
Cannot we delude the eyes
Of a few poor household spies?
Or his easier ears beguile,
Thus removéd by our wile?
'T is no sin love's fruits to steal;
But the sweet theft to reveal,
To be taken, to be seen,
These have crimes accounted been.

TO CELIA

Drink to me only with thine eyes,
And I will pledge with mine;
Or leave a kiss but in the cup,
And I'll not look for wine.
The thirst that from the soul doth rise
Doth ask a drink divine;
But might I of Jove's nectar sup,
I would not change for thine.

I sent thee late a rosy wreath,
Not so much honoring thee

As giving it a hope, that there
  It could not withered be.
But thou thereon didst only breathe,
  And sent'st it back to me;
Since when it grows, and smells, I swear,
  Not of itself, but thee.

SONG: THAT WOMEN ARE BUT MEN'S SHADOWS

Follow a shadow, it still flies you,
  Seem to fly it, it will pursue:
So court a mistress, she denies you;
  Let her alone, she will court you.
Say are not women truly, then,
Styled but the shadows of us men?

At morn and even shades are longest;
  At noon they are or short, or none:
So men at weakest, they are strongest,
  But grant us perfect, they're not known.
Say are not women truly, then,
Styled but the shadows of us men?

STILL TO BE NEAT

Still to be neat, still to be drest,
As you were going to a feast;
Still to be powdered, still perfumed;—
Lady, it is to be presumed,
Though art's hid causes are not found,
All is not sweet, all is not sound.

Give me a look, give me a face,
That makes simplicity a grace;
Robes loosely flowing, hair as free:
Such sweet neglect more taketh me
Than all th' adulteries of art;
They strike mine eyes, but not my heart.

HER TRIUMPH

See the chariot at hand here of Love,
  Wherein my Lady rideth!
Each that draws is a swan or a dove,
  And well the car Love guideth.
As she goes, all hearts do duty
    Unto her beauty;
And enamored, do wish, so they might
    But enjoy such a sight,
That they still were to run by her side,
Through swords, through seas, whither she
  would ride.

Do but look on her eyes, they do light
  All that Love's world compriseth!
Do but look on her hair, it is bright
  As Love's star when it riseth!
Do but mark, her forehead's smoother
    Than words that soothe her;
And from her arched brows, such a grace
    Sheds itself through the face
As alone there triumphs to the life
All the gain, all the good, of the elements'
  strife.

Have you seen but a bright lily grow
  Before rude hands have touched it?
Have you marked but the fall of the snow
  Before the soil hath smutched[1] it?
Have you felt the wool of the beaver?
    Or swan's down ever?
Or have smelt o' the bud of the briar?
    Or the nard in the fire?
Or have tasted the bag of the bee!
O so white! O so soft! O so sweet is she!

AN ODE

  High-spirited friend,
I send nor balms, nor corsives to your wound;
  Your faith hath found
A gentler, and more agile hand, to tend
The cure of that which is but corporal,
And doubtful days, which were named critical,
  Have made their fairest flight,
  And now are out of sight.
Yet doth some wholesome physic for the mind,
  Wrapt in this paper lie,
Which in the taking if you misapply,
    You are unkind.

  Your covetous hand,
Happy in that fair honor it hath gained,
  Must now be reined.
True valor doth her own renown command
In one full action; nor have you now more
To do, than be a husband of that store.
  Think but how dear you bought
  This same which you have caught,
Such thoughts will make you more in love
  with truth:
  'Tis wisdom, and that high,
For men to use their fortune reverently,
    Even in youth.

A SONG

O do not wanton with those eyes,
  Lest I be sick with seeing;
Nor cast them down, but let them rise,
  Lest shame destroy their being.

O be not angry with those fires,
  For then their threats will kill me;
Nor look too kind on my desires,
  For then my hopes will spill me.

[1]Dirtied.

O do not steep them in thy tears,
For so will sorrow slay me;
Nor spread them as distract with fears;
Mine own enough betray me.

A NYMPH'S PASSION

I LOVE, and he loves me again,
Yet dare I not tell who;
For if the nymphs should know my swain,
I fear they'd love him too;
Yet if he be not known,
The pleasure is as good as none,
For that's a narrow joy is but our own.

I'll tell, that if they be not glad,
They yet may envy me;
But then if I grow jealous mad,
And of them pitied be,
It were a plague 'bove scorn:
And yet it cannot be forborn,
Unless my heart would, as my thought, be torn.

He is, if they can find him, fair,
And fresh and fragrant too,
As summer's sky, or purgéd air,
And looks as lilies do
That are this morning blown;
Yet, yet I doubt he is not known,
And fear much more, that more of him be shown.

But he hath eyes so round, and bright,
As make away my doubt,
Where Love may all his torches light
Though hate had put them out:
But then, t' increase my fears,
What nymph soe'er his voice but hears,
Will be my rival, though she have but ears.

I'll tell no more, and yet I love,
And he loves me; yet no
One unbecoming thought doth move
From either heart, I know;
But so exempt from blame,
As it would be to each a fame,
If love or fear would let me tell his name.

TO THE MEMORY OF MY BELOVED MASTER WILLIAM SHAKESPEARE

To DRAW no envy, Shakespeare, on thy name,
Am I thus ample to thy book and fame;
While I confess thy writings to be such
As neither man, nor muse, can praise too much.
'T is true, and all men's suffrage. But these ways
Were not the paths I meant unto thy praise;
For silliest ignorance on these may light,
Which, when it sounds at best, but echoes right;
Or blind affection, which doth ne'er advance
The truth, but gropes, and urgeth all by chance;
Or crafty malice might pretend this praise,
And think to ruin, where it seemed to raise.
These are, as some infamous bawd or whore
Should praise a matron. What could hurt her more?
But thou art proof against them, and, indeed,
Above the ill fortune of them, or the need.
I therefore will begin. Soul of the age!
The applause, delight, the wonder of our stage!
My Shakespeare, rise! I will not lodge thee by
Chaucer, or Spenser, or bid Beaumont lie
A little further, to make thee a room:
Thou art a monument without a tomb,
And art alive still while thy book doth live
And we have wits to read and praise to give.
That I not mix thee so, my brain excuses,
I mean with great, but disproportioned Muses;
For if I thought my judgment were of years,
I should commit thee surely with thy peers,
And tell how far thou didst our Lyly outshine,
Or sporting Kyd, or Marlowe's mighty line.
And though thou hadst small Latin and less Greek,
From thence to honor thee, I would not seek
For names; but call forth thundering Æschylus,
Euripides, and Sophocles to us;
Pacuvius,[1] Accius,[1] him of Cordova[2] dead,
To life again, to hear thy buskin[3] tread,
And shake a stage; or, when thy socks[4] were on,
Leave thee alone for the comparison
Of all that insolent Greece or haughty Rome
Sent forth, or since did from their ashes come.
Triumph, my Britain, thou hast one to show
To whom all scenes of Europe homage owe.
He was not of an age, but for all time!
And all the Muses still were in their prime,
When, like Apollo, he came forth to warm
Our ears, or like a Mercury to charm!
Nature herself was proud of his designs
And joyed to wear the dressing of his lines!
Which were so richly spun, and woven so fit,
As, since, she will vouchsafe no other wit.
The merry Greek, tart Aristophanes,
Neat Terence, witty Plautus, now not please;
But antiquated and deserted lie,
As they were not of Nature's family.
Yet must I not give Nature all; thy art,
My gentle Shakespeare, must enjoy a part.

[1]Roman tragic poet. [2]Seneca the tragic poet.
[3]The high boot worn in classical times by actors in tragedy.
[4]Light shoes worn in classical times by actors in comedy.

For though the poet's matter nature be,
His art doth give the fashion; and, that he
Who casts to write a living line, must sweat,
(Such as thine are) and strike the second heat
Upon the Muses' anvil; turn the same
(And himself with it) that he thinks to frame,
Or, for the laurel, he may gain a scorn;
For a good poet's made, as well as born.
And such wert thou! Look how the father's face
Lives in his issue, even so the race
Of Shakespeare's mind and manners brightly shines
In his well turnéd, and true filéd lines;
In each of which he seems to shake a lance,
As brandished at the eyes of ignorance.
Sweet Swan of Avon! what a sight it were
To see thee in our waters yet appear,
And make those flights upon the banks of Thames,
That so did take Eliza, and our James![1]
But stay, I see thee in the hemisphere
Advanced, and made a constellation there!
Shine forth, thou Star of poets, and with rage
Or influence, chide or cheer the drooping stage,
Which, since thy flight from hence, hath mourned like night,
And despairs day, but for thy volume's light

A PINDARIC ODE

TO THE IMMORTAL MEMORY AND FRIENDSHIP OF THAT NOBLE PAIR, SIR LUCIUS CARY AND SIR H. MORISON.[2]

I

The Strophe, or Turn

BRAVE infant of Saguntum,[3] clear
Thy coming forth in that great year,
When the prodigious Hannibal did crown
His rage with razing your immortal town.
Thou looking then about,
Ere thou were half got out,
Wise child, didst hastily return,
And mad'st thy mother's womb thine urn.
How summed[4] a circle didst thou leave mankind
Of deepest lore, could we the center find!

The Antistrophe, or Counter-Turn

Did wiser nature draw thee back,
From out the horror of that sack;
Where shame, faith, honor, and regard of right,
Lay trampled on? the deeds of death and night
Urged, hurried forth, and hurled
Upon the affrighted world;
Fire, famine, and fell fury met,
And all on utmost ruin set:
As, could they but life's miseries foresee,
No doubt all infants would return like thee.

The Epode, or Stand

For what is life, if measured by the space,
Not by the act?
Or maskéd man, if valued by his face,
Above his fact?[5]
Here's one outlived his peers
And told forth fourscore years:
He vexéd time, and busied the whole state:
Troubled both foes and friends;
But ever to no ends:
What did this stirrer but die late?
How well at twenty had he fallen or stood![6]
For three of his four score he did no good.

II

The Strophe, or Turn

He entered well by virtuous parts,
Got up, and thrived with honest arts,
He purchased friends, and fame, and honors then,
And had his noble name advanced with men;
But weary of that flight,
He stooped in all men's sight
To sordid flatteries, acts of strife,
And sunk in that dead sea of life,
So deep, as he did then death's waters sup,
But that the cork of title buoyed him up.

The Antistrophe, or Counter-Turn

Alas! but Morison fell young!
He never fell,—thou fall'st, my tongue.
He stood a soldier to the last right end,
A perfect patriot and a noble friend;
But most, a virtuous son.
All offices were done
By him, so ample, full, and round,
In weight, in measure, number, sound,
As, though his age imperfect might appear,
His life was of humanity the sphere.[7]

---

[1]Queen Elizabeth and James I.

[2]Pindar was the greatest of Greek lyric poets. This poem is modeled upon his odes in its stanzaic structure, and to some extent in its style and tone. Sir Lucius Cary, Viscount Falkland, was himself a poet and the friend of men of letters, who visited him freely at his country house near Oxford. He married the sister of Sir Henry Morison. Morison died in 1629, shortly before Jonson's ode was written.

[3]A city in Spain captured by Hannibal after a painful siege (219 B. C.). The story told by Jonson is recorded by Pliny, *Natural History*, VII, iii.

[4]Complete.

[5]Deed. [6]Stopped.

[7]*I. e.*, included all that humanity may achieve.

The Epode, or Stand

Go now, and tell[1] our days summed up with fears,
And make them years;
Produce thy mass of miseries on the stage,
To swell thine age;
Repeat of things a throng,
To show thou hast been long,
Not lived; for life doth her great actions spell
By what was done and wrought
In season, and so brought
To light: her measures are, how well
Each syllabe answered, and was formed how fair;
These make the lines of life, and that's her air!

III

The Strophe, or Turn

It is not growing like a tree
In bulk, doth make men better be;
Or standing long an oak, three hundred year,
To fall a log at last, dry, bald, and sear:
A lily of a day,
Is fairer far, in May,
Although it fall and die that night;
It was the plant and flower of light.
In small proportions we just beauties see;
And in short measures life may perfect be.

The Antistrophe, or Counter-Turn

Call, noble Lucius, then, for wine,
And let thy looks with gladness shine;
Accept this garland, plant it on thy head,
And think, nay know, thy Morison's now dead.
He leaped the present age,
Possest with holy rage,
To see that bright eternal day;
Of which we priests and poets say
Such truths as we expect for happy men;
And there he lives with memory and Ben

The Epode, or Stand

Jonson, who sung this of him, ere he went,
Himself, to rest,
Or taste a part of that full joy he meant
To have exprest,
In this bright asterism;[2]
Where it were friendship's schism,
Were not his Lucius long with us to tarry,
To separate these twi-
Lights, the Dioscuri;[3]
And keep the one half from his Harry.

[1]Count. [2]Constellation.
[3]Castor and Pollux, children of Zeus.

But fate doth so alternate the design,
Whilst that in heaven, this light on earth must shine.

IV

The Strophe, or Turn

And shine as you exalted are;
Two names of friendship, but one star:
Of hearts the union, and those not by chance
Made, or indenture, or leased out t' advance
The profits for a time.
No pleasures vain did chime,
Of rimes, or riots, at your feasts,
Orgies of drink, or feigned protests;
But simple love of greatness and of good,
That knits brave minds and manners more than blood.

The Antistrophe, or Counter-Turn

This made you first to know the why
You liked, then after, to apply
That liking; and approach so one the t' other,
Till either grew a portion of the other;
Each stylèd by his end,
The copy of his friend.
You lived to be the great sir-names
And titles by which all made claims
Unto the Virtue: nothing perfect done,
But as a Cary or a Morison.

The Epode, or Stand

And such a force the fair example had,
As they that saw
The good and durst not practice it, were glad
That such a law
Was left yet to mankind;
Where they might read and find
Friendship, indeed, was written not in words;
And with the heart, not pen,
Of two so early men,
Whose lines her rolls were, and records;
Who, ere the first down bloomèd on the chin,
Had sowed these fruits, and got the harvest in.

EPITAPH ON ELIZABETH, L. H.

Would'st thou hear what man can say
In a little? Reader, stay.
Underneath this stone doth lie
As much beauty as could die:
Which in life did harbor give
To more virtue than doth live.

If at all she had a fault,
Leave it buried in this vault.
One name was Elizabeth,
The other, let it sleep with death!

Fitter, where it died, to tell,
Than that it lived at all. Farewell!

EPITAPH ON SALATHIEL PAVY

Weep with me, all you that read
  This little story:
And know, for whom a tear you shed
  Death's self is sorry.
'T was a child that so did thrive
  In grace and feature,
As heaven and nature seemed to strive
  Which owned the creature.
Years he numbered scarce thirteen
  When fates turned cruel,
Yet three filled zodiacs[1] had he been
  The stage's jewel;
And did act, what now we moan,
  Old men so duly,
As, sooth, the Parcæ[2] thought him one,
  He played so truly.
So, by error, to his fate
  They all consented;
But viewing him since, alas, too late!
  They have repented;
And have sought, to give new birth,
  In baths to steep him;
But being so much too good for earth,
  Heaven vows to keep him.

JOHN DONNE
(1573–1631)

SONG

Go and catch a falling star,
  Get with child a mandrake root,[3]
Tell me where all past years are,
  Or who cleft the devil's foot;
Teach me to hear mermaids singing,
Or to keep off envy's stinging,
    And find
    What wind
Serves to advance an honest mind.

If thou be'st born to strange sights,
  Things invisible to see,
Ride ten thousand days and nights
  Till age snow white hairs on thee;
Thou, when thou return'st, wilt tell me
All strange wonders that befell thee,
    And swear
    No where
Lives a woman true and fair.

If thou find'st one, let me know;
  Such a pilgrimage were sweet.
Yet do not; I would not go,
  Though at next door we might meet.
Though she were true when you met her,
And last till you write your letter,
    Yet she
    Will be
False, ere I come, to two or three.

THE INDIFFERENT

I can love both fair and brown;
Her whom abundance melts, and her whom want betrays;
Her who loves loneness best, and her who masks and plays;
Her whom the country formed, and whom the town;
Her who believes, and her who tries;
Her who still weeps with spongy eyes,
And her who is dry cork and never cries.
I can love her, and her, and you, and you;
I can love any, so she be not true.

Will no other vice content you?
Will it not serve your turn to do as did your mothers?
Or have you all old vices spent and now would find out others?
Or doth a fear that men are true torment you?
O we are not, be not you so;
Let me—and do you—twenty know;
Rob me, but bind me not, and let me go.
Must I, who came to travel thorough you,
Grow your fixed subject, because you are true?

Venus heard me sigh this song;
And by love's sweetest part, variety, she swore,
She heard not this till now; it should be so no more.
She went, examined, and returned ere long,
And said, "Alas! some two or three
Poor heretics in love there be,
Which think to stablish dangerous constancy.
But I have told them, 'Since you will be true,
You shall be true to them who're false to you.'"

LOVERS' INFINITENESS

If yet I have not all thy love,
Dear, I shall never have it all,
I cannot breathe one other sigh, to move,
Nor can intreat one other tear to fall,

[1]Full years. [2]The Fates.

[3]This root has a shape somewhat like that of the human body.

And all my treasure, which should purchase thee,
Sighs, tears, and oaths, and letters, I have spent.
Yet no more can be due to me,
Than at the bargain made was meant;
If then thy gift of love were partial,
That some to me, some should to others fall,
  Dear, I shall never have thee all.

Or if then thou gavest me all,
All was but all, which thou hadst then;
But if in thy heart, since, there be or shall,
New love created be, by other men,
Which have their stocks entire, and can in tears,
In sighs, in oaths, and letters outbid me,
This new love may beget new fears,
For, this love was not vowed by thee;
And yet it was, thy gift being general,
The ground, thy heart is mine, what ever shall
  Grow there, dear; I should have it all.

Yet I would not have all yet;
He that hath all can have no more,
And since my love doth every day admit
New growth, thou shouldst have new rewards in store;
Thou canst not every day give me thy heart,
If thou canst give it, then thou never gavest it:
Love's riddles are, that though thy heart depart,
It stays at home, and thou with losing savest it:
But we will have a way more liberal,
Than changing hearts, to join them, so we shall
  Be one, and one another's all.

THE DREAM

DEAR love, for nothing less than thee
Would I have broke this happy dream;
    It was a theme
For reason, much too strong for fantasy.
Therefore thou waked'st me wisely; yet
My dream thou brok'st not, but continued'st it.
Thou art so true that thoughts of thee suffice
To make dreams truths and fables histories;
Enter these arms, for since thou thought'st it best
Not to dream all my dream, let's act the rest.

As lightning, or a taper's light,
Thine eyes, and not thine noise, waked me;
    Yet I thought thee—
For thou lov'st truth—an angel, at first sight;
But when I saw thou saw'st my heart,
And knew'st my thoughts beyond an angel's art,
When thou knew'st what I dreamt, when thou knew'st when
Excess of joy would wake me, and cam'st then,
I must confess it could not choose but be
Profane to think thee anything but thee.

Coming and staying showed thee thee,
But rising makes me doubt that now
    Thou art not thou.
That love is weak where fear's as strong as he;
'T is not all spirit pure and brave
If mixture it of fear, shame, honor have.
Perchance as torches, which must ready be,
Men light and put out, so thou deal'st with me.
Thou cam'st to kindle, go'st to come: then I
Will dream that hope again, but else would die.

THE ECSTASY

WHERE, like a pillow on a bed,
  A pregnant bank swelled up, to rest
The violet's reclining head,
  Sat we two, one another's best.
Our hands were firmly cemented
  With a fast balm, which thence did spring,
Our eye-beams twisted, and did thread
  Our eyes, upon one double string;
So t' intergraft our hands, as yet
  Was all the means to make us one,
And pictures in our eyes to get
  Was all our propagation.
As 'twixt two equal armies, fate
  Suspends uncertain victory,
Our souls (which to advance their state,
  Were gone out) hung 'twixt her, and me.
And whil'st our souls negotiate there,
  We like sepulchral statues lay;
All day, the same our postures were,
  And we said nothing, all the day.
If any, so by love refined
  That he soul's language understood,
And by good love were grown all mind,
  Within convenient distance stood,
He (though he knew not which soul spake,
  Because both meant, both spake the same)
Might thence a new concoction take,
  And part far purer than he came.
This Ecstasy doth unperplex
  (We said) and tell us what we love;
We see by this, it was not sex,
  We see, we saw not what did move:[1]
But as all several souls contain
  Mixture of things, they know not what,
Love, these mixed souls, doth mix again,
  And makes both one, each this and that.
A single violet transplant,
  The strength, the color, and the size,
(All which before was poor, and scant)
  Redoubles still, and multiplies.

[1] We see now that we did not before know the true source of our love.

When love, with one another so
  Interinanimates two souls,
That abler soul, which thence doth flow,
  Defects of loneliness controls.
We then, who are this new soul, know
  Of what we are composed, and made,
For, th' atomies of which we grow,
  Are souls, whom no change can invade.
But O alas, so long, so far
  Our bodies why do we forbear?
They are ours, though they are not we; we are
  The intelligences, they the sphere.
We owe them thanks, because they thus,
  Did us, to us, at first convey,
Yielded their forces, sense, to us,
  Nor are dross to us, but allay.[1]
On man heaven's influence works not so,
  But that it first imprints the air,
So soul into the soul may flow,
  Though it to body first repair.
As our blood labors to beget
  Spirits, as like souls as it can,
Because such fingers need to knit
  That subtle knot, which makes us man:
So must pure lovers' souls descend
  T' affections, and to faculties,
Which sense may reach and apprehend,
  Else a great prince in prison lies.
T' our bodies turn we then, that so
  Weak men on love revealed may look;
Love's mysteries in souls do grow,
  But yet the body is his book.
And if some lover, such as we,
  Have heard this dialogue of one,
Let him still mark us, he shall see
  Small change, when we're to bodies gone.

[1]Alloy.

THE FUNERAL

Whoever comes to shroud me, do not harm
  Nor question much
That subtle wreath of hair about mine arm;
The mystery, the sign you must not touch,
  For 'tis my outward soul,
Viceroy to that which, unto heav'n being gone,
  Will leave this to control
And keep these limbs, her provinces, from dissolution.

For if the sinewy thread my brain lets fall
  Through every part
Can tie those parts, and make me one of all;
Those hairs which upward grew, and strength and art
  Have from a better brain,
Can better do't: except she meant that I
  By this should know my pain,
As prisoners then are manacled, when they're condemned to die.

Whate'er she meant by 't, bury it with me:
  For since I am
Love's martyr, it might breed idolatry
If into other hands these relics came;
  As 'twas humility
To afford to it all that a soul can do,
  So 'tis some bravery
That, since you would have none of me, I bury some of you.

HOLY SONNET

Death, be not proud, though some have callèd thee
Mighty and dreadful, for thou art not so;
For those whom thou think'st thou dost overthrow
Die not, poor Death; nor yet canst thou kill me.
From rest and sleep, which but thy picture be,
Much pleasure; then from thee much more must flow;
And soonest our best men with thee do go—
Rest of their bones and souls' delivery!
Thou'rt slave to fate, chance, kings, and desperate men,
And dost with poison, war, and sickness dwell;
And poppy or charms can make us sleep as well
And better than thy stroke. Why swell'st thou then?
One short sleep past, we wake eternally,
And Death shall be no more: Death, thou shalt die!

A HYMN TO GOD THE FATHER

Wilt thou forgive that sin where I begun,
  Which was my sin, though it were done before?
Wilt thou forgive that sin through which I run,
  And do run still, though still I do deplore?
When thou hast done, thou hast not done;
    For I have more.

Wilt thou forgive that sin which I have won
  Others to sin, and made my sins their door?
Wilt thou forgive that sin which I did shun
  A year or two, but wallowed in a score?
When thou hast done, thou hast not done;
    For I have more.

I have a sin of fear, that when I've spun
  My last thread, I shall perish on the shore;
But swear by thyself that at my death thy Son
  Shall shine as he shines now and heretofore;
And having done that, thou hast done;
    I fear no more.

ROBERT HERRICK
(1591-1674)

THE ARGUMENT OF HIS BOOK

I SING of brooks, of blossoms, birds and bowers,
Of April, May, of June and July-flowers;
I sing of May-poles, hock-carts, wassails, wakes,[1]
Of bridegrooms, brides, and of their bridal cakes;
I write of youth, of love, and have access
By these to sing of cleanly wantonness;
I sing of dews, of rains, and, piece by piece,
Of balm, of oil, of spice and ambergris;
I sing of times trans-shifting, and I write
How roses first came red and lilies white;
I write of groves, of twilights, and I sing
The court of Mab, and of the Fairy King;
I write of hell; I sing (and ever shall)
Of heaven, and hope to have it after all.

UPON THE LOSS OF HIS MISTRESSES

I HAVE lost, and lately, these
Many dainty mistresses:
Stately Julia, prime of all;
Sapho next, a principal;
Smooth Anthea, for a skin
White and heaven-like crystalline;
Sweet Electra, and the choice
Myrha, for the lute and voice.
Next, Corinna, for her wit,
And the graceful use of it;
With Perilla: all are gone,
Only Herrick's left alone,
For to number sorrow by
Their departures hence, and die.

CHERRY-RIPE

CHERRY-RIPE, ripe, ripe, I cry,
Full and fair ones; come and buy!
If so be you ask me where
They do grow, I answer, there,
Where my Julia's lips do smile;
There's the land, or cherry-isle,
Whose plantations fully show
All the year where cherries grow.

DELIGHT IN DISORDER

A SWEET disorder in the dress
Kindles in clothes a wantonness.
A lawn about the shoulders thrown
Into a fine distraction;
An erring lace, which here and there
Enthralls the crimson stomacher;[2]
A cuff neglectful, and thereby
Ribbons to flow confusedly;
A winning wave (deserving note)
In the tempestuous petticoat;
A careless shoe-string, in whose tie
I see a wild civility;—
Do more bewitch me than when art
Is too precise in every part.

CORINNA'S GOING A-MAYING

GET up, get up for shame, the blooming morn
Upon her wings presents the god unshorn.
See how Aurora throws her fair
Fresh-quilted colors through the air:
Get up, sweet slug-a-bed, and see
The dew bespangling herb and tree.
Each flower has wept and bowéd toward the east
Above an hour since: yet you not dressed;
Nay! not so much as out of bed?
When all the birds have matins said
And sung their thankful hymns, 'tis sin,
Nay, profanation, to keep in,
Whenas a thousand virgins on this day
Spring, sooner than the lark, to fetch in May.

Rise, and put on your foliage, and be seen
To come forth, like the spring-time, fresh and green,
And sweet as Flora.[3] Take no care
For jewels for your gown or hair:
Fear not; the leaves will strew
Gems in abundance upon you:
Besides, the childhood of the day has kept,
Against you come, some orient pearls unwept;
Come and receive them while the light
Hangs on the dew-locks of the night:
And Titan[4] on the eastern hill
Retires himself, or else stands still
Till you come forth. Wash, dress, be brief in praying:
Few beads[5] are best when once we go a-Maying.

Come, my Corinna, come; and, coming mark
How each field turns a street, each street a park

[1]A hock-cart is the last cart drawn from the field at harvest. Wassail is a drinking-bout. Wake is a merry-making or fair held on the anniversary of the dedication of a church.

[2]Front-piece of woman's dress.

[3]Goddess of flowers.

[4]The sun.

[5]Prayers.

Made green and trimmed with trees; see how
Devotion gives each house a bough
Or branch: each porch, each door ere this
An ark, a tabernacle is,
Made up of white-thorn, neatly interwove;
As if here were those cooler shades of love.
Can such delights be in the street
And open fields and we not see 't?
Come, we'll abroad; and let's obey
The proclamation made for May:
And sin no more, as we have done, by staying;
But, my Corinna, come, let's go a-Maying.

There's not a budding boy or girl this day
But is got up, and gone to bring in May.
A deal of youth, ere this, is come
Back, and with white-thorn laden home.
Some have dispatched their cakes and cream
Before that we have left to dream:
And some have wept, and wooed, and plighted troth,
And chose their priest, ere we can cast off sloth:
Many a green-gown[1] has been given;
Many a kiss, both odd and even:
Many a glance too has been sent
From out the eye, love's firmament;
Many a jest told of the keys betraying
This night, and locks picked, yet we're not a-Maying.

Come, let us go while we are in our prime;
And take the harmless folly of the time.
We shall grow old apace, and die
Before we know our liberty.
Our life is short, and our days run
As fast away as does the sun;
And, as a vapor or a drop of rain,
Once lost, can ne'er be found again,
So when or you or I are made
A fable, song, or fleeting shade,
All love, all liking, all delight
Lies drowned with us in endless night.
Then while time serves, and we are but decaying,
Come, my Corinna, come let's go a-Maying.

TO THE VIRGINS TO MAKE MUCH OF TIME

GATHER ye rosebuds while ye may,
Old Time is still a-flying;
And this same flower that smiles to-day,
To-morrow will be dying.

The glorious lamp of heaven, the sun,
The higher he's a-getting,
The sooner will his race be run,
And nearer he's to setting.

That age is best which is the first,
When youth and blood are warmer;
But being spent, the worse and worst
Times still succeed the former.

Then be not coy, but use your time,
And while ye may, go marry;
For, having lost but once your prime,
You may forever tarry.

[1]Many a tumble on the grass.

TO MUSIC, TO BECALM HIS FEVER

CHARM me asleep, and melt me so
With thy delicious numbers,
That being ravished, hence I go
Away in easy slumbers.
Ease my sick head,
And make my bed,
Thou power that canst sever
From me this ill;
And quickly still,
Though thou not kill
My fever.

Thou sweetly canst convert the same
From a consuming fire,
Into a gentle-licking flame,
And make it thus expire.
Then make me weep
My pains asleep,
And give me such reposes,
That I, poor I,
May think, thereby,
I live and die
'Mongst roses.

Fall on me like a silent dew,
Or like those maiden showers,
Which, by the peep of day, do strew
A baptism o'er the flowers.
Melt, melt my pains
With thy soft strains;
That having ease me given,
With full delight,
I leave this light,
And take my flight
For heaven.

TO ANTHEA, WHO MAY COMMAND HIM ANYTHING

BID me to live, and I will live
Thy protestant to be:
Or bid me love, and I will give
A loving heart to thee.

A heart as soft, a heart as kind,
A heart as sound and free
As in the whole world thou canst find,
That heart I'll give to thee.

Bid that heart stay, and it will stay,
To honor thy decree:
Or bid it languish quite away,
And 't shall do so for thee.

Bid me to weep, and I will weep,
While I have eyes to see:
And having none, yet I will keep
A heart to weep for thee.

Bid me despair, and I'll despair,
Under that cypress tree:
Or bid me die, and I will dare
E'en death, to die for thee.

Thou art my life, my love, my heart,
The very eyes of me,
And hast command of every part,
To live and die for thee.

UPON A CHILD THAT DIED

Here she lies, a pretty bud,
Lately made of flesh and blood:
Who as soon fell fast asleep,
As her little eyes did peep.
Give her strewings, but not stir
The earth that lightly covers her.

TO DAFFODILS

Fair Daffodils, we weep to see
You haste away so soon;
As yet the early rising sun
Has not attained his noon.
Stay, stay,
Until the hasting day
Has run
But to the even-song;
And, having prayed together, we
Will go with you along.

We have short time to stay, as you,
We have as short a spring;
As quick a growth to meet decay,
As you, or anything.
We die
As your hours do, and dry
Away,
Like to the summer's rain;
Or as the pearls of morning's dew,
Ne'er to be found again.

TO DAISIES, NOT TO SHUT SO SOON

Shut not so soon; the dull-eyed night
Has not as yet begun
To make a seizure on the light,
Or to seal up the sun.

No marigolds yet closéd are,
No shadows great appear;
Nor doth the early shepherd's star
Shine like a spangle here.

Stay but till my Julia close
Her life-begetting eye;
And let the whole world then dispose
Itself to live or die.

TO ENJOY THE TIME

While fates permit us, let's be merry:
Pass all we must the fatal ferry;
And this our life too whirls away
With the rotation of the day.

HIS WINDING-SHEET

Come thou, who art the wine and wit
Of all I've writ;
The grace, the glory, and the best
Piece of the rest.
Thou art, of what I did intend,
The all and end;
And what was made, was made to meet
Thee, thee, my sheet.
Come then, and be to my chaste side
Both bed and bride.
We, two, as relics left will have
One rest, one grave;
And, hugging close, we will not fear
Lust ent'ring here,
Where all desires are dead, or cold
As is the mold,
And all affections are forgot,
Or trouble not.
Here, here the slaves and pris'ners be
From shackles free,
And weeping widows, long oppressed,
Do here find rest.
The wrongéd client ends his laws
Here, and his cause;
Here those long suits of chancery lie
Quiet, or die,
And all star-chamber bills do cease,
Or hold their peace.
Here needs no court for our request,
Where all are best;
All wise, all equal, and all just,
Alike i' th' dust;
Nor need we here to fear the frown
Of court, or crown;

Where fortune bears no sway o'er things,
  There all are kings.
In this securer place we'll keep,
  As lulled asleep;
Or for a little time we'll lie,
  As robes laid by,
To be another day re-worn,—
  Turned, but not torn:
Or like old testaments engrossed,
  Locked up, not lost:
And for a while lie here concealed,
  To be revealed
Next at that great Platonic year,[1]
  And then meet here.

ART ABOVE NATURE. TO JULIA

When I behold a forest spread
With silken trees upon thy head,
And when I see that other dress
Of flowers set in comeliness;
When I behold another grace
In the ascent of curious lace,
Which like a pinnacle doth show
The top, and the top-gallant too;
Then, when I see thy tresses bound
Into an oval, square, or round,
And knit in knots far more than I
Can tell by tongue, or true-love tie;
Next, when those lawny films I see
Play with a wild civility,
And all those airy silks to flow,
Alluring me, and tempting so:
I must confess, mine eye and heart
Dotes less on nature than on art.

THE PRIMROSE

  Ask me why I send you here
This sweet infanta of the year?
  Ask me why I send to you
This primrose, thus bepearled with dew?
  I will whisper to your ears,
The sweets of love are mixed with tears.

  Ask me why this flower does show
So yellow-green, and sickly too?
  Ask me why the stalk is weak
And bending, yet it doth not break?
  I will answer, these discover
What fainting hopes are in a lover.

THE NIGHT-PIECE, TO JULIA

Her eyes the glow-worm lend thee,
The shooting stars attend thee;
  And the elves also,
  Whose little eyes glow
Like the sparks of fire, befriend thee.

No Will-o'-th'-Wisp mis-light thee,
Nor snake nor slow-worm bite thee;
  But on, on thy way,
  Not making a stay,
Since ghost there's none to affright thee.

Let not the dark thee cumber;
What though the moon does slumber?
  The stars of the night
  Will lend thee their light,
Like tapers clear without number.

Then, Julia, let me woo thee,
Thus, thus, to come unto me·
  And when I shall meet
  Thy silvery feet
My soul I'll pour into thee.

TO ELECTRA

I dare not ask a kiss;
  I dare not beg a smile;
Lest having that or this,
  I might grow proud the while.

No, no, the utmost share
  Of my desire shall be,
Only to kiss that air.
  That lately kisséd thee.

AN ODE FOR BEN JONSON

Ah, Ben!
Say how or when
Shall we, thy guests,
Meet at those lyric feasts,
Made at the Sun,
The Dog, the Triple Tun;[2]
Where we such clusters had,
As made us nobly wild, not mad?
And yet each verse of thine
Out-did the meat, out-did the frolic wine.

My Ben!
Or come again,
Or send to us
Thy wit's great overplus;
But teach us yet
Wisely to husband it,
Lest we that talent spend;
And having once brought to an end
That precious stock, the store
Of such a wit the world should have no more.

COMFORT TO A YOUTH THAT HAD LOST HIS LOVE

What needs complaints,
  When she a place
Has with the race
  Of saints?

[1]The year in which everything will return to its original state.

[2]Names of London taverns.

In endless mirth,
She thinks not on
What's said or done
In earth.
She sees no tears,
Or any tone
Of thy deep groan
She hears:
Nor does she mind,
Or think on't now,
That ever thou
Wast kind.
But changed above,
She likes not there,
As she did here,
Thy love.
Forbear therefore,
And lull asleep
Thy woes, and weep
No more.

HIS LITANY, TO THE HOLY SPIRIT

IN THE hour of my distress,
When temptations me oppress,
And when I my sins confess,
Sweet Spirit, comfort me!

When I lie within my bed,
Sick in heart, and sick in head,
And with doubts discomforted,
Sweet Spirit, comfort me!

When the house doth sigh and weep,
And the world is drowned in sleep,
Yet mine eyes the watch do keep,
Sweet Spirit, comfort me!

When the artless doctor sees
No one hope, but of his fees,
And his skill runs on the lees,
Sweet Spirit, comfort me!

When his potion and his pill,
Has or none or little skill,
Meet for nothing but to kill,
Sweet Spirit, comfort me!

When the passing-bell doth toll,
And the furies in a shoal
Come to fright a parting soul,
Sweet Spirit, comfort me!

When the tapers now burn blue,
And the comforters are few,
And that number more than true,
Sweet Spirit, comfort me!

When the priest his last hath prayed,
And I nod to what is said,
'Cause my speech is now decayed,
Sweet Spirit, comfort me!

When, God knows, I'm tossed about,
Either with despair or doubt,
Yet before the glass be out,
Sweet Spirit, comfort me!

When the Tempter me pursu'th
With the sins of all my youth,
And half damns me with untruth,
Sweet Spirit, comfort me!

When the flames and hellish cries
Fright mine ears and fright mine eyes,
And all terrors me surprise,
Sweet Spirit, comfort me!

When the judgment is revealed,
And that opened which was sealed,
When to thee I have appealed,
Sweet Spirit, comfort me!

A GRACE FOR A CHILD

HERE, a little child, I stand,
Heaving up my either hand:
Cold as paddocks though they be,
Here I lift them up to thee,
For a benison to fall
On our meat, and on us all. Amen.

GEORGE HERBERT

(1593–1633)

THE COLLAR

I STRUCK the board, and cried, "No more; I will abroad!
What! shall I ever sigh and pine?
My lines and life are free; free as the road,
Loose as the wind, as large as store.[1]
Shall I be still in suit?
Have I no harvest but a thorn
To let me blood, and not restore
What I have lost with cordial fruit?
Sure there was wine
Before my sighs did dry it; there was corn
Before my tears did drown it;
Is the year only lost to me?
Have I no bays to crown it,
No flowers, no garlands gay? all blasted,

[1] An abundance.

All wasted?
Not so, my heart, but there is fruit,
And thou hast hands.
Recover all thy sigh-blown age
On double pleasures; leave thy cold dispute
Of what is fit and not; forsake thy cage,
Thy rope of sands
Which petty thoughts have made, and made to thee
Good cable, to enforce and draw,
And be thy law,
While thou didst wink and wouldst not see.
Away! take heed;
I will abroad.
Call in thy death's head there, tie up thy fears;
He that forbears
To suit and serve his need
Deserves his load."
But as I raved, and grew more fierce and wild
At every word,
Methought I heard one calling, "Child";
And I replied, "My Lord."

DISCIPLINE

THROW away thy rod,
Throw away thy wrath:
O my God,
Take the gentle path.

For my heart's desire
Unto thine is bent:
I aspire
To a full consent.[1]

Not a word or look
I affect to own,
But by book,
And thy book alone.

Though I fail, I weep:
Though I halt in pace,
Yet I creep
To the throne of grace.

Then let wrath remove;
Love will do the deed:
For with love
Stony hearts will bleed.

Love is swift of foot;
Love's a man of war,
And can shoot,
And can hit from far.

Who can scape his bow?
That which wrought on thee,
Brought thee low,
Needs must work on me.

Throw away thy rod;
Though man frailties hath,
Thou art God:
Throw away thy wrath.

THE PULLEY

WHEN God at first made man,
Having a glass of blessing standing by;
"Let us," said he, "pour on him all we can:
Let the world's riches, which disperséd lie,
Contract into a span."

So Strength first made a way;
Then Beauty flowed; then Wisdom, Honor, Pleasure.
When almost all was out, God made a stay,
Perceiving that alone, of all his treasure,
Rest in the bottom lay.

"For if I should," said he,
"Bestow this jewel also on my creature,
He would adore my gifts instead of me,
And rest in Nature, not the God of Nature;
So both should losers be.

"Yet let him keep the rest,
But keep them with repining restlessness;
Let him be rich and weary, that at least,
If goodness lead him not, yet weariness
May toss him to my breast."

LOVE

LOVE bade me welcome; yet my soul drew back,
Guilty of dust and sin.
But quick-eyed Love, observing me grow slack
From my first entrance in,
Drew nearer to me, sweetly questioning,
If I lacked anything.

"A guest," I answered, "worthy to be here:"
Love said, "You shall be he."
"I, the unkind, ungrateful? Ah, my dear,
I cannot look on thee!"
Love took my hand and smiling did reply,
"Who made the eyes but I?"

"Truth, Lord; but I have marred them: let my shame
Go where it doth deserve."
"And know you not," says Love, "who bore the blame?"
"My dear, then I will serve."
"You must sit down," says Love, "and taste my meat."
So I did sit and eat.

[1]Harmony.

EDMUND WALLER
(1606–1687)

GO, LOVELY ROSE!

Go, lovely Rose!
Tell her that wastes her time and me,
That now she knows,
When I resemble her to thee,
How sweet and fair she seems to be.

Tell her that's young,
And shuns to have her graces spied,
That hadst thou sprung
In deserts, where no men abide,
Thou must have uncommended died.

Small is the worth
Of beauty from the light retired;
Bid her come forth,
Suffer herself to be desired,
And not blush so to be admired.

Then die! that she
The common fate of all things rare
May read in thee;
How small a part of time they share
That are so wondrous sweet and fair!

SIR JOHN SUCKLING
(1609–1642)

A DOUBT OF MARTYRDOM

O for some honest lover's ghost,
Some kind unbodied post
Sent from the shades below!
I strangely long to know
Whether[1] the noble chaplets wear,
Those that their mistress' scorn did bear
Or those that were used kindly.

For whatso'er they tell us here
To make those sufferings dear,
'Twill there, I fear, be found
That to the being crowned
T' have loved alone will not suffice,
Unless we also have been wise
And have our loves enjoyed.

What posture can we think him in
That, here unloved, again
Departs, and 's thither gone
Where each sits by his own?
Or how can that Elysium be
Where I my mistress still must see
Circled in other's arms?

For there the judges all are just,
And Sophonisba[2] must
Be his whom she held dear,
Not his who loved her here.
The sweet Philoclea,[3] since she died,
Lies by her Pirocles his side,
Not by Amphialus.

Some bays, perchance, or myrtle bough
For difference crowns the brow
Of those kind souls that were
The noble martyrs here:
And if that be the only odds
(As who can tell?) ye kinder gods,
Give me the woman here!

[1]Which.

[2]A Carthaginian. She was betrothed to a Numidian prince but married another; later, however, she married the Numidian when he conquered her husband.

[3]Philoclea and the two following are characters in Sir Philip Sidney's *Arcadia*.

THE CONSTANT LOVER

Out upon it, I have loved
Three whole days together!
And am like to love three more,
If it prove fair weather.

Time shall molt away his wings
Ere he shall discover
In the whole wide world again
Such a constant lover.

But the spite on't is, no praise
Is due at all to me:
Love with me had made no stays,
Had it any been but she.

Had it any been but she,
And that very face,
There had been at least ere this
A dozen dozen in her place.

WHY SO PALE AND WAN?

Why so pale and wan, fond lover?
Prithee, why so pale?
Will, when looking well can't move her,
Looking ill prevail?
Prithee, why so pale?

Why so dull and mute, young sinner?
  Prithee, why so mute?
Will, when speaking well can't win her,
  Saying nothing do 't?
  Prithee, why so mute?

Quit, quit for shame! This will not move;
  This cannot take her.
If of herself she will not love,
  Nothing can make her:
  The devil take her!

RICHARD LOVELACE

(1618–1658)

TO ALTHEA, FROM PRISON

When Love with unconfinéd wings
  Hovers within my gates,
And my divine Althea brings
  To whisper at the grates;
When I lie tangled in her hair
  And fettered to her eye,
The birds that wanton in the air
  Know no such liberty.

When flowing cups run swiftly round
  With no allaying Thames,
Our careless heads with roses bound,
  Our hearts with loyal flames;
When thirsty grief in wine we steep,
  When healths and draughts go free,
Fishes that tipple in the deep
  Know no such liberty.

When, like committed linnets, I
  With shriller throat will sing
The sweetness, mercy, majesty,
  And glories of my king;
When I shall voice aloud how good
  He is, how great should be,
Enlargéd winds, that curl the flood,
  Know no such liberty.

Stone walls do not a prison make,
  Nor iron bars a cage;
Minds innocent and quiet take
  That for an hermitage;
If I have freedom in my love
  And in my soul am free,
Angels alone, that soar above,
  Enjoy such liberty.

ANDREW MARVELL

(1621–1678)

AN HORATIAN ODE UPON CROMWELL'S RETURN FROM IRELAND

The forward youth that would appear
Must now forsake his muses dear,
  Nor in the shadows sing
  His numbers languishing:

'Tis time to leave the books in dust,
And oil the unused armor's rust,
  Removing from the wall
  The corselet of the hall.

So restless Cromwell would not cease
In the inglorious arts of peace,
  But through adventurous war
  Urgéd his active star;

And, like the three-forked lightning, first
Breaking the clouds where it was nursed,
  Did thorough his own side
  His fiery way divide;[1]

For 'tis all one to courage high,
The emulous, or enemy,
  And with such to inclose,
  Is more than to oppose.

Then burning through the air he went,
And palaces and temples rent;
  And Cæsar's[2] head at last
  Did through his laurels[3] blast.

'Tis madness to resist or blame
The face of angry heaven's flame;
  And if we would speak true,
  Much to the man is due,

Who from his private gardens, where
He lived reservéd and austere,
  As if his highest plot
  To plant the bergamot,[4]

Could by industrious valor climb
To ruin the great work of Time,
  And cast the kingdoms old,
  Into another mold,

[1] The allusion is to differences which arose between the puritan army and the puritan parliament—differences which Cromwell forcibly resolved by bringing the army to London.

[2] Charles I's. [3] Spite of his crown.

[4] A variety of pear.

Though Justice against Fate complain,
And plead the ancient rights in vain;
But those do hold or break,
As men are strong or weak.

Nature, that hateth emptiness,
Allows of penetration less,
And therefore must make room
Where greater spirits come.

What field of all the civil war,
Where his were not the deepest scar?
And Hampton[1] shows what part
He had of wiser art;

Where, twining subtle fears with hope,
He wove a net of such a scope
That Charles himself might chase
To Caresbrooke's narrow case,

That thence the royal actor borne
The tragic scaffold might adorn,
While round the armèd bands
Did clap their bloody hands.

He[2] nothing common did, or mean,
Upon that memorable scene,
But with his keener eye
The ax's edge did try;

Nor called the gods with vulgar spite
To vindicate his helpless right,
But bowed his comely head
Down, as upon a bed.

This was that memorable hour,
Which first assured the forcèd power;
So, when they did design
The capitol's first line,

A bleeding head, where they begun,
Did fright the architects to run;[3]
And yet in that the state
Foresaw its happy fate.

And now the Irish are ashamed
To see themselves in one year tamed;
So much one man can do,
That does both act and know.

They can affirm his praises best,
And have, though overcome, confessed
How good he is, how just,
And fit for highest trust;

Nor yet grown stiffer with command,
But still in the republic's hand,
How fit he is to sway,
That can so well obey!

He to the Common's feet presents
A kingdom[4] for his first year's rents;
And, what he may, forbears
His fame, to make it theirs;

And has his sword and spoils ungirt,
To lay them at the public's skirt:
So when the falcon high
Falls heavy from the sky,

She, having killed, no more doth search,
But on the next green bough to perch;
Where, when he first does lure,
The falconer has her sure.

What may not then our isle presume,
While victory his crest does plume?
What may not others fear,
If thus he crowns each year?

As Cæsar, he, ere long, to Gaul,
To Italy a Hannibal,
And to all states not free
Shall climacteric be.[5]

The Pict[6] no shelter now shall find
Within his parti-colored[7] mind,
But, from this valor sad,[8]
Shrink underneath the plaid;

Happy if in the tufted brake
The English hunter him mistake,
Nor lay his hounds in near
The Caledonian deer.

But thou, the war's and Fortune's son,
March undefatigably on;
And for the least effect,
Still keep the sword erect;

Besides the force it has to fright
The spirits of the shady night,
The same arts that did gain
A power, must it maintain.

TO HIS COY MISTRESS

HAD we but world enough, and time,
This coyness, Lady, were no crime,
We would sit down and think which way
To walk and pass our long love's day.

---

[1]Hampton Court. Marvell shared the belief of other contemporaries (as the following lines show) that Cromwell tacitly abetted Charles I's flight from Hampton Court to Carisbrooke Castle.

[2]Charles I.

[3]Pliny tells this story (*Natural History*, XXVIII, 4).

[4]Ireland. [5]Shall be a dangerous menace.

[6]The Scot. [7]*I. e.*, fickle. [8]Resolute.

Thou by the Indian Ganges' side
Shouldst rubies find; I by the tide
Of Humber would complain. I would
Love you ten years before the Flood,
And you should, if you please, refuse
Till the conversion of the Jews.
My vegetable love should grow
Vaster than empires, and more slow;
An hundred years should go to praise
Thine eyes and on thy forehead gaze;
Two hundred to adore each breast,
But thirty thousand to the rest;
An age at least to every part,
And the last age should show your heart.
For, Lady, you deserve this state,
Nor would I love at lower rate.
  But at my back I always hear
Time's wingéd chariot hurrying near;
And yonder all before us lie
Deserts of vast eternity.
Thy beauty shall no more be found,
Nor, in thy marble vault, shall sound
My echoing song; then worms shall try
That long preserved virginity,
And your quaint honor turn to dust,
And into ashes all my lust:
The grave's a fine and private place,
But none, I think, do there embrace.
  Now therefore, while the youthful hue
Sits on thy skin like morning dew,
And while thy willing soul transpires
At every pore with instant fires,
Now let us sport us while we may,
And now, like amorous birds of prey,
Rather at once our time devour
Than languish in his slow-chapt[1] power.
Let us roll all our strength and all
Our sweetness up into one ball,
And tear our pleasures with rough strife
Thorough the iron gates of life:
Thus, though we cannot make our sun
Stand still, yet we will make him run.

BERMUDAS

WHERE the remote Bermudas ride,
In the ocean's bosom unespied,
From a small boat, that rowed along,
The listening winds received this song:[2]
"What should we do but sing his praise,
That led us through the watery maze,
Unto an isle so long unknown,
And yet far kinder than our own?
Where he the huge sea-monsters wracks,
That lift the deep upon their backs,
He lands us on a grassy stage,
Safe from the storms' and prelates' rage.
He gave us this eternal spring,
Which here enamels everything,
And sends the fowls to us in care,
On daily visits through the air;
He hangs in shades the orange bright,
Like golden lamps in a green night,
And does in the pomegranates close
Jewels more rich than Ormus[3] shows;
He makes the figs our mouths to meet,
And throws the melons at our feet,
But apples[4] plants of such a price,
No tree could ever bear them twice;
With cedars chosen by his hand
From Lebanon, he stores the land,
And makes the hollow seas, that roar,
Proclaim the ambergris on shore;
He cast (of which we rather boast)
The Gospel's pearl upon our coast,
And in these rocks for us did frame
A temple, where to sound his name.
Oh! let our voice his praise exalt,
Till it arrive at heaven's vault,
Which, thence (perhaps) rebounding, may
Echo beyond the Mexique Bay."
Thus sung they, in the English boat,
A holy and a cheerful note,
And all the way, to guide their chime,
With falling oars they kept the time.

HENRY VAUGHAN

(1622–1695)

THE WORLD[5]

I SAW Eternity the other night,
Like a great ring of pure and endless light,
    All calm, as it was bright;
And round beneath it, Time, in hours, days,
  years,
    Driv'n by the spheres
Like a vast shadow moved; in which the world
    And all her train were hurled.
The doting lover in his quaintest strain
    Did there complain;
Near him, his lute, his fancy, and his flights,
    Wit's four delights,
With gloves, and knots, the silly snares of
  pleasure,
    Yet his dear treasure,

[1]Perhaps, slowly consuming.

[2]The Bermudas were settled early in the seventeenth century by Englishmen who, like those who came to New England, sought to escape tyranny at home.

[3]An island in the Persian Gulf.

[4]Pineapples.

[5]Vaughan printed 1 John, ii, 16–17, at the end of this poem.

All scattered lay, while he his eyes did pour
Upon a flower.

The darksome statesman, hung with weights and woe,
Like a thick midnight-fog, moved there so slow,
He did not stay, nor go;
Condemning thoughts, like sad eclipses, scowl
Upon his soul,
And clouds of crying witnesses without
Pursued him with one shout.
Yet digged the mole, and lest his ways be found,
Worked under ground,
Where he did clutch his prey; but one did see
That policy:
Churches and altars fed him; perjuries
Were gnats and flies;
It rained about him blood and tears, but he
Drank them as free.[1]

The fearful miser on a heap of rust
Sat pining all his life there, did scarce trust
His own hands with the dust,
Yet would not place one piece above,[2] but lives
In fear of thieves.
Thousands there were as frantic as himself,
And hugged each one his pelf;
The downright epicure placed heaven in sense,
And scorned pretense;
While others, slipt into a wide excess,
Said little less;
The weaker sort, slight, trivial wares enslave,
Who think them brave;
And poor, despiséd Truth sat counting by
Their victory.

Yet some, who all this while did weep and sing,
And sing and weep, soared up into the ring;
But most would use no wing.
O fools, said I, thus to prefer dark night
Before true light!
To live in grots and caves, and hate the day
Because it shows the way,
The way, which from this dead and dark abode
Leads up to God;
A way where you might tread the sun, and be
More bright than he!
But, as I did their madness so discuss,
One whispered thus,
"This ring the Bridegroom did for none provide
But for his bride."

THE RETREAT

Happy those early days, when I
Shined in my angel-infancy!
Before I understood this place
Appointed for my second race,
Or taught my soul to fancy aught
But a white, celestial thought;
When yet I had not walked above
A mile or two from my first love,
And looking back at that short space,
Could see a glimpse of his bright face;
When on some gilded cloud or flower
My gazing soul would dwell an hour,
And in those weaker glories spy
Some shadows of eternity;
Before I taught my tongue to wound
My conscience with a sinful sound,
Or had the black art to dispense,
A several sin to every sense,
But felt through all this fleshly dress
Bright shoots of everlastingness.
O, how I long to travel back,
And tread again that ancient track,
That I might once more reach that plain,
Where first I felt my glorious train;
From whence the enlightened spirit sees
That shady city of palm trees.[3]
But ah! my soul with too much stay
Is drunk, and staggers in the way!
Some men a forward motion love,
But I by backward steps would move;
And when this dust falls to the urn,
In that state I came, return.

MAN

Weighing the steadfastness and state
Of some mean things which here below reside,
Where birds like watchful clocks the noiseless date
And intercourse of times divide,
Where bees at night get home and hive, and flowers
Early, as well as late,
Rise with the sun, and set in the same bowers;

I would (said I) my God would give
The staidness of these things to man! for these
To his divine appointments ever cleave,
And no new business breaks their peace;
The birds nor sow, nor reap, yet sup and dine,
The flowers without clothes live,
Yet Solomon was never dressed so fine.

Man hath still either toys, or care,
He hath no root, nor to one place is tied,
But ever restless and irregular
About this earth doth run and ride,
He knows he hath a home, but scarce knows where,
He says it is so far
That he hath quite forgot how to go there.

[1] As freely as if it had not rained blood and tears.
[2] In heaven.
[3] *I. e.*, Jericho.

He knocks at all doors, strays and roams,
Nay hath not so much wit as some stones[1] have
Which in the darkest nights point to their homes,
By some hid sense their Maker gave;
Man is the shuttle, to whose winding quest
And passage through these looms
God ordered motion, but ordained no rest.

ASCENSION HYMN

They are all gone into the world of light!
And I alone sit ling'ring here;
Their very memory is fair and bright,
And my sad thoughts doth clear.

It glows and glitters in my cloudy breast
Like stars upon some gloomy grove,
Or those faint beams in which this hill is drest,
After the sun's remove.

I see them walking in an air of glory,
Whose light doth trample on my days:
My days, which are at best but dull and hoary,
Mere glimmering and decays.

O holy hope! and high humility,
High as the heavens above!
These are your walks, and you have showed them me
To kindle my cold love.

Dear, beauteous death! the jewel of the just,
Shining nowhere, but in the dark;
What mysteries do lie beyond thy dust;
Could man outlook that mark!

He that hath found some fledged bird's nest may know
At first sight, if the bird be flown;
But what fair well[2] or grove he sings in now,
That is to him unknown.

And yet, as angels in some brighter dreams
Call to the soul, when man doth sleep:
So some strange thoughts transcend our wonted themes,
And into glory peep.

If a star were confined into a tomb
Her captive flames must needs burn there;
But when the hand that locked her up gives room,
She'll shine through all the sphere.

O Father of eternal life, and all
Created glories under thee!
Resume thy spirit from this world of thrall
Into true liberty.

Either disperse these mists, which blot and fill
My perspective (still) as they pass,
Or else remove me hence unto that hill,
Where I shall need no glass.

[1] Loadstones. [2] Spring or fountain.

THE WATERFALL

With what deep murmurs through time's silent stealth
Doth thy transparent, cool and wat'ry wealth
Here flowing fall,
And chide, and call,
As if his liquid, loose retinue stayed
Ling'ring, and were of this steep place afraid;
The common pass
Where, clear as glass,
All must descend
Not to an end,
But, quickened by this deep and rocky grave,
Rise to a longer course more bright and brave.

Dear stream! dear bank, where often I
Have sat, and pleased my pensive eye:
Why, since each drop of thy quick store
Runs thither, whence it flowed before,
Should poor souls fear a shade or night,
Who came (sure) from a sea of light?
Or since those drops are all sent back
So sure to thee, that none doth lack,
Why should frail flesh doubt any more
That what God takes, he'll not restore?

O useful element and clear!
My sacred wash and cleanser here.
My first consigner unto those
Fountains of life, where the Lamb goes![3]
What sublime truths, and wholesome themes,
Lodge in thy mystical, deep streams!—
Such as dull man can never find
Unless that Spirit lead his mind,
Which first upon thy face did move,
And hatched all with his quick'ning love.
As this loud brook's incessant fall
In streaming rings restagnates all,
Which reach by course the bank, and then
Are no more seen, just so pass men.
O my invisible estate,
My glorious liberty, still late!
Thou art the channel my soul seeks,
Not this with cataracts and creeks.

[3] *I. e.*, in baptism.

SIR THOMAS BROWNE (1605–1682)

Sir Thomas Browne was born on 19 October, 1605. His father was a London mercer. Browne was sent to Winchester School in 1616, and in 1623 he went thence to Broadgates Hall (now Pembroke College), Oxford. He took his B. A. in 1626, his M. A. in 1629, and little else is known about his Oxford years. In 1630 he began a period of travel and study on the Continent, going first to Montpellier, in the south of France, then famous for its medical school. He continued his medical studies at Padua, and then at Leyden, where it is thought he obtained a medical degree. In 1633 he returned to England and settled himself near Halifax. He was made doctor of medicine at Oxford in 1637. Soon after this he began to practice medicine at Norwich, where he remained until his death. He married, in 1641, Dorothy Mileham, "a lady of such symmetrical proportion to her worthy husband, both in the graces of her body and mind, that they seemed to come together by a kind of natural magnetism." About 1635 Browne had written, "at leisurable hours," for his "private exercise and satisfaction," his famous confession of faith, the *Religio Medici*. He apparently had no intention of publishing this, but allowed friends to read it in manuscript and to make copies of it; and thus, being admired, it came to be widely known (there are at least five manuscripts of the book extant, or were in the early nineteenth century). The result was that in 1642 an unauthorized edition was printed from one of these copies and so quickly sold out that a second edition was printed within a few months. This troubled Browne because the book was about so serious a subject as religion, and was now being much more widely read, and not only read but criticized, in a form very different from what he had actually written. The copy which reached the press was, Browne wrote, "most depraved," as the result of successive transcriptions, and so in 1643 he published as a kind of duty the first authorized edition of the book. The general scandal of his profession, Browne said, might help to persuade the world that he had no religion at all, but it was not so. On the contrary he was disposed rather to wish, if for anything, for more curious tests of his faith than Christianity afforded. "Methinks," he says, "there be not impossibilities enough in religion for an active faith; the deepest mysteries ours contains have not only been illustrated, but maintained, by syllogism and the rule of reason. I love to lose myself in a mystery, to pursue my reason to an *O altitudo!* 'Tis my solitary recreation to pose my apprehension with those involved enigmas and riddles of the Trinity, with Incarnation, and Resurrection." In this Browne told the simple truth; a touch of mystery fired his mind and sent it soaring on its speculative way. Whatever was odd or strange was food for him, and he became one of the most curiously learned men of any age. At the same time his wide reading helped him to clothe his grave meditations in a style which for richness and dignity is not surpassed even by any other of the great prose-writers of his own century.

Browne was a royalist, but lived through the Civil War without, apparently, being much disturbed by outward events. In 1646 he published an eminently characteristic book, his *Pseudodoxia Epidemica or Enquiries into very many received Tenets and commonly presumed Truths, which examined prove but Vulgar and Common Errors*. Some years later certain urns were unearthed in Norfolk, which were exactly the sort of thing to set his mind in motion, and the result was that he wrote and, in 1658, published *Hydriotaphia*, in which the qualities of his mind and of his personality are finely exhibited. Two other works, *A Letter to a Friend* and *Christian Morals*, were not published until after his death. In 1671 Browne was knighted, in consequence of the singular modesty of the then mayor of Norwich. Charles II was visiting Norwich and proposed to confer knighthood on the mayor, who declined it and begged that it be conferred instead on Browne, as the citizen of Norwich who most deserved the honor.

HYDRIOTAPHIA,

URN-BURIAL

CHAPTER I

In the deep discovery of the subterranean world, a shallow part would satisfy some inquirers; who, if two or three yards were open about the surface, would not care to rake the bowels of Potosi,[1] and regions towards the center. Nature hath furnished one part of the earth, and man another. The treasures of time lie high, in urns, coins, and monuments, scarce below the roots of some vegetables. Time hath endless rarities, and shows of all

[1] Silver mines in Bolivia.

varieties; which reveals old things in heaven, makes new discoveries in earth, and even earth itself a discovery. That great antiquity America lay buried for thousands of years, and a large part of the earth is still in the urn[1] unto us.

Though, if Adam were made out of an extract of the earth, all parts might challenge a restitution, yet few have returned their bones far lower than they might receive them; not affecting the graves of giants, under hilly and heavy coverings, but content with less than their own depth, have wished their bones might lie soft, and the earth be light upon them. Even such as hope to rise again, would not be content with central interment, or so desperately to place their relics as to lie beyond discovery, and in no way to be seen again; which happy contrivance hath made communication with our forefathers, and left unto our view some parts, which they never beheld themselves.

Though earth hath engrossed[2] the name, yet water hath proved the smartest grave; which in forty days swallowed almost mankind, and the living creation; fishes not wholly escaping, except the salt ocean were handsomely[3] contempered by a mixture of the fresh element.

Many have taken voluminous pains to determine the state of the soul upon disunion; but men have been most fantastical in the singular contrivances of their corporal dissolution: whilst the soberest nations have rested in two ways, of simple inhumation[4] and burning.

That carnal interment or burying was of the elder date, the old examples of Abraham and the patriarchs are sufficient to illustrate; and were without competition, if it could be made out that Adam was buried near Damascus, or Mount Calvary, according to some tradition. God himself, that buried but one, was pleased to make choice of this way, collectible from Scripture expression, and the hot contest[5] between Satan and the arch-angel, about discovering the body of Moses. But the practice of burning was also of great antiquity, and of no slender extent. For (not to derive the same from Hercules) noble descriptions there are hereof in the Grecian funerals of Homer, in the formal obsequies of Patroclus and Achilles; and somewhat elder in the Theban war, and solemn combustion of Meneceus, and Archemorus, contemporary unto Jair the eighth judge of Israel. Confirmable also among the Trojans, from the funeral pyre of Hector, burned before the gates of Troy: and the burning of Penthesilea the Amazonian queen: and long continuance of that practice, in the inward countries of Asia; while as low as the reign of Julian, we find that the king of Chionia[6] burned the body of his son, and interred the ashes in a silver urn.

The same practice extended also far west; and, besides Herulians, Getes, and Thracians, was in use with most of the Celtæ, Sarmatians, Germans, Gauls, Danes, Swedes, Norwegians; not to omit some use thereof among Carthaginians and Americans. Of greater antiquity among the Romans than most opinion, or Pliny seems to allow: for (beside the old Table Laws of burning or burying within the city, of making the funeral fire with planed wood, or quenching the fire with wine), Manlius the consul burned the body of his son: Numa, by special clause of his will, was not burned but buried; and Remus was solemnly burned, according to the description of Ovid.

Cornelius Sylla was not the first whose body was burned in Rome, but of the Cornelian family; which, being indifferently, not frequently used before, from that time spread, and became the prevalent practice. Not totally pursued in the highest run of cremation; for when even crows were funerally burned, Poppæa the wife of Nero found a peculiar grave interment. Now as all customs were founded upon some bottom of reason, so there wanted not grounds for this; according to several apprehensions of the most rational dissolution. Some being of the opinion of Thales, that water was the original of all things, thought it most equal to submit unto the principle of putrefaction, and conclude in a moist relentment.[7] Others conceived it most natural to end in fire, as due unto the master principle in the composition, according to the doctrine of Heraclitus; and therefore heaped up large piles, more actively to waft them toward that element, whereby they also declined[8] a visible degeneration into worms, and left a lasting parcel of their composition.

[1]Still undiscovered. [2]Monopolized. [3]Suitably. [4]Burying. [5]*Cf.* Jude, 9.

[6]According to Browne, a country near Persia. [7]Dissolution. [8]Avoided.

Some apprehended a purifying virtue in fire, refining the grosser conmixture, and firing out the ethereal particles so deeply immersed in it. And such as by tradition or rational conjecture held any hint of the final pyre of all things, or that this element at last must be too hard for all the rest, might conceive most naturally of the fiery dissolution. Others pretending no natural grounds, politicly declined the malice of enemies upon their buried bodies. Which consideration led Sylla unto this practice; who having thus served the body of Marius, could not but fear a retaliation upon his own; entertained after in the civil wars, and revengeful contentions of Rome.

But, as many nations embraced, and many left it indifferent, so others too much affected, or strictly declined this practice. The Indian Brahmans seemed too great friends unto fire, who burned themselves alive, and thought it the noblest way to end their days in fire; according to the expression of the Indian, burning himself at Athens, in his last words upon the pyre unto the amazed spectators, "Thus I make myself immortal."

But the Chaldeans, the great idolaters of fire, abhorred the burning of their carcases, as a pollution of that deity. The Persian magi declined it upon the like scruple, and being only solicitous about their bones, exposed their flesh to the prey of birds and dogs. And the Parsees now in India, which expose their bodies unto vultures, and endure not so much as *feretra* or biers of wood, the proper fuel of fire, are led on with such niceties. But whether the ancient Germans, who burned their dead, held any such fear to pollute their deity of Herthus, or the Earth, we have no authentic conjecture.

The Egyptians were afraid of fire, not as a deity, but a devouring element, mercilessly consuming their bodies, and leaving too little of them; and therefore by precious embalmments, depositure in dry earths, or handsome inclosure in glasses, contrived the notablest ways of integral conservation. And from such Egyptian scruples, imbibed by Pythagoras, it may be conjectured that Numa and the Pythagorical sect first waved[1] the fiery solution.

The Scythians, who swore by wind and sword, that is, by life and death, were so far from burning their bodies, that they declined all interment, and made their graves in the air: and the Ichthyophagi, or fish-eating nations about Egypt, affected the sea for their grave; thereby declining visible corruption, and restoring the debt of their bodies. Whereas the old heroes, in Homer, dreaded nothing more than water or drowning; probably upon the old opinion of the fiery substance of the soul, only extinguishable by that element; and therefore the poet emphatically implieth the total destruction in this kind of death, which happened to Ajax Oileus.[2]

The old Balearians[3] had a peculiar mode, for they used great urns and much wood, but no fire in their burials, while they bruised the flesh and bones of the dead, crowded them into urns, and laid heaps of wood upon them. And the Chinese without cremation or urnal interment of their bodies, make use of trees and much burning, while they plant a pine-tree by their grave, and burn great numbers of printed draughts[4] of slaves and horses over it, civilly content with their companies *in effigy*, which barbarous nations exact unto reality.

Christians abhorred this way of obsequies, and though they sticked[5] not to give their bodies to be burned in their lives, detested that mode after death; affecting rather a depositure than absumption,[6] and properly submitting unto the sentence of God, to return not unto ashes but unto dust again, conformable unto the practice of the patriarchs, the interment of our Savior, of Peter, Paul, and the ancient martyrs. And so far at last declining promiscuous interment with Pagans, that some have suffered ecclesiastical censures, for making no scruple thereof.

The Musselman believers will never admit this fiery resolution. For they hold a present[7] trial from their black and white angels in the grave; which they must have made so hollow, that they may rise upon their knees.

The Jewish nation, though they entertained the old way of inhumation, yet sometimes admitted this practice. For the men of Jabesh burned the body of Saul; and by no prohibited practice, to avoid contagion or pollution, in time of pestilence, burned the bodies of their friends. And when they burned not their dead bodies, yet sometimes used great burn-

[1]Forsook.

[2]Browne refers to *Odyssey*, IV, 511.

[3]Dwellers in the Balearic Islands.

[4]Drawings.

[5]Hesitated.

[6]A wasting away.

[7]An immediate

ings near and about them, deducible from the expressions concerning Jehoram, Zedechias, and the sumptuous pyre of Asa. And were so little averse from Pagan burning, that the Jews lamenting the death of Cæsar, their friend and revenger on Pompey, frequented the place where his body was burned for many nights together. And as they raised noble monuments and mausoleums, for their own nation, so they were not scrupulous in erecting some for others, according to the practice of Daniel, who left that lasting sepulchral pile in Ecbatana, for the Median and Persian kings.

But even in times of subjection and hottest use, they conformed not unto the Roman practice of burning; whereby the prophecy was secured concerning the body of Christ, that it should not see corruption, or a bone should not be broken; which we believe was also providentially prevented, from the soldier's spear and nails that passed by the little bones both in his hands and feet; not of ordinary contrivance, that it should not corrupt on the cross, according to the laws of Roman crucifixion; or an hair of his head perish, though observable in Jewish customs, to cut the hairs of malefactors.

Nor in their long cohabitation with[1] Egyptians, crept into a custom of their exact embalming, wherein deeply slashing the muscles, and taking out the brains and entrails, they had broken the subject of so entire a resurrection, nor fully answered the types of Enoch, Elijah, or Jonah, which yet to prevent or restore, was of equal facility unto that rising power, able to break the fasciations[2] and bands of death, to get clear out of the cerecloth, and an hundred pounds of ointment, and out of the sepulcher before the stone was rolled from it.

But though they embraced not this practice of burning, yet entertained they many ceremonies agreeable unto Greek and Roman obsequies. And he that observeth their funeral feasts, their lamentations at the grave, their music, and weeping mourners; how they closed the eyes of their friends, how they washed, anointed, and kissed the dead; may easily conclude these were not mere Pagan civilities. But whether that mournful burthen, and treble calling out after Absalom,[3] had any reference unto the last conclamation,[4] and triple valediction, used by other nations, we hold but a wavering conjecture.

Civilians[5] make sepulture but of the law of nations, others do naturally found it and discover it also in animals. They that are so thick-skinned as still to credit the story of the *Phœnix*,[6] may say something for animal burning. More serious conjectures find some examples of sepulture in elephants, cranes, the sepulchral cells of pismires,[7] and practice of bees,—which civil society carrieth out their dead, and hath exequies, if not interments.

CHAPTER II

THE solemnities, ceremonies, rites of their cremation or interment, so solemnly delivered by authors, we shall not disparage our reader to repeat. Only the last and lasting part in their urns, collected bones and ashes, we cannot wholly omit, or decline that subject, which occasion lately presented, in some discovered among us.

In a field of Old Walsingham,[8] not many months past, were digged up between forty and fifty urns, deposited in a dry and sandy soil, not a yard deep, nor far from one another. Not all strictly of one figure, but most answering these described:[9] some containing two pounds of bones, distinguishable in skulls, ribs, jaws, thigh bones, and teeth, with fresh impressions of their combustion; besides the extraneous substances, like pieces of small boxes, or combs handsomely wrought, handles of small brass instruments, brazen nippers, and in one some kind of opal.

Near the same plot of ground, for about six yards' compass, were digged up coals and incinerated substances, which begat conjecture that this was the *ustrina* or place of burning their bodies, or some sacrificing place unto the *manes*,[10] which was properly below the surface of the ground, as the *aræ* and altars unto the gods and heroes above it.

That these were the urns of Romans[11] from

[1] Living in the same land with. [2] Bandages.
[3] *Cf.* 2 Samuel, xviii, 33. [4] Loud general shout.

[5] Writers on civil law.
[6] The story that it renewed its life through fire.
[7] Ants.
[8] In northern Norfolk, south of Wells.
[9] Pictured. Browne published a plate containing drawings of four urns.
[10] *Di manes* were deified spirits of the dead, gods of the lower world.
[11] Modern antiquaries say that these urns were of Saxon origin.

the common custom and place where they were found, is no obscure conjecture, not far from a Roman garrison, and but five miles from Brancaster, set down by ancient record under the name of Brannodunum. And where the adjoining town, containing seven parishes, in no very different sound, but Saxon termination, still retains the name of Burnham, which being an early station, it is not improbable the neighbor parts were filled with habitations, either of Romans themselves, or Britons Romanized, which observed the Roman customs.

Nor is it improbable, that the Romans early possessed this country. For though we meet not with such strict particulars of these parts before the new institution of Constantine and military charge of the count of the Saxon shore, and that about the Saxon invasions, the Dalmatian horsemen were in the garrison of Brancaster; yet in the time of Claudius, Vespasian, and Severus, we find no less than three legions dispersed through the province of Britain. And as high as the reign of Claudius a great overthrow was given unto the Iceni, by the Roman lieutenant Ostorius. Not long after, the country was so molested, that, in hope of a better state, Prasutagus bequeathed his kingdom unto Nero and his daughters; and Boadicea, his queen, fought the last decisive battle with Paulinus. After which time, and conquest of Agricola, the lieutenant of Vespasian, probable it is, they wholly possessed this country, ordering it into garrisons or habitations best suitable with their securities; and so some Roman habitations not improbable in these parts, as high as the time of Vespasian, where the Saxons after seated, in whose thin-filled maps we yet find the name of Walsingham. Now if the Iceni were but Gammadims, Anconians, or men that lived in an angle, wedge, or elbow of Britain, according to the original etymology, this country will challenge the emphatical appellation, as most properly making the elbow or *iken* of Icenia.

That Britain was notably populous is undeniable, from that expression of Cæsar.[1] That the Romans themselves were early in no small numbers, seventy thousand, with their associates, slain by Boadicea, affords a sure account. And though not many Roman habitations are now known, yet some, by old works, rampiers,[2] coins, and urns, do testify their possessions. Some urns have been found at Castor, some also about Southcreak, and, not many years past, no less than ten in a field at Buxton, not near any recorded garrison. Nor is it strange to find Roman coins of copper and silver among us; of Vespasian, Trajan, Adrian, Commodus, Antoninus, Severus, *etc.;* but the greater number of Dioclesian, Constantine, Constans, Valens, with many of Victorinus, Posthumius, Tetricus, and the thirty tyrants in the reign of Gallienus; and some as high as Adrianus have been found about Thetford, or Sitomagus, mentioned in the *Itinerary* of Antoninus, as the way from Venta or Castor unto London.[3] But the most frequent discovery is made at the two Castors by Norwich and Yarmouth, at Burghcastle, and Brancaster.

Besides the Norman, Saxon, and Danish pieces of Cuthred, Canutus, William, Matilda, and others, some British coins of gold have been dispersedly found, and no small number of silver pieces near Norwich, with a rude head upon the obverse, and an ill-formed horse on the reverse, with inscriptions *Ic. Duro. T.;* whether implying Iceni, Durotriges, Tascia, or Trinobantes, we leave to higher conjecture. Vulgar chronology will have Norwich Castle as old as Julius Cæsar; but his distance from these parts, and its gothic[4] form of structure, abridgeth such antiquity. The British coins afford conjecture of early habitation in these parts, though the city of Norwich arose from the ruins of Venta; and though, perhaps, not without some habitation before, was enlarged, builded, and nominated by the Saxons. In what bulk or populosity it stood in the old East-Angle monarchy tradition and history are silent. Considerable it was in the Danish eruptions, when Sueno burned Thetford and Norwich, and Ulfketel, the governor thereof, was able to make some resistance, and after endeavored to burn the Danish navy.

How the Romans left so many coins in countries of their conquests seems of hard resolution; except we consider how they buried them under ground when, upon barbarous invasions, they were fain to desert their habita-

[1]Browne quotes part of Cæsar's account of Britain (*Concerning the Gallic War*, v, 10).

[2]Roman roads (as the word is here used by Browne).

[3]Venta Browne thought to be the Roman name for Norwich. Castor is Caistor St. Edmund's. The second Castor mentioned below is Caistor-on-Sea.

[4]Its architecture is really Norman. It was built c. 1100.

tions in most part of their empire, and the strictness of their laws forbidding to transfer them to any other uses: wherein the Spartans were singular, who, to make their copper money useless, contempered it with vinegar. That the Britons left any, some wonder, since their money was iron and iron rings before Cæsar; and those of after-stamp by permission, and but small in bulk and bigness. That so few of the Saxons remain, because, overcome by succeeding conquerors upon the place, their coins, by degrees, passed into other stamps and the marks of after-ages.

Than the time of these urns deposited, or precise antiquity of these relics, nothing of more uncertainty; for since the lieutenant of Claudius seems to have made the first progress into these parts, since Boadicea was overthrown by the forces of Nero, and Agricola put a full end to these conquests, it is not probable the country was fully garrisoned or planted before; and, therefore, however these urns might be of later date, not likely of higher antiquity.

And the succeeding emperors desisted not from their conquests in these and other parts, as testified by history and medal-inscription yet extant: the province of Britain, in so divided a distance from Rome, beholding the faces of many imperial persons, and in large account, no fewer than Cæsar, Claudius, Britannicus, Vespasian, Titus, Adrian, Severus, Commodus, Geta, and Caracalla.

A great obscurity herein, because no medal or emperor's coin enclosed, which might denote the date of their interments; observable in many urns, and found in those of Spitalfields, by London, which contained the coins of Claudius, Vespasian, Commodus, Antoninus, attended with lacrymatories,[1] lamps, bottles of liquor, and other appurtenances of affectionate superstition, which in these rural interments were wanting.

Some uncertainty there is from the period or term of burning, or the cessation of that practice. Macrobius affirmeth it was disused in his days;[2] but most agree, though without authentic record, that it ceased with the Antonini—most safely to be understood after the reign of those emperors which assumed the name of Antoninus, extending unto Heliogabalus. Not strictly after Marcus; for about fifty years later, we find the magnificent burning and consecration of Severus; and, if we so fix this period or cessation, these urns will challenge above thirteen hundred years.

But whether this practice was only then left by emperors and great persons, or generally about Rome, and not in other provinces, we hold not authentic account; for after Tertullian, in the days of Minucius, it was obviously objected upon Christians, that they condemned the practice of burning. And we find a passage in Sidonius, which asserteth that practice in France unto a lower account.[3] And, perhaps, not fully discussed till Christianity fully established, which gave the final extinction to these sepulchral bonfires.

Whether they were the bones of men, or women, or children, no authentic decision from ancient custom in distinct places of burial. Although not improbably conjectured, that the double sepulture or burying-place of Abraham, had in it such intention. But from exility[4] of bones, thinness of skulls, smallness of teeth, ribs, and thigh bones, not improbable that many thereof were persons of minor age, or women. Confirmable also from things contained in them. In most were found substances resembling combs, plates like boxes, fastened with iron pins, and handsomely overwrought like the necks or bridges of musical instruments; long brass plates overwrought like the handles of neat implements; brazen nippers, to pull away hair; and in one a kind of opal, yet maintaining a bluish color.

Now that they accustomed to burn or bury with them, things wherein they excelled, delighted, or which were dear unto them, either as farewells unto all pleasure, or vain apprehension that they might use them in the other world, is testified by all antiquity, observable from the gem or beryl ring upon the finger of Cynthia, the mistress of Propertius, when after her funeral pyre her ghost appeared unto him; and notably illustrated from the contents of that Roman urn preserved by Cardinal Farnese, wherein besides great number of gems with heads of gods and goddesses, were found an ape of agath, a grasshopper, an elephant of amber, a crystal ball, three glasses, two spoons, and six nuts of crystal; and beyond the content of urns, in the monument of

[1]Tear-bottles, *i. e.*, small bottles of glass, alabaster and other substances found in ancient Roman tombs.

[2]About A. D. 400.

[3]At a later date.

[4]Smallness.

Childeric the First,[1] and fourth king from Pharamond, casually discovered three years past at Tournay, restoring unto the world much gold richly adorning his sword, two hundred rubies, many hundred imperial coins, three hundred golden bees, the bones and horse-shoes of his horse interred with him, according to the barbarous magnificence of those days in their sepulchral obsequies. Although, if we steer by the conjecture of many[2] and Septuagint[3] expression, some trace thereof may be found even with the ancient Hebrews, not only from the sepulchral treasure of David, but the circumcision knives which Joshua also buried.

Some men, considering the contents of these urns, lasting pieces and toys included in them, and the custom of burning with many other nations, might somewhat doubt whether all urns found among us, were properly Roman relics, or some not belonging unto our British, Saxon, or Danish forefathers.

In the form of burial among the ancient Britons, the large discourses of Cæsar, Tacitus, and Strabo are silent. For the discovery whereof, with other particulars, we much deplore the loss of that letter which Cicero expected or received from his brother Quintus, as a resolution of British customs; or the account which might have been made by Scribonius Largus, the physician, accompanying the Emperor Claudius, who might have also discovered that frugal bit[4] of the old Britons, which in the bigness of a bean could satisfy their thirst and hunger.

But that the Druids and ruling priests used to burn and bury, is expressed by Pomponius; that Bellinus, the brother of Brennus, and king of Britons, was burned, is acknowledged by Polydorus, as also by Amandus Zierexensis[5] in *Historia*, and Pineda in his *Universa Historia* (Spanish). That they held that practice in Gallia, Cæsar expressly delivereth. Whether the Britons (probably descended from them, of like religion, language, and manners) did not sometimes make use of burning, or whether at least such as were after civilized unto the Roman life and manners, conformed not unto this practice, we have no historical assertion or denial. But since, from the account of Tacitus, the Romans early wrought so much civility upon the British stock, that they brought them to build temples, to wear the gown, and study the Roman laws and language, that they conformed also unto their religious rites and customs in burials seems no improbable conjecture.

That burning the dead was used in Sarmatia is affirmed by Gaguinus; that the Sueons and Gothlanders used to burn their princes and great persons, is delivered by Saxo and Olaus;[6] that this was the old German practice, is also asserted by Tacitus. And though we are bare in historical particulars of such obsequies in this island, or that the Saxons, Jutes, and Angles burned their dead, yet came they from parts where 'twas of ancient practice; the Germans using it, from whom they were descended. And even in Jutland and Sleswick in Anglia Cymbrica, urns with bones were found not many years before us.

But the Danish and northern nations have raised an era or point of compute from their custom of burning their dead: some deriving it from Unguinus, some from Frotho the Great, who ordained by law, that princes and chief commanders should be committed unto the fire, though the common sort had the common grave interment. So Starkatterus, that old hero, was burned, and Ringo royally burned the body of Harold the king slain by him.[7]

What time this custom generally expired in that nation, we discern no assured period; whether it ceased before Christianity, or upon their conversion, by Ansgarius the Gaul, in the time of Ludovicus Pius[8] the son of Charles the Great, according to good computes; or whether it might not be used by some persons, while for an hundred and eighty years Paganism and Christianity were promiscuously embraced among them, there is no assured conclusion. About which times the Danes were busy in England, and particularly infested this country; where many castles and strongholds were built by them, or against them, and great number of names and families still derived from them. But since this custom was

[1] Died A. D. 481; was king of the Salian Franks.

[2] *I. e.*, many writers.

[3] Greek version of the Old Testament, which differs in some respects from the accepted Hebrew text—for example, in mentioning the circumcision knives of which Browne speaks.

[4] *I. e.*, small quantity of food.

[5] A Dutch writer.

[6] Saxo Grammaticus and Olaus Wormius.

[7] Those named in this paragraph are all mentioned in the *Danish History* of Saxo Grammaticus.

[8] Louis the Pious reigned A. D. 814–840.

probably disused before their invasion or conquest, and the Romans confessedly practiced the same since their possession of this island, the most assured account will fall upon the Romans, or Britons Romanized.

However, certain it is, that urns conceived of no Roman original, are often digged up both in Norway and Denmark, handsomely described, and graphically represented by the learned physician Wormius. And, in some parts of Denmark in no ordinary number, as stands delivered by authors exactly describing those countries. And they contained not only bones, but many other substances in them, as knives, pieces of iron, brass, and wood, and one of Norway a brass gilded jew's-harp.

Nor were they confused or careless in disposing the noblest sort, while they placed large stones in circle about the urns or bodies which they interred: somewhat answerable unto the monument of Rollrich stones in England, or sepulchral monument probably erected by Rollo,[1] who after conquered Normandy; where 'tis not improbable somewhat might be discovered. Meanwhile to what nation or person belonged that large urn found at Ashbury, containing mighty bones, and a buckler; what those large urns found at Little Massingham; or why the Anglesea urns are placed with their mouths downward, remains yet undiscovered.

CHAPTER III

PLASTERED and whited sepulchers were anciently affected in cadaverous and corruptive burials;[2] and the rigid Jews were wont to garnish the sepulchers of the righteous. Ulysses, in Hecuba, cared not how meanly he lived, so he might find a noble tomb after death. Great persons affected great monuments; and the fair and larger urns contained no vulgar ashes, which makes that disparity in those which time discovereth among us. The present urns were not of one capacity, the largest containing above a gallon, some not much above half that measure; nor all of one figure, wherein there is no strict conformity in the same or different countries; observable from those represented by Casalius, Bosio, and others, though all found in Italy; while many have handles, ears, and long necks, but most imitate a circular figure, in a spherical and round composure; whether from any mystery, best duration or capacity,[3] were but a conjecture. But the common form with necks was a proper figure, making our last bed like our first; nor much unlike the urns of our nativity while we lay in the nether part of the earth, and inward vault of our microcosm. Many urns are red, these but of a black color, somewhat smooth, and dully sounding, which begat some doubt, whether they were burned, or only baked in oven or sun, according to the ancient way, in many bricks, tiles, pots, and testaceous[4] works; and, as the word *testa* is properly to be taken, when occurring without addition and chiefly intended by Pliny, when he commendeth bricks and tiles of two years old, and to make them in the spring. Nor only these concealed pieces, but the open magnificence of antiquity, ran much in the artifice of clay. Hereof the house of Mausolus was built, thus old Jupiter stood in the Capitol, and the *statua*[5] of Hercules, made in the reign of Tarquinius Priscus, was extant in Pliny's days. And such as declined burning or funeral urns, affected coffins of clay, according to the mode of Pythagoras, and way preferred by Varro. But the spirit of great ones was above these circumscriptions,[6] affecting copper, silver, gold, and porphyry urns, wherein Severus lay, after a serious view and sentence on that which should contain him. Some of these urns were thought to have been silvered over, from sparklings in several pots, with small tinsel parcels; uncertain whether from the earth, or the first mixture in them.

Among these urns we could obtain no good account of their coverings; only one seemed arched over with some kind of brick-work. Of those found at Buxton, some were covered with flints, some, in other parts, with tiles; those at Yarmouth Caster were closed with Roman bricks, and some have proper earthen covers adapted and fitted to them. But in the Homerical urn of Patroclus, whatever was the solid tegument,[7] we find the immediate covering to be a purple piece of silk: and such as had no covers might have the earth closely

[1]Territory in northern France was ceded to Rolf in 912. The stones mentioned are in reality prehistoric. They are in Oxfordshire, in the parish of Little Rollright.

[2]Burials of the whole corruptible body.

[3]Whether because this shape has any mysterious significance, or endures best, or has the largest capacity.

[4]Earthenware.

[5]Statue.

[6]Boundaries.

[7]Covering.

pressed into them, after which disposure were probably some of these, wherein we found the bones and ashes half mortared unto the sand and sides of the urn, and some long roots of quich, or dog's-grass, wreathed about the bones.

No lamps, included[1] liquors, lacrymatories, or tear bottles, attended these rural urns, either as sacred unto the *manes*, or passionate expressions of their surviving friends. While with rich flames, and hired tears, they solemnized their obsequies, and in the most lamented monuments made one part of their inscriptions.[2] Some find sepulchral vessels containing liquors, which time hath incrassated[3] into jellies. For, besides these lacrymatories, notable lamps, with vessels of oils, and aromatical liquors, attended noble ossuaries;[4] and some yet retaining a vinosity and spirit in them, which, if any have tasted, they have far exceeded the palates of antiquity. Liquors not to be computed by years of annual magistrates, but by great conjunctions and the fatal periods of kingdoms. The draughts of consulary date were but crude unto these, and Opimian wine but in the must[5] unto them.

In sundry graves and sepulchers we meet with rings, coins, and chalices. Ancient frugality was so severe, that they allowed no gold to attend the corpse, but only that which served to fasten their teeth. Whether the Opaline stone in this were burned upon the finger of the dead, or cast into the fire by some affectionate friend, it will consist with either custom. But other incinerable[6] substances were found so fresh, that they could feel no singe from fire. These, upon view, were judged to be wood; but, sinking in water, and tried by the fire, we found them to be bone or ivory. In their hardness and yellow color they most resembled box, which, in old expressions, found the epithet of eternal, and perhaps in such conservatories might have passed uncorrupted.

That bay leaves were found green in the tomb of S. Humbert, after an hundred and fifty years, was looked upon as miraculous. Remarkable it was unto old spectators, that the cypress of the temple of Diana lasted so many hundred years. The wood of the ark and olive-rod of Aaron, were older at the captivity; but the cypress of the ark of Noah was the greatest vegetable of antiquity, if Josephus were not deceived by some fragments of it in his days: to omit the moor logs and fir trees found under-ground in many parts of England; the undated ruins of winds, floods, or earthquakes, and which in Flanders still show from what quarter they fell, as generally lying in a northeast position.

But though we found not these pieces to be wood, according to first apprehensions, yet we missed not altogether of some woody substance; for the bones were not so clearly picked but some coals were found amongst them; a way to make wood perpetual, and a fit associate for metal, whereon was laid the foundation of the great Ephesian temple,[7] and which were made the lasting tests of old boundaries and landmarks. Whilst we look on these, we admire not observations of coals found fresh after four hundred years. In a long-deserted habitation even egg-shells have been found fresh, not tending to corruption.

In the monument of King Childeric the iron relics were found all rusty and crumbling into pieces; but our little iron pins, which fastened the ivory works, held well together, and lost not their magnetical quality, though wanting a tenacious moisture for the firmer union of parts; although it be hardly drawn into fusion, yet that metal soon submitteth unto rust and dissolution. In the brazen pieces we admired not the duration, but the freedom from rust, and ill savor, upon the hardest attrition; but now exposed unto the piercing atoms of air, in the space of a few months, they begin to spot and betray their green entrails.[8] We conceive not these urns to have descended thus naked as they appear, or to have entered their graves without the old habit[9] of flowers. The urn of Philopœmen was so laden with flowers and ribbons, that it afforded no sight of itself. The rigid Lycurgus allowed olive and myrtle. The Athenians might fairly except against the practice of Democritus, to be buried up in honey, as fearing to embezzle[10] a great com-

[1]Enclosed.

[2]In the monuments showing the greatest lamentation part of the inscription stated that the dead were placed there with tears.

[3]Thickened.

[4]Receptacles for bones.

[5]But sour. The meaning is that these wines had attained an age far greater than any the ancients drank, and presumably a correspondingly finer flavor.

[6]Reducible by fire to ashes.

[7]The temple of Diana at Ephesus, one of the "seven wonders" of the ancient world.

[8]The green rust of brass. [9]Adornment. [10]Squander.

modity of their country, and the best of that kind in Europe. But Plato seemed too frugally politic, who allowed no larger monument than would contain four heroic verses, and designed the most barren ground for sepulture: though we cannot commend the goodness of that sepulchral ground which was set at no higher rate than the mean salary of Judas. Though the earth had confounded the ashes of these ossuaries, yet the bones were so smartly burned, that some thin plates of brass were found half melted among them. Whereby we apprehend they were not of the meanest carcases, perfunctorily fired, as sometimes in military, and commonly in pestilence, burnings; or after the manner of abject corpses, huddled forth and carelessly burned, without the Esquiline Port at Rome; which was an affront continued upon Tiberius, while they but half burned his body, and in the amphitheater, according to the custom in notable malefactors; whereas Nero seemed not so much to fear his death as that his head should be cut off and his body not burned entire.

Some, finding many fragments of skulls in these urns, suspected a mixture of bones; in none we searched was there cause of such conjecture, though sometimes they declined not that practice.—The ashes of Domitian were mingled with those of Julia; of Achilles with those of Patroclus. All urns contained not single ashes; without confused burnings they affectionately compounded their bones; passionately endeavoring to continue their living unions. And when distance of death denied such conjunctions, unsatisfied affections conceived some satisfaction to be neighbors in the grave, to lie urn by urn, and touch but in their names. And many were so curious to continue their living relations, that they contrived large and family urns, wherein the ashes of their nearest friends and kindred might successively be received, at least some parcels thereof, while their collateral memorials[1] lay in minor vessels about them.

Antiquity held too light thoughts from objects of mortality, while some drew provocatives of mirth from anatomies,[2] and jugglers showed tricks with skeletons; when fiddlers made not so pleasant mirth as fencers, and men could sit with quiet stomachs, while hanging was played before them. Old considerations made few mementos by skulls and bones upon their monuments. In the Egyptian obelisks and hieroglyphical figures it is not easy to meet with bones. The sepulchral lamps speak nothing less than[3] sepulture, and in their literal draughts[4] prove often obscene and antic pieces. Where we find *D. M.*[5] it is obvious[6] to meet with sacrificing *pateras* and vessels of libation upon old sepulchral monuments. In the Jewish hypogæum and subterranean cell at Rome, was little observable beside the variety of lamps and frequent draughts of the holy candlestick. In authentic draughts of Anthony and Jerome we meet with thigh bones and death's-heads, but the cemeterial cells of ancient Christians and martyrs were filled with draughts of Scripture stories; not declining the flourishes of cypress palms, and olive, and the mystical figures of peacocks, doves, and cocks; but iterately[7] affecting the portraits of Enoch, Lazarus, Jonas, and the vision of Ezekiel, as hopeful draughts, and hinting imagery of the resurrection, which is the life of the grave, and sweetens our habitations in the land of moles and pismires.

Gentile inscriptions precisely delivered the extent of men's lives, seldom the manner of their deaths, which history itself so often leaves obscure in the records of memorable persons. There is scarce any philosopher but dies twice or thrice in Laërtius; nor almost any life without two or three deaths in Plutarch; which makes the tragical ends of noble persons more favorably resented[8] by compassionate readers who find some relief in the election of such differences.

The certainty of death is attended with uncertainties, in time, manner, places. The variety of monuments hath often obscured true graves; and cenotaphs confounded[9] sepulchers. For beside their real tombs, many have found honorary and empty sepulchers. The variety of Homer's monuments made him of various countries. Euripides had his tomb in Attica, but his sepulture in Macedonia. And Severus found his real sepulcher in Rome, but his empty grave in Gallia.

He that lay in a golden urn eminently above the earth, was not like to find the quiet of his bones. Many of these urns were broke by a

[1]Memorials of collateral relatives.
[2]Skeletons.

[3]Anything but. [4]Realistic pictures.
[5]Abbreviation for *Dis Manibus*. [6]Common.
[7]Repeatedly. [8]Received. [9]Caused doubt about.

vulgar discoverer in hope of enclosed treasure. The ashes of Marcellus were lost above ground, upon the like account. Where profit hath prompted, no age hath wanted such miners; for which the most barbarous expilators[1] found the most civil rhetoric:—"Gold once out of the earth is no more due unto it;—what was unreasonably committed to the ground, is reasonably resumed from it;—let monuments and rich fabrics, not riches, adorn men's ashes;—the commerce of the living is not to be transferred unto the dead;—it is not injustice to take that which none complains to lose, and no man is wronged where no man is possessor."

What virtue yet sleeps in this *terra damnata*[2] and aged cinders, were petty magic to experiment. These crumbling relics and long fired particles superannuate[3] such expectations; bones, hairs, nails, and teeth of the dead, were the treasures of old sorcerers. In vain we revive such practices; present superstition too visibly perpetuates the folly of our forefathers, wherein unto old observation[4] this island was so complete, that it might have instructed Persia.

Plato's historian of the other world[5] lies twelve days incorrupted, while his soul was viewing the large stations of the dead. How to keep the corpse seven days from corruption by anointing and washing, without exenteration,[6] were an hazardable piece of art, in our choicest practice. How they made distinct separation of bones and ashes from fiery admixture, hath found no historical solution; though they seemed to make a distinct collection, and overlooked not Pyrrhus his toe.[7] Some provision they might make by fictile[8] vessels, coverings, tiles, or flat stones, upon and about the body (and in the same field, not far from these urns, many stones were found under ground), as also by careful separation of extraneous matter, composing and raking up the burned bones with forks, observable in that notable lamp of Galvanus. Marlianus, who had the sight of the *vas ustrinum* or vessel wherein they burned the dead, found in the Esquiline field at Rome, might have afforded clearer solution. But their insatisfaction herein begat that remarkable invention in the funeral pyres of some princes, by incombustible sheets made with a texture of asbestos, incremable flax, or salamander's wool,[9] which preserved their bones and ashes incommixed.

How the bulk of a man should sink into so few pounds of bones and ashes, may seem strange unto any who considers not its constitution, and how slender a mass will remain upon an open and urging fire of the carnal composition. Even bones themselves, reduced into ashes, do abate a notable proportion. And consisting much of a volatile salt, when that is fired out, make a light kind of cinders. Although their bulk be disproportionable to their weight, when the heavy principle of salt is fired out, and the earth almost only remaineth; observable in sallow, which makes more ashes than oak, and discovers the common fraud of selling ashes by measure, and not by ponderation.

Some bones make best skeletons, some bodies quick and speediest ashes. Who would expect a quick flame from hydropical Heraclitus? The poisoned soldier when his belly brake, put out two pyres in Plutarch. But in the plague of Athens, one private pyre served two or three intruders; and the Saracens burned in large heaps, by the king of Castile, showed how little fuel sufficeth. Though the funeral pyre of Patroclus took up an hundred foot, a piece of an old boat burned Pompey; and if the burthen of Isaac were sufficient for an holocaust, a man may carry his own pyre.

From animals are drawn good burning lights, and good medicines against burning.[10] Though the seminal humor seems of a contrary nature to fire, yet the body completed proves a combustible lump, wherein fire finds flame even from bones, and some fuel almost from all parts; though the metropolis of humidity[11] seems least disposed unto it, which might render the skulls of these urns less burned than other bones. But all flies or sinks before fire almost in all bodies: when the common ligament is dissolved, the attenuable

[1]Pillagers.

[2]Condemned earth;—an alchemical term, meaning what remains after all else has been removed by burning, distilling, and the like.

[3]Are too old for.

[4]*I. e.*, to Pliny, to whom Browne refers in a note (*Natural History*, xxx, 4).

[5]Er the Pamphylian, *Republic*, x, 614.

[6]Disemboweling.

[7]Which was incombustible.

[8]Clay.

[9]Amianthus, a kind of asbestos.

[10]Browne's note appears to indicate that he was thinking of sperm oil and white of egg.

[11]The brain.

parts ascend, the rest subside in coal, calx,[1] or ashes.

To burn the bones of the king of Edom for lime, seems no irrational ferity;[2] but to drink of the ashes of dead relations, a passionate prodigality. He that hath the ashes of his friend, hath an everlasting treasure; where fire taketh leave, corruption slowly enters. In bones well burned, fire makes a wall against itself; experimented[3] in cupels,[4] and tests of metals, which consist of such ingredients. What the sun compoundeth, fire analyzeth, not transmuteth. That devouring agent leaves almost always a morsel for the earth, whereof all things are but a colony; and which, if time permits, the mother element will have in their primitive mass again.

He that looks for urns and old sepulchral relics, must not seek them in the ruins of temples, where no religion anciently placed them. These were found in a field, according to ancient custom, in noble or private burial; the old practice of the Canaanites, the family of Abraham, and the burying-place of Joshua, in the borders of his possessions; and also agreeable unto Roman practice to bury by highways, whereby their monuments were under eye;—memorials of themselves, and mementos of mortality unto living passengers; whom the epitaphs of great ones were fain to beg to stay and look upon them,—a language though sometimes used, not so proper in church inscriptions. The sensible rhetoric of the dead, to exemplarity of good life, first admitted the bones of pious men and martyrs within church walls, which in succeeding ages crept into promiscuous practice: while Constantine was peculiarly favored to be admitted into the church porch, and the first thus buried in England, was in the days of Cuthred.

Christians dispute how their bodies should lie in the grave. In urnal interment they clearly escaped this controversy. Though we decline the religious consideration, yet in cemeterial and narrower burying-places, to avoid confusion and cross-position, a certain posture were to be admitted: which even Pagan civility observed. The Persians lay north and south; the Megarians and Phœnicians placed their heads to the east; the Athenians, some think, towards the west, which Christians still retain. And Beda will have it to be the posture of our Savior. That he was crucified with his face toward the west, we will not contend with tradition and probable account; but we applaud not the hand of the painter, in exalting his cross so high above those on either side: since hereof we find no authentic account in history, and even the crosses found by Helena, pretend no such distinction from longitude or dimension.

To be gnawed out of our graves, to have our skulls made drinking-bowls, and our bones turned into pipes, to delight and sport our enemies, are tragical abominations escaped in burning burials.

Urnal interments and burned relics lie not in fear of worms, or to be an heritage for serpents. In carnal sepulture, corruptions seem peculiar unto parts; and some speak of snakes out of the spinal marrow. But while we suppose common worms in graves, 'tis not easy to find any there; few in churchyards above a foot deep, fewer or none in churches though in fresh-decayed bodies. Teeth, bones, and hair, give the most lasting defiance to corruption. In an hydropical[5] body, ten years buried in the churchyard, we[6] met with a fat concretion, where the niter of the earth, and the salt and lixivious[7] liquor of the body, had coagulated large lumps of fat into the consistence of the hardest Castile soap, whereof part remaineth with us. After a battle with the Persians, the Roman corpses decayed in few days, while the Persian bodies remained dry and uncorrupted. Bodies in the same ground do not uniformly dissolve, nor bones equally molder; whereof in the opprobrious disease, we expect no long duration. The body of the Marquis of Dorset seemed sound and handsomely cereclothed, that after seventy-eight years was found uncorrupted. Common tombs preserve not beyond powder: a firmer consistence and compage[8] of parts might be expected from arefaction,[9] deep burial, or charcoal. The greatest antiquities of mortal bodies may remain in putrefied bones, whereof, though we take not in the pillar of Lot's wife, or metamorphosis of Ortelius, some may be older than pyramids, in the putrefied relics

[1]Powder remaining after all else has been consumed by burning or roasting; an alchemical term.

[2]Barbarity.

[3]As is shown.

[4]Refining vessels made of bone-ash, used in refining gold and silver.

[5]Dropsical. [6]*I. e.*, Browne. [7]Alkaline.

[8]Coherence. [9]Drying.

of the general inundation. When Alexander opened the tomb of Cyrus, the remaining bones discovered his proportion, whereof urnal fragments afford but a bad conjecture, and have this disadvantage of grave interments, that they leave us ignorant of most personal discoveries. For since bones afford not only rectitude and stability but figure unto the body, it is no impossible physiognomy to conjecture at fleshy appendencies, and after what shape the muscles and carnous parts might hang in their full consistencies. A full-spread *cariola*[1] shows a well-shaped horse behind; handsome formed skulls give some analogy to fleshy resemblance. A critical view of bones makes a good distinction of sexes. Even color is not beyond conjecture, since it is hard to be deceived in the distinction of Negroes' skulls. Dante's[2] characters are to be found in skulls as well as faces. Hercules is not only known by his foot. Other parts make out their comproportions and inferences upon whole or parts. And since the dimensions of the head measure the whole body, and the figure thereof gives conjecture of the principal faculties, physiognomy outlives ourselves and ends not in our graves.

Severe contemplators, observing these lasting relics, may think them good monuments of persons past, little advantage to future beings; and, considering that power which subdueth all things unto itself, that can resume the scattered atoms, or identify out of anything, conceive it superfluous to expect a resurrection out of relics: but the soul subsisting, other matter, clothed with due accidents,[3] may salve the individuality. Yet the saints, we observe, arose from graves and monuments about the holy city. Some think the ancient patriarchs so earnestly desired to lay their bones in Canaan, as hoping to make a part of that resurrection; and, though thirty miles from Mount Calvary, at least to lie in that region which should produce the first fruits of the dead. And if, according to learned conjecture, the bodies of men shall rise where their greatest relics remain, many are not like to err in the topography of their resurrection, though their bones or bodies be after translated by angels into the field of Ezekiel's vision, or as some will order it, into the valley of judgment, or Jehosaphat.

[1]The haunch-bones of a horse.

[2]Dante in his view of purgatory, found gluttons so meager, and extenuated, that he conceived them to have been in the siege of Jerusalem, and that it was easy to have discovered Homo or Omo in their faces. M being made by the two lines of their cheeks, arching over the eyebrows to the nose, and their sunk eyes making OO which makes up Omo (Browne's note).

[3]Qualities.

CHAPTER IV

CHRISTIANS have handsomely glossed the deformity of death by careful consideration of the body, and civil rites which take off brutal terminations: and though they conceived all reparable by a resurrection, cast not off all care of interment. And since the ashes of sacrifices burned upon the altar of God were carefully carried out by the priests, and deposed[4] in a clean field; since they acknowledged their bodies to be the lodging of Christ, and temples of the Holy Ghost, they devolved not all upon the sufficiency of soul-existence; and therefore with long services and full solemnities, concluded their last exequies, wherein to all distinctions the Greek devotion seems most pathetically ceremonious.

Christian invention hath chiefly driven at rites, which speak hopes of another life, and hints of a resurrection. And if the ancient Gentiles held not the immortality of their better part, and some subsistence after death, in several rites, customs, actions, and expressions, they contradicted their own opinions: wherein Democritus went high, even to the thought of a resurrection, as scoffingly recorded by Pliny. What can be more express than the expression of Phocylides? Or who would expect from Lucretius a sentence of Ecclesiastes? Before Plato could speak, the soul had wings in Homer, which fell not, but flew out of the body into the mansions of the dead; who also observed that handsome distinction of Demas and Soma, for the body conjoined to the soul, and body separated from it. Lucian spoke much truth in jest, when he said that part of Hercules which proceeded from Alcmena perished, that from Jupiter remained immortal. Thus Socrates was content that his friends should bury his body, so they would not think they buried Socrates; and, regarding only his immortal part, was indifferent to be burned or buried. From such considerations, Diogenes might contemn sepulture, and, being satisfied that

[4]Deposited.

the soul could not perish, grow careless of corporal interment. The Stoics, who thought the souls of wise men had their habitation about the moon, might make slight account of subterraneous deposition; whereas the Pythagoreans and transcorporating[1] philosophers, who were to be often buried, held great care of their interment. And the Platonics rejected not a due care of the grave, though they put their ashes to unreasonable expectations, in their tedious term of return and long set revolution.[2]

Men have lost their reason in nothing so much as their religion, wherein stones and clouts make martyrs; and, since the religion of one seems madness unto another, to afford an account or rational of old rites requires no rigid reader. That they kindled the pyre aversely, or turning their face from it, was an handsome symbol of unwilling ministration. That they washed their bones with wine and milk; that the mother wrapped them in linen, and dried them in her bosom, the first fostering part and place of their nourishment; that they opened their eyes towards heaven before they kindled the fire, as the place of their hopes or original, were no improper ceremonies. Their last valediction, thrice uttered by the attendants, was also very solemn, and somewhat answered by Christians, who thought it too little, if they threw not the earth thrice upon the interred body. That, in strewing their tombs, the Romans affected the rose; the Greeks amaranthus and myrtle: that the funeral pyre consisted of sweet fuel, cypress, fir, larix,[3] yew, and trees perpetually verdant, lay silent expressions of their surviving hopes. Wherein Christians, who deck their coffins with bays, have found a more elegant emblem; for that tree, seeming dead, will restore itself from the root, and its dry and exsuccous[4] leaves resume their verdure again; which, if we mistake not, we have also observed in furze. Whether the planting of yew in churchyards hold not its original from ancient funeral rites, or as an emblem of resurrection, from its perpetual verdure, may also admit conjecture.

They made use of music to excite or quiet the affections of their friends, according to different harmonies. But the secret and symbolical hint was the harmonical nature of the soul; which, delivered from the body, went again to enjoy the primitive harmony of heaven, from whence it first descended; which, according to its progress traced by antiquity, came down by Cancer, and ascended by Capricornus.[5]

They burned not children before their teeth appeared, as apprehending their bodies too tender a morsel for fire, and that their gristly bones would scarce leave separable relics after the pyral combustion. That they kindled not fire in their houses for some days after was a strict memorial of the late afflicting fire. And mourning without hope, they had an happy fraud against excessive lamentation, by a common opinion that deep sorrows disturb their ghosts.

That they buried their dead on their backs, or in a supine position, seems agreeable unto profound sleep, and common posture of dying; contrary to the most natural way of birth; nor unlike our pendulous posture, in the doubtful[6] state of the womb. Diogenes was singular, who preferred a prone situation in the grave; and some Christians like neither, who decline the figure of rest, and make choice of an erect posture.

That they carried them out of the world with their feet forward, not inconsonant unto reason, as contrary unto the native posture of man, and his production first into it; and also agreeable unto their opinions, while they bid adieu unto the world, not to look again upon it; whereas Mahometans who think to return to a delightful life again, are carried forth with their heads forward, and looking toward their houses.

They closed their eyes, as parts which first die, or first discover the sad effects of death. But their iterated clamations[7] to excitate[8] their dying or dead friends, or revoke them unto life again, was a vanity of affection; as not presumably ignorant of the critical tests of death, by apposition of feathers, glasses, and reflection of figures, which dead eyes represent not: which, however not strictly verifiable in fresh and warm *cadavers*,[9] could hardly elude the test, in corpses of four or five days.

That they sucked in the last breath of their expiring friends, was surely a practice of no

[1] Believers in the doctrine of the transmigration of souls.
[2] The period was perhaps 25,000 years.
[3] Larch
[4] Sapless.
[5] Signs of the zodiac.
[6] Obscure.
[7] Outcries.
[8] Arouse.
[9] Dead bodies.

medical institution, but a loose opinion that the soul passed out that way, and a fondness of affection, from some Pythagorical foundation, that the spirit of one body passed into another, which they wished might be their own.

That they poured oil upon the pyre, was a tolerable practice, while the intention rested in facilitating the accension.[1] But to place good omens in the quick and speedy burning, to sacrifice unto the winds for a dispatch in this office, was a low form of superstition.

The archimime, or jester, attending the funeral train, and imitating the speeches, gesture, and manners of the deceased, was too light for such solemnities, contradicting their funeral orations and doleful rites of the grave.

That they buried a piece of money with them as a fee of the Elysian ferryman, was a practice full of folly. But the ancient custom of placing coins in considerable urns, and the present practice of burying medals in the noble foundations of Europe, are laudable ways of historical discoveries, in actions, persons, chronologies; and posterity will applaud them.

We examine not the old laws of sepulture, exempting certain persons from burial or burning. But hereby we apprehend that these were not the bones of persons planet-struck or burned with fire from heaven; no relics of traitors to their country, self-killers, or sacrilegious malefactors; persons in old apprehension unworthy of the earth: condemned unto the Tartarus of hell, and bottomless pit of Plato, from whence there was no redemption.

Nor were only many customs questionable in order to their obsequies, but also sundry practices, fictions, and conceptions, discordant or obscure, of their state and future beings. Whether unto eight or ten bodies of men to add one of a woman, as being more inflammable, and unctuously constituted for the better pyral combustion, were any rational practice; or whether the complaint of Periander's wife be tolerable, that wanting her funeral burning, she suffered intolerable cold in hell, according to the constitution of the infernal house of Plato, wherein cold makes a great part of their tortures, it cannot pass without some question.

Why the female ghosts appear unto Ulysses, before the heroes and masculine spirits,—why the Psyche or soul of Tiresias is of the masculine gender, who, being blind on earth, sees more than all the rest in hell; why the funeral suppers consisted of eggs, beans, smallage,[2] and lettuce, since the dead are made to eat asphodels about the Elysian meadows,—why, since there is no sacrifice acceptable, nor any propitiation for the covenant of the grave, men set up the deity of Morta,[3] and fruitlessly adored divinities without ears, it cannot escape some doubt.

The dead seem all alive in the human Hades of Homer, yet cannot well speak, prophesy, or know the living, except they drink blood, wherein is the life of man. And therefore the souls of Penelope's paramours, conducted by Mercury, chirped like bats, and those which followed Hercules, made a noise but like a flock of birds.

The departed spirits know things past and to come; yet are ignorant of things present. Agamemnon foretells what should happen unto Ulysses; yet ignorantly inquires what is become of his own son. The ghosts are afraid of swords in Homer; yet Sibylla tells Æneas in Virgil, the thin habit of spirits was beyond the force of weapons. The spirits put off their malice with their bodies, and Cæsar and Pompey accord in Latin hell; yet Ajax, in Homer, endures not a conference with Ulysses: and Deiphobus appears all mangled in Virgil's ghosts, yet we meet with perfect shadows among the wounded ghosts of Homer.

Since Charon in Lucian applauds his condition among the dead, whether it be handsomely said of Achilles, that living contemner of death, that he had rather be a plowman's servant, than emperor of the dead? How Hercules his soul is in hell, and yet in heaven; and Julius his soul in a star, yet seen by Æneas in hell?—except the ghosts were but images and shadows of the soul, received in higher mansions, according to the ancient division of body, soul, and image, or *simulacrum* of them both. The particulars of future beings must needs be dark unto ancient theories, which Christian philosophy yet determines but in a cloud of opinions. A dialogue between two infants in the womb concerning the state of this world, might handsomely illustrate our ignorance of the next, whereof methinks we

[1] Ignition.

[2] Wild celery.

[3] One of the Fates, goddess of death.

yet discourse in Plato's den, and are but embryon[1] philosophers.

Pythagoras escapes in the fabulous Hell of Dante, among that swarm of philosophers, wherein whilst we meet with Plato and Socrates, Cato is to be found in no lower place than purgatory. Among all the set, Epicurus is most considerable, whom men make honest without an Elysium, who contemned life without encouragement of immortality, and making nothing after death, yet made nothing of the king of terrors.

Were the happiness of the next world as closely apprehended as the felicities of this, it were a martyrdom to live; and unto such as consider none hereafter, it must be more than death to die, which makes us amazed at those audacities that durst be nothing and return into their chaos again. Certainly such spirits as could contemn death, when they expected no better being after, would have scorned to live, had they known any. And therefore we applaud not the judgment of Machiavel, that Christianity makes men cowards, or that with the confidence of but half-dying, the despised virtues of patience and humility have abased the spirits of men, which Pagan principles exalted; but rather regulated the wildness of audacities, in the attempts, grounds, and eternal sequels of death; wherein men of the boldest spirits are often prodigiously temerarious.[2] Nor can we extenuate the valor of ancient martyrs, who contemned death in the uncomfortable scene of their lives, and in their decrepit martyrdoms did probably lose not many months of their days, or parted with life when it was scarce worth the living. For (beside that long time past holds no consideration unto a slender time to come) they had no small disadvantage from the constitution of old age, which naturally makes men fearful; complexionally superannuated from the bold and courageous thoughts of youth and fervent years. But the contempt of death from corporal animosity,[3] promoteth not our felicity.[4] They may sit in the orchestra, and noblest seats of heaven, who have held up shaking hands[5] in the fire, and humanly[6] contended for glory.

Meanwhile Epicurus lies deep in Dante's Hell, wherein we meet with tombs enclosing souls which denied their immortalities. But whether the virtuous heathen, who lived better than he spake, or erring in the principles of himself, yet lived above philosophers of more specious[7] maxims, lie so deep as he is placed, at least so low as not to rise against Christians, who believing or knowing that truth, have lastingly denied it in their practice and conversation—were a query too sad to insist on.

But all or most apprehensions rested in opinions of some future being, which, ignorantly or coldly believed, begat those perverted conceptions, ceremonies, sayings, which Christians pity or laugh at. Happy are they which live not in that disadvantage of time, when men could say little for futurity, but from reason: whereby the noblest minds fell often upon doubtful deaths, and melancholy dissolutions. With these hopes, Socrates warmed his doubtful spirits against that cold potion;[8] and Cato, before he durst give the fatal stroke, spent part of the night in reading the Immortality of Plato, thereby confirming his wavering hand unto the animosity of that attempt.

It is the heaviest stone that melancholy can throw at a man, to tell him he is at the end of his nature; or that there is no further state to come, unto which this seems progressional, and otherwise made in vain. Without this accomplishment,[9] the natural expectation and desire of such a state, were but a fallacy in nature; unsatisfied considerators would quarrel the justice of their constitutions, and rest content that Adam had fallen lower; whereby, by knowing no other original, and deeper ignorance of themselves, they might have enjoyed the happiness of inferior creatures, who in tranquillity possess their constitutions, as having not the apprehension to deplore their own natures, and, being framed below the circumference of these hopes, or cognition of better being, the wisdom of God hath necessitated their contentment: but the superior ingredient and obscured part of ourselves, where to all present felicities afford no resting contentment, will be able at last to tell us, we are more than our present selves, and evacuate such hopes in the fruition of their own accomplishments.

[1] Rudimentary. [2] Foolhardy. [3] High spirits.
[4] Does not bring us a higher reward in heaven.
[5] Shaking, *i. e.*, for fear. [6] With human weakness.

[7] Splendid.
[8] The hemlock, which Socrates had to drink when condemned to death by the Athenians.
[9] Fulfillment.

CHAPTER V

Now since these dead bones have already out-lasted the living ones of Methuselah, and in a yard under ground, and thin walls of clay, out-worn all the strong and specious buildings above it, and quietly rested under the drums and tramplings of three conquests: what prince can promise such diuturnity[1] unto his relics, or might not gladly say,

Sic ego componi versus in ossa velim?[2]

Time, which antiquates antiquities, and hath an art to make dust of all things, hath yet spared these minor monuments.

In vain we hope to be known by open and visible conservatories,[3] when to be unknown was the means of their continuation, and obscurity their protection. If they died by violent hands, and were thrust into their urns, these bones become considerable, and some old philosophers would honor them, whose souls they conceived most pure, which were thus snatched from their bodies, and to retain a stronger propension unto them; whereas they weariedly left a languishing corpse, and with faint desires of re-union. If they fell by long and aged decay, yet wrapped up in the bundle of time, they fall into indistinction,[4] and make but one blot with infants. If we begin to die when we live, and long life be but a prolongation of death, our life is a sad composition; we live with death, and die not in a moment. How many pulses made up the life of Methuselah, were work for Archimedes: common counters sum up the life of Moses his man.[5] Our days become considerable, like petty sums, by minute accumulations; where numerous fractions make up but small round numbers; and our days of a span long, make not one little finger.

If the nearness of our last necessity brought a nearer conformity into it, there were a happiness in hoary hairs, and no calamity in half-senses. But the long habit of living indisposeth us for dying; when avarice makes us the sport of death, when even David grew politicly cruel and Solomon could hardly be said to be the wisest of men. But many are too early old, and before the date of age. Adversity stretcheth our days, misery makes Alcmena's nights,[6] and time hath no wings unto it. But the most tedious being is that which can unwish itself, content to be nothing, or never to have been, which was beyond the malcontent of Job, who cursed not the day of his life, but his nativity; content to have so far been, as to have a title to future being, although he had lived here but in an hidden state of life, and as it were an abortion.

What song the Syrens sang, or what name Achilles assumed when he hid himself among women, though puzzling questions,[7] are not beyond all conjecture. What time the persons of these ossuaries entered the famous nations of the dead, and slept with princes and counselors, might admit a wide solution. But who were the proprietaries of these bones, or what bodies these ashes made up, were a question above antiquarism; not to be resolved by man, nor easily perhaps by spirits, except we consult the provincial guardians, or tutelary observators.[8] Had they made as good provision for their names, as they have done for their relics, they had not so grossly erred in the art of perpetuation. But to subsist in bones, and be but pyramidally[9] extant, is a fallacy in duration. Vain ashes which in the oblivion of names, persons, times, and sexes, have found unto themselves a fruitless continuation, and only arise unto late posterity, as emblems of mortal vanities, antidotes against pride, vain-glory, and madding vices. Pagan vain-glories which thought the world might last for ever, had encouragement for ambition; and, finding no Atropos[10] unto the immortality of their names, were never damped with the necessity of oblivion. Even old ambitions had the advantage of ours, in the attempts of their vain-glories, who acting early, and before the probable meridian of time, have by this time found great accomplishment of their designs, whereby the ancient heroes have already out-lasted their monuments and mechanical preservations. But in this latter scene of time, we cannot ex-

---

[1]Lastingness.

[2]Thus I should wish to be buried when turned to bones (Tibullus, III, ii, 26).

[3]Repositories. [4]Obscurity.

[5]The allusion is to Psalms, xc, 10, where the normal life of man is said to be 70 years.

[6]One night as long as three (Browne's note).

[7]Browne says in a note that these are two of the three questions which Tiberius put to grammarians.

[8]Protecting spirits of the place.

[9]After the manner of a mummy.

[10]One of the Fates. She cut the thread of life.

pect such mummies unto our memories, when ambition may fear the prophecy of Elias, and Charles the Fifth can never hope to live within two Methuselahs of Hector.

And therefore, restless unquiet for the diuturnity of our memories unto present considerations seems a vanity almost out of date, and superannuated piece of folly. We cannot hope to live so long in our names, as some have done in their persons. One face of Janus holds no proportion unto the other. 'Tis too late to be ambitious. The great mutations of the world are acted, or time may be too short for our designs. To extend our memories by monuments, whose death we daily pray for, and whose duration we cannot hope, without injury to our expectations in the advent of the last day, were a contradiction to our beliefs. We whose generations are ordained in this setting part of time, are providentially taken off from such imaginations; and, being necessitated to eye the remaining particle of futurity, are naturally constituted unto thoughts of the next world, and cannot excusably decline the consideration of that duration, which maketh pyramids pillars of snow, and all that's past a moment.

Circles and right lines limit and close all bodies, and the mortal right-lined circle must conclude and shut up all. There is no antidote against the opium of time, which temporally considereth all things: our fathers find their graves in our short memories, and sadly tell us how we may be buried in our survivors. Gravestones tell truth scarce forty years. Generations pass while some trees stand, and old families last not three oaks. To be read by bare inscriptions like many in Gruter,[1] to hope for eternity by enigmatical epithets or first letters of our names, to be studied by antiquaries, who we were, and have new names given us like many of the mummies, are cold consolations unto the students of perpetuity, even by everlasting languages.

To be content that times to come should only know there was such a man, not caring whether they knew more of him, was a frigid ambition in Cardan;[2] disparaging his horoscopical inclination and judgment of himself. Who cares to subsist like Hippocrates' patients, or Achilles' horses in Homer, under naked nominations, without deserts and noble acts, which are the balsam[3] of our memories, the *entelechia*[4] and soul of our subsistences? To be nameless in worthy deeds, exceeds an infamous history. The Canaanitish woman lives more happily without a name, than Herodias with one. And who had not rather been the good thief than Pilate?

But the iniquity of oblivion blindly scattereth her poppy, and deals with the memory of men without distinction to merit of perpetuity. Who can but pity the founder of the pyramids? Herostratus lives that burned the temple of Diana; he is almost lost that built it. Time hath spared the epitaph of Adrian's horse, confounded that of himself. In vain we compute our felicities by the advantage of our good names, since bad have equal durations, and Thersites is like to live as long as Agamemnon. Who knows whether the best of men be known, or whether there be not more remarkable persons forgot, than any that stand remembered in the known account of time? Without the favor of the everlasting register, the first man had been as unknown as the last, and Methuselah's long life had been his only chronicle.

Oblivion is not to be hired. The greater part must be content to be as though they had not been, to be found in the register of God, not in the record of man. Twenty-seven names make up the first story,[5] and the recorded names ever since contain not one living century. The number of the dead long exceedeth all that shall live. The night of time far surpasseth the day, and who knows when was the equinox? Every hour adds unto that current arithmetic,[6] which scarce stands one moment. And since death must be the *Lucina*[7] of life, and even Pagans could doubt, whether thus to live were to die; since our longest sun sets at right descensions, and makes but winter arches, and therefore it cannot be long before we lie down in darkness, and have our light in ashes; since the brother of death daily haunts us with dying mementos, and time that grows old in itself, bids us hope no long duration;—diuturnity is a dream and folly of expectation.

Darkness and light divide the course of time, and oblivion shares with memory a great

[1] A Dutch philologer.

[2] An Italian mathematician, physician, and philosopher.

[3] Preservative.

[4] Entelechy, the soul.

[5] The time before the Flood.

[6] That running account—*i. e.*, continuously moving time.

[7] Goddess of childbirth.

part even of our living beings; we slightly remember our felicities, and the smartest strokes of affliction leave but short smart upon us. Sense endureth no extremities, and sorrows destroy us or themselves. To weep into stones are fables. Afflictions induce callosities;[1] miseries are slippery, or fall like snow upon us, which notwithstanding is no unhappy stupidity. To be ignorant of evils to come, and forgetful of evils past, is a merciful provision in nature, whereby we digest the mixture of our few and evil days, and, our delivered senses not relapsing into cutting remembrances, our sorrows are not kept raw by the edge of repetitions. A great part of antiquity contented their hopes of subsistency with a transmigration of their souls,—a good way to continue their memories, while having the advantage of plural successions, they could not but act something remarkable in such variety of beings, and enjoying the fame of their passed selves, make accumulation of glory unto their last durations. Others, rather than be lost in the uncomfortable night of nothing, were content to recede into the common being, and make one particle of the public soul of all things, which was no more than to return into their unknown and divine original again. Egyptian ingenuity was more unsatisfied, contriving their bodies in sweet consistencies, to attend the return of their souls. But all was vanity, feeding the wind, and folly. The Egyptian mummies, which Cambyses or time hath spared, avarice now consumeth. Mummy is become merchandise,[2] Mizraim[3] cures wounds, and Pharaoh is sold for balsams.

In vain do individuals hope for immortality, or any patent from oblivion, in preservations below the moon; men have been deceived even in their flatteries above the sun, and studied conceits to perpetuate their names in heaven. The various cosmography of that part hath already varied the names of contrived constellations; Nimrod is lost in Orion, and Osyris in the Dog-star. While we look for incorruption in the heavens, we find they are but like the earth;—durable in their main bodies, alterable in their parts; whereof, beside comets and new stars, perspectives[4] begin to tell tales, and the spots that wander about the sun, with Phaeton's favor, would make clear conviction.

There is nothing strictly immortal, but immortality. Whatever hath no beginning, may be confident of no end (all others have a dependent being and within the reach of destruction); which is the peculiar of that necessary Essence that cannot destroy itself; and the highest strain of omnipotency, to be so powerfully constituted as not to suffer even from the power of itself. But the sufficiency of Christian immortality frustrates all earthly glory, and the quality of either state after death, makes a folly of posthumous memory. God who can only[5] destroy our souls, and hath assured our resurrection, either of our bodies or names hath directly promised no duration. Wherein there is so much of chance, that the boldest expectants have found unhappy frustration; and to hold long subsistence, seems but a scape in oblivion.[6] But man is a noble animal, splendid in ashes, and pompous in the grave, solemnizing nativities and deaths with equal luster, nor omitting ceremonies of bravery in the infamy of his nature.

Life is a pure flame, and we live by an invisible sun within us. A small fire sufficeth for life, great flames seemed too little after death, while men vainly affected precious pyres, and to burn like Sardanapalus; but the wisdom of funeral laws found the folly of prodigal blazes, and reduced undoing fires unto the rule of sober obsequies, wherein few could be so mean as not to provide wood, pitch, a mourner, and an urn.

Five languages secured not the epitaph of Gordianus. The man of God lives longer without a tomb, than any by one, invisibly interred by angels, and adjudged to obscurity, though not without some marks directing human discovery. Enoch and Elias, without either tomb or burial, in an anomalous state of being, are the great examples of perpetuity, in their long and living memory, in strict account being still on this side death, and having a late part yet to act upon this stage of earth. If in the decretory term of the world,[7] we shall not all die but be changed, according to received translation, the last day will make but few graves; at least quick resurrections will anticipate lasting sepultures. Some

[1]Cause insensibility.

[2]The substance of mummies was in use as a medicine in Browne's day and before.

[3]Hebrew name of Egypt.

[4]Telescopes.

[5]*I. e.*, who only can.

[6]But a chance of escaping oblivion.

[7]If at the day of judgment.

graves will be opened before they be quite closed, and Lazarus be no wonder. When many that feared to die, shall groan that they can die but once, the dismal state is the second and living death, when life puts despair on the damned; when men shall wish the coverings of mountains, not of monuments, and annihilations shall be courted.

While some have studied monuments, others have studiously declined them, and some have been so vainly boisterous,[1] that they durst not acknowledge their graves; wherein Alaricus seems most subtle, who had a river turned to hide his bones at the bottom. Even Sylla, that thought himself safe in his urn, could not prevent revenging tongues, and stones thrown at his monument. Happy are they whom privacy makes innocent, who deal so with men in this world, that they are not afraid to meet them in the next; who, when they die, make no commotion among the dead, and are not touched with that poetical taunt of Isaiah.[2]

Pyramids, arches, obelisks, were but the irregularities of vain-glory, and wild enormities of ancient magnanimity. But the most magnanimous resolution rests in the Christian religion, which trampleth upon pride, and sits on the neck of ambition, humbly pursuing that infallible perpetuity, unto which all others must diminish their diameters, and be poorly seen in angles of contingency.

[1]Turbulent.

[2]*Cf.* Isaiah, xiv, 9, and following verses.

Pious spirits who passed their days in raptures of futurity, made little more of this world, than the world that was before it, while they lay obscure in the chaos of preordination, and night of their fore-beings. And if any have been so happy as truly to understand Christian annihilation, ecstasies, exolution, liquefaction, transformation, the kiss of the spouse, gustation of God, and ingression into the divine shadow,[3] they have already had an handsome anticipation of heaven; the glory of the world is surely over, and the earth in ashes unto them.

To subsist in lasting monuments, to live in their productions, to exist in their names and predicament of chimæras,[4] was large satisfaction unto old expectations, and made one part of their Elysiums. But all this is nothing in the metaphysics of true belief. To live indeed, is to be again ourselves, which being not only an hope, but an evidence in noble believers, 'tis all one to lie in St. Innocents' church-yard, as in the sands of Egypt. Ready to be anything, in the ecstasy of being ever, and as content with six foot as the *moles* of Adrianus.[5]

—tabesne cadavera solvat,
An rogus, haud refert.[6]

[3]These terms are descriptive of the experiences of mystics.

[4]Condition of unfounded conceptions.

[5]The monument of Hadrian, now known in its altered form as the castle of St. Angelo.

[6]It matters not whether our bodies rot in the grave or are consumed by the funeral pyre (Lucan, *Pharsalia*, VII, 809–810).

IZAAK WALTON (1593–1683)

Walton was born at Stafford on 9 August, 1593. Of his youth and education nothing is known—and indeed little enough is known of the whole course of his long life. He obeyed a text which he more than once used: "Study to be quiet, and to do your own business" (I Thessalonians, iv, 11). He was in London by 1611, and in 1618 was admitted a "free brother" of the Ironmongers' Company. He followed his trade in Fleet Street and in Chancery Lane for many years, though just when he abandoned active connection with it cannot be determined. He left his house in Chancery Lane in 1644, because it had become a dangerous neighborhood "for honest men"—that is, for Royalists. But he probably did not then leave London. He is said to have been living in Clerkenwell in 1650. Meanwhile on 27 December, 1626, he had married Rachel Floud of Canterbury. Their carved marriage-chest, for which Walton wrote an inscription, is now in the hall of Warwick Castle. Rachel Walton died in 1640, having borne her husband six children, all of whom died in infancy. In 1646 Walton married Anne Ken, a half-sister of Bishop Ken of Winchester, who bore him three children, of whom a daughter and a son survived him. Anne Walton died at Worcester in 1662. George Morley, then Bishop of Worcester, later Bishop of Winchester, had appointed Walton his steward, and much of his time during his later years was spent at Farnham Castle, the bishop's residence. During these years he also lived at times with his daughter, whose husband was Prebendary of Winchester, and in her home he died on 15 December, 1683. He was buried in a chapel of the Cathedral, in accordance with a request in his will: "I desire my burial may be near the place of my death; and free from any ostentation or charge, but privately."

Walton must have been from his youth interested in literature, and he must also have been, all his life, a reading man. He was besides, as everybody knows, a devoted fisherman. Guileless, simple, easy, charming, he had a genius for friendship, though—as his younger friend Charles Cotton said plainly—he was not everybody's friend: "My father Walton will be seen twice in no man's company he does not like, and likes none but such as he believes to be very honest men." Amongst these "very honest men" were Ben Jonson, Michael Drayton, John Hales of Eton, Henry King, Thomas Fuller; Sir Henry Wotton, and John Donne. And out of his friendships and "the contemplative man's recreation" issued Walton's unassuming and singularly perfect writings. When he began to write cannot be known, but his earliest publication was an elegy on Donne, printed in the first edition of Donne's *Poems* in 1633. Thereafter he collected material for a biography of Donne which their common friend Sir Henry Wotton intended to write. But Wotton died without having written it, and Walton then took up the task, and his *Life of Donne* was published with Donne's *LXXX Sermons*, 1640. Eleven years later the *Life of Wotton* was published in *Reliquiae Wottonianae*, and in 1653 appeared the first edition of *The Compleat Angler*. Walton modestly thought, "Most readers may receive so much pleasure or profit by it as may make it worthy the time of their perusal, if they be not very busy men." He disallowed "severe, sour-complexioned men" to be competent judges of his book, and these have in fact held their peace; for no dissenting voice has marred the chorus of grateful and affectionate praise which has followed the quiet angler and biographer down the years. The *Life of Hooker* was first published in 1665, the *Life of Herbert* in 1670, and the *Life of Bishop Sanderson* in 1678. Walton had seen Herbert, but did not know him; yet this, to some readers, remains the most vivid and charming of the *Lives*.

THE LIFE OF MR. GEORGE HERBERT[1] (1670)

George Herbert was born the third day of April, in the Year of our Redemption 1593. The place of his birth was near to the town of Montgomery, and in that Castle that did then bear the name of that town and county; that Castle was then a place of state and strength, and had been successively happy in the family of the Herberts, who had long possessed it; and with it, a plentiful estate, and hearts as

[1]In the main Walton gives the facts correctly, and his few unimportant mistakes are here allowed to pass uncorrected. But it should be remembered that "he paints us the Saint of Bemerton. And while too honest to conceal discordant facts from him who will search his pages, he contrives to throw so strong a light on Herbert's three consecrated years that few readers notice how unlike these are to his vacillating thirty-six." (G. H. Palmer.)

liberal to their poor neighbors. A family, that hath been blessed with men of remarkable wisdom, and a willingness to serve their country, and, indeed, to do good to all mankind; for which they are eminent: But alas! this family did in the late rebellion suffer extremely in their estates; and the heirs of that Castle saw it laid level with that earth, that was too good to bury those wretches that were the cause of it.

The father of our George was Richard Herbert, the son of Edward Herbert, Knight, the son of Richard Herbert, Knight, the son of the famous Sir Richard Herbert of Colebrook, in the County of Monmouth, Banneret, who was the youngest brother of that memorable William Herbert, Earl of Pembroke, that lived in the reign of our King Edward the Fourth.

His mother was Magdalen Newport, the youngest daughter of Sir Richard, and sister to Sir Francis Newport of High-Arkall, in the County of Salop, Knight, and grandfather of Francis Lord Newport, now Controller of his Majesty's Household. A family that for their loyalty have suffered much in their estates, and seen the ruin of that excellent structure, where their ancestors have long lived, and been memorable for their hospitality.

This mother of George Herbert—of whose person, and wisdom, and virtue I intend to give a true account in a seasonable place—was the happy mother of seven sons and three daughters, which she would often say was Job's number, and Job's distribution; and as often bless God, that they were neither defective in their shapes, or in their reason; and very often reprove them that did not praise God for so great a blessing. I shall give the reader a short account of their names, and not say much of their fortunes.

Edward, the eldest, was first made Knight of the Bath, at that glorious time of our late Prince Henry's being installed Knight of the Garter; and after many years' useful travel, and the attainment of many languages, he was by King James sent Ambassador resident to the then French King, Lewis the Thirteenth. There he continued about two years; but he could not subject himself to a compliance with the humors of the Duke de Luisnes, who was then the great and powerful favorite at Court: so that upon a complaint to our King, he was called back into England in some displeasure; but at his return he gave such an honorable account of his employment, and so justified his comportment to the Duke and all the Court, that he was suddenly sent back upon the same Embassy, from which he returned in the beginning of the reign of our good King Charles the First, who made him first Baron of Castle-Island, and not long after of Cherbury, in the County of Salop. He was a man of great learning and reason, as appears by his printed book, *De Veritate*, and by his *History of the Reign of King Henry the Eighth*, and by several other tracts.

The second and third brothers were Richard and William, who ventured their lives to purchase honor in the wars of the Low Countries, and died officers in that employment. Charles was the fourth, and died fellow of New College in Oxford. Henry was the sixth, who became a menial servant to the Crown in the days of King James, and hath continued to be so for fifty years; during all which time he hath been Master of the Revels; a place that requires a diligent wisdom, with which God hath blessed him. The seventh son was Thomas, who, being made captain of a ship in that fleet with which Sir Robert Mansell was sent against Algiers, did there show a fortunate and true English valor. Of the three sisters I need not say more than that they were all married to persons of worth, and plentiful fortunes; and lived to be examples of virtue, and to do good in their generations.

I now come to give my intended account of George, who was the fifth of those seven brothers.

George Herbert spent much of his childhood in a sweet content under the eye and care of his prudent mother, and the tuition of a chaplain, or tutor to him and two of his brothers, in her own family—for she was then a widow—where he continued till about the age of twelve years; and being at that time well instructed in the rules of grammar, he was not long after commended to the care of Dr. Neale, who was then Dean of Westminster; and by him to the care of Mr. Ireland, who was then Chief Master of that School; where the beauties of his pretty behavior and wit shined, and became so eminent and lovely in this his innocent age, that he seemed to be marked out for piety, and to become the care of Heaven, and of a particular good angel to guard and guide him. And thus he continued in that School, till he came to be perfect in the learned languages, and especially in the Greek tongue, in which he after proved an excellent critic.

About the age of fifteen—he being then a King's Scholar—he was elected out of that School for Trinity College in Cambridge, to which place he was transplanted about the year 1608; and his prudent mother, well knowing that he might easily lose or lessen that virtue and innocence which her advice and example had planted in his mind, did therefore procure the generous and liberal Dr. Nevil, who was then Dean of Canterbury, and Master of that College, to take him into his particular care, and provide him a tutor; which he did most gladly undertake, for he knew the excellencies of his mother, and how to value such a friendship.

This was the method of his education, till he was settled in Cambridge; where we will leave him in his study, till I have paid my promised account of his excellent mother; and I will endeavor to make it short.

I have told her birth, her marriage, and the number of her children, and have given some short account of them. I shall next tell the reader that her husband died when our George was about the age of four years: I am next to tell, that she continued twelve years a widow; that she then married happily to a noble gentleman, the brother and heir of the Lord Danvers, Earl of Danby, who did highly value both her person and the most excellent endowments of her mind.

In this time of her widowhood, she being desirous to give Edward, her eldest son, such advantages of learning, and other education, as might suit his birth and fortune, and thereby make him the more fit for the service of his country, did, at his being of a fit age, remove from Montgomery Castle with him, and some of her younger sons, to Oxford; and having entered Edward into Queen's College, and provided him a fit tutor, she commended him to his care, yet she continued there with him, and still kept him in a moderate awe of herself, and so much under her own eye as to see and converse with him daily: but she managed this power over him without any such rigid sourness as might make her company a torment to her child; but with such a sweetness and compliance with the recreations and pleasures of youth, as did incline him willingly to spend much of his time in the company of his dear and careful mother; which was to her great content: for she would often say, "That as our bodies take a nourishment suitable to the meat on which we feed; so our souls do as insensibly take in vice by the example or conversation with wicked company": and would therefore as often say, "That ignorance of vice was the best preservation of virtue; and that the very knowledge of wickedness was as tinder to inflame and kindle sin and to keep it burning." For these reasons she endeared him to her own company, and continued with him in Oxford four years; in which time her great and harmless wit, her cheerful gravity, and her obliging behavior, gained her an acquaintance and friendship with most of any eminent worth or learning, that were at that time in or near that University; and particularly with Mr. John Donne, who then came accidentally to that place, in this time of her being there. It was that John Donne who was after Dr. Donne, and Dean of St. Paul's, London: and he, at his leaving Oxford, writ and left there, in verse, a character of the beauties of her body and mind: of the first he says,

No Spring nor Summer-beauty has such grace
As I have seen in an Autumnal face.

Of the latter he says,

In all her words to every hearer fit,
You may at revels, or at council sit.

The rest of her character may be read in his printed poems, in that elegy which bears the name of *The Autumnal Beauty*. For both he and she were then past the meridian of man's life.

This amity, begun at this time and place, was not an amity that polluted their souls; but an amity made up of a chain of suitable inclinations and virtues; an amity like that of St. Chrysostom's to his dear and virtuous Olympias; whom, in his letters, he calls his Saint: or an amity, indeed, more like that of St. Jerome to his Paula; whose affection to her was such that he turned poet in his old age, and then made her epitaph: wishing all his body were turned into tongues, that he might declare her just praises to posterity. And this amity betwixt her and Mr. Donne was begun in a happy time for him, he being then near to the fortieth year of his age (which was some years before he entered into Sacred Orders), a time when his necessities needed a daily supply for the support of his wife, seven children, and a family. And in this time she proved one of his most bountiful benefactors; and he as grateful an acknowledger of it.[1] * * *

And much more might be said of her great prudence and piety: but my design was not to write hers, bat the life of her son; and therefore I shall only tell my reader that [twenty years thereafter] I saw and heard this Mr. John Donne—who was then Dean of St. Paul's—weep, and preach her Funeral Sermon, in the Parish Church of Chelsea, near London, where she now rests in her quiet grave: and where we must now leave her, and return to her son George, whom we left in his study in Cambridge.

And in Cambridge we may find our George Herbert's behavior to be such that we may conclude he consecrated the first-fruits of his early age to virtue, and a serious study of learning. And that he did so, this following letter and sonnet, which were, in the first year of his going to Cambridge, sent his dear mother for a New-Year's gift, may appear to be some testimony.

But I fear the heat of my late ague hath dried up those springs, by which scholars say the Muses use to take up their habitations. However, I need not their help to reprove the vanity of those many love-poems that are daily writ, and consecrated to Venus; nor to bewail that so few are writ that look towards God and Heaven. For my own part, my meaning—dear Mother—is, in these sonnets, to declare my resolution to be, that my poor abilities in poetry shall be all and ever consecrated to God's glory: and I beg you to receive this as one testimony.

My God, where is that ancient heat towards thee,
  Wherewith whole shoals of martyrs once did burn,
  Besides their other flames? Doth Poetry
Wear Venus' livery? only serve her turn?
Why are not sonnets made of thee? and lays
  Upon thine altar burned? Cannot thy love
  Heighten a spirit to sound out thy praise
As well as any she? Cannot thy Dove
Outstrip their Cupid easily in flight?
  Or, since thy ways are deep, and still the same,
  Will not a verse run smooth that bears thy name?
Why doth that fire, which by thy power and might
  Each breast does feel, no braver fuel choose
  Than that, which one day, worms may chance refuse?
Sure, Lord, there is enough in thee to dry
  Oceans of ink; for as the Deluge did
  Cover the earth, so doth thy Majesty;
Each cloud distils thy praise, and doth forbid
Poets to turn it to another use.
  Roses and lilies speak Thee; and to make
  A pair of cheeks of them, is thy abuse.
Why should I women's eyes for crystal take?
Such poor invention burns in their low mind
  Whose fire is wild, and doth not upward go
  To praise, and on thee, Lord, some ink bestow.
Open the bones, and you shall nothing find
  In the best face but filth; when, Lord, in Thee
  The beauty lies in the discovery.

G. H.

This was his resolution at the sending this letter to his dear mother, about which time he was in the seventeenth year of his age: and as he grew older, so he grew in learning, and more and more in favor both with God and man: insomuch that, in this morning of that short day of his life, he seemed to be marked out for virtue, and to become the care of Heaven; for God still kept his soul in so holy a frame that he may, and ought to be, a pattern of virtue to all posterity, and especially to his brethren of the clergy, of which the reader may expect a more exact account in what will follow.

I need not declare that he was a strict student, because, that he was so, there will be many testimonies in the future part of his life. I shall therefore only tell that he was made Bachelor of Arts in the year 1611; Major Fellow of the College, March 15, 1615: and that in that year he was also made Master of Arts, he being then in the twenty-second year of his age; during all which time, all, or the greatest diversion from his study, was the practice of music, in which he became a great master; and of which he would say, "That it did relieve his drooping spirits, compose his distracted thoughts, and raised his weary soul so far above earth that it gave him an earnest of the joys of Heaven, before he possessed them." And it may be noted, that from his first entrance into the College, the generous Dr. Nevil was a cherisher of his studies, and such a lover of his person, his behavior, and the excellent endowments of his mind, that he took him often into his own company; by

[1] A letter from Donne bearing witness to his gratitude, and also a poem of his, follow; but are here omitted.

which he confirmed his native gentleness: and if during this time he expressed any error, it was that he kept himself too much retired, and at too great a distance with all his inferiors; and his clothes seemed to prove that he put too great a value on his parts and parentage.

This may be some account of his disposition, and of the employment of his time till he was Master of Arts, which was *anno* 1615, and in the year 1619 he was chosen Orator for the University. His two precedent Orators were Sir Robert Naunton, and Sir Francis Nethersole. The first was not long after made Secretary of State, and Sir Francis, not very long after his being Orator, was made Secretary to the Lady Elizabeth, Queen of Bohemia. In this place of Orator our George Herbert continued eight years; and managed it with as becoming and grave a gayety, as any had ever before or since his time. For "he had acquired great learning, and was blessed with a high fancy, a civil and sharp wit; and with a natural elegance, both in his behavior, his tongue, and his pen." Of all which there might be very many particular evidences; but I will limit myself to the mention of but three.

And the first notable occasion of showing his fitness for this employment of Orator was manifested in a letter to King James, upon the occasion of his sending that University his book called *Basilicon Doron;* and their Orator was to acknowledge this great honor, and return their gratitude to his Majesty for such a condescension; at the close of which letter he writ,

Quid Vaticanam Bodleianamque objicis, hospes!
Unicus est nobis Bibliotheca Liber.[1]

This letter was writ in such excellent Latin, was so full of conceits, and all the expressions so suited to the genius of the King, that he inquired the Orator's name, and then asked William, Earl of Pembroke, if he knew him? whose answer was, "That he knew him very well, and that he was his kinsman; but he loved him more for his learning and virtue than for that he was of his name and family." At which answer the King smiled, and asked the Earl leave "that he might love him too, for he took him to be the jewel of that University."

[1]What though you reproach us with [the superiority of] the Vatican and Bodleian [libraries], O stranger! This single book is a library to us.

The next occasion he had and took to show his great abilities was, with them, to show also his great affection to that Church in which he received his baptism, and of which he professed himself a member; and the occasion was this: There was one Andrew Melvin,[2] a Minister of the Scotch Church, and Rector of St. Andrew's; who, by a long and constant converse with a discontented part of that Clergy which opposed Episcopacy, became at last to be a chief leader of that faction; and had proudly appeared to be so to King James, when he was but King of that nation, who, the second year after his coronation in England, convened a part of the Bishops, and other learned Divines of his Church, to attend him at Hampton Court, in order to a friendly conference with some dissenting brethren, both of this and the Church of Scotland: of which Scotch party Andrew Melvin was one; and he being a man of learning, and inclined to satirical poetry, had scattered many malicious, bitter verses against our liturgy, our ceremonies, and our church-government; which were by some of that party so magnified for the wit, that they were therefore brought into Westminster School, where Mr. George Herbert then, and often after, made such answers to them, and such reflections on him and his Kirk, as might unbeguile any man that was not too deeply pre-engaged in such a quarrel.—But to return to Mr. Melvin at Hampton Court Conference; he there appeared to be a man of an unruly wit, of a strange confidence, of so furious a zeal, and of so ungoverned passions, that his insolence to the King, and others at this Conference, lost him both his Rectorship of St. Andrew's and his liberty too; for his former verses, and his present reproaches there used against the Church and State, caused him to be committed prisoner to the Tower of London; where he remained very angry for three years. At which time of his commitment, he found the Lady Arabella[3] an innocent prisoner there; and he pleased himself much in sending, the next day after his commitment, these two verses to the good lady; which I will under-

[2]Properly, Andrew Melville (1545–1622).

[3]The Lady Arabella Stuart (*c.* 1575–1615), daughter of the younger brother of King James's father (Darnley), and thought to be a probable heir to the crown. She incurred James's displeasure by marrying William Seymour (1610) and was from that time confined to the Tower until her death.

write, because they may give the reader a taste of his others, which were like these.

Causa tibi mecum est communis, carceris, Ara-
Bella, tibi causa est, Araque sacra mihi.[1]

I shall not trouble my reader with an account of his enlargement from that prison, or his death; but tell him Mr. Herbert's verses were thought so worthy to be preserved that Dr. Duport, the learned Dean of Peterborough, hath lately collected and caused many of them to be printed, as an honorable memorial of his friend Mr. George Herbert, and the cause he undertook.

And in order to my third and last observation of his great abilities, it will be needful to declare that about this time King James came very often to hunt at Newmarket and Royston, and was almost as often invited to Cambridge, where his entertainment was comedies, suited to his pleasant humor; and where Mr. George Herbert was to welcome him with gratulations, and the applauses of an Orator; which he always performed so well that he still grew more into the King's favor, insomuch that he had a particular appointment to attend his Majesty at Royston; where, after a discourse with him, his Majesty declared to his kinsman, the Earl of Pembroke, "that he found the Orator's learning and wisdom much above his age or wit." The year following, the King appointed to end his progress at Cambridge, and to stay there certain days; at which time he was attended by the great Secretary of Nature and all learning, Sir Francis Bacon, Lord Verulam, and by the ever-memorable and learned Dr. Andrews, Bishop of Winchester, both which did at that time begin a desired friendship with our Orator. Upon whom, the first put such a value on his judgment, that he usually desired his approbation before he would expose any of his books to be printed; and thought him so worthy of his friendship that, having translated many of the Prophet David's Psalms into English verse, he made George Herbert his patron, by a public dedication of them to him, as the best judge of Divine Poetry. And for the learned Bishop, it is observable, that at that time there fell to be a modest debate betwixt them two about predestination, and sanctity of life; of both of which the Orator did, not long after, send the Bishop some safe and useful aphorisms, in a long letter, written in Greek; which letter was so remarkable for the language and reason of it, that, after the reading it, the Bishop put it into his bosom, and did often show it to many scholars, both of this and foreign nations; but did always return it back to the place where he first lodged it, and continued it so near his heart till the last day of his life.

To these I might add the long and entire friendship betwixt him and Sir Henry Wotton, and Dr. Donne; but I have promised to contract myself, and shall therefore only add one testimony to what is also mentioned in the *Life* of Dr. Donne; namely, that a little before his death he caused many seals to be made, and in them to be engraven the figure of Christ, crucified on an Anchor—the emblem of hope—and of which Dr. Donne would often say, "*Crux mihi anchora.*"[2]—These seals he gave or sent to most of those friends on which he put a value: and, at Mr. Herbert's death, these verses were found wrapped up with that seal which was by the Doctor given to him:

When my dear friend could write no more,
He gave this *Seal* and so gave o'er.

When winds and waves rise highest I am sure,
This *Anchor* keeps my faith, that, me secure.

At this time of being Orator, he had learned to understand the Italian, Spanish, and French tongues very perfectly: hoping, that as his predecessors, so he might in time attain the place of a Secretary of State, he being at that time very high in the King's favor, and not meanly valued and loved by the most eminent and most powerful of the Court Nobility. This, and the love of a Court-conversation, mixed with a laudable ambition to be something more than he then was, drew him often from Cambridge, to attend the King wheresoever the Court was, who then gave him a sinecure, which fell into his Majesty's disposal, I think, by the death of the Bishop of St. Asaph. It was the same that Queen Elizabeth had formerly given to her favorite Sir Philip Sidney, and valued to be worth an hundred and twenty pounds *per annum.* With this, and his annuity, and the

[1]The cause of our imprisonment, Arabella, is common to us both; the cause of yours, and of mine, is a sacred altar.

[2]The Cross is my anchor.

advantage of his College, and of his Oratorship, he enjoyed hi genteel humor for clothes, and Court-like company, and seldom looked towards Cambridge, unless the King were there, but then he never failed; and, at other times, left the manage of his Orator's place to his learned friend, Mr. Herbert Thorndike, who is now Prebend of Westminster.

I may not omit to tell that he had often designed to leave the University, and decline all study, which he thought did impair his health; for he had a body apt to a consumption, and to fevers, and other infirmities, which he judged were increased by his studies; for he would often say, "He had too thoughtful a wit; a wit like a penknife in too narrow a sheath, too sharp for his body." But his mother would by no means allow him to leave the University, or to travel; and though he inclined very much to both, yet he would by no means satisfy his own desires at so dear a rate as to prove an undutiful son to so affectionate a mother; but did always submit to her wisdom. And what I have now said may partly appear in a copy of verses in his printed poems; 'tis one of those that bear the title of *Affliction*;[1] and it appears to be a pious reflection on God's providence, and some passages of his life, in which he says:

Whereas my birth and spirit rather took
  The way that takes the town:
Thou didst betray me to a lingering book,
  And wrap me in a gown:
I was entangled in a world of strife,
Before I had the power to change my life.

Yet, for I threatened oft the siege to raise,
  Not simpering all mine age;
Thou often didst with academic praise
  Melt and dissolve my rage:
I took the sweetened pill, till I came where
I could not go away, nor persevere.

Yet, lest perchance I should too happy be
  In my unhappiness,
Turning my purge to food, thou throwest me
  Into more sicknesses.
Thus dost thy power cross-bias me, not making
Thine own gifts good, yet me from my ways taking.

Now I am here, what thou wilt do with me
  None of my books will show.
I read, and sigh, and wish I were a tree,
  For then sure I should grow
To fruit or shade, at least some bird would trust
Her household with me, and I would be just.

Yet, though thou troublest me, I must be meek,
  In weakness must be stout,
Well, I will change my service, and go seek
  Some other master out;
Ah, my dear God! though I am clean forgot,
Let me not love thee, if I love thee not.

G. H.

In this time of Mr. Herbert's attendance and expectation of some good occasion to remove from Cambridge to Court, God, in whom there is an unseen chain of causes, did in a short time put an end to the lives of two of his most obliging and most powerful friends, Lodowick, Duke of Richmond, and James, Marquis of Hamilton; and not long after him King James died also, and with them all Mr. Herbert's Court-hopes: so that he presently betook himself to a retreat from London, to a friend in Kent, where he lived very privately, and was such a lover of solitariness, as was judged to impair his health, more than his study had done. In this time of retirement, he had many conflicts with himself, whether he should return to the painted pleasures of a Court-life, or betake himself to a study of Divinity, and enter into Sacred Orders, to which his dear mother had often persuaded him. These were such conflicts as they only can know that have endured them; for ambitious desires, and the outward glory of this world, are not easily laid aside; but at last God inclined him to put on a resolution to serve at his altar.

He did, at his return to London, acquaint a Court-friend with his resolution to enter into Sacred Orders, who persuaded him to alter it, as too mean an employment, and too much below his birth, and the excellent abilities and endowments of his mind. To whom he replied, "It hath been formerly judged that the domestic servants of the King of Heaven should be of the noblest families on earth. And though the iniquity of the late times have made clergymen meanly valued, and the sacred name of priest contemptible; yet I will labor to make it honorable, by consecrating all my learning, and all my poor abilities to advance the glory of that God that gave them; knowing that I can never do too much for him, that hath done so much for me as to make me a Christian. And I will labor to

[1]Five of Herbert's poems bear this title. Walton quotes stanzas 7–11 of the one beginning: "When first thou didst entice."

be like my Savior, by making humility lovely in the eyes of all men, and by following the merciful and meek example of my dear Jesus."

This was then his resolution; and the God of constancy, who intended him for a great example of virtue, continued him in it, for within that year he was made Deacon, but the day when, or by whom, I cannot learn; but that he was about that time made Deacon is most certain; for I find by the Records of Lincoln, that he was made Prebend of Layton Ecclesia, in the Diocese of Lincoln, July 15th, 1626, and that this Prebend was given him by John, then Lord Bishop of that See. And now he had a fit occasion to show that piety and bounty that was derived from his generous mother, and his other memorable ancestors, and the occasion was this.

This Layton Ecclesia is a village near to Spalden, in the County of Huntington, and the greatest part of the parish church was fallen down, and that of it which stood was so decayed, so little, and so useless, that the parishioners could not meet to perform their duty to God in public prayer and praises; and thus it had been for almost twenty years, in which time there had been some faint endeavors for a public collection to enable the parishioners to rebuild it; but with no success, till Mr. Herbert undertook it; and he, by his own, and the contribution of many of his kindred, and other noble friends, undertook the re-edification of it; and made it so much his whole business, that he became restless till he saw it finished as it now stands; being for the workmanship, a costly mosaic; for the form, an exact cross; and for the decency and beauty, I am assured, it is the most remarkable parish church that this nation affords. He lived to see it so wainscoted as to be exceeded by none; and, by his order, the reading pew and pulpit were a little distant from each other, and both of an equal height; for he would often say, "They should neither have a precedency or priority of the other; but that prayer and preaching, being equally useful, might agree like brethren, and have an equal honor and estimation."

Before I proceed farther, I must look back to the time of Mr. Herbert's being made Prebend, and tell the reader that not long after, his mother being informed of his intentions to rebuild that church, and apprehending the great trouble and charge that he was like to draw upon himself, his relations and friends, before it could be finished, sent for him from London to Chelsea—where she then dwelt—and at his coming, said, "George, I sent for you, to persuade you to commit simony, by giving your patron as good a gift as he has given to you; namely, that you give him back his prebend; for, George, it is not for your weak body, and empty purse, to undertake to build churches." Of which, he desired he might have a day's time to consider, and then make her an answer. And at his return to her the next day, when he had first desired her blessing, and she given it him, his next request was, "That she would at the age of thirty-three years, allow him to become an undutiful son: for he had made a vow to God, that, if he were able, he would rebuild that church." And then showed her such reasons for his resolution, that she presently subscribed to be one of his benefactors; and undertook to solicit William, Earl of Pembroke, to become another, who subscribed for fifty pounds; and not long after, by a witty and persuasive letter from Mr. Herbert, made it fifty pounds more. And in this nomination of some of his benefactors, James, Duke of Lenox, and his brother, Sir Henry Herbert, ought to be remembered; as also the bounty of Mr. Nicholas Farrer,[1] and Mr. Arthur Woodnot: the one a gentleman in the neighborhood of Layton, and the other a goldsmith in Foster Lane, London, ought not to be forgotten: for the memory of such men ought to outlive their lives. Of Mr. Farrer, I shall hereafter give an account in a more seasonable place; but before I proceed farther, I will give this short account of Mr. Arthur Woodnot.

He was a man that had considered overgrown estates do often require more care and watchfulness to preserve than get them, and considered that there be many discontents, that riches cure not; and did therefore set limits to himself, as to desire of wealth. And having attained so much as to be able to show some mercy to the poor, and preserve a competence for himself, he dedicated the remaining part of his life to the service of God, and to be useful for his friends; and he proved to be so to Mr. Herbert; for besides his own bounty, he collected and returned most of the money that was paid for the re-

[1]Properly, Ferrar (1593–1637).

building of that church; he kept all the account of the charges, and would often go down to state them, and see all the workmen paid. When I have said that this good man was a useful friend to Mr. Herbert's father, and to his mother, and continued to be so to him, till he closed his eyes on his death-bed; I will forbear to say more, till I have the next fair occasion to mention the holy friendship that was betwixt him and Mr. Herbert. From whom Mr. Woodnot carried to his mother this following letter, and delivered it to her in a sickness, which was not long before that which proved to be her last.

A LETTER OF MR. GEORGE HERBERT TO HIS MOTHER IN HER SICKNESS.

MADAM,

At my last parting from you, I was the better content, because I was in hope I should myself carry all sickness out of your family: but since I know I did not and that your share continues, or rather increaseth, I wish earnestly that I were again with you; and would quickly make good my wish, but that my employment does fix me here, it being now but a month to our commencement: wherein my absence, by how much it naturally augmenteth suspicion, by so much shall it make my prayers the more constant and the more earnest for you to the God of all consolation.—In the mean time, I beseech you to be cheerful, and comfort yourself in the God of all comfort, who is not willing to behold any sorrow but for sin.—What hath affliction grievous in it more than for a moment? or why should our afflictions here have so much power or boldness as to oppose the hope of our joys hereafter?—Madam, as the earth is but a point in respect of the heavens, so are earthly troubles compared to heavenly joys; therefore, if either age or sickness lead you to those joys, consider what advantage you have over youth and health, who are now so near those true comforts. Your last letter gave me earthly preferment, and I hope kept heavenly for yourself: but would you divide and choose too? Our College customs allow not that: and I should account myself most happy, if I might change with you; for I have always observed the thread of life to be like other threads or skeins of silk, full of snarls and encumbrances. Happy is he, whose bottom is wound up, and laid ready for work in the New Jerusalem.—For myself, dear Mother, I always feared sickness more than death, because sickness hath made me unable to perform those offices for which I came into the world, and must yet be kept in it; but you are freed from that fear, who have already abundantly discharged that part, having both ordered your family and so brought up your children, that they have attained to the years of discretion, and competent maintenance. So that now, if they do not well, the fault cannot be charged on you, whose example and care of them will justify you both to the world and your own conscience; insomuch that, whether you turn your thoughts on the life past, or on the joys that are to come, you have strong preservatives against all disquiet. And for temporal afflictions, I beseech you consider, all that can happen to you are either afflictions of estate, or body, or mind. For those of estate, of what poor regard ought they to be? since, if we had riches, we are commanded to give them away: so that the best use of them is, having, not to have them. But perhaps, being above the common people, our credit and estimation calls on us to live in a more splendid fashion: but, O God! how easily is that answered, when we consider that the blessings in the holy Scripture are never given to the rich, but to the poor. I never find "Blessed be the rich," or "Blessed be the noble"; but, "Blessed be the meek," and, "Blessed be the poor," and, "Blessed be the mourners, for they shall be comforted."—And yet, O God! most carry themselves so, as if they not only not desired, but even feared to be blessed.—And for afflictions of the body, dear Madam, remember the holy martyrs of God, how they have been burned by thousands, and have endured such other tortures as the very mention of them might beget amazement: but their fiery trials have had an end; and yours—which, praised be God, are less—are not like to continue long. I beseech you, let such thoughts as these moderate your present fear and sorrow; and know that if any of yours should prove a Goliah-like trouble, yet you may say with David, "That God, who hath delivered me out of the paws of the lion and bear, will also deliver me out of the hands of this uncircumcised Philistine."—Lastly, for those afflictions of the soul; consider that God intends that to be as a Sacred Temple for himself to dwell in, and will not allow any room there for such an inmate as grief; or allow that any sadness shall be his competitor. And, above all, if any care of future things molest you, remember those admirable words of the Psalmist: "Cast thy care on the Lord, and he shall nourish thee." To which join that of St. Peter, "Casting all your care on the Lord, for he careth for you." What an admirable thing is this, that God puts his shoulder to our burden, and entertains our care for us, that we may the more quietly intend his service! To conclude, let me commend only one place more to you: Philipp. iv. 4. St. Paul saith there, "Rejoice in the Lord always: and again I say, rejoice." He doubles it to take away the scruple of those that might say, What, shall we rejoice in afflictions? Yes, I say again, rejoice; so that it is not left to us to rejoice, or not rejoice; but, whatsoever befalls us, we must always, at all times, rejoice in the Lord, who taketh care for us. And it follows in the next verse: "Let your moderation appear to all men: The Lord is at hand: Be careful for nothing." What can be said more comfortably? Trouble not yourselves; God is at hand, to deliver us from all, or in all.—Dear Madam, pardon my boldness, and accept the good meaning of

Your most obedient son,
GEORGE HERBERT.

TRINITY COLLEGE, May 25, 1622.

About the year 1629, and the thirty-fourth of his age, Mr. Herbert was seized with a sharp quotidian ague, and thought to remove it by the change of air; to which end, he went to Woodford in Essex, but thither more chiefly to enjoy the company of his beloved brother, Sir Henry Herbert, and other friends then of that family. In his house he remained about twelve months, and there became his own physician, and cured himself of his ague, by forbearing drink, and not eating any meat, no not mutton, nor a hen, or pigeon, unless they were salted; and by such a constant diet he removed his ague, but with inconveniences that were worse; for he brought upon himself a disposition to rheums, and other weaknesses, and a supposed consumption. And it is to be noted that in the sharpest of his extreme fits he would often say, "Lord, abate my great affliction, or increase my patience: but Lord, I repine not; I am dumb, Lord, before thee, because thou doest it." By which, and a sanctified submission to the will of God, he showed he was inclinable to bear the sweet yoke of Christian discipline, both then and in the latter part of his life, of which there will be many true testimonies.

And now his care was to recover from his consumption, by a change from Woodford into such an air as was most proper to that end. And his remove was to Dauntsey in Wiltshire, a noble house, which stands in a choice air; the owner of it then was the Lord Danvers, Earl of Danby, who loved Mr. Herbert so very much that he allowed him such an apartment in it as might best suit with his accommodation and liking. And in this place, by a spare diet, declining all perplexing studies, moderate exercise, and a cheerful conversation, his health was apparently improved to a good degree of strength and cheerfulness. And then he declared his resolution both to marry, and to enter into the Sacred Orders of Priesthood. These had long been the desires of his mother, and his other relations; but she lived not to see either, for she died in the year 1627. And though he was disobedient to her about Layton Church, yet, in conformity to her will, he kept his Orator's place till after her death, and then presently declined it; and the more willingly, that he might be succeeded by his friend Robert Creighton, who now is Dr. Creighton, and the worthy Bishop of Wells.

I shall now proceed to his marriage; in order to which, it will be convenient that I first give the reader a short view of his person, and then an account of his wife, and of some circumstances concerning both.—He was for his person of a stature inclining towards tallness; his body was very straight, and so far from being cumbered with too much flesh, that he was lean to an extremity. His aspect was cheerful, and his speech and motion did both declare him a gentleman; for they were all so meek and obliging, that they purchased love and respect from all that knew him.

These, and his other visible virtues, begot him much love from a gentleman of a noble fortune, and a near kinsman to his friend the Earl of Danby; namely, from Mr. Charles Danvers of Bainton, in the County of Wilts, Esq. This Mr. Danvers, having known him long, and familiarly, did so much affect him, that he often and publicly declared a desire that Mr. Herbert would marry any of his nine daughters—for he had so many—but rather his daughter Jane than any other, because Jane was his beloved daughter. And he had often said the same to Mr. Herbert himself; and that if he could like her for a wife, and she him for a husband, Jane should have a double blessing: and Mr. Danvers had so often said the like to Jane, and so much commended Mr. Herbert to her, that Jane became so much a platonic[1] as to fall in love with Mr. Herbert unseen.

This was a fair preparation for a marriage; but, alas! her father died before Mr. Herbert's retirement to Dauntsey: yet some friends to both parties procured their meeting; at which time a mutual affection entered into

[1]The word is used in a sense made current in England in the second quarter of the 17th century. Queen Henrietta Maria (married Charles I, 1625) brought with her from France a cult of so-called spiritual love, misnamed Platonic, which was responsible for much affectation. It also provoked a reaction, illustrated in some of the poems of Suckling.

both their hearts, as a conqueror enters into a surprised city; and love having got such possession, governed, and made there such laws and resolutions, as neither party was able to resist; insomuch, that she changed her name into Herbert the third day after this first interview.

This haste might in others be thought a love-frenzy, or worse; but it was not, for they had wooed so like princes, as to have select proxies; such as were true friends to both parties, such as well understood Mr. Herbert's and her temper of mind, and also their estates, so well before this interview, that the suddenness was justifiable by the strictest rules of prudence; and the more, because it proved so happy to both parties; for the eternal lover of mankind made them happy in each other's mutual and equal affections, and compliance; indeed, so happy, that there never was any opposition betwixt them, unless it were a contest which should most incline to a compliance with the other's desires. And though this begot, and continued in them, such a mutual love, and joy, and content, as was no way defective; yet this mutual content, and love, and joy, did receive a daily augmentation, by such daily obligingness to each other as still added such new affluences to the former fullness of these divine souls, as was only improvable in Heaven, where they now enjoy it.

About three months after his marriage, Dr. Curle, who was then Rector of Bemerton, in Wiltshire, was made Bishop of Bath and Wells, and not long after translated to Winchester, and by that means the presentation of a Clerk to Bemerton did not fall to the Earl of Pembroke—who was the undoubted patron of it—but to the King, by reason of Dr. Curle's advancement: but Philip, then Earl of Pembroke—for William was lately dead—requested the King to bestow it upon his kinsman George Herbert; and the King said, "Most willingly to Mr. Herbert, if it be worth his acceptance"; and the Earl as willingly and suddenly sent it him, without seeking. But though Mr. Herbert had formerly put on a resolution for the clergy; yet, at receiving this presentation, the apprehension of the last great account that he was to make for the cure of so many souls, made him fast and pray often, and consider for not less than a month: in which time he had some resolutions to decline both the priesthood and that living. And in this time of considering, "he endured," as he would often say, "such spiritual conflicts, as none can think, but only those that have endured them."

In the midst of these conflicts, his old and dear friend, Mr. Arthur Woodnot, took a journey to salute him at Bainton—where he then was, with his wife's friends and relations—and was joyful to be an eye-witness of his health and happy marriage. And after they had rejoiced together some few days, they took a journey to Wilton, the famous seat of the Earls of Pembroke; at which time the King, the Earl, and the whole Court were there, or at Salisbury, which is near to it. And at this time Mr. Herbert presented his thanks to the Earl, for his presentation to Bemerton, but had not yet resolved to accept it, and told him the reason why: but that night the Earl acquainted Dr. Laud, then Bishop of London, and after Archbishop of Canterbury, with his kinsman's irresolution. And the Bishop did the next day so convince Mr. Herbert that the refusal of it was a sin, that a tailor was sent for to come speedily from Salisbury to Wilton, to take measure, and make him canonical clothes against next day; which the tailor did: and Mr. Herbert being so habited, went with his presentation to the learned Dr. Davenant, who was then Bishop of Salisbury, and he gave him institution immediately—for Mr. Herbert had been made Deacon some years before—and he was also the same day—which was April 26, 1630—inducted into the good, and more pleasant than healthful, parsonage of Bemerton; which is a mile from Salisbury.

I have now brought him to the parsonage of Bemerton, and to the thirty-sixth year of his age, and must stop here, and bespeak the reader to prepare for an almost incredible story, of the great sanctity of the short remainder of his holy life; a life so full of charity, humility, and all Christian virtues, that it deserves the eloquence of St. Chrysostom to commend and declare it: a life, that if it were related by a pen like his, there would then be no need for this age to look back into times past for the examples of primitive piety; for they might be all found in the life of George Herbert. But now, alas! who is fit to undertake it? I confess I am not; and am not pleased with myself that I must; and profess myself amazed, when I consider how few of the clergy lived like him then, and how many live so unlike him now. But it becomes not me to censure: my design is rather to assure the reader that I have used very great diligence to inform myself, that I might inform him of the truth of what follows; and though I cannot adorn it with eloquence, yet I will do it with sincerity.

When at his induction he was shut into Bemerton Church, being left there alone to toll the bell—as the law requires him—he stayed so much longer than an ordinary time, before he returned to those friends that stayed expecting him at the church-door, that his friend Mr. Woodnot looked in at the church-window, and saw him lie prostrate on the ground before the altar; at which time and place—as he after told Mr. Woodnot—he set some rules to himself, for the future manage of his life; and then and there made a vow to labor to keep them.

And the same night that he had his induction, he said to Mr. Woodnot, "I now look back upon my aspiring thoughts, and think myself more happy than if I had attained what then I so ambitiously thirsted for. And I can now behold the Court with an impartial eye, and see plainly that it is made up of fraud and titles, and flattery, and many other such empty, imaginary, painted pleasures; pleasures, that are so empty, as not to satisfy when they are enjoyed. But in God, and his service, is a fullness of all joy and pleasure, and no satiety. And I will now use all my endeavors to bring my relations and dependents to a love and reliance on Him, who never fails those that trust him. But above all, I will be sure to live well, because the virtuous life of a clergyman is the most powerful eloquence to persuade all that see it to reverence and love, and at least to desire to live like him. And this I will do, because I know we live in an age that hath more need of good examples than precepts. And I beseech that God, who hath honored me so much as to call me to serve him at his altar, that as by his special grace he hath put into my heart these good desires and resolutions; so he will, by his assisting grace, give me ghostly strength to bring the same to good effect. And I beseech him that my humble and charitable life may so win upon others, as to bring glory to my Jesus, whom I have this day taken to be my Master and Governor; and I am so proud of his service that I will always observe, and obey, and do his will; and always call him, Jesus my Master; and I will always contemn my birth, or any title or dignity that can be conferred upon me, when I shall compare them with my title of being a Priest, and serving at the altar of Jesus my Master."

And that he did so, may appear in many parts of his book of Sacred Poems: especially in that which he calls *The Odor*. In which he seems to rejoice in the thoughts of that word Jesus, and say that the adding these words, my Master, to it, and the often repetition of them, seemed to perfume his mind, and leave an oriental fragrancy in his very breath. And for his unforced choice to serve at God's altar, he seems in another place of his poems (*The Pearl*, Matthew xiii) to rejoice and say, "He knew the ways of learning; knew what nature does willingly, and what, when 'tis forced by fire; knew the ways of honor, and when glory inclines the soul to noble expressions; knew the Court; knew the ways of pleasure, of love, of wit, of music, and upon what terms he declined all these for the service of his Master Jesus"; and then concludes, saying:

That, through these labyrinths, not my groveling wit,
But thy silk twist, let down from Heaven to me,
Did both conduct, and teach me, how by it
To climb to thee.

The third day after he was made Rector of Bemerton, and had changed his sword and silk clothes into a canonical coat, he returned so habited with his friend Mr. Woodnot to Bainton; and immediately after he had seen and saluted his wife he said to her, "You are now a minister's wife, and must now so far forget your father's house as not to claim a precedence of any of your parishioners; for you are to know that a priest's wife can challenge no precedence or place, but that which she purchases by her obliging humility; and I am sure, places so purchased do best become them. And let me tell you, that I am so good a herald, as to assure you that this is truth." And she was so meek a wife, as to assure him, "It was no vexing news to her, and that he should see her observe it with a cheerful willingness." And, indeed, her unforced humility, that humility that was in her so original, as to be born with her, made her so happy as to do so; and her doing so begot her an unfeigned love, and a serviceable respect from all that conversed with her; and this love followed her in all places, as inseparably as shadows follow substances in sunshine.

It was not many days before he returned back to Bemerton, to view the church, and repair the chancel: and indeed to rebuild almost three parts of his house, which was fallen down, or decayed by reason of his predecessor's living at a better parsonage-house; namely, at Minal, sixteen or twenty miles from this place. At which time of Mr. Herbert's coming alone to Bemerton, there came to him a poor old woman, with an intent to acquaint him with her necessitous condition, as also with some troubles of her mind: but after she had spoke some few words to him, she was surprised with a fear, and that begot a shortness of breath, so that her spirits and speech failed her; which he perceiving, did so compassionate her, and was so humble, that he took her by the hand, and said, "Speak, good mother; be not afraid to speak to me; for I am a man that will hear you with patience; and will relieve your necessities too, if I be able: and this I will do willingly, and therefore, mother, be not afraid to acquaint me with what you desire." After which comfortable speech, he again took her by the hand, made her sit down by him, and understanding she was of his parish, he told her, "He would be acquainted with her, and take her into his care." And having with patience heard and understood her wants—and it is some relief for a poor body to be but heard with patience—he, like a Christian clergyman, comforted her by his meek behavior and counsel: but because that cost him nothing, he relieved her with money too, and so sent her home with a cheerful heart, praising God, and praying for him. Thus worthy, and—like David's blessed man—thus lowly, was Mr. George Herbert in his own eyes, and thus lovely in the eyes of others.

At his return that night to his wife at Bainton, he gave her an account of the passages 'twixt him and the poor woman; with which she was so affected that she went next day to Salisbury, and there bought a pair of blankets, and sent them as a token of her love to the poor woman; and with them a message, "That she would see and be acquainted with her, when her house was built at Bemerton."

There be many such passages both of him and his wife, of which some few will be related: but I shall first tell, that he hasted to get the parish church repaired; then to beautify the chapel—which stands near his house—and that at his own great charge. He then proceeded to rebuild the greatest part of the parsonage-house, which he did also very completely, and at his own charge; and having done this good work, he caused these verses to be writ upon, or engraven in, the mantel of the chimney in his hall.

TO MY SUCCESSOR

If thou chance for to find
A new house to thy mind,
And built without thy cost;
  Be good to the poor,
  As God gives thee store,
And then my labor's not lost.

We will now, by the reader's favor, suppose him fixed at Bemerton, and grant him to have seen the church repaired, and the chapel belonging to it very decently adorned at his own great charge—which is a real truth; and having now fixed him there, I shall proceed to give an account of the rest of his behavior, both to his parishioners, and those many others that knew and conversed with him.

Doubtless Mr. Herbert had considered, and given rules to himself for his Christian carriage both to God and man, before he entered into Holy Orders. And 'tis not unlike, but that he renewed those resolutions at his prostration before the holy altar, at his induction into the church of Bemerton: but as yet he was but a Deacon, and therefore longed for the next Ember-week, that he might be ordained Priest, and made capable of administering both the sacraments. At which time the reverend Dr. Humphrey Henchman, now Lord Bishop of London—who does not mention him but with some veneration for his life and excellent learning—tells me, "He laid his hand on Mr. Herbert's head, and, alas! within less than three years, lent his shoulder to carry his dear friend to his grave."

And that Mr. Herbert might the better preserve those holy rules which such a priest as he intended to be, ought to observe; and that time might not insensibly blot them out of his memory, but that the next year might show him his variations from this year's resolutions; he therefore did set down his rules, then resolved upon, in that order as the world now sees them printed in a little book, called *The Country Parson;*[1] in which some of his rules are:

The Parson's knowledge.
The Parson on Sundays.
The Parson praying.
The Parson preaching.
The Parson's charity.
The Parson comforting the sick.
The Parson arguing.
The Parson condescending.
The Parson in his journey.
The Parson in his mirth.
The Parson with his Churchwardens.
The Parson blessing the people.

And his behavior towards God and man may be said to be a practical comment on these and the other holy rules set down in that useful book: a book so full of plain, prudent, and useful rules, that that country parson, that can spare twelve pence, and yet wants it, is scarce excusable; because it will both direct him what he ought to do, and convince him for not having done it.

At the death of Mr. Herbert, this book fell into the hands of his friend Mr. Woodnot; and he commended it into the trusty hands of Mr. Barnabas Oley, who published it with a most conscientious and excellent preface; from which I have had some of those truths, that are related in this life of Mr. Herbert. The text for his first sermon was taken out of Solomon's Proverbs, and the words were, "Keep thy heart with all diligence." In which first sermon he gave his parishioners many necessary, holy, safe rules for the discharge of a good conscience, both to God and man; and delivered his sermon after a most florid manner, both with great learning and eloquence; but, at the close of this sermon, told them, "That should not be his constant way of preaching; for since Almighty God does not intend to lead men to Heaven by hard questions, he would not therefore fill their heads with unnecessary notions; but that, for their sakes, his language and his expressions should be more plain and practical in his future sermons." And he then made it his humble request, "That they would be constant to the afternoon's service, and catechizing": and showed them convincing reasons why he desired it; and his obliging example and persuasions brought them to a willing conformity to his desires.

The texts for all his future sermons—which, God knows, were not many—were constantly taken out of the Gospel for the day; and he did as constantly declare why the Church did appoint that portion of Scripture to be that day read; and in what manner the collect for every Sunday does refer to the Gospel or to the Epistle then read to them; and, that they might pray with understanding, he did usually take occasion to explain, not only the collect for every particular Sunday, but the reasons of all the other collects and responses in our Church-service; and made it appear to them, that the whole service of the Church was a reasonable and therefore an acceptable sacrifice to God: as namely, that we begin with "Confession of ourselves to be vile, miserable sinners"; and that we begin so, because, till we have confessed ourselves to be such, we are not capable of that mercy which we acknowledge we need, and pray for: but having, in the prayer of our Lord, begged pardon for those sins which we have confessed; and hoping, that as the priest hath declared our absolution, so by our public confession, and real repentance, we have obtained that pardon; then we dare and do proceed to beg of the Lord, "to open our lips, that our mouths may show forth his praise"; for till then we are neither able nor worthy to praise him. But this being supposed, we are then fit to say, "Glory be to the Father, and to the Son, and to the Holy Ghost"; and fit to proceed to a further service of our God, in the collects, and psalms, and lauds, that follow in the service.

And as to the psalms and lauds, he proceeded to inform them why they were so often, and some of them daily, repeated in our Church-service; namely, the psalms every month, because they be an historical and thankful repetition of mercies past, and such a composition of prayers and praises, as ought to be repeated often, and publicly; for "with such sacrifices God is honored and well-pleased." This for the psalms.

[1] First published in 1652, with certain other of Herbert's works; first separately published in 1671.

And for the hymns and lauds appointed to be daily repeated or sung after the first and second lessons are read to the congregation; he proceeded to inform them that it was most reasonable, after they have heard the will and goodness of God declared or preached by the priest in his reading the two chapters, that it was then a seasonable duty to rise up, and express their gratitude to Almighty God, for those his mercies to them, and to all mankind; and then to say with the Blessed Virgin, "that their souls do magnify the Lord, and that their spirits do also rejoice in God their Savior": and that it was their duty also to rejoice with Simeon in his song, and say with him, "That their eyes have" also "seen their salvation"; for they have seen that salvation which was but prophesied till his time: and he then broke out into those expressions of joy that he did see it; but they live to see it daily in the history of it, and therefore ought daily to rejoice, and daily to offer up their sacrifices of praise to their God, for that particular mercy. A service, which is now the constant employment of that Blessed Virgin and Simeon, and all those blessed saints that are possessed of Heaven: and where they are at this time interchangeably and constantly singing, "Holy, holy, holy, Lord God; glory be to God on high, and on earth peace." And he taught them, that to do this was an acceptable service to God, because the Prophet David says in his Psalms, "He that praiseth the Lord honoreth him."

He made them to understand how happy they be that are freed from the encumbrances of that law which our forefathers groaned under: namely, from the legal sacrifices, and from the many ceremonies of the Levitical law; freed from circumcision, and from the strict observation of the Jewish Sabbath, and the like. And he made them know that having received so many and so great blessings, by being born since the days of our Savior, it must be an acceptable sacrifice to Almighty God for them to acknowledge those blessings daily, and stand up and worship, and say as Zacharias did, "Blessed be the Lord God of Israel, for he hath—in our days—visited and redeemed his people; and he hath—in our days—remembered, and showed that mercy, which by the mouth of the Prophets he promised to our forefathers"; and this he hath done "according to his holy covenant made with them." And he made them to understand that we live to see and enjoy the benefit of it, in his birth, in his life, his passion, his resurrection, and ascension into Heaven, where he now sits sensible of all our temptations and infirmities; and where he is at this present time making intercession for us, to his and our Father: and therefore they ought daily to express their public gratulations, and say daily with Zacharias, "Blessed be that Lord God of Israel, that hath thus visited and thus redeemed his people."—These were some of the reasons by which Mr. Herbert instructed his congregation for the use of the psalms and hymns appointed to be daily sung or said in the Church-service.

He informed them also, when the priest did pray only for the congregation, and not for himself; and when they did only pray for him; as namely, after the repetition of the creed before he proceeds to pray the Lord's Prayer, or any of the appointed collects, the priest is directed to kneel down, and pray for them, saying, "The Lord be with you"; and when they pray for him, saying, "And with thy spirit"; and then they join together in the following collects: and he assured them that when there is such mutual love, and such joint prayers offered for each other, then the holy angels look down from Heaven, and are ready to carry such charitable desires to God Almighty, and he as ready to receive them; and that a Christian congregation calling thus upon God with one heart, and one voice, and in one reverent and humble posture, looks as beautifully as Jerusalem, that is at peace with itself.

He instructed them also why the prayer of our Lord was prayed often in every full service of the Church; namely, at the conclusion of the several parts of that service; and prayed then, not only because it was composed and commanded by our Jesus that made it, but as a perfect pattern for our less perfect forms of prayer, and therefore fittest to sum up and conclude all our imperfect petitions.

He instructed them also, that as by the second commandment we are required not to bow down, or worship an idol, or false god; so, by the contrary rule, we are to bow down and kneel, or stand up and worship the true God. And he instructed them why the Church required the congregation to stand up at the repetition of the creeds; namely, because they did thereby declare both their obedience to the Church, and an assent to that faith into which they had been baptized. And he taught them that in that shorter creed or doxology, so often repeated daily, they also stood up to testify their belief to be, that "the God that they trusted in was one God, and three persons; the Father, the Son, and the Holy Ghost; to whom they and the priest gave glory." And because there had been heretics that had denied some of these three persons to be God, therefore the congregation stood up and honored him, by confessing and saying, "It was so in the beginning, is now so, and shall ever be so world without end." And all gave their assent to this belief, by standing up and saying, Amen.

He instructed them also what benefit they had by the Church's appointing the celebration of holidays and the excellent use of them, namely, that they were set apart for particular commemorations of particular mercies received from Almighty God; and—as Reverend Mr. Hooker[1] says—to be the landmarks to distinguish times; for by them we are taught to take notice how time passes by us, and that we ought not to let the years pass without a celebration of praise for those mercies which those days give us occasion to remember, and therefore they were to note that the year is appointed to begin the 25th day of March; a day in which we commemorate the angel's appearing to the Blessed Virgin, with the joyful tidings that "she should conceive and bear a son, that should be the Redeemer of mankind." And she did so forty weeks after this joyful salutation; namely, at our Christmas: a day in which we commemorate his birth with joy and praise: and that eight days after this happy birth we celebrate his circumcision; namely, in that which we call New Year's Day. And that, upon that day which we call Twelfth Day, we commemorate the manifestation of the unsearchable riches of Jesus to the Gentiles: and that that day we also celebrate the memory of his goodness in sending a star to guide the three Wise Men from the east to Bethlehem, that they might there worship, and present him with their oblations of gold, frankincense, and myrrh. And he—Mr. Herbert—instructed them, that Jesus was forty days after his birth presented by his blessed mother in the temple; namely, on that day which we call, "The Purification of the Blessed Virgin, Saint Mary." And he instructed them, that by the Lent-fast we imitate and commemorate our Savior's humiliation in fasting forty days; and that we ought to endeavor to be like him in purity: and that on Good Friday we commemorate and condole his crucifixion; and at Easter commemorate his glorious resurrection. And he taught them that after Jesus had manifested himself to his disciples to be "that Christ that was crucified, dead, and buried"; and by his appearing and conversing with his disciples for the space of forty days after his resurrection, he then, and not till then, ascended into Heaven in the sight of those disciples; namely, on that day which we call the ascension, or Holy Thursday. And that we then celebrate the performance of the promise which he made to his disciples at or before his ascension; namely, "that though he left them, yet he would send them the Holy Ghost to be their Comforter"; and that he did so on that day which the Church calls Whitsunday.—Thus the Church keeps an historical and circular commemoration of times, as they pass by us; of such times as ought to incline us to occasional praises, for the particular blessings which we do or might receive, by those holy commemorations.

He made them know also why the Church hath appointed Ember weeks; and to know the reason why the commandments, and the Epistles and Gospels, were to be read at the altar or communion table: why the priest was to pray the litany kneeling; and why to pray some collects standing: and he gave them many other observations, fit for his plain congregation, but not fit for me now to mention; for I must set limits to my pen, and not make that a treatise which I intended to be a much shorter account than I have made it: but I have done, when I have told the reader that he was constant in catechizing every Sunday in the afternoon, and that his catechizing was after his Second Lesson, and in the pulpit; and that he never exceeded his half hour, and was always so happy as to have an obedient and a full congregation.

And to this I must add that if he were at

[1]Richard Hooker (1554–1600), author of the treatise *Of the Laws of Ecclesiastical Polity* (Bks. I–IV, 1593; Bk. V, 1597; Bks. VI–VIII, concerning whose genuineness in their present state there is some question, 1648, 1651, 1662).

any time too zealous in his sermons, it was in reproving the indecencies of the people's behavior in the time of divine service; and of those ministers that huddled up the church-prayers, without a visible reverence and affection; namely, such as seemed to say the Lord's prayer, or a collect, in a breath. But for himself, his custom was to stop betwixt every collect, and give the people time to consider what they had prayed, and to force their desires affectionately to God, before he engaged them into new petitions.

And by this account of his diligence to make his parishioners understand what they prayed, and why they praised and adored their Creator, I hope I shall the more easily obtain the reader's belief to the following account of Mr. Herbert's own practice; which was to appear constantly with his wife and three nieces—the daughters of a deceased sister—and his whole family, twice every day at the church-prayers in the chapel, which does almost join to his parsonage-house. And for the time of his appearing, it was strictly at the canonical hours of ten and four: and then and there he lifted up pure and charitable hands to God in the midst of the congregation. And he would joy to have spent that time in that place, where the honor of his Master Jesus dwelleth; and there, by that inward devotion which he testified constantly by an humble behavior and visible adoration, he, like Joshua, brought not only "his own household thus to serve the Lord"; but brought most of his parishioners, and many gentlemen in the neighborhood, constantly to make a part of his congregation twice a day: and some of the meaner sort of his parish did so love and reverence Mr. Herbert that they would let their plow rest when Mr. Herbert's Saint's-bell rung to prayers, that they might also offer their devotions to God with him; and would then return back to their plow. And his most holy life was such that it begot such reverence to God, and to him, that they thought themselves the happier when they carried Mr. Herbert's blessing back with them to their labor. Thus powerful was his reason and example to persuade others to a practical piety and devotion.

And his constant public prayers did never make him to neglect his own private devotions, nor those prayers that he thought himself bound to perform with his family, which always were a set form, and not long; and he did always conclude them with that collect which the Church hath appointed for the day or week.—"Thus he made every day's sanctity a step towards that kingdom, where impurity cannot enter."

His chiefest recreation was music, in which heavenly art he was a most excellent master, and did himself compose many divine hymns and anthems, which he set and sung to his lute or viol: and though he was a lover of retiredness, yet his love to music was such that he went usually twice every week, on certain appointed days, to the Cathedral Church in Salisbury; and at his return would say, "That his time spent in prayer, and cathedral music, elevated his soul, and was his Heaven upon earth." But before his return thence to Bemerton, he would usually sing and play his part at an appointed private music-meeting; and, to justify this practice, he would often say, "Religion does not banish mirth, but only moderates and sets rules to it."

And as his desire to enjoy his Heaven upon earth drew him twice every week to Salisbury, so his walks thither were the occasion of many happy accidents to others; of which I will mention some few.

In one of his walks to Salisbury he overtook a gentleman that is still living in that city; and in their walk together, Mr. Herbert took a fair occasion to talk with him, and humbly begged to be excused, if he asked him some account of his faith; and said, "I do this the rather, because though you are not of my parish, yet I receive tithe from you by the hand of your tenant; and, Sir, I am the bolder to do it, because I know there be some sermon-hearers that be like those fishes that always live in salt water, and yet are always fresh."

After which expression, Mr. Herbert asked him some needful questions, and having received his answer, gave him such rules for the trial of his sincerity, and for a practical piety, and in so loving and meek a manner, that the gentleman did so fall in love with him, and his discourse, that he would often contrive to meet him in his walk to Salisbury, or to attend him back to Bemerton; and still mentions the name of Mr. George Herbert with veneration, and still praiseth God for the occasion of knowing him.

In another of his Salisbury walks, he met

with a neighbor minister; and after some friendly discourse betwixt them, and some condolement for the decay of piety, and too general contempt of the clergy, Mr. Herbert took occasion to say:

"One cure for these distempers would be for the clergy themselves to keep the Ember weeks strictly, and beg of their parishioners to join with them in fasting and prayers for a more religious clergy.

"And another cure would be, for themselves to restore the great and neglected duty of catechizing, on which the salvation of so many of the poor and ignorant lay-people does depend; but principally, that the clergy themselves would be sure to live unblameably; and that the dignified clergy especially which preach temperance, would avoid surfeiting and take all occasions to express a visible humility and charity in their lives; for this would force a love and an imitation, and an unfeigned reverence from all that knew them to be such." (And for proof of this, we need no other testimony than the life and death of Dr. Lake, late Lord Bishop of Bath and Wells.) "This," said Mr. Herbert, "would be a cure for the wickedness and growing atheism of our age. And, my dear brother, till this be done by us, and done in earnest, let no man expect a reformation of the manners of the laity; for 'tis not learning, but this, this only that must do it; and, till then, the fault must lie at our doors."

In another walk to Salisbury, he saw a poor man with a poorer horse, that was fallen under his load: they were both in distress, and needed present help; which Mr. Herbert perceiving, put off his canonical coat, and helped the poor man to unload, and after to load, his horse. The poor man blessed him for it, and he blessed the poor man; and was so like the Good Samaritan that he gave him money to refresh both himself and his horse; and told him, "That if he loved himself he should be merciful to his beast." Thus he left the poor man: and at his coming to his musical friends at Salisbury, they began to wonder that Mr. George Herbert, which used to be so trim and clean, came into that company so soiled and discomposed: but he told them the occasion. And when one of the company told him, "He had disparaged himself by so dirty an employment," his answer was, "That the thought of what he had done would prove music to him at midnight; and that the omission of it would have upbraided and made discord in his conscience, whensoever he should pass by that place: for if I be bound to pray for all that be in distress, I am sure that I am bound, so far as it is in my power, to practice what I pray for. And though I do not wish for the like occasion every day, yet let me tell you, I would not willingly pass one day of my life without comforting a sad soul, or showing mercy; and I praise God for this occasion. And now let's tune our instruments."

Thus, as our blessed Savior, after his resurrection, did take occasion to interpret the Scripture to Cleopas, and that other disciple, which he met with and accompanied in their journey to Emmaus; so Mr. Herbert, in his path toward Heaven, did daily take any fair occasion to instruct the ignorant, or comfort any that were in affliction; and did always confirm his precepts, by showing humility and mercy, and ministering grace to the hearers.

And he was most happy in his wife's unforced compliance with his acts of charity, whom he made his almoner, and paid constantly into her hand a tenth penny of what money he received for tithe, and gave her power to dispose that to the poor of his parish, and with it a power to dispose a tenth part of the corn that came yearly into his barn: which trust she did most faithfully perform, and would often offer to him an account of her stewardship, and as often beg an enlargement of his bounty; for she rejoiced in the employment: and this was usually laid out by her in blankets and shoes for some such poor people as she knew to stand in most need of them. This as to her charity.—And for his own, he set no limits to it: nor did ever turn his face from any that he saw in want, but would relieve them; especially his poor neighbors; to the meanest of whose houses he would go, and inform himself of their wants, and relieve them cheerfully, if they were in distress; and would always praise God, as much for being willing, as for being able to do it. And when he was advised by a friend to be more frugal, because he might have children, his answer was, "He would not see the danger of want so far off: but being the Scripture does so commend charity, as to tell us that charity is the top of Christian virtues, the covering of sins, the fulfilling of the law, the life of faith; and that charity hath a promise of the blessings of this life, and of a reward in that life which is to come: being these, and more excellent things are in Scripture spoken of thee, O Charity! and that, being all my tithes and church-dues are a deodate from thee, O my God! make me, O my God! so far to trust thy promise, as to return them back to thee; and by thy grace I will do so, in distributing them to any of thy poor members that are in distress, or do but bear the image of Jesus my Master." "Sir," said he to his friend, "my wife hath a competent maintenance secured her after my death; and therefore, as this is my prayer, so this my resolution shall, by God's grace, be unalterable."

This may be some account of the excellencies of the active part of his life; and thus he continued, till a consumption so weakened him as to confine him to his house, or to the chapel, which does almost join to it; in which he continued to read prayers constantly twice every day, though he were very weak: in one of which times of his reading his wife observed him to read in pain, and told him so, and that it wasted his spirits, and weakened him; and he confessed it did, but said, "His life could not be better spent, than in the service of his Master Jesus, who had done and suffered so much for him. But," said he, "I will not be willful; for though my spirit be willing, yet I find my flesh is weak; and therefore Mr. Bostock shall be appointed to read prayers for me to-morrow; and I shall now be only a hearer of them, till this mortal shall put on immortality." And Mr. Bostock did the next day undertake and continue this happy employment, till Mr. Herbert's death. This Mr. Bostock was a learned and virtuous man, an old friend of Mr. Herbert's, and then his curate to the church of Fulston, which is a mile from Bemerton, to which church Bemerton is but a chapel of ease. And this Mr. Bostock did also constantly supply the church-service for Mr. Herbert in that chapel, when the music-meeting at Salisbury caused his absence from it.

About one month before his death, his friend Mr. Farrer—for an account of whom I am by promise indebted to the reader, and intend to make him sudden payment—hearing of Mr. Herbert's sickness, sent Mr. Edmund Duncon—who is now Rector of Friar Barnet in the County of Middlesex—from his house of Gidden Hall, which is near to Huntingdon, to see Mr. Herbert, and to assure him he wanted not his daily prayers for his recovery; and Mr. Duncon was to return back to Gidden, with an account of Mr. Herbert's condition. Mr. Duncon found him weak, and at that time lying on his bed, or on a pallet; but at his seeing Mr. Duncon he raised himself vigorously, saluted him, and with some earnestness inquired the health of his brother Farrer; of which Mr. Duncon satisfied him, and after some discourse of Mr. Farrer's holy life, and the manner of his constant serving God, he said to Mr. Duncon, "Sir, I see by your habit that you are a priest, and I desire you to pray with me": which being granted, Mr. Duncon asked him, "What prayers?" To which Mr. Herbert's answer was, "O, Sir! the prayers of my mother, the Church of England: no other prayers are equal to them! But at this time, I beg of you to pray only the litany, for I am weak and faint": and Mr. Duncon did so. After which, and some other discourse of Mr. Farrer, Mrs. Herbert provided Mr. Duncon a plain supper, and a clean lodging, and he betook himself to rest. This Mr. Duncon tells me; and tells me, that at his first view of Mr. Herbert he saw majesty and humility so reconciled in his looks and behavior, as begot in him an awful reverence for his person; and says, "his discourse was so pious, and his motion so genteel and meek, that after almost forty years, yet they remain still fresh in his memory."

The next morning Mr. Duncon left him, and betook himself to a journey to Bath, but with a promise to return back to him within five days; and he did so;[1] * * * and then found Mr. Herbert much weaker than he left him; and therefore their discourse could not be long; but at Mr. Duncon's parting with him, Mr. Herbert spoke to this purpose: "Sir, I pray give my brother Farrer an account of the decaying condition of my body, and tell him I beg him to continue his daily prayers for me; and let him know that I have considered that God only is what he would be; and that I am, by his grace, become now so like him as to be pleased with what pleaseth him; and tell him that I do not repine, but am pleased with my want of health: and tell him, my heart is fixed on that place where

[1]Walton's promised account of Nicholas Ferrar is here omitted.

true joy is only to be found; and that I long to be there, and do wait for my appointed change with hope and patience." Having said this, he did, with so sweet a humility as seemed to exalt him, bow down to Mr. Duncon, and with a thoughtful and contented look, say to him, "Sir, I pray deliver this little book to my dear brother Farrer, and tell him he shall find in it a picture of the many spiritual conflicts that have passed betwixt God and my soul, before I could subject mine to the will of Jesus my Master: in whose service I have now found perfect freedom. Desire him to read it; and then, if he can think it may turn to the advantage of any dejected poor soul, let it be made public; if not, let him burn it; for I and it are less than the least of God's mercies." Thus meanly did this humble man think of this excellent book, which now bears the name of *The Temple; or, Sacred Poems and Private Ejaculations;* of which Mr. Farrer would say, "There was in it the picture of a divine soul in every page: and that the whole book was such a harmony of holy passions, as would enrich the world with pleasure and piety." And it appears to have done so; for there have been more than twenty thousand of them sold since the first impression.

And this ought to be noted, that when Mr. Farrer sent this book to Cambridge to be licensed for the press, the Vice-Chancellor would by no means allow the two so much noted verses,

> Religion stands a tiptoe in our land,
> Ready to pass to the American strand,

to be printed; and Mr. Farrer would by no means allow the book to be printed and want them. But after some time, and some arguments for and against their being made public, the Vice-Chancellor said, "I knew Mr. Herbert well, and know that he had many heavenly speculations, and was a divine poet: but I hope the world will not take him to be an inspired prophet, and therefore I license the whole book." So that it came to be printed without the diminution or addition of a syllable, since it was delivered into the hands of Mr. Duncon, save only that Mr. Farrer hath added that excellent preface that is printed before it.[1]

At the time of Mr. Duncon's leaving Mr. Herbert—which was about three weeks before his death—his old and dear friend Mr. Woodnot came from London to Bemerton, and never left him till he had seen him draw his last breath, and closed his eyes on his deathbed. In this time of his decay, he was often visited and prayed for by all the clergy that lived near to him, especially by his friends the Bishop and Prebends of the Cathedral Church in Salisbury; but by none more devoutly than his wife, his three nieces—then a part of his family—and Mr. Woodnot, who were the sad witnesses of his daily decay; to whom he would often speak to this purpose: "I now look back upon the pleasures of my life past, and see the content I have taken in beauty, in wit, in music, and pleasant conversation, are now all passed by me like a dream, or as a shadow that returns not, and are now all become dead to me, or I to them; and I see, that as my father and generation hath done before me, so I also shall now suddenly (with Job) make my bed also in the dark; and I praise God I am prepared for it; and I praise him that I am not to learn patience now I stand in such need of it; and that I have practiced mortification, and endeavored to die daily, that I might not die eternally; and my hope is, that I shall shortly leave this valley of tears, and be free from all fevers and pain; and, which will be a more happy condition, I shall be free from sin, and all the temptations and anxieties that attend it: and this being past, I shall dwell in the New Jerusalem; dwell there with men made perfect; dwell where these eyes shall see my Master and Savior Jesus; and with him see my dear mother, and all my relations and friends. But I must die, or not come to that happy place. And this is my content, that I am going daily towards it: and that every day which I have lived hath taken a part of my appointed time from me; and that I shall live the less time for having lived this and the day past." These, and the like expressions, which he uttered often, may be said to be his enjoyment of Heaven before he enjoyed it. The Sunday before his death he rose suddenly from his bed or couch, called for one of his instruments, took it into his hand and said:

> My God, my God,
> My music shall find thee,
> And every string
> Shall have his attribute to sing.

[1]The book was first published at Cambridge in 1633.

And having tuned it, he played and sung:

> The Sundays of man's life,
> Threaded together on time's string,
> Make bracelets to adorn the wife
> Of the eternal glorious King:
> On Sundays Heaven's door stands ope;
> Blessings are plentiful and rife,
> More plentiful than hope.

Thus he sung on earth such hymns and anthems as the angels, and he, and Mr. Farrer, now sing in Heaven.

Thus he continued meditating, and praying, and rejoicing, till the day of his death; and on that day said to Mr. Woodnot, "My dear friend, I am sorry I have nothing to present to my merciful God but sin and misery; but the first is pardoned, and a few hours will now put a period to the latter; for I shall suddenly go hence, and be no more seen." Upon which expression Mr. Woodnot took occasion to remember him of the re-edifying Layton Church, and his many acts of mercy. To which he made answer, saying, "They be good works, if they be sprinkled with the blood of Christ, and not otherwise." After this discourse he became more restless, and his soul seemed to be weary of her earthly tabernacle; and this uneasiness became so visible that his wife, his three nieces, and Mr. Woodnot, stood constantly about his bed, beholding him with sorrow, and an unwillingness to lose the sight of him whom they could not hope to see much longer. As they stood thus beholding him, his wife observed him to breathe faintly, and with much trouble, and observed him to fall into a sudden agony; which so surprised her that she fell into a sudden passion, and required of him to know how he did. To which his answer was, "That he had passed a conflict with his last enemy, and had overcome him by the merits of his Master Jesus." After which answer he looked up, and saw his wife and nieces weeping to an extremity, and charged them, if they loved him, to withdraw into the next room, and there pray every one alone for him; for nothing but their lamentations could make his death uncomfortable. To which request their sighs and tears would not suffer them to make any reply; but they yielded him a sad obedience, leaving only with him Mr. Woodnot and Mr. Bostock. Immediately after they had left him, he said to Mr. Bostock, "Pray, Sir, open that door, then look into that cabinet, in which you may easily find my last Will, and give it into my hand": which being done, Mr. Herbert delivered it into the hand of Mr. Woodnot, and said, "My old friend, I here deliver you my last Will, in which you will find that I have made you my sole executor for the good of my wife and nieces; and I desire you to show kindness to them, as they shall need it: I do not desire you to be just; for I know you will be so for your own sake; but I charge you, by the religion of our friendship, to be careful of them." And having obtained Mr. Woodnot's promise to be so, he said, "I am now ready to die." After which words, he said, "Lord, forsake me not now my strength faileth me: but grant me mercy for the merits of my Jesus. And now, Lord—Lord, now receive my soul." And with those words he breathed forth his divine soul, without any apparent disturbance, Mr. Woodnot and Mr. Bostock attending his last breath, and closing his eyes.

Thus he lived, and thus he died, like a saint, unspotted of the world, full of alms-deeds, full of humility, and all the examples of a virtuous life; which I cannot conclude better than with this borrowed observation:

> —All must to their cold graves:
> But the religious actions of the just
> Smell sweet in death, and blossom in the dust.[1]

Mr. George Herbert's have done so to this, and will doubtless do so to succeeding generations.—I have but this to say more of him; that if Andrew Melvin died before him, then George Herbert died without an enemy. I wish—if God shall be so pleased—that I may be so happy as to die like him.

---

[1]Borrowed from the dirge in *The Contention of Ajax and Ulysses* (1659), Scene III, by James Shirley. Shirley's lines are:

> "Your heads must come
> To the cold tomb,
> Only the actions of the just
> Smell sweet, and blossom in their dust."

JOHN MILTON (1608–1674)

Milton was born in London on 9 December, 1608. His father was a scrivener or solicitor, and a convinced puritan. There was indeed so much feeling behind his puritanism as to have caused him to break with his family on this account, Milton's grandfather having been a Catholic recusant in the reign of Elizabeth. It should be remembered, however, that puritanism had not yet become the narrow, ascetic, intolerant force that we generally associate with the name, and Milton, as a matter of fact, was brought up in an environment of cultivation in which music and poetry were ever-present realities. As a boy he attended St. Paul's School in London, and went thence to Christ's College, Cambridge, in 1625. There he remained for seven years, reading widely and deeply, laying the foundations of his immense learning, commencing his work as a poet with his ode *On the Morning of Christ's Nativity* (1629) and other shorter poems, and exhibiting already that spirit of independence which remained throughout his life a major characteristic. The immediate circumstances, it is true, of Milton's trouble with his college tutor are obscure, but it is at least a probable supposition that his independent spirit had something to do with his temporary banishment from Cambridge and his transference to another tutor on his return. In 1632 Milton left Cambridge and went to Horton, in Buckinghamshire, where his father had retired from his London business. Here he spent six years, perhaps the happiest years of his life, continuing his studies with the conscious purpose of preparing himself for some great poetical achievement. For Milton was a dedicated spirit; from an early time aware of his great powers, he proceeded deliberately to make himself fit for the execution of his high purpose, the creation of a noble monument in verse. Many years later he expressed what was his abiding conviction from youth to old age, when he said that "he who would not be frustrate of his hope to write well hereafter in laudable things ought himself to be a true poem . . . not presuming to sing high praises of heroic men or famous cities unless he have in himself the experience and practice of all that which is praiseworthy." During the years at Horton, too, Milton not only read himself into the spirit of great poetry in ages past, but also sent forth those trial barks which remain still among the loveliest of their kind in English verse. For at Horton he wrote *L'Allegro*, *Il Penseroso*, *Comus*, and *Lycidas*, as well as other of his so-called minor poems. In 1638 he left England to travel southward to Italy, where he spent some months in pleasant intercourse with learned and cultivated men in several Italian towns. He was planning to travel farther, to Greece and Palestine, when the news of Charles's first expedition against the Scots reached him and determined him to turn his steps homeward. He knew the political situation in England well enough to realize that this was probably the beginning of worse things, and he wrote afterwards, "I thought it base to be traveling for amusement abroad while my fellow citizens were fighting for liberty at home." On his way back he had the opportunity of meeting Galileo—then old, blind, and in partial confinement at the hand of the Inquisition—at Florence.

Milton reached England in August, 1639, and proceeded to become a schoolmaster. This result of his anxiety to share in his countrymen's fight for liberty has, certainly, the air of anti-climax, but his serious purpose was to fight in the way he best could, with his pen, and his teaching was punctuated by the writing of controversial pamphlets, some of which won him appointment in 1649 as Latin Secretary in the puritan government. He never made himself, however, the instrument of a party. His guiding star was liberty, and he was ready to turn against the puritans themselves when they seemed to him in danger of deserting that principle for which, as he thought, they fundamentally stood. In 1641 and 1642 he wrote five pamphlets against episcopacy, or government of the church by bishops, fighting therein for religious liberty. In 1643 he began a series of pamphlets in which he contended passionately for easy divorce. The immediate occasion of these was his own unhappy marriage in that year, but the battle he waged was entirely consistent with his previously formed conviction that liberty was essential to human well-being. In 1644 he wrote his tract on liberal education, designed to principle the mind in virtue, "the only genuine source of political and individual liberty"; and also his *Areopagitica*, an eloquent defense of freedom of speech, in the course of which he uttered his celebrated praise of Spenser, "our sage and serious poet." After three years of work as Latin Secretary Milton's devotion to his duties in the service of the Commonwealth caused his blindness, though he did not allow this to stop either his official work or his controversial writing, any more than he allowed it to prevent the later accomplishment of his purpose of writing a great poem. That purpose he never relinquished through all the central years of his life when the cause of liberty and public duty claimed his energy. And before the Restoration in 1660 he had begun the writing of *Paradise Lost.* There is no reason for thinking that either the theme or his execution of it in the poem was influenced by the decay of the Commonwealth and Charles II's return, bitter blows to Milton though both were. The theme was chosen after long hesitation simply on the ground that it was the most heroic in its proportions of all possible subjects. Milton was subjected to surprisingly little annoyance by the new government, and lived his remaining years quietly enough, save for disturbances within his family, at work upon various tasks, but chiefly *Paradise Lost, Paradise Regained,* and *Samson Agonistes.* The first was finished by the summer of 1665 and was published in 1667. *Paradise Regained* and *Samson Agonistes* were published in 1671. *Paradise Lost* in the first edition has ten books; in the year of his death Milton published a second edition in which two of the original ten books were divided, making the twelve in which the poem has ever since been printed.

ON TIME

Fly, envious Time, till thou run out thy race:
Call on the lazy leaden-stepping Hours,
Whose speed is but the heavy plummet's pace;[1]
And glut thyself with what thy womb devours,
Which is no more than what is false and vain,
And merely mortal dross;
So little is our loss,
So little is thy gain!
For, when as each thing bad thou hast entombed,
And, last of all, thy greedy self consumed,
Then long Eternity shall greet our bliss
With an individual kiss,
And Joy shall overtake us as a flood;
When everything that is sincerely good,
And perfectly divine,
With Truth, and Peace, and Love, shall ever shine
About the supreme throne
Of him, to whose happy-making sight alone
When once our heavenly-guided soul shall climb,
Then, all this earthly grossness quit,
Attired with stars we shall for ever sit,
Triumphing over Death, and Chance, and thee, O Time!

AT A SOLEMN MUSIC

Blest pair of Sirens, pledges of Heaven's joy,
Sphere-born harmonious sisters, Voice and Verse,
Wed your divine sounds, and mixed power employ,
Dead things with inbreathed sense able to pierce;
And to our high-raised fantasy present
That undisturbéd song of pure consent,[2]
Aye sung before the sapphire-colored throne
To him that sits thereon,
With saintly shout and solemn jubilee;
Where the bright Seraphim in burning row
Their loud uplifted angel-trumpets blow,
And the Cherubic host in thousand quires,[3]
Touch their immortal harps of golden wires,
With those just Spirits that wear victorious palms,
Hymns devout and holy psalms
Singing everlastingly:
That we on Earth, with undiscording voice,
May rightly answer that melodious noise;
As once we did, till disproportioned sin
Jarred against nature's chime, and with harsh din
Broke the fair music that all creatures made
To their great Lord, whose love their motion swayed
In perfect diapason,[4] whilst they stood
In first obedience, and their state of good.
O, may we soon again renew that song,
And keep in tune with Heaven, till God ere long
To his celestial consort[5] us unite,
To live with him, and sing in endless morn of light!

ON SHAKESPEARE

What needs my Shakespeare for his honored bones
The labor of an age in piléd stones?
Or that his hallowed relics should be hid
Under a star-ypointing pyramid?
Dear son of memory, great heir of fame,
What need'st thou such weak witness of thy name?
Thou in our wonder and astonishment
Has built thyself a livelong monument.
For whilst, to the shame of slow-endeavoring art,
Thy easy numbers flow, and that each heart
Hath from the leaves of thy unvalued[6] book
Those Delphic[7] lines with deep impression took,

[1] *I. e.,* the gradual descent of the weights in a clock.
[2] Harmony.
[3] Choirs.
[4] Combination of notes or parts in harmonious whole.
[5] Symphony. [6] Invaluable. [7] Inspired.

Then thou, our fancy of itself bereaving,
Dost make us marble with too much conceiving,
And so sepúlchered in such pomp dost lie
That kings for such a tomb would wish to die.

L'ALLEGRO

HENCE, loathéd Melancholy,
Of Cerberus and blackest Midnight born
In Stygian cave forlorn
'Mongst horrid shapes, and shrieks, and sights unholy!
Find out some uncouth[1] cell,
Where brooding Darkness spreads his jealous wings,
And the night-raven sings;
There, under ebon[2] shades and low-browed rocks,
As ragged as thy locks,
In dark Cimmerian desert[3] ever dwell.
But come, thou Goddess fair and free,
In heaven yclept[4] Euphrosyne,
And by men heart-easing Mirth;
Whom lovely Venus, at a birth,
With two sister Graces more,
To ivy-crownéd Bacchus bore:
Or whether (as some sager sing)
The frolic wind that breathes the spring,
Zephyr, with Aurora playing,
As he met her once a-Maying,
There, on beds of violets blue,
And fresh-blown roses washed in dew,
Filled her with thee, a daughter fair,
So buxom, blithe, and debonair.
Haste thee, Nymph, and bring with thee
Jest, and youthful Jollity,
Quips and cranks and wanton wiles,
Nods and becks and wreathéd smiles,
Such as hang on Hebe's cheek,
And love to live in dimple sleek;
Sport that wrinkled Care derides,
And Laughter holding both his sides.
Come, and trip it, as you go,
On the light fantastic toe;
And in thy right hand lead with thee
The mountain-nymph, sweet Liberty;
And, if I give thee honor due,
Mirth, admit me of thy crew,
To live with her, and live with thee,
In unreprovéd[5] pleasures free;
To hear the lark begin his flight,
And, singing, startle the dull night,
From his watch-tower in the skies,
Till the dappled dawn doth rise;
Then to come, in spite of sorrow,

[1]Unknown, strange. [2]Black.
[3]A mythical land involved in perpetual mist and darkness (*Odyssey*, XI, 14).
[4]Called. [5]Innocent.

And at my window bid good-morrow,
Through the sweet-briar or the vine,
Or the twisted eglantine;
While the cock, with lively din,
Scatters the rear of darkness thin;
And to the stack, or the barn-door,
Stoutly struts his dames before:
Oft listening how the hounds and horn
Cheerly rouse the slumbering morn,
From the side of some hoar hill,
Through the high wood echoing shrill:
Sometime walking, not unseen,
By hedgerow elms, on hillocks green,
Right against the eastern gate
Where the great Sun begins his state,
Robed in flames and amber light,
The clouds in thousand liveries dight;[6]
While the plowman, near at hand,
Whistles o'er the furrowed land,
And the milkmaid singeth blithe,
And the mower whets his scythe,
And every shepherd tells his tale[7]
Under the hawthorn in the dale.
Straight mine eye hath caught new pleasures
Whilst the landscape round it measures:
Russet lawns, and fallows gray,
Where the nibbling flocks do stray,
Mountains on whose barren breast
The laboring clouds do often rest;
Meadows trim, with daisies pied;
Shallow brooks, and rivers wide;
Towers and battlements it sees
Bosomed high in tufted trees,
Where perhaps some beauty lies,
The cynosure[8] of neighboring eyes.
Hard by a cottage chimney smokes
From betwixt two agéd oaks,
Where Corydon and Thyrsis[9] met
Are at their savory dinner set
Of herbs and other country messes,
Which the neat-handed Phyllis dresses;
And then in haste her bower she leaves,
With Thestylis to bind the sheaves;
Or, if the earlier season lead,
To the tanned haycock in the mead.
Sometimes, with secure[10] delight,
The upland hamlets will invite,
When the merry bells ring round,
And the jocund rebecks[11] sound
To many a youth and many a maid
Dancing in the checkered shade,
And young and old come forth to play
On a sunshine holiday,
Till the livelong daylight fail:
Then to a spicy nut-brown ale,
With stories told of many a feat,

[6]Adorned. [7]Counts his sheep. [8]Center of admiration.
[9]These and the two other names in following lines are conventional names drawn from pastoral poetry.
[10]Carefree. [11]Fiddles.

How Faery Mab the junkets eat.
She was pinched and pulled, she said;
And he, by Friar's lantern[1] led,
Tells how the drudging goblin[2] sweat
To earn his cream-bowl duly set,
When in one night, ere glimpse of morn,
His shadowy flail hath threshed the corn
That ten day-laborers could not end;
Then lies him down, the lubber[3] fiend,
And, stretched out all the chimney's length,
Basks at the fire his hairy strength,
And crop-full out of doors he flings,
Ere the first cock his matin rings.
Thus done the tales, to bed they creep,
By whispering winds soon lulled asleep.
Towered cities please us then,
And the busy hum of men,
Where throngs of knights and barons bold,
In weeds[4] of peace, high triumphs hold,
With store of ladies, whose bright eyes
Rain influence, and judge the prize
Of wit or arms, while both contend
To win her grace whom all commend.
There let Hymen oft appear
In saffron robe, with taper clear,
And pomp, and feast, and revelry,
With mask and antique pageantry;
Such sights as youthful poets dream
On summer eves by haunted stream.
Then to the well-trod stage anon,
If Jonson's learnéd sock[5] be on,
Or sweetest Shakespeare, Fancy's child,
Warble his native wood-notes wild.
And ever, against eating cares,
Lap me in soft Lydian airs,
Married to immortal verse,
Such as the meeting soul may pierce,
In notes with many a winding bout[6]
Of linkéd sweetness long drawn out
With wanton heed and giddy cunning,
The melting voice through mazes running,
Untwisting all the chains that tie
The hidden soul of harmony;
That Orpheus' self may heave his head
From golden slumber on a bed
Of heaped Elysian flowers, and hear
Such strains as would have won the ear
Of Pluto to have quite set free
His half-regained Eurydice.
These delights if thou canst give,
Mirth, with thee I mean to live.

IL PENSEROSO

HENCE, vain deluding Joys,
  The brood of Folly without father bred!
How little you bested,[7]
  Or fill the fixéd mind with all your toys!
Dwell in some idle brain,
  And fancies fond[8] with gaudy shapes possess,
As thick and numberless
  As the gay motes that people the sunbeam,
Or likest hovering dreams,
  The fickle pensioners of Morpheus' train.
But, hail! thou Goddess sage and holy!
Hail, divinest Melancholy!
Whose saintly visage is too bright
To hit the sense of human sight,
And therefore to our weaker view
O'erlaid with black, staid Wisdom's hue;
Black, but such as in esteem
Prince Memnon's sister might beseem,
Or that starred Ethiop queen[9] that strove
To set her beauty's praise above
The Sea-Nymphs, and their powers offended.
Yet thou art higher far descended:
Thee bright-haired Vesta long of yore
To solitary Saturn bore;
His daughter she; in Saturn's reign
Such mixture was not held a stain.
Oft in glimmering bowers and glades
He met her, and in secret shades
Of woody Ida's inmost grove,
Whilst yet there was no fear of Jove.
Come, pensive Nun, devout and pure,
Sober, steadfast, and demure,
All in a robe of darkest grain,[10]
Flowing with majestic train,
And sable stole of cypress lawn[11]
Over thy decent shoulders drawn.
Come; but keep thy wonted state,
With even step, and musing gait,
And looks commercing with the skies,
Thy rapt soul sitting in thine eyes:
There, held in holy passion still,
Forget thyself to marble, till
With a sad leaden downward cast
Thou fix them on the earth as fast.
And join with thee calm Peace and Quiet,
Spare Fast, that oft with gods doth diet,
And hears the Muses in a ring
Aye round about Jove's altar sing;
And add to these retiréd Leisure,
That in trim gardens takes his pleasure;
But, first and chiefest, with thee bring
Him that yon soars on golden wing,
Guiding the fiery-wheeléd throne,
The Cherub Contemplation;
And the mute Silence hist along,
'Less Philomel[12] will deign a song,
In her sweetest saddest plight,
Smoothing the rugged brow of Night,

[1]Will-o'-the-wisp. [2]Robin Goodfellow.
[3]Clumsy. [4]Garments.
[5]The light shoe worn in classical times by actors in comedy.
[6]Turn.

[7]Profit. [8]Foolish.
[9]Cassiopeia, who was placed among the stars.
[10]Purple color. [11]A light crape. [12]The nightingale.

While Cynthia[1] checks her dragon yoke
Gently o'er the accustomed oak.
Sweet bird, that shunn'st the noise of folly,
Most musical, most melancholy!
Thee, chauntress, oft the woods among
I woo, to hear thy even-song;
And, missing thee, I walk unseen
On the dry smooth-shaven green
To behold the wandering moon,
Riding near her highest noon,
Like one that had been led astray
Through the heaven's wide pathless way,
And oft, as if her head she bowed,
Stooping through a fleecy cloud.
Oft, on a plat of rising ground,
I hear the far-off curfew sound,
Over some wide-watered shore,
Swinging slow with sullen roar;
Or, if the air will not permit,
Some still removéd place will fit,
Where glowing embers through the room
Teach light to counterfeit a gloom,
Far from all resort of mirth,
Save the cricket on the hearth,
Or the bellman's drowsy charm
To bless the doors from nightly harm.
Or let my lamp, at midnight hour,
Be seen in some high lonely tower,
Where I may oft outwatch the Bear,[2]
With thrice great Hermes,[3] or unsphere[4]
The spirit of Plato, to unfold
What worlds or what past regions hold
The immortal mind that hath forsook
Her mansion in this fleshly nook;
And of those demons that are found
In fire, air, flood, or underground,
Whose power hath a true consent[5]
With planet or with element.
Sometimes let gorgeous Tragedy
In sceptered pall come sweeping by,
Presenting Thebes, or Pelops' line,
Or the tale of Troy divine,
Or what (though rare) of later age
Ennobled hath the buskined[6] stage.
But, O sad Virgin! that thy power
Might raise Musæus from his bower;
Or bid the soul of Orpheus sing
Such notes as, warbled to the string,
Drew iron tears down Pluto's cheek,
And made Hell grant what love did seek;
Or call up him[7] that left half-told

[1]The moon.

[2]The Great Bear never sets in England, consequently he would have to sit up until dawn.

[3]Hermes Trismegistus, a fabled Egyptian ruler to whom were ascribed many books.

[4]Call his spirit from the sphere where it abides.

[5]Sympathy.

[6]Tragic (the buskin was the heavy boot worn by tragic actors in classical times).

[7]Chaucer (the allusion is to the uncompleted Squire's Tale).

The story of Cambuscan bold,
Of Camball, and of Algarsife,
And who had Canace to wife,
That owned the virtuous ring and glass,
And of the wondrous horse of brass
On which the Tartar king did ride;
And if aught else great bards beside
In sage and solemn tunes have sung,
Of turneys, and of trophies hung,
Of forests, and enchantments drear,
Where more is meant than meets the ear.[8]
Thus, Night, oft see me in thy pale career,
Till civil-suited Morn appear,
Not tricked and frounced, as she was wont
With the Attic boy[9] to hunt,
But kerchiefed in a comely cloud,
While rocking winds are piping loud,
Or ushered with a shower still,
When the gust hath blown his fill,
Ending on the rustling leaves,
With minute-drops from off the eaves.
And, when the sun begins to fling
His flaring beams, me, Goddess, bring
To archéd walks of twilight groves,
And shadows brown, that Sylvan loves,
Of pine, or monumental oak,
Where the rude ax with heavéd stroke
Was never heard the nymphs to daunt,
Or fright them from their hallowed haunt.
There, in close covert, by some brook,
Where no profaner eye may look,
Hide me from day's garish eye,
While the bee with honeyed thigh,
That at her flowery work doth sing,
And the waters murmuring,
With such consort as they keep,
Entice the dewy-feathered Sleep.
And let some strange mysterious dream
Wave at his wings, in airy stream
Of lively portraiture displayed,
Softly on my eyelids laid;
And, as I wake, sweet music breathe
Above, about, or underneath,
Sent by some Spirit to mortals good,
Or the unseen Genius of the wood.
But let my due feet never fail
To walk the studious cloister's pale,[10]
And love the high embowéd roof,
With antique pillars massy-proof,
And storied windows richly dight,[11]
Casting a dim religious light.
There let the pealing organ blow,
To the full-voiced quire below,
In service high and anthems clear,
As may with sweetness, through mine ear,
Dissolve me into ecstasies,

[8]The allusion is probably to Spenser.

[9]Cephalus, loved by Aurora.

[10]Enclosure.

[11]Windows richly adorned with stories (from the Bible).

And bring all Heaven before mine eyes.
And may at last my weary age
Find out the peaceful hermitage,
The hairy gown and mossy cell,
Where I may sit and rightly spell[1]
Of every star that heaven doth shew,
And every herb that sips the dew,
Till old experience do attain
To something like prophetic strain.
These pleasures, Melancholy, give;
And I with thee will choose to live.

LYCIDAS[2]

YET once more, O ye laurels, and once more,
Ye myrtles brown, with ivy never sere,
I come to pluck your berries harsh and crude,
And with forced fingers rude
Shatter your leaves before the mellowing year.[3]
Bitter constraint and sad occasion dear
Compels me to disturb your season due;
For Lycidas[4] is dead, dead ere his prime,
Young Lycidas, and hath not left his peer.
Who would not sing for Lycidas? he knew
Himself to sing, and build the lofty rime.
He must not float upon his watery bier
Unwept, and welter to the parching wind,
Without the meed of some melodious tear.
Begin, then, Sisters of the sacred well[5]
That from beneath the seat of Jove doth spring;
Begin, and somewhat loudly sweep the string.
Hence with denial vain and coy excuse:
So may some gentle Muse
With lucky words favor *my* destined urn,
And as he passes turn,
And bid fair peace be to my sable shroud!
For we were nursed upon the self-same hill,
Fed the same flock, by fountain, shade, and rill;
Together both, ere the high lawns appeared
Under the opening eyelids of the Morn,
We drove a-field, and both together heard
What time the gray-fly winds her sultry horn,
Battening[6] our flocks with the fresh dews of night,
Oft till the star that rose at evening bright
Toward heaven's descent had sloped his westering wheel.
Meanwhile the rural ditties were not mute;
Tempered to the oaten flute,
Rough Satyrs danced, and Fauns with cloven heel
From the glad sound would not be absent long;
And old Damœtas[7] loved to hear our song.
But, oh! the heavy change, now thou art gone,
Now thou art gone and never must return!
Thee, Shepherd, thee the woods and desert caves,
With wild thyme and the gadding vine o'ergrown,
And all their echoes, mourn.
The willows, and the hazel copses green,
Shall now no more be seen
Fanning their joyous leaves to thy soft lays.
As killing as the canker to the rose,
Or taint-worm to the weanling herds that graze,
Or frost to flowers, that their gay wardrobe wear,
When first the white-thorn blows;
Such, Lycidas, thy loss to shepherd's ear.
Where were ye, Nymphs, when the remorseless deep
Closed o'er the head of your loved Lycidas?
For neither were ye playing on the steep
Where your old bards, the famous Druids, lie,
Nor on the shaggy top of Mona high,
Nor yet where Deva spreads her wizard stream.
Ay me! I fondly[8] dream
"Had ye been there," . . . for what could that have done?
What could the Muse[9] herself that Orpheus bore,
The Muse herself, for her enchanting son,
Whom universal nature did lament,
When, by the rout that made the hideous roar,
His gory visage down the stream was sent,
Down the swift Hebrus to the Lesbian shore?
Alas! what boots[10] it with uncessant care
To tend the homely, slighted, shepherd's trade,
And strictly meditate the thankless Muse?
Were it not better done, as others use,
To sport with Amaryllis in the shade,
Or with the tangles of Neæra's hair?
Fame is the spur that the clear spirit doth raise
(That last infirmity of noble mind)
To scorn delights and live laborious days;

[1] Read.

[2] In this monody the author bewails a learned friend, unfortunately drowned in his passage from Chester on the Irish seas, 1637, and by occasion foretells the ruin of our corrupted clergy, then in their height (Milton's note). Milton's learned friend was Edward King of Christ's College, Cambridge.

[3] *I. e.*, Milton was forced to break his resolution not to write until his powers were fully matured.

[4] The name occurs in the seventh Idyll of Theocritus.

[5] Muses of the Pierian spring.

[6] Feeding.

[7] A conventional name drawn from pastoral poetry. Probably some fellow or the master of Christ's College is meant.

[8] Foolishly.

[9] Calliope. Orpheus was torn to pieces by Thracian women, and his head was thrown into the river Hebrus.

[10] Avails.

But the fair guerdon when we hope to find,
And think to burst out into sudden blaze,
Comes the blind Fury[1] with the abhorréd shears,
And slits the thin-spun life. "But not the praise,"
Phœbus replied, and touched my trembling ears:
"Fame is no plant that grows on mortal soil,
Nor in the glistening foil[2]
Set off to the world, nor in broad rumor lies,
But lives and spreads aloft by those pure eyes
And perfect witness of all-judging Jove;
As he pronounces lastly on each deed,
Of so much fame in heaven expect thy meed."
O fountain Arethuse, and thou honored flood,
Smooth-sliding Mincius, crowned with vocal reeds,
That strain I heard was of a higher mood.
But now my oat[3] proceeds,
And listens to the Herald of the Sea,
That came in Neptune's plea.
He asked the waves, and asked the felon winds,
What hard mishap hath doomed this gentle swain?
And questioned every gust of rugged wings
That blows from off each beakéd promontory.
They knew not of his story;
And sage Hippotades[4] their answer brings,
That not a blast was from his dungeon strayed:
The air was calm, and on the level brine
Sleek Panope[5] with all her sisters played.
It was that fatal[6] and perfidious bark,
Built in the eclipse, and rigged with curses dark,
That sunk so low that sacred head of thine.
Next, Camus,[7] reverend sire, went footing slow,
His mantle hairy, and his bonnet sedge,
Inwrought with figures dim, and on the edge
Like to that sanguine flower inscribed with woe.[8]
"Ah! who hath reft," quoth he, "my dearest pledge?"[9]
Last came, and last did go,
The Pilot of the Galilean Lake;[10]
Two massy keys he bore of metals twain[11]
(The golden opes, the iron shuts amain[12]).

[1]Atropos, a Fate. Milton here calls her a Fury because of his anger.
[2]Tinsel. [3]Shepherd s pipe.
[4]Æolus, god of winds.
[5]One of the Nereids. [6]Fated.
[7]The god of the Cam, the river at Cambridge.
[8]The hyacinth, whose leaves have certain markings, said by the ancients to be AI, AI (alas!), in mourning for Hyacinthus.
[9]Bereaved me of my dearest child.
[10]St. Peter. [11]*Cf.* St. Matthew, xvi, 19.
[12]With force.

He shook his mitered locks, and stern bespake:—
"How well could I have spared for thee, young swain,
Enow of such as, for their bellies' sake,
Creep, and intrude, and climb into the fold!
Of other care they little reckoning make
Than how to scramble at the shearers' feast,
And shove away the worthy bidden guest.
Blind mouths! that scarce themselves know how to hold
A sheep-hook, or have learned aught else the least
That to the faithful herdman's art belongs!
What recks[13] it them? What need they? They are sped;[14]
And, when they list, their lean and flashy songs
Grate on their scrannel[15] pipes of wretched straw;
The hungry sheep look up, and are not fed,
But, swoln with wind and the rank mist they draw,
Rot inwardly, and foul contagion spread;
Besides what the grim wolf with privy paw
Daily devours apace, and nothing said.
But that two-handed engine[16] at the door
Stands ready to smite once, and smite no more."
Return, Alpheus;[17] the dread voice is past
That shrunk thy streams; return, Sicilian Muse,
And call the vales, and bid them hither cast
Their bells and flowerets of a thousand hues.
Ye valleys low, where the mild whispers use
Of shades, and wanton winds, and gushing brooks,
On whose fresh lap the swart star[18] sparely looks,
Throw hither all your quaint enameled eyes
That on the green turf suck the honeyed showers,
And purple all the ground with vernal flowers.
Bring the rathe[19] primrose that forsaken dies,
The tufted crow-toe, and pale jessamine,
The white pink, and the pansy freaked[20] with jet,
The growing violet,
The musk rose, and the well-attired woodbine,
With cowslips wan that hang the pensive head,
And every flower that sad embroidery wears;
Bid amaranthus all his beauty shed,
And daffadillies fill their cups with tears,

[13]Concerns. [14]Provided for. [15]Thin.
[16]Perhaps the ax of St. Matthew, iii, 10, and St. Luke, iii, 9.
[17]River of Arcadia, whose spirit loved Arethusa.
[18]The dog-star, supposed to be injurious to plants.
[19]Early. [20]Sprinkled.

To strew the laureate hearse where Lycid lies.
For so, to interpose a little ease,
Let our frail thoughts dally with false surmise,
Ay me! whilst thee the shores and sounding seas
Wash far away, where'er thy bones are hurled;
Whether beyond the stormy Hebrides,
Where thou perhaps under the whelming tide
Visit'st the bottom of the monstrous world;[1]
Or whether thou, to our moist vows denied,
Sleep'st by the fable of Bellerus old,[2]
Where the great Vision of the guarded mount[3]
Looks toward Namancos and Bayona's hold.[4]
Look homeward, Angel, now, and melt with ruth:[5]
And, O ye dolphins, waft the hapless youth.
Weep no more, woeful shepherds, weep no more,
For Lycidas, your sorrow, is not dead,
Sunk though he be beneath the watery floor.
So sinks the day-star in the ocean bed,
And yet anon repairs his drooping head,
And tricks[6] his beams, and with new-spangled ore[7]
Flames in the forehead of the morning sky:
So Lycidas sunk low, but mounted high,
Through the dear might of him that walked the waves,
Where, other groves and other streams along,
With nectar pure his oozy locks he laves,
And hears the unexpressive[8] nuptial song,
In the blest kingdoms meek of joy and love.
There entertain him all the Saints above,
In solemn troops, and sweet societies,
That sing, and singing in their glory move,
And wipe the tears for ever from his eyes.
Now, Lycidas, the shepherds weep no more;
Henceforth thou art the Genius of the shore,
In thy large recompense, and shalt be good
To all that wander in that perilous flood.
Thus sang the uncouth swain to the oaks and rills,
While the still morn went out with sandals gray:
He touched the tender stops of various quills,[9]
With eager thought warbling his Doric lay:[10]
And now the sun had stretched out all the hills,
And now was dropped into the western bay.
At last he rose, and twitched his mantle blue:
To-morrow to fresh woods, and pastures new.

[1]World of monsters. [2]Land's End.
[3]St. Michael's Mount, near Land's End.
[4]In Spain, near Cape Finisterre.
[5]Pity. [6]Adorns. [7]Brightness.
[8]Inexpressible. [9]Reeds, *i. e.*, pipes.
[10]Pastoral poem.

SONNETS[11]

VII

How soon hath Time, the subtle thief of youth,
Stolen on his wing my three-and-twentieth year!
My hasting days fly on with full career,
But my late spring no bud or blossom shew'th.
Perhaps my semblance might deceive the truth
That I to manhood am arrived so near;
And inward ripeness doth much less appear,
That some more timely-happy spirits endu'th.
Yet, be it less or more, or soon or slow,
It shall be still in strictest measure even
To that same lot, however mean or high,
Toward which Time leads me, and the will of Heaven;
All is, if I have grace to use it so,
As ever in my great Task-Master's eye.

VIII[12]

Captain or Colonel, or Knight in Arms,
Whose chance on these defenseless doors may seize,
If deed of honor did thee ever please,
Guard them, and him within protect from harms:
He can requite thee, for he knows the charms
That call fame on such gentle acts as these;
And he can spread thy name o'er lands and seas,
Whatever clime the sun's bright circle warms.
Lift not thy spear against the Muses' bower:
The great Emathian conqueror[13] bid spare
The house of Pindarus, when temple and tower
Went to the ground; and the repeated air
Of sad Electra's poet[14] had the power
To save the Athenian walls from ruin bare.

IX

Lady, that in the prime of earliest youth
Wisely hast shunned the broad way and the green,
And with those few art eminently seen
That labor up the hill of heavenly Truth,
The better part with Mary and with Ruth,
Chosen thou hast; and they that overween,
And at thy growing virtues fret their spleen,
No anger find in thee, but pity and ruth.

[11]The Sonnets are numbered as in H. C. Beeching's edition.
[12]Written in the fall of 1642 when the army of Charles I was advancing on London.
[13]Alexander the Great, when he sacked Thebes.
[14]Euripedes.

Thy care is fixed, and zealously attends
To fill thy odorous lamp with deeds of light,
And hope that reaps not shame. Therefore be sure
Thou, when the Bridegroom with his feastful friends
Passes to bliss at the mid-hour of night,
Hast gained thy entrance, Virgin wise and pure.

XI

A BOOK was writ of late called *Tetrachordon*,[1]
And woven close, both matter, form, and style;
The subject new: it walked the town a while,
Numbering good intellects; now seldom pored on.
Cries the stall-reader, "Bless us! what a word on
A title-page is this!"; and some in file
Stand spelling false, while one might walk to Mile-
End Green. Why, is it harder, sirs, than *Gordon*,
Colkitto, or *Macdonnel*, or *Galasp*?[2]
Those rugged names to our like mouths grow sleek,
That would have made Quintilian stare and gasp.
Thy age, like ours, O soul of Sir John Cheek,
Hated not learning worse than toad or asp,
When thou taught'st Cambridge and King Edward Greek.

XII

ON THE SAME

I DID but prompt the age to quit their clogs
By the known rules of ancient liberty,
When straight a barbarous noise environs me
Of owls and cuckoos, asses, apes, and dogs;
As when those hinds that were transformed to frogs
Railed at Latona's twin-born progeny,[3]
Which after held the Sun and Moon in fee.
But this is got by casting pearl to hogs,
That bawl for freedom in their senseless mood,
And still revolt when Truth would set them free.
Licence they mean when they cry Liberty;
For who loves that must first be wise and good:
But from that mark how far they rove we see,
For all this waste of wealth and loss of blood.

XV

ON THE LATE MASSACRE IN PIEDMONT[4]

AVENGE, O Lord, thy slaughtered saints, whose bones
Lie scattered on the Alpine mountains cold;
Even them who kept thy truth so pure of old,
When all our fathers worshiped stocks and stones,
Forget not: in thy book record their groans
Who were thy sheep, and in their ancient fold
Slain by the bloody Piemontese, that rolled
Mother with infant down the rocks. Their moans
The vales redoubled to the hills, and they
To heaven. Their martyred blood and ashes sow
O'er all th' Italian fields, where still doth sway
The triple Tyrant;[5] that from these may grow
A hundred fold, who, having learned thy way,
Early may fly the Babylonian woe.

XVI

WHEN I consider how my light is spent
Ere half my days in this dark world and wide,
And that one talent which is death to hide
Lodged with me useless, though my soul more bent
To serve therewith my Maker, and present
My true account, lest He returning chide,
"Doth God exact day-labor, light denied?"
I fondly ask. But Patience, to prevent
That murmur, soon replies, "God doth not need
Either man's work or his own gifts. Who best
Bear his mild yoke, they serve him best. His state
Is kingly: thousands at his bidding speed,
And post o'er land and ocean without rest;
They also serve who only stand and wait."

XVII

LAWRENCE, of virtuous father virtuous son,
Now that the fields are dank, and ways are mire,
Where shall we sometimes meet, and by the fire
Help waste a sullen day, what may be won

[1] One of Milton's pamphlets on divorce.

[2] Names of Scottish generals during the war of 1644–1645.

[3] Apollo and Diana.

[4] In 1655 the Count of Turin subjected the protestants of Piedmont to bitter persecution, cruelly killing a number of them.

[5] The pope. The puritans identified Rome with Babylon (*Cf.* Revelation, xvii, 5).

From the hard season gaining? Time will run
On smoother, till Favonius[1] reinspire
The frozen earth, and clothe in fresh attire
The lily and rose, that neither sowed nor spun.
What neat repast shall feast us, light and choice,
Of Attic taste, with wine, whence we may rise,
To hear the lute well touched, or artful voice
Warble immortal notes and Tuscan air?
He who of those delights can judge, and spare
To interpose them oft, is not unwise.

XVIII

CYRIACK, whose grandsire[2] on the royal bench
Of British Themis,[3] with no mean applause,
Pronounced, and in his volumes taught, our laws,
Which others at their bar so often wrench,
To-day deep thoughts resolve with me to drench
In mirth that after no repenting draws;
Let Euclid rest, and Archimedes pause,
And what the Swede intend, and what the French.[4]
To measure life learn thou betimes, and know
Towards solid good what leads the nearest way;
For other things mild Heaven a time ordains,
And disapproves that care, though wise in show,
That with superfluous burden loads the day,
And, when God sends a cheerful hour, refrains.

XIX

METHOUGHT I saw my late espousèd saint[5]
Brought to me like Alcestis from the grave,
Whom Jove's great son[6] to her glad husband gave,
Rescued from Death by force, though pale and faint.
Mine, as whom washed from spot of child-bed taint
Purification in the Old Law[7] did save,
And such as yet once more I trust to have
Full sight of her in Heaven without restraint,
Came vested all in white, pure as her mind.
Her face was veiled; yet to my fancied sight
Love, sweetness, goodness, in her person shined
So clear as in no face with more delight.
But, oh! as to embrace me she inclined,
I waked, she fled, and day brought back my night.

[1]The spring wind from the southwest.

[2]Sir Edward Coke. [3]Goddess of justice.

[4]Charles X of Sweden was at war with Poland and Russia, and Louis XIV was fighting the Spanish in the Netherlands.

[5]Catherine Woodcock, Milton's second wife, who died in childbirth in February, 1658.

[6]Hercules. [7]Leviticus, xii.

TO THE LORD GENERAL CROMWELL MAY, 1652

ON THE PROPOSALS OF CERTAIN MINISTERS AT THE COMMITTEE FOR PROPAGATION OF THE GOSPEL

CROMWELL, our chief of men, who through a cloud
Not of war only, but detractions rude,
Guided by faith and matchless fortitude,
To peace and truth thy glorious way hast plowed,
And on the neck of crownéd Fortune proud
Hast reared God's trophies, and his work pursued,
While Darwen stream, with blood of Scots imbrued,
And Dunbar field, resounds thy praises loud,
And Worcester's laureate wreath: yet much remains
To conquer still; Peace hath her victories
No less renowned than War: new foes arise,
Threatening to bind our souls with secular chains.[8]
Help us to save free conscience from the paw
Of hireling wolves, whose Gospel is their maw.

TO MR. CYRIACK SKINNER

UPON HIS BLINDNESS

CYRIACK, this three years' day these eyes, though clear
To outward view, of blemish or of spot,
Bereft of light, their seeing have forgot;
Nor to their idle orbs doth sight appear
Of sun, or moon, or star, throughout the year,
Or man, or woman. Yet I argue not
Against Heaven's hand or will, nor bate a jot
Of heart or hope, but still bear up and steer
Right onward. What supports me, dost thou ask?
The conscience, friend, to have lost them overplied

[8]Government control. The proposals to which Milton objected were that puritan ministers be supported by the state.

In Liberty's defense, my noble task,
Of which all Europe rings from side to side
This thought might lead me through the world's vain mask
Content, though blind, had I no better guide.

PARADISE LOST

THE VERSE

The measure is English heroic verse without rime, as that of Homer in Greek, and of Virgil in Latin; rime being no necessary adjunct or true ornament of poem or good verse, in longer works especially, but the invention of a barbarous age to set off wretched matter and lame meter; graced indeed since by the use of some famous modern poets, carried away by custom, but much to their own vexation, hindrance, and constraint to express many things otherwise, and for the most part worse, than else they would have expressed them. Not without cause therefore, some both Italian and Spanish poets of prime note have rejected rime both in longer and shorter works, as have long since our best English tragedies; as a thing of itself, to all judicious ears, trivial and of no true musical delight; which consists only in apt numbers, fit quantity of syllables, and the sense variously drawn out from one verse into another; not in the jingling sound of like endings, a fault avoided by the learned ancients both in poetry and all good oratory. This neglect then of rime so little is to be taken for a defect, though it may seem so perhaps to vulgar readers, that it is rather to be esteemed an example set, the first in English, of ancient liberty recovered to heroic poem, from the troublesome and modern bondage of riming.

BOOK I

THE ARGUMENT

This First Book proposes, first in brief, the whole subject—Man's disobedience, and the loss thereupon of Paradise, wherein he was placed: then touches the prime cause of his fall—the Serpent, or rather Satan in the Serpent; who, revolting from God, and drawing to his side many legions of Angels, was, by the command of God, driven out of Heaven, with all his crew, into the great Deep. Which action passed over, the Poem hastens into the midst of things; presenting Satan, with his Angels, now fallen into Hell—described here not in the Center (for heaven and earth may be supposed as yet not made, certainly not yet accursed), but in a place of utter darkness, fitliest called Chaos. Here Satan, with his Angels lying on the burning lake, thunderstruck and astonished, after a certain space recovers, as from confusion; calls up him who, next in order and dignity, lay by him: they confer of their miserable fall. Satan awakens all his legions, who lay till then in the same manner confounded. They rise: their numbers; array of battle; their chief leaders named, according to the idols known afterwards in Canaan and the countries adjoining. To these Satan directs his speech; comforts them with hope yet of regaining Heaven; but tells them, lastly, of a new world and new kind of creature to be created, according to an ancient prophecy, or report, in Heaven—for that Angels were long before this visible creation was the opinion of many ancient Fathers. To find out the truth of this prophecy, and what to determine thereon, he refers to a full council. What his associates thence attempt. Pandemonium, the palace of Satan, rises, suddenly built out of the Deep: the infernal Peers there sit in council.

Of man's first disobedience, and the fruit
Of that forbidden tree whose mortal taste
Brought death into the World, and all our woe,
With loss of Eden, till one greater Man
Restore us, and regain the blissful seat,
Sing, Heavenly Muse, that, on the secret top
Of Oreb, or of Sinai, didst inspire
That shepherd who first taught the chosen seed
In the beginning how the heavens and earth
Rose out of Chaos: or, if Sion hill
Delight thee more, and Siloa's brook that flowed
Fast[1] by the oracle of God,[2] I thence
Invoke thy aid to my adventrous song,
That with no middle flight intends to soar
Above the Aonian mount,[3] while it pursues
Things unattempted yet in prose or rime.
And chiefly thou, O Spirit, that does prefer
Before all temples the upright heart and pure,
Instruct me, for thou know'st; thou from the first
Wast present, and, with mighty wings outspread,
Dove-like sat'st brooding on the vast Abyss,
And mad'st it pregnant: what in me is dark
Illumine, what is low raise and support;
That, to the highth of this great argument,
I may assert[4] Eternal Providence,
And justify the ways of God to men.
Say first—for Heaven hides nothing from thy view,
Nor the deep tract of Hell—say first what cause

[1]Close. [2]The temple of Jerusalem.
[3]Helicon, home of the muses. [4]Vindicate.

Moved our grand[1] Parents, in that happy state,
Favored of Heaven so highly, to fall off
From their Creator, and transgress his will
For[2] one restraint, lords of the World besides.
Who first seduced them to that foul revolt?
  The infernal Serpent; he it was whose guile,
Stirred up with envy and revenge, deceived
The mother of mankind, what time his pride
Had cast him out from Heaven, with all his host
Of rebel Angels, by whose aid, aspiring
To set himself in glory above his peers,
He trusted to have equaled the Most High,
If he opposed, and, with ambitious aim
Against the throne and monarchy of God,
Raised impious war in Heaven and battle proud,
With vain attempt. Him the Almighty Power
Hurled headlong flaming from the ethereal sky,
With hideous ruin and combustion, down
To bottomless perdition, there to dwell
In adamantine chains and penal fire,
Who durst defy the Omnipotent to arms.[3]
  Nine times the space that measure day and night
To mortal men, he, with his horrid crew,
Lay vanquished, rolling in the fiery gulf,
Confounded, though immortal. But his doom
Reserved him to more wrath; for now the thought
Both of lost happiness and lasting pain
Torments him: round he throws his baleful eyes,
That witnessed huge affliction and dismay,
Mixed with obdurate pride and steadfast hate.
At once, as far as Angels ken, he views
The dismal situation waste and wild.

[1]First. [2]Because of.

[3]Milton's conception of the universe and of its relation to heaven and hell should be grasped at the outset. He follows the Ptolemaic system, according to which the earth is the center of the universe, about which the other bodies revolve. These (sun, moon, *etc.*) are supposed to be fastened in a series of hollow spheres, made of some transparent substance, which move around the earth as a common center. The hollow spheres were, in medieval and early modern times, supposed to be ten in number, the outermost being the *primum mobile*, or "first moved." Thus the starry universe has the form of a large globe, and it is suspended from the wall of heaven by a golden chain. Heaven is the region lying entirely outside the starry universe and immediately above it. Surrounding the universe and separated from heaven by a wall is chaos, the region of unformed, warring elements through which Satan and his host were hurled from heaven. At the bottom of this region of chaos is hell, the place of punishment prepared for Satan and his followers when they rebelled. Hell, then, is under the universe and is separated from it by a distance through chaos equal to the distance from the center of the earth to the *primum mobile* (see where Milton says the distance from heaven to hell is three times the radius of the universe).

A dungeon horrible, on all sides round,
As one great furnace flamed; yet from those flames
No light; but rather darkness visible
Served only to discover sights of woe,
Regions of sorrow, doleful shades, where peace
And rest can never dwell, hope never comes
That comes to all, but torture without end
Still urges, and a fiery deluge, fed
With ever-burning sulphur unconsumed.
Such place Eternal Justice had prepared
For those rebellious; here their prison ordained
In utter darkness, and their portion set,
As far removed from God and light of Heaven
As from the center thrice to the utmost pole.
Oh how unlike the place from whence they fell!
There the companions of his fall, o'erwhelmed
With floods and whirlwinds of tempestuous fire,
He soon discerns; and, weltering by his side,
One next himself in power, and next in crime,
Long after known in Palestine, and named
BEËLZEBUB. To whom the Arch-Enemy,
And thence in Heaven called SATAN,[4] with bold words
Breaking the horrid silence, thus began:—
  "If thou beest he—but Oh how fallen! how changed
From him!—who, in the happy realms of light,
Clothed with transcendent brightness, didst outshine
Myriads, though bright—if he whom mutual league,
United thoughts and counsels, equal hope
And hazard in the glorious enterprise,
Joined with me once, now misery hath joined
In equal ruin; into what pit thou seest
From what highth fallen: so much the stronger proved
He with his thunder: and till then who knew
The force of those dire arms? Yet not for those,
Nor what the potent Victor in his rage
Can else inflict, do I repent, or change,
Though changed in outward luster, that fixed mind,
And high disdain from sense of injured merit,
That with the Mightiest raised me to contend,
And to the fierce contention brought along
Innumerable force of Spirits armed,
That durst dislike his reign, and, me preferring,
His utmost power with adverse power opposed
In dubious battle on the plains of Heaven,
And shook his throne. What though the field be lost?
All is not lost—the unconquerable will,

[4]A Hebrew word meaning adversary.

And study of revenge, immortal hate,
And courage never to submit or yield;
And what is else not to be overcome?
That glory never shall his wrath or might
Extort from me. To bow and sue for grace
With suppliant knee, and deify his power
Who, from the terror of this arm, so late
Doubted[1] his empire—that were low indeed;
That were an ignominy and shame beneath
This downfall; since, by fate, the strength of Gods,
And this empyreal substance, cannot fail;
Since, through experience of this great event,
In arms not worse, in foresight much advanced,
We may with more successful hope resolve
To wage by force or guile eternal war,
Irreconcilable to our grand Foe,
Who now triumphs, and in the excess of joy
Sole reigning holds the tyranny of Heaven."
So spake the apostate Angel, though in pain,
Vaunting aloud, but racked with deep despair;
And him thus answered soon his bold compeer:—
"O Prince, O Chief of many thronéd Powers
That led the embattled Seraphim to war
Under thy conduct, and, in dreadful deeds
Fearless, endangered Heaven's perpetual King,
And put to proof his high supremacy,
Whether upheld by strength, or chance, or fate,
Too well I see and rue the dire event
That, with sad overthrow and foul defeat,
Hath lost us Heaven, and all this mighty host
In horrible destruction laid thus low,
As far as Gods and Heavenly Essences
Can perish: for the mind and spirit remains
Invincible, and vigor soon returns,
Though all our glory extinct, and happy state
Here swallowed up in endless misery.
But what if he our Conqueror (whom I now
Of force believe almighty, since no less
Than such could have o'erpowered such force as ours)
Have left us this our spirit and strength entire,
Strongly to suffer and support our pains,
That we may so suffice[2] his vengeful ire,
Or do him mightier service as his thralls
By right of war, whate'er his business be,
Here in the heart of Hell to work in fire,
Or do his errands in the gloomy Deep?
What can it then avail though yet we feel
Strength undiminished, or eternal being
To undergo eternal punishment?"
Whereto with speedy words the Arch-Fiend replied:—
"Fallen Cherub, to be weak is miserable,
Doing or suffering: but of this be sure—
To do ought good never will be our task,
But ever to do ill our sole delight,
As being the contrary to his high will
Whom we resist. If then his providence
Out of our evil seek to bring forth good,
Our labor must be to pervert that end,
And out of good still to find means of evil;
Which ofttimes may succeed so as perhaps
Shall grieve him, if I fail not,[3] and disturb
His inmost counsels from their destined aim.
But see! the angry Victor hath recalled
His ministers of vengeance and pursuit
Back to the gates of Heaven: the sulphurous hail,
Shot after us in storm, o'erblown hath laid
The fiery surge that from the precipice
Of Heaven received us falling; and the thunder,
Winged with red lightning and impetuous rage,
Perhaps hath spent his shafts, and ceases now
To bellow through the vast and boundless Deep.
Let us not slip the occasion, whether scorn
Or satiate fury yield it from our Foe.
Seest thou yon dreary plain, forlorn and wild,
The seat of desolation, void of light,
Save what the glimmering of these livid flames
Casts pale and dreadful? Thither let us tend
From off the tossing of these fiery waves;
There rest, if any rest can harbor there;
And, re-assembling our afflicted powers,
Consult how we may henceforth most offend
Our enemy, our own loss how repair,
How overcome this dire calamity,
What reinforcement we may gain from hope,
If not, what resolution from despair."
Thus Satan, talking to his nearest mate,
With head uplift above the wave, and eyes
That sparkling blazed; his other parts besides
Prone on the flood, extended long and large,
Lay floating many a rood, in bulk as huge
As whom the fables name of monstrous size,
Titanian or Earth-born, that warred on Jove,[4]
Briareos or Typhon, whom the den
By ancient Tarsus held, or that sea-beast
Leviathan, which God of all his works
Created hugest that swim the ocean-stream.
Him, haply slumbering on the Norway foam,
The pilot of some small night-foundered[5] skiff,
Deeming some island, oft, as seamen tell,
With fixéd anchor in his scaly rind,
Moors by his side under the lee, while night
Invests the sea, and wishéd morn delays.

[1]Feared for. [2]Satisfy.

[3]If I mistake not.

[4]The Titans warred on Uranus, the Giants (earth-born) on Jove (Zeus). Briareos was a Titan, Typhon a Giant.

[5]Overtaken by night and so brought to a stand.

So stretched out huge in length the Arch-Fiend lay,
Chained on the burning lake; nor ever thence
Had risen, or heaved his head, but that the will
And high permission of all-ruling Heaven
Left him at large to his own dark designs,
That with reiterated crimes he might
Heap on himself damnation, while he sought
Evil to others, and enraged might see
How all his malice served but to bring forth
Infinite goodness, grace, and mercy, shown
On Man by him seduced, but on himself
Treble confusion, wrath, and vengeance poured.
  Forthwith upright he rears from off the pool
His mighty stature; on each hand the flames
Driven backward slope their pointing spires, and, rolled
In billows, leave i'the midst a horrid vale.
Then with expanded wings he steers his flight
Aloft, incumbent on the dusky air,
That felt unusual weight; till on dry land
He lights—if it were land that ever burned
With solid, as the lake with liquid fire,
And such appeared in hue as when the force
Of subterranean wind transports a hill
Torn from Pelorus, or the shattered side
Of thundering Ætna, whose combustible
And fueled entrails, thence conceiving fire,
Sublimed with mineral fury, aid the winds,
And leave a singéd bottom all involved
With stench and smoke. Such resting found the sole
Of unblest feet. Him followed his next mate;
Both glorying to have scaped the Stygian flood
As gods, and by their own recovered strength,
Not by the sufferance of supernal power.
  "Is this the region, this the soil, the clime,"
Said then the lost Archangel, "this the seat
That we must change for Heaven?—this mournful gloom
For that celestial light? Be it so, since he
Who now is sovran can dispose and bid
What shall be right: farthest from him is best,
Whom reason hath equaled, force hath made supreme
Above his equals. Farewell, happy fields,
Where joy for ever dwells! Hail, horrors! hail,
Infernal World! and thou, profoundest Hell,
Receive thy new possessor—one who brings
A mind not to be changed by place or time.
The mind is its own place, and in itself
Can make a Heaven of Hell, a Hell of Heaven.
What matter where, if I be still the same,
And what I should be, all but less than[1] he
Whom thunder hath made greater? Here at least
We shall be free; the Almighty hath not built
Here for his envy, will not drive us hence:
Here we may reign secure; and, in my choice,
To reign is worth ambition, though in Hell:
Better to reign in Hell than serve in Heaven.
But wherefore let we then our faithful friends,
The associates and co-partners of our loss,
Lie thus astonished on the oblivious pool,[2]
And call them not to share with us their part
In this unhappy mansion, or once more
With rallied arms to try what may be yet
Regained in Heaven, or what more lost in Hell?"
  So Satan spake; and him Beëlzebub
Thus answered:—"Leader of those armies bright
Which, but the Omnipotent, none could have foiled!
If once they hear that voice, their liveliest pledge
Of hope in fears and dangers—heard so oft
In worst extremes, and on the perilous edge
Of battle, when it raged, in all assaults
Their surest signal—they will soon resume
New courage and revive, though now they lie
Groveling and prostrate on yon lake of fire,
As we erewhile, astounded and amazed;
No wonder, fallen such a pernicious highth!"
  He scarce had ceased when the superior Fiend
Was moving toward the shore; his ponderous shield,
Ethereal temper, massy, large, and round,
Behind him cast. The broad circumference
Hung on his shoulders like the moon, whose orb
Through optic glass[3] the Tuscan artist views
At evening, from the top of Fesolé,
Or in Valdarno, to descry new lands,
Rivers, or mountains, in her spotty globe.
His spear—to equal which the tallest pine
Hewn on Norwegian hills, to be the mast
Of some great ammiral,[4] were but a wand—
He walked with, to support uneasy steps
Over the burning marl, not like those steps
On Heaven's azure; and the torrid clime
Smote on him sore besides, vaulted with fire.
Nathless[5] he so endured, till on the beach
Of that inflaméd sea he stood, and called
His legions—Angel Forms, who lay entranced
Thick as autumnal leaves that strow the brooks

[1] *I. e.*, only less than.

[2] Lie thus thunderstruck on the benumbing pool.

[3] The telescope, greatly improved by Galileo (the Tuscan artist). Fiesole is a hill just outside of Florence; Val d'Arno the valley in which Florence lies.

[4] Chief vessel in a fleet.

[5] Nevertheless.

In Vallombrosa,[1] where the Etrurian shades
High over-arched embower; or scattered sedge
Afloat, when with fierce winds Orion armed
Hath vexed the Red-Sea coast, whose waves o'erthrew
Busiris and his Memphian chivalry,[2]
While with perfidious hatred they pursued
The sojourners of Goshen, who beheld
From the safe shore their floating carcases
And broken chariot-wheels. So thick bestrown,
Abject and lost, lay these, covering the flood,
Under amazement of their hideous change.
He called so loud that all the hollow deep
Of Hell resounded:—"Princes, Potentates,
Warriors, the Flower of Heaven—once yours; now lost,
If such astonishment as this can seize
Eternal Spirits! Or have ye chosen this place
After the toil of battle to repose
Your wearied virtue,[3] for the ease you find
To slumber here, as in the vales of Heaven?
Or in this abject posture have ye sworn
To adore the Conqueror, who now beholds
Cherub and Seraph rolling in the flood
With scattered arms and ensigns, till anon
His swift pursuers from Heaven-gates discern
The advantage, and, descending, tread us down
Thus drooping, or with linkéd thunderbolts
Transfix us to the bottom of this gulf?—
Awake, arise, or be for ever fallen!"
  They heard, and were abashed, and up they sprung
Upon the wing, as when men wont to watch,
On duty sleeping found by whom they dread,
Rouse and bestir themselves ere well awake.
Nor did they not perceive[4] the evil plight
In which they were, or the fierce pains not feel;
Yet to their General's voice they soon obeyed
Innumerable. As when the potent rod
Of Amram's son,[5] in Egypt's evil day,
Waved round the coast, up-called a pitchy cloud
Of locusts, warping on the eastern wind,
That o'er the realm of impious Pharaoh hung
Like Night, and darkened all the land of Nile;
So numberless were those bad Angels seen
Hovering on wing under the cope of Hell,
'Twixt upper, nether, and surrounding fires;
Till, as a signal given, the uplifted spear
Of their great Sultan waving to direct
Their course, in even balance down they light
On the firm brimstone, and fill all the plain:
A multitude like which the populous North
Poured never from her frozen loins to pass
Rhene or the Danaw,[6] when her barbarous sons
Came like a deluge on the South, and spread
Beneath Gibraltar to the Libyan sands.
Forthwith, from every squadron and each band,
The heads and leaders thither haste where stood
Their great Commander—godlike Shapes, and Forms
Excelling human; princely Dignities;
And Powers that erst[7] in Heaven sat on thrones,
Though of their names in Heavenly records now
Be no memorial, blotted out and razed
By their rebellion from the Books of Life.
Nor had they yet among the sons of Eve
Got them new names, till, wandering o'er the earth,
Through God's high sufferance for the trial of man,
By falsities and lies the greatest part
Of mankind they corrupted to forsake
God their Creator, and the invisible
Glory of him that made them, to transform
Oft to the image of a brute, adorned
With gay religions full of pomp and gold,
And devils to adore for deities:
Then were they known to men by various names,
And various idols through the Heathen World.
  Say, Muse, their names then known, who first, who last,
Roused from the slumber on that fiery couch,
At their great Emperor's call, as next in worth
Came singly where he stood on the bare strand,
While the promiscuous crowd stood yet aloof.
  The chief were those who, from the pit of Hell
Roaming to seek their prey on Earth, durst fix
Their seats, long after, next the seat of God,
Their altars by his altar, gods adored
Among the nations round, and durst abide
Jehovah thundering out of Sion, throned
Between the Cherubim; yea, often placed
Within his sanctuary itself their shrines,
Abominations; and with curséd things
His holy rites and solemn feasts profaned,
And with their darkness durst affront his light.
First, *Moloch*, horrid king, besmeared with blood
Of human sacrifice, and parents' tears;
Though, for the noise of drums and timbrels loud,
Their children's cries unheard that passed through fire

[1] Eighteen miles from Florence.

[2] Busiris, Pharaoh; Memphian, Egyptian.

[3] Courage.

[4] Nor did they fail to perceive.

[5] Aaron.

[6] Rhine or the Danube.

[7] Formerly.

To his grim idol. Him the Ammonite
Worshiped in Rabba and her watery plain,
In Argob and in Basan, to the stream
Of utmost Arnon. Nor content with such
Audacious neighborhood, the wisest heart
Of Solomon he led by fraud to build
His temple right against the temple of God
On that opprobrious hill,[1] and made his grove
The pleasant valley of Hinnom, Tophet thence
And black Gehenna called, the type of Hell.
Next *Chemos*, the obscene dread of Moab's sons,
From Aroar to Nebo and the wild
Of southmost Abarim; in Hesebon
And Horonaim, Seon's realm, beyond
The flowery dale of Sibma clad with vines,
And Elealé to the Asphaltic Pool:[2]
Peor his other name, when he enticed
Israel in Sittim on their march from Nile,
To do him wanton rites, which cost them woe.
Yet thence his lustful orgies he enlarged
Even to that hill of scandal, by the grove
Of Moloch homicide, lust hard by hate,
Till good Josiah drove them thence to Hell.
With these came they who, from the bordering flood
Of old Euphrates to the brook that parts
Egypt from Syrian ground, had general names
Of *Baälim* and *Ashtaroth*—those male,
These feminine. For spirits, when they please,
Can either sex assume, or both; so soft
And uncompounded is their essence pure,
Not tied or manacled with joint or limb,
Nor founded on the brittle strength of bones,
Like cumbrous flesh; but, in what shape they choose,
Dilated or condensed, bright or obscure,
Can execute their aery purposes,
And works of love or enmity fulfill.
For those the race of Israel oft forsook
Their Living Strength, and unfrequented left
His righteous altar, bowing lowly down
To bestial gods; for which their heads, as low
Bowed down in battle, sunk before the spear
Of despicable foes. With these in troop
Came *Astoreth*, whom the Phœnicians called
Astarté, queen of heaven, with crescent horns;
To whose bright image nightly by the moon
Sidonian virgins paid their vows and songs;
In Sion also not unsung, where stood
Her temple on the offensive mountain, built
By that uxorious king[3] whose heart, though large,
Beguiled by fair idolatresses, fell
To idols foul. *Thammuz* came next behind,
Whose annual wound in Lebanon allured
The Syrian damsels to lament his fate
In amorous ditties all a summer's day,
While smooth Adonis[4] from his native rock
Ran purple to the sea, supposed with blood,
Of Thammuz yearly wounded: the love-tale
Infected Sion's daughters with like heat,
Whose wanton passions in the sacred porch
Ezekiel saw, when, by the vision led,
His eye surveyed the dark idolatries
Of alienated Judah. Next came one
Who mourned in earnest, when the captive ark
Maimed his brute image, head and hands lopped off,
In his own temple, on the grunsel[5] edge,
Where he fell flat and shamed his worshipers:
Dagon his name, sea-monster, upward man
And downward fish; yet had his temple high
Reared in Azotus, dreaded through the coast
Of Palestine, in Gath and Ascalon,
And Accaron and Gaza's frontier bounds.
Him followed *Rimmon*, whose delightful seat
Was fair Damascus, on the fertile banks
Of Abbana and Pharphar, lucid streams.
He also against the house of God was bold:
A leper[6] once he lost, and gained a king—
Ahaz, his sottish conqueror, whom he drew
God's altar to disparage and displace
For one of Syrian mode, whereon to burn
His odious offerings, and adore the gods
Whom he had vanquished. After these appeared
A crew who, under names of old renown—
Osiris, *Isis*, *Orus*, and their train—
With monstrous shapes and sorceries abused
Fanatic Egypt and her priests to seek
Their wandering gods disguised in brutish forms
Rather than human. Nor did Israel scape
The infection, when their borrowed gold[7] composed
The calf in Oreb; and the rebel king[8]
Doubled that sin in Bethel and in Dan,
Likening his Maker to the grazéd ox—
Jehovah, who, in one night, when he[9] passed
From Egypt marching, equaled[10] with one stroke
Both her first-born and all her bleating gods.
Belial came last; than whom a Spirit more lewd
Fell not from Heaven, or more gross to love
Vice for itself. To him no temple stood
Or altar smoked; yet who more oft than he
In temples and at altars, when the priest
Turns atheist, as did Eli's sons, who filled
With lust and violence the house of God?
In courts and palaces he also reigns,

[1]The Mount of Olives, later called the Mount of Offense.
[2]The Dead Sea. [3]Solomon.

[4]A river in Phœnicia whose waters are colored by the soil through which it flows.
[5]Threshold. [6]Naaman.
[7]"Borrowed" from the Egyptians. [8]Jeroboam.
[9]*I. e.*, Israel. [10]Struck down.

And in luxurious cities, where the noise
Of riot ascends above their loftiest towers,
And injury and outrage; and, when night
Darkens the streets, then wander forth the sons
Of Belial, flown[1] with insolence and wine.
Witness the streets of Sodom, and that night
In Gibeah, when the hospitable door
Exposed a matron, to avoid worse rape.
These were the prime in order and in might:
The rest were long to tell; though far renowned
The Ionian gods—of Javan's issue held
Gods, yet confessed later than Heaven and Earth,
Their boasted parents;—*Titan*, Heaven's first-born,
With his enormous brood, and birthright seized
By younger *Saturn:* he from mightier Jove,
His own and Rhea's son, like measure found;
So *Jove* usurping reigned. These, first in Crete
And Ida known, thence on the snowy top
Of cold Olympus ruled the middle air,
Their highest heaven; or on the Delphian cliff,
Or in Dodona, and through all the bounds
Of Doric land; or who with Saturn old
Fled over Adria to the Hesperian fields,
And o'er the Celtic roamed the utmost Isles.
All these and more came flocking; but with looks
Downcast and damp;[2] yet such wherein appeared
Obscure some glimpse of joy to have found their Chief
Not in despair, to have found themselves not lost
In loss itself; which on his countenance cast
Like doubtful hue. But he, his wonted pride
Soon recollecting,[3] with high words, that bore
Semblance of worth, not substance, gently raised
Their fainting courage, and dispelled their fears:
Then straight commands that, at the warlike sound
Of trumpets loud and clarions, be upreared
His mighty standard. That proud honor claimed
Azazel as his right, a Cherub tall:
Who forthwith from the glittering staff unfurled
The imperial ensign; which, full high advanced,
Shone like a meteor streaming to the wind,
With gems and golden luster rich emblazed,
Seraphic arms and trophies; all the while
Sonorous metal blowing martial sounds:

[1]Flushed. [2]Depressed. [3]Regaining.

At which the universal host up-sent
A shout that tore Hell's concave, and beyond
Frighted the reign of Chaos and old Night.
All in a moment through the gloom were seen
Ten thousand banners rise into the air,
With orient[4] colors waving: with them rose
A forest huge of spears; and thronging helms
Appeared, and serried shields in thick array
Of depth immeasurable. Anon they move
In perfect phalanx to the Dorian mood[5]
Of flutes and soft recorders[6]—such as raised
To highth of noblest temper heroes old
Arming to battle, and instead of rage
Deliberate valor breathed, firm, and unmoved[7]
With dread of death to flight or foul retreat;
Nor wanting power to mitigate and swage[8]
With solemn touches troubled thoughts, and chase
Anguish and doubt and fear and sorrow and pain
From mortal or immortal minds. Thus they,
Breathing united force with fixéd thought,
Moved on in silence to soft pipes that charmed
Their painful steps o'er the burnt soil. And now
Advanced in view they stand—a horrid[9] front
Of dreadful length and dazzling arms, in guise
Of warriors old, with ordered spear and shield,
Awaiting what command their mighty Chief
Had to impose. He through the armed files
Darts his experienced eye, and soon traverse[10]
The whole battalion views—their order due,
Their visages and stature as of gods;
Their number last he sums. And now his heart
Distends with pride, and, hardening in his strength,
Glories: for never, since created Man,[11]
Met such embodied force as, named with these,
Could merit more than that small infantry
Warred on by cranes[12]—though all the giant brood
Of Phlegra with the heroic race were joined
That fought at Thebes and Ilium, on each side
Mixed with auxiliar gods; and what resounds
In fable or romance of Uther's son[13]
Begirt with British and Armoric[14] knights;
And all who since, baptized or infidel,
Jousted in Aspramont, or Montalban,
Damasco, or Marocco, or Trebisond,

[4]Bright.

[5]It was grave, or even stern, in character—suitable for soldiers.

[6]A kind of flute. [7]Immovable.

[8]Assuage. [9]Bristling. [10]Across.

[11]Since man's creation.

[12]The Pygmies (*Iliad*, III, 5).

[13]King Arthur. [14]Breton.

Or whom Biserta sent from Afric shore
When Charlemagne with all his peerage fell
By Fontarabbia. Thus far these beyond
Compare of mortal prowess, yet observed[1]
Their dread Commander. He, above the rest
In shape and gesture proudly eminent,
Stood like a tower. His form had yet not lost
All her original brightness, nor appeared
Less than Archangel ruined, and the excess
Of glory obscured: as when the sun new-risen
Looks through the horizontal misty air
Shorn of his beams, or from behind the moon,
In dim eclipse, disastrous twilight sheds
On half the nations, and with fear of change
Perplexes monarchs. Darkened so, yet shone
Above them all the Archangel: but his face
Deep scars of thunder had intrenched, and care
Sat on his faded cheek, but under brows
Of dauntless courage, and considerate[2] pride
Waiting revenge. Cruel his eye, but cast
Signs of remorse and passion,[3] to behold
The fellows of his crime, the followers rather
(Far other once beheld in bliss), condemned
For ever now to have their lot in pain—
Millions of Spirits for his fault amerced[4]
Of Heaven, and from eternal splendors flung
For his revolt—yet faithful how they stood,
Their glory withered; as, when heaven's fire
Hath scathed[5] the forest oaks or mountain pines,
With singéd top their stately growth, though bare,
Stands on the blasted heath. He now prepared
To speak; whereat their doubled ranks they bend
From wing to wing, and half enclose him round
With all his peers: Attention held them mute.
Thrice he assayed, and thrice, in spite of scorn,
Tears, such as angels weep, burst forth: at last
Words interwove with sighs found out their way:—
"O myriads of immortal Spirits! O Powers
Matchless, but with the Almighty!—and that strife
Was not inglorious, though the event[6] was dire,
As this place testifies, and this dire change,
Hateful to utter. But what power of mind,
Foreseeing or presaging, from the depth
Of knowledge past or present, could have feared
How such united force of gods, how such
As stood like these, could ever know repulse?
For who can yet believe, though after loss,
That all these puissant legions, whose exile
Hath emptied Heaven, shall fail to re-ascend,
Self-raised, and re-possess their native seat?
For me, be witness all the host of Heaven,
If counsels different, or danger shunned
By me, have lost our hopes. But he who reigns
Monarch in Heaven till then as one secure
Sat on his throne, upheld by old repute,
Consent or custom, and his regal state
Put forth at full, but still his strength concealed—
Which tempted our attempt, and wrought our fall.
Henceforth his might we know, and know our own,
So as not either to provoke, or dread
New war provoked: our better part remains
To work in close design, by fraud or guile,
What force effected not; that he no less
At length from us may find, who overcomes
By force hath overcome but half his foe.
Space may produce new Worlds; whereof so rife
There went a fame in Heaven that he ere long
Intended to create, and therein plant
A generation whom his choice regard
Should favor equal to the Sons of Heaven.
Thither, if but to pry, shall be perhaps
Our first eruption—thither, or elsewhere;
For this infernal pit shall never hold
Celestial Spirits in bondage, nor the Abyss
Long under darkness cover. But these thoughts
Full counsel must mature. Peace is despaired;
For who can think submission? War, then, war
Open or understood,[7] must be resolved."
He spake; and, to confirm his words, outflew
Millions of flaming swords, drawn from the thighs
Of mighty Cherubim; the sudden blaze
Far round illumined Hell. Highly they raged
Against the Highest, and fierce with graspéd arms
Clashed on their sounding shields the din of war,
Hurling defiance toward the vault of Heaven
There stood a hill not far, whose grisly top
Belched fire and rolling smoke; the rest entire
Shone with a glossy scurf—undoubted sign
That in his womb was hid metallic ore,
The work of sulphur.[8] Thither, winged with speed,
A numerous brigad hastened: as when bands

[1]Obeyed. [2]Thoughtful. [3]Pity and strong emotion. [4]Punished by loss. [5]Injured. [6]Result.

[7]Not openly declared.

[8]Sulphur was formerly believed to be the formative element of metals.

Of pioneers, with spade and pickax armed,
Forerun the royal camp, to trench a field,
Or cast a rampart. Mammon led them on—
Mammon, the least erected Spirit that fell
From Heaven; for even in Heaven his looks and thoughts
Were always downward bent, admiring more
The riches of Heaven's pavement, trodden gold,
Than aught divine or holy else enjoyed
In vision beatific. By him first
Men also, and by his suggestion taught,
Ransacked the center,[1] and with impious hands
Rifled the bowels of their mother earth
For treasures better hid. Soon had his crew
Opened into the hill a spacious wound,
And digged out ribs[2] of gold. Let none admire[3]
That riches grow in Hell; that soil may best
Deserve the precious bane. And here let those
Who boast in mortal things, and wondering tell
Of Babel, and the works of Memphian kings,[4]
Learn how their greatest monuments of fame
And strength, and art, are easily outdone
By Spirits reprobate, and in an hour
What in an age they, with incessant toil
And hands innumerable, scarce perform.
Nigh on the plain, in many cells prepared,
That underneath had veins of liquid fire
Sluiced from the lake, a second multitude
With wondrous art founded[5] the massy ore,
Severing each kind, and scummed the bullion-dross.
A third as soon had formed within the ground
A various mold, and from the boiling cells
By strange conveyance filled each hollow nook;
As in an organ, from one blast of wind,
To many a row of pipes the sound-board breathes.
Anon out of the earth a fabric huge
Rose like an exhalation, with the sound
Of dulcet symphonies and voices sweet—
Built like a temple, where pilasters round
Were set, and Doric pillars overlaid[6]
With golden architrave; nor did there want
Cornice or frieze, with bossy[7] sculptures graven;
The roof was fretted[8] gold. Not Babylon
Nor great Alcairo such magnificence
Equaled in all their glories, to enshrine
Belus or Serapis their gods, or seat
Their kings, when Egypt with Assyria strove
In wealth and luxury. The ascending pile
Stood fixed her stately highth; and straight the doors,
Opening their brazen folds, discover, wide
Within, her ample spaces o'er the smooth
And level pavement: from the archéd roof,
Pendent by subtle magic, many a row
Of starry lamps and blazing cressets, fed
With naphtha and asphaltus, yielded light
As from a sky. The hasty multitude
Admiring entered; and the work some praise,
And some the architect. His hand was known
In Heaven by many a towered structure high,
Where sceptered Angels held their residence,
And sat as Princes, whom the supreme King
Exalted to such power, and gave to rule,
Each in his hierarchy. the Orders bright.
Nor was his name unheard or unadored
In ancient Greece; and in Ausonian land[9]
Men called him Mulciber; and how he fell
From Heaven they fabled, thrown by angry Jove
Sheer o'er the crystal battlements: from morn
To noon he fell, from noon to dewy eve,
A summer's day, and with the setting sun
Dropped from the zenith, like a falling star,
On Lemnos, the Ægæan isle. Thus they relate,
Erring; for he with this rebellious rout
Fell long before; nor aught availed him now
To have built in Heaven high towers; nor did he scape
By all his engines,[10] but was headlong sent,
With his industrious crew, to build in Hell.

Meanwhile the wingéd heralds, by command
Of sovran power, with awful ceremony
And trumpet's sound, throughout the host proclaim
A solemn council forthwith to be held
At Pandemonium,[11] the high capital
Of Satan and his peers. Their summons called
From every band and squaréd regiment
By place or choice the worthiest: they anon
With hundreds and with thousands trooping came
Attended. All access was thronged; the gates
And porches wide, but chief the spacious hall
(Though like a covered field, where champions bold
Wont ride in armed, and at the soldan's[12] chair
Defied the best of paynim[13] chivalry
To mortal combat, or career with lance),
Thick swarmed, both on the ground and in the air,
Brushed with the hiss of rustling wings. As bees
In spring-time, when the Sun with Taurus[14] rides,

[1] The earth. [2] Bars. [3] Wonder. [4] The pyramids. [5] Melted. [6] Surmounted. [7] Projecting. [8] Checkered; or adorned with embossed designs.

[9] Italy. [10] Contrivances. [11] Abode of all demons. [12] Sultan's. [13] Pagan. [14] Sign of the zodiac (the time is 19 April to 20 May).

Pour forth their populous youth about the hive
In clusters; they among fresh dews and flowers
Fly to and fro, or on the smoothéd plank,
The suburb of their straw-built citadel,
New rubbed with balm, expatiate,[1] and confer[2]
Their state-affairs: so thick the aery crowd
Swarmed and were straitened; till, the signal given,
Behold a wonder! They but now who seemed
In bigness to surpass earth's giant sons,
Now less than smallest dwarfs, in narrow room
Throng numberless—like that pygmean race
Beyond the Indian mount; or faery elves,
Whose midnight revels, by a forest-side
Or fountain, some belated peasant sees,
Or dreams he sees, while overhead the Moon
Sits arbitress,[3] and nearer to the earth
Wheels her pale course: they, on their mirth and dance
Intent, with jocund music charm his ear;
At once with joy and fear his heart rebounds.
Thus incorporeal Spirits to smallest forms
Reduced their shapes immense, and were at large,
Though without number still, amidst the hall
Of that infernal court. But far within,
And in their own dimensions like themselves,
The great Seraphic Lords and Cherubim
In close recess[4] and secret conclave sat,
A thousand demi-gods on golden seats,
Frequent[5] and full. After short silence then,
And summons read, the great consult[6] began.

BOOK II

THE ARGUMENT

THE consultation begun, Satan debates whether another battle be to be hazarded for the recovery of Heaven: some advise it, others dissuade. A third proposal is preferred, mentioned before by Satan—to search the truth of that prophecy or tradition in Heaven concerning another world, and another kind of creature, equal, or not much inferior, to themselves, about this time to be created. Their doubt who shall be sent on this difficult search: Satan, their chief, undertakes alone the voyage; is honored and applauded. The council thus ended, the rest betake them several ways and to several employments, as their inclinations lead them, to entertain the time till Satan return. He passes on his journey to Hell-gates; finds them shut, and who sat there to guard them; by whom at length they are opened, and discover to him the great gulf between Hell and Heaven. With what difficulty he passes through, directed by Chaos, the Power of that place, to the sight of this new World which he sought.

HIGH on a throne of royal state, which far
Outshone the wealth of Ormus[7] and of Ind,
Or where the gorgeous East with richest hand
Showers on her kings barbaric pearl and gold,
Satan exalted sat, by merit raised
To that bad eminence; and, from despair
Thus high uplifted beyond hope, aspires
Beyond thus high, insatiate to pursue
Vain war with Heaven; and, by success[8] untaught,
His proud imaginations thus displayed:—
"Powers and Dominions, Deities of Heaven!—
For, since no deep within her gulf can hold
Immortal vigor, though oppressed and fallen,
I give not Heaven for lost: from this descent
Celestial Virtues rising will appear
More glorious and more dread than from no fall,
And trust themselves to fear no second fate!—
Me though just right, and the fixed laws of Heaven,
Did first create your leader—next, free choice,
With what besides in council or in fight
Hath been achieved of merit—yet this loss,
Thus far at least recovered, hath much more
Established in a safe, unenvied throne,
Yielded with full consent. The happier state
In Heaven, which follows dignity, might draw
Envy from each inferior; but who here
Will envy whom the highest place exposes
Foremost to stand against the Thunderer's aim
Your bulwark, and condemns to greatest share
Of endless pain? Where there is, then, no good
For which to strive, no strife can grow up there
From faction: for none sure will claim in Hell
Precedence; none whose portion is so small
Of present pain that with ambitious mind
Will covet more! With this advantage, then,
To union, and firm faith, and firm accord,
More than can be in Heaven, we now return
To claim our just inheritance of old,
Surer to prosper than prosperity
Could have assured us; and by what best way,
Whether of open war or covert guile,
We now debate. Who can advise may speak."

He ceased; and next him Moloch, sceptered king,
Stood up—the strongest and the fiercest Spirit
That fought in Heaven, now fiercer by despair.
His trust was with the Eternal to be deemed
Equal in strength, and rather than be less

[1]Walk abroad. [2]Discuss. [3]Witness.
[4]Retirement. [5]Numerous. [6]Consultation.

[7]An island in the Persian Gulf. [8]Experience.

Cared not to be at all; with that care lost
Went all his fear: of God, or Hell, or worse,
He recked[1] not, and these words thereafter spake:—
"My sentence is for open war. Of wiles,
More unexpert,[2] I boast not: them let those
Contrive who need, or when they need; not now.
For, while they sit contriving, shall the rest—
Millions that stand in arms, and longing wait
The signal to ascend—sit lingering here,
Heaven's fugitives, and for their dwelling-place
Accept this dark opprobrious den of shame,
The prison of his tyranny who reigns
By our delay? No! let us rather choose,
Armed with Hell-flames and fury, all at once
O'er Heaven's high towers to force resistless way,
Turning our tortures into horrid arms
Against the Torturer; when, to meet the noise
Of his almighty engine, he shall hear
Infernal thunder, and, for lightning, see
Black fire and horror shot with equal rage
Among his Angels, and his throne itself
Mixed with Tartarean[3] sulphur and strange fire,
His own invented torments. But perhaps
The way seems difficult, and steep to scale
With upright wing against a higher foe!
Let such bethink them, if the sleepy drench
Of that forgetful lake benumb not still,
That in our proper[4] motion we ascend
Up to our native seat; descent and fall
To us is adverse. Who but felt of late,
When the fierce foe hung on our broken rear
Insulting, and pursued us through the Deep,
With what compulsion and laborious flight
We sunk thus low? The ascent is easy, then;
The event[5] is feared! Should we again provoke
Our stronger, some worse way his wrath may find
To our destruction, if there be in Hell
Fear to be worse destroyed! What can be worse
Than to dwell here, driven out from bliss, condemned
In this abhorréd deep to utter woe!
Where pain of unextinguishable fire
Must exercise[6] us without hope of end
The vassals of his anger, when the scourge
Inexorably, and the torturing hour,
Calls us to penance? More destroyed than thus,
We should be quite abolished, and expire.
What fear we then? what doubt we to incense
His utmost ire? which, to the highth enraged,
Will either quite consume us, and reduce
To nothing this essential[7]—happier far
Than miserable to have eternal being!—
Or, if our substance be indeed divine,
And cannot cease to be, we are at worst
On this side nothing; and by proof we feel
Our power sufficient to disturb his Heaven
And with perpetual inroads to alarm,
Though inaccessible, his fatal throne:
Which, if not victory, is yet revenge."
He ended frowning, and his look denounced[8]
Desperate revenge, and battle dangerous
To less than gods. On the other side up rose
Belial, in act more graceful and humane.
A fairer person lost not Heaven; he seemed
For dignity composed, and high exploit.
But all was false and hollow; though his tongue
Dropped manna, and could make the worse appear
The better reason, to perplex and dash
Maturest counsels: for his thoughts were low—
To vice industrious, but to nobler deeds
Timorous and slothful. Yet he pleased the ear,
And with persuasive accent thus began:—
"I should be much for open war, O Peers,
As not behind in hate, if what was urged
Main reason to persuade immediate war
Did not dissuade me most, and seem to cast
Ominous conjecture on the whole success;
When he who most excels in fact[9] of arms,
In what he counsels and in what excels
Mistrustful, grounds his courage on despair
And utter dissolution, as the scope
Of all his aim, after some dire revenge.
First, what revenge? The towers of Heaven are filled
With arméd watch, that render all access
Impregnable: oft on the bordering Deep
Encamp their legions, or with obscure wing
Scout far and wide into the realm of Night,
Scorning surprise. Or, could we break our way
By force, and at our heels all Hell should rise
With blackest insurrection to confound
Heaven's purest light, yet our great Enemy,
All incorruptible, would on his throne
Sit unpolluted, and the ethereal mold,[10]
Incapable of stain, would soon expel
Her mischief, and purge off the baser fire,
Victorious. Thus repulsed, our final hope
Is flat despair: we must exasperate
The Almighty Victor to spend all his rage;
And that must end us; that must be our cure—
To be no more. Sad cure! for who would lose,

[1]Cared. [2]Inexperienced. [3]Infernal.
[4]Natural. [5]Its result. [6]Torment.

[7]Substance (adjective for substantive, as frequently with Milton).
[8]Indicated. [9]Deeds. [10]Substance.

Though full of pain, this intellectual being,
Those thoughts that wander through eternity,
To perish rather, swallowed up and lost
In the wide womb of uncreated Night,
Devoid of sense and motion? And who knows,
Let this be good, whether our angry Foe
Can give it, or will ever? How he can
Is doubtful; that he never will is sure.
Will he, so wise, let loose at once his ire,
Belike[1] through impotence or unaware,
To give his enemies their wish, and end
Them in his anger whom his anger saves
To punish endless? 'Wherefore cease we, then?'
Say they who counsel war; 'we are decreed,
Reserved, and destined to eternal woe;
Whatever doing, what can we suffer more,
What can we suffer worse?' Is this, then, worst—
Thus sitting, thus consulting, thus in arms?
What when we fled amain, pursued and strook
With Heaven's afflicting thunder, and besought
The Deep to shelter us? This Hell then seemed
A refuge from those wounds. Or when we lay
Chained on the burning lake? That sure was worse.
What if the breath that kindled those grim fires,
Awaked, should blow them into sevenfold rage
And plunge us in the flames; or from above
Should intermitted vengeance arm again
His red right hand to plague us? What if all
Her stores were opened, and this firmament
Of Hell should spout her cataracts of fire,
Impendent horrors, threatening hideous fall
One day upon our heads; while we perhaps,
Designing or exhorting glorious war
Caught in a fiery tempest, shall be hurled,
Each on his rock transfixed, the sport and prey
Of racking whirlwinds, or for ever sunk
Under yon boiling ocean, wrapped in chains,
There to converse with everlasting groans,
Unrespited, unpitied, unreprieved,
Ages of hopeless end? This would be worse.
War, therefore, open or concealed, alike
My voice dissuades; for what can force or guile
With him, or who deceive his mind, whose eye
Views all things at one view? He from Heaven's highth
All these our motions vain sees and derides,
Not more almighty to resist our might
Than wise to frustrate all our plots and wiles.
Shall we, then, live thus vile—the race of Heaven,
Thus trampled, thus expelled, to suffer here
Chains and these torments? Better these than worse,
By my advice; since fate inevitable
Subdues us, and omnipotent decree,
The Victor's will. To suffer, as to do,
Our strength is equal; nor the law unjust
That so ordains. This was at first resolved,
If we were wise, against so great a foe
Contending, and so doubtful what might fall.
I laugh when those who at the spear are bold
And venturous, if that fail them, shrink, and fear
What yet they know must follow—to endure
Exile, or ignominy, or bonds, or pain,
The sentence of their conqueror. This is now
Our doom; which if we can sustain and bear,
Our Supreme Foe in time may much remit
His anger, and perhaps, thus far removed,
Not mind us not offending, satisfied
With what is punished; whence these raging fires
Will slacken, if his breath stir not their flames.
Our purer essence then will overcome
Their noxious vapor; or, inured, not feel;
Or, changed at length, and to the place conformed
In temper and in nature, will receive
Familiar the fierce heat; and, void of pain,
This horror will grow mild, this darkness light;
Besides what hope the never-ending flight
Of future days may bring, what chance, what change
Worth waiting—since our present lot appears
For happy though but ill, for ill not worst,[2]
If we procure not to ourselves more woe."
  Thus Belial, with words clothed in reason's garb,
Counseled ignoble ease and peaceful sloth,
Not peace; and after him thus Mammon spake:—
  "Either to disenthrone the King of Heaven
We war, if war be best, or to regain
Our own right lost. Him to unthrone we then
May hope, when everlasting Fate shall yield
To fickle Chance, and Chaos judge the strife.
The former, vain to hope, argues as vain
The latter; for what place can be for us
Within Heaven's bound, unless Heaven's Lord Supreme
We overpower? Suppose he should relent,
And publish grace to all, on promise made
Of new subjection; with what eyes could we
Stand in his presence humble, and receive
Strict laws imposed, to celebrate his throne
With warbled hymns, and to his Godhead sing
Forced Halleluiahs, while he lordly sits
Our envied sovran, and his altar breathes
Ambrosial odors and ambrosial flowers,

[1]Probably

[2]Since our present lot appears ill, indeed, compared with happiness, yet not so bad as it might be.

Our servile offerings? This must be our task
In Heaven, this our delight. How wearisome
Eternity so spent in worship paid
To whom we hate! Let us not then pursue,
By force impossible, by leave obtained
Unacceptable, though in Heaven, our state
Of splendid vassalage; but rather seek
Our own good from ourselves, and from our own
Live to ourselves, though in this vast recess,
Free and to none accountable, preferring
Hard liberty before the easy yoke
Of servile pomp. Our greatness will appear
Then most conspicuous when great things of small,
Useful of hurtful, prosperous of adverse,
We can create, and in what place soe'er
Thrive under evil, and work ease out of pain
Through labor and endurance. This deep world
Of darkness do we dread? How oft amidst
Thick clouds and dark doth Heaven's all-ruling Sire
Choose to reside, his glory unobscured,
And with the majesty of darkness round
Covers his throne, from whence deep thunders roar,
Mustering their rage, and Heaven resembles Hell!
As he our darkness, cannot we his light
Imitate when we please? This desert soil
Wants not her hidden luster, gems and gold;
Nor want we skill or art from whence to raise
Magnificence; and what can Heaven show more?
Our torments also may, in length of time,
Become our elements, these piercing fires
As soft as now severe, our temper changed
Into their temper; which must needs remove
The sensible[1] of pain. All things invite
To peaceful counsels, and the settled state
Of order, how in safety best we may
Compose our present evils, with regard
Of what we are and where, dismissing quite
All thoughts of war. Ye have what I advise."
He scarce had finished, when such murmur filled
The assembly as when hollow rocks retain
The sound of blustering winds, which all night long
Had roused the sea, now with hoarse cadence lull
Seafaring men o'erwatched,[2] whose bark by chance,
Or pinnace, anchors in a craggy bay
After the tempest. Such applause was heard
As Mammon ended, and his sentence pleased,
Advising peace: for such another field[3]
They dreaded worse than Hell; so much the fear
Of thunder and the sword of Michaël
Wrought still within them; and no less desire
To found this nether empire, which might rise,
By policy and long process of time,
In emulation opposite to Heaven.
Which when Beëlzebub perceived—than whom,
Satan except, none higher sat—with grave
Aspect he rose, and in his rising seemed
A pillar of state. Deep on his front engraven
Deliberation sat, and public care;
And princely counsel in his face yet shone,
Majestic, though in ruin. Sage he stood,
With Atlantean shoulders,[4] fit to bear
The weight of mightiest monarchies; his look
Drew audience and attention still as night
Or summer's noontide air, while thus he spake:—
"Thrones and Imperial Powers, Offspring of Heaven,
Ethereal Virtues! or these titles now
Must we renounce, and, changing style, be called
Princes of Hell? for so the popular vote
Inclines—here to continue, and build up here
A growing empire; doubtless! while we dream,
And know not that the King of Heaven hath doomed
This place our dungeon—not our safe retreat
Beyond his potent arm, to live exempt
From Heaven's high jurisdiction, in new league
Banded against his throne, but to remain
In strictest bondage, though thus far removed,
Under the inevitable curb, reserved
His captive multitude. For He, be sure,
In highth or depth, still first and last will reign
Sole king, and of his kingdom lose no part
By our revolt, but over Hell extend
His empire, and with iron scepter rule
Us here, as with his golden those in Heaven.
What sit we then projecting peace and war?
War hath determined[5] us and foiled with loss
Irreparable; terms of peace yet none
Vouchsafed or sought; for what peace will be given
To us enslaved, but custody severe,
And stripes and arbitrary punishment
Inflicted? and what peace can we return,
But, to[6] our power, hostility and hate,
Untamed reluctance, and revenge, though slow,
Yet ever plotting how the Conqueror least
May reap his conquest, and may least rejoice
In doing what we most in suffering feel?

[1]Sense. [2]Wearied with watching. [3]Battle.

[4]Shoulders like those of Atlas, who supported the columns on which the heavens rest.

[5]Undone. [6]To the limit of.

Nor will occasion want, nor shall we need
With dangerous expedition to invade
Heaven, whose high walls fear no assault or siege,
Or ambush from the Deep. What if we find
Some easier enterprise? There is a place
(If ancient and prophetic fame[1] in Heaven
Err not)—another World, the happy seat
Of some new race, called Man, about this time
To be created like to us, though less
In power and excellence, but favored more
Of him who rules above; so was his will
Pronounced among the gods, and by an oath
That shook Heaven's whole circumference confirmed.
Thither let us bend all our thoughts, to learn
What creatures there inhabit, of what mold
Or substance, how endued, and what their power.
And where their weakness: how attempted best
By force or subtlety. Though Heaven be shut,
And Heaven's high Arbitrator sit secure
In his own strength, this place may lie exposed,
The utmost border of his kingdom, left
To their defense who hold it: here, perhaps,
Some advantageous act may be achieved
By sudden onset—either with Hell-fire
To waste his whole creation, or possess
All as our own, and drive, as we are driven,
The puny habitants; or, if not drive,
Seduce them to our party, that their God
May prove their foe, and with repenting hand
Abolish his own works. This would surpass
Common revenge, and interrupt his joy
In our confusion, and our joy upraise
In his disturbance; when his darling sons,
Hurled headlong to partake with us, shall curse
Their frail original, and faded bliss—
Faded so soon! Advise[2] if this be worth
Attempting, or to sit in darkness here
Hatching vain empires." Thus Beëlzebub
Pleaded his devilish counsel—first devised
By Satan, and in part proposed: for whence,
But from the author of all ill, could spring
So deep a malice, to confound the race
Of mankind in one root, and Earth with Hell
To mingle and involve, done all to spite
The great Creator? But their spite still serves
His glory to augment. The bold design
Pleased highly those Infernal States,[3] and joy
Sparkled in all their eyes: with full assent
They vote: whereat his speech he thus renews:—
"Well have ye judged, well ended long debate,
Synod of Gods, and, like to what ye are,
Great things resolved, which from the lowest deep
Will once more lift us up, in spite of fate,
Nearer our ancient seat—perhaps in view
Of those bright confines, whence, with neighboring arms,
And opportune excursion, we may chance
Re-enter Heaven; or else in some mild zone
Dwell, not unvisited of Heaven's fair light,
Secure, and at the brightening orient beam
Purge off this gloom: the soft delicious air,
To heal the scar of these corrosive fires,
Shall breathe her balm. But, first, whom shall we send
In search of this new World? whom shall we find
Sufficient? who shall tempt[4] with wandering feet
The dark, unbottomed, infinite Abyss,
And through the palpable obscure[5] find out
His uncouth[6] way, or spread his aery flight,
Upborne with indefatigable wings
Over the vast Abrupt,[7] ere he arrive
The happy Isle? What strength, what art, can then
Suffice, or what evasion bear him safe,
Through the strict senteries and stations thick
Of Angels watching round? Here he had need
All circumspection: and we now no less
Choice[8] in our suffrage; for on whom we send
The weight of all, and our last hope, relies."
This said, he sat; and expectation held
His look suspense,[9] awaiting who appeared
To second, or oppose, or undertake
The perilous attempt. But all sat mute,
Pondering the danger with deep thoughts; and each
In other's countenance read his own dismay,
Astonished. None among the choice and prime
Of those Heaven-warring champions could be found
So hardy as to proffer or accept,
Alone, the dreadful voyage; till, at last,
Satan, whom now transcendent glory raised
Above his fellows, with monarchal pride
Conscious of highest worth, unmoved thus spake:—
"O Progeny of Heaven! Empyreal Thrones!
With reason hath deep silence and demur[10]
Seized us, though undismayed. Long is the way
And hard, that out of Hell leads up to Light.
Our prison strong, this huge convex of fire,
Outrageous to devour, immures us round

[1]Report. [2]Consider. [3]Councilors.

[4]Try. [5]Obscurity. [6]Unknown.
[7]The region of chaos. [8]Care.
[9]In suspense. [10]Hesitancy.

Ninefold; and gates of burning adamant,
Barred over us, prohibit all egress.
These passed, if any pass, the void profound
Of unessential[1] Night receives him next,
Wide-gaping, and with utter loss of being
Threatens him, plunged in that abortive[2] gulf.
If thence he scape, into whatever world,
Or unknown region, what remains[3] him less
Than unknown dangers, and as hard escape?
But I should ill become this throne, O Peers,
And this imperial sovranty, adorned
With splendor, armed with power, if aught proposed
And judged of public moment in the shape
Of difficulty or danger, could deter
Me from attempting. Wherefore do I assume
These royalties, and not refuse to reign,
Refusing to accept as great a share
Of hazard as of honor, due alike
To him who reigns, and so much to him due
Of hazard more as he above the rest
High honored sits? Go, therefore, mighty Powers,
Terror of Heaven, though fallen: intend[4] at home,
While here shall be our home, what best may ease
The present misery, and render Hell
More tolerable; if there be cure or charm
To respite, or deceive,[5] or slack the pain
Of this ill mansion: intermit no watch
Against a wakeful foe, while I abroad
Through all the coasts of dark destruction seek
Deliverance for us all. This enterprise
None shall partake with me." Thus saying, rose
The Monarch, and prevented all reply;
Prudent lest, from his resolution raised,[6]
Others among the chief might offer now,
Certain to be refused, what erst they feared,
And, so refused, might in opinion stand
His rivals, winning cheap the high repute
Which he through hazard huge must earn. But they
Dreaded not more the adventure than his voice
Forbidding; and at once with him they rose.
Their rising all at once was as the sound
Of thunder heard remote. Towards him they bend
With awful reverence prone, and as a God
Extol him equal to the Highest in Heaven.
Nor failed they to express how much they praised
That for the general safety he despised
His own: for neither do the Spirits damned
Lose all their virtue; lest bad men should boast
Their specious deeds on earth, which glory excites,
Or close[7] ambition varnished o'er with zeal.
Thus they their doubtful consultations dark
Ended, rejoicing in their matchless Chief:
As, when from mountain-tops the dusky clouds
Ascending, while the North-wind sleeps, o'erspread
Heaven's cheerful face, the louring element
Scowls o'er the darkened landscape snow or shower,
If chance the radiant sun, with farewell sweet,
Extend his evening beam, the fields revive,
The birds their notes renew, and bleating herds
Attest their joy, that hill and valley rings.
O shame to men! Devil with devil damned
Firm concord holds; men only disagree
Of creatures rational, though under hope
Of heavenly grace, and, God proclaiming peace,
Yet live in hatred, enmity, and strife
Among themselves, and levy cruel wars
Wasting the earth, each other to destroy:
As if (which might induce us to accord)
Man had not hellish foes enow[8] besides,
That day and night for his destruction wait!
The Stygian council thus dissolved; and forth
In order came the grand Infernal Peers:
Midst came their mighty Paramount,[9] and seemed
Alone the antagonist of Heaven, nor less
Than Hell's dread Emperor, with pomp supreme,
And god-like imitated state: him round
A globe of fiery Seraphim enclosed
With bright emblazonry, and horrent[10] arms.
Then of their session ended they bid cry
With trumpet's regal sound the great result:
Toward the four winds four speedy Cherubim
Put to their mouths the sounding alchemy,[11]
By herald's voice explained;[12] the hollow Abyss
Heard far and wide, and all the host of Hell
With deafening shout returned them loud acclaim.
Thence more at ease their minds, and somewhat raised
By false presumptuous hope, the rangéd Powers
Disband; and, wandering, each his several way
Pursues, as inclination or sad choice
Leads him perplexed, where he may likeliest find
Truce to his restless thoughts, and entertain
The irksome hours, till his great Chief return.
Part on the plain, or in the air sublime,

[1]Void of being. [2]Dangerous. [3]Awaits.
[4]Consider. [5]Divert us from.
[6]Lest, encouraged by his bravery.

[7]Secret. [8]Enough. [9]Chief.
[10]Bristling. [11]Trumpets.
[12]*I. e.*, the herald states the meaning of the trumpet blasts.

Upon the wing or in swift race contend,
As at the Olympian games or Pythian fields;
Part curb their fiery steeds, or shun the goal
With rapid wheels, or fronted brigads form:
As when, to warn proud cities, war appears
Waged in the troubled sky, and armies rush
To battle in the clouds; before each van
Prick[1] forth the aery knights, and couch their spears,
Till thickest legions close; with feats of arms
From either end of heaven the welkin[2] burns.
Others, with vast Typhœan rage, more fell,
Rend up both rocks and hills, and ride the air
In whirlwind; Hell scarce holds the wild uproar:—
As when Alcides,[3] from Œchalia crowned
With conquest, felt the envenomed robe, and tore
Through pain up by the roots Thessalian pines,
And Lichas from the top of Œta threw
Into the Euboic sea. Others, more mild,
Retreated in a silent valley, sing
With notes angelical to many a harp
Their own heroic deeds, and hapless fall
By doom of battle, and complain that Fate
Free Virtue should enthrall to Force or Chance.
Their song was partial; but the harmony
(What could it less when Spirits immortal sing?)
Suspended Hell, and took with ravishment
The thronging audience. In discourse more sweet
(For Eloquence the Soul, Song charms the Sense)
Others apart sat on a hill retired,
In thoughts more elevate, and reasoned high
Of Providence, Foreknowledge, Will, and Fate—
Fixed fate, free will, foreknowledge absolute,
And found no end, in wandering mazes lost.
Of good and evil much they argued then,
Of happiness and final misery,
Passion and apathy, and glory and shame:
Vain wisdom all, and false philosophy!—
Yet, with a pleasing sorcery, could charm
Pain for a while or anguish, and excite
Fallacious hope, or arm the obdurẽd breast
With stubborn patience as with triple steel.
Another part, in squadrons and gross[4] bands,
On bold adventure to discover wide
That dismal world, if any clime perhaps
Might yield them easier habitation, bend
Four ways their flying march, along the banks
Of four infernal rivers, that disgorge
Into the burning lake their baleful streams—
Abhorrẽd Styx, the flood of deadly hate;
Sad Acheron of sorrow, black and deep;
Cocytus, named of lamentation loud
Heard on the rueful stream; fierce Phlegeton,
Whose waves of torrent fire inflame with rage.
Far off from these, a slow and silent stream,
Lethe, the river of oblivion, rolls
Her watery labyrinth, whereof who drinks
Forthwith his former state and being forgets—
Forgets both joy and grief, pleasure and pain.
Beyond this flood a frozen continent
Lies dark and wild, beat with perpetual storms
Of whirlwind and dire hail, which on firm land
Thaws not, but gathers heap, and ruin seems
Of ancient pile; all else deep snow and ice,
A gulf profound as that Serbonian bog
Betwixt Damiata and Mount Casius old,[5]
Where armies whole have sunk: the parching air
Burns frore,[6] and cold performs the effect of fire.
Thither, by harpy-footed Furies haled,
At certain revolutions all the damned
Are brought; and feel by turns the bitter change
Of fierce extremes, extremes by change more fierce,
From beds of raging fire to starve in ice
Their soft ethereal warmth, and there to pine
Immovable, infixed, and frozen round
Periods of time—thence hurried back to fire.
They ferry over this Lethean sound
Both to and fro, their sorrow to augment,
And wish and struggle, as they pass, to reach
The tempting stream, with one small drop to lose
In sweet forgetfulness all pain and woe,
All in one moment, and so near the brink;
But Fate withstands, and, to oppose the attempt,
Medusa with Gorgonian terror guards
The ford, and of itself the water flies
All taste of living wight,[7] as once it fled
The lip of Tantalus. Thus roving on
In confused march forlorn, the adventurous bands,
With shuddering horror pale, and eyes aghast,
Viewed first[8] their lamentable lot, and found
No rest. Through many a dark and dreary vale
They passed, and many a region dolorous,
O'er many a frozen, many a fiery Alp,
Rocks, caves, lakes, fens, bogs, dens, and shades of death—

[1]Ride. [2]Sky.

[3]Hercules. The robe is the poisoned shirt which his wife obtained from the centaur Nessus and sent to him by his servant Lichas.

[4]Large.

[5]*I. e.*, in Egypt. [6]Frozen. [7]Living being.

[8]Viewed for the first time.

A universe of death, which God by curse
Created evil, for evil only good;
Where all life dies, death lives, and Nature breeds,
Perverse, all monstrous, all prodigious things,
Abominable, inutterable, and worse
Than fables yet have feigned or fear conceived,
Gorgons, and Hydras, and Chimæras dire.
  Meanwhile the Adversary of God and Man,
Satan, with thoughts inflamed of highest design,
Puts on swift wings, and toward the gates of Hell
Explores his solitary flight: sometimes
He scours the right hand coast, sometimes the left;
Now shaves with level wing the deep, then soars
Up to the fiery concave towering high.
As when far off at sea a fleet descried
Hangs in the clouds, by equinoctial winds
Close sailing from Bengala, or the isles
Of Ternate and Tidore,[1] whence merchants bring
Their spicy drugs; they on the trading flood,
Through the wide Ethiopian to the Cape,[2]
Ply stemming nightly toward the pole:[3] so seemed
Far off the flying Fiend. At last appear
Hell-bounds, high reaching to the horrid roof,
And thrice threefold the gates; three folds were brass,
Three iron, three of adamantine rock,
Impenetrable, impaled with circling fire,
Yet unconsumed. Before the gates there sat
On either side a formidable Shape,
The one seemed woman to the waist, and fair,
But ended foul in many a scaly fold,
Voluminous and vast—a serpent armed
With mortal sting. About her middle round
A cry[4] of Hell-hounds never-ceasing barked
With wide Cerberean mouths full loud, and rung
A hideous peal; yet, when they list, would creep,
If aught disturbed their noise, into her womb,
And kennel there; yet there still barked and howled
Within unseen. Far less abhorred[5] than these
Vexed Scylla, bathing in the sea that parts
Calabria from the hoarse Trinacrian shore;[6]
Nor uglier follow the night-hag, when, called
In secret, riding through the air she comes,
Lured with the smell of infant blood, to dance
With Lapland witches,[7] while the laboring moon
Eclipses at their charms. The other Shape—
If shape it might be called that shape had none
Distinguishable in member, joint, or limb;
Or substance might be called that shadow seemed,
For each seemed either—black it stood as Night,
Fierce as ten Furies, terrible as Hell,
And shook a dreadful dart: what seemed his head
The likeness of a kingly crown had on.
Satan was now at hand, and from his seat
The monster moving onward came as fast
With horrid strides; Hell trembled as he strode.
The undaunted Fiend what this might be admired[8]—
Admired, not feared (God and his Son except,
Created thing naught valued he nor shunned),
And with disdainful look thus first began:—
  "Whence and what art thou, execrable Shape,
That dar'st, though grim and terrible, advance
Thy miscreated front athwart my way
To yonder gates? Through them I mean to pass,
That be assured, without leave asked of thee.
Retire; or taste thy folly, and learn by proof,
Hell-born, not to contend with Spirits of Heaven."
  To whom the Goblin,[9] full of wrath, replied:—
"Art thou that Traitor-Angel, art thou he,
Who first broke peace in Heaven and faith, till then
Unbroken, and in proud rebellious arms
Drew after him the third part of Heaven's sons,
Conjured[10] against the Highest—for which both thou
And they, outcast from God, are here condemned
To waste eternal days in woe and pain?
And reckon'st thou thyself with Spirits of Heaven,
Hell-doomed, and breath'st defiance here and scorn,
Where I reign king, and, to enrage thee more,
Thy king and lord? Back to thy punishment,
False fugitive; and to thy speed add wings,
Lest with a whip of scorpions I pursue
Thy lingering, or with one stroke of this dart
Strange horror seize thee, and pangs unfelt before."

[1]Two of the Moluccas.
[2]Through the Indian Ocean to the Cape of Good Hope.
[3]The South Pole. [4]Pack. [5]Less to be abhorred.
[6]The sea between Italy and Sicily.
[7]Lapland was believed to be a favorite home of witches.
[8]Wondered. [9]*I. e.*, demon, or fiend.
[10]Banded by oath.

So spake the grisly Terror, and in shape,
So speaking and so threatening, grew tenfold
More dreadful and deform. On the other side,
Incensed with indignation, Satan stood
Unterrified, and like a comet burned,
That fires the length of Ophiuchus[1] huge
In the arctic sky, and from his horrid hair
Shakes pestilence and war. Each at the head
Leveled his deadly aim; their fatal hands
No second stroke intend; and such a frown
Each cast at the other as when two black clouds,
With heaven's artillery fraught, come rattling on
Over the Caspian—then stand front to front
Hovering a space, till winds the signal blow
To join their dark encounter in mid-air.
So frowned the mighty combatants that Hell
Grew darker at their frown; so matched they stood;
For never but once more was either like
To meet so great a foe.[2] And now great deeds
Had been achieved, whereof all Hell had rung,
Had not the snaky Sorceress, that sat
Fast by Hell-gate and kept the fatal key,
Risen, and with hideous outcry rushed between.
"O father, what intends thy hand," she cried,
"Against thy only son? What fury, O son,
Possesses thee to bend that mortal dart
Against thy father's head? And know'st for whom;[3]
For him who sits above, and laughs the while
At thee, ordained his drudge to execute
Whate'er his wrath, which he calls justice, bids—
His wrath, which one day will destroy ye both!"
She spake, and at her words the hellish Pest
Forbore: then these to her Satan returned:—
"So strange thy outcry, and thy words so strange
Thou interposest, that my sudden hand,
Prevented, spares to tell thee yet by deeds
What it intends, till first I know of thee
What thing thou art, thus double-formed, and why,
In this infernal vale first met, thou call'st
Me father, and that phantasm call'st my son.
I know thee not, nor ever saw till now
Sight more detestable than him and thee."
To whom thus the Portress of Hell-gate replied:—
"Hast thou forgot me, then; and do I seem
Now in thine eye so foul?—once deemed so fair
In Heaven, when at the assembly, and in sight
Of all the Seraphim with thee combined
In bold conspiracy against Heaven's King,
All on a sudden miserable pain
Surprised thee, dim thine eyes and dizzy swum
In darkness, while thy head flames thick and fast
Threw forth, till on the left side opening wide,
Likest to thee in shape and countenance bright,
Then shining heavenly fair, a goddess armed,
Out of thy head I sprung. Amazement seized
All the host of Heaven; back they recoiled afraid
At first, and called me *Sin*, and for a sign
Portentous held me; but, familiar grown,
I pleased, and with attractive graces won
The most averse—thee chiefly, who, full oft
Thyself in me thy perfect image viewing,
Becam'st enamored; and such joy thou took'st
With me in secret that my womb conceived
A growing burden. Meanwhile war arose,
And fields were fought in Heaven: wherein remained
(For what could else?) to our Almighty Foe
Clear victory; to our part loss and rout
Through all the Empyrean. Down they fell,
Driven headlong from the pitch of Heaven, down
Into this Deep; and in the general fall
I also: at which time this powerful key
Into my hands was given, with charge to keep
These gates for ever shut, which none can pass
Without my opening. Pensive here I sat
Alone; but long I sat not, till my womb,
Pregnant by thee, and now excessive grown,
Prodigious motion felt and rueful throes.
At last this odious offspring whom thou seest,
Thine own begotten, breaking violent way,
Tore through my entrails, that, with fear and pain
Distorted, all my nether shape thus grew
Transformed: but he my inbred enemy
Forth issued, brandishing his fatal dart,
Made to destroy. I fled, and cried out *Death!*
Hell trembled at the hideous name, and sighed
From all her caves, and back resounded *Death!*
I fled; but he pursued (though more, it seems,
Inflamed with lust than rage), and, swifter far,
Me overtook, his mother, all dismayed,
And, in embraces forcible and foul
Engendering with me, of that rape begot
These yelling monsters, that with ceaseless cry
Surround me, as thou saw'st—hourly conceived
And hourly born, with sorrow infinite
To me; for, when they list, into the womb

[1]A large constellation.

[2]Christ (*Cf.* 1 Corinthians, xv, 26, and Hebrews, ii, 14).

[3]*I. e.*, and though thou knowest for whom.

That bred them they return, and howl, and
gnaw
My bowels, their repast; then, bursting forth
Afresh, with conscious terrors vex me round,
That rest or intermission none I find.
Before mine eyes in opposition sits
Grim Death, my son and foe, who sets them
on,
And me, his parent, would full soon devour
For want of other prey, but that he knows
His end with mine involved, and knows that I
Should prove a bitter morsel, and his bane,
Whenever that shall be: so Fate pronounced.
But thou, O father, I forewarn thee, shun
His deadly arrow; neither vainly hope
To be invulnerable in those bright arms,
Though tempered heavenly; for that mortal
dint,[1]
Save he who reigns above, none can resist."
She finished; and the subtle Fiend his lore
Soon learned, now milder, and thus answered
smooth:—
"Dear daughter—since thou claim'st me
for thy sire,
And my fair son here show'st me, the dear
pledge
Of dalliance had with thee in Heaven, and joys
Then sweet, now sad to mention, through dire
change
Befallen us unforeseen, unthought-of—know,
I come no enemy, but to set free
From out this dark and dismal house of pain
Both him and thee, and all the Heavenly
host
Of Spirits that, in our just pretenses[2] armed,
Fell with us from on high. From them I go
This uncouth[3] errand sole, and one for all
Myself expose, with lonely steps to tread
The unfounded[4] Deep, and through the void
immense
To search, with wandering quest, a place
foretold
Should be—and, by concurring signs, ere now
Created vast and round—a place of bliss
In the purlieus[5] of Heaven; and therein placed
A race of upstart creatures, to supply
Perhaps our vacant room, though more re-
moved,
Lest Heaven, surcharged with potent multi-
tude,
Might hap to move new broils. Be this, or
aught
Than this more secret, now designed, I haste
To know; and, this once known, shall soon
return,
And bring ye to the place where thou and
Death
Shall dwell at ease, and up and down unseen
Wing silently the buxom[6] air, embalmed
With odors. There ye shall be fed and filled
Immeasurably; all things shall be your prey."
He ceased; for both seemed highly pleased,
and Death
Grinned horrible a ghastly smile, to hear
His famine should be filled, and blessed his
maw
Destined to that good hour. No less rejoiced
His mother bad, and thus bespake her sire:—
"The key of this infernal Pit, by due
And by command of Heaven's all-powerful
king,
I keep, by him forbidden to unlock
These adamantine gates; against all force
Death ready stands to interpose his dart,
Fearless to be o'ermatched by living might.
But what owe I to his commands above,
Who hates me, and hath hither thrust me
down
Into this gloom of Tartarus profound,
To sit in hateful office here confined,
Inhabitant of Heaven and heavenly born
Here in perpetual agony and pain,
With terrors and with clamors compassed
round
Of mine own brood, that on my bowels feed?
Thou art my father, thou my author, thou
My being gav'st me; whom should I obey
But thee? whom follow? Thou wilt bring me
soon
To that new world of light and bliss, among
The gods who live at ease, where I shall reign
At thy right hand voluptuous, as beseems
Thy daughter and thy darling, without end."
Thus saying, from her side the fatal key,
Sad instrument of all our woe, she took;
And, towards the gate rolling her bestial train,
Forthwith the huge portcullis[7] high up-drew,
Which, but herself, not all the Stygian Powers
Could once have moved; then in the key-hole
turns
The intricate wards,[8] and every bolt and bar
Of massy iron or solid rock with ease
Unfastens. On a sudden open fly,
With impetuous recoil and jarring sound,
The infernal doors, and on their hinges grate
Harsh thunder, that the lowest bottom shook
Of Erebus. She opened; but to shut
Excelled her power: the gates wide open stood,
That with extended wings a bannered host,
Under spread ensigns marching, might pass
through
With horse and chariots ranked in loose
array;
So wide they stood, and like a furnace-mouth

[1]Blow. [2]Claims. [3]Unknown, strange.
[4]Without foundation. [5]Suburbs.

[6]Yielding.
[7]Heavy grating sliding up and down in grooves placed at sides of gateway.
[8]Notches and projections in key and lock.

Cast forth redounding[1] smoke and ruddy flame.
Before their eyes in sudden view appear
The secrets of the hoary Deep—a dark
Illimitable ocean, without bound,
Without dimension; where length, breadth, and highth,
And time, and place, are lost; where eldest Night
And Chaos, ancestors of Nature, hold
Eternal anarchy, amidst the noise
Of endless wars, and by confusion stand.
For Hot, Cold, Moist, and Dry,[2] four champions fierce,
Strive here for mastery, and to battle bring
Their embryon atoms: they around the flag
Of each his faction, in their several clans,
Light-armed or heavy, sharp, smooth, swift, or slow,
Swarm populous, unnumbered as the sands
Of Barca or Cyrene's[3] torrid soil,
Levied to side with warring winds, and poise
Their lighter wings. To whom these most adhere
He rules a moment: Chaos umpire sits,
And by decision more embroils the fray
By which he reigns: next him, high arbiter,
Chance governs all. Into this wild Abyss,
The womb of Nature, and perhaps her grave,
Of neither Sea, nor Shore, nor Air, nor Fire,[4]
But all these in their pregnant causes mixed
Confusedly, and which thus must ever fight,
Unless the Almighty Maker them ordain
His dark materials to create more worlds—
Into this wild Abyss the wary Fiend
Stood on the brink of Hell and looked a while,
Pondering his voyage; for no narrow frith[5]
He had to cross. Nor was his ear less pealed
With noises loud and ruinous (to compare
Great things with small) than when Bellona[6] storms
With all her battering engines, bent to raze
Some capital city; or less than if this frame
Of Heaven were falling, and these elements
In mutiny had from her axle torn
The steadfast Earth. At last his sail-broad vans[7]
He spread for flight, and, in the surging smoke
Uplifted, spurns the ground; thence many a league,
As in a cloudy chair, ascending rides
Audacious; but, that seat soon failing, meets
A vast vacuity. All unawares,
Fluttering his pennons vain, plumb-down he drops
Ten thousand fathom deep, and to this hour
Down had been falling, had not, by ill chance,
The strong rebuff of some tumultuous cloud,
Instinct with fire and niter, hurried him
As many miles aloft. That fury stayed—
Quenched in a boggy Syrtis,[8] neither sea,
Nor good dry land—nigh foundered, on he fares,
Treading the crude consistence, half on foot,
Half flying; behoves him now both oar and sail.
As when a gryphon through the wilderness
With wingéd course, o'er hill or moory dale,
Pursues the Arimaspian,[9] who by stealth
Had from his wakeful custody purloined
The guarded gold; so eagerly the Fiend
O'er bog or steep, through strait, rough, dense, or rare,
With head, hands, wings, or feet, pursues his way,
And swims, or sinks, or wades, or creeps, or flies.
At length a universal hubbub wild
Of stunning sounds, and voices all confused,
Borne through the hollow dark, assaults his ear
With loudest vehemence. Thither he plies
Undaunted, to meet there whatever Power
Or Spirit of the nethermost Abyss
Might in that noise reside, of whom to ask
Which way the nearest coast of darkness lies
Bordering on light; when straight behold the throne
Of *Chaos*, and his dark pavilion spread
Wide on the wasteful Deep! With him enthroned
Sat sable-vested *Night*, eldest of things,
The consort of his reign; and by them stood
Orcus and Ades, and the dreaded name
Of Demogorgon; Rumor next, and Chance,
And Tumult, and Confusion, all embroiled,
And Discord with a thousand various mouths.
To whom Satan, turning boldly, thus:—"Ye Powers
And Spirits of this nethermost Abyss,
Chaos and ancient Night, I come no spy
With purpose to explore or to disturb
The secrets of your realm; but, by constraint
Wandering this darksome desert, as my way
Lies through your spacious empire up to light,
Alone and without guide, half lost, I seek,
What readiest path leads where your gloomy bounds
Confine with Heaven; or, if some other place,
From your dominion won, the Ethereal King
Possesses lately, thither to arrive

[1]Rolling in billows.

[2]The four humors of medieval medicine.

[3]Cities of northern Africa.

[4]The four elements of the older physical science.

[5]Arm of the sea. [6]Goddess of war. [7]Wings.

[8]The Syrtes were two quicksands off the north coast of Africa.

[9]The Arimaspians were a one-eyed people of Scythia who, according to ancient writers, were continually fighting the griffins for the sake of the gold guarded by the latter.

I travel this profound. Direct my course:
Directed, no mean recompense it brings
To your behoof,[1] if I that region lost,
All usurpation thence expelled, reduce
To her original darkness and your sway
(Which is my present journey[2]), and once more
Erect the standard there of ancient Night.
Yours be the advantage all, mine the revenge!"
  Thus Satan; and him thus the Anarch old,
With faltering speech and visage incomposed,
Answered:—"I know thee, stranger, who thou art—
That mighty leading Angel, who of late
Made head against Heaven's King, though overthrown.
I saw and heard; for such a numerous host
Fled not in silence through the frighted Deep,
With ruin upon ruin, rout on rout,
Confusion worse confounded; and Heaven-gates
Poured out by millions her victorious bands.
Pursuing. I upon my frontiers here
Keep residence; if all I can will serve
That little which is left so to defend,
Encroached on still through our intestine broils
Weakening the scepter of old Night: first, Hell,
Your dungeon, stretching far and wide beneath,
Now lately Heaven and Earth, another world
Hung o'er my realm, linked in a golden chain
To that side Heaven from whence your legions fell!
If that way be your walk, you have not far;
So much the nearer danger. Go, and speed;
Havoc, and spoil, and ruin, are my gain."
  He ceased; and Satan stayed not to reply,
But, glad that now his sea should find a shore,
With fresh alacrity and force renewed
Springs upward, like a pyramid of fire,
Into the wild expanse, and through the shock
Of fighting elements, on all sides round
Environed, wins his way; harder beset
And more endangered than when Argo[3] passed
Through Bosporus betwixt the justling rocks,[4]
Or when Ulysses on the larboard shunned
Charybdis, and by the other whirlpool steered.
So he with difficulty and labor hard
Moved on. With difficulty and labor he;
But, he once passed, soon after, when Man fell,
Strange alteration! Sin and Death amain,[5]
Following his track (such was the will of Heaven)
Paved after him a broad and beaten way
Over the dark Abyss, whose boiling gulf
Tamely endured a bridge of wondrous length,
From Hell continued, reaching the utmost Orb[6]
Of this frail World; by which the Spirits perverse
With easy intercourse pass to and fro
To tempt or punish mortals, except whom
God and good Angels guard by special grace.
  But now at last the sacred influence
Of light appears, and from the walls of Heaven
Shoots far into the bosom of dim Night
A glimmering dawn. Here Nature first begins
Her farthest verge, and Chaos to retire,
As from her outmost works, a broken foe,
With tumult less and with less hostile din;
That[7] Satan with less toil, and now with ease,
Wafts on the calmer wave by dubious light,
And, like a weather-beaten vessel, holds[8]
Gladly the port, though shrouds and tackle torn;
Or in the emptier waste, resembling air,
Weighs his spread wings, at leisure to behold
Far off the empyreal Heaven, extended wide
In circuit, undetermined square or round,
With opal towers and battlements adorned
Of living sapphire, once his native seat,
And, fast by, hanging in a golden chain,
This pendent World, in bigness as a star
Of smallest magnitude close by the moon.
Thither, full fraught with mischievous revenge,
Accursed, and in a cursèd hour, he hies.

[1]Advantage. [2]Work.
[3]The boat in which Jason went to Colchis for the golden fleece.
[4]The Symplegades, at the entrance of the Black Sea.
[5]In great haste.
[6]The outermost of the concentric spheres surrounding the earth.
[7]So that. [8]Makes for.

OF EDUCATION

TO MASTER SAMUEL HARTLIB[1] (1644)

MASTER HARTLIB:

I AM long since persuaded that to say or do aught worth memory and imitation, no purpose or respect[2] should sooner move us than simply the love of God and of mankind. Nevertheless to write now the reforming of education, though it be one of the greatest and noblest designs that can be thought on, and for the want whereof this nation perishes, I had not yet at this time been induced but by your earnest entreaties and serious conjurements; as having my mind for the present half diverted in the pursuance of some other assertions, the knowledge and the use of which cannot but be a great furtherance both to the enlargement of truth, and honest living, with much more peace. Nor should the laws of any private friendship have prevailed with me to divide thus or transpose my former thoughts, but that I see those aims, those actions which have won you with me the esteem of a person sent hither by some good providence from a far country to be the occasion and the incitement of great good to this island.

And, as I hear, you have obtained the same repute with men of most approved wisdom, and some of highest authority among us; not to mention the learned correspondence which you hold in foreign parts, and the extraordinary pains and diligence which you have used in this matter, both here and beyond the seas; either by the definite will of God so ruling, or the peculiar sway of nature, which also is God's working. Neither can I think that, so reputed and so valued as you are, you would, to the forfeit of your own discerning ability, impose upon me an unfit and overponderous argument; but that the satisfaction which you profess to have received from those incidental discourses which we have wandered into, hath pressed and almost constrained you into a persuasion that what you require from me in this point, I neither ought, nor can in conscience, defer beyond this time both of so much need at once, and so much opportunity to try what God hath determined.

I will not resist, therefore, whatever it is either of divine or human obligement, that you lay upon me; but will forthwith set down in writing, as you request me, that voluntary idea, which hath long in silence presented itself to me, of a better education, in extent and comprehension far more large, and yet of time far shorter and of attainment far more certain than hath been yet in practice. Brief I shall endeavor to be; for that which I have to say, assuredly this nation hath extreme need should be done sooner than spoken. To tell you, therefore, what I have benefited herein among old renowned authors, I shall spare; and to search what many modern Januas and Didactics,[3] more than ever I shall read, have projected, my inclination leads me not. But if you can accept of these few observations which have flowered off, and are as it were the burnishing of many studious and contemplative years altogether spent in the search of religious and civil knowledge, and such as pleased you so well in the relating, I here give you them to dispose of.

The end, then, of learning is to repair the ruins of our first parents by regaining to know God aright, and out of that knowledge to love him, to imitate him, to be like him, as we may the nearest by possessing our souls of true virtue, which, being united to the heavenly grace of faith, makes up the highest perfection. But because our understanding cannot in this body found itself but on sensible things, nor arrive so clearly to the knowledge of God and things invisible, as by orderly conning over the visible and inferior creature, the same method is necessarily to be followed in all discreet teaching. And seeing every nation affords not experience and tradition enough for all kind of learning, therefore we are chiefly taught the languages of those people who have at any time been most industrious after wisdom; so that language is but the instrument conveying to us

[1]Born in Prussia (*c.* 1600; died *c.* 1670), his father Polish, his mother English. He became a merchant in London, and was constantly busy with various projects for public reform. It has often and truly been said that Milton's program of education, from its extent, is impossible of execution, calling for a race of young Miltons. This, however, does not at all lessen the value of the letter as a discussion of principles and method.

[2]Consideration.

[3]Milton thus refers to two treatises by the Moravian educational reformer, John Amos Comenius (1592–1671), *Janua Linguarum Reserata*, and *Didactica Magna*. Comenius spent a year in London (1641–1642) and was intimate with Hartlib, who eagerly espoused his plans of educational reform. They were in fact similar to Milton's, though the latter's way of speaking would not lead one to suppose so.

things useful to be known. And though a linguist should pride himself to have all the tongues that Babel cleft the world into, yet if he have not studied the solid things in them, as well as the words and lexicons, he were nothing so much to be esteemed a learned man as any yeoman or tradesman competently wise in his mother-dialect only.

Hence appear the many mistakes which have made learning generally so unpleasing and so unsuccessful; first, we do amiss to spend seven or eight years merely in scraping together so much miserable Latin and Greek as might be learned otherwise easily and delightfully in one year. And that which casts our proficiency therein so much behind is our time lost partly in too oft idle vacancies given both to schools and universities; partly in a preposterous exaction, forcing the empty wits of children to compose themes, verses, and orations, which are the acts of ripest judgment, and the final work of a head filled by long reading and observing with elegant maxims and copious invention. These are not matters to be wrung from poor striplings, like blood out of the nose, or the plucking of untimely fruit. Besides the ill habit which they get of wretched barbarizing against the Latin and Greek idiom with their untutored Anglicisms, odious to be read, yet not to be avoided without a well-continued and judicious conversing among pure authors, digested, which they scarce taste. Whereas, if after some preparatory grounds of speech by their certain forms got into memory, they were led to the praxis thereof in some chosen short book lessoned thoroughly to them, they might then forthwith proceed to learn the substance of good things, and arts in due order, which would bring the whole language quickly into their power. This I take to be the most rational and most profitable way of learning languages, and whereby we may best hope to give account to God of our youth spent herein.

And for the usual method of teaching arts,[1] I deem it to be an old error of universities, not yet well recovered from the scholastic grossness of barbarous ages, that instead of beginning with arts most easy (and those be such as are most obvious to the sense), they present their young unmatriculated novices at first coming with the most intellective abstractions of logic and metaphysics; so that they having but newly left those grammatic flats and shallows, where they stuck unreasonably to learn a few words with lamentable construction, and now on the sudden transported under another climate, to be tossed and turmoiled with their unballasted wits in fathomless and unquiet deeps of controversy, do for the most part grow into hatred and contempt of learning, mocked and deluded all this while with ragged notions and babblements, while they expected worthy and delightful knowledge; till poverty or youthful years call them importunately their several ways, and hasten them, with the sway of friends, either to an ambitious and mercenary, or ignorantly zealous divinity: some allured to the trade of law, grounding their purposes not on the prudent and heavenly contemplation of justice and equity, which was never taught them, but on the promising and pleasing thoughts of litigious terms, fat contentions, and flowing fees; others betake them to state affairs, with souls so unprincipled in virtue and true generous breeding that flattery, and court shifts, and tyrannous aphorisms appear to them the highest points of wisdom, instilling their barren hearts with a conscientious slavery, if, as I rather think, it be not feigned. Others, lastly, of a more delicious and airy spirit, retire themselves (knowing no better) to the enjoyments of ease and luxury, living out their days in feast and jollity; which, indeed, is the wisest and the safest course of all these, unless they were with more integrity undertaken. And these are the errors, and these are the fruits of misspending our prime youth at the schools and universities as we do, either in learning mere words, or such things chiefly as were better unlearned.

I shall detain you now no longer in the demonstration of what we should not do, but straight conduct ye to a hillside, where I will point ye out the right path of a virtuous and noble education; laborious indeed at the first ascent, but else so smooth, so green, so full of goodly prospect and melodious sounds on every side that the harp of Orpheus was not more charming. I doubt not but ye shall have more ado to drive our dullest and laziest youth, our stocks and stubs, from the infinite desire of such a happy nurture, than we have

[1] Liberal arts, leading to the degrees of A.B. and A.M.

now to hale and drag our choicest and hopefullest wits to that asinine feast of sowthistles and brambles which is commonly set before them as all the food and entertainment of their tenderest and most docible age. I call, therefore, a complete and generous education, that which fits a man to perform justly, skillfully, and magnanimously all the offices, both private and public, of peace and war. And how all this may be done between twelve and one-and-twenty, less time than is now bestowed in pure trifling at grammar and sophistry, is to be thus ordered:

First, to find out a spacious house and ground about it fit for an academy, and big enough to lodge a hundred and fifty persons, whereof twenty or thereabout may be attendants, all under the government of one who shall be thought of desert sufficient, and ability either to do all, or wisely to direct and oversee it done. This place should be at once both school and university, not needing a remove to any other house of scholarship, except it be some peculiar college of law, or physic, where they mean to be practitioners; but as for those general studies which take up all our time from Lily[1] to the commencing,[2] as they term it, master of art, it should be absolute. After this pattern, as many edifices may be converted to this use as shall be needful in every city throughout this land, which would tend much to the increase of learning and civility everywhere. This number, less or more, thus collected, to the convenience of a foot-company, or interchangeably two troops of cavalry, should divide their day's work into three parts as it lies orderly: their studies, their exercise, and their diet.

For their studies: first, they should begin with the chief and necessary rules of some good grammar,[3] either that now used, or any better; and while this is doing, their speech is to be fashioned to a distinct and clear pronunciation, as near as may be to the Italian, especially in the vowels. For we Englishmen, being far northerly, do not open our mouths in the cold air wide enough to grace a southern tongue; but are observed by all other nations to speak exceeding close and inward, so that to smatter[4] Latin with an English mouth is as ill a hearing as law French. Next, to make them expert in the usefullest points of grammar, and withal to season them and win them early to the love of virtue and true labor, ere any flattering seducement or vain principle seize them wandering, some easy and delightful book of education would be read to them, whereof the Greeks have store, as Cebes,[5] Plutarch,[6] and other Socratic discourses. But in Latin we have none of classic authority extant, except the two or three first books of Quintilian,[7] and some select pieces elsewhere.

But here the main skill and groundwork will be to temper them such lectures and explanations, upon every opportunity, as may lead and draw them in willing obedience, inflamed with the study of learning and the admiration of virtue; stirred up with high hopes of living to be brave men and worthy patriots, dear to God, and famous to all ages: that they may despise and scorn all their childish and ill-taught qualities, to delight in manly and liberal exercises, which he who hath the art and proper eloquence to catch them with, what with mild and effectual persuasions, and what with the intimation of some fear, if need be, but chiefly by his own example, might in a short space gain them to an incredible diligence and courage, infusing into their young breasts such an ingenuous and noble ardor as would not fail to make many of them renowned and matchless men. At the same time, some other hour of the day, might be taught them the rules of arithmetic; and soon after the elements of geometry, even playing, as the old manner was. After evening repast, till bedtime, their thoughts will be best taken up in the easy grounds of religion, and the story of Scripture.

The next step would be to the authors of

[1]The name denotes the *Latin Grammar* of William Lily (*c.* 1468–1522), who became master of Colet's school in St. Paul's churchyard in 1512. He had studied in Italy, was one of the earliest teachers of Greek in England, and had the aid of Erasmus in compiling his Latin syntax (1513). This was the foundation of all Latin grammars which have been used in England until comparatively recent times.

[2]Taking the degree of.

[3]Latin grammar.

[4]To utter without proper knowledge; but Milton seems rather to have in mind the older meaning, "to defile," or the dialectal, "to smash."

[5]A Theban, of the school of Socrates. Milton refers to a brief philosophical work, very popular in the later 16th, and in the 17th, centuries, which is, however, falsely attributed to Cebes. It was popular, in fact, because of its graphic, literary presentation of some elements of Stoic morality.

[6]The author of *Moral Essays*, besides the famous *Parallel Lives*.

[7]A celebrated teacher in Rome (flourished A. D. 65), author of the *Institutes of Oratory*, here referred to.

agriculture, Cato, Varro, and Columella, for the matter is most easy; and if the language be difficult, so much the better; it is not a difficulty above their years. And here will be an occasion of inciting and enabling them hereafter to improve the tillage of their country, to recover the bad soil, and to remedy the waste that is made of good; for this was one of Hercules' praises. Ere half these authors be read (which will soon be with plying hard and daily), they cannot choose but be masters of any ordinary prose: so that it will be then seasonable for them to learn in any modern author the use of the globes, and all the maps, first with the old names, and then with the new; or they might be then capable to read any compendious method of natural philosophy;—and at the same time might be entering into the Greek tongue, after the same manner as was before prescribed in the Latin; whereby the difficulties of grammar being soon overcome, all the historical physiology of Aristotle and Theophrastus[1] are open before them, and, as I may say, under contribution. The like access will be to Vitruvius;[2] to Seneca's *Natural Questions*, to Mela, Celsus, Pliny, or Solinus.[3] And having thus passed the principles of arithmetic, geometry, astronomy, and geography, with a general compact of physics, they may descend in mathematics to the instrumental science of trigonometry, and from thence to fortification, architecture, enginery, or navigation. And in natural philosophy they may proceed leisurely from the history of meteors, minerals, plants, and living creatures, as far as anatomy.

Then also in course might be read to them, out of some not tedious writer, the institution of physic,[4] that they may know the tempers, the humors, the seasons, and how to manage a crudity;[5] which he who can wisely and timely do, is not only a great physician to himself and to his friends, but also may, at some time or other, save an army by this frugal and expenseless means only; and not let the healthy and stout bodies of young men rot away under him for want of this discipline, which is a great pity, and no less a shame to the commander. To set forward all these proceedings in nature and mathematics, what hinders but that they may procure, as oft as shall be needful, the helpful experiences of hunters, fowlers, fishermen, shepherds, gardeners, apothecaries; and in the other sciences, architects, engineers, mariners, anatomists; who doubtless would be ready, some for reward, and some to favor such a hopeful seminary. And this will give them such a real tincture of natural knowledge as they shall never forget, but daily augment with delight. Then also those poets which are now counted most hard will be both facile and pleasant, Orpheus,[6] Hesiod, Theocritus, Aratus,[7] Nicander,[8] Oppian,[9] Dionysius;[10] and in Latin, Lucretius, Manilius,[11] and the rural part of Virgil.

By this time, years and good general precepts will have furnished them more distinctly with that act of reason which in ethics is called proairesis,[12] that they may with some judgment contemplate upon moral good and evil. Then will be required a special reinforcement of constant and sound indoctrinating, to set them right and firm, instructing them more amply in the knowledge of virtue and the hatred of vice; while their young and pliant affections are led through all the moral works of Plato, Xenophon, Cicero, Plutarch, Laertius,[13] and those Locrian remnants;[14] but still to be reduced[15] in their nightward studies wherewith they close the day's work, under the determinate sentence of David or Solomon, or the evangels and apostolic Scrip-

[1]Pupil of Aristotle and his successor at the Lyceum, famous for his treatises on botany.

[2]Roman architect and engineer (contemporary with Quintilian), author of an influential treatise on architecture.

[3]Seneca's work deals chiefly with meteorology and astronomy. The others named are authors, respectively, of works on geography, medicine, natural science, and, in the case of Solinus, "memorable things," chiefly retold from Pliny.

[4]The first principles of medicine.

[5]Indigestion.

[6]A mythical Thracian, to whom were formerly attributed several poems. Perhaps Milton refers to the *Lithica*, a poem treating of the properties of stones.

[7]Author (*c.* 270 B. C.) of two astronomical poems.

[8]Author (2nd century B. C.) of poems dealing with venomous animals and with poisons and their antidotes.

[9]Formerly thought to be the author of poems on fishing and on hunting.

[10]Author of a poetical description of the then known earth (*c.* A. D. 300).

[11]Author of an astronomical or, more correctly, astrological poem (edited in recent years by A. E. Housman).

[12]Choice between good and evil.

[13]Diogenes Laertius (*c.* A. D. 150) whose *Lives and Opinions of Eminent Philosophers* is a great storehouse of anecdote often, though not always, edifying.

[14]Timaeus of Locri (in Italy) was formerly thought to be author of a treatise *On the Soul of the World.* Nothing is known of him save what can be learned from Plato's ***Timaeus.***

[15]Led back.

tures. Being perfect in the knowledge of personal duty, they may then begin the study of economics. And either now or before this they may have easily learned, at any odd hour, the Italian tongue. And soon after, but with wariness and good antidote, it would be wholesome enough to let them taste some choice comedies, Greek, Latin, or Italian; those tragedies also that treat of household matters, as *Trachiniæ*, *Alcestis*,[1] and the like.

The next remove must be to the study of politics; to know the beginning, end, and reasons of political societies, that they may not, in a dangerous fit of the commonwealth, be such poor, shaken, uncertain reeds, of such a tottering conscience, as many of our great counselors have lately shown themselves, but steadfast pillars of the state. After this, they are to dive into the grounds of law, and legal justice; delivered first and with best warrant by Moses; and, as far as human prudence can be trusted, in those extolled remains of Grecian lawgivers, Lycurgus, Solon, Zaleucus,[2] Charondas;[3] and thence to all the Roman edicts and tables, with their Justinian; and so down to the Saxon and common laws of England, and the statutes.

Sundays also and every evening may be now understandingly spent in the highest matters of theology, and church history, ancient and modern; and ere this time the Hebrew tongue at a set hour might have been gained, that the Scriptures may be now read in their own original; whereto it would be no impossibility to add the Chaldee and the Syrian dialect. When all these employments are well conquered, then will the choice histories, heroic poems, and Attic tragedies of stateliest and most regal argument, with all the famous political orations, offer themselves; which, if they were not only read, but some of them got by memory, and solemnly pronounced with right accent and grace, as might be taught, would endue them even with the spirit and vigor of Demosthenes or Cicero, Euripides or Sophocles.

And now, lastly, will be the time to read with them those organic[4] arts which enable men to discourse and write perspicuously, elegantly, and according to the fitted style of lofty, mean,[5] or lowly. Logic, therefore, so much as is useful, is to be referred to this due place with all her well-couched heads and topics, until it be time to open her contracted palm into a graceful and ornate rhetoric, taught out of the rule of Plato, Aristotle, Phalereus,[6] Cicero, Hermogenes,[7] Longinus. To which poetry would be made subsequent, or indeed rather precedent, as being less subtle and fine, but more simple, sensuous, and passionate. I mean not here the prosody of a verse, which they could not but have hit on before among the rudiments of grammar; but that sublime art which in Aristotle's *Poetics*, in Horace, and the Italian commentaries of Castelvetro, Tasso, Mazzoni,[8] and others, teaches what the laws are of a true epic poem, what of a dramatic, what of a lyric, what decorum[9] is, which is the grand masterpiece[10] to observe. This would make them soon perceive what despicable creatures our common rimers and play-writers be; and show them what religious, what glorious and magnificent use, might be made of poetry, both in divine and human things.

From hence, and not till now, will be the right season of forming them to be able writers and composers in every excellent matter, when they shall be thus fraught with an universal insight into things. Or whether they be to speak in parliament or council, honor and attention would be waiting on their lips. There would then also appear in pulpits other visages, other gestures, and stuff otherwise wrought than what we now sit under, oft-times to as great trial of our patience as any other that they preach to us. These are the studies wherein our noble and our gentle youth ought to bestow their time in a disciplinary way from twelve to one-and-twenty, unless they rely more upon their ancestors dead than upon themselves living. In which methodical course it is so supposed they must proceed by the steady pace of learning on-

---

[1]By Sophocles and Euripides, respectively.

[2]Lawgiver of the Locrians, about 700 B. C.

[3]Lawgiver of Catana (in Sicily) and of other cities nearby, about 485 B. C.

[4]Instrumental.

[5]Intermediate.

[6]Known as a late Athenian orator (345–283 B. C.), formerly thought to be the author of an extant treatise on elocution.

[7]Greek rhetorician (flourished A. D. 170) whose works were long used in the schools.

[8]All of the 16th century.

[9]Fitness or appropriateness, as of characters to the action, of style to the theme, *etc.*

[10]The most important point.

ward, as at convenient times, for memory's sake, to retire back into the middle ward, and sometimes into the rear of what they have been taught, until they have confirmed and solidly united the whole body of their perfected knowledge, like the last embattling of a Roman legion. Now will be worth the seeing what exercises and what recreations may best agree and become these studies.

The course of study hitherto briefly described is, what I can guess by reading, likest to those ancient and famous schools of Pythagoras, Plato, Isocrates, Aristotle, and such others, out of which were bred up such a number of renowned philosophers, orators, historians, poets, and princes all over Greece, Italy, and Asia, besides the flourishing studies of Cyrene and Alexandria. But herein it shall exceed them, and supply a defect as great as that which Plato noted in the commonwealth of Sparta. Whereas that city trained up their youth most for war, and these in their academies and Lyceum all for the gown,[1] this institution of breeding which I here delineate shall be equally good both for peace and war. Therefore about an hour and a half ere they eat at noon should be allowed them for exercise, and due rest afterwards; but the time for this may be enlarged at pleasure according as their rising in the morning shall be early.

The exercise which I commend first is the exact use of their weapon,[2] to guard, and to strike safely with edge or point. This will keep them healthy, nimble, strong, and well in breath; is also the likeliest means to make them grow large and tall, and to inspire them with a gallant and fearless courage, which being tempered with seasonable lectures and precepts to them of true fortitude and patience, will turn into a native and heroic valor and make them hate the cowardice of doing wrong. They must be also practiced in all the locks and gripes of wrestling, wherein Englishmen were wont to excel, as need may often be in fight to tug, to grapple, and to close. And this perhaps will be enough, wherein to prove and heat their single strength.

The interim of unsweating themselves[3] regularly, and convenient rest before meat, may, both with profit and delight, be taken up in recreating and composing their travailed spirits with the solemn and divine harmonies of music, heard or learned; either while the skillful organist plies his grave and fancied descant in lofty fugues, or the whole symphony with artful and unimaginable touches adorn and grace the well-studied chords of some choice composer; sometimes the lute or soft organ-stop waiting on elegant voices, either to religious, martial, or civil ditties; which, if wise men and prophets be not extremely out, have a great power over dispositions and manners, to smooth and make them gentle from rustic harshness and distempered passions. The like also would not be unexpedient after meat, to assist and cherish nature in her first concoction,[4] and send their minds back to study in good tune and satisfaction. Where having followed it under vigilant eyes till about two hours before supper, they are, by a sudden alarum or watchword, to be called out to their military motions, under sky or covert, according to the season, as was the Roman wont; first on foot, then, as their age permits, on horseback, to all the art of cavalry; that having in sport, but with much exactness and daily muster, served out the rudiments of their soldiership in all the skill of embattling, marching, encamping, fortifying, besieging, and battering, with all the helps of ancient and modern stratagems, tactics, and warlike maxims, they may as it were out of a long war come forth renowned and perfect commanders in the service of their country. They would not then, if they were trusted with fair and hopeful armies, suffer them, for want of just and wise discipline, to shed away from about them like sick feathers, though they be never so oft supplied; they would not suffer their empty and unrecruitable[5] colonels of twenty men in a company to quaff out or convey into secret hoards the wages of a delusive list[6] and a miserable remnant; yet in the meanwhile to be overmastered with a score or two of drunkards, the only soldiery left about them, or else to comply with all rapines and violences. No, certainly, if they knew aught of that knowledge that belongs to good men or good governors they would not suffer these things.

[1]That is, for civil pursuits.

[2]Fencing.

[3]That is, of allowing their bodies to cool, following the exercises above prescribed.

[4]Digestion.

[5]Unable to obtain recruits.

[6]Wages drawn for men who existed only on a fictitious list of company-members.

But to return to our own institute: besides these constant exercises at home, there is another opportunity of gaining experience to be won from pleasure itself abroad; in those vernal seasons of the year when the air is calm and pleasant, it were an injury and sullenness against nature not to go out and see her riches, and partake in her rejoicing with heaven and earth. I should not, therefore, be a persuader to them of studying much then, after two or three years that they have well laid their grounds, but to ride out in companies, with prudent and staid guides, to all the quarters of the land; learning and observing all places of strength, all commodities[1] of building and of soil, for towns and tillage, harbors and ports for trade. Sometimes taking sea as far as to our navy, to learn there also what they can in the practical knowledge of sailing and of sea-fight.

These ways would try all their peculiar gifts of nature; and if there were any secret excellence among them would fetch it out, and give it fair opportunities to advance itself by, which could not but mightily redound to the good of this nation, and bring into fashion again those old admired virtues and excellencies, with far more advantage now in this purity of Christian knowledge. Nor shall we then need the monsieurs of Paris to take our hopeful youth into their slight and prodigal custodies, and send them over back again transformed into mimics, apes, and kickshaws.[2] But if they desire to see other countries at three or four and twenty years of age, not to learn principles, but to enlarge experience and make wise observation, they will by that time be such as shall deserve the regard and honor of all men where they pass, and the society and friendship of those in all places who are best and most eminent. And perhaps then other nations will be glad to visit us for their breeding, or else to imitate us in their own country.

Now, lastly, for their diet there cannot be much to say, save only that it would be best in the same house; for much time else would be lost abroad, and many ill habits got; and that it should be plain, healthful, and moderate, I suppose is out of controversy.

Thus, Mr. Hartlib, you have a general view in writing, as your desire was, of that which at several times I had discoursed with you concerning the best and noblest way of education; not beginning, as some have done, from the cradle, which yet might be worth many considerations, if brevity had not been my scope. Many other circumstances also I could have mentioned, but this, to such as have the worth in them to make trial, for light and direction may be enough. Only I believe that this is not a bow for every man to shoot in[3] that counts himself a teacher, but will require sinews almost equal to those which Homer gave Ulysses; yet I am withal persuaded that it may prove much more easy in the assay[4] than it now seems at distance, and much more illustrious; howbeit, not more difficult than I imagine, and that imagination presents me with nothing but very happy, and very possible according to best wishes, if God have so decreed, and this age have spirit and capacity enough to apprehend.

[1]Suitable properties. [2]Trifling persons.

[3]With. [4]Trial.

JOHN BUNYAN (1628–1688)

The Bunyan family was settled in Bedfordshire from at least the end of the twelfth century. Bunyan's grandfather was a "petty chapman," or small retail trader. Thomas, Bunyan's father, called himself a "brazier";—he made and mended pots and kettles, but did not belong to the more or less disreputable tribe of wandering tinkers. Bunyan carried on the same trade. His father married three times, and Bunyan was the first child of his second wife, and was born at the village of Elstow, about a mile south of the town of Bedford, in November, 1628. His baptism was recorded on 30 November. As a child he had some schooling, learning to read and to write, probably at Elstow. In 1644 he became a soldier in the Commonwealth army, fighting against his king until July, 1647. Towards the close of 1648 or the beginning of 1649 he married. No record of his marriage remains, and the name of his wife is not known; but she came of a godly family and, though she brought little else, she contributed to the new household two books inherited from her father—*The Plain Man's Pathway to Heaven* and *The Practice of Piety*. Her own devout conversation and the former of these books combined to send Bunyan off on that quest of the spirit for religious certitude and for the right pathway to salvation which ended by making him a nonconformist preacher, a writer for edification, and—something that he himself never suspected and would not have desired—one of the great figures in the annals of English literature. Sensitive, highly strung, vividly imaginative, he came to manhood at a time of general religious excitement, and could scarcely in any event have escaped its influence. His long and agonized conflict with himself and final victory he described years later in a book which (though not trustworthy as a record of fact) is a classic of spiritual autobiography: *Grace Abounding to the Chief of Sinners: or, A Brief and Faithful Relation of the Exceeding Mercy of God in Christ to his Poor Servant, John Bunyan; Wherein is particularly showed the manner of his conversion, his sight and trouble for sin, his dreadful temptations, also how he despaired of God's mercy, and how the Lord at length through Christ did deliver him from all the guilt and terror that lay upon him. Whereunto is added a brief relation of his call to the work of the ministry, of his temptations therein, as also what he hath met with in prison. All which was written by his own hand there, and now published for the support of the weak and tempted people of God* (1666).

This was not Bunyan's first book; it was in fact his twelfth publication. In 1653 he had joined a nonconformist body meeting in St. John's Church, at Bedford, and had moved there in 1655. Soon thereafter he lost his wife, who had borne him four children. About the same time he was made a deacon, and in 1656 he published (at Newport Pagnell, where he had been stationed while in the army) his first book, *Some Gospel Truths Opened*, written in confutation of the Quakers. In the following year his calling as a preacher was formally recognized, and his fame began to spread. In 1658 he published his third book, *A Few Sighs from Hell, or the Groans of a Damned Soul*. Probably late in 1659 he married a second time. In the next year, after the accession of Charles II, steps were taken to restore the Church of England to her former position, and Bunyan's preaching at public assemblies became illegal. He determined, however, to persist, and was accordingly arrested on 12 November at the hamlet of Lower Samsell by Harlington (about 13 miles south of Bedford). He was imprisoned for the next 12 years, with the exception, probably, of a brief interval in 1666. While in jail he made long tagged laces to support his family. During part of this period he was allowed much freedom, was often present at church meetings in Bedford, and even went to "see Christians in London." In 1672, following Charles's Declaration of Indulgence, he was pardoned, but was again imprisoned in 1675;—and it was during this period of confinement that he wrote the first part of *The Pilgrim's Progress* (published in 1678). Thereafter, though he continued to be active in preaching, and ran some risks, he escaped molestation. *The Life and Death of Mr. Badman* was published in 1680, *The Holy War*, in 1682, and the second part of *The Pilgrim's Progress* in 1684. In 1688 he was caught in a severe storm while riding to London after aiding in the reconciliation of a father and son. He came down with a severe cold followed by a fever, and died on 31 August. He was buried in Bunhill Fields, Finsbury.

In all, Bunyan wrote 60 books and tracts. It is thought that no fewer than 100,000 copies of *The Pilgrim's Progress* were sold before his death; and during the first century of the book's existence 33 editions of Part I were published, and 59 editions of Parts I and II together. There are said to be versions of the book in no less than 108 languages and dialects. No book has had a comparable circulation save the Bible. And on the

Bible, almost alone, Bunyan was nourished, and its language and rhythms mingle pleasantly with the homelier speech of the seventeenth-century English countryside in his great allegory of the spiritual life. Bunyan was no poet, but he chose to tell in verse the genesis of his book, and one may best learn from his own words one reason for its enduring vitality:

> "When at the first I took my pen in hand
> Thus for to write, I did not understand
> That I at all should make a little Book
> In such a mode. Nay, I had undertook
> To make another; which when almost done,
> Before I was aware, I this begun;
> . . . . . but yet I did not think
> To show to all the world my pen and ink
> In such a mode. I only thought to make
> I knew not what; nor did I undertake
> Thereby to please my neighbor. No, not I,
> I did it mine own self to gratify."

When he had been humanized by a full experience of life, knowing the workings of the human heart and mind as few in any age are given to know them, he wrote this book, not of set purpose nor expressly for the improvement of mankind, but almost in his own despite—just because it so "gratified" him to dramatize the spiritual conflict within the soul's dark habitation. And thus was one of the world's few great books born.

PASSAGES FROM
THE PILGRIM'S PROGRESS

FROM THIS WORLD TO THAT WHICH IS TO COME: DELIVERED UNDER THE SIMILITUDE OF A DREAM

THE FIRST PART (1678)

I

As I walked through the wilderness of this world, I lighted on a certain place where was a Den, and I laid me down in that place to sleep: and as I slept I dreamed a dream. I dreamed, and behold, I saw a man clothed with rags, standing in a certain place, with his face from his own house, a book in his hand, and a great burden upon his back. I looked, and saw him open the book, and read therein; and, as he read, he wept, and trembled; and, not being able longer to contain, he brake out with a lamentable cry, saying, What shall I do?

In this plight, therefore, he went home and refrained himself as long as he could, that his wife and children should not perceive his distress; but he could not be silent long, because that his trouble increased. Wherefore at length he brake his mind to his wife and children; and thus he began to talk to them: O my dear wife, said he, and you the children of my bowels, I, your dear friend, am in myself undone by reason of a burden that lieth hard upon me; moreover, I am for certain informed that this our city will be burned with fire from heaven; in which fearful overthrow, both myself, with thee my wife, and you my sweet babes, shall miserably come to ruin, except (the which yet I see not) some way of escape can be found, whereby we may be delivered. At this his relations were sore amazed; not for that they believed that what he had said to them was true, but because they thought that some frenzy distemper had got into his head; therefore, it drawing towards night, and they hoping that sleep might settle his brains, with all haste they got him to bed. But the night was as troublesome to him as the day; wherefore, instead of sleeping, he spent it in sighs and tears. So, when the morning was come, they would know how he did. He told them, Worse and worse: he also set to talking to them again; but they began to be hardened. They also thought to drive away his distemper by harsh and surly carriages to him; sometimes they would deride, sometimes they would chide, and sometimes they would quite neglect him. Wherefore he began to retire himself to his chamber, to pray for and pity them, and also to condole his own misery; he would also walk solitarily in the fields, sometimes reading, and sometimes praying: and thus for some days he spent his time.

Now, I saw, upon a time, when he was walking in the fields, that he was, as he was wont, reading in this book, and greatly distressed in his mind; and, as he read, he burst out, as he had done before, crying, What shall I do to be saved?

I saw also that he looked this way and that way, as if he would run; yet he stood still, because, as I perceived, he could not tell which way to go. I looked then, and saw a man named *Evangelist* coming to him, and asked, Wherefore dost thou cry?

He answered, Sir, I perceive by the book in my hand, that I am condemned to die, and after that to come to judgment; and I find that I am not willing to do the first, nor able to do the second.

Then said *Evangelist,* Why not willing to die, since this life is attended with so many evils? The man answered, Because I fear that this burden that is upon my back will sink me lower than the grave, and I shall fall into Tophet. And, Sir, if I be not fit to go to prison, I am not fit to go to judgment, and from thence to execution; and the thoughts of these things make me cry.

Then said *Evangelist,* If this be thy condition, why standest thou still? He answered, Because I know not whither to go. Then he gave him a parchment roll, and there was written within, Fly from the wrath to come.

The man, therefore, read it, and looking upon *Evangelist* very carefully, said, Whither must I fly? Then said *Evangelist,* pointing with his finger over a very wide field, Do you see yonder wicket-gate? The man said, No. Then said the other, Do you see yonder shining light? He said, I think I do. Then said *Evangelist,* Keep that light in your eye, and go up directly thereto: so shalt thou see the gate; at which, when thou knockest, it shall be told thee what thou shalt do. So I saw in my dream that the man began to run. Now, he had not run far from his own door, but his wife and children, perceiving it, began to cry after him to return; but the man put his fingers in his ears, and ran on, crying, Life! life! eternal life! So he looked not behind him, but fled towards the middle of the plain.

The neighbors also came out to see him run; and, as he ran, some mocked, others threatened, and some cried after him to return; and, among those that did so, there were two that resolved to fetch him back by force. The name of the one was *Obstinate,* and the name of the other *Pliable.* Now, by this time, the man was got a good distance from them; but, however, they were resolved to pursue him, which they did, and in a little time they overtook him. Then said the man, Neighbors, wherefore are you come? They said, To persuade you to go back with us. But he said, That can by no means be; you dwell, said he, in the *City of Destruction,* the place also where I was born: I see it to be so; and, dying there, sooner or later, you will sink lower than the grave, into a place that burns with fire and brimstone: be content, good neighbors, and go along with me.

OBST. What! said *Obstinate,* and leave our friends and our comforts behind us?

CHR. Yes, said *Christian,* for that was his name, because that ALL which you shall forsake is not worthy to be compared with a little of that, that I am seeking to enjoy; and, if you will go along with me, and hold it, you shall fare as I myself; for there, where I go, is enough and to spare. Come away, and prove my words.

OBST. What are the things you seek, since you leave all the world to find them?

CHR. I seek an inheritance incorruptible, undefiled, and that fadeth not away, and it is laid up in heaven, and safe there, to be bestowed, at the time appointed, on them that diligently seek it. Read it so, if you will, in my book.

OBST. Tush! said *Obstinate,* away with your book; will you go back with us or no?

CHR. No, not I, said the other, because I have laid my hand to the plow.

OBST. Come, then, neighbor *Pliable,* let us turn again, and go home without him; there is a company of these crazed-headed coxcombs, that, when they take a fancy by the end, are wiser in their own eyes than seven men that can render a reason.

PLI. Then said *Pliable,* Don't revile; if what the good *Christian* says is true, the things he looks after are better than ours: my heart inclines to go with my neighbor.

OBST. What! more fools still? Be ruled by me, go back; who knows whither such a brain-sick fellow will lead you? Go back, go back, and be wise.

CHR. Nay, but do thou come with thy neighbor, *Pliable;* there are such things to be had which I spoke of, and many more glories besides. If you believe not me, read here in this book; and for the truth of what is expressed therein, behold, all is confirmed by the blood of Him that made it.

PLI. Well, neighbor *Obstinate,* saith *Pliable,* I begin to come to a point; I intend to go along with this good man, and to cast in my lot with him: but, my good companion, do you know the way to this desired place?

CHR. I am directed by a man, whose name is *Evangelist,* to speed me to a little gate that is before us, where we shall receive instructions about the way.

PLI. Come, then, good neighbor, let us be going. Then they went both together.

OBST. And I will go back to my place, said *Obstinate;* I will be no companion of such misled, fantastical fellows.

Now I saw in my dream, that when *Obstinate* was gone back, *Christian* and *Pliable* went talking over the plain; and thus they began their discourse.

CHR. Come, neighbor *Pliable*, how do you do? I am glad you are persuaded to go along with me. Had even *Obstinate* himself but felt what I have felt of the powers and terrors of what is yet unseen, he would not thus lightly have given us the back.

PLI. Come, neighbor *Christian*, since there is none but us two here, tell me now further what the things are, and how to be enjoyed, whither we are going.

CHR. I can better conceive of them with my mind, than speak of them with my tongue: but yet, since you are desirous to know, I will read of them in my book.

PLI. And do you think that the words of your book are certainly true?

CHR. Yes, verily; for it was made by Him that cannot lie.

PLI. Well said; what things are they?

CHR. There is an endless kingdom to be inhabited, and everlasting life to be given us, that we may inhabit that kingdom for ever.

PLI. Well said; and what else?

CHR. There are crowns of glory to be given us, and garments that will make us shine like the sun in the firmament of heaven.

PLI. This is very pleasant; and what else?

CHR. There shall be no more crying, nor sorrow: for He that is owner of the place will wipe all tears from our eyes.

PLI. And what company shall we have there?

CHR. There we shall be with seraphims and cherubims, creatures that will dazzle your eyes to look on them. There also you shall meet with thousands and ten thousands that have gone before us to that place; none of them are hurtful, but loving and holy; every one walking in the sight of God, and standing in his presence with acceptance for ever. In a word, there we shall see the elders with their golden crowns, there we shall see the holy virgins with their golden harps, there we shall see men that by the world were cut in pieces, burnt in flames, eaten of beasts, drowned in the seas, for the love that they bear to the Lord of the place; all well, and clothed with immortality as with a garment.

PLI. The hearing of this is enough to ravish one's heart. But are these things to be enjoyed? How shall we get to be sharers thereof?

CHR. The Lord, the Governor of the country, hath recorded that in this book; the substance of which is, If we be truly willing to have it, he will bestow it upon us freely.

PLI. Well, my good companion, glad am I to hear of these things: come on, let us mend our pace.

CHR. I cannot go so fast as I would, by reason of this burden that is on my back.

Now I saw in my dream, that just as they had ended this talk they drew near to a very miry slough, that was in the midst of the plain; and they, being heedless, did both fall suddenly into the bog. The name of the slough was *Despond*. Here, therefore, they wallowed for a time, being grievously bedaubed with dirt; and *Christian*, because of the burden that was on his back, began to sink in the mire.

PLI. Then said *Pliable*, Ah! neighbor *Christian*, where are you now?

CHR. Truly, said *Christian*, I do not know.

PLI. At that *Pliable* began to be offended, and angrily said to his fellow, Is this the happiness you have told me all this while of? If we have such ill speed at our first setting out, what may we expect betwixt this and our journey's end? May I get out again with my life, you shall possess the brave country alone for me. And, with that, he gave a desperate struggle or two, and got out of the mire on that side of the slough which was next to his own house: so away he went, and *Christian* saw him no more.

Wherefore *Christian* was left to tumble in the *Slough of Despond* alone: but still he endeavored to struggle to that side of the slough that was further from his own house, and next to the wicket-gate; the which he did, but could not get out, because of the burden that was upon his back: but I beheld in my dream, that a man came to him, whose name was *Help*, and asked him, What he did there?

CHR. Sir, said *Christian*, I was bid go this way by a man called *Evangelist*, who directed me also to yonder gate, that I might escape the wrath to come; and as I was going thither I fell in here.

Help. But why did not you look for the steps?

Chr. Fear followed me so hard, that I fled the next way, and fell in.

Help. Then said he, Give me thy hand: so he gave him his hand, and he drew him out, and set him upon sound ground, and bid him go on his way.

Then I stepped to him that plucked him out, and said, Sir, wherefore, since over this place is the way from the *City of Destruction* to yonder gate, is it that this plat is not mended, that poor travelers might go thither with more security? And he said unto me, This miry slough is such a place as cannot be mended; it is the descent whither the scum and filth that attends conviction for sin doth continually run, and therefore it was called the *Slough of Despond;* for still, as the sinner is awakened about his lost condition, there ariseth in his soul many fears, and doubts, and discouraging apprehensions, which all of them get together, and settle in this place. And this is the reason of the badness of this ground.

It is not the pleasure of the King that this place should remain so bad. His laborers also have, by the direction of His Majesty's surveyors, been for above these sixteen hundred years employed about this patch of ground, if perhaps it might have been mended: yea, and to my knowledge, said he, here have been swallowed up at least twenty thousand cart-loads, yea, millions of wholesome instructions, that have at all seasons been brought from all places of the King's dominions, and they that can tell, say they are the best materials to make good ground of the place; if so be, it might have been mended, but it is the *Slough of Despond* still, and so will be when they have done what they can.

True, there are, by the direction of the Law-giver, certain good and substantial steps, placed even through the very midst of this slough; but at such time as this place doth much spew out its filth, as it doth against change of weather, these steps are hardly seen; or, if they be, men, through the dizziness of their heads, step beside, and then they are bemired to purpose, notwithstanding the steps be there; but the ground is good when they are once got in at the gate.

Now, I saw in my dream, that by this time *Pliable* was got home to his house, so his neighbors came to visit him; and some of them called him wise man for coming back, and some called him fool for hazarding himself with *Christian:* others again did mock at his cowardliness; saying, Surely, since you began to venture, I would not have been so base to have given out for a few difficulties. So *Pliable* sat sneaking among them. But at last he got more confidence, and then they all turned their tales, and began to deride poor *Christian* behind his back. And thus much concerning *Pliable.*

Now, as *Christian* was walking solitarily by himself, he espied one afar off, come crossing over the field to meet him; and their hap was to meet just as they were crossing the way of each other. The gentleman's name that met him was Mr. *Worldly Wiseman;* he dwelt in the town of *Carnal Policy,* a very great town, and also hard by from whence *Christian* came. This man, then, meeting with *Christian,* and having some inkling of him—for *Christian's* setting forth from the *City of Destruction* was much noised abroad, not only in the town where he dwelt, but also it began to be the town talk in some other places—Master *Worldly Wiseman,* therefore, having some guess of him, by beholding his laborious going, by observing his sighs and groans, and the like, began thus to enter into some talk with *Christian.*

World. How now, good fellow, whither away after this burdened manner?

Chr. A burdened manner, indeed, as ever, I think, poor creature had! And whereas you ask me, Whither away? I tell you, Sir, I am going to yonder wicket-gate before me; for there, as I am informed, I shall be put into a way to be rid of my heavy burden.

World. Hast thou a wife and children?

Chr. Yes; but I am so laden with this burden that I cannot take that pleasure in them as formerly; methinks I am as if I had none.

World. Wilt thou hearken to me if I give thee counsel?

Chr. If it be good, I will; for I stand in need of good counsel.

World. I would advise thee, then, that thou with all speed get thyself rid of thy burden; for thou wilt never be settled in thy mind till then; nor canst thou enjoy the benefits of the blessing which God hath bestowed upon thee till then.

Chr. That is that which I seek for, even to be rid of this heavy burden; but get it off myself, I cannot; nor is there any man in our country that can take it off my shoulders; therefore am I going this way, as I told you, that I may be rid of my burden.

World. Who bid you go this way to be rid of your burden?

Chr. A man that appeared to me to be a very great and honorable person; his name, as I remember, is *Evangelist.*

World. I beshrew him for his counsel! there is not a more dangerous and troublesome way in the world than is that unto which he hath directed thee; and that thou shalt find, if thou wilt be ruled by his counsel. Thou hast met with something, as I perceive already; for I see the dirt of the *Slough of Despond* is upon thee; but that slough is the beginning of the sorrows that do attend those that go on in that way. Hear me, I am older than thou; thou art like to meet with, in the way which thou goest, wearisomeness, painfulness, hunger, perils, nakedness, sword, lions, dragons, darkness, and, in a word, death, and what not! These things are certainly true, having been confirmed by many testimonies. And should a man so carelessly cast away himself, by giving heed to a stranger?

Chr. Why, Sir, this burden upon my back is more terrible to me than are all these things which you have mentioned; nay, methinks I care not what I meet with in the way, if so be I can also meet with deliverance from my burden.

World. How camest thou by the burden at first?

Chr. By reading this book in my hand.

World. I thought so; and it is happened unto thee as to other weak men, who, meddling with things too high for them, do suddenly fall into thy distractions; which distractions do not only unman men, as thine, I perceive, has done thee, but they run them upon desperate ventures to obtain they know not what.

Chr. I know what I would obtain; it is ease for my heavy burden.

II

Then he went on till he came to the house of the *Interpreter*, where he knocked over and over; at last one came to the door, and asked who was there.

Chr. Sir, here is a traveler, who was bid by an acquaintance of the good-man of this house to call here for my profit; I would therefore speak with the master of the house. So he called for the master of the house, who, after a little time, came to *Christian*, and asked him what he would have.

Chr. Sir, said *Christian*, I am a man that am come from the *City of Destruction*, and am going to the Mount *Zion;* and I was told by the man that stands at the gate, at the head of this way, that if I called here, you would show me excellent things, such as would be an help to me in my journey.

Inter. Then said the *Interpreter*, Come in; I will show that which will be profitable to thee. So he commanded his man to light the candle, and bid *Christian* follow him: so he had him into a private room, and bid his man open a door; the which when he had done, *Christian* saw the picture of a very grave person hang up against the wall; and this was the fashion of it. It had eyes lifted up to heaven, the best of books in his hand, the law of truth was written upon its lips, the world was behind his back. It stood as if it pleaded with men, and a crown of gold did hang over its head.

Chr. Then said *Christian*, What meaneth this?

Inter. The man whose picture this is, is one of a thousand; he can beget children, travail in birth with children, and nurse them himself when they are born. And whereas thou seest him with his eyes lift up to heaven, the best of books in his hand, and the law of truth writ on his lips, it is to show thee that his work is to know and unfold dark things to sinners; even as also thou seest him stand as if he pleaded with men: and whereas thou seest the world as cast behind him, and that a crown hangs over his head, that is to show thee that slighting and despising the things that are present, for the love that he hath to his Master's service, he is sure in the world that comes next to have glory for his reward. Now, said the *Interpreter*, I have showed thee this picture first, because the man whose picture this is, is the only man whom the Lord of the place whither thou art going, hath authorized to be thy guide in all difficult places thou mayest meet with in the way; wherefore, take good heed to what I have showed thee, and bear well in thy mind what thou hast seen, lest in thy journey thou meet with some that pretend to lead thee right, but their way goes down to death.

Then he took him by the hand, and led him into a very large parlor that was full of dust, because never swept; the which after he had reviewed a little while, the *Interpreter* called for a man to sweep. Now, when he began to sweep, the dust began so abundantly to fly about, that *Christian* had almost therewith been choked. Then said the *Interpreter* to a damsel that stood by, Bring hither water, and sprinkle the room; the which, when she had done, it was swept and cleansed with pleasure.

CHR. Then said *Christian*, What means this?

INTER. The *Interpreter* answered, This parlor is the heart of a man that was never sanctified by the sweet grace of the gospel; the dust is his original sin and inward corruptions, that have defiled the whole man. He that began to sweep at first, is the *Law;* but she that brought water, and did sprinkle it, is the *Gospel.* Now, whereas thou sawest, that so soon as the first began to sweep, the dust did so fly about that the room by him could not be cleansed, but that thou wast almost choked therewith; this is to show thee, that the law, instead of cleansing the heart (by its working) from sin, doth revive, put strength into, and increase it in the soul, even as it doth discover and forbid it, for it doth not give power to subdue.

Again, as thou sawest the damsel sprinkle the room with water, upon which it was cleansed with pleasure; this is to show thee, that when the gospel comes in the sweet and precious influences thereof to the heart, then, I say, even as thou sawest the damsel lay the dust by sprinkling the floor with water, so is sin vanquished and subdued, and the soul made clean through the faith of it, and consequently fit for the King of glory to inhabit.

I saw, moreover, in my dream, that the *Interpreter* took him by the hand, and had him into a little room, where sat two little children, each one in his chair. The name of the eldest was *Passion*, and the name of the other *Patience*. *Passion* seemed to be much discontented; but *Patience* was very quiet. Then *Christian* asked, What is the reason of the discontent of *Passion?* The *Interpreter* answered, The Governor of them would have him stay for his best things till the beginning of the next year; but he will have all now: but *Patience* is willing to wait.

Then I saw that one came to *Passion*, and brought him a bag of treasure, and poured it down at his feet, the which he took up and rejoiced therein, and withal laughed *Patience* to scorn. But I beheld but a while, and he had lavished all away, and had nothing left him but rags.

CHR. Then said *Christian* to the *Interpreter*, Expound this matter more fully to me.

INTER. So he said, These two lads are figures: *Passion*, of the men of this world; and *Patience*, of the men of that which is to come; for as here thou seest, *Passion* will have all now this year, that is to say, in this world; so are the men of this world, they must have all their good things now, they cannot stay till next year, that is until the next world, for their portion of good. That proverb, "A bird in the hand is worth two in the bush," is of more authority with them than are all the Divine testimonies of the good of the world to come. But as thou sawest that he had quickly lavished all away, and had presently left him nothing but rags; so will it be with all such men at the end of this world.

CHR. Then said *Christian*, Now I see that *Patience* has the best wisdom, and that upon many accounts. First, because he stays for the best things. Second, and also because he will have the glory of his, when the other had nothing but rags.

INTER. Nay, you may add another, to wit, the glory of the next world will never wear out; but these are suddenly gone. Therefore *Passion* had not so much reason to laugh at *Patience*, because he had his good things first, as *Patience* will have to laugh at *Passion*, because he had his best things last; for first must give place to last, because last must have his time to come; but last gives place to nothing; for there is not another to succeed. He, therefore, that hath his portion first, must needs have a time to spend it; but he that has his portion last, must have it lastingly; therefore it is said of Dives, In thy lifetime thou receivedst thy good things, and likewise Lazarus evil things; but now he is comforted, and thou art tormented.

CHR. Then I perceive 'tis not best to covet things that are now, but to wait for things to come.

INTER. You say the truth: For the things that are seen are temporal; but the things which are not seen are eternal. But though this be so, yet since things present and our fleshly appetite are such near neighbors one to another; and again, because things to come, and carnal sense, are such strangers one to another; therefore it is that the first of these so suddenly fall into amity, and that distance is so continually between the second.

Then I saw in my dream that the *Interpreter* took *Christian* by the hand, and led him into a place where was a fire burning against a wall, and one standing by it, always casting much water upon it, to quench it; yet did the fire burn higher and hotter.

Then said *Christian*, What means this?

The *Interpreter* answered, This fire is the work of grace that is wrought in the heart; he that casts water upon it, to extinguish and put it out, is the Devil; but in that thou seest the fire notwithstanding burn higher and hotter, thou shalt also see the reason of that. So he had him about to the backside of the wall, where he saw a man with a vessel of oil in his hand, of the which he did also continually cast, but secretly, into the fire.

Then said *Christian*, What means this?

The *Interpreter* answered, This is Christ, who continually, with the oil of his grace, maintains the work already begun in the heart: by the means of which, notwithstanding what the devil can do, the souls of his people prove gracious still. And in that thou sawest that the man stood behind the wall to maintain the fire, this is to teach thee that it is hard for the tempted to see how this work of grace is maintained in the soul.

I saw also, that the *Interpreter* took him again by the hand, and led him into a pleasant place, where was builded a stately palace, beautiful to behold; at the sight of which *Christian* was greatly delighted. He saw also, upon the top thereof, certain persons walking, who were clothed all in gold.

Then said *Christian*, May we go in thither?

Then the *Interpreter* took him, and led him up towards the door of the palace; and behold, at the door stood a great company of men, as desirous to go in, but durst not. There also sat a man at a little distance from the door, at a table-side, with a book and his inkhorn before him, to take the name of him that should enter therein; he saw also, that in the doorway stood many men in armor to keep it, being resolved to do to the men that would enter what hurt and mischief they could. Now was *Christian* somewhat in amaze. At last, when every man started back for fear of the armed men, *Christian* saw a man of a very stout countenance come up to the man that sat there to write, saying, Set down my name, Sir: the which when he had done, he saw the man draw his sword, and put an helmet upon his head, and rush toward the door upon the armed men, who laid upon him with deadly force; but the man, not at all discouraged, fell to cutting and hacking most fiercely. So after he had received and given many wounds to those that attempted to keep him out, he cut his way through them all, and pressed forward into the palace, at which there was a pleasant voice heard from those that were within, even of those that walked upon the top of the palace, saying—

> Come in, come in;
> Eternal glory thou shalt win.

So he went in, and was clothed with such garments as they. Then *Christian* smiled and said, I think verily I know the meaning of this.

Now, said *Christian*, let me go hence. Nay, stay, said the *Interpreter*, till I have showed thee a little more, and after that thou shalt go on thy way. So he took him by the hand again, and led him into a very dark room, where there sat a man in an iron cage.

Now the man, to look on, seemed very sad; he sat with his eyes looking down to the ground, his hands folded together, and he sighed as if he would break his heart. Then said *Christian*, What means this? At which the *Interpreter* bid him talk with the man.

Then said *Christian* to the man, What art thou? The man answered, I am what I was not once.

CHR. What wast thou once?

MAN. The man said, I was once a fair and flourishing professor,[1] both in mine own eyes, and also in the eyes of others; I once was, as I thought, fair for the *Celestial City*, and had then even joy at the thoughts that I should get thither.

[1]Professing Christian.

CHR. Well, but what art thou now?

MAN. I am now a man of despair, and am shut up in it, as in this iron cage. I cannot get out. Oh, now I cannot!

CHR. But how camest thou in this condition?

MAN. I left off to watch and be sober; I laid the reins upon the neck of my lusts; I sinned against the light of the Word and the goodness of God; I have grieved the Spirit, and he is gone; I tempted the devil, and he is come to me; I have provoked God to anger, and he has left me: I have so hardened my heart, that I cannot repent.

Then said *Christian* to the *Interpreter*, But is there no hopes for such a man as this? Ask him, said the *Interpreter*.

CHR. Then said *Christian*, Is there no hope, but you must be kept in the iron cage of despair?

MAN. No, none at all.

CHR. Why, the Son of the Blessed is very pitiful.

MAN. I have crucified him to myself afresh; I have despised his person; I have despised his righteousness; I have counted his blood an unholy thing; I have done despite to the Spirit of grace. Therefore I have shut myself out of all the promises, and there now remains to me nothing but threatenings, dreadful threatenings, faithful threatenings, of certain judgment and fiery indignation, which shall devour me as an adversary.

CHR. For what did you bring yourself into this condition?

MAN. For the lusts, pleasures, and profits of this world; in the enjoyment of which I did then promise myself much delight; but now every one of those things also bite me, and gnaw me like a burning worm.

CHR. But canst thou not now repent and turn?

MAN. God hath denied me repentance. His Word gives me no encouragement to believe; yea, himself hath shut me up in this iron cage; nor can all the men in the world let me out. O eternity, eternity! how shall I grapple with the misery that I must meet with in eternity!

INTER. Then said the *Interpreter* to *Christian*, Let this man's misery be remembered by thee, and be an everlasting caution to thee.

CHR. Well, said *Christian*, this is fearful! God help me to watch and be sober, and to pray that I may shun the cause of this man's misery! Sir, is it not time for me to go on my way now?

INTER. Tarry till I shall show thee one thing more, and then thou shalt go on thy way.

So he took *Christian* by the hand again, and led him into a chamber, where there was one rising out of bed; and as he put on his raiment he shook and trembled. Then said *Christian*, Why doth this man thus tremble? The *Interpreter* then bid him tell to *Christian* the reason of his so doing. So he began and said, This night, as I was in my sleep, I dreamed, and behold the heavens grew exceeding black; also it thundered and lightened in most fearful wise, that it put me into an agony; so I looked up in my dream, and saw the clouds rack at an unusual rate, upon which I heard a great sound of a trumpet, and saw also a man sit upon a cloud, attended with the thousands of heaven; they were all in flaming fire: also the heavens were in a burning flame. I heard then a voice saying, Arise, ye dead, and come to judgment; and with that the rocks rent, the graves opened, and the dead that were therein came forth. Some of them were exceeding glad, and looked upward; and some sought to hide themselves under the mountains. Then I saw the man that sat upon the cloud open the book, and bid the world draw near. Yet there was, by reason of a fierce flame that issued out and came before him, a convenient distance betwixt him and them, as betwixt the judge and the prisoners at the bar. I heard it also proclaimed to them that attended on the man that sat on the cloud, Gather together the tares, the chaff, and stubble, and cast them into the burning lake. And with that, the bottomless pit opened, just whereabout I stood; out of the mouth of which there came, in an abundant manner, smoke and coals of fire, with hideous noises. It was also said to the same persons, Gather my wheat into the garner. And with that I saw many catched up and carried away into the clouds, but I was left behind. I also sought to hide myself, but I could not, for the man that sat upon the cloud still kept his eye upon me; my sins also came into my mind; and my conscience did accuse me on every side. Upon this I awaked from my sleep.

CHR. But what is it that made you so afraid of this sight?

MAN. Why, I thought that the day of judgment was come, and that I was not ready for it: but this frighted me most, that the angels gathered up several, and left me behind; also the pit of hell opened her mouth just where I stood. My conscience, too, afflicted me; and, as I thought, the Judge had always his eye upon me, showing indignation in his countenance.

Then said the *Interpreter* to *Christian*, Hast thou considered all these things?

CHR. Yes, and they put me in hope and fear.

INTER. Well, keep all things so in thy mind that they may be as a goad in thy sides, to prick thee forward in the way thou must go. Then *Christian* began to gird up his loins, and to address himself to his journey. Then said the *Interpreter*, The Comforter be always with thee, good *Christian*, to guide thee in the way that leads to the City.

So *Christian* went on his way, saying—

Here I have seen things rare and profitable;
Things pleasant, dreadful, things to make me stable
In what I have began to take in hand;
Then let me think on them and understand
Wherefore they showed me were, and let me be
Thankful, O good *Interpreter*, to thee.

Now I saw in my dream, that the highway up which *Christian* was to go, was fenced on either side with a wall, and that wall was called *Salvation*. Up this way, therefore, did burdened *Christian* run, but not without great difficulty, because of the load on his back.

He ran thus till he came at a place somewhat ascending, and upon that place stood a cross, and a little below, in the bottom, a sepulcher. So I saw in my dream, that just as *Christian* came up with the cross, his burden loosed from off his shoulders, and fell from off his back, and began to tumble, and so continued to do, till it came to the mouth of the sepulcher, where it fell in, and I saw it no more.

Then was *Christian* glad and lightsome, and said, with a merry heart, He hath given me rest by his sorrow, and life by his death. Then he stood still awhile to look and wonder; for it was very surprising to him, that the sight of the cross should thus ease him of his burden. He looked therefore, and looked again, even till the springs that were in his head sent the waters down his cheeks. Now, as he stood looking and weeping, behold three Shining Ones came to him and saluted him with, Peace be unto thee. So the first said to him, Thy sins be forgiven thee; the second stripped him of his rags, and clothed him with change of raiment; the third also set a mark in his forehead, and gave him a roll with a seal upon it, which he bade him look on as he ran, and that he should give it in at the *Celestial Gate*.

III

So he went on, and *Apollyon* met him. Now the monster was hideous to behold; he was clothed with scales, like a fish (and they are his pride); he had wings like a dragon, feet like a bear, and out of his belly came fire and smoke, and his mouth was as the mouth of a lion. When he was come up to *Christian*, he beheld him with a disdainful countenance, and thus began to question with him.

APOL. Whence come you? and whither are you bound?

CHR. I am come from the *City of Destruction*, which is the place of all evil, and am going to the *City of Zion*.

APOL. By this I perceive thou art one of my subjects, for all that country is mine, and I am the prince and god of it. How is it, then, that thou hast run away from thy king? Were it not that I hope thou mayest do me more service, I would strike thee now, at one blow, to the ground.

CHR. I was born, indeed, in your dominions, but your service was hard, and your wages such as a man could not live on, for the wages of sin is death; therefore, when I was come to years, I did, as other considerate persons do, look out, if, perhaps, I might mend myself.

APOL. There is no prince that will thus lightly lose his subjects, neither will I as yet lose thee; but since thou complainest of thy service and wages, be content to go back: what our country will afford, I do here promise to give thee.

CHR. But I have let myself to another, even to the King of princes; and how can I, with fairness, go back with thee?

APOL. Thou hast done in this, according to the proverb, "Change a bad for a worse"; but it is ordinary for those that have professed themselves his servants, after a while to give him the slip, and return again to me. Do thou so too, and all shall be well.

CHR. I have given him my faith, and sworn my allegiance to him; how, then, can I go back from this, and not be hanged as a traitor?

APOL. Thou didst the same by me, and yet I am willing to pass by all, if now thou wilt yet turn again and go back.

CHR. What I promised thee was in my nonage; and, besides, I count that the Prince under whose banner now I stand is able to absolve me; yea, and to pardon also what I did as to my compliance with thee; and besides, O thou destroying *Apollyon!* to speak truth, I like his service, his wages, his servants, his government, his company, and country, better than thine; and, therefore, leave off to persuade me further; I am his servant, and I will follow him.

APOL. Consider, again, when thou art in cool blood, what thou art like to meet with in the way that thou goest. Thou knowest that, for the most part, his servants come to an ill end, because they are transgressors against me and my way. How many of them have been put to shameful death! and, besides, thou countest his service better than mine, whereas he never came yet from the place where he is to deliver any that served him out of their hands; but as for me, how many times, as all the world very well knows, have I delivered, either by power, or fraud, those that have faithfully served me, from him and his, though taken by them; and so I will deliver thee.

CHR. His forbearing at present to deliver them is on purpose to try their love, whether they will cleave to him to the end; and as for the ill end thou sayest they come to, that is most glorious in their account; for, for present deliverance, they do not much expect it, for they stay for their glory, and then they shall have it when their Prince comes in his and the glory of the angels.

APOL. Thou hast already been unfaithful in thy service to him; and how dost thou think to receive wages of him?

CHR. Wherein, O *Apollyon!* have I been unfaithful to him?

APOL. Thou didst faint at first setting out, when thou wast almost choked in the *Gulf of Despond;* thou didst attempt wrong ways to be rid of thy burden, whereas thou shouldst have stayed till thy Prince had taken it off; thou didst sinfully sleep and lose thy choice things; thou wast, also, almost persuaded to go back at the sight of the lions; and when thou talkest of thy journey, and of what thou hast heard and seen, thou art inwardly desirous of vain-glory in all that thou sayest or doest.

CHR. All this is true, and much more which thou hast left out; but the Prince whom I serve and honor is merciful, and ready to forgive; but, besides, these infirmities possessed me in thy country, for there I sucked them in; and I have groaned under them, being sorry for them, and have obtained pardon of my Prince.

APOL. Then *Apollyon* broke out into a grievous rage, saying, I am an enemy to this Prince; I hate his person, his laws, and people; I am come out on purpose to withstand thee.

CHR. *Apollyon*, beware what you do; for I am in the King's highway, the way of holiness; therefore take heed to yourself.

APOL. Then *Apollyon* straddled quite over the whole breadth of the way, and said, I am void of fear in this matter: prepare thyself to die; for I swear by my infernal den, that thou shalt go no further; here will I spill thy soul.

And with that he threw a flaming dart at his breast; but *Christian* had a shield in his hand, with which he caught it, and so prevented the danger of that.

Then did *Christian* draw, for he saw it was time to bestir him; and *Apollyon* as fast made at him, throwing darts as thick as hail; by the which, notwithstanding all that *Christian* could do to avoid it, *Apollyon* wounded him in his head, his hand, and foot. This made *Christian* give a little back; *Apollyon*, therefore, followed his work amain, and *Christian* again took courage, and resisted as manfully as he could. This sore combat lasted for above half a day, even till *Christian* was almost quite spent; for you must know that *Christian*, by reason of his wounds, must needs grow weaker and weaker.

Then *Apollyon*, espying his opportunity, began to gather up close to *Christian*, and wrestling with him, gave him a dreadful fall; and with that *Christian's* sword flew out of his hand. Then said *Apollyon*, I am sure of thee now. And with that he had almost pressed him to death, so that *Christian* began to despair of life; but as God would have it, while *Apollyon* was fetching his last blow, thereby to make a full end of this good man, *Christian* nimbly stretched out his hand for his sword, and caught it, saying, Rejoice not against me, O mine enemy; when I fall I shall arise; and with that gave him a deadly thrust, which made him give back, as one that had received his mortal wound. *Christian* perceiving that, made at him again, saying, Nay, in all these things we are more than conquerors through him that loved us. And with that *Apollyon* spread forth his dragon's wings, and sped him away, that *Christian* saw him no more.

In this combat no man can imagine, unless he had seen and heard as I did, what yelling and hideous roaring *Apollyon* made all the time of the fight—he spake like a dragon; and, on the other side, what sighs and groans burst from *Christian's* heart. I never saw him all the while give so much as one pleasant look, till he perceived he had wounded *Apollyon* with his two-edged sword; then, indeed, he did smile, and look upward; but it was the dreadfulest sight that ever I saw.

So when the battle was over, *Christian* said, I will here give thanks to him that delivered me out of the mouth of the lion, to him that did help me against *Apollyon*. And so he did, saying—

> Great Beelzebub, the captain of this fiend,
> Designed my ruin; therefore to this end
> He sent him harnessed out: and he with rage
> That hellish was, did fiercely me engage.
> But blessed Michael helpêd me, and I,
> By dint of sword, did quickly make him fly.
> Therefore to him let me give lasting praise,
> And thanks, and bless his holy name always.

Then there came to him an hand, with some of the leaves of the tree of life, the which Christian took, and applied to the wounds that he had received in the battle, and was healed immediately. He also sat down in that place to eat bread, and to drink of the bottle that was given him a little before; so, being refreshed, he addressed himself to his journey, with his sword drawn in his hand; for he said, I know not but some other enemy may be at hand. But he met with no other affront from *Apollyon* quite through this valley.

Now, at the end of this valley was another, called the *Valley of the Shadow of Death*, and *Christian* must needs go through it, because the way to the *Celestial City* lay through the midst of it. Now, this valley is a very solitary place. The prophet Jeremiah thus describes it:—A wilderness, a land of deserts and of pits, a land of drought, and of the shadow of death, a land that no man (but a Christian) passeth through, and where no man dwelt.

Now here *Christian* was worse put to it than in his fight with *Apollyon*, as by the sequel you shall see.

I saw then in my dream, that when *Christian* was got on the borders of the *Shadow of Death*, there met him two men, children of them that brought up an evil report of the good land, making haste to go back; to whom *Christian* spake as follows:—

CHR. Whither are you going?

MEN. They said, Back! back! and we would have you do so too, if either life or peace is prized by you.

CHR. Why, what's the matter? said *Christian*.

MEN. Matter! said they; we were going that way as you are going, and went as far as we durst; and indeed we were almost past coming back; for had we gone a little further, we had not been here to bring the news to thee.

CHR. But what have you met with? said *Christian*.

MEN. Why, we were almost in the *Valley of the Shadow of Death;* but that, by good hap, we looked before us, and saw the danger before we came to it.

CHR. But what have you seen? said *Christian*.

MEN. Seen! Why, the Valley itself, which is as dark as pitch; we also saw there the hobgoblins, satyrs, and dragons of the pit; we heard also in that Valley a continual howling and yelling, as of a people under unutterable misery, who were sat down in affliction and irons; and over that Valley hangs the discouraging clouds of confusion. Death also doth always spread his wings over it. In a word, it is every whit dreadful, being utterly without order.

CHR. Then, said *Christian*, I perceive not yet, by what you have said, but that this is my way to the desired heaven.

MEN. Be it thy way; we will not choose it for ours. So they parted, and *Christian* went on his way, but still with his sword drawn in his hand, for fear lest he should be assaulted.

I saw then in my dream, so far as this valley reached, there was on the right hand a very deep ditch; that ditch is it into which the blind hath led the blind in all ages, and have both there miserably perished. Again, behold, on the left hand, there was a very dangerous quag, into which, if even a good man falls, he finds no bottom for his foot to stand on. Into this quag King David once did fall, and had no doubt there been smothered, had not He that is able plucked him out.

The pathway was here also exceeding narrow, and therefore good *Christian* was the more put to it; for when he sought, in the dark, to shun the ditch on the one hand, he was ready to tip over into the mire on the other; also when he sought to escape the mire, without great carefulness he would be ready to fall into the ditch. Thus he went on, and I heard him here sigh bitterly; for, besides the danger mentioned above, the pathway was here so dark, that ofttimes, when he lift up his foot to go forward, he knew not where or upon what he should set it next.

About the midst of this valley, I perceived the mouth of hell to be, and it stood also hard by the way-side. Now, thought *Christian*, what shall I do? And ever and anon the flame and smoke would come out in such abundance, with sparks and hideous noises (things that cared not for *Christian's* sword, as did *Apollyon* before), that he was forced to put up his sword, and betake himself to another weapon called *all-prayer*. So he cried, in my hearing, O Lord, I beseech thee, deliver my soul! Thus he went on a great while, yet still the flames would be reaching towards him. Also he heard doleful voices, and rushings to and fro, so that sometimes he thought he should be torn in pieces, or trodden down like mire in the streets. This frightful sight was seen, and these dreadful noises were heard by him for several miles together; and, coming to a place where he thought he heard a company of fiends coming forward to meet him, he stopped, and began to muse what he had best to do. Sometimes he had half a thought to go back; then again he thought he might be half way through the valley; he remembered also how he had already vanquished many a danger, and that the danger of going back might be much more than for to go forward; so he resolved to go on. Yet the fiends seemed to come nearer and nearer; but when they were come even almost at him, he cried out with a most vehement voice, I will walk in the strength of the Lord God!—so they gave back, and came no further.

One thing I would not let slip; I took notice that now poor *Christian* was so confounded, that he did not know his own voice; and thus I perceived it. Just when he was come over against the mouth of the burning pit, one of the wicked ones got behind him, and stepped up softly to him, and whisperingly suggested many grievous blasphemies to him, which he verily thought had proceeded from his own mind. This put *Christian* more to it than anything that he met with before, even to think that he should now blaspheme him that he loved so much before; yet, if he could have helped it, he would not have done it; but he had not the discretion neither to stop his ears, nor to know from whence these blasphemies came.

When *Christian* had traveled in this disconsolate condition some considerable time, he thought he heard the voice of a man, going before him, saying, Though I walk through the valley of the shadow of death, I will fear none ill, for thou art with me.

Then was he glad.

IV

Then I saw in my dream, that when they[1] were got out the wilderness, they presently saw a town before them, and the name of that town is *Vanity;* and at the town there is a fair kept, called *Vanity Fair:* it is kept all the year long; it beareth the name of *Vanity Fair,* because the town where it is kept is lighter than vanity; and also because all that is there sold, or that cometh thither, is vanity. As is the saying of the wise, all that cometh is vanity.

This fair is no new-erected business, but a thing of ancient standing; I will show you the original of it.

Almost five thousand years agone, there

[1] Shortly after he had passed through the *Valley of the Shadow of Death*, *Christian* met *Faithful*, journeying likewise towards the *Celestial City*, and they went on together.

were pilgrims walking to the *Celestial City*, as these two honest persons are: and *Beelzebub*, *Apollyon*, and *Legion*, with their companions, perceiving by the path that the pilgrims made, that their way to the city lay through this town of *Vanity*, they contrived here to set up a fair; a fair wherein should be sold all sorts of vanity, and that it should last all the year long: therefore at this fair are all such merchandise sold, as houses, lands, trades, places, honors, preferments, titles, countries, kingdoms, lusts, pleasures, and delights of all sorts, as whores, bawds, wives, husbands, children, masters, servants, lives, blood, bodies, souls, silver, gold, pearls, precious stones, and what not.

And, moreover, at this fair there is at all times to be seen jugglings, cheats, games, plays, fools, apes, knaves, and rogues, and that of every kind.

Here are to be seen, too, and that for nothing, thefts, murders, adulteries, false swearers, and that of a blood-red color.

And, as in other fairs of less moment, there are several rows and streets, under their proper names, where such wares are vended; so here likewise you have the proper places, rows, streets (*viz.*, countries and kingdoms), where the wares of this fair are soonest to be found. Here is the *Britain Row*, the *French Row*, the *Italian Row*, the *Spanish Row*, the *German Row*, where several sorts of vanities are to be sold. But, as in other fairs, some one commodity is as the chief of all the fair, so the ware of *Rome* and her merchandise is greatly promoted in this fair; only our *English* nation, with some others, have taken a dislike thereat.

Now, as I said, the way to the *Celestial City* lies just through this town where this lusty fair is kept; and he that will go to the city, and yet not go through this town, must needs go out of the world. The Prince of princes himself, when here, went through this town to his own country, and that upon a fair day too; yea, and as I think, it was *Beelzebub*, the chief lord of this fair, that invited him to buy of his vanities; yea, would have made him lord of the fair, would he but have done him reverence as he went through the town. Yea, because he was such a person of honor, *Beelzebub* had him from street to street, and showed him all the kingdoms of the world in a little time, that he might, if possible, allure that Blessed One to cheapen and buy some of his vanities; but he had no mind to the merchandise, and therefore left the town, without laying out so much as one farthing upon these vanities. This fair, therefore, is an ancient thing, of long standing, and a very great fair. Now these pilgrims, as I said, must needs go through this fair. Well, so they did: but, behold, even as they entered into the fair, all the people in the fair were moved, and the town itself as it were in a hubbub about them; and that for several reasons: for—

First, the Pilgrims were clothed with such kind of raiment as was diverse from the raiment of any that traded in that fair. The people, therefore, of the fair, made a great gazing upon them: some said they were fools, some they were bedlams, and some they were outlandish men.

Secondly, And as they wondered at their apparel, so they did likewise at their speech; for few could understand what they said; they naturally spoke the language of Canaan, but they that kept the fair were the men of this world; so that, from one end of the fair to the other, they seemed barbarians each to the other.

Thirdly, But that which did not a little amuse the merchandisers was, that these pilgrims set very light by all their wares; they cared not so much as to look upon them; and if they called upon them to buy, they would put their fingers in their ears, and cry, Turn away mine eyes from beholding vanity, and look upwards, signifying that their trade and traffic was in heaven.

One chanced mockingly, beholding the carriages of the men, to say unto them, What will ye buy? But they, looking gravely upon him, said, We buy the truth. At that there was an occasion taken to despise the men the more; some mocking, some taunting, some speaking reproachfully, and some calling upon others to smite them. At last things came to an hubbub and great stir in the fair, insomuch that all order was confounded. Now was word presently brought to the great one of the fair, who quickly came down, and deputed some of his most trusty friends to take these men into examination, about whom the fair was almost overturned. So the men were brought to examination; and they that sat upon them, asked them whence they came, whither they went, and what they did there, in such an unusual garb? The men told them that they were pilgrims and strangers in the world, and that they were going to their own country, which was the heavenly *Jerusalem*, and that they had given no occasion to the men of the town, nor yet to the merchandisers, thus to abuse them, and to let[1] them in their journey, except it was for that, when one asked them what they would buy, they said they would buy the truth. But they that were appointed to examine them did not believe them to be any other than bedlams and mad, or else such as came to put all things into a confusion in the fair. Therefore they took them and beat them, and besmeared them with dirt, and then put them into the cage, that they might be made a spectacle to all the men of the fair.

There, therefore, they lay for some time, and were made the objects of any man's sport, or malice, or revenge, the great one of the fair laughing still at all that befell them. But the men being patient, and not rendering railing for railing, but contrariwise, blessing, and giving good words for bad, and kindness for injuries done, some men in the fair that were more observing, and less prejudiced than the rest, began to check and blame the baser sort for their continual abuses done by them to the men; they, therefore, in angry manner, let fly at them again, counting them as bad as the men in the cage, and telling them that they seemed confederates, and should be made partakers of their misfortunes. The other replied that, for aught they could see, the men were quiet, and sober, and intended nobody any harm; and that there were many that traded in their fair that were more worthy to be put into the cage, yea, and pillory too, than were the men that they had abused. Thus, after divers words had passed on both sides, the men behaving themselves all the while very wisely and soberly before them, they fell to some blows among themselves, and did harm one to another. Then were these two poor men brought before their examiners again, and there charged as being guilty of the late hubbub that had been in the fair. So they beat them pitifully, and hanged irons upon them, and led them in chains up and down the fair, for an example and a terror to others, lest any should speak in their behalf, or join themselves unto them. But *Christian* and *Faithful* behaved themselves yet more wisely, and received the ignominy and shame that was cast upon them with so much meekness and patience, that it won to their side, though but few in comparison of the rest, several of the men in the fair. This put the other party yet into a greater rage, insomuch that they concluded the death of these two men. Wherefore they threatened, that neither the cage nor irons should serve their turn, but that they should die, for the abuse they had done, and for deluding the men of the fair.

Then were they remanded to the cage again, until further order should be taken with them. So they put them in, and made their feet fast in the stocks.

Here, therefore, they called again to mind what they had heard from their faithful friend *Evangelist*, and were the more confirmed in their way and sufferings by what he told them would happen to them. They also now comforted each other, that whose lot it was to suffer, even he should have the best on't; therefore each man secretly wished that he might have that preferment: but committing themselves to the all-wise dispose of Him that ruleth all things, with much content, they abode in the condition in which they were, until they should be otherwise disposed of.

Then a convenient time being appointed, they brought them forth to their trial, in order to their condemnation. When the time was come, they were brought before their enemies and arraigned. The judge's name was Lord *Hate-good*. Their indictment was one and the same in substance, though somewhat varying in form, the contents whereof was this:—

That they were enemies to and disturbers of their trade; that they had made commotions and divisions in the town, and had won a party to their own most dangerous opinions, in contempt of the law of their prince.

Then *Faithful* began to answer, that he had only set himself against that which hath set itself against Him that is higher than the highest. And, said he, as for disturbance, I make none, being myself a man of peace; the parties that were won to us, were won by beholding our truth and innocence,

[1]To hinder.

Good piece of Narrative; suspense; specific descriptions.

and they are only turned from the worse to the better. And as to the king you talk of, since he is *Beelzebub*, the enemy of our Lord, I defy him and all his angels.

Then proclamation was made, that they that had aught to say for their lord the king against the prisoner at the bar, should forthwith appear and give in their evidence. So there came in three witnesses, to wit, *Envy*, *Superstition*, and *Pickthank*. They were then asked, if they knew the prisoner at the bar; and what they had to say for their lord the king against him.

Then stood forth *Envy*, and said to this effect: My Lord, I have known this man a long time, and will attest upon my oath before this honorable bench that he is—

JUDGE. Hold! Give him his oath. So they sware him. Then he said—

ENVY. My Lord, this man, notwithstanding his plausible name, is one of the vilest men in our country. He neither regardeth prince nor people, law nor custom; but doth all that he can to possess all men with certain of his disloyal notions, which he in the general calls principles of faith and holiness. And, in particular, I heard him once myself affirm that Christianity and the customs of our town of *Vanity* were diametrically opposite, and could not be reconciled. By which saying, my Lord, he doth at once not only condemn all our laudable doings, but us in the doing of them.

JUDGE. Then did the Judge say unto him, Hast thou any more to say?

ENVY. My Lord, I could say much more, only I would not be tedious to the court. Yet, if need be, when the other gentlemen have given in their evidence, rather than anything shall be wanting that will dispatch him, I will enlarge my testimony against him. So he was bid to stand by.

Then they called *Superstition*, and bid him look upon the prisoner. They also asked, what he could say for their lord the king against him. Then they sware him; so he began.

SUPER. My Lord, I have no great acquaintance with this man, nor do I desire to have farther knowledge of him; however, this I know, that he is a very pestilent fellow, from some discourse that, the other day, I had with him in this town; for then, talking with him, I heard him say, that our religion was nought, and such by which a man could by no means please God. Which saying of his, my Lord, your Lordship very well knows, what necessarily thence will follow, to wit, that we still do worship in vain, are yet in our sins, and finally shall be damned; and this is that which I have to say.

Then was *Pickthank* sworn, and bid say what he knew, in behalf of their lord the king, against the prisoner at the bar.

PICK. My Lord, and you gentlemen all, This fellow I have known of a long time, and have heard him speak things that ought not to be spoke; for he hath railed on our noble prince *Beelzebub*, and hath spoken contemptible of his honorable friends, whose names are the Lord *Old Man*, the Lord *Carnal Delight*, the Lord *Luxurious*, the Lord *Desire of Vain Glory*, my old Lord *Lechery*, Sir *Having Greedy*, with all the rest of our nobility; and he hath said, moreover, That if all men were of his mind, if possible, there is not one of these noblemen should have any longer a being in this town. Besides, he hath not been afraid to rail on you, my Lord, who are now appointed to be his judge, calling you an ungodly villain, with many other such like vilifying terms, with which he hath bespattered most of the gentry of our town.

When this *Pickthank* had told his tale, the Judge directed his speech to the prisoner at the bar, saying, Thou runagate, heretic, and traitor, hast thou heard what these honest gentlemen have witnessed against thee?

FAITH. May I speak a few words in my own defense?

JUDGE. Sirrah! sirrah! thou deservest to live no longer, but to be slain immediately upon the place; yet, that all men may see our gentleness towards thee, let us hear what thou, vile runagate, hast to say.

FAITH. 1. I say, then, in answer to what Mr. *Envy* hath spoken, I never said aught but this, That what rule, or laws, or custom, or people, were flat against the Word of God, are diametrically opposite to Christianity. If I have said amiss in this, convince me of my error, and I am ready here before you to make my recantation.

2. As to the second, to wit, Mr. *Superstition*, and his charge against me, I said only this, That in the worship of God there is required a Divine faith; but there can be no Divine faith without a Divine revelation of

the will of God. Therefore, whatever is thrust into the worship of God that is not agreeable to Divine revelation, cannot be done but by a humane faith, which faith will not be profitable to eternal life.

3. As to what Mr. *Pickthank* hath said, I say (avoiding terms, as that I am said to rail, and the like) that the prince of this town, with all the rabblement, his attendants, by this gentleman named, are more fit for being in hell, than in this town and country: and so, the Lord have mercy upon me!

Then the Judge called to the jury (who all this while stood by, to hear and observe): Gentlemen of the jury, you see this man about whom so great an uproar hath been made in this town. You have also heard what these worthy gentlemen have witnessed against him. Also you have heard his reply and confession. It lieth now in your breast to hang him or save his life; but yet I think meet to instruct you in our law.

There was an Act made in the days of Pharaoh the Great, servant to our prince, that lest those of a contrary religion should multiply and grow too strong for him, their males should be thrown into the river. There was an Act also made in the days of Nebuchadnezzar the Great, another of his servants, that whoever would not fall down and worship his golden image, should be thrown into a fiery furnace. There was also an Act made in the days of Darius, that whoso, for some time, called upon any god but him, should be cast into the lions' den. Now the substance of these laws this rebel has broken, not only in thought (which is not to be borne), but also in word and deed, which must therefore needs be intolerable.

For that of Pharaoh, his law was made upon supposition, to prevent mischief, no crime yet being apparent; but here is a crime apparent. For the second and third, you see he disputeth against our religion; and for the treason he hath confessed, he deserveth to die the death.

Then went the jury out, whose names were, Mr. *Blind-man*, Mr. *No-good*, Mr. *Malice*, Mr. *Love-lust*, Mr. *Live-loose*, Mr. *Heady*, Mr. *High-mind*, Mr. *Enmity*, Mr. *Liar*, Mr. *Cruelty*, Mr. *Hate-light*, and Mr. *Implacable;* who every one gave in his private verdict against him among themselves, and afterwards unanimously concluded to bring him in guilty before the Judge. And first, among themselves, Mr. *Blind-Man*, the foreman, said, I see clearly that this man is a heretic. Then said Mr. *No-good*, Away with such a fellow from the earth. Ay, said Mr. *Malice*, for I hate the very looks of him. Then said Mr. *Love-lust*, I could never endure him. Nor I, said Mr. *Live-loose*, for he would always be condemning my way. Hang him, hang him, said Mr. *Heady*. A sorry scrub, said Mr. *High-mind*. My heart riseth against him, said Mr. *Enmity*. He is a rogue, said Mr. *Liar*. Hanging is too good for him, said Mr. *Cruelty*. Let's dispatch him out of the way, said Mr. *Hate-light*. Then said Mr. *Implacable*, Might I have all the world given me, I could not be reconciled to him; therefore, let us forthwith bring him in guilty of death. And so they did; therefore he was presently condemned to be had from the place where he was, to the place from whence he came, and there to be put to the most cruel death that could be invented.

They, therefore, brought him out, to do with him according to their law; and, first, they scourged him, then they buffeted him, then they lanced his flesh with knives; after that, they stoned him with stones, then pricked him with their swords; and, last of all, they burned him to ashes at the stake. Thus came *Faithful* to his end.

Now I saw that there stood behind the multitude a chariot and a couple of horses, waiting for *Faithful*, who (so soon as his adversaries had dispatched him) was taken up into it, and straightway was carried up through the clouds, with sound of trumpet, the nearest way to the *Celestial Gate*.

But as for *Christian*, he had some respite, and was remanded back to prison. So he there remained for a space; but He that overrules all things, having the power of their rage in his own hand, so wrought it about, that *Christian* for that time escaped them, and went his way.

V

Now there was, not far from the place where they[1] lay, a castle called *Doubting Castle*, the

[1]At his escape from *Vanity Fair*, "*Christian* went not forth alone, for there was one whose name was *Hopeful* (being so made by the beholding of *Christian* and *Faithful* in their words and behavior, in their sufferings at the *Fair*), who joined himself unto him."

owner whereof was *Giant Despair;* and it was in his grounds they were now sleeping: wherefore he, getting up in the morning early, and walking up and down in his fields, caught *Christian* and *Hopeful* asleep in his grounds. Then, with a grim and surly voice, he bid them awake; and asked them whence they were, and what they did in his grounds. They told him they were pilgrims, and that they had lost their way. Then said the Giant, You have this night trespassed on me, by trampling in and lying on my ground, and therefore you must go along with me. So they were forced to go, because he was stronger than they. They also had but little to say, for they knew themselves in a fault. The Giant, therefore, drove them before him, and put them into his castle, into a very dark dungeon, nasty and stinking to the spirits of these two men. Here, then, they lay from Wednesday morning till Saturday night, without one bit of bread, or drop of drink, or light, or any to ask how they did; they were, therefore, here in evil case, and were far from friends and acquaintance. Now in this place *Christian* had double sorrow, because 'twas through his unadvised counsel that they were brought into this distress.

Now, *Giant Despair* had a wife, and her name was *Diffidence.* So when he was gone to bed, he told his wife what he had done; to wit, that he had taken a couple of prisoners and cast them into his dungeon, for trespassing on his grounds. Then he asked her also what he had best to do further to them. So she asked what they were, whence they came, and whither they were bound; and he told her. Then she counseled him that when he arose in the morning he should beat them without mercy. So, when he arose, he getteth him a grievous crab-tree cudgel, and goes down into the dungeon to them, and there first falls to rating of them as if they were dogs, although they gave him never a word of distaste. Then he falls upon them, and beats them fearfully, in such sort that they were not able to help themselves, or to turn them upon the floor. This done, he withdraws and leaves them, there to condole their misery and to mourn under their distress. So all that day they spent the time in nothing but sighs and bitter lamentations. The next night, she, talking with her husband about them further, and understanding that they were yet alive, did advise him to counsel them to make away themselves. So when morning was come, he goes to them in a surly manner as before, and perceiving them to be very sore with the stripes that he had given them the day before, he told them, that since they were never like to come out of that place, their only way would be forthwith to make an end of themselves, either with knife, halter, or poison, for why, said he, should you choose life, seeing it is attended with so much bitterness? But they desired him to let them go. With that he looked ugly upon them, and, rushing to them, had doubtless made an end of them himself, but that he fell into one of his fits (for he sometimes, in sunshiny weather, fell into fits), and lost for a time the use of his hand; wherefore he withdrew, and left them as before, to consider what to do. Then did the prisoners consult between themselves whether 'twas best to take his counsel or no; and thus they began to discourse:—

Chr. Brother, said *Christian*, what shall we do? The life that we now live is miserable. For my part I know not whether is best, to live thus, or to die out of hand. My soul chooseth strangling rather than life, and the grave is more easy for me than this dungeon. Shall we be ruled by the Giant?

Hope. Indeed, our present condition is dreadful, and death would be far more welcome to me than thus for ever to abide; but yet, let us consider, the Lord of the country to which we are going hath said, Thou shalt do no murder: no, not to another man's person; much more, then, are we forbidden to take his counsel to kill ourselves. Besides, he that kills another, can but commit murder upon his body; but for one to kill himself is to kill body and soul at once. And, moreover, my brother, thou talkest of ease in the grave; but hast thou forgotten the hell, whither for certain the murderers go? For no murderer hath eternal life, *etc.* And let us consider, again, that all the law is not in the hand of *Giant Despair*. Others, so far as I can understand, have been taken by him, as well as we; and yet have escaped out of his hand. Who knows, but that God that made the world may cause that *Giant Despair* may die? or that, at some time or other, he may forget to lock us in? or but he may, in a short time, have another of his fits before us, and may lose the use of his limbs? and if ever that should come to pass again, for my part, I am resolved to pluck up the heart of a man, and to try my utmost to get from under his hand. I was a fool that I did not try to do it before; but, however, my brother, let us be patient, and endure a while. The time may come that may give us a happy release; but let us not be our own murderers. With these words *Hopeful* at present did moderate the mind of his brother; so they continued together (in the dark) that day, in their sad and doleful condition.

Well, towards evening, the Giant goes down into the dungeon again, to see if his prisoners had taken his counsel; but when he came there he found them alive; and truly, alive was all; for now, what for want of bread and water, and by reason of the wounds they received when he beat them, they could do little but breathe. But, I say, he found them alive; at which he fell into a grievous rage, and told them that, seeing they had disobeyed his counsel, it should be worse with them than if they had never been born.

At this they trembled greatly, and I think that *Christian* fell into a swoon; but, coming a little to himself again, they renewed their discourse about the Giant's counsel; and whether yet they had best take it or no. Now *Christian* again seemed to be for doing it, but *Hopeful* made his second reply as followeth:—

HOPE. My brother, said he, rememberest thou not how valiant thou hast been heretofore? *Apollyon* could not crush thee, nor could all that thou didst hear, or see, or feel, in the *Valley of the Shadow of Death*. What hardship, terror, and amazement hast thou already gone through! And art thou now nothing but fears? Thou seest that I am in the dungeon with thee, a far weaker man by nature than thou art; also, this Giant has wounded me as well as thee, and hath also cut off the bread and water from my mouth; and with that I mourn without the light. But let's exercise a little more patience; remember how thou playedest the man at *Vanity Fair*, and wast neither afraid of the chain or cage, nor yet of bloody death. Wherefore let us (at least to avoid the shame, that becomes not a Christian to be found in) bear up with patience as well as we can.

Now, night being come again, and the Giant and his wife being in bed, she asked him concerning the prisoners, and if they had taken his counsel. To which he replied, They are sturdy rogues, they choose rather to bear all hardship, than to make away themselves. Then said she, Take them into the castle-yard to-morrow, and show them the bones and skulls of those that thou hast already dispatched, and make them believe, ere a week comes to an end, thou also wilt tear them in pieces, as thou hast done their fellows before them.

So when the morning was come, the Giant goes to them again, and takes them into the castle-yard, and shows them, as his wife had bidden him. These, said he, were pilgrims as you are, once, and they trespassed in my grounds, as you have done; and when I thought fit, I tore them in pieces, and so, within ten days, I will do you. Get you down into your den again; and with that he beat them all the way thither. They lay, therefore, all day on Saturday in a lamentable case, as before. Now, when night was come, and when Mrs. *Diffidence* and her husband, the Giant, were got to bed, they began to renew their discourse of their prisoners; and withal the old Giant wondered, that he could neither by his blows nor his counsel bring them to an end. And with that his wife replied, I fear, said she, that they live in hopes that some will come to relieve them, or that they have picklocks about them, by the means of which they hope to escape. And sayest thou so, my dear? said the Giant; I will, therefore, search them in the morning.

Well, on Saturday, about midnight, they began to pray, and continued in prayer till almost break of day.

Now, a little before it was day, good *Christian*, as one half amazed, brake out in this passionate speech:—What a fool, quoth he, am I, thus to lie in a stinking dungeon, when I may as well walk at liberty! I have a key in my bosom, called *Promise*, that will, I am persuaded, open any lock in *Doubting Castle*. Then said *Hopeful*, That's good news, good brother; pluck it out of thy bosom, and try.

Then *Christian* pulled it out of his bosom, and began to try at the dungeon door, whose bolt (as he turned the key) gave back, and the door flew open with ease, and *Christian* and *Hopeful* both came out. Then he went to the outward door that leads into the castle-yard, and, with his key, opened that door also. After, he went to the iron gate, for that must be opened too; but that lock went damnable hard, yet the key did open it. Then they thrust open the gate to make their escape with speed, but that gate, as it opened, made such a cracking, that it waked *Giant Despair*, who, hastily rising to pursue his prisoners, felt his limbs to fail, for his fits took him again, so that he could by no means go after them. Then they went on, and came to the King's highway, and so were safe, because they were out of his jurisdiction.

VI

They went then till they came to the *Delectable Mountains*, which mountains belong to the Lord of that hill of which we have spoken before; so they went up to the mountains, to behold the gardens and orchards, the vineyards and fountains of water; where also they drank and washed themselves, and did freely eat of the vineyards. Now there were on the tops of these mountains Shepherds feeding their flocks, and they stood by the highway side. The Pilgrims therefore went to them, and leaning upon their staves (as is common with weary pilgrims when they stand to talk with any by the way), they asked, Whose *Delectable Mountains* are these? And whose be the sheep that feed upon them?

SHEP. These mountains are *Immanuel's Land*, and they are within sight of His city; and the sheep also are His, and He laid down His life for them.

CHR. Is this the way to the *Celestial City?*

SHEP. You are just in your way.

CHR. How far is it thither?

SHEP. Too far for any but those that shall get thither indeed.

CHR. Is the way safe or dangerous?

SHEP. Safe for those for whom it is to be safe; but transgressors shall fall therein.

JOHN DRYDEN (1631–1700)

Dryden was born on 9 August, 1631, at Aldwinkle, a Northamptonshire village. His parents belonged to good families which had been conspicuous for their puritanism. Dryden was sent to Westminster School, in London, and in 1650 entered Trinity College, Cambridge. Like Milton, Dryden did not escape trouble with his college authorities. He took his B. A. in 1654. Dryden's first notable poem was his *Heroic Stanzas consecrated to the Memory of his Highness Oliver Cromwell*, written in 1658. It is significant of much in Dryden's life and character that he was, two years later, among the first to celebrate the return of Charles II, in his poem called *Astraea Redux*. If Dryden changed, Dr. Johnson said, he changed with the nation, which of course is true; but it is also true that Dryden as a working man of letters was dependent for his livelihood upon the favor of the great. This was an influence constantly determining what he should write, and how he should write, and it was undeniably harmful to him as a poet. Moreover, if Dryden's own sense of personal integrity did not suffer from the life of dependence he was condemned to lead this was only because his warmly felt interests were specifically literary rather than broadly human, which after all is merely another way of saying that Dryden suffered from essentially the same kind of moral obtuseness as did Bacon. Dryden was dramatist as well as poet, but here too his need of money drove him into close dependence on the taste of his day, with harmful results which are particularly evident in his comedies. The serious plays of the Restoration were of the so-called heroic type. They tended to sensationalism in plot, they were sentimental in conception, and in form they were more or less obedient to classical rule as that was laid down by seventeenth-century criticism. French influences were strong in England after 1660, and played a part in the development of Restoration drama, though the relative strength of the French and native influences entering into the drama of this period is still a debated question. The more notable of Dryden's heroic plays are *The Indian Emperor* (1665), *Tyrannic Love* (1669), *The Conquest of Granada* (in two parts, 1670–1672), and *Aurengzebe* (1675). All of these were written in rimed couplets, a practice which Dryden defended in his *Essay of Dramatic Poesy* (1668). In *All for Love* (1678), however, Dryden returned to blank verse. Some of his comedies are *The Rival Ladies* (1664), *Sir Martin Mar-All* (1667), *Marriage à la Mode* (1672), and *The Spanish Friar* (1681).

In 1670 Dryden attained office, being made historiographer-royal and poet laureate, and some years later he was made collector of customs for the port of London, posts which to some extent relieved his financial burdens until the Revolution of 1688, when he lost all his offices and was again reduced to the necessity of earning his living by his pen. The satires for which Dryden is best known as a poet were written in 1681 and 1682—*Absalom and Achitophel*, *MacFlecknoe*, and *The Medal*. In 1682 he also published his defense of the Church of England, *Religio Laici*. In 1686 Dryden became a Roman Catholic, and in the following year published a defense of his new faith in the form of a beast-fable, *The Hind and the Panther*. The latter part of the seventeenth century was little favorable to lyric poetry, nor did Dryden attempt to write much in that kind, though his ode, *Alexander's Feast*, written in 1697, is a brilliant performance. One can hardly escape astonishment at the range of Dryden's power, successfully exerted despite the handicaps of his circumstances and character. In panegyric and satire, in comedy and heroic play and tragedy, in criticism and translation—in all these he excelled; and as England's greatest and most fully representative man of letters in the latter years of the seventeenth century he amply deserved the dictatorship of literature which he attained in his old age.

ABSALOM AND ACHITOPHEL (1681)

Si propius stes
Te capiat magis.[1]

TO THE READER

'TIS not my intention to make an apology for my poem: some will think it needs no excuse, and others will receive none. The design, I am sure, is honest; but he who draws his pen for one party must expect to make enemies of the other. For wit and fool are consequents of Whig and Tory; and every man is a knave or an ass to the contrary side. There's a treasury of merits in the Fanatic Church, as well as in the Papist; and a pennyworth to be had of saintship, honesty, and poetry, for the lewd, the factious, and the blockheads; but the longest chapter in Deuteronomy has not

[1] The closer you stand, the more it takes your fancy (Horace, *Art of Poetry*, 361).

curses enough for an anti-Bromingham.[2] My comfort is, their manifest prejudice to my cause will render their judgment of less authority against me. Yet if a poem have a genius, it will force its own reception in the world; for there's a sweetness in good verse, which tickles even while it hurts, and no man can be heartily angry with him who pleases him against his will. The commendation of adversaries is the greatest triumph of a writer, because it never comes unless extorted. But I can be satisfied on more easy terms: if I happen to please the more moderate sort, I shall be sure of an honest party, and, in all probability, of the best judges; for the least concerned are commonly the least corrupt. And, I confess, I have laid in for those, by rebating[3] the satire (where justice would allow it) from carrying too sharp an edge. They who can criticize so weakly, as to imagine I have done my worst, may be convinced, at their own cost, that I can write severely with more ease than I can gently. I have but laughed at some men's follies, when I could have declaimed against their vices; and other men's virtues I have commended, as freely as I have taxed their crimes. And now, if you are a malicious reader, I expect you should return upon me that I affect to be thought more impartial than I am. But if men are not to be judged by their professions, God forgive you commonwealth's-men for professing so plausibly for the government. You cannot be so unconscionable as to charge me for not subscribing of my name; for that would reflect too grossly upon your own party, who never dare, though they have the advantage of a jury to secure them. If you like not my poem, the fault may, possibly, be in my writing (though 'tis hard for an author to judge against himself); but, more probably, 'tis in your morals, which cannot bear the truth of it. The violent, on both sides, will condemn the character of Absalom, as either too favorably or too hardly drawn. But they are not the violent whom I desire to please. The fault on the right hand is to extenuate, palliate, and indulge; and, to

[2]Anti-Whig.

[3]Blunting.

confess freely, I have endeavored to commit it. Besides the respect which I owe his birth I have a greater for his heroic virtues; and David himself could not be more tender of the young man's life than I would be of his reputation. But since the most excellent natures are always the most easy, and, as being such, are the soonest perverted by ill counsels, especially when baited with fame and glory; 't is no more a wonder that he withstood not the temptations of Achitophel, than it was for Adam not to have resisted the two devils, the serpent and the woman. The conclusion of the story I purposely forbore to prosecute, because I could not obtain from myself to show Absalom unfortunate. The frame of it was cut out but for a picture to the waist, and if the draught be so far true, 't is as much as I designed.

Were I the inventor, who am only the historian, I should certainly conclude the piece with the reconcilement of Absalom to David. And who knows but this may come to pass? Things were not brought to an extremity where I left the story; there seems yet to be room left for a composure; hereafter there may only be for pity. I have not so much as an uncharitable wish against Achitophel, but am content to be accused of a good-natured error, and to hope with Origen, that the Devil himself may at last be saved. For which reason, in this poem, he is neither brought to set his house in order, nor to dispose of his person afterwards as he in wisdom shall think fit. God is infinitely merciful; and his vicegerent is only not so, because he is not infinite.

The true end of satire is the amendment of vices by correction. And he who writes honestly is no more an enemy to the offender, than the physician to the patient, when he prescribes harsh remedies to an inveterate disease; for those are only in order to prevent the chirurgeon's work of an *ense rescindendum*,[4] which I wish not to my very enemies. To conclude all; if the body politic have any analogy to the natural, in my weak judgment an act of oblivion were as necessary in a hot, distempered state, as an opiate would be in a raging fever.

[4]Cutting out with the knife (Ovid, *Metamorphoses*, I, 191).

ABSALOM AND ACHITOPHEL[1]

IN PIOUS times, ere priestcraft did begin,
Before polygamy was made a sin;
When man on many multiplied his kind,
Ere one to one was cursedly confined;
When nature prompted, and no law denied
Promiscuous use of concubine and bride;
Then Israel's monarch[2] after Heaven's own heart,
His vigorous warmth did variously impart
To wives and slaves; and, wide as his command,
Scattered his Maker's image through the land.
Michal[3] of royal blood, the crown did wear;
A soil ungrateful to the tiller's care:
Not so the rest; for several mothers bore
To godlike David several sons before.
But since like slaves his bed they did ascend,
No true succession could their seed attend.
Of all this numerous progeny was none
So beautiful, so brave, as Absalon:[4]
Whether, inspired by some diviner lust,
His father got him with a greater gust;
Or that his conscious destiny made way,
By manly beauty, to imperial sway.
Early in foreign fields he won renown
With kings and states allied to Israel's crown;
In peace the thoughts of war he could remove,
And seemed as he were only born for love.
Whate'er he did, was done with so much ease,
In him alone 't was natural to please:
His motions all accompanied with grace;
And paradise was opened in his face.
With secret joy indulgent David viewed
His youthful image in his son renewed:
To all his wishes nothing he denied;
And made the charming Annabel[5] his bride.
What faults he had (for who from faults is free?)
His father could not or he would not see.
Some warm excesses which the law forbore,
Were construed youth that purged by boiling o'er,
And Amnon's murder, by a specious name,
Was called a just revenge for injured fame.
Thus praised and loved the noble youth remained,
While David, undisturbed, in Sion[6] reigned.
But life can never be sincerely blest;
Heav'n punishes the bad, and proves the best.
The Jews,[7] a headstrong, moody, murm'ring race,
As ever tried th' extent and stretch of grace;
God's pampered people, whom, debauched with ease,
No king could govern, nor no God could please
(Gods they had tried of every shape and size,
That god-smiths could produce, or priests devise);
These Adam-wits, too fortunately free,
Began to dream they wanted liberty;
And when no rule, no precedent was found,
Of men by laws less circumscribed and bound;
They led their wild desires to woods and caves,
And thought that all but savages were slaves.
They who, when Saul[8] was dead, without a blow,
Made foolish Ishbosheth[9] the crown forgo;
Who banished David did from Hebron[10] bring,
And with a general shout proclaimed him king:
Those very Jews, who, at their very best,
Their humor more than loyalty expressed,
Now wondered why so long they had obeyed
An idol monarch, which their hands had made;
Thought they might ruin him they could create,
Or melt him to that golden calf, a State.
But these were random bolts; no formed design,
Nor interest made the factious crowd to join:
The sober part of Israel, free from stain,
Well knew the value of a peaceful reign;
And, looking backward with a wise affright,
Saw seams of wounds, dishonest to the sight:
In contemplation of whose ugly scars
They cursed the memory of civil wars.
The moderate sort of men, thus qualified,
Inclined the balance to the better side;
And David's mildness managed it so well,
The bad found no occasion to rebel.
But when to sin our biased nature leans,
The careful Devil is still at hand with means;
And providently pimps for ill desires:
The Good Old Cause, revived, a plot requires.
Plots, true or false, are necessary things,
To raise up commonwealths and ruin kings.
  Th' inhabitants of old Jerusalem
Were Jebusites;[11] the town so called from them;

[1]As Dryden's preface indicates, this is a political poem. The Biblical story of the revolt of Absalom (2 Samuel, xiii-xviii) was used as a thin veil for satire in support of the king and the Tories. Charles II's rightful successor to the throne was his brother James, Duke of York, who was, however, opposed by the Whigs because he was a Roman Catholic. The Whig leader, the first Earl of Shaftesbury, wished to make James, Duke of Monmouth, an illegitimate son of Charles, his successor. It was against this project that Dryden directed his satire.

[2]David; Charles II.

[3]Catharine of Portugal, Charles II's queen.

[4]James, Duke of Monmouth.

[5]Anne Scott, Countess of Buccleuch.

[6]London. [7]The English.

[8]Oliver Cromwell. [9]Richard Cromwell.

[10]Apparently Scotland, though one would expect it here to mean Brussels.

[11]Roman Catholics.

And theirs the native right.
But when the chosen people grew more strong,
The rightful cause at length became the wrong;
And every loss the men of Jebus bore,
They still were thought God's enemies the more.
Thus worn and weakened, well or ill content,
Submit they must to David's government:
Impoverished and deprived of all command,
Their taxes doubled as they lost their land;
And, what was harder yet to flesh and blood,
Their gods disgraced, and burned like common wood.
This set the heathen priesthood in a flame;
For priests of all religions are the same:
Of whatsoe'er descent their godhead be,
Stock, stone, or other homely pedigree,
In his defense his servants are as bold,
As if he had been born of beaten gold.
The Jewish rabbins,[1] though their enemies,
In this conclude them honest men and wise:
For 'twas their duty, all the learnéd think,
T' espouse his cause, by whom they eat and drink.
From hence began that Plot, the nation's curse,
Bad in itself, but represented worse,
Raised in extremes, and in extremes decried,
With oaths affirmed, with dying vows denied,
Not weighed or winnowed by the multitude;
But swallowed in the mass, unchewed and crude.
Some truth there was, but dashed and brewed with lies,
To please the fools, and puzzle all the wise:
Succeeding times did equal folly call,
Believing nothing, or believing all.
Th' Egyptian[2] rites the Jebusites embraced;
Where gods were recommended by their taste.
Such sav'ry deities must needs be good,
As served at once for worship and for food.
By force they could not introduce these gods,
For ten to one in former days was odds;
So fraud was used (the sacrificer's trade):
Fools are more hard to conquer than persuade.
Their busy teachers mingled with the Jews,
And raked for converts e'en the court and stews:
Which Hebrew priests[3] the more unkindly took,
Because the fleece accompanies the flock.
Some thought they God's anointed meant to slay
By guns, invented since full many a day:

[1]Doctors of the Anglican Church.
[2]French (the immediate reference is to transubstantiation).
[3]Clergymen of the Anglican Church.

Our author swears it not; but who can know
How far the Devil and Jebusites may go?
This Plot, which failed for want of common sense,
Had yet a deep and dangerous consequence:
For, as when raging fevers boil the blood,
The standing lake soon floats into a flood,
And every hostile humor, which before
Slept quiet in its channels, bubbles o'er;
So several factions from this first ferment
Work up to foam, and threat the government.
Some by their friends, more by themselves thought wise,
Opposed the power to which they could not rise.
Some had in courts been great, and thrown from thence,
Like fiends were hardened in impenitence.
Some, by their monarch's fatal mercy, grown
From pardoned rebels kinsmen to the throne,
Were raised in power and public office high;
Strong bands, if bands ungrateful men could tie.
Of these the false Achitophel[4] was first;
A name to all succeeding ages curst:
For close[5] designs and crooked counsels fit;
Sagacious, bold, and turbulent of wit;
Restless, unfixed in principles and place;
In power unpleased, impatient of disgrace:
A fiery soul, which, working out its way,
Fretted the pigmy body to decay,
And o'er-informed the tenement of clay.
A daring pilot in extremity;
Pleased with the danger, when the waves went high,
He sought the storms; but, for a calm unfit,
Would steer too nigh the sands, to boast his wit.
Great wits are sure to madness near allied,
And thin partitions do their bounds divide;
Else why should he, with wealth and honor blest,
Refuse his age the needful hours of rest?
Punish a body which he could not please;
Bankrupt of life, yet prodigal of ease?
And all to leave what with his toil he won,
To that unfeathered two-legg'd thing, a son;
Got, while his soul did huddled notions try
And born a shapeless lump, like anarchy.
In friendship false, implacable in hate;
Resolved to ruin or to rule the State.
To compass this the triple bond he broke,
The pillars of the public safety shook;
And fitted Israel for a foreign yoke;[6]

[4]Anthony Ashley Cooper, Earl of Shaftesbury.
[5]Secret.
[6]Dryden here refers to England's alliance with France against Holland in 1670. The broken "triple bond" was an alliance made in 1667 between England, Holland, and Sweden, which was directed against France. As a matter of fact Shaftesbury had nothing to do with the alliance of 1670, but Dryden did not know this.

Then seized with fear, yet still affecting fame,
Usurped a patriot's all-atoning name.
So easy still it proves in factious times,
With public zeal to cancel private crimes.
How safe is treason, and how sacred ill,
Where none can sin against the people's will!
Where crowds can wink, and no offense be known,
Since in another's guilt they find their own!
Yet fame deserved no enemy can grudge;
The statesman we abhor, but praise the judge.
In Israel's courts ne'er sat an Abbethdin[1]
With more discerning eyes, or hands more clean;
Unbribed, unsought, the wretched to redress;
Swift of dispatch, and easy of access.
Oh, had he been content to serve the crown,
With virtues only proper to the gown;
Or had the rankness of the soil been freed
From cockle, that oppressed the noble seed;
David for him his tuneful harp had strung,
And Heav'n had wanted[2] one immortal song.
But wild Ambition loves to slide, not stand,
And Fortune's ice prefers to Virtue's land.
Achitophel, grown weary to possess
A lawful fame, and lazy happiness,
Disdained the golden fruit to gather free,
And lent the crowd his arm to shake the tree.
Now, manifest of crimes contrived long since,
He stood at bold defiance with his prince;
Held up the buckler of the people's cause
Against the crown, and skulked behind the laws.
The wished occasion of the Plot he takes;
Some circumstances finds, but more he makes.
By buzzing emissaries fills the ears
Of list'ning crowds with jealousies and fears
Of arbitrary counsels brought to light,
And proves the king himself a Jebusite.
Weak arguments! which yet he knew full well
Were strong with people easy to rebel.
For, governed by the moon, the giddy Jews
Tread the same track when she the prime renews;
And once in twenty years, their scribes record,
By natural instinct they change their lord.
Achitophel still wants a chief, and none
Was found so fit as warlike Absalon:
Not that he wished his greatness to create,
For politicians neither love nor hate,
But, for he knew his title not allowed,
Would keep him still depending on the crowd,
That kingly pow'r, thus ebbing out, might be
Drawn to the dregs of a democracy.
Him he attempts with studied arts to please,
And sheds his venom in such words as these:
"Auspicious prince, at whose nativity
Some royal planet ruled the southern sky;
Thy longing country's darling and desire;
Their cloudy pillar and their guardian fire:
Their second Moses, whose extended wand
Divides the seas, and shows the promised land;
Whose dawning day in every distant age
Has exercised the sacred prophets' rage;
The people's prayer, the glad diviners' theme,
The young men's vision, and the old men's dream!
Thee, Savior, thee, the nation's vows confess,
And, never satisfied with seeing, bless:
Swift unbespoken pomps thy steps proclaim,
And stammering babes are taught to lisp thy name.
How long wilt thou the general joy detain,
Starve and defraud the people of thy reign?
Content ingloriously to pass thy days
Like one of Virtue's fools that feeds on praise;
Till thy fresh glories, which now shine so bright,
Grow stale and tarnish with our daily sight.
Believe me, royal youth, thy fruit must be
Or gathered ripe, or rot upon the tree.
Heav'n has to all allotted, soon or late,
Some lucky revolution of their fate;
Whose motions if we watch and guide with skill
(For human good depends on human will),
Our Fortune rolls as from a smooth descent,
And from the first impression takes the bent;
But, if unseized, she glides away like wind,
And leaves repenting Folly far behind.
Now, now she meets you with a glorious prize,
And spreads her locks before her as she flies.
Had thus old David, from whose loins you spring,
Not dared, when Fortune called him, to be king,
At Gath[3] an exile he might still remain,
And Heaven's anointing oil had been in vain.
Let his successful youth your hopes engage;
But shun th' example of declining age:
Behold him setting in his western skies,
The shadows lengthening as the vapors rise.
He is not now, as when on Jordan's sand[4]
The joyful people thronged to see him land,
Cov'ring the beach, and black'ning all the strand;
But, like the Prince of Angels, from his height
Comes tumbling downward with diminished light;
Betrayed by one poor plot to public scorn,
(Our only blessing since his curst return;)
Those heaps of people which one sheaf did bind,
Blown off and scattered by a puff of wind.

[1]Judge. [2]Lacked.

[3]Brussels.

[4]Jordan represents the sea surrounding England.

What strength can he to your designs oppose,
Naked of friends and round beset with foes?
If Pharaoh's[1] doubtful succor he should use,
A foreign aid would more incense the Jews:
Proud Egypt would dissembled friendship bring;
Foment the war, but not support the king:
Nor would the royal party e'er unite
With Pharaoh's arms t'assist the Jebusite;
Or if they should, their interest soon would break,
And with such odious aid make David weak.
All sorts of men by my successful arts,
Abhorring kings, estrange their altered hearts
From David's rule: and 't is the general cry,
'Religion, commonwealth, and liberty.'
If you, as champion of the public good,
Add to their arms a chief of royal blood,
What may not Israel hope, and what applause
Might such a general gain by such a cause?
Not barren praise alone, that gaudy flower
Fair only to the sight, but solid power;
And nobler is a limited command,
Giv'n by the love of all your native land,
Than a successive title, long and dark,
Drawn from the moldy rolls of Noah's ark."

What cannot praise effect in mighty minds,
When flattery soothes, and when ambition blinds!
Desire of power, on earth a vicious weed,
Yet, sprung from high, is of celestial seed:
In God 't is glory; and when men aspire,
'T is but a spark too much of heavenly fire.
Th' ambitious youth, too covetous of fame,
Too full of angels' metal in his frame,
Unwarily was led from virtue's ways,
Made drunk with honor, and debauched with praise.
Half loath, and half consenting to the ill—
For loyal blood within him struggled still—
He thus replied: "And what pretense have I
To take up arms for public liberty?
My father governs with unquestioned right;
The faith's defender, and mankind's delight;
Good, gracious, just, observant of the laws:
And Heav'n by wonders has espoused his cause.
Whom has he wronged in all his peaceful reign?
Who sues for justice to his throne in vain?
What millions has he pardoned of his foes,
Whom just revenge did to his wrath expose?
Mild, easy, humble, studious of our good;
Inclined to mercy, and averse from blood;
If mildness ill with stubborn Israel suit,
His crime is God's belovéd attribute.
What could he gain, his people to betray,
Or change his right for arbitrary sway?
Let haughty Pharaoh curse with such a reign
His fruitful Nile, and yoke a servile train.
If David's rule Jerusalem displease,
The Dog-star heats their brains to this disease.
Why then should I, encouraging the bad,
Turn rebel and run popularly mad?
Were he a tyrant, who, by lawless might
Oppressed the Jews, and raised the Jebusite,
Well might I mourn; but nature's holy bands
Would curb my spirits and restrain my hands:
The people might assert their liberty;
But what was right in them were crime in me.
His favor leaves me nothing to require,
Prevents[2] my wishes, and outruns desire.
What more can I expect while David lives?
All but his kingly diadem he gives:
And that"—But there he paused; then sighing, said—
"Is justly destined for a worthier head.
For when my father from his toils shall rest,
And late augment the number of the blest,
His lawful issue shall the throne ascend,
Or the collat'ral line, where that shall end.
His brother, though oppressed with vulgar spite,
Yet dauntless, and secure of native right,
Of every royal virtue stands possessed,
Still dear to all the bravest and the best.
His courage foes, his friends his truth proclaim;
His loyalty the king, the world his fame.
His mercy e'en th' offending crowd will find;
For sure he comes of a forgiving kind.
Why should I then repine at Heav'n's decree,
Which gives me no pretense to royalty?
Yet O that fate, propitiously inclined,
Had raised my birth, or had debased my mind;
To my large soul not all her treasure lent,
And then betrayed it to a mean descent!
I find, I find my mounting spirits bold,
And David's part disdains my mother's mold.
Why am I scanted by a niggard birth?
My soul disclaims the kindred of her earth;
And, made for empire, whispers me within,
'Desire of greatness is a godlike sin.'"

Him staggering so when hell's dire agent found,
While fainting Virtue scarce maintained her ground,
He pours fresh forces in, and thus replies:

"Th' eternal God, supremely good and wise,
Imparts not these prodigious gifts in vain:
What wonders are reserved to bless your reign!
Against your will, your arguments have shown,
Such virtue's only giv'n to guide a throne.

[1]Louis XIV of France (Egypt).

[2]Anticipates.

Not that your father's mildness I contemn;
But manly force becomes the diadem.
'T is true he grants the people all they crave;
And more, perhaps, than subjects ought to have:
For lavish grants suppose a monarch tame,
And more his goodness than his wit proclaim.
But when should people strive their bonds to break,
If not when kings are negligent or weak?
Let him give on till he can give no more,
The thrifty Sanhedrin[1] shall keep him poor;
And every shekel which he can receive,
Shall cost a limb of his prerogative.
To ply him with new plots shall be my care;
Or plunge him deep in some expensive war;
Which when his treasure can no more supply,
He must, with the remains of kingship, buy.
His faithful friends, our jealousies and fears
Call Jebusites, and Pharaoh's pensioners;
Whom when our fury from his aid has torn,
He shall be naked left to public scorn.
The next successor, whom I fear and hate,
My arts have made obnoxious to the State;
Turned all his virtues to his overthrow,
And gained our elders to pronounce a foe.
His right, for sums of necessary gold,
Shall first be pawned, and afterwards be sold;
Till time shall ever-wanting David draw,
To pass your doubtful title into law:
If not, the people have a right supreme
To make their kings; for kings are made for them.
All empire is no more than power in trust,
Which, when resumed, can be no longer just.
Succession, for the general good designed,
In its own wrong a nation cannot bind;
If altering that the people can relieve,
Better one suffer than a nation grieve.
The Jews well know their power: ere Saul they chose,
God was their king, and God they durst depose.[2]
Urge now your piety, your filial name,
A father's right, and fear of future fame;
The public good, that universal call,
To which e'en Heav'n submitted, answers all.
Nor let his love enchant your generous mind;
'T is Nature's trick to propagate her kind.
Our fond begetters, who would never die,
Love but themselves in their posterity.
Or let his kindness by th' effects be tried,
Or let him lay his vain pretense aside.
God said he loved your father; could he bring
A better proof, than to anoint him king?
It surely showed he loved the shepherd well,
Who gave so fair a flock as Israel.
Would David have you thought his darling son?
What means he then, to alienate the crown?
The name of godly he may blush to bear;
'T is after God's own heart to cheat his heir.
He to his brother gives supreme command;
To you a legacy of barren land,
Perhaps th' old harp, on which he thrums his lays,
Or some dull Hebrew ballad in your praise.
Then the next heir, a prince severe and wise,
Already looks on you with jealous eyes;
Sees through the thin disguises of your arts,
And marks your progress in the people's hearts.
Though now his mighty soul its grief contains,
He meditates revenge who least complains;
And, like a lion, slumb'ring in the way,
Or sleep dissembling, while he waits his prey,
His fearless foes within his distance draws,
Constrains his roaring, and contracts his paws;
Till at the last, his time for fury found,
He shoots with sudden vengeance from the ground;
The prostrate vulgar passes o'er and spares,
But with a lordly rage his hunters tears.
Your case no tame expedients will afford:
Resolve on death, or conquest by the sword,
Which for no less a stake than life you draw;
And self-defense is nature's eldest law.
Leave the warm people no considering time;
For then rebellion may be thought a crime.
Prevail[3] yourself of what occasion gives,
But try your title while your father lives;
And that your arms may have a fair pretense,
Proclaim you take them in the king's defense;
Whose sacred life each minute would expose
To plots, from seeming friends, and secret foes.
And who can sound the depth of David's soul?
Perhaps his fear his kindness may control.
He fears his brother, though he loves his son,
For plighted vows too late to be undone.
If so, by force he wishes to be gained,
Like women's lechery, to seem constrained.
Doubt not: but, when he most affects the frown,
Commit a pleasing rape upon the crown.
Secure his person to secure your cause:
They who possess the prince, possess the laws."

He said, and this advice above the rest,
With Absalom's mild nature suited best:
Unblamed of life (ambition set aside),
Not stained with cruelty, nor puffed with pride,

[1]Parliament.

[2]The government of the Commonwealth previous to Cromwell's protectorate is represented as a theocracy.

[3]Avail.

How happy had he been, if destiny
Had higher placed his birth, or not so high!
His kingly virtues might have claimed a throne,
And blessed all other countries but his own.
But charming greatness since so few refuse,
'T is juster to lament him than accuse.
Strong were his hopes a rival to remove,
With blandishments to gain the public love;
To head the faction while their zeal was hot,
And popularly prosecute the Plot.
To further this, Achitophel unites
The malcontents of all the Israelites;
Whose differing parties he could wisely join,
For several ends, to serve the same design:
The best (and of the princes some were such),
Who thought the pow'r of monarchy too much;
Mistaken men, and patriots in their hearts;
Not wicked, but seduced by impious arts.
By these the springs of property were bent,
And wound so high, they cracked the government.
The next for interest sought t' embroil the State,
To sell their duty at a dearer rate;
And make their Jewish markets of the throne,
Pretending public good, to serve their own.
Others thought kings an useless heavy load,
Who cost too much, and did too little good.
These were for laying honest David by,
On principles of pure good husbandry.
With them joined all th' haranguers of the throng,
That thought to get preferment by the tongue.
Who follow next, a double danger bring,
Not only hating David, but the king:
The Solymæan rout,[1] well-versed of old
In godly faction, and in treason bold;
Cow'ring and quaking at a conqu'ror's sword,
But lofty to a lawful prince restored,
Saw with disdain an Ethnic plot[2] begun,
And scorned by Jebusites to be outdone.
Hot Levites[3] headed these; who, pulled before
From th' ark, which in the Judges' days they bore,
Resumed their cant, and with a zealous cry
Pursued their old belov'd Theocracy:
Where Sanhedrin and priest enslaved the nation,
And justified their spoils by inspiration:
For who so fit for reign as Aaron's race,[4]
If once dominion they could find in grace?
These led the pack; though not of surest scent,
Yet deepest mouthed against the government.
A numerous host of dreaming saints succeed,
Of the true old enthusiastic breed:
'Gainst form and order they their power employ,
Nothing to build, and all things to destroy.
But far more numerous was the herd of such,
Who think too little, and who talk too much.
These, out of mere instinct, they knew not why,
Adored their fathers' God and property;
And, by the same blind benefit of fate,
The Devil and the Jebusite did hate:
Born to be saved, even in their own despite,
Because they could not help believing right.
Such were the tools; but a whole Hydra more
Remains, of sprouting heads too long to score.
Some of their chiefs were princes of the land:
In the first rank of these did Zimri[5] stand;
A man so various, that he seemed to be
Not one, but all mankind's epitome:
Stiff in opinions, always in the wrong;
Was everything by starts, and nothing long;
But, in the course of one revolving moon,
Was chemist, fiddler, statesman, and buffoon:
Then all for women, painting, riming, drinking,
Besides ten thousand freaks that died in thinking.
Blest madman, who could every hour employ,
With something new to wish, or to enjoy!
Railing and praising were his usual themes;
And both (to show his judgment) in extremes:
So over-violent, or over-civil,
That every man, with him, was God or Devil.
In squand'ring wealth was his peculiar art:
Nothing went unrewarded but desert.
Beggared by fools, whom still he found too late,
He had his jest, and they had his estate.
He laughed himself from court; then sought relief
By forming parties, but could ne'er be chief;
For, spite of him, the weight of business fell
On Absalom and wise Achitophel:
Thus, wicked but in will, of means bereft,
He left not faction, but of that was left.
Titles and names 't were tedious to rehearse
Of lords, below the dignity of verse.
Wits, warriors, commonwealth's-men, were the best;
Kind husbands, and mere nobles, all the rest.
And therefore, in the name of dullness, be
The well-hung Balaam[6] and cold Caleb[7] free;

[1] The London rabble.

[2] The Popish Plot.

[3] Presbyterian ministers, who had been displaced after the Restoration.

[4] The clergy.

[5] George Villiers, Duke of Buckingham.

[6] The Earl of Huntingdon.

[7] Lord Grey of Wark.

And canting Nadab[1] let oblivion damn,
Who made new porridge for the paschal lamb.
Let friendship's holy band some names assure;
Some their own worth, and some let scorn secure.
Nor shall the rascal rabble here have place,
Whom kings no titles gave, and God no grace:
Not bull-faced Jonas[2] who could statutes draw
To mean rebellion, and make treason law.
But he, though bad, is followed by a worse,
The wretch who Heav'n's anointed dared to curse:
Shimei,[3] whose youth did early promise bring
Of zeal to God and hatred to his king,
Did wisely from expensive sins refrain,
And never broke the Sabbath, but for gain;
Nor ever was he known an oath to vent,
Or curse, unless against the government.
Thus heaping wealth, by the most ready way
Among the Jews, which was to cheat and pray,
The city, to reward his pious hate
Against his master, chose him magistrate.
His hand a vare[4] of justice did uphold;
His neck was loaded with a chain of gold.
During his office, treason was no crime;
The sons of Belial had a glorious time;
For Shimei, though not prodigal of pelf,
Yet loved his wicked neighbor as himself.
When two or three were gathered to declaim
Against the monarch of Jerusalem,
Shimei was always in the midst of them;
And if they cursed the king when he was by,
Would rather curse than break good company.
If any durst his factious friends accuse,
He packed a jury of dissenting Jews;
Whose fellow-feeling in the godly cause
Would free the suff'ring saint from human laws.
For laws are only made to punish those
Who serve the king, and to protect his foes.
If any leisure time he had from power,
(Because 't is sin to misemploy an hour,)
His bus'ness was, by writing, to persuade
That kings were useless, and a clog to trade;
And, that his noble style he might refine,
No Rechabite more shunned the fumes of wine.
Chaste were his cellars, and his shrieval board[5]
The grossness of a city feast abhorred:
His cooks, with long disuse, their trade forgot;
Cool was his kitchen, though his brains were hot.
Such frugal virtue malice may accuse,
But sure 't was necessary to the Jews;
For towns once burned such magistrates require
As dare not tempt God's providence by fire.
With spiritual food he fed his servants well,
But free from flesh that made the Jews rebel;
And Moses' laws he held in more account,
For forty days of fasting in the mount.
To speak the rest, who better are forgot,
Would tire a well-breathed witness of the Plot.
Yet, Corah,[6] thou shalt from oblivion pass:
Erect thyself, thou monumental brass,
High as the serpent of thy metal made,
While nations stand secure beneath thy shade.
What though his birth were base, yet comets rise
From earthy vapors, ere they shine in skies.
Prodigious actions may as well be done
By weaver's issue, as by prince's son.
This arch-attestor for the public good
By that one deed ennobles all his blood.
Who ever asked the witnesses' high race,
Whose oath with martyrdom did Stephen grace?
Ours was a Levite, and as times went then,
His tribe were God Almighty's gentlemen.
Sunk were his eyes, his voice was harsh and loud,
Sure signs he neither choleric was nor proud:
His long chin proved his wit; his saintlike grace
A church vermilion, and a Moses' face.
His memory, miraculously great,
Could plots, exceeding man's belief, repeat;
Which therefore cannot be accounted lies,
For human wit could never such devise.
Some future truths are mingled in his book;
But where the witness failed, the prophet spoke:
Some things like visionary flights appear;
The spirit caught him up, the Lord knows where;
And gave him his rabbinical degree,
Unknown to foreign university.[7]
His judgment yet his mem'ry did excel;
Which pieced his wondrous evidence so well,
And suited to the temper of the times,
Then groaning under Jebusitic crimes.
Let Israel's foes suspect his heav'nly call,
And rashly judge his writ apocryphal;
Our laws for such affronts have forfeits made;
He takes his life, who takes away his trade.

[1]Lord Howard of Escrick (the allusion in the following line is to the story that Howard had taken the Sacrament in "lamb's wool"—ale poured on roasted apples and sauce—instead of wine).

[2]Sir William Jones.

[3]Slingsby Bethel, a sheriff of London in 1680.

[4]Wand.

[5]His table when he was a sheriff.

[6]Titus Oates.

[7]Oates pretended to have the degree of D.D. from Salamanca.

Were I myself in witness Corah's place,
The wretch who did me such a dire disgrace,
Should whet my memory, though once forgot,
To make him an appendix of my plot.
His zeal to Heav'n made him his prince despise,
And load his person with indignities;
But zeal peculiar privilege affords,
Indulging latitude to deeds and words;
And Corah might for Agag's[1] murder call,
In terms as coarse as Samuel used to Saul.
What others in his evidence did join
(The best that could be had for love or coin),
In Corah's own predicament will fall;
For *witness* is a common name to all.
Surrounded thus with friends of every sort,
Deluded Absalom forsakes the court;
Impatient of high hopes, urged with renown,
And fired with near possession of a crown.
Th' admiring crowd are dazzled with surprise,
And on his goodly person feed their eyes.
His joy concealed, he sets himself to show,
On each side bowing popularly low;
His looks, his gestures, and his words he frames,
And with familiar ease repeats their names.
Thus formed by nature, furnished out with arts,
He glides unfelt into their secret hearts.
Then, with a kind compassionating look,
And sighs, bespeaking pity ere he spoke,
Few words he said; but easy those and fit,
More slow than Hybla-drops, and far more sweet.
"I mourn, my countrymen, your lost estate;
Though far unable to prevent your fate:
Behold a banished man,[2] for your dear cause
Exposed a prey to arbitrary laws!
Yet oh, that I alone could be undone,
Cut off from empire, and no more a son!
Now all your liberties a spoil are made;
Egypt and Tyrus[3] intercept your trade,
And Jebusites your sacred rites invade.
My father, whom with reverence yet I name,
Charmed into ease, is careless of his fame;
And, bribed with petty sums of foreign gold,
Is grown in Bathsheba's[4] embraces old;
Exalts his enemies, his friends destroys;
And all his power against himself employs.
He gives, and let him give, my right away;
But why should he his own and yours betray?
He, only he, can make the nation bleed,
And he alone from my revenge is freed.
Take then my tears (with that he wiped his eyes),
'T is all the aid my present power supplies:
No court-informer can these arms accuse;
These arms may sons against their fathers use:
And 't is my wish, the next successor's reign
May make no other Israelite complain."
Youth, beauty, graceful action seldom fail;
But common interest always will prevail;
And pity never ceases to be shown
To him who makes the people's wrongs his own.
The crowd, that still believe their kings oppress,
With lifted hands their young Messiah bless:
Who now begins his progress to ordain
With chariots, horsemen, and a num'rous train;
From east to west his glories he displays,
And, like the sun, the promised land surveys.
Fame runs before him as the morning star,
And shouts of joy salute him from afar:
Each house receives him as a guardian god,
And consecrates the place of his abode.
But hospitable treats did most commend
Wise Issachar,[5] his wealthy western friend.
This moving court, that caught the people's eyes,
And seemed but pomp, did other ends disguise:
Achitophel had formed it, with intent
To sound the depths, and fathom, where it went,
The people's hearts; distinguish friends from foes,
And try their strength, before they came to blows.
Yet all was colored with a smooth pretense
Of specious love, and duty to their prince.
Religion, and redress of grievances,
Two names that always cheat and always please,
Are often urged; and good King David's life
Endangered by a brother and a wife.
Thus in a pageant show a plot is made,
And peace itself is war in masquerade.
O foolish Israel! never warned by ill!
Still the same bait, and circumvented still!
Did ever men forsake their present ease,
In midst of health imagine a disease;
Take pains contingent mischiefs to foresee,
Make heirs for monarchs, and for God decree?
What shall we think! Can people give away,
Both for themselves and sons, their native sway?

---

[1]Sir Edmund Bury Godfrey, before whom Oates testified concerning the Popish Plot, and who was soon thereafter murdered.

[2]Monmouth had been sent from England in 1679, but had returned.

[3]France and Holland.

[4]Louise de Querouaille, Duchess of Portsmouth, Charles's mistress.

[5]Thomas Thynne of Longleat.

Then they are left defenseless to the sword
Of each unbounded, arbitrary lord:
And laws are vain, by which we right enjoy,
If kings unquestioned can those laws destroy.
Yet if the crowd be judge of fit and just,
And kings are only officers in trust,
Then this resuming cov'nant was declared
When kings were made, or is for ever barred.
If those who gave the scepter could not tie
By their own deed their own posterity,
How then could Adam bind his future race?
How could his forfeit on mankind take place?
Or how could heavenly justice damn us all,
Who ne'er consented to our father's fall?
Then kings are slaves to those whom they command,
And tenants to their people's pleasure stand.
Add, that the power for property allowed
Is mischievously seated in the crowd;
For who can be secure of private right,
If sovereign sway may be dissolved by might?
Nor is the people's judgment always true:
The most may err as grossly as the few;
And faultless kings run down, by common cry,
For vice, oppression, and for tyranny.
What standard is there in a fickle rout,
Which, flowing to the mark, runs faster out?
Nor only crowds, but Sanhedrins may be
Infected with this public lunacy,
And share the madness of rebellious times,
To murder monarchs for imagined crimes.
If they may give and take whene'er they please,
Not kings alone (the Godhead's images),
But government itself at length must fall
To nature's state, where all have right to all.
Yet, grant our lords the people kings can make,
What prudent men a settled throne would shake?
For whatsoe'er their sufferings were before,
That change they covet makes them suffer more.
All other errors but disturb a state,
But innovation is the blow of fate.
If ancient fabrics nod and threat to fall,
To patch the flaws and buttress up the wall,
Thus far 't is duty: but here fix the mark;
For all beyond it is to touch our ark.
To change foundations, cast the frame anew,
Is work for rebels, who base ends pursue,
At once divine and human laws control,
And mend the parts by ruin of the whole.
The tamp'ring world is subject to this curse,
To physic their disease into a worse.
Now what relief can righteous David bring?
How fatal 't is to be too good a king!
Friends he has few, so high the madness grows:
Who dare be such, must be the people's foes.
Yet some there were, e'en in the worst of days;
Some let me name, and naming is to praise.
In this short file Barzillai[1] first appears;
Barzillai, crowned with honor and with years.
Long since, the rising rebels he withstood
In regions waste, beyond the Jordan's flood:
Unfortunately brave to buoy the State;
But sinking underneath his master's fate:
In exile with his godlike prince he mourned;
For him he suffered, and with him returned.
The court he practiced, not the courtier's art:
Large was his wealth, but larger was his heart,
Which well the noblest objects knew to choose,
The fighting warrior, and recording Muse.
His bed could once a fruitful issue boast;
Now more than half a father's name is lost.
His eldest hope, with every grace adorned,
By me (so Heav'n will have it) always mourned,
And always honored, snatched in manhood's prime
B' unequal fates, and Providence's crime;
Yet not before the goal of honor won,
All parts fulfilled of subject and of son:
Swift was the race, but short the time to run.
O narrow circle, but of power divine,
Scanted in space, but perfect in thy line!
By sea, by land, thy matchless worth was known,
Arms thy delight, and war was all thy own:
Thy force, infused, the fainting Tyrians propped;
And haughty Pharaoh found his fortune stopped.
O ancient honor! O unconquered hand,
Whom foes unpunished never could withstand!
But Israel was unworthy of thy name;
Short is the date of all immoderate fame.
It looks as Heav'n our ruin had designed,
And durst not trust thy fortune and thy mind.
Now, free from earth, thy disencumbered soul
Mounts up, and leaves behind the clouds and starry pole:
From thence thy kindred legions may'st thou bring,
To aid the guardian angel of thy king.
Here stop, my Muse, here cease thy painful flight;
No pinions can pursue immortal height:
Tell good Barzillai thou canst sing no more,
And tell thy soul she should have fled before:
Or fled she with his life, and left this verse
To hang on her departed patron's hearse?
Now take thy steepy flight from heav'n, and see
If thou canst find on earth another he:

[1]The Duke of Ormond.

Another he would be too hard to find;
See then whom thou canst see not far behind.
Zadoc[1] the priest, whom, shunning power and place,
His lowly mind advanced to David's grace.
With him the Sagan of Jerusalem,[2]
Of hospitable soul, and noble stem;
Him of the western dome,[3] whose weighty sense
Flows in fit words and heavenly eloquence.
The prophets' sons, by such example led,
To learning and to loyalty were bred:
For colleges on bounteous kings depend,
And never rebel was to arts a friend.
To these succeed the pillars of the laws;
Who best could plead, and best can judge a cause.
Next them a train of loyal peers ascend;
Sharp-judging Adriel,[4] the Muses' friend;
Himself a Muse—in Sanhedrin's debate
True to his prince, but not a slave of state:
Whom David's love with honors did adorn,
That from his disobedient son were torn.
Jotham[5] of piercing wit, and pregnant thought;
Endued by nature, and by learning taught
To move assemblies, who but only tried
The worse a while, then chose the better side:
Nor chose alone, but turned the balance too;
So much the weight of one brave man can do.
Hushai,[6] the friend of David in distress;
In public storms, of manly steadfastness:
By foreign treaties he informed his youth,
And joined experience to his native truth.
His frugal care supplied the wanting throne;
Frugal for that, but bounteous of his own:
'T is easy conduct when exchequers flow,
But hard the task to manage well the low;
For sovereign power is too depressed or high,
When kings are forced to sell, or crowds to buy.
Indulge one labor more, my weary Muse,
For Amiel:[7] who can Amiel's praise refuse?
Of ancient race by birth, but nobler yet
In his own worth, and without title great:
The Sanhedrin long time as chief he ruled,
Their reason guided, and their passion cooled:
So dext'rous was he in the crown's defense,
So formed to speak a loyal nation's sense,
That, as their band was Israel's tribes in small,
So fit was he to represent them all.

[1]William Sancroft, Archbishop of Canterbury.

[2]Henry Compton, Bishop of London.

[3]John Dolben, Bishop of Rochester and Dean of Westminster. The "western dome" is Westminster Abbey.

[4]John Sheffield, Earl of Mulgrave, later Duke of Buckinghamshire.

[5]George Savile, Marquis of Halifax.

[6]Lawrence Hyde, after 1682 Earl of Rochester.

[7]Edward Seymour, Speaker of the House of Commons from 1673 to 1679.

Now rasher charioteers the seat ascend,
Whose loose careers his steady skill commend:
They, like th' unequal ruler of the day,[8]
Misguide the seasons, and mistake the way;
While he withdrawn at their mad labor smiles,
And safe enjoys the sabbath of his toils.
These were the chief, a small but faithful band
Of worthies, in the breach who dared to stand,
And tempt th' united fury of the land.
With grief they viewed such powerful engines bent,
To batter down the lawful government:
A numerous faction, with pretended frights,
In Sanhedrins to plume[9] the regal rights;
The true successor from the court removed;
The Plot, by hireling witnesses, improved.
These ills they saw, and, as their duty bound,
They showed the king the danger of the wound;
That no concessions from the throne would please,
But lenitives fomented the disease;
That Absalom, ambitious of the crown,
Was made the lure to draw the people down;
That false Achitophel's pernicious hate
Had turned the Plot to ruin Church and State;
The council violent, the rabble worse;
That Shimei taught Jerusalem to curse.
With all these loads of injuries oppressed,
And long revolving in his careful breast
Th' event of things, at last, his patience tired,
Thus from his royal throne, by Heav'n inspired,
The godlike David spoke: with awful fear
His train their Maker in their master hear.
"Thus long have I, by native mercy swayed,
My wrongs dissembled, my revenge delayed;
So willing to forgive th' offending age;
So much the father did the king assuage.
But now so far my clemency they slight,
Th' offenders question my forgiving right.
That one was made for many, they contend;
But 'tis to rule; for that's a monarch's end.
They call my tenderness of blood, my fear;
Though manly tempers can the longest bear.
Yet, since they will divert my native course,
'T is time to show I am not good by force.
Those heaped affronts that haughty subjects bring,
Are burdens for a camel, not a king.
Kings are the public pillars of the State,
Born to sustain and prop the nation's weight;
If my young Samson will pretend a call
To shake the column, let him share the fall:

[8]Phaeton. [9]*I. e.*, to pluck out.

But O that yet he would repent and live!
How easy 't is for parents to forgive!
With how few tears a pardon might be won
From nature, pleading for a darling son!
Poor pitied youth, by my paternal care
Raised up to all the height his frame could bear!
Had God ordained his fate for empire born,
He would have giv'n his soul another turn:
Gulled with a patriot's name, whose modern sense
Is one that would by law supplant his prince;
The people's brave, the politician's tool;
Never was patriot yet, but was a fool.
Whence comes it that religion and the laws
Should more be Absalom's than David's cause?
His old instructor, ere he lost his place,
Was never thought indued with so much grace.
Good heav'ns, how faction can a patriot paint!
My rebel ever proves my people's saint.
Would *they* impose an heir upon the throne?
Let Sanhedrins be taught to give their own.
A king's at least a part of government,
And mine as requisite as their consent;
Without my leave a future king to choose,
Infers a right the present to depose.
True, they petition me t'approve their choice;
But Esau's hands suit ill with Jacob's voice.
My pious subjects for my safety pray;
Which to secure, they take my power away.
From plots and treasons Heav'n preserve my years,
But save me most from my petitioners!
Unsatiate as the barren womb or grave;
God cannot grant so much as they can crave.
What then is left, but with a jealous eye
To guard the small remains of royalty?
The law shall still direct my peaceful sway,
And the same law teach rebels to obey:
Votes shall no more established power control—
Such votes as make a part exceed the whole:
No groundless clamors shall my friends remove,
Nor crowds have power to punish ere they prove;
For gods and godlike kings their care express,
Still to defend their servants in distress.
O that my power to saving were confined!
Why am I forced, like Heav'n, against my mind,
To make examples of another kind?
Must I at length the sword of justice draw?
O curst effects of necessary law!
How ill my fear they by my mercy scan!
Beware the fury of a patient man.
Law they require, let Law then show her face;
They could not be content to look on Grace,
Her hinder parts, but with a daring eye
To tempt the terror of her front and die.
By their own arts, 't is righteously decreed,
Those dire artificers of death shall bleed.
Against themselves their witnesses will swear,
Till viper-like their mother Plot they tear;
And suck for nutriment that bloody gore,
Which was their principle of life before.
Their Belial with their Belzebub will fight;
Thus on my foes, my foes shall do me right.
Nor doubt th' event; for factious crowds engage,
In their first onset, all their brutal rage.
Then let 'em take an unresisted course;
Retire, and traverse, and delude their force;
But, when they stand all breathless, urge the fight,
And rise upon 'em with redoubled might;
For lawful power is still superior found;
When long driv'n back, at length it stands the ground."
He said. Th' Almighty, nodding, gave consent;
And peals of thunder shook the firmament.
Henceforth a series of new time began,
The mighty years in long procession ran:
Once more the godlike David was restored,
And willing nations knew their lawful lord.

MAC FLECKNOE

OR, A SATIRE UPON THE TRUE-BLUE-PROTESTANT POET T. S.[1] (1682)

All human things are subject to decay,
And when fate summons, monarchs must obey.
This Flecknoe[2] found, who, like Augustus, young
Was called to empire, and had governed long;
In prose and verse was owned, without dispute,
Through all the realms of Nonsense absolute.
This aged prince, now flourishing in peace,
And bless'd with issue of a large increase;
Worn out with business, did at length debate
To settle the succession of the State;
And, pond'ring which of all his sons was fit
To reign, and wage immortal war with wit,
Cried: "'T is resolved; for nature pleads, that he
Should only rule, who most resembles me.

[1]Dryden published *The Medal* in the spring of 1682. One of the answers to it was *The Medal of John Bayes*, by Thomas Shadwell. Dryden and Shadwell had once been friends, but Shadwell was a strong Whig, the two were now enemies, and Shadwell's poem was savagely abusive. *Mac Flecknoe* was Dryden's reply.

[2]Flecknoe died in 1678. He was a Roman Catholic priest before the restoration of Charles II. At one time he was entertained at Lisbon by King John of Portugal.

Sh—— alone my perfect image bears,
Mature in dullness from his tender years:
Sh—— alone, of all my sons, is he
Who stands confirmed in full stupidity.
The rest to some faint meaning make pretense,
But Sh—— never deviates into sense.
Some beams of wit on other souls may fall,
Strike through, and make a lucid interval;
But Sh——'s genuine night admits no ray,
His rising fogs prevail upon the day.
Besides, his goodly fabric fills the eye,
And seems designed for thoughtless majesty;
Thoughtless as monarch oaks that shade the plain,
And, spread in solemn state, supinely reign.
Heywood and Shirley[1] were but types of thee,
Thou last great prophet of tautology.
Even I, a dunce of more renown than they,
Was sent before but to prepare thy way;
And, coarsely clad in Norwich drugget, came
To teach the nations in thy greater name.
My warbling lute, the lute I whilom strung,
When to King John of Portugal I sung,
Was but the prelude to that glorious day,
When thou on silver Thames didst cut thy way,
With well-timed oars before the royal barge,
Swelled with the pride of thy celestial charge;
And big with hymn, commander of a host,
The like was ne'er in Epsom blankets tossed.[2]
Methinks I see the new Arion[3] sail,
The lute still trembling underneath thy nail.
At thy well-sharpened thumb from shore to shore
The treble squeaks for fear, the basses roar;
Echoes from Pissing Alley Sh—— call,
And Sh—— they resound from Aston Hall.
About thy boat the little fishes throng,
As at the morning toast that floats along.
Sometimes, as prince of thy harmonious band,
Thou wield'st thy papers in thy threshing hand.
St. André's[4] feet ne'er kept more equal time,
Not e'en the feet of thy own *Psyche's*[5] rime;
Though they in number as in sense excel:
So just, so like tautology, they fell,
That, pale with envy, Singleton[6] forswore
The lute and sword, which he in triumph bore,
And vowed he ne'er would act Villerius[7] more."

[1]Thomas Heywood and James Shirley, both dramatists of the early seventeenth century.

[2]A play of Shadwell's was entitled *Epsom Wells;* tossing in a blanket is also the punishment given a character in Shadwell's *The Virtuoso.*

[3]A Greek musician of the eighth century, B. C. Shadwell was a musician as well as a poet.

[4]A French dancing-master.

[5]An opera in rime by Shadwell.

[6]A singer of the day.

[7]A character in Davenant's *Siege of Rhodes.*

Here stopped the good old sire, and wept for joy
In silent raptures of the hopeful boy.
All arguments, but most his plays, persuade,
That for anointed dullness he was made.
Close to the walls which fair Augusta[8] bind
(The fair Augusta much to fears inclined),
An ancient fabric raised t' inform the sight,
There stood of yore, and Barbican it hight:
A watchtower once; but now, so fate ordains,
Of all the pile an empty name remains.
From its old ruins brothel-houses rise,
Scenes of lewd loves, and of polluted joys,
Where their vast courts the mother-strumpets keep,
And, undisturbed by watch, in silence sleep.
Near these a Nursery[9] erects its head,
Where queens are formed, and future heroes bred;
Where unfledged actors learn to laugh and cry,
Where infant punks their tender voices try,
And little Maximins[10] the gods defy.
Great Fletcher never treads in buskins here,
Nor greater Jonson dares in socks appear;
But gentle Simkin[11] just reception finds
Amidst this monument of vanished minds:
Pure clinches[12] the suburbian Muse affords,
And Panton waging harmless war with words.
Here Flecknoe, as a place to fame well known,
Ambitiously designed his Sh——'s throne;
For ancient Dekker prophesied long since,
That in this pile should reign a mighty prince,
Born for a scourge of wit, and flail of sense;
To whom true dullness should some *Psyches* owe,
But worlds of *Misers* from his pen should flow;
Humorists and hypocrites it should produce,
Whole Raymond families, and tribes of Bruce.[13]
Now Empress Fame had published the renown
Of Sh——'s coronation through the town.
Roused by report of Fame, the nations meet,
From near Bunhill, and distant Watling Street.
No Persian carpets spread th' imperial way,
But scattered limbs of mangled poets lay;
From dusty shops neglected authors come,
Martyrs of pies, and relics of the bum.

[8]London, at the time fearful of the King and Roman Catholicism.

[9]A theater for the training of young actors.

[10]The name of the chief character in Dryden's *Tyrannic Love.*

[11]A clown.

[12]Puns. Panton is said to have been a celebrated punster.

[13]*The Miser* and *The Humorists* are plays by Shadwell Raymond is a character in the latter, Bruce a character in Shadwell's *The Virtuoso.*

Much Heywood, Shirley, Ogleby[1] there lay,
But loads of Sh—— almost choked the way.
Bilked stationers for yeomen stood prepared,
And Herringman[2] was captain of the guard.
The hoary prince in majesty appeared,
High on a throne of his own labors reared.
At his right hand our young Ascanius sate,
Rome's other hope, and pillar of the State.
His brows thick fogs, instead of glories, grace,
And lambent dullness played around his face.
As Hannibal did to the altars come,
Sworn by his sire a mortal foe to Rome;
So Sh—— swore, nor should his vow be vain,
That he till death true dullness would maintain;
And, in his father's right, and realm's defense,
Ne'er to have peace with wit, nor truce with sense.
The king himself the sacred unction made,
As king by office, and as priest by trade.
In his sinister hand, instead of ball,
He placed a mighty mug of potent ale;
Love's Kingdom[3] to his right he did convey,
At once his scepter, and his rule of sway;
Whose righteous lore the prince had practiced young,
And from whose loins recorded *Psyche* sprung.
His temples, last, with poppies were o'erspread,
That nodding seemed to consecrate his head.
Just at that point of time, if fame not lie,
On his left hand twelve reverend owls did fly.
So Romulus, 't is sung, by Tiber's brook,
Presage of sway from twice six vultures took.
Th' admiring throng loud acclamations make,
And omens of his future empire take.
The sire then shook the honors of his head,
And from his brows damps of oblivion shed
Full on the filial dullness: long he stood,
Repelling from his breast the raging god;
At length burst out in this prophetic mood:
"Heavens bless my son, from Ireland let him reign
To far Barbadoes on the western main;
Of his dominion may no end be known,
And greater than his father's be his throne;
Beyond *Love's Kingdom* let him stretch his pen!"
He paused, and all the people cried, "Amen."
Then thus continued he: "My son, advance
Still in new impudence, new ignorance.
Success let others teach, learn thou from me
Pangs without birth, and fruitless industry.
Let *Virtuosos* in five years be writ;
Yet not one thought accuse thy toil of wit.
Let gentle George[4] in triumph tread the stage,
Make Dorimant betray, and Loveit rage;
Let Cully, Cockwood, Fopling, charm the pit,
And in their folly show the writer's wit.
Yet still thy fools shall stand in thy defense,
And justify their author's want of sense.
Let 'em be all by thy own model made
Of dullness, and desire no foreign aid;
That they to future ages may be known,
Not copies drawn, but issue of thy own.
Nay, let thy men of wit too be the same,
All full of thee, and differing but in name.
But let no alien S—dl—y[5] interpose,
To lard with wit thy hungry *Epsom* prose.
And when false flowers of rhetoric thou wouldst cull,
Trust nature, do not labor to be dull;
But write thy best, and top; and, in each line,
Sir Formal's[6] oratory will be thine:
Sir Formal, though unsought, attends thy quill,
And does thy northern dedications[7] fill.
Nor let false friends seduce thy mind to fame,
By arrogating Jonson's hostile name.[8]
Let father Flecknoe fire thy mind with praise,
And uncle Ogleby thy envy raise.
Thou art my blood, where Jonson has no part:
What share have we in nature, or in art?
Where did his wit on learning fix a brand,
And rail at arts he did not understand?
Where made he love in Prince Nicander's[9] vein,
Or swept the dust in *Psyche's* humble strain?
Where sold he bargains, 'whip-stitch, kiss my arse,'[10]
Promised a play and dwindled to a farce?
When did his Muse from Fletcher scenes purloin,
As thou whole Eth'rege dost transfuse to thine?
But so transfused as oil on water's flow,
His always floats above, thine sinks below.
This is thy province, this thy wondrous way,
New humors to invent for each new play:
This is that boasted bias of thy mind,
By which one way, to dullness, 't is inclined;
Which makes thy writings lean on one side still,
And, in all changes, that way bends thy will.
Nor let thy mountain-belly make pretense
Of likeness; thine's a tympany of sense.

[1]Ogleby had been a dancing-master and had afterwards translated Homer, Virgil, and Æsop, besides writing other poems.

[2]A London publisher.

[3]A play by Flecknoe.

[4]Sir George Etheredge. The names in the two following lines are those of characters in Etheredge's plays.

[5]Sir Charles Sedley, who had written the prologue for Shadwell's *Epsom Wells*, and who probably, as Dryden suggests, gave Shadwell other assistance.

[6]Sir Formal Trifle is a character in Shadwell's *Virtuoso*.

[7]An allusion to Shadwell's dedication of various books to the Duke of Newcastle and members of his family.

[8]Shadwell frequently eulogized Jonson.

[9]A character in Shadwell's *Psyche*.

[10]Such phrases are used by Sir Samuel Hearty in Shadwell's *Virtuoso*.

A tun of man in thy large bulk is writ,
But sure thou 'rt but a kilderkin of wit.
Like mine, thy gentle numbers feebly creep;
Thy tragic Muse gives smiles, thy comic sleep.
With whate'er gall thou sett'st thyself to write,
Thy inoffensive satires never bite.
In thy felonious heart though venom lies,
It does but touch thy Irish pen, and dies.
Thy genius calls thee not to purchase fame
In keen iambics, but mild anagram.
Leave writing plays, and choose for thy command
Some peaceful province in acrostic land.
There thou may'st wings display and altars raise,
And torture one poor word ten thousand ways.
Or, if thou wouldst thy diff'rent talents suit,
Set thy own songs, and sing them to thy lute."
He said: but his last words were scarcely heard;
For Bruce and Longvil had a trap prepared,[1]
And down they sent the yet declaiming bard.
Sinking he left his drugget robe behind,
Borne upwards by a subterranean wind.
The mantle fell to the young prophet's part,
With double portion of his father's art.

A SONG FOR ST. CECILIA'S DAY[2] (1687)

I

FROM harmony, from heav'nly harmony
This universal frame began:
When Nature underneath a heap
Of jarring atoms lay,
And could not heave her head,
The tuneful voice was heard from high:
"Arise, ye more than dead."
Then cold, and hot, and moist, and dry,
In order to their stations leap,
And Music's pow'r obey.
From harmony, from heav'nly harmony
This universal frame began:
From harmony to harmony
Through all the compass of the notes it ran,
The diapason closing full in Man.

II

What passion cannot Music raise and quell!
When Jubal[3] struck the corded shell,
His list'ning brethren stood around,
And, wond'ring, on their faces fell
To worship that celestial sound.
Less than a god they thought there could not dwell
Within the hollow of that shell
That spoke so sweetly and so well.
What passion cannot Music raise and quell!

III

The Trumpet's loud clangor
Excites us to arms,
With shrill notes of anger,
And mortal alarms.
The double double double beat
Of the thund'ring Drum
Cries: "Hark! the foes come;
Charge, charge, 't is too late to retreat."

IV

The soft complaining Flute
In dying notes discovers
The woes of hopeless lovers,
Whose dirge is whispered by the warbling Lute.

V

Sharp Violins proclaim
Their jealous pangs, and desperation,
Fury, frantic indignation,
Depth of pains, and height of passion,
For the fair, disdainful dame.

VI

But O! what art can teach,
What human voice can reach,
The sacred Organ's praise?
Notes inspiring holy love,
Notes that wing their heav'nly ways
To mend the choirs above.

VII

Orpheus could lead the savage race;
And trees unrooted left their place,
Sequacious of the lyre;
But bright Cecilia raised the wonder high'r:
When to her Organ vocal breath was giv'n,
An angel heard, and straight appeared,
Mistaking earth for heav'n.

GRAND CHORUS

As from the pow'r of sacred lays
The spheres began to move,
And sung the great Creator's praise
To all the blest above;
So, when the last and dreadful hour
This crumbling pageant shall devour,
The Trumpet shall be heard on high,
The dead shall live, the living die,
And Music shall untune the sky.

[1]These characters thus make Sir Formal Trifle disappear in Shadwell's *Virtuoso*.

[2]St. Cecilia is said to have invented the organ, and was canonized as the patron saint of music. A musical society was organized in London in 1683 for the celebration of St. Cecilia's day, 22 November, and each year an ode, composed for the occasion, was sung. This and the following poem were written by Dryden for this purpose.

[3]See Genesis, iv, 21.

ALEXANDER'S FEAST

OR, THE POWER OF MUSIC; AN ODE IN HONOR OF ST. CECILIA'S DAY

(1697)

I

'T WAS at the royal feast, for Persia won
By Philip's warlike son:[1]
Aloft in awful state
The godlike hero sate
On his imperial throne:
His valiant peers were placed around;
Their brows with roses and with myrtles bound
(So should desert in arms be crowned).
The lovely Thais, by his side,
Sate like a blooming Eastern bride
In flow'r of youth and beauty's pride.
Happy, happy, happy pair!
None but the brave,
None but the brave,
None but the brave deserves the fair.

CHORUS

Happy, happy, happy pair!
None but the brave,
None but the brave,
None but the brave deserves the fair.

II

Timotheus,[2] placed on high
Amid the tuneful choir,
With flying fingers touched the lyre:
The trembling notes ascend the sky,
And heav'nly joys inspire.
The song began from Jove,
Who left his blissful seats above
(Such is the power of mighty love).
A dragon's fiery form belied the god:
Sublime on radiant spires he rode,
When he to fair Olympia pressed;
And while he sought her snowy breast:
Then, round her slender waist he curled,
And stamped an image of himself, a sov'reign of the world.
The list'ning crowd admire the lofty sound;
"A present deity," they shout around;
"A present deity," the vaulted roofs rebound:
With ravished ears
The monarch hears,
Assumes the god,
Affects to nod,
And seems to shake the spheres.

CHORUS

With ravished ears
The monarch hears,
Assumes the god,
Affects to nod,
And seems to shake the spheres.

III

The praise of Bacchus then the sweet musician sung,
Of Bacchus ever fair and ever young:
The jolly god in triumph comes;
Sound the trumpets; beat the drums;
Flushed with a purple grace
He shows his honest face:
Now give the hautboys breath; he comes, he comes.
Bacchus, ever fair and young,
Drinking joys did first ordain;
Bacchus' blessings are a treasure.
Drinking is the soldier's pleasure:
Rich the treasure,
Sweet the pleasure,
Sweet is pleasure after pain.

CHORUS

Bacchus' blessings are a treasure,
Drinking is the soldier's pleasure:
Rich the treasure,
Sweet the pleasure,
Sweet is pleasure after pain.

IV

Soothed with the sound, the king grew vain;
Fought all his battles o'er again;
And thrice he routed all his foes; and thrice he slew the slain.
The master saw the madness rise;
His glowing cheeks, his ardent eyes;
And, while he heav'n and earth defied,
Changed his hand, and checked his pride.
He chose a mournful Muse,
Soft pity to infuse:
He sung Darius[3] great and good,
By too severe a fate,
Fallen, fallen, fallen, fallen,
Fallen from his high estate,
And welt'ring in his blood;
Deserted, at his utmost need,
By those his former bounty fed;
On the bare earth exposed he lies,
With not a friend to close his eyes.
With downcast looks the joyless victor sate,
Revolving in his altered soul
The various turns of chance below;
And, now and then, a sigh he stole;
And tears began to flow.

---

[1]Alexander the Great.

[2]A Bœotian musician, a favorite of Alexander.

[3]The Persian monarch conquered by Alexander.

CHORUS

Revolving in his altered soul
The various turns of chance below;
And, now and then, a sigh he stole;
And tears began to flow.

V

The mighty master smiled, to see
That love was in the next degree:
'Twas but a kindred sound to move,
For pity melts the mind to love.
Softly sweet, in Lydian measures,
Soon he soothed his soul to pleasures.
"War," he sung, "is toil and trouble;
Honor, but an empty bubble;
Never ending, still beginning,
Fighting still, and still destroying;
If the world be worth thy winning,
Think, O think it worth enjoying;
Lovely Thais sits beside thee,
Take the good the gods provide thee."
The many rend the skies with loud applause;
So Love was crowned, but Music won the cause.
The prince, unable to conceal his pain,
Gazed on the fair
Who caused his care,
And sighed and looked, sighed and looked,
Sighed and looked, and sighed again:
At length, with love and wine at once oppressed,
The vanquished victor sunk upon her breast.

CHORUS

The prince, unable to conceal his pain,
Gazed on the fair
Who caused his care,
And sighed and looked, sighed and looked,
Sighed and looked, and sighed again:
At length, with love and wine at once oppressed,
The vanquished victor sunk upon her breast.

VI

Now strike the golden lyre again:
A louder yet, and yet a louder strain.
Break his bands of sleep asunder,
And rouse him, like a rattling peal of thunder.
Hark, hark, the horrid sound
Has raised up his head:
As awaked from the dead,
And amazed, he stares around.
"Revenge, revenge!" Timotheus cries,
"See the Furies arise!
See the snakes that they rear,
How they hiss in their hair,
And the sparkles that flash from their eyes!
Behold a ghastly band,
Each a torch in his hand!
Those are Grecian ghosts, that in battle were slain,
And unburied remain
Inglorious on the plain:
Give the vengeance due
To the valiant crew.
Behold how they toss their torches on high,
How they point to the Persian abodes,
And glitt'ring temples of their hostile gods!"
The princes applaud, with a furious joy;
And the king seized a flambeau with zeal to destroy;
Thais led the way,
To light him to his prey,
And, like another Helen, fired another Troy.

CHORUS

And the king seized a flambeau with zeal to destroy;
Thais led the way,
To light him to his prey,
And, like another Helen, fired another Troy.

VII

Thus, long ago,
Ere heaving bellows learned to blow,
While organs yet were mute;
Timotheus, to his breathing flute,
And sounding lyre,
Could swell the soul to rage, or kindle soft desire.
At last, divine Cecilia came,
Inventress of the vocal frame;[1]
The sweet enthusiast, from her sacred store,
Enlarged the former narrow bounds,
And added length to solemn sounds,
With nature's mother wit, and arts unknown before.
Let old Timotheus yield the prize,
Or both divide the crown;
He raised a mortal to the skies;
She drew an angel down.

GRAND CHORUS

At last, divine Cecilia came,
Inventress of the vocal frame;
The sweet enthusiast, from her sacred store,
Enlarged the former narrow bounds,
And added length to solemn sounds,
With nature's mother wit, and arts unknown before.
Let old Timotheus yield the prize,
Or both divide the crown;
He raised a mortal to the skies;
She drew an angel down.

[1] *I. e.*, organ.

PREFACE TO THE *FABLES*[1]
(1700)

'Tis with a Poet, as with a man who designs to build, and is very exact, as he supposes, in casting up the cost beforehand; but, generally speaking, he is mistaken in his account, and reckons short of the expense he first intended. He alters his mind as the work proceeds, and will have this or that convenience more, of which he had not thought when he began. So has it happened to me; I have built a house, where I intended but a lodge; yet with better success than a certain nobleman,[2] who, beginning with a dog-kennel, never lived to finish the palace he had contrived.

From translating the first of Homer's *Iliads* (which I intended as an essay to the whole work), I proceeded to the translation of the twelfth book of Ovid's *Metamorphoses*, because it contains, among other things, the causes, the beginning, and ending, of the Trojan war. Here I ought in reason to have stopped; but the speeches of Ajax and Ulysses lying next in my way, I could not balk 'em. When I had compassed them, I was so taken with the former part of the fifteenth book (which is the masterpiece of the whole *Metamorphoses*), that I enjoined myself the pleasing task of rendering it into English. And now I found, by the number of my verses, that they began to swell into a little volume; which gave me an occasion of looking backward on some beauties of my author, in his former books: there occurred to me the *Hunting of the Boar*, *Cinyras and Myrrha*, the good-natured story of *Baucis and Philemon*, with the rest, which I hope I have translated closely enough, and given them the same turn of verse which they had in the original; and this, I may say, without vanity, is not the talent of every poet. He who has arrived the nearest to it, is the ingenious and learned Sandys,[3] the best versifier of the former age; if I may properly call it by that name, which was the former part of this concluding century. For Spenser and Fairfax[4] both flourished in the reign of Queen Elizabeth; great masters in our language, and who saw much further into the beauties of our numbers than those who immediately followed them. Milton was the poetical son of Spenser, and Mr. Waller of Fairfax; for we have our lineal descents and clans as well as other families. Spenser more than once insinuates that the soul of Chaucer was transfused into his body;[5] and that he was begotten by him two hundred years after his decease. Milton has acknowledged to me, that Spenser was his original; and many besides myself have heard our famous Waller own that he derived the harmony of his numbers from *Godfrey of Bulloign*, which was turned into English by Mr. Fairfax.

But to return: having done with Ovid for this time, it came into my mind that our old English poet, Chaucer, in many things resembled him, and that with no disadvantage on the side of the modern author, as I shall endeavor to prove when I compare them; and as I am, and always have been, studious to promote the honor of my native country, so I soon resolved to put their merits to the trial, by turning some of the *Canterbury Tales* into our language, as it is now refined; for by this means, both the poets being set in the same light, and dressed in the same English habit, story to be compared with story, a certain judgment may be made betwixt them by the reader, without obtruding my opinion on him. Or, if I seem partial to my countryman and predecessor in the laurel, the friends of antiquity are not few; and, besides many of the learned, Ovid has almost all the beaux, and the whole fair sex, his declared patrons. Perhaps I have assumed somewhat more to myself than they allow me, because I have adventured to sum up the evidence; but the readers are the jury, and their privilege remains entire, to decide according to the merits of the cause; or, if they please, to bring it to another hearing

[1]Full title: *Fables Ancient and Modern; translated into verse, from Homer, Ovid, Boccace, and Chaucer; with Original Poems. The Preface*, "addressed to the Duke of Ormond, is a piece of work of which it is hard to speak except in some such terms as those which Dryden himself employs in it when he has to write about Chaucer. . . . [It] is more full of life than anything else in Dryden's prose; . . . while nothing, either in prose or verse, brings out more admirably or to better advantage the qualities of Dryden as the great English man of letters. For this is what he was, rather than essentially a poet; his genius is one that commands both vehicles of expression, it is not one that is specially inclined to verse; and the free movement of his mind and speech is scarcely less wonderful in a prose tract like this *Preface* than in the verse of *Absalom and Achitophel*." (W. P. Ker.)

[2]The Duke of Buckingham (Zimri in *Absalom and Achitophel*).

[3]George Sandys (1578–1644), who translated Ovid's *Metamorphoses*.

[4]Edward Fairfax (died 1635) published his translation of Tasso's *Godfrey of Bulloigne, or the Recovery of Jerusalem* in 1600.

[5]See *Faerie Queene*, Bk. IV, 2, 34.

before some other court. In the mean time, to follow the thread of my discourse (as thoughts, according to Mr. Hobbes,[1] have always some connection), so from Chaucer I was led to think on Boccaccio, who was not only his contemporary, but also pursued the same studies; wrote novels in prose, and many works in verse; particularly is said to have invented the octave rime, or stanza of eight lines, which ever since has been maintained by the practice of all Italian writers who are, or at least assume the title of, heroic poets. He and Chaucer, among other things, had this in common, that they refined their mother-tongues; but with this difference, that Dante had begun to file their language, at least in verse, before the time of Boccaccio, who likewise received no little help from his master Petrarch; but the reformation of their prose was wholly owing to Boccaccio himself, who is yet the standard of purity in the Italian tongue, though many of his phrases are become obsolete, as in process of time it must needs happen. Chaucer (as you have formerly been told by our learned Mr. Rymer[2]) first adorned and amplified our barren tongue from the Provençal, which was then the most polished of all the modern languages; but this subject has been copiously treated by that great critic, who deserves no little commendation from us his countrymen. For these reasons of time, and resemblance of genius, in Chaucer and Boccaccio, I resolved to join them in my present work; to which I have added some original papers of my own, which whether they are equal or inferior to my other poems, an author is the most improper judge; and therefore I leave them wholly to the mercy of the reader. I will hope the best, that they will not be condemned; but if they should, I have the excuse of an old gentleman, who, mounting on horseback before some ladies, when I was present, got up somewhat heavily, but desired of the fair spectators that they would count fourscore and eight before they judged him. By the mercy of God, I am already come within twenty years of his number; a cripple in my limbs, but what decays are in my mind the reader must determine. I think myself as vigorous as ever in the faculties of my soul, excepting only my memory, which is not impaired to any great degree; and if I lose not more of it, I have no great reason to complain. What judgment I had, increases rather than diminishes; and thoughts, such as they are, come crowding in so fast upon me that my only difficulty is to choose or to reject, to run them into verse, or to give them the other harmony of prose: I have so long studied and practiced both, that they are grown into a habit, and become familiar to me. In short, though I may lawfully plead some part of the old gentleman's excuse, yet I will reserve it till I think I have greater need, and ask no grains of allowance for the faults of this my present work, but those which are given of course to human frailty. I will not trouble my reader with the shortness of time in which I writ it, or the several intervals of sickness. They who think too well of their own performances are apt to boast in their prefaces how little time their works have cost them, and what other business of more importance interfered; but the reader will be as apt to ask the question, why they allowed not a longer time to make their works more perfect? and why they had so despicable an opinion of their judges as to thrust their indigested stuff upon them, as if they deserved no better?

With this account of my present undertaking, I conclude the first part of this discourse: in the second part, as at a second sitting, though I alter not the draft, I must touch the same features over again, and change the dead-coloring of the whole. In general I will only say, that I have written nothing which savors of immorality or profaneness; at least, I am not conscious to myself of any such intention. If there happen to be found an irreverent expression, or a thought too wanton, they are crept into my verses through my inadvertency; if the searchers find any in the cargo, let them be staved[3] or forfeited, like counterbanded goods; at least, let their au-

[1]Thomas Hobbes (1588–1679). The reference is to Pt. I, Chap. 3, of the *Leviathan.*

[2]Thomas Rymer (1641–1713), author of *The Tragedies of the Last Age* (1678) and of *A Short View of Tragedy* (1693). It is in the latter that Rymer puts forward his notion that Chaucer belongs to the "Provençal School": "They who attempted verse in English, down till Chaucer's time, made an heavy pudder, and are always miserably put to 't for a word to clink; which commonly fall so awkward and unexpectedly as dropping from the clouds by some machine or miracle. Chaucer found an Herculean labor on his hands; and did perform to admiration. He seizes all Provençal, French, and Latin that came in his way, gives them a new garb and livery, and mingles them amongst our English: turns out English, gouty or superannuated, to place in their room the foreigners fit for service, trained and accustomed to poetical discipline."

[3]Destroyed, as contraband hogsheads were, by breaking holes in them.

thors be answerable for them, as being but imported merchandise, and not of my own manufacture. On the other side, I have endeavored to choose such fables, both ancient and modern, as contain in each of them some instructive moral; which I could prove by induction, but the way is tedious, and they leap foremost into sight, without the reader's trouble of looking after them. I wish I could affirm, with a safe conscience, that I had taken the same care in all my former writings; for it must be owned, that supposing verses are never so beautiful or pleasing, yet, if they contain anything which shocks religion or good manners, they are at best what Horace says of good numbers without good sense, *Versus inopes rerum, nugæque canoræ.*[1] Thus far, I hope, I am right in court, without renouncing to my other right of self-defense, where I have been wrongfully accused, and my sense wire-drawn into blasphemy or bawdry, as it has often been by a religious lawyer,[2] in a late pleading against the stage; in which he mixes truth with falsehood, and has not forgotten the old rule of calumniating strongly, that something may remain.

I resume the thread of my discourse with the first of my translations, which was the first *Iliad* of Homer. If it shall please God to give me longer life, and moderate health, my intentions are to translate the whole *Ilias;* provided still that I meet with those encouragements from the public which may enable me to proceed in my undertaking with some cheerfulness. And this I dare assure the world beforehand, that I have found, by trial, Homer a more pleasing task than Virgil, though I say not the translation will be less laborious; for the Grecian is more according to my genius than the Latin poet. In the works of the two authors we may read their manners, and natural inclinations, which are wholly different. Virgil was of a quiet, sedate temper; Homer was violent, impetuous, and full of fire. The chief talent of Virgil was propriety of thoughts, and ornament of words: Homer was rapid in his thoughts, and took all the liberties, both of numbers and of expressions, which his language, and the age in which he lived, allowed him. Homer's invention was more copious, Virgil's more confined; so that if Homer had not led the way, it was not in Virgil to have begun heroic poetry; for nothing can be more evident than that the Roman poem is but the second part of the *Ilias;* a continuation of the same story, and the persons already formed. The manners of Æneas are those of Hector, superadded to those which Homer gave him. The adventures of Ulysses in the *Odysseis* are imitated in the first six books of Virgil's *Æneis;* and though the accidents are not the same (which would have argued him of a servile copying, and total barrenness of invention), yet the seas were the same in which both the heroes wandered; and Dido cannot be denied to be the poetical daughter of Calypso. The six latter books of Virgil's poem are the four-and-twenty *Iliads* contracted; a quarrel occasioned by a lady, a single combat, battles fought, and a town besieged. I say not this in derogation to Virgil, neither do I contradict anything which I have formerly said in his just praise; for his episodes are almost wholly of his own invention, and the form which he has given to the telling makes the tale his own, even though the original story had been the same. But this proves, however, that Homer taught Virgil to design; and if invention be the first virtue of an epic poet, then the Latin poem can only be allowed the second place. Mr. Hobbes, in the preface to his own bald translation of the *Ilias* (studying poetry as he did mathematics, when it was too late), Mr. Hobbes, I say, begins the praise of Homer where he should have ended it. He tells us that the first beauty of an epic poem consists in diction; that is, in the choice of words, and harmony of numbers. Now the words are the coloring of the work, which, in the order of nature, is last to be considered. The design, the disposition, the manners, and the thoughts, are all before it: where any of those are wanting or imperfect, so much wants or is imperfect in the imitation of human life, which is in the very definition of a poem. Words, indeed, like glaring colors, are the first beauties that arise and strike the sight; but, if the draft be false or lame, the figures ill disposed, the manners obscure or inconsistent, or the thoughts unnatural, then the finest colors are but daubing, and the piece is a beautiful monster at the best. Neither Virgil nor Homer were deficient in any of the former beauties; but in this

[1] Verses lacking substance, and melodious trumpery. (*De Arte Poetica,* 322.)

[2] Jeremy Collier (1650–1726), in his *Short View of the Immorality and Profaneness of the English Stage* (1698).

last, which is expression, the Roman poet is at least equal to the Grecian, as I have said elsewhere; supplying the poverty of his language by his musical ear, and by his diligence.

But to return: our two great poets being so different in their tempers, one choleric and sanguine, the other phlegmatic and melancholic; that which makes them excel in their several ways is, that each of them has followed his own natural inclination, as well in forming the design, as in the execution of it. The very heroes show their authors: Achilles is hot, impatient, revengeful—

Impiger, iracundus, inexorabilis, acer, etc.,[1]

Æneas patient, considerate, careful of his people, and merciful to his enemies; ever submissive to the will of heaven—

. . . *quo fata trahunt retrahuntque, sequamur.*[2]

I could please myself with enlarging on this subject, but am forced to defer it to a fitter time. From all I have said, I will only draw this inference, that the action of Homer, being more full of vigor than that of Virgil, according to the temper of the writer, is of consequence more pleasing to the reader. One warms you by degrees; the other sets you on fire all at once, and never intermits his heat. 'Tis the same difference which Longinus makes betwixt the effects of eloquence in Demosthenes and Tully;[3] one persuades, the other commands. You never cool while you read Homer, even not in the second book (a graceful flattery to his countrymen); but he hastens from the ships, and concludes not that book till he has made you an amends by the violent playing of a new machine.[4] From thence he hurries on his action with variety of events, and ends it in less compass than two months. This vehemence of his, I confess, is more suitable to my temper; and, therefore, I have translated his first book with greater pleasure than any part of Virgil; but it was not a pleasure without pains. The continual agitations of the spirits must needs be a weakening of any constitution, especially in age; and many pauses are required for refreshment betwixt the heats; the *Iliad* of itself being a third part longer than all Virgil's works together.

This is what I thought needful in this place to say of Homer. I proceed to Ovid and Chaucer, considering the former only in relation to the latter. With Ovid ended the golden age of the Roman tongue; from Chaucer the purity of the English tongue began. The manners of the poets were not unlike. Both of them were well-bred, well-natured, amorous, and libertine, at least in their writings; it may be, also in their lives. Their studies were the same, philosophy and philology.[5] Both of them were knowing in astronomy; of which Ovid's books of the *Roman Feasts*, and Chaucer's *Treatise of the Astrolabe*, are sufficient witnesses. But Chaucer was likewise an astrologer, as were Virgil, Horace, Persius, and Manilius. Both writ with wonderful facility and clearness; neither were great inventors: for Ovid only copied the Grecian fables, and most of Chaucer's stories were taken from his Italian contemporaries, or their predecessors. Boccaccio his *Decameron* was first published, and from thence our Englishman has borrowed many of his *Canterbury Tales*:[6] yet that of *Palamon and Arcite* was written, in all probability, by some Italian wit, in a former age, as I shall prove hereafter. The tale of *Griselda* was the invention of Petrarch; by him sent to Boccaccio,[7] from whom it came to Chaucer. *Troilus and Cressida* was also written by a Lombard author,[8] but much amplified by our English translator, as well as beautified; the genius of our countrymen, in general, being rather to improve an invention than to invent themselves, as is evident not only in our poetry, but in many of our manufactures. I find I have anticipated already, and taken up from Boccaccio before I come to him: but there is so much less behind; and I am of the temper of most kings, who love to be in debt, are all for present

[1]Impatient, fiery, ruthless, keen (Horace, *De Arte Poetica*, 121).

[2]Whither the Fates, in their ebb and flow, draw us, let us follow. (Virgil, *Æneid*, V, 709.)

[3]M. Tullius Cicero.

[4]This is a slip. The dream of Agamemnon (referred to at the end of the sentence) *precedes* the catalogue of the ships in Bk. II.

[5]The word here denotes all studies connected with literature.

[6]"In all probability, Chaucer was unacquainted with" the *Decameron*. (R. K. Root, *The Poetry of Chaucer*.)

[7]"What Petrarch sent to Boccaccio was a Latin version of Boccaccio's story of Griselda in the *Decameron*." (W. P. Ker.) Chaucer took the tale from Petrarch's version.

[8]The *Filostrato*, by Boccaccio, was Chaucer's immediate source. Dryden was misled by Chaucer's reference to one Lollius as his authority. This Lollius seems to be the *Maxime Lolli* of Horace's Second *Epistle* (Bk. I). Chaucer, probably, saw the first verse without its context, and mistakenly inferred that "Lollius was the name of a writer on the Trojan war." (Skeat.)

money, no matter how they pay it afterwards: besides, the nature of a preface is rambling, never wholly out of the way, nor in it. This I have learned from the practice of honest Montaigne, and return at my pleasure to Ovid and Chaucer, of whom I have little more to say.

Both of them built on the inventions of other men; yet since Chaucer had something of his own, as *The Wife of Bath's Tale*, *The Cock and the Fox*,[1] which I have translated, and some others, I may justly give our countryman the precedence in that part; since I can remember nothing of Ovid which was wholly his. Both of them understood the manners; under which name I comprehend the passions, and, in a larger sense, the descriptions of persons, and their very habits. For an example, I see Baucis and Philemon as perfectly before me, as if some ancient painter had drawn them; and all the Pilgrims in the *Canterbury Tales*, their humors, their features, and the very dress, as distinctly as if I had supped with them at the *Tabard* in Southwark. Yet even there, too, the figures of Chaucer are much more lively, and set in a better light; which though I have not time to prove, yet I appeal to the reader, and am sure he will clear me from partiality. The thoughts and words remain to be considered, in the comparison of the two poets, and I have saved myself one-half of the labor, by owning that Ovid lived when the Roman tongue was in its meridian; Chaucer, in the dawning of our language: therefore that part of the comparison stands not on an equal foot, any more than the diction of Ennius and Ovid, or of Chaucer and our present English. The words are given up, as a post not to be defended in our poet, because he wanted the modern art of fortifying. The thoughts remain to be considered; and they are to be measured only by their propriety; that is, as they flow more or less naturally from the persons described, on such and such occasions. The vulgar judges, which are nine parts in ten of all nations, who call conceits and jingles wit, who see Ovid full of them, and Chaucer altogether without them, will think me little less than mad for preferring the Englishman to the Roman. Yet, with their leave, I must presume to say that the things they admire are only glittering trifles, and so far from being witty, that in a serious poem they are nauseous, because they are unnatural. Would any man, who is ready to die for love, describe his passion like Narcissus? Would he think of *inopem me copia fecit*,[2] and a dozen more of such expressions, poured on the neck of one another, and signifying all the same thing? If this were wit, was this a time to be witty, when the poor wretch was in the agony of death? This is just John Littlewit, in *Bartholomew Fair*,[3] who had a conceit (as he tells you) left him in his misery; a miserable conceit. On these occasions the poet should endeavor to raise pity; but, instead of this, Ovid is tickling you to laugh. Virgil never made use of such machines when he was moving you to commiserate the death of Dido: he would not destroy what he was building. Chaucer makes Arcite violent in his love, and unjust in the pursuit of it; yet, when he came to die, he made him think more reasonably: he repents not of his love, for that had altered his character; but acknowledges the injustice of his proceedings, and resigns Emilia to Palamon. What would Ovid have done on this occasion? He would certainly have made Arcite witty on his deathbed; he had complained he was further off from possession, by being so near, and a thousand such boyisms, which Chaucer rejected as below the dignity of the subject. They who think otherwise, would, by the same reason, prefer Lucan and Ovid to Homer and Virgil, and Martial to all four of them. As for the turn of words, in which Ovid particularly excels all poets, they are sometimes a fault, and sometimes a beauty, as they are used properly or improperly; but in strong passions always to be shunned, because passions are serious, and will admit no playing. The French have a high value for them; and, I confess, they are often what they call delicate, when they are introduced with judgment; but Chaucer writ with more simplicity, and followed Nature more closely than to use them. I have thus far, to the best of my knowledge, been an upright judge betwixt the parties in competition, not meddling with the design nor the disposition of it; because the design

---

[1]Chaucer invented neither of these tales. Both contain traditional matter—though Chaucer's immediate sources remain still unknown, and are probably lost.

[2]My very riches have made me poor. (Ovid, *Metamorphoses*, III, 466.)

[3]By Ben Jonson. Dryden's memory betrays him, not as to Jonson's intention, but as to Littlewit's words.

was not their own; and in the disposing of it they were equal. It remains that I say somewhat of Chaucer in particular.

In the first place, as he is the father of English poetry, so I hold him in the same degree of veneration as the Grecians held Homer, or the Romans Virgil. He is a perpetual fountain of good sense; learned in all sciences; and, therefore, speaks properly on all subjects. As he knew what to say, so he knows also when to leave off; a continence which is practiced by few writers, and scarcely by any of the ancients, excepting Virgil and Horace. One of our late great poets[1] is sunk in his reputation, because he could never forgive any conceit which came in his way; but swept like a drag-net, great and small. There was plenty enough, but the dishes were ill sorted; whole pyramids of sweetmeats for boys and women, but little of solid meat for men. All this proceeded not from any want of knowledge, but of judgment. Neither did he want that in discerning the beauties and faults of other poets, but only indulged himself in the luxury of writing; and perhaps knew it was a fault, but hoped the reader would not find it. For this reason, though he must always be thought a great poet, he is no longer esteemed a good writer; and for ten impressions which his works have had in so many successive years, yet at present a hundred books are scarcely purchased once a twelvemonth; for, as my last Lord Rochester said, though somewhat profanely, "Not being of God, he could not stand."

Chaucer followed Nature everywhere, but was never so bold to go beyond her; and there is a great difference of being *poeta* and *nimis poeta*, if we may believe Catullus,[2] as much as betwixt a modest behavior and affectation. The verse of Chaucer, I confess, is not harmonious to us; but 'tis like the eloquence of one whom Tacitus commends, it was *auribus istius temporis accommodata*:[3] they who lived with him, and some time after him, thought it musical; and it continues so, even in our judgment, if compared with the numbers of Lidgate and Gower, his contemporaries: there is the rude sweetness of a Scotch tune in it, which is natural and pleasing, though not perfect. 'Tis true, I cannot go so far as he who published the last edition of him;[4] for he would make us believe the fault is in our ears, and that there were really ten syllables in a verse where we find but nine: but this opinion is not worth confuting; 'tis so gross and obvious an error, that common sense (which is a rule in everything but matters of Faith and Revelation) must convince the reader, that equality of numbers, in every verse which we call *heroic*, was either not known, or not always practiced, in Chaucer's age. It were an easy matter to produce some thousands of his verses, which are lame for want of half a foot, and sometimes a whole one, and which no pronunciation can make otherwise. We can only say, that he lived in the infancy of our poetry, and that nothing is brought to perfection at the first. We must be children before we grow men. There was an Ennius, and in process of time a Lucilius, and a Lucretius, before Virgil and Horace; even after Chaucer there was a Spenser, a Harrington,[5] a Fairfax, before Waller and Denham[6] were in being; and our numbers were in their nonage till these last appeared. I need say little of his parentage, life, and fortunes; they are to be found at large in all the editions of his works. He was employed abroad, and favored, by Edward the Third, Richard the Second, and Henry the Fourth, and was poet, as I suppose, to all three of them. In Richard's time, I doubt, he was a little dipped in the rebellion of the Commons; and being brother-in-law to John of Gaunt, it was no wonder if he followed the fortunes of that family; and was well with Henry the Fourth when he had deposed his predecessor. Neither is it to be admired, that Henry, who was a wise as well as a valiant prince, who claimed by succession, and was sensible that his title was not sound, but was rightfully in Mortimer, who had married the heir of York; it was not to be admired, I say, if that great politician should be pleased to have the greatest Wit of those times in his

[1] Abraham Cowley (1618–1667).

[2] Another slip. The man "too much a poet" is admonished by Martial, *Epigrams*, III, 44.

[3] Well suited to the taste of that time. (*De Oratoribus*, 21, where, however, Tacitus has *auribus judicum*, "to the taste of a law-court.')

[4] Thomas Speght, 1598. This edition was reprinted with additions in 1602, and again reprinted in 1687. As everybody now knows, Speght was right;—though it should be remembered in Dryden's favor that the text of Chaucer was very imperfectly printed in Speght's edition, and that the principles of Chaucerian pronunciation were unknown in the 17th century.

[5] Sir John Harington (1561–1612), whose translation of Ariosto's *Orlando Furicso* was published in 1591.

[6] Sir John Denham (1618–1669).

interests, and to be the trumpet of his praises. Augustus had given him the example, by the advice of Mæcenas, who recommended Virgil and Horace to him; whose praises helped to make him popular while he was alive, and after his death have made him precious to posterity. As for the religion of our poet, he seems to have some little bias towards the opinions of Wyclif, after John of Gaunt his patron; somewhat of which appears in the tale of *Piers Plowman*:[1] yet I cannot blame him for inveighing so sharply against the vices of the clergy in his age: their pride, their ambition, their pomp, their avarice, their worldly interest, deserved the lashes which he gave them, both in that, and in most of his *Canterbury Tales.* Neither has his contemporary Boccaccio spared them: yet both those poets lived in much esteem with good and holy men in orders; for the scandal which is given by particular priests reflects not on the sacred function. Chaucer's Monk, his Canon, and his Friar, took not from the character of his Good Parson. A satirical poet is the check of the laymen on bad priests. We are only to take care, that we involve not the innocent with the guilty in the same condemnation. The good cannot be too much honored, nor the bad too coarsely used; for the corruption of the best becomes the worst. When a clergyman is whipped, his gown is first taken off, by which the dignity of his order is secured. If he be wrongfully accused, he has his action of slander; and 'tis at the poet's peril if he transgress the law. But they will tell us that all kind of satire, though never so well deserved by particular priests, yet brings the whole order into contempt. Is then the peerage of England anything dishonored when a peer suffers for his treason? If he be libeled, or any way defamed, he has his *scandalum magnatum*[2] to punish the offender. They who use this kind of argument, seem to be conscious to themselves of somewhat which has deserved the poet's lash, and are less concerned for their public capacity than for their private; at least there is pride at the bottom of their reasoning. If the faults of men in orders are only to be judged among themselves, they are all in some sort parties; for, since they say the honor of their order is concerned in every member of it, how can we be sure that they will be impartial judges? How far I may be allowed to speak my opinion in this case, I know not; but I am sure a dispute of this nature caused mischief in abundance betwixt a King of England and an Archbishop of Canterbury;[3] one standing up for the laws of his land, and the other for the honor (as he called it) of God's Church; which ended in the murder of the prelate, and in the whipping of his Majesty from post to pillar for his penance. The learned and ingenious Dr. Drake[4] has saved me the labor of inquiring into the esteem and reverence which the priests have had of old; and I would rather extend than diminish any part of it: yet I must needs say that when a priest provokes me without any occasion given him, I have no reason, unless it be the charity of a Christian, to forgive him: *prior læsit*[5] is justification sufficient in the civil law. If I answer him in his own language, self-defense I am sure must be allowed me; and if I carry it further, even to a sharp recrimination, somewhat may be indulged to human frailty. Yet my resentment has not wrought so far but that I have followed Chaucer, in his character of a holy man, and have enlarged on that subject with some pleasure; reserving to myself the right, if I shall think fit hereafter, to describe another sort of priests, such as are more easily to be found than the Good Parson; such as have given the last blow to Christianity in this age, by a practice so contrary to their doctrine. But this will keep cold till another time. In the meanwhile, I take up Chaucer where I left him.

He must have been a man of a most wonderful comprehensive nature, because, as it has been truly observed of him, he has taken into the compass of his *Canterbury Tales* the various manners and humors (as we now call them) of the whole English nation, in his age. Not a single character has escaped him. All his pilgrims are severally distinguished from each other; and not only in their inclinations, but in their very physiognomies and persons. Baptista Porta[6] could not have described their natures better than by the marks which the

[1]That is, the *Plowman's Tale*, which Dryden found in Speght's edition. It was not, however, written by Chaucer, but by the unknown author of the *Plowman's Creed*.

[2]The offense of defaming magnates of the realm.

[3]Henry II and Thomas à Becket.

[4]James Drake (1667–1707) wrote an answer to Jeremy Collier, *The Ancient and Modern Stages Reviewed*, 1699.

[5]He gave the provocation. (Terence, *Eunuchus*, Prologue 6.)

[6]A famous Italian physiognomist, born 1538, died 1615.

poet gives them. The matter and manner of their tales, and of their telling, are so suited to their different educations, humors, and callings, that each of them would be improper in any other mouth. Even the grave and serious characters are distinguished by their several sorts of gravity: their discourses are such as belong to their age, their calling, and their breeding; such as are becoming of them, and of them only. Some of his persons are vicious, and some virtuous; some are unlearned, or (as Chaucer calls them) lewd, and some are learned. Even the ribaldry of the low characters is different: the Reeve, the Miller, and the Cook, are several men, and distinguished from each other as much as the mincing Lady-Prioress and the broad-speaking, gap-toothed Wife of Bath. But enough of this; there is such a variety of game springing up before me that I am distracted in my choice, and know not which to follow. 'Tis sufficient to say, according to the proverb, that "Here is God's plenty." We have our forefathers and great-grand-dames all before us, as they were in Chaucer's days: their general characters are still remaining in mankind, and even in England, though they are called by other names than those of Monks, and Friars, and Canons, and Lady Abbesses, and Nuns; for mankind is ever the same, and nothing lost out of Nature, though everything is altered. May I have leave to do myself the justice (since my enemies will do me none, and are so far from granting me to be a good poet, that they will not allow me so much as to be a Christian, or a moral man), may I have leave, I say, to inform my reader, that I have confined my choice to such tales of Chaucer as savor nothing of immodesty. If I had desired more to please than to instruct, the Reeve, the Miller, the Shipman, the Merchant, the Sumner, and, above all, the Wife of Bath, in the *Prologue* to her *Tale*, would have procured me as many friends and readers as there are beaux and ladies of pleasure in the town. But I will no more offend against good manners: I am sensible as I ought to be of the scandal I have given by my loose writings; and make what reparation I am able, by this public acknowledgment. If anything of this nature, or of profaneness, be crept into these poems, I am so far from defending it, that I disown it. *Totum hoc indictum volo.*[1] Chaucer makes another manner of apology for his broad speaking, and Boccaccio makes the like; but I will follow neither of them. Our countryman, in the end of his Characters, before the *Canterbury Tales*, thus excuses the ribaldry, which is very gross in many of his novels:—

But firste, I pray you, of your courtesy,
That ye ne arrete it not my vil any,
Though that I plainly speak in this mattere,
To tellen you her words, and eke her chere:
Ne though I speak her words properly,
For this ye knowen as well as I,
Who shall tellen a tale after a man,
He mote rehearse as nye as ever he can:
Everich word of it ben in his charge,
All speke he, never so rudely, ne large:
Or else he mote tellen his tale untrue,
Or feine things, or find words new:
He may not spare, altho he were his brother,
He mote as wel say o word as another.
Crist spake himself ful broad in holy Writ,
And well I wote no villany is it,
Eke Plato saith, who so can him rede,
The words mote been cousin to the dede.

Yet if a man should have inquired of Boccaccio or of Chaucer, what need they had of introducing such characters, where obscene words were proper in their mouths, but very indecent to be heard; I know not what answer they could have made; for that reason, such tales shall be left untold by me. You have here a specimen of Chaucer's language, which is so obsolete, that his sense is scarce to be understood; and you have likewise more than one example of his unequal numbers, which were mentioned before. Yet many of his verses consist of ten syllables, and the words not much behind our present English: as for example, these two lines, in the description of the Carpenter's young wife:—

Wincing she was, as is a jolly colt,
Long as a mast, and upright as a bolt.[2]

I have almost done with Chaucer, when I have answered some objections relating to my present work. I find some people are offended that I have turned these tales into modern English; because they think them unworthy of my pains, and look on Chaucer as a dry, old-fashioned wit, not worth reviving. I have often heard the late Earl of Leicester say, that Mr. Cowley himself was of that opinion; who,

[1] I wish this wholly unsaid.

[2] *The Miller's Tale*, ll. 77–78.

having read him over at my Lord's request, declared he had no taste of him. I dare not advance my opinion against the judgment of so great an author; but I think it fair, however, to leave the decision to the public. Mr. Cowley was too modest to set up for a dictator; and being shocked perhaps with his old style, never examined into the depth of his good sense. Chaucer, I confess, is a rough diamond, and must first be polished, ere he shines. I deny not likewise, that, living in our early days of poetry, he writes not always of a piece; but sometimes mingles trivial things with those of greater moment. Sometimes also, though not often, he runs riot, like Ovid, and knows not when he has said enough. But there are more great wits besides Chaucer, whose fault is their excess of conceits, and those ill sorted. An author is not to write all he can, but only all he ought. Having observed this redundancy in Chaucer (as it is an easy matter for a man of ordinary parts to find a fault in one of greater), I have not tied myself to a literal translation; but have often omitted what I judged unnecessary, or not of dignity enough to appear in the company of better thoughts. I have presumed further, in some places, and added somewhat of my own where I thought my author was deficient, and had not given his thoughts their true luster, for want of words in the beginning of our language. And to this I was the more emboldened, because (if I may be permitted to say it of myself) I found I had a soul congenial to his, and that I had been conversant in the same studies. Another poet, in another age, may take the same liberty with my writings; if at least they live long enough to deserve correction. It was also necessary sometimes to restore the sense of Chaucer, which was lost or mangled in the errors of the press. Let this example suffice at present: in the story of *Palamon and Arcite*, where the temple of Diana is described, you find these verses in all the editions of our author:—

There saw I Danè turned unto a tree,
I mean not the goddess Diane,
But Venus daughter, which that hight Danè[1]

Which, after a little consideration, I knew was to be reformed into this sense, that Daphne, the daughter of Peneus, was turned into a tree. I durst not make thus bold with Ovid, lest some future Milbourne[2] should arise, and say, I varied from my author, because I understood him not.

But there are other judges, who think I ought not to have translated Chaucer into English, out of a quite contrary notion: they suppose there is a certain veneration due to his old language; and that it is little less than profanation and sacrilege to alter it. They are farther of opinion, that somewhat of his good sense will suffer in this transfusion, and much of the beauty of his thoughts will infallibly be lost, which appear with more grace in their old habit. Of this opinion was that excellent person, whom I mentioned, the late Earl of Leicester, who valued Chaucer as much as Mr. Cowley despised him. My Lord dissuaded me from this attempt (for I was thinking of it some years before his death), and his authority prevailed so far with me as to defer my undertaking while he lived, in deference to him; yet my reason was not convinced with what he urged against it. If the first end of a writer be to be understood, then, as his language grows obsolete, his thoughts must grow obscure:—

Multa renascentur, quæ nunc cecidere; cadentque
Quæ nunc sunt in honore vocabula, si volet usus,
Quem penes arbitrium est et jus et norma loquendi.[3]

When an ancient word, for its sound and significancy, deserves to be revived, I have that reasonable veneration for antiquity to restore it. All beyond this is superstition. Words are not like landmarks, so sacred as never to be removed; customs are changed, and even statutes are silently repealed, when the reason ceases for which they were enacted. As for the other part of the argument, that his thoughts will lose of their original beauty by the innovation of words; in the first place, not only their beauty, but their being is lost, where they are no longer understood, which is the present case. I grant that something must be lost in all transfusion, that is, in all translations; but the sense will remain, which would otherwise be lost, or at least be maimed,

[1]*The Knight's Tale*, ll. 1204–1206.

[2]Luke Milbourne (1649–1720), author of *Notes on Dryden's Virgil*, 1698.

[3]. . . Words long faded may again revive,
And words may fade now blooming and alive,
If usage wills it so, to whom belongs
The rule, the law, the government of tongues.
(Horace, *De Arte Poetica*, ll. 70–72. Conington's translation. In the first line *nunc* should be *jam*.)

when it is scarce intelligible, and that but to a few. How few are there, who can read Chaucer, so as to understand him perfectly? And if imperfectly, then with less profit, and no pleasure. It is not for the use of some old Saxon friends[1] that I have taken these pains with him: let them neglect my version, because they have no need of it. I made it for their sakes who understand sense and poetry as well as they, when that poetry and sense is put into words which they understand. I will go farther, and dare to add, that what beauties I lose in some places, I give to others which had them not originally: but in this I may be partial to myself; let the reader judge, and I submit to his decision. Yet I think I have just occasion to complain of them who, because they understand Chaucer, would deprive the greater part of their countrymen of the same advantage, and hoard him up, as misers do their grandam gold, only to look on it themselves, and hinder others from making use of it. In sum, I seriously protest that no man ever had, or can have, a greater veneration for Chaucer than myself. I have translated some part of his works, only that I might perpetuate his memory, or at least refresh it, amongst my countrymen. If I have altered him anywhere for the better, I must at the same time acknowledge that I could have done nothing without him. *Facile est inventis addere*[2] is no great commendation; and I am not so vain to think I have deserved a greater. I will conclude what I have to say of him singly, with this one remark: A lady of my acquaintance, who keeps a kind of correspondence with some authors of the fair sex in France, has been informed by them, that Mademoiselle de Scudery,[3] who is as old as Sibyl, and inspired like her by the same God of Poetry, is at this time translating Chaucer into modern French. From which I gather that he has been formerly translated into the old Provençal;[4] for how she should come to understand old English, I know not. But the matter of fact being true, it makes me think that there is something in it like fatality; that, after certain periods of time, the fame and memory of great wits should be renewed, as Chaucer is both in France and England. If this be wholly chance, 'tis extraordinary; and I dare not call it more, for fear of being taxed with superstition.

Boccaccio comes last to be considered, who, living in the same age with Chaucer, had the same genius, and followed the same studies. Both writ novels, and each of them cultivated his mother-tongue. But the greatest resemblance of our two modern authors being in their familiar style, and pleasing way of relating comical adventures, I may pass it over, because I have translated nothing from Boccaccio of that nature. In the serious part of poetry, the advantage is wholly on Chaucer's side; for though the Englishman has borrowed many tales from the Italian, yet it appears that those of Boccaccio were not generally of his own making, but taken from authors of former ages, and by him only modeled; so that what there was of invention, in either of them, may be judged equal. But Chaucer has refined on Boccaccio, and has mended the stories which he has borrowed, in his way of telling; though prose allows more liberty of thought, and the expression is more easy when unconfined by numbers. Our countryman carries weight, and yet wins the race at disadvantage. I desire not the reader should take my word; and, therefore, I will set two of their discourses, on the same subject, in the same light, for every man to judge betwixt them. I translated Chaucer first, and, amongst the rest, pitched on *The Wife of Bath's Tale;* not daring, as I have said, to adventure on her *Prologue*, because 'tis too licentious. There Chaucer introduces an old woman, of mean parentage, whom a youthful knight, of noble blood, was forced to marry, and consequently loathed her. The crone being in bed with him on the wedding-night, and finding his aversion, endeavors to win his affection by reason, and speaks a good word for herself (as who could blame her?), in hope to mollify the sullen bridegroom. She takes her topics from the benefits of poverty, the advantages of old age and ugliness, the vanity of youth, and the silly pride of ancestry and titles, without inherent virtue, which is the true nobility. When I had closed Chaucer, I returned to Ovid, and translated some more

---

[1]That is, friends acquainted with very early English, the study of which was making progress at this time, through the industry of several antiquaries.

[2]It is easy to make additions to inventions.

[3]Madeleine de Scudéry (1607–1701), poet and author of huge romances (*Artamenes, Clelia, Cleopatra*) which live now only in the histories.

[4]Here, as earlier in the *Preface*, Dryden supposes Provençal to be identical with early French.

of his fables; and, by this time, had so far forgotten *The Wife of Bath's Tale* that, when I took up Boccaccio, unawares I fell on the same argument, of preferring virtue to nobility of blood and titles, in the story of *Sigismonda*; which I had certainly avoided, for the resemblance of the two discourses, if my memory had not failed me. Let the reader weigh them both; and, if he thinks me partial to Chaucer, 'tis in him to right Boccaccio.

I prefer, in our countryman, far above all his other stories, the noble poem of *Palamon and Arcite*, which is of the epic kind, and perhaps not much inferior to the *Ilias*, or the *Æneis*. The story is more pleasing than either of them, the manners as perfect, the diction as poetical, the learning as deep and various, and the disposition full as artful: only it includes a greater length of time, as taking up seven years at least; but Aristotle has left undecided the duration of the action; which yet is easily reduced into the compass of a year, by a narration of what preceded the return of Palamon to Athens. I had thought, for the honor of our narration, and more particularly for his, whose laurel, though unworthy, I have worn after him, that this story was of English growth, and Chaucer's own: but I was undeceived by Boccaccio; for, casually looking on the end of his seventh *Giornata*,[1] I found Dioneo (under which name he shadows himself), and Fiametta (who represents his mistress, the natural daughter of Robert, King of Naples), of whom these words are spoken: *Dioneo e Fiametta gran pezza cantarono insieme d'Arcita, e di Palemone*;[2] by which it appears that this story was written before the time of Boccaccio; but the name of its author being wholly lost, Chaucer is now become an original; and I question not but the poem has received many beauties, by passing through his noble hands. Besides this tale, there is another of his own invention, after the manner of the Provençals, called *The Flower and the Leaf*,[3] with which I was so particularly pleased, both for the invention and the moral, that I cannot hinder myself from recommending it to the reader.

As a corollary to this preface, in which I have done justice to others, I owe somewhat to myself; not that I think it worth my time to enter the lists with one M——, and one B——,[4] but barely to take notice that such men there are, who have written scurrilously against me, without any provocation. M——, who is in orders, pretends, amongst the rest, this quarrel to me, that I have fallen foul on priesthood: if I have, I am only to ask pardon of good priests, and am afraid his part of the reparation will come to little. Let him be satisfied, that he shall not be able to force himself upon me for an adversary. I contemn him too much to enter into competition with him. His own translations of Virgil have answered his criticisms on mine. If (as they say, he has declared in print), he prefers the version of Ogilby to mine, the world has made him the same compliment; for 'tis agreed, on all hands, that he writes even below Ogilby. That, you will say, is not easily to be done; but what cannot M—— bring about? I am satisfied, however, that, while he and I live together, I shall not be thought the worst poet of the age. It looks as if I had desired him underhand to write so ill against me; but upon my honest word I have not bribed him to do me this service, and am wholly guiltless of his pamphlet. 'Tis true, I should be glad if I could persuade him to continue his good offices, and write such another critique on anything of mine; for I find, by experience, he has a great stroke with the reader, when he condemns any of my poems, to make the world have a better opinion of them. He has taken some pains with my poetry; but nobody will be persuaded to take the same with his. If I had taken to the Church, as he affirms, but which was never in my thoughts, I should have had more sense, if not more grace, than to have turned myself out of my benefice, by writing libels on my parishioners. But his account of my manners and my principles are of a piece with his cavils and his poetry; and so I have done with him for ever.

As for the City Bard, or Knight Physician, I hear his quarrel to me is, that I was the author of *Absalom and Achitophel*, which, he thinks, is a little hard on his fanatic patrons in London.

But I will deal the more civilly with his two

[1] Day (in the *Decameron*).

[2] Dioneo and Fiammetta sang together a great while of Arcite and Palamon. (Dryden did not know Boccaccio's *Teseide*, the immediate source of *The Knight's Tale*.)

[3] It has now been shown that Chaucer did not write this.

[4] Milbourne; and Sir Richard Blackmore (died 1729), author of *Prince Arthur* (1695), *King Arthur* (1697), and other poetical pieces.

poems, because nothing ill is to be spoken of the dead; and therefore peace be to the *Manes* of his *Arthurs*. I will only say that it was not for this noble Knight that I drew the plan of an epic poem on King Arthur, in my preface to the translation of Juvenal. The Guardian Angels of kingdoms were machines too ponderous for him to manage; and therefore he rejected them, as Dares did the whirl-bats of Eryx when they were thrown before him by Entellus:[1] yet from that preface, he plainly took his hint; for he began immediately upon the story, though he had the baseness not to acknowledge his benefactor, but instead of it, to traduce me in a libel.

I shall say the less of Mr. Collier, because in many things he has taxed me justly; and I have pleaded guilty to all thoughts and expressions of mine, which can be truly argued of obscenity, profaneness, or immorality, and retract them. If he be my enemy, let him triumph; if he be my friend, as I have given him no personal occasion to be otherwise, he will be glad of my repentance. It becomes me not to draw my pen in the defense of a bad cause, when I have so often drawn it for a good one. Yet it were not difficult to prove that in many places he has perverted my meaning by his glosses, and interpreted my words into blasphemy and bawdry, of which they were not guilty. Besides that, he is too much given to horse-play in his raillery, and comes to battle like a dictator from the plow. I will not say, "The zeal of God's house has eaten him up"; but I am sure it has devoured some part of his good manners and civility. It might also be doubted, whether it were altogether zeal which prompted him to this rough manner of proceeding; perhaps, it became not one of his function to rake into the rubbish of ancient and modern plays: a divine might have employed his pains to better purpose, than in the nastiness of Plautus and Aristophanes, whose examples, as they excuse not me, so it might be possibly supposed that he read them not without some pleasure. They who have written commentaries on those poets, or on Horace, Juvenal, and Martial, have explained some vices, which, without their interpretation, had been unknown to modern times. Neither has he judged impartially betwixt the former age and us. There is more bawdry in one play of Fletcher's, called *The Custom of the Country*, than in all ours together. Yet this has been often acted on the stage, in my remembrance. Are the times so much more reformed now, than they were five-and-twenty years ago? If they are, I congratulate the amendment of our morals. But I am not to prejudice the cause of my fellow poets, though I abandon my own defense: they have some of them answered for themselves; and neither they nor I can think Mr. Collier so formidable an enemy that we should shun him. He has lost ground, at the latter end of the day, by pursuing his point too far, like the Prince of Condé, at the battle of Senneph:[2] from immoral plays to no plays, *ab abusu ad usum, non valet consequentia*.[3] But, being a party, I am not to erect myself into a judge. As for the rest of those who have written against me, they are such scoundrels, that they deserve not the least notice to be taken of them. B—— and M—— are only distinguished from the crowd by being remembered to their infamy:—

> . . . *Demetri, teque, Tigelli,*
> *Discipulorum inter jubeo plorare cathedras*.[4]

[1]See *Æneid*, V, 400.

[2]At this battle (11 August, 1674) Condé attacked the rearguard of the Prince of Orange, then in retreat between Charleroi and Mons.

[3]The argument from abuse against use is weak.

[4]Demetrius, and you, Tigellius, go weep amidst your pupils' chairs. (Horace, *Satires*, I, x, 90–91. Horace has ***discipularum***.)

WILLIAM CONGREVE (1670–1729)

Congreve came of an old and well-connected Staffordshire family, but was born at Bardsey, near Leeds. He was baptized on 10 February, 1670. Soon thereafter his father, an officer in the army, was sent to Ireland to command the garrison at Youghal. He later removed to Lismore. Congreve "received the first tincture of letters at the great school of Kilkenny." "While at school he gave several instances of his genius for poetry; but the most peculiar one was a very pretty copy of verses which he made upon the death of his master's magpie." Here, perhaps, he made the acquaintance of Swift; certainly, at any rate, the two knew each other at Trinity College, Dublin, to which Congreve was admitted on 5 April, 1685. Probably towards the close of 1688, as a consequence of the Revolution, Congreve, like Swift, went over to England. In March, 1691, he was admitted to the Middle Temple. If he had any real intention of studying the law, he soon abandoned it for literature, and early in 1692 published *Incognita, or Love and Duty Reconciled.* This is a tale, of the type "best exemplified by the work of Aphra Behn," though "in its expression and atmosphere it undoubtedly is derived from" Dryden's comedy, *The Assignation, or Love in a Nunnery* (Montague Summers). It shows distinctly the dramatic bent of its young author. In the same year Congreve published several poems, two of which (one a translation of Juvenal's *Eleventh Satire*) signalized his friendship with Dryden. *The Old Bachelor*, his first play, was performed in January, 1693 (published in the same year), and was enthusiastically received. Dryden, we are told, declared that "he never saw such a first play in his life." *The Double Dealer* was acted in November, 1693 (published in December, but dated 1694), and some were at first shocked, but its success was assured after Queen Mary came to see it. *Love for Love* was performed (and published) in April, 1695. *The Mourning Bride*, Congreve's only tragedy, was acted early in 1697 (published in March), was universally liked, and long held the stage; though since the close of the eighteenth century few have given it high praise. Dr. Johnson extravagantly maintained that if he were "required to select from the whole mass of English poetry the most poetical paragraph," it would be Almeria's description of the cathedral, near the beginning of Act II.

In March, 1698, Jeremy Collier, a non-juring clergyman and an able writer, published his *Short View of the Immorality and Profaneness of the English Stage, together with the Sense of Antiquity upon this Argument*, in which Congreve, together with practically every other contemporary dramatist, was vigorously attacked. The book made a deep impression; it was in large part, as Dryden acknowledged, unanswerable; and it deserves much of the praise which Macaulay gave it in the nineteenth century. It called forth a number of replies, among them Congreve's ill-considered and not very successful *Amendments of Mr. Collier's False and Imperfect Citations* (1698). Collier persisted, answering Congreve and others, and before he was through lost his temper, grossly abused his opponents, and went far to justify the bad reputation he has had with posterity. But meanwhile the man had a pronounced influence in reforming the stage, and there can be no doubt that Congreve felt the blow. His next and last and best play, *The Way of the World*, was acted (and published) in 1700, when it was comparatively a failure. It "is the best-written, the most dazzling, the most intellectually accomplished of all English comedies, perhaps of all the comedies of the world. But it has the defects of the very qualities which make it so brilliant. . . . In no play of Congreve's is the literature so consummate, in none is the human interest in movement and surprise so utterly neglected, as in *The Way of the World*. . . . We have slow, elaborate dialogue, spread out like some beautiful endless tapestry, and no action whatever. . . . With an experienced audience, prepared for an intellectual pleasure, the wit . . . would no doubt encourage a cultivation of patience through less lively portions of the play, but to spectators coming perfectly fresh to the piece, and expecting rattle and movement, this series of still-life pictures may easily be conceived to be exasperating, especially as the satire contained in them was exceedingly sharp and direct." (E. Gosse, *Congreve.*)

After this experience of the limitations and fickleness of his theatrical public, Congreve wrote nothing of great importance. Some connection with the play-houses he maintained until after 1705; he aided in the translation of a farce by Molière; he composed two stage-pieces for music; he joined in the management of a new theater; but he wrote no more comedies, and very little else. After the death of Dryden he was generally proclaimed the leading man of letters of the time; he was universally liked; he was welcome in the noblest houses, and counted Swift, Pope, Gay, Steele, Addison, Vanbrugh—indeed nearly every writer of the early eighteenth century—among his friends. He was in easy circumstances, and became through legacies, gifts, and sinecures in the latter part of his life a wealthy man. He never married, but was not lonely. The accomplished and lovely Mrs. Bracegirdle, an actress who had a leading part in each of his plays, was devoted to him; and in his elder time the second Duchess of Marlborough became virtually his slave. It is related that after his death she expended a large portion of the £10,000 he left her upon a splendid diamond necklace, and with the remainder had made in his likeness a wax, or perhaps ivory, figure, which she dressed in his clothes, and kept near her, and talked to, and offered food, and caused to be attended by a physician. Whether the tale be wholly true or not, the slavery of the Duchess was patent to contemporaries, and aids one—with the other circumstances mentioned above—to understand how her master, who was, besides, a socially-inclined, good-humored man of pleasure, should easily have sunk into a life of idleness. There was, moreover, an added reason for Congreve's idleness, which has not always been taken sufficiently into account. Swift said Congreve "had the misfortune to squander away a very good constitution in his younger days"; and, whatever the basis of that statement, in fact we hear of him enduring "a fit of sickness" from which he made a slow recovery when he was scarcely more than twenty, of his being attacked by gout when he was only twenty-five, and of his being constantly subject to that disease, with recurrent attacks of great severity, from his thirtieth year on. Nor was this all; in October, 1710, Swift wrote to Stella: "I was to-day to see Mr. Congreve, who is almost blind with cataracts growing on his eyes; and his case is, that he must wait two or three years, until the cataracts are riper, and till he is quite blind, and then he must have them couched; and besides he is never rid of the gout, yet he looks young and fresh, and is as cheerful as ever. He is younger by three years or more than I, and I am twenty years younger than he. He gave me a pain in the great toe, by mentioning the gout."

Congreve preserved his good humor until the end, though his infirmities might well have daunted a stronger man, and though they may have had their share in causing him to think slightingly of his early compositions. In 1726 Voltaire came to see him, and after Congreve's death (on 19 January, 1729) wrote: "The late Mr. Congreve raised the glory of comedy to a greater height than any English writer before or since his time. He wrote only a few plays, but they are all excellent in their kind. The laws of the drama are strictly observed in them; they abound with characters all which are shadowed with the utmost delicacy, and we don't meet with so much as one low or coarse jest. The language is everywhere that of men of honor, but their actions are those of knaves; a proof that he was perfectly well acquainted with human nature, and frequented what we call polite company. He was infirm, and come to the verge of life when I knew him. Mr. Congreve had one defect, which was, his entertaining too mean an idea of his first profession (that of a writer), though 'twas to this he owed his fame and fortune. He spoke of his works as of trifles that were beneath him; and hinted to me in our first conversation that I should visit him upon no other foot than that of a gentleman who led a life of plainness and simplicity. I answered that had he been so unfortunate as to be a mere gentleman I should never have ome to see him; and I was very much disgusted at so unseasonable a piece of vanity." It is not altogether surprising that the world should generally have credited Voltaire's discovery of vanity where, in truth, there was a composed and unembittered disillusionment conducive to modesty and, perhaps, to wisdom.

THE WAY OF THE WORLD

A COMEDY (1700)

To the Right Honorable Ralph, Earl of Montague, etc.

My Lord,

Whether the world will arraign me of vanity or not, that I have presumed to dedicate this comedy to your Lordship, I am yet in doubt; though, it may be, it is some degree of vanity even to doubt of it. One who has at any time had the honor of your Lordship's conversation, cannot be supposed to think very meanly of that which he would prefer to your perusal; yet it were to incur the imputation of too much sufficiency, to pretend to such a merit as might abide the test of your Lordship's censure.

Whatever value may be wanting to this play while yet it is mine, will be sufficiently made up to it when it is once become your Lordship's; and it is my security that I cannot have overrated it more by my dedication, than your Lordship will dignify it by your patronage.

That it succeeded on the stage, was almost beyond my expectation; for but little of it was prepared for that general taste which seems now to be predominant in the palates of our audience.

Those characters which are meant to be ridiculous in most of our comedies, are of fools so gross, that, in my humble opinion, they should rather disturb than divert the well-natured and reflecting part of an audience; they are rather objects of charity than contempt; and instead of moving our mirth, they ought very often to excite our compassion.

This reflection moved me to design some characters which should appear ridiculous, not so much through a natural folly (which is incorrigible, and therefore not proper for the stage) as through an affected wit; a wit which at the same time that it is affected, is also false. As there is some difficulty in the formation of a character of this nature, so there is some hazard which attends the progress of its success upon the stage; for many come to a play so overcharged with criticism, that they very often let fly their censure, when through their rashness they have mistaken their aim. This I had occasion lately to observe; for this play had been acted two or three days before some of these hasty judges could find the leisure to distinguish betwixt the character of a Witwoud and a Truewit.

I must beg your Lordship's pardon for this digression from the true course of this epistle; but that it may not seem altogether impertinent, I beg that I may plead the occasion of it, in part of that excuse of which I stand in need, for recommending this comedy to your protection. It is only by the countenance of your Lordship and the *few* so qualified, that such who write with care and pains can hope to be distinguished; for the prostituted name of *poet* promiscuously levels all that bear it.

Terence, the most correct writer in the world, had a Scipio and a Lælius, if not to assist him, at least to support him in his reputation; and notwithstanding his extraordinary merit, it may be their countenance was not more than necessary.

The purity of his style, the delicacy of his turns, and the justness of his characters, were all of them beauties which the greater part of his audience were incapable of tasting; some of the coarsest strokes of Plautus, so severely censured by Horace, were more likely to affect the multitude—such who come with expectation to laugh at the last act of a play, and are better entertained with two or three unseasonable jests, than with the artful solution of the *fable*.

As Terence excelled in his performances, so had he great advantages to encourage his undertakings; for he built most on the foundations of Menander; his plots were generally modeled, and his characters ready drawn to his hand. He copied Menander, and Menander had no less light in the formation of his characters, from the observations of Theophrastus, of whom he was a disciple; and Theophrastus, it is known, was not only the disciple, but the immediate successor, of Aristotle, the first and greatest judge of poetry. These were great models to design by; and the further advantage which Terence possessed, towards giving his plays the due ornaments of purity of style and justness of manners, was not less considerable, from the freedom of conversation which was permitted him with Lælius and Scipio, two of the greatest and most polite men of his age. And indeed the privilege of such a conversation is the only certain means of attaining to the perfection of dialogue.

If it has happened in any part of this comedy that I have gained a turn of style or expression more correct, or at least, more corrigible, than in those which I have formerly written, I must, with equal pride and gratitude, ascribe it to the honor of your Lordship's admitting me into your conversation, and that of a society where everybody else was so well worthy of you, in your retirement last summer from the town; for it was immediately after that this comedy was written. If I have failed in my performance, it is only to be regretted, where there were so many not inferior either to a Scipio or a Lælius, that there should be one wanting equal in capacity to a Terence.

If I am not mistaken, poetry is almost the only art which has not yet laid claim to your Lordship's patronage. Architecture and painting, to the great honor of our country, have flourished under your influence and protection. In the meantime, poetry, the eldest sister of all arts, and parent of most, seems to have resigned her birthright, by having neglected to pay her duty to your Lordship, and by permitting others of a later extraction to prepossess that place in your esteem to which none can pretend a better title. Poetry, in its nature, is sacred to the good and great; the relation between them is reciprocal, and they are ever propitious to it. It is the privilege of poetry to address to them, and it is their prerogative alone to give it protection.

This received maxim is a general apology for all writers who consecrate their labors to great men: but I could wish at this time, that this address were exempted from the common pretense of all dedications; and that as I can distinguish your Lordship even among the most deserving, so this offering might become remarkable by some particular instance of respect which should assure your Lordship that I am, with all due sense of your extreme worthiness and humanity, my Lord, your Lordship's most obedient, and most obliged humble servant,

Will. Congreve

PROLOGUE

Of those few fools who with ill stars are cursed,
Sure scribbling fools, called poets, fare the worst:
For they're a sort of fools which Fortune makes,
And after she has made 'em fools, forsakes.
With Nature's oafs 'tis quite a different case,
For Fortune favors all her idiot-race.
In her own nest the cuckoo-eggs we find,
O'er which she broods to hatch the changeling-kind.
No portion for her own she has to spare,
So much she dotes on her adopted care.
Poets are bubbles, by the town drawn in,
Suffered at first some trifling stakes to win;
But what unequal hazards do they run!
Each time they write they venture all they've won:
The squire that's buttered[1] still, is sure to be undone.
This author heretofore has found your favor;
But pleads no merit from his past behavior.
To build on that might prove a vain presumption,
Should grants, to poets made, admit resumption:
And in Parnassus he must lose his seat,
If that be found a forfeited estate.
He owns with toil he wrought the following scenes;
But, if they're naught, ne'er spare him for his pains:
Damn him the more; have no commiseration
For dullness on mature deliberation.
He swears he'll not resent one hissed-off scene,
Nor, like those peevish wits, his play maintain,
Who, to assert their sense, your taste arraign.
Some plot we think he has, and some new thought;
Some humor too, no farce—but that's a fault.
Satire, he thinks, you ought not to expect;
For so reformed a town who dares correct?
To please, this time, has been his sole pretense,
He'll not instruct, lest it should give offense.
Should he by chance a knave or fool expose,
That hurts none here; sure, here are none of those.
In short, our play shall (with your leave to show it)
Give you one instance of a passive poet,
Who to your judgments yields all resignation;
So save or damn, after your own discretion.

[1]Flattered lavishly.

DRAMATIS PERSONÆ

Fainall, *in love with Mrs. Marwood*[2]
Mirabell, *in love with Mrs. Millamant*
Witwoud, Petulant } *followers of Mrs. Millamant*
Sir Wilfull Witwoud, *half-brother to Witwoud, and nephew to Lady Wishfort*
Waitwell, *servant to Mirabell*
Lady Wishfort, *enemy to Mirabell, for having falsely pretended love to her*
Mrs. Millamant, *a fine lady, niece to Lady Wishfort, and loves Mirabell*
Mrs. Marwood, *friend to Mr. Fainall, and likes Mirabell*
Mrs. Fainall, *daughter to Lady Wishfort, and wife to Fainall, formerly friend to Mirabell*
Foible, *woman to Lady Wishfort*
Mincing, *woman to Mrs. Millamant*
Dancers, Footmen, and Attendants

Scene, *London*
The Time equal to that of the Presentation

ACT I

SCENE I. *A Chocolate-House*

Mirabell *and* Fainall *rising from cards.* Betty *waiting*

Mirabell. You are a fortunate man, Mr. Fainall!

Fainall. Have we done?

[2]In the 17th and 18th centuries "Mrs." (originally an abbreviation of "Mistress") was prefixed to the names of all women who had no superior title. It was not confined, as at present, to married women.

MIRABELL. What you please: I'll play on to entertain you.

FAINALL. No, I'll give you your revenge another time, when you are not so indifferent; you are thinking of something else now, and play too negligently. The coldness of a losing gamester lessens the pleasure of the winner. I'd no more play with a man that slighted his ill fortune than I'd make love to a woman who undervalued the loss of her reputation.

MIRABELL. You have a taste extremely delicate, and are for refining on your pleasures.

FAINALL. Prithee, why so reserved? Something has put you out of humor.

MIRABELL. Not at all. I happen to be grave to-day, and you are gay; that's all.

FAINALL. Confess, Millamant and you quarreled last night after I left you; my fair cousin has some humors that would tempt the patience of a Stoic. What, some coxcomb came in, and was well received by her, while you were by?

MIRABELL. Witwoud and Petulant; and what was worse, her aunt, your wife's mother, my evil genius; or to sum up all in her own name, my old Lady Wishfort came in.

FAINALL. Oh, there it is then! She has a lasting passion for you, and with reason.—What, then my wife was there?

MIRABELL. Yes, and Mrs. Marwood, and three or four more, whom I never saw before. Seeing me, they all put on their grave faces, whispered one another, then complained aloud of the vapors, and after fell into a profound silence.

FAINALL. They had a mind to be rid of you.

MIRABELL. For which reason I resolved not to stir. At last the good old lady broke through her painful taciturnity with an invective against long visits. I would not have understood her, but Millamant joining in the argument I rose, and, with a constrained smile, told her I thought nothing was so easy as to know when a visit began to be troublesome. She reddened, and I withdrew without expecting[1] her reply.

FAINALL. You were to blame to resent what she spoke only in compliance with her aunt.

MIRABELL. She is more mistress of herself than to be under the necessity of such a resignation.

FAINALL. What! though half her fortune depends upon her marrying with my lady's approbation?

MIRABELL. I was then in such a humor, that I should have been better pleased if she had been less discreet.

FAINALL. Now I remember, I wonder not they were weary of you; last night was one of their cabal nights. They have 'em three times a-week, and meet by turns at one another's apartments, where they come together like the coroner's inquest, to sit upon the murdered reputations of the week. You and I are excluded, and it was once proposed that all the male sex should be excepted; but somebody moved that, to avoid scandal, there might be one man of the community, upon which motion Witwoud and Petulant were enrolled members.

MIRABELL. And who may have been the foundress of this sect?—my Lady Wishfort, I warrant, who publishes her detestation of mankind, and, full of the vigor of fifty-five, declares for a friend and ratafia;[2] and let posterity shift for itself, she'll breed no more.

FAINALL. The discovery of your sham addresses to her, to conceal your love to her niece, has provoked this separation; had you dissembled better, things might have continued in the state of nature.

MIRABELL. I did as much as man could, with any reasonable conscience; I proceeded to the very last act of flattery with her, and was guilty of a song in her commendation. Nay, I got a friend to put her into a lampoon and compliment her with the imputation of an affair with a young fellow, which I carried so far that I told her the malicious town took notice that she was grown fat of a sudden; and when she lay in of a dropsy, persuaded her she was reported to be in labor. The devil's in't, if an old woman is to be flattered further, unless a man should endeavor downright personally to debauch her; and that my virtue forbade me. But for the discovery of this amour I am indebted to your friend, or your wife's friend, Mrs. Marwood.

FAINALL. What should provoke her to be your enemy unless she has made you advances which you have slighted? Women do not easily forgive omissions of that nature.[3]

[1]Awaiting.

[2]Cherry brandy flavored with peach and apricot kernels.

[3]"Heaven has no rage like love to hatred turned,
Nor Hell a fury like a woman scorned."
(*The Mourning Bride*, end of Act III.)

MIRABELL. She was always civil to me till of late.—I confess I am not one of those coxcombs who are apt to interpret a woman's good manners to her prejudice, and think that she who does not refuse 'em everything, can refuse 'em nothing.

FAINALL. You are a gallant man, Mirabell; and though you may have cruelty enough not to satisfy a lady's longing, you have too much generosity not to be tender of her honor. Yet you speak with an indifference which seems to be affected and confesses you are conscious of a negligence.

MIRABELL. You pursue the argument with a distrust that seems to be unaffected and confesses you are conscious of a concern for which the lady is more indebted to you than is your wife.

FAINALL. Fie, fie, friend! If you grow censorious I must leave you.—I'll look upon the gamesters in the next room.

MIRABELL. Who are they?

FAINALL. Petulant and Witwoud.—(*To* BETTY) Bring me some chocolate. [*Exit.*

MIRABELL. Betty, what says your clock?

BETTY. Turned of the last canonical hour,[1] sir. [*Exit.*

MIRABELL. How pertinently the jade answers me! Ha! almost one o'clock!—(*Looking on his watch*)—Oh, y'are come!

Enter a Servant

Well, is the grand affair over? You have been something tedious.

SERVANT. Sir, there's such coupling at Pancras[2] that they stand behind one another, as 'twere in a country dance. Ours was the last couple to lead up, and no hopes appearing of dispatch—besides, the parson growing hoarse, we were afraid his lungs would have failed before it came to our turn; so we drove round to Duke's-place,[3] and there they were riveted in a trice.

MIRABELL. So, so! You are sure they are married?

SERVANT. Married and bedded, sir; I am witness.

MIRABELL. Have you the certificate?

SERVANT. Here it is, sir.

MIRABELL. Has the tailor brought Waitwell's clothes home, and the new liveries?

SERVANT. Yes, sir.

MIRABELL. That's well. Do you go home again, d'ye hear, and adjourn the consummation till farther order. Bid Waitwell shake his ears, and Dame Partlet[4] rustle up her feathers and meet me at one o'clock by Rosamond's Pond,[5] that I may see her before she returns to her lady; and as you tender your ears be secret. [*Exit Servant.*

Re-enter FAINALL *and* BETTY

FAINALL. Joy of your success, Mirabell; you look pleased.

MIRABELL. Aye; I have been engaged in a matter of some sort of mirth, which is not yet ripe for discovery. I am glad this is not a cabal night. I wonder, Fainall, that you, who are married and of consequence should be discreet, will suffer your wife to be of such a party.

FAINALL. Faith, I am not jealous. Besides, most who are engaged are women and relations; and for the men, they are of a kind too contemptible to give scandal.

MIRABELL. I am of another opinion. The greater the coxcomb, always the more the scandal; for a woman who is not a fool, can have but one reason for associating with a man who is one.

FAINALL. Are you jealous as often as you see Witwoud entertained by Millamant?

MIRABELL. Of her understanding I am, if not of her person.

FAINALL. You do her wrong; for, to give her her due, she has wit.

MIRABELL. She has beauty enough to make any man think so, and complaisance enough not to contradict him who shall tell her so.

FAINALL. For a passionate lover, methinks you are a man somewhat too discerning in the failings of your mistress.

MIRABELL. And for a discerning man, somewhat too passionate a lover; for I like her with all her faults—nay, like her for her faults. Her follies are so natural, or so artful, that they become her; and those affectations which in another woman would be odious, serve but to make her more agreeable. I'll tell thee, Fainall, she once used me with that insolence, that in revenge I took her to pieces, sifted her,

[1]Hours appointed for prayer, and for the celebration of marriage.

[2]A church at which, it was currently said, irregular marriages took place.

[3]*I. e.*, to St. James's, another church notorious for irregular marriages.

[4]Pertelote, the hen (Chaucer's *Nun's Priest's Tale*).

[5]In St. James's Park.

and separated her failings. I studied 'em, and got 'em by rote. The catalogue was so large that I was not without hopes one day or other to hate her heartily: to which end I so used myself to think of 'em, that at length, contrary to my design and expectation, they gave me every hour less and less disturbance, till in a few days it became habitual to me to remember 'em without being displeased. They are now grown as familiar to me as my own frailties, and, in all probability, in a little time longer I shall like 'em as well.

FAINALL. Marry her, marry her! Be half as well acquainted with her charms as you are with her defects, and my life on't, you are your own man again.

MIRABELL. Say you so?

FAINALL. Aye, aye, I have experience: I have a wife, and so forth.

Enter Messenger

MESSENGER. Is one Squire Witwoud here?

BETTY. Yes, what's your business?

MESSENGER. I have a letter for him from his brother Sir Wilfull, which I am charged to deliver into his own hands.

BETTY. He's in the next room, friend—that way. [*Exit Messenger.*

MIRABELL. What, is the chief of that noble family in town—Sir Wilfull Witwoud?

FAINALL. He is expected to-day. Do you know him?

MIRABELL. I have seen him; he promises to be an extraordinary person. I think you have the honor to be related to him.

FAINALL. Yes; he is half-brother to this Witwoud by a former wife, who was sister to my Lady Wishfort, my wife's mother. If you marry Millamant, you must call cousins too.

MIRABELL. I had rather be his relation than his acquaintance.

FAINALL. He comes to town in order to equip himself for travel.

MIRABELL. For travel? Why, the man that I mean is above forty.

FAINALL. No matter for that; 'tis for the honor of England, that all Europe should know we have blockheads of all ages.

MIRABELL. I wonder there is not an act of Parliament to save the credit of the nation, and prohibit the exportation of fools.

FAINALL. By no means; 'tis better as 'tis. 'Tis better to trade with a little loss, than to be quite eaten up with being overstocked.

MIRABELL. Pray, are the follies of this knight-errant and those of the squire his brother anything related?

FAINALL. Not at all; Witwoud grows by the knight, like a medlar grafted on a crab. One will melt in your mouth, and t'other set your teeth on edge; one is all pulp, and the other all core.

MIRABELL. So one will be rotten before he be ripe, and the other will be rotten without ever being ripe at all.

FAINALL. Sir Wilfull is an odd mixture of bashfulness and obstinacy.—But when he's drunk he's as loving as the monster in *The Tempest*,[1] and much after the same manner. To give t'other his due, he has something of good nature, and does not always want wit.

MIRABELL. Not always; but as often as his memory fails him, and his commonplace[2] of comparisons. He is a fool with a good memory and some few scraps of other folks' wit. He is one whose conversation can never be approved; yet it is now and then to be endured. He has indeed one good quality—he is not exceptious; for he so passionately affects the reputation of understanding raillery, that he will construe an affront into a jest, and call downright rudeness and ill language satire and fire.

FAINALL. If you have a mind to finish his picture, you have an opportunity to do it at full length.—Behold the original!

Enter WITWOUD

WITWOUD. Afford me your compassion, my dears! Pity me, Fainall! Mirabell, pity me!

MIRABELL. I do, from my soul.

FAINALL. Why, what's the matter?

WITWOUD. —No letters for me, Betty?

BETTY. Did not the messenger bring you one but now, sir?

WITWOUD. Aye, but no other?

BETTY. No, sir.

WITWOUD. That's hard, that's very hard.—A messenger!—A mule, a beast of burden! He has brought me a letter from the fool my brother, as heavy as a panegyric in a funeral sermon, or a copy of commendatory verses from one poet to another. And what's worse, 'tis as sure a forerunner of the author as an epistle dedicatory.

[1]Sycorax, Caliban's sister, in Davenant and Dryden's *The Tempest*. (See Act III.)

[2]Collection.

Close contact of all characters.

MIRABELL. A fool, and your brother, Witwoud!

WITWOUD. Aye, aye, my half-brother. My half-brother he is; no nearer, upon honor.

MIRABELL. Then 'tis possible he may be but half a fool.

WITWOUD. Good, good, Mirabell, *le drôle!* Good, good; hang him, don't let's talk of him. —Fainall, how does your lady? Gad, I say anything in the world to get this fellow out of my head. I beg pardon that I should ask a man of pleasure and the town, a question at once so foreign and domestic. But I talk like an old maid at a marriage; I don't know what I say. But she's the best woman in the world.

FAINALL. 'Tis well you don't know what you say, or else your commendation would go near to make me either vain or jealous.

WITWOUD. No man in town lives well with a wife but Fainall.—Your judgment, Mirabell?

MIRABELL. You had better step and ask his wife if you would be credibly informed.

WITWOUD. Mirabell?

MIRABELL. Aye.

WITWOUD. My dear, I ask ten thousand pardons—gad, I have forgot what I was going to say to you!

MIRABELL. I thank you heartily, heartily.

WITWOUD. No! But prithee, excuse me; —my memory is such a memory.

MIRABELL. Have a care of such apologies, Witwoud; for I never knew a fool but he affected to complain either of the spleen or his memory.

FAINALL. What have you done with Petulant?

WITWOUD. He's reckoning his money—my money it was. I have no luck to-day.

FAINALL. You may allow him to win of you at play, for you are sure to be too hard for him at repartee. Since you monopolize the wit that is between you, the fortune must be his, of course.

MIRABELL. I don't find that Petulant confesses the superiority of wit to be your talent, Witwoud.

WITWOUD. Come, come, you are malicious now, and would breed debates.—Petulant's my friend, and a very honest fellow, and a very pretty fellow, and has a smattering— faith and troth, a pretty deal of an odd sort of a small wit. Nay, I'll do him justice. I'm his friend; I won't wrong him.—And if he had any judgment in the world, he would not be altogether contemptible. Come, come, don't detract from the merits of my friend.

FAINALL. You don't take your friend to be over-nicely bred?

WITWOUD. No, no, hang him! The rogue has no manners at all, that I must own—no more breeding than a bumbaily,[1] that I grant you—'tis pity; the fellow has fire and life.

MIRABELL. What, courage?

WITWOUD. Hum, faith I don't know as to that; I can't say as to that. Yes, faith, in a controversy, he'll contradict anybody.

MIRABELL. —Though 'twere a man whom he feared, or a woman whom he loved?

WITWOUD. Well, well, he does not always think before he speaks—we have all our failings: you are too hard upon him—you are, faith. Let me excuse him. I can defend most of his faults, except one or two. One he has, that's the truth on't; if he were my brother, I could not acquit him—that, indeed, I could wish were otherwise.

MIRABELL. Aye, marry, what's that, Witwoud?

WITWOUD. O pardon me!—Expose the infirmities of my friend?—No, my dear, excuse me there.

FAINALL. What! I warrant he's unsincere, or 'tis some such trifle.

WITWOUD. No, no!—What if he be? 'Tis no matter for that; his wit will excuse that. A wit should no more be sincere than a woman constant; one argues a decay of parts, as t'other of beauty.

MIRABELL. Maybe you think him too positive?

WITWOUD. No, no, his being positive is an incentive to argument, and keeps up conversation.

FAINALL. Too illiterate?

WITWOUD. That? that's his happiness: his want of learning gives him the more opportunities to show his natural parts.

MIRABELL. He wants words?

WITWOUD. Aye: but I like him for that, now; for his want of words gives me the pleasure very often to explain his meaning.

FAINALL. He's impudent?

WITWOUD. No, that's not it.

MIRABELL. Vain?

WITWOUD. No.

[1]Bailiff employed for making arrests. (In arresting debtors, the bailiff touched them on the back.)

MIRABELL. What! He speaks unseasonable truths sometimes, because he has not wit enough to invent an evasion?

WITWOUD. Truths! ha! ha! ha! No, no; since you will have it—I mean, he never speaks truth at all—that's all. He will lie like a chambermaid, or a woman of quality's porter. Now, that is a fault.

Enter Coachman

COACHMAN. Is Master Petulant here, mistress?

BETTY. Yes.

COACHMAN. Three gentlewomen in the coach would speak with him.

FAINALL. O brave Petulant!—three!

BETTY. I'll tell him.

COACHMAN. You must bring two dishes of chocolate and a glass of cinnamon-water.[1]

[*Exit.*

WITWOUD. That should be for two fasting strumpets, and a bawd troubled with wind. Now you may know what the three are.

MIRABELL. You are very free with your friend's acquaintance.

WITWOUD. Aye, aye; friendship without freedom is as dull as love without enjoyment, or wine without toasting. But to tell you a secret, these are trulls whom he allows coach-hire, and something more, by the week, to call on him once a day at public places.

MIRABELL. How!

WITWOUD. You shall see he won't go to 'em, because there's no more company here to take notice of him.—Why, this is nothing to what he used to do; before he found out this way, I have known him call for himself.

FAINALL. —Call for himself! What dost thou mean?

WITWOUD. Mean! Why, he would slip you out of this chocolate-house just when you had been talking to him; as soon as your back was turned—whip, he was gone!—then trip to his lodging, clap on a hood and scarf and a mask, slap into a hackney-coach, and drive hither to the door again in a trice, where he would send in for himself—that is, I mean—call for himself, wait for himself; nay, and what's more, not finding himself, sometimes leave a letter for himself.

MIRABELL. I confess this is something extraordinary.—I believe he waits for himself now, he is so long a-coming.—Oh! I ask his pardon.

Enter PETULANT

BETTY. Sir, the coach stays.

PETULANT. Well, well; I come.—'Sbud, a man had as good be a professed midwife as a professed whoremaster, at this rate! To be knocked up and raised at all hours, and in all places! Pox on 'em, I won't come!—D'ye hear, tell 'em I won't come—let 'em snivel and cry their hearts out.

FAINALL. You are very cruel, Petulant.

PETULANT. All's one, let it pass. I have a humor to be cruel.

MIRABELL. I hope they are not persons of condition that you use at this rate.

PETULANT. Condition! condition's a dried fig if I am not in humor!—By this hand, if they were your—a—a—your what-d'ye-call-'ems themselves, they must wait or rub off[2] if I want appetite.

MIRABELL. What-d'ye-call-'ems! What are they, Witwoud?

WITWOUD. Empresses, my dear: by your what-d'ye-call-'ems he means sultana queens.

PETULANT. Aye, Roxolanas.[3]

MIRABELL. Cry you mercy!

FAINALL. Witwoud says they are—

PETULANT. What does he say th' are?

WITWOUD. I? Fine ladies, I say.

PETULANT. Pass on, Witwoud.—Hark'ee, by this light, his relations—two coheiresses, his cousins, and an old aunt who loves caterwauling better than a conventicle.

WITWOUD. Ha! ha! ha! I had a mind to see how the rogue would come off.—Ha! ha! ha! Gad, I can't be angry with him if he had said they were my mother and my sisters.

MIRABELL. No?

WITWOUD. No; the rogue's wit and readiness of invention charm me. Dear Petulant!

BETTY. They are gone, sir, in great anger.

PETULANT. Enough; let 'em trundle. Anger helps complexion—saves paint.

FAINALL. This continence is all dissembled; this is in order to have something to brag of the next time he makes court to Millamant and swear he has abandoned the whole sex for her sake.

---

[1] A digestive cordial.

[2] *I. e.*, clear out.

[3] Roxolana is the wife of Solyman the Magnificent in Davenant's *Siege of Rhodes*.

MIRABELL. Have you not left off your impudent pretensions there yet? I shall cut your throat some time or other, Petulant, about that business.

PETULANT. Aye, aye, let that pass—there are other throats to be cut.

MIRABELL. Meaning mine, sir?

PETULANT. Not I—I mean nobody—I know nothing: but there are uncles and nephews in the world—and they may be rivals.—What then? All's one for that.

MIRABELL. How! Hark'ee, Petulant; come hither—explain, or I shall call your interpreter.

PETULANT. Explain? I know nothing. Why, you have an uncle, have you not, lately come to town, and lodges by my Lady Wishfort's?

MIRABELL. True.

PETULANT. Why, that's enough—you and he are not friends; and if he should marry and have a child you may be disinherited, ha?

MIRABELL. Where hast thou stumbled upon all this truth?

PETULANT. All's one for that; why, then, say I know something.

MIRABELL. Come, thou art an honest fellow, Petulant, and shalt make love to my mistress; thou sha't, faith. What hast thou heard of my uncle?

PETULANT. I? Nothing, I. If throats are to be cut, let swords clash! snug's the word; I shrug and am silent.

MIRABELL. Oh, raillery, raillery! Come, I know thou art in the women's secrets.—What, you're a cabalist; I know you stayed at Millamant's last night after I went. Was there any mention made of my uncle or me? Tell me. If thou hadst but good nature equal to thy wit, Petulant, Tony Witwoud, who is now thy competitor in fame, would show as dim by thee as a dead whiting's eye by a pearl of orient; he would no more be seen by thee than Mercury is by the sun. Come, I'm sure thou wo't tell me.

PETULANT. If I do, will you grant me common sense then for the future?

MIRABELL. Faith, I'll do what I can for thee, and I'll pray that Heaven may grant it thee in the meantime.

PETULANT. Well, hark'ee.

(MIRABELL *and* PETULANT *talk apart*)

FAINALL. Petulant and you both will find Mirabell as warm a rival as a lover.

WITWOUD. Pshaw! pshaw! that she laughs at Petulant is plain. And for my part, but that it is almost a fashion to admire her, I should—hark'ee—to tell you a secret, but let it go no further—between friends, I shall never break my heart for her.

FAINALL. How!

WITWOUD. She's handsome; but she's a sort of an uncertain woman.

FAINALL. I thought you had died for her.

WITWOUD. Umh—no—

FAINALL. She has wit.

WITWOUD. 'Tis what she will hardly allow anybody else now, demme! I should hate her, if she were as handsome as Cleopatra. Mirabell is not so sure of her as he thinks for.

FAINALL. Why do you think so?

WITWOUD. We stayed pretty late there last night, and heard something of an uncle to Mirabell, who is lately come to town—and is between him and the best part of his estate. Mirabell and he are at some distance, as my Lady Wishfort has been told; and you know she hates Mirabell worse than a Quaker hates a parrot, or than a fishmonger hates a hard frost. Whether this uncle has seen Mrs. Millamant or not, I cannot say, but there were items of such a treaty being in embryo; and if it should come to life, poor Mirabell would be in some sort unfortunately fobbed,[1] i'faith.

FAINALL. 'Tis impossible Millamant should hearken to it.

WITWOUD. Faith, my dear, I can't tell; she's a woman, and a kind of a humorist.[2]

MIRABELL. [*To* PETULANT] And this is the sum of what you could collect last night?

PETULANT. The quintessence. Maybe Witwoud knows more; he stayed longer. Besides, they never mind him; they say anything before him.

MIRABELL. I thought you had been the greatest favorite.

PETULANT. Aye, *tête-à-tête*, but not in public, because I make remarks.

MIRABELL. Do you?

PETULANT. Aye; aye; pox, I'm malicious, man! Now, he's soft, you know; they are not in awe of him—the fellow's well-bred; he's what you call a what-d'ye-call-'em, a fine gentleman—but he's silly withal.

MIRABELL. I thank you. I know as much

[1]Cheated.

[2]A whimsical person, subject to fancies

as my curiosity requires.—Fainall, are you for the Mall?

FAINALL. Aye, I'll take a turn before dinner.

WITWOUD. Aye, we'll all walk in the Park; the ladies talked of being there.

MIRABELL. I thought you were obliged to watch for your brother Sir Wilfull's arrival.

WITWOUD. No, no; he comes to his aunt's, my Lady Wishfort. Pox on him! I shall be troubled with him, too; what shall I do with the fool?

PETULANT. Beg him for his estate, that I may beg you afterwards, and so have but one trouble with you both.

WITWOUD. Oh, rare Petulant! Thou art as quick as fire in a frosty morning. Thou shalt to the Mall with us, and we'll be very severe.

PETULANT. Enough! I'm in a humor to be severe.

MIRABELL. Are you? Pray then, walk by yourselves: let not us be accessory to your putting the ladies out of countenance with your senseless ribaldry, which you roar out aloud as often as they pass by you; and when you have made a handsome woman blush, then you think you have been severe.

PETULANT. What, what! Then let 'em either show their innocence by not understanding what they hear, or else show their discretion by not hearing what they would not be thought to understand.

MIRABELL. But hast not thou then sense enough to know that thou oughtest to be most ashamed thyself when thou hast put another out of countenance?

PETULANT. Not I, by this hand!—I always take blushing either for a sign of guilt or ill breeding.

MIRABELL. I confess you ought to think so. You are in the right, that you may plead the error of your judgment in defense of your practice.

Where modesty's ill manners, 'tis but fit
That impudence and malice pass for wit.

[*Exeunt.*

ACT II

SCENE I. *St. James's Park*

Enter MRS. FAINALL *and* MRS. MARWOOD

MRS. FAINALL. Aye, aye, dear Marwood; if we will be happy, we must find the means in ourselves and among ourselves. Men are ever in extremes—either doting or averse. While they are lovers, if they have fire and sense, their jealousies are insupportable; and when they cease to love, (we ought to think at least) they loathe; they look upon us with horror and distaste; they meet us like the ghosts of what we were, and as from such, fly from us.

MRS. MARWOOD. True, 'tis an unhappy circumstance of life, that love should ever die before us and that the man so often should outlive the lover. But say what you will, 'tis better to be left than never to have been loved. To pass our youth in dull indifference, to refuse the sweets of life because they once must leave us, is as preposterous as to wish to have been born old because we one day must be old. For my part, my youth may wear and waste, but it shall never rust in my possession.

MRS. FAINALL. Then it seems you dissemble an aversion to mankind only in compliance to my mother's humor?

MRS. MARWOOD. Certainly. To be free; I have no taste of those insipid dry discourses with which our sex of force must entertain themselves apart from men. We may affect endearments to each other, profess eternal friendships, and seem to dote like lovers; but 'tis not in our natures long to persevere. Love will resume his empire in our breasts and every heart, or soon or late, receive and readmit him as its lawful tyrant.

MRS. FAINALL. Bless me, how have I been deceived! Why, you profess a libertine.

MRS. MARWOOD. You see my friendship by my freedom. Come, be as sincere; acknowledge that your sentiments agree with mine.

MRS. FAINALL. Never!

MRS. MARWOOD. You hate mankind?

MRS. FAINALL. Heartily, inveterately.

MRS. MARWOOD. Your husband?

MRS. FAINALL. Most transcendently; aye, though I say it, meritoriously.

MRS. MARWOOD. Give me your hand upon it.

MRS. FAINALL. There.

MRS. MARWOOD. I join with you; what I have said has been to try you.

MRS. FAINALL. Is it possible? Dost thou hate those vipers, men?

MRS. MARWOOD. I have done hating 'em, and am now come to despise 'em; the next thing I have to do, is eternally to forget 'em.

Dialogue brings out the fondness of each woman for Mirabel.

Mrs. Fainall. There spoke the spirit of an Amazon, a Penthesilea![1]

Mrs. Marwood. And yet I am thinking sometimes to carry my aversion further.

Mrs. Fainall. How?

Mrs. Marwood. Faith, by marrying; if I could but find one that loved me very well and would be thoroughly sensible of ill usage, I think I should do myself the violence of undergoing the ceremony.

Mrs. Fainall. You would not make him a cuckold!

Mrs. Marwood. No; but I'd make him believe I did, and that's as bad.

Mrs. Fainall. Why had not you as good do it?

Mrs. Marwood. Oh, if he should ever discover it, he would then know the worst and be out of his pain; but I would have him ever to continue upon the rack of fear and jealousy.

Mrs. Fainall. Ingenious mischief! would thou wert married to Mirabell.

Mrs. Marwood. Would I were!

Mrs. Fainall. You change color.

Mrs. Marwood. Because I hate him.

Mrs. Fainall. So do I, but I can hear him named. But what reason have you to hate him in particular?

Mrs. Marwood. I never loved him; he is, and always was, insufferably proud.

Mrs. Fainall. By the reason you give for your aversion, one would think it dissembled; for you have laid a fault to his charge, of which his enemies must acquit him.

Mrs. Marwood. Oh, then it seems you are one of his favorable enemies! Methinks you look a little pale—and now you flush again.

Mrs. Fainall. Do I? I think I am a little sick o' the sudden.

Mrs. Marwood. What ails you?

Mrs. Fainall. My husband. Don't you see him? He turned short upon me unawares, and has almost overcome me.

Enter Fainall *and* Mirabell

Mrs. Marwood. Ha! ha! ha! He comes opportunely for you.

Mrs. Fainall. For you, for he has brought Mirabell with him.

Fainall. My dear!

Mrs. Fainall. My soul!

Fainall. You don't look well to-day, child.

Mrs. Fainall. D'ye think so?

Mirabell. He is the only man that does, madam.

Mrs. Fainall. The only man that would tell me so, at least, and the only man from whom I could hear it without mortification.

Fainall. Oh, my dear, I am satisfied of your tenderness; I know you cannot resent anything from me, especially what is an effect of my concern.

Mrs. Fainall. Mr. Mirabell, my mother interrupted you in a pleasant relation last night; I would fain hear it out.

Mirabell. The persons concerned in that affair have yet a tolerable reputation.—I am afraid Mr. Fainall will be censorious.

Mrs. Fainall. He has a humor more prevailing than his curiosity, and will willingly dispense with the hearing of one scandalous story, to avoid giving an occasion to make another by being seen to walk with his wife. This way, Mr. Mirabell, and I dare promise you will oblige us both.

[*Exeunt* Mrs. Fainall *and* Mirabell.

Fainall. Excellent creature! Well, sure if I should live to be rid of my wife, I should be a miserable man.

Mrs. Marwood. Aye?

Fainall. For having only that one hope, the accomplishment of it, of consequence, must put an end to all my hopes; and what a wretch is he who must survive his hopes! Nothing remains when that day comes but to sit down and weep like Alexander when he wanted other worlds to conquer.

Mrs. Marwood. Will you not follow 'em?

Fainall. Faith, I think not.

Mrs. Marwood. Pray, let us; I have a reason.

Fainall. You are not jealous?

Mrs. Marwood. Of whom?

Fainall. Of Mirabell.

Mrs. Marwood. If I am, is it inconsistent with my love to you that I am tender of your honor?

Fainall. You would intimate, then, as if there were a fellow-feeling between my wife and him.

Mrs. Marwood. I think she does not hate him to that degree she would be thought.

Fainall. But he, I fear, is too insensible.

Mrs. Marwood. It may be you are deceived.

[1]She fought on the Trojan side until slain by Achilles.

Fainall. It may be so. I do not now begin to apprehend it.

Mrs. Marwood. What?

Fainall. That I have been deceived, madam, and you are false.

Mrs. Marwood. That I am false! What mean you?

Fainall. To let you know I see through all your little arts.—Come, you both love him, and both have equally dissembled your aversion. Your mutual jealousies of one another have made you clash till you have both struck fire. I have seen the warm confession reddening on your cheeks and sparkling from your eyes.

Mrs. Marwood. You do me wrong.

Fainall. I do not. 'Twas for my ease to oversee and willfully neglect the gross advances made him by my wife, that by permitting her to be engaged, I might continue unsuspected in my pleasures and take you oftener to my arms in full security. But could you think, because the nodding husband would not wake, that e'er the watchful lover slept?

Mrs. Marwood. And wherewithal can you reproach me?

Fainall. With infidelity, with loving another—with love of Mirabell.

Mrs. Marwood. 'Tis false! I challenge you to show an instance that can confirm your groundless accusation. I hate him!

Fainall. And wherefore do you hate him? He is insensible, and your resentment follows his neglect. An instance?—the injuries you have done him are a proof—your interposing in his love. What cause had you to make discoveries of his pretended passion?—to undeceive the credulous aunt, and be the officious obstacle of his match with Millamant?

Mrs. Marwood. My obligations to my lady urged me. I had professed a friendship to her, and could not see her easy nature so abused by that dissembler.

Fainall. What, was it conscience, then? Professed a friendship! Oh, the pious friendships of the female sex!

Mrs. Marwood. More tender, more sincere, and more enduring than all the vain and empty vows of men, whether professing love to us or mutual faith to one another.

Fainall. Ha! ha! ha! You are my wife's friend, too.

Mrs. Marwood. Shame and ingratitude! Do you reproach me?—You, you upbraid me? Have I been false to her, through strict fidelity to you, and sacrificed my friendship to keep my love inviolate? And have you the baseness to charge me with the guilt, unmindful of the merit? To you it should be meritorious that I have been vicious: and do you reflect that guilt upon me which should lie buried in your bosom?

Fainall. You misinterpret my reproof. I meant but to remind you of the slight account you once could make of strictest ties when set in competition with your love to me.

Mrs. Marwood. 'Tis false; you urged it with deliberate malice! 'Twas spoken in scorn, and I never will forgive it.

Fainall. Your guilt, not your resentment, begets your rage. If yet you loved, you could forgive a jealousy; but you are stung to find you are discovered.

Mrs. Marwood. It shall be all discovered. —You too shall be discovered; be sure you shall. I can but be exposed.—If I do it myself I shall prevent your baseness.

Fainall. Why, what will you do?

Mrs. Marwood. Disclose it to your wife; own what has passed between us.

Fainall. Frenzy!

Mrs. Marwood. By all my wrongs I'll do't!—I'll publish to the world the injuries you have done me, both in my fame and fortune! With both I trusted you,—you bankrupt in honor, as indigent of wealth.

Fainall. Your fame I have preserved: your fortune has been bestowed as the prodigality of your love would have it, in pleasures which we both have shared. Yet, had not you been false, I had ere this repaid it—'tis true. Had you permitted Mirabell with Millamant to have stolen their marriage, my lady had been incensed beyond all means of reconcilement; Millamant had forfeited the moiety of her fortune, which then would have descended to my wife—and wherefore did I marry but to make lawful prize of a rich widow's wealth, and squander it on love and you?

Mrs. Marwood. Deceit and frivolous pretense!

Fainall. —Death, am I not married? What's pretense? Am I not imprisoned, fettered? Have I not a wife?—nay, a wife that was a widow, a young widow, a handsome widow; and would be again a widow, but that I have a heart of proof, and something of a constitution to bustle through the ways of wedlock and this world! Will you yet be reconciled to truth and me?

MRS. MARWOOD. Impossible. Truth and you are inconsistent: I hate you, and shall for ever.

FAINALL. For loving you?

MRS. MARWOOD. I loathe the name of love after such usage; and next to the guilt with which you would asperse me, I scorn you most. Farewell!

FAINALL. Nay, we must not part thus.

MRS. MARWOOD. Let me go.

FAINALL. Come, I'm sorry.

MRS. MARWOOD. I care not—let me go—break my hands, do! I'd leave 'em to get loose.

FAINALL. I would not hurt you for the world. Have I no other hold to keep you here?

MRS. MARWOOD. Well, I have deserved it all.

FAINALL. You know I love you.

MRS. MARWOOD. Poor dissembling!—Oh, that—well, it is not yet—

FAINALL. What? What is it not? What is it not yet? It is not yet too late—

MRS. MARWOOD. No, it is not yet too late—I have that comfort.

FAINALL. It is, to love another.

MRS. MARWOOD. But not to loathe, detest, abhor mankind, myself, and the whole treacherous world.

FAINALL. Nay, this is extravagance!—Come, I ask your pardon—no tears—I was to blame; I could not love you and be easy in my doubts. Pray, forbear—I believe you; I'm convinced I've done you wrong, and anyway, every way will make amends. I'll hate my wife yet more, damn her! I'll part with her, rob her of all she's worth, and we'll retire somewhere—anywhere—to another world. I'll marry thee—be pacified.—'Sdeath, they come! Hide your face, your tears.—You have a mask; wear it a moment. This way, this way—be persuaded. [*Exeunt.*

Enter MIRABELL *and* MRS. FAINALL

MRS. FAINALL. They are here yet.

MIRABELL. They are turning into the other walk.

MRS. FAINALL. While I only hated my husband, I could bear to see him; but since I have despised him, he's too offensive.

MIRABELL. Oh, you should hate with prudence.

MRS. FAINALL. Yes, for I have loved with indiscretion.

MIRABELL. You should have just so much disgust for your husband as may be sufficient to make you relish your lover.

MRS. FAINALL. You have been the cause that I have loved without bounds, and would you set limits to that aversion of which you have been the occasion? Why did you make me marry this man?

MIRABELL. Why do we daily commit disagreeable and dangerous actions? To save that idol, reputation. If the familiarities of our loves had produced that consequence of which you were apprehensive, where could you have fixed a father's name with credit but on a husband? I knew Fainall to be a man lavish of his morals, an interested and professing friend, a false and a designing lover, yet one whose wit and outward fair behavior have gained a reputation with the town enough to make that woman stand excused who has suffered herself to be won by his addresses. A better man ought not to have been sacrificed to the occasion, a worse had not answered to the purpose. When you are weary of him, you know your remedy.

MRS. FAINALL. I ought to stand in some degree of credit with you, Mirabell.

MIRABELL. In justice to you, I have made you privy to my whole design, and put it in your power to ruin or advance my fortune.

MRS. FAINALL. Whom have you instructed to represent your pretended uncle?

MIRABELL. Waitwell, my servant.

MRS. FAINALL. He is an humble servant to Foible my mother's woman, and may win her to your interest.

MIRABELL. Care is taken for that—she is won and worn by this time. They were married this morning.

MRS. FAINALL. Who?

MIRABELL. Waitwell and Foible. I would not tempt my servant to betray me by trusting him too far. If your mother, in hopes to ruin me, should consent to marry my pretended uncle, he might, like Mosca in *The Fox*,[1] stand upon terms; so I made him sure beforehand.

MRS. FAINALL. So if my poor mother is caught in a contract, you will discover the im-

[1]Ben Jonson's *Volpone*.

posture betimes, and release her by producing a certificate of her gallant's former marriage?

MIRABELL. Yes, upon condition that she consent to my marriage with her niece, and surrender the moiety of her fortune in her possession.

MRS. FAINALL. She talked last night of endeavoring at a match between Millamant and your uncle.

MIRABELL. That was by Foible's direction and my instruction, that she might seem to carry it more privately.

MRS. FAINALL. Well, I have an opinion of your success; for I believe my lady will do anything to get a husband, and when she has this which you have provided for her, I suppose she will submit to anything to get rid of him.

MIRABELL. Yes, I think the good lady would marry anything that resembled a man, though 'twere no more than what a butler could pinch out of a napkin.

MRS. FAINALL. Female frailty! We must all come to it if we live to be old and feel the craving of a false appetite when the true is decayed.

MIRABELL. An old woman's appetite is depraved like that of a girl—'tis the green sickness of a second childhood, and, like the faint offer of a latter spring, serves but to usher in the fall and withers in an affected bloom.

MRS. FAINALL. Here's your mistress.

Enter MRS. MILLAMANT, WITWOUD, MINCING

MIRABELL. Here she comes, i'faith, full sail, with her fan spread and streamers out, and a shoal of fools for tenders. Ha, no, I cry her mercy!

MRS. FAINALL. I see but one poor empty sculler, and he tows her woman after him.

MIRABELL. You seem to be unattended, madam. You used to have the *beau monde*[1] throng after you, and a flock of gay fine perukes[2] hovering round you.

WITWOUD. Like moths about a candle.—I had like to have lost my comparison for want of breath.

MRS. MILLAMANT. Oh, I have denied myself airs to-day. I have walked as fast through the crowd—

WITWOUD. As a favorite just disgraced, and with as few followers.

MRS. MILLAMANT. Dear Mr. Witwoud, truce with your similitudes; for I am as sick of 'em—

WITWOUD. As a physician of a good air.—I cannot help it, madam, though 'tis against myself.

MRS. MILLAMANT. Yet again! Mincing, stand between me and his wit.

WITWOUD. Do, Mrs. Mincing, like a screen before a grate fire.—I confess I do blaze to-day; I am too bright.

MRS. FAINALL. But, dear Millamant, why were you so long?

MRS. MILLAMANT. Long? Lord, have I not made violent haste? I have asked every living thing I met for you; I have inquired after you as after a new fashion.

WITWOUD. Madam, truce with your similitudes.—No, you met her husband, and did not ask him for her.

MRS. MILLAMANT. By your leave, Witwoud, that were like inquiring after an old fashion, to ask a husband for his wife.

WITWOUD. Hum, a hit! a hit! a palpable hit! I confess it.

MRS. FAINALL. You were dressed before I came abroad.

MRS. MILLAMANT. Aye, that's true.—Oh, but then I had—Mincing, what had I? Why was I so long?

MINCING. O mem, your la'ship stayed to peruse a packet of letters.

MRS. MILLAMANT. Oh, aye, letters—I had letters—I am persecuted with letters—I hate letters.—Nobody knows how to write letters—and yet one has 'em, one does not know why. They serve one to pin up one's hair.

WITWOUD. Is that the way? Pray, madam, do you pin up your hair with all your letters? I find I must keep copies.

MRS. MILLAMANT. Only with those in verse, Mr. Witwoud; I never pin up my hair with prose. I think I tried once, Mincing.

MINCING. O mem, I shall never forget it.

MRS. MILLAMANT. Aye, poor Mincing tift[3] and tift all the morning.

MINCING. Till I had the cremp in my fingers, I'll vow, mem; and all to no purpose. But when your la'ship pins it up with poetry, it sits so pleasant the next day as anything and is so pure and so crips.[4]

WITWOUD. Indeed, so "crips"?

---

[1]Fashionable world. [2]Wigs, then worn by men. [3]Arranged it [4]Crisp.

MINCING. You're such a critic, Mr. Witwoud.

MRS. MILLAMANT. Mirabell, did you take exceptions last night? Oh, aye, and went away.—Now I think on't I'm angry—no, now I think on't I'm pleased—for I believe I gave you some pain.

MIRABELL. Does that please you?

MRS. MILLAMANT. Infinitely; I love to give pain.

MIRABELL. You would affect a cruelty which is not in your nature; your true vanity is in the power of pleasing.

MRS. MILLAMANT. Oh, I ask your pardon for that—one's cruelty is one's power; and when one parts with one's cruelty, one parts with one's power; and when one has parted with that, I fancy one's old and ugly.

MIRABELL. Aye, aye, suffer your cruelty to ruin the object of your power, to destroy your lover—and then how vain, how lost a thing you'll be! Nay, 'tis true: you are no longer handsome when you've lost your lover; your beauty dies upon the instant, for beauty is the lover's gift. 'Tis he bestows your charms—your glass is all a cheat. The ugly and the old, whom the looking-glass mortifies, yet after commendation can be flattered by it and discover beauties in it; for that reflects our praises, rather than your face.

MRS. MILLAMANT. Oh, the vanity of these men!—Fainall, d'ye hear him? If they did not commend us, we were not handsome! Now you must know they could not commend one, if one was not handsome. Beauty the lover's gift!—Lord, what is a lover, that it can give? Why, one makes lovers as fast as one pleases, and they live as long as one pleases, and they die as soon as one pleases: and then, if one pleases, one makes more.

WITWOUD. Very pretty. Why, you make no more of making of lovers, madam, than of making so many card-matches.

MRS. MILLAMANT. One no more owes one's beauty to a lover, than one's wit to an echo. They can but reflect what we look and say—vain empty things if we are silent or unseen, and want a being.

MIRABELL. Yet to those two vain empty things you owe two the greatest pleasures of your life.

MRS. MILLAMANT. How so?

MIRABELL. To your lover you owe the pleasure of hearing yourselves praised, and to an echo the pleasure of hearing yourselves talk.

WITWOUD. But I know a lady that loves talking so incessantly, she won't give an echo fair play; she has that everlasting rotation of tongue, that an echo must wait till she dies before it can catch her last words.

MRS. MILLAMANT. Oh, fiction!—Fainall, let us leave these men.

MIRABELL. (*Aside to* MRS. FAINALL) Draw off Witwoud.

MRS. FAINALL. Immediately.—I have a word or two for Mr. Witwoud.

[*Exeunt* WITWOUD *and* MRS. FAINALL.

MIRABELL. I would beg a little private audience too.—You had the tyranny to deny me last night, though you knew I came to impart a secret to you that concerned my love.

MRS. MILLAMANT. You saw I was engaged.

MIRABELL. Unkind! You had the leisure to entertain a herd of fools—things who visit you from their excessive idleness, bestowing on your easiness that time which is the encumbrance of their lives. How can you find delight in such society? It is impossible they should admire you; they are not capable—or if they were, it should be to you as a mortification, for sure to please a fool is some degree of folly.

MRS. MILLAMANT. I please myself: besides, sometimes to converse with fools is for my health.

MIRABELL. Your health! Is there a worse disease than the conversation of fools?

MRS. MILLAMANT. Yes, the vapors; fools are physic for it, next to asafœtida.

MIRABELL. You are not in a course of fools?

MRS. MILLAMANT. Mirabell, if you persist in this offensive freedom, you'll displease me.—I think I must resolve, after all, not to have you; we shan't agree.

MIRABELL. Not in our physic, it may be.

MRS. MILLAMANT. And yet our distemper, in all likelihood, will be the same; for we shall be sick of one another. I shan't endure to be reprimanded nor instructed: 'tis so dull to act always by advice, and so tedious to be told of one's faults—I can't bear it. Well, I won't have you, Mirabell,—I'm resolved—I think—you may go.—Ha! ha! ha! What would you give, that you could help loving me?

MIRABELL. I would give something that you did not know I could not help it.

MRS. MILLAMANT. Come, don't look grave, then. Well, what do you say to me?

MIRABELL. I say that a man may as soon make a friend by his wit, or a fortune by his honesty, as win a woman by plain dealing and sincerity.

MRS. MILLAMANT. Sententious Mirabell!—Prithee, don't look with that violent and inflexible wise face, like Solomon at the dividing of the child in an old tapestry hanging.[1]

MIRABELL. You are merry, madam, but I would persuade you for a moment to be serious.

MRS. MILLAMANT. What, with that face? No, if you keep your countenance, 'tis impossible I should hold mine. Well, after all, there is something very moving in a lovesick face. Ha! ha! ha!—Well, I won't laugh; don't be peevish—Heigho! now I'll be melancholy—as melancholy as a watch-light. Well, Mirabell, if ever you will win me, woo me now.—Nay, if you are so tedious, fare you well; I see they are walking away.

MIRABELL. Can you not find in the variety of your disposition one moment—

MRS. MILLAMANT. To hear you tell me Foible's married, and your plot like to speed? No.

MIRABELL. But how came you to know it?

MRS. MILLAMANT. Without the help of the devil, you can't imagine—unless she should tell me herself. Which of the two it may have been I will leave you to consider; and when you have done thinking of that, think of me. [*Exit.*

MIRABELL. I have something more!—Gone!—Think of you? To think of a whirlwind, though 'twere in a whirlwind, were a case of more steady contemplation—a very tranquillity of mind and mansion. A fellow that lives in a windmill, has not a more whimsical dwelling than the heart of a man that is lodged in a woman. There is no point of the compass to which they cannot turn, and by which they are not turned—and by one as well as another. For motion, not method, is their occupation. To know this, and yet continue to be in love, is to be made wise from the dictates of reason, and yet persevere to play the fool by the force of instinct.—Oh, here come my pair of turtles!—What, billing so sweetly! Is not Valentine's Day over with you yet?

[1]Wall-coverings with such representations were then common.

Enter WAITWELL *and* FOIBLE

Sirrah Waitwell; why, sure you think you were married for your own recreation, and not for my conveniency.

WAITWELL. Your pardon, sir. With submission, we have indeed been solacing in lawful delights; but still with an eye to business, sir. I have instructed her as well as I could. If she can take your directions as readily as my instructions, sir, your affairs are in a prosperous way.

MIRABELL. Give you joy, Mrs. Foible.

FOIBLE. Oh, 'las, sir, I'm so ashamed!—I'm afraid my lady has been in a thousand inquietudes for me. But I protest, sir, I made as much haste as I could.

WAITWELL. That she did indeed, sir. It was my fault that she did not make more.

MIRABELL. That I believe.

FOIBLE. But I told my lady as you instructed me, sir, that I had a prospect of seeing Sir Rowland, your uncle; and that I would put her ladyship's picture in my pocket to show him—which I'll be sure to say has made him so enamored of her beauty, that he burns with impatience to lie at her ladyship's feet and worship the original.

MIRABELL. Excellent Foible! Matrimony has made you eloquent in love.

WAITWELL. I think she has profited, sir; I think so.

FOIBLE. You have seen Madam Millamant, sir?

MIRABELL. Yes.

FOIBLE. I told her, sir, because I did not know that you might find an opportunity; she had so much company last night.

MIRABELL. Your diligence will merit more—in the meantime— (*Gives money*)

FOIBLE. O dear sir, your humble servant!

WAITWELL. [*Putting forth hand*] Spouse.

MIRABELL. Stand off, sir, not a penny!—Go on and prosper, Foible—the lease shall be made good and the farm stocked if we succeed.

FOIBLE. I don't question your generosity, sir, and you need not doubt of success. If you have no more commands, sir, I'll be gone; I'm sure my lady is at her toilet, and can't dress till I come.—Oh, dear, (*Looking out*) I'm sure that was Mrs. Marwood that went by in a mask! If she has seen me with you, I'm sure she'll tell my lady. I'll make haste home and prevent her. Your servant, sir.—B'w'y,[1] Waitwell. [*Exit.*

WAITWELL. Sir Rowland, if you please.—The jade's so pert upon her preferment she forgets herself.

MIRABELL. Come, sir, will you endeavor to forget yourself, and transform into Sir Rowland?

WAITWELL. Why, sir, it will be impossible I should remember myself.—Married, knighted, and attended all in one day! 'tis enough to make any man forget himself. The difficulty will be how to recover my acquaintance and familiarity with my former self, and fall from my transformation to a reformation into Waitwell. Nay, I shan't be quite the same Waitwell neither; for now, I remember me, I'm married and can't be my own man again.

Aye, there's my grief; that's the sad change of life,
To lose my title, and yet keep my wife.
[*Exeunt.*

ACT III

SCENE I. *A Room in* LADY WISHFORT'S *House*

LADY WISHFORT *at her toilet*, PEG *waiting*

LADY WISHFORT. Merciful! no news of Foible yet?

PEG. No, madam.

LADY WISHFORT. I have no more patience.—If I have not fretted myself till I am pale again, there's no veracity in me! Fetch me the red—the red, do you hear, sweetheart?—An arrant ash-color, as I'm a person! Look you how this wench stirs!—Why dost thou not fetch me a little red? Didst thou not hear me, Mopus?[2]

PEG. The red ratafia, does your ladyship mean, or the cherry-brandy?

LADY WISHFORT. Ratafia, fool! No, fool.—Not the ratafia, fool—grant me patience!—I mean the Spanish paper,[3] idiot—complexion, darling. Paint, paint, paint!—dost thou understand that, changeling, dangling thy hands like bobbins before thee? Why dost thou not stir, puppet? Thou wooden thing upon wires!

PEG. Lord, madam, your ladyship is so impatient!—I cannot come at the paint, madam; Mrs. Foible has locked it up and carried the key with her.

LADY WISHFORT. A pox take you both!—Fetch me the cherry-brandy then. [*Exit* PEG. I'm as pale and as faint, I look like Mrs. Qualmsick, the curate's wife, that's always breeding.—Wench! Come, come, wench, what art thou doing? Sipping, tasting?—Save thee, dost thou not know the bottle?

Enter PEG *with a bottle and china cup*

PEG. Madam, I was looking for a cup.

LADY WISHFORT. A cup, save thee! and what a cup hast thou brought!—Dost thou take me for a fairy, to drink out of an acorn? Why didst thou not bring thy thimble? Hast thou ne'er a brass thimble clinking in thy pocket with a bit of nutmeg?—I warrant thee. Come, fill, fill!—So—again.—(*One knocks*)—See who that is.—Set down the bottle first—here, here, under the table.—What, wouldst thou go with the bottle in thy hand, like a tapster? As I'm a person, this wench has lived in an inn upon the road before she came to me, like Maritornes the Asturian in *Don Quixote!*—No Foible yet?

PEG. No, madam; Mrs. Marwood.

LADY WISHFORT. Oh, Marwood; let her come in.—Come in, good Marwood.

Enter MRS. MARWOOD

MRS. MARWOOD. I'm surprised to find your ladyship in dishabille at this time of day.

LADY WISHFORT. Foible's a lost thing—has been abroad since morning, and never heard of since.

MRS. MARWOOD. I saw her but now as I came masked through the park, in conference with Mirabell.

LADY WISHFORT. With Mirabell!—You call my blood into my face, with mentioning that traitor. She durst not have the confidence! I sent her to negotiate an affair in which, if I'm detected, I'm undone. If that wheedling villain has wrought upon Foible to detect me, I'm ruined. Oh, my dear friend, I'm a wretch of wretches if I'm detected.

MRS. MARWOOD. O madam, you cannot suspect Mrs. Foible's integrity!

LADY WISHFORT. Oh, he carries poison in his tongue that would corrupt integrity itself! If she has given him an opportunity, she has as good as put her integrity into his hands.

[1] God be with you.
[2] A name for a stupid person.
[3] Rouge.

Ah, dear Marwood, what's integrity to an opportunity?—Hark! I hear her! [*To* PEG] Go, you thing, and send her in. [*Exit* PEG. Dear friend, retire into my closet, that I may examine her with more freedom.—You'll pardon me, dear friend; I can make bold with you. —There are books over the chimney—Quarles and Prynne, and *The Short View of the Stage*,[1] with Bunyan's works, to entertain you.

[*Exit* MRS. MARWOOD.

Enter FOIBLE

LADY WISHFORT. O Foible, where hast thou been? What hast thou been doing?

FOIBLE. Madam, I have seen the party.

LADY WISHFORT. But what hast thou done?

FOIBLE. Nay, 'tis your ladyship has done, and are to do; I have only promised. But a man so enamored—so transported!—Well, here it is, all that is left—all that is not kissed away.—Well, if worshiping of pictures be a sin—poor Sir Rowland, I say—

LADY WISHFORT. The miniature has been counted like—but hast thou not betrayed me, Foible? Hast thou not detected me to that faithless Mirabell?—What hadst thou to do with him in the Park? Answer me; has he got nothing out of thee?

FOIBLE. [*Aside*] So the devil has been beforehand with me. What shall I say?—Alas, madam, could I help it if I met that confident thing? Was I in fault? If you had heard how he used me, and all upon your ladyship's account, I'm sure you would not suspect my fidelity. Nay, if that had been the worst, I could have borne; but he had a fling at your ladyship too. And then I could not hold, but i'faith I gave him his own.

LADY WISHFORT. Me? What did the filthy fellow say?

FOIBLE. Oh, madam! 'tis a shame to say what he said—with his taunts and his fleers, tossing up his nose. Humph! (says he) what, you are a hatching some plot (says he), you are so early abroad, or catering (says he), ferreting for some disbanded officer, I warrant. —Half-pay is but thin subsistence (says he)—well, what pension does your lady propose? Let me see (says he); what, she must come down pretty deep now, she's superannuated (says he) and—

LADY WISHFORT. Odds my life, I'll have him—I'll have him murdered! I'll have him poisoned! Where does he eat?—I'll marry a drawer to have him poisoned in his wine. I'll send for Robin from Locket's[2] immediately.

FOIBLE. Poison him! poisoning's too good for him. Starve him, madam, starve him: marry Sir Rowland, and get him disinherited. Oh, you would bless yourself to hear what he said!

LADY WISHFORT. A villain! Superannuated!

FOIBLE. Humph (says he), I hear you are laying designs against me too (says he), and Mrs. Millamant is to marry my uncle (he does not suspect a word of your ladyship); but (says he) I'll fit you for that. I warrant you (says he) I'll hamper you for that (says he)—you and your old frippery[3] too (says he); I'll handle you—

LADY WISHFORT. Audacious villain! Handle me! would he durst!—Frippery! old frippery! Was there ever such a foul-mouthed fellow? I'll be married to-morrow; I'll be contracted to-night.

FOIBLE. The sooner the better, madam.

LADY WISHFORT. Will Sir Rowland be here, sayest thou? When, Foible?

FOIBLE. Incontinently, madam. No new sheriff's wife expects the return of her husband after knighthood with that impatience in which Sir Rowland burns for the dear hour of kissing your ladyship's hand after dinner.

LADY WISHFORT. Frippery! superannuated frippery! I'll frippery the villain; I'll reduce him to frippery and rags! a tatterdemalion! I hope to see him hung with tatters, like a Long-lane penthouse[4] or a gibbet thief. A slander-mouthed railer! I warrant the spendthrift prodigal's in debt as much as the million lottery, or the whole court upon a birthday.[5] I'll spoil his credit with his tailor. Yes, he shall have my niece with her fortune, he shall.

FOIBLE. He! I hope to see him lodge in Ludgate first, and angle into Blackfriars for brass farthings with an old mitten.[6]

---

[1]Francis Quarles (1592–1644), whose sacred poems were held "in wonderful veneration among the vulgar," the puritanical sort, for at least a century after his death.

William Prynne (1600–1669), puritan writer and statesman, author of *Histriomastix* (1633), an attack on the stage.

The *Short View* is Jeremy Collier s book.

[2]A tavern. [3]Old-clothes shop.

[4]A shed in Long Lane (West Smithfield to Barbican), where rag-sellers displayed their wares.

[5]Because of the gifts which had to be presented on a royal birthday.

[6]Ludgate was a debtors' prison, the condition of whose inmates was extremely wretched.

LADY WISHFORT. Aye, dear Foible; thank thee for that, dear Foible. He has put me out of all patience. I shall never recompose my features to receive Sir Rowland with any economy[1] of face. This wretch has fretted me that I am absolutely decayed. Look, Foible.

FOIBLE. Your ladyship has frowned a little too rashly, indeed, madam. There are some cracks discernible in the white varnish.

LADY WISHFORT. Let me see the glass.—Cracks, sayest thou?—why, I am arrantly flayed—I look like an old peeled wall. Thou must repair me, Foible, before Sir Rowland comes, or I shall never keep up to my picture.

FOIBLE. I warrant you, madam, a little art once made your picture like you, and now a little of the same art must make you like your picture. Your picture must sit for you, madam.

LADY WISHFORT. But art thou sure Sir Rowland will not fail to come? Or will he not fail, when he does come? Will he be importunate, Foible, and push? For if he should not be importunate, I shall never break decorums—I shall die with confusion if I am forced to advance.—Oh, no, I can never advance!—I shall swoon if he should expect advances. No, I hope Sir Rowland is better bred than to put a lady to the necessity of breaking her forms. I won't be too coy, neither.—I won't give him despair—but a little disdain is not amiss; a little scorn is alluring.

FOIBLE. A little scorn becomes your ladyship.

LADY WISHFORT. Yes, but tenderness becomes me best—a sort of a dyingness—you see that picture has a sort of a—ha, Foible? a swimmingness in the eyes—yes, I'll look so.—My niece affects it, but she wants features. Is Sir Rowland handsome? Let my toilet be removed—I'll dress above. I'll receive Sir Rowland here.—Is he handsome? Don't answer me. I won't know; I'll be surprised. I'll be taken by surprise.

FOIBLE. By storm, madam! Sir Rowland's a brisk man.

LADY WISHFORT. Is he? Oh, then he'll importune, if he's a brisk man. I shall save decorums if Sir Rowland importunes. I have a mortal terror at the apprehension of offending against decorums. Oh, I'm glad he's a brisk man!—Let my things be removed, good Foible. [*Exit.*

Enter MRS. FAINALL

MRS. FAINALL. Oh, Foible, I have been in a fright lest I should come too late! That devil Marwood saw you in the Park with Mirabell, and I'm afraid will discover it to my lady.

FOIBLE. Discover what, madam?

MRS. FAINALL. Nay, nay, put not on that strange face! I am privy to the whole design, and know that Waitwell, to whom thou wert this morning married, is to personate Mirabell's uncle, and as such, winning my lady, to involve her in those difficulties from which Mirabell only must release her, by his making his conditions to have my cousin and her fortune left to her own disposal.

FOIBLE. Oh, dear madam, I beg your pardon. It was not my confidence in your ladyship that was deficient, but I thought the former good correspondence between your ladyship and Mr. Mirabell might have hindered his communicating this secret.

MRS. FAINALL. Dear Foible, forget that.

FOIBLE. O dear madam, Mr. Mirabell is such a sweet, winning gentleman—but your ladyship is the pattern of generosity.—Sweet lady, to be so good! Mr. Mirabell cannot choose but be grateful. I find your ladyship has his heart still. Now, madam, I can safely tell your ladyship our success: Mrs. Marwood had told my lady, but I warrant I managed myself. I turned it all for the better. I told my lady that Mr. Mirabell railed at her; I laid horrid things to his charge, I'll vow; and my lady is so incensed that she'll be contracted to Sir Rowland to-night, she says. I warrant I worked her up, that he may have her for asking for, as they say of a Welsh maidenhead.

MRS. FAINALL. O rare Foible!

FOIBLE. Madam, I beg your ladyship to acquaint Mr. Mirabell of his success. I would be seen as little as possible to speak to him: besides, I believe Madam Marwood watches me.—She has a month's mind;[2] but I know Mr. Mirabell can't abide her.—John!—remove my lady's toilet.— [*Enter* FOOTMAN. Madam, your servant: my lady is so impatient I fear she'll come for me if I stay.

MRS. FAINALL. I'll go with you up the backstairs lest I should meet her. [*Exeunt.*

[1]Good order.

[2]A strong desire.

Enter MRS. MARWOOD

MRS. MARWOOD. Indeed, Mrs. Engine, is it thus with you? Are you become a go-between of this importance?—Yes, I shall watch you. Why this wench is the *passe-partout*[1]—a very master-key to everybody's strong-box. My friend Fainall, have you carried it so swimmingly? I thought there was something in it, but it seems it's over with you. Your loathing is not from a want of appetite, then, but from a surfeit.—Else you could never be so cool to fall from a principal to be an assistant, to procure for him! A pattern of generosity, that, I confess. Well, Mr. Fainall, you have met with your match.—O man, man! Woman, woman! The devil's an ass: if I were a painter, I would draw him like an idiot, a driveler with bib and bells. Man should have his head and horns, and woman the rest of him. Poor simple fiend!—"Madam Marwood has a month's mind, but he can't abide her."—'Twere better for him you had not been his confessor in that affair, without you could have kept his counsel closer. I shall not prove another pattern of generosity; he has not obliged me to that with those excesses of himself! And now I'll have none of him.—Here comes the good lady, panting ripe, with a heart full of hope, and a head full of care, like any chemist upon the day of projection.[2]

Enter LADY WISHFORT

LADY WISHFORT. Oh, dear Marwood, what shall I say for this rude forgetfulness?—but my dear friend is all goodness.

MRS. MARWOOD. No apologies, dear madam; I have been very well entertained.

LADY WISHFORT. As I'm a person, I am in a very chaos to think I should so forget myself: but I have such an olio of affairs, really I know not what to do.—(*Calls*) Foible!—I expect my nephew, Sir Wilfull, every moment too.—Why, Foible!—He means to travel for improvement.

MRS. MARWOOD. Methinks Sir Wilfull should rather think of marrying than traveling, at his years. I hear he is turned of forty.

LADY WISHFORT. Oh, he's in less danger of being spoiled by his travels—I am against my nephew's marrying too young. It will be time enough when he comes back and has acquired discretion to choose for himself.

MRS. MARWOOD. Methinks Mrs. Millamant and he would make a very fit match. He may travel afterwards.—'Tis a thing very usual with young gentlemen.

LADY WISHFORT. I promise you I have thought on't—and since 'tis your judgment, I'll think on't again. I assure you I will. I value your judgment extremely. On my word, I'll propose it.

Enter FOIBLE

LADY WISHFORT. Come, come, Foible—I had forgot my nephew will be here before dinner. I must make haste.

FOIBLE. Mr. Witwoud and Mr. Petulant are come to dine with your ladyship.

LADY WISHFORT. Oh, dear, I can't appear till I'm dressed!—Dear Marwood, shall I be free with you again, and beg you to entertain 'em? I'll make all imaginable haste. Dear friend, excuse me.

[*Exeunt* LADY WISHFORT *and* FOIBLE.

Enter MRS. MILLAMANT *and* MINCING

MRS. MILLAMANT. Sure never anything was so unbred as that odious man!—Marwood, your servant.

MRS. MARWOOD. You have a color; what's the matter?

MRS. MILLAMANT. That horrid fellow, Petulant, has provoked me into a flame: I have broke my fan.—Mincing, lend me yours. Is not all the powder out of my hair?

MRS. MARWOOD. No. What has he done?

MRS. MILLAMANT. Nay, he has done nothing; he has only talked—nay, he has said nothing neither, but he has contradicted everything that has been said. For my part, I thought Witwoud and he would have quarreled.

MINCING. I vow, mem, I thought once they would have fit.

MRS. MILLAMANT. Well, 'tis a lamentable thing, I swear, that one has not the liberty of choosing one's acquaintance as one does one's clothes.

MRS. MARWOOD. If we had that liberty, we should be as weary of one set of acquaintance, though never so good, as we are of one suit though never so fine. A fool and a doily stuff

[1]Master-key.

[2]Like any alchemist on the day of his crucial experiment.

would now and then find days of grace, and be worn for variety.

MRS. MILLAMANT. I could consent to wear 'em if they would wear alike; but fools never wear out—they are such *Drap-du-Berry*[1] things! Without one could give 'em to one's chambermaid after a day or two!

MRS. MARWOOD. 'Twere better so indeed. Or what think you of the playhouse? A fine, gay, glossy fool should be given there, like a new masking habit, after the masquerade is over and we have done with the disguise. For a fool's visit is always a disguise, and never admitted by a woman of wit but to blind her affair with a lover of sense. If you would but appear barefaced now, and own Mirabell, you might as easily put off Petulant and Witwoud as your hood and scarf. And indeed, 'tis time, for the town has found it; the secret is grown too big for the pretense. 'Tis like Mrs. Primly's great belly; she may lace it down before, but it burnishes on her hips. Indeed, Millamant, you can no more conceal it than my Lady Strammel can her face—that goodly face, which, in defiance of her Rhenish wine tea, will not be comprehended in a mask.

MRS. MILLAMANT. I'll take my death, Marwood, you are more censorious than a decayed beauty or a discarded toast.—Mincing, tell the men they may come up.—My aunt is not dressing here; their folly is less provoking than your malice. [*Exit* MINCING. —The town has found it! what has it found? That Mirabell loves me is no more a secret than it is a secret that you discovered it to my aunt, or than the reason why you discovered it is a secret.

MRS. MARWOOD. You are nettled.

MRS. MILLAMANT. You're mistaken. Ridiculous!

MRS. MARWOOD. Indeed, my dear, you'll tear another fan if you don't mitigate those violent airs.

MRS. MILLAMANT. Oh, silly! ha! ha! ha! I could laugh immoderately.—Poor Mirabell! His constancy to me has quite destroyed his complaisance for all the world beside. I swear, I never enjoined it him to be so coy. If I had the vanity to think he would obey me, I would command him to show more gallantry—'tis hardly well-bred to be so particular on one hand, and so insensible on the other. But I despair to prevail, and so let him follow his own way. Ha! ha! ha! Pardon me, dear creature, I must laugh—ha! ha! ha!—though I grant you 'tis a little barbarous—ha! ha! ha!

MRS. MARWOOD. What pity 'tis, so much fine raillery and delivered with so significant gesture, should be so unhappily directed to miscarry!

MRS. MILLAMANT. Ha? Dear creature, I ask your pardon. I swear, I did not mind you.

MRS. MARWOOD. Mr. Mirabell and you both may think it a thing impossible, when I shall tell him by telling you—

MRS. MILLAMANT. Oh dear, what? for it is the same thing if I hear it—ha! ha! ha!

MRS. MARWOOD. That I detest him, hate him, madam.

MRS. MILLAMANT. O madam! why, so do I—and yet the creature loves me—ha! ha! ha! How can one forbear laughing to think of it. —I am a sibyl if I am not amazed to think what he can see in me. I'll take my death, I think you are handsomer—and within a year or two as young; if you could but stay for me, I should overtake you—but that cannot be.—Well, that thought makes me melancholic.—Now I'll be sad.

MRS. MARWOOD. Your merry note may be changed sooner than you think.

MRS. MILLAMANT. D'ye say so? Then I'm resolved I'll have a song to keep up my spirits.

Enter MINCING

MINCING. The gentlemen stay but to comb,[2] madam, and will wait on you.

MRS. MILLAMANT. Desire Mrs. —— that is in the next room to sing the song I would have learned yesterday.—You shall hear it, madam—not that there's any great matter in it, but 'tis agreeable to my humor.

SONG[3]

I

Love's but the frailty of the mind,
When 'tis not with ambition joined;
A sickly flame, which, if not fed, expires,
And feeding, wastes in self-consuming fires.

[1]Woolen cloth formerly made at Berry, France.

[2]To comb their wigs.

[3]As the preceding speech indicates, this was sung by one who had no speaking part (by Mrs. Hodgson at the original performance).

2

'Tis not to wound a wanton boy
Or amorous youth, that gives the joy;
But 'tis the glory to have pierced a swain,
For whom inferior beauties sighed in vain.

3

Then I alone the conquest prize,
When I insult a rival's eyes:
If there's delight in love, 'tis when I see
That heart, which others bleed for, bleed for me.

Enter PETULANT, WITWOUD

MRS. MILLAMANT. Is your animosity composed, gentlemen?

WITWOUD. Raillery, raillery, madam; we have no animosity—we hit off a little wit now and then, but no animosity.—The falling out of wits is like the falling out of lovers. We agree in the main,[1] like treble and bass.—Ha, Petulant?

PETULANT. Aye, in the main—but when I have a humor to contradict—

WITWOUD. Aye, when he has a humor to contradict, then I contradict too. What, I know my cue. Then we contradict one another like two battledores; for contradictions beget one another like Jews.

PETULANT. If he says black's black—if I have a humor to say 'tis blue—let that pass—all's one for that. If I have a humor to prove it, it must be granted.

WITWOUD. Not positively must—but it may—it may.

PETULANT. Yes, it positively must, upon proof positive.

WITWOUD. Aye, upon proof positive it must; but upon proof presumptive it only may.—That's a logical distinction now, madam.

MRS. MARWOOD. I perceive your debates are of importance and very learnedly handled.

PETULANT. Importance is one thing, and learning's another. But a debate's a debate; that I assert.

WITWOUD. Petulant's an enemy to learning; he relies altogether on his parts.

PETULANT. No, I'm no enemy to learning. It hurts not me.

MRS. MARWOOD. That's a sign indeed 'tis no enemy to you.

[1]In the middle (tenor) part.

PETULANT. No, no, it's no enemy to anybody but them that have it.

MRS. MILLAMANT. Well, an illiterate man's my aversion. I wonder at the impudence of any illiterate man to offer to make love.

WITWOUD. That I confess I wonder at too.

MRS. MILLAMANT. Ah! to marry an ignorant that can hardly read or write!

PETULANT. Why should a man be any further from being married, though he can't read, than he is from being hanged? The ordinary's[2] paid for setting the psalm, and the parish priest for reading the ceremony. And for the rest which is to follow in both cases, a man may do it without book—so all's one for that.

MRS. MILLAMANT. D'ye hear the creature?—Lord, here's company; I'll be gone.

[*Exeunt* MRS. MILLAMANT *and* MINCING.

Enter SIR WILFULL WITWOUD *in a country riding habit, and Servant to* LADY WISHFORT

WITWOUD. In the name of Bartlemew and his fair, what have we here?

MRS. MARWOOD. 'Tis your brother, I fancy. Don't you know him?

WITWOUD. Not I.—Yes, I think it is he—I've almost forgot him; I have not seen him since the Revolution.[3]

SERVANT. Sir, my lady's dressing. Here's company; if you please to walk in, in the meantime.

SIR WILFULL. Dressing! What, 'tis but morning here I warrant, with you in London; we should count it towards afternoon in our parts, down in Shropshire.—Why then, belike, my aunt han't dined yet,—ha, friend?

SERVANT. Your aunt, sir?

SIR WILFULL. My aunt, sir! Yes, my aunt, sir, and your lady, sir; your lady is my aunt, sir.—Why, what! Dost thou not know me, friend? Why, then send somebody hither that does. How long hast thou lived with thy lady, fellow,—ha?

SERVANT. A week, sir—longer than anybody in the house, except my lady's woman.

SIR WILFULL. Why, then belike thou dost not know thy lady, if thou seest her,—ha, friend?

SERVANT. Why, truly, sir, I cannot safely

[2]A diocesan officer appointed to give criminals their neck-verses, and to prepare them for death.

[3]Of 1688.

swear to her face in a morning, before she is dressed. 'Tis like I may give a shrewd guess at her by this time.

SIR WILFULL. Well, prithee try what thou canst do; if thou canst not guess, inquire her out,—dost hear, fellow?—and tell her, her nephew, Sir Wilfull Witwoud, is in the house.

SERVANT. I shall, sir.

SIR WILFULL. —Hold ye; hear me, friend—a word with you in your ear. Prithee, who are these gallants?

SERVANT. Really, sir, I can't tell; here come so many here, 'tis hard to know 'em all. [*Exit Servant.*

SIR WILFULL. Oons, this fellow knows less than a starling; I don't think a' knows his own name.

MRS. MARWOOD. Mr. Witwoud, your brother is not behindhand in forgetfulness—I fancy he has forgot you too.

WITWOUD. I hope so—the devil take him that remembers first, I say.

SIR WILFULL. Save you, gentlemen and lady!

MRS. MARWOOD. For shame, Mr. Witwoud; why don't you speak to him?—[*To* SIR WILFULL] And you, sir.

WITWOUD. Petulant, speak.

PETULANT. [*To* SIR WILFULL] And you, sir.

SIR WILFULL. No offense, I hope. (*Salutes* MRS. MARWOOD)

MRS. MARWOOD. No, sure, sir.

WITWOUD. [*Aside*] This is a vile dog, I see that already. No offense! ha! ha! ha!—To him; to him, Petulant, smoke him.[1]

PETULANT. [*Surveying him round*] It seems as if you had come a journey, sir;—hem, hem.

SIR WILFULL. Very likely, sir, that it may seem so.

PETULANT. No offense, I hope, sir.

WITWOUD. [*Aside*] Smoke the boots, the boots!—Petulant, the boots! Ha! ha! ha!

SIR WILFULL. May be not, sir; thereafter, as 'tis meant, sir.

PETULANT. Sir, I presume upon the information of your boots.

SIR WILFULL. Why, 'tis like you may, sir: if you are not satisfied with the information of my boots, sir, if you will step to the stable, you may inquire further of my horse, sir.

PETULANT. Your horse, sir? your horse is an ass, sir!

SIR WILFULL. Do you speak by way of offense, sir?

MRS. MARWOOD. The gentleman's merry, that's all, sir.—(*Aside*) 'Slife, we shall have a quarrel betwixt an horse and an ass before they find one another out.—(*Aloud*) You must not take anything amiss from your friends, sir. You are among your friends here, though it may be you don't know it.—If I am not mistaken, you are Sir Wilfull Witwoud.

SIR WILFULL. Right, lady; I am Sir Wilfull Witwoud. So I write myself. No offense to anybody, I hope—and nephew to the Lady Wishfort of this mansion.

MRS. MARWOOD. Don't you know this gentleman, sir?

SIR WILFULL. Hum! What, sure 'tis not—yea by'r Lady, but 'tis—'sheart, I know not whether 'tis or no—yea, but 'tis, by the Wrekin.[2] Brother Anthony! What, Tony, i'faith!—what, dost thou not know me? By'r Lady, nor I thee, thou art so becravated, and so beperiwigged!—'Sheart, why dost not speak? art thou o'erjoyed?

WITWOUD. Odso, brother, is it you?—your servant, brother.

SIR WILFULL. Your servant!—why yours, sir. Your servant again—'sheart, and your friend and servant to that—and a—and a—flap-dragon for your service, sir! and a hare's foot and a hare's scut[3] for your service, sir! an you be so cold and so courtly.

WITWOUD. No offense, I hope, brother.

SIR WILFULL. 'Sheart, sir, but there is, and much offense!—A pox, is this your Inns o' Court breeding, not to know your friends and your relations, your elders and your betters?

WITWOUD. Why, brother Wilfull of Salop,[4] you may be as short as a Shrewsbury-cake, if you please. But I tell you 'tis not modish to know relations in town: you think you're in the country, where great lubberly brothers slabber and kiss one another when they meet, like a call of sergeants—'tis not the fashion here; 'tis not indeed, dear brother.

SIR WILFULL. The fashion's a fool; and you're a fop, dear brother. 'Sheart, I've suspected this—by'r Lady, I conjectured you were a fop since you began to change the style of your letters, and write in a scrap of paper gilt round the edges, no bigger than a *subpœna*. I might expect this when you left off

[1]Make fun of him.

[2]Hill in Shropshire.

[3]Hare's tail.

[4]Shropshire.

"Honored Brother," and "hoping you are in good health," and so forth—to begin with a "Rat me, knight, I'm so sick of a last night's debauch—'ods heart," and then tell a familiar tale of a cock and a bull, and a whore and a bottle, and so conclude.—You could write news before you were out of your time,[1] when you lived with honest Pumple Nose, the attorney of Furnival's Inn—you could entreat to be remembered then to your friends round the Wrekin. We could have gazettes, then, and Dawks's Letter,[2] and the Weekly Bill, till of late days.

PETULANT. 'Slife, Witwoud, were you ever an attorney's clerk? of the family of the Furnivals? Ha! ha! ha!

WITWOUD. Aye, aye, but that was but for a while—not long, not long. Pshaw! I was not in my own power then; an orphan, and this fellow was my guardian. Aye, aye, I was glad to consent to that, man, to come to London. He had the disposal of me then. If I had not agreed to that, I might have been bound 'prentice to a felt-maker in Shrewsbury; this fellow would have bound me to a maker of felts.

SIR WILFULL. 'Sheart, and better than to be bound to a maker of fops—where, I suppose, you have served your time, and now you may set up for yourself.

MRS. MARWOOD. You intend to travel, sir, as I'm informed.

SIR WILFULL. Belike I may, madam. I may chance to sail upon the salt seas, if my mind hold.

PETULANT. And the wind serve.

SIR WILFULL. Serve or not serve, I shan't ask license of you, sir; nor the weathercock your companion. I direct my discourse to the lady, sir.—'Tis like my aunt may have told you, madam—yes, I have settled my concerns, I may say now, and am minded to see foreign parts—if an how that the peace holds, whereby that is, taxes abate.

MRS. MARWOOD. I thought you had designed for France at all adventures.

SIR WILFULL. I can't tell that; 'tis like I may, and 'tis like I may not. I am somewhat dainty in making a resolution because when I make it I keep it. I don't stand shill I, shall I,[3] then; if I say't, I'll do't. But I have thoughts to tarry a small matter in town to learn somewhat of your lingo first, before I cross the seas. I'd gladly have a spice of your French, as they say, whereby to hold discourse in foreign countries.

MRS. MARWOOD. Here's an academy in town for that use.

SIR WILFULL. There is? 'Tis like there may.

MRS. MARWOOD. No doubt you will return very much improved.

WITWOUD. Yes, refined, like a Dutch skipper from a whale-fishing.

Enter LADY WISHFORT *and* FAINALL

LADY WISHFORT. Nephew, you are welcome.

SIR WILFULL. Aunt, your servant.

FAINALL. Sir Wilfull, your most faithful servant.

SIR WILFULL. Cousin Fainall, give me your hand.

LADY WISHFORT. Cousin Witwoud, your servant; Mr. Petulant, your servant; nephew, you are welcome again. Will you drink anything after your journey, nephew, before you eat? Dinner's almost ready.

SIR WILFULL. I'm very well, I thank you, aunt—however, I thank you for your courteous offer. 'Sheart, I was afraid you would have been in the fashion too, and have remembered to have forgot your relations. Here's your cousin Tony; belike, I mayn't call him brother for fear of offense.

LADY WISHFORT. Oh, he's a rallier, nephew—my cousin's a wit. And your great wits always rally their best friends to choose.[4] When you have been abroad, nephew, you'll understand raillery better.

(FAINALL *and* MRS. MARWOOD *talk apart*)

SIR WILFULL. Why then, let him hold his tongue in the meantime, and rail when that day comes.

Enter MINCING

MINCING. Mem, I am come to acquaint your la'ship that dinner is impatient.

SIR WILFULL. Impatient? why then, belike it won't stay till I pull off my boots.—Sweet-

[1]Before you had completed your period of service. Furnival's Inn was formerly an inn of chancery and a part of Lincoln's Inn.

[2]A news-letter printed to resemble script, with space left blank for personal additions. "Weekly Bill": Bill of Mortality within the city of London.

[3]Hesitating (shilly-shallying).

[4]At will.

heart, can you help me to a pair of slippers?—My man's with his horses, I warrant.

Lady Wishfort. Fie, fie, nephew! you would not pull off your boots here?—Go down into the hall—dinner shall stay for you.

[*Exit* Sir Wilfull.

My nephew's a little unbred; you'll pardon him, madam.—Gentlemen, will you walk?—Marwood?

Mrs. Marwood. I'll follow you, madam—before Sir Wilfull is ready.

(*Exeunt all but* Mrs. Marwood *and* Fainall)

Fainall. Why then, Foible's a bawd—an arrant, rank, match-making bawd. And I, it seems, am a husband, a rank husband; and my wife a very arrant, rank wife—all in the way of the world. 'Sdeath, to be an anticipated cuckold, a cuckold in embryo! Sure, I was born with budding antlers, like a young satyr or a citizen's child. 'Sdeath! to be out-witted—to be out-jilted—out-matrimony'd!—If I had kept my speed like a stag, 'twere somewhat—but to crawl after, with my horns, like a snail, and beout stripped by my wife—'tis scurvy wedlock.

Mrs. Marwood. Then shake it off. You have often wished for an opportunity to part, and now you have it. But first prevent their plot—the half of Millamant's fortune is too considerable to be parted with to a foe—to Mirabell.

Fainall. Damn him! that had been mine, had you not made that fond discovery—that had been forfeited, had they been married. My wife had added luster to my horns by that increase of fortune; I could have worn 'em tipped with gold, though my forehead had been furnished like a deputy-lieutenant's hall.

Mrs. Marwood. They may prove a cap of maintenance[1] to you still, if you can away with your wife. And she's no worse than when you had her—I dare swear she had given up her game before she was married.

Fainall. Hum! that may be. She might throw up her cards, but I'll be hanged if she did not put pam[2] in her pocket.

Mrs. Marwood. You married her to keep you; and if you can contrive to have her keep you better than you expected, why should you not keep her longer than you intended?

Fainall. The means, the means?

Mrs. Marwood. Discover to my lady your wife's conduct; threaten to part with her! My lady loves her, and will come to any composition to save her reputation. Take the opportunity of breaking it just upon the discovery of this imposture. My lady will be enraged beyond bounds, and sacrifice niece, and fortune, and all, at that conjuncture. And let me alone to keep her warm; if she should flag in her part, I will not fail to prompt her.

Fainall. Faith, this has an appearance.

Mrs. Marwood. I'm sorry I hinted to my lady to endeavor a match between Millamant and Sir Wilfull; that may be an obstacle.

Fainall. Oh, for that matter, leave me to manage him. I'll disable him for that; he will drink like a Dane. After dinner I'll set his hand in.

Mrs. Marwood. Well, how do you stand affected towards your lady?

Fainall. Why, faith, I'm thinking of it.—Let me see—I am married already, so that's over. My wife has played the jade with me—well, that's over too. I never loved her, or if I had, why that would have been over too by this time.—Jealous of her I cannot be, for I am certain; so there's an end of jealousy: weary of her I am, and shall be—no, there's no end of that—no, no, that were too much to hope.—Thus far concerning my repose; now for my reputation. As to my own, I married not for it, so that's out of the question; and as to my part in my wife's—why, she had parted with hers before; so bringing none to me, she can take none from me. 'Tis against all rule of play that I should lose to one who has not wherewithal to stake.

Mrs. Marwood. Besides, you forget marriage is honorable.

Fainall. Hum, faith, and that's well thought on. Marriage is honorable, as you say; and if so, wherefore should cuckoldom be a discredit, being derived from so honorable a root?

Mrs. Marwood. Nay, I know not; if the root be honorable, why not the branches?

Fainall. So, so; why, this point's clear—well, how do we proceed?

Mrs. Marwood. I will contrive a letter which shall be delivered to my lady at the time when that rascal who is to act Sir Rowland is with her. It shall come as from an

---

[1]Heraldic term: a cap with two points like horns behind, borne in the arms of some families.

[2]Knave of Clubs in certain games in which this is the highest trump.

unknown hand—for the less I appear to know of the truth, the better I can play the incendiary. Besides, I would not have Foible provoked if I could help it—because you know she knows some passages—nay, I expect all will come out. But let the mine be sprung first, and then I care not if I am discovered.

FAINALL. If the worst come to the worst, I'll turn my wife to grass. I have already a deed of settlement of the best part of her estate, which I wheedled out of her, and that you shall partake at least.

MRS. MARWOOD. I hope you are convinced that I hate Mirabell now: you'll be no more jealous?

FAINALL. Jealous! No, by this kiss. Let husbands be jealous, but let the lover still believe; or, if he doubt, let it be only to endear his pleasure, and prepare the joy that follows when he proves his mistress true. But let husbands' doubts convert to endless jealousy; or, if they have belief, let it corrupt to superstition and blind credulity. I am single, and will herd no more with 'em. True, I wear the badge, but I'll disown the order. And since I take my leave of 'em, I care not if I leave 'em a common motto to their common crest:

All husbands must or pain or shame endure;
The wise too jealous are, fools too secure.

[*Exeunt.*

ACT IV

SCENE I. [*Scene continues*]

Enter LADY WISHFORT *and* FOIBLE

LADY WISHFORT. Is Sir Rowland coming, sayest thou, Foible? And are things in order?

FOIBLE. Yes, madam, I have put wax lights in the sconces, and placed the footmen in a row in the hall, in their best liveries, with the coachman and postilion to fill up the equipage.

LADY WISHFORT. Have you pulvilled[1] the coachman and postilion, that they may not stink of the stable when Sir Rowland comes by?

FOIBLE. Yes, madam.

LADY WISHFORT. And are the dancers and the music ready, that he may be entertained in all points with correspondence to his passion?

FOIBLE. All is ready, madam.

LADY WISHFORT. And—well—and how do I look, Foible?

FOIBLE. Most killing well, madam.

LADY WISHFORT. Well, and how shall I receive him? in what figure shall I give his heart the first impression? There is a great deal in the first impression. Shall I sit?—no, I won't sit—I'll walk—aye, I'll walk from the door upon his entrance, and then turn full upon him—no, that will be too sudden. I'll lie,—aye, I'll lie down—I'll receive him in my little dressing-room; there's a couch—yes, yes, I'll give the first impression on a couch.—I won't lie neither, but loll and lean upon one elbow with one foot a little dangling off, jogging in a thoughtful way—yes—and then as soon as he appears, start, aye, start and be surprised, and rise to meet him in a pretty disorder—yes.—Oh, nothing is more alluring than a levee from a couch, in some confusion; it shows the foot to advantage, and furnishes with blushes, and recomposing airs beyond comparison. Hark! there's a coach.

FOIBLE. 'Tis he, madam.

LADY WISHFORT. Oh, dear!—Has my nephew made his addresses to Millamant? I ordered him.

FOIBLE. Sir Wilfull is set in to drinking, madam, in the parlor.

LADY WISHFORT. Odds my life, I'll send him to her. Call her down, Foible; bring her hither. I'll send him as I go—when they are together, then come to me, Foible, that I may not be too long alone with Sir Rowland.

[*Exit.*

Enter MRS. MILLAMANT *and* MRS. FAINALL

FOIBLE. Madam, I stayed here to tell your ladyship that Mr. Mirabell has waited this half-hour for an opportunity to talk with you—though my lady's orders were to leave you and Sir Wilfull together. Shall I tell Mr. Mirabell that you are at leisure?

MRS. MILLAMANT. No. What would the dear man have? I am thoughtful, and would amuse myself—bid him come another time.

(*Repeating, and walking about*)

There never yet was woman made
Nor shall, but to be cursed.[2]

That's hard!

MRS. FAINALL. You are very fond of Sir John Suckling to-day, Millamant, and the poets.

[1]Perfumed.

[2]Opening lines of a poem by Sir John Suckling. (*Works*, ed. A. H. Thompson, p. 18.)

MRS. MILLAMANT. He? Aye, and filthy verses—so I am.

FOIBLE. Sir Wilfull is coming, madam. Shall I send Mr. Mirabell away?

MRS. MILLAMANT. Aye, if you please, Foible, send him away, or send him hither—just as you will, dear Foible.—I think I'll see him—shall I? Aye, let the wretch come.

[*Exit* FOIBLE.

(*Repeating*)

Thyrsis, a youth of the inspirèd train.[1]

Dear Fainall, entertain Sir Wilfull—thou hast philosophy to undergo a fool. Thou art married and hast patience—I would confer with my own thoughts.

MRS. FAINALL. I am obliged to you that you would make me your proxy in this affair, but I have business of my own.

Enter SIR WILFULL

MRS. FAINALL. O Sir Wilfull, you are come at the critical instant. There's your mistress up to the ears in love and contemplation; pursue your point now or never.

SIR WILFULL. Yes; my aunt will have it so—I would gladly have been encouraged with a bottle or two, because I'm somewhat wary at first before I am acquainted.—(*This while* MILLAMANT *walks about repeating to herself*)—But I hope, after a time, I shall break my mind—that is, upon further acquaintance—so for the present, cousin, I'll take my leave. If so be you'll be so kind to make my excuse, I'll return to my company—

MRS. FAINALL. Oh, fie, Sir Wilfull! What! You must not be daunted.

SIR WILFULL. Daunted! No, that's not it; it is not so much for that—for if so be that I set on't, I'll do't. But only for the present, 'tis sufficient till further acquaintance, that's all—your servant.

MRS. FAINALL. Nay, I'll swear you shall never lose so favorable an opportunity if I can help it. I'll leave you together, and lock the door. [*Exit.*

SIR WILFULL. Nay, nay, cousin—I have forgot my gloves!—What d'ye do?—'Sheart, a' has locked the door indeed, I think. Nay, Cousin Fainall, open the door! Pshaw, what a vixen trick is this?—Nay, now a' has seen me too.—Cousin, I made bold to pass through as it were—I think this door's enchanted!

MRS. MILLAMANT. (*Repeating*)

I prithee spare me, gentle boy,
Press me no more for that slight toy.[2]

SIR WILFULL. Anan?[3] Cousin, your servant.

MRS. MILLAMANT. (*Repeating*)

That foolish trifle of a heart.[4]

Sir Wilfull?

SIR WILFULL. Yes—your servant. No offense, I hope, cousin.

MRS. MILLAMANT. (*Repeating*)

I swear it will not do its part,
Though thou dost thine, employ'st thy power and art.

Natural, easy Suckling!

SIR WILFULL. Anan? Suckling? no such suckling neither, cousin, nor stripling: I thank Heaven, I'm no minor.

MRS. MILLAMANT. Ah, rustic, ruder than Gothic!

SIR WILFULL. Well, well, I shall understand your lingo one of these days, cousin; in the meanwhile I must answer in plain English.

MRS. MILLAMANT. Have you any business with me, Sir Wilfull?

SIR WILFULL. Not at present, cousin.—Yes, I made bold to see, to come and know if that how you were disposed to fetch a walk this evening; if so be that I might not be troublesome, I would have sought a walk with you.

MRS. MILLAMANT. A walk? what then?

SIR WILFULL. Nay, nothing—only for the walk's sake, that's all.

MRS. MILLAMANT. I nauseate walking; 'tis a country diversion. I loathe the country, and everything that relates to it.

SIR WILFULL. Indeed! ha! Look ye, look ye—you do? Nay, 'tis like you may—here are choice of pastimes here in town, as plays and the like; that must be confessed, indeed.

MRS. MILLAMANT. *Ah, l'étourdi!*[5] I hate the town too.

SIR WILFULL. Dear heart, that's much—ha! that you should hate 'em both! Ha! 'tis like you may; there are some can't relish the

[1]Opening line of Edmund Waller's *Story of Phoebus and Daphne, Applied.*

[2]Suckling, *Works*, p. 20.

[3]What did you say?

[4]Suckling. This line and the following two repeated by Millamant complete the stanza begun with "I prithee."

[5]Blunderer.

town, and others can't away with the country—'tis like you may be one of those, cousin.

MRS. MILLAMANT. Ha! ha! ha! yes, 'tis like I may.—You have nothing further to say to me?

SIR WILFULL. Not at present, cousin.—'Tis like when I have an opportunity to be more private—I may break my mind in some measure—I conjecture you partly guess—however, that's as time shall try—but spare to speak and spare to speed, as they say.

MRS. MILLAMANT. If it is of no great importance, Sir Wilfull, you will oblige me to leave me; I have just now a little business—

SIR WILFULL. Enough, enough, cousin: yes, yes, all a case.—When you're disposed, when you're disposed. Now's as well as another time, and another time as well as now. All's one for that—yes, yes, if your concerns call you, there's no haste; it will keep cold, as they say.—Cousin, your servant.—I think this door's locked.

MRS. MILLAMANT. You may go this way, sir.

SIR WILFULL. Your servant; then with your leave I'll return to my company. [*Exit.*

MRS. MILLAMANT. Aye, aye; ha! ha! ha!

Like Phœbus sung the no less amorous boy.[1]

Enter MIRABELL

MIRABELL. "Like Daphne she, as lovely and as coy." Do you lock yourself up from me, to make my search more curious, or is this pretty artifice contrived to signify that here the chase must end, and my pursuit be crowned? For you can fly no further.

MRS. MILLAMANT. Vanity! no—I'll fly, and be followed to the last moment. Though I am upon the very verge of matrimony, I expect you should solicit me as much as if I were wavering at the grate of a monastery, with one foot over the threshold. I'll be solicited to the very last—nay, and afterwards.

MIRABELL. What, after the last?

MRS. MILLAMANT. Oh, I should think I was poor and had nothing to bestow, if I were reduced to an inglorious ease and freed from the agreeable fatigues of solicitation.

MIRABELL. But do not you know that when favors are conferred upon instant and tedious solicitation, that they diminish in their value, and that both the giver loses the grace, and the receiver lessens his pleasure?

MRS. MILLAMANT. It may be in things of common application; but never, sure, in love. Oh, I hate a lover that can dare to think he draws a moment's air, independent on the bounty of his mistress. There is not so impudent a thing in nature as the saucy look of an assured man, confident of success. The pedantic arrogance of a very husband has not so pragmatical an air. Ah! I'll never marry unless I am first made sure of my will and pleasure.

MIRABELL. Would you have 'em both before marriage? or will you be contented with the first now, and stay for the other till after grace?

MRS. MILLAMANT. Ah! don't be impertinent.—My dear liberty, shall I leave thee? my faithful solitude, my darling contemplation, must I bid you then adieu? Ay-h adieu—my morning thoughts, agreeable wakings, indolent slumbers, all ye *douceurs*, ye *sommeils du matin*,[2] *adieu*.—I can't do't, 'tis more than impossible—positively, Mirabell, I'll lie abed in a morning as long as I please.

MIRABELL. Then I'll get up in a morning as early as I please.

MRS. MILLAMANT. Ah! idle creature, get up when you will—and d'ye hear, I won't be called names after I'm married; positively, I won't be called names.

MIRABELL. Names!

MRS. MILLAMANT. Aye,—as wife, spouse, my dear, joy, jewel, love, sweetheart, and the rest of that nauseous cant, in which men and their wives are so fulsomely familiar—I shall never bear that. Good Mirabell, don't let us be familiar or fond, nor kiss before folks, like my Lady Fadler and Sir Francis; nor go to Hyde Park together the first Sunday in a new chariot, to provoke eyes and whispers, and then never be seen there together again—as if we were proud of one another the first week, and ashamed of one another ever after. Let us never visit together, nor go to a play together; but let us be very strange and well-bred. Let us be as strange as if we had been married a great while, and as well-bred as if we were not married at all.

MIRABELL. Have you any more conditions to offer? Hitherto your demands are pretty reasonable.

[1]Waller. L. 3 of the poem above named. Mirabell repeats l. 4.

[2]Sweets, ye morning naps.

MRS. MILLAMANT. Trifles—as liberty to pay and receive visits to and from whom I please; to write and receive letters, without interrogatories or wry faces on your part; to wear what I please, and choose conversation with regard only to my own taste; to have no obligation upon me to converse with wits that I don't like, because they are your acquaintance: or to be intimate with fools, because they may be your relations.—Come to dinner when I please; dine in my dressing-room when I'm out of humor, without giving a reason. To have my closet inviolate; to be sole empress of my tea-table, which you must never presume to approach without first asking leave. And lastly, wherever I am, you shall always knock at the door before you come in. These articles subscribed, if I continue to endure you a little longer, I may by degrees dwindle into a wife.

MIRABELL. Your bill of fare is something advanced in this latter account.—Well, have I liberty to offer conditions—that when you are dwindled into a wife, I may not be beyond measure enlarged into a husband?

MRS. MILLAMANT. You have free leave. Propose your utmost; speak and spare not.

MIRABELL. I thank you.—*Imprimis*[1] then, I covenant that your acquaintance be general; that you admit no sworn confidant or intimate of your own sex—no she-friend to screen her affairs under your countenance, and tempt you to make trial of a mutual secrecy. No decoy-duck to wheedle you—a fop, scrambling to the play in a mask—then bring you home in a pretended fright, when you think you shall be found out—and rail at me for missing the play and disappointing the frolic which you had, to pick me up and prove my constancy.

MRS. MILLAMANT. Detestable *imprimis!* I go to the play in a mask!

MIRABELL. *Item*, I article, that you continue to like your own face, as long as I shall; and while it passes current with me, that you endeavor not to new-coin it. To which end, together with all vizards for the day, I prohibit all masks for the night, made of oiled-skins and I know not what—hogs' bones, hares' gall, pig-water, and the marrow of a roasted cat. In short, I forbid all commerce with the gentlewoman in what-d'ye-call-it Court. *Item*, I shut my doors against all bawds with baskets, and pennyworths of muslin, china, fans, atlases,[2] *etc.—Item*, when you shall be breeding—

MRS. MILLAMANT. Ah! name it not.

MIRABELL. Which may be presumed, with a blessing on our endeavors—

MRS. MILLAMANT. Odious endeavors!

MIRABELL. I denounce against all strait lacing, squeezing for a shape, till you mold my boy's head like a sugar-loaf, and instead of a man-child, make me father to a crooked billet. Lastly, to the dominion of the tea-table I submit—but with proviso, that you exceed not in your province, but restrain yourself to native and simple tea-table drinks, as tea, chocolate, and coffee; as likewise to genuine and authorized tea-table talk—such as mending of fashions, spoiling reputations, railing at absent friends, and so forth—but that on no account you encroach upon the men's prerogative, and presume to drink healths, or toast fellows: for prevention of which I banish all foreign forces, all auxiliaries to the tea-table, as orange-brandy, all aniseed, cinnamon, citron, and Barbadoes waters, together with ratafia, and the most noble spirit of clary[3]—but for cowslip wine, poppy water, and all dormitives, those I allow.—These provisos admitted, in other things I may prove a tractable and complying husband.

MRS. MILLAMANT. O horrid provisos! filthy strong-waters!—I toast fellows!—odious men! I hate your odious provisos.

MIRABELL. Then we're agreed! Shall I kiss your hand upon the contract? And here comes one to be a witness to the sealing of the deed.

Enter MRS. FAINALL

MRS. MILLAMANT. Fainall, what shall I do? Shall I have him?—I think I must have him.

MRS. FAINALL. Aye, aye, take him, take him; what should you do?

MRS. MILLAMANT. Well then—I'll take my death, I'm in a horrid fright.—Fainall, I shall never say it—well—I think—I'll endure you.

MRS. FAINALL. Fie! fie! Have him, have him, and tell him so in plain terms; for I am sure you have a mind to him.

MRS. MILLAMANT. Are you? I think I have—and the horrid man looks as if he

[1]First.

[2]Rich satins, from the East.

[3]All of these are cordials, and very potent.

thought so too. Well, you ridiculous thing you, I'll have you—I won't be kissed, nor I won't be thanked—here, kiss my hand though. —So, hold your tongue now; don't say a word.

Mrs. Fainall. Mirabell, there's a necessity for your obedience; you have neither time to talk nor stay. My mother is coming, and in my conscience if she should see you, would fall into fits, and maybe not recover time enough to return to Sir Rowland, who, as Foible tells me, is in a fair way to succeed. Therefore spare your ecstasies for another occasion, and slip down the backstairs, where Foible waits to consult you.

Mrs. Millamant. Aye, go, go. In the meantime I suppose you have said something to please me.

Mirabell. I am all obedience.

[*Exit* Mirabell.

Mrs. Fainall. Yonder, Sir Wilfull's drunk, and so noisy that my mother has been forced to leave Sir Rowland to appease him; but he answers her only with singing and drinking. What they may have done by this time I know not, but Petulant and he were upon quarreling as I came by.

Mrs. Millamant. Well, if Mirabell should not make a good husband, I am a lost thing, for I find I love him violently.

Mrs. Fainall. So it seems, for you mind not what's said to you.—If you doubt him, you had best take up with Sir Wilfull.

Mrs. Millamant. How can you name that superannuated lubber?—Foh!

Enter Witwoud *from drinking*

Mrs. Fainall. So! Is the fray made up, that you have left 'em?

Witwoud. Left 'em? I could stay no longer. I have laughed like ten christ'nings—I am tipsy with laughing. If I had stayed any longer I should have burst—I must have been let out and pieced in the sides like an unfixed camlet.[1]—Yes, yes, the fray is composed; my lady came in like a *noli prosequi*,[2] and stopped the proceedings.

Mrs. Millamant. What was the dispute?

Witwoud. That's the jest; there was no dispute. They could neither of 'em speak for rage, and so fell a sputtering at one another like two roasting apples.

Enter Petulant, *drunk*

Now, Petulant, all's over, all's well. Gad, my head begins to whim it about—Why dost thou not speak? Thou art both as drunk and as mute as a fish.

Petulant. Look you, Mrs. Millamant—if you can love me, dear nymph, say it—and that's the conclusion. Pass on, or pass off—that's all.

Witwoud. Thou hast uttered volumes, folios, in less than *decimo sexto*, my dear Lacedemonian.[3] Sirrah Petulant, thou art an epitomizer of words.

Petulant. Witwoud—you are an annihilator of sense.

Witwoud. Thou art a retailer of phrases, and dost deal in remnants of remnants, like a maker of pincushions—thou art in truth (metaphorically speaking) a speaker of shorthand.

Petulant. Thou art (without a figure) just one-half of an ass, and Baldwin[4] yonder, thy half-brother, is the rest.—A Gemini[5] of asses split would make just four of you.

Witwoud. Thou dost bite, my dear mustard seed; kiss me for that.

Petulant. Stand off!—I'll kiss no more males—I have kissed your twin yonder in a humor of reconciliation, till he (*Hiccup*) rises upon my stomach like a radish.

Mrs. Millamant. Eh! filthy creature!—What was the quarrel?

Petulant. There was no quarrel—there might have been a quarrel.

Witwoud. If there had been words enow between 'em to have expressed provocation, they had gone together by the ears like a pair of castanets.

Petulant. You were the quarrel.

Mrs. Millamant. Me!

Petulant. If I have a humor to quarrel, I can make less matters conclude premises.—If you are not handsome, what then, if I have a humor to prove it? If I shall have my reward, say so; if not, fight for your face that next time yourself. I'll go sleep.

Witwoud. Do; wrap thyself up like a woodlouse, and dream revenge—and hear me; if thou canst learn to write by to-morrow morning, pen me a challenge.—I'll carry it for thee.

---

[1]Unstiffened cheap cloth.

[2]Stay of prosecution.

[3]The Spartans were famous in antiquity for their brevity of speech.

[4]The name of the ass in *Reynard the Fox*.

[5]The Twins (constellation Castor and Pollux).

PETULANT. Carry your mistress's monkey a spider!—Go flea dogs, and read romances!—I'll go to bed to my maid. [*Exit.*

MRS. FAINALL. He's horridly drunk.—How came you all in this pickle?

WITWOUD. A plot! a plot! to get rid of the knight—your husband's advice, but he sneaked off.

Enter LADY *and* SIR WILFULL, *drunk*

LADY WISHFORT. Out upon't, out upon't! At years of discretion, and comport yourself at this rantipole[1] rate!

SIR WILFULL. No offense, aunt.

LADY WISHFORT. Offense! as I'm a person, I'm ashamed of you. Foh! how you stink of wine! D'ye think my niece will ever endure such a Borachio![2] you're an absolute Borachio.

SIR WILFULL. Borachio?

LADY WISHFORT. At a time when you should commence an amour and put your best foot foremost—

SIR WILFULL. 'Sheart, an you grutch[3] me your liquor, make a bill—give me more drink, and take my purse—(*Sings*)

Prithee fill me the glass,
 Till it laugh in my face,
With ale that is potent and mellow;
 He that whines for a lass,
 Is an ignorant ass,
For a bumper has not its fellow.

But if you would have me marry my cousin—say the word, and I'll do't. Wilfull will do't; that's the word. Wilfull will do't; that's my crest—My motto I have forgot.

LADY WISHFORT. [*To* MRS. MILLAMANT] My nephew's a little overtaken, cousin, but 'tis with drinking your health.—O' my word, you are obliged to him.

SIR WILFULL. *In vino veritas*,[4] aunt.—If I drunk your health to-day, cousin—I am a Borachio. But if you have a mind to be married, say the word, and send for the piper; Wilfull will do't. If not, dust it away, and let's have t'other round.—Tony!—Odds heart, where's Tony!—Tony's an honest fellow; but he spits after a bumper, and that's a fault.—(*Sings*)

We'll drink, and we'll never have done, boys,
 Put the glass then around with the sun, boys,

[1]Wild, disorderly. [2]Drunkard.
[3]Grudge. [4]There is truth in wine.

Let Apollo's example invite us;
 For he's drunk every night,
 And that makes him so bright,
That he's able next morning to light us.

The sun's a good pimple,[5] an honest soaker; he has a cellar at your Antipodes. If I travel, aunt, I touch at your Antipodes.—Your Antipodes are a good, rascally sort of topsy-turvy fellows: if I had a bumper, I'd stand upon my head and drink a health to 'em.—A match or no match, cousin with the hard name?—Aunt, Wilfull will do't. If she has her maidenhead, let her look to't; if she has not, let her keep her own counsel in the meantime, and cry out at the nine months' end.

MRS. MILLAMANT. Your pardon, madam, I can stay no longer—Sir Wilfull grows very powerful.—Eh! how he smells! I shall be overcome, if I stay.—Come, cousin.

[*Exeunt* MRS. MILLAMANT *and* MRS. FAINALL.

LADY WISHFORT. Smells! He would poison a tallow-chandler and his family! Beastly creature, I know not what to do with him!—Travel, quotha! Aye, travel, travel—get thee gone, get thee gone; get thee but far enough, to the Saracens, or the Tartars, or the Turks!—for thou art not fit to live in a Christian commonwealth, thou beastly pagan!

SIR WILFULL. Turks? No; no Turks, aunt. Your Turks are infidels, and believe not in the grape. Your Mahometan, your Mussulman, is a dry stinkard—no offense, aunt. My map says that your Turk is not so honest a man as your Christian. I cannot find by the map that your Mufti is orthodox—whereby it is a plain case that orthodox is a hard word, aunt, and (*Hiccup*)—Greek for claret.—(*Sings*)

To drink is a Christian diversion,
Unknown to the Turk or the Persian:
 Let Mahometan fools
 Live by heathenish rules,
And be damned over tea-cups and coffee.
 But let British lads sing,
 Crown a health to the king,
And a fig for your sultan and sophy!

Ah, Tony!

Enter FOIBLE *and whispers to* LADY

LADY WISHFORT. [*Aside to* FOIBLE]—Sir Rowland impatient? Good lack! what shall I do with this beastly tumbril?—[*Aloud*] Go

[5]Boon companion.

lie down and sleep, you sot!—or, as I'm a person, I'll have you bastinadoed with broomsticks.—Call up the wenches. [*Exit* FOIBLE.

SIR WILFULL. Ahey! wenches; where are the wenches?

LADY WISHFORT. Dear Cousin Witwoud, get him away, and you will bind me to you inviolably. I have an affair of moment that invades me with some precipitation—you will oblige me to all futurity.

WITWOUD. Come, knight.—Pox on him, I don't know what to say to him.—Will you go to a cock-match?

SIR WILFULL. With a wench, Tony? Is she a shakebag,[1] sirrah? Let me bite your cheek for that.

WITWOUD. Horrible! he has a breath like a bagpipe!—Aye, aye; come, will you march, my Salopian?

SIR WILFULL. Lead on, little Tony—I'll follow thee, my Anthony, my Tantony.[2] Sirrah, thou shalt be my Tantony, and I'll be thy pig. (*Sings*)

And a fig for your sultan and sophy.

[*Exeunt* SIR WILFULL *and* WITWOUD.

LADY WISHFORT. This will never do. It will never make a match—at least before he has been abroad.

Enter WAITWELL, *disguised as for* SIR ROWLAND

LADY WISHFORT. Dear Sir Rowland, I am confounded with confusion at the retrospection of my own rudeness!—I have more pardons to ask than the pope distributes in the year of jubilee. But I hope, where there is likely to be so near an alliance, we may unbend the severity of decorum and dispense with a little ceremony.

WAITWELL. My impatience, madam, is the effect of my transport; and till I have the possession of your adorable person, I am tantalized on the rack; and do but hang, madam, on the tenter of expectation.

LADY WISHFORT. You have excess of gallantry, Sir Rowland, and press things to a conclusion with a most prevailing vehemence.—But a day or two for decency of marriage—

WAITWELL. For decency of funeral, madam! The delay will break my heart—or, if that should fail, I shall be poisoned. My nephew will get an inkling of my designs, and poison me; and I would willingly starve him before I die—I would gladly go out of the world with that satisfaction.—That would be some comfort to me, if I could but live so long as to be revenged on that unnatural viper!

LADY WISHFORT. Is he so unnatural, say you? Truly, I would contribute much, both to the saving of your life and the accomplishment of your revenge—not that I respect myself, though he has been a perfidious wretch to me.

WAITWELL. Perfidious to you?

LADY WISHFORT. O Sir Rowland, the hours that he has died away at my feet, the tears that he has shed, the oaths that he has sworn, the palpitations that he has felt, the trances and the tremblings, the ardors and the ecstasies, the kneelings and the risings, the heartheavings and the handgripings, the pangs and the pathetic regards of his protesting eyes!—Oh, no memory can register!

WAITWELL. What, my rival! is the rebel my rival?—a' dies!

LADY WISHFORT. No, don't kill him at once, Sir Rowland; starve him gradually, inch by inch.

WAITWELL. I'll do't. In three weeks he shall be barefoot; in a month out at knees with begging an alms.—He shall starve upward and upward, till he has nothing living but his head, and then go out in a stink like a candle's end upon a save-all.[3]

LADY WISHFORT. Well, Sir Rowland, you have the way—you are no novice in the labyrinth of love; you have the clue.—But as I am a person, Sir Rowland, you must not attribute my yielding to any sinister appetite, or indigestion of widowhood; nor impute my complacency to any lethargy of continence. I hope you do not think me prone to any iteration of nuptials—

WAITWELL. Far be it from me—

LADY WISHFORT. If you do, I protest I must recede—or think that I have made a prostitution of decorums; but in the vehemence of compassion, and to save the life of a person of so much importance—

WAITWELL. I esteem it so—

[1]"A shakebag is a cock turned out of the bag to fight another cock, unsight, unseen, or unmatched; a battle at a venture." (Holme, *Armory*, 1688.) Sir Wilfull uses the word in a transferred sense.

[2]Contraction from St. Anthony, patron saint of swine-herds.

[3]A device for burning candle-ends until completely consumed.

Lady Wishfort. Or else you wrong my condescension.

Waitwell. I do not, I do not!

Lady Wishfort. Indeed you do.

Waitwell. I do not, fair shrine of virtue!

Lady Wishfort. If you think the least scruple of carnality was an ingredient,—

Waitwell. Dear madam, no. You are all camphor and frankincense, all chastity and odor.

Lady Wishfort. Or that-

Enter Foible

Foible. Madam, the dancers are ready; and there's one with a letter, who must deliver it into your own hands.

Lady Wishfort. Sir Rowland, will you give me leave? Think favorably, judge candidly, and conclude you have found a person who would suffer racks in honor's cause, dear Sir Rowland, and will wait on you incessantly. [*Exit.*

Waitwell. Fie, fie!—What a slavery have I undergone! Spouse, hast thou any cordial? I want spirits.

Foible. What a washy rogue art thou, to pant thus for a quarter of an hour's lying and swearing to a fine lady!

Waitwell. Oh, she is the antidote to desire! Spouse, thou wilt fare the worse for't—I shall have no appetite to iteration of nuptials this eight-and-forty hours.—By this hand I'd rather be a chairman in the dog-days than act Sir Rowland till this time to-morrow!

Enter Lady *with a letter*

Lady Wishfort. Call in the dancers.—Sir Rowland, we'll sit, if you please, and see the entertainment. (*A dance*) Now, with your permission, Sir Rowland, I will peruse my letter.—I would open it in your presence, because I would not make you uneasy. If it should make you uneasy, I would burn it.—Speak, if it does—but you may see by the superscription it is like a woman's hand.

Foible. (*Aside to* Waitwell) By Heaven! Mrs. Marwood's, I know it.—My heart aches—get it from her.

Waitwell. A woman's hand? No, madam, that's no woman's hand; I see that already. That's somebody whose throat must be cut.

Lady Wishfort. Nay, Sir Rowland, since you give me a proof of your passion by your jealousy, I promise you I'll make a return by a frank communication.—You shall see it—we'll open it together—look you here.—(*Reads*)—"Madam, though unknown to you"—Look you there, 'tis from nobody that I know—"I have that honor for your character, that I think myself obliged to let you know you are abused. He who pretends to be Sir Rowland, is a cheat and a rascal."—Oh, heavens! what's this?

Foible. [*Aside*] Unfortunate! all's ruined!

Waitwell. How, how! Let me see, let me see!—(*Reads*) "A rascal, and disguised and suborned for that imposture,"—O villainy! O villainy!—"by the contrivance of—"

Lady Wishfort. I shall faint!—I shall die!—Oh!

Foible. (*Aside to* Waitwell) Say 'tis your nephew's hand—quickly, his plot,—swear, swear it!

Waitwell. Here's a villain! Madam, don't you perceive it? Don't you see it?

Lady Wishfort. Too well, too well! I have seen too much.

Waitwell. I told you at first I knew the hand.—A woman's hand! The rascal writes a sort of a large hand—your Roman hand.—I saw there was a throat to be cut presently. If he were my son, as he is my nephew, I'd pistol him!

Foible. O treachery!—But are you sure, Sir Rowland, it is his writing?

Waitwell. Sure?—Am I here? Do I live?—Do I love this pearl of India? I have twenty letters in my pocket from him in the same character.

Lady Wishfort. How!

Foible. Oh, what luck it is, Sir Rowland, that you were present at this juncture!—This was the business that brought Mr. Mirabell disguised to Madam Millamant this afternoon. I thought something was contriving when he stole by me and would have hid his face.

Lady Wishfort. How, how!—I heard the villain was in the house, indeed; and now I remember, my niece went away abruptly when Sir Wilfull was to have made his addresses.

Foible. Then, then, madam, Mr. Mirabell waited for her in her chamber! but I would not tell your ladyship to discompose you when you were to receive Sir Rowland.

WAITWELL. Enough; his date is short.

FOIBLE. No, good Sir Rowland, don't incur the law.

WAITWELL. Law! I care not for law. I can but die and 'tis in a good cause.—My lady shall be satisfied of my truth and innocence, though it cost me my life.

LADY WISHFORT. No, dear Sir Rowland, don't fight. If you should be killed, I must never show my face; or hanged—oh, consider my reputation, Sir Rowland!—No, you shan't fight.—I'll go in and examine my niece; I'll make her confess. I conjure you, Sir Rowland, by all your love, not to fight.

WAITWELL. I am charmed, madam; I obey. But some proof you must let me give you; I'll go for a black box which contains the writings of my whole estate, and deliver that into your hands.

LADY WISHFORT. Aye, dear Sir Rowland, that will be some comfort. Bring the black box.

WAITWELL. And may I presume to bring a contract to be signed this night? May I hope so far?

LADY WISHFORT. Bring what you will, but come alive. Pray, come alive! Oh, this is a happy discovery!

WAITWELL. Dead or alive I'll come—and married we will be in spite of treachery—aye, and get an heir that shall defeat the last remaining glimpse of hope in my abandoned nephew. Come, my buxom widow:

Ere long you shall substantial proof receive,
That I'm an errant knight—

FOIBLE. Or arrant knave.

[*Exeunt.*

ACT V

SCENE I [*Scene continues*]

LADY WISHFORT *and* FOIBLE

LADY WISHFORT. Out of my house! Out of my house, thou viper! thou serpent, that I have fostered! thou bosom traitress, that I raised from nothing!—Begone! begone! begone!—go! go!—That I took from washing of old gauze and weaving of dead hair, with a bleak blue nose over a chafing-dish of starved embers, and dining behind a traverse rag,[1] in a shop no bigger than a bird-cage!—Go, go! Starve again! Do, do!

[1]A ragged curtain shutting off part of the shop from the public.

FOIBLE. Dear madam, I'll beg pardon on my knees.

LADY WISHFORT. Away! out! out!—Go, set up for yourself again!—Do, drive a trade! do, with your three-pennyworth of small ware, flaunting upon a packthread under a brandy-seller's bulk, or against a dead wall by a ballad-monger! Go, hang out an old Frisoneer gorget,[2] with a yard of yellow colbertine[3] again! Do! An old gnawed mask, two rows of pins, and a child's fiddle; a glass necklace with the beads broken, and a quilted night-cap with one ear! Go, go, drive a trade!—These were your commodities, you treacherous trull! this was the merchandise you dealt in when I took you into my house, placed you next myself, and made you governant of my whole family!—You have forgot this, have you, now you have feathered your nest?

FOIBLE. No, no, dear madam. Do but hear me; have but a moment's patience. I'll confess all. Mr. Mirabell seduced me. I am not the first that he has wheedled with his dissembling tongue; your ladyship's own wisdom has been deluded by him—then how should I, a poor ignorant, defend myself? O madam, if you knew but what he promised me, and how he assured me your ladyship should come to no damage!—Or else the wealth of the Indies should not have bribed me to conspire against so good, so sweet, so kind a lady as you have been to me.

LADY WISHFORT. No damage! What, to betray me, and marry me to a cast[4] serving-man! to make me a receptacle, an hospital for a decayed pimp! No damage! O thou frontless impudence, more than a big-bellied actress!

FOIBLE. Pray, do but hear me, madam! He could not marry your ladyship, madam.—No, indeed; his marriage was to have been void in law, for he was married to me first, to secure your ladyship. He could not have bedded your ladyship; for if he had consummated with your ladyship, he must have run the risk of the law, and been put upon his clergy.[5]—Yes, indeed, I inquired of the law in that case before I would meddle or make.[6]

[2]A coarse woolen wimple.

[3]An open lace of inferior quality.

[4]Discharged.

[5]All who could read might plead "benefit of clergy" and thus obtain exemption from sentence for a first conviction.

[6]Interfere.

LADY WISHFORT. What, then I have been your property, have I? I have been convenient to you, it seems!—While you were catering for Mirabell, I have been broker for you! What, have you made a passive bawd of me?—This exceeds all precedent; I am brought to fine uses, to become a botcher of second-hand marriages between Abigails and Andrews!—I'll couple you!—Yes, I'll baste you together, you and your Philander! I'll Duke's-place[1] you, as I'm a person! Your turtle is in custody already: you shall coo in the same cage if there be constable or warrant in the parish. [*Exit.*

FOIBLE. Oh, that ever I was born! Oh, that I was ever married!—A bride!—aye, I shall be a Bridewell-bride.—Oh!

Enter MRS. FAINALL

MRS. FAINALL. Poor Foible, what's the matter?

FOIBLE. O madam, my lady's gone for a constable! I shall be had to a justice and put to Bridewell to beat hemp. Poor Waitwell's gone to prison already.

MRS. FAINALL. Have a good heart, Foible; Mirabell's gone to give security for him. This is all Marwood's and my husband's doing.

FOIBLE. Yes, yes; I know it, madam. She was in my lady's closet, and overheard all that you said to me before dinner. She sent the letter to my lady, and that missing effect, Mr. Fainall laid this plot to arrest Waitwell when he pretended to go for the papers, and in the meantime Mrs. Marwood declared all to my lady.

MRS. FAINALL. Was there no mention made of me in the letter? My mother does not suspect my being in the confederacy? I fancy Marwood has not told her, though she has told my husband.

FOIBLE. Yes, madam, but my lady did not see that part; we stifled the letter before she read so far—Has that mischievous devil told Mr. Fainall of your ladyship, then?

MRS. FAINALL. Aye, all's out—my affair with Mirabell—everything discovered. This is the last day of our living together, that's my comfort.

FOIBLE. Indeed, madam; and so 'tis a comfort if you knew all—he has been even with your ladyship, which I could have told you long enough since, but I love to keep peace and quietness by my goodwill. I had rather bring friends together than set 'em at distance. But Mrs. Marwood and he are nearer related than ever their parents thought for.

MRS. FAINALL. Sayest thou so, Foible? Canst thou prove this?

FOIBLE. I can take my oath of it, madam; so can Mrs. Mincing. We have had many a fair word from Madam Marwood, to conceal something that passed in our chamber one evening when you were at Hyde Park, and we were thought to have gone a-walking, but we went up unawares—though we were sworn to secrecy, too; Madam Marwood took a book and swore us upon it, but it was but a book of verses and poems. So long as it was not a Bible oath, we may break it with a safe conscience.

MRS. FAINALL. This discovery is the most opportune thing I could wish.—Now, Mincing!

Enter MINCING

MINCING. My lady would speak with Mrs. Foible, mem. Mr. Mirabell is with her; he has set your spouse at liberty, Mrs. Foible, and would have you hide yourself in my lady's closet till my old lady's anger is abated. Oh, my old lady is in a perilous passion at something Mr. Fainall has said; he swears, and my old lady cries. There's a fearful hurricane, I vow. He says, mem, how that he'll have my lady's fortune made over to him, or he'll be divorced.

MRS. FAINALL. Does your lady or Mirabell know that?

MINCING. Yes, mem; they have sent me to see if Sir Wilfull be sober, and to bring him to them. My lady is resolved to have him, I think, rather than lose such a vast sum as six thousand pound.—Oh, come, Mrs. Foible, I hear my old lady.

MRS. FAINALL. Foible, you must tell Mincing that she must prepare to vouch when I call her.

FOIBLE. Yes, yes, madam.

MINCING. Oh, yes, mem, I'll vouch anything for your ladyship's service, be what it will. [*Exeunt* MINCING *and* FOIBLE.

Enter LADY *and* MRS. MARWOOD

LADY WISHFORT. Oh, my dear friend, how can I enumerate the benefits that I have re-

[1]Marry.

ceived from your goodness! To you I owe the timely discovery of the false vows of Mirabell; to you I owe the detection of the impostor Sir Rowland.—And now you are become an intercessor with my son-in-law, to save the honor of my house and compound for the frailties of my daughter. Well, friend, you are enough to reconcile me to the bad world, or else I would retire to deserts and solitudes, and feed harmless sheep by groves and purling streams. Dear Marwood, let us leave the world, and retire by ourselves and be shepherdesses.

MRS. MARWOOD. Let us first dispatch the affair in hand, madam. We shall have leisure to think of retirement afterwards. Here is one who is concerned in the treaty.

LADY WISHFORT. Oh, daughter, daughter! is it possible thou shouldst be my child, bone of my bone, and flesh of my flesh, and, as I may say, another me, and yet transgress the most minute particle of severe virtue? Is it possible you should lean aside to iniquity, who have been cast in the direct mold of virtue? I have not only been a mold but a pattern for you and a model for you, after you were brought into the world.

MRS. FAINALL. I don't understand your ladyship.

LADY WISHFORT. Not understand? Why, have you not been taught? have you not been sophisticated? Not understand! here I am ruined to compound for your caprices and your cuckoldoms. I must pawn my plate and my jewels, and ruin my niece, and all little enough—

MRS. FAINALL. I am wronged and abused, and so are you. 'Tis a false accusation—as false as hell, as false as your friend there, aye, or your friend's friend, my false husband!

MRS. MARWOOD. My friend, Mrs. Fainall! —Your husband my friend? What do you mean?

MRS. FAINALL. I know what I mean, madam, and so do you; and so shall the world at a time convenient.

MRS. MARWOOD. I am sorry to see you so passionate, madam. More temper would look more like innocence. But I have done. I am sorry my zeal to serve your ladyship and family should admit of misconstruction, or make me liable to affronts. You will pardon me, madam, if I meddle no more with an affair in which I am not personally concerned.

LADY WISHFORT. O dear friend, I am so ashamed that you should meet with such returns!—[*To* MRS. FAINALL] You ought to ask pardon on your knees, ungrateful creature! she deserves more from you than all your life can accomplish.—[*To* MRS. MARWOOD] Oh, don't leave me destitute in this perplexity!—no, stick to me, my good genius.

MRS. FAINALL. I tell you, madam, you're abused.—Stick to you! aye, like a leech, to suck your best blood—she'll drop off when she's full. Madam, you shan't pawn a bodkin, nor part with a brass counter,[1] in composition for me. I defy 'em all. Let 'em prove their aspersions; I know my own innocence, and dare stand a trial. [*Exit.*

LADY WISHFORT. Why—if she should be innocent, if she should be wronged after all—ha!—I don't know what to think—and I promise you her education has been unexceptionable—I may say it; for I chiefly made it my own care to initiate her very infancy in the rudiments of virtue, and to impress upon her tender years a young odium and aversion to the very sight of men. Aye, friend, she would ha' shrieked if she had but seen a man, till she was in her teens. As I'm a person, 'tis true—she was never suffered to play with a male child, though but in coats; nay, her very babies[2] were of the feminine gender. Oh, she never looked a man in the face but her own father, or the chaplain, and him we made a shift to put upon her for a woman, by the help of his long garments and his sleek face, till she was going in her fifteen.

MRS. MARWOOD. 'Twas much she should be deceived so long.

LADY WISHFORT. I warrant you, or she would never have borne to have been catechized by him; and have heard his long lectures against singing and dancing, and such debaucheries; and going to filthy plays, and profane music-meetings, where the lewd trebles squeak nothing but bawdy, and the basses roar blasphemy. Oh, she would have swooned at the sight or name of an obscene play-book!—and can I think, after all this, that my daughter can be naught? What, a whore? and thought it excommunication to set her foot within the door of a playhouse! O dear friend, I can't believe it. No, no! As she says, let him prove it—let him prove it.

[1]A token used to represent a real coin.

[2]Dolls.

MRS. MARWOOD. Prove it, madam? What, and have your name prostituted in a public court—yours and your daughter's reputation worried at the bar by a pack of bawling lawyers! To be ushered in with an "O yez" of scandal, and have your case opened by an old fumbling lecher in a quoif[1] like a man-midwife; to bring your daughter's infamy to light; to be a theme for legal punsters and quibblers by the statute; and become a jest against a rule of court, where there is no precedent for a jest in any record—not even in Domesday Book; to discompose the gravity of the bench, and provoke naughty interrogatories in more naughty law Latin; while the good judge, tickled with the proceeding, simpers under a gray beard, and fidgets off and on his cushion as if he had swallowed cantharides, or sat upon cow-itch!

LADY WISHFORT. Oh, 'tis very hard!

MRS. MARWOOD. And then to have my young revelers of the Temple take notes, like 'prentices at a conventicle; and after talk it over again in commons, or before drawers in an eating-house.

LADY WISHFORT. Worse and worse!

MRS. MARWOOD. Nay, this is nothing; if it would end here, 'twere well. But it must, after this, be consigned by the shorthand writers to the public press; and from thence be transferred to the hands, nay into the throats and lungs of hawkers, with voices more licentious than the loud flounder-man's.[2] And this you must hear till you are stunned—nay, you must hear nothing else for some days.

LADY WISHFORT. Oh, 'tis insupportable! No, no, dear friend, make it up, make it up; aye, aye, I'll compound. I'll give up all, myself and my all, my niece and her all—anything, everything for composition.

MRS. MARWOOD. Nay, madam, I advise nothing; I only lay before you, as a friend, the inconveniences which perhaps you have overseen. Here comes Mr. Fainall. If he will be satisfied to huddle up all in silence, I shall be glad. You must think I would rather congratulate than condole with you.

LADY WISHFORT. Aye, aye, I do not doubt it, dear Marwood; no, no, I do not doubt it.

[1]White cap formerly worn by lawyers.

[2]"From King William's days to almost the end of George I, there was a fellow who distinguished himself above all others in crying flounders in the streets of London. His voice was loud, but not unmusical." (Davies, *Dramatic Miscellanies*. Quoted by Summers.)

Enter FAINALL

FAINALL. Well, madam, I have suffered myself to be overcome by the importunity of this lady, your friend; and am content you shall enjoy your own proper estate during life, on condition you oblige yourself never to marry, under such penalty as I think convenient.

LADY WISHFORT. Never to marry!

FAINALL. No more Sir Rowlands; the next imposture may not be so timely detected.

MRS. MARWOOD. That condition, I dare answer, my lady will consent to without difficulty; she has already but too much experienced the perfidiousness of men.—Besides, madam, when we retire to our pastoral solitude we shall bid adieu to all other thoughts.

LADY WISHFORT. Aye, that's true; but in case of necessity, as of health, or some such emergency—

FAINALL. Oh, if you are prescribed marriage, you shall be considered; I will only reserve to myself the power to choose for you. If your physic be wholesome, it matters not who is your apothecary. Next, my wife shall settle on me the remainder of her fortune not made over already, and for her maintenance depend entirely on my discretion.

LADY WISHFORT. This is most inhumanly savage, exceeding the barbarity of a Muscovite husband.[3]

FAINALL. I learned it from his Czarish majesty's retinue, in a winter evening's conference over brandy and pepper, amongst other secrets of matrimony and policy as they are at present practiced in the northern hemisphere. But this must be agreed unto, and that positively. Lastly, I will be endowed, in right of my wife, with that six thousand pound which is the moiety of Mrs. Millamant's fortune in your possession, and which she has forfeited (as will appear by the last will and testament of your deceased husband, Sir Jonathan Wishfort) by her disobedience in contracting herself against your consent or knowledge and by refusing the offered match with Sir Wilfull Witwoud, which you, like a careful aunt, had provided for her.

LADY WISHFORT. My nephew was *non compos*, and could not make his addresses.

FAINALL. I come to make demands—I'll hear no objections.

[3]Peter the Great had visited England in 1697, giving Englishmen the opportunity to see barbarous Russians.

LADY WISHFORT. You will grant me time to consider?

FAINALL. Yes, while the instrument is drawing, to which you must set your hand till more sufficient deeds can be perfected—which I will take care shall be done with all possible speed. In the meanwhile I will go for the said instrument, and till my return you may balance this matter in your own discretion. [*Exit* FAINALL.

LADY WISHFORT. This insolence is beyond all precedent, all parallel. Must I be subject to this merciless villain?

MRS. MARWOOD. 'Tis severe indeed, madam, that you should smart for your daughter's wantonness.

LADY WISHFORT. 'Twas against my consent that she married this barbarian, but she would have him, though her year was not out.—Ah! her first husband, my son Languish, would not have carried it thus! Well, that was my choice, this is hers: she is matched now with a witness.—I shall be mad!—Dear friend, is there no comfort for me? must I live to be confiscated at this rebel-rate?—Here come two more of my Egyptian plagues too.

Enter MRS. MILLAMANT *and* SIR WILFULL WITWOUD

SIR WILFULL. Aunt, your servant.

LADY WISHFORT. Out, caterpillar! Call not me aunt! I know thee not!

SIR WILFULL. I confess I have been a little in disguise,[1] as they say.—'Sheart! and I'm sorry for't. What would you have? I hope I committed no offense, aunt—and if I did I am willing to make satisfaction; and what can a man say fairer? If I have broke anything, I'll pay for't, an it cost a pound. And so let that content for what's past, and make no more words. For what's to come, to pleasure you I'm willing to marry my cousin; so pray let's all be friends. She and I are agreed upon the matter before a witness.

LADY WISHFORT. How's this, dear niece?—Have I any comfort? Can this be true?

MRS. MILLAMANT. I am content to be a sacrifice to your repose, madam, and to convince you that I had no hand in the plot, as you were misinformed. I have laid my commands on Mirabell to come in person and be a witness that I give my hand to this flower of knighthood; and for the contract that passed between Mirabell and me, I have obliged him to make a resignation of it in your ladyship's presence. He is without, and waits your leave for admittance.

LADY WISHFORT. Well, I'll swear I am something revived at this testimony of your obedience, but I cannot admit that traitor.—I fear I cannot fortify myself to support his appearance. He is as terrible to me as a gorgon; if I see him I fear I shall turn to stone, petrify incessantly.

MRS. MILLAMANT. If you disoblige him, he may resent your refusal and insist upon the contract still. Then 'tis the last time he will be offensive to you.

LADY WISHFORT. Are you sure it will be the last time?—If I were sure of that—shall I never see him again?

MRS. MILLAMANT. Sir Wilfull, you and he are to travel together, are you not?

SIR WILFULL. 'Sheart, the gentleman's a civil gentleman, aunt; let him come in. Why, we are sworn brothers and fellow-travelers.—We are to be Pylades and Orestes, he and I.—He is to be my interpreter in foreign parts. He has been over-seas once already, and with proviso that I marry my cousin, will cross 'em once again only to bear me company.—'Sheart, I'll call him in. An I set on't once, he shall come in; and see who'll hinder him. [*Exit.*

MRS. MARWOOD. This is precious fooling, if it would pass; but I'll know the bottom of it.

LADY WISHFORT. O dear Marwood, you are not going?

MRS. MARWOOD. Not far, madam; I'll return immediately. [*Exit.*

Re-enter SIR WILFULL *and* MIRABELL

SIR WILFULL. Look up, man, I'll stand by you. 'Sbud an she do frown, she can't kill you; besides—harkee, she dare not frown desperately, because her face is none of her own. 'Sheart, an she should, her forehead would wrinkle like the coat of a cream-cheese; but mum for that, fellow-traveler.

MIRABELL. If a deep sense of the many injuries I have offered to so good a lady, with a sincere remorse and a hearty contrition, can but obtain the least glance of compassion, I

[1] Disordered by drink.

am too happy.—Ah, madam, there was a time!—but let it be forgotten—I confess I have deservedly forfeited the high place I once held, of sighing at your feet. Nay, kill me not, by turning from me in disdain. I come not to plead for favor—nay, not for pardon; I am a suppliant only for pity. I am going where I never shall behold you more—

SIR WILFULL. How, fellow-traveler! you shall go by yourself then.

MIRABELL. Let me be pitied first, and afterwards forgotten.—I ask no more.

SIR WILFULL. By'r Lady, a very reasonable request, and will cost you nothing, aunt! Come, come, forgive and forget, aunt. Why, you must, an you are a Christian.

MIRABELL. Consider, madam, in reality you could not receive much prejudice. It was an innocent device; though I confess it had a face of guiltiness, it was at most an artifice which love contrived. And errors which love produces have ever been accounted venial. At least think it is punishment enough that I have lost what in my heart I hold most dear, that to your cruel indignation I have offered up this beauty, and with her my peace and quiet—nay, all my hopes of future comfort.

SIR WILFULL. An he does not move me, would I may never be o' the quorum! An it were not as good a deed as to drink, to give her to him again, I would I might never take shipping!—Aunt, if you don't forgive quickly, I shall melt, I can tell you that. My contract went no farther than a little mouth glue, and that's hardly dry—one doleful sigh more from my fellow-traveler, and 'tis dissolved.

LADY WISHFORT. Well, nephew, upon your account—Ah, he has a false insinuating tongue!—Well sir, I will stifle my just resentment at my nephew's request.—I will endeavor what I can to forget, but on proviso that you resign the contract with my niece immediately.

MIRABELL. It is in writing, and with papers of concern; but I have sent my servant for it, and will deliver it to you with all acknowledgments for your transcendent goodness.

LADY WISHFORT. (*Aside*) Oh, he has witchcraft in his eyes and tongue!—When I did not see him, I could have bribed a villain to his assassination; but his appearance rakes the embers which have so long lain smothered in my breast.

Enter FAINALL *and* MRS. MARWOOD

FAINALL. Your date of deliberation, madam, is expired. Here is the instrument; are you prepared to sign?

LADY WISHFORT. If I were prepared, I am not impowered. My niece exerts a lawful claim, having matched herself by my direction to Sir Wilfull.

FAINALL. That sham is too gross to pass on me—though 'tis imposed on you, madam.

MRS. MILLAMANT. Sir, I have given my consent.

MIRABELL. And, sir, I have resigned my pretensions.

SIR WILFULL. And, sir, I assert my right and will maintain it in defiance of you, sir, and of your instrument. 'Sheart, an you talk of an instrument, sir, I have an old fox[1] by my thigh shall hack your instrument of ram vellum to shreds, sir! It shall not be sufficient for a mittimus[2] or a tailor's measure. Therefore withdraw your instrument, sir, or by'r Lady, I shall draw mine.

LADY WISHFORT. Hold, nephew, hold!

MRS. MILLAMANT. Good Sir Wilfull, respite your valor!

FAINALL. Indeed! Are you provided of your guard, with your single beef-eater there? But I'm prepared for you, and insist upon my first proposal. You shall submit your own estate to my management, and absolutely make over my wife's to my sole use, as pursuant to the purport and tenor of this other covenant.—[*To* MRS. MILLAMANT] I suppose, madam, your consent is not requisite in this case; nor, Mr. Mirabell, your resignation; nor, Sir Wilfull, your right.—You may draw your fox if you please, sir, and make a bear-garden flourish somewhere else, for here it will not avail. This, my Lady Wishfort, must be subscribed, or your darling daughter's turned adrift, like a leaky hulk, to sink or swim, as she and the current of this lewd town can agree.

LADY WISHFORT. Is there no means, no remedy to stop my ruin? Ungrateful wretch! dost thou not owe thy being, thy subsistence, to my daughter's fortune?

FAINALL. I'll answer you when I have the rest of it in my possession.

MIRABELL. But that you would not accept

[1] Sword.

[2] Warrant of commitment to prison.

of a remedy from my hands—I own I have not deserved you should owe any obligation to me—or else perhaps I could advise—

LADY WISHFORT. Oh, what?—what? To save me and my child from ruin, from want, I'll forgive all that's past; nay, I'll consent to anything to come, to be delivered from this tyranny.

MIRABELL. Aye, madam, but that is too late; my reward is intercepted. You have disposed of her who only could have made me a compensation for all my services. But be it as it may, I am resolved I'll serve you! You shall not be wronged in this savage manner.

LADY WISHFORT. How, dear Mr. Mirabell, can you be so generous at last? But it is not possible. Harkee, I'll break my nephew's match; you shall have my niece yet, and all her fortune, if you can but save me from this imminent danger.

MIRABELL. Will you? I'll take you at your word. I ask no more. I must have leave for two criminals to appear.

LADY WISHFORT. Aye, aye;—anybody, anybody!

MIRABELL. Foible is one, and a penitent.

Enter MRS. FAINALL, FOIBLE, *and* MINCING

MRS. MARWOOD. (*Aside to* FAINALL) Oh, my shame! (MIRABELL *and* LADY WISHFORT *go to* MRS. FAINALL *and* FOIBLE) These corrupt things are brought hither to expose me.

FAINALL. If it must all come out, why let 'em know it; 'tis but the way of the world. That shall not urge me to relinquish or abate one tittle of my terms; no, I will insist the more.

FOIBLE. Yes, indeed, madam, I'll take my Bible oath of it.

MINCING. And so will I, mem.

LADY WISHFORT. O Marwood, Marwood, art thou false? My friend deceive me? Hast thou been a wicked accomplice with that profligate man?

MRS. MARWOOD. Have you so much ingratitude and injustice to give credit against your friend to the aspersions of two such mercenary trulls?

MINCING. Mercenary, mem? I scorn your words. 'Tis true we found you and Mr. Fainall in the blue garret; by the same token, you swore us to secrecy upon Messalina's poems.[1] Mercenary! No, if we would have been mercenary, we should have held our tongues; you would have bribed us sufficiently.

FAINALL. Go, you are an insignificant thing! —Well, what are you the better for this? Is this Mr. Mirabell's expedient? I'll be put off no longer.—You, thing that was a wife, shall smart for this! I will not leave thee wherewithal to hide thy shame; your body shall be naked as your reputation.

MRS. FAINALL. I despise you and defy your malice!—You have aspersed me wrongfully—I have proved your falsehood! Go, you and your treacherous—I will not name it, but—starve together. Perish!

FAINALL. Not while you are worth a groat, indeed, my dear.—Madam, I'll be fooled no longer.

LADY WISHFORT. Ah, Mr. Mirabell, this is small comfort, the detection of this affair.

MIRABELL. Oh, in good time. Your leave for the other offender and penitent to appear, madam.

Enter WAITWELL *with a box of writings*

LADY WISHFORT. O Sir Rowland!—Well, rascal!

WAITWELL. What your ladyship pleases. I have brought the black box at last, madam.

MIRABELL. Give it me.—Madam, you remember your promise?

LADY WISHFORT. Aye, dear sir.

MIRABELL. Where are the gentlemen?

WAITWELL. At hand, sir, rubbing their eyes —just risen from sleep.

FAINALL. 'Sdeath, what's this to me? I'll not wait your private concerns.

Enter PETULANT *and* WITWOUD

PETULANT. How now! What's the matter? Whose hand's out?

WITWOUD. Heyday! What, are you all got together like players at the end of the last act?

MIRABELL. You may remember, gentlemen, I once requested your hands as witnesses to a certain parchment.

WITWOUD. Aye, I do; my hand I remember —Petulant set his mark.

MIRABELL. You wrong him. His name is fairly written, as shall appear.—(*Undoing the box*) You do not remember, gentlemen, anything of what that parchment contained?

WITWOUD. No.

PETULANT. Not I; I writ, I read nothing.

[1] *I. e.*, Miscellaneous Poems, pronounced as Mincing remembers it.

MIRABELL. Very well, now you shall know.—Madam, your promise.

LADY WISHFORT. Aye, aye, sir, upon my honor.

MIRABELL. Mr. Fainall, it is now time that you should know that your lady, while she was at her own disposal, and before you had by your insinuations wheedled her out of a pretended settlement of the greatest part of her fortune—

FAINALL. Sir! pretended!

MIRABELL. Yes, sir. I say that this lady while a widow, having it seems received some cautions respecting your inconstancy and tyranny of temper, which from her own partial opinion and fondness of you she could never have suspected—she did, I say, by the wholesome advice of friends and of sages learned in the laws of this land, deliver this same as her act and deed to me in trust, and to the uses within mentioned. You may read if you please—(*Holding out the parchment*) though perhaps what is written on the back may serve your occasions.

FAINALL. Very likely, sir. What's here?—Damnation! (*Reads*) "A deed of conveyance of the whole estate real of Arabella Languish, widow, in trust to Edward Mirabell."—Confusion!

MIRABELL. Even so, sir; 'tis the way of the world, sir,—of the widows of the world. I suppose this deed may bear an elder date than what you have obtained from your lady?

FAINALL. Perfidious fiend! then thus I'll be revenged. (*Offers to run at* MRS. FAINALL)

SIR WILFULL. Hold, sir! Now you may make your bear-garden flourish somewhere else, sir.

FAINALL. Mirabell, you shall hear of this, sir, be sure you shall.—Let me pass, oaf! [*Exit.*

MRS. FAINALL. Madam, you seem to stifle your resentment; you had better give it vent.

MRS. MARWOOD. Yes, it shall have vent—and to your confusion, or I'll perish in the attempt. [*Exit.*

LADY WISHFORT. O daughter, daughter! 'Tis plain thou hast inherited thy mother's prudence.

MRS. FAINALL. Thank Mr. Mirabell, a cautious friend, to whose advice all is owing.

LADY WISHFORT. Well, Mr. Mirabell, you have kept your promise—and I must perform mine.—First, I pardon, for your sake, Sir Rowland there, and Foible; the next thing is to break the matter to my nephew—and how to do that—

MIRABELL. For that, madam, give yourself no trouble; let me have your consent. Sir Wilfull is my friend. He has had compassion upon lovers, and generously engaged a volunteer in this action for our service, and now designs to prosecute his travels.

SIR WILFULL. 'Sheart, aunt, I have no mind to marry. My cousin's a fine lady, and the gentleman loves her, and she loves him, and they deserve one another. My resolution is to see foreign parts—I have set on't—and when I'm set on't I must do't. And if these two gentlemen would travel too, I think they may be spared.

PETULANT. For my part, I say little—I think things are best off or on.

WITWOUD. Egad, I understand nothing of the matter; I'm in a maze yet, like a dog in a dancing-school.

LADY WISHFORT. [*To* MIRABELL] Well, sir, take her, and with her all the joy I can give you.

MRS. MILLAMANT. Why does not the man take me? Would you have me give myself to you over again?

MIRABELL. Aye, and over and over again; (*Kisses her hand*) I would have you as often as possibly I can. Well, Heaven grant I love you not too well; that's all my fear.

SIR WILFULL. 'Sheart, you'll have time enough to toy after you're married; or if you will toy now, let us have a dance in the meantime, that we who are not lovers may have some other employment besides looking on.

MIRABELL. With all my heart, dear Sir Wilfull. What shall we do for music?

FOIBLE. Oh, sir, some that were provided for Sir Rowland's entertainment are yet within call. (*A dance*)

LADY WISHFORT. As I am a person, I can hold out no longer. I have wasted my spirits so to-day already, that I am ready to sink under the fatigue, and I cannot but have some fears upon me yet, that my son Fainall will pursue some desperate course.

MIRABELL. Madam, disquiet not yourself on that account; to my knowledge his circumstances are such he must of force comply. For my part, I will contribute all that in me lies to a reunion; in the meantime, madam—(*To* MRS. FAINALL) let me before these wit nesses restore to you this deed of trust. It may be a means, well-managed, to make you live easily together.

From hence let those be warned who mean
to wed,
Lest mutual falsehood stain the bridal bed;
For each deceiver to his cost may find
That marriage-frauds too oft are paid in
kind. [*Exeunt Omnes.*

EPILOGUE

After our Epilogue this crowd dismisses,
I'm thinking how this play'll be pulled to
pieces.
But pray consider, ere you doom its fall,
How hard a thing 'twould be to please you all.
There are some critics so with spleen diseased,
They scarcely come inclining to be pleased:
And sure he must have more than mortal
skill,
Who pleases anyone against his will.
Then, all bad poets we are sure are foes,
And how their number's swelled, the town
well knows:
In shoals I've marked 'em judging in the
pit;
Though they're on no pretense for judg-
ment fit,
But that they have been damned for want
of wit.
Since when, they by their own offenses
taught,
Set up for spies on plays and finding fault.
Others there are whose malice we'd pre-
vent;
Such who watch plays with scurrilous
intent
To mark out who by characters are meant.
And though no perfect likeness they can
trace,
Yet each pretends to know the copied face.
These with false glosses feed their own ill
nature,
And turn to libel what was meant a satire.
May such malicious fops this fortune find,
To think themselves alone the fools de-
signed—
If any are so arrogantly vain,
To think they singly can support a scene,
And furnish fool enough to entertain.
For well the learn'd and the judicious
know
That satire scorns to stoop so meanly low
As any one abstracted fop to show.
For, as when painters form a matchless face,
They from each fair one catch some different
grace,
And shining features in one portrait blend,
To which no single beauty must pretend;
So poets oft do in one piece expose
Whole *belles-assemblées* of coquettes and
beaux.

JOSEPH ADDISON (1672–1719) AND SIR RICHARD STEELE (1672–1729)

Addison was born at Milston, Wiltshire, on 1, May, 1672. His father was a clergyman and the boy was brought up in a cultivated environment. He was sent to the Charterhouse School, and then to Queen's College, Oxford. At Oxford he distinguished himself both as a scholar and as a writer of smooth English and Latin verse, and he won a fellowship at Magdalen College which he held until 1699. His Latin poem on the peace of Ryswick, together with his general ability as a man of letters, won him a pension from the Whigs, who wished to secure his continued support. This enabled him to spend four years in travel and study on the continent. Immediately on his return in 1704 he was asked to write a poem celebrating Marlborough's victory at Blenheim. He wrote *The Campaign*, which was at once successful and which ensured his political position. He was somewhat reserved and cautious in temperament, yet nevertheless became intimate with many of the "wits" of the day. He wrote several plays which would hardly be remembered now were it not that one of them, *Cato*, which was put on the stage in 1713, attained a remarkable factitious success. It had a long run, not because of its dramatic interest or power, but because it was believed to contain good Whig doctrine. When the Whigs returned to power in 1714, Addison was made Chief Secretary for Ireland. Later he became Commissioner for Trade and the Colonies, and finally Secretary of State, in 1717. After he had held this post for only a few months he resigned it, chiefly because of ill-health. He died on 17 June, 1719, and was buried in Westminster Abbey.

Richard Steele was born in Dublin in March, 1672. He was sent to Charterhouse, where he became acquainted with Addison; and like Addison he went up to Oxford. He entered Christ Church, at Oxford, in 1690, but left without a degree to become a soldier. His career in the army was not without irregularities, but he rose to a captaincy by 1700. In the following year he began writing for the theater, his first play being *The Funeral, or Grief à la Mode*. In 1703 *The Lying Lover* was produced at Drury Lane, and in 1705 *The Tender Husband*. In these plays Steele attempted to reform the taste of the day; he proved successfully that a comedy could be genuinely amusing without descending to ribaldry and the exhibition of gross immorality, and thus he foreshadowed one of the prominent aims of later work which he and Addison were to do together. In 1707 Steele was appointed Gazetteer, a post which he lost in 1710. In 1713 he sat in Parliament for Stockbridge, but in the following spring was expelled from the House of Commons for uttering seditious sentiments—a charge without real foundation, the vote on which served to show, not Steele's guilt, but simply the solid Tory majority in the House. On the accession of George I in the fall of 1714 Steele was rewarded for his support of the Hanoverian succession by the gift of several offices, and in 1715 he was again elected to Parliament, and was knighted. He also became in that year the Patentee, or manager, of Drury Lane Theater. In spite, however, of these and other turns of fortune in his favor, Steele, owing to his reckless expenditures, was never out of financial difficulties, and his difficulties of this sort grew worse as he grew older. In the fall of 1723 he left London for Bath, then lived for a time at Hereford, and finally retired to Carmarthen in Wales—all this being done in pursuit of an arrangement designed to aid his creditors. At Carmarthen he died on 1 September, 1729, and was buried there in St. Peter's Church.

Both Steele and Addison are remembered to-day for their two periodicals, the *Tatler* and the *Spectator*. While Steele was editing the *Gazette*, an official government paper, he conceived the idea of a livelier periodical than that organ, and in 1709 began the *Tatler*. Addison soon joined him in writing for it, and the paper ran successfully until they stopped it in January, 1711, in order a few months later to begin the *Spectator* on a somewhat different plan. The *Spectator* was issued daily until 6 December, 1712, reaching a total of 555 numbers. The purposes of Steele and Addison are indicated by themselves in numbers of the two papers printed below. Briefly, their most general aim was the reformation of manners, and to this end they freely employed good-humored satire. Their style was marked by simplicity, as the content of their papers was marked by common sense. Of the two writers Addison was easily the superior, his style exhibiting a fine urbanity and quiet distinction which Steele could not attain. Addison, too, extended the *Spectator's* reforming activities to the sphere of taste, and made effective attacks on pedantry which have not yet lost either their force or their applicability. It should be remembered, however, that the whole design was of Steele's invention, and that Steele's reputation has suffered in a sense unfairly from the constant comparison of his essays with those of Addison.

THE TATLER

No. 1. Tuesday, 12 April, 1709.

[Steele.]

Quicquid agunt homines——
nostri est farrago libelli.[1]
—Juv. *Sat.* i. 85, 86.

Though the other papers, which are published for the use of the good people of England, have certainly very wholesome effects, and are laudable in their particular kinds, they do not seem to come up to the main design of such narrations, which, I humbly presume, should be principally intended for the use of politic persons, who are so public-spirited as to neglect their own affairs to look into transactions of state. Now these gentlemen, for the most part, being persons of strong zeal, and weak intellects, it is both a charitable and necessary work to offer something, whereby such worthy and well-affected members of the commonwealth may be instructed, after their reading, what to think; which shall be the end and purpose of this my paper, wherein I shall, from time to time, report and consider all matters of what kind soever that shall occur to me, and publish such my advices and reflections every Tuesday, Thursday, and Saturday in the week, for the convenience of the post. I resolve to have something which may be of entertainment to the fair sex, in honor of whom I have invented the title of this paper. I therefore earnestly desire all persons, without distinction, to take it in for the present *gratis*, and hereafter at the price of one penny, forbidding all hawkers to take more for it at their peril. And I desire all persons to consider, that I am at a very great charge for proper materials for this work, as well as that, before I resolved upon it, I had settled a correspondence in all parts of the known and knowing world. And forasmuch as this globe is not trodden upon by mere drudges of business only, but that men of spirit and genius are justly to be esteemed as considerable agents in it, we shall not, upon a dearth of news, present you with musty foreign edicts, and dull proclamations, but shall divide our relation of the passages which occur in action or discourse throughout this town, as well as elsewhere, under such dates of places as may prepare you for the matter you are to expect in the following manner.

All accounts of gallantry, pleasure, and entertainment, shall be under the article of White's Chocolate-house; poetry under that of Will's Coffee-house; Learning, under the title of Grecian; foreign and domestic news, you will have from St. James's Coffee-house;[2] and what else I have to offer on any other subject shall be dated from my own Apartment.

I once more desire my reader to consider, that as I cannot keep an ingenious man to go daily to Will's under two-pence each day, merely for his charges; to White's under six-pence; nor to the Grecian, without allowing him some plain Spanish,[3] to be as able as others at the learned table; and that a good observer cannot speak with even Kidney[4] at St. James's without clean linen; I say, these considerations will, I hope, make all persons willing to comply with my humble request (when my *gratis* stock is exhausted) of a penny apiece; especially since they are sure of some proper amusement, and that it is impossible for me to want means to entertain them, having, besides the force of my own parts, the power of divination, and that I can, by casting a figure, tell you all that will happen before it comes to pass.

But this last faculty I shall use very sparingly, and speak but of few things until they are passed, for fear of divulging matters which may offend our superiors.

No. 25. Tuesday, 7 June, 1709.

[Steele.]

A letter from a young lady, written in the most passionate terms, wherein she laments the misfortune of a gentleman, her lover, who was lately wounded in a duel, has turned my thoughts to that subject, and inclined me to examine into the causes which precipitate men into so fatal a folly. And as it has been proposed to treat of subjects of gallantry in the article from hence,[5] and no one point in nature is more proper to be considered by the

[1]Whate'er men do, or say, or think, or dream,
Our motley paper seizes for its theme. (Pope.)

[2]These famous institutions occupied an important place in London life in the late seventeenth and early eighteenth centuries, serving as informal clubs and as centers of social, political, and literary influence. Steele indicates in a general way the kinds of people who frequented the four he mentions.

[3]Wine.

[4]One of the waiters at St. James's.

[5]This number of the *Tatler* is dated from White's Chocolate-House.

company who frequent this place than that of duels, it is worth our consideration to examine into this chimerical groundless humor, and to lay every other thought aside, until we have stripped it of all its false pretenses to credit and reputation amongst men.

But I must confess, when I consider what I am going about, and run over in my imagination all the endless crowd of men of honor who will be offended at such a discourse; I am undertaking, methinks, a work worthy an invulnerable hero in romance, rather than a private gentleman with a single rapier: but as I am pretty well acquainted by great opportunities with the nature of man, and know of a truth that all men fight against their will, the danger vanishes, and resolution rises upon this subject. For this reason, I shall talk very freely on a custom which all men wish exploded, though no man has courage enough to resist it.

But there is one unintelligible word, which I fear will extremely perplex my dissertation, and I confess to you I find very hard to explain, which is the term "satisfaction." An honest country gentleman had the misfortune to fall into company with two or three modern men of honor, where he happened to be very ill-treated; and one of the company, being conscious of his offense, sends a note to him in the morning, and tells him, he was ready to give him satisfaction. "This is fine doing," says the plain fellow; "last night he sent me away cursedly out of humor, and this morning he fancies it would be a satisfaction to be run through the body."

As the matter at present stands, it is not to do handsome actions denominates a man of honor; it is enough if he dares to defend ill ones. Thus you often see a common sharper in competition with a gentleman of the first rank; though all mankind is convinced, that a fighting gamester is only a pickpocket with the courage of an highwayman. One cannot with any patience reflect on the unaccountable jumble of persons and things in this town and nation, which occasions very frequently, that a brave man falls by a hand below that of a common hangman, and yet his executioner escapes the clutches of the hangman for doing it. I shall therefore hereafter consider, how the bravest men in other ages and nations have behaved themselves upon such incidents as we decide by combat; and show, from their practice, that this resentment neither has its foundation from true reason or solid fame; but is an imposture, made of cowardice, falsehood, and want of understanding. For this work, a good history of quarrels would be very edifying to the public, and I apply myself to the town for particulars and circumstances within their knowledge, which may serve to embellish the dissertation with proper cuts. Most of the quarrels I have ever known, have proceeded from some valiant coxcomb's persisting in the wrong, to defend some prevailing folly, and preserve himself from the ingenuousness of owning a mistake.

By this means it is called "giving a man satisfaction," to urge your offense against him with your sword; which puts me in mind of Peter's order to the keeper, in *The Tale of a Tub:*[1] "If you neglect to do all this, damn you and your generation for ever: and so we bid you heartily farewell." If the contradiction in the very terms of one of our challenges were as well explained and turned into downright English, would it not run after this manner?

"SIR,

"Your extraordinary behavior last night, and the liberty you were pleased to take with me, makes me this morning give you this, to tell you, because you are an ill-bred puppy, I will meet you in Hyde-park, an hour hence; and because you want both breeding and humanity, I desire you would come with a pistol in your hand, on horseback, and endeavor to shoot me through the head, to teach you more manners. If you fail of doing me this pleasure, I shall say, you are a rascal, on every post in town: and so, sir, if you will not injure me more, I shall never forgive what you have done already. Pray, sir, do not fail of getting everything ready; and you will infinitely oblige, sir, your most obedient humble servant, *etc.*"

No. 85. TUESDAY, 25 OCTOBER, 1709.

[STEELE.]

MY BROTHER Tranquillus, who is a man of business, came to me this morning into my study, and after very many civil expressions in return for what good offices I had done him, told me, "he desired to carry his wife,

[1] By Jonathan Swift.

my sister, that very morning, to his own house." I readily told him, "I would wait upon him," without asking why he was so impatient to rob us of his good company. He went out of my chamber, and I thought seemed to have a little heaviness upon him, which gave me some disquiet. Soon after my sister came to me, with a very matron-like air, and most sedate satisfaction in her looks, which spoke her very much at ease; but the traces of her countenance seemed to discover that she had been lately in a passion, and that air of content to flow from a certain triumph upon some advantage obtained. She no sooner sat down by me, but I perceived she was one of those ladies who begin to be managers within the time of their being brides. Without letting her speak, which I saw she had a mighty inclination to do, I said, "Here has been your husband, who tells me he has a mind to go home this very morning, and I have consented to it." "It is well," said she, "for you must know ——" "Nay, Jenny," said I. "I beg your pardon, for it is you must know—— You are to understand, that now is the time to fix or alienate your husband's heart for ever; and I fear you have been a little indiscreet in your expressions or behavior towards him, even here in my house." "There has," says she, "been some words; but I will be judged by you if he was not in the wrong; nay I need not be judged by anybody, for he gave it up himself, and said not a word when he saw me grow passionate, but, 'Madam, you are perfectly in the right of it'; as you shall judge——" "Nay, Madam," said I, "I am judge already, and tell you that you are perfectly in the wrong of it; for if it was a matter of importance, I know he has better sense than you; if a trifle, you know what I told you on your wedding-day, that you were to be above little provocations." She knows very well I can be sour upon occasion, therefore gave me leave to go on.

"Sister," said I, "I will not enter into the dispute between you, which I find his prudence put an end to before it came to extremity; but charge you to have a care of the first quarrel, as you tender your happiness; for then it is that the mind will reflect harshly upon every circumstance that has ever passed between you. If such an accident is ever to happen, which I hope never will, be sure to keep to the circumstance before you; make no allusions to what is passed, or conclusions referring to what is to come: do not show a hoard of matter for dissension in your breast: but, if it is necessary, lay before him the thing as you understand it, candidly, without being ashamed of acknowledging an error, or proud of being in the right. If a young couple be not careful in this point, they will get into a habit of wrangling: and when to displease is thought of no consequence, to please is always of as little moment. There is a play, Jenny, I have formerly been at when I was a student: we got into a dark corner with a porringer of brandy, and threw raisins into it, then set it on fire. My chamber-fellow and I diverted ourselves with the sport of venturing our fingers for the raisins; and the wantonness of the thing was to see each other look like a demon, as we burned ourselves, and snatched out the fruit. This fantastical mirth was called Snap-Dragon. You may go into many a family, where you see the man and wife at this sport; every word at their table alludes to some passage between themselves; and you see by the paleness and emotion in their countenances, that it is for your sake, and not their own, that they forbear playing out the whole game in burning each other's fingers. In this case, the whole purpose of life is inverted, and the ambition turns upon a certain contention who shall contradict best, and not upon an inclination to excel in kindnesses and good offices. Therefore, dear Jenny, remember me, and avoid Snap-Dragon."

"I thank you, brother," said she, "but you do not know how he loves me; I find I can do anything with him." "If you can so, why should you desire to do anything but please him? but I have a word or two more before you go out of the room; for I see you do not like the subject I am upon: let nothing provoke you to fall upon an imperfection he cannot help; for, if he has a resenting spirit, he will think your aversion as immovable as the imperfection with which you upbraid him. But, above all, dear Jenny, be careful of one thing, and you will be something more than woman; that is, a levity you are almost all guilty of, which is, to take a pleasure in your power to give pain. It is even in a mistress an argument of meanness of spirit, but in a wife it is injustice and ingratitude. When a sensible man once observes this in a woman, he must have a very great, or very little spirit, to overlook it. A woman ought, therefore, to consider very often, how few men there are who will regard a meditated offense as a weakness of temper."

I was going on in my confabulation, when Tranquillus entered. She cast all her eyes upon him with much shame and confusion, mixed with great complacency and love, and went up to him. He took her in his arms, and looked so many soft things at one glance, that I could see he was glad I had been talking to her, sorry she had been troubled, and angry at himself that he could not disguise the concern he was in an hour before. After which he says to me, with an air awkward enough, but, methought, not unbecoming, "I have altered my mind, brother; we will live upon you a day or two longer." I replied, "That is what I have been persuading Jenny to ask of you, but she is resolved never to contradict your inclination, and refused me."

We were going on in that way which one hardly knows how to express; as when two people mean the same thing in a nice case, but come at it by talking as distantly from it as they can; when very opportunely came in upon us an honest inconsiderable fellow Tim Dapper, a gentleman well known to us both. Tim is one of those who are very necessary, by being very inconsiderable. Tim dropped in at an incident when we knew not how to fall into either a grave or a merry way. My sister took this occasion to make off, and Dapper gave us an account of all the company he has been in to-day, who was and was not at home where he visited. This Tim is the head of a species; he is a little out of his element in this town; but he is a relation of Tranquillus, and his neighbor in the country, which is the true place of residence for this species. The habit of a Dapper, when he is at home, is a light broadcloth, with calamanco[1] or red waistcoat and breeches; and it is remarkable that their wigs seldom hide the collar of their coats. They have always a peculiar spring in their arms, a wriggle in their bodies, and a trip in their gait. All which motions they express at once in their drinking, bowing, or saluting ladies; for a distant imitation of a forward fop, and a resolution to overtop him in his way, are the distinguishing marks of a Dapper. These under-characters of men, are parts of the sociable world by no means to be neglected: they are like pegs in a building; they make no figure in it, but hold the structure together, and are as absolutely necessary as the pillars and columns. I am sure we found it so this morning; for Tranquillus and I should, perhaps, have looked cold at each other the whole day, but Dapper fell in with his brisk way, shook us both by the hand, rallied the bride, mistook the acceptance he met with amongst us for extraordinary perfection in himself, and heartily pleased, and was pleased all the while he stayed. His company left us all in good humor, and we were not such fools as to let it sink, before we confirmed it by great cheerfulness and openness in our carriage the whole evening.

[1]A woolen material.

No. 132. SATURDAY, 11 FEBRUARY, 1710.

[STEELE.]

Habeo senectuti magnam gratiam, quæ mihi sermonis aviditatem auxit, potionis et cibi sustulit.[2]
—TULL. *de Sen.*

AFTER having applied my mind with more than ordinary attention to my studies, it is my usual custom to relax and unbend it in the conversation of such, as are rather easy than shining companions. This I find particularly necessary for me before I retire to rest, in order to draw my slumbers upon me by degrees, and fall asleep insensibly. This is the particular use I make of a set of heavy honest men, with whom I have passed many hours with much indolence, though not with great pleasure. Their conversation is a kind of preparative for sleep; it takes the mind down from its abstractions, leads it into the familiar traces of thought, and lulls it into that state of tranquillity which is the condition of a thinking man, when he is but half awake. After this, my reader will not be surprised to hear the account, which I am about to give of a club of my own contemporaries, among whom I pass two or three hours every evening. This I look upon as taking my first nap before I go to bed. The

[2]I owe much gratitude to old age, which has sharpened my appetite for conversation and dulled my appetite for food and drink (Cicero, *De Senectute*).

truth of it is, I should think myself unjust to posterity, as well as to the society at the Trumpet, of which I am a member, did not I in some part of my writings give an account of the persons among whom I have passed almost a sixth part of my time for these last forty years. Our club consisted originally of fifteen; but, partly by the severity of the law in arbitrary times, and partly by the natural effects of old age, we are at present reduced to a third part of that number: in which, however, we hear this consolation, that the best company is said to consist of five persons. I must confess, besides the aforementioned benefit which I meet with in the conversation of this select society, I am not the less pleased with the company, in that I find myself the greatest wit among them, and am heard as their oracle in all points of learning and difficulty.

Sir Jeoffrey Notch, who is the oldest of the club, has been in possession of the right-hand chair time out of mind, and is the only man among us that has the liberty of stirring the fire. This our foreman is a gentleman of an ancient family, that came to a great estate some years before he had discretion, and run it out in hounds, horses, and cock-fighting; for which reason he looks upon himself as an honest, worthy gentleman, who has had misfortunes in the world, and calls every thriving man a pitiful upstart.

Major Matchlock is the next senior, who served in the last civil wars, and has all the battles by heart. He does not think any action in Europe worth talking of since the fight of Marston Moor; and every night tells us of his having been knocked off his horse at the rising of the London apprentices; for which he is in great esteem among us.

Honest old Dick Reptile is the third of our society. He is a good-natured indolent man, who speaks little himself, but laughs at our jokes; and brings his young nephew along with him, a youth of eighteen years old, to show him good company, and give him a taste of the world. This young fellow sits generally silent; but whenever he opens his mouth, or laughs at anything that passes, he is constantly told by his uncle, after a jocular manner, "Ay, ay, Jack, you young men think us fools; but we old men know you are."

The greatest wit of our company, next to myself, is a Bencher of the neighboring Inn, who in his youth frequented the ordinaries about Charing Cross, and pretends to have been intimate with Jack Ogle. He has about ten distichs of Hudibras without book, and never leaves the club until he has applied them all. If any modern wit be mentioned, or any town-frolic spoken of, he shakes his head at the dullness of the present age, and tells us a story of Jack Ogle.

For my own part, I am esteemed among them, because they see I am something respected by others; though at the same time I understand by their behavior, that I am considered by them as a man of a great deal of learning, but no knowledge of the world; insomuch, that the Major sometimes, in the height of his military pride, calls me the Philosopher: and Sir Jeoffrey, no longer ago than last night, upon a dispute what day of the month it was then in Holland, pulled his pipe out of his mouth, and cried, "What does the scholar say to it?"

Our club meets precisely at *six o'clock in the evening;* but I did not come last night until half an hour after seven, by which means I escaped the battle of Naseby, which the Major usually begins at about three-quarters after six: I found also, that my good friend the Bencher had already spent three of his distichs; and only waited an opportunity to hear a sermon spoken of, that he might introduce the couplet where "a stick" rimes to "ecclesiastic." At my entrance into the room, they were naming a red petticoat and a cloak, by which I found that the Bencher had been diverting them with a story of Jack Ogle.

I had no sooner taken my seat, but Sir Jeoffrey, to show his good-will towards me, gave me a pipe of his own tobacco, and stirred up the fire. I look upon it as a point of morality, to be obliged by those who endeavor to oblige me; and therefore, in requital for his kindness, and to set the conversation a-going, I took the best occasion I could to put him upon telling us the story of old Gantlett, which he always does with very particular concern. He traced up his descent on both sides for several generations, describing his diet and manner of life, with his several battles, and particularly that in which he fell. This Gantlett was a gamecock, upon whose head the knight, in his youth, had won five hundred pounds, and lost two thousand. This naturally set the Major upon the account of Edge Hill fight, and ended in a duel of Jack Ogle's.

Old Reptile was extremely attentive to all that was said, though it was the same he had heard every night for these twenty years, and, upon all occasions, winked upon his nephew to mind what passed.

This may suffice to give the world a taste of our innocent conversation, which we spun out until about ten of the clock, when my maid came with a lantern to light me home. I could not but reflect with myself, as I was going out, upon the talkative humor of old men, and the little figure which that part of life makes in one who cannot employ his natural propensity in discourses which would make him venerable. I must own, it makes me very melancholy in company, when I hear a young man begin a story; and have often observed, that one of a quarter of an hour long in a man of five-and-twenty, gathers circumstances every time he tells it, until it grows into a long Canterbury tale of two hours by that time he is threescore.

The only way of avoiding such a trifling and frivolous old age is, to lay up in our way to it such stores of knowledge and observation, as may make us useful and agreeable in our declining years. The mind of man in a long life will become a magazine of wisdom or folly, and will consequently discharge itself in something impertinent or improving. For which reason, as there is nothing more ridiculous than an old trifling story-teller, so there is nothing more venerable, than one who has turned his experience to the entertainment and advantage of mankind.

In short, we, who are in the last stage of life, and are apt to indulge ourselves in talk, ought to consider, if what we speak be worth being heard, and endeavor to make our discourse like that of Nestor, which Homer compares to the flowing of honey for its sweetness.

I am afraid I shall be thought guilty of this excess I am speaking of, when I cannot conclude without observing, that Milton certainly thought of this passage in Homer, when, in his description of an eloquent spirit, he says, "His tongue dropped manna."[1]

[1]Said of Belial, *Paradise Lost*, II. 112–113.

No. 158. Thursday, 13 April, 1710.

[Addison.]

Faciunt næ intelligendo, ut nihil intelligant.[2]
—Ter.

Tom Folio is a broker in learning, employed to get together good editions, and stock the libraries of great men. There is not a sale of books begins until Tom Folio is seen at the door. There is not an auction where his name is not heard, and that too in the very nick of time, in the critical moment, before the last decisive stroke of the hammer. There is not a subscription goes forward in which Tom is not privy to the first rough draught of the proposals; nor a catalogue printed, that doth not come to him wet from the press. He is an universal scholar, so far as the title-page of all authors; knows the manuscripts in which they were discovered, the editions through which they have passed, with the praises or censures which they have received from the several members of the learned world. He has a greater esteem for Aldus and Elzevir, than for Virgil and Horace. If you talk of Herodotus, he breaks out into a panegyric upon Harry Stephens. He thinks he gives you an account of an author, when he tells you the subject he treats of, the name of the editor, and the year in which it was printed. Or if you draw him into farther particulars, he cries up the goodness of the paper, extols the diligence of the corrector, and is transported with the beauty of the letter. This he looks upon to be sound learning, and substantial criticism. As for those who talk of the fineness of style, and the justness of thought, or describe the brightness of any particular passages; nay, though they themselves write in the genius and spirit of the author they admire; Tom looks upon them as men of superficial learning, and flashy parts.

I had yesterday morning a visit from this learned *idiot*, for *that* is the light in which I consider every pedant, when I discovered in him some little touches of the coxcomb, which I had not before observed. Being very full of the figure which he makes in the republic of letters, and wonderfully satisfied with his great stock of knowledge, he gave me broad intimations, that he did not be-

[2]While they pretend to know more than others, they really know nothing (Terence, *Andr.* Prol. 17).

lieve in all points as his forefathers had done. He then communicated to me a thought of a certain author upon a passage of Virgil's account of the dead, which I made the subject of a late paper. This thought hath taken very much among men of Tom's pitch and understanding, though universally exploded by all that know how to construe Virgil, or have any relish of antiquity. Not to trouble my reader with it, I found, upon the whole, that Tom did not believe a future state of rewards and punishments, because Æneas, at his leaving the empire of the dead, passed through the gate of ivory, and not through that of horn. Knowing that Tom had not sense enough to give up an opinion which he had once received, that I might avoid wrangling, I told him "that Virgil possibly had his oversights as well as another author." "Ah! Mr. Bickerstaff,"[1] says he, "you would have another opinion of him, if you would read him in Daniel Heinsius's edition. I have perused him myself several times in that edition," continued he; "and after the strictest and most malicious examination, could find but two faults in him; one of them is in the Æneids, where there are two commas instead of a parenthesis; and another in the third Georgic, where you may find a semicolon turned upside down." "Perhaps," said I, "these were not Virgil's faults, but those of the transcriber." "I do not design it," says Tom, "as a reflection on Virgil; on the contrary, I know that all the manuscripts declaim against such a punctuation. Oh! Mr. Bickerstaff," says he, "what would a man give to see one simile of Virgil writ in his own hand?" I asked him which was the simile he meant; but was answered, any simile in Virgil. He then told me all the secret history in the commonwealth of learning; of modern pieces that had the names of ancient authors annexed to them; of all the books that were now writing or printing in the several parts of Europe; of many amendments which are made, and not yet published, and a thousand other particulars, which I would not have my memory burdened with for a Vatican.

[1]The *Tatler* papers, it was pretended, were written by Isaac Bickerstaff, a fictitious astrologer invented several years before by Swift for the purpose of making fun of one Partridge, an astrologer who published predictions much after the manner of the old-fashioned almanac still occasionally to be met with.

At length, being fully persuaded that I thoroughly admired him, and looked upon him as a prodigy of learning, he took his leave. I know several of Tom's class, who are professed admirers of Tasso, without understanding a word of Italian: and one in particular, that carries a *Pastor Fido* in his pocket, in which, I am sure, he is acquainted with no other beauty but the clearness of the character.

There is another kind of pedant, who, with all Tom Folio's impertinences, hath greater superstructures and embellishments of Greek and Latin; and is still more insupportable than the other, in the same degree as he is more learned. Of this kind very often are editors, commentators, interpreters, scholiasts, and critics; and, in short, all men of deep learning without common sense. These persons set a greater value on themselves for having found out the meaning of a passage in Greek, than upon the author for having written it; nay, will allow the passage itself not to have any beauty in it, at the same time that they would be considered as the greatest men of the age, for having interpreted it. They will look with contempt on the most beautiful poems that have been composed by any of their contemporaries; but will lock themselves up in their studies for a twelvemonth together, to correct, publish, and expound such trifles of antiquity, as a modern author would be contemned for. Men of the strictest morals, severest lives, and the gravest professions, will write volumes upon an idle sonnet, that is originally in Greek or Latin; give editions of the most immoral authors; and spin out whole pages upon the various readings of a lewd expression. All that can be said in excuse for them is, that their works sufficiently show they have no taste of their authors; and that what they do in this kind, is out of their great learning, and not out of any levity or lasciviousness of temper.

A pedant of this nature is wonderfully well described in six lines of Boileau, with which I shall conclude his character:

Un Pédant enyvré de sa vaine science,
Tout herissé de Grec, tout bouffi d'arrogance;
Et qui de mille auteurs retenus mot pour mot,
Dans sa tête entassés n'a souvent fait qu'un sot,
Croit qu'un livre fait tout, et que sans Aristote
La raison ne voit goute, et le bon sens radote.

Brim-full of learning see that pedant stride,
Bristling with horrid Greek, and puffed with pride!
A thousand authors he in vain has read,
And with their maxims stuffed his empty head;
And thinks that, without Aristotle's rule,
Reason is blind, and common sense a fool.

THE SPECTATOR

No. 1. Thursday, 1 March, 1711.
[Addison.]

Non fumum ex fulgore, sed ex fumo dare lucem
Cogitat, ut speciosa dehinc miracula promat.[1]
—Horace.

I have observed that a reader seldom peruses a book with pleasure till he knows whether the writer of it be a black or a fair man, of a mild or choleric disposition, married or a bachelor, with other particulars of the like nature that conduce very much to the right understanding of an author. To gratify this curiosity, which is so natural to a reader, I design this paper and my next as prefatory discourses to my following writings, and shall give some account in them of the several persons that are engaged in this work. As the chief trouble of compiling, digesting, and correcting will fall to my share, I must do myself the justice to open the work with my own history. I was born to a small hereditary estate, which, according to the tradition of the village where it lies, was bounded by the same hedges and ditches in William the Conqueror's time that it is at present, and has been delivered down from father to son whole and entire, without the loss or acquisition of a single field or meadow, during the space of six hundred years. There runs a story in the family, that my mother dreamed that she was brought to bed of a judge: whether this might proceed from a lawsuit which was then depending in the family, or my father's being a justice of the peace, I cannot determine; for I am not so vain as to think it presaged any dignity that I should arrive at in my future life, though that was the interpretation which the neighborhood put upon it. The gravity of my behavior at my very first appearance in the world seemed to favor my mother's dream: for, as she has often told me, I threw away my rattle before I was two months old, and would not make use of my coral till they had taken away the bells from it.

As for the rest of my infancy, there being nothing in it remarkable, I shall pass it over in silence. I find that, during my nonage, I had the reputation of a very sullen youth, but was always a favorite of my schoolmaster, who used to say *that my parts were solid and would wear well.* I had not been long at the University before I distinguished myself by a most profound silence; for during the space of eight years, excepting in the public exercises of the college, I scarce uttered the quantity of an hundred words; and indeed do not remember that I ever spoke three sentences together in my whole life. Whilst I was in this learned body, I applied myself with so much diligence to my studies that there are very few celebrated books, either in the learned or the modern tongues, which I am not acquainted with.

Upon the death of my father I was resolved to travel into foreign countries, and therefore left the University with the character of an odd, unaccountable fellow, that had a great deal of learning if I would but show it. An insatiable thirst after knowledge carried me into all the countries of Europe in which there was anything new or strange to be seen; nay, to such a degree was my curiosity raised, that having read the controversies of some great men concerning the antiquities of Egypt, I made a voyage to Grand Cairo, on purpose to take the measure of a pyramid; and as soon as I had set myself right in that particular, returned to my native country with great satisfaction.

I have passed my latter years in this city, where I am frequently seen in most public places, though there are not above half a dozen of my select friends that know me; of whom my next paper shall give a more particular account. There is no place of general sort wherein I do not often make my appearance; sometimes I am seen thrusting my head into a round of politicians at Will's, and listening with great attention to the narratives that are made in those little circular audiences. Sometimes I smoke a pipe at Child's, and whilst I seem attentive to nothing but *The Postman*, overhear the conversation of every table in the room. I appear on Sunday nights at St. James's Coffee-house,

[1]Not smoke from fire his object is to bring,
But fire from smoke, a very different thing.
(*Art of Poetry*, 143–144; Conington's translation.)

and sometimes join the little committee of politics in the Inner room, as one who comes there to hear and improve. My face is likewise very well known at the Grecian, the Cocoa-Tree, and in the theaters both of Drury Lane and the Hay-Market. I have been taken for a merchant upon the Exchange for above these ten years, and sometimes pass for a Jew in the assembly of stock-jobbers at Jonathan's. In short, wherever I see a cluster of people, I always mix with them, though I never open my lips but in my own club.

Thus I live in the world rather as a SPECTATOR of mankind than as one of the species; by which means I have made myself a speculative statesman, soldier, merchant, and artisan, without ever meddling with any practical part in life. I am very well versed in the theory of an husband or a father, and can discern the errors in the economy, business, and diversion of others better than those who are engaged in them; as standers-by discover blots which are apt to escape those who are in the game. I never espoused any party with violence, and am resolved to observe an exact neutrality between the Whigs and Tories, unless I shall be forced to declare myself by the hostilities of either side. In short, I have acted in all the parts of my life as a looker-on, which is the character I intend to preserve in this paper.

I have given the reader just so much of my history and character as to let him see I am not altogether unqualified for the business I have undertaken. As for other particulars in my life and adventures, I shall insert them in following papers as I shall see occasion. In the meantime, when I consider how much I have seen, read, and heard, I began to blame my own taciturnity: and since I have neither time nor inclination to communicate the fullness of my heart in speech, I am resolved to do it in writing, and to print myself out, if possible, before I die. I have been often told by my friends that it is a pity so many useful discoveries which I have made, should be in the possession of a silent man. For this reason, therefore, I shall publish a sheetful of thoughts every morning for the benefit of my contemporaries; and if I can in any way contribute to the diversion or improvement of the country in which I live, I shall leave it, when I am summoned out of it, with the secret satisfaction of thinking that I have not lived in vain.

There are three very material points which I have not spoken to in this paper, and which, for several important reasons, I must keep to myself, at least for some time: I mean, an account of my name, my age, and my lodgings. I must confess, I would gratify my reader in anything that is reasonable; but, as for these three particulars, though I am sensible they might tend very much to the embellishment of my paper, I cannot yet come to a resolution of communicating them to the public. They would indeed draw me out of that obscurity which I have enjoyed for many years, and expose me in public places to several salutes and civilities which have been always very disagreeable to me; for the greatest pain I can suffer is the being talked to and being stared at. It is for this reason, likewise, that I keep my complexion and dress as very great secrets, though it is not impossible but I may make discoveries of both in the progress of the work I have undertaken.

After having been thus particular upon myself, I shall in to-morrow's paper give an account of those gentlemen who are concerned with me in this work; for, as I have before intimated, a plan of it is laid and concerted (as all other matters of importance are) in a club. However, as my friends have engaged me to stand in the front, those who have a mind to correspond with me may direct their letters *To The Spectator, at Mr. Buckley's, in Little Britain.* For I must further acquaint the reader that, though our club meets only on Tuesdays and Thursdays, we have appointed a committee to sit every night for the inspection of all such papers as may contribute to the advancement of the public weal.

No. 2. FRIDAY, 2 MARCH, 1711.

[STEELE.]

——Haec alii sex
Vel plures uno conclamant ore.[1]
—JUVENAL.

THE first of our society is a gentleman of Worcestershire, of ancient descent, a baronet, his name Sir Roger de Coverley. His

[1]Six others and more cry out with one voice (*Satires*, VII, 167).

great-grandfather was inventor of that famous country-dance which is called after him. All who know that shire are very well acquainted with the parts and merits of Sir Roger. He is a gentleman that is very singular in his behavior, but his singularities proceed from his good sense, and are contradictions to the manners of the world only as he thinks the world is in the wrong. However, this humor creates him no enemies, for he does nothing with sourness of obstinacy; and his being unconfined to modes and forms, makes him but the readier and more capable to please and oblige all who know him. When he is in town, he lives in Soho Square. It is said he keeps himself a bachelor by reason he was crossed in love by a perverse, beautiful widow of the next county to him. Before this disappointment, Sir Roger was what you call a fine gentleman, had often supped with my Lord Rochester and Sir George Etherege, fought a duel upon his first coming to town, and kicked Bully Dawson in a public coffee-house for calling him "youngster." But being ill-used by the above-mentioned widow, he was very serious for a year and a half; and though, his temper being naturally jovial, he at last got over it, he grew careless of himself, and never dressed afterward. He continues to wear a coat and doublet of the same cut that were in fashion at the time of his repulse, which, in his merry humors, he tells us, has been in and out twelve times since he first wore it. 'Tis said Sir Roger grew humble in his desires after he had forgot this cruel beauty; but this is looked upon by his friends rather as matter of raillery than truth. He is now in his fifty-sixth year, cheerful, gay, and hearty; keeps a good house in both town and country; a great lover of mankind; but there is such a mirthful cast in his behavior that he is rather beloved than esteemed. His tenants grow rich, his servants look satisfied, all the young women profess love to him, and the young men are glad of his company; when he comes into a house he calls the servants by their names, and talks all the way up stairs to a visit. I must not omit that Sir Roger is a justice of the quorum; that he fills the chair at a quarter-session with great abilities; and, three months ago, gained universal applause by explaining a passage in the Game Act.

The gentleman next in esteem and authority among us is another bachelor, who is a member of the Inner Temple; a man of great probity, wit, and understanding; but he has chosen his place of residence rather to obey the direction of an old humorsome father, than in pursuit of his own inclinations. He was placed there to study the laws of the land, and is the most learned of any of the house in those of the stage. Aristotle and Longinus are much better understood by him than Littleton or Coke. The father sends up, every post, questions relating to marriage-articles, leases, and tenures, in the neighborhood; all which questions he agrees with an attorney to answer and take care of in the lump. He is studying the passions themselves, when he should be inquiring into the debates among men which arise from them. He knows the argument of each of the orations of Demosthenes and Tully,[1] but not one case in the reports of our own courts. No one ever took him for a fool, but none, except his intimate friends, know he has a great deal of wit. This turn makes him at once both disinterested and agreeable; as few of his thoughts are drawn from business, they are most of them fit for conversation. His taste of books is a little too just for the age he lives in; he has read all, but approves of very few. His familiarity with the customs, manners, actions, and writings of the ancients makes him a very delicate observer of what occurs to him in the present world. He is an excellent critic, and the time of the play is his hour of business; exactly at five he passes through New Inn, crosses through Russell Court, and takes a turn at Will's till the play begins; he has his shoes rubbed and his periwig powdered at the barber's as you go into the Rose. It is for the good of the audience when he is at a play, for the actors have an ambition to please him.

The person of next consideration is Sir Andrew Freeport, a merchant of great eminence in the city of London, a person of indefatigable industry, strong reason, and great experience. His notions of trade are noble and generous, and (as every rich man has usually some sly way of jesting which would make no great figure were he not a rich man) he calls the sea the British Common. He is acquainted with commerce in all its parts, and will tell you that it is a stupid and barbarous way to extend dominion by arms; for true

[1]Cicero.

power is to be got by arts and industry. He will often argue that if this part of our trade were well cultivated, we should gain from one nation; and if another, from another. I have heard him prove that diligence makes more lasting acquisitions than valor, and that sloth has ruined more nations than the sword. He abounds in several frugal maxims, among which the greatest favorite is, "A penny saved is a penny got." A general trader of good sense is pleasanter company than a general scholar; and Sir Andrew having a natural unaffected eloquence, the perspicuity of his discourse gives the same pleasure that wit would in another man. He has made his fortunes himself, and says that England may be richer than other kingdoms by as plain methods as he himself is richer than other men; though at the same time I can say this of him, that there is not a point in the compass but blows home a ship in which he is an owner.

Next to Sir Andrew in the club-room sits Captain Sentry, a gentleman of great courage, good understanding, but invincible modesty. He is one of those that deserve very well, but are very awkward at putting their talents within the observation of such as should take notice of them. He was some years a captain, and behaved himself with great gallantry in several engagements and at several sieges; but having a small estate of his own, and being next heir to Sir Roger, he has quitted a way of life in which no man can rise suitably to his merit who is not something of a courtier as well as a soldier. I have heard him often lament that in a profession where merit is placed in so conspicuous a view, impudence should get the better of modesty. When he has talked to this purpose I never heard him make a sour expression, but frankly confess that he left the world because he was not fit for it. A strict honesty and an even, regular behavior are in themselves obstacles to him that must press through crowds who endeavor at the same end with himself,—the favor of a commander. He will, however, in this way of talk, excuse generals for not disposing according to men's desert, or inquiring into it, "For," says he, "that great man who has a mind to help me, has as many to break through to come at me as I have to come at him"; therefore he will conclude that the man who would make a figure, especially in a military way, must get over all false modesty, and assist his patron against the importunity of other pretenders by a proper assurance in his own vindication. He says it is a civil cowardice to be backward in asserting what you ought to expect, as it is a military fear to be slow in attacking when it is your duty. With this candor does the gentleman speak of himself and others. The same frankness runs through all his conversation. The military part of his life has furnished him with many adventures, in the relation of which he is very agreeable to the company; for he is never overbearing, though accustomed to command men in the utmost degree below him; nor ever too obsequious from an habit of obeying men highly above him.

But that our society may not appear a set of humorists unacquainted with the gallantries and pleasures of the age, we have among us the gallant Will Honeycomb, a gentleman who, according to his years, should be in the decline of his life, but having ever been very careful of his person, and always had a very easy fortune, time has made but very little impression either by wrinkles on his forehead or traces in his brain. His person is well turned and of a good height. He is very ready at that sort of discourse with which men usually entertain women. He has all his life dressed very well, and remembers habits as others do men. He can smile when one speaks to him, and laughs easily. He knows the history of every mode, and can inform you from which of the French king's wenches our wives and daughters had this manner of curling their hair, that way of placing their hoods; whose frailty was covered by such a sort of petticoat, and whose vanity to show her foot made that part of the dress so short in such a year. In a word, all his conversation and knowledge has been in the female world. As other men of his age will take notice to you what such a minister said upon such and such an occasion, he will tell you when the Duke of Monmouth danced at court such a woman was then smitten, another was taken with him at the head of his troop in the Park. In all these important relations, he has ever about the same time received a kind glance or a blow of a fan from some celebrated beauty, mother of the present Lord Such-a-one. If you speak of a young commoner that said a lively thing in the House, he starts up: "He has good blood in his veins; Tom Mirabell, the rogue, cheated me in that affair; that young fellow's mother used me more like a dog than any woman I ever made advances to." This way of talking of his very much enlivens the conversation among us of a more sedate turn; and I find there is not one of the company but myself, who rarely speak at all, but speaks of him as of that sort of man who is usually called a well-bred, fine gentleman. To conclude his character, where women are not concerned, he is an honest, worthy man.

I cannot tell whether I am to account him whom I am next to speak of as one of our company, for he visits us but seldom; but when he does, it adds to every man else a new enjoyment of himself. He is a clergyman, a very philosophic man, of general learning, great sanctity of life, and the most exact good breeding. He has the misfortune to be of a very weak constitution, and consequently cannot accept of such cares and business as preferments in his function would oblige him to; he is therefore among divines what a chamber-counselor is among lawyers. The probity of his mind and the integrity of his life create him followers, as being eloquent or loud advances others. He seldom introduces the subject he speaks upon; but we are so far gone in years that he observes, when he is among us, an earnestness to have him fall on some divine topic, which he always treats with much authority, as one who has no interest in this world, as one who is hastening to the object of all his wishes and conceives hope from his decays and infirmities. These are my ordinary companions.

No. 10. Monday, 12 March, 1711.
[Addison.]

Non aliter quam qui adverso vix flumine lembum
Remigiis subigit, si brachia forte remisit,
Atque illum in præceps prono rapit alveus amni.[1]
—Virg.

It is with much satisfaction that I hear this great city inquiring day by day after these my papers, and receiving my morning lectures with a becoming seriousness and attention. My publisher tells me that there are already three thousand of them distributed every day. So that if I allow twenty readers to every paper, which I look upon as a modest computation, I may reckon about three-score thousand disciples in London and Westminster, who I hope will take care to distinguish themselves from the thoughtless herd of their ignorant and unattentive brethren. Since I have raised to myself so great an audience, I shall spare no pains to make their instruction agreeable, and their diversion useful. For which reasons I shall endeavor to enliven morality with wit, and to temper wit with morality, that my readers may, if possible, both ways find their account in the speculation of the day. And to the end that their virtue and discretion may not be short, transient, intermitting starts of thought, I have resolved to refresh their memories from day to day, till I have recovered them out of that desperate state of vice and folly into which the age is fallen. The mind that lies fallow but a single day, sprouts up in follies that are only to be killed by a constant and assiduous culture. It was said of Socrates, that he brought philosophy down from heaven, to inhabit among men; and I shall be ambitious to have it said of me, that I have brought philosophy out of closets and libraries, schools and colleges, to dwell in clubs and assemblies, at tea-tables and in coffee-houses.

I would therefore in a very particular manner recommend these my speculations to all well-regulated families, that set apart an hour in every morning for tea and bread and butter; and would earnestly advise them for their good to order this paper to be punctually served up, and to be looked upon as a part of the tea-equipage.

Sir Francis Bacon observes, that a well written book, compared with its rivals and antagonists, is like Moses' serpent, that immediately swallowed up and devoured those of the Egyptians. I shall not be so vain as to think, that where *The Spectator* appears, the other public prints will vanish; but shall leave it to my reader's consideration, whether, is it not much better to be let into the knowledge of one's self, than to hear what passes in Muscovy or Poland; and to amuse ourselves with such writings as tend to the wearing out of ignorance, passion, and prejudice,

[1]Like a man whose oars can barely force the boat upstream, and if he relaxes his arms the current carries it headlong down the river (*Georgics*, I, 201).

than such as naturally conduce to inflame hatreds, and make enmities irreconcilable?

In the next place, I would recommend this paper to the daily perusal of those gentlemen whom I cannot but consider as my good brothers and allies, I mean the fraternity of spectators, who live in the world without having anything to do in it; and either by the affluence of their fortunes, or laziness of their dispositions, have no other business with the rest of mankind, but to look upon them. Under this class of men are comprehended all contemplative tradesmen, titular physicians, fellows of the Royal Society, Templars that are not given to be contentious, and statesmen that are out of business; in short, every one that considers the world as a theater, and desires to form a right judgment of those who are the actors on it.

There is another set of men that I must likewise lay a claim to, whom I have lately called the blanks of society, as being altogether unfurnished with ideas, till the business and conversation of the day has supplied them. I have often considered these poor souls with an eye of great commiseration, when I have heard them asking the first man they have met with, whether there was any news stirring? and by that means gathering together materials for thinking. These needy persons do not know what to talk of, till about twelve o'clock in the morning; for by that time they are pretty good judges of the weather, know which way the wind sits, and whether the Dutch mail be come in. As they lie at the mercy of the first man they meet, and are grave or impertinent all the day long, according to the notions which they have imbibed in the morning, I would earnestly entreat them not to stir out of their chambers till they have read this paper, and do promise them that I will daily instil into them such sound and wholesome sentiments, as shall have a good effect on their conversation for the ensuing twelve hours.

But there are none to whom this paper will be more useful, than to the female world. I have often thought there has not been sufficient pains taken in finding out proper employments and diversions for the fair ones. Their amusements seem contrived for them, rather as they are women, than as they are reasonable creatures; and are more adapted to the sex than to the species. The toilet is their great scene of business, and the right adjusting of their hair the principal employment of their lives. The sorting of a suit of ribbons is reckoned a very good morning's work; and if they make an excursion to a mercer's or a toy-shop, so great a fatigue makes them unfit for anything else all the day after. Their more serious occupations are sewing and embroidery, and their greatest drudgery the preparation of jellies and sweetmeats. This, I say, is the state of ordinary women; though I know there are multitudes of those of a more elevated life and conversation, that move in an exalted sphere of knowledge and virtue, that join all the beauties of the mind to the ornaments of dress, and inspire a kind of awe and respect, as well as love, into their male beholder. I hope to increase the number of these by publishing this daily paper, which I shall always endeavor to make an innocent if not an improving entertainment, and by that means at least divert the minds of my female readers from greater trifles. At the same time, as I would fain give some finishing touches to those which are already the most beautiful pieces in human nature, I shall endeavor to point out all those imperfections that are the blemishes, as well as those virtues which are the embellishments of the sex. In the meanwhile I hope these my gentle readers, who have so much time on their hands, will not grudge throwing away a quarter of an hour in a day on this paper, since they may do it without any hindrance to business.

I know several of my friends and well-wishers are in great pain for me, lest I should not be able to keep up the spirit of a paper which I oblige myself to furnish every day: but to make them easy in this particular, I will promise them faithfully to give it over as soon as I grow dull. This I know will be matter of great raillery to the small wits; who will frequently put me in mind of my promise, desire me to keep my word, assure me that it is high time to give over, with many other little pleasantries of the like nature, which men of a little smart genius cannot forbear throwing out against their best friends, when they have such a handle given them of being witty. But let them remember that I do hereby enter my caveat against this piece of raillery.

No. 81. SATURDAY, 2 JUNE, 1711.
[ADDISON.]

Qualis ubi audito venantum murmure tigris
Horruit in maculas—[1]

—STATIUS.

ABOUT the middle of last winter I went to see an opera at the theater in the Haymarket, where I could not but take notice of two parties of very fine women, that had placed themselves in the opposite side-boxes, and seemed drawn up in a kind of battle array one against another. After a short survey of them, I found they were patched differently; the faces on one hand being spotted on the right side of the forehead, and those upon the other on the left. I quickly perceived that they cast hostile glances upon one another; and that their patches were placed in those different situations, as party-signals to distinguish friends from foes. In the middle boxes, between these two opposite bodies, were several ladies who patched indifferently on both sides of their faces, and seemed to sit there with no other intention but to see the opera. Upon inquiry I found, that the body of Amazons on my right hand, were Whigs, and those on my left, Tories; and that those who had placed themselves in the middle boxes were a neutral party, whose faces had not yet declared themselves. These last, however, as I afterwards found, diminished daily, and took their party with one side or the other; insomuch that I observed in several of them, the patches, which were before dispersed equally, are now all gone over to the Whig or Tory side of the face. The censorious say, that the men, whose hearts are aimed at, are very often the occasions that one part of the face is thus dishonored, and lies under a kind of disgrace, while the other is so much set off and adorned by the owner; and that the patches turn to the right or to the left, according to the principles of the man who is most in favor. But whatever may be the motives of a few fantastical coquettes, who do not patch for the public good so much as for their own private advantage, it is certain, that there are several women of honor who patch out of principle, and with an eye to the interest of their country. Nay, I am informed that some of them adhere so steadfastly to their party, and are so far from sacrificing their zeal for the public to their passion for any particular person, that in a late draft of marriage articles a lady has stipulated with her husband, that, whatever his opinions are, she shall be at liberty to patch on which side she pleases.

I must here take notice, that Rosalinda, a famous Whig partisan, has most unfortunately a very beautiful mole on the Tory part of her forehead; which being very conspicuous, has occasioned many mistakes, and given a handle to her enemies to misrepresent her face, as though it had revolted from the Whig interest. But, whatever this natural patch may seem to intimate, it is well-known that her notions of government are still the same. This unlucky mole, however, has misled several coxcombs; and like the hanging out of false colors, made some of them converse with Rosalinda in what they thought the spirit of her party, when on a sudden she has given them an unexpected fire, that has sunk them all at once. If Rosalinda is unfortunate in her mole, Nigranilla is as unhappy in a pimple, which forces her, against her inclinations, to patch on the Whig side.

I am told that many virtuous matrons, who formerly have been taught to believe that this artificial spotting of the face was unlawful, are now reconciled by a zeal for their cause, to what they could not be prompted by a concern for their beauty. This way of declaring war upon one another, puts me in mind of what is reported of the tigress, that several spots rise in her skin when she is angry, or as Mr. Cowley has imitated the verses that stand as the motto on this paper,

——She swells with angry pride,
And calls forth all her spots on ev'ry side.[2]

When I was in the theater the time abovementioned, I had the curiosity to count the patches on both sides, and found the Tory patches to be about twenty stronger than the Whig; but to make amends for this small inequality, I the next morning found the whole puppet-show filled with faces spotted after the Whiggish manner. Whether or no the ladies had retreated hither in order to rally their forces I cannot tell; but the next night

[1]Like the tigress when, at the sound of the hunters, spots appear upon her skin (*Theb.* II, 128).

[2]*Davideis*, III, 403–404.

they came in so great a body to the opera, that they outnumbered the enemy.

This account of party patches will, I am afraid, appear improbable to those who live at a distance from the fashionable world; but as it is a distinction of a very singular nature, and what perhaps may never meet with a parallel, I think I should not have discharged the office of a faithful Spectator had I not recorded it.

I have, in former papers, endeavored to expose this party-rage in women, as it only serves to aggravate the hatreds and animosities that reign among men, and in a great measure deprive the fair sex of those peculiar charms with which nature has endowed them.

When the Romans and Sabines were at war, and just upon the point of giving battle, the women, who were allied to both of them, interposed with so many tears and entreaties, that they prevented the mutual slaughter which threatened both parties, and united them together in a firm and lasting peace.

I would recommend this noble example to our British ladies, at a time when their country is torn with so many unnatural divisions, that if they continue, it will be a misfortune to be born in it. The Greeks thought it so improper for women to interest themselves in competitions and contentions, that for this reason, among others, they forbade them, under pain of death, to be present at the Olympic games, notwithstanding these were the public diversions of all Greece.

As our English women excel those of all nations in beauty, they should endeavor to outshine them in all other accomplishments proper to the sex, and to distinguish themselves as tender mothers, and faithful wives, rather than as furious partisans. Female virtues are of a domestic turn. The famil is the proper province for private women to shine in. If they must be showing their zeal for the public, let it not be against those who are perhaps of the same family, or at least of the same religion or nation, but against those who are the open, professed, undoubted enemies of their faith, liberty, and country. When the Romans were pressed with a foreign enemy, the ladies voluntarily contributed all their rings and jewels to assist the government under a public exigence, which appeared so laudable an action in the eyes of their countrymen, that from thenceforth it was permitted by a law to pronounce public orations at the funeral of a woman in praise of the deceased person, which till that time was peculiar to men. Would our English ladies, instead of sticking on a patch against those of their own country, show themselves so truly public-spirited as to sacrifice every one her necklace against the common enemy, what decrees ought not to be made in favor of them?

Since I am recollecting upon this subject such passages as occur to my memory out of ancient authors, I cannot omit a sentence in the celebrated funeral oration of Pericles, which he made in honor of those brave Athenians that were slain in a fight with the Lacedæmonians. After having addressed himself to the several ranks and orders of his countrymen, and shown them how they should behave themselves in the public cause, he turns to the female part of his audience: "And as for you (says he) I shall advise you in very few words: Aspire only to those virtues that are peculiar to your sex; follow your natural modesty, and think it your greatest commendation not to be talked of one way or other."[1]

No. 112. Monday, 9 July, 1711.

[Addison.]

'Αθανάτους μὲν πρῶτα θεοὺς, νόμῳ ὡς διάκειται, Τίμα.[2]

—Pythagoras.

I am always very well pleased with a country Sunday, and think, if keeping holy the seventh day were only a human institution, it would be the best method that could have been thought of for the polishing and civilizing of mankind. It is certain the country people would soon degenerate into a kind of savages and barbarians were there not such frequent returns of a stated time, in which the whole village meet together with their best faces, and in their cleanliest habits, to converse with one another upon indifferent subjects, hear their duties explained to them, and join together in adoration of the Supreme Being. Sunday clears away the rust of the whole week, not only as it refreshes in their minds the notions of re-

[1]Thucydides, II, xlv.

[2]First reverence the immortal gods. as custom decrees (*Carmina Aurea*, 1–2).

ligion, but as it puts both the sexes upon appearing in their most agreeable forms, and exerting all such qualities as are apt to give them a figure in the eye of the village. A country fellow distinguishes himself as much in the churchyard as a citizen does upon the 'Change, the whole parish politics being generally discussed in that place either after sermon or before the bell rings.

My friend Sir Roger, being a good churchman, has beautified the inside of his church with several texts of his own choosing; he has likewise given a handsome pulpit-cloth, and railed in the communion-table at his own expense. He has often told me that, at his coming to his estate, he found his parishioners very irregular; and that, in order to make them kneel and join in the responses, he gave every one of them a hassock and a common-prayer-book, and at the same time employed an itinerant singing-master, who goes about the country for that purpose, to instruct them rightly in the tunes of the Psalms; upon which they now very much value themselves, and indeed outdo most of the country churches that I have ever heard.

As Sir Roger is landlord to the whole congregation, he keeps them in very good order, and will suffer nobody to sleep in it besides himself; for, if by chance he has been surprised into a short nap at sermon, upon recovering out of it he stands up and looks about him, and, if he sees anybody else nodding, either wakes them himself, or sends his servant to them. Several other of the old knight's particularities break out upon these occasions; sometimes he will be lengthening out a verse in the Singing-Psalms half a minute after the rest of the congregation have done with it; sometimes, when he is pleased with the matter of his devotion, he pronounces "Amen" three or four times to the same prayer; and sometimes stands up when everybody else is upon their knees, to count the congregation, or see if any of his tenants are missing.

I was yesterday very much surprised to hear my old friend, in the midst of the service, calling out to one John Matthews to mind what he was about, and not disturb the congregation. This John Matthews, it seems, is remarkable for being an idle fellow, and at that time was kicking his heels for his diversion. This authority of the knight, though exerted in that odd manner which accompanies him in all circumstances of life, has a very good effect upon the parish, who are not polite enough to see anything ridiculous in his behavior; besides that the general good sense and worthiness of his character makes his friends observe these little singularities as foils that rather set off than blemish his good qualities.

As soon as the sermon is finished, nobody presumes to stir till Sir Roger is gone out of the church. The knight walks down from his seat in the chancel between a double row of his tenants, that stand bowing to him on each side, and every now and then inquires how such an one's wife, or mother, or son, or father do, whom he does not see at church,—which is understood as a secret reprimand to the person that is absent.

The chaplain has often told me that, upon a catechizing day, when Sir Roger had been pleased with a boy that answers well, he has ordered a Bible to be given him next day for his encouragement, and sometimes accompanies it with a flitch of bacon to his mother. Sir Roger has likewise added five pounds a year to the clerk's place; and, that he may encourage the young fellows to make themselves perfect in the church service, has promised, upon the death of the present incumbent, who is very old, to bestow it according to merit.

The fair understanding between Sir Roger and his chaplain, and their mutual concurrence in doing good, is the more remarkable because the very next village is famous for the differences and contentions that rise between the parson and the squire, who live in a perpetual state of war. The parson is always preaching at the squire, and the squire, to be revenged on the parson, never comes to church. The squire has made all his tenants atheists and tithe-stealers; while the parson instructs them every Sunday in the dignity of his order, and insinuates to them in almost every sermon that he is a better man than his patron. In short, matters are come to such an extremity that the squire has not said his prayers either in public or private this half year; and that the parson threatens him, if he does not mend his manners, to pray for him in the face of the whole congregation.

Feuds of this nature, though too frequent

in the country, are very fatal to the ordinary people, who are so used to be dazzled with riches that they pay as much deference to the understanding of a man of an estate as of a man of learning; and are very hardly brought to regard any truth, how important soever it may be, that is preached to them, when they know there are several men of five hundred a year who do not believe it.

No. 122. Friday, 20 July, 1711.

[Addison.]

Comes jucundus in via pro vehiculo est.[1]

—Publ. Syr.

A man's first care should be to avoid the reproaches of his own heart; his next, to escape the censures of the world. If the last interferes with the former, it ought to be entirely neglected; but otherwise there cannot be a greater satisfaction to an honest mind than to see those approbations which it gives itself seconded by the applauses of the public. A man is more sure of his conduct when the verdict which he passes upon his own behavior is thus warranted and confirmed by the opinion of all that know him.

My worthy friend Sir Roger is one of those who is not only at peace within himself but beloved and esteemed by all about him. He receives a suitable tribute for his universal benevolence to mankind in the returns of affection and good-will which are paid him by every one that lives within his neighborhood. I lately met with two or three odd instances of that general respect which is shown to the good old knight. He would needs carry Will Wimble and myself with him to the county assizes. As we were upon the road, Will Wimble joined a couple of plain men who rid before us, and conversed with them for some time, during which my friend Sir Roger acquainted me with their characters.

"The first of them," says he, "that has a spaniel by his side, is a yeoman of about an hundred pounds a year, an honest man. He is just within the Game Act, and qualified to kill an hare or a pheasant. He knocks down a dinner with his gun twice or thrice a week; and by that means lives much cheaper than those who have not so good an estate as himself. He would be a good neighbor if he did not destroy so many partridges; in short he is a very sensible man, shoots flying, and has been several times foreman of the petty-jury.

"The other that rides along with him is Tom Touchy, a fellow famous for taking the law of everybody. There is not one in the town where he lives that he has not sued for a quarter-sessions. The rogue had once the impudence to go to law with the widow. His head is full of costs, damages, and ejectments; he plagued a couple of honest gentlemen so long for a trespass in breaking one of his hedges, till he was forced to sell the ground it enclosed to defray the charges of the prosecution. His father left him fourscore pounds a year, but he has cast and been cast so often that he is not now worth thirty. I suppose he is going upon the old business of the willow tree."

As Sir Roger was giving me this account of Tom Touchy, Will Wimble and his two companions stopped short till we came up to them. After having paid their respects to Sir Roger, Will told him that Mr. Touchy and he must appeal to him upon a dispute that arose between them. Will, it seems, had been giving his fellow-traveler an account of his angling one day in such a hole; when Tom Touchy, instead of hearing out his story, told him that Mr. Such-an-one, if he pleased, might take the law of him for fishing in that part of the river. My friend Sir Roger heard them both, upon a round trot; and, after having paused some time, told them, with the air of a man who would not give his judgment rashly, *that much might be said on both sides*. They were neither of them dissatisfied with the knight's determination, because neither of them found himself in the wrong by it. Upon which we made the best of our way to the assizes.

The court was sat before Sir Roger came; but notwithstanding all the justices had taken their places upon the bench, they made room for the old knight at the head of them; who, for his reputation in the country, took occasion to whisper in the judge's ear that he was glad his lordship had met with so much good weather in his circuit. I was listening to the proceeding of the court with

[1]A pleasant comrade on a journey is as good as a carriage (Publilius Syrus, *Fragments*).

much attention, and infinitely pleased with that great appearance and solemnity which so properly accompanies such a public administration of our laws, when, after about an hour's sitting, I observed, to my great surprise, in the midst of a trial, that my friend Sir Roger was getting up to speak. I was in some pain for him, till I found he had acquitted himself of two or three sentences, with a look of much business and great intrepidity.

Upon his first rising the court was hushed, and a general whisper ran among the country people that Sir Roger was up. The speech he made was so little to the purpose that I shall not trouble my readers with an account of it; and I believe was not so much designed by the knight himself to inform the court, as to give him a figure in my eye, and keep up his credit in the country.

I was highly delighted, when the court rose, to see the gentlemen of the country gathering about my old friend, and striving who should compliment him most; at the same time that the ordinary people gazed upon him at a distance, not a little admiring his courage that was not afraid to speak to the judge.

In our return home we met with a very odd accident, which I cannot forbear relating, because it shows how desirous all who know Sir Roger are of giving him marks of their esteem. When we were arrived upon the verge of his estate, we stopped at a little inn to rest ourselves and our horses. The man of the house had, it seems, been formerly a servant in the knight's family; and, to do honor to his old master, had some time since, unknown to Sir Roger, put him up in a signpost before the door; so that the knight's head had hung out upon the road about a week before he himself knew anything of the matter. As soon as Sir Roger was acquainted with it, finding that his servant's indiscretion proceeded wholly from affection and goodwill, he only told him that he had made him too high a compliment; and when the fellow seemed to think that could hardly be, added, with a more decisive look, that it was too great an honor for any man under a duke; but told him at the same time that it might be altered with a very few touches, and that he himself would be at the charge of it. Accordingly they got a painter, by the knight's directions, to add a pair of whiskers to the face, and by a little aggravation to the features to change it into the Saracen's Head. I should not have known this story had not the inn-keeper, upon Sir Roger's alighting, told him in my hearing that his honor's head was brought back last night with the alterations that he had ordered to be made in it. Upon this, my friend, with his usual cheerfulness, related the particulars above mentioned, and ordered the head to be brought into the room. I could not forbear discovering greater expressions of mirth than ordinary upon the appearance of this monstrous face, under which, notwithstanding it was made to frown and stare in a most extraordinary manner, I could still discover a distant resemblance of my old friend. Sir Roger, upon seeing me laugh, desired me to tell him truly if I thought it possible for people to know him in that disguise. I at first kept my usual silence; but upon the knight's conjuring me to tell him whether it was not still more like himself than a Saracen, I composed my countenance in the best manner I could, and replied that much might be said on both sides.

These several adventures, with the knight's behavior in them, gave me as pleasant a day as ever I met with in any of my travels.

No. 159. Saturday, 1 September, 1711.

[Addison.]

—Omnem, quæ nunc obducta tuenti
Mortales hebetat visus tibi, et humida circum
Caligat, nubem eripiam—[1]

—Virg.

When I was at Grand Cairo, I picked up several Oriental manuscripts, which I have still by me. Among others I met with one entitled The Visions of Mirza, which I have read over with great pleasure. I intend to give it to the public when I have no other entertainment for them; and shall begin with the first vision, which I have translated word for word as follows:—

"On the fifth day of the moon, which according to the custom of my forefathers I always keep holy, after having washed myself, and offered up my morning devotions, I ascended the high hills of Bagdad, in order

[1] All the cloud which, drawn across your eyes, now dulls your mortal vision and shrouds you in mist, I shall snatch away (*Æneid*, II, 604–606).

to pass the rest of the day in meditation and prayer. As I was here airing myself on the tops of the mountains, I fell into a profound contemplation on the vanity of human life; and passing from one thought to another, 'Surely,' said I, 'man is but a shadow, and life a dream.' Whilst I was thus musing, I cast my eyes towards the summit of a rock that was not far from me, where I discovered one in the habit of a shepherd, with a musical instrument in his hand. As I looked upon him he applied it to his lips, and began to play upon it. The sound of it was exceedingly sweet, and wrought into a variety of tunes that were inexpressibly melodious, and altogether different from anything I had ever heard. They put me in mind of those heavenly airs that are played to the departed souls of good men upon their first arrival in Paradise, to wear out the impressions of their last agonies, and qualify them for the pleasures of that happy place. My heart melted away in secret raptures.

"I had been often told that the rock before me was the haunt of a Genius; and that several had been entertained with music who had passed by it, but never heard that the musician had before made himself visible. When he had raised my thoughts by those transporting airs which he played to taste the pleasures of his conversation, as I looked upon him like one astonished, he beckoned to me, and by the waving of his hand directed me to approach the place where he sat. I drew near with that reverence which is due to a superior nature; and as my heart was entirely subdued by the captivating strains I had heard, I fell down at his feet and wept. The Genius smiled upon me with a look of compassion and affability that familiarized him to my imagination, and at once dispelled all the fears and apprehensions with which I approached him. He lifted me from the ground, and taking me by the hand, 'Mirza,' said he, 'I have heard thee in thy soliloquies; follow me.'

"He then led me to the highest pinnacle of the rock, and placing me on the top of it, 'Cast thy eyes eastward,' said he, 'and tell me what thou seest.' 'I see,' said I, 'a huge valley, and a prodigious tide of water rolling through it.' 'The valley that thou seest,' said he, 'is the Vale of Misery, and the tide of water that thou seest is part of the great Tide of Eternity.' 'What is the reason,' said I, 'that the tide I see rises out of a thick mist at one end, and again loses itself in a thick mist at the other?' 'What thou seest,' said he, 'is that portion of eternity which is called time, measured out by the sun, and reaching from the beginning of the world to its consummation. Examine now,' said he, 'this sea that is bounded with darkness at both ends, and tell me what thou discoverest in it.' 'I see a bridge,' said I, 'standing in the midst of the tide.' 'The bridge thou seest,' said he, 'is Human Life: consider it attentively.' Upon a more leisurely survey of it, I found that it consisted of three-score and ten entire arches, with several broken arches, which added to those that were entire, made up the number about a hundred. As I was counting the arches, the Genius told me that this bridge consisted at first of a thousand arches; but that a great flood swept away the rest, and left the bridge in the ruinous condition I now beheld it. 'But tell me farther,' said he, 'what thou discoverest on it.' 'I see multitudes of people passing over it,' said I, 'and a black cloud hanging on each end of it.' As I looked more attentively, I saw several of the passengers dropping through the bridge into the great tide that flowed underneath it; and upon farther examination, perceived there were innumerable trap-doors that lay concealed in the bridge, which the passengers no sooner trod upon, but they fell through them into the tide, and immediately disappeared. These hidden pitfalls were set very thick at the entrance of the bridge, so that throngs of people no sooner broke through the cloud, but many of them fell into them. They grew thinner towards the middle, but multiplied and lay closer together towards the end of the arches that were entire.

"There were indeed some persons, but their number was very small, that continued a kind of hobbling march on the broken arches, but fell through one after another, being quite tired and spent with so long a walk.

"I passed some time in the contemplation of this wonderful structure, and the great variety of objects which it presented. My heart was filled with a deep melancholy to see several dropping unexpectedly in the midst of mirth and jollity, and catching at everything that stood by them to save themselves. Some were looking up towards the heavens in a thoughtful posture, and in the midst of a speculation stumbled and fell out of sight. Multitudes were very busy in the pursuit of bubbles that glittered in their eyes and danced before them; but often when they thought themselves within the reach of them, their footing failed and down they sunk. In this confusion of objects, I observed some with scimitars in their hands, and others with urinals, who ran to and fro upon the bridge, thrusting several persons on trap-doors which did not seem to lie in their way, and which they might have escaped had they not been thus forced upon them.

"The Genius seeing me indulge myself on this melancholy prospect, told me I had dwelt long enough upon it. 'Take thine eyes off the bridge,' said he, 'and tell me if thou yet seest anything thou dost not comprehend.' Upon looking up, 'What mean,' said I, 'those great flights of birds that are perpetually hovering about the bridge, and settling upon it from time to time? I see vultures, harpies, ravens, cormorants, and among many other feathered creatures several little winged boys, that perch in great numbers upon the middle arches.' 'These,' said the Genius, 'are Envy, Avarice, Superstition, Despair, Love, with the like cares and passions that infest human life.'

"I here fetched a deep sigh. 'Alas,' said I, 'Man was made in vain! how is he given away to misery and mortality! tortured in life, and swallowed up in death!' The Genius being moved with compassion towards me, bid me quit so uncomfortable a prospect. 'Look no more,' said he, 'on man in the first stage of his existence, in his setting out for eternity; but cast thine eye on that thick mist into which the tide bears the several generations of mortals that fall into it.' I directed my sight as I was ordered, and (whether or no the good Genius strengthened it with any supernatural force, or dissipated part of the mist that was before too thick for the eye to penetrate) I saw the valley opening at the farther end, and spreading forth into an immense ocean, that had a huge rock of adamant running through the midst of it, and dividing it into two equal parts. The clouds still rested on one half of it, insomuch that I could discover nothing in it; but the other appeared to me a vast ocean planted with innumerable islands, that were covered with fruits and flowers, and interwoven with a thousand little shining seas that ran among them. I could see persons dressed in glorious habits with garlands upon their heads, passing among the trees, lying down by the sides of fountains, or resting on beds of flowers; and could hear a confused harmony of singing birds, falling waters, human voices, and musical instruments. Gladness grew in me upon the discovery of so delightful a scene. I wished for the wings of an eagle, that I might fly away to those happy seats; but the Genius told me there was no passage to them, except through the gates of death that I saw opening every moment upon the bridge. 'The islands,' said he, 'that lie so fresh and green before thee, and with which the whole face of the ocean appears spotted as far as thou canst see, are more in number than the sands on the seashore: there are myriads of islands behind those which thou here discoverest, reaching farther than thine eye, or even thine imagination can extend itself. These are the mansions of good men after death, who, according to the degree and kinds of virtue in which they excelled, are distributed among these several islands, which abound with pleasures of different kinds and degrees, suitable to the relishes and perfections of those who are settled in them: every island is a paradise accommodated to its respective inhabitants. Are not these, O Mirza, habitations worth contending for? Does life appear miserable that gives thee opportunities of earning such a reward? Is death to be feared that will convey thee to so happy an existence? Think not man was made in vain, who has such an eternity reserved for him.' I gazed with inexpressible pleasure on these happy islands. At length, said I, 'Show me now, I beseech thee, the secrets that lie hid under those dark clouds which cover the ocean on the other side of the rock of adamant.' The Genius making me no answer, I turned me about to address myself to him a second time, but I found that he had left me; I then turned again to the vision which I had been so long contemplating; but instead of the rolling tide, the arched bridge, and the happy islands, I saw nothing but the long hollow valley of Bagdad, with oxen, sheep, and camels grazing upon the sides of it."

No. 323. TUESDAY, 11 MARCH, 1712.
[ADDISON.]

Modo vir, modo femina.[1]
—OVID.

THE Journal with which I presented my readers on Tuesday last,[2] has brought me in several letters with accounts of many private lives cast into that form. I have the Rake's Journal, the Sot's Journal, the Whoremaster's Journal, and among several others a very curious piece, entitled, The Journal of a Mohock.[3] By these instances I find that the intention of my last Tuesday's paper has been mistaken by many of my readers. I did not design so much to expose vice as idleness, and aimed at those persons who pass away their time rather in trifles and impertinence, than in crimes and immoralities. Offenses of this later kind are not to be dallied with, or treated in so ludicrous a manner. In short, my journal only holds up folly to the light, and shows the disagreeableness of such actions as are indifferent in themselves, and blamable only as they proceed from creatures endowed with reason.

My following correspondent, who calls herself Clarinda, is such a journalist as I require: she seems by her letter to be placed in a modish state of indifference between vice and virtue, and to be susceptible of either, were there proper pains taken with her. Had her journal been filled with gallantries, or such occurrences as had shown her wholly divested of her natural innocence, notwithstanding it might have been more pleasing to the generality of readers, I should not have published it; but as it is only the picture of a life filled with a fashionable kind of gayety and laziness, I shall set down five days of it, as I have received it from the hand of my correspondent.

DEAR MR. SPECTATOR,

You having set your readers an exercise in one of your last week's papers, I have performed mine according to your orders, and herewith send it you enclosed. You must know, Mr. Spectator, that I am a maiden lady of a good fortune, who have had several matches offered me for these ten years last past, and have at present warm applications made to me by a very pretty fellow. As I am at my own disposal, I come up to town every winter, and pass my time after the manner you will find in the following journal, which I began to write upon the very day after your *Spectator* upon that subject.

TUESDAY *night.* Could not go to sleep till one in the morning for thinking of my journal.

WEDNESDAY. *From Eight till Ten.* Drank two dishes of chocolate in bed, and fell asleep after them.

From Ten to Eleven. Eat a slice of bread and butter, drank a dish of bohea,[4] read *The Spectator.*

From Eleven to One. At my toilette, tried a new head.[5] Gave orders for Veny to be combed and washed. Mem. I look best in blue.

From One till half an hour after Two. Drove to the Change. Cheapened a couple of fans.

Till Four. At dinner. Mem. Mr. Froth passed by in his new liveries.

From Four to Six. Dressed, paid a visit to old Lady Blithe and her sister, having before heard they were gone out of town that day.

From Six to Eleven. At basset. Mem. Never set again upon the ace of diamonds.

THURSDAY. *From Eleven at night to Eight in the morning.* Dreamed that I punted to Mr. Froth.

From Eight to Ten. Chocolate. Read two acts in *Aurenzebe*[6] a-bed.

From Ten to Eleven. Tea-table. Sent to borrow Lady Faddle's Cupid for Veny. Read the play-bills. Received a letter from Mr. Froth. Mem. Locked it up in my strong box.

Rest of the morning. Fontange,[7] the tire-woman, her account of my Lady Blithe's wash. Broke a tooth in my little tortoise-shell comb. Sent Frank to know how my

---

[1]Sometimes a man, sometimes a woman (*Metamorphoses*, IV, 280).

[2]*Spectator* No. 317. The journal was that of a "sober citizen," "of greater consequence in his own thoughts than in the eye of the world."

[3]The name given to the ruffians and thieves who infested London and terrorized many at night. They had formerly been called "Hectors."

[4]Tea. [5]*I. e.*, head-dress. [6]Heroic play by Dryden.

[7]Mlle. de Fontange introduced a new type of head-dress which was fashionable among Englishwomen at the end of the seventeenth century.

Lady Hectic rested after her monkey's leaping out at window. Looked pale. Fontange tells me my glass is not true. Dressed by Three.

From Three to Four. Dinner cold before I sat down.

From Four to Eleven. Saw company. Mr. Froth's opinion of Milton. His account of the Mohocks. His fancy for a pin-cushion. Picture in the lid of his snuff-box. Old Lady Faddle promises me her woman to cut my hair. Lost five guineas at crimp.

Twelve a clock at night. Went to bed.

FRIDAY. *Eight in the morning.* A-bed. Read over all Mr. Froth's letters. Cupid and Veny.

Ten a clock. Stayed within all day, not at home.

From Ten to Twelve. In conference with my mantua-maker. Sorted a suit of ribands. Broke my blue china cup.

From Twelve to One. Shut myself up in my chamber, practiced Lady Betty Modely's skuttle.

One in the afternooon. Called for my flowered handkerchief. Worked half a violet leaf in it. Eyes ached and head out of order. Threw by my work, and read over the remaining part of *Aurenzebe.*

From Three to Four. Dined.

From Four to Twelve. Changed my mind, dressed, went abroad, and played at crimp till midnight. Found Mrs. Spitely at home. Conversation: Mrs. Brilliant's necklace false stones. Old Lady Loveday going to be married to a young fellow that is not worth a groat. Miss Prue gone into the country. Tom Townley has red hair. Mem. Mrs. Spitely whispered in my ear that she had something to tell me about Mr. Froth; I am sure it is not true.

Between Twelve and One. Dreamed that Mr. Froth lay at my feet, and called me Indamora.[1]

SATURDAY. Rose at eight a clock in the morning. Sat down to my toilette.

From Eight to Nine. Shifted a patch for half an hour before I could determine it. Fixed it above my left eyebrow.

From Nine to Twelve. Drank my tea, and dressed.

From Twelve to Two. At Chapel. A great deal of good company. Mem. The third air in the new opera. Lady Blithe dressed frightfully.

From Three to Four. Dined. Mrs. Kitty called upon me to go to the opera before I was risen from table.

From dinner to Six. Drank tea. Turned off a footman for being rude to Veny.

Six a clock. Went to the opera. I did not see Mr. Froth till the beginning of the second act. Mr. Froth talked to a gentleman in a black wig. Bowed to a lady in the front box. Mr. Froth and his friend clapped Nicolini[2] in the third act. Mr. Froth cried out Ancora.[3] Mr. Froth led me to my chair. I think he squeezed my hand.

Eleven at night. Went to bed. Melancholy dreams. Methought Nicolini said he was Mr. Froth.

SUNDAY. Indisposed.

MONDAY. *Eight a clock.* Waked by Miss Kitty. *Aurenzebe* lay upon the chair by me. Kitty repeated without book the eight best lines in the play. Went in our mobs to the dumb man, according to appointment. Told me that my lover's name began with a G. Mem. The conjurer was within a letter of Mr. Froth's name, *etc.*

Upon looking back into this my journal, I find that I am at a loss to know whether I pass my time well or ill; and indeed never thought of considering how I did it, before I perused your speculation upon that subject. I scarce find a single action in these five days that I can thoroughly approve of, except the working upon the violet leaf, which I am resolved to finish the first day I am at leisure. As for Mr. Froth and Veny, I did not think they took up so much of my time and thoughts, as I find they do upon my journal. The latter of them I will turn off if you insist upon it; and if Mr. Froth does not bring matters to a conclusion very suddenly, I will not let my life run away in a dream.

Your humble servant,
CLARINDA.

[1]The "Captive Queen" in Dryden's *Aureng-Zebe.*

[2]Nicolino Grimaldi, a famous Italian singer, who came to England in 1708.

[3]*I. e.*, Encore.

To resume one of the morals of my first paper, and to confirm Clarinda in her good inclinations, I would have her consider what a pretty figure she would make among posterity, were the history of her whole life published like these five days of it. I shall conclude my paper with an epitaph written by an uncertain author[1] on Sir Philip Sidney's sister, a lady who seems to have been of a temper very much different from that of Clarinda. The last thought of it is so very noble, that I daré say my reader will pardon the quotation.

ON THE COUNTESS DOWAGER OF PEMBROKE

Underneath this marble hearse
Lies the subject of all verse,
Sidney's sister, Pembroke's mother;
Death, ere thou hast killed another,
Fair and learn'd and good as she,
Time shall throw a dart at thee.

No. 377. Tuesday, 13 May, 1712. [Addison.]

Quid quisque vitet, nunquam homini satis
Cautum est in horas.[2]

—Hor.

Love was the mother of poetry, and still produces, among the most ignorant and barbarous, a thousand imaginary distresses and poetical complaints. It makes a footman talk like Oroondates,[3] and converts a brutal rustic into a gentle swain. The most ordinary plebeian or mechanic in love bleeds and pines away with a certain elegance and tenderness of sentiments which this passion naturally inspires.

These inward languishings of a mind infected with this softness have given birth to a phrase which is made use of by all the melting tribe, from the highest to the lowest, I mean that of *dying for love*.

Romances, which owe their very being to this passion, are full of these metaphorical deaths. Heroes and heroines, knights, squires, and damsels, are all of them in a dying condition. There is the same kind of mortality in our modern tragedies, where every one gasps, faints, bleeds, and dies. Many of the poets, to describe the execution which is done by this passion, represent the fair sex as Basilisks that destroy with their eyes; but I think Mr. Cowley has with great justness of thought compared a beautiful woman to a porcupine, that sends an arrow from every part.

I have often thought, that there is no way so effectual for the cure of this general infirmity, as a man's reflecting upon the motives that produce it. When the passion proceeds from the sense of any virtue or perfection in the person beloved, I would by no means discourage it; but if a man considers that all his heavy complaints of wounds and deaths rise from some little affectations of coquetry, which are improved into charms by his own fond imagination, the very laying before himself the cause of his distemper may be sufficient to effect the cure of it.

It is in this view that I have looked over the several bundles of letters which I have received from dying people, and composed out of them the following bill of mortality, which I shall lay before my reader without any further preface, as hoping that it may be useful to him in discovering those several places where there is most danger, and those fatal arts which are made use of to destroy the heedless and unwary.

Lysander, slain at a puppet-show on the 3rd of September.

Thyrsis, shot from a casement in Pickadilly.

T. S., wounded by Zelinda's scarlet stocking as she was stepping out of a coach.

Will. Simple, smitten at the opera by the glance of an eye that was aimed at one who stood by him.

Tho. Vainlove, lost his life at a ball.

Tim. Tattle, killed by the tap of a fan on his left shoulder by Coquetilla, as he was talking carelessly with her in a bow-window.

Sir Simon Softly, murdered at the playhouse in Drury Lane by a frown.

Philander, mortally wounded by Cleora, as she was adjusting her tucker.

Ralph Gapely, Esq., hit by a random shot at the ring.

F. R., caught his death upon the water, April the 31st.

[1]The poem (of which Addison quotes only the first half) has been generally ascribed to Ben Jonson, but in recent years has been claimed for William Browne of Tavistock.

[2]The dangers of the hour! no thought
We give them.
(Horace, *Odes*, II, xiii, 13–14. Conington's translation.)

[3]A character in de Scudéry's romance of *Artamène ou le Grand Cyrus*.

W. W., killed by an unknown hand, that was playing, with the glove off, upon the side of the front box in Drury Lane.

Sir Christopher Crazy, Bar., hurt by the brush of a whalebone petticoat.

Sylvius, shot through the sticks of a fan at St. James's Church.

Damon, struck through the heart by a diamond necklace.

Thomas Trusty, Francis Goosequill, William Meanwell, Edward Callow, Esqrs., standing in a row, fell all four at the same time by an ogle of the Widow Trapland.

Tom Rattle, chancing to tread upon a lady's tail as he came out of the playhouse, she turned full upon him, and laid him dead upon the spot.

Dick Tastewell, slain by a blush from the Queen's box in the third act of the *Trip to the Jubilee.*

Samuel Felt, Haberdasher, wounded in his walk to Islington by Mrs. Susannah Crossstitch, as she was clambering over a stile.

R. F. T., W. S. I., M. P., etc., put to death in the last birthday massacre.

Roger Blinko, cut off in the twenty-first year of his age by a white-wash.

Musidorus, slain by an arrow that flew out of a dimple in Belinda's left cheek.

Ned Courtly, presenting Flavia with her glove (which she had dropped on purpose) she received it, and took away his life with a curtsy.

John Gosselin, having received a slight hurt from a pair of blue eyes, as he was making his escape was dispatched by a smile.

Strephon, killed by Clarinda as she looked down into the pit.

Charles Careless, shot flying by a girl of fifteen who unexpectedly popped her head upon him out of a coach.

Josiah Wither, aged threescore and three, sent to his long home by Elizabeth Jettwell, spinster.

Jack Freelave, murdered by Melissa in her hair.

William Wiseaker, Gent., drowned in a flood of tears by Moll Common.

John Pleadwell, Esq., of the Middle Temple, barrister at law, assassinated in his chambers the sixth instant by Kitty Sly, who pretended to come to him for his advice.

JONATHAN SWIFT (1667–1745)

One of the things Swift was heard to say to himself in his dreadful last days was "I am what I am; I am what I am." This has been difficult for many, particularly for comfortable people, to believe, and Swift has often been explained away. Yet he lives on, not merely in the minds and hearts of children who, by a consummate irony, find Lilliput amusing, but as a man speaking to men. For Swift, by virtue of a simplicity of outlook which has its parallel only in the lives and words of a few of the world's great religious figures, attained an insight into human folly which pierces the hearts of men by its profound truth. Uneasily men may squirm, attempting to minimize or to disregard his words, but they do not succeed; for in the end they cannot deny that beneath his coarseness and exaggeration, beneath the trappings of his age in which he clothed his thoughts and his pictures of life, Swift was essentially right. Swift wrote satirically in accordance with his own bent and the temper of his age, but he does not live simply as the prose counterpart of Pope; not alone for his mastery of satire, nor for its unexampled fierceness, nor yet for the downright plainness and directness and demonic force of his speech does he live, but because he was what he was, beneath all else a noble personality, deeply sensitive to the confused splendor and misery of humankind.

The first blow of adverse fortune which Swift had to endure came with his birth, for he always considered it an indignity that, though his parents were English, he happened to be born in Ireland, which he hated. He was born on 30 November, 1667, in Dublin. His father had died a short time before his birth, leaving his mother practically destitute. The consequence was that Swift was dependent through his early years on the charity of an uncle—a kind of dependence which was inevitably galling to him, though there is no evidence that his uncle treated him worse than victims of charity are generally treated. In 1673 he was sent to Kilkenny School; in 1681 he proceeded to Trinity College, Dublin, from which he was graduated in 1685, with a poor academic record. In 1689 he was employed as an amanuensis and secretary by Sir William Temple, a kinsman and a man now largely forgotten, though of great note in his day. Temple was a man of the world and had been a diplomat; he was on intimate terms with many of the great and influential people of the time, and he was a smooth and polished writer. There can be no doubt that he did much for Swift, whose association with him lasted, with several interruptions, until Temple's death in 1699. Through Temple's influence Swift was in 1692 admitted an M. A. at Oxford, and in 1694 he took holy orders. He had earlier considered this method of making a living, but had refused to take the step as long as he could not at least say that he had other alternatives and so had not entered the priesthood simply for the sake of income. It was during Swift's stay with Temple that he experimented until he learned how to write and what he could best do. He began apparently with poems, but was told by Dryden that he would never be a poet—a blunt verdict which may have been wrong and which Swift never forgave, although he acted on it and devoted himself chiefly thereafter to prose. It was as a result, too, of a controversy into which Temple had got over the relative merits of the ancients and the moderns that Swift wrote one of his most effective satirical pamphlets, *The Battle of the Books*, chiefly composed in 1697. And, moreover, it was while he was living with Temple that he first met Esther Johnson, the Stella of the famous *Journal*, whose devoted friend he remained, spite of passing attachments to other women, and spite of Hester Vanhomrigh's love for him, until Stella's death in 1728. It has been maintained that Swift was secretly married to Stella, and the truth about this cannot be determined. It is not, however, a matter of very great importance, it being sufficiently plain that only the ceremony is in question, the relations between the two having been simply those of close friends. In 1699 Swift returned to Ireland and in the following year was made Vicar of Laracor. He became attached to the place and did much to improve the living, though he never remained there very long at a time. From 1701, indeed, until 1714 he was much in England. He returned in the first instance to present to the government certain grievances of the Irish clergy, but, particularly after the publication of *A Tale of a Tub* and *The Battle of the Books* in 1704, it was recognized that he would make a powerful political writer and both Whigs and Tories made bids for his support. In the end he threw himself in with the Tories and for several years worked hard and brilliantly for them. His reward, however, was not the bishopric he desired and thought he deserved, nor even a lesser post in England, but the Deanery of St. Patrick's Cathedral, in Dublin. Thus, to his bitter disappointment, was Swift's exile perpetuated, and after 1714—save for two visits to England in 1726 and 1727—he remained in Ireland until his death. He never ceased to hate Ireland, but in the course of time he was moved by the wretched condition of the island and the character of English misrule to write indignantly in support of Irish causes, as, for example, in the *Drapier's Letters*. Gulliver's *Travels into several remote Nations of the World*—unquestionably Swift's greatest and most fully representative book—was also written during these years, being published in 1726. It comprises four voyages, all intended "to vex the world rather than divert it." During the last years of his life Swift became hopelessly mad. He died on 19 October, 1745, and was buried in his own cathedral.

GULLIVER'S TRAVELS

(1726)

THE PUBLISHER TO THE READER

THE author of these Travels, Mr. Lemuel Gulliver, is my ancient and intimate friend; there is likewise some relation between us by the mother's side. About three years ago, Mr. Gulliver growing weary of the concourse of curious people coming to him at his house in Redriff, made a small purchase of land, with a convenient house, near Newark, in Nottinghamshire, his native country; where he now lives retired, yet in good esteem among his neighbors.

Although Mr. Gulliver was born in Nottinghamshire, where his father dwelt, yet I have heard him say his family came from Oxfordshire; to confirm which, I have observed in the churchyard at Banbury, in that county, several tombs and monuments of the Gullivers.

Before he quitted Redriff, he left the custody of the following papers in my hands, with the liberty to dispose of them as I should think fit. I have carefully perused them three times: the style is very plain and simple; and the only fault I find is, that the author, after the manner of travelers, is a little too circumstantial. There is an air of truth apparent through the whole; and indeed the author was so distinguished for his veracity, that it became a sort of proverb among his neighbors at Redriff, when any one affirmed a thing, to say it was as true as if Mr. Gulliver had spoke it.

By the advice of several worthy persons, to whom, with the author's permission, I communicated these papers, I now venture to send them into the world, hoping they may be at least, for some time, a better entertainment to our young noblemen, than the common scribbles of politics and party.

This volume would have been at least twice as large, if I had not made bold to strike out innumerable passages relating to the winds and tides, as well as to the variations and bearings in the several voyages; together with the minute descriptions of the management of the ship in storms, in the style of sailors: likewise the account of longitudes and latitudes; wherein I have reason to apprehend that Mr. Gulliver may be a little dissatisfied: but I was resolved to fit the work as much as possible to the general capacity of readers. However, if my own ignorance in sea-affairs shall have led me to commit some mistakes, I alone am answerable for them: and if any traveler hath a curiosity to see the whole work at large, as it came from the hand of the author, I will be ready to gratify him.

As for any further particulars relating to the author, the reader will receive satisfaction from the first pages of the book.

RICHARD SYMPSON.

PART I

A VOYAGE TO LILLIPUT[1]

CHAPTER I

The Author gives some account of himself and family, his first inducements to travel. He is shipwrecked, and swims for his life, gets safe on shore in the country of Lilliput, *is made a prisoner, and is carried up country.*

MY FATHER had a small estate in Nottinghamshire; I was the third of five sons. He sent me to Emanuel College in Cambridge, at fourteen years old, where I resided three years, and applied myself close to my studies; but the charge of maintaining me (although I had a very scanty allowance) being too great for a narrow fortune, I was bound apprentice to Mr. James Bates, an eminent surgeon in London, with whom I continued four years; and my father now and then sending me small sums of money, I laid them out

---

[1]Lilliput means "little fellow."

in learning navigation, and other parts of the mathematics, useful to those who intend to travel, as I always believed it would be some time or other my fortune to do. When I left Mr. Bates, I went down to my father; where, by the assistance of him and my uncle John, and some other relations, I got forty pounds, and a promise of thirty pounds a year to maintain me at Leyden: there I studied physic two years and seven months, knowing it would be useful in long voyages.

Soon after my return from Leyden, I was recommended by my good master, Mr. Bates, to be surgeon to the *Swallow*, Captain Abraham Pannell, commander; with whom I continued three years and a half, making a voyage or two into the Levant, and some other parts. When I came back, I resolved to settle in London, to which Mr. Bates, my master, encouraged me, and by him I was recommended to several patients. I took part of a small house in the Old Jury; and being advised to alter my condition, I married Mrs. Mary Burton, second daughter to Mr. Edmund Burton, hosier, in Newgate-Street, with whom I received four hundred pounds for a portion.

But, my good master Bates dying in two years after, and I having few friends, my business began to fail; for my conscience would not suffer me to imitate the bad practice of too many among my brethren. Having therefore consulted with my wife, and some of my acquaintance, I determined to go again to sea. I was surgeon successively in two ships, and made several voyages, for six years, to the East and West Indies, by which I got some addition to my fortune. My hours of leisure I spent in reading the best authors, ancient and modern, being always provided with a good number of books; and when I was ashore, in observing the manners and dispositions of the people, as well as learning their language, wherein I had a great facility by the strength of my memory.

The last of these voyages not proving very fortunate, I grew weary of the sea, and intended to stay at home with my wife and family. I removed from the Old Jury to Fetter-Lane, and from thence to Wapping, hoping to get business among the sailors; but it would not turn to account. After three years' expectation that things would mend, I accepted an advantageous offer from Captain William Prichard, master of the *Antelope*, who was making a voyage to the South Sea. We set sail from Bristol, May 4, 1699, and our voyage at first was very prosperous.

It would not be proper, for some reasons, to trouble the reader with the particulars of our adventures in those seas; let it suffice to inform him, that in our passage from thence to the East Indies, we were driven by a violent storm to the north-west of Van Diemen's Land.[1] By an observation, we found ourselves in the latitude of 30 degrees 2 minutes south. Twelve of our crew were dead by immoderate labor, and ill food, the rest were in a very weak condition. On the fifth of November, which was the beginning of summer in those parts, the weather being very hazy, the seamen spied a rock, within half a cable's length of the ship; but the wind was so strong, that we were driven directly upon it, and immediately split. Six of the crew, of whom I was one, having let down the boat into the sea, made a shift to get clear of the ship, and the rock. We rowed, by my computation, about three leagues, till we were able to work no longer, being already spent with labor while we were in the ship. We therefore trusted ourselves to the mercy of the waves, and in about half an hour the boat was overset by a sudden flurry from the north. What became of my companions in the boat, as well as of those who escaped on the rock, or were left in the vessel, I cannot tell; but conclude they were all lost. For my own part, I swam as fortune directed me, and was pushed forward by wind and tide. I often let my legs drop, and could feel no bottom: but when I was almost gone, and able to struggle no longer, I found myself within my depth; and by this time the storm was much abated. The declivity was so small, that I walked near a mile before I got to the shore, which I conjectured was about eight o'clock in the evening. I then advanced forward near half a mile, but could not discover any sign of houses or inhabitants; at least I was in so weak a condition, that I did not observe them. I was extremely tired, and with that, and the heat

[1]Perhaps Tasmania is meant, or a part of New Zealand. The latitude mentioned in the next sentence would indicate that Swift meant Australia, were it not for the fact that western Australia was very vaguely known in the early eighteenth century.

of the weather, and about half a pint of brandy that I drank as I left the ship, I found myself much inclined to sleep. I lay down on the grass, which was very short and soft, where I slept sounder than ever I remember to have done in my life; and, as I reckoned, above nine hours; for when I awaked, it was just day-light. I attempted to rise, but was not able to stir: for as I happened to lie on my back, I found my arms and legs were strongly fastened on each side to the ground; and my hair, which was long and thick, tied down in the same manner. I likewise felt several slender ligatures across my body, from my arm-pits to my thighs. I could only look upwards, the sun began to grow hot, and the light offended my eyes. I heard a confused noise about me, but in the posture I lay, could see nothing except the sky. In a little time I felt something alive moving on my left leg, which advancing gently forward over my breast, came almost up to my chin; when bending my eyes downwards as much as I could, I perceived it to be a human creature not six inches high, with a bow and arrow in his hands, and a quiver at his back. In the mean time, I felt at least forty more of the same kind (as I conjectured) following the first. I was in the utmost astonishment, and roared so loud, that they all ran back in a fright; and some of them as I was afterwards told, were hurt with the falls they got by leaping from my sides upon the ground. However, they soon returned, and one of them, who ventured so far as to get a full sight of my face, lifting up his hands and eyes by way of admiration, cried out in a shrill, but distinct voice, *Hekinah degul:* the others repeated the same words several times, but then I knew not what they meant. I lay all this while, as the reader may believe, in great uneasiness: at length, struggling to get loose, I had the fortune to break the strings, and wrench out the pegs that fastened my left arm to the ground; for, by lifting it up to my face, I discovered the methods they had taken to bind me, and at the same time with a violent pull, which gave me excessive pain, I a little loosened the strings that tied down my hair on the left side, so that I was just able to turn my head about two inches. But the creatures ran off a second time, before I could seize them; whereupon there was a great shout in a very shrill accent, and after it ceased, I heard one of them cry aloud *Tolgo phonac;* when in an instant I felt above an hundred arrows discharged on my left hand, which pricked me like so many needles; and besides, they shot another flight into the air, as we do bombs in Europe, whereof many, I suppose, fell on my body (though I felt them not), and some on my face, which I immediately covered with my left hand. When this shower of arrows was over, I fell a groaning with grief and pain, and then striving again to get loose, they discharged another volley larger than the first, and some of them attempted with spears to stick me in the sides; but, by good luck, I had on a buff jerkin, which they could not pierce. I thought it the most prudent method to lie still, and my design was to continue so till night, when, my left hand being already loose, I could easily free myself: and as for the inhabitants, I had reason to believe I might be a match for the greatest armies they could bring against me, if they were all of the same size with him that I saw. But fortune disposed otherwise of me. When the people observed I was quiet, they discharged no more arrows; but, by the noise I heard, I knew their numbers increased; and about four yards from me, over-against my right ear, I heard a knocking for above an hour, like that of people at work; when turning my head that way, as well as the pegs and strings would permit me, I saw a stage erected, about a foot and a half from the ground, capable of holding four of the inhabitants, with two or three ladders to mount it: from whence one of them, who seemed to be a person of quality, made me a long speech, whereof I understood not one syllable. But I should have mentioned, that before the principal person began his oration, he cried out three times, *Langro dehul san* (these words and the former were afterwards repeated and explained to me). Whereupon immediately about fifty of the inhabitants came and cut the strings that fastened the left side of my head, which gave me the liberty of turning it to the right, and of observing the person and gesture of him that was to speak. He appeared to be of a middle age, and taller than any of the other three who attended him, whereof one was a page that held up his train, and seemed to be somewhat longer than my middle finger; the other two stood one on each side to support him. He acted every part of an orator, and I could observe many periods of threatenings, and others of promises, pity, and kindness. I answered in a few words, but in the most submissive manner, lifting up my left hand, and both my eyes to the sun, as calling him for a witness; and being almost famished with hunger, having not eaten a morsel for some hours before I left the ship, I found the demands of nature so strong upon me, that I could not forbear showing my impatience (perhaps against the strict rules of decency) by putting my finger frequently on my mouth to signify that I wanted food. The *Hurgo* (for so they call a great lord, as I afterwards learned) understood me very well. He descended from the stage, and commanded that several ladders should be applied to my sides, on which above an hundred of the inhabitants mounted and walked towards my mouth, laden with baskets full of meat, which had been provided and sent thither by the King's orders, upon the first intelligence he received of me. I observed there was the flesh of several animals, but could not distinguish them by the taste. There were shoulders, legs, and loins, shaped like those of mutton, and very well dressed, but smaller than the wings of a lark. I ate them by two or three at a mouthful, and took three loaves at a time, about the bigness of musket bullets. They supplied me as fast as they could, showing a thousand marks of wonder and astonishment at my bulk and appetite. I then made another sign that I wanted drink. They found by my eating, that a small quantity would not suffice me: and being a most ingenious people, they slung up with great dexterity one of their largest hogsheads, then rolled it towards my hand, and beat out the top; I drank it off at a draught, which I might well do, for it did not hold half a pint, and tasted like a small wine of Burgundy, but much more delicious. They brought me a second hogshead, which I drank in the same manner, and made signs for more, but they had none to give me. When I had performed these wonders, they shouted for joy, and danced upon my breast, repeating several times as they did at first, *Hekinah degul.* They made me a sign that I should throw down the two hogsheads, but first warning the people below to stand out of the way, crying aloud, *Borach mivola*, and when they saw the vessels in the air, there was an universal shout of *Hekinah degul.* I confess I was often tempted while they were passing backwards and forwards on my body, to seize forty or fifty of the first that came in my reach, and dash them against the ground. But the remembrance of what I had felt, which probably might not be the worst they could do, and the promise of honor I made them, for so I interpreted my submissive behavior, soon drove out these imaginations. Besides, I now considered myself as bound by the laws of hospitality to a people who had treated me with so much expense and magnificence. However, in my thoughts, I could not sufficiently wonder at the intrepidity of these diminutive mortals, who durst venture to mount and walk upon my body, while one of my hands was at liberty, without trembling at the very sight of so prodigious a creature as I must appear to them. After some time, when they observed that I made no more demands for meat, there appeared before me a person of high rank from his Imperial Majesty. His Excellency, having mounted on the small of my right leg, advanced forwards up to my face, with about a dozen of his retinue. And producing his credentials under the Signet Royal, which he applied close to my eyes, spoke about ten minutes, without any signs of anger, but with a kind of determinate resolution; often pointing forwards, which, as I afterwards found, was towards the capital city, about half a mile distant, whither it was agreed by his Majesty in council that I must be conveyed. I answered in few words, but to no purpose, and made a sign with my hand that was loose, putting it to the other (but over his Excellency's head for fear of hurting him or his train), and then to my own head and body, to signify that I desired my liberty. It appeared that he understood me well enough, for he shook his head by way of disapprobation, and held his hand in a posture to show that I must be carried as a prisoner. However, he made other signs to let me understand that I should have meat and drink enough, and very good treatment. Whereupon I once more thought of attempting to break my bonds; but again, when I felt the smart of their arrows, upon my face and hands, which were all in blisters, and many of the darts still sticking in them, and observing likewise that the number of my enemies increased, I gave tokens to let them know that they might do with me what they pleased. Upon this, the *Hurgo* and his train withdrew, with much civility and cheerful countenances. Soon after I heard a general shout, with frequent repetitions of the words, *Peplom selan*, and I felt great numbers of people on my left side relaxing the cords to such a degree, that I was able to turn upon my right, and to ease myself with making water; which I very plentifully did, to the great astonishment of the people, who conjecturing by my motions what I was going to do, immediately opened to the right and left on that side to avoid the torrent which fell with such noise and violence from me. But before this, they had daubed my face and both my hands with a sort of ointment very pleasant to the smell, which in a few minutes removed all the smart of their arrows. These circumstances, added to the refreshment I had received by their victuals and drink, which were very nourishing, disposed me to sleep. I slept about eight hours, as I was afterwards assured; and it was no wonder, for the physicians, by the Emperor's order, had mingled a sleepy potion in the hogshead of wine.

It seems that upon the first moment I was discovered sleeping on the ground after my landing, the Emperor had early notice of it by an express; and determined in council that I should be tied in the manner I have related (which was done in the night while I slept), that plenty of meat and drink should be sent to me, and a machine prepared to carry me to the capital city.

This resolution perhaps may appear very bold and dangerous, and I am confident would not be imitated by any prince in Europe on the like occasion; however, in my opinion, it was extremely prudent, as well as generous: for supposing these people had endeavored to kill me with their spears and arrows while I was asleep, I should certainly have awaked with the first sense of smart, which might so far have roused my rage and strength, as to have enabled me to break the strings wherewith I was tied; after which, as they were not able to make resistance, so they could expect no mercy.

These people are most excellent mathematicians, and arrived to a great perfection in mechanics, by the countenance and encouragement of the Emperor, who is a renowned patron of learning. This prince hath several machines fixed on wheels, for the carriage of trees and other great weights. He often builds his largest men of war, whereof some are nine foot long, in the woods where the timber grows, and has them carried on these engines three or four hundred yards to the sea. Five hundred carpenters and engineers were immediately set at work to prepare the greatest engine they had. It was a frame of wood raised three inches from the ground, about seven foot long and four wide, moving upon twenty-two wheels. The shout I heard was upon the arrival of this engine, which it seems set out in four hours after my landing. It was brought parallel to me as I lay. But the principal difficulty was to raise and place me in this vehicle. Eighty poles, each of one foot high, were erected for this purpose, and very strong cords of the bigness of packthread were fastened by hooks to many bandages, which the workmen had girt round my neck, my hands, my body, and my legs. Nine hundred of the strongest men were employed to draw up these cords by many pulleys fastened on the poles, and thus, in less than three hours, I was raised and slung into the engine, and there tied fast. All this I was told, for, while the whole operation was performing, I lay in a profound sleep, by the force of that soporiferous medicine infused into my liquor. Fifteen hundred of the Emperor's largest horses, each about four inches and a half high, were employed to draw me towards the metropolis, which, as I said, was half a mile distant.

About four hours after we began our journey, I awaked by a very ridiculous accident; for the carriage being stopped a while to adjust something that was out of order, two or three of the young natives had the curiosity to see how I looked when I was asleep; they climbed up into the engine, and advancing very softly to my face, one of them, an officer in the guards, put the sharp end of his half-pike a good way up into my left nostril, which tickled my nose like a straw, and made me sneeze violently: whereupon they stole off unperceived, and it was three weeks before I knew the cause of my awakening so suddenly. We made a long march the remaining part of that day, and rested at night with five hundred guards on each side of me, half with torches, and half with bows and arrows, ready to shoot me if I should offer to stir. The next morning at sun-rise we continued our march, and arrived within two hundred yards of the city gates about noon. The Emperor, and all his court, came out to meet us; but his great officers would by no means suffer his Majesty to endanger his person by mounting on my body.

At the place where the carriage stopped, there stood an ancient temple, esteemed to be the largest in the whole kingdom; which having been polluted some years before by an unnatural murder, was, according to the zeal of those people, looked upon as profane, and therefore had been applied to common uses, and all the ornaments and furniture carried away. In this edifice it was determined I should lodge. The great gate fronting to the north was about four foot high, and almost two foot wide, through which I could easily creep. On each side of the gate was a small window not above six inches from the ground: into that on the left side, the King's smiths conveyed fourscore and eleven chains, like those that hang to a lady's watch in Europe, and almost as large, which were locked to my left leg with six and thirty padlocks. Over-against this temple, on t'other side of the great highway, at twenty foot distance, there was a turret at least five foot high. Here the Emperor ascended, with many principal lords of his court, to have an opportunity of viewing me, as I was told, for I could not see them. It was reckoned that above an hundred thousand inhabitants came out of the town upon the same errand; and, in spite of my guards, I believe there could not be fewer than ten thousand at several times, who mounted my body by the help of ladders. But a proclamation was soon issued to forbid it upon pain of death. When the workmen found it was impossible for me to break loose, they cut all the strings that bound me; whereupon I rose up, with as melancholy a disposition as ever I had in my life. But the noise and astonishment of the people at seeing me rise and walk, are not to be expressed. The chains that held my left leg were about two yards long, and gave me not only the liberty of walking backwards and forwards in a semicircle; but, being fixed within four inches of the gate, allowed me to creep in, and lie at my full length in the temple.

CHAPTER II

The Emperor of Lilliput, *attended by several of the nobility, comes to see the Author in his confinement. The Emperor's person and habit described. Learned men appointed to teach the Author their language. He gains favor by his mild disposition. His pockets are searched, and his sword and pistols taken from him.*

When I found myself on my feet, I looked about me, and must confess I never beheld a more entertaining prospect. The country round appeared like a continued garden, and the inclosed fields, which were generally forty foot square, resembled so many beds of flowers. These fields were intermingled with woods of half a stang,[1] and the tallest trees, as I could judge, appeared to be seven foot high. I viewed the town on my left hand, which looked like the painted scene of a city in a theater.

I had been for some hours extremely pressed by the necessities of nature; which was no wonder, it being almost two days since I had last disburdened myself. I was under great difficulties between urgency and shame. The best expedient I could think on, was to creep into my house, which I accordingly did; and shutting the gate after me, I went as far as the length of my chain would suffer, and discharged my body of that uneasy load. But this was the only time I was ever guilty of so uncleanly an action; for which I cannot but hope the candid reader will give some allowance, after he hath maturely and impartially considered my case, and the distress I was in. From this time my constant practice was, as soon as I rose, to perform that business in open air, at the full extent of my chain, and due care was taken every morning before company came, that the offensive matter should be carried off in wheel-barrows, by two servants appointed for that purpose. I would not have dwelt so long upon a circumstance, that perhaps at first sight may appear not very

[1] *I. e.*, half a square rod.

momentous, if I had not thought it necessary to justify my character in point of cleanliness to the world; which I am told some of my maligners have been pleased, upon this and other occasions, to call in question.

When this adventure was at an end, I came back out of my house, having occasion for fresh air. The Emperor was already descended from the tower, and advancing on horseback towards me, which had like to have cost him dear; for the beast, though very well trained, yet wholly unused to such a sight, which appeared as if a mountain moved before him, reared up on his hinder feet: but that prince, who is an excellent horseman, kept his seat, till his attendants ran in, and held the bridle, while his Majesty had time to dismount. When he alighted, he surveyed me round with great admiration, but kept beyond the length of my chain. He ordered his cooks and butlers, who were already prepared, to give me victuals and drink, which they pushed forward in a sort of vehicles upon wheels, till I could reach them. I took these vehicles, and soon emptied them all; twenty of them were filled with meat, and ten with liquor; each of the former afforded me two or three good mouthfuls, and I emptied the liquor of ten vessels, which was contained in earthen vials, into one vehicle, drinking it off at a draught; and so I did with the rest. The Empress, and young Princes of the blood of both sexes, attended by many ladies, sat at some distance in their chairs; but upon the accident that happened to the Emperor's horse, they alighted, and came near his person, which I am now going to describe. He is taller by almost the breadth of my nail, than any of his court; which alone is enough to strike an awe into the beholders. His features are strong and masculine, with an Austrian lip and arched nose, his complexion olive, his countenance erect, his body and limbs well proportioned, all his motions graceful, and his deportment majestic. He was then past his prime, being twenty-eight years and three-quarters old, of which he had reigned about seven, in great felicity, and generally victorious. For the better convenience of beholding him, I lay on my side, so that my face was parallel to his, and he stood but three yards off: however, I have had him since many times in my hand, and therefore cannot be deceived in the description. His dress was very plain and simple, and the fashion of it between the Asiatic and the European: but he had on his head a light helmet of gold, adorned with jewels, and a plume on the crest. He held his sword drawn in his hand, to defend himself, if I should happen to break loose; it was almost three inches long, the hilt and scabbard were gold enriched with diamonds. His voice was shrill, but very clear and articulate, and I could distinctly hear it when I stood up. The ladies and courtiers were all most magnificently clad, so that the spot they stood upon seemed to resemble a petticoat spread on the ground, embroidered with figures of gold and silver. His Imperial Majesty spoke often to me, and I returned answers, but neither of us could understand a syllable. There were several of his priests and lawyers present (as I conjectured by their habits) who were commanded to address themselves to me, and I spoke to them in as many languages as I had the least smattering of, which were High and Low Dutch, Latin, French, Spanish, Italian, and Lingua Franca;[1] but all to no purpose. After about two hours the court retired, and I was left with a strong guard, to prevent the impertinence, and probably the malice of the rabble, who were very impatient to crowd about me as near as they durst, and some of them had the impudence to shoot their arrows at me as I sat on the ground by the door of my house, whereof one very narrowly missed my left eye. But the colonel ordered six of the ringleaders to be seized, and thought no punishment so proper as to deliver them bound into my hands, which some of his soldiers accordingly did, pushing them forwards with the butt-ends of their pikes into my reach; I took them all in my right hand, put five of them into my coat-pocket, and as to the sixth, I made a countenance as if I would eat him alive. The poor man squalled terribly, and the colonel and his officers were in much pain, especially when they saw me take out my pen-knife: but I soon put them out of fear: for, looking mildly, and immediately cutting the strings he was bound with, I set him gently on the ground, and away he ran. I

[1]The mixed language used in communication between European travelers and the Greeks and others at the eastern end of the Mediterranean.

treated the rest in the same manner, taking them one by one out of my pocket, and I observed both the soldiers and people were highly obliged at this mark of my clemency, which was represented very much to my advantage at court.

Towards night I got with some difficulty into my house, where I lay on the ground, and continued to do so about a fortnight; during which time the Emperor gave orders to have a bed prepared for me. Six hundred beds of the common measure were brought in carriages, and worked up in my house; an hundred and fifty of their beds sewn together made up the breadth and length, and these were four double, which however kept me but very indifferently from the hardness of the floor, that was of smooth stone. By the same computation they provided me with sheets, blankets, and coverlets, tolerable enough for one who had been so long inured to hardships as I.

As the news of my arrival spread through the kingdom, it brought prodigious numbers of rich, idle, and curious people to see me; so that the villages were almost emptied, and great neglect of tillage and household affairs must have ensued, if his Imperial Majesty had not provided, by several proclamations and orders of state, against this inconveniency. He directed that those who had already beheld me should return home, and not presume to come within fifty yards of my house without license from court; whereby the secretaries of state got considerable fees.

In the mean time, the Emperor held frequent councils to debate what course should be taken with me; and I was afterwards assured by a particular friend, a person of great quality, who was looked upon to be as much in the secret as any, that the court was under many difficulties concerning me. They apprehended my breaking loose, that my diet would be very expensive, and might cause a famine. Sometimes they determined to starve me, or at least to shoot me in the face and hands with poisoned arrows, which would soon dispatch me; but again they considered, that the stench of so large a carcass might produce a plague in the metropolis, and probably spread through the whole kingdom. In the midst of these consultations, several officers of the army went to the door of the great council-chamber; and two of them being admitted, gave an account of my behavior to the six criminals abovementioned, which made so favorable an impression in the breast of his Majesty and the whole board, in my behalf, that an Imperial Commission was issued out, obliging all the villages nine hundred yards round the city, to deliver in every morning six beeves, forty sheep, and other victuals for my sustenance; together with a proportionable quantity of bread, and wine, and other liquors; for the due payment of which his Majesty gave assignments upon his treasury. For this prince lives chiefly upon his own demesnes, seldom, except upon great occasions, raising any subsidies upon his subjects, who are bound to attend him in his wars at their own expense. An establishment was also made of six hundred persons to be my domestics, who had board-wages allowed for their maintenance, and tents built for them very conveniently on each side of my door. It was likewise ordered, that three hundred tailors should make me a suit of clothes after the fashion of the country: that six of his Majesty's greatest scholars should be employed to instruct me in their language: and, lastly, that the Emperor's horses, and those of the nobility, and troops of guards, should be frequently exercised in my sight, to accustom themselves to me. All these orders were duly put in execution, and in about three weeks I made a great progress in learning their language; during which time, the Emperor frequently honored me with his visits, and was pleased to assist my masters in teaching me. We began already to converse together in some sort; and the first words I learned were to express my desire that he would please give me my liberty, which I every day repeated on my knees. His answer, as I could comprehend it, was, that this must be a work of time, not to be thought on without the advice of his council, and that first I must *Lumos kelmin pesso desmar lon Emposo;* that is, swear a peace with him and his kingdom. However, that I should be used with all kindness; and he advised me to acquire, by my patience and discreet behavior, the good opinion of himself and his subjects. He desired I would not take it ill, if he gave orders to certain proper officers to search me; for probably I might carry about me several weapons, which must needs be dangerous things, if they answered the bulk of so prodigious a person. I said, his Majesty should be satisfied, for I was ready to strip myself, and turn up my pockets before him. This I delivered part in words, and part in signs. He replied, that by the laws of the kingdom I must be searched by two of his officers; that he knew this could not be done without my consent and assistance; that he had so good an opinion of my generosity and justice, as to trust their persons in my hands: that whatever they took from me should be returned when I left the country, or paid for at the rate which I would set upon them. I took up the two officers in my hands, put them first into my coat-pockets, and then into every other pocket about me, except my two fobs, and another secret pocket which I had no mind should be searched, wherein I had some little necessaries that were of no consequence to any but myself. In one of my fobs there was a silver watch, and in the other a small quantity of gold in a purse. These gentlemen, having pen, ink, and paper about them, made an exact inventory of everything they saw; and when they had done, desired I would set them down, that they might deliver it to the Emperor. This inventory I afterwards translated into English, and is word for word as follows:

Imprimis, In the right coat-pocket of the Great Man-Mountain (for so I interpret the words *Quinbus Flestrin*) after the strictest search, we found only one great piece of coarse cloth, large enough to be a foot-cloth for your Majesty's chief room of state. In the left pocket we saw a huge silver chest, with a cover of the same metal, which we, the searchers, were not able to lift. We desired it should be opened, and one of us stepping into it, found himself up to the mid leg in a sort of dust, some part whereof flying up to our faces, set us both a sneezing for several times together. In his right waistcoat-pocket we found a prodigious bundle of white thin substances, folded one over another, about the bigness of three men, tied with a strong cable, and marked with black figures, which we humbly conceive to be writings, every letter almost half as large as the palm of our hands. In the left there was a sort of engine, from the back of which were extended twenty long poles, resembling the palisadoes before your Majesty's court; wherewith we conjecture the Man-Mountain combs his head; for we did not always trouble him with questions, because we found it a great difficulty to make him understand us. In the large pocket on the right side of his middle cover (so I translate the word *ranfulo*, by which they meant my breeches) we saw a hollow pillar of iron, about the length of a man, fastened to a strong piece of timber, larger than the pillar; and upon one side of the pillar were huge pieces of iron sticking out, cut into strange figures, which we know not what to make of. In the left pocket, another engine of the same kind. In the smaller pocket on the right side, were several round flat pieces of white and red metal, of different bulk; some of the white, which seemed to be silver, were so large and heavy, that my comrade and I could hardly lift them. In the left pocket were two black pillars irregularly shaped: we could not, without difficulty, reach the top of them as we stood at the bottom of his pocket. One of them was covered, and seemed all of a piece: but at the upper end of the other, there appeared a white round substance, about twice the bigness of our heads. Within each of these was enclosed a prodigious plate of steel; which, by our orders, we obliged him to show us, because we apprehended they might be dangerous engines. He took them out of their cases, and told us, that in his own country his practice was to shave his beard with one of these, and cut his meat with the other. There were two pockets which we could not enter: these he called his fobs; they were two large slits cut into the top of his middle cover, but squeezed close by the pressure of his belly. Out of the right fob hung a great silver chain, with a wonderful kind of engine at the bottom. We directed him to draw out whatever was fastened to that chain; which appeared to be a globe, half silver, and half of some transparent metal; for, on the transparent side, we saw certain strange figures circularly drawn, and thought we could touch them, till we found our fingers stopped by that lucid substance. He put this engine to our ears, which made an incessant noise like that of a water-mill. And we conjecture it is either some unknown animal, or the god that he worships; but we are more inclined to the latter opinion, because he assured us (if we understood him right, for he expressed himself very imperfectly), that he seldom did anything without consulting it. He called it his oracle, and said it pointed out the time for every action of his life. From the left fob he took out a net almost large enough for a fisherman, but contrived to open and shut like a purse, and served him for the same use: we found therein several massy pieces of yellow metal, which, if they be real gold, must be of immense value.

Having thus, in obedience to your Majesty's commands, diligently searched all his pockets, we observed a girdle about his waist made of the hide of some prodigious animal; from which, on the left side, hung a sword of the length of five men; and on the right, a bag or pouch divided into two cells, each cell capable of holding three of your Majesty's subjects. In one of these cells were several globes or balls of a most ponderous metal, about the bigness of our heads, and requiring a strong hand to lift them: the other cell contained a heap of certain black grains, but of no great bulk or weight, for we could hold above fifty of them in the palms of our hands.

This is an exact inventory of what we found about the body of the Man-Mountain, who used us with great civility, and due respect to your Majesty's Commission. Signed and sealed on the fourth day of the eighty-ninth moon of your Majesty's auspicious reign.

Clefrin Frelock, Marsi Frelock.

When this inventory was read over to the Emperor, he directed me, although in very gentle terms, to deliver up the several particulars. He first called for my scimitar, which I took out, scabbard and all. In the mean time he ordered three thousand of his choicest troops (who then attended him) to surround me at a distance, with their bows and arrows just ready to discharge: but I did not observe it, for my eyes were wholly fixed upon his Majesty. He then desired me to draw my scimitar, which, although it had got some rust by the sea-water, was in most parts exceeding bright. I did so, and immediately all the troops gave a shout between terror and surprise; for the sun shone clear, and the reflection dazzled their eyes, as I waved the scimitar to and fro in my hand. His Majesty, who is a most magnanimous prince, was less daunted than I could expect; he ordered me to return it into the scabbard, and cast it on the ground as gently as I could, about six foot from the end of my chain. The next thing he demanded, was one of the hollow iron pillars, by which he meant my pocket-pistols. I drew it out, and at his desire, as well as I could, expressed to him the use of it; and charging it only with powder, which, by the closeness of my pouch, happened to escape wetting in the sea (an inconvenience against which all prudent mariners take special care to provide), I first cautioned the Emperor not to be afraid, and then I let it off in the air. The astonishment here was much greater than at the sight of my scimitar. Hundreds fell down, as if they had been struck dead; and even the Emperor, although he stood his ground, could not recover himself in some time. I delivered up both my pistols in the same manner as I had done my scimitar, and then my pouch of powder and bullets; begging him that the former might be kept from fire, for it would kindle with the smallest spark, and blow up his imperial palace into the air. I likewise delivered up my watch, which the Emperor was very curious to see, and commanded two of his tallest yeomen of the guards to bear it on a pole upon their shoulders, as draymen in England do a barrel of ale. He was amazed at the continual noise it made, and the motion of the minute-hand, which he could easily discern; for their sight is much more acute than ours: and asked the opinions of his learned men about him, which were various and remote,[1] as the reader may well imagine without my repeating; although indeed I could not very perfectly understand them. I then gave up my silver and copper money, my purse, with nine large pieces of gold, and some smaller ones; my knife and razor, my comb and silver snuff-box, my handkerchief and journal-book. My scimitar, pistols, and pouch, were conveyed in carriages to his Majesty's stores; but the rest of my goods were returned to me.

I had, as I before observed, one private pocket which escaped their search, wherein

---

[1]Recondite.

there was a pair of spectacles (which I sometimes use for the weakness of my eyes), a pocket perspective, and several other little conveniences; which being of no consequence to the Emperor, I did not think myself bound in honor to discover, and I apprehended they might be lost or spoiled if I ventured them out of my possession.

CHAPTER III

The Author diverts the Emperor, and his nobility of both sexes, in a very uncommon manner. The diversions of the court of Lilliput *described. The Author has his liberty granted him upon certain conditions.*

My gentleness and good behavior had gained so far on the Emperor and his court, and indeed upon the army and people in general, that I began to conceive hopes of getting my liberty in a short time. I took all possible methods to cultivate this favorable disposition. The natives came by degrees to be less apprehensive of any danger from me. I would sometimes lie down, and let five or six of them dance on my hand. And at last the boys and girls would venture to come and play at hide and seek in my hair. I had now made a good progress in understanding and speaking their language. The Emperor had a mind one day to entertain me with several of the country shows, wherein they exceed all nations I have known, both for dexterity and magnificence. I was diverted with none so much as that of the rope-dancers, performed upon a slender white thread, extended about two foot, and twelve inches from the ground. Upon which I shall desire liberty, with the reader's patience, to enlarge a little.

This diversion is only practiced by those persons who are candidates for great employments, and high favor, at court.[1] They are trained in this art from their youth, and are not always of noble birth, or liberal education. When a great office is vacant, either by death or disgrace (which often happens), five or six of those candidates petition the Emperor to entertain his Majesty and the court with a dance on the rope, and whoever jumps the highest without falling succeeds in the office. Very often the chief ministers themselves are commanded to show their skill, and to convince the Emperor that they have not lost their faculty. Flimnap,[2] the Treasurer, is allowed to cut a caper on the straight rope, at least an inch higher than any other lord in the whole empire. I have seen him do the summerset several times together upon a trencher fixed on the rope, which is no thicker than a common packthread in England. My friend Reldresal, principal Secretary for Private Affairs, is, in my opinion, if I am not partial, the second after the Treasurer; the rest of the great officers are much upon a par.

These diversions are often attended with fatal accidents, whereof great numbers are on record. I myself have seen two or three candidates break a limb. But the danger is much greater when the ministers themselves are commanded to show their dexterity; for, by contending to excel themselves and their fellows, they strain so far, that there is hardly one of them who hath not received a fall, and some of them two or three. I was assured that a year or two before my arrival, Flimnap would have infallibly broke his neck, if one of the King's cushions, that accidentally lay on the ground, had not weakened the force of his fall.

There is likewise another diversion, which is only shown before the Emperor and Empress, and first minister, upon particular occasions. The Emperor lays on the table three fine silken threads of six inches long.[3] One is blue, the other red, and the third green. These threads are proposed as prizes for those persons whom the Emperor hath a mind to distinguish by a peculiar mark of his favor. The ceremony is performed in his Majesty's great chamber of state, where the candidates are to undergo a trial of dexterity very different from the former, and such as I have not observed the least resemblance of in any other country of the old or the new world. The Emperor holds a stick in his hands, both ends parallel to the horizon, while the candidates advancing one by one, sometimes leap over the stick, sometimes creep under it backwards and forwards sev-

[1] Swift, of course, has the English court in mind.

[2] Sir Robert Walpole, a Whig. One should remember, however, that the analogies with English affairs cannot be pushed too far.

[3] The ribbons of the Garter, the Thistle, and the Bath.

eral times, according as the stick is advanced or depressed. Sometimes the Emperor holds one end of the stick, and his first minister the other; sometimes the minister has it entirely to himself. Whoever performs his part with most agility, and holds out the longest in leaping and creeping, is rewarded with the blue-colored silk; the red is given to the next, and the green to the third, which they all wear girt twice round about the middle; and you see few great persons about this court, who are not adorned with one of these girdles.

The horses of the army, and those of the royal stables, having been daily led before me, were no longer shy, but would come up to my very feet without starting. The riders would leap them over my hand as I held it on the ground, and one of the Emperor's huntsmen, upon a large courser, took my foot, shoe and all; which was indeed a prodigious leap. I had the good fortune to divert the Emperor one day after a very extraordinary manner. I desired he would order several sticks of two foot high, and the thickness of an ordinary cane, to be brought me; whereupon his Majesty commanded the master of his woods to give directions accordingly; and the next morning six woodmen arrived with as many carriages, drawn by eight horses to each. I took nine of these sticks, fixing them firmly in the ground in a quadrangular figure, two foot and a half square. I took four other sticks, and tied them parallel at each corner, about two foot from the ground; then I fastened my handkerchief to the nine sticks that stood erect, and extended it on all sides, till it was tight as the top of a drum; and the four parallel sticks rising about five inches higher than the handkerchief, served as ledges on each side. When I had finished my work, I desired the Emperor to let a troop of his best horse, twenty-four in number, come and exercise upon this plain. His Majesty approved of the proposal, and I took them up, one by one, in my hands, ready mounted and armed, with the proper officers to exercise them. As soon as they got into order, they divided into two parties, performed mock skirmishes, discharged blunt arrows, drew their swords, fled and pursued, attacked and retired, and in short discovered the best military discipline I ever beheld. The parallel sticks secured them and their horses from falling over the stage; and the Emperor was so much delighted that he ordered this entertainment to be repeated several days, and once was pleased to be lifted up and give the word of command; and, with great difficulty, persuaded even the Empress herself to let me hold her in her close chair within two yards of the stage, from whence she was able to take a full view of the whole performance. It was my good fortune that no ill accident happened in these entertainments, only once a fiery horse, that belonged to one of the captains, pawing with his hoof, struck a hole in my handkerchief, and his foot slipping, he overthrew his rider and himself; but I immediately relieved them both, and covering the hole with one hand, I set down the troop with the other, in the same manner as I took them up. The horse that fell was strained in the left shoulder, but the rider got no hurt, and I repaired my handkerchief as well as I could: however, I would not trust to the strength of it any more in such dangerous enterprises.

About two or three days before I was set at liberty, as I was entertaining the court with these kind of feats, there arrived an express to inform his Majesty, that some of his subjects riding near the place where I was first taken up, had seen a great black substance lying on the ground, very oddly shaped, extending its edges round as wide as his Majesty's bedchamber, and rising up in the middle as high as a man; that it was no living creature, as they at first apprehended, for it lay on the grass without motion, and some of them had walked round it several times: that by mounting upon each other's shoulders, they had got to the top, which was flat and even, and stamping upon it they found it was hollow within; that they humbly conceived it might be something belonging to the Man-Mountain; and if his Majesty pleased, they would undertake to bring it with only five horses. I presently knew what they meant, and was glad at heart to receive this intelligence. It seems upon my first reaching the shore after our ship-wreck, I was in such confusion, that before I came to the place where I went to sleep, my hat, which I had fastened with a string to my head while I was rowing, and had stuck on all the time I was swimming, fell off after I came to land; the string, as I conjecture, breaking by some accident which

I never observed, but thought my hat had been lost at sea. I entreated his Imperial Majesty to give orders it might be brought to me as soon as possible, describing to him the use and the nature of it: and the next day the wagoners arrived with it, but not in a very good condition; they had bored two holes in the brim, within an inch and half of the edge, and fastened two hooks in the holes; these hooks were tied by a long cord to the harness, and thus my hat was dragged along for above half an English mile; but the ground in that country being extremely smooth and level, it received less damage than I expected.

Two days after this adventure, the Emperor having ordered that part of his army which quarters in and about his metropolis to be in readiness, took a fancy of diverting himself in a very singular manner. He desired I would stand like a Colossus, with my legs as far asunder as I conveniently could. He then commanded his General (who was an old experienced leader, and a great patron of mine) to draw up the troops in close order, and march them under me; the foot by twenty-four in a breast, and the horse by sixteen, with drums beating, colors flying, and pikes advanced. This body consisted of three thousand foot, and a thousand horse. His Majesty gave orders, upon pain of death, that every soldier in his march should observe the strictest decency with regard to my person; which, however, could not prevent some of the younger officers from turning up their eyes as they passed under me. And, to confess the truth, my breeches were at that time in so ill a condition, that they afforded some opportunities for laughter and admiration.

I had sent so many memorials and petitions for my liberty, that his Majesty at length mentioned the matter, first in the cabinet, and then in a full council; where it was opposed by none, except Skyresh Bolgolam, who was pleased, without any provocation, to be my mortal enemy. But it was carried against him by the whole board, and confirmed by the Emperor. That minister was *Galbet*, or Admiral of the Realm, very much in his master's confidence, and a person well versed in affairs, but of a morose and sour complexion. However, he was at length persuaded to comply; but prevailed that the articles and conditions upon which I should be set free, and to which I must swear, should be drawn up by himself. These articles were brought to me by Skyresh Bolgolam in person, attended by two under-secretaries, and several persons of distinction. After they were read, I was demanded to swear to the performance of them; first in the manner of my own country, and afterwards in the method prescribed by their laws; which was to hold my right foot in my left hand, to place the middle finger of my right hand on the crown of my head, and my thumb on the tip of my right ear. But because the reader may be curious to have some idea of the style and manner of expression peculiar to that people, as well as to know the articles upon which I recovered my liberty, I have made a translation of the whole instrument word for word, as near as I was able, which I here offer to the public.

Golbasto Momarem Evlame Gurdilo Shefin Mully Ully Gue, most mighty Emperor of Lilliput, delight and terror of the universe, whose dominions extend five thousand *blustrugs* (about twelve miles in circumference) to the extremities of the globe; monarch of all monarchs, taller than the sons of men; whose feet press down to the center, and whose head strikes against the sun; at whose nod the princes of the earth shake their knees; pleasant as the spring, comfortable as the summer, fruitful as autumn, dreadful as winter. His most sublime Majesty proposeth to the Man-Mountain, lately arrived to our celestial dominions, the following articles, which by a solemn oath he shall be obliged to perform.

First, The Man-Mountain shall not depart from our dominions, without our license under our great seal.

2d, He shall not presume to come into our metropolis, without our express order; at which time, the inhabitants shall have two hours' warning to keep within their doors.

3rd, The said Man-Mountain shall confine his walks to our principal high-roads, and not offer to walk or lie down in a meadow or field of corn.

4th, As he walks the said roads, he shall take the utmost care not to trample upon the bodies of any of our loving subjects, their horses, or carriages, nor take any of our subjects into his hands, without their own consent.

5th, If an express requires extraordinary dispatch, the Man-Mountain shall be obliged to carry in his pocket the messenger and horse a six days' journey once in every moon, and return the said messenger back (if so required) safe to our Imperial Presence.

6th, He shall be our ally against our enemies in the Island of Blefuscu,[1] and do his utmost to destroy their fleet, which is now preparing to invade us.

7th, That the said Man-Mountain shall, at his times of leisure, be aiding and assisting our workmen, in helping to raise certain great stones, towards covering the wall of the principal park, and other our royal buildings.

8th, That the said Man-Mountain shall, in two moons' time, deliver in an exact survey of the circumference of our dominions by a computation of his own paces round the coast.

Lastly, That upon his solemn oath to observe all the above articles, the said Man-Mountain shall have a daily allowance of meat and drink sufficient for the support of 1728 of our subjects, with free access to our Royal Person, and other marks of our favor. Given at our Palace at Belfaborac the twelfth day of the ninety-first moon of our reign.

I swore and subscribed to these articles with great cheerfulness and content, although some of them were not so honorable as I could have wished; which proceeded wholly from the malice of Skyresh Bolgolam, the High-Admiral: whereupon my chains were immediately unlocked, and I was at full liberty; the Emperor himself in person did me the honor to be by at the whole ceremony. I made my acknowledgments by prostrating myself at his Majesty's feet: but he commanded me to rise; and after many gracious expressions, which, to avoid the censure of vanity, I shall not repeat, he added, that he hoped I should prove a useful servant, and well deserve all the favors he had already conferred upon me, or might do for the future.

The reader may please to observe, that in the last article for the recovery of my liberty, the Emperor stipulates to allow me a quantity of meat and drink sufficient for the support of 1728 Lilliputians. Some time after, asking a friend at court how they came to fix on that determinate number; he told me that his Majesty's mathematicians, having taken the height of my body by the help of a quadrant, and finding it to exceed theirs in the proportion of twelve to one, they concluded from the similarity of their bodies, that mine must contain at least 1728 of theirs, and consequently would require as much food as was necessary to support that number of Lilliputians. By which, the reader may conceive an idea of the ingenuity of that people, as well as the prudent and exact economy of so great a prince.

CHAPTER IV

Mildendo, *the metropolis of* Lilliput, *described, together with the Emperor's palace. A conversation between the Author and a principal Secretary, concerning the affairs of that empire. The Author's offer to serve the Emperor in his wars.*

THE first request I made after I had obtained my liberty, was, that I might have license to see Mildendo, the metropolis; which the Emperor easily granted me, but with a special charge to do no hurt either to the inhabitants or their houses. The people had notice by proclamation of my design to visit the town. The wall which encompassed it, is two foot and an half high, and at least eleven inches broad, so that a coach and horses may be driven very safely round it; and it is flanked with strong towers at ten foot distance. I stepped over the great Western Gate, and passed very gently, and sideling through the two principal streets, only in my short waistcoat, for fear of damaging the roofs and eaves of the houses with the skirts of my coat. I walked with the utmost circumspection, to avoid treading on any stragglers, that might remain in the

[1]This country probably represents France under Louis XIV.

streets, although the orders were very strict, that all people should keep in their houses, at their own peril. The garret windows and tops of houses were so crowded with spectators, that I thought in all my travels I had not seen a more populous place. The city is an exact square, each side of the wall being five hundred foot long. The two great streets, which run cross and divide it into four quarters, are five foot wide. The lanes and alleys, which I could not enter, but only viewed them as I passed, are from twelve to eighteen inches. The town is capable of holding five hundred thousand souls. The houses are from three to five stories. The shops and markets well provided.

The Emperor's palace is in the center of the city, where the two great streets meet. It is enclosed by a wall of two foot high, and twenty foot distant from the buildings. I had his Majesty's permission to step over this wall; and the space being so wide between that and the palace, I could easily view it on every side. The outward court is a square of forty foot, and includes two other courts: in the inmost are the royal apartments, which I was very desirous to see, but found it extremely difficult; for the great gates, from one square into another, were but eighteen inches high, and seven inches wide. Now the buildings of the outer court were at least five foot high, and it was impossible for me to stride over them without infinite damage to the pile, though the walls were strongly built of hewn stone, and four inches thick. At the same time the Emperor had a great desire that I should see the magnificence of his palace; but this I was not able to do till three days after, which I spent in cutting down with my knife some of the largest trees in the royal park, about an hundred yards distant from the city. Of these trees I made two stools, each about three foot high, and strong enough to bear my weight. The people having received notice a second time, I went again through the city to the palace, with my two stools in my hands. When I came to the side of the outer court, I stood upon one stool, and took the other in my hand: this I lifted over the roof, and gently set it down on the space between the first and second court, which was eight foot wide. I then stepped over the buildings very conveniently from one stool to the other, and drew up the first after me with a hooked stick. By this contrivance I got into the inmost court; and lying down upon my side, I applied my face to the windows of the middle stories, which were left open on purpose, and discovered the most splendid apartments that can be imagined. There I saw the Empress and the young Princes, in their several lodgings, with their chief attendants about them. Her Imperial Majesty[1] was pleased to smile very graciously upon me, and gave me out of the window her hand to kiss.

But I shall not anticipate the reader with farther descriptions of this kind, because I reserve them for a greater work, which is now almost ready for the press, containing a general description of this empire, from its first erection, through a long series of Princes, with a particular account of their wars and politics, laws, learning, and religion: their plants and animals, their peculiar manners and customs, with other matters very curious and useful; my chief design at present being only to relate such events and transactions as happened to the public, or to myself, during a residence of about nine months in that empire.

One morning, about a fortnight after I had obtained my liberty, Reldresal, principal Secretary (as they style him) of Private Affairs, came to my house attended only by one servant. He ordered his coach to wait at a distance, and desired I would give him an hour's audience; which I readily consented to, on account of his quality and personal merits, as well as the many good offices he had done me during my solicitations at court. I offered to lie down, that he might the more conveniently reach my ear; but he chose rather to let me hold him in my hand during our conversation. He began with compliments on my liberty; said he might pretend to some merit in it: but, however, added, that if it had not been for the present situation of things at court, perhaps I might not have obtained it so soon. For, said he, as flourishing a condition as we may appear to be in to foreigners, we labor under two mighty evils; a violent faction at home, and the danger of an invasion by a most potent enemy from abroad. As to the first, you are to understand, that for about seventy moons

[1]Probably Queen Anne.

past there have been two struggling parties in this empire, under the names of *Tramecksan* and *Slamecksan*, from the high and low heels on their shoes,[1] by which they distinguish themselves. It is alleged indeed, that the high heels are most agreeable to our ancient constitution; but, however this be, his Majesty hath determined to make use of only low heels in the administration of the government, and all offices in the gift of the Crown, as you cannot but observe; and particularly, that his Majesty's Imperial heels are lower at least by a *drurr* than any of his court (*drurr* is a measure about the fourteenth part of an inch). The animosities between these two parties run so high, that they will neither eat nor drink, nor talk with each other. We compute the *Tramecksan*, or High-Heels, to exceed us in number; but the power is wholly on our side. We apprehend his Imperial Highness, the Heir to the Crown, to have some tendency towards the High-Heels;[2] at least we can plainly discover one of his heels higher than the other, which gives him a hobble in his gait. Now, in the midst of these intestine disquiets, we are threatened with an invasion from the Island of Blefuscu, which is the other great empire of the universe, almost as large and powerful as this of his Majesty. For as to what we have heard you affirm, that there are other kingdoms and states in the world inhabited by human creatures as large as yourself, our philosophers are in much doubt, and would rather conjecture that you dropped from the moon, or one of the stars; because it is certain, that an hundred mortals of your bulk would, in a short time, destroy all the fruits and cattle of his Majesty's dominions. Besides, our histories of six thousand moons make no mention of any other regions, than the two great empires of Lilliput and Blefuscu. Which two mighty powers have, as I was going to tell you, been engaged in a most obstinate war for six and thirty moons past. It began upon the following occasion. It is allowed on all hands, that the primitive way of breaking eggs before we eat them, was upon the larger end: but his present Majesty's grandfather, while he was a boy going to eat an egg, and breaking it according to the ancient practice, happened to cut one of his fingers. Whereupon the Emperor his father published an edict, commanding all his subjects, upon great penalties, to break the smaller end of their eggs.[3] The people so highly resented this law, that our histories tell us there have been six rebellions raised on that account; wherein one Emperor lost his life, and another his crown. These civil commotions were constantly fomented by the monarchs of Blefuscu; and when they were quelled, the exiles always fled for refuge to that empire. It is computed, that eleven thousand persons have, at several times, suffered death, rather than submit to break their eggs at the smaller end. Many hundred large volumes have been published upon this controversy: but the books of the Big-Endians have been long forbidden, and the whole party rendered incapable by law of holding employments. During the course of these troubles, the Emperors of Blefuscu did frequently expostulate by their ambassadors, accusing us of making a schism in religion, by offending against a fundamental doctrine of our great prophet Lustrog, in the fifty-fourth chapter of the Blundecral (which is their Alcoran). This, however, is thought to be a mere strain upon the text: for the words are these; *That all true believers break their eggs at the convenient end:* and which is the convenient end, seems, in my humble opinion, to be left to every man's conscience, or at least in the power of the chief magistrate to determine. Now the Big-Endian exiles have found so much credit in the Emperor of Blefuscu's court, and so much private assistance and encouragement from their party here at home, that a bloody war has been carried on between the two empires for six and thirty moons with various success; during which time we have lost forty capital ships, and a much greater number of smaller vessels, together with thirty thousand of our best sea-

[1]This and what follows is a satire upon party government, but it is a mistake to suppose, from Swift's terms, that it refers specially to the High and Low Church parties in England.

[2]This probably refers to intrigues of the Prince of Wales (later George II) directed against his father's policies.

[3]This controversy is usually said to refer to the troubles between Catholics and protestants in England, and no doubt correctly; though the full force of the satire is lost, here and elsewhere in the book, if we tend to think of it as having only, or even chiefly, a particular application. The Little-Endians are explained to be the protestants, the Big-Endians the Catholics. The Emperor's grandfather is thus Henry VIII and, in the next sentence, the Emperor who lost his life is Charles I, he who lost his crown James II. France (Blefuscu), of course, encouraged the English Catholics.

men and soldiers; and the damage received by the enemy is reckoned to be somewhat greater than ours. However, they have now equipped a numerous fleet, and are just preparing to make a descent upon us; and his Imperial Majesty, placing great confidence in your valor and strength, has commanded me to lay this account of his affairs before you.

I desired the Secretary to present my humble duty to the Emperor, and to let him know, that I thought it would not become me, who was a foreigner, to interfere with parties; but I was ready, with the hazard of my life, to defend his person and state against all invaders.

CHAPTER V

The Author, by an extraordinary stratagem, prevents an invasion. A high title of honor is conferred upon him. Ambassadors arrive from the Emperor of Blefuscu, *and sue for peace. The Emperor's apartment on fire by an accident; the Author instrumental in saving the rest of the palace.*

THE Empire of Blefuscu is an island situated to the north north-east side of Lilliput, from whence it is parted only by a channel of eight hundred yards wide. I had not yet seen it, and upon this notice of an intended invasion, I avoided appearing on that side of the coast, for fear of being discovered by some of the enemy's ships, who had received no intelligence of me, all intercourse between the two empires having been strictly forbidden during the war, upon pain of death, and an embargo laid by our Emperor upon all vessels whatsoever. I communicated to his Majesty a project I had formed of seizing the enemy's whole fleet: which, as our scouts assured us, lay at anchor in the harbor ready to sail with the first fair wind. I consulted the most experienced seamen, upon the depth of the channel, which they had often plumbed, who told me, that in the middle at high-water it was seventy *glumgluffs* deep, which is about six foot of European measure; and the rest of it fifty *glumgluffs* at most. I walked towards the north-east coast over against Blefuscu; and lying down behind a hillock, took out my small pocket perspective-glass, and viewed the enemy's fleet at anchor, consisting of about fifty men of war, and a great number of transports: I then came back to my house, and gave order (for which I had a warrant) for a great quantity of the strongest cable and bars of iron. The cable was about as thick as packthread, and the bars of the length and size of a knitting-needle. I trebled the cable to make it stronger, and for the same reason I twisted three of the iron bars together, binding the extremities into a hook. Having thus fixed fifty hooks to as many cables, I went back to the north-east coast, and putting off my coat, shoes, and stockings, walked into the sea in my leathern jerkin, about half an hour before high water. I waded with what haste I could, and swam in the middle about thirty yards till I felt ground; I arrived at the fleet in less than half an hour. The enemy was so frighted when they saw me, that they leaped out of their ships, and swam to shore, where there could not be fewer than thirty thousand souls. I then took my tackling, and fastening a hook to the hole at the prow of each, I tied all the cords together at the end. While I was thus employed, the enemy discharged several thousand arrows, many of which stuck in my hands and face; and besides the excessive smart, gave me much disturbance in my work. My greatest apprehension was for my eyes, which I should have infallibly lost, if I had not suddenly thought of an expedient. I kept among other little necessaries a pair of spectacles in a private pocket, which, as I observed before, had scaped the Emperor's searchers. These I took out and fastened as strongly as I could upon my nose, and thus armed went on boldly with my work in spite of the enemy's arrows, many of which struck against the glasses of my spectacles, but without any other effect, further than a little to discompose them. I had now fastened all the hooks, and taking the knot in my hand, began to pull; but not a ship would stir, for they were all too fast held by their anchors, so that the boldest part of my enterprise remained. I therefore let go the cord, and leaving the hooks fixed to the ships, I resolutely cut with my knife the cables that fastened the anchors, receiving about two hundred shots in my face and hands; then I took up the knotted end of the cables, to which my hooks were tied, and with great ease drew fifty of the enemy's largest men of war after me.

The Blefuscudians, who had not the least imagination of what I intended, were at first confounded with astonishment. They had seen me cut the cables, and thought my design was only to let the ships run adrift, or fall foul on each other: but when they perceived the whole fleet moving in order, and saw me pulling at the end, they set up such a scream of grief and despair, that it is almost impossible to describe or conceive. When I had got out of danger, I stopped awhile to pick out the arrows that stuck in my hands and face; and rubbed on some of the same ointment that was given me at my first arrival, as I have formerly mentioned. I then took off my spectacles, and waiting about an hour, till the tide was a little fallen, I waded through the middle with my cargo, and arrived safe at the royal port of Lilliput.

The Emperor and his whole court stood on the shore, expecting the issue of this great adventure. They saw the ships move forward in a large half-moon, but could not discern me, who was up to my breast in water. When I advanced in the middle of the channel, they were yet in more pain, because I was under water to my neck. The Emperor concluded me to be drowned, and that the enemy's fleet was approaching in a hostile manner: but he was soon eased of his fears, for the channel growing shallower every step I made, I came in a short time within hearing, and holding up the end of the cable by which the fleet was fastened, I cried in a loud voice, *Long live the most puissant Emperor of Lilliput!* This great prince received me at my landing with all possible encomiums, and created me a *Nardac* upon the spot, which is the highest title of honor among them.

His Majesty desired I would take some other opportunity of bringing all the rest of his enemy's ships into his ports. And so unmeasurable is the ambition of princes, that he seemed to think of nothing less than reducing the whole empire of Blefuscu into a province, and governing it by a viceroy; of destroying the Big-Endian exiles, and compelling the people to break the smaller end of their eggs, by which he would remain the sole monarch of the whole world. But I endeavored to divert him from this design, by many arguments drawn from the topics of policy as well as justice; and I plainly protested, that I would never be an instrument of bringing a free and brave people into slavery. And when the matter was debated in council, the wisest part of the ministry were of my opinion.

This open bold declaration of mine was so opposite to the schemes and politics of his Imperial Majesty, that he could never forgive it; he mentioned it in a very artful manner at council, where I was told that some of the wisest appeared, at least by their silence, to be of my opinion; but others, who were my secret enemies, could not forbear some expressions, which by a side-wind reflected on me. And from this time began an intrigue between his Majesty and a junto of ministers maliciously bent against me, which broke out in less than two months, and had like to have ended in my utter destruction. Of so little weight are the greatest services to princes, when put into the balance with a refusal to gratify their passions.

About three weeks after this exploit, there arrived a solemn embassy from Blefuscu, with humble offers of a peace; which was soon concluded upon conditions very advantageous to our Emperor, wherewith I shall not trouble the reader. There were six ambassadors, with a train of about five hundred persons, and their entry was very magnificent, suitable to the grandeur of their master, and the importance of their business. When their treaty was finished, wherein I did them several good offices by the credit I now had, or at least appeared to have at court, their Excellencies, who were privately told how much I had been their friend, made me a visit in form. They began with many compliments upon my valor and generosity, invited me to that kingdom in the Emperor their master's name, and desired me to show them some proofs of my prodigious strength, of which they had heard so many wonders; wherein I readily obliged them, but shall not trouble the reader with the particulars.

When I had for some time entertained their Excellencies, to their infinite satisfaction and surprise, I desired they would do me the honor to present my most humble respects to the Emperor their master, the renown of whose virtues had so justly filled the whole world with admiration, and whose royal person I resolved to attend before I returned to my own country: accordingly, the next time I had the honor to see our Emperor, I desired his general license to wait on the Blefuscudian monarch, which he was pleased to grant me, as I could perceive, in a very cold manner; but could not guess the reason, till I had a whisper from a certain person that Flimnap and Bolgolam had represented my intercourse with those ambassadors as a mark of disaffection, from which I am sure my heart was wholly free. And this was the first time I began to conceive some imperfect idea of courts and ministers.

It is to be observed, that these ambassadors spoke to me by an interpreter, the languages of both empires differing as much from each other as any two in Europe, and each nation priding itself upon the antiquity, beauty, and energy of their own tongues, with an avowed contempt for that of their neighbor; yet our Emperor, standing upon the advantage he had got by the seizure of their fleet, obliged them to deliver their credentials, and make their speech in the Lilliputian tongue. And it must be confessed, that from the great intercourse of trade and commerce between both realms, from the continual reception of exiles, which is mutual among them, and from the custom in each empire to send their young nobility and richer gentry to the other, in order to polish themselves by seeing the world, and understanding men and manners; there are few persons of distinction, or merchants, or seamen, who dwell in the maritime parts, but what can hold conversation in both tongues; as I found some weeks after, when I went to pay my respects to the Emperor of Blefuscu, which in the midst of great misfortunes, through the malice of my enemies, proved a very happy adventure to me, as I shall relate in its proper place.

The reader may remember, that when I signed those articles upon which I recovered my liberty, there were some which I disliked upon account of their being too servile, neither could anything but an extreme necessity have forced me to submit. But being now a *Nardac* of the highest rank in that empire, such offices were looked upon as below my dignity, and the Emperor (to do him justice) never once mentioned them to me. However, it was not long before I had an opportunity of doing his Majesty, at least, as I then thought, a most signal service. I was alarmed at midnight with the cries of many hundred people at my door; by which being suddenly awaked, I was in some kind of terror. I heard the word *burglum* repeated incessantly: several of the Emperor's court, making their way through the crowd, entreated me to come immediately to the palace, where her Imperial Majesty's apartment was on fire, by the carelessness of a maid of honor, who fell asleep while she was reading a romance. I got up in an instant; and orders being given to clear the way before me, and it being likewise a moonshine night, I made a shift to get to the Palace without trampling on any of the people. I found they had already applied ladders to the walls of the apartment, and were well provided with buckets, but the water was at some distance. These buckets were about the size of a large thimble, and the poor people supplied me with them as fast as they could; but the flame was so violent that they did little good. I might easily have stifled it with my coat, which I unfortunately left behind me for haste, and came away only in my leathern jerkin. The case seemed wholly desperate and deplorable; and this magnificent palace would have infallibly been burned down to the ground, if, by a presence of mind, unusual to me, I had not suddenly thought of an expedient. I had the evening before drunk plentifully of a most delicious wine, called *glimigrim* (the Blefuscudians call it *flunec*, but ours is esteemed the better sort), which is very diuretic. By the luckiest chance in the world, I had not discharged myself of any part of it. The heat I had contracted by coming very near the flames, and by laboring to quench them, made the wine begin to operate by urine; which I voided in such a quantity, and applied so well to the proper places, that in three minutes the fire was wholly extinguished, and the rest of that noble pile, which had cost so many ages in erecting, preserved from destruction.

It was now day-light, and I returned to my house without waiting to congratulate with the Emperor: because, although I had done a very eminent piece of service, yet I could not tell how his Majesty might resent the manner by which I had performed it: for, by the fundamental laws of the realm, it is capital in any person, of what quality soever, to make water within the precincts of the palace. But I was a little comforted by a message from his Majesty, that he would give orders to the Grand Justiciary for passing my pardon in form; which, however, I could not obtain. And I was privately assured, that the Empress, conceiving the greatest abhorrence of what I had done, removed to the most distant side of the court, firmly resolved that those buildings should never be repaired for her use: and, in the presence of her chief confidents could not forbear vowing revenge.[1]

CHAPTER VI

Of the inhabitants of Lilliput; *their learning, laws, and customs, the manner of educating their children. The Author's way of living in that country. His vindication of a great lady.*

Although I intend to leave the description of this empire to a particular treatise, yet in the mean time I am content to gratify the curious reader with some general ideas. As the common size of the natives is somewhat under six inches high, so there is an exact proportion in all other animals, as well as plants and trees: for instance, the tallest horses and oxen are between four and five inches in height, the sheep an inch and a half, more or less: their geese about the bigness of a sparrow, and so the several gradations downwards till you come to the smallest, which, to my sight, were almost invisible; but nature hath adapted the eyes of the Lilliputians to all objects proper for their view: they see with great exactness, but at no great distance. And to show the sharpness of their sight towards objects that are near, I have been much pleased with observing a cook pulling a lark, which was not so large as a common fly; and a young girl threading an invisible needle with invisible silk. Their tallest trees are about seven foot high: I mean some of those in the great royal park, the tops whereof I could but just reach with my fist clinched. The other vegetables are in the same proportion; but this I leave to the reader's imagination.

I shall say but little at present of their learning, which for many ages hath flourished in all its branches among them: but their manner of writing is very peculiar, being neither from the left to the right, like the Europeans; nor from the right to the left, like the Arabians; nor from up to down, like the Chinese; nor from down to up, like the Cascagians; but aslant from one corner of the paper to the other, like ladies in England.

They bury their dead with their heads directly downwards, because they hold an opinion, that in eleven thousand moons they are all to rise again, in which period the earth (which they conceive to be flat) will turn upside down, and by this means they shall, at their resurrection, be found ready standing on their feet. The learned among them confess the absurdity of this doctrine, but the practice still continues, in compliance to the vulgar.

There are some laws and customs in this empire very peculiar; and if they were not so directly contrary to those of my own dear country, I should be tempted to say a little in their justification. It is only to be wished, that they were as well executed. The first I shall mention, relates to informers. All crimes against the state are punished here with the utmost severity; but if the person accused maketh his innocence plainly to appear upon his trial, the accuser is immediately put to an ignominious death; and out of his goods or lands, the innocent person is quadruply recompensed for the loss of his time, for the danger he underwent, for the hardship of his imprisonment, and for all the charges he hath been at in making his defense. Or, if that fund be deficient, it is largely supplied by the Crown. The Emperor does also confer on him some public mark of his favor, and proclamation is made of his innocence through the whole city.

They look upon fraud as a greater crime than theft, and therefore seldom fail to punish it with death; for they allege, that care and vigilance, with a very common understanding, may preserve a man's goods from thieves, but honesty has no fence against superior cunning; and since it is necessary that there should be a perpetual intercourse of buying and selling, and dealing upon credit, where fraud is permitted and connived at, or hath no law to punish it, the honest dealer is always undone, and the knave gets the advantage. I remember when I was once interceding with the Emperor for a criminal who had wronged his master of a great sum of money, which he had received by order, and ran away with; and happening to tell his Majesty, by way of extenuation, that it was only a breach of trust;

[1]This episode may have reference to Swift's failure to obtain a bishopric because of his authorship of *A Tale of a Tub.*

the Emperor thought it monstrous in me to offer, as a defense, the greatest aggravation of the crime: and truly I had little to say in return, farther than the common answer, that different nations had different customs; for, I confess, I was heartily ashamed.

Although we usually call reward and punishment the two hinges upon which all government turns, yet I could never observe this maxim to be put in practice by any nation except that of Lilliput. Whoever can there bring sufficient proof that he hath strictly observed the laws of his country for seventy-three moons, hath a claim to certain privileges, according to his quality and condition of life, with a proportionable sum of money out of a fund appropriated for that use: he likewise acquires the title of *Snilpall*, or Legal, which is added to his name, but does not descend to his posterity. And these people thought it a prodigious defect of policy among us, when I told them that our laws were enforced only by penalties, without any mention of reward. It is upon this account that the image of Justice, in their courts of judicature, is formed with six eyes, two before, as many behind, and on each side one, to signify circumspection; with a bag of gold open in her right hand, and a sword sheathed in her left, to show she is more disposed to reward than to punish.

In choosing persons for all employments, they have more regard to good morals than to great abilities; for, since government is necessary to mankind, they believe that the common size of human understandings is fitted to some station or other, and that Providence never intended to make the management of public affairs a mystery, to be comprehended only by a few persons of sublime genius, of which there seldom are three born in an age: but they suppose truth, justice, temperance, and the like, to be in every man's power; the practice of which virtues, assisted by experience and a good intention, would qualify any man for the service of his country, except where a course of study is required. But they thought the want of moral virtues was so far from being supplied by superior endowments of the mind, that employments could never be put into such dangerous hands as those of persons so qualified; and at least, that the mistakes committed by ignorance in a virtuous disposition, would never be of such fatal consequence to the public weal, as the practices of a man whose inclinations led him to be corrupt, and had great abilities to manage, and multiply, and defend his corruptions.

In like manner, the disbelief of a Divine Providence renders a man uncapable of holding any public station; for, since kings avow themselves to be the deputies of Providence, the Lilliputians think nothing can be more absurd than for a prince to employ such men as disown the authority under which he acts.

In relating these and the following laws, I would only be understood to mean the original institutions, and not the most scandalous corruptions into which these people are fallen by the degenerate nature of man. For as to that infamous practice of acquiring great employments by dancing on the ropes, or badges of favor and distinction by leaping over sticks and creeping under them, the reader is to observe, that they were first introduced by the grandfather of the Emperor now reigning, and grew to the present height, by the gradual increase of party and faction.

Ingratitude is among them a capital crime, as we read it to have been in some other countries: for they reason thus, that whoever makes ill returns to his benefactor, must needs be a common enemy to the rest of mankind, from whom he hath received no obligation, and therefore such a man is not fit to live.

Their notions relating to the duties of parents and children differ extremely from ours. For, since the conjunction of male and female is founded upon the great law of nature, in order to propagate and continue the species, the Lilliputians will needs have it, that men and women are joined together like other animals, by the motives of concupiscence; and that their tenderness towards their young proceeds from the like natural principle: for which reason they will never allow, that a child is under any obligation to his father for begetting him, or to his mother for bringing him into the world, which, considering the miseries of human life, was neither a benefit in itself, nor intended so by his parents, whose thoughts in their love-encounters were otherwise employed. Upon these, and the like reasonings, their opinion is, that parents are the last of all others to be trusted with the education of their own children; and therefore they have in every town public nurseries, where all parents, except cottagers and laborers, are obliged to send their infants of both sexes to be reared and educated when they come to the age of twenty moons, at which time they are supposed to have some rudiments of docility. These schools are of several kinds, suited to different qualities, and to both sexes. They have certain professors well skilled in preparing children for such a condition of life as befits the rank of their parents, and their own capacities as well as inclinations. I shall first say something of the male nurseries, and then of the female.

The nurseries for males of noble or eminent birth, are provided with grave and learned professors, and their several deputies. The clothes and food of the children are plain and simple. They are bred up in the principles of honor, justice, courage, modesty, clemency, religion, and love of their country; they are always employed in some business, except in the times of eating and sleeping, which are very short, and two hours for diversions, consisting of bodily exercises. They are dressed by men till four years of age, and then are obliged to dress themselves, although their quality be ever so great; and the women attendants, who are aged proportionably to ours at fifty, perform only the most menial offices. They are never suffered to converse with servants, but go together in small or greater numbers to take their diversions, and always in the presence of a professor, or one of his deputies; whereby they avoid those early bad impressions of folly and vice to which our children are subject. Their parents are suffered to see them only twice a year; the visit is to last but an hour. They are allowed to kiss the child at meeting and parting; but a professor, who always stands by on those occasions, will not suffer them to whisper, or use any fondling expressions, or bring any presents of toys, sweetmeats, and the like.

The pension from each family for the education and entertainment of a child, upon failure of due payment, is levied by the Emperor's officers.

The nurseries for children of ordinary gentlemen, merchants, traders, and handicrafts, are managed proportionably after the same manner; only those designed for trades, are put out apprentices at eleven years old, whereas those of persons of quality continue in their exercises till fifteen, which answers to one and twenty with us: but the confinement is gradually lessened for the last three years.

In the female nurseries, the young girls of quality are educated much like the males, only they are dressed by orderly servants of their own sex; but always in the presence of a professor or deputy, till they come to dress themselves, which is at five years old. And if it be found that these nurses ever presume to entertain the girl with frightful or foolish stories, or the common follies practiced by chambermaids among us, they are publicly whipped thrice about the city, imprisoned for a year, and banished for life to the most desolate part of the country. Thus the young ladies there are as much ashamed of being cowards and fools, as the men, and despise all personal ornaments beyond decency and cleanliness: neither did I perceive any difference in their education, made by their difference of sex, only that the exercises of the females were not altogether so robust; and that some rules were given them relating to domestic life, and a smaller compass of learning was enjoined them: for their maxim is, that among people of quality, a wife should be always a reasonable and agreeable companion, because she cannot always be young. When the girls are twelve years old, which among them is the marriageable age, their parents or guardians take them home, with great expressions of gratitude to the professors, and seldom without tears of the young lady and her companions.

In the nurseries of females of the meaner sort, the children are instructed in all kinds of works proper for their sex, and their several degrees: those intended for apprentices, are dismissed at seven years old, the rest are kept to eleven.

The meaner families who have children at these nurseries, are obliged, besides their annual pension, which is as low as possible, to return to the steward of the nursery a small monthly share of their gettings, to be a portion for the child; and therefore all parents are limited in their expenses by the law. For the Lilliputians think nothing can be more unjust, than for people, in subservience to their own appetites, to bring children into the world, and leave the burden of supporting them on the public. As to persons of quality, they give security to appropriate a certain sum for each child, suitable to their condition; and these funds are always managed with good husbandry, and the most exact justice.

The cottagers and laborers keep their children at home, their business being only to till and cultivate the earth, and therefore their education is of little consequence to the public; but the old and diseased among them are supported by hospitals: for begging is a trade unknown in this empire.

And here it may perhaps divert the curious reader, to give some account of my domestic, and my manner of living in this country, during a residence of nine months and thirteen days. Having a head mechanically turned, and being likewise forced by necessity, I had made for myself a table and chair convenient enough, out of the largest trees in the royal park. Two hundred sempstresses were employed to make me shirts, and linen for my bed and table, all of the strongest and coarsest kind they could get; which, however, they were forced to quilt together in several folds, for the thickest was some degrees finer than lawn. Their linen was usually three inches wide, and three foot make a piece. The sempstresses took my measure as I lay on the ground, one standing at my neck, and another at my mid-leg, with a strong cord extended, that each held by the end, while the third measured the length of the cord with a rule of an inch long. Then they measured my right thumb, and desired no more; for by a mathematical computation, that twice round the thumb is once round the wrist, and so on to the neck and the waist, and by the help of my old shirt, which I displayed on the ground before them for a pattern, they fitted me exactly. Three hundred tailors were employed in the same manner to make me clothes; but they had another contrivance for taking my measure. I kneeled down, and they raised a ladder from the ground to my neck; upon this ladder one of them mounted, and let fall a plumb-line from my collar to the floor, which just answered the length of my coat: but my waist and arms I measured myself. When my clothes were finished, which was done in my house, (for the largest of their would not have been able to hold them) they looked like the patchwork made by the ladies in England, only that mine were all of a color.

I had three hundred cooks to dress my victuals, in little convenient huts built about my house, where they and their families lived, and prepared me two dishes apiece. I took up twenty waiters in my hand, and placed them on the table: an hundred more attended below on the ground, some with dishes of meat, and some with barrels of wine, and other liquors, slung on their shoulders; all which the waiters above drew up as I wanted, in a very ingenious manner, by certain cords, as we draw the bucket up a well in Europe. A dish of their meat was a good mouthful, and a barrel of their liquor a reasonable draught. Their mutton yields to ours, but their beef is excellent. I have had a sirloin so large, that I have been forced to make three bites of it; but this is rare. My servants were astonished to see me eat it bones and all, as in our country we do the leg of a lark. Their geese and turkeys I usually ate at a mouthful, and I must confess they far exceed ours. Of their smaller fowl I could take up twenty or thirty at the end of my knife.

One day his Imperial Majesty, being informed of my way of living, desired that himself and his Royal Consort, with the young Princes of the blood of both sexes, might have the happiness (as he was pleased to call it) of dining with me. They came accordingly, and I placed them in chairs of state on my table, just over against me, with their guards about them. Flimnap, the Lord High Treasurer, attended there likewise with his white staff; and I observed he often looked on me with a sour countenance, which I would not seem to regard, but ate more than usual, in honor to my dear country, as well as to fill the court with admiration. I have some private reasons to believe, that this visit from his Majesty gave Flimnap an opportunity of doing me ill offices to his master. That minister had always been my secret enemy, though he outwardly caressed me more than was usual to the moroseness of his nature. He represented to the Emperor the low condition of his treasury; that he was forced to take up money at great discount; that exchequer bills would not circulate under nine *per cent.* below par; that in short I had cost his Majesty above a million and a half of *sprugs* (their greatest gold coin, about the bigness of a spangle); and upon the whole, that it would be advisable in the Emperor to take the first fair occasion of dismissing me.

I am here obliged to vindicate the reputation of an excellent lady, who was an innocent sufferer upon my account. The Treasurer took a fancy to be jealous of his wife, from the malice of some evil tongues, who informed him that her Grace had taken a violent affection for my person; and the court-scandal ran for some time, that she once came privately to my lodging. This I solemnly declare to be a most infamous falsehood, without any grounds, farther than that her Grace was pleased to treat me with all innocent marks of freedom and friendship. I own she came often to my house, but always publicly, nor ever without three more in the coach, who were usually her sister and young daughter, and some particular acquaintance; but this was common to many other ladies of the court. And I still appeal to my servants round, whether they at any time saw a coach at my door without knowing what persons were in it. On those occasions, when a servant had given me notice, my custom was to go immediately to the door; and, after paying my respects, to take up the coach and two horses very carefully in my hands (for, if there were six horses, the postillion always unharnessed four), and place them on a table, where I had fixed a moveable rim quite round, of five inches high, to prevent accidents. And I have often had four coaches and horses at once on my table full of company, while I sat in my chair leaning my face towards them; and when I was engaged with one set, the coachmen would gently drive the others round my table. I have passed many an afternoon very agreeably in these conversations. But I defy the Treasurer, or his two informers (I will name them, and let them make their best of it) Clustril and Drunlo, to prove that any person ever came to me *incognito*, except the secretary Reldresal, who was sent by express command of his Imperial Majesty, as I have before related. I should not have dwelt so long upon this particular, if it had not been a point wherein the reputation of a great lady is so nearly concerned, to say nothing of my own; though I then had the honor to be a *Nardac*, which the Treasurer himself is not; for all the world knows he is only a *Clumglum*, a title inferior by one degree, as that of a Marquis is to a Duke in England, although I allow he preceded me in right of his post. These false informations, which I afterwards came to the knowledge of, by an accident not proper to mention, made Flimnap, the Treasurer, show his lady for some time an ill countenance, and me a worse; and although he were at last undeceived and reconciled to her, yet I lost all credit with him, and found my interest decline very fast with the Emperor himself, who was indeed too much governed by that favorite.

CHAPTER VII

The Author, being informed of a design to accuse him of high treason, makes his escape to Blefuscu. His reception there.

Before I proceed to give an account of my leaving this kingdom, it may be proper to inform the reader of a private intrigue which had been for two months forming against me.

I had been hitherto all my life a stranger to courts, for which I was unqualified by the meanness of my condition. I had indeed heard and read enough of the dispositions of great princes and ministers; but never expected to have found such terrible effects of them in so remote a country, governed, as I thought, by very different maxims from those in Europe.

When I was just preparing to pay my attendance on the Emperor of Blefuscu, a considerable person at court (to whom I had been very serviceable at a time when he lay under the highest displeasure of his Imperial Majesty) came to my house very privately at night in a close chair, and without sending his name, desired admittance. The chairmen were dismissed; I put the chair, with his Lordship in it, into my coat-pocket: and giving orders to a trusty servant to say I was indisposed and gone to sleep, I fastened the door of my house, placed the chair on the table, according to my usual custom, and sat down by it. After the common salutations were over, observing his Lordship's countenance full of concern, and inquiring into the reason, he desired I would hear him with patience in a matter that highly concerned my honor and my life. His speech was to the following effect, for I took notes of it as soon as he left me.

You are to know, said he, that several Committees of Council have been lately called in the most private manner on your account; and it is but two days since his Majesty came to a full resolution.

You are very sensible that Skyresh Bolgolam (*Galbet*, or High-Admiral) hath been your mortal enemy almost ever since your arrival. His original reasons I know not; but his hatred is much increased since your great success against Blefuscu, by which his glory, as Admiral, is obscured. This Lord, in conjunction with Flimnap the High-Treasurer, whose enmity against you is notorious on account of his lady, Limtoc the General, Lalcon the Chamberlain, and Balmuff the Grand Justiciary, have prepared articles of impeachment against you, for treason, and other capital crimes.

This preface made me so impatient, being conscious of my own merits and innocence, that I was going to interrupt; when he entreated me to be silent, and thus proceeded.

Out of gratitude for the favors you have done me, I procured information of the whole proceedings, and a copy of the articles, wherein I venture my head for your service.

Articles of Impeachment against Quinbus Flestrin (the Man-Mountain)

ARTICLE I

Whereas, by a statute made in the reign of his Imperial Majesty Calin Deffar Plune, it is enacted, that whoever shall make water within the precincts of the royal palace, shall be liable to the pains and penalties of high treason; notwithstanding, the said Quinbus Flestrin, in open breach of the said law, under color of extinguishing the fire kindled in the apartment of his Majesty's most dear Imperial Consort, did maliciously, traitorously, and devilishly, by discharge of his urine, put out the said fire kindled in the said apartment, lying and being within the precincts of the said royal palace, against the statute in that case provided, *etc.*, against the duty, *etc.*

ARTICLE II

That the said Quinbus Flestrin having brought the imperial fleet of Blefuscu into the royal port, and being afterwards commanded by his Imperial Majesty to seize all the other ships of the said empire of Blefuscu, and reduce that empire to a province, to be governed by a viceroy from hence, and to destroy and put to death not only all the Big-Endian exiles, but likewise all the people of that empire, who would not immediately forsake the Big-Endian heresy: He, the said Flestrin, like a false traitor against his most Auspicious, Serene, Imperial Majesty, did petition to be excused from the said service, upon pretense of unwillingness to force the consciences, or destroy the liberties and lives of an innocent people.

ARTICLE III

That, whereas certain ambassadors arrived from the court of Blefuscu, to sue for peace in his Majesty's court: He, the said Flestrin, did, like a false traitor, aid, abet, comfort, and divert the said ambassadors, although he knew them to be servants to a Prince who was lately an open enemy to his Imperial Majesty, and in open war against his said Majesty.

ARTICLE IV

That the said Quinbus Flestrin, contrary to the duty of a faithful subject, is now preparing to make a voyage to the court and empire of Blefuscu, for which he hath received only verbal license from his Imperial Majesty; and under color of the said license, doth falsely and traitorously intend to take the said voyage, and thereby to aid, comfort, and abet the Emperor of Blefuscu, so late an enemy, and in open war with his Imperial Majesty aforesaid.

There are some other articles, but these are the most important, of which I have read you an abstract.

In the several debates upon this impeachment, it must be confessed that his Majesty gave many marks of his great lenity, often urging the services you had done him, and endeavoring to extenuate your crimes. The Treasurer and Admiral insisted that you should be put to the most painful and ignominious death, by setting fire on your house at night, and the General was to attend with twenty thousand men armed with poisoned arrows to shoot you on the face and hands. Some of your servants were to have private orders to strew a poisonous juice on your shirts, which would soon make you tear your own flesh, and die in the utmost torture. The General came into the same opinion; so that for a long time there was a majority against you. But his Majesty resolving, if possible, to spare your life, at last brought off the Chamberlain.

Upon this incident, Reldresal, principal Secretary for Private Affairs, who always approved himself your true friend, was commanded by the Emperor to deliver his opinion, which he accordingly did; and therein justified the good thoughts you have of him. He allowed your crimes to be great, but that still there was room for mercy, the most commendable virtue in a prince, and for which his Majesty was so justly celebrated. He said, the friendship between you and him was so well known to the world, that perhaps the most honorable board might think him partial: however, in obedience to the command he had received, he would freely offer his sentiments. That if his Majesty, in consideration of your services, and pursuant to his own merciful disposition, would please to spare your life, and only give orders to put out both your eyes, he humbly conceived, that by this expedient, justice might in some measure be satisfied, and all the world would applaud the lenity of the Emperor, as well as the fair and generous proceedings of those who have the honor to be his counselors. That the loss of your eyes would be no impediment to your bodily strength, by which you might still be useful to his Majesty. That blindness is an addition to courage, by concealing dangers from us; that the fear you had for your eyes, was the greatest difficulty in bringing over the enemy's fleet, and it would be sufficient for you to see by the eyes of the ministers, since the greatest princes do no more.

This proposal was received with the utmost disapprobation by the whole board. Bolgolam, the Admiral, could not preserve his temper; but rising up in fury, said, he wondered how the Secretary durst presume to give his opinion for preserving the life of a traitor: that the services you had performed, were, by all true reasons of state, the great aggravation of your crimes; that you, who were able to extinguish the fire, by discharge of urine in her Majesty's apartment (which he mentioned with horror), might, at another time, raise an inundation by the same means, to drown the whole palace; and the same strength which enabled you to bring over the enemy's fleet, might serve, upon the first discontent, to carry it back: that he had good reasons to think you were a Big-Endian in your heart; and as treason begins in the heart, before it appears in overt acts, so he accused you as a traitor on that account, and therefore insisted you should be put to death.

The Treasurer was of the same opinion; he showed to what straits his Majesty's revenue was reduced by the charge of maintaining you, which would soon grow insupportable: that the Secretary's expedient of putting out your eyes was so far from being a remedy against this evil, that it would probably increase it, as it is manifest from the common practice of blinding some kind of fowl, after which they fed the faster, and grew sooner fat: that his sacred Majesty and the Council, who are your judges, were in their own consciences fully convinced of your guilt, which was a sufficient argument to condemn you to death, without the formal proofs required by the strict letter of the law.

But his Imperial Majesty, fully determined against capital punishment, was graciously pleased to say, that since the Council thought the loss of your eyes too easy a censure, some other may be inflicted hereafter. And your friend the Secretary humbly desiring to be heard again, in answer to what the Treasurer had objected concerning the great charge his Majesty was at in maintaining you, said, that his Excellency, who had the sole disposal of the Emperor's revenue, might easily provide against that evil, by gradually lessening your establishment; by which, for want of sufficient food, you would grow weak and faint, and lose your appetite, and consequently decay and consume in a few months; neither would the stench of your carcass be then so dangerous, when it should become more than half diminished; and immediately upon your death, five or six thousand of his Majesty's subjects might, in two or three days, cut your flesh from your bones, take it away by cart-loads, and bury it in distant parts to prevent infection, leaving the skeleton as a monument of admiration to posterity.

Thus by the great friendship of the Secretary, the whole affair was compromised. It was strictly enjoined, that the project of starving you by degrees should be kept a secret, but the sentence of putting out your eyes was entered on the books; none dissenting except Bolgolam the Admiral, who, being a creature of the Empress, was perpetually instigated by her Majesty to insist upon your death, she having borne perpetual malice against you, on account of that infamous and illegal method you took to extinguish the fire in her apartment.

In three days your friend the Secretary will be directed to come to your house, and read before you the articles of impeachment; and then to signify the great lenity and favor of his Majesty and Council, whereby you are only condemned to the loss of your eyes, which his Majesty doth not question you will gratefully and humbly submit to; and twenty of his Majesty's surgeons will attend, in order to see the operation well performed, by discharging very sharp-pointed arrows into the balls of your eyes, as you lie on the ground.

I leave to your prudence what measures you will take; and to avoid suspicion, I must immediately return in as private a manner as I came.

His Lordship did so, and I remained alone, under many doubts and perplexities of mind.

It was a custom introduced by this prince and his ministry (very different, as I have been assured, from the practices of former times), that after the court had decreed any cruel execution, either to gratify the monarch's resentment, or the malice of a favorite, the Emperor always made a speech to his whole Council, expressing his great lenity and tenderness, as qualities known and confessed by all the world. This speech was immediately published through the kingdom; nor did anything terrify the people so much as those encomiums on his Majesty's mercy; because it was observed, that the more these praises were enlarged and insisted on, the more inhuman was the punishment, and the sufferer more innocent. And as to myself, I must confess, having never been designed for a courtier either by my birth or education, I was so ill a judge of things, that I could not discover the lenity and favor of his sentence, but conceived it (perhaps erroneously) rather to be rigorous than gentle. I sometimes thought of standing my trial, for although I could not deny the facts alleged in the several articles, yet I hoped they would admit of some extenuations. But having in my life perused many state-trials, which I ever observed to terminate as the judges thought fit to direct, I durst not rely on so dangerous a decision, in so critical a juncture, and against such powerful enemies. Once I was strongly bent upon resistance, for while I had liberty, the whole strength of that empire could hardly subdue me, and I might easily with stones pelt the metropolis to pieces; but I soon rejected that project with horror, by remembering the oath I had made to the Emperor, the favors I received from him, and the high title of *Nardac* he conferred upon me. Neither had I so soon learned the gratitude of courtiers, to persuade myself that his Majesty's present severities acquitted me of all past obligations.

At last I fixed upon a resolution, for which it is probable I may incur some censure, and not unjustly; for I confess I owe the preserving my eyes, and consequently my liberty, to my own great rashness and want of experience: because if I had then known the nature of princes and ministers, which I have since observed in many other courts, and their methods of treating criminals less obnoxious than myself, I should with great alacrity and readiness have submitted to so easy a punishment. But hurried on by the precipitancy of youth, and having his Imperial Majesty's license to pay my attendance upon the Emperor of Blefuscu, I took this opportunity, before the three days were elapsed, to send a letter to my friend the Secretary, signifying my resolution of setting out that morning for Blefuscu pursuant to the leave I had got; and without waiting for an answer, I went to that side of the island where our fleet lay. I seized a large man of war, tied a cable to the prow, and, lifting up the anchors, I stripped myself, put my clothes (together with my coverlet, which I brought under my arm) into the vessel, and drawing it after me between wading and swimming, arrived at the royal port of Blefuscu, where the people had long expected me: they lent me two guides to direct me to the capital city, which is of the same name. I held them in my hands till I came within two hundred yards of the gate, and desired them to signify my arrival to one of the secretaries, and let him know, I there waited his Majesty's command. I had an answer in about an hour, that his Majesty, attended by the Royal Family, and great officers of the court, was coming out to receive me. I advanced a hundred yards. The Emperor and his train alighted from their horses, the Empress and ladies from their coaches, and I did not perceive they were in any fright or concern. I lay on the ground to kiss his Majesty's and the Empress's hands. I told his Majesty, that I was come according to my promise, and with the license of the Emperor my master, to have the honor of seeing so mighty a monarch, and to offer him any service in my power, consistent with my duty to my own prince; not mentioning a word of my disgrace, because I had hitherto no regular information of it, and might suppose myself wholly ignorant of any such design; neither could I reasonably conceive that the Emperor would discover the secret while I was out of his power: wherein, however, it soon appeared I was deceived.

I shall not trouble the reader with the particular account of my reception at this court, which was suitable to the generosity of so great a prince; nor of the difficulties I was in for want of a house and bed, being forced to lie on the ground, wrapped up in my coverlet.

CHAPTER VIII

The Author, by a lucky accident, finds means to leave Blefuscu: *and, after some difficulties, returns safe to his native country.*

THREE days after my arrival, walking out of curiosity to the north-east coast of the island, I observed, about half a league off, in the sea, somewhat that looked like a boat overturned. I pulled off my shoes and stockings, and wading two or three hundred yards, I found the object to approach nearer by force of the tide; and then plainly saw it to be a real boat, which I supposed might, by some tempest, have been driven from a ship; whereupon I returned immediately towards the city, and desired his Imperial Majesty to lend me twenty of the tallest vessels he had left after the loss of his fleet, and three thousand seamen under the command of his Vice-Admiral. This fleet sailed round, while I went back the shortest way to the coast where I first discovered the boat; I found the tide had driven it still nearer. The seamen were all provided with cordage, which I had beforehand twisted to a sufficient strength. When the ships came up, I stripped myself, and waded till I came within an hundred yards of the boat, after which I was forced to swim till I got up to it. The seamen threw me the end of the cord, which I fastened to a hole in the fore-part of the boat, and the other end to a man of war; but I found all my labor to little purpose; for being out of my depth, I was not able to work. In this necessity, I was forced to swim behind, and push the boat forwards as often as I could, with one of my hands; and the tide favoring me, I advanced so far, that I could just hold up my chin and feel the ground. I rested two or three minutes, and then gave the boat another shove, and so on till the sea was no higher than my arm-pits; and now the most laborious part being over, I took out my other cables, which were stowed in one of the ships, and fastening them first to the boat, and then to nine of the vessels which attended me; the wind being favorable, the seamen towed, and I shoved till we arrived within forty yards of the shore; and waiting till the tide was out, I got dry to the boat, and by the assistance of two thousand men, with ropes and engines, I made a shift to turn it on its bottom, and found it was but little damaged.

I shall not trouble the reader with the difficulties I was under by the help of certain paddles, which cost me ten days making, to get my boat to the royal port of Blefuscu, where a mighty concourse of people appeared upon my arrival, full of wonder at the sight of so prodigious a vessel. I told the Emperor that my good fortune had thrown this boat in my way, to carry me to some place from whence I might return into my native country, and begged his Majesty's orders for getting materials to fit it up, together with his license to depart; which, after some kind expostulations, he was pleased to grant.

I did very much wonder, in all this time, not to have heard of any express relating to me from our Emperor to the court of Blefuscu. But I was afterwards given privately to understand, that his Imperial Majesty, never imagining I had the least notice of his designs, believed I was only gone to Blefuscu in performance of my promise, according to the license he had given me, which was well known at our court, and would return in a few days when that ceremony was ended. But he was at last in pain at my long absence; and after consulting with the Treasurer, and the rest of that cabal, a person of quality was dispatched with the copy of the articles against me. This envoy had instructions to represent to the monarch of Blefuscu, the great lenity of his master, who was content to punish me no farther than with the loss of my eyes; that I had fled from justice, and if I did not return in two hours, I should be deprived of my title of *Nardac*, and declared a traitor. The envoy further added, that in order to maintain the peace and amity between both empires, his master expected that his brother of Blefuscu would give orders to have me sent back to Lilliput, bound hand and foot, to be punished as a traitor.

The Emperor of Blefuscu having taken three days to consult, returned an answer consisting of many civilities and excuses. He said, that as for sending me bound, his brother knew it was impossible; that although I had deprived him of his fleet, yet he owed great obligations to me for many good offices I had done him in making the peace. That, however, both their Majesties would soon be made easy; for I had found a prodigious vessel on the shore, able to carry me on the sea, which he had given order to fit up with my own assistance and direction and he hoped in a few weeks both empires would be freed from so insupportable an incumbrance.

With this answer the envoy returned to Lilliput, and the monarch of Blefuscu related to me all that had passed; offering me at the same time (but under the strictest confidence) his gracious protection, if I would continue in his service; wherein although I believed him sincere, yet I resolved never more to put any confidence in princes or ministers, where I could possibly avoid it; and therefore, with all due acknowledgments for his favorable intentions, I humbly begged to be excused. I told him, that since fortune, whether good or evil, had thrown a vessel in my way, I was resolved to venture myself in the ocean, rather than be an occasion of difference between two such mighty monarchs. Neither did I find the Emperor at all displeased; and I discovered by a certain accident, that he was very glad of my resolution, and so were most of his ministers.

These considerations moved me to hasten my departure somewhat sooner than I intended; to which the court, impatient to have me gone, very readily contributed. Five hundred workmen were employed to make two sails to my boat, according to my directions, by quilting thirteen fold of their strongest linen together. I was at the pains of making ropes and cables, by twisting ten, twenty, or thirty of the thickest and strongest of theirs. A great stone that I happened to find, after a long search, by the sea-shore, served me for an anchor. I had the tallow of three hundred cows for greasing my boat, and other uses. I was at incredible pains in cutting down some of the largest timber-trees for oars and masts, wherein I was, however, much assisted by his Majesty's ship-carpenters, who helped me in smoothing them, after I had done the rough work.

In about a month, when all was prepared, I sent to receive his Majesty's commands, and take my leave. The Emperor and Royal Family came out of the palace; I lay down on my face to kiss his hand, which he very graciously gave me: so did the Empress and young Princes of the blood. His Majesty presented me with fifty purses of two hundred *sprugs* apiece, together with his picture at full length, which I put immediately into one of my gloves, to keep it from being hurt. The ceremonies at my departure were too many to trouble the reader with at this time.

I stored the boat with the carcasses of an hundred oxen, and three hundred sheep, with bread and drink proportionable, and as much meat ready dressed as four hundred cooks could provide. I took with me six cows and two bulls alive, with as many ewes and rams, intending to carry them into my own country, and propagate the breed. And to feed them on board, I had a good bundle of hay, and a bag of corn. I would gladly have taken a dozen of the natives, but this was a thing the Emperor would by no means permit; and besides a diligent search into my pockets, his Majesty engaged my honor not to carry away any of his subjects, although with their own consent and desire.

Having thus prepared all things as well as I was able, I set sail on the twenty-fourth day of September, 1701, at six in the morning; and when I had gone about four leagues to the northward, the wind being at southeast, at six in the evening I descried a small island about half a league to the north-west. I advanced forward, and cast anchor on the lee-side of the island, which seemed to be uninhabited. I then took some refreshment, and went to my rest. I slept well, and as I conjecture at least six hours, for I found the day broke in two hours after I awaked. It was a clear night. I ate my breakfast before the sun was up; and heaving anchor, the wind being favorable, I steered the same course that I had done the day before, wherein I was directed by my pocket-compass. My intention was to reach, if possible, one of those islands, which I had reason to believe lay to the north-east of Van Diemen's Land. I discovered nothing all that day; but upon the next, about three in the afternoon, when I had by my computation made twenty-four leagues from Blefuscu, I descried a sail steering to the south-east; my course was due east. I hailed her, but could get no answer; yet I found I gained upon her, for the wind slackened. I made all the sail I could, and in half an hour she spied me, then hung out her ancient, and discharged a gun. It is not easy to express the joy I was in upon the unexpected hope of once more seeing my beloved country, and the dear pledges I had left in it. The ship slackened her sails, and I came up with her between five and six in the evening, September 26; but my heart leaped within me to see her English colors. I put my cows and sheep into my coat-pockets, and got on board with all my little cargo of provisions. The vessel was an English merchantman returning from Japan by the North and South Seas; the Captain, Mr. John Biddel of Deptford, a very civil man, and an excellent sailor. We were now in the latitude of 30 degrees south; there were about fifty men in the ship; and here I met an old comrade of mine, one Peter Williams, who gave me a good character to the Captain. This gentleman treated me with kindness, and desired I would let him know what place I came from last, and whither I was bound; which I did in a few words, but he thought I was raving, and that the dangers I underwent had disturbed my head; whereupon I took my black cattle and sheep out of my pocket, which, after great astonishment, clearly convinced him of my veracity. I then showed him the gold given me by the Emperor of Blefuscu, together with his Majesty's picture at full length, and some other rarities of that country. I gave him two purses of two hundred *sprugs* each, and promised, when we arrived in England, to make him a present of a cow and a sheep big with young.

I shall not trouble the reader with a particular account of this voyage, which was very prosperous for the most part. We arrived in the Downs on the 13th of April, 1702. I had only one misfortune, that the rats on board carried away one of my sheep; I found her bones in a hole, picked clean from the flesh. The rest of my cattle I got safe on shore, and set them a grazing in a bowling-green at Greenwich, where the fineness of the grass made them feed very heartily, though I had always feared the contrary: neither could I possibly have preserved them in so long a voyage, if the Captain had not allowed me some of his best biscuit, which, rubbed to powder, and mingled with water, was their constant food. The short time I continued in England, I made a considerable profit by showing my cattle to many persons of quality, and others: and before I began my second voyage, I sold them for six hundred pounds. Since my last return, I find the breed is considerably increased, especially the sheep; which I hope will prove much to the advantage of the woolen manufacture, by the fineness of the fleeces.

I stayed but two months with my wife and family; for my insatiable desire of seeing foreign countries would suffer me to continue no longer. I left fifteen hundred pounds with my wife, and fixed her in a good house at Redriff. My remaining stock I carried with me, part in money, and part in goods, in hopes to improve my fortunes. My eldest uncle John had left me an estate in land, near Epping, of about thirty pounds a year; and I had a long lease of the Black Bull in Fetter-Lane, which yielded me as much more; so that I was not in any danger of leaving my family upon the parish. My son Johnny, named so after his uncle, was at the Grammar School, and a towardly child. My daughter Betty (who is now well married, and has children) was then at her needle-work. I took leave of my wife, and boy and girl, with tears on both sides, and went on board the *Adventure*, a merchant-ship of three hundred tons, bound for Surat, Captain John Nicholas, of Liverpool, Commander. But my account of this voyage must be referred to the second part of my Travels.

ALEXANDER POPE (1688–1744)

What Dryden was in the latter part of the seventeenth century Pope became in the first half of the eighteenth—the foremost man of letters of the age and the acknowledged arbiter of literary taste. Pope was born in the year of the Revolution, on 21 May. His father was a London merchant and a Roman Catholic. The latter fact colored Pope's whole life, because for many years after the Revolution Catholics suffered oppressive disabilities, both social and legal, which marked them as a class apart from the rest of the nation and almost forced them to live in an atmosphere of suspicion, intrigue, and evasion of the law. Among other things, they were debarred from the universities, they were burdened with heavy taxes, and they could hold no public offices. Pope, moreover, always refused to change his religion, although the heaviest inducements were held before him from time to time, and although, too, his adherence to Catholicism was merely formal, the result rather of filial piety than of personal conviction. It is doubtful, however, if Pope would have been able to attend one of the universities, even had his parents been Church-of-England people, for from his birth he was deformed, and delicate in health. In his *Epistle to Arbuthnot* he described his life as one long disease, which was scarcely an exaggeration, as there must have been hardly a day when he was free from pain and his face was lined and contorted from his intense sufferings. His education was largely got through his own eager and wide reading in classical and English poetry, with the result that his scholarship remained always seriously defective and that he had no methodical training save such as was administered by his father in the correction of his youthful verses. He was a precocious boy, and determined at an early age to be a poet. At an early age, too, he succeeded in attracting the interest of several men of taste and cultivation, at least one of whom, William Walsh, deserves to be mentioned in any account of Pope. For "knowing Walsh," whether he exerted a decisive influence or not, marked out precisely the direction in which Pope was to travel. "He used to encourage me much," Pope in later years wrote to a friend, "and used to tell me there was one way left of excelling: for though we had several great poets, we never had any one great poet that was *correct;* and he desired me to make that my study and aim." Pope did so; and in correctness of form, in clarity, pointed wit, polish, studied concision, smoothness, and metrical precision, Pope excelled remarkably, as is witnessed, for example, by the number of familiar sayings he has given to the English-speaking world, and as no one who reads more than a few pages of him needs to be told.

Pope's *Pastorals* were his first published poems, printed in 1709, but written, as he always claimed, when he was only sixteen years old. These were followed by his *Essay on Criticism* in 1711 and by his *Rape of the Lock,* in its earlier form, in 1712. These poems made his reputation immediately, placing him by general consent at the head of living poets. He was, however, poor, and could not expect, on account of his Catholicism, either public office or a pension, the usual rewards bestowed on successful and useful men of letters by the government in his day. Consequently Pope had to find some new way of securing an income, and he found it. In 1713 he issued proposals for a translation of the *Iliad,* inviting immediate subscriptions in support of the project, Warm friends helped him with enthusiasm to secure subscriptions, a publisher offered him a large sum for the right of publication, and, as the combined result of his reputation and of his persistent hard work with the translation, Pope managed to clear over £5000 on the work, and later made another large sum when, with the help of assistants, he translated the *Odyssey.* Such profits from literary work were unprecedented, and they were sufficient to enable Pope to buy a country house with a small estate at Twickenham and to live there comfortably through the remainder of his life, independent of private patronage or the favor of public men.

The *Essay on Criticism,* though didactic in character, had shown Pope's gift as a satirist, and his greatest success came in that field, particularly in the *Dunciad* and in the poems collected under the title, *Satires and Epistles.* Pope's satire was never, like Dryden's, political; and though in *The Rape of the Lock* his ridicule was general, he chiefly devoted himself to personal satire. In this he was biting, even venomous, and he has often been blamed for the number and virulence of his enmities, for his spitefulness, and for his treachery. It cannot be pretended that Pope's character had many edifying qualities, yet no one who has not read widely in the literature of the early eighteenth century can know the extent and kind of provocation he had for his angry retorts. And despite all blemishes and all limitations he remains an arresting figure in his own right, besides embodying more completely than any of his contemporaries the classicism of his age.

ODE ON SOLITUDE[1]

Happy the man whose wish and care
 A few paternal acres bound,
Content to breathe his native air
 In his own ground.

Whose herds with milk, whose fields with bread,
 Whose flocks supply him with attire,
Whose trees in summer yield him shade,
 In winter fire.

Bless'd, who can unconcern'dly find
 Hours, days, and years slide soft away,
In health of body, peace of mind,
 Quiet by day,

Sound sleep by night; study and ease
 Together mixed; sweet recreation;
And Innocence, which most does please,
 With meditation.

Thus let me live, unseen, unknown,
 Thus unlamented let me die;
Steal from the world, and not a stone
 Tell where I lie.

AN ESSAY ON CRITICISM[2]

CONTENTS

Part I

Introduction. That 'tis as great a fault to judge ill, as to write ill, and a more dangerous one to the public, v. 1. That a true Taste is as rare to be found, as a true Genius, v. 9 to 18. That most men are born with some Taste, but spoiled by false Education, v. 19 to 25. The multitude of Critics, and causes of them, v. 26 to 45. That we are to study our own Taste, and know the Limits of it, v. 46 to 67. Nature the best guide of Judgment, v. 68 to 87. Improved by Art and Rules, which are but methodized Nature, 88. Rules derived from the Practice of the Ancient Poets, *v. id.* to 110. That therefore the Ancients are necessary to be studied, by a Critic, particularly Homer and Virgil, v. 120 to 138. Of Licenses, and the use of them by the Ancients, v. 140 to 180. Reverence due to the Ancients, and praise of them, v. 181, *etc.*

Part II. Ver. 201, *etc.*

Causes hindering a true Judgment. 1. Pride, v. 208. 2. Imperfect Learning, v. 215. 3. Judging by parts, and not by the whole, v. 233 to 288. Critics in Wit, Language, Versification, only, v. 288, 305, 399, *etc.* 4. Being too hard to please, or too apt to admire, v. 384. 5. Partiality—too much Love to a Sect—to the Ancients or Moderns, v. 394. 6. Prejudice or Prevention, v. 408. 7. Singularity, v. 424. 8. Inconstancy, v. 430. 9. Party Spirit, v. 452, *etc.* 10. Envy, v. 466. Against Envy, and in praise of Good-nature, v. 508, *etc.* When Severity is chiefly to be used by Critics, v. 526, *etc.*

Part III. Ver. 560, *etc.*

Rules for the Conduct of Manners in a Critic. 1. Candor, v. 563. Modesty, v. 566. Good-breeding, v. 572. Sincerity, and Freedom of advice, v. 578. 2. When one's Counsel is to be restrained, v. 584. Character of an incorrigible Poet, v. 600. And of an impertinent Critic, v. 610, *etc.* Character of a good Critic, v. 629. The History of Criticism, and Characters of the best Critics, Aristotle, v. 645. Horace, v. 653. Dionysius, v. 665. Petronius, v. 667. Quintilian, v. 670. Longinus, v. 675. Of the Decay of Criticism, and its Revival. Erasmus, v. 693. Vida, v. 705. Boileau, v. 714. Lord Roscommon, *etc.*, v. 725. Conclusion.

PART I

'Tis hard to say, if greater want of skill
Appear in writing or in judging ill;
But, of the two, less dang'rous is th' offense
To tire our patience, than mislead our sense.
Some few in that, but numbers err in this,
Ten censure wrong for one who writes amiss;
A fool might once himself alone expose,
Now one in verse makes many more in prose.
 'Tis with our judgments as our watches, none
Go just alike, yet each believes his own.
In Poets as true genius is but rare,
True Taste as seldom is the Critic's share;
Both must alike from Heav'n derive their light,
These born to judge, as well as those to write.
Let such teach others who themselves excel,
And censure freely who have written well.
Authors are partial to their wit, 'tis true,
But are not Critics to their judgment too?
 Yet if we look more closely, we shall find
Most have the seeds of judgment in their mind:
Nature affords at least a glimm'ring light;
The lines, though touched but faintly, are drawn right.

[1] According to Pope himself this poem was written when he was only twelve years old, in 1700. Pope's statements about the dates of his earlier works are unreliable, and it seems unlikely that this one can be true. In any case, however, this is in all probability the earliest poem by Pope which has been preserved.

[2] Pope began to write the *Essay* perhaps as early as 1707. It was finished in 1709, and published in 1711.

But as the slightest sketch, if justly traced,
Is by ill-coloring but the more disgraced,
So by false learning is good sense defaced:
Some are bewildered in the maze of schools,
And some made coxcombs Nature meant but fools.
In search of wit these lose their common sense,
And then turn Critics in their own defense:
Each burns alike, who can, or cannot write,
Or with a Rival's, or an Eunuch's spite.
All fools have still an itching to deride,
And fain would be upon the laughing side.
If Mævius[1] scribble in Apollo's spite,
There are who judge still worse than he can write.

Some have at first for Wits, then Poets passed,
Turned Critics next, and proved plain fools at last.
Some neither can for Wits nor Critics pass,
As heavy mules are neither horse nor ass.
Those half-learn'd witlings, num'rous in our isle,
As half-formed insects on the banks of Nile;
Unfinished things, one knows not what to call,
Their generation's so equivocal:
To tell 'em, would a hundred tongues require,
Or one vain wit's, that might a hundred tire.

But you who seek to give and merit fame,
And justly bear a Critic's noble name,
Be sure yourself and your own reach to know,
How far your genius, taste, and learning go;
Launch not beyond your depth, but be discreet,
And mark that point where sense and dullness meet.

Nature to all things fixed the limits fit,
And wisely curbed proud man's pretending wit.
As on the land while here the ocean gains,
In other parts it leaves wide sandy plains;
Thus in the soul while memory prevails,
The solid pow'r of understanding fails;
Where beams of warm imagination play,
The memory's soft figures melt away.
One science only will one genius fit;
So vast is art, so narrow human wit:
Not only bounded to peculiar arts,
But oft in those confined to single parts.
Like kings we lose the conquests gained before,
By vain ambition still to make them more;
Each might his sev'ral province well command,
Would all but stoop to what they understand.

First follow Nature, and your judgment frame
By her just standard, which is still the same:
Unerring Nature, still divinely bright,
One clear, unchanged, and universal light,
Life, force, and beauty, must to all impart,
At once the source, and end, and test of Art.
Art from that fund each just supply provides,
Works without show, and without pomp presides:
In some fair body thus th' informing soul
With spirits feeds, with vigor fills the whole,
Each motion guides, and ev'ry nerve sustains;
Itself unseen, but in th' effects, remains.
Some, to whom Heav'n in wit has been profuse,
Want as much more, to turn it to its use;
For wit and judgment often are at strife,
Though meant each other's aid, like man and wife.
'Tis more to guide, than spur the Muse's steed;
Restrain his fury, than provoke his speed;
The wingéd courser, like a gen'rous horse,
Shows most true mettle when you check his course.

Those Rules of old discovered, not devised,
Are Nature still, but Nature methodized;
Nature, like liberty, is but restrained
By the same laws which first herself ordained.

Hear how learn'd Greece her useful rules indites,
When to repress, and when indulge our flights.
High on Parnassus' top her sons she showed,
And pointed out those arduous paths they trod;
Held from afar, aloft, th' immortal prize,
And urged the rest by equal steps to rise.
Just precepts thus from great examples giv'n,
She drew from them what they derived from Heav'n.
The gen'rous Critic fanned the Poet's fire,
And taught the world with reason to admire.
Then Criticism the Muse's handmaid proved,
To dress her charms, and make her more belov'd:
But following wits from that intention strayed,
Who could not win the mistress, wooed the maid;
Against the Poets their own arms they turned,
Sure to hate most the men from whom they learned.
So modern 'Pothecaries, taught the art
By Doctors' bills to play the Doctor's part,
Bold in the practice of mistaken rules,
Prescribe, apply, and call their masters fools.
Some on the leaves of ancient authors prey,
Nor time nor moths e'er spoiled so much as they.
Some dryly plain, without invention's aid,
Write dull receipts how poems may be made.
These leave the sense, their learning to display,

[1]A Roman poet of no ability, whose name has been preserved by Virgil and Horace.

criticism of lack of methodizing in Shakespeare; he did not adhere to rules.
As Romantic writers come there is deffinite breaking from laws.

And those explain the meaning quite away.
You then whose judgment the right course would steer,
Know well each Ancient's proper character;
His fable, subject, scope in ev'ry page;
Religion, Country, genius of his Age:
Without all these at once before your eyes,
Cavil you may, but never criticize.
Be Homer's works your study and delight,
Read them by day, and meditate by night;
Thence form your judgment, thence your maxims bring,
And trace the Muses upward to their spring.
Still with itself compared, his text peruse;
And let your comment be the Mantuan Muse.
When first young Maro[1] in his boundless mind
A work t' outlast immortal Rome designed,
Perhaps he seemed above the critic's law,
And but from Nature's fountains scorned to draw:
But when t' examine every part he came,
Nature and Homer were, he found, the same.
Convinced, amazed, he checks the bold design;
And rules as strict his labored work confine,
As if the Stagirite[2] o'erlooked each line.
Learn hence for ancient rules a just esteem;
To copy nature is to copy them.
Some beauties yet no Precepts can declare,
For there's a happiness as well as care.
Music resembles Poetry, in each
Are nameless graces which no methods teach,
And which a master-hand alone can reach.
If, where the rules not far enough extend
(Since rules were made but to promote their end),
Some lucky License answer to the full
Th' intent proposed, that License is a rule.
Thus Pegasus, a nearer way to take,
May boldly deviate from the common track;
From vulgar bounds with brave disorder part,
And snatch a grace beyond the reach of art,
Which without passing through the judgment, gains
The heart, and all its end at once attains.
In prospects thus, some objects please our eyes,
Which out of nature's common order rise,
The shapeless rock, or hanging precipice.
Great wits sometimes may gloriously offend,
And rise to faults true Critics dare not mend.
But though the Ancients thus their rules invade
(As Kings dispense with laws themselves have made),
Moderns, beware! or if you must offend
Against the precept, ne'er transgress its End;
Let it be seldom, and compelled by need;
And have, at least, their precedent to plead.
The Critic else proceeds without remorse,
Seizes your fame, and puts his laws in force.
I know there are, to whose presumptuous thoughts
Those freer beauties, e'en in them, seem faults.
Some figures monstrous and mis-shaped appear,
Considered singly, or beheld too near,
Which, but proportioned to their light, or place,
Due distance reconciles to form and grace.
A prudent chief not always must display
His powers in equal ranks, and fair array.
But with th' occasion and the place comply,
Conceal his force, nay seem sometimes to fly.
Those oft are stratagems which error seem,
Nor is it Homer nods, but we that dream.
Still green with bays each ancient Altar stands,
Above the reach of sacrilegious hands;
Secure from Flames, from Envy's fiercer rage,
Destructive War, and all-involving Age.
See, from each clime the learn'd their incense bring!
Hear, in all tongues consenting Pæans ring!
In praise so just let ev'ry voice be joined,
And fill the gen'ral chorus of mankind.
Hail, Bards triumphant! born in happier days;
Immortal heirs of universal praise!
Whose honors with increase of ages grow,
As streams roll down, enlarging as they flow;
Nations unborn your mighty names shall sound,
And worlds applaud that must not yet be found!
Oh may some spark of your celestial fire,
The last, the meanest of your sons inspire
(That on weak wings, from far, pursues your flights;
Glows while he reads, but trembles as he writes),
To teach vain Wits a science little known,
T' admire superior sense, and doubt their own!

PART II

Of all the Causes which conspire to blind
Man's erring judgment, and misguide the mind,
What the weak head with strongest bias rules,
Is Pride, the never-failing voice of fools.
Whatever nature has in worth denied,
She gives in large recruits of needful pride;
For as in bodies, thus in souls, we find
What wants in blood and spirits, swelled with wind:
Pride, where wit fails, steps in to our defense,
And fills up all the mighty Void of sense.
If once right reason drives that cloud away,
Truth breaks upon us with resistless day.

[1] Virgil. [2] Aristotle

Trust not yourself; but your defects to know,
Make use of ev'ry friend—and ev'ry foe.
A little learning is a dang'rous thing;
Drink deep, or taste not the Pierian spring.[1]
There shallow draughts intoxicate the brain,
And drinking largely sobers us again
Fired at first sight with what the Muse imparts,
In fearless youth we tempt the heights of Arts,
While from the bounded level of our mind
Short views we take, nor see the lengths behind;
But more advanced, behold with strange surprise
New distant scenes of endless science rise!
So pleased at first the tow'ring Alps we try,
Mount o'er the vales, and seem to tread the sky,
Th' eternal snows appear already past,
And the first clouds and mountains seem the last;
But, those attained, we tremble to survey
The growing labors of the lengthened way,
Th' increasing prospect tires our wand'ring eyes,
Hills peep o'er hills, and Alps on Alps arise!
A perfect Judge will read each work of Wit
With the same spirit that its author writ:
Survey the Whole, nor seek slight faults to find
Where nature moves, and rapture warms the mind;
Nor lose, for that malignant dull delight,
The gen'rous pleasure to be charmed with Wit.
But in such lays as neither ebb, nor flow,
Correctly cold, and regularly low,
That, shunning faults, one quiet tenor keep,
We cannot blame indeed—but we may sleep.
In wit, as nature, what affects our hearts
Is not th' exactness of peculiar parts;
'Tis not a lip, or eye, we beauty call,
But the joint force and full result of all.
Thus when we view some well-proportioned dome
(The world's just wonder, and e'en thine, O Rome![2]),
No single parts unequally surprise,
All comes united to th' admiring eyes;
No monstrous height, or breadth, or length appear;
The Whole at once is bold and regular.
Whoever thinks a faultless piece to see,
Thinks what ne'er was, nor is, nor e'er shall be.
In every work regard the writer's End,
Since none can compass more than they intend;
And if the means be just, the conduct true,
Applause, in spite of trivial faults, is due;
As men of breeding, sometimes men of wit,
T' avoid great errors, must the less commit:
Neglect the rules each verbal Critic lays,
For not to know some trifles is a praise.
Most Critics, fond of some subservient art,
Still make the Whole depend upon a Part:
They talk of principles, but notions prize,
And all to one loved Folly sacrifice.
Once on a time, La Mancha's Knight,[3] they say,
A certain bard encount'ring on the way,
Discoursed in terms as just, with looks as sage,
As e'er could Dennis[4] of the Grecian stage;
Concluding all were desp'rate sots and fools,
Who durst depart from Aristotle's rules.
Our Author, happy in a judge so nice,
Produced his Play, and begged the Knight's advice;
Made him observe the subject, and the plot,
The manners, passions, unities; what not?
All which, exact to rule, were brought about,
Were but a Combat in the lists left out.
"What! leave the Combat out?" exclaims the Knight;
Yes, or we must renounce the Stagirite.
"Not so, by Heav'n" (he answers in a rage),
"Knights, squires, and steeds, must enter on the stage."
So vast a throng the stage can ne'er contain.
"Then build a new, or act it in a plain."
Thus Critics, of less judgment than caprice,
Curious, not knowing, not exact but nice,
Form short Ideas; and offend in arts
(As most in manners) by a love to parts.
Some to Conceit alone their taste confine,
And glitt'ring thoughts struck out at ev'ry line;
Pleased with a work where nothing 's just or fit;
One glaring Chaos and wild heap of wit.
Poets like painters, thus, unskilled to trace
The naked nature and the living grace,
With gold and jewels cover ev'ry part,
And hide with ornaments their want of art.
True Wit is Nature to advantage dressed,
What oft was thought, but ne'er so well expressed;
Something, whose truth convinced at sight we find,
That gives us back the image of our mind.
As shades more sweetly recommend the light,
So modest plainness sets off sprightly wit.
For works may have more wit than does 'em good,
As bodies perish through excess of blood.
Others for Language all their care express,
And value books, as women men, for Dress:

[1]Pieria was said to be the birthplace of the muses.
[2]St. Peter's.

[3]Don Quixote.
[4]John Dennis, critic and playwright contemporary with Pope.

Their praise is still—the Style is excellent:
The Sense, they humbly take upon content.
Words are like leaves; and where they most abound,
Much fruit of sense beneath is rarely found,
False Eloquence, like the prismatic glass,
Its gaudy colors spreads on ev'ry place;
The face of Nature we no more survey,
All glares alike, without distinction gay:
But true expression, like th' unchanging Sun,
Clears and improves whate'er it shines upon,
It gilds all objects, but it alters none.
Expression is the dress of thought, and still
Appears more decent, as more suitable;
A vile conceit in pompous words expressed,
Is like a clown in regal purple dressed:
For diff'rent styles with diff'rent subjects sort,
As several garbs with country, town, and court.
Some by old words to fame have made pretense,
Ancients in phrase, mere moderns in their sense;
Such labored nothings, in so strange a style,
Amaze th' unlearn'd, and make the learnéd smile.
Unlucky, as Fungoso[1] in the play,
These sparks with awkward vanity display
What the fine gentleman wore yesterday;
And but so mimic ancient wits at best,
As apes our grandsires, in their doublets dressed.
In words, as fashions, the same rule will hold;
Alike fantastic, if too new, or old:
Be not the first by whom the new are tried,
Nor yet the last to lay the old aside.
But most by Numbers judge a Poet's song;
And smooth or rough, with them is right or wrong:
In the bright Muse though thousand charms conspire,
Her voice is all these tuneful fools admire;
Who haunt Parnassus but to please their ear,
Not mend their minds; as some to Church repair,
Not for the doctrine, but the music there.
These equal syllables alone require,
Though oft the ear the open vowels tire;
While expletives their feeble aid do join;
And ten low words oft creep in one dull line:
While they ring round the same unvaried chimes,
With sure returns of still expected rimes;
Where'er you find "the cooling western breeze,"
In the next line, it "whispers through the trees":
If crystal streams "with pleasing murmurs creep,"
The reader's threatened (not in vain) with "sleep";
Then, at the last and only couplet fraught
With some unmeaning thing they call a thought,
A needless Alexandrine ends the song
That, like a wounded snake, drags its slow length along.
Leave such to tune their own dull rimes, and know
What's roundly smooth or languishingly slow;
And praise the easy vigor of a line,
Where Denham's strength, and Waller's sweetness join.[2]
True ease in writing comes from art, not chance,
As those move easiest who have learned to dance.
'T is not enough no harshness gives offense,
The sound must seem an echo to the sense:
Soft is the strain when Zephyr gently blows,
And the smooth stream in smoother numbers flows;
But when loud surges lash the sounding shore,
The hoarse, rough verse should like the torrent roar:
When Ajax strives some rock's vast weight to throw,
The line too labors, and the words move slow;
Not so, when swift Camilla scours the plain,
Flies o'er th' unbending corn, and skims along the main.
Hear how Timotheus' varied lays surprise,
And bid alternate passions fall and rise![3]
While, at each change, the son of Libyan Jove
Now burns with glory, and then melts with love,
Now his fierce eyes with sparkling fury glow,
Now sighs steal out, and tears begin to flow:
Persians and Greeks like turns of nature found,
And the world's victor stood subdued by Sound!
The pow'r of Music all our hearts allow,
And what Timotheus was, is Dryden now.
Avoid Extremes; and shun the fault of such,
Who still are pleased too little or too much.
At ev'ry trifle scorn to take offense,
That always shows great pride, or little sense;
Those heads, as stomachs, are not sure the best,
Which nauseate all, and nothing can digest.
Yet let not each gay Turn thy rapture move;
For fools admire, but men of sense approve:

---

[1]A character in Ben Jonson's *Every Man out of His Humor.*

[2]Both poets of the mid-seventeenth century, long highly praised as the "fathers" of the plain style and the closed couplet which Dryden developed and Pope perfected.

[3]The reference in these and the following lines is to Dryden's *Alexander's Feast.*

As things seem large which we through mists descry,
Dullness is ever apt to magnify.
  Some foreign writers, some our own despise;
The Ancients only, or the Moderns prize.
Thus Wit, like Faith, by each man is applied
To one small sect, and all are damned beside.
Meanly they seek the blessing to confine,
And force that sun but on a part to shine,
Which not alone the southern wit sublimes,
But ripens spirits in cold northern climes;
Which from the first has shone on ages past,
Enlights the present, and shall warm the last;
Though each may feel increases and decays,
And see now clearer and now darker days.
Regard not then if Wit be old or new,
But blame the false, and value still the true.
  Some ne'er advance a Judgment of their own,
But catch the spreading notion of the Town;
They reason and conclude by precedent,
And own stale nonsense which they ne'er invent.
Some judge of author's names, not works, and then
Nor praise nor blame the writings, but the men.
Of all this servile herd the worst is he
That in proud dullness joins with Quality,
A constant Critic at the great man's board,
To fetch and carry nonsense for my Lord.
What woeful stuff this madrigal would be,
In some starved hackney sonneteer, or me!
But let a Lord once own the happy lines,
How the wit brightens! how the style refines!
Before his sacred name flies ev'ry fault,
And each exalted stanza teems with thought!
  The Vulgar thus through Imitation err;
As oft the Learn'd by being singular;
So much they scorn the crowd, that if the throng
By chance go right, they purposely go wrong;
So Schismatics the plain believers quit,
And are but damned for having too much wit.
Some praise at morning what they blame at night;
But always think the last opinion right.
A Muse by these is like a mistress used,
This hour she's idolized, the next abused;
While their weak heads like towns unfortified,
'Twixt sense and nonsense daily change their side.
Ask them the cause; they're wiser still, they say;
And still to-morrow's wiser than to-day.
We think our fathers fools, so wise we grow,
Our wiser sons, no doubt, will think us so.
Once School-divines this zealous isle o'erspread;
Who knew most Sentences,[1] was deepest read;
Faith, Gospel, all, seemed made to be disputed,
And none had sense enough to be confuted:
Scotists and Thomists,[2] now, in peace remain,
Amidst their kindred cobwebs in Duck-lane.
If Faith itself has different dresses worn,
What wonder modes in Wit should take their turn?
Oft', leaving what is natural and fit,
The current folly proves the ready wit;
And authors think their reputation safe,
Which lives as long as fools are pleased to laugh.
  Some valuing those of their own side or mind,
Still make themselves the measure of mankind:
Fondly we think we honor merit then,
When we but praise ourselves in other men.
Parties in Wit attend on those of State,
And public faction doubles private hate.
Pride, Malice, Folly, against Dryden rose,
In various shapes of Parsons, Critics, Beaus;
But sense survived, when merry jests were past;
For rising merit will buoy up at last.
Might he return, and bless once more our eyes,
New Blackmores and new Milbourns must arise:[3]
Nay should great Homer lift his awful head,
Zoilus[4] again would start up from the dead.
Envy will merit, as its shade, pursue;
But like a shadow, proves the substance true;
For envied Wit, like Sol eclipsed, makes known
Th' opposing body's grossness, not its own,
When first that sun too powerful beams displays,
It draws up vapors which obscure its rays;
But e'en those clouds at last adorn its way,
Reflect new glories, and augment the day.
  Be thou the first true merit to befriend;
His praise is lost, who stays till all commend.
Short is the date, alas, of modern rimes,
And 't is but just to let them live betimes.
No longer now that golden age appears,
When Patriarch-wits survived a thousand years:
Now length of Fame (our second life) is lost,
And bare threescore is all e'en that can boast;
Our sons their fathers' failing language see,
And such as Chaucer is, shall Dryden be.

---

[1]The reference is to the *Book of Sentences* of Peter Lombard.

[2]Followers of Duns Scotus and St. Thomas Aquinas, scholastic philosophers of the thirteenth century. Duck Lane was a London street where second-hand books were formerly sold.

[3]Blackmore was a physician and a dull poet, Milbourn a clergyman; both attacked Dryden.

[4]Greek critic (fourth century, B. C.) who attacked Homer.

So when the faithful pencil has designed
Some bright Idea of the master's mind,
Where a new world leaps out at his command,
And ready Nature waits upon his hand;
When the ripe colors soften and unite,
And sweetly melt into just shade and light;
When mellowing years their full perfection give,
And each bold figure just begins to live,
The treach'rous colors the fair art betray,
And all the bright creation fades away!
Unhappy Wit, like most mistaken things,
Atones not for that envy which it brings.
In youth alone its empty praise we boast,
But soon the short-lived vanity is lost:
Like some fair flow'r the early spring supplies,
That gaily blooms, but e'en in blooming dies.
What is this Wit, which must our cares employ?
The owner's wife, that other men enjoy;
Then most our trouble still when most admired,
And still the more we give, the more required;
Whose fame with pains we guard, but lose with ease,
Sure some to vex, but never all to please;
'Tis what the vicious fear, the virtuous shun,
By fools 'tis hated, and by knaves undone!
If Wit so much from Ign'rance undergo,
Ah, let not Learning too commence its foe!
Of old, those met rewards who could excel,
And such were praised who but endeavored well:
Though triumphs were to gen'rals only due,
Crowns were reserved to grace the soldiers too.
Now, they who reach Parnassus' lofty crown,
Employ their pains to spurn some others down;
And while self-love each jealous writer rules,
Contending wits become the sport of fools:
But still the worst with most regret commend,
For each ill Author is as bad a Friend.
To what base ends, and by what abject ways,
Are mortals urged through sacred lust of praise!
Ah ne'er so dire a thirst of glory boast,
Nor in the Critic let the Man be lost.
Good-nature and good-sense must ever join;
To err is human, to forgive, divine.
But if in noble minds some dregs remain
Not yet purged off, of spleen and sour disdain;
Discharge that rage on more provoking crimes,
Nor fear a dearth in these flagitious times.
No pardon vile Obscenity should find,
Though wit and art conspire to move your mind;
But Dullness with Obscenity must prove
As shameful sure as Impotence in love.
In the fat age of pleasure, wealth, and ease
Sprung the rank weed, and thrived with large increase:
When love was all an easy Monarch's care;
Seldom at council, never in a war:
Jilts ruled the state, and statesmen farces writ;
Nay wits had pensions, and young Lords had wit:
The Fair sate panting at a Courtier's play,
And not a Mask[1] went unimproved away:
The modest fan was lifted up no more,
And Virgins smiled at what they blushed before.
The following license of a Foreign reign
Did all the dregs of bold Socinus[2] drain;
Then unbelieving priests reformed the nation,
And taught more pleasant methods of salvation;
Where Heav'n's free subjects might their rights dispute,
Lest God himself should seem too absolute:
Pulpits their sacred satire learned to spare,
And Vice admired[3] to find a flatt'rer there!
Encouraged thus, Wit's Titans braved the skies,
And the press groaned with licensed blasphemies.
These monsters, Critics! with your darts engage,
Here point your thunder, and exhaust your rage!
Yet shun their fault, who, scandalously nice,
Will needs mistake an author into vice;
All seems infected that th' infected spy,
As all looks yellow to the jaundiced eye.

PART III

LEARN then what Morals Critics ought to show,
For 'tis but half a Judge's task, to know.
'Tis not enough, taste, judgment, learning, join;
In all you speak, let truth and candor shine:
That not alone what to your sense is due
All may allow; but seek your friendship too.
Be silent always when you doubt your sense;
And speak, though sure, with seeming diffidence:
Some positive, persisting fops we know,
Who, if once wrong, will needs be always so;
But you, with pleasure own your errors past,
And make each day a Critic on the last.
'Tis not enough, your counsel still be true;
Blunt truths more mischief than nice falsehoods do;
Men must be taught as if you taught them not,
And things unknown proposed as things forgot.

[1] *I. e.*, woman wearing a mask.

[2] The name of two Italians of the sixteenth century who revived Arianism and may be regarded as forerunners of modern unitarianism.

[3] Wondered.

Without Good Breeding, truth is disapproved;
That only makes superior sense beloved.

Be niggards of advice on no pretense;
For the worst avarice is that of sense.
With mean complacence ne'er betray your trust,
Nor be so civil as to prove unjust.
Fear not the anger of the wise to raise;
Those best can bear reproof, who merit praise.

'Twere well might critics still this freedom take,
But Appius[1] reddens at each word you speak,
And stares, tremendous, with a threat'ning eye,
Like some fierce Tyrant in old tapestry.
Fear most to tax an Honorable fool,
Whose right it is, uncensured, to be dull;
Such, without wit, are Poets when they please,
As without learning they can take Degrees.
Leave dang'rous truths to unsuccessful Satires,
And flattery to fulsome Dedicators,
Whom, when they praise, the world believes no more,
Than when they promise to give scribbling o'er.
'Tis best sometimes your censure to restrain,
And charitably let the dull be vain:
Your silence there is better than your spite,
For who can rail so long as they can write!
Still humming on, their drowsy course they keep,
And lashed so long, like tops, are lashed asleep.
False steps but help them to renew the race,
As, after stumbling, Jades will mend their pace.
What crowds of these, impenitently bold,
In sounds and jingling syllables grown old,
Still run on Poets, in a raging vein,
E'en to the dregs and squeezings of the brain,
Strain out the last dull droppings of their sense,
And rime with all the rage of Impotence.

Such shameless Bards we have; and yet 'tis true,
There are as mad abandoned Critics too.
The bookful blockhead, ignorantly read,
With loads of learnéd lumber in his head,
With his own tongue still edifies his ears,
And always list'ning to himself appears.
All books he reads, and all he reads assails,
From Dryden's Fables down to Durfey's Tales.
With him, most authors steal their works, or buy;
Garth did not write his own Dispensary.
Name a new Play, and he's the Poet's friend,
Nay showed his faults—but when would Poets mend?
No place so sacred from such fops is barred,
Nor is Paul's church more safe than Paul's churchyard:
Nay, fly to Altars; there they'll talk you dead:
For Fools rush in where Angels fear to tread.
Distrustful sense with modest caution speaks,
It still looks home, and short excursions makes;
But rattling nonsense in full volleys breaks,
And never shocked, and never turned aside,
Bursts out, resistless, with a thund'ring tide.

But where's the man, who counsel can bestow,
Still pleased to teach, and yet not proud to know?
Unbiassed, or by favor, or by spite;
Not dully prepossessed, nor blindly right;
Though learn'd, well-bred; and though well-bred, sincere,
Modestly bold, and humanly severe:
Who to a friend his faults can freely show,
And gladly praise the merit of a foe?
Bless'd with a taste exact, yet unconfined;
A knowledge both of books and human kind:
Gen'rous converse; a soul exempt from pride;
And love to praise, with reason on his side?

Such once were Critics; such the happy few,
Athens and Rome in better ages knew.
The mighty Stagirite first left the shore,
Spread all his sails, and durst the deeps explore:
He steered securely, and discovered far,
Led by the light of the Mæonian Star.[2]
Poets, a race long unconfined, and free,
Still fond and proud of savage liberty,
Received his laws; and stood convinced 'twas fit,
Who conquered Nature, should preside o'er Wit.

Horace still charms with graceful negligence,
And without method talks us into sense,
Will, like a friend, familiarly convey
The truest notions in the easiest way.
He, who supreme in judgment, as in wit,
Might boldly censure, as he boldly writ,
Yet judged with coolness, though he sung with fire;
His Precepts teach but what his works inspire.
Our Critics take a contrary extreme,
They judge with fury, but they write with fle'me:[3]
Nor suffers Horace more in wrong Translations
By Wits, than Critics in as wrong Quotations.

See Dionysius[4] Homer's thoughts refine,
And call new beauties forth from every line!

---

[1] *I. e.*, John Dennis. The name was taken from his tragedy, *Appius and Virginia.*

[2] Homer.

[3] Phlegm, *i. e.*, dullness.

[4] Dionysius of Halicarnassus, Greek critic.

Fancy and art in gay Petronius please,
The scholar's learning, with the courtier's ease.
In grave Quintilian's copious work, we find
The justest rules, and clearest method joined:
Thus useful arms in magazines we place,
All ranged in order, and disposed with grace,
But less to please the eye, than arm the hand,
Still fit for use, and ready at command.
Thee, bold Longinus! all the Nine[1] inspire,
And bless their Critic with a Poet's fire.
An ardent Judge, who zealous in his trust,
With warmth gives sentence, yet is always just;
Whose own example strengthens all his laws;
And is himself that great Sublime he draws.
Thus long succeeding Critics justly reigned,
License repressed, and useful laws ordained.
Learning and Rome alike in empire grew;
And Arts still followed where her Eagles flew;
From the same foes, at last, both felt their doom,
And the same age saw Learning fall, and Rome.
With Tyranny, then Superstition joined,
As that the body, this enslaved the mind;
Much was believed, but little understood,
And to be dull was construed to be good;
A second deluge Learning thus o'er-run,
And the Monks finished what the Goths begun.
At length Erasmus, that great injured name
(The glory of the Priesthood, and the shame!),
Stemmed the wild torrent of a barb'rous age,
And drove those holy Vandals off the stage.
But see! each Muse, in Leo's[2] golden days,
Starts from her trance, and trims her withered bays,
Rome's ancient Genius, o'er its ruins spread,
Shakes off the dust, and rears his rev'rend head.
Then Sculpture and her sister-arts revive;
Stones leaped to form, and rocks began to live;
With sweeter notes each rising Temple rung;
A Raphael painted, and a Vida sung.
Immortal Vida: on whose honored brow
The Poet's bays and Critic's ivy grow:
Cremona now shall ever boast thy name,
As next in place to Mantua, next in fame!
But soon by impious arms from Latium chased,
Their ancient bounds the banished Muses passed;
Thence Arts o'er all the northern world advance,
But Critic-learning flourished most in France:
The rules a nation, born to serve, obeys;
And Boileau still in right of Horace sways.
But we, brave Britons, foreign laws despised,
And kept unconquered, and uncivilized;
Fierce for the liberties of wit, and bold,
We still defied the Romans, as of old.
Yet some there were, among the sounder few
Of those who less presumed, and better knew,
Who durst assert the juster ancient cause,
And here restored Wit's fundamental laws.
Such was the Muse, whose rules and practice tell,
"Nature's chief Master-piece is writing well."
Such was Roscommon,[3] not more learn'd than good,
With manners gen'rous as his noble blood;
To him the wit of Greece and Rome was known,
And ev'ry author's merit, but his own.
Such late was Walsh[4]—the Muse's judge and friend,
Who justly knew to blame or to commend:
To failings mild, but zealous for desert;
The clearest head, and the sincerest heart.
This humble praise, lamented shade! receive,
This praise at least a grateful Muse may give:
The Muse, whose early voice you taught to sing,
Prescribed her heights, and pruned her tender wing
(Her guide now lost), no more attempts to rise,
But in low numbers short excursions tries:
Content, if hence th' unlearn'd their wants may view,
The learn'd reflect on what before they knew:
Careless of censure, nor too fond of fame;
Still pleased to praise, yet not afraid to blame,
Averse alike to flatter, or offend;
Not free from faults, nor yet too vain to mend.

[1]The muses. [2]Leo X.

THE RAPE OF THE LOCK[5]

AN HEROI-COMICAL POEM

Nolueram, Belinda, tuos violare capillos;
Sed juvat, hoc precibus me tribuisse tuis.[6] MART.

TO MRS. ARABELLA FERMOR

MADAM,

It will be in vain to deny that I have some regard for this piece, since I dedicate it to You.

[3]Wentworth Dillon, Earl of Roscommon.

[4]See the introductory account of Pope above.

[5]First published in 1712, but rewritten and published in its present form in 1714. The occasion of the poem was as follows: Lord Petre had in a moment of fun cut off a lock of Miss Arabella Fermor's hair. Miss Fermor became angry, the families of both took up the quarrel, and serious consequences seemed likely to follow. At this point a common friend, Mr. John Caryll, suggested to Pope that he write a poem to make a jest of the whole affair. The result was the earlier version of the *Rape of the Lock*, which is said to have succeeded in its immediate purpose.

[6]I did not want, Belinda, to do violence to your lock, but I am glad to yield this gift to your entreaties (Martial, *Epigrams*, xii, 84. Pope alters the name).

Yet you may bear me witness, it was intended only to divert a few young Ladies, who have good sense and good humor enough to laugh not only at their sex's little unguarded follies, but at their own. But as it was communicated with the air of a Secret, it soon found its way into the world. An imperfect copy having been offered to a Bookseller, you had the good nature for my sake to consent to the publication of one more correct: This I was forced to, before I had executed half my design, for the Machinery was entirely wanting to complete it.

The Machinery, Madam, is a term invented by the Critics, to signify that part which the Deities, Angels, or Demons are made to act in a Poem: For the ancient Poets are in one respect like many modern Ladies: let an action be never so trivial in itself, they always make it appear of the utmost importance. These Machines I determined to raise on a very new and odd foundation, the Rosicrucian doctrine of Spirits.

I know how disagreeable it is to make use of hard words before a Lady; but 'tis so much the concern of a Poet to have his works understood, and particularly by your Sex, that you must give me leave to explain two or three difficult terms.

The Rosicrucians are a people I must bring you acquainted with. The best account I know of them is in a French book called *Le Comte de Gabalis*, which both in its title and size is so like a Novel, that many of the Fair Sex have read it for one by mistake. According to these Gentlemen, the four Elements are inhabited by Spirits, which they call Sylphs, Gnomes, Nymphs, and Salamanders. The Gnomes or Demons of Earth delight in mischief; but the Sylphs, whose habitation is in the Air, are the best-conditioned creatures imaginable. For, they say, any mortals may enjoy the most intimate familiarities with these gentle Spirits, upon a condition very easy to all true Adepts, an inviolate preservation of Chastity.

As to the following Cantos, all the passages of them are as fabulous as the Vision at the beginning, or the Transformation at the end (except the loss of your Hair, which I always mention with reverence). The Human persons are as fictitious as the airy ones; and the character of Belinda, as it is now managed, resembles you in nothing but in Beauty.

If this Poem had as many Graces as there are in your Person, or in your Mind, yet I could never hope it should pass through the world half so Uncensured as You have done. But let its fortune be what it will, mine is happy enough, to have given me this occasion of assuring you that I am, with the truest esteem, MADAM;

Your most obedient, Humble Servant,

A. POPE.

CANTO I

WHAT dire offense from am'rous causes springs,
What mighty contests rise from trivial things,
I sing—This verse to Caryl, Muse! is due:
This, e'en Belinda may vouchsafe to view:
Slight is the subject, but not so the praise,
If She inspire, and He approve my lays.
Say what strange motive, Goddess! could compel
A well-bred Lord t' assault a gentle Belle?
O say what stranger cause, yet unexplored,
Could make a gentle Belle reject a Lord?
In tasks so bold, can little men engage,
And in soft bosoms dwells such mighty Rage?
Sol through white curtains shot a tim'rous ray,
And oped those eyes that must eclipse the day:
Now lap-dogs give themselves the rousing shake,
And sleepless lovers, just at twelve, awake:
Thrice rung the bell, the slipper knocked the ground,[1]
And the pressed watch returned a silver sound.
Belinda still her downy pillow pressed,
Her guardian Sylph prolonged the balmy rest:
'Twas He had summoned to her silent bed
The morning-dream that hovered o'er her head;
A Youth more glitt'ring than a Birth-night Beau
(That e'en in slumber caused her cheek to glow),
Seemed to her ear his winning lips to lay,
And thus in whispers said, or seemed to say:
"Fairest of mortals, thou distinguished care
Of thousand bright Inhabitants of Air!
If e'er one vision touched thy infant thought,
Of all the Nurse and all the Priest have taught;
Of airy Elves by moonlight shadows seen,
The silver token, and the circled green,
Or virgins visited by Angel-pow'rs,
With golden crowns and wreaths of heav'nly flow'rs;
Hear and believe! thy own importance know,
Nor bound thy narrow views to things below.
Some secret truths, from learnéd pride concealed,
To Maids alone and Children are revealed:
What though no credit doubting Wits may give?
The Fair and Innocent shall still believe.
Know, then, unnumbered Spirits round thee fly,
The light Militia of the lower sky:
These, though unseen, are ever on the wing,
Hang o'er the Box, and hover round the Ring.

[1]To call her maid, who had not come when the bell was rung.

Think what an equipage thou hast in Air,
And view with scorn two Pages and a Chair.
As now your own, our beings were of old,
And once enclosed in Woman's beauteous mold;
Thence, by a soft transition, we repair
From earthly Vehicles to these of air.
Think not, when Woman's transient breath is fled,
That all her vanities at once are dead;
Succeeding vanities she still regards,
And though she plays no more, o'erlooks the cards.
Her joy in gilded Chariots, when alive,
And love of Ombre, after death survive.
For when the Fair in all their pride expire,
To their first Elements their Souls retire:
The Sprites of fiery Termagants in Flame
Mount up, and take a Salamander's name.
Soft yielding minds to Water glide away,
And sip, with Nymphs, their elemental Tea.
The graver Prude sinks downward to a Gnome,
In search of mischief still on Earth to roam.
The light Coquettes in Sylphs aloft repair,
And sport and flutter in the fields of Air.
"Know further yet; whoever fair and chaste
Rejects mankind, is by some Sylph embraced:
For Spirits, freed from mortal laws, with ease
Assume what sexes and what shapes they please.
What guards the purity of melting Maids,
In courtly balls, and midnight masquerades,
Safe from the treach'rous friend, the daring spark,
The glance by day, the whisper in the dark,
When kind occasion prompts their warm desires,
When music softens, and when dancing fires?
'Tis but their Sylph, the wise Celestials know,
Though Honor is the word with Men below.
Some nymphs there are, too conscious of their face,
For life predestined to the Gnomes' embrace.
These swell their prospects and exalt their pride,
When offers are disdained, and love denied:
Then gay Ideas crowd the vacant brain,
While Peers, and Dukes, and all their sweeping train,
And Garters, Stars, and Coronets appear,
And in soft sounds, Your Grace salutes their ear.
'Tis these that early taint the female soul,
Instruct the eyes of young Coquettes to roll,
Teach Infant-cheeks a bidden blush to know,
And little hearts to flutter at a Beau.
"Oft, when the world imagine women stray,
The Sylphs through mystic mazes guide their way,
Through all the giddy circle they pursue,
And old impertinence expel by new.
What tender maid but must a victim fall
To one man's treat, but for another's ball?
When Florio speaks what virgin could withstand,
If gentle Damon did not squeeze her hand?
With varying vanities, from ev'ry part,
They shift the moving Toyshop of their heart;
Where wigs with wigs, with sword-knots sword-knots strive,
Beaux banish beaux, and coaches coaches drive.
This erring mortals Levity may call;
Oh blind to truth! the Sylphs contrive it all.
"Of these am I, who thy protection claim,
A watchful sprite, and Ariel is my name.
Late, as I ranged the crystal wilds of air,
In the clear Mirror of thy ruling Star
I saw, alas! some dread event impend,
Ere to the main this morning sun descend,
But heav'n reveals not what, or how, or where:
Warned by the Sylph, oh pious maid, beware!
This to disclose is all thy guardian can:
Beware of all, but most beware of Man!"
He said; when Shock, who thought she slept too long,
Leaped up, and waked his mistress with his tongue.
'Twas then, Belinda, if report say true,
Thy eyes first opened on a Billet-doux;
Wounds, Charms, and Ardors were no sooner read,
But all the Vision vanished from thy head.
And now, unveiled, the Toilet stands displayed,
Each silver Vase in mystic order laid.
First, robed in white, the Nymph intent adores,
With head uncovered, the Cosmetic pow'rs.
A heav'nly image in the glass appears,
To that she bends, to that her eyes she rears;
Th' inferior Priestess, at her altar's side,
Trembling begins the sacred rites of Pride.
Unnumbered treasures ope at once, and here
The various off'rings of the world appear;
From each she nicely culls with curious toil,
And decks the Goddess with the glitt'ring spoil.
This casket India's glowing gems unlocks,
And all Arabia breathes from yonder box.
The Tortoise here and Elephant unite,
Transformed to combs, the speckled, and the white.
Here files of pins extend their shining rows,
Puffs, Powders, Patches, Bibles, Billet-doux.
Now awful Beauty puts on all its arms;
The fair each moment rises in her charms,
Repairs her smiles, awakens ev'ry grace,
And calls forth all the wonders of her face;
Sees by degrees a purer blush arise,
And keener lightnings quicken in her eyes.
The busy Sylphs surround their darling care,
These set the head, and those divide the hair,

Some fold the sleeve, whilst others plait the gown;
And Betty's[1] praised for labors not her own.

CANTO II

Not with more glories, in th' etherial plain,
The Sun first rises o'er the purple main,
Than, issuing forth, the rival of his beams
Launched on the bosom of the silver Thames.
Fair Nymphs, and well-dressed Youths around her shone,
But ev'ry eye was fixed on her alone.
On her white breast a sparkling Cross she wore,
Which Jews might kiss, and Infidels adore.
Her lively looks a sprightly mind disclose,
Quick as her eyes, and as unfixed as those:
Favors to none, to all she smiles extends;
Oft she rejects, but never once offends.
Bright as the sun, her eyes the gazers strike,
And, like the sun, they shine on all alike.
Yet graceful ease, and sweetness void of pride,
Might hide her faults, if Belles had faults to hide:
If to her share some female errors fall,
Look on her face, and you'll forget 'em all.
This Nymph, to the destruction of mankind,
Nourished two Locks which graceful hung behind
In equal curls, and well conspired to deck
With shining ringlets the smooth iv'ry neck.
Love in these labyrinths his slaves detains,
And mighty hearts are held in slender chains.
With hairy springes we the birds betray,
Slight lines of hair surprise the finny prey,
Fair tresses man's imperial race ensnare,
And beauty draws us with a single hair.
Th' advent'rous Baron the bright locks admired;
He saw, he wished, and to the prize aspired.
Resolved to win, he meditates the way,
By force to ravish, or by fraud betray;
For when success a Lover's toil attends,
Few ask, if fraud or force attained his ends.
For this, ere Phœbus rose, he had implored
Propitious heav'n, and every pow'r adored,
But chiefly Love—to Love an Altar built,
Of twelve vast French Romances, neatly gilt.
There lay three garters, half a pair of gloves;
And all the trophies of his former loves;
With tender Billet-doux he lights the pyre,
And breathes three am'rous sighs to raise the fire.
Then prostrate falls, and begs with ardent eyes
Soon to obtain, and long possess the prize:
The pow'rs gave ear, and granted half his pray'r,
The rest, the winds dispersed in empty air.

[1]Belinda's maid.

But now secure the painted vessel glides,
The sun-beams trembling on the floating tides:
While melting music steals upon the sky,
And softened sounds along the waters die;
Smooth flow the waves, the Zephyrs gently play,
Belinda smiled, and all the world was gay.
All but the Sylph—with careful thoughts oppressed,
Th' impending woe sat heavy on his breast.
He summons straight his Denizens of air;
The lucid squadrons round the sails repair:
Soft o'er the shrouds aërial whispers breathe,
That seemed but Zephyrs to the train beneath.
Some to the sun their insect-wings unfold,
Waft on the breeze, or sink in clouds of gold;
Transparent forms, too fine for mortal sight,
Their fluid bodies half dissolved in light,
Loose to the wind their airy garments flew,
Thin glitt'ring textures of the filmy dew,
Dipped in the richest tincture of the skies,
Where light disports in ever-mingling dyes,
While ev'ry beam new transient colors flings,
Colors that change whene'er they wave their wings.
Amid the circle, on the gilded mast,
Superior by the head, was Ariel placed;
His purple pinions op'ning to the sun,
He raised his azure wand, and thus begun:
"Ye Sylphs and Sylphids, to your chief give ear!
Fays, Fairies, Genii, Elves, and Demons, hear!
Ye know the spheres and various tasks assigned
By laws eternal to th' aërial kind.
Some in the fields of purest ether play,
And bask and whiten in the blaze of day.
Some guide the course of wand'ring orbs on high,
Or roll the planets through the boundless sky.
Some less refined, beneath the moon's pale light
Pursue the stars that shoot athwart[2] the night,
Or suck the mists in grosser air below,
Or dip their pinions in the painted bow,
Or brew fierce tempests on the wintry main,
Or o'er the glebe distil the kindly rain.
Others on earth o'er human race preside,
Watch all their ways, and all their actions guide:
Of these the chief the care of Nations own,
And guard with Arms divine the British Throne.
"Our humbler province is to tend the Fair,
Not a less pleasing, though less glorious care;
To save the powder from too rude a gale,
Nor let th' imprisoned essences exhale;
To draw fresh colors from the vernal flow'rs;

[2]Across.

To steal from rainbows e'er they drop in show'rs
A brighter wash; to curl their waving hairs,
Assist their blushes, and inspire their airs;
Nay oft, in dreams, invention we bestow,
To change a Flounce, or add a Furbelow.
"This day, black Omens threat the brightest Fair,
That e'er deserved a watchful spirit's care;
Some dire disaster, or by force, or slight;
But what, or where, the fates have wrapped in night.
Whether the nymph shall break Diana's law,
Or some frail China jar receive a flaw;
Or stain her honor or her new brocade;
Forget her pray'rs, or miss a masquerade;
Or lose her heart, or necklace, at a ball;
Or whether Heav'n has doomed that Shock must fall.
Haste, then, ye spirits! to your charge repair:
The flutt'ring fan be Zephyretta's care;
The drops[1] to thee, Brillante, we consign;
And, Momentilla, let the watch be thine;
Do thou, Crispissa, tend her fav'rite Lock;
Ariel himself shall be the guard of Shock.
"To fifty chosen Sylphs, of special note,
We trust th' important charge, the Petticoat:
Oft have we known that seven-fold fence to fail,
Though stiff with hoops, and armed with ribs of whale;
Form a strong line about the silver bound,
And guard the wide circumference around.
"Whatever spirit, careless of his charge,
His post neglects, or leaves the fair at large,
Shall feel sharp vengeance soon o'ertake his sins,
Be stopped in vials, or transfixed with pins;
Or plunged in lakes of bitter washes lie,
Or wedged whole ages in a bodkin's eye:
Gums and Pomatums shall his flight restrain,
While clogged he beats his silken wings in vain;
Or Alum styptics with contracting pow'r
Shrink his thin essence like a riveled[2] flow'r:
Or, as Ixion fixed, the wretch shall feel
The giddy motion of the whirling Mill,
In fumes of burning Chocolate shall glow,
And tremble at the sea that froths below!"
He spoke; the spirits from the sails descend;
Some, orb in orb, around the nymph extend;
Some thread the mazy ringlets of her hair;
Some hang upon the pendants of her ear:
With beating hearts the dire event they wait,
Anxious, and trembling for the birth of Fate.

CANTO III

CLOSE by those meads, for ever crowned with flow'rs,
Where Thames with pride surveys his rising tow'rs,
There stands a structure of majestic frame,[3]
Which from the neighb'ring Hampton takes its name.
Here Britain's statesmen oft the fall foredoom
Of foreign Tyrants and of Nymphs at home;
Here thou, great Anna! whom three realms obey,
Dost sometimes counsel take—and sometimes Tea.
Hither the heroes and the nymphs resort,
To taste awhile the pleasures of a Court;
In various talk th' instructive hours they passed,
Who gave the ball, or paid the visit last;
One speaks the glory of the British Queen,
And one describes a charming Indian screen;
A third interprets motions, looks, and eyes;
At ev'ry word a reputation dies.
Snuff, or the fan, supply each pause of chat,
With singing, laughing, ogling, *and all that.*
Meanwhile, declining from the noon of day,
The sun obliquely shoots his burning ray;
The hungry Judges soon the sentence sign,
And wretches hang that jurymen may dine;
The merchant from th' Exchange returns in peace,
And the long labors of the Toilet cease.
Belinda now, whom thirst of fame invites,
Burns to encounter two advent'rous Knights,
At Ombre[4] singly to decide their doom;
And swells her breast with conquests yet to come.
Straight the three bands prepare in arms to join,
Each band the number of the sacred nine.
Soon as she spreads her hand, th' aërial guard
Descend, and sit on each important card:
First Ariel perched upon a Matadore,
Then each, according to the rank they bore;
For Sylphs, yet mindful of their ancient race,
Are, as when women, wondrous fond of place.
Behold, four Kings in majesty revered,
With hoary whiskers and a forky beard;
And four fair Queens whose hands sustain a flow'r,
Th' expressive emblem of their softer pow'r;
Four Knaves in garbs succinct, a trusty band,
Caps on their heads, and halberts in their hand;

[1]Earrings. [2]Shrunken.

[3]Hampton Court, a royal palace.

[4]A game of cards, of Spanish origin, usually played by three people. Each player received nine cards. The one who declared the trump became the "ombre" and played against the other two. If one of these took more tricks than the "ombre" the latter was defeated, which was called "codille." The three highest cards were called "matadores." They were, in the order of their value, "Spadillio" (ace of spades), "Manillio" (when trumps were black, the two of trumps; when red the seven of trumps), and "Basto" (ace of clubs).

And particolored troops, a shining train,
Draw forth to combat on the velvet plain.
The skillful Nymph reviews her force with care:
"Let Spades be trumps!" she said, and trumps they were.
Now move to war her sable Matadores,
In show like leaders of the swarthy Moors.
Spadillio first, unconquerable Lord!
Led off two captive trumps, and swept the board.
As many more Manillio forced to yield,
And marched a victor from the verdant field.
Him Basto followed, but his fate more hard
Gained but one trump and one plebeian card.
With his broad saber next, a chief in years,
The hoary Majesty of Spades appears,
Puts forth one manly leg, to sight revealed,
The rest, his many-colored robe concealed.
The rebel Knave, who dares his prince engage,
Proves the just victim of his royal rage.
E'en mighty Pam,[1] that Kings and Queens o'erthrew
And mowed down armies in the fights of Lu,
Sad chance of war! now destitute of aid,
Falls undistinguished by the victor spade!
Thus far both armies to Belinda yield;
Now to the Baron fate inclines the field.
His warlike Amazon her host invades,
Th' imperial consort of the crown of Spades.
The Club's black Tyrant first her victim died,
Spite of his haughty mien, and barb'rous pride:
What boots the regal circle on his head,
His giant limbs, in state unwieldy spread;
That long behind he trails his pompous robe,
And, of all monarchs, only grasps the globe?
The Baron now his Diamonds pours apace;
Th' embroidered King who shows but half his face,
And his refulgent Queen, with pow'rs combined
Of broken troops an easy conquest find.
Clubs, Diamonds, Hearts, in wild disorder seen,
With throngs promiscuous strew the level green.
Thus when dispersed a routed army runs,
Of Asia's troops, and Afric's sable sons,
With like confusion different nations fly,
Of various habit, and of various dye,
The pierced battalions dis-united fall,
In heaps on heaps; one fate o'erwhelms them all.
The Knave of Diamonds tries his wily arts,
And wins (oh shameful chance!) the Queen of Hearts.
At this, the blood the virgin's cheek forsook,
A livid paleness spreads o'er all her look;
She sees, and trembles at th' approaching ill,
Just in the jaws of ruin, and Codille.
And now (as oft in some distempered State)
On one nice Trick depends the gen'ral fate.
An Ace of Hearts steps forth: The King unseen
Lurked in her hand, and mourned his captive Queen:
He springs to Vengeance with an eager pace,
And falls like thunder on the prostrate Ace.
The nymph exulting fills with shouts the sky;
The walls, the woods, and long canals reply.
O thoughtless mortals! ever blind to fate,
Too soon dejected, and too soon elate.
Sudden, these honors shall be snatched away,
And cursed for ever this victorious day.
For lo! the board with cups and spoons is crowned,
The berries crackle, and the mill turns round;
On shining Altars of Japan they raise
The silver lamp; the fiery spirits blaze:
From silver spouts the grateful liquors glide,
While China's earth receives the smoking tide:
At once they gratify their scent and taste,
And frequent cups prolong the rich repast.
Straight hover round the Fair her airy band;
Some, as she sipped, the fuming liquor fanned,
Some o'er her lap their careful plumes displayed,
Trembling, and conscious of the rich brocade.
Coffee (which makes the politician wise,
And see through all things with his half-shut eyes),
Sent up in vapors to the Baron's brain
New Stratagems, the radiant Lock to gain.
Ah cease, rash youth! desist ere 't is too late,
Fear the just Gods, and think of Scylla's Fate!
Changed to a bird, and sent to flit in air,
She dearly pays for Nisus' injured hair!
But when to mischief mortals bend their will,
How soon they find fit instruments of ill!
Just then, Clarissa drew with tempting grace
A two-edged weapon from her shining case:
So Ladies in Romance assist their Knight,
Present the spear, and arm him for the fight.
He takes the gift with rev'rence, and extends
The little engine on his fingers' ends;
This just behind Belinda's neck he spread,
As o'er the fragrant steams she bends her head.
Swift to the Lock a thousand Sprites repair,
A thousand wings, by turns, blow back the hair;
And thrice they twitched the diamond in her ear;
Thrice she looked back, and thrice the foe drew near.
Just in that instant, anxious Ariel sought
The close recesses of the Virgin's thought;
As on the nosegay in her breast reclined,
He watched th' Ideas rising in her mind,
Sudden he viewed, in spite of all her art,

[1]Knave of clubs, highest card in the game of loo.

An earthly Lover lurking at her heart.
Amazed, confused, he found his pow'r expired,
Resigned to fate, and with a sigh retired.
The Peer now spreads the glitt'ring Forfex wide,
T' enclose the Lock; now joins it, to divide.
E'en then, before the fatal engine closed,
A wretched Sylph too fondly interposed;
Fate urged the shears, and cut the Sylph in twain
(But airy substance soon unites again),
The meeting points the sacred hair dissever
From the fair head, for ever, and for ever!
Then flashed the living lightning from her eyes,
And screams of horror rend th' affrighted skies.
Not louder shrieks to pitying heav'n are cast,
When husbands, or when lapdogs breathe their last;
Or when rich China vessels fall'n from high,
In glitt'ring dust and painted fragments lie!
Let wreaths of triumph now my temples twine
(The victor cried) the glorious Prize is mine!
While fish in streams, or birds delight in air,
Or in a coach and six the British Fair,
As long as Atalantis[1] shall be read,
Or the small pillow grace a Lady's bed,
While visits shall be paid on solemn days,
When num'rous wax-lights in bright order blaze,
While nymphs take treats, or assignations give,
So long my honor, name, and praise shall live!
What Time would spare, from Steel receives its date,
And monuments, like men, submit to fate!
Steel could the labor of the Gods destroy,
And strike to dust th' imperial towers of Troy;
Steel could the works of mortal pride confound,
And hew triumphal arches to the ground.
What wonder then, fair nymph! thy hairs should feel,
The conqu'ring force of unresisted steel?

CANTO IV

BUT anxious cares the pensive nymph oppressed,
And secret passions labored in her breast.
Not youthful kings in battle seized alive,
Not scornful virgins who their charms survive,
Not ardent lovers robbed of all their bliss,
Not ancient ladies when refused a kiss,
Not tyrants fierce that unrepenting die,
Not Cynthia when her manteau's pinned awry,
E'er felt such rage, resentment, and despair,
As thou, sad Virgin! for thy ravished Hair.
For, that sad moment, when the Sylphs withdrew
And Ariel weeping from Belinda flew,
Umbriel, a dusky, melancholy sprite,
As ever sullied the fair face of light,
Down to the central earth, his proper scene,
Repaired to search the gloomy Cave of Spleen.[2]
Swift on his sooty pinions flits the Gnome,
And in a vapor reached the dismal dome.
No cheerful breeze this sullen region knows,
The dreaded East is all the wind that blows.
Here in a grotto, sheltered close from air,
And screened in shades from day's detested glare,
She sighs for ever on her pensive bed,
Pain at her side, and Megrim[3] at her head.
Two handmaids wait the throne: alike in place,
But diff'ring far in figure and in face.
Here stood Ill-nature like an ancient maid,
Her wrinkled form in black and white arrayed;
With store of pray'rs, for mornings, nights, and noons,
Her hand is filled; her bosom with lampoons.
There Affectation, with a sickly mien,
Shows in her cheek the roses of eighteen,
Practiced to lisp, and hang the head aside,
Faints into airs, and languishes with pride,
On the rich quilt sinks with becoming woe,
Wrapped in a gown, for sickness, and for show.
The fair ones feel such maladies as these,
When each new night-dress gives a new disease.
A constant Vapor o'er the palace flies;
Strange phantoms rising as the mists arise;
Dreadful, as hermit's dreams in haunted shades,
Or bright, as visions of expiring maids.
Now glaring fiends, and snakes on rolling spires,
Pale specters, gaping tombs, and purple fires:
Now lakes of liquid gold, Elysian scenes,
And crystal domes, and angels in machines.[4]
Unnumbered throngs on every side are seen,
Of bodies changed to various forms by Spleen.
Here living Tea-pots stand, one arm held out,
One bent; the handle this, and that the spout:
A Pipkin[5] there, like Homer's Tripod walks;
Here sighs a Jar, and there a Goose-pie talks;
Men prove with child, as powerful fancy works,
And maids turned bottles, call aloud for corks.

[1]*The New Atalantis* by Mrs. Manley (published in 1709), a voluminous work which chronicled contemporary scandal.

[2]Low spirits, or ill temper.

[3]Headache, but the word was used in the early eighteenth century (as was "vapors") for what we should call "the blues."

[4]The "*deus ex machina.*"

[5]A small jar. "Homer's tripod" is one of the self-moving tripods made by Vulcan, described in the *Iliad* (XVIII, 373–377).

Safe passed the Gnome through this fantastic band,
A branch of healing Spleenwort in his hand.
Then thus addressed the pow'r: "Hail, wayward Queen!
Who rule the sex to fifty from fifteen:
Parent of vapors and of female wit,
Who give th' hysteric, or poetic fit,
On various tempers act by various ways,
Make some take physic, others scribble plays;
Who cause the proud their visits to delay,
And send the godly in a pet to pray.
A nymph there is, that all thy pow'r disdains,
And thousands more in equal mirth maintains.
But oh! if e'er thy Gnome could spoil a grace,
Or raise a pimple on a beauteous face,
Like Citron-waters matrons' cheeks inflame,
Or change complexions at a losing game;
If e'er with airy horns I planted heads,
Or rumpled petticoats, or tumbled beds,
Or caused suspicion when no soul was rude,
Or discomposed the head-dress of a Prude,
Or e'er to costive lap-dog gave disease,
Which not the tears of brightest eyes could ease:
Hear me, and touch Belinda with chagrin,
That single act gives half the world the spleen."
The Goddess with a discontented air
Seems to reject him, though she grants his pray'r.
A wondrous Bag with both her hands she binds,
Like that where once Ulysses held the winds;
There she collects the force of female lungs,
Sighs, sobs, and passions, and the war of tongues.
A Vial next she fills with fainting fears,
Soft sorrows, melting griefs, and flowing tears.
The Gnome rejoicing bears her gifts away,
Spreads his black wings, and slowly mounts to day.
Sunk in Thalestris'[1] arms the nymph he found,
Her eyes dejected and her hair unbound.
Full o'er their heads the swelling bag he rent,
And all the Furies issued at the vent.
Belinda burns with more than mortal ire,
And fierce Thalestris fans the rising fire.
"O wretched maid!" she spread her hands, and cried
(While Hampton's echoes, "Wretched maid!" replied),
"Was it for this you took such constant care
The bodkin, comb, and essence to prepare?
For this your locks in paper durance bound,
For this with tort'ring irons wreathed around?

[1]A friend of Belinda's, said to be a Mrs. Morley.

For this with fillets strained your tender head,
And bravely bore the double loads of lead?[2]
Gods! shall the ravisher display your hair,
While the Fops envy, and the Ladies stare!
Honor forbid! at whose unrivaled shrine
Ease, pleasure, virtue, all our sex resign.
Methinks already I your tears survey,
Already hear the horrid things they say,
Already see you a degraded toast,[3]
And all your honor in a whisper lost!
How shall I, then, your helpless fame defend?
'Twill then be infamy to seem your friend!
And shall this prize, th' inestimable prize,
Exposed through crystal to the gazing eyes,
And heightened by the diamond's circling rays,
On that rapacious hand for ever blaze?
Sooner shall grass in Hyde-park Circus grow,
And wits take lodgings in the sound of Bow;[4]
Sooner let earth, air, sea, to Chaos fall,
Men, monkeys, lap-dogs, parrots, perish all!"
She said; then raging to Sir Plume[5] repairs,
And bids her Beau demand the precious hairs:
(Sir Plume of amber snuff-box justly vain,
And the nice conduct of a clouded cane)
With earnest eyes, and round unthinking face,
He first the snuff-box opened, then the case,
And thus broke out—"My Lord, why, what the devil?
Z—ds! damn the lock! 'fore Gad, you must be civil!
Plague on 't! 'tis past a jest—nay prithee, pox!
Give her the hair"—he spoke, and rapped his box.
"It grieves me much" (replied the Peer again)
"Who speaks so well should ever speak in vain.
But by this Lock, this sacred Lock I swear
(Which never more shall join its parted hair;
Which never more its honors shall renew,
Clipped from the lovely head where late it grew),
That while my nostrils draw the vital air,
This hand, which won it, shall for ever wear."
He spoke, and speaking, in proud triumph spread
The long-contended honors of her head.
But Umbriel, hateful Gnome! forbears not so;
He breaks the Vial whence the sorrows flow.

[2]Fastenings for curl-papers.

[3]A slang term for a woman whose health was drunk by her admirers.

[4]The bells of the church of St. Mary le Bow, in Cheapside, an unfashionable quarter of the city.

[5]Sir George Brown, brother of Mrs. Morley. He is said to have threatened Pope with violence for the picture of him which follows.

Then see! the nymph in beauteous grief appears,
Her eyes half-languishing, half-drowned in tears;
On her heaved bosom hung her drooping head,
Which, with a sigh, she raised; and thus she said:
"For ever cursed be this detested day,
Which snatched my best, my fav'rite curl away!
Happy! ah, ten times happy had I been,
If Hampton Court these eyes had never seen!
Yet am not I the first mistaken maid,
By love of Courts to num'rous ills betrayed.
O had I rather un-admired remained
In some lone isle, or distant Northern land;
Where the gilt Chariot never marks the way,
Where none learn Ombre, none e'er taste Bohea![1]
There kept my charms concealed from mortal eye,
Like roses, that in deserts bloom and die.
What moved my mind with youthful Lords to roam?
O had I stayed, and said my pray'rs at home!
'T was this, the morning omens seemed to tell,
Thrice from my trembling hand the patch-box[2] fell;
The tott'ring China shook without a wind,
Nay, Poll sat mute, and Shock was most unkind!
A Sylph too warned me of the threats of fate,
In mystic visions, now believed too late!
See the poor remnants of these slighted hairs!
My hands shall rend what e'en thy rapine spares:
These in two sable ringlets taught to break,
Once gave new beauties to the snowy neck;
The sister-lock now sits uncouth, alone,
And in its fellow's fate foresees its own;
Uncurled it hangs, the fatal shears demands,
And tempts once more thy sacrilegious hands.
O hadst thou, cruel! been content to seize
Hairs less in sight, or any hairs but these!"

CANTO V

SHE said: the pitying audience melt in tears.
But Fate and Jove had stopped the Baron's ears.
In vain Thalestris with reproach assails,
For who can move when fair Belinda fails?
Not half so fixed the Trojan[3] could remain,
While Anna begged and Dido raged in vain.
Then grave Clarissa graceful waved her fan;
Silence ensued, and thus the nymph began:
"Say why are Beauties praised and honored most,
The wise man's passion, and the vain man's toast?
Why decked with all that land and sea afford,
Why Angels called, and Angel-like adored?
Why round our coaches crowd the white-gloved Beaux,
Why bows the side-box from its inmost rows;
How vain are all these glories, all our pains,
Unless good sense preserve what beauty gains;
That men may say, when we the front-box grace:
'Behold the first in virtue as in face!'
Oh! if to dance all night, and dress all day,
Charmed the small-pox, or chased old age away;
Who would not scorn what housewife's cares produce,
Or who would learn one earthly thing of use?
To patch, nay ogle, might become a Saint,
Nor could it sure be such a sin to paint.
But since, alas! frail beauty must decay,
Curled or uncurled, since Locks will turn to gray;
Since painted, or not painted, all shall fade,
And she who scorns a man, must die a maid;
What then remains but well our pow'r to use,
And keep good-humor still whate'er we lose?
And trust me, dear! good-humor can prevail,
When airs, and flights, and screams, and scolding fail.
Beauties in vain their pretty eyes may roll;
Charms strike the sight, but merit wins the soul."
So spoke the Dame, but no applause ensued;
Belinda frowned, Thalestris called her Prude.
"To arms, to arms!" the fierce Virago cries,
And swift as lightning to the combat flies.
All side in parties, and begin th' attack;
Fans clap, silks rustle, and tough whalebones crack;
Heroes' and Heroines' shouts confus'dly rise,
And bass, and treble voices strike the skies.
No common weapons in their hands are found,
Like Gods they fight, nor dread a mortal wound.
So when bold Homer makes the Gods engage,
And heav'nly breasts with human passions rage;
'Gainst Pallas, Mars; Latona, Hermes arms;
And all Olympus rings with loud alarms:
Jove's thunder roars, heav'n trembles all around,
Blue Neptune storms, the bellowing deeps resound:
Earth shakes her nodding tow'rs, the ground gives way,

[1]Tea.
[2]Box which held patches of sticking plaster for the face.
[3]Æneas.

And the pale ghosts start at the flash of day!
Triumphant Umbriel on a sconce's height
Clapped his glad wings, and sat to view the fight:
Propped on the bodkin spears, the Sprites survey
The growing combat, or assist the fray.
While through the press enraged Thalestris flies,
And scatters death around from both her eyes,
A Beau and Witling perished in the throng,
One died in metaphor, and one in song.
"O cruel nymph! a living death I bear,"
Cried Dapperwit, and sunk beside his chair.
A mournful glance Sir Fopling upwards cast,
"Those eyes are made so killing"—was his last.
Thus on Mæander's flowery margin lies
Th' expiring Swan, and as he sings he dies.
When bold Sir Plume had drawn Clarissa down,
Chloe stepped in, and killed him with a frown;
She smiled to see the doughty hero slain,
But, at her smile, the Beau revived again.
Now Jove suspends his golden scales in air,
Weighs the Men's wits against the Lady's hair;
The doubtful beam long nods from side to side;
At length the wits mount up, the hairs subside.
See, fierce Belinda on the Baron flies,
With more than usual lightning in her eyes:
Nor feared the Chief th' unequal fight to try,
Who sought no more than on his foe to die.
But this bold Lord with manly strength endued,
She with one finger and a thumb subdued:
Just where the breath of life his nostrils drew,
A charge of Snuff the wily virgin threw;
The Gnomes direct, to ev'ry atom just,
The pungent grains of titillating dust.
Sudden, with starting tears each eye o'erflows,
And the high dome re-echoes to his nose.
"Now meet thy fate," incensed Belinda cried,
And drew a deadly bodkin from her side.
(The same, his ancient personage to deck,
Her great great grandsire wore about his neck,
In three seal-rings; which after, melted down,
Formed a vast buckle for his widow's gown:
Her infant grandame's whistle next it grew,
The bells she jingled, and the whistle blew;
Then in a bodkin graced her mother's hairs,
Which long she wore, and now Belinda wears.)
"Boast not my fall" (he cried) "insulting foe!
Thou by some other shalt be laid as low,
Nor think, to die dejects my lofty mind:
All that I dread is leaving you behind!
Rather than so, ah, let me still survive,
And burn in Cupid's flames—but burn alive."
"Restore the Lock!" she cries; and all around
"Restore the Lock!" the vaulted roofs rebound.
Not fierce Othello in so loud a strain
Roared for the handkerchief that caused his pain.
But see how oft ambitious aims are crossed,
And chiefs contend 'till all the prize is lost!
The Lock, obtained with guilt, and kept with pain,
In every place is sought, but sought in vain:
With such a prize no mortal must be bless'd,
So heav'n decrees! with heav'n who can contest?
Some thought it mounted to the Lunar sphere,
Since all things lost on earth are treasured there.
There Heroes' wits are kept in pond'rous vases,
And beaux' in snuff-boxes and tweezer-cases.
There broken vows and death-bed alms are found,
And lovers' hearts with ends of riband bound,
The courtier's promises, and sick man's pray'rs,
The smiles of harlots, and the tears of heirs,
Cages for gnats, and chains to yoke a flea,
Dried butterflies, and tomes of casuistry.
But trust the Muse—she saw it upward rise,
Though marked by none but quick, poetic eyes
(So Rome's great founder[1] to the heav'ns withdrew,
To Proculus alone confessed in view);
A sudden Star, it shot through liquid air,
And drew behind a radiant trail of hair.
Not Berenice's[2] Locks first rose so bright,
The heav'ns bespangling with disheveled light.
The Sylphs behold it kindling as it flies,
And pleased pursue its progress through the skies.
This the Beau monde shall from the Mall[3] survey,
And hail with music its propitious ray.
This the bless'd Lover shall for Venus take,
And send up vows from Rosamonda's lake.[4]
This Partridge[5] soon shall view in cloudless skies,
When next he looks through Galileo's eyes;

---

[1]Romulus (the legend Pope alludes to is to be found in Livy, I, xvi).

[2]An Egyptian queen who dedicated a lock of hair for her husband's safe return from war. It was said to have become a constellation.

[3]Upper side of St. James's Park, London.

[4]A pond in St. James's Park.

[5]An astrologer who published predictions. Swift made fun of him in his Bickerstaff papers, foretelling his death, and later pretending that the astrologer had duly died at the appointed time.

And hence th' egregious wizard shall foredoom
The fate of Louis, and the fall of Rome.[1]
Then cease, bright Nymph! to mourn thy ravished hair,
Which adds new glory to the shining sphere!
Not all the tresses that fair head can boast,
Shall draw such envy as the Lock you lost.
For, after all the murders of your eye,
When, after millions slain, yourself shall die:
When those fair suns shall set, as set they must,
And all those tresses shall be laid in dust,
This Lock, the Muse shall consecrate to fame,
And 'midst the stars inscribe Belinda's name.

AN ESSAY ON MAN[2]

TO

H. ST. JOHN LORD BOLINGBROKE

ARGUMENT OF EPISTLE I

Of the Nature and State of Man, with Respect to the Universe.

Of Man in the abstract. I. That we can judge only with regard to our own system, being ignorant of the relations of systems and things, v. 17, *etc.* II. That Man is not to be deemed imperfect, but a Being suited to his place and rank in the creation, agreeable to the general Order of things, and conformable to Ends and Relations to him unknown, v. 35, *etc.* III. That it is partly upon his ignorance of future events, and partly upon the hope of a future state, that all his happiness in the present depends, v. 77, *etc.* IV. The pride of aiming at more knowledge, and pretending to more Perfection, the cause of Man's error and misery. The impiety of putting himself in the place of God, and judging of the fitness or unfitness, perfection or imperfection, justice or injustice of his dispensations, v. 109, *etc.* V. The absurdity of conceiting himself the final cause of the creation, or expecting that perfection in the moral world, which is not in the natural, v. 131, *etc.* VI. The unreasonableness of his complaints against Providence, while on the one hand he demands the Perfections of the Angels, and on the other the bodily qualifications of the Brutes; though, to possess any of the sensitive faculties in a higher degree, would render him miserable, v. 173, *etc.* VII. That throughout the whole visible world, an universal order and gradation in the sensual and mental faculties is observed, which causes a subordination of creature to creature, and of all creatures to Man. The gradations of sense, instinct, thought, reflection, reason; that Reason alone countervails all the other faculties, v. 207. VIII. How much further this order and subordination of living creatures may extend, above and below us; were any part of which broken, not that part only, but the whole connected creation must be destroyed, v. 233. IX. The extravagance, madness, and pride of such a desire, v. 250. X. The consequence of all, the absolute submission due to Providence, both as to our present and future state, v. 281, *etc.* to the end.

EPISTLE I

AWAKE, my ST. JOHN! leave all meaner things
To low ambition, and the pride of Kings.
Let us (since Life can little more supply
Than just to look about us and to die)
Expatiate[3] free o'er all this scene of Man;
A mighty maze! but not without a plan;[4]
A Wild, where weeds and flow'rs promiscuous shoot;
Or Garden, tempting with forbidden fruit.
Together let us beat this ample field,
Try what the open, what the covert yield;
The latent tracts, the giddy heights, explore
Of all who blindly creep, or sightless soar;
Eye Nature's walks, shoot Folly as it flies,
And catch the Manners living as they rise;
Laugh where we must, be candid where we can;
But vindicate the ways of God to Man.
I. Say first, of God above, or Man below,
What can we reason, but from what we know?
Of Man, what see we but his station here,
From which to reason, or to which refer?
Through worlds unnumbered though the God be known,
'T is ours to trace him only in our own.
He, who through vast immensity can pierce,
See worlds on worlds compose one universe,
Observe how system into system runs,
What other planets circle other suns,
What varied Being peoples ev'ry star,
May tell why Heav'n has made us as we are.
But of this frame the bearings, and the ties,
The strong connections, nice dependencies,

[1]Louis XIV and the Papacy.

[2]The first epistle, all that is here printed, was written in 1732, though the complete work (four epistles) was not finished and published until 1734. The *Essay* purports to be a philosophical poem, an aim characteristic of the age. Pope, however, had not a philosophic mind, and the interest of the poem lies in its detached sayings. It has even been claimed that Pope merely put into verse material given him by Lord Bolingbroke, his "guide, philosopher, and friend," to whom the poem is addressed. Though this can hardly be true, at least in the literal sense of the words, doubtless the matter of the poem was a subject of frequent discussion between the two.

[3]Wander.

[4]This line in the original editions stood,
"A mighty maze of walks without a plan;"
and it has been remarked (by Lowell) that "perhaps this came nearer Pope's real opinion than the verse he substituted for it."

Gradations just, has thy pervading soul
Looked through? or can a part contain the whole?
  Is the great chain, that draws all to agree,
And drawn supports, upheld by God, or thee?
II. Presumptuous Man! the reason wouldst thou find,
Why formed so weak, so little, and so blind?
First, if thou canst, the harder reason guess,
Why formed no weaker, blinder, and no less?
Ask of thy mother earth, why oaks are made
Taller or stronger than the weeds they shade?
Or ask of yonder argent fields above,
Why Jove's satellites are less than Jove?
  Of Systems possible, if 'tis confessed
That Wisdom infinite must form the best,
Where all must full or not coherent be,
And all that rises, rise in due degree;
Then, in the scale of reas'ning life, 'tis plain,
There must be, somewhere, such a rank as Man:
And all the question (wrangle e'er so long)
Is only this, if God has placed him wrong?
  Respecting Man, whatever wrong we call,
May, must be right, as relative to all.
In human works, though labored on with pain,
A thousand movements scarce one purpose gain;
In God's, one single can its end produce;
Yet serves to second too some other use.
So Man, who here seems principal alone,
Perhaps acts second to some sphere unknown,
Touches some wheel, or verges to some goal:
'Tis but a part we see, and not a whole.
  When the proud steed shall know why Man restrains
His fiery course, or drives him o'er the plains:
When the dull Ox, why now he breaks the clod,
Is now a victim, and now Egypt's God:
Then shall Man's pride and dullness comprehend
His actions', passions', being's, use and end;
Why doing, suff'ring, checked, impelled; and why
This hour a slave, the next a deity.
  Then say not Man's imperfect, Heav'n in fault;
Say rather, Man's as perfect as he ought:
His knowledge measured to his state and place;
His time a moment, and a point his space.
If to be perfect in a certain sphere,
What matter, soon or late, or here or there?
The bless'd to-day is as completely so,
As who began a thousand years ago.
III. Heav'n from all creatures hides the book of Fate,
All but the page prescribed, their present state:
From brutes what men, from men what spirits know:
Or who could suffer Being here below?
The lamb thy riot dooms to bleed to-day,
Had he thy Reason, would he skip and play?
Pleased to the last, he crops the flow'ry food,
And licks the hand just raised to shed his blood.
O blindness to the future! kindly giv'n,
That each may fill the circle marked by Heav'n:
Who sees with equal eye, as God of all,
A hero perish, or a sparrow fall,
Atoms or systems into ruin hurled,
And now a bubble burst, and now a world.
  Hope humbly then; with trembling pinions soar;
Wait the great teacher Death: and God adore.
What future bliss, he gives not thee to know,
But gives that Hope to be thy blessing now.
Hope springs eternal in the human breast:
Man never Is, but always To be bless'd:
The soul, uneasy and confined from home,
Rests and expatiates in a life to come.
  Lo, the poor Indian! whose untutored mind
Sees God in clouds, or hears him in the wind:
His soul proud Science never taught to stray
Far as the solar walk, or milky way;
Yet simple Nature to his hope has giv'n,
Behind the cloud-topped hill, an humbler heav'n;
Some safer world in depth of woods embraced,
Some happier island in the watry waste,
Where slaves once more their native land behold,
No fiends torment, no Christians thirst for gold.
To Be, contents his natural desire,
He asks no Angel's wing, no Seraph's fire;
But thinks, admitted to that equal[1] sky,
His faithful dog shall bear him company.
IV. Go, wiser thou! and, in thy scale of sense,
Weigh thy Opinion against Providence;
Call imperfection what thou fanci'st such,
Say, here he gives too little, there too much:
Destroy all Creatures for thy sport or gust,[2]
Yet cry, If Man's unhappy, God's unjust;
If Man alone engross not Heav'n's high care,
Alone made perfect here, immortal there:
Snatch from his hand the balance and the rod,
Re-judge his justice, be the God of God.
In Pride, in reas'ning Pride, our error lies;
All quit their sphere, and rush into the skies.
Pride still is aiming at the bless'd abodes,
Men would be Angels, Angels would be Gods
Aspiring to be Gods, if Angels fell,
Aspiring to be Angels, Men rebel:

---

[1]Impartial. [2]Pleasure.

And who but wishes to invert the laws
Of Order, sins against th' Eternal Cause.
V. Ask for what end the heav'nly bodies shine,
Earth for whose use? Pride answers, "'Tis for mine:
For me kind Nature wakes her genial Pow'r,
Suckles each herb, and spreads out ev'ry flow'r;
Annual for me, the grape, the rose renew
The juice nectareous, and the balmy dew;
For me, the mine a thousand treasures brings;
For me, health gushes from a thousand springs;
Seas roll to waft me, suns to light me rise;
My foot-stool earth, my canopy the skies."
But errs not Nature from his gracious end,
From burning suns when livid deaths descend,
When earthquakes swallow, or when tempests sweep
Towns to one grave, whole nations to the deep?
"No," ('tis replied) "the first Almighty Cause
Acts not by partial, but by gen'ral laws;
Th' exceptions few; some change since all began:
And what created perfect?"—Why then Man?
If the great end be human Happiness,
Then Nature deviates; and can Man do less?
As much that end a constant course requires
Of show'rs and sun-shine, as of Man's desires;
As much eternal springs and cloudless skies,
As Men for ever temp'rate, calm, and wise.
If plagues or earthquakes break not Heav'n's design,
Why then a Borgia, or a Catiline?
Who knows but he, whose hand the lightning forms,
Who heaves old Ocean, and who wings the storms;
Pours fierce Ambition in a Cæsar's mind,
Or turns young Ammon,[1] loose to scourge mankind?
From pride, from pride, our very reas'ning springs;
Account for moral as for nat'ral things:
Why charge we Heav'n in those, in these acquit?
In both, to reason right is to submit.
Better for Us, perhaps, it might appear,
Were there all harmony, all virtue here;
That never air or ocean felt the wind;
That never passion discomposed the mind.
But all subsists by elemental strife;
And Passions are the elements of Life.
The gen'ral Order, since the whole began
Is kept in Nature, and is kept in Man.

[1]Alexander the Great, who allowed himself to be called the son of Jupiter Ammon.

VI. What would this Man? Now upward will he soar,
And, little less than Angel, would be more;
Now looking downwards, just as grieved appears
To want the strength of bulls, the fur of bears.
Made for his use all creatures if he call,
Say what their use, had he the pow'rs of all?
Nature to these, without profusion, kind,
The proper organs, proper pow'rs assign'd;
Each seeming want compensated of course,
Here with degrees of swiftness, there of force;
All in exact proportion to the state;
Nothing to add, and nothing to abate.
Each beast, each insect, happy in its own:
Is Heav'n unkind to Man, and Man alone?
Shall he alone, whom rational we call,
Be pleased with nothing, if not bless'd with all?
The bliss of Man (could Pride that blessing find)
Is not to act or think beyond mankind;
No pow'rs of body or of soul to share,
But what his nature and his state can bear.
Why has not Man a microscopic eye?
For this plain reason, Man is not a Fly.
Say what the use, were finer optics giv'n,
T' inspect a mite, not comprehend the heav'n?
Or touch, if tremblingly alive all o'er,
To smart and agonize at every pore?
Or quick effluvia darting through the brain,
Die of a rose in aromatic pain?
If Nature thundered in his op'ning ears,
And stunned him with the music of the spheres,
How would he wish that Heav'n had left him still
The whisp'ring Zephyr, and the purling rill?
Who finds not Providence all good and wise,
Alike in what it gives, and what denies?
VII. Far as Creation's ample range extends,
The scale of sensual, mental pow'rs ascends:
Mark how it mounts, to Man's imperial race,
From the green myriads in the peopled grass:
What modes of sight betwixt each wide extreme,
The mole's dim curtain, and the lynx's beam:
Of smell, the headlong lioness between,
And hound sagacious on the tainted green:
Of hearing, from the life that fills the Flood,
To that which warbles through the vernal wood:
The spider's touch, how exquisitely fine!
Feels at each thread, and lives along the line:
In the nice bee, what sense so subtly true
From pois'nous herbs extracts the healing dew?
How Instinct varies in the grov'ling swine,
Compared, half-reas'ning elephant, with thine!

'Twixt that, and Reason, what a nice barrier,
For ever sep'rate, yet for ever near!
Remembrance and Reflection how allied;
What thin partitions Sense from Thought divide:
And Middle natures, how they long to join,
Yet never pass th' insuperable line!
Without this just gradation, could they be
Subjected, these to those, or all to thee?
The pow'rs of all subdued by thee alone,
Is not thy Reason all these pow'rs in one?

VIII. See, through this air, this ocean, and this earth,
All matter quick, and bursting into birth.
Above, how high progressive life may go!
Around, how wide! how deep extend below!
Vast chain of Being! which from God began,
Natures ethereal, human, angel, man,
Beast, bird, fish, insect, what no eye can see,
No glass can reach; from Infinite to thee,
From thee to Nothing.—On superior pow'rs
Were we to press, inferior might on ours:
Or in the full creation leave a void,
Where, one step broken, the great scale's destroyed:
From Nature's chain whatever link you strike,
Tenth or ten-thousandth, breaks the chain alike.

And, if each system in gradation roll
Alike essential to th' amazing Whole,
The least confusion but in one, not all
That system only, but the Whole must fall.
Let Earth unbalanced from her orbit fly,
Planets and Suns run lawless through the sky;
Let ruling Angels from their spheres be hurled,
Being on Being wrecked, and world on world;
Heav'n's whole foundations to their center nod,
And Nature tremble to the throne of God.
All this dread Order break—for whom? for thee?
Vile worm!—O Madness! Pride! Impiety!

IX. What if the foot, ordained the dust to tread,
Or hand, to toil, aspired to be the head?
What if the head, the eye, or ear repined
To serve mere engines to the ruling Mind?
Just as absurd for any part to claim
To be another, in this gen'ral frame:
Just as absurd, to mourn the tasks or pains,
The great directing Mind of all ordains.

All are but parts of one stupendous whole,
Whose body Nature is, and God the soul;
That, changed through all, and yet in all the same;
Great in the earth, as in th' ethereal frame;
Warms in the sun, refreshes in the breeze,
Glows in the stars, and blossoms in the trees,
Lives through all life, extends through all extent,
Spreads undivided, operates unspent;
Breathes in our soul, informs our mortal part,
As full, as perfect, in a hair as heart:
As full, as perfect, in vile Man that mourns,
As the rapt Seraph that adores and burns:
To him no high, no low, no great, no small;
He fills, he bounds, connects, and equals all.

X. Cease then, nor Order Imperfection name:
Our proper bliss depends on what we blame.
Know thy own point: This kind, this due degree
Of blindness, weakness, Heav'n bestows on thee.
Submit.—In this, or any other sphere,
Secure to be as bless'd as thou canst bear:
Safe in the hand of one disposing Pow'r,
Or in the natal, or the mortal hour.
All Nature is but Art, unknown to thee;
All Chance, Direction, which thou canst not see;
All Discord, Harmony not understood;
All partial Evil, universal Good:
And, spite of Pride, in erring Reason's spite,
One truth is clear, *Whatever is, is right.*

EPISTLE TO DR. ARBUTHNOT[1]

ADVERTISEMENT TO THE FIRST PUBLICATION OF THIS *EPISTLE*

THIS paper is a sort of bill of complaint, begun many years since, and drawn up by snatches, as the several occasions offered. I had no thoughts of publishing it, till it pleased some Persons of Rank and Fortune (the Authors of *Verses to the Imitator of Horace*, and of an *Epistle to a Doctor of Divinity from a Nobleman at Hampton Court*) to attack, in a very extraordinary manner, not only my Writings (of which, being public, the Public is judge), but my Person, Morals, and Family, whereof, to those who know me not, a truer information may be requisite. Being divided between the necessity to say something of myself, and my own laziness to undertake so awkward a task, I thought it the shortest way to put

[1]Pope indicates, in the "Advertisement" printed above, the purpose of this *Epistle*, but his statement concerning the time of its composition cannot be taken literally. A few passages were written earlier than 1734 (the portraits of Addison and Bufo, and the reference to his mother), but the *Epistle* as a whole dates from this year, or from 1735. Its immediate occasion was the abusive attack on Pope contained in the two poems he mentions in the "Advertisement." The first of these is said to have been written by Lady Mary Wortley Montague and Lord John Hervey together; the second was written by Hervey. Dr. John Arbuthnot was both physician and man of letters, and Pope's close friend until his death in 1735, only a short time after the publication of the *Epistle*. The poem is cast in the form of a dialogue between Pope himself and Arbuthnot.

the last hand to this Epistle. If it have anything pleasing, it will be that by which I am most desirous to please, the Truth and the Sentiment; and if anything offensive, it will be only to those I am least sorry to offend, the vicious or the ungenerous.

Many will know their own pictures in it, there being not a circumstance but what is true; but I have, for the most part, spared their Names, and they may escape being laughed at, if they please.

I would have some of them know, it was owing to the request of the learned and candid Friend to whom it is inscribed, that I make not as free use of theirs as they have done of mine. However, I shall have this advantage, and honor, on my side, that whereas, by their proceeding, any abuse may be directed at any man, no injury can possibly be done by mine, since a nameless character can never be found out, but by its truth and likeness. P.

P. SHUT, shut the door, good John![1] fatigued, I said,
Tie up the knocker, say I'm sick, I'm dead.
The Dog-star rages! nay 'tis past a doubt,
All Bedlam, or Parnassus, is let out:
Fire in each eye, and papers in each hand,
They rave, recite, and madden round the land.
What walls can guard me, or what shade can hide?
They pierce my thickets, through my Grot[2] they glide;
By land, by water, they renew the charge;
They stop the chariot, and they board the barge.
No place is sacred, not the Church is free;
E'en Sunday shines no Sabbath-day to me;
Then from the Mint[3] walks forth the Man of rime,
Happy to catch me just at Dinner-time.
Is there a Parson, much bemused in beer,
A maudlin Poetess, a riming Peer,
A Clerk,[4] foredoomed his father's soul to cross,
Who pens a Stanza, when he should *engross?*
Is there, who, locked from ink and paper, scrawls
With desp'rate charcoal round his darkened walls?
All fly to Twit'nam,[5] and in humble strain
Apply to me, to keep them mad or vain.
Arthur,[6] whose giddy son neglects the Laws,
Imputes to me and my damned works the cause:
Poor Cornus[7] sees his frantic wife elope,
And curses Wit, and Poetry, and Pope.
Friend to my Life (which did not you prolong,
The world had wanted many an idle song)
What Drop or Nostrum can this plague remove?
Or which must end me, a Fool's wrath or love?
A dire dilemma! either way I'm sped,[8]
If foes, they write, if friends, they read me dead.
Seized and tied down to judge, how wretched I!
Who can't be silent, and who will not lie.
To laugh, were want of goodness and of grace,
And to be grave, exceeds all Pow'r of face.
I sit with sad civility, I read
With honest anguish, and an aching head;
And drop at last, but in unwilling ears,
This saving counsel, "Keep your piece nine years."[9]
"Nine years!" cries he, who high in Drury-Lane,
Lulled by soft Zephyrs through the broken pane,
Rimes ere he wakes, and prints before Term ends,[10]
Obliged by hunger, and request of friends:
"The piece, you think, is incorrect? why, take it,
I'm all submission, what you'd have it, make it."
Three things another's modest wishes bound,
My Friendship, and a Prologue, and ten pound.
Pitholeon sends to me: "You know his Grace,
I want a Patron; ask him for a Place."
Pitholeon libeled me—"but here's a letter
Informs you, Sir, 'twas when he knew no better.
Dare you refuse him? Curll[11] invites to dine,
He'll write a *Journal*, or he'll turn Divine."
Bless me! a packet.—"'Tis a stranger sues,
A Virgin Tragedy, an Orphan Muse."
If I dislike it, "Furies, death and rage!"
If I approve, "Commend it to the Stage."
There (thank my stars) my whole Commission ends,
The Play'rs and I are, luckily, no friends,
Fired that the house reject him, "'Sdeath I'll print it,

[1]John Searl, Pope's body-servant.

[2]An artificial grotto that formed a passage-way under a road which ran through Pope's grounds at Twickenham. This grotto and its ornamentation gave Pope a particular pleasure.

[3]A district in London where debtors could not be arrested; nor could they be arrested anywhere on Sundays.

[4]Law clerk.

[5]Twickenham, where Pope lived.

[6]Arthur Moore, a politician.

[7]Robert, Lord Walpole.

[8]Done for.

[9]Horace's advice in his *Art of Poetry* (line 388).

[10]*I. e.*, before the season is over.

[11]A piratical publisher and an enemy of Pope.

And shame the fools——Your Int'rest, Sir, with Lintot!"[1]
Lintot, dull rogue! will think your price too much:
"Not, Sir, if you revise it, and retouch."
All my demurs but double his Attacks;
At last he whispers, "Do; and we go snacks."
Glad of a quarrel, straight I clap the door,
Sir, let me see your works and you no more.
'Tis sung, when Midas' Ears began to spring
(Midas, a sacred person and a king),
His very Minister who spied them first,
(Some say his Queen) was forced to speak, or burst.
And is not mine, my friend, a sorer case,
When ev'ry coxcomb perks them in my face?
A. Good friend, forbear! you deal in dang'rous things.
I'd never name Queens, Ministers, or Kings;
Keep close to Ears, and those let asses prick;
'Tis nothing— P. Nothing? if they bite and kick?
Out with it, *Dunciad!* let the secret pass,
That secret to each fool, that he's an Ass:
The truth once told (and wherefore should we lie?)
The Queen of Midas slept, and so may I.
You think this cruel? take it for a rule,
No creature smarts so little as a fool.
Let peals of laughter, Codrus! round thee break,
Thou unconcerned canst hear the mighty crack:
Pit, Box, and gall'ry in convulsions hurled,
Thou stand'st unshook amidst a bursting world.
Who shames a Scribbler? break one cobweb through,
He spins the slight, self-pleasing thread anew:
Destroy his fib or sophistry, in vain,
The creature's at his dirty work again,
Throned in the center of his thin designs,
Proud of a vast extent of flimsy lines!
Whom have I hurt? has Poet yet, or Peer,
Lost the arched eye-brow, or Parnassian sneer?
And has not Colley[2] still his Lord and Whore?
His butchers Henley? his freemasons Moore?
Does not one table Bavius still admit?
Still to one Bishop Philips[3] seem a wit?
Still Sappho[4]— A. Hold! for God's sake—you'll offend,
No Names!—be calm!—learn prudence of a friend!
I too could write, and I am twice as tall;
But foes like these— P. One Flatt'rer's worse than all.

[1]Another publisher, who published much of Pope's work.
[2]Colley Cibber. [3]Ambrose Philips.
[4]Lady Mary Wortley Montague.

Of all mad creatures, if the learn'd are right,
It is the slaver kills, and not the bite.
A fool quite angry is quite innocent:
Alas! 'tis ten times worse when they *repent.*
One dedicates in high heroic prose,
And ridicules beyond a hundred foes:
One from all Grubstreet will my fame defend,
And, more abusive, calls himself my friend.
This prints my *Letters*, that expects a bribe,
And others roar aloud, "Subscribe, subscribe."
There are, who to my person pay their court:
I cough like Horace, and, though lean, am short,
Ammon's[5] great son one shoulder had too high,
Such Ovid's nose, and "Sir! you have an Eye"—
Go on, obliging creatures, make me see
All that disgraced my Betters, met in me.
Say for my comfort, languishing in bed,
"Just so immortal Maro[6] held his head:"
And when I die, be sure you let me know
Great Homer died three thousand years ago.
Why did I write? what sin to me unknown
Dipped me in ink, my parents', or my own?
As yet a child, nor yet a fool to fame,
I lisped in numbers, for the numbers came.
I left no calling for this idle trade,
No duty broke, no father disobeyed.
The Muse but served to ease some friend, not Wife,
To help me through this long disease, my Life,
To second, Arbuthnot! thy Art and Care,
And teach the Being you preserved, to bear.
But why then publish? Granville[7] the polite,
And knowing Walsh,[8] would tell me I could write;
Well-natured Garth[9] inflamed with early praise;
And Congreve loved, and Swift endured my lays;
The courtly Talbot, Somers, Sheffield,[10] read;
E'en mitered Rochester[11] would nod the head,
And St. John's self (great Dryden's friends before)
With open arms received one Poet more.
Happy my studies, when by these approved!
Happier their author, when by these belov'd!
From these the world will judge of men and books,
Not from the Burnets, Oldmixons, and Cookes.[12]

[5]Alexander the Great. [6]Virgil.
[7]George Granville, Lord Lansdowne.
[8]See introductory account of Pope above.
[9]Samuel Garth, physician and man of letters.
[10]All statesmen and patrons of letters.
[11]Francis Atterbury, Bishop of Rochester.
[12]Authors of secret and scandalous history (Pope's note).

Soft were my numbers; who could take offense,
While pure Description held the place of Sense?
Like gentle Fanny's[1] was my flow'ry theme,
A painted mistress, or a purling stream.
Yet then did Gildon draw his venal quill;—
I wished the man a dinner, and sat still.
Yet then did Dennis[2] rave in furious fret;
I never answered,—I was not in debt.
If want provoked, or madness made them print,
I waged no war with Bedlam or the Mint.
Did some more sober Critic come abroad;
If wrong, I smiled; if right, I kissed the rod.
Pains, reading, study, are their just pretense,
And all they want is spirit, taste, and sense.
Commas and points they set exactly right,
And 'twere a sin to rob them of their mite.
Yet ne'er one sprig of laurel graced these ribalds,
From slashing Bentley down to pidling Tibalds:[3]
Each wight, who reads not, and but scans and spells,
Each Word-catcher, that lives on syllables,
E'en such small Critics some regard may claim,
Preserved in Milton's or in Shakespeare's name.
Pretty! in amber to observe the forms
Of hairs, or straws, or dirt, or grubs, or worms!
The things, we know, are neither rich nor rare,
But wonder how the devil they got there.
Were others angry: I excused them too;
Well might they rage, I gave them but their due.
A man's true merit 'tis not hard to find;
But each man's secret standard in his mind,
That Casting-weight pride adds to emptiness,
This, who can gratify? for who can guess?
The Bard[4] whom pilfered Pastorals renown,
Who turns a Persian tale for half a Crown,
Just writes to make his barrenness appear,
And strains, from hard-bound brains, eight lines a year;
He, who still wanting, though he lives on theft,
Steals much, spends little, yet has nothing left:
And He, who now to sense, now nonsense leaning,
Means not, but blunders round about a meaning:
And He, whose fustian's so sublimely bad,
It is not Poetry, but prose run mad:
All these, my modest Satire bade translate,
And owned that nine such Poets made a Tate.[5]
How did they fume, and stamp, and roar, and chafe!
And swear, not Addison himself was safe.
Peace to all such! but were there One whose fires
True Genius kindles, and fair Fame inspires;
Bless'd with each talent and each art to please,
And born to write, converse, and live with ease:
Should such a man, too fond to rule alone,
Bear, like the Turk, no brother near the throne,
View him with scornful, yet with jealous eyes,
And hate for arts that caused himself to rise;
Damn with faint praise, assent with civil leer,
And without sneering, teach the rest to sneer;
Willing to wound, and yet afraid to strike,
Just hint a fault, and hesitate dislike;
Alike reserved to blame, or to commend,
A tim'rous foe, and a suspicious friend;
Dreading e'en fools, by Flatterers besieged,
And so obliging, that he ne'er obliged;
Like Cato, give his little Senate laws,
And sit attentive to his own applause;
While Wits and Templars ev'ry sentence raise,
And wonder with a foolish face of praise:—
Who but must laugh, if such a man there be?
Who would not weep, if Atticus[6] were he?
What though my Name stood rubric[7] on the walls
Or plastered posts, with claps,[8] in capitals?
Or smoking forth, a hundred hawkers' load,
On wings of winds came flying all abroad?
I sought no homage from the Race that write;
I kept, like Asian Monarchs, from their sight:
Poems I heeded (now be-rimed so long)
No more than thou, great George! a birthday song.
I ne'er with wits or witlings passed my days,
To spread about the itch of verse and praise;
Nor like a puppy, daggled through the town,
To fetch and carry sing-song up and down;
Nor at Rehearsals sweat, and mouthed, and cried,
With handkerchief and orange at my side;
But sick of fops, and poetry, and prate,
To Bufo,[9] left the whole Castalian state.

[1]Lord Hervey.

[2]Gildon and Dennis were critics of the day.

[3]Bentley was a famous classical scholar who published an edition of *Paradise Lost;* Theobald a scholar and editor of Shakespeare.

[4]Ambrose Philips.

[5]Nahum Tate, at the time poet laureate.

[6]Addison.

[7]The reference is to Lintot's practice of posting on the walls of his shop the titles of new books in red letters.

[8]Posters.

[9]Probably Lord Halifax (the following portrait is said to have been intended, when first written, for Bubb Dodington).

Proud as Apollo on his forkéd hill,
Sat full-blown Bufo, puffed by ev'ry quill;
Fed with soft Dedication all day long,
Horace and he went hand in hand in song.
His Library (where busts of Poets dead
And a true Pindar stood without a head),
Received of wits an undistinguished race,
Who first his judgment asked, and then a place:
Much they extolled his pictures, much his seat,
And flattered ev'ry day, and some days eat:
Till grown more frugal in his riper days,
He paid some bards with port, and some with praise:
To some a dry rehearsal saw assigned,
And others (harder still) he paid in kind.
Dryden alone (what wonder?) came not nigh,
Dryden alone escaped this judging eye:
But still the Great have kindness in reserve,
He helped to bury whom he helped to starve.
May some choice patron bless each gray goose quill!
May ev'ry Bavius have his Bufo still!
So, when a Statesman wants a day's defense,
Or Envy holds a whole week's war with Sense,
Or simple pride for flatt'ry makes demands,
May dunce by dunce be whistled off my hands!
Bless'd be the Great! for those they take away,
And those they left me; for they left me Gay;[1]
Left me to see neglected Genius bloom,
Neglected die, and tell it on his tomb:
Of all thy blameless life the sole return
My Verse, and Queensb'ry weeping o'er thy urn.
Oh, let me live my own, and die so too!
(To live and die is all I have to do)
Maintain a Poet's dignity and ease,
And see what friends, and read what books I please;
Above a Patron, though I condescend
Sometimes to call a minister my friend.
I was not born for Courts or great affairs;
I pay my debts, believe, and say my pray'rs;
Can sleep without a Poem in my head;
Nor know, if Dennis be alive or dead.
Why am I asked what next shall see the light?
Heav'ns! was I born for nothing but to write?
Has Life no joys for me? or (to be grave)
Have I no friend to serve, no soul to save?
"I found him close with Swift"—"Indeed? no doubt"
(Cries prating Balbus), "something will come out."
'Tis all in vain, deny it as I will.
"No, such a Genius never can lie still;"

[1]John Gay, the poet.

And then for mine obligingly mistakes
The first Lampoon Sir Will or Bubo[2] makes.
Poor guiltless I! and can I choose but smile,
When ev'ry Coxcomb knows me by my Style?
Cursed be the verse, how well soe'er it flow,
That tends to make one worthy man my foe,
Give Virtue scandal, Innocence a fear,
Or from the soft-eyed Virgin steal a tear!
But he who hurts a harmless neighbor's peace,
Insults fall'n worth, or Beauty in distress,
Who loves a Lie, lame slander helps about,
Who writes a Libel, or who copies out:
That Fop, whose pride affects a patron's name,
Yet absent, wounds an author's honest fame:
Who can your merit selfishly approve,
And show the sense of it without the love;
Who has the vanity to call you friend,
Yet wants the honor, injured, to defend;
Who tells whate'er you think, whate'er you say,
And, if he lie not, must at least betray:
Who to the Dean, and silver bell can swear,
And sees at Canons what was never there;
Who reads, but with a lust to misapply,
Make Satire a Lampoon, and Fiction, Lie.
A lash like mine no honest man shall dread,
But all such babbling blockheads in his stead.
Let Sporus[3] tremble— A. What? that thing of silk,
Sporus, that mere white curd of Ass's milk!
Satire or sense, alas! can Sporus feel?
Who breaks a butterfly upon a wheel?
P. Yet let me flap this bug with gilded wings,
This painted child of dirt, that stinks and stings;
Whose buzz the witty and the fair annoys,
Yet wit ne'er tastes, and beauty ne'er enjoys:
So well-bred spaniels civilly delight
In mumbling of the game they dare not bite.
Eternal smiles his emptiness betray,
As shallow streams run dimpling all the way.
Whether in florid impotence he speaks,
And, as the prompter breathes, the puppet squeaks;
Or at the ear of Eve, familiar Toad,
Half froth, half venom, spits himself abroad,
In puns, or politics, or tales, or lies,
Or spite, or smut, or rimes, or blasphemies.
His wit all see-saw, between that and this,
Now high, now low, now master up, now miss,
And he himself one vile Antithesis.
Amphibious thing! that acting either part,
The trifling head or the corrupted heart,
Fop at the toilet, flatt'rer at the board,
Now trips a Lady, and now struts a Lord.
Eve's tempter thus the Rabbins have expressed,
A Cherub's face, a reptile all the rest;

[2]Sir William Yonge and Bubb Doddington.
[3]John, Lord Hervey.

Beauty that shocks you, parts that none will trust;
Wit that can creep, and pride that licks the dust.
  Not Fortune's worshiper, nor fashion's fool,
Not Lucre's madman, nor Ambition's tool,
Not proud, nor servile;—be one Poet's praise,
That, if he pleased, he pleased by manly ways:
That Flatt'ry, e'en to Kings, he held a shame,
And thought a Lie in verse or prose the same.
That not in Fancy's maze he wandered long,
But stooped to Truth, and moralized his song:
That not for Fame, but Virtue's better end,
He stood the furious foe, the timid friend,
The damning critic, half approving wit,
The coxcomb hit, or fearing to be hit;
Laughed at the loss of friends he never had,
The dull, the proud, the wicked, and the mad;
The distant threats of vengeance on his head,
The blow unfelt, the tear he never shed;
The tale revived, the lie so oft o'erthrown,
Th' imputed trash, and dullness not his own;
The morals blackened when the writings 'scape,
The libeled person, and the pictured shape;
Abuse, on all he loved, or loved him, spread,
A friend in exile, or a father dead;
The whisper, that to greatness still too near,
Perhaps, yet vibrates on his Sov'reign's ear:—
Welcome for thee, fair Virtue! all the past;
For thee, fair Virtue! welcome e'en the last!
  A. But why insult the poor, affront the great?
P. A knave's a knave, to me, in ev'ry state:
Alike my scorn, if he succeed or fail,
Sporus at court, or Japhet[1] in a jail,
A hireling scribbler, or a hireling peer,
Knight of the post corrupt, or of the shire;
If on a Pillory, or near a Throne,
He gain his Prince's ear, or lose his own.
  Yet soft by nature, more a dupe than wit,
Sappho can tell you how this man was bit;
This dreaded Sat'rist Dennis will confess
Foe to his pride, but friend to his distress:
So humble, he has knocked at Tibbald's door,
Has drunk with Cibber, nay has rimed for Moore.
Full ten years slandered, did he once reply?
Three thousand suns went down on Welsted's[2] lie.
To please a Mistress one aspersed his life;
He lashed him not, but let her be his wife.
Let Budgell[3] charge low Grubstreet on his quill,
And write whate'er he pleased, except his Will;
Let the two Curlls[4] of Town and Court, abuse
His father, mother, body, soul, and muse.
Yet why? that Father held it for a rule,
It was a sin to call our neighbor fool;
That harmless Mother thought no wife a whore:
Hear this, and spare his family, James Moore!
Unspotted names, and memorable long!
If there be force in Virtue, or in Song.
  Of gentle blood (part shed in Honor's cause,
While yet in Britain Honor had applause)
Each parent sprung— A. What fortune, pray?— P. Their own,
And better got, than Bestia's from the throne.
Born to no Pride, inheriting no Strife,
Nor marrying Discord in a noble wife,
Stranger to civil and religious rage,
The good man walked innoxious through his age.
Nor Courts he saw, no suits would ever try,
Nor dared an Oath, nor hazarded a Lie.
Unlearn'd, he knew no schoolman's subtle art,
No language, but the language of the heart.
By Nature honest, by Experience wise,
Healthy by temp'rance, and by exercise:
His life, though long, to sickness past unknown,
His death was instant, and without a groan.
O grant me, thus to live, and thus to die!
Who sprung from Kings shall know less joy than I.
  O Friend! may each domestic bliss be thine!
Be no unpleasing Melancholy mine:
Me, let the tender office long engage,
To rock the cradle of reposing Age,
With lenient arts extend a Mother's breath,
Make Languor smile, and smooth the bed of Death,
Explore the thought, explain the asking eye,
And keep a while one parent from the sky!
On cares like these if length of days attend,
May Heav'n, to bless those days, preserve my friend,
Preserve him social, cheerful, and serene,
And just as rich as when he served a Queen.[5]
A. Whether that blessing be denied or giv'n,
Thus far was right, the rest belongs to Heav'n.

[1]Japhet Crooke, a forger.

[2]A hack-writer of the day.

[3]Budgell was charged with forging a will, to his own profit.

[4]The bookseller and Lord Hervey.

[5]Arbuthnot had been physician to Queen Anne.

Rea

JAMES THOMSON (1700–1748) K

Thomson's father was a minister in the Scottish Kirk, and both parents were natives of Roxburghshire. The poet, their fourth child, was born in the village of Ednam, on 7 or 11 September (there is no record, and biographers differ, though the latter date was regarded by Thomson's relatives as his birthday). Two months later Thomson's father was called to the church at Southdean, "situated close to the Cheviots, on the upper stream of the 'sylvan Jed,' a locality which combines bleak mountain scenery with the charm of prettily wooded valleys: and it was here that the first impressions of external nature were received by the growing boy." (G. C. Macaulay, *Thomson*, p. 2.) He attended a grammar school at Jedburgh, some eight miles from Southdean. In 1715 he entered Edinburgh University. In the following year his father died suddenly while exorcizing a ghost for one of his parishioners, and the poet's family soon after removed to Edinburgh. Thomson was designed for the ministry, but from a very early time he had been given to versifying, and one of his teachers finally told him that his bent was for literature rather than for useful preaching. Early in 1725 he turned to "the noblest prospect which a Scotchman ever sees"—journeying, however, from Leith by sea—and was soon seeking his literary fortune in London. He managed, for a time, to exist by acting as a tutor, and meanwhile composed *Winter*, which was published in 1726. The poem was, says one of Thomson's earliest biographers, Patrick Murdoch, "no sooner read than universally admired, those only excepted who had not been used to feel or to look for anything in poetry beyond a *point* of satirical or epigrammatic wit, a smart *antithesis* richly trimmed with rime, or the softness of an elegiac complaint. To such his manly, classical spirit could not readily recommend itself, till after a more attentive perusal they had got the better of their prejudices and either acquired or affected a truer taste."

From this time Thomson's path lay clear before him, and his success seemed assured, though his circumstances were not yet easy. In 1727, upon the death of Sir Isaac Newton, he published a poem to his memory, and in the same year published *Summer*. *Spring* followed in 1728, and *Britannia* in 1729 (written, however, two years earlier). In 1730 *Autumn* was published, and the *Hymn on the Seasons*, in the first collected edition of *The Seasons;* and in this year also the tragedy of *Sophonisba* was successfully acted at Drury Lane, and was published. In all, Thomson wrote five tragedies—none of them of any great interest today, though their blank verse has a quality of ease which shows the capable workman. Towards the close of 1730 he went abroad, as traveling tutor and companion to the young son of Charles Talbot. He spent some time in Paris, where he called on Voltaire, and traveled through Italy, returning to England in December, 1731. In 1733 he received, through Talbot, then Lord Chancellor, a sinecure which he held until 1737. Meanwhile he published (1735–1736) his unsuccessful poem *Liberty*, which Dr. Johnson found himself unable to read, and in 1736 took a house in Kew Lane, Richmond, where he lived during the remainder of his life. In 1737 he made the acquaintance of George Lyttelton, through whose good offices he received a pension from the Prince of Wales and, later, a sinecure post—the Surveyor-Generalship of the Leeward Islands. In 1740 he wrote *Rule, Britannia!* for *The Masque of Alfred*, in the composition of which he and David Mallet joined hands. In May, 1748, *The Castle of Indolence* was published (two cantos in Spenserian stanzas), and on 27 August Thomson died.

Many stories have been told of his growing indolence through his later years, but with little or no foundation in fact. He may have been in the habit of eating the sunny side from the peaches in his garden with his hands in his pockets, too indolent to pluck the fruit; and he did usually rise at noon—because, however, he generally composed his verses at night, and often remained at work until near morning. He was careless of his clothes, and uninviting, perhaps positively disagreeable, in appearance. But he was good-humored, sensitive, generous, high-minded, had a cultivated taste, and was warmly loved by many friends. He was devoted to Elizabeth Young—the "Amanda" of his poems—but was not considered a sufficiently good match by her mother, and so never married. As a poet his great distinction is that of having thrown open a new world, the world of natural scenery and of country employments. Though Thomson's originality was not absolute, still, it may be said that in *The Seasons* for the first time the realm of external nature, regarded in and for itself, became the sufficient subject of a long poem. Yet this fact does not make Thomson—as Wordsworth and certain critics following his lead have pretended—"a herald of the romantic revival. . . . He was essentially a representative of his own age, and that was also the age of Pope. . . . His representations are broadly objective, not lyrical or personal, and he does not by preference select for treatment that which is wild or awful in nature." (Macaulay, p. 93.)

THE SEASONS

WINTER[1]

THE ARGUMENT.—The subject proposed. Address to the Earl of Wilmington. First approach of Winter. According to the natural course of the season, various storms described. Rain. Wind. Snow. The driving of the snows: a man perishing among them; whence reflections on the wants and miseries of human life. The wolves descending from the Alps and Apennines. A winter evening described: as spent by philosophers; by the country people; in the city. Frost. A view of Winter within the polar circle. A thaw. The whole concluding with moral reflections on a future state.

SEE, Winter comes to rule the varied year,
Sullen and sad, with all his rising train—
Vapors, and clouds, and storms. Be these my theme;
These, that exalt the soul to solemn thought
And heavenly musing. Welcome, kindred glooms!
Cogenial[2] horrors, hail! With frequent foot,
Pleased have I, in my cheerful morn of life,
When nursed by careless solitude I lived
And sung of Nature with unceasing joy,
Pleased have I wandered through your rough domain;
Trod the pure virgin-snows, myself as pure;
Heard the winds roar, and the big torrent burst;
Or seen the deep-fermenting tempest brewed
In the grim evening-sky. Thus passed the time,
Till through the lucid chambers of the south
Looked out the joyous Spring—looked out and smiled.
To thee, the patron of this first essay,
The muse, O Wilmington![3] renews her song.
Since has she rounded the revolving year:
Skimmed the gay Spring; on eagle-pinions borne,
Attempted through the Summer-blaze to rise;
Then swept o'er Autumn with the shadowy gale.
And now among the Wintry clouds again,
Rolled in the doubling storm, she tries to soar,
To swell her note with all the rushing winds,
To suit her sounding cadence to the floods;
As is her theme, her numbers wildly great.
Thrice happy, could she fill thy judging ear
With bold description and with manly thought!
Nor art thou skilled in awful schemes alone,
And how to make a mighty people thrive;
But equal goodness, sound integrity,
A firm, unshaken, uncorrupted soul
Amid a sliding age, and burning strong,
Not vainly blazing, for thy country's weal,
A steady spirit, regularly free—
These, each exalting each, the statesman light
Into the patriot; these, the public hope
And eye to thee converting, bid the Muse
Record what envy dares not flattery call.
Now, when the cheerless empire of the sky
To Capricorn the Centaur-Archer[4] yields,
And fierce Aquarius stains the inverted year—
Hung o'er the farthest verge of heaven, the sun
Scarce spreads o'er ether the dejected day.
Faint are his gleams, and ineffectual shoot
His struggling rays in horizontal lines
Through the thick air; as clothed in cloudy storm,
Weak, wan, and broad, he skirts the southern sky;
And, soon descending, to the long dark night,
Wide-shading all, the prostrate world resigns.
Nor is the night unwished; while vital heat,
Light, life, and joy the dubious day forsake.
Meantime, in sable cincture, shadows vast,
Deep-tinged and damp, and congregated clouds,
And all the vapory turbulence of heaven
Involve the face of things. Thus Winter falls,
A heavy gloom oppressive o'er the world,
Through Nature shedding influence malign,
And rouses up the seeds of dark disease.
The soul of man dies in him, loathing life,
And black with more than melancholy views.
The cattle droop; and o'er the furrowed land,
Fresh from the plow, the dun discolored flocks,
Untended spreading, crop the wholesome root.
Along the woods, along the moorish fens,
Sighs the sad genius of the coming storm;
And up among the loose disjointed cliffs

[1]The text is that of the last edition in Thomson's lifetime, 1746. When first published, *Winter* contained 405 lines, which were increased to 1069 in successive revisions. Thomson "cherished a passion for corrrecting and improving. As long as he lived, and had the leisure (he never wanted the inclination), he was revising and altering." (J. L. Robertson.) It has been thought that in his revision for the edition of 1744 he was aided by Pope, but it has now been established that the suggestions in question—many of which were adopted—came from Thomson's friend Lyttelton. Doubt has sometimes been expressed as to the happiness of Thomson's frequent alterations and additions, but it is the opinion of the most thorough and competent student of the subject (G. C. Macaulay) that "few poets have been so successful as Thomson in the revision of their work." The same critic says: "*Winter* is on the whole the most successful of the four poems in producing a single harmonious impression. . . . It is the only poem of the series in which the season is successfully personified."

[2]Modern editors alter to "congenial," but "cogenial" is what Thomson wrote, meaning "familiar from birth."

[3]On its first publication *Winter* was dedicated to Sir Spencer Compton (*c.* 1673–1743), Speaker of the House of Commons. In 1730 he was created Earl of Wilmington.

[4]Sagittarius. The sun leaves the sign of Sagittarius and enters that of Capricorn on 21 December, and a month later enters that of Aquarius.

And fractured mountains wild, the brawling brook
And cave, presageful, send a hollow moan,
Resounding long in listening fancy's ear.
 Then comes the father of the tempest forth,
Wrapped in black glooms. First, joyless rains obscure
Drive through the mingling skies with vapor foul,
Dash on the mountain's brow, and shake the woods
That grumbling wave below. The unsightly plain
Lies a brown deluge; as the low-bent clouds
Pour flood on flood, yet unexhausted still
Combine, and, deepening into night, shut up
The day's fair face. The wanderers of heaven,
Each to his home, retire; save those that love
To take their pastime in the troubled air,
Or skimming flutter round the dimply pool.
The cattle from the untasted fields return
And ask, with meaning low, their wonted stalls,
Or ruminate in the contiguous shade.
Thither the household feathery people crowd,
The crested cock, with all his female train,
Pensive and dripping; while the cottage-hind
Hangs o'er the enlivening blaze, and taleful there
Recounts his simple frolic: much he talks,
And much he laughs, nor recks the storm that blows
Without, and rattles on his humble roof.
 Wide o'er the brim, with many a torrent swelled,
And the mixed ruin of its banks o'erspread,
At last the roused-up river pours along:
Resistless, roaring, dreadful, down it comes,
From the rude mountain and the mossy wild,
Tumbling through rocks abrupt, and sounding far;
Then o'er the sanded valley floating spreads,
Calm, sluggish, silent; till again, constrained
Between two meeting hills, its bursts a way
Where rocks and woods o'erhang the turbid stream;
There, gathering triple force, rapid and deep,
It boils, and wheels, and foams, and thunders through.
 Nature! great parent! whose unceasing hand
Rolls round the Seasons of the changeful year,
How mighty, how majestic are thy works!
With what a pleasing dread they swell the soul,
That sees astonished, and astonished sings!
Ye too, ye winds! that now begin to blow
With boisterous sweep, I raise my voice to you.
Where are your stores, ye powerful beings! say,
Where your aerial magazines reserved
To swell the brooding terrors of the storm?
In what far-distant region of the sky,
Hushed in deep silence, sleep you when 'tis calm?
 When from the pallid sky the Sun descends,
With many a spot, that o'er his glaring orb
Uncertain wanders, stained; red fiery streaks
Begin to flush around. The reeling clouds
Stagger with dizzy poise, as doubting yet
Which master to obey; while, rising slow,
Blank in the leaden-colored east, the moon
Wears a wan circle round her blunted horns.
Seen through the turbid, fluctuating air,
The stars obtuse emit a shivering ray;
Or frequent seem to shoot athwart the gloom,
And long behind them trail the whitening blaze.
Snatched in short eddies, plays the withered leaf;
And on the flood the dancing feather floats.
With broadened nostrils to the sky upturned,
The conscious heifer snuffs the stormy gale.
E'en as the matron, at her nightly task,
With pensive labor draws the flaxen thread,
The wasted taper and the crackling flame
Foretell the blast. But chief the plumy race,
The tenants of the sky, its changes speak.
Retiring from the downs, where all day long
They picked their scanty fare, a blackening train
Of clamorous rooks thick-urge their weary flight,
And seek the closing shelter of the grove.
Assiduous, in his bower, the wailing owl
Plies his sad song. The cormorant on high
Wheels from the deep, and screams along the land.
Loud shrieks the soaring hern; and with wild wing
The circling sea-fowl cleave the flaky clouds.
Ocean, unequal pressed, with broken tide
And blind commotion heaves; while from the shore,
Eat into caverns by the restless wave,
And forest-rustling mountain comes a voice
That, solemn-sounding, bids the world prepare.
Then issues forth the storm with sudden burst,
And hurls the whole precipitated air
Down in a torrent. On the passive main
Descends the ethereal force, and with strong gust
Turns from its bottom the discolored deep.
Through the black night that sits immense around,
Lashed into foam, the fierce-conflicting brine
Seems o'er a thousand raging waves to burn.
Meantime the mountain-billows, to the clouds
In dreadful tumult swelled, surge above surge,
Burst into chaos with tremendous roar,
And anchored navies from their stations drive
Wild as the winds, across the howling waste
Of mighty waters: now the inflated wave

Straining they scale, and now impetuous shoot
Into the secret chambers of the deep,
The wintry Baltic thundering o'er their head.
Emerging thence again, before the breath
Of full-exerted heaven they wing their course,
And dart on distant coasts—if some sharp rock
Or shoal insidious break not their career,
And in loose fragments fling them floating round.

Nor less at land the loosened tempest reigns.
The mountain thunders, and its sturdy sons
Stoop to the bottom of the rocks they shade.
Lone on the midnight steep, and all aghast,
The dark wayfaring stranger breathless toils,
And, often falling, climbs against the blast.
Low waves the rooted forest, vexed, and sheds
What of its tarnished honors yet remain—
Dashed down and scattered, by the tearing wind's
Assiduous fury, its gigantic limbs.
Thus struggling through the dissipated grove,
The whirling tempest raves along the plain;
And, on the cottage thatched or lordly roof
Keen-fastening, shakes them to the solid base.
Sleep frighted flies; and round the rocking dome,
For entrance eager, howls the savage blast.
Then too, they say, through all the burdened air
Long groans are heard, shrill sounds, and distant sighs,
That, uttered by the demon of the night,
Warn the devoted wretch of woe and death.

Huge uproar lords it wide. The clouds, commixed
With stars swift-gliding, sweep along the sky.
All Nature reels: till Nature's King, who oft
Amid tempestuous darkness dwells alone,
And on the wings of the careering wind
Walks dreadfully serene, commands a calm;
Then straight air, sea, and earth are hushed at once.

As yet 'tis midnight deep. The weary clouds,
Slow-meeting, mingle into solid gloom.
Now, while the drowsy world lies lost in sleep,
Let me associate with the serious Night,
And Contemplation, her sedate compeer;
Let me shake off the intrusive cares of day,
And lay the meddling senses all aside.

Where now, ye lying vanities of life!
Ye ever-tempting, ever-cheating train!
Where are you now? and what is your amount?
Vexation, disappointment, and remorse.
Sad, sickening thought! and yet deluded man,
A scene of crude disjointed visions past,
And broken slumbers, rises still resolved,
With new-flushed hopes, to run the giddy round.

Father of light and life! thou Good Supreme!
O teach me what is good! teach me Thyself!
Save me from folly, vanity, and vice,
From every low pursuit; and feed my soul
With knowledge, conscious peace, and virtue pure—
Sacred, substantial, never-fading bliss!

The keener tempests come: and, fuming dun
From all the livid east or piercing north,
Thick clouds ascend, in whose capacious womb
A vapory deluge lies, to snow congealed.[1]
Heavy they roll their fleecy world along,
And the sky saddens with the gathered storm.
Through the hushed air the whitening shower descends,
At first thin-wavering; till at last the flakes
Fall broad and wide and fast, dimming the day
With a continual flow. The cherished fields
Put on their winter-robe of purest white.
'Tis brightness all; save where the new snow melts
Along the mazy current. Low the woods
Bow their hoar head; and, ere the languid sun
Faint from the west emits his evening ray,
Earth's universal face, deep-hid and chill,
Is one wild dazzling waste, that buries wide
The works of man. Drooping, the laborer-ox
Stands covered o'er with snow, and then demands
The fruit of all his toil. The fowls of heaven,
Tamed by the cruel season, crowd around
The winnowing store, and claim the little boon
Which Providence assigns them. One alone,
The redbreast, sacred to the household gods,
Wisely regardful of the embroiling sky,
In joyless fields and thorny thickets leaves
His shivering mates, and pays to trusted man
His annual visit. Half afraid, he first
Against the window beats; then brisk alights
On the warm hearth; then, hopping o'er the floor,
Eyes all the smiling family askance,
And pecks, and starts, and wonders where he is—
Till, more familiar grown, the table-crumbs
Attract his slender feet. The foodless wilds
Pour forth their brown inhabitants. The hare,
Though timorous of heart, and hard beset
By death in various forms, dark snares, and dogs,
And more unpitying men, the garden seeks,
Urged on by fearless want. The bleating kind
Eye the bleak heaven, and next the glistening earth,
With looks of dumb despair; then, sad-dispersed,

[1]"His presentation of a snowstorm is Thomson's highest achievement in natural description. . . . It is a perfect picture of its kind, unmatched for clearness and delicate accuracy of detail." (J. L. Robertson.)

Dig for the withered herb through heaps of snow.
Now, shepherds, to your helpless charge be kind:
Baffle the raging year, and fill their pens
With food at will; lodge them below the storm,
And watch them strict: for, from the bellowing east,
In this dire season, oft the whirlwind's wing
Sweeps up the burden of whole wintry plains
In one wide waft, and o'er the hapless flocks,
Hid in the hollow of two neighboring hills,
The billowy tempest whelms; till, upward urged,
The valley to a shining mountain swells,
Tipped with a wreath high-curling in the sky.
As thus the snows arise, and, foul and fierce,
All Winter drives along the darkened air,
In his own loose-revolving fields the swain
Disastered stands; sees other hills ascend,
Of unknown joyless brow; and other scenes,
Of horrid prospect, shag the trackless plain;
Nor finds the river nor the forest, hid
Beneath the formless wild; but wanders on
From hill to dale, still more and more astray—
Impatient flouncing through the drifted heaps,
Stung with the thoughts of home: the thoughts of home
Rush on his nerves and call their vigor forth
In many a vain attempt. How sinks his soul!
What black despair, what horror fills his heart,
When, for the dusky spot which fancy feigned
His tufted cottage rising through the snow,
He meets the roughness of the middle waste,
Far from the track and blest abode of man;
While round him night resistless closes fast,
And every tempest, howling o'er his head,
Renders the savage wilderness more wild.
Then throng the busy shapes into his mind
Of covered pits, unfathomably deep,
A dire descent! beyond the power of frost;
Of faithless bogs; of precipices huge,
Smoothed up with snow; and (what is land unknown,
What water) of the still unfrozen spring,
In the loose marsh or solitary lake,
Where the fresh fountain from the bottom boils.
These check his fearful steps; and down he sinks
Beneath the shelter of the shapeless drift,
Thinking o'er all the bitterness of death,
Mixed with the tender anguish nature shoots
Through the wrung bosom of the dying man—
His wife, his children, and his friends unseen.
In vain for him the officious wife prepares
The fire fair-blazing, and the vestment warm;
In vain his little children, peeping out
Into the mingling storm, demand their sire
With tears of artless innocence. Alas!
Nor wife nor children more shall he behold,
Nor friends, nor sacred home. On every nerve
The deadly Winter seizes, shuts up sense,
And, o'er his inmost vitals creeping cold,
Lays him along the snows a stiffened corse,
Stretched out, and bleaching in the northern blast.
Ah! little think the gay licentious proud,
Whom pleasure, power, and affluence surround—
They, who their thoughtless hours in giddy mirth,
And wanton, often cruel, riot waste—
Ah! little think they, while they dance along,
How many feel, this very moment, death
And all the sad variety of pain;
How many sink in the devouring flood,
Or more devouring flame; how many bleed,
By shameful variance betwixt man and man;
How many pine in want, and dungeon-glooms,
Shut from the common air and common use
Of their own limbs; how many drink the cup
Of baleful grief, or eat the bitter bread
Of misery; sore pierced by wintry winds,
How many shrink into the sordid hut
Of cheerless poverty; how many shake
With all the fiercer tortures of the mind,
Unbounded passion, madness, guilt, remorse—
Whence, tumbled headlong from the height of life,
They furnish matter for the tragic muse;
Even in the vale, where wisdom loves to dwell,
With friendship, peace, and contemplation joined,
How many, racked with honest passions, droop
In deep retired distress; how many stand
Around the death-bed of their dearest friends,
And point the parting anguish! Thought fond man
Of these, and all the thousand nameless ills
That one incessant struggle render life,
One scene of toil, of suffering, and of fate,
Vice in his high career would stand appalled,
And heedless rambling Impulse learn to think;
The conscious heart of Charity would warm,
And her wide wish Benevolence dilate;
The social tear would rise, the social sigh;
And, into clear perfection, gradual bliss,
Refining still, the social passions work.
And here can I forget the generous band[1]
Who, touched with human woe, redressive searched
Into the horrors of the gloomy jail?
Unpitied and unheard where misery moans,
Where sickness pines, where thirst and hunger burn,

[1]The Jail Committee, in the year 1729. (Thomson.)

And poor misfortune feels the lash of vice;
While in the land of liberty—the land
Whose every street and public meeting glow
With open freedom—little tyrants raged,
Snatched the lean morsel from the starving mouth,
Tore from cold wintry limbs the tattered weed,
E'en robbed them of the last of comforts, sleep,
The free-born Briton to the dungeon chained
Or, as the lust of cruelty prevailed,
At pleasure marked him with inglorious stripes,
And crushed out lives, by secret barbarous ways,
That for their country would have toiled or bled.
O great design! if executed well,
With patient care and wisdom-tempered zeal.
Ye sons of mercy! yet resume the search;
Drag forth the legal monsters into light,
Wrench from their hands Oppression's iron rod,
And bid the cruel feel the pains they give.
Much still untouched remains; in this rank age,
Much is the patriot's weeding hand required.
The toils of law—what dark insidious men
Have cumbrous added to perplex the truth
And lengthen simple justice into trade—
How glorious were the day that saw these broke,
And every man within the reach of right!
  By wintry famine roused, from all the tract
Of horrid mountains which the shining Alps,
And wavy Apennines, and Pyrenees
Branch out stupendous into distant lands,
Cruel as death, and hungry as the grave!
Burning for blood, bony, and gaunt, and grim!
Assembling wolves in raging troops descend;
And, pouring o'er the country, bear along,
Keen as the north-wind sweeps the glossy snow.
All is their prize. They fasten on the steed,
Press him to earth, and pierce his mighty heart.
Nor can the bull his awful front defend,
Or shake the murdering savages away.
Rapacious, at the mother's throat they fly,
And tear the screaming infant from her breast.
The godlike face of man avails him naught.
Even Beauty, force divine! at whose bright glance
The generous lion stands in softened gaze,
Here bleeds, a hapless undistinguished prey.
But if, apprised of the severe attack,
The country be shut up, lured by the scent,
On churchyards drear (inhuman to relate!)
The disappointed prowlers fall, and dig
The shrouded body from the grave; o'er which,
Mixed with foul shades and frighted ghosts, they howl.
  Among those hilly regions, where, embraced
In peaceful vales, the happy Grisons[1] dwell,
Oft, rushing sudden from the loaded cliffs,
Mountains of snow their gathering terrors roll.
From steep to steep, loud thundering, down they come,
A wintry waste in dire commotion all;
And herds, and flocks, and travelers, and swains,
And sometimes whole brigades of marching troops,
Or hamlets sleeping in the dead of night,
Are deep beneath the smothering ruin whelmed.
  Now, all amid the rigors of the year,
In the wild depth of winter while without
The ceaseless winds blow ice, be my retreat,
Between the groaning forest and the shore,
Beat by the boundless multitude of waves,
A rural, sheltered, solitary scene;
Where ruddy fire and beaming tapers join
To cheer the gloom. There studious let me sit,
And hold high converse with the mighty dead—
Sages of ancient time, as gods revered,
As gods beneficent, who blessed mankind
With arts and arms, and humanized a world.
Roused at the inspiring thought, I throw aside
The long-lived volume, and deep-musing hail
The sacred shades that slowly rising pass
Before my wondering eyes. First Socrates,
Who, firmly good in a corrupted state,
Against the rage of tyrants single stood,
Invincible! calm reason's holy law,
That voice of God within the attentive mind,
Obeying, fearless or in life or death:
Great moral teacher! wisest of mankind!
Solon the next, who built his commonweal
On equity's wide base; by tender laws
A lively people curbing, yet undamped
Preserving still that quick peculiar fire,
Whence in the laureled field of finer arts,
And of bold freedom, they unequaled shone,
The pride of smiling Greece and human-kind.
Lycurgus then, who bowed beneath the force
Of strictest discipline, severely wise,
All human passions. Following him I see,
As at Thermopylae he glorious fell,
The firm devoted chief,[2] who proved by deeds
The hardest lesson which the other taught.
Then Aristides lifts his honest front;
Spotless of heart, to whom the unflattering voice
Of freedom gave the noblest name of Just;

[1]Inhabitants of what is now the easternmost canton of Switzerland.

[2]Leonidas. (Thomson.)

In pure majestic poverty revered;
Who, even his glory to his country's weal
Submitting, swelled a haughty rival's[1] fame.
Reared by his care, of softer ray appears
Cimon, sweet-souled; whose genius, rising strong,
Shook off the load of young debauch; abroad
The scourge of Persian pride, at home the friend
Of every worth and every splendid art;
Modest and simple in the pomp of wealth.
Then the last worthies of declining Greece,
Late-called to glory, in unequal times,
Pensive appear. The fair Corinthian boast,
Timoleon, tempered happy, mild, and firm,
Who wept the brother while the tyrant bled;
And, equal to the best, the Theban pair,[2]
Whose virtues, in heroic concord joined,
Their country raised to freedom, empire, fame.
He too, with whom Athenian honor sunk,
And left a mass of sordid lees behind,—
Phocion the Good; in public life severe,
To virtue still inexorably firm;
But when, beneath his low illustrious roof,
Sweet peace and happy wisdom smoothed his brow,
Not friendship softer was, nor love more kind.
And he, the last of old Lycurgus' sons,
The generous victim to that vain attempt
To save a rotten state—Agis, who saw
E'en Sparta's self to servile avarice sunk.
The two Achaian heroes close the train—
Aratus, who a while relumed the soul
Of fondly lingering liberty in Greece;
And he, her darling, as her latest hope,
The gallant Philopoemen, who to arms
Turned the luxurious pomp he could not cure,
Or toiling in his farm, a simple swain,
Or bold and skillful thundering in the field.
  Of rougher front, a mighty people come,
A race of heroes! in those virtuous times
Which knew no stain, save that with partial flame
Their dearest country they too fondly loved.
Her better founder first, the Light of Rome,
Numa, who softened her rapacious sons;
Servius, the king who laid the solid base
On which o'er earth the vast republic spread.
Then the great consuls venerable rise:
The public father[3] who the private quelled,
As on the dread tribunal, sternly sad;
He, whom his thankless country could not lose,
Camillus, only vengeful to her foes;
Fabricius, scorner of all-conquering gold,
And Cincinnatus, awful from the plow;
Thy willing victim,[4] Carthage! bursting loose
From all that pleading Nature could oppose,
From a whole city's tears, by rigid faith
Imperious called, and honor's dire command;
Scipio, the gentle chief, humanely brave,
Who soon the race of spotless glory ran,
And, warm in youth, to the poetic shade
With friendship and philosophy retired;
Tully,[5] whose powerful eloquence a while
Restrained the rapid fate of rushing Rome;
Unconquered Cato, virtuous in extreme;
And thou, unhappy Brutus, kind of heart,
Whose steady arm, by awful virtue urged,
Lifted the Roman steel against thy friend.
Thousands besides the tribute of a verse
Demand; but who can count the stars of heaven?
Who sing their influence on this lower world?
  Behold, who yonder comes! in sober state,
Fair, mild, and strong as is a vernal sun:
'Tis Phoebus' self, or else the Mantuan swain![6]
Great Homer too appears, of daring wing,
Parent of song! and equal by his side,
The British Muse; joined hand in hand they walk,
Darkling, full up the middle steep to fame.
Nor absent are those shades, whose skillful touch
Pathetic drew the impassioned heart, and charmed
Transported Athens with the moral scene;
Nor those who, tuneful, waked the enchanting lyre.
  First of your kind! society divine!
Still visit thus my nights, for you reserved,
And mount my soaring soul to thoughts like yours.
Silence, thou lonely power! the door be thine;
See on the hallowed hour that none intrude,
Save a few chosen friends, who sometimes deign
To bless my humble roof, with sense refined,
Learning digested well, exalted faith,
Unstudied wit, and humor ever gay.
Or from the Muses' hill will Pope descend,
To raise the sacred hour, to bid it smile,
And with the social spirit warm the heart;
For, though not sweeter his own Homer sings,
Yet is his life the more endearing song.
  Where art thou, Hammond?[7] thou the darling pride,
The friend and lover of the tuneful throng!

[1]Themistocles. (Thomson.)

[2]Pelopidas and Epaminondas. (Thomson.)

[3]Marcus Junius Brutus. (Thomson.) As consul, he tried and condemned his sons, Titus and Tiberius, for participating in a conspiracy, and beheld their execution.

[4]Regulus. (Thomson.) Captured by the Carthaginians, he was sent to Rome (250 B. C.) with their ambassadors to negotiate a peace, which would have brought about his liberation; but he prevailed upon the Romans to decline the terms, and so was carried back to Carthage, where he died a prisoner.

[5]Marcus Tullius Cicero.

[6]Virgil.

[7]James Hammond (1710–1742), Equerry to Frederick, Prince of Wales.

Ah! why, dear youth, in all the blooming prime
Of vernal genius, where, disclosing fast,
Each active worth, each manly virtue lay,
Why wert thou ravished from our hope so soon?
What now avails that noble thirst of fame,
Which stung thy fervent breast? that treasured store
Of knowledge, early gained? that eager zeal
To serve thy country, glowing in the band
Of youthful patriots who sustain her name?
What now, alas! that life-diffusing charm
Of sprightly wit? that rapture for the muse,
That heart of friendship, and that soul of joy,
Which bade with softest light thy virtues smile?
Ah! only showed to check our fond pursuits,
And teach our humbled hopes that life is vain.
 Thus in some deep retirement would I pass
The winter-glooms with friends of pliant soul,
Or blithe or solemn, as the theme inspired:
With them would search if nature's boundless frame
Was called, late-rising, from the void of night,
Or sprung eternal from the Eternal Mind;
Its life, its laws, its progress, and its end.
Hence larger prospects of the beauteous whole
Would gradual open on our opening minds;
And each diffusive harmony unite
In full perfection to the astonished eye.
Then would we try to scan the moral world,
Which, though to us it seems embroiled, moves on
In higher order, fitted and impelled
By wisdom's finest hand, and issuing all
In general good. The sage historic muse
Should next conduct us through the deeps of time,
Show us how empire grew, declined, and fell
In scattered states; what makes the nations smile,
Improves their soil, and gives them double suns;
And why they pine beneath the brightest skies
In nature's richest lap. As thus we talked,
Our hearts would burn within us, would inhale
That portion of divinity, that ray
Of purest heaven, which lights the public soul
Of patriots and of heroes. But, if doomed
In powerless humble fortune to repress
These ardent risings of the kindling soul,
Then, e'en superior to ambition, we
Would learn the private virtues—how to glide
Through shades and plains along the smoothest stream
Of rural life: or, snatched away by hope
Through the dim spaces of futurity,
With earnest eye anticipate those scenes
Of happiness and wonder. where the mind,
In endless growth and infinite ascent,
Rises from state to state, and world to world.
But, when with these the serious thought is foiled,
We, shifting for relief, would play the shapes
Of frolic fancy; and incessant form
Those rapid pictures, that assembled train
Of fleet ideas, never joined before,
Whence lively wit excites to gay surprise,
Or folly-painting humor, grave himself,
Calls laughter forth, deep-shaking every nerve.
 Meantime the village rouses up the fire;
While, well attested, and as well believed,
Heard solemn, goes the goblin-story round,
Till superstitious horror creeps o'er all.
Or frequent in the sounding hall they wake
The rural gambol. Rustic mirth goes round—
The simple joke that takes the shepherd's heart,
Easily pleased; the long loud laugh sincere;
The kiss, snatched hasty from the sidelong maid
On purpose guardless, or pretending sleep;
The leap, the slap, the haul; and, shook to notes
Of native music, the respondent dance.
Thus jocund fleets with them the winter-night.[1]
 The city swarms intense. The public haunt,
Full of each theme and warm with mixed discourse,
Hums indistinct. The sons of riot flow
Down the loose stream of false enchanted joy
To swift destruction. On the rankled soul
The gaming fury falls; and in one gulf
Of total ruin, honor, virtue, peace,
Friends, families, and fortune headlong sink.
Up springs the dance along the lighted dome,
Mixed and evolved a thousand sprightly ways.
The glittering court effuses every pomp;
The circle deepens; beamed from gaudy robes,
Tapers, and sparkling gems, and radiant eyes,
A soft effulgence o'er the palace waves—
While, a gay insect in his summer shine,
The fop, light-fluttering, spreads his mealy wings.
 Dread o'er the scene the ghost of Hamlet stalks;
Othello rages; poor Monimia[2] mourns;
And Belvidera pours her soul in love.
Terror alarms the breast; the comely tear
Steals o'er the cheek: or else the comic muse
Holds to the world a picture of itself,
And raises sly the fair impartial laugh.

---

[1]Thomson's indebtedness to Milton, here and elsewhere, is obvious. He consciously looked to Milton as his poetical model.

[2]The Orphan in Thomas Otway's play so entitled. Belvidera is a character in the same writer's *Venice Preserved*.

Sometimes she lifts her strain, and paints the scenes
Of beauteous life—whate'er can deck mankind,
Or charm the heart, in generous Bevil[1] showed.
O thou, whose wisdom, solid yet refined,
Whose patriot virtues, and consummate skill
To touch the finer springs that move the world,
Joined to whate'er the graces can bestow,
And all Apollo's animating fire
Give thee with pleasing dignity to shine
At once the guardian, ornament, and joy
Of polished life—permit the rural muse,
O Chesterfield, to grace with thee her song.
Ere to the shades again she humbly flies,
Indulge her fond ambition, in thy train
(For every muse has in thy train a place)
To mark thy various full-accomplished mind—
To mark that spirit which with British scorn
Rejects the allurements of corrupted power;
That elegant politeness which excels,
Even in the judgment of presumptuous France,
The boasted manners of her shining court;
That wit, the vivid energy of sense,
The truth of nature, which with Attic point,
And kind well-tempered satire, smoothly keen,
Steals through the soul and without pain corrects.
Or, rising thence with yet a brighter flame,
O let me hail thee on some glorious day,
When to the listening senate ardent crowd
Britannia's sons to hear her pleaded cause!
Then, dressed by thee, more amiably fair,
Truth the soft robe of mild persuasion wears;
Thou to assenting reason giv'st again
Her own enlightened thoughts; called from the heart,
The obedient passions on thy voice attend;
And even reluctant party feels a while
Thy gracious power, as through the varied maze
Of eloquence, now smooth, now quick, now strong,
Profound and clear, you roll the copious flood.
To thy loved haunt return, my happy muse:
For now, behold! the joyous Winter days,
Frosty, succeed; and through the blue serene,
For sight too fine, the ethereal niter flies,
Killing infectious damps, and the spent air
Storing afresh with elemental life.
Close crowds the shining atmosphere; and binds
Our strengthened bodies in its cold embrace,
Constringent; feeds, and animates our blood;
Refines our spirits, through the new-strung nerves
In swifter sallies darting to the brain—
Where sits the soul, intense, collected, cool,
Bright as the skies, and as the season keen.
All nature feels the renovating force
Of Winter—only to the thoughtless eye
In ruin seen. The frost-concocted glebe
Draws in abundant vegetable soul,
And gathers vigor for the coming year;
A stronger glow sits on the lively cheek
Of ruddy fire; and luculent along
The purer rivers flow; their sullen deeps,
Transparent, open to the shepherd's gaze,
And murmur hoarser at the fixing frost.
What art thou, frost? and whence are thy keen stores
Derived, thou secret all-invading power,
Whom even the illusive fluid cannot fly?
Is not thy potent energy, unseen,
Myriads of little salts, or hooked, or shaped
Like double wedges, and diffused immense
Through water, earth, and ether? Hence at eve,
Steamed eager from the red horizon round,
With the fierce rage of Winter deep suffused,
An icy gale, oft shifting, o'er the pool
Breathes a blue film, and in its mid-career
Arrests the bickering stream. The loosened ice,
Let down the flood and half dissolved by day,
Rustles no more; but to the sedgy bank
Fast grows, or gathers round the pointed stone,
A crystal pavement, by the breath of heaven
Cemented firm; till, seized from shore to shore,
The whole imprisoned river growls below,
Loud rings the frozen earth, and hard reflects
A double noise; while, at his evening watch,
The village-dog deters the nightly thief;
The heifer lows; the distant waterfall
Swells in the breeze; and with the hasty tread
Of traveler the hollow-sounding plain
Shakes from afar. The full ethereal round,
Infinite worlds disclosing to the view,
Shines out intensely keen, and, all one cope
Of starry glitter, glows from pole to pole.
From pole to pole the rigid influence falls
Through the still night incessant, heavy, strong,
And seizes nature fast. It freezes on,
Till morn, late-rising o'er the drooping world,
Lifts her pale eye unjoyous. Then appears
The various labor of the silent night—
Prone from the dripping eave, and dumb cascade,
Whose idle torrents only seem to roar,
The pendent icicle; the frost-work fair,
Where transient hues and fancied figures rise;
Wide-spouted o'er the hill the frozen brook,
A livid tract, cold-gleaming on the morn,
The forest bent beneath the plumy wave;
And by the frost refined the whiter snow
Incrusted hard, and sounding to the tread

[1]A character in *The Conscious Lovers*, written by Sir Richard Steele. (Thomson.)

Of early shepherd, as he pensive seeks
His pining flock, or from the mountain top,
Pleased with the slippery surface, swift descends.
On blithesome frolics bent, the youthful swains,
While every work of man is laid at rest,
Fond o'er the river crowd, in various sport
And revelry dissolved; where, mixing glad,
Happiest of all the train! the raptured boy
Lashes the whirling top. Or, where the Rhine
Branched out in many a long canal extends,
From every province swarming, void of care,
Batavia rushes forth; and, as they sweep
On sounding skates a thousand different ways
In circling poise swift as the winds along,
The then gay land is maddened all to joy.
Nor less the northern courts, wide o'er the snow,
Pour a new pomp. Eager, on rapid sleds,
Their vigorous youth in bold contention wheel
The long-resounding course. Meantime, to raise
The manly strife, with highly blooming charms,
Flushed by the season, Scandinavia's dames
Or Russia's buxom daughters glow around.
Pure, quick, and sportful is the wholesome day;
But soon elapsed. The horizontal sun
Broad o'er the south hangs at his utmost noon;
And ineffectual strikes the gelid cliff.
His azure gloss the mountain still maintains,
Nor feels the feeble touch. Perhaps the vale
Relents awhile to the reflected ray;
Or from the forest falls the clustered snow,
Myriads of gems, that in the waving gleam
Gay-twinkle as they scatter. Thick around
Thunders the sport of those who with the gun,
And dog impatient bounding at the shot,
Worse than the season desolate the fields,
And, adding to the ruins of the year,
Distress the footed or the feathered game.
But what is this? Our infant Winter sinks
Divested of his grandeur should our eye
Astonished shoot into the frigid zone,
Where for relentless months continual night
Holds o'er the glittering waste her starry reign.
There, through the prison of unbounded wilds,
Barred by the hand of nature from escape,
Wide roams the Russian exile. Naught around
Strikes his sad eye but deserts lost in snow,
And heavy-loaded groves, and solid floods
That stretch athwart the solitary vast
Their icy horrors to the frozen main,
And cheerless towns far distant—never bless'd,
Save when its annual course the caravan
Bends to the golden coast of rich Cathay,[1]
With news of human-kind. Yet there life glows;
Yet, cherished there, beneath the shining waste
The furry nations harbor—tipped with jet,
Fair ermines spotless as the snows they press;
Sables of glossy black; and, dark-embrowned,
Or beauteous freaked with many a mingled hue,
Thousands besides, the costly pride of courts.
There, warm together pressed, the trooping deer
Sleep on the new-fallen snows; and, scarce his head
Raised o'er the heapy wreath, the branching elk
Lies slumbering sullen in the white abyss.
The ruthless hunter wants nor dogs nor toils,
Nor with the dread of sounding bows he drives
The fearful flying race—with ponderous clubs,
As weak against the mountain-heaps they push
Their beating breast in vain, and piteous bray,
He lays them quivering on the ensanguined snows,
And with loud shouts rejoicing bears them home.
There, through the piny forest half-absorbed,
Rough tenant of these shades, the shapeless bear,
With dangling ice all horrid, stalks forlorn;
Slow-paced, and sourer as the storms increase,
He makes his bed beneath the inclement drift,
And, with stern patience, scorning weak complaint,
Hardens his heart against assailing want.
Wide o'er the spacious regions of the north,
That see Boötes[2] urge his tardy wain,
A boisterous race, by frosty Caurus[3] pierced,
Who little pleasure know and fear no pain,
Prolific swarm. They once relumed the flame
Of lost mankind in polished slavery sunk;
Drove martial horde on horde, with dreadful sweep
Resistless rushing o'er the enfeebled south,
And gave the vanquished world another form.
Not such the sons of Lapland: wisely they
Despise the insensate barbarous trade of war;
They ask no more than simple Nature gives;
They love their mountains and enjoy their storms.
No false desires, no pride-created wants,
Disturb the peaceful current of their time,
And through the restless ever-tortured maze
Of pleasure or ambition bid it rage.

[1] The old name of China. (Thomson.)

[2] A small star near the Great Bear.

[3] The north-west wind. (Thomson.)

[4] The wandering Scythian clans. (Thomson.)

Their reindeer form their riches. These their tents,
Their robes, their beds, and all their homely wealth
Supply, their wholesome fare, and cheerful cups.
Obsequious at their call, the docile tribe
Yield to the sled their necks, and whirl them swift
O'er hill and dale, heaped into one expanse
Of marbled snow, or, far as eye can sweep,
With a blue crust of ice unbounded glazed.
By dancing meteors then, that ceaseless shake
A waving blaze refracted o'er the heavens,
And vivid moons, and stars that keener play
With doubled luster from the radiant waste,
Even in the depth of polar night they find
A wondrous day—enough to light the chase
Or guide their daring steps to Finland fairs.
Wished spring returns; and from the hazy south,
While dim Aurora slowly moves before,
The welcome sun, just verging up at first,
By small degrees extends the swelling curve;
Till, seen at last for gay rejoicing months,
Still round and round his spiral course he winds,
And, as he nearly dips his flaming orb,
Wheels up again and re-ascends the sky.
In that glad season, from the lakes and floods,
Where pure Niëmi's fairy mountains[1] rise,
And fringed with roses Tenglio rolls his stream,[2]
They draw the copious fry. With these at eve
They cheerful-loaded to their tents repair,
Where, all day long in useful cares employed,
Their kind unblemished wives the fire prepare.
Thrice happy race! by poverty secured
From legal plunder and rapacious power,
In whom fell interest never yet has sown
The seeds of vice, whose spotless swains ne'er knew
Injurious deed, nor, blasted by the breath
Of faithless love, their blooming daughters woe.
Still pressing on, beyond Tornêa's lake,
And Hecla flaming through a waste of snow,
And farthest Greenland, to the pole itself,
Where, failing gradual, life at length goes out,
The muse expands her solitary flight;
And, hovering o'er the wild stupendous scene,
Beholds new seas beneath another sky.[3]
Throned in his palace of cerulean ice,
Here Winter holds his unrejoicing court;
And through his airy hall the loud misrule
Of driving tempest is for ever heard:
Here the grim tyrant meditates his wrath;
Here arms his winds with all-subduing frost;
Molds his fierce hail, and treasures up his snows,
With which he now oppresses half the globe.
Thence winding eastward to the Tartar's coast,
She sweeps the howling margin of the main;
Where, undissolving from the first of time,
Snows swell on snows amazing to the sky;
And icy mountains high on mountains piled
Seem to the shivering sailor from afar,
Shapeless and white, an atmosphere of clouds.
Projected huge and horrid o'er the surge,
Alps frown on Alps; or, rushing hideous down,
As if old Chaos was again returned,
Wide-rend the deep and shake the solid pole.
Ocean itself no longer can resist
The binding fury: but, in all its rage
Of tempest taken by the boundless frost,
Is many a fathom to the bottom chained,
And bid to roar no more—a bleak expanse
Shagged o'er with wavy rocks, cheerless, and void
Of every life, that from the dreary months
Flies conscious southward. Miserable they!
Who, here entangled in the gathering ice,
Take their last look of the descending sun;
While, full of death and fierce with tenfold frost,
The long, long night, incumbent o'er their heads,
Falls horrible! Such was the Briton's[4] fate,
As with first prow (what have not Britons dared?)
He for the passage sought, attempted since
So much in vain, and seeming to be shut
By jealous nature with eternal bars.
In these fell regions, in Arzina caught,
And to the stony deep his idle ship
Immediate sealed, he with his hapless crew,
Each full exerted at his several task,
Froze into statues—to the cordage glued
The sailor, and the pilot to the helm.
Hard by these shores, where scarce his freezing stream
Rolls the wild Oby, live the last of men;
And, half enlivened by the distant sun,
That rears and ripens man as well as plants,
Here human nature wears its rudest form.
Deep from the piercing Season sunk in caves,

[1]M. de Maupertuis, in his book on the figure of the Earth, after having described the beautiful lake and mountain of Niëmi in Lapland, says: "From this height we had occasion several times to see those vapors rise from the lake which the people of the country call *Haltios*, and which they deem to be the guardian spirits of the mountains. We had been frighted with stories of bears that haunted this place, but saw none. It seemed rather a place of resort for fairies and genii than bears." (Thomson.)

[2]The same author observes: "I was surprised to see upon the banks of this river (the Tenglio) roses of as lively a red as any that are in our gardens." (Thomson.)

[3]The other hemisphere. (Thomson.)

[4]Sir Hugh Willoughby, sent by Queen Elizabeth to discover the north-east passage. (Thomson.)

Here by dull fires and with unjoyous cheer
They waste the tedious gloom: immersed in furs
Doze the gross race—nor sprightly jest, nor song,
Nor tenderness they know, nor aught of life
Beyond the kindred bears that stalk without—
Till Morn at length, her roses drooping all,
Sheds a long twilight brightening o'er their fields
And calls the quivered savage to the chase.
What cannot active government perform,
New-molding man? Wide-stretching from these shores,
A people savage from remotest time,
A huge neglected empire, one vast mind
By heaven inspired, from Gothic darkness called.
Immortal Peter! first of monarchs! He
His stubborn country tamed,—her rocks, her fens,
Her floods, her seas, her ill-submitting sons;
And, while the fierce barbarian he subdued,
To more exalted soul he raised the man.
Ye shades of ancient heroes, ye who toiled
Through long successive ages to build up
A laboring plan of state, behold at once
The wonder done! behold the matchless prince!
Who left his native throne, where reigned till then
A mighty shadow of unreal power;
Who greatly spurned the slothful pomp of courts;
And, roaming every land, in every port
His scepter laid aside, with glorious hand
Unwearied plying the mechanic tool,
Gathered the seeds of trade, of useful arts,
Of civil wisdom, and of martial skill.
Charged with the stores of Europe home he goes!
Then cities rise amid the illumined waste;
O'er joyless deserts smiles the rural reign;
Far-distant flood to flood is social joined;
The astonished Euxine hears the Baltic roar;
Proud navies ride on seas that never foamed
With daring keel before; and armies stretch
Each way their dazzling files, repressing here
The frantic Alexander of the north,[1]
And awing there stern Othman's shrinking sons.
Sloth flies the land, and ignorance and vice,
Of old dishonor proud: it glows around,
Taught by the royal hand that roused the whole,
One scene of arts, of arms, of rising trade—
For, what his wisdom planned and power enforced,
More potent still his great example showed.
Muttering, the winds at eve with blunted point
Blow hollow-blustering from the south. Subdued,
The frost resolves into a trickling thaw.
Spotted the mountains shine: loose sleet descends,
And floods the country round. The rivers swell,
Of bonds impatient. Sudden from the hills,
O'er rocks and woods, in broad brown cataracts,
A thousand snow-fed torrents shoot at once;
And, where they rush, the wide-resounding plain
Is left one slimy waste. Those sullen seas,
That washed the ungenial pole, will rest no more
Beneath the shackles of the mighty north,
But, rousing all their waves, resistless heave.
And, hark! the lengthening roar continuous runs
Athwart the rifted deep: at once it bursts,
And piles a thousand mountains to the clouds.
Ill fares the bark, with trembling wretches charged,
That, tossed amid the floating fragments, moors
Beneath the shelter of an icy isle,
While night o'erwhelms the sea, and horror looks
More horrible. Can human force endure
The assembled mischiefs that besiege them round?—
Heart-gnawing hunger, fainting weariness,
The roar of winds and waves, the crush of ice,
Now ceasing, now renewed with louder rage,
And in dire echoes bellowing round the main.
More to embroil the deep, Leviathan
And his unwieldy train in dreadful sport
Tempest the loosened brine; while through the gloom
Far from the bleak inhospitable shore,
Loading the winds, is heard the hungry howl
Of famished monsters, there awaiting wrecks.
Yet Providence, that ever-waking Eye,
Looks down with pity on the feeble toil
Of mortals lost to hope, and lights them safe
Through all this dreary labyrinth of fate.
'Tis done! Dread Winter spreads his latest glooms,
And reigns tremendous o'er the conquered year.
How dead the vegetable kingdom lies!
How dumb the tuneful! Horror wide extends
His desolate domain. Behold, fond man!
See here thy pictured life; pass some few years,
Thy flowering Spring, thy Summer's ardent strength,

[1]Charles XII, of Sweden.

Thy sober Autumn fading into age,
And pale concluding Winter comes at last
And shuts the scene. Ah! whither now are fled
Those dreams of greatness? those unsolid hopes
Of happiness? those longings after fame?
Those restless cares? those busy bustling days?
Those gay-spent festive nights? those veering thoughts,
Lost between good and ill, that shared thy life?
All now are vanished! Virtue sole survives—
Immortal, never-failing friend of man,
His guide to happiness on high. And see!
'Tis come, the glorious morn! the second birth
Of heaven and earth! awakening nature hears
The new-creating word, and starts to life
In every heightened form, from pain and death
For ever free. The great eternal scheme,
Involving all, and in a perfect whole
Uniting, as the prospect wider spreads,
To reason's eye refined clears up apace.
Ye vainly wise! ye blind presumptuous! now,
Confounded in the dust, adore that Power
And Wisdom—oft arraigned: see now the cause
Why unassuming worth in secret lived
And died neglected: why the good man's share
In life was gall and bitterness of soul:
Why the lone widow and her orphans pined
In starving solitude; while luxury
In palaces lay straining her low thought
To form unreal wants: why heaven-born truth
And moderation fair wore the red marks
Of superstition's scourge; why licensed pain,
That cruel spoiler, that embosomed foe,
Embittered all our bliss. Ye good distressed!
Ye noble few! who here unbending stand
Beneath life's pressure, yet bear up a while,
And what your bounded view, which only saw
A little part, deemed evil is no more:
The storms of wintry time will quickly pass,
And one unbounded Spring encircle all.

A HYMN ON THE SEASONS[1]

THESE, as they change, Almighty Father! these
Are but the varied God. The rolling year
Is full of thee. Forth in the pleasing Spring
Thy beauty walks, thy tenderness and love.
Wide flush the fields; the softening air is balm;
Echo the mountains round; the forest smiles;
And every sense, and every heart, is joy.
Then comes thy glory in the Summer-months,
With light and heat refulgent. Then thy sun
Shoots full perfection through the swelling year:
And oft thy voice in dreadful thunder speaks,
And oft, at dawn, deep noon, or falling eve,
By brooks and groves, in hollow-whispering gales.
Thy bounty shines in Autumn unconfined,
And spreads a common feast for all that lives.
In Winter awful thou! with clouds and storms
Around thee thrown, tempest o'er tempest rolled,
Majestic darkness! On the whirlwind's wing
Riding sublime, thou bidst the world adore,
And humblest nature with thy northern blast.
Mysterious round! what skill, what force divine,
Deep-felt in these appear! a simple train,
Yet so delightful mixed, with such kind art,
Such beauty and beneficence combined,
Shade unperceived so softening into shade,
And all so forming an harmonious whole
That, as they still succeed, they ravish still.
But, wandering oft with brute unconscious gaze,
Man marks not thee, marks not the mighty hand
That, ever busy, wheels the silent spheres,
Works in the secret deep, shoots steaming thence
The fair profusion that o'erspreads the Spring,
Flings from the sun direct the flaming day,
Feeds every creature, hurls the tempest forth,
And, as on earth this grateful change revolves,
With transport touches all the springs of life.
Nature, attend! join, every living soul
Beneath the spacious temple of the sky,
In adoration join; and ardent raise
One general song! To him, ye vocal gales,
Breathe soft, whose spirit in your freshness breathes:
Oh! talk of him in solitary glooms,
Where, o'er the rock, the scarcely-waving pine
Fills the brown shade with a religious awe.
And ye, whose bolder note is heard afar,
Who shake the astonished world, lift high to Heaven
The impetuous song, and say from whom you rage.
His praise, ye brooks, attune, ye trembling rills;
And let me catch it as I muse along.
Ye headlong torrents, rapid and profound;
Ye softer floods, that lead the humid maze
Along the vale; and thou, majestic main,
A secret world of wonders in thyself,
Sound his stupendous praise, whose greater voice
Or bids you roar or bids your roarings fall.
Soft roll your incense, herbs, and fruits, and flowers,

[1]The text is that of the edition of 1746.

In mingled clouds to him, whose sun exalts,
Whose breath perfumes you, and whose pencil paints.
Ye forests, bend; ye harvests, wave to him—
Breathe your still song into the reaper's heart
As home he goes beneath the joyous moon.
Ye that keep watch in heaven, as earth asleep
Unconscious lies, effuse your mildest beams,
Ye constellations! while your angels strike
Amid the spangled sky the silver lyre.
Great source of day! best image here below
Of thy Creator, ever pouring wide
From world to world the vital ocean round!
On nature write with every beam his praise.
The thunder rolls: be hushed the prostrate world,
While cloud to cloud returns the solemn hymn.
Bleat out afresh, ye hills; ye mossy rocks,
Retain the sound; the broad responsive low,
Ye valleys, raise; for the Great Shepherd reigns,
And his unsuffering kingdom yet will come.
Ye woodlands all, awake: a boundless song
Burst from the groves; and, when the restless day,
Expiring, lays the warbling world asleep,
Sweetest of birds, sweet Philomela![1] charm
The listening shades, and teach the night his praise!
Ye, chief, for whom the whole creation smiles,
At once the head, the heart, the tongue of all,
Crown the great hymn! In swarming cities vast,
Assembled men, to the deep organ join
The long-resounding voice, oft breaking clear
At solemn pauses through the swelling bass;
And, as each mingling flame increases each,
In one united ardor rise to heaven.
Or, if you rather choose the rural shade,
And find a fane in every sacred grove,
There let the shepherd's flute, the virgin's lay,
The prompting seraph, and the poet's lyre
Still sing the God of Seasons as they roll.
For me, when I forget the darling theme,
Whether the blossom blows, the summer-ray
Russets the plain, inspiring autumn gleams,
Or winter rises in the blackening east,
Be my tongue mute, may fancy paint no more,
And, dead to joy, forget my heart to beat!
Should fate command me to the farthest verge
Of the green earth, to distant barbarous climes,
Rivers unknown to song, where first the sun
Gilds Indian mountains, or his setting beam
Flames on the Atlantic isles, 'tis nought to me;
Since God is ever present, ever felt,
In the void waste as in the city full,
And where he vital spreads there must be joy.
When even at last the solemn hour shall come,
And wing my mystic flight to future worlds,
I cheerful will obey; there, with new powers,
Will rising wonders sing: I cannot go
Where universal love not smiles around,
Sustaining all yon orbs and all their sons;
From seeming evil still educing good,
And better thence again, and better still,
In infinite progression. But I lose
Myself in him, in light ineffable!
Come then, expressive Silence, muse his praise.

[1]The nightingale.

RULE, BRITANNIA!

WHEN Britain first, at Heaven's command,
Arose from out the azure main,
This was the charter of the land,
And guardian angels sung this strain—
"Rule, Britannia, rule the waves;
Britons never will be slaves."

The nations, not so bless'd as thee,
Must in their turns to tyrants fall,
While thou shalt flourish great and free,
The dread and envy of them all.
"Rule," *etc.*

Still more majestic shalt thou rise,
More dreadful from each foreign stroke;
As the loud blast that tears the skies
Serves but to root thy native oak.
"Rule," *etc.*

Thee haughty tyrants ne'er shall tame;
All their attempts to bend thee down
Will but arouse thy generous flame,
But work their woe and thy renown.
"Rule," *etc.*

To thee belongs the rural reign;
Thy cities shall with commerce shine;
All thine shall be the subject main,
And every shore it circles thine.
"Rule," *etc.*

The Muses, still with freedom found,
Shall to thy happy coast repair:
Bless'd isle! with matchless beauty crowned,
And manly hearts to guard the fair.
"Rule, Britannia, rule the waves;
Britons never will be slaves."

WILLIAM COLLINS (1721–1759)

Collins was born in Chichester, coming of a family of tradesmen long established there. The date of his birth is not known, though there is a tradition that he was born on Christmas day. As a boy he probably attended the prebendal school at Chichester, and in 1753 he was sent to Winchester, where he came to know several youths afterwards eminent, among them Joseph Warton. Collins showed already at Winchester a pronounced turn for verse-writing, and there is ground for believing that he also distinguished himself for scholarship. In 1740 he was entered at Queen's College, Oxford, and after the summer of the following year he was at Magdalen College. He took his B. A. in 1743. Our knowledge of his Oxford years is meager, but it appears that, while he made some real progress in his studies, he began to exhibit there the indolence and taste for dissipation which marked his later years in London. Collins's father had died, leaving little or no money, in 1734, and he derived his chief means of support from allowances made by his uncle. It was apparently intended that he should provide for himself by taking holy orders, but instead he went to London to support himself by literature. "He was romantic enough," says his college friend White, "to suppose that his superior abilities would draw the attention of the great world, by means of whom he was to make his fortune." He had many plans both for historical work and for play-writing, and he might have made, not a fortune, but at least a competency had he ever seriously attempted to carry them out. He contented himself, however, largely with talk, while he bought fine clothes when he could, enjoyed the gayety of London, and drank intemperately. His actual performance consisted only of his *Persian Eclogues*, said by Joseph Warton to have been written at Winchester when Collins was only seventeen (published in 1742), his *Epistle Addressed to Sir Thomas Hanmer*, an editor of Shakespeare (1743), and a small number of lyrical poems, chiefly odes (*Odes on Several Descriptive and Allegoric Subjects*, 1747; *Ode Occasioned by the Death of Mr. Thomson*, 1749; *Ode on the Popular Superstitions of the Highlands of Scotland*, not published until 1788). In 1749 Collins's days of poverty ended, his uncle dying in that year and leaving him a large sum of money. Shortly afterwards he apparently left London, to live in Chichester through the remaining years of his life. His mind was still full of projects, but it soon became evident that there was less hope than ever of their being carried out. For Collins soon began to show signs of mental break-down. These gradually increased, leaving him weak and helpless even when he was in possession of his faculties, and he was insane practically from 1754 until the time of his death.

Small though the quantity of Collins's poetry is, his odes are of so singularly fine a quality as to give his name lasting interest. He was one of the few men of his period who had lyrical power of a high order, and he wrote at least enough to give this enduring, if not full, expression. In the nineteenth century he was looked upon with increased interest as a real, if largely unconscious, forerunner of the romantic movement of the early years of that century. Collins was "romantic" in that to some extent he shared the growing antiquarian interests of his age, and in that his descriptions of natural scenery show some freshness, while it is evident that he could only with difficulty bring his imaginative powers into relation with real life. On the other hand, as some of Collins's odes show in their stanzaic structure the influence of classical example, so does his poetic style exhibit classical restraint, proportion, finish, ease, and simplicity. When at his best, Collins shows a considerable degree of emancipation from the conventional classicism of his age, in favor of a truer classicism of form induced by independent study of the Greeks, particularly of the Greek dramatists.

DIRGE IN *CYMBELINE*

SUNG BY GUIDERUS AND ARVIRAGUS OVER FIDELE, SUPPOSED TO BE DEAD (1744)

To FAIR Fidele's grassy tomb
  Soft maids and village hinds shall bring
Each op'ning sweet, of earliest bloom,
  And rifle all the breathing Spring.

No wailing ghost shall dare appear,
  To vex with shrieks this quiet grove;
But shepherd lads assemble here,
  And melting virgins own their love.

No withered witch shall here be seen,
  No goblins lead their nightly crew;
The female fays shall haunt the green,
  And dress thy grave with pearly dew.

The red-breast oft at ev'ning hours
  Shall kindly lend his little aid,
With hoary moss, and gathered flow'rs,
  To deck the ground where thou art laid.

When howling winds, and beating rain,
  In tempests shake the sylvan cell,
Or 'midst the chase on ev'ry plain,
  The tender thought on thee shall dwell.

Each lonely scene shall thee restore,
  For thee the tear be duly shed:
Belov'd till life can charm no more,
  And mourned, till Pity's self be dead.

ODE TO SIMPLICITY[1]

O THOU by Nature taught
  To breathe her genuine thought,
In numbers warmly pure, and sweetly strong:
  Who first, on mountains wild,
  In Fancy, loveliest child,
Thy babe or Pleasure's, nursed the pow'rs of song!

  Thou who with hermit heart
  Disdain'st the wealth of art,
And gauds, and pageant weeds, and trailing pall,
  But com'st a decent maid
  In Attic robe arrayed,
O chaste, unboastful nymph, to thee I call!

  By all the honeyed store
  On Hybla's thymy shore,
By all her blooms, and mingled murmurs dear,
  By her[2] whose lovelorn woe
  In ev'ning musings slow
Soothed sweetly sad Electra's poet's[3] ear:

  By old Cephisus[4] deep,
  Who spread his wavy sweep
In warbled wand'rings round thy green retreat,
  On whose enameled side
  When holy Freedom died,
No equal haunt allured thy future feet:

  O sister meek of Truth,
  To my admiring youth
Thy sober aid and native charms infuse!
  The flow'rs that sweetest breathe,
  Though Beauty culled the wreath,
Still ask thy hand to range their ordered hues.

  While Rome could none esteem
  But virtue's patriot theme,
You loved her hills, and led her laureate band:
  But stayed to sing alone
  To one distinguished throne,[5]
And turned thy face, and fled her altered land.

  No more, in hall or bow'r,
  The passions own thy pow'r;
Love, only love, her forceless numbers mean:
  For thou hast left her shrine;
  Nor olive more, nor vine,
Shall gain thy feet to bless the servile scene.

  Though taste, though genius bless
  To some divine excess,
Faints the cold work till thou inspire the whole;
  What each, what all supply,
  May court, may charm our eye,
Thou, only thou, canst raise the meeting soul!

  Of these let others ask,
  To aid some mighty task;
I only seek to find thy temp'rate vale:
  Where oft my reed might sound
  To maids and shepherds round,
And all thy sons, O Nature, learn my tale.

ODE ON THE POETICAL CHARACTER

STROPHE

As ONCE, if not with light regard
I read aright that gifted bard[6]
(Him whose school above the rest
His loveliest Elfin Queen has bless'd),
One, only one, unrivaled fair
Might hope the magic girdle wear,
At solemn tourney hung on high,
The wish of each love-darting eye;
Lo! to each other nymph in turn applied,
  As if, in air unseen, some hov'ring hand,
Some chaste and angel friend to virgin fame,
  With whispered spell had burst the starting band,
It left unbless'd her loathed, dishonored side;
  Happier hopeless fair, if never
  Her baffled hand with vain endeavor
Had touched that fatal zone to her denied!
Young Fancy thus, to me divinest name,
  To whom, prepared and bathed in heav'n,
  The cest[7] of amplest pow'r is giv'n,
  To few the godlike gift assigns,
  To gird their bless'd, prophetic loins,
And gaze her visions wild, and feel unmixed her flame!

[1]This and all the following poems were published in 1747 (this is the date on the title-page of the first edition, though the volume actually appeared in December, 1746).

[2]The nightingale.

[3]Sophocles.

[4]River of Attica.

[5]The throne of Augustus, patron of Virgil and Horace.

[6]Spenser. [7]Girdle.

EPODE

The band, as fairy legends say,
Was wove on that creating day
When He who called with thought to birth
Yon tented sky, this laughing earth,
And dressed with springs and forests tall,
And poured the main engirting all,
Long by the loved enthusiast wooed,
Himself in some diviner mood,
Retiring, sate with her alone,
And placed her on his sapphire throne,
The whiles, the vaulted shrine around,
Seraphic wires were heard to sound,
Now sublimest triumph swelling,
Now on love and mercy dwelling;
And she, from out the veiling cloud,
Breathed her magic notes aloud:
And thou, thou rich-haired Youth of Morn,
And all thy subject life, was born!
The dang'rous Passions kept aloof,
Far from the sainted growing woof:
But near it sat ecstatic Wonder,
List'ning the deep applauding thunder;
And Truth, in sunny vest arrayed,
By whose the tarsel's[1] eyes were made;
All the shad'wy tribes of mind
In braided dance their murmurs joined,
And all the bright uncounted Powers
Who feed on heav'n's ambrosial flowers.
Where is the bard whose soul can now
Its high presuming hopes avow?
Where he who thinks, with rapture blind,
This hallowed work for him designed?

ANTISTROPHE

High on some cliff, to heav'n up-piled,
Of rude access, of prospect wild,
Where, tangled round the jealous steep,
Strange shades o'er-brow the valleys deep,
And holy genii guard the rock,
Its glooms embrown, its springs unlock,
While on its rich ambitious head
An Eden, like his own, lies spread,
I view that oak, the fancied glades among,
By which as Milton lay, his ev'ning ear,
From many a cloud that dropped ethereal dew,
Nigh sphered in heav'n its native strains could hear,
On which that ancient trump he reached was hung:
Thither oft, his glory greeting,
From Waller's myrtle shades retreating,
With many a vow from Hope's aspiring tongue,
My trembling feet his guiding steps pursue;
In vain—such bliss to one alone
Of all the sons of soul was known,
And Heav'n and Fancy, kindred powers,
Have now o'erturned th' inspiring bowers,
Or curtained close such scene from ev'ry future view.

[1] Male falcon.

ODE

WRITTEN IN THE BEGINNING OF THE YEAR 1746

How sleep the brave who sink to rest
By all their country's wishes bless'd!
When Spring, with dewy fingers cold,
Returns to deck their hallowed mold,
She there shall dress a sweeter sod
Than Fancy's feet have ever trod.

By fairy hands their knell is rung,
By forms unseen their dirge is sung;
There Honor comes, a pilgrim gray,
To bless the turf that wraps their clay;
And Freedom shall awhile repair,
To dwell a weeping hermit there!

ODE TO LIBERTY

STROPHE

Who shall awake the Spartan fife,
And call in solemn sounds to life
The youths whose locks divinely spreading,
Like vernal hyacinths in sullen hue,
At once the breath of fear and virtue shedding,
Applauding Freedom loved of old to view?
What new Alcæus, fancy-bless'd,
Shall sing the sword, in myrtles dressed,
At Wisdom's shrine awhile its flame concealing
(What place so fit to seal a deed renowned?),
Till she her brightest lightnings round revealing,
It leaped in glory forth, and dealt her prompted wound?
O goddess, in that feeling hour,
When most its sounds would court thy ears,
Let not my shell's misguided pow'r
E'er draw thy sad, thy mindful tears.
No, Freedom, no, I will not tell
How Rome, before thy weeping face,
With heaviest sound, a giant statue, fell,
Pushed by a wild and artless race
From off its wide ambitious base,
When Time his Northern sons of spoil awoke,
And all the blended work of strength and grace,
With many a rude repeated stroke,
And many a barb'rous yell, to thousand fragments broke.

EPODE

Yet e'en where'er the least appeared,
Th' admiring world thy hand revered;
Still, midst the scattered states around,
Some remnants of her strength were found;
They saw, by what escaped the storm,
How wondrous rose her perfect form,
How in the great, the labored whole,
Each mighty master poured his soul!
For sunny Florence, seat of Art,
Beneath her vines preserved a part,
Till they[1] whom Science loved to name
(O who could fear it?) quenched her flame.
And lo, an humbler relic laid
In jealous Pisa's olive shade!
See, small Marino joins the theme,
Though least, not last in thy esteem.
Strike, louder strike th' ennobling strings
To those[2] whose merchant sons were kings;
To him[3] who, decked with pearly pride,
In Adria weds his green-haired bride.
Hail, port of glory, wealth, and pleasure!
Ne'er let me change this Lydian measure,
Nor e'er her former pride relate
To sad Liguria's[4] bleeding state.
Ah no! more pleased thy haunts I seek,
On Wild Helvetia's[5] mountains bleak
(Where, when the favored of thy choice,
The daring archer,[6] heard thy voice,
Forth from his eyrie roused in dread,
The rav'ning eagle[7] northward fled):
Or dwell in willowed meads more near,
With those[8] to whom thy stork is dear;
Those whom the rod of Alva bruised,
Whose crown a British queen[9] refused!
The magic works, thou feel'st the strains,
One holier name alone remains;
The perfect spell shall then avail:
Hail nymph, adored by Britain, hail!

ANTISTROPHE

Beyond the measure vast of thought,
The works the wizard Time has wrought!
The Gaul, 't is held of antique story,
Saw Britain linked to his now adverse strand;
No sea between, nor cliff sublime and hoary,
He passed with unwet feet through all our land.
To the blown Baltic then, they say,
The wild waves found another way,
Where Orcas howls, his wolfish mountains rounding;
Till all the banded West at once 'gan rise,
A wide wild storm e'en Nature's self confounding,
With'ring her giant sons with strange uncouth surprise.
This pillared earth so firm and wide,
By winds and inward labors torn,
In thunders dread was pushed aside,
And down the should'ring billows borne.
And see, like gems, her laughing train,
The little isles on every side!
Mona, once hid from those who search the main,
Where thousand elfin shapes abide,
And Wight, who checks the west'ring tide;
For thee consenting Heav'n has each bestowed,
A fair attendant on her sov'reign pride.
To thee this bless'd divorce she owed,
For thou hast made her vales thy loved, thy last abode!

SECOND EPODE

Then too, 'tis said, an hoary pile,
Midst the green navel of our isle,
Thy shrine in some religious wood,
O soul-enforcing goddess, stood!
There oft the painted native's feet
Were wont thy form celestial meet:
Though now with hopeless toil we trace
Time's backward rolls to find its place;
Whether the fiery-tressèd Dane
Or Roman's self o'erturned the fane,
Or in what heaven-left age it fell,
'Twere hard for modern song to tell.
Yet still, if truth those beams infuse
Which guide at once and charm the Muse,
Beyond yon braided clouds that lie,
Paving the light-embroidered sky,
Amidst the bright pavilioned plains,
The beauteous model still remains.
There, happier than in islands bless'd,[10]
Or bow'rs by Spring or Hebe dressed,
The chiefs who fill our Albion's story,
In warlike weeds, retired in glory,
Hear their consorted druids sing
Their triumphs to th' immortal string.
How may the poet now unfold
What never tongue or numbers told?
How learn, delighted and amazed,
What hands unknown that fabric raised?
E'en now, before his favored eyes,
In Gothic pride it seems to rise!
Yet Græcia's graceful orders join,
Majestic through the mixed design;
The secret builder knew to choose
Each sphere-found gem of richest hues:
Whate'er heav'n's purer mold contains,
When nearer suns emblaze its veins;
There on the walls the patriot's sight
May ever hang with fresh delight,

[1]The Medici. "Science" is used as a synonym for learning.
[2]The Venetians. [3]The Doge of Venice. [4]Genoa.
[5]Switzerland. [6]William Tell. [7]Austria.
[8]The Dutch. [9]Queen Elizabeth (in 1575).

[10]The Happy Islands, abode of the souls of heroes.

And, graved with some prophetic rage,
Read Albion's fame through ev'ry age.
  Ye forms divine, ye laureate band,
That near her inmost altar stand,
Now sooth her to her blissful train
Blithe Concord's social form to gain:
Concord, whose myrtle wand can steep
E'en Anger's bloodshot eyes in sleep:
Before whose breathing bosom's balm
Rage drops his steel, and storms grow calm.
Her let our sires and matrons hoar
Welcome to Britain's ravaged shore;
Our youths, enamored of the fair,
Play with the tangles of her hair;
Till, in one loud applauding sound,
The nations shout to her around,
"O how supremely art thou bless'd!
Thou, lady, thou shalt rule the West!"

ODE TO EVENING

If aught of oaten stop, or pastoral song,
May hope, chaste Eve, to soothe thy modest ear,
  Like thy own solemn springs,
  Thy springs and dying gales,

O nymph reserved, while now the bright-haired sun
Sits in yon western tent, whose cloudy skirts,
  With brede[1] ethereal wove,
  O'erhang his wavy bed:

Now air is hushed, save where the weak-eyed bat,
With short shrill shriek, flits by on leathern wing,
  Or where the beetle winds
  His small but sullen horn,

As oft he rises 'midst the twilight path,
Against the pilgrim borne in heedless hum:
  Now teach me, maid composed,
  To breathe some softened strain,

Whose numbers, stealing through thy dark'ning vale,
May not unseemly with its stillness suit,
  As, musing slow, I hail
  Thy genial loved return!

For when thy folding-star arising shows
His paly circlet, at his warning lamp
  The fragrant Hours, and elves
  Who slept in flowers the day,

And many a nymph who wreaths her brows with sedge,
And sheds the fresh'ning dew, and, lovelier still,
  The pensive Pleasures sweet,
  Prepare thy shadowy car.

Then lead, calm vot'ress, where some sheety lake
Cheers the lone heath, or some time-hallowed pile
  Or upland fallows gray
  Reflect its last cool gleam.

But when chill blust'ring winds, or driving rain,
Forbid my willing feet, be mine the hut
  That from the mountain's side
  Views wilds, and swelling floods,

And hamlets brown, and dim-discovered spires,
And hears their simple bell, and marks o'er all
  Thy dewy fingers draw
  The gradual dusky veil.

While Spring shall pour his show'rs, as oft he wont,
And bathe thy breathing tresses, meekest Eve;
  While Summer loves to sport
  Beneath thy ling'ring light;

While sallow Autumn fills thy lap with leaves;
Or Winter, yelling through the troublous air,
  Affrights thy shrinking train,
  And rudely rends thy robes;

So long, sure-found beneath the sylvan shed,
Shall Fancy, Friendship, Science, rose-lipped Health,
  Thy gentlest influence own,
  And hymn thy fav'rite name!

THE PASSIONS

AN ODE FOR MUSIC

When Music, heav'nly maid, was young,
While yet in early Greece she sung,
The Passions oft, to hear her shell,
Thronged around her magic cell,
Exulting, trembling, raging, fainting,
Possessed beyond the Muse's painting;
By turns they felt the glowing mind
Disturbed, delighted, raised, refined:
Till once, 'tis said, when all were fired,
Filled with fury, rapt, inspired,
From the supporting myrtles round
They snatched her instruments of sound;

[1]Embroidery.

And as they oft had heard apart
Sweet lessons of her forceful art,
Each—for madness ruled the hour—
Would prove his own expressive pow'r.

First Fear his hand, its skill to try,
  Amid the chords bewildered laid,
And back recoiled, he knew not why,
  E'en at the sound himself had made.

Next Anger rushed; his eyes, on fire,
  In lightnings owned his secret stings;
In one rude clash he struck the lyre,
  And swept with hurried hand the strings.

With woeful measures wan Despair
  Low sullen sounds his grief beguiled;
A solemn, strange, and mingled air;
  'Twas sad by fits, by starts 'twas wild.

But thou, O Hope, with eyes so fair,
  What was thy delightful measure?
Still it whispered promised pleasure,
  And bade the lovely scenes at distance hail!
Still would her touch the strain prolong,
  And from the rocks, the woods, the vale,
She called on Echo still through all the song;
  And where her sweetest theme she chose,
  A soft responsive voice was heard at ev'ry close,
And Hope enchanted smiled, and waved her golden hair.

And longer had she sung,—but with a frown
    Revenge impatient rose;
He threw his blood-stained sword in thunder down
    And with a with'ring look
  The war-denouncing[1] trumpet took,
And blew a blast so loud and dread,
Were ne'er prophetic sounds so full of woe.
    And ever and anon he beat
    The doubling drum with furious heat;
  And though sometimes, each dreary pause between,
    Dejected Pity, at his side,
    Her soul-subduing voice applied,
  Yet still he kept his wild unaltered mien,
While each strained ball of sight seemed bursting from his head.

Thy numbers, Jealousy, to nought were fixed,
  Sad proof of thy distressful state;
Of diff'ring themes the veering song was mixed,
  And now it courted Love, now raving called on Hate.

[1]War-announcing.

With eyes upraised, as one inspired,
Pale Melancholy sat retired,
And from her wild sequestered seat,
In notes by distance made more sweet,
Poured through the mellow horn her pensive soul:
  And, dashing soft from rocks around,
  Bubbling runnels joined the sound;
Through glades and glooms the mingled measure stole;
  Or o'er some haunted stream with fond delay
    Round an holy calm diffusing,
    Love of peace and lonely musing,
  In hollow murmurs died away.

But O how altered was its sprightlier tone,
When Cheerfulness, a nymph of healthiest hue,
  Her bow across her shoulder flung,
  Her buskins gemmed with morning dew,
Blew an inspiring air, that dale and thicket rung,
  The hunter's call to faun and dryad known!
  The oak-crowned sisters, and their chaste-eyed queen,[2]
  Satyrs, and sylvan boys, were seen,
  Peeping from forth their alleys green;
Brown Exercise rejoiced to hear,
  And Sport leaped up, and seized his beechen spear.

Last came Joy's ecstatic trial.
He, with viny crown advancing,
  First to the lively pipe his hand addressed;
But soon he saw the brisk awak'ning viol,
  Whose sweet entrancing voice he loved the best.
    They would have thought, who heard the strain,
    They saw in Tempe's vale[3] her native maids,
    Amidst the festal sounding shades,
To some unwearied minstrel dancing,
  While, as his flying fingers kissed the strings,
  Love framed with Mirth a gay fantastic round;
  Loose were her tresses seen, her zone unbound,
  And he, amidst his frolic play,
As if he would the charming air repay,
Shook thousand odors from his dewy wings.

O Music, sphere-descended maid,
Friend of Pleasure, Wisdom's aid,
Why, goddess, why, to us denied,
Lay'st thou thy ancient lyre aside?

[2]The wood-nymphs and Diana.
[3]A valley in Thessaly.

As in that loved Athenian bower
You learned an all-commanding power,
Thy mimic soul, O nymph endeared,
Can well recall what then it heard.
Where is thy native simple heart,
Devote to Virtue, Fancy, Art?
Arise as in that elder time,
Warm, energic, chaste, sublime!
Thy wonders, in that godlike age,
Fill thy recording sister's page—
'Tis said, and I believe the tale,
Thy humblest reed could more prevail,
Had more of strength, diviner rage,
Than all which charms this laggard age,
E'en all at once together found,
Cecilia's[1] mingled world of sound.
O bid our vain endeavors cease,
Revive the just designs of Greece,
Return in all thy simple state,
Confirm the tales her sons relate!

[1]St. Cecilia was said to have invented the organ.

THOMAS GRAY (1716–1771)

Gray was born in Cornhill, London, on 26 December, 1716. When he was about eleven years old he was sent to Eton, where he formed close friendships with Horace Walpole, Richard West, whose early death in 1742 caused him deep grief, and Thomas Ashton. In 1734 he entered Peterhouse, Cambridge. He made but few acquaintances there, his life-long habit of reserve already asserting itself, and he left Cambridge in 1738 without taking a degree, because of his hatred of mathematics. In 1739 he went with Horace Walpole to travel on the continent, and they spent some months together very agreeably, though in Italy there arose a difference between them which caused them to part company, Gray returning home alone in the summer of 1741. He spent about a year living with his mother at Stoke Poges, and then in 1742 returned to Peterhouse. He made some efforts to study the law, and was given the bachelor's degree in law in 1743, but he never took any steps looking to active practice. Instead he settled down to a life of study at Cambridge, where he remained, save for one interruption, through the rest of his life. In consequence of some disturbance he moved from Peterhouse to Pembroke in 1756, and in a life outwardly so quiet as his this was a great event. When the British Museum was opened in 1759 he took lodgings in London and remained there two years, studying manuscripts and old books in the Museum. He is said to have become one of the most learned men in Europe in his time, his studies including classical literature, history, modern languages and literatures, architecture, botany, and music. He made extensive collections and notes for a history of English poetry, but gave over his design when he learned that Thomas Warton was engaged on the same subject. His few poems he wrote slowly and with difficulty, and he had no ambition for fame. He was occupied with the famous *Elegy* for about eight years before he completed it, and then was induced to publish it in 1751 only when he learned that a mutilated copy was about to be printed without his permission. Nevertheless the few poems he published in 1753 and 1757 won him immediate recognition, and he was offered the post of poet laureate in the latter year. This he refused without hesitation, regarding it, in view of the character of recent incumbents, as a questionable honor, and as in any case one which he did not care for. In 1768 he was made professor of modern history at Cambridge, a post which in his day did not necessarily carry any duties with it and, though he planned to deliver some lectures, he never did so. Gray died on 30 July, 1771, and was buried at Stoke Poges, by the side of his mother.

Gray's poems are almost as few in number as those of Collins, and like Collins's they are characterized by an exquisite sense of form. Gray's fastidious classicism of style and form issued from qualities of temperament which were reënforced by his close study of the Greeks and, among English poets, of Milton and Dryden. Gray's antiquarianism, which found expression in the *Bard* and in his Norse and other Welsh poems, together with admiration which he felt for rugged natural scenery, has caused him to be regarded as a forerunner of the romantic poets of the early nineteenth century. This to a certain extent he was, but the point may be unduly insisted on to the obscuration of his more important qualities. His interesting letters are of a piece with his poems in showing that he was "romantic" in only a very partial and external sense.

ODE ON THE DEATH OF A FAVORITE CAT,

DROWNED IN A TUB OF GOLD FISHES[1]

'TWAS on a lofty vase's side,
Where China's gayest art had dyed
  The azure flowers, that blow;
Demurest of the tabby kind,
The pensive Selima reclined,
  Gazed on the lake below.

Her conscious tail her joy declared;
The fair round face, the snowy beard,
  The velvet of her paws,
Her coat, that with the tortoise vies,
Her ears of jet, and emerald eyes,
  She saw; and purred applause.

Still had she gazed; but 'midst the tide
Two angel forms were seen to glide,
  The Genii of the stream:
Their scaly armor's Tyrian hue
Through richest purple to the view
  Betrayed a golden gleam:

The hapless Nymph with wonder saw:
A whisker first and then a claw,

[1]Written early in 1747; first published in 1748.

With many an ardent wish,
She stretched in vain to reach the prize.
What female heart can gold despise?
What Cat's averse to fish?

Presumptuous Maid! with looks intent
Again she stretched, again she bent,
Nor knew the gulf between.
(Malignant Fate sat by, and smiled)
The slipp'ry verge her feet beguiled,
She tumbled headlong in.

Eight times emerging from the flood
She mewed to ev'ry wat'ry God,
Some speedy aid to send.
No Dolphin came, no Nereid stirred:
Nor cruel Tom, nor Susan heard.
A Fav'rite has no friend!

From hence, ye Beauties, undeceived,
Know, one false step is ne'er retrieved,
And be with caution bold.
Not all that tempts your wand'ring eyes
And heedless hearts, is lawful prize;
Nor all, that glisters, gold.

ODE ON A DISTANT PROSPECT OF ETON COLLEGE[1]

Ἄνθρωπος· ἱκανὴ πρόφασις εἰς τὸ δυστυχεῖν.[2]
—MENANDER.

YE DISTANT spires, ye antique towers,
That crown the wat'ry glade,
Where grateful Science still adores
Her Henry's[3] holy Shade;
And ye, that from the stately brow
Of Windsor's[4] heights th' expanse below
Of grove, of lawn, of mead survey,
Whose turf, whose shade, whose flowers among
Wanders the hoary Thames along
His silver-winding way.

Ah happy hills, ah pleasing shade,
Ah fields belov'd in vain,
Where once my careless childhood strayed,
A stranger yet to pain!
I feel the gales, that from ye blow,
A momentary bliss bestow,
As waving fresh their gladsome wing,
My weary soul they seem to sooth,
And, redolent of joy and youth,
To breathe a second spring.

Say, Father Thames, for thou hast seen
Full many a sprightly race
Disporting on thy margent green
The paths of pleasure trace,
Who foremost now delight to cleave
With pliant arm thy glassy wave?
The captive linnet which enthrall?
What idle progeny succeed
To chase the rolling circle's speed,
Or urge the flying ball?

While some on earnest business bent
Their murm'ring labors ply
'Gainst graver hours, that bring constraint
To sweeten liberty:
Some bold adventurers disdain
The limits of their little reign,
And unknown regions dare descry:
Still as they run they look behind,
They hear a voice in every wind,
And snatch a fearful joy.

Gay hope is theirs by fancy fed,
Less pleasing when possessed;
The tear forgot as soon as shed,
The sunshine of the breast:
Theirs buxom health of rosy hue,
Wild wit, invention ever-new,
And lively cheer of vigor born;
The thoughtless day, the easy night,
The spirits pure, the slumbers light,
That fly th' approach of morn.

Alas, regardless of their doom,
The little victims play!
No sense have they of ills to come,
Nor care beyond to-day:
Yet see how all around 'em wait
The Ministers of human fate,
And black Misfortune's baleful train!
Ah, show them where in ambush stand
To seize their prey the murd'rous band!
Ah, tell them, they are men!

These shall the fury Passions tear,
The vultures of the mind,
Disdainful Anger, pallid Fear,
And Shame that skulks behind;
Or pining Love shall waste their youth,
Or Jealousy with rankling tooth,
That inly gnaws the secret heart,
And Envy wan, and faded Care,
Grim-visaged comfortless Despair,
And Sorrow's piercing dart.

Ambition this shall tempt to rise,
Then whirl the wretch from high,
To bitter Scorn a sacrifice,
And grinning Infamy.

---

[1]Written in 1742; first published in 1747.
[2]A human being: sufficient cause for misery.
[3]Henry VI, founder of Eton College (1440).
[4]Windsor Castle, a royal palace near Eton.

The stings of Falsehood those shall try,
And hard Unkindness' altered eye,
  That mocks the tear it forced to flow;
And keen Remorse with blood defiled,
And moody Madness laughing wild
  Amid severest woe.

Lo, in the vale of years beneath
  A grisly troop are seen,
The painful family of Death,
  More hideous than their Queen:
This racks the joints, this fires the veins,
That every laboring sinew strains,
  Those in the deeper vitals rage:
Lo, Poverty, to fill the band,
That numbs the soul with icy hand,
  And slow-consuming Age.

To each his suff'rings: all are men,
  Condemned alike to groan;
The tender for another's pain,
  Th' unfeeling for his own.
Yet ah! why should they know their fate?
Since sorrow never comes too late,
  And happiness too swiftly flies.
Thought would destroy their paradise.
No more; where ignorance is bliss,
  'Tis folly to be wise.

HYMN TO ADVERSITY[1]

—Ζῆνα
τὸν φρονεῖν βροτοὺς ὁδώ-
σαντα, τῷ πάθει μαθὰν
θέντα κυρίως ἔχειν.[2]
ÆSCHYLUS, *Agamemnon.*

DAUGHTER of Jove, relentless Power,
Thou Tamer of the human breast,
Whose iron scourge and tort'ring hour,
The Bad affright, afflict the Best!
Bound in thy adamantine chain
The Proud are taught to taste of pain,
And purple Tyrants vainly groan
With pangs unfelt before, unpitied and alone.

When first thy Sire to send on earth
Virtue, his darling Child, designed,
To thee he gave the heav'nly Birth,
And bade to form her infant mind.
Stern rugged Nurse! thy rigid lore
With patience many a year she bore:
What sorrow was, thou bad'st her know,
And from her own she learned to melt at others' woe.

[1]Written in 1742; first published in 1753.

[2]Zeus has set men on the way to wisdom and decreed that they shall learn through suffering (lines 167–171).

Scared at thy frown terrific, fly
Self-pleasing Folly's idle brood,
Wild Laughter, Noise, and thoughtless Joy,
And leave us leisure to be good.
Light they disperse, and with them go
The summer Friend, the flatt'ring Foe;
By vain Prosperity received,
To her they vow their truth, and are again believed.

Wisdom in sable garb arrayed
Immersed in rapt'rous thought profound,
And Melancholy, silent maid
With leaden eye, that loves the ground,
Still on thy solemn steps attend:
Warm Charity, the gen'ral Friend,
With Justice to herself severe,
And Pity dropping soft the sadly-pleasing tear.

Oh, gently on thy Suppliant's head,
Dread Goddess, lay thy chast'ning hand!
Not in thy Gorgon terrors clad,[3]
Nor circled with the vengeful Band
(As by the Impious thou art seen)
With thund'ring voice, and threat'ning mien,
With screaming Horror's funeral cry,
Despair, and fell Disease, and ghastly Poverty.

Thy form benign, O Goddess, wear,
Thy milder influence impart,
Thy philosophic Train be there
To soften, not to wound my heart,
The gen'rous spark extinct revive,
Teach me to love and to forgive,
Exact my own defects to scan,
What others are, to feel, and know myself a Man.

THE PROGRESS OF POESY,[4]

A PINDARIC ODE

Φωνᾶντα συνετοῖσιν· ἐς
Δὲ τὸ πὰν ἑρμηνέων χατίζει.[5]
—PINDAR, *Olymp. II.*

I. STROPHE

AWAKE, Æolian lyre,[6] awake,
And give to rapture all thy trembling strings.
From Helicon's harmonious springs
A thousand rills their mazy progress take:

[3]Gorgon means dreadful; the reference is to the image on the shield of Pallas Athene. In the next line "the vengeful Band" are the Furies.

[4]Written in 1754; first published in 1757.

[5]A voice intelligible to the wise, but one that needs interpreters for the rabble (lines 153–154).

[6]The lyre of Pindar.

The laughing flowers, that round them blow,
Drink life and fragrance as they flow.
Now the rich stream of music winds along
Deep, majestic, smooth, and strong,
Through verdant vales, and Ceres' golden reign:[1]
Now rolling down the steep amain,
Headlong, impetuous, see it pour:
The rocks, and nodding groves rebellow to the roar.

ANTISTROPHE

Oh! Sovereign of the willing soul,
Parent of sweet and solemn-breathing airs,
Enchanting shell![2] the sullen Cares,
And frantic Passions hear thy soft control.
On Thracia's hills the Lord of War,[3]
Has curbed the fury of his car,
And dropped his thirsty lance at thy command.
Perching on the sceptered hand
Of Jove, thy magic lulls the feathered king[4]
With ruffled plumes, and flagging wing:
Quenched in dark clouds of slumber lie
The terror of his beak, and lightnings of his eye.

EPODE

Thee the voice, the dance, obey,
Tempered to thy warbled lay.
O'er Idalia's[5] velvet-green
The rosy-crownéd Loves are seen
On Cytherea's day
With antic Sports, and blue-eyed Pleasures,
Frisking light in frolic measures;
Now pursuing, now retreating,
Now in circling troops they meet:
To brisk notes in cadence beating
Glance their many-twinkling feet.
Slow melting strains their Queen's approach declare:
Where'er she turns the Graces homage pay.
With arms sublime, that float upon the air,
In gliding state she wins her easy way:
O'er her warm cheek, and rising bosom, move
The bloom of young Desire, and purple light of Love.

II. STROPHE

Man's feeble race what Ills await,
Labor and Penury, the racks of Pain,
Disease, and Sorrow's weeping train,
And Death, sad refuge from the storms of Fate!

[1]Fields over which Ceres reigns.

[2]The lyre was said to have been made first by Hermes from a tortoise shell.

[3]Mars. Thrace was thought to be his favorite abode.

[4]The eagle.

[5]A town in Cyprus containing a temple to Venus, or Cytherea, as she was sometimes called.

The fond complaint, my Song, disprove,
And justify the laws of Jove.
Say, has he giv'n in vain the heav'nly Muse?
Night, and all her sickly dews,
Her Specters wan, and Birds of boding cry,
He gives to range the dreary sky:
Till down the eastern cliffs afar
Hyperion's march[6] they spy, and glitt'ring shafts of war.

ANTISTROPHE

In climes beyond the solar road,
Where shaggy forms o'er ice-built mountains roam,
The Muse has broke the twilight-gloom
To cheer the shiv'ring Native's dull abode.
And oft, beneath the od'rous shade
Of Chili's boundless forests laid,
She deigns to hear the savage Youth repeat
In loose numbers wildly sweet
Their feather-cintured Chiefs, and dusky Loves.
Her track, where'er the Goddess roves,
Glory pursue, and generous Shame,
Th' unconquerable Mind, and Freedom's holy flame.

EPODE

Woods, that wave o'er Delphi's steep,
Isles, that crown th' Ægean deep,
Fields, that cool Ilissus[7] laves,
Or where Mæander's[8] amber waves
In lingering Lab'rinths creep,
How do your tuneful Echoes languish,
Mute, but to the voice of Anguish?
Where each old poetic Mountain
Inspiration breathed around:
Ev'ry shade and hallowed Fountain
Murmured deep a solemn sound:
Till the sad Nine in Greece's evil hour
Left their Parnassus for the Latian plains.
Alike they scorn the pomp of tyrant-Power,
And coward Vice, that revels in her chains.
When Latium had her lofty spirit lost,
They sought, O Albion! next thy sea-encircled coast.[9]

[6]The sunrise.

[7]A stream flowing through Athens.

[8]A river in Asia Minor.

[9]Gray's note on this epode is as follows: Progress of poetry from Greece to Italy, and from Italy to England. Chaucer was not unacquainted with the writings of Dante or of Petrarch. The Earl of Surrey and Sir Tho. Wyatt had traveled in Italy [Gray is wrong about Surrey, who was never in Italy, though he spent some time in France], and formed their taste there; Spenser imitated the Italian writers; Milton improved on them: but this school expired soon after the Restoration and a new one arose on the French model, which has subsisted ever since.

III. STROPHE

Far from the sun and summer-gale,
In thy green lap was Nature's Darling[1] laid,
What time, where lucid Avon strayed,
To Him the mighty Mother did unveil
Her awful face: The dauntless Child
Stretched forth his little arms, and smiled.
This pencil take (she said) whose colors clear
Richly paint the vernal year:
Thine too these golden keys, immortal Boy!
This can unlock the gates of Joy;
Of Horror that, and thrilling Fears,
Or ope the sacred source of sympathetic Tears.

ANTISTROPHE

Nor second He,[2] that rode sublime
Upon the seraph-wings of Ecstasy,
The secrets of th' Abyss to spy.
He passed the flaming bounds of Place and Time:
The living Throne, the sapphire-blaze,
Where Angels tremble, while they gaze,
He saw; but blasted with excess of light,
Closed his eyes in endless night.
Behold, where Dryden's less presumptuous car,
Wide o'er the fields of Glory bear
Two Coursers of ethereal race,
With necks in thunder clothed, and long-resounding pace.

EPODE

Hark, his hands the lyre explore!
Bright-eyed Fancy hovering o'er
Scatters from her pictured urn
Thoughts that breathe, and words that burn.
But ah! 'tis heard no more——
Oh! Lyre divine, what daring Spirit
Wakes thee now? though he inherit
Nor the pride, nor ample pinion,
That the Theban Eagle bear[3]
Sailing with supreme dominion
Through the azure deep of air:
Yet oft before his infant eyes would run
Such forms, as glitter in the Muse's ray
With orient hues, unborrowed of the Sun:
Yet shall he mount, and keep his distant way
Beyond the limits of a vulgar fate,
Beneath the Good how far—but far above the Great.

[1]Shakespeare. [2]Milton.

[3]Pindar compares himself to that bird, and his enemies to ravens that croak and clamor in vain below, while it pursues its flight, regardless of their noise (Gray's note).

THE BARD,[4]

A PINDARIC ODE

ADVERTISEMENT

The following Ode is founded on a Tradition current in Wales, that Edward the First, when he completed the conquest of that country, ordered all the Bards that fell into his hands to be put to death.[5]

I. STROPHE

"RUIN seize thee, ruthless King!
Confusion on thy banners wait,
Though fanned by Conquest's crimson wing
They mock the air with idle state.
Helm, nor Hauberk's twisted mail,
Nor even thy virtues, Tyrant, shall avail
To save thy secret soul from nightly fears,
From Cambria's[6] curse, from Cambria's tears!"
Such were the sounds, that o'er the crested pride
Of the first Edward scattered wild dismay,
As down the steep of Snowdon's[7] shaggy side
He wound with toilsome march his long array.
Stout Glo'ster[8] stood aghast in speechless trance;
To arms! cried Mortimer,[9] and couched his quiv'ring lance.

ANTISTROPHE

On a rock, whose haughty brow
Frowns o'er old Conway's foaming flood,
Robed in the sable garb of woe,
With haggard eyes the Poet stood;
(Loose his beard, and hoary hair
Streamed, like a meteor, to the troubled air)
And with a Master's hand, and Prophet's fire,
Struck the deep sorrows of his lyre.
"Hark, how each giant-oak, and desert cave,
Sighs to the torrent's awful voice beneath!
O'er thee, O King! their hundred arms they wave,
Revenge on thee in hoarser murmurs breathe;
Vocal no more, since Cambria's fatal day,
To high-born Hoel's harp, or soft Llewellyn's lay.

[4]Begun in 1754 and finished in 1757, when it was first published.

[5]This tradition has no foundation in fact. Edward I reigned from 1272 to 1307.

[6]Wales.

[7]A name given by the Saxons to that mountainous tract which the Welsh themselves call *Craigian-eryri:* it included all the highlands of Carnarvonshire and Merionethshire, as far east as the river Conway (Gray's note).

[8]Gilbert de Clare, surnamed the Red, Earl of Gloucester and Hertford, son-in-law to King Edward (Gray's note).

[9]Edmond de Mortimer, Lord of Wigmore. They were both Lords-Marchers, whose lands lay on the borders of Wales, and probably accompanied the king in this expedition (Gray's note).

EPODE

"Cold is Cadwallo's tongue,
That hushed the stormy main:
Brave Urien sleeps upon his craggy bed:
Mountains, ye mourn in vain
Modred, whose magic song
Made huge Plinlimmon[1] bow his cloud-topped head.
On dreary Arvon's shore they lie,[2]
Smeared with gore, and ghastly pale:
Far, far aloof th' affrighted ravens sail;
The famished Eagle screams, and passes by.
Dear lost companions of my tuneful art,
Dear, as the light that visits these sad eyes,
Dear, as the ruddy drops that warm my heart,
Ye died amidst your dying country's cries—
No more I weep. They do not sleep.
On yonder cliffs, a grisly band,
I see them sit, they linger yet,
Avengers of their native land:
With me in dreadful harmony they join,
And weave with bloody hands the tissue of thy line.

II. STROPHE

"'Weave the warp, and weave the woof,
The winding-sheet of Edward's race.
Give ample room, and verge enough
The characters of hell to trace.
Mark the year, and mark the night,
When Severn shall re-echo with affright
The shrieks of death, through Berkeley's roofs that ring,
Shrieks of an agonizing King![3]
She-Wolf[4] of France, with unrelenting fangs,
That tear'st the bowels of thy mangled Mate,
From thee be born, who o'er thy country hangs[5]
The scourge of Heav'n. What Terrors round him wait!
Amazement in his van, with Flight combined,
And sorrow's faded form, and solitude behind.

ANTISTROPHE

"'Mighty Victor, mighty Lord,
Low on his funeral couch he lies!
No pitying heart, no eye, afford
A tear to grace his obsequies.
Is the sable Warrior[6] fled?
Thy son is gone. He rests among the Dead.
The Swarm, that in thy noon-tide beam were born?
Gone to salute the rising Morn.
Fair laughs[7] the Morn, and soft the Zephyr blows,
While proudly riding o'er the azure realm
In gallant trim the gilded Vessel goes;
Youth on the prow, and Pleasure at the helm;
Regardless of the sweeping Whirlwind's sway,
That, hushed in grim repose, expects his evening prey.

EPODE

"'Fill high the sparkling bowl,
The rich repast prepare,
Reft of a crown, he yet may share the feast:
Close by the regal chair
Fell Thirst and Famine scowl
A baleful smile upon their baffled Guest.
Heard ye the din of battle bray,
Lance to lance, and horse to horse?
Long Years of havoc[8] urge their destined course,
And through the kindred squadrons mow their way.
Ye Towers of Julius,[9] London's lasting shame,
With many a foul and midnight murder fed,
Revere his Consort's[10] faith, his Father's[11] fame,
And spare the meek Usurper's[12] holy head.
Above, below, the rose[13] of snow,
Twined with her blushing foe, we spread:
The bristled Boar[14] in infant gore
Wallows beneath the thorny shade.
Now, Brothers, bending o'er th' accurséd loom
Stamp we our vengeance deep, and ratify his doom.

III. STROPHE

"'Edward, lo! to sudden fate
(Weave we the woof. The thread is spun.)
Half of thy heart we consecrate.
(The web is wove. The work is done.)'
Stay, O stay! nor thus forlorn
Leave me unblessed, unpitied, here to mourn:
In yon bright track, that fires the western skies,
They melt, they vanish from my eyes.
But oh! what solemn scenes on Snowdon's height

[1]A mountain in Wales.

[2]The shores of Carnarvonshire opposite to the isle of Anglesey (Gray's note).

[3]Edward II, murdered in Berkeley Castle, 1327.

[4]Isabel of France, Edward II's adulterous queen (Gray's note).

[5]Edward III. The reference is to his triumphs in France.

[6]The Black Prince.

[7]These lines describe the reign of Richard II and (in the epode) his death by starvation.

[8]The Wars of the Roses.

[9]The Tower of London. The oldest part of that structure is vulgarly attributed to Julius Cæsar (Gray's note).

[10]Margaret of Anjou.

[11]Henry V.

[12]Henry VI, who was "very near being canonized" (Gray).

[13]The white and red roses, devices of York and Lancaster (Gray).

[14]The silver boar was the device of Richard III (Gray). The "infant gore" is that of the murdered princes.

Descending slow their glitt'ring skirts unroll?
Visions of glory, spare my aching sight,
Ye unborn Ages, crowd not on my soul!
No more our long-lost Arthur we bewail.
All-hail, ye genuine Kings,[1] Britannia's Issue,
hail!

ANTISTROPHE

"Girt with many a Baron bold
Sublime their starry fronts they rear;
And gorgeous Dames, and Statesmen old
In bearded majesty, appear.
In the midst a Form divine![2]
Her eye proclaims her of the Briton-Line;
Her lion-port, her awe-commanding face,
Attempered sweet to virgin grace.
What strings symphonious tremble in the air,
What strains of vocal transport round her
play!
Hear from the grave, great Taliessin, hear:
They breathe a soul to animate thy clay.
Bright Rapture calls, and soaring, as she sings,
Waves in the eye of Heav'n her many-colored
wings.

EPODE

"The verse adorn again
Fierce War, and faithful Love,
And Truth severe, by fairy Fiction dressed.[3]
In buskined measures move
Pale Grief, and pleasing Pain,
With Horror, Tyrant of the throbbing breast.[4]
A Voice, as of the Cherub-Choir,
Gales from blooming Eden bear;[5]
And distant warblings lessen on my ear,
That lost in long futurity expire.[6]
Fond impious Man, think'st thou, yon
sanguine cloud,
Raised by thy breath, has quenched the Orb
of day?
To-morrow he repairs the golden flood,
And warms the nations with redoubled ray.
Enough for me: With joy I see
The different doom our Fates assign.
Be thine Despair, and sceptered Care,
To triumph, and to die, are mine."
He spoke, and headlong from the mountain's
height
Deep in the roaring tide he plunged to endless
night.

[1]Both Merlin and Taliessin [Cymric bard, sixth century] had prophesied that the Welsh should regain their sovereignty over this island, which seemed to be accomplished in the House of Tudor [beginning with Henry VII] (Gray).

[2]Queen Elizabeth.

[3]The reference is to Spenser's *Faerie Queene.*

[4]Shakespeare.

[5]Milton.

[6]The succession of poets after Milton's time (Gray).

THE FATAL SISTERS

AN ODE[7]

PREFACE

In the Eleventh Century Sigurd, Earl of the Orkney Islands, went with a fleet of ships and a considerable body of troops into Ireland to the assistance of Sictryg with the silken beard, who was then making war on his father-in-law Brian, King of Dublin: the Earl and all his forces were cut to pieces, and Sictryg was in danger of a total defeat; but the enemy had a greater loss by the death of Brian, their King, who fell in action. On Christmas day (the day of the battle), a Native of Caithness in Scotland saw at a distance a number of persons on horseback riding full speed towards a hill, and seeming to enter into it. Curiosity led him to follow them, till looking through an opening in the rocks he saw twelve gigantic figures resembling women: they were all employed about a loom; and as they wove, they sung the following dreadful Song; which when they had finished, they tore the web into twelve pieces, and (each taking her portion) galloped Six to the North and as many to the South.

Now the storm begins to lower
(Haste, the loom of Hell prepare),
Iron-sleet of arrowy shower
Hurtles in the darkened air.

Glitt'ring lances are the loom,
Where the dusky warp we strain,
Weaving many a Soldier's doom,
Orkney's woe, and Randver's bane.

See the grisly texture grow
('Tis of human entrails made),
And the weights, that play below,
Each a gasping Warrior's head.

Shafts for shuttles, dipped in gore,
Shoot the trembling cords along.
Sword, that once a Monarch bore,
Keep the tissue close and strong.

[7]Written in 1761; first published in 1768. Gray made this version from a Latin translation of an Old Norse poem. The original text, with an English prose translation, is to be found in Vigfusson and Powell's *Corpus Poeticum Boreale*, I, 281–283. The prose which precedes and follows the poem Gray embodied in the Preface printed above. The event which it celebrates is the Battle of Clontarf, fought 23 April (not on Christmas day, as Gray says), 1014. Sictryg, it may be noted, was King of Dublin, Brian, King of Ireland. Brian was Sictryg's stepfather, which may be what Gray means when he says "father-in-law." The "gigantic figures resembling women" are the Valkyries, who in the poem are represented as weaving the web of battle.

Mista black, terrific Maid,
Sangrida, and Hilda[1] see,
Join the wayward work to aid:
'Tis the woof of victory.

Ere the ruddy sun be set,
Pikes must shiver, javelins sing,
Blade with clattering buckler meet,
Hauberk crash, and helmet ring.

(Weave the crimson web of war)
Let us go, and let us fly,
Where our Friends the conflict share,
Where they triumph, where they die.

As the paths of fate we tread,
Wading through th' ensanguined field:
Gondula, and Geira, spread
O'er the youthful King your shield.

We the reins to slaughter give,
Ours to kill, and ours to spare:
Spite of danger he shall live.
(Weave the crimson web of war.)

They, whom once the desert-beach
Pent within its bleak domain,
Soon their ample sway shall stretch
O'er the plenty of the plain.

Low the dauntless Earl is laid,
Gored with many a gaping wound:
Fate demands a nobler head;
Soon a King shall bite the ground.[2]

Long his loss shall Eirin[3] weep,
Ne'er again his likeness see;
Long her strains in sorrow steep,
Strains of Immortality!

Horror covers all the heath,
Clouds of carnage blot the sun.
Sisters, weave the web of death;
Sisters, cease, the work is done.

Hail the task, and hail the hands!
Songs of joy and triumph sing!
Joy to the victorious bands;
Triumph to the younger King.

Mortal, thou that hear'st the tale,
Learn the tenor of our song.
Scotland, through each winding vale
Far and wide the notes prolong.

Sisters, hence with spurs of speed:
Each her thundering falchion[4] wield;
Each bestride her sable steed.
Hurry, hurry to the field.

[1] These are names of Valkyries, as are also the names in the third stanza below.

[2] *I. e.*, Brian. [3] Ireland. [4] Short sword.

ELEGY

WRITTEN IN A COUNTRY CHURCH-YARD[5]

The Curfew tolls the knell of parting day,
The lowing herd wind slowly o'er the lea,
The plowman homeward plods his weary way,
And leaves the world to darkness and to me.

Now fades the glimmering landscape on the sight,
And all the air a solemn stillness holds,
Save where the beetle wheels his droning flight,
And drowsy tinklings lull the distant folds;

Save that from yonder ivy-mantled tower
The moping owl does to the moon complain
Of such, as wand'ring near her secret bower,
Molest her ancient solitary reign.

Beneath those rugged elms, that yew-tree's shade,
Where heaves the turf in many a mold'ring heap,
Each in his narrow cell for ever laid,
The rude Forefathers of the hamlet sleep.

The breezy call of incense-breathing Morn,
The swallow twitt'ring from the straw-built shed,
The cock's shrill clarion, or the echoing horn,
No more shall rouse them from their lowly bed.

For them no more the blazing hearth shall burn,
Or busy housewife ply her evening care:
No children run to lisp their sire's return,
Or climb his knees the envied kiss to share.

Oft did the harvest to their sickle yield,
Their furrow oft the stubborn glebe has broke;
How jocund did they drive their team afield!
How bowed the woods beneath their sturdy stroke!

Let not Ambition mock their useful toil,
Their homely joys, and destiny obscure;
Nor Grandeur hear with a disdainful smile,
The short and simple annals of the poor.

The boast of heraldry, the pomp of pow'r,
And all that beauty, all that wealth e'er gave,
Awaits alike th' inevitable hour.
The paths of glory lead but to the grave.

[5] Completed in 1750; first published in 1751.

Nor you, ye Proud, impute to These the fault,
If Mem'ry o'er their Tomb no Trophies raise,
Where through the long-drawn isle and fretted vault
The pealing anthem swells the note of praise.

Can storied urn or animated bust
Back to its mansion call the fleeting breath?
Can Honor's voice provoke the silent dust,
Or Flatt'ry sooth the dull cold ear of Death?

Perhaps in this neglected spot is laid
Some heart once pregnant with celestial fire;
Hands, that the rod of empire might have swayed,
Or waked to ecstasy the living lyre.

But Knowledge to their eyes her ample page
Rich with the spoils of time did ne'er unroll;
Chill Penury repressed their noble rage,
And froze the genial current of the soul.

Full many a gem of purest ray serene,
The dark unfathomed caves of ocean bear:
Full many a flower is born to blush unseen,
And waste its sweetness on the desert air.

Some village-Hampden,[1] that with dauntless breast
The little Tyrant of his fields withstood;
Some mute inglorious Milton here may rest,
Some Cromwell guiltless of his country's blood.

Th' applause of list'ning senates to command,
The threats of pain and ruin to despise,
To scatter plenty o'er a smiling land,
And read their hist'ry in a nation's eyes,

Their lot forbade: nor circumscribed alone
Their growing virtues, but their crimes confined;
Forbade to wade through slaughter to a throne,
And shut the gates of mercy on mankind,

The struggling pangs of conscious truth to hide,
To quench the blushes of ingenuous shame,
Or heap the shrine of Luxury and Pride
With incense kindled at the Muse's flame.

Far from the madding crowd's ignoble strife,
Their sober wishes never learned to stray;
Along the cool sequestered vale of life
They kept the noiseless tenor of their way.

Yet e'en these bones from insult to protect
Some frail memorial still erected nigh,
With uncouth rimes and shapeless sculpture decked,
Implores the passing tribute of a sigh.

Their name, their years, spelt by th' unlettered muse,
The place of fame and elegy supply:
And many a holy text around she strews,
That teach the rustic moralist to die.

For who to dumb Forgetfulness a prey,
This pleasing anxious being e'er resigned,
Left the warm precincts of the cheerful day,
Nor cast one longing ling'ring look behind?

On some fond breast the parting soul relies,
Some pious drops the closing eye requires;
E'en from the tomb the voice of Nature cries,
E'en in our Ashes live their wonted Fires.

For thee, who mindful of th' unhonored Dead
Dost in these lines their artless tale relate;
If chance, by lonely contemplation led,
Some kindred Spirit shall inquire thy fate,

Haply some hoary-headed Swain may say,
"Oft have we seen him at the peep of dawn
Brushing with hasty steps the dews away
To meet the sun upon the upland lawn.

"There at the foot of yonder nodding beech
That wreathes its old fantastic roots so high,
His listless length at noontide would he stretch,
And pore upon the brook that babbles by.

"Hard by yon wood, now smiling as in scorn,
Mutt'ring his wayward fancies he would rove,
Now drooping, woeful wan, like one forlorn,
Or crazed with care, or crossed in hopeless love.

"One morn I missed him on the customed hill,
Along the heath and near his fav'rite tree;
Another came; nor yet beside the rill,
Nor up the lawn, nor at the wood was he;

[1] John Hampden, who in 1636 refused to pay the ship-money demanded by Charles I.

"The next with dirges due in sad array
Slow through the church-way path we saw him borne.
Approach and read (for thou can'st read) the lay,
Graved on the stone beneath yon agéd thorn."

THE EPITAPH

Here rests his head upon the lap of Earth
A Youth to Fortune and to Fame unknown.
Fair Science frowned not on his humble birth,
And Melancholy marked him for her own.

Large was his bounty, and his soul sincere,
Heav'n did a recompense as largely send:
He gave to Mis'ry all he had, a tear,
He gained from Heav'n ('twas all he wished) a friend.

No farther seek his merits to disclose,
Or draw his frailties from their dread abode
(There they alike in trembling hope repose),
The bosom of his Father and his God.

SONNET

ON THE DEATH OF RICHARD WEST[1]

IN VAIN to me the smiling Mornings shine,
And redd'ning Phoebus lifts his golden Fire:
The Birds in vain their amorous Descant join;
Or cheerful Fields resume their green Attire:
These Ears, alas! for other Notes repine,
A different Object do these Eyes require
My lonely Anguish melts no Heart, but mine;
And in my Breast the imperfect Joys expire.
Yet Morning smiles the busy Race to cheer,
And new-born Pleasure brings to happier Men:
The Fields to all their wonted Tribute bear;
To warm their little Loves the Birds complain;
I fruitless mourn to him that cannot hear,
And weep the more, because I weep in vain.

[1]Written in 1742; first published in 1775.

SKETCH OF HIS OWN CHARACTER[2]

Too poor for a bribe, and too proud to importune;
He had not the method of making a fortune;
Could love, and could hate, so was thought somewhat odd;
No very great wit, he believed in a God.
A Post or a Pension he did not desire,
But left Church and State to Charles Townshend and Squire.[3]

[2]Written in 1761; first published in 1775.

[3]Townshend was Chancellor of the Exchequer in 1767; he was a politician, orator, and man of the world. Samuel Squire was a fellow of St. John's College, Cambridge; in 1761 he was Bishop of St. David's.

SAMUEL JOHNSON (1709–1784)

Johnson's father was a bookseller doing business in Lichfield, and there Johnson was born on 18 September, 1709. There was little money in the family, and Johnson's struggle with poverty began almost with his birth. The one fortunate circumstance of his youth was the fact that he had the freedom of his father's shop; and his early education was got largely from wide reading in the books which the people of Lichfield did not buy. In 1728 Johnson entered Pembroke College, Oxford, but was able to remain there only fourteen months. He then did not know where to turn for a living. He took a position in a school, but such were schools in that time that after a few months "he relinquished a situation which all his life long he recollected with the strongest aversion, and even a degree of horror." He next made unsuccessful attempts to obtain appointment to headmasterships, and almost equally unsuccessful attempts to earn money by literary hackwork. When he was twenty-six he married Mrs. Porter, a widow who was many years older than himself, whom he regarded with true and undiminished affection until her death in 1752, and whose loss he did not cease to lament until his own death. With a little money which his wife had, Johnson opened a school at Edial, near Lichfield—a school which was never attended by more than three pupils and which he soon abandoned. Other efforts having failed, he now determined to try his fortune in London, whither he went in the company of one of his three former pupils, David Garrick, who was to become the greatest of English actors.

Johnson found employment in London, managing to make a bare living, often enough to do little better than escape starvation, by means of hackwriting for the booksellers. In 1738 he published *London*, a satirical poem imitated from Juvenal after the manner of Pope's imitations of Horace, which won him immediate recognition from the best judges of the day, including Pope himself, but which brought him very little money. Gradually he became known, but could not cease struggling, by means of all kinds of literary work that offered, for a bare subsistence. In 1745 he projected a new edition of Shakespeare, but did not actually publish it until 1765. In 1747 he announced his plan for what was his greatest work, though a work which has now little more than historical interest and one whose value it is not entirely easy for us to grasp. This was his *Dictionary of the English Language*, which it took him and his assistants eight years of hard work to complete. Meanwhile Johnson had published *The Vanity of Human Wishes* in 1749, had seen his classical tragedy, *Irene*, acted with little success, and had published two series of periodical essays, *The Rambler* (1750–1752) and *The Adventurer* (1753). A third series, *The Idler*, was written from 1758 to 1760. Early in 1759 occurred the death of his mother, and it was to meet the expenses of her illness and death that he wrote *Rasselas*. His need was urgent, and he wrote the tale within the space of a single week, or, at the most, if we are to accept O. F. Emerson's criticism of Boswell's account, within a period of ten days—a period during which he was distracted by fears and sorrow and was expecting daily to hear the news of his mother's death. Though Johnson all his life had a pronounced tendency to indolence, his mind could on occasion work, as this instance proves, with astonishing rapidity. A few years later, however, on the accession of George III in 1762, Johnson's long struggle with poverty ceased. The Tories at that time returned to power, and Johnson, who was strongly attached to the Tory party, was granted a pension of £300, which was sufficient to make him fairly comfortable through the remainder of his life. After this, until within a few years of the end of his life, he wrote but little. These years after 1762 were the years of his famous talk. It was in 1763 that he met Boswell, who was to record it all in the greatest of English biographies, and it was in 1764 that the Club (later called the Literary Club) was founded, which brought together at once some of Johnson's closest friends and a remarkable group of the men of that age whose names time has not obliterated—Sir Joshua Reynolds, Edmund Burke, Garrick, Boswell, Goldsmith, Charles James Fox, Thomas and Joseph Warton, Edward Gibbon, and others, including R. B. Sheridan and Bishop Percy. These were the happiest years of Johnson's life, and at the close they were crowned by a great achievement. In the late 1770's a group of booksellers planned to issue a collection of the works of the English poets, and Johnson undertook to write biographical and critical notices of the poets included in the series. The result was his *Lives of the Poets*, which contains some of his best and easiest writing, and which, as a monument of the man and of his type of criticism, remains of lasting interest and importance.

Johnson's fame remains secure, as secure as that of any man in the annals of English literature.

As a writer, he has had the curious fate to be overshadowed by his own biography, but the day has now happily passed when one can think that one sufficiently knows Johnson from the pages of Boswell. The man, truly enough, was greater than any of his works; yet those works have a vitality which Johnson's enemies have belittled in vain. In them still lives a man "who cared passionately for truth and nothing at all for novelty." And one must go to the writer, as well as to the talker, if one is to understand what Sir Joshua Reynolds gratefully said of his friend: "I acknowledge the highest obligations to him. He may be said to have formed my mind, and to have brushed from it a great deal of rubbish. . . . He qualified my mind to think justly."

THE RAMBLER

No. 50. SATURDAY, 8 SEPTEMBER, 1750.

Credebant hoc grande nefas, et morte piandum,
Si juvenis vetulo non assurrexerat, atque
Barbato cuicunque puer, licet ipse videret
Plura domi fraga, et majores glandis acervos.
—JUVENAL.[1]

And had not men the hoary head revered,
And boys paid rev'rence when a man appeared,
Both must have died, though richer skids they wore,
And saw more heaps of acorns in their store.
—CREECH.

I HAVE always thought it the business of those who turn their speculations upon the living world, to commend the virtues, as well as to expose the faults of their contemporaries, and to confute a false as well as to support a just accusation; not only because it is peculiarly the business of a monitor to keep his own reputation untainted, lest those who can once charge him with partiality, should indulge themselves afterwards in disbelieving him at pleasure; but because he may find real crimes sufficient to give full employment to caution or repentance, without distracting the mind by needless scruples and vain solicitudes.

There are certain fixed and stated reproaches that one part of mankind has in all ages thrown upon another, which are regularly transmitted through continued successions, and which he that has once suffered them is certain to use with the same undistinguishing vehemence, when he has changed his station, and gained the prescriptive right of inflicting on others what he had formerly endured himself.

To these hereditary imputations, of which no man sees the justice, till it becomes his interest to see it, very little regard is to be shown; since it does not appear that they are produced by ratiocination or inquiry, but received implicitly, or caught by a kind of instantaneous contagion, and supported rather by willingness to credit, than ability to prove, them.

It has been always the practice of those who are desirous to believe themselves made venerable by length of time, to censure the new comers into life, for want of respect to gray hairs and sage experience, for heady confidence in their own understandings, for hasty conclusions upon partial views, for disregard of counsels, which their fathers and grandsires are ready to afford them, and a rebellious impatience of that subordination to which youth is condemned by nature, as necessary to its security from evils into which it would be otherwise precipitated, by the rashness of passion, and the blindness of ignorance.

Every old man complains of the growing depravity of the world, of the petulance and insolence of the rising generation. He recounts the decency and regularity of former times, and celebrates the discipline and sobriety of the age in which his youth was passed; a happy age, which is now no more to be expected, since confusion has broken in upon the world and thrown down all the boundaries of civility and reverence.

It is not sufficiently considered how much he assumes who dares to claim the privilege of complaining; for as every man has, in his own opinion, a full share of the miseries of life, he is inclined to consider all clamorous uneasiness, as a proof of impatience rather than of affliction, and to ask, What merit has this man to show, by which he has acquired a right to repine at the distributions of nature? Or, why does he imagine that exemptions should be granted him from the general condition of man? We find ourselves excited rather to captiousness than pity, and instead of being in haste to soothe his complaints by sympathy and tenderness, we inquire, whether the pain be proportionate to the lamentation; and

[1] *Satires*, XIII, 54–57. In the 2nd line *atque* should be *et si*. Often Johnson's quotations are somewhat inexact, but these unimportant slips will not be noted here.

whether, supposing the affliction real, it is not the effect of vice and folly, rather than calamity.

The querulousness and indignation which is observed so often to disfigure the last scene of life, naturally leads us to inquiries like these. For surely it will be thought at the first view of things, that if age be thus contemned and ridiculed, insulted and neglected, the crime must at least be equal on either part. They who have had opportunities of establishing their authority over minds ductile and unresisting, they who have been the protectors of helplessness, and the instructors of ignorance, and who yet retain in their own hands the power of wealth, and the dignity of command, must defeat their influence by their own misconduct, and make use of all these advantages with very little skill, if they cannot secure to themselves an appearance of respect, and ward off open mockery, and declared contempt.

The general story of mankind will evince, that lawful and settled authority is very seldom resisted when it is well employed. Gross corruption, or evident imbecility, is necessary to the suppression of that reverence with which the majority of mankind look upon their governors, and on those whom they see surrounded by splendor, and fortified by power. For though men are drawn by their passions into forgetfulness of invisible rewards and punishments, yet they are easily kept obedient to those who have temporal dominion in their hands, till their veneration is dissipated by such wickedness and folly as can neither be defended nor concealed.

It may, therefore, very reasonably be suspected that the old draw upon themselves the greatest part of those insults which they so much lament, and that age is rarely despised but when it is contemptible. If men imagine that excess of debauchery can be made reverend by time, that knowledge is the consequence of long life, however idly or thoughtlessly employed, that priority of birth will supply the want of steadiness or honesty, can it raise much wonder that their hopes are disappointed, and that they see their posterity rather willing to trust their own eyes in their progress into life, than enlist themselves under guides who have lost their way?

There are indeed, many truths which time necessarily and certainly teaches, and which might, by those who have learned them from experience, be communicated to their successors at a cheaper rate; but dictates, though liberally enough bestowed, are generally without effect, the teacher gains few proselytes by instruction which his own behavior contradicts; and young men miss the benefit of counsel, because they are not very ready to believe that those who fall below them in practice, can much excel them in theory. Thus the progress of knowledge is retarded, the world is kept long in the same state, and every new race is to gain the prudence of their predecessors by committing and redressing the same miscarriages.

To secure to the old that influence which they are willing to claim, and which might so much contribute to the improvement of the arts of life, it is absolutely necessary that they give themselves up to the duties of declining years; and contentedly resign to youth its levity, its pleasures, its frolics, and its fopperies. It is a hopeless endeavor to unite the contrarieties of spring and winter; it is unjust to claim the privileges of age, and retain the playthings of childhood. The young always form magnificent ideas of the wisdom and gravity of men, whom they consider as placed at a distance from them in the ranks of existence, and naturally look on those whom they find trifling with long beards, with contempt and indignation, like that which women feel at the effeminacy of men. If dotards will contend with boys in those performances in which boys must always excel them; if they will dress crippled limbs in embroidery, endeavor at gayety with faltering voices, and darken assemblies of pleasure with the ghastliness of disease, they may well expect those who find their diversions obstructed will hoot them away; and that if they descend to competition with youth, they must bear the insolence of successful rivals.

Lusisti satis, edisti satis atque bibisti:
Tempus abire tibi est.[1]

You've had your share of mirth, of meat and drink;
'Tis time to quit the scene—'tis time to think.

—Elphinston

Another vice of age, by which the rising generation may be alienated from it, is severity and censoriousness, that gives no allowance

[1] Horace, *Epistles*, II, ii, 214–215.

to the failings of early life, that expects artfulness[1] from childhood, and constancy from youth, that is peremptory in every command, and inexorable to every failure. There are many who live merely to hinder happiness, and whose descendants can only tell of long life, that it produces suspicion, malignity, peevishness, and persecution; and yet even these tyrants can talk of the ingratitude of the age, curse their heirs for impatience, and wonder that young men cannot take pleasure in their father's company.

He that would pass the latter part of life with honor and decency, must, when he is young, consider that he shall one day be old; and remember, when he is old, that he has once been young. In youth, he must lay up knowledge for his support, when his powers of acting shall forsake him; and in age forbear to animadvert with rigor on faults which experience only can correct.

No. 59. Tuesday, 9 October, 1750.

Est aliquid fatale malum per verba levare:
Hoc querulam Prognen Halcyonenque facit.
Hoc erat, in solo quare Pœantius antro
Voce fatigaret Lemnia saxa sua.
Strangulat inclusus dolor, atque excæstuat intus;
Cogitur et vires multiplicare suas.

—Ovid.[2]

Complaining oft gives respite to our grief;
From hence the wretched Progne sought relief,
Hence the Paeantian chief his fate deplores,
And vents his sorrow to the Lemnian shores;
In vain by secrecy we would assuage
Our cares; concealed they gather tenfold rage.

—F. Lewis.

It is common to distinguish men by the names of animals which they are supposed to resemble. Thus a hero is frequently termed a lion, and a statesman a fox, an extortioner gains the appellation of vulture, and a fop the title of monkey. There is also among the various anomalies of character, which a survey of the world exhibits, a species of beings in human form, which may be properly marked out as the screech-owls of mankind.

These screech-owls seem to be settled in an opinion that the great business of life is to complain, and that they were born for no other purpose than to disturb the happiness of others, to lessen the little comforts, and shorten the short pleasures of our condition, by painful remembrances of the past, or melancholy prognostics of the future; their only care is to crush the rising hope, to damp the kindling transport, and allay the golden hours of gayety with the hateful dross of grief and suspicion.

To those whose weakness of spirits, or timidity of temper, subjects them to impressions from others, and who are to suffer by fascination, and catch the contagion of misery, it is extremely unhappy to live within the compass of a screech-owl's voice; for it will often fill their ears in the hour of dejection, terrify them with apprehensions, which their own thoughts would never have produced, and sadden, by intruded sorrows, the day which might have been passed in amusements or in business; it will burden the heart with unnecessary discontents, and weaken for a time that love of life which is necessary to the vigorous prosecution of any undertaking.

Though I have, like the rest of mankind, many failings and weaknesses, I have not yet, by either friends or enemies, been charged with superstition; I never count the company which I enter, and I look at the new moon indifferently over either shoulder. I have, like most other philosophers, often heard the cuckoo without money in my pocket, and have been sometimes reproached as foolhardy for not turning down my eyes when a raven flew over my head. I never go home abruptly because a snake crosses my way, nor have any particular dread of a climacterical year;[3] yet I confess that, with all my scorn of old women, and their tales, I consider it as an unhappy day when I happen to be greeted, in the morning, by Suspirius the screech-owl.

I have now known Suspirius fifty-eight years and four months, and have never yet passed an hour with him in which he has not made some attack upon my quiet. When we were first acquainted, his great topic was the misery of youth without riches; and whenever we walked out together, he solaced me with a long enumeration of pleasures, which, as they were beyond the reach of my fortune, were without the verge of my desires, and which I should never have considered as the objects of

[1]Skill. [2]*Tristia*, V, i, 59–64.

[3]"Certain observable years are supposed to be attended with some considerable change in the body; as the 7th year; the 21st, made up of three times seven; the 49th, made up of seven times seven; the 63rd, being nine times seven; and the 81st, which is nine times nine; which two last are called the grand climacterics." (Johnson's *Dictionary*.)

a wish, had not his unseasonable representations placed them in my sight.

Another of his topics is the neglect of merit, with which he never fails to amuse[1] every man whom he sees not eminently fortunate. If he meets with a young officer, he always informs him of gentlemen whose personal courage is unquestioned, and whose military skill qualifies them to command armies, that have, notwithstanding all their merit, grown old with subaltern commissions. For a genius in the church, he is always provided with a curacy for life. The lawyer he informs of many men of great parts and deep study, who have never had an opportunity to speak in the courts: And meeting Serenus the physician, "Ah, doctor," says he, "what, a-foot still, when so many blockheads are rattling in their chariots? I told you seven years ago that you would never meet with encouragement, and I hope you will now take more notice, when I tell you that your Greek, and your diligence, and your honesty, will never enable you to live like yonder apothecary, who prescribes to his own shop, and laughs at the physician."

Suspirius has, in his time, intercepted fifteen authors in their way to the stage; persuaded nine and thirty merchants to retire from a prosperous trade for fear of bankruptcy, broke off an hundred and thirteen matches by prognostications of unhappiness, and enabled the smallpox to kill nineteen ladies, by perpetual alarm of the loss of beauty.

Whenever my evil stars bring us together, he never fails to represent to me the folly of my pursuits, and informs me that we are much older than when we began our acquaintance, that the infirmities of decrepitude are coming fast upon me, that whatever I now get, I shall enjoy but a little time, that fame is to a man tottering on the edge of the grave of very little importance, and that the time is at hand when I ought to look for no other pleasures than a good dinner and an easy chair.

Thus he goes on in his unharmonious strain, displaying present miseries, and foreboding more, *νυκτικόραξ ᾄδει θανατηφόρον*,[2] every syllable is loaded with misfortune, and death is always brought nearer to the view. Yet, what always raises my resentment and indignation, I do not perceive that his mournful meditations have much effect upon himself. He talks and has long talked of calamities, without discovering otherwise than by the tone of his voice, that he feels any of the evils which he bewails or threatens, but has the same habit of uttering lamentations, as others of telling stories, and falls into expressions of condolence for past, or apprehension of future mischiefs, as all men studious of their ease have recourse to those subjects upon which they can most fluently or copiously discourse.

It is reported of the Sybarites, that they destroyed all their cocks, that they might dream out their morning dreams without disturbance. Though I would not so far promote effeminacy as to propose the Sybarites for an example, yet since there is no man so corrupt or foolish, but something useful may be learned from him, I could wish that, in imitation of a people not often to be copied, some regulations might be made to exclude screech-owls from all company, as the enemies of mankind, and confine them to some proper receptacle, where they may mingle sighs at leisure, and thicken the gloom of one another.

"Thou prophet of evil," says Homer's Agamemnon, "thou never foretellest me good, but the joy of thy heart is to predict misfortunes."[3] Whoever is of the same temper, might there find the means of indulging his thoughts, and improving his vein of denunciation, and the flock of screech-owls might hoot together without injury to the rest of the world.

Yet, though I have so little kindness for this dark generation, I am very far from intending to debar the soft and tender mind from the privilege of complaining, when the sigh arises from the desire not of giving pain, but of gaining ease. To hear complaints with patience, even when complaints are vain, is one of the duties of friendship; and though it must be allowed that he suffers most like a hero that hides his grief in silence,

Spem vultu simulat, premit altum corde dolorem,[4]

His outward smiles concealed his inward smart.
—DRYDEN.

yet it cannot be denied, that he who complains acts like a man, like a social being, who looks

[1]To engage the attention of.

[2]The night-raven's song bodes death. (*Greek Anthology*, XI, Satirical Epigrams, 186. In one of his sleepless nights Johnson turned this epigram into Latin verse.)

[3]*Iliad*, I, 106.

[4]*Æneid*, I, 209.

for help from his fellow-creatures. Pity is to many of the unhappy a source of comfort in hopeless distresses, as it contributes to recommend them to themselves, by proving that they have not lost the regard of others; and heaven seems to indicate the duty even of barren compassion, by inclining us to weep for evils which we cannot remedy.

No. 137. Tuesday, 9 July, 1751.

Dum vitant stulti vitia, in contraria currunt.
—Horace.[1]

——— Whilst fools one vice condemn,
They run into the opposite extreme.
—Creech.

That wonder is the effect of ignorance, has been often observed. The awful stillness of attention, with which the mind is overspread at the first view of an unexpected effect, ceases when we have leisure to disentangle complications and investigate causes. Wonder is a pause of reason, a sudden cessation of the mental progress, which lasts only while the understanding is fixed upon some single idea, and is at an end when it recovers force enough to divide the object into its parts, or mark the intermediate gradations from the first agent to the last consequence.

It may be remarked with equal truth, that ignorance is often the effect of wonder. It is common for those who have never accustomed themselves to the labor of inquiry, nor invigorated their confidence by conquests over difficulty, to sleep in the gloomy quiescence of astonishment, without any effort to animate inquiry or dispel obscurity. What they cannot immediately conceive, they consider as too high to be reached, or too extensive to be comprehended; they therefore content themselves with the gaze of folly, forbear to attempt what they have no hopes of performing, and resign the pleasure of rational contemplation to more pertinacious study or more active faculties.

Among the productions of mechanic art, many are of a form so different from that of their first materials, and many consist of parts so numerous and so nicely adapted to each other, that it is not possible to view them without amazement. But when we enter the shops of artificers, observe the various tools by which every operation is facilitated, and trace the progress of a manufacture through the different hands, that, in succession to each other, contribute to its perfection, we soon discover that every single man has an easy task, and that the extremes, however remote, of natural rudeness and artificial elegance, are joined by a regular concatenation of effects, of which every one is introduced by that which precedes it, and equally introduces that which is to follow.

The same is the state of intellectual and manual performances. Long calculations or complex diagrams affright the timorous and unexperienced from a second view; but if we have skill sufficient to analyze them into simple principles, it will be discovered that our fear was groundless. *Divide and Conquer*, is a principle equally just in science as in policy. Complication is a species of confederacy which, while it continues united, bids defiance to the most active and vigorous intellect; but of which every member is separately weak, and which may therefore be quickly subdued, if it can once be broken.

The chief art of learning, as Locke has observed, is to attempt but little at a time.[2] The widest excursions of the mind are made by short flights frequently repeated; the most lofty fabrics of science are formed by the continued accumulation of single propositions.

It often happens, whatever be the cause, that impatience of labor, or dread of miscarriage, seizes those who are most distinguished for quickness of apprehension; and that they who might with greatest reason promise themselves victory, are least willing to hazard the encounter. This diffidence, where the attention is not laid asleep by laziness, or dissipated by pleasures, can arise only from confused and general views, such as negligence snatches in haste, or from the disappointment of the first hopes formed by arrogance without reflection. To expect that the intricacies of science will be pierced by a careless glance, or the eminences of fame ascended without labor, is to expect a particular privilege, a power denied to the rest of mankind; but to suppose that the maze is inscrutable to diligence, or the heights inaccessible to perseverance, is to sub-

---

[1] *Satires*, I, ii, 24.

[2] See *Some Thoughts concerning Education*, Sect. 160, Writing.

mit tamely to the tyranny of fancy, and enchain the mind in voluntary shackles.

It is the proper ambition of the heroes in literature to enlarge the boundaries of knowledge by discovering and conquering new regions of the intellectual world. To the success of such undertakings perhaps some degree of fortuitous happiness is necessary, which no man can promise or procure to himself; and therefore doubt and irresolution may be forgiven in him that ventures into the unexplored abysses of truth, and attempts to find his way through the fluctuations of uncertainty, and the conflicts of contradiction. But when nothing more is required than to pursue a path already beaten, and to trample obstacles which others have demolished, why should any man so much distrust his own intellect as to imagine himself unequal to the attempt?

It were to be wished that they who devote their lives to study would at once believe nothing too great for their attainment, and consider nothing as too little for their regard; that they would extend their notice alike to science and to life; and unite some knowledge of the present world to their acquaintance with past ages and remote events.

Nothing has so much exposed men of learning to contempt and ridicule, as their ignorance of things which are known to all but themselves. Those who have been taught to consider the institutions of the schools[1] as giving the last perfection to human abilities, are surprised to see men wrinkled with study, yet wanting to be instructed in the minute circumstances of propriety, or the necessary forms of daily transaction; and quickly shake off their reverence for modes of education which they find to produce no ability above the rest of mankind.

"Books," says Bacon, "can never teach the use of books."[2] The student must learn by commerce with mankind to reduce his speculations to practice, and accommodate his knowledge to the purposes of life.

It is too common for those who have been bred to scholastic professions, and passed much of their time in academies where nothing but learning confers honors, to disregard every other qualification, and to imagine that they shall find mankind ready to pay homage to their knowledge, and to crowd about them for instruction. They therefore step out from their cells into the open world with all the confidence of authority and dignity of importance; they look round about them at once with ignorance and scorn on a race of beings to whom they are equally unknown and equally contemptible, but whose manners they must imitate, and with whose opinions they must comply, if they desire to pass their time happily among them.

To lessen that disdain with which scholars are inclined to look on the common business of the world, and the unwillingness with which they condescend to learn what is not to be found in any system of philosophy, it may be necessary to consider that though admiration is excited by abstruse researches and remote discoveries, yet pleasure is not given, nor affection conciliated, but by softer accomplishments, and qualities more easily communicable to those about us. He that can only converse upon questions about which only a small part of mankind has knowledge sufficient to make them curious, must lose his days in unsocial silence, and live in the crowd of life without a companion. He that can be only useful on great occasions may die without exerting his abilities, and stand a helpless spectator of a thousand vexations which fret away happiness, and which nothing is required to remove but a little dexterity of conduct and readiness of expedients.

No degree of knowledge attainable by man is able to set him above the want of hourly assistance, or to extinguish the desire of fond endearments, and tender officiousness;[3] and therefore, no one should think it unnecessary to learn those arts by which friendship may be gained. Kindness is preserved by a constant reciprocation of benefits or interchange of pleasures; but such benefits only can be bestowed, as others are capable to receive, and such pleasures only imparted, as others are qualified to enjoy.

By this descent from the pinnacles of art no honor will be lost; for the condescensions of learning are always overpaid by gratitude. An elevated genius employed in little things, appears, to use the simile of Longinus, like the sun in his evening declination, he remits his splendor but retains his magnitude, and pleases more though he dazzles less.

[1]*I. e.*, of the university.

[2]See *Essays*, *Of Studies* ("They teach not their own use").

[3]Readiness in doing good offices.

No. 191. Tuesday, 14 January, 1752.

Cereus in vitium flecti, monitoribus asper.
—Horace.[1]

The youth——
Yielding like wax, th' impressive folly bears;
Rough to reproof, and slow to future cares.
—Francis.

TO THE RAMBLER

Dear Mr. Rambler:

I have been four days confined to my chamber by a cold, which has already kept me from three plays, nine sales, five shows, and six card-tables, and put me seventeen visits behindhand; and the doctor tells my mamma, that if I fret and cry, it will settle in my head, and I shall not be fit to be seen these six weeks. But, dear Mr. Rambler, how can I help it? At this very time Melissa is dancing with the prettiest gentleman; she will breakfast with him to-morrow, and then run to two auctions, and hear compliments, and have presents; then she will be dressed, and visit, and get a ticket to the play; then go to cards and win, and come home with two flambeaux before her chair. Dear Mr. Rambler, who can bear it?

My aunt has just brought me a bundle of your papers for my amusement. She says, you are a philosopher, and will teach me to moderate my desires, and look upon the world with indifference. But, dear sir, I do not wish, nor intend, to moderate my desires, nor can I think it proper to look upon the world with indifference, till the world looks with indifference on me. I have been forced, however, to sit this morning a whole quarter of an hour with your paper before my face; but just as my aunt came in, Phyllida had brought me a letter from Mr. Trip, which I put within the leaves; and read about "absence" and "inconsolableness," and "ardor," and "irresistible passion," and "eternal constancy," while my aunt imagined that I was puzzling myself with your philosophy, and often cried out, when she saw me look confused, "If there is any word that you do not understand, child, I will explain it."

Dear soul! How old people that think themselves wise may be imposed upon! But it is fit that they should take their turn, for I am sure, while they can keep poor girls close in the nursery, they tyrannize over us in a very shameful manner, and fill our imaginations with tales of terror, only to make us live in quiet subjection, and fancy that we can never be safe but by their protection.

I have a mamma and two aunts, who have all been formerly celebrated for wit and beauty, and are still generally admired by those that value themselves upon their understanding, and love to talk of vice and virtue, nature and simplicity, and beauty and propriety; but if there was not some hope of meeting me, scarcely a creature would come near them that wears a fashionable coat. These ladies, Mr. Rambler, have had me under their government fifteen years and a half, and have all that time been endeavoring to deceive me by such representations of life as I now find not to be true; but I know not whether I ought to impute them to ignorance or malice, as it is possible the world may be much changed since they mingled in general conversation.

Being desirous that I should love books, they told me that nothing but knowledge could make me an agreeable companion to men of sense, or qualify me to distinguish the superficial glitter of vanity from the solid merit of understanding; and that a habit of reading would enable me to fill up the vacuities of life without the help of silly or dangerous amusements, and preserve me from the snares of idleness and the inroads of temptation.

But their principal intention was to make me afraid of men; in which they succeeded so well for a time, that I durst not look in their faces, or be left alone with them in a parlor; for they made me fancy that no man ever spoke but to deceive, or looked but to allure; that the girl who suffered him that had once squeezed her hand, to approach her a second time, was on the brink of ruin; and that she who answered a billet, without consulting her relations, gave love such power over her that she would certainly become either poor or infamous.

From the time that my leading-strings were taken off, I scarce heard any mention of my beauty but from the milliner, the mantua-maker, and my own maid; for my mamma never said more, when she heard me commended, but "The girl is very well," and then endeavored to divert my attention by some inquiry after my needle, or my book.

It is now three months since I have been

[1]*De Arte Poetica*, 163.

suffered to pay and receive visits, to dance at public assemblies, to have a place kept for me in the boxes, and to play at Lady Racket's rout; and you may easily imagine what I think of those who have so long cheated me with false expectations, disturbed me with fictitious terrors, and concealed from me all that I have found to make the happiness of woman.

I am so far from perceiving the usefulness or necessity of books, that if I had not dropped all pretensions to learning, I should have lost Mr. Trip, whom I once frighted into another box, by retailing some of Dryden's remarks upon a tragedy; for Mr. Trip declares that he hates nothing like hard words, and, I am sure, there is not a better partner to be found; his very walk is a dance. I have talked once or twice among ladies about principles and ideas, but they put their fans before their faces, and told me I was too wise for them, who for their part never pretended to read anything but the play-bill, and then asked me the price of my best head.[1]

Those vacancies of time which are to be filled up with books I have never yet obtained; for, consider, Mr. Rambler, I go to bed late, and therefore cannot rise early; as soon as I am up, I dress for the gardens; then walk in the park; then always go to some sale or show, or entertainment at the little theater; then must be dressed for dinner; then must pay my visits; then walk in the park; then hurry to the play; and from thence to the card-table. This is the general course of the day, when there happens nothing extraordinary; but sometimes I ramble into the country, and come back again to a ball; sometimes I am engaged for a whole day and part of the night. If, at any time, I can gain an hour by not being at home, I have so many things to do, so many orders to give to the milliner, so many alterations to make in my clothes, so many visitants' names to read over, so many invitations to accept or refuse, so many cards to write, and so many fashions to consider, that I am lost in confusion, forced at last to let in company or step into my chair, and leave half my affairs to the direction of my maid.

This is the round of my day; and when shall I either stop my course, or so change it as to want a book? I suppose it cannot be imagined, that any of these diversions will soon be at an end. There will always be gardens, and a park, and auctions, and shows, and play-houses, and cards; visits will always be paid, and clothes always be worn; and how can I have time unemployed upon my hands?

But I am most at a loss to guess for what purpose they related such tragic stories of the cruelty, perfidy, and artifices of men, who, if they ever were so malicious and destructive, have certainly now reformed their manners. I have not, since my entrance into the world, found one who does not profess himself devoted to my service, and ready to live or die as I shall command him. They are so far from intending to hurt me, that their only contention is, who shall be allowed most closely to attend, and most frequently to treat me. When different places of entertainment or schemes of pleasure are mentioned, I can see the eye sparkle and the cheeks glow of him whose proposals obtain my approbation; he then leads me off in triumph, adores my condescension, and congratulates himself that he has lived to the hour of felicity. Are these, Mr. Rambler, creatures to be feared? Is it likely that any injury will be done me by those who can enjoy life only while I favor them with my presence?

As little reason can I yet find to suspect them of stratagems and fraud. When I play at cards, they never take advantage of my mistakes, nor exact from me a rigorous observation of the game. Even Mr. Shuffle, a grave gentleman, who has daughters older than myself, plays with me so negligently that I am sometimes inclined to believe he loses his money by design, and yet he is so fond of play, that he says he will one day take me to his house in the country, that we may try by ourselves who can conquer. I have not yet promised him; but when the town grows a little empty, I shall think upon it, for I want some trinkets, like Letitia's, to my watch. I do not doubt my luck, but must study some means of amusing[2] my relations.

For all these distinctions I find myself indebted to that beauty which I was never suffered to hear praised, and of which, therefore, I did not before know the full value. The concealment was certainly an intentional fraud, for my aunts have eyes like other people, and I am every day told that nothing

[1] *I. e.*, head-dress.

[2] Of distracting the attention of.

but blindness can escape the influence of my charms. Their whole account of that world which they pretend to know so well has been only one fiction entangled with another; and though the modes of life oblige me to continue some appearances of respect, I cannot think that they, who have been so clearly detected in ignorance or imposture, have any right to the esteem, veneration, or obedience of,

Sir, Yours,

Bellaria.

THE IDLER

No. 16. Saturday, 29 July, 1758.

I paid a visit yesterday to my old friend Ned Drugget, at his country lodgings. Ned began trade with a very small fortune; he took a small house in an obscure street, and for some years dealt only in remnants. Knowing that *light gains make a heavy purse*, he was content with moderate profit; having observed or heard the effects of civility, he bowed down to the counter-edge at the entrance and departure of every customer, listened without impatience to the objections of the ignorant, and refused without resentment the offers of the penurious. His only recreation was to stand at his own door and look into the street. His dinner was sent him from a neighboring alehouse, and he opened and shut the shop at a certain hour with his own hands.

His reputation soon extended from one end of the street to the other; and Mr. Drugget's exemplary conduct was recommended by every master to his apprentice, and by every father to his son. Ned was not only considered as a thriving trader, but as a man of elegance and politeness, for he was remarkably neat in his dress, and would wear his coat threadbare without spotting it; his hat was always brushed, his shoes glossy, his wig nicely curled, and his stockings without a wrinkle. With such qualifications it was not very difficult for him to gain the heart of Miss Comfit, the only daughter of Mr. Comfit the confectioner.

Ned is one of those whose happiness marriage has increased. His wife had the same disposition with himself; and his method of life was very little changed, except that he dismissed the lodgers from the first floor,[1] and took the whole house into his own hands.

He had already, by his parsimony, accumulated a considerable sum, to which the fortune of his wife was now added. From this time he began to grasp at greater acquisitions, and was always ready, with money in his hand, to pick up the refuse of a sale, or to buy the stock of a trader who retired from business. He soon added his parlor to his shop, and was obliged a few months afterwards to hire a warehouse.

He had now a shop splendidly and copiously furnished with everything that time had injured, or fashion had degraded, with fragments of tissues, odd yards of brocade, vast bales of faded silk, and innumerable boxes of antiquated ribbons. His shop was soon celebrated through all quarters of the town, and frequented by every form of ostentatious poverty. Every maid, whose misfortune it was to be taller than her lady, matched[2] her gown at Mr. Drugget's; and many a maiden, who had passed a winter with her aunt in London, dazzled the rustics, at her return, with cheap finery which Drugget had supplied. His shop was often visited in a morning by ladies who left their coaches in the next street, and crept through the alley in linen gowns. Drugget knows the rank of his customers by their bashfulness; and, when he finds them unwilling to be seen, invites them upstairs, or retires with them to the back window.

I rejoiced at the increasing prosperity of my friend, and imagined, that as he grew rich, he was growing happy. His mind has partaken the enlargement of his fortune. When I stepped in for the first five years, I was welcomed only with a shake of the hand; in the next period of his life, he beckoned across the way for a pot of beer; but for six years past, he invites me to dinner; and if he bespeaks me the day before, never fails to regale me with a fillet of veal.

His riches neither made him uncivil nor negligent; he rose at the same hour, attended with the same assiduity, and bowed with the same gentleness. But for some years he has been much inclined to talk of the fatigues of business, and the confinement of a shop, and to wish that he had been so happy as to have renewed his uncle's lease of a farm, that he might have lived without noise and hurry, in

[1] *I. e.*, the first floor above the ground-floor.

[2] *I. e.*, shopped for; found one there which (in this instance) accorded with her height

a pure air, in the artless society of honest villagers, and the contemplation of the works of nature.

I soon discovered the cause of my friend's philosophy. He thought himself grown rich enough to have a lodging in the country, like the mercers on Ludgate Hill, and was resolved to enjoy himself in the decline of life. This was a revolution not to be made suddenly. He talked three years of the pleasures of the country, but passed every night over his own shop. But at last he resolved to be happy, and hired a lodging in the country, that he may steal some hours in the week from business; for, says he, *when a man advances in life, he loves to entertain himself sometimes with his own thoughts.*

I was invited to this seat of quiet and contemplation among those whom Mr. Drugget considers as his most reputable friends, and desires to make the first witnesses of his elevation to the highest dignities of a shopkeeper. I found him at Islington, in a room which overlooked the high road, amusing himself with looking through the window, which the clouds of dust would not suffer him to open. He embraced me, told me I was welcome into the country, and asked me, if I did not feel myself refreshed. He then desired that dinner might be hastened, for fresh air always sharpened his appetite, and ordered me a toast and a glass of wine after my walk. He told me much of the pleasure he found in retirement, and wondered what had kept him so long out of the country. After dinner, company came in, and Mr. Drugget again repeated the praises of the country, recommended the pleasures of meditation, and told them, that he had been all the morning at the window, counting the carriages as they passed before him.

No. 19. Saturday, 19 August, 1758.

Some of those ancient sages that have exercised their abilities in the inquiry after the *supreme good*, have been of opinion, that the highest degree of earthly happiness is quiet; a calm repose both of mind and body undisturbed by the sight of folly or the noise of business, the tumults of public commotion, or the agitations of private interest; a state in which the mind has no other employment but to observe and regulate her own motions, to trace thought from thought, combine one image with another, raise systems of science and form theories of virtue.

To the scheme of these solitary speculatists, it has been justly objected, that if they are happy, they are happy only by being useless. That mankind is one vast republic, where every individual receives many benefits from the labors of others, which, by laboring in his turn for others, he is obliged to repay; and that where the united efforts of all are not able to exempt all from misery, none have a right to withdraw from their task of vigilance, or to be indulged in idle wisdom, or solitary pleasures.

It is common for controvertists, in the heat of disputation, to add one position to another till they reach the extremities of knowledge, where truth and falsehood lose their distinction. Their admirers follow them to the brink of absurdity, and then start back from each side towards the middle point. So it has happened in this great disquisition. Many perceive alike the force of the contrary arguments, find quiet shameful, and business dangerous, and therefore pass their lives between them, in bustle without business, and negligence without quiet.

Among the principal names of this moderate set is that great philosopher Jack Whirler,[1] whose business keeps him in perpetual motion, and whose motion always eludes his business; who is always to do what he never does, who cannot stand still because he is wanted in another place, and who is wanted in many places because he stays in none.

Jack has more business than he can conveniently transact in one house; he has therefore one habitation near Bow Church, and another about a mile distant. By this ingenious distribution of himself between two houses, Jack has contrived to be found at neither. Jack's trade is extensive, and he has many dealers; his conversation is sprightly, and he has many companions; his disposition is kind, and he has many friends. Jack neither forbears pleasure for business, nor omits business for pleasure, but is equally invisible to his friends and his customers; to him that comes with an invitation to a club, and to him that waits to settle an account.

[1] It is said that John Newbery, a bookseller (and one of the publishers of the collected edition of *The Idler*), was the original of Whirler.

When you call at his house, his clerk tells you, that Mr. Whirler was just stepped out, but will be at home exactly at two; you wait at a coffee-house till two, and then find that he has been at home, and is gone out again, but left word that he should be at the Half Moon Tavern at seven, where he hopes to meet you. At seven you go to the tavern. At eight in comes Mr. Whirler to tell you that he is glad to see you, and only begs leave to run for a few minutes to a gentleman that lives near the Exchange, from whom he will return before supper can be ready. Away he runs to the Exchange, to tell those who are waiting for him, that he must beg them to defer the business till to-morrow, because his time is come at the Half Moon.

Jack's cheerfulness and civility rank him among those whose presence never gives pain, and whom all receive with fondness and caresses. He calls often on his friends, to tell them, that he will come again to-morrow; on the morrow he comes again, to tell them how an unexpected summons hurries him away. When he enters a house, his first declaration is, that he cannot sit down; and so short are his visits, that he seldom appears to have come for any other reason but to say, He must go.

The dogs of Egypt, when thirst brings them to the Nile, are said to run as they drink for fear of the crocodiles. Jack Whirler always dines at full speed. He enters, finds the family at table, sits familiarly down, and fills his plate; but while the first morsel is in his mouth, hears the clock strike, and rises; then goes to another house, sits down again, recollects another engagement; has only time to taste the soup, makes a short excuse to the company, and continues through another street his desultory dinner.

But, overwhelmed as he is with business, his chief desire is to have still more. Every new proposal takes possession of his thoughts; he soon balances probabilities, engages in the project, brings it almost to completion, and then forsakes it for another, which he catches with some alacrity, urges with the same vehemence, and abandons with the same coldness.

Every man may be observed to have a certain strain of lamentation, some peculiar theme of complaint on which he dwells in his moments of dejection. Jack's topic of sorrow is the want of time. Many an excellent design languishes in empty theory for want of time. For the omission of any civilities, want of time is his plea to others; for the neglect of any affairs, want of time is his excuse to himself. That he wants time, he sincerely believes; for he once pined away many months with a lingering distemper, for want of time to attend his health.

Thus Jack Whirler lives in perpetual fatigue without proportionate advantage, because he does not consider that no man can see all with his own eyes, or do all with his own hands; that whoever is engaged in multiplicity of business, must transact much by substitution, and leave something to hazard: and that he who attempts to do all, will waste his life in doing little.

No. 48. Saturday, 17 March, 1759.

There is no kind of idleness by which we are so easily seduced, as that which dignifies itself by the appearance of business, and, by making the loiterer imagine that he has something to do which must not be neglected, keeps him in perpetual agitation, and hurries him rapidly from place to place.

He that sits still, or reposes himself upon a couch, no more deceives himself than he deceives others; he knows that he is doing nothing, and has no other solace of his insignificance than the resolution, which the lazy hourly make, of changing his mode of life.

To do nothing every man is ashamed: and to do much almost every man is unwilling or afraid. Innumerable expedients have therefore been invented to produce motion without labor, and employment without solicitude. The greater part of those whom the kindness of fortune has left to their own direction, and whom want does not keep chained to the counter or the plow, play throughout life with the shadows of business, and know not at last what they have been doing.

These imitators of action are of all denominations. Some are seen at every auction without intention to purchase; others appear punctually at the Exchange, though they are known there only by their faces. Some are always making parties to visit collections for which they have no taste; and some neglect every pleasure and every duty to hear questions, in which they have no interest, debated in parliament.

These men never appear more ridiculous than in the distress which they imagine themselves to feel, from some accidental interruption of those empty pursuits. A tiger newly imprisoned is indeed more formidable, but not more angry, than Jack Tulip withheld from a florist's feast, or Tom Distich hindered from seeing the first representation of a play.

As political affairs are the highest and most extensive of temporal concerns, the mimic of a politician is more busy and important than any other trifler. Monsieur le Noir, a man who, without property or importance in any corner of the earth, has, in the present confusion of the world, declared himself a steady adherent to the French, is made miserable by a wind that keeps back the packet-boat, and still more miserable by every account of a Malouin privateer[1] caught in his cruise; he knows well that nothing can be done or said by him which can produce any effect but that of laughter, that he can neither hasten nor retard good or evil, that his joys and sorrows have scarcely any partakers; yet such is his zeal, and such his curiosity, that he would run barefooted to Gravesend, for the sake of knowing first that the English had lost a tender, and would ride out to meet every mail from the continent if he might be permitted to open it.

Learning is generally confessed to be desirable, and there are some who fancy themselves always busy in acquiring it. Of these ambulatory students, one of the most busy is my friend Tom Restless.[2]

Tom has long had a mind to be a man of knowledge, but he does not care to spend much time among authors; for he is of opinion that few books deserve the labor of perusal, that they give the mind an unfashionable cast, and destroy that freedom of thought and easiness of manners indispensably requisite to acceptance in the world. Tom has therefore found another way to wisdom. When he rises he goes into a coffee-house, where he creeps so near to men whom he takes to be reasoners as to hear their discourse, and endeavors to remember something which, when it has been strained through Tom's head, is so near to nothing, that what it once was cannot be discovered. This he carries round from friend to friend through a circle of visits, till, hearing what each says upon the question, he becomes able at dinner to say a little himself; and, as every great genius relaxes himself among his inferiors, meets with some who wonder how so young a man can talk so wisely.

At night he has a new feast prepared for his intellects; he always runs to a disputing society, or a speaking club, where he half hears what, if he had heard the whole, he would but half understand; goes home pleased with the consciousness of a day well spent, lies down full of ideas, and rises in the morning empty as before.

No. 60. Saturday, 9 June, 1759.

Criticism is a study by which men grow important and formidable at a very small expense. The power of invention has been conferred by nature upon few, and the labor of learning those sciences which may by mere labor be obtained is too great to be willingly endured; but every man can exert such judgment as he has upon the works of others; and he whom nature has made weak, and idleness keeps ignorant, may yet support his vanity by the name of a Critic.

I hope it will give comfort to great numbers who are passing through the world in obscurity, when I inform them how easily distinction may be obtained. All the other powers of literature are coy and haughty, they must be long courted, and at last are not always gained; but Criticism is a goddess easy of access and forward of advance, who will meet the slow, and encourage the timorous; the want of meaning she supplies with words, and the want of spirit she recompenses with malignity.

This profession has one recommendation peculiar to itself, that it gives vent to malignity without real mischief. No genius was ever blasted by the breath of critics. The poison, which, if confined, would have burst the heart, fumes away in empty hisses, and malice is set at ease with very little danger to merit. The Critic is the only man whose triumph is without another's pain, and whose greatness does not rise upon another's ruin.

[1] A privateer of St. Malo.

[2] Johnson said that Restless was meant for Thomas Tyers, son of the founder of Vauxhall Gardens. He was "bred to the law; but, having a handsome fortune, vivacity of temper, and eccentricity of mind, he could not confine himself to the regularity of practice. He therefore ran about the world with a pleasant carelessness, amusing everybody by his desultory conversation." (Boswell, *Life of Johnson.*)

To a study at once so easy and so reputable, so malicious and so harmless, it cannot be necessary to invite my readers by a long or labored exhortation; it is sufficient, since all would be Critics if they could, to show by one eminent example that all can be critics if they will.

Dick Minim, after the common course of puerile studies, in which he was no great proficient, was put an apprentice to a brewer, with whom he had lived two years, when his uncle died in the city, and left him a large fortune in the stocks. Dick had for six months before used the company of the lower players, of whom he had learned to scorn a trade, and, being now at liberty to follow his genius, he resolved to be a man of wit and humor. That he might be properly initiated in his new character, he frequented the coffee-houses near the theaters, where he listened very diligently, day after day, to those who talked of language and sentiments, and unities and catastrophes, till by slow degrees he began to think that he understood something of the stage, and hoped in time to talk himself.

But he did not trust so much to natural sagacity as wholly to neglect the help of books. When the theaters were shut, he retired to Richmond with a few select writers,[1] whose opinions he impressed upon his memory by unwearied diligence; and, when he returned with other wits to the town, was able to tell, in very proper phrases, that the chief business of art is to copy nature; that a perfect writer is not to be expected, because genius decays as judgment increases; that the great art is the art of blotting; and that, according to the rule of Horace, every piece should be kept nine years.

Of the great authors he now began to display the characters, laying down as an universal position, that all had beauties and defects. His opinion was, that Shakespeare, committing himself wholly to the impulse of nature, wanted that correctness which learning would have given him; and that Jonson, trusting to learning, did not sufficiently cast his eye on nature. He blamed the *stanza* of Spenser, and could not bear the *hexameters* of Sidney. Denham and Waller he held the first reformers of English numbers; and thought that if Waller could have obtained the strength of Denham, or Denham the sweetness of Waller, there had been nothing wanting to complete a poet. He often expressed his commiseration of Dryden's poverty, and his indignation at the age which suffered him to write for bread; he repeated with rapture the first lines of *All for Love*, but wondered at the corruption of taste which could bear anything so unnatural as riming tragedies. In Otway he found uncommon powers of moving the passions, but was disgusted by his general negligence, and blamed him for making a conspirator his hero; and never concluded his disquisition, without remarking how happily the sound of the clock is made to alarm the audience. Southern[2] would have been his favorite, but that he mixes comic with tragic scenes, intercepts the natural course of the passions, and fills the mind with a wild confusion of mirth and melancholy. The versification of Rowe he thought too melodious for the stage, and too little varied in different passions. He made it the great fault of Congreve, that all his persons were wits, and that he always wrote with more art than nature. He considered *Cato* rather as a poem than a play, and allowed Addison to be the complete master of allegory and grave humor, but paid no great deference to him as a critic. He thought the chief merit of Prior was in his easy tales and lighter poems, though he allowed that his *Solomon* had many noble sentiments elegantly expressed. In Swift he discovered an inimitable vein of irony, and an easiness which all would hope and few would attain. Pope he was inclined to degrade from a poet to a versifier, and thought his numbers rather luscious than sweet. He often lamented the neglect of *Phædra and Hippolitus*,[3] and wished to see the stage under better regulations.

These assertions passed commonly uncontradicted; and if now and then an opponent started up, he was quickly repressed by the suffrages of the company, and Minim went away from every dispute with elation of heart and increase of confidence.

He now grew conscious of his abilities, and began to talk of the present state of dramatic poetry; wondered what was become of the comic genius which supplied our ancestors

[1]The opinions which follow come from these writers—from Pope chiefly, but also from Collins's *Epistle to Hanmer*, from Dryden, from Addison, and from Joseph Warton.

[2]Thomas Southerne (1660–1746).

[3]A tragedy by Edmund Smith (1672–1710), which pleased Addison, but not the public.

with wit and pleasantry, and why no writer could be found that durst now venture beyond a farce. He saw no reason for thinking that the vein of humor was exhausted, since we live in a country where liberty suffers every character to spread itself to its utmost bulk, and which therefore produces more originals than all the rest of the world together. Of tragedy he concluded business to be the soul, and yet often hinted that love predominates too much upon the modern stage.

He was now an acknowledged critic, and had his own seat in a coffee-house, and headed a party in the pit. Minim has more vanity than ill-nature, and seldom desires to do much mischief; he will perhaps murmur a little in the ear of him that sits next him, but endeavors to influence the audience to favor, by clapping when an actor exclaims "Ye gods!" or laments the misery of his country.

By degrees he was admitted to rehearsals, and many of his friends are of opinion that our present poets are indebted to him for their happiest thoughts; by his contrivance the bell was rung twice in *Barbarossa*,[1] and by his persuasion the author of *Cleone*[2] concluded his play without a couplet; for what can be more absurd, said Minim, than that part of a play should be rimed, and part written in blank verse? and by what acquisition of faculties is the speaker, who never could find rimes before, enabled to rime at the conclusion of an act?

He is the great investigator of hidden beauties, and is particularly delighted when he finds *the sound an echo to the sense*. He has read all our poets with particular attention to this delicacy of versification, and wonders at the supineness with which their works have been hitherto perused, so that no man has found the sound of a drum in this distich:

> When pulpit, drum ecclesiastic,
> Was beat with fist instead of a stick;[3]

and that the wonderful lines upon honor and a bubble have hitherto passed without notice:

> Honor is like the glassy bubble,
> Which cost philosophers such trouble;
> Where, one part cracked, the whole does fly,
> And wits are cracked to find out why.[4]

In these verses, says Minim, we have two striking accommodations of the sound to the sense. It is impossible to utter the two lines emphatically without an act like that which they describe; *bubble* and *trouble* causing a momentary inflation of the cheeks by the retention of the breath, which is afterwards forcibly emitted, as in the practice of *blowing bubbles*. But the greatest excellence is in the third line, which is *cracked* in the middle to express a crack, and then shivers into monosyllables. Yet has this diamond laid neglected with common stones, and among the innumerable admirers of *Hudibras* the observation of this superlative passage has been reserved for the sagacity of Minim.

No. 61. Saturday, 15 June, 1759.

Mr. Minim had now advanced himself to the zenith of critical reputation; when he was in the pit, every eye in the boxes was fixed upon him; when he entered his coffee-house, he was surrounded by circles of candidates, who passed their novitiate of literature under his tuition; his opinion was asked by all who had no opinion of their own, and yet loved to debate and decide; and no composition was supposed to pass in safety to posterity, till it had been secured by Minim's approbation.

Minim professes great admiration of the wisdom and munificence by which the academies of the continent were raised; and often wishes for some standard of taste, for some tribunal, to which merit may appeal from caprice, prejudice, and malignity. He has formed a plan for an academy of criticism, where every work of imagination may be read before it is printed, and which shall authoritatively direct the theaters what pieces to receive or reject, to exclude or to revive.

Such an institution would, in Dick's opinion, spread the fame of English literature over Europe, and make London the metropolis of elegance and politeness, the place to which the learned and ingenious of all countries would repair for instruction and improvement, where nothing would any longer be applauded or

[1]A tragedy by Dr. John Brown (1715–1766).

[2]A tragedy by Robert Dodsley (1703–1764). "Mr. Langton, when a very young man," read this play to Johnson. At the end of an act, Johnson said: "Come, let's have some more, let's go into the slaughter-house again, Lanky. But I am afraid there is more blood than brains." (Boswell, *Life of Johnson*.)

[3]Samuel Butler's *Hudibras*, I, i, 11–12.

[4]*Ibid.*, II, ii, 385–388. The "bubble" (Prince Rupert's drop) of which Butler speaks is made of glass, and the "philosophers" whom it puzzled were the members of the Royal Society.

endured that was not conformed to the nicest rules, and finished with the highest elegance.

Till some happy conjunction of the planets shall dispose our princes or ministers to make themselves immortal by such an academy, Minim contents himself to preside four nights in a week in a critical society selected by himself, where he is heard without contradiction, and whence his judgment is disseminated through the great vulgar and the small.[1]

When he is placed in the chair of criticism, he declares loudly for the noble simplicity of our ancestors, in opposition to the petty refinements, and ornamental luxuriance. Sometimes he is sunk in despair, and perceives false delicacy daily gaining ground, and sometimes brightens his countenance with a gleam of hope, and predicts the revival of the true sublime. He then fulminates his loudest censures against the monkish barbarity of rime; wonders how beings that pretend to reason can be pleased with one line always ending like another; tells how unjustly and unnaturally sense is sacrificed to sound; how often the best thoughts are mangled by the necessity of confining or extending them to the dimensions of a couplet; and rejoices that genius has, in our days, shaken off the shackles which had encumbered it so long. Yet he allows that rime may sometimes be borne, if the lines be often broken, and the pauses judiciously diversified.

From blank verse he makes an easy transition to Milton, whom he produces as an example of the slow advance of lasting reputation. Milton is the only writer in whose books Minim can read for ever without weariness. What cause it is that exempts this pleasure from satiety he has long and diligently inquired, and believes it to consist in the perpetual variation of the numbers, by which the ear is gratified and the attention awakened. The lines that are commonly thought rugged and unmusical, he conceives to have been written to temper the melodious luxury of the rest, or to express things by a proper cadence: for he scarcely finds a verse that has not this favorite beauty; he declares that he could shiver in a hot-house when he reads that

> The ground
> Burns frore, and cold performs th' effect of fire;[2]

and that, when Milton bewails his blindness, the verse,

> So thick a drop serene has quenched these orbs,[3]

has, he knows not how, something that strikes him with an obscure sensation like that which he fancies would be felt from the sound of darkness.

Minim is not so confident of his rules of judgment as not very eagerly to catch new light from the name of the author. He is commonly so prudent as to spare those whom he cannot resist, unless, as will sometimes happen, he finds the public combined against them. But a fresh pretender to fame he is strongly inclined to censure, till his own honor requires that he commend him. Till he knows the success of a composition, he intrenches himself in general terms; there are some new thoughts and beautiful passages, but there is likewise much which he would have advised the author to expunge. He has several favorite epithets, of which he has never settled the meaning, but which are very commodiously applied to books which he has not read, or cannot understand. One is *manly*, another is *dry*, another *stiff*, and another *flimsy;* sometimes he discovers delicacy of style, and sometimes meets with *strange expressions.*

He is never so great, or so happy, as when a youth of promising parts is brought to receive his directions for the prosecution of his studies. He then puts on a very serious air; he advises the pupil to read none but the best authors, and, when he finds one congenial to his own mind, to study his beauties, but avoid his faults; and, when he sits down to write, to consider how his favorite author would think at the present time on the present occasion. He exhorts him to catch those moments when he finds his thoughts expanded and his genius exalted, but to take care lest imagination hurry him beyond the bounds of nature. He holds diligence the mother of success; yet enjoins him, with great earnestness, not to read more than he can digest, and not to confuse his mind by pursuing studies of contrary tendencies. He tells him, that every man has his genius, and that Cicero could never be a poet. The boy retires illuminated, resolves to follow his genius, and to think how Milton would have thought: and Minim feasts upon his own beneficence till another day brings another pupil.

[1]See Abraham Cowley, *Several Discourses by Way of Essays, in Verse and Prose,* 6. Of Greatness (at end, imitation of Horace, *Odes,* III, i, 2).

[2]*Paradise Lost,* II, 594–595.

[3]*Ibid.,* III, 25.

ON THE DEATH OF MR. ROBERT LEVET, A PRACTICER IN PHYSIC[1]

Condemned to Hope's delusive mine,
As on we toil from day to day,
By sudden blasts, or slow decline,
Our social comforts drop away.

Well tried through many a varying year,
See Levet to the grave descend,
Officious,[2] innocent, sincere,
Of every friendless name the friend.

Yet still he fills affection's eye,
Obscurely wise and coarsely kind;
Nor lettered arrogance deny
Thy praise to merit unrefined.

When fainting nature called for aid,
And hovering death prepared the blow,
His vigorous remedy displayed
The power of art without the show.

In misery's darkest cavern known,
His useful care was ever nigh,
Where hopeless anguish poured his groan,
And lonely want retired to die.

No summons mocked by chill delay,
No petty gain disdained by pride;
The modest wants of every day
The toil of every day supplied.

His virtues walked their narrow round,
Nor made a pause, nor left a void;
And sure th' Eternal master found
The single talent well employed.

The busy day—the peaceful night,
Unfelt, uncounted, glided by;
His frame was firm—his powers were bright,
Though now his *eightieth* year was nigh.

Then with no fiery throbbing pain,
No cold gradations of decay,
Death broke at once the vital chain,
And freed his soul the nearest way.

[1]Levett died on 17 January, 1782. Johnson wrote this poem in the same year. It was published in the *Gentleman's Magazine*, August, 1783. Boswell says: He was "an obscure practicer in physic amongst the lower people. . . . It appears from Johnson's diary that their acquaintance commenced about the year 1746." For many years Levett "had an apartment in his house, or his chambers, and waited upon him every morning, through the whole course of his late and tedious breakfast. He was of a strange, grotesque appearance, stiff and formal in his manner, and seldom said a word while any company was present."

[2]Ready in doing good offices.

W. Irving's "Life of Goldsmith".

JAMES BOSWELL (1740–1795)

Boswell's parents were both members of distinguished and ancient Scottish families. His father, Alexander Boswell, was an able lawyer and judge and, moreover, the master of Auchinleck, in Ayrshire—an estate conferred by James IV upon his ancestor, Thomas Boswell, in 1504. James was born at Edinburgh on 29 October, 1740. He was educated privately and at the Edinburgh High School, proceeding thence to Edinburgh University. His father designed him for the law, and to pursue that study he went to Glasgow in November, 1759, "where he also attended the lectures of Dr. Adam Smith on moral philosophy and rhetoric." James's own inclination was not for the law, however, but for the army, and for a characteristic reason. He discovered in soldiers "an animation and relish of existence" unequaled except, perhaps, amongst actors; and he also "had acquired, from reading and conversation, an almost enthusiastic notion of the felicity of London" —a notion which experience did not disappoint. Hence he "was now earnest to have a commission as an officer of the Guards," in order at once to gratify his love of London and of the most animated society. Early in 1760 his father took him to the metropolis, apparently yielding to martial ardor, but continuing to press the claims of the law. After a year, a commission not being obtained, Boswell returned to Edinburgh and legal studies. But he was again in London in the autumn of 1762, still trying to obtain a commission. In the following spring, on 16 May, he was introduced to Dr. Johnson. During the summer he finally agreed to follow the law and in August, 1763, left for Utrecht to continue his studies. In the summer of 1764 he was in Berlin, and thereafter in Switzerland, where he contrived to meet both Rousseau and Voltaire. Thence he journeyed to Italy, where he managed to renew his acquaintance with John Wilkes, then a political exile, and whence he traveled to Corsica, armed with an introduction from Rousseau to General Paoli. He returned to England in February, 1766, and became an advocate at the Scottish bar in the same year. On 25 November, 1769, he married his cousin Margaret Montgomery. He was already the father of two natural children. His wife bore him four sons (two dying in infancy) and three daughters.

In 1772 Boswell was again in London, and saw much of Johnson. From this time, indeed, he was with him as much as possible, spending long periods in London in 1773, 1775, 1776, 1778, 1779, 1781, 1783, and 1784. He was kept in Scotland by lack of money—of which he never had enough to free him from embarrassments—in 1774, 1780, and 1782. In April, 1773, he was elected a member of the Literary Club, despite some opposition. In August of the same year Johnson went to Scotland and journeyed with Boswell to the Hebrides. Boswell also met Johnson at Ashbourne in September, 1777. It has been calculated that, in all, Boswell saw Johnson on 276 days. Meanwhile he had begun in 1775 to keep terms at the Inner Temple, and in 1786 (two years after Johnson's death) he was called to the English bar. In 1788 he was in London, and in the following year took a house there. And in London he died, on 19 May, 1795.

Boswell commenced author very early, publishing in 1760 a pamphlet which "is a rather strained imitation of the style of Sterne," with whom he had been intimate in London during his first visit. Other minor publications followed rapidly, including in 1761 *An Ode to Tragedy* which Boswell gaily dedicated to himself, and in 1763 a series of letters "which is the first considerable example of his life-long willingness to be indiscreet provided thereby he could be interesting." (F. A. Pottle, *Literary Career of Boswell.*) Through many years he contributed steadily and voluminously to periodicals; and one series of his essays, numbering 70—originally published in the *London Magazine*, 1777–1783—has recently been reprinted (*The Hypochondriack*, edited by Margery Bailey, 2 vols., 1928). The mass of his publications is in fact very large, though only three of his books give him any claim to remembrance: *An Account of Corsica* (1768); *The Journal of a Tour to the Hebrides with Samuel Johnson, LL. D.* (1785); and *The Life of Samuel Johnson, LL.D.* (1791). It is for the last, of course, that he *is* remembered; because, as Macaulay has splendidly and truly said: "Homer is not more decidedly the first of heroic poets, Shakespeare is not more decidedly the first of dramatists, Demosthenes is not more decidedly the first of orators, than Boswell is the first of biographers. He has no second. He has distanced all his competitors so decidedly that it is not worth while to place them. Eclipse is first, and the rest nowhere."

Yet Boswell, despite his literary genius, and despite the amiable qualities which endeared him to Johnson and which enabled him all his life to gratify his passion for association with the great, has never attained a place amongst English writers commensurate with his magnificent achievement. A contemporary, echoing a very general feeling, asked: "Who would purchase fame as an author, or in any other way, on such terms as this creature, Boswell?" His close friend and devoted correspondent, William Johnston Temple, considered him the most thinking man he ever knew, but, nevertheless, confided to his Diary (25 May, 1783): "Boswell irregular in his conduct and manners, selfish, indelicate, thoughtless, no sensibility or feeling for others who have not his coarse and rustic strength and spirits. Sorry I came to town to meet him. Detaining me here to no purpose. Seems often absurd and almost mad I think. No composure or rational view of things. Years do not improve him." Macaulay, paying every tribute to his great *book*, thought the *man* "one of the smallest that ever lived," and "of the meanest and feeblest intellect": "servile and impertinent, shallow and pedantic, a bigot and a sot; bloated with family pride, and eternally blustering about the dignity of a born gentleman, yet stooping to be a talebearer, an eavesdropper, a common butt in the taverns of London; so curious to know everybody who was talked about that, Tory and high Churchman as he was, he maneuvered, we have been told, for an introduction to Tom Paine; so vain of the most childish distinctions that, when he had been to court, he drove to the office where his book was printing without changing his clothes, and summoned all the printer's devils to admire his new ruffles and sword; such was this man, and such he was content and proud to be." And Macaulay's accusations cannot be disputed, though his strong language has been of late years universally deplored, as taking into account only one side of a complex nature. The other side has been presented by the accomplished editor of Boswell's *Letters* (2 vols., 1924), Professor C. B. Tinker, in a volume of frank special-pleading (*Young Boswell*, 1922). Probably the case for Boswell has best been stated by Raleigh: "He had simplicity, candor, fervor, a warmly affectionate nature, a quick intelligence, and a passion for telling all that he knew. These are qualities which make for good literature. They enabled Boswell to portray Johnson with an intimacy and truth that has no parallel in any language." (*Six Essays on Johnson.*)

PASSAGES FROM

THE

LIFE OF SAMUEL JOHNSON, LL.D.

(1791)

THE DICTIONARY (1747–1756)

THE year 1747 is distinguished as the epoch when Johnson's arduous and important work, his DICTIONARY OF THE ENGLISH LANGUAGE was announced to the world, by the publication of its Plan or *Prospectus*.

How long this immense undertaking had been the object of his contemplation, I do not know. I once asked him by what means he had attained to that astonishing knowledge of our language, by which he was enabled to realize a design of such extent, and accumulated difficulty. He told me, that "it was not the effect of particular study; but that it had grown up in his mind insensibly." I have been informed by Mr. James Dodsley, that several years before this period, when Johnson was one day sitting in his brother Robert's shop, he heard his brother suggest to him, that a Dictionary of the English Language would be a work that would be well received by the public; that Johnson seemed at first to catch at the proposition, but, after a pause, said, in his abrupt decisive manner, "I believe I shall not undertake it." That he, however, had bestowed much thought upon the subject, before he published his *Plan*, is evident from the enlarged, clear, and accurate views which it exhibits; and we find him mentioning in that tract, that many of the writers whose testimonies were to be produced as authorities, were selected by Pope; which proves that he had been furnished, probably by Mr. Robert Dodsley, with whatever hints that eminent poet had contributed towards a great literary project, that had been the subject of important consideration in a former reign.

The booksellers who contracted with Johnson, single and unaided, for the execution of a work, which in other countries has not been effected but by the co-operating exertions of many, were Mr. Robert Dodsley, Mr. Charles Hitch, Mr. Andrew Millar, the two Messieurs Longman, and the two Messieurs Knapton. The price stipulated was fifteen hundred and seventy-five pounds.

The *Plan* was addressed to Philip Dormer, Earl of Chesterfield, then one of his Majesty's Principal Secretaries of State; a nobleman who was very ambitious of literary distinction, and who, upon being informed of the design, had expressed himself in terms very favorable to its success. There is, perhaps in everything of any consequence, a secret history which it would be amusing to know, could we have it authentically communicated. Johnson told me, "Sir, the way in which the *Plan* of my *Dictionary* came to be inscribed to Lord Chesterfield, was this: I had neglected to write it by the time appointed. Dodsley suggested a desire to have it addressed to Lord Chesterfield. I laid hold of this as a pretext for delay, that it might be better done, and let Dodsley have his desire. I said to my friend, Dr. Bathurst, 'Now if any good comes of my addressing to Lord Chesterfield, it will be ascribed to deep policy, when, in fact, it was only a casual excuse for laziness.'" * * *

Dr. Adams found him one day busy at his *Dictionary*, when the following dialogue ensued. "ADAMS. This is a great work, Sir. How are you to get all the etymologies? JOHNSON. Why, Sir, here is a shelf with Junius, and Skinner, and others; and there is a Welsh gentleman who has published a collection of Welsh proverbs, who will help me with the Welsh. ADAMS. But, Sir, how can you do this in three years? JOHNSON. Sir, I have no doubt that I can do it in three years. ADAMS. But the French Academy, which consists of forty members, took forty years to compile their Dictionary. JOHNSON. Sir, thus it is. This is the proportion. Let me see; forty times forty is sixteen hundred. As three to sixteen hundred, so is the proportion of an Englishman to a Frenchman." With so much ease and pleasantry could he talk of that prodigious labor which he had undertaken to execute. * * *

For the mechanical part he employed, as he told me, six amanuenses; and let it be remembered by the natives of North-Britain, to whom he is supposed to have been so hostile, that five of them were of that country. * * *

1754: ÆTAT. 45.] * * * The *Dictionary*, we may believe, afforded Johnson full occupation this year. As it approached to its conclusion, he probably worked with redoubled vigor, as seamen increase their exertion and alacrity when they have a near prospect of their haven.

Lord Chesterfield, to whom Johnson had paid the high compliment of addressing to his Lordship the *Plan* of his *Dictionary*, had behaved to him in such a manner as to excite his contempt and indignation. The world has been for many years amused with a story confidently told, and as confidently repeated with additional circumstances, that a sudden disgust was taken by Johnson upon occasion of his having been one day kept long in waiting in his Lordship's antechamber, for which the reason assigned was, that he had company with him; and that at last, when the door opened, out walked Colley Cibber; and that Johnson was so violently provoked when he found for whom he had been so long excluded, that he went away in a passion, and never would return. I remember having mentioned this story to George Lord Lyttelton, who told me, he was very intimate with Lord Chesterfield; and holding it as a well-known truth, defended Lord Chesterfield, by saying, that "Cibber, who had been introduced familiarly by the back-stairs, had probably not been there above ten minutes." It may seem strange even to entertain a doubt concerning a story so long and so widely current, and thus implicitly adopted, if not sanctioned, by the authority which I have mentioned; but Johnson himself assured me that there was not the least foundation for it. He told me that there never was any particular incident which produced a quarrel between Lord Chesterfield and him; but that his Lordship's continued neglect was the reason why he resolved to have no connection with him. When the *Dictionary* was upon the eve of publication, Lord Chesterfield, who, it is said, had flattered himself with expectations that Johnson would dedicate the work to him, attempted, in a courtly manner, to soothe, and insinuate himself with the Sage, conscious, as it should seem, of the cold indifference with which he had treated its learned author; and further attempted to conciliate him, by writing two papers in *The World*, in recommendation of the work; and it must be confessed, that they contain some studied compliments, so finely turned, that if there had been no previous offense, it is probable that Johnson would have been highly delighted. Praise, in general, was pleasing to him; but by praise from a man of rank and elegant accomplishments, he was peculiarly gratified. * * *

This courtly device failed of its effect. Johnson, who thought that "all was false and hollow," despised the honeyed words, and was even indignant that Lord Chesterfield should, for a moment, imagine that he could be the dupe of such an artifice. His expression to me concerning Lord Chesterfield, upon this occasion, was, "Sir, after making great professions, he had, for many years, taken no notice of me; but when my *Dictionary* was coming out, he fell a scribbling in *The World* about it. Upon which, I wrote him a letter expressed in civil terms, but such as might show him that I did not mind what he said or wrote, and that I had done with him."

This is that celebrated letter of which so much has been said, and about which curiosity has been so long excited, without being gratified. I for many years solicited Johnson to favor me with a copy of it, that so excellent a composition might not be lost to posterity. He delayed from time to time to give it me; till at last in 1781, when we were on a visit at Mr. Dilly's, at Southill in Bedfordshire, he was pleased to dictate it to me from memory. He afterwards found among his papers a copy of it, which he had dictated to Mr. Baretti, with its title and corrections, in his own handwriting. This he gave to Mr. Langton; adding that if it were to come into print, he wished it to be from that copy. By Mr. Langton's kindness, I am enabled to enrich my work with a perfect transcript of what the world has so eagerly desired to see.

TO THE RIGHT HONORABLE THE EARL OF CHESTERFIELD.

February 7, 1755.

MY LORD, I have been lately informed, by the proprietor of *The World*, that two papers, in which my Dictionary is recommended to the public, were written by your Lordship. To be so distinguished, is an honor, which, being very little accustomed to favors from the great, I know not well how to receive, or in what terms to acknowledge.

When, upon some slight encouragement, I first visited your Lordship, I was overpowered, like the rest of mankind, by the enchantment of your address; and could not forbear to wish that I might boast myself *Le vainqueur du vainqueur de la terre;*[1]—that I might obtain that regard for which I saw the world contending; but I found my attendance so little encouraged, that neither pride nor modesty would suffer me to continue it. When I had once addressed your Lordship in public, I had exhausted all the art of pleasing which a retired and uncourtly scholar can possess. I had done all that I could; and no man is well pleased to have his all neglected, be it ever so little.

[1]The conqueror of the conqueror of the earth. (Boileau, *L'Art Poétique*, III, 272.)

Seven years, my Lord, have now passed, since I waited in your outward rooms, or was repulsed from your door; during which time I have been pushing on my work through difficulties, of which it is useless to complain, and have brought it, at last, to the verge of publication, without one act of assistance, one word of encouragement, or one smile of favor. Such treatment I did not expect, for I never had a Patron before.

The shepherd in Virgil grew at last acquainted with Love, and found him a native of the rocks.[2]

Is not a Patron, my Lord, one who looks with unconcern on a man struggling for life in the water, and, when he has reached ground, encumbers him with help? The notice which you have been pleased to take of my labors, had it been early, had been kind; but it has been delayed till I am indifferent, and cannot enjoy it; till I am solitary,[3] and cannot impart it; till I am known, and do not want it. I hope it is no very cynical asperity not to confess obligations where no benefit has been received, or to be unwilling that the Public should consider me as owing that to a Patron, which Providence has enabled me to do for myself.

Having carried on my work thus far with so little obligation to any favorer of learning, I shall not be disappointed though I should conclude it, if less be possible, with less; for I have been long wakened from that dream of hope, in which I once boasted myself with so much exultation, my Lord, your Lordship's most humble, most obedient servant,

SAM. JOHNSON.

* * *

The *Dictionary*, with a *Grammar and History of the English Language*, being now at length published, in two volumes folio, the world contemplated with wonder so stupendous a work achieved by one man, while other countries had thought such undertakings fit only for whole academies. Vast as his powers were, I cannot but think that his imagination deceived him, when he supposed that by constant application he might have performed the task in three years. * * *

The extensive reading which was absolutely necessary for the accumulation of authorities, and which alone may account for Johnson's retentive mind being enriched with a very large and various store of knowledge and imagery, must have occupied several years. The Preface furnishes an eminent instance of a double talent, of which Johnson was fully conscious. Sir Joshua Reynolds heard him

[2]*Eclogues*, VIII, 43.

[3]Johnson's wife had died on 17 March, 1752.

say, "There are two things which I am confident I can do very well: one is an introduction to any literary work, stating what it is to contain, and how it should be executed in the most perfect manner; the other is a conclusion, showing from various causes why the execution has not been equal to what the author promised to himself and to the public." * * *

A few of his definitions must be admitted to be erroneous. Thus, *Windward* and *Leeward*, though directly of opposite meaning, are defined identically the same way; as to which inconsiderable specks it is enough to observe, that his Preface announces that he was aware there might be many such in so immense a work; nor was he at all disconcerted when an instance was pointed out to him. A lady once asked him how he came to define *Pastern* the *knee* of a horse: instead of making an elaborate defense, as she expected, he at once answered, "Ignorance, Madam, pure ignorance." His definition of *Network*[1] has been often quoted with sportive malignity, as obscuring a thing in itself very plain. But to these frivolous censures no other answer is necessary than that with which we are furnished by his own Preface. * * *

His introducing his own opinions, and even prejudices, under general definitions of words, while at the same time the original meaning of the words is not explained, as his *Tory*, *Whig*, *Pension*, *Oats*, *Excise*,[2] and a few more, cannot be fully defended, and must be placed to the account of capricious and humorous indulgence. Talking to me upon this subject when we were at Ashbourne in 1777, he mentioned a still stronger instance of the predominance of his private feelings in the composition of this work, than any now to be found in it. "You know, Sir, Lord Gower forsook the old Jacobite interest. When I came to the word *Renegado*, after telling that it meant 'one who deserts to the enemy, a revolter,' I added, *Sometimes we say a* GOWER. Thus it went to the press; but the printer had more wit than I, and struck it out."

Let it, however, be remembered, that this indulgence does not display itself only in sarcasm towards others, but sometimes in playful allusion to the notions commonly entertained of his own laborious task. Thus: "*Grub-street*, the name of a street in London, much inhabited by writers of small histories, *dictionaries*, and temporary poems; whence any mean production is called *Grub-street*."—"*Lexicographer*, a writer of dictionaries, a *harmless drudge*." * * *

He had spent, during the progress of the work, the money for which he had contracted to write his *Dictionary*. We have seen that the reward of his labor was only fifteen hundred and seventy-five pounds; and when the expense of amanuenses and paper, and other articles are deducted, his clear profit was very inconsiderable. I once said to him, "I am sorry, Sir, you did not get more for your *Dictionary*." His answer was, "I am sorry, too. But it was very well. The booksellers are generous, liberal-minded men." He, upon all occasions, did ample justice to their character in this respect. He considered them as the patrons of literature; and, indeed, although they have eventually been considerable gainers by his *Dictionary*, it is to them that we owe its having been undertaken and carried through at the risk of great expense, for they were not absolutely sure of being indemnified.

CHRISTOPHER SMART (1763)

CONCERNING this unfortunate poet, Christopher Smart, who was confined in a mad-house, he had, at another time, the following conversation with Dr. Burney:—BURNEY. "How does poor Smart do, Sir; is he likely to recover?" JOHNSON. "It seems as if his mind had ceased to struggle with the disease; for he grows fat upon it." BURNEY. "Perhaps, Sir, that may be from want of exercise." JOHNSON. "No, Sir; he has partly as much exercise as he used to have, for he digs in the garden. Indeed, before his confinement, he used for exercise to walk to the ale-house; but he was *carried* back again. I did not think he ought to be shut up. His infirmities were not noxious to society. He insisted on people praying with him; and I'd as lief pray with Kit Smart as any one else. Another charge was,

[1] "Anything reticulated or decussated, at equal distances, with interstices between the intersections."

[2] *Tory:* "One who adheres to the ancient constitution of the state, and the apostolical hierarchy of the Church of England; opposed to a whig." *Whig:* "The name of a faction." *Pension:* "An allowance made to any one without an equivalent. In England it is generally understood to mean pay given to a state hireling for treason to his country." *Oats:* "A grain which in England is generally given to horses, but in Scotland supports the people." *Excise:* "A hateful tax levied upon commodities, and adjudged not by the common judges of property, but wretches hired by those to whom Excise is paid."

that he did not love clean linen; and I have no passion for it."—Johnson continued. "Mankind have a great aversion to intellectual labor; but even supposing knowledge to be easily attainable, more people would be content to be ignorant than would take even a little trouble to acquire it."

THE SOCIAL ORDER (1763)

I DESCRIBED to him an impudent fellow from Scotland, who affected to be a savage, and railed at all established systems. JOHNSON. "There is nothing surprising in this, Sir. He wants to make himself conspicuous. He would tumble in a hog-sty, as long as you looked at him and called to him to come out. But let him alone, never mind him, and he'll soon give it over."

I added, that the same person maintained that there was no distinction between virtue and vice. JOHNSON. "Why, Sir, if the fellow does not think as he speaks, he is lying; and I see not what honor he can propose to himself from having the character of a liar. But if he does really think that there is no distinction between virtue and vice, why, Sir, when he leaves our houses let us count our spoons." * * *

He recommended to me to keep a journal of my life, full and unreserved. He said it would be a very good exercise, and would yield me great satisfaction when the particulars were faded from my remembrance. I was uncommonly fortunate in having had a previous coincidence of opinion with him upon this subject, for I had kept such a journal for some time; and it was no small pleasure to me to have this to tell him, and to receive his approbation. He counseled me to keep it private, and said I might surely have a friend who would burn it in case of my death. From this habit I have been enabled to give the world so many anecdotes, which would otherwise have been lost to posterity. I mentioned that I was afraid I put into my journal too many little incidents. JOHNSON. "There is nothing, Sir, too little for so little a creature as man. It is by studying little things that we attain the great art of having as little misery and as much happiness as possible."

Next morning Mr. Dempster happened to call on me, and was so much struck even with the imperfect account which I gave him of Dr. Johnson's conversation, that to his honor be it recorded, when I complained that drinking port and sitting up late with him affected my nerves for some time after, he said, "One had better be palsied at eighteen than not keep company with such a man."

On Tuesday, July 18, I found tall Sir Thomas Robinson sitting with Johnson. Sir Thomas said, that the king of Prussia valued himself upon three things;—upon being a hero, a musician, and an author. JOHNSON. "Pretty well, Sir, for one man. As to his being an author, I have not looked at his poetry; but his prose is poor stuff. He writes just as you might suppose Voltaire's footboy to do, who has been his amanuensis. He has such parts as the valet might have, and about as much of the coloring of the style as might be got by transcribing his works." When I was at Ferney, I repeated this to Voltaire, in order to reconcile him somewhat to Johnson, whom he, in affecting the English mode of expression, had previously characterized as "a superstitious dog"; but after hearing such a criticism on Frederick the Great, with whom he was then on bad terms, he exclaimed, "An honest fellow!" * * *

Mr. Levet[1] this day showed me Dr. Johnson's library, which was contained in two garrets over his Chambers, where Lintot, son of the celebrated bookseller of that name, had formerly his warehouse. I found a number of good books, but very dusty and in great confusion. The floor was strewed with manuscript leaves, in Johnson's own handwriting, which I beheld with a degree of veneration, supposing they perhaps might contain portions of *The Rambler* or of *Rasselas*. I observed an apparatus for chemical experiments, of which Johnson was all his life very fond. The place seemed to be very favorable for retirement and meditation. Johnson told me that he went up thither without mentioning it to his servant, when he wanted to study, secure from interruption; for he would not allow his servant to say he was not at home when he really was. "A servant's strict regard for truth (said he), must be weakened by such a practice. A philosopher may know that it is merely a form of denial; but few servants are such nice distinguishers. If I accustom a servant to tell a lie for *me*, have I not

[1] See Johnson's poem on his death, and the note there printed concerning him, p. 647, above.

reason to apprehend that he will tell many lies for *himself?*" * * *

Mr. Temple,[1] now vicar of St. Gluvias, Cornwall, who had been my intimate friend for many years, had at this time chambers in Farrar's Buildings, at the bottom of Inner Temple Lane, which he kindly lent me upon my quitting my lodgings, he being to return to Trinity Hall, Cambridge. I found them particularly convenient for me, as they were so near Dr. Johnson's.

On Wednesday, July 20, Dr. Johnson, Mr. Dempster, and my uncle Dr. Boswell, who happened to be now in London, supped with me at these Chambers. JOHNSON. "Pity is not natural to man. Children are always cruel. Savages are always cruel. Pity is acquired and improved by the cultivation of reason. We may have uneasy sensations from seeing a creature in distress, without pity; for we have not pity unless we wish to relieve them. When I am on my way to dine with a friend, and finding it late, have bid the coachman make haste, if I happen to attend when he whips his horses, I may feel unpleasantly that the animals are put to pain, but I do not wish him to desist. No, Sir, I wish him to drive on." * * *

Rousseau's treatise on the inequality of mankind was at this time a fashionable topic. It gave rise to an observation by Mr. Dempster, that the advantages of fortune and rank were nothing to a wise man, who ought to value only merit. JOHNSON. "If man were a savage, living in the woods by himself, this might be true; but in civilized society we all depend upon each other, and our happiness is very much owing to the good opinion of mankind. Now, Sir, in civilized society, external advantages make us more respected. A man with a good coat upon his back meets with a better reception than he who has a bad one. Sir, you may analyze this, and say what is there in it? But that will avail you nothing, for it is a part of a general system. Pound St. Paul's Church into atoms, and consider any single atom; it is, to be sure, good for nothing: but, put all these atoms together, and you have St. Paul's Church. So it is with human felicity, which is made up of many ingredients, each of which may be shown to be very insignificant. In civilized society, personal merit will not serve you so much as money will. Sir, you may make the experiment. Go into the street, and give one man a lecture on morality, and another a shilling, and see which will respect you most. If you wish only to support nature, Sir William Petty fixes your allowance at three pounds a year; but as times are much altered, let us call it six pounds. This sum will fill your belly, shelter you from the weather, and even get you a strong lasting coat, supposing it to be made of good bull's hide. Now, Sir, all beyond this is artificial, and is desired in order to obtain a greater degree of respect from our fellow-creatures. And, Sir, if six hundred pounds a year procure a man more consequence, and, of course, more happiness than six pounds a year, the same proportion will hold as to six thousand, and so on as far as opulence can be carried. Perhaps he who has a large fortune may not be so happy as he who has a small one; but that must proceed from other causes than from his having the large fortune: for, *cæteris paribus*,[2] he who is rich in a civilized society, must be happier than he who is poor; as riches, if properly used (and it is a man's own fault if they are not), must be productive of the highest advantages. Money, to be sure, of itself is of no use; for its only use is to part with it. Rousseau, and all those who deal in paradoxes, are led away by a childish desire of novelty. When I was a boy, I used always to choose the wrong side of a debate, because most ingenious things, that is to say, most new things, could be said upon it. Sir, there is nothing for which you may not muster up more plausible arguments, than those which are urged against wealth and other external advantages. Why, now, there is stealing; why should it be thought a crime? When we consider by what unjust methods property has been often acquired, and that what was unjustly got it must be unjust to keep, where is the harm in one man's taking the property of another from him? Besides, Sir, when we consider the bad use that many people make of their property, and how much better use the thief may make of it, it may be defended as a very allowable practice. Yet, Sir, the experience of mankind has discovered stealing to be so very bad a thing, that they make no scruple to hang a man for it. When I was running about this town a very poor fellow, I was a great arguer for the advantages of poverty; but I was, at the same

[1] William Johnston Temple (1739–1796).

[2] Other things being equal.

time, very sorry to be poor. Sir, all the arguments which are brought to represent poverty as no evil, show it to be evidently a great evil. You never find people laboring to convince you that you may live very happily upon a plentiful fortune.—So you hear people talking how miserable a King must be; and yet they all wish to be in his place."

It was suggested that Kings must be unhappy, because they are deprived of the greatest of all satisfactions, easy and unreserved society. JOHNSON. "That is an ill-founded notion. Being a King does not exclude a man from such society. Great Kings have always been social. The King of Prussia, the only great King at present, is very social. Charles the Second, the last King of England who was a man of parts, was social; and our Henrys and Edwards were all social."

Mr. Dempster having endeavored to maintain that intrinsic merit *ought* to make the only distinction amongst mankind. JOHNSON. "Why, Sir, mankind have found that this cannot be. How shall we determine the proportion of intrinsic merit? Were that to be the only distinction amongst mankind, we should soon quarrel about the degrees of it. Were all distinctions abolished, the strongest would not long acquiesce, but would endeavor to obtain a superiority by their bodily strength. But, Sir, as subordination is very necessary for society, and contentions for superiority very dangerous, mankind, that is to say, all civilized nations, have settled it upon a plain invariable principle. A man is born to hereditary rank; or his being appointed to certain offices, gives him a certain rank. Subordination tends greatly to human happiness. Were we all upon an equality, we should have no other enjoyment than mere animal pleasure." * * *

He took care to guard himself against any possible suspicion that his settled principles of reverence for rank and respect for wealth were at all owing to mean or interested motives; for he asserted his own independence as a literary man. "No man (said he) who ever lived by literature, has lived more independently than I have done."

YOUNG PEOPLE (1763)

"SIR, I love the acquaintance of young people; because, in the first place, I don't like to think myself growing old. In the next place, young acquaintances must last longest, if they do last; and then, Sir, young men have more virtue than old men: they have more generous sentiments in every respect. I love the young dogs of this age: they have more wit and humor and knowledge of life than we had; but then the dogs are not so good scholars. Sir, in my early years I read very hard. It is a sad reflection, but a true one, that I knew almost as much at eighteen as I do now. My judgment, to be sure, was not so good; but I had all the facts. I remember very well, when I was at Oxford, an old gentleman said to me, 'Young man, ply your book diligently now, and acquire a stock of knowledge; for when years come upon you, you will find that poring upon books will be but an irksome task.'"

A WOMAN'S PREACHING (1763)

NEXT day, Sunday, July 31, I told him I had been that morning at a meeting of the people called Quakers, where I had heard a woman preach. JOHNSON. "Sir, a woman's preaching is like a dog's walking on his hinder legs. It is not done well; but you are surprised to find it done at all."

GEORGE III (1767)

IN FEBRUARY, 1767, there happened one of the most remarkable incidents of Johnson's life, which gratified his monarchical enthusiasm, and which he loved to relate with all its circumstances, when requested by his friends. This was his being honored by a private conversation with his Majesty, in the library at the Queen's house. He had frequently visited those splendid rooms and noble collection of books, which he used to say was more numerous and curious than he supposed any person could have made in the time which the King had employed. Mr. Barnard, the librarian, took care that he should have every accommodation that could contribute to his ease and convenience, while indulging his literary taste in that place; so that he had here a very agreeable resource at leisure hours.

His Majesty having been informed of his occasional visits, was pleased to signify a desire that he should be told when Dr. Johnson came next to the library. Accordingly, the next time that Johnson did come, as soon as he was fairly engaged with a book, on which, while he sat by the fire, he seemed quite intent, Mr. Barnard stole round to the apartment where the King was, and, in obedience to his Majesty's commands, mentioned that Dr. Johnson was then in the library. His Majesty said he was at leisure, and would go to him; upon which Mr. Barnard took one of the candles that stood on the King's table, and lighted his Majesty through a suite of rooms, till they came to a private door into the library, of which his Majesty had the key. Being entered, Mr. Barnard stepped forward hastily to Dr. Johnson, who was still in a profound study, and whispered him, "Sir, here is the King." Johnson started up, and stood still. His Majesty approached him, and at once was courteously easy.

His Majesty began by observing, that he understood he came sometimes to the library; and then mentioning his having heard that the Doctor had been lately at Oxford, asked him if he was not fond of going thither. To which Johnson answered, that he was indeed fond of going to Oxford sometimes, but was likewise glad to come back again. The King then asked him what they were doing at Oxford. Johnson answered, he could not much commend their diligence, but that in some respects they were mended, for they had put their press under better regulations, and were at that time printing Polybius. He was then asked whether there were better libraries at Oxford or Cambridge. He answered, he believed the Bodleian was larger than any they had at Cambridge; at the same time adding, "I hope, whether we have more books or not than they have at Cambridge, we shall make as good use of them as they do." Being asked whether All-Souls or Christ-Church library was the largest, he answered, "All-Souls library is the largest we have, except the Bodleian." "Aye (said the King), that is the public library."

His Majesty inquired if he was then writing anything. He answered, he was not, for he had pretty well told the world what he knew, and must now read to acquire more knowledge. The King, as it should seem with a view to urge him to rely on his own stores as an original writer, and to continue his labors, then said "I do not think you borrow much from anybody." Johnson said, he thought he had already done his part as a writer. "I should have thought so too (said the King), if you had not written so well."—Johnson observed to me, upon this, that "No man could have paid a handsomer compliment; and it was fit for a King to pay. It was decisive." When asked by another friend, at Sir Joshua Reynolds's, whether he made any reply to this high compliment, he answered, "No, Sir. When the King had said it, it was to be so. It was not for me to bandy civilities with my Sovereign." Perhaps no man who had spent his whole life in courts could have shown a more nice and dignified sense of true politeness, than Johnson did in this instance.

His Majesty having observed to him that he supposed he must have read a great deal; Johnson answered, that he thought more than he read; that he had read a great deal in the early part of his life, but having fallen into ill health, he had not been able to read much, compared with others: for instance, he said he had not read much, compared with Dr. Warburton. Upon which the King said, that he heard Dr. Warburton was a man of such general knowledge that you could scarce talk with him on any subject on which he was not qualified to speak; and that his learning resembled Garrick's acting, in its universality. His Majesty then talked of the controversy between Warburton and Lowth,[1] which he seemed to have read, and asked Johnson what he thought of it. Johnson answered, "Warburton has most general, most scholastic learning; Lowth is the more correct scholar. I do not know which of them calls names best." The King was pleased to say he was of the same opinion; adding, "You do not think, then, Dr. Johnson, that there was much argument in the case." Johnson said, he did not think there was. "Why truly (said the King), when once it comes to calling names, argument is pretty well at an end."

CRITICISM (1769)

Mrs. Montagu, a lady distinguished for having written an Essay on Shakespeare, being mentioned; Reynolds. "I think that essay does her honor." Johnson. "Yes, Sir; it does *her* honor, but it would do nobody else honor. I have, indeed, not read it all But when I take up the end of a web, and find it packthread, I do not expect, by looking

[1]See Gibbon's *Memoirs of my Life and Writings*, "Oxford."

further, to find embroidery. Sir, I will venture to say, there is not one sentence of true criticism in her book." GARRICK. "But, Sir, surely it shows how much Voltaire has mistaken Shakespeare, which nobody else has done." JOHNSON. "Sir, nobody else has thought it worth while. And what merit is there in that? You may as well praise a schoolmaster for whipping a boy who has construed ill. No, Sir, there is no real criticism in it: none showing the beauty of thought, as formed on the workings of the human heart."

The admirers of this Essay may be offended at the slighting manner in which Johnson spoke of it; but let it be remembered, that he gave his honest opinion unbiased by any prejudice, or any proud jealousy of a woman intruding herself into the chair of criticism; for Sir Joshua Reynolds has told me, that when the Essay first came out, and it was not known who had written it, Johnson wondered how Sir Joshua could like it. At this time Sir Joshua himself had received no information concerning the author, except being assured by one of our most eminent literati, that it was clear its author did not know the Greek tragedies in the original. One day at Sir Joshua's table, when it was related that Mrs. Montagu, in an excess of compliment to the author of a modern tragedy, had exclaimed, "I tremble for Shakespeare"; Johnson said, "When Shakespeare has got —— for his rival, and Mrs. Montagu for his defender, he is in a poor state indeed."

Johnson proceeded: "The Scotchman[1] has taken the right method in his *Elements of Criticism*. I do not mean that he has taught us anything; but he has told us old things in a new way." MURPHY. "He seems to have read a great deal of French criticism, and wants to make it his own; as if he had been for years anatomizing the heart of man, and peeping into every cranny of it." GOLDSMITH. "It is easier to write that book, than to read it." JOHNSON. "We have an example of true criticism in Burke's *Essay on the Sublime and Beautiful;* and, if I recollect, there is also Du Bos; and Bouhours, who shows all beauty to depend on truth. There is no great merit in telling how many plays have ghosts in them, and how this Ghost is better than that. You must show how terror is impressed on the human heart. In the description of night in *Macbeth*, the beetle and the bat detract from the general idea of darkness,—inspissated gloom."

[1]Henry Home, Lord Kames (1696–1782).

SYMPATHY (1769)

TALKING of our feeling for the distresses of others;—JOHNSON. "Why, Sir, there is much noise made about it, but it is greatly exaggerated. No, Sir, we have a certain degree of feeling to prompt us to do good: more than that, Providence does not intend. It would be misery to no purpose." BOSWELL. "But suppose now, Sir, that one of your intimate friends were apprehended for an offense for which he might be hanged." JOHNSON. "I should do what I could to bail him, and give him any other assistance; but if he were once fairly hanged, I should not suffer." BOSWELL. "Would you eat your dinner that day, Sir?" JOHNSON. "Yes, Sir; and eat it as if he were eating it with me. Why, there's Baretti, who is to be tried for his life to-morrow, friends have risen up for him on every side; yet if he should be hanged, none of them will eat a slice of plum-pudding the less. Sir, that sympathetic feeling goes a very little way in depressing the mind."

I told him that I had dined lately at Foote's, who showed me a letter which he had received from Tom Davies, telling him that he had not been able to sleep from the concern which he felt on account of "This sad affair of Baretti," begging of him to try if he could suggest anything that might be of service; and, at the same time, recommending to him an industrious young man who kept a pickle-shop. JOHNSON. "Ay, Sir, here you have a specimen of human sympathy; a friend hanged, and a cucumber pickled. We know not whether Baretti or the pickle-man has kept Davies from sleep; nor does he know himself. And as to his not sleeping, Sir; Tom Davies is a very great man; Tom has been upon the stage, and knows how to do those things. I have not been upon the stage, and cannot do those things." BOSWELL. "I have often blamed myself, Sir, for not feeling for others as sensibly as many say they do." JOHNSON. "Sir, don't be duped by them any more. You will find these very feeling people are not very ready to do you good. They *pay* you by *feeling*."

GOOD BEINGS (1772)

I TALKED of the recent expulsion of six students from the University of Oxford, who were methodists and would not desist from publicly praying and exhorting. JOHNSON. "Sir, that expulsion was extremely just and proper. What have they to do at an University who are not willing to be taught, but will presume to teach? Where is religion to be learned but at an University? Sir, they were examined, and found to be mighty ignorant fellows." BOSWELL. "But, was it not hard, Sir, to expel them, for I am told they were good beings?" JOHNSON. "I believe they might be good beings; but they were not fit to be in the University of Oxford. A cow is a very good animal in the field; but we turn her out of a garden." Lord Elibank used to repeat this as an illustration uncommonly happy.

READING (1773)

ON MONDAY, April 19, he called on me with Mrs. Williams, in Mr. Strahan's coach, and carried me out to dine with Mr. Elphinston, at his academy at Kensington. A printer having acquired a fortune sufficient to keep his coach, was a good topic for the credit of literature. Mrs. Williams said, that another printer, Mr. Hamilton, had not waited so long as Mr. Strahan, but had kept his coach several years sooner. JOHNSON. "He was in the right. Life is short. The sooner that a man begins to enjoy his wealth the better."

Mr. Elphinston talked of a new book that was much admired, and asked Dr. Johnson if he had read it. JOHNSON. "I have looked into it." "What (said Elphinston), have you not read it through?" Johnson, offended at being thus pressed, and so obliged to own his cursory mode of reading, answered tartly, "No, Sir, do *you* read books *through?*"

OSSIAN (1775)

MR. BOSWELL TO DR. JOHNSON.

Edinburgh, Feb. 2, 1775.

. . . AS TO Macpherson,[1] I am anxious to have from yourself a full and pointed account of what has passed between you and him. It is confidently told here, that before your book came out he sent to you, to let you know that he understood you meant to deny the authenticity of Ossian's poems; that the originals were in his possession; that you might have inspection of them, and might take the evidence of people skilled in the Erse language; and that he hoped, after this fair offer, you would not be so uncandid as to assert that he had refused reasonable proof. That you paid no regard to his message, but published your strong attack upon him; and then he wrote a letter to you, in such terms as he thought suited to one who had not acted as a man of veracity. * * *

TO JAMES BOSWELL, ESQ.

MY DEAR BOSWELL,—I am surprised that, knowing as you do the disposition of your countrymen to tell lies in favor of each other,[2] you can be at all affected by any reports that circulate among them. Macpherson never in his life offered me a sight of any original or of any evidence of any kind; but thought only of intimidating me by noise and threats, till my last answer—that I would not be deterred from detecting what I thought a cheat, by the menaces of a ruffian—put an end to our correspondence.

The state of the question is this. He, and Dr. Blair, whom I consider as deceived, say, that he copied the poem from old manuscripts. His copies, if he had them, and I believe him to have none, are nothing. Where are the manuscripts? They can be shown if they exist, but they were never shown. *De non existentibus et non apparentibus*, says our law, *eadem est ratio*.[3] No man has a claim to credit upon his own word, when better evidence, if he had it, may be easily produced. But, so far as we can find, the Erse language was never written till very lately for the purposes of religion. A nation that cannot write, or a language that was never written, has no manuscripts.

But whatever he has he never offered to show. If old manuscripts should now be mentioned, I should, unless there were more evidence than can be easily had, suppose them another proof of Scotch conspiracy in national falsehood.

Do not censure the expression; you know it to be true. * * *

My compliments to Madam and Veronica.

I am, Sir, Your most humble servant,

SAM. JOHNSON.

February 7, 1775.

[1]James Macpherson (1736–1796) had in 1760 begun publishing what he claimed were translations of ancient poetry composed in the Gaelic (or Erse) tongue by Ossian. These "translations" (it is now agreed they were forgeries) were eagerly accepted in Scotland, were popular on the continent, and occupy an important place in the rise of Romanticism. Macpherson's prose translation of the *Iliad* of Homer was published in 1773.

[2]My friend has, in this letter, relied upon my testimony, with a confidence, of which the ground has escaped my recollection. (Boswell.)

[3]Reasoning is identical, says our law, concerning the nonexistent and concerning the invisible.

What words were used by Mr. Macpherson in his letter to the venerable Sage, I have never heard; but they are generally said to have been of a nature very different from the language of literary contest. Dr. Johnson's answer appeared in the newspapers of the day, and has since been frequently republished; but not with perfect accuracy. I give it as dictated to me by himself, written down in his presence, and authenticated by a note in his own handwriting, "This, I think, is a true copy."

Mr. James Macpherson,—I received your foolish and impudent letter. Any violence offered me I shall do my best to repel; and what I cannot do for myself, the law shall do for me. I hope I shall never be deterred from detecting what I think a cheat, by the menaces of a ruffian.

What would you have me retract? I thought your book an imposture; I think it an imposture still. For this opinion I have given my reasons to the public, which I here dare you to refute. Your rage I defy. Your abilities, since your Homer, are not so formidable; and what I hear of your morals, inclines me to pay regard not to what you shall say, but to what you shall prove. You may print this if you will.

Sam. Johnson.

Mr. Macpherson little knew the character of Dr. Johnson, if he supposed that he could be easily intimidated; for no man was ever more remarkable for personal courage. He had, indeed, an awful dread of death, or rather, "of something after death"; and what rational man, who seriously thinks of quitting all that he has ever known, and going into a new and unknown state of being, can be without that dread? But his fear was from reflection; his courage natural. His fear, in that one instance, was the result of philosophical and religious consideration. He feared death, but he feared nothing else, not even what might occasion death. Many instances of his resolution may be mentioned. One day, at Mr. Beauclerk's house in the country, when two large dogs were fighting, he went up to them, and beat them till they separated; and at another time, when told of the danger there was that a gun might burst if charged with many balls, he put in six or seven, and fired it off against a wall. Mr. Langton told me, that when they were swimming together near Oxford, he cautioned Dr. Johnson against a pool, which was reckoned particularly dangerous; upon which Johnson directly swam into it. He told me himself that one night he was attacked in the street by four men, to whom he would not yield, but kept them all at bay, till the watch came up, and carried both him and them to the round-house. In the playhouse at Lichfield, as Mr. Garrick informed me, Johnson having for a moment quitted a chair which was placed for him between the side-scenes, a gentleman took possession of it, and when Johnson on his return civilly demanded his seat, rudely refused to give it up; upon which Johnson laid hold of it, and tossed him and the chair into the pit. Foote, who so successfully revived the old comedy, by exhibiting living characters, had resolved to imitate Johnson on the stage, expecting great profits from his ridicule of so celebrated a man. Johnson being informed of his intention, and being at dinner at Mr. Thomas Davies's the bookseller, from whom I had the story, he asked Mr. Davies "what was the common price of an oak stick"; and being answered six-pence, "Why then, Sir (said he), give me leave to send your servant to purchase me a shilling one. I'll have a double quantity; for I am told Foote means to *take me off*, as he calls it, and I am determined the fellow shall not do it with impunity." Davies took care to acquaint Foote of this, which effectually checked the wantonness of the mimic. Mr. Macpherson's menaces made Johnson provide himself with the same implement of defense; and had he been attacked, I have no doubt that, old as he was, he would have made his corporal prowess be felt as much as his intellectual.

THE IRISH (1775)

My much-valued friend Dr. Barnard, now Bishop of Killaloe, having once expressed to him an apprehension, that if he should visit Ireland he might treat the people of that country more unfavorably than he had done the Scotch, he answered, with strong pointed double-edged wit, "Sir, you have no reason to be afraid of me. The Irish are not in a conspiracy to cheat the world by false representations of the merits of their countrymen. No, Sir; the Irish are a fair people;—they never speak well of one another."

THE INDISTINCT RELATER (1775)

I VISITED him by appointment in the evening, and we drank tea with Mrs. Williams. He told me that he had been in the company of a gentleman whose extraordinary travels had been much the subject of conversation. But I found that he had not listened to him with that full confidence, without which there is little satisfaction in the society of travelers. I was curious to hear what opinion so able a judge as Johnson had formed of his abilities, and I asked if he was not a man of sense. JOHNSON. "Why, Sir, he is not a distinct relater; and I should say, he is neither abounding nor deficient in sense. I did not perceive any superiority of understanding." BOSWELL. "But will you not allow him a nobleness of resolution, in penetrating into distant regions?" JOHNSON. "That, Sir, is not to the present purpose. We are talking of his sense. A fighting cock has a nobleness of resolution."

A GOOD THING (1775)

NO MORE of his conversation for some days appears in my journal, except that when a gentleman told him he had bought a suit of lace for his lady, he said, "Well, Sir, you have done a good thing and a wise thing." "I have done a good thing (said the gentleman), but I do not know that I have done a wise thing." JOHNSON. "Yes, Sir; no money is better spent than what is laid out for domestic satisfaction. A man is pleased that his wife is dressed as well as other people; and a wife is pleased that she is dressed."

THE FELICITY OF ENGLAND IN ITS TAVERNS (1776)

WE DINED at an excellent inn at Chapel House, where he expatiated on the felicity of England in its taverns and inns, and triumphed over the French for not having, in any perfection, the tavern life. "There is no private house (said he), in which people can enjoy themselves so well, as at a capital tavern. Let there be ever so great plenty of good things, ever so much grandeur, ever so much elegance, ever so much desire that everybody should be easy; in the nature of things it cannot be: there must always be some degree of care and anxiety. The master of the house is anxious to entertain his guests; the guests are anxious to be agreeable to him: and no man, but a very impudent dog indeed, can as freely command what is in another man's house, as if it were his own. Whereas, at a tavern, there is a general freedom from anxiety. You are sure you are welcome: and the more noise you make, the more trouble you give, the more good things you call for, the welcomer you are. No servants will attend you with the alacrity which waiters do, who are incited by the prospect of an immediate reward in proportion as they please. No, Sir; there is nothing which has yet been contrived by man, by which so much happiness is produced as by a good tavern or inn."[1] He then repeated, with great emotion, Shenstone's lines:—

> Whoe'er has traveled life's dull round,
> Where'er his stages may have been,
> May sigh to think he still has found
> The warmest welcome at an inn.

MARRIAGE (1776)

WHEN he again talked of Mrs. Careless tonight, he seemed to have had his affection revived; for he said, "If I had married her, it might have been as happy for me." BOSWELL. "Pray, Sir, do you not suppose that there are fifty women in the world, with any one of whom a man may be as happy, as with any one woman in particular?" JOHNSON. "Ay, Sir, fifty thousand." BOSWELL. "Then, Sir, you are not of opinion with some who imagine that certain men and certain women are made for each other; and that they cannot be happy if they miss their counterparts?" JOHNSON. "To be sure not, Sir. I believe marriages would in general be as happy, and often more so, if they were all made by the Lord Chancellor, upon a due consideration of characters and circumstances, without the parties having any choice in the matter."

---

[1]Sir John Hawkins has preserved very few *Memorabilia* of Johnson. There is, however, to be found, in his bulky tome, a very excellent one upon this subject:—"In contradiction to those, who, having a wife and children, prefer domestic enjoyments to those which a tavern affords, I have heard him assert, *that a tavern chair was the throne of human felicity*.—'As soon,' said he, 'as I enter the door of a tavern, I experience an oblivion of care, and a freedom from solicitude: when I am seated, I find the master courteous, and the servants obsequious to my call; anxious to know and ready to supply my wants: wine there exhilarates my spirits, and prompts me to free conversation and an interchange of discourse with those whom I most love. I dogmatize and am contradicted, and in this conflict of opinions and sentiments I find delight.'" (Boswell.)

THE REVIEWS (1776)

"The Monthly Reviewers (said he) are not Deists; but they are Christians with as little Christianity as may be; and are for pulling down all establishments. The Critical Reviewers are for supporting the constitution both in church and state. The Critical Reviewers, I believe, often review without reading the books through; but lay hold of a topic, and write chiefly from their own minds. The Monthly Reviewers are duller men, and are glad to read the books through."

JOHN WILKES (1776)

My desire of being acquainted with celebrated men of every description had made me, much about the same time, obtain an introduction to Dr. Samuel Johnson and to John Wilkes, Esq.[1] Two men more different could perhaps not be selected out of all mankind. They had even attacked one another with some asperity in their writings; yet I lived in habits of friendship with both. I could fully relish the excellence of each; for I have ever delighted in that intellectual chemistry, which can separate good qualities from evil in the same person.

Sir John Pringle, "mine own friend and my Father's friend," between whom and Dr. Johnson I in vain wished to establish an acquaintance, as I respected and lived in intimacy with both of them, observed to me once, very ingeniously, "It is not in friendship as in mathematics, where two things, each equal to a third, are equal between themselves. You agree with Johnson as a middle quality, and you agree with me as a middle quality; but Johnson and I should not agree." Sir John was not sufficiently flexible; so I desisted; knowing, indeed, that the repulsion was equally strong on the part of Johnson; who, I know not from what cause, unless his being a Scotchman, had formed a very erroneous opinion of Sir John. But I conceived an irresistible wish, if possible, to bring Dr. Johnson and Mr. Wilkes together. How to manage it, was a nice and difficult matter.

My worthy booksellers and friends, Messieurs Dilly in the Poultry, at whose hospitable and well-covered table I have seen a greater number of literary men, than at any other, except that of Sir Joshua Reynolds, had invited me to meet Mr. Wilkes and some more gentlemen on Wednesday, May 15. "Pray (said I), let us have Dr. Johnson."—"What, with Mr. Wilkes? not for the world (said Mr. Edward Dilly): Dr. Johnson would never forgive me."—"Come (said I), if you'll let me negotiate for you, I will be answerable that all shall go well." Dilly. "Nay, if you will take it upon you, I am sure I shall be very happy to see them both here."

Notwithstanding the high veneration which I entertained for Dr. Johnson, I was sensible that he was sometimes a little actuated by the spirit of contradiction, and by means of that I hoped I should gain my point. I was persuaded that if I had come upon him with a direct proposal, "Sir, will you dine in company with Jack Wilkes?" he would have flown into a passion, and would probably have answered, "Dine with Jack Wilkes, Sir! I'd as soon dine with Jack Ketch." I therefore, while we were sitting quietly by ourselves at his house in an evening, took occasion to open my plan thus:—"Mr. Dilly, Sir, sends his respectful compliments to you, and would be happy if you would do him the honor to dine with him on Wednesday next along with me, as I must soon go to Scotland." Johnson. "Sir, I am obliged to Mr. Dilly. I will wait upon him—" Boswell. "Provided, Sir, I suppose, that the company which he is to have, is agreeable to you." Johnson. "What do you mean, Sir? What do you take me for? Do you think I am so ignorant of the world as to imagine that I am to prescribe to a gentleman what company he is to have at his table?" Boswell. "I beg your pardon, Sir, for wishing to prevent you from meeting people whom you might not like. Perhaps he may have some of what he calls his patriotic friends with him." Johnson. "Well, Sir, and what then? What care *I* for his *patriotic friends?* Poh!" Boswell. "I should not be surprised to find Jack Wilkes there." Johnson. "And if Jack Wilkes *should* be there, what is that to *me*, Sir? My dear

[1] Demagogue and man of loose life (1727–1797); editor of the political periodical *The North Briton*, for one number of which he suffered a brief imprisonment, which helped to make him popular. Later he was outlawed, but in 1768 returned to England and was elected to Parliament for Middlesex. He was then imprisoned and in 1769 expelled from Parliament. He was several times reëlected, but each time declared ineligible. In 1774 he became lord mayor of London, and, again elected to Parliament, he was now allowed to sit, and remained a member until 1790.

friend, let us have no more of this. I am sorry to be angry with you; but really it is treating me strangely to talk to me as if I could not meet any company whatever, occasionally." Boswell. "Pray forgive me, Sir: I meant well. But you shall meet whoever comes, for me." Thus I secured him, and told Dilly that he would find him very well pleased to be one of his guests on the day appointed.

Upon the much-expected Wednesday, I called on him about half an hour before dinner, as I often did when we were to dine out together, to see that he was ready in time, and to accompany him. I found him buffeting his books, as upon a former occasion, covered with dust, and making no preparation for going abroad. "How is this, Sir? (said I). Don't you recollect that you are to dine at Mr. Dilly's?" Johnson. "Sir, I did not think of going to Dilly's: it went out of my head. I have ordered dinner at home with Mrs. Williams." Boswell. "But, my dear Sir, you know you were engaged to Mr. Dilly, and I told him so. He will expect you, and will be much disappointed if you don't come." Johnson. "You must talk to Mrs. Williams about this."

Here was a sad dilemma. I feared that what I was so confident I had secured would yet be frustrated. He had accustomed himself to show Mrs. Williams such a degree of humane attention, as frequently imposed some restraint upon him; and I knew that if she should be obstinate, he would not stir. I hastened down stairs to the blind lady's room, and told her I was in great uneasiness, for Dr. Johnson had engaged to me to dine this day at Mr. Dilly's, but that he had told me he had forgotten his engagement, and had ordered dinner at home. "Yes, Sir (said she, pretty peevishly), Dr. Johnson is to dine at home."—"Madam (said I), his respect for you is such, that I know he will not leave you unless you absolutely desire it. But as you have so much of his company, I hope you will be good enough to forgo it for a day; as Mr. Dilly is a very worthy man, has frequently had agreeable parties at his house for Dr. Johnson, and will be vexed if the Doctor neglects him to-day. And then, Madam, be pleased to consider my situation; I carried the message, and I assured Mr. Dilly that Dr. Johnson was to come, and no doubt he has made a dinner, and invited a company, and boasted of the honor he expected to have. I shall be quite disgraced if the Doctor is not there." She gradually softened to my solicitations, which were certainly as earnest as most entreaties to ladies upon any occasion, and was graciously pleased to empower me to tell Dr. Johnson, "That all things considered, she thought he should certainly go." I flew back to him, still in dust, and careless of what should be the event, "indifferent in his choice to go or stay"; but as soon as I had announced to him Mrs. Williams's consent, he roared, "Frank, a clean shirt," and was very soon dressed. When I had him fairly seated in a hackney-coach with me, I exulted as much as a fortune-hunter who has got an heiress into a post-chaise with him to set out for Gretna Green.

When we entered Mr. Dilly's drawing room, he found himself in the midst of a company he did not know. I kept myself snug and silent, watching how he would conduct himself. I observed him whispering to Mr. Dilly, "Who is that gentleman, Sir?"—"Mr. Arthur Lee."—Johnson. "Too, too, too" (under his breath), which was one of his habitual mutterings. Mr. Arthur Lee could not but be very obnoxious to Johnson, for he was not only a *patriot* but an *American*. He was afterwards minister from the United States at the court of Madrid. "And who is the gentleman in lace?"—"Mr. Wilkes, Sir." This information confounded him still more; he had some difficulty to restrain himself, and taking up a book, sat down upon a window-seat and read, or at least kept his eye upon it intently for some time, till he composed himself. His feelings, I dare say, were awkward enough. But he no doubt recollected his having rated me for supposing that he could be at all disconcerted by any company, and he, therefore, resolutely set himself to behave quite as an easy man of the world, who could adapt himself at once to the disposition and manners of those whom he might chance to meet.

The cheering sound of "Dinner is upon the table," dissolved his reverie, and we *all* sat down without any symptom of ill humor. There were present, beside Mr. Wilkes, and Mr. Arthur Lee, who was an old companion of mine when he studied physic at Edinburgh, Mr. (now Sir John) Miller, Dr. Lettsom, and Mr. Slater the druggist. Mr. Wilkes placed himself next to Dr. Johnson, and behaved to him with so much attention and politeness, that he gained upon him insensibly. No man ate more heartily than Johnson, or loved better what was nice and delicate. Mr. Wilkes was very assiduous in helping him to some fine veal. "Pray give me leave, Sir:—It is better here—A little of the brown—Some fat, Sir—A little of the stuffing—Some gravy—Let me have the pleasure of giving you some butter—Allow me to recommend a squeeze of this orange;—or the lemon, perhaps, may have more zest."—"Sir, Sir, I am obliged to you, Sir," cried Johnson, bowing, and turning his head to him with a look for some time of "surly virtue," but, in a short while, of complacency.

Foote being mentioned, Johnson said, "He is not a good mimic." One of the company added, "A merry Andrew, a buffoon." JOHNSON. "But he has wit too, and is not deficient in ideas, or in fertility and variety of imagery, and not empty of reading; he has knowledge enough to fill up his part. One species of wit he has in an eminent degree, that of escape. You drive him into a corner with both hands; but he's gone, Sir, when you think you have got him—like an animal that jumps over your head. Then he has a great range for wit; he never lets truth stand between him and a jest, and he is sometimes mighty coarse. Garrick is under many restraints from which Foote is free." WILKES. "Garrick's wit is more like Lord Chesterfield's." JOHNSON. "The first time I was in company with Foote was at Fitzherbert's. Having no good opinion of the fellow, I was resolved not to be pleased; and it is very difficult to please a man against his will. I went on eating my dinner pretty sullenly, affecting not to mind him. But the dog was so very comical, that I was obliged to lay down my knife and fork, throw myself back upon my chair, and fairly laugh it out. No, Sir, he was irresistible. He upon one occasion experienced, in an extraordinary degree, the efficacy of his powers of entertaining. Amongst the many and various modes which he tried of getting money, he became a partner with a small-beer brewer, and he was to have a share of the profits for procuring customers amongst his numerous acquaintance. Fitzherbert was one who took his small-beer; but it was so bad that the servants resolved not to drink it. They were at some loss how to notify their resolution, being afraid of offending their master, who they knew liked Foote much as a companion. At last they fixed upon a little black boy, who was rather a favorite, to be their deputy, and deliver their remonstrance; and having invested him with the whole authority of the kitchen, he was to inform Mr. Fitzherbert, in all their names, upon a certain day, that they would drink Foote's small-beer no longer. On that day Foote happened to dine at Fitzherbert's, and this boy served at table; he was so delighted with Foote's stories, and merriment, and grimace, that when he went down stairs, he told them, 'This is the finest man I have ever seen. I will not deliver your message. I will drink his small-beer.'"

Somebody observed that Garrick could not have done this. WILKES. "Garrick would have made the small-beer still smaller. He is now leaving the stage; but he will play *Scrub* all his life." I knew that Johnson would let nobody attack Garrick but himself, as Garrick once said to me, and I had heard him praise his liberality; so to bring out his commendation of his celebrated pupil, I said, loudly, "I have heard Garrick is liberal." JOHNSON. "Yes, Sir, I know that Garrick has given away more money than any man in England that I am acquainted with, and that not from ostentatious views. Garrick was very poor when he began life; so when he came to have money, he probably was very unskillful in giving away, and saved when he should not. But Garrick began to be liberal as soon as he could; and I am of opinion, the reputation of avarice which he has had, has been very lucky for him, and prevented his having many enemies. You despise a man for avarice, but do not hate him. Garrick might have been much better attacked for living with more splendor than is suitable to a player: if they had had the wit to have assaulted him in that quarter, they might have galled him more. But they have kept clamoring about his avarice, which has rescued him from much obloquy and envy."

Talking of the great difficulty of obtaining authentic information for biography, Johnson told us, "When I was a young fellow I wanted to write the *Life of Dryden*, and in order to get materials, I applied to the only two persons then alive who had seen him; these were old Swinney, and old Cibber. Swinney's information was no more than this, 'That at Will's coffee-house Dryden had a particular chair for himself, which was set by the fire in winter, and was then called his winter-chair; and that it was carried out for him to the balcony in summer, and was then called his summer-chair.' Cibber could tell no more but 'That he remembered him a decent old man, arbiter of critical disputes at Will's.' You are to consider that Cibber was then at a great distance from Dryden, had perhaps one leg only in the room, and durst not draw in the other." BOSWELL. "Yet Cibber was a man of observation?" JOHNSON. "I think not." BOSWELL. "You will allow his *Apology* to be well done." JOHNSON. "Very well done, to be sure, Sir. That book is a striking proof of the justice of Pope's remark:

Each might his several province well command,
Would all but stoop to what they understand."[1]

BOSWELL. "And his plays are good." JOHNSON. "Yes; but that was his trade; *l'esprit du corps:* he had been all his life among players and play-writers. I wondered that he had so little to say in conversation, for he had kept the best company, and learned all that can be got by the ear. He abused Pindar to me, and then showed me an Ode of his own, with an absurd couplet, making a linnet soar on an eagle's wing. I told him that when the ancients made a simile, they always made it like something real."

Mr. Wilkes remarked, that "among all the bold flights of Shakespeare's imagination, the boldest was making Birnam Wood march to Dunsinane; creating a wood where there never was a shrub; a wood in Scotland! ha! ha! ha!" And he also observed, that "the clannish slavery of the Highlands of Scotland was the single exception to Milton's remark of 'The Mountain Nymph, sweet Liberty,' being worshiped in all hilly countries."—"When I was at Inverary (said he) on a visit to my old friend, Archibald, Duke of Argyle, his dependents congratulated me on being such a favorite of his Grace. I said, 'It is then, gentlemen, truly lucky for me; for if I had displeased the Duke, and he had wished it, there is not a Campbell among you but would have been ready to bring John Wilkes's head to him in a charger. It would have been only

Off with his head! So much for Aylesbury.'

I was then member for Aylesbury." * * *

[1] *Essay on Criticism*, I, 66–67.

Mr. Arthur Lee mentioned some Scotch who had taken possession of a barren part of America, and wondered why they should choose it. JOHNSON. "Why, Sir, all barrenness is comparative. The *Scotch* would not know it to be barren." BOSWELL. "Come, come, he is flattering the English. You have now been in Scotland, Sir, and say if you did not see meat and drink enough there." JOHNSON. "Why yes, Sir; meat and drink enough to give the inhabitants sufficient strength to run away from home." All these quick and lively sallies were said sportively, quite in jest, and with a smile, which showed that he meant only wit. Upon this topic he and Mr. Wilkes could perfectly assimilate; here was a bond of union between them, and I was conscious that as both of them had visited Caledonia, both were fully satisfied of the strange narrow ignorance of those who imagine that it is a land of famine. But they amused themselves with persevering in the old jokes. When I claimed a superiority for Scotland over England in one respect, that no man can be arrested there for a debt merely because another swears it against him; but there must first be the judgment of a court of law ascertaining its justice; and that a seizure of the person, before judgment is obtained, can take place only if his creditor should swear that he is about to fly from the country, or, as it is technically expressed, is *in meditatione fugæ:* WILKES. "That, I should think, may be safely sworn of all the Scotch nation." JOHNSON. (to Mr. Wilkes) "You must know, Sir, I lately took my friend Boswell and showed him genuine civilized life in an English provincial town. I turned him loose at Lichfield, my native city, that he might see for once real civility: for you know he lives among savages in Scotland, and among rakes in London." WILKES. "Except when he is with grave, sober, decent people like you and me." JOHNSON. (smiling) "And we ashamed of him."

A BAD STYLE OF POETRY (1777)

HE OBSERVED, that a gentleman of eminence in literature had got into a bad style of poetry of late. "He puts (said he) a very common thing in a strange dress till he does not know it himself, and thinks other people do not know it." BOSWELL. "That is owing to his being so much versant in old English poetry." JOHNSON. "What is that to the purpose, Sir? If I say a man is drunk, and you tell me it is owing to his taking much drink, the matter is not mended. No, Sir, ——[1] has taken to an odd mode. For example, he'd write thus:

Hermit hoar, in solemn cell,
Wearing out life's evening gray.

Gray evening is common enough; but *evening gray* he'd think fine.—Stay;—we'll make out the stanza:

Hermit hoar, in solemn cell,
Wearing out life's evening gray;
Smite thy bosom, sage, and tell,
What is bliss? and which the way?"

BOSWELL. "But why smite his bosom, Sir?" JOHNSON. "Why, to show he was in earnest" (smiling).—He at an after period added the following stanza:

Thus I spoke; and speaking sighed;
—Scarce repressed the starting tear;—
When the smiling sage replied—
—Come, my lad, and drink some beer.

HAPPINESS (1777)

IN OUR way, Johnson strongly expressed his love of driving fast in a post-chaise. "If (said he) I had no duties, and no reference to futurity, I would spend my life in driving briskly in a post-chaise with a pretty woman; but she should be one who could understand me, and would add something to the conversation."

LONDON (1777)

WE ENTERED seriously upon a question of much importance to me, which Johnson was pleased to consider with friendly attention. I had long complained to him that I felt myself discontented in Scotland, as too narrow a sphere, and that I wished to make my chief residence in London, the great scene of ambition, instruction, and amusement: a scene, which was to me, comparatively speaking, a heaven upon earth. JOHNSON. "Why, Sir, I never knew any one who had such a *gust* for London as you have: and I cannot blame you for your wish to live there: yet, Sir, were I in your father's place, I should not consent to your settling there; for I have the old feudal notions, and I should be afraid that Auchinleck would be deserted, as you would soon find it more desirable to have a country-seat in a better climate." * * *

I suggested a doubt, that if I were to reside in London, the exquisite zest with which I relished it in occasional visits might go off, and I might grow tired of it. JOHNSON. "Why, Sir, you find no man, at all intellectual, who is willing to leave London. No, Sir, when a man is tired of London, he is tired of life; for there is in London all that life can afford."

OLIVER EDWARDS (1778)

AND now I am to give a pretty full account of one of the most curious incidents in Johnson's life, of which he himself has made the following minute on this day: "In my return from church, I was accosted by Edwards, an old fellow-collegian, who had not seen me since 1729. He knew me, and asked if I remembered one Edwards; I did not at first recollect the name, but gradually as we walked along, recovered it, and told him a conversation that had passed at an ale-house between us. My purpose is to continue our acquaintance."

It was in Butcher Row that this meeting happened. Mr. Edwards, who was a decent-looking elderly man in gray clothes, and a wig of many curls, accosted Johnson with familiar confidence, knowing who he was, while Johnson returned his salutation with a courteous formality, as to a stranger. But as soon as Edwards had brought to his recollection their having been at Pembroke College together nine-and-forty years ago, he seemed much pleased, asked where he lived, and said he should be glad to see him in Bolt Court. EDWARDS. "Ah, Sir! we are old men now." JOHNSON. (who never liked to think of being old), "Don't let us discourage one another." EDWARDS. "Why, Doctor, you look stout and hearty, I am happy to see you so; for the newspapers told us you were very ill." JOHNSON. "Ay, Sir, they are always telling lies of *us old fellows*."

Wishing to be present at more of so singular a conversation as that between two fellow-collegians, who had lived forty years in London without ever having chanced to meet, I whispered to Mr. Edwards that Dr. Johnson

[1]Thomas Warton (1728–1790).

was going home, and that he had better accompany him now. So Edwards walked along with us, I eagerly assisting to keep up the conversation. Mr. Edwards informed Dr. Johnson that he had practiced long as a solicitor in Chancery, but that he now lived in the country upon a little farm, about sixty acres, just by Stevenage in Hertfordshire, and that he came to London (to Barnard's Inn, No. 6), generally twice a week. Johnson appearing to me in a reverie, Mr. Edwards addressed himself to me, and expatiated on the pleasure of living in the country. BOSWELL. "I have no notion of this, Sir. What you have to entertain you, is, I think, exhausted in half an hour." EDWARDS. "What? don't you love to have hope realized? I see my grass, and my corn, and my trees growing. Now, for instance, I am curious to see if this frost has not nipped my fruit-trees." JOHNSON. (who we did not imagine was attending) "You find, Sir, you have fears as well as hopes."—So well did he see the whole, when another saw but the half of a subject.

When we got to Dr. Johnson's house, and were seated in his library, the dialogue went on admirably. EDWARDS. "Sir, I remember you would not let us say *prodigious* at College. For even then, Sir (turning to me), he was delicate in language, and we all feared him."[1] JOHNSON. (to Edwards) "From your having practiced the law long, Sir, I presume you must be rich." EDWARDS. "No, Sir; I got a good deal of money; but I had a number of poor relations to whom I gave a great part of it." JOHNSON. "Sir, you have been rich in the most valuable sense of the word." EDWARDS. "But I shall not die rich." JOHNSON. "Nay, sure, Sir, it is better to *live* rich than to *die* rich." EDWARDS. "I wish I had continued at College." JOHNSON. "Why do you wish that, Sir?" EDWARDS. "Because I think I should have had a much easier life than mine has been. I should have been a parson, and had a good living, like Bloxam and several others, and lived comfortably." JOHNSON. "Sir, the life of a parson, of a conscientious clergyman, is not easy. I have always considered a clergyman as the father of a larger family than he is able to maintain. I would rather have Chancery suits upon my hands than the cure of souls. No, Sir, I do not envy a clergyman's life as an easy life, nor do I envy the clergyman who makes it an easy life." Here taking himself up all of a sudden, he exclaimed, "O! Mr. Edwards! I'll convince you that I recollect you. Do you remember our drinking together at an alehouse near Pembroke gate? At that time, you told me of the Eton boy, who, when verses on our SAVIOR's turning water into wine were prescribed as an exercise, brought up a single line, which was highly admired,—

Vidit et erubuit lympha pudica DEUM,[2]

and I told you of another fine line in Camden's *Remains*, an eulogy upon one of our Kings, who was succeeded by his son, a prince of equal merit:—

Mira cano, Sol occubuit, nox nulla secuta est."[3]

EDWARDS. "You are a philosopher, Dr. Johnson. I have tried too in my time to be a philosopher; but, I don't know how, cheerfulness was always breaking in."—Mr. Burke, Sir Joshua Reynolds, Mr. Courtenay, Mr. Malone, and, indeed, all the eminent men to whom I have mentioned this, have thought it an exquisite trait of character. The truth is, that philosophy, like religion, is too generally supposed to be hard and severe, at least so grave as to exclude all gayety.

EDWARDS. "I have been twice married, Doctor. You, I suppose, have never known what it was to have a wife." JOHNSON. "Sir, I have known what it was to have a wife, and (in a solemn, tender, faltering tone) I have known what it was to *lose a wife.*—It had almost broke my heart."

EDWARDS. "How do you live, Sir? For my part, I must have my regular meals, and a glass of good wine. I find I require it." JOHNSON. "I now drink no wine, Sir. Early in life I drank wine: for many years I drank none. I then for some years drank a great deal." EDWARDS. "Some hogsheads, I warrant you." JOHNSON. "I then had a severe

[1] Johnson said to me afterwards, "Sir, they respected me for my literature; and yet it was not great but by comparison. Sir, it is amazing how little literature there is in the world." (Boswell)

[2] The line is really lifted (as the "Mr. Malone" of the next paragraph later discovered) from an epigram, on the miracle of the water turned into wine, by Richard Crashaw: "The modest spring has seen her God and blushed."

[3] Camden says that some ascribe this line, written to "honor King Henry II, then departed, and King Richard succeeding," to Giraldus Cambrensis: "I sing of wonders, the Sun has set, yet no night has followed."

illness, and left it off, and I have never begun it again. I never felt any difference upon myself from eating one thing rather than another, nor from one kind of weather rather than another. There are people, I believe, who feel a difference; but I am not one of them. And as to regular meals, I have fasted from the Sunday's dinner to the Tuesday's dinner, without any inconvenience. I believe it is best to eat just as one is hungry: but a man who is in business, or a man who has a family, must have stated meals. I am a straggler. I may leave this town and go to Grand Cairo, without being missed here or observed there." EDWARDS. "Don't you eat supper, Sir?" JOHNSON. "No, Sir." EDWARDS. "For my part, now, I consider supper as a turnpike through which one must pass, in order to get to bed."

JOHNSON. "You are a lawyer, Mr. Edwards. Lawyers know life practically. A bookish man should always have them to converse with. They have what he wants." EDWARDS. "I am grown old: I am sixty-five." JOHNSON. "I shall be sixty-eight next birthday. Come, Sir, drink water, and put in for a hundred." * * *

This interview confirmed my opinion of Johnson's most humane and benevolent heart. His cordial and placid behavior to an old fellow-collegian, a man so different from himself; and his telling him that he would go down to his farm and visit him, showed a kindness of disposition very rare at an advanced age. He observed, "how wonderful it was that they had both been in London forty years, without having ever once met, and both walkers in the street too!" Mr. Edwards, when going away, again recurred to his consciousness of senility, and looking full in Johnson's face, said to him, "You'll find in Dr. Young,

O my coevals! remnants of yourselves."[1]

Johnson did not relish this at all; but shook his head with impatience. Edwards walked off, seemingly highly pleased with the honor of having been thus noticed by Dr. Johnson. When he was gone, I said to Johnson, I thought him but a weak man. JOHNSON. "Why, yes, Sir. Here is a man who has passed through life without experience: yet I would rather have him with me than a more sensible man who will not talk readily. This man is always willing to say what he has to say." Yet Dr. Johnson had himself by no means that willingness which he praised so much, and I think so justly; for who has not felt the painful effect of the dreary void, when there is a total silence in a company, for any length of time; or, which is as bad, or perhaps worse, when the conversation is with difficulty kept up by a perpetual effort?

Johnson once observed to me, "Tom Tyers described me the best: 'Sir (said he), you are like a ghost: you never speak till you are spoken to.'"

BAD MANAGEMENT (1778)

ON MONDAY, April 20, I found him at home in the morning. We talked of a gentleman who we apprehended was gradually involving his circumstances by bad management. JOHNSON. "Wasting a fortune is evaporation by a thousand imperceptible means. If it were a stream, they'd stop it. You must speak to him. It is really miserable. Were he a gamester, it could be said he had hopes of winning. Were he a bankrupt in trade, he might have grown rich; but he has neither spirit to spend nor resolution to spare. He does not spend fast enough to have pleasure from it. He has the crime of prodigality, and the wretchedness of parsimony. If a man is killed in a duel, he is killed as many a one has been killed; but it is a sad thing for a man to lie down and die; to bleed to death, because he has not fortitude enough to sear the wound, or even to stitch it up." I cannot but pause a moment to admire the fecundity of fancy, and choice of language, which in this instance, and, indeed, on almost all occasions, he displayed. It was well observed by Dr. Percy, now Bishop of Dromore, "The conversation of Johnson is strong and clear, and may be compared to an antique statue, where every vein and muscle is distinct and bold. Ordinary conversation resembles an inferior cast."

THE FIRST WHIG (1778)

BOSWELL. "I drank chocolate, Sir, this morning with Mr. Eld; and, to my no small surprise, found him to be a *Staffordshire Whig*, a being which I did not believe had existed." JOHNSON. "Sir, there are rascals in all

[1]*Night Thoughts*, IV, 109.

countries." BOSWELL. "Eld said, a Tory was a creature generated between a non-juring parson and one's grandmother." JOHNSON. "And I have always said, the first Whig was the Devil." BOSWELL. "He certainly was, Sir. The Devil was impatient of subordination; he was the first who resisted power:—

Better to reign in Hell, than serve in Heaven."[1]

KINDNESS (1783)

JOHNSON'S love of little children, which he discovered upon all occasions, calling them "pretty dears," and giving them sweetmeats, was an undoubted proof of the real humanity and gentleness of his disposition.

His uncommon kindness to his servants, and serious concern, not only for their comfort in this world, but their happiness in the next, was another unquestionable evidence of what all, who were intimately acquainted with him, knew to be true.

Nor would it be just, under this head, to omit the fondness which he showed for animals which he had taken under his protection. I never shall forget the indulgence with which he treated Hodge, his cat: for whom he himself used to go out and buy oysters, lest the servants having that trouble should take a dislike to the poor creature. I am, unluckily, one of those who have an antipathy to a cat, so that I am uneasy when in the room with one; and I own, I frequently suffered a good deal from the presence of this same Hodge. I recollect him one day scrambling up Dr. Johnson's breast, apparently with much satisfaction, while my friend smiling and half-whistling, rubbed down his back, and pulled him by the tail; and when I observed he was a fine cat, saying, "Why yes, Sir, but I have had cats whom I liked better than this"; and then as if perceiving Hodge to be out of countenance, adding, "but he is a very fine cat, a very fine cat indeed."

This reminds me of the ludicrous account which he gave Mr. Langton, of the despicable state of a young Gentleman of good family. "Sir, when I heard of him last, he was running about town shooting cats." And then in a sort of kindly reverie, he bethought himself of his own favorite cat, and said, "But Hodge shan't be shot; no, no, Hodge shall not be shot."

[1]*Paradise Lost*, I, 263.

CANT (1783)

BOSWELL. "I wish much to be in Parliament, Sir." JOHNSON. "Why, Sir, unless you come resolved to support any administration, you would be the worse for being in Parliament, because you would be obliged to live more expensively." BOSWELL. "Perhaps, Sir, I should be the less happy for being in Parliament. I never would sell my vote, and I should be vexed if things went wrong." JOHNSON. "That's cant, Sir. It would not vex you more in the House, than in the gallery: public affairs vex no man." BOSWELL. "Have not they vexed yourself a little, Sir? Have not you been vexed by all the turbulence of this reign, and by that absurd vote of the House of Commons, 'That the influence of the Crown has increased, is increasing, and ought to be diminished?'" JOHNSON. "Sir, I have never slept an hour less, nor eat an ounce less meat. I would have knocked the factious dogs on the head, to be sure; but I was not *vexed*." BOSWELL. "I declare, Sir, upon my honor, I did imagine I was vexed, and took a pride in it; but it *was*, perhaps, cant; for I own I neither ate less, nor slept less." JOHNSON. "My dear friend, clear your *mind* of cant. You may *talk* as other people do: you may say to a man, 'Sir, I am your most humble servant.' You are *not* his most humble servant. You may say, 'These are bad times; it is a melancholy thing to be reserved to such times.' You don't mind the times. You tell a man, 'I am sorry you had such bad weather the last day of your journey, and were so much wet.' You don't care six-pence whether he is wet or dry. You may *talk* in this manner; it is a mode of talking in Society: but don't *think* foolishly."

OLIVER GOLDSMITH (1728–1774)

Goldsmith's family was of English origin, but had long been settled in Ireland when he was born there on 10 November, 1728. Goldsmith's father was a clergyman and farmer, with a small income and a large family. Oliver has sketched his father's character in the narrative of the Man in Black in *The Citizen of the World*, and it is said that all members of the family were "equally generous, credulous, simple," and improvident. The greater part of Oliver's boyhood was passed in the village of Lissoy, where he was given some rather irregular instruction, and whence he proceeded in 1744 to Trinity College, Dublin. There he was entered as a poor scholar, or "sizar," a position humiliating to one of his sensitiveness of temper. He was also unfortunate in having a tutor who delighted in two subjects which Goldsmith detested—logic and mathematics—and who was apparently rather brutal besides. In addition, Goldsmith's awkwardness, ungainly appearance, and mental unreadiness—not to speak of his infractions of collegiate rules—all made against his academic success. He did, however, manage to obtain the degree of B. A. in 1749. His relatives wanted him to become a clergyman and he unwillingly undertook to prepare himself for ordination, but when he presented himself to Bishop Synge of Elphin he was rejected, because, according to tradition, he was wearing a pair of flaming scarlet breeches. A period of uncertain groping for a career followed, in which money was spent or lost which Goldsmith's relatives and now widowed mother could ill afford. Finally, early in 1753, Goldsmith reached Edinburgh to study medicine. There he attended some lectures, probably not working overmuch, and then went to Leyden to continue his studies. From Leyden he presently set out, "with one shirt in his pocket and a devout reliance on Providence," as Sir Walter Scott says, to travel through Europe on foot. By one means or another he succeeded in procuring subsistence as he walked through Flanders, France, Germany, Switzerland, and Italy, learning much which he afterwards put to literary use, and obtaining, it is said, a medical degree at either Louvain or Padua. Early in 1756 he was back again in England, living miserably in London, and trying with little or no success to earn a bare living by various occupations. By 1760 he had drifted into hackwriting for the booksellers, and this he continued until his death on 4 April, 1774. Goldsmith was the master of an easy, finished style—he touched no branch of literature that he did not adorn, wrote Dr. Johnson in the Latin epitaph inscribed on his monument in Westminster Abbey—and, despite his irregular habits, the booksellers found him a profitable servant. He compiled histories of Rome, Greece, and England, *A History of the Earth and Animated Nature*, and many another work which cannot here even be mentioned. Of the *Animated Nature* Dr. Johnson said: "He is now writing a Natural History, and will make it as interesting as a Persian tale." According to Lee Lewes, an actor, Goldsmith used to say that of all his compilations "his *Selections of English Poetry* showed more 'the art of profession.' Here he did nothing but mark the particular passages with a red lead pencil, and for this he got *two hundred pounds*—but then he used to add, 'a man shows his judgment in these selections, and he may be often twenty years of his life cultivating that judgment.'" It has been estimated that in the later years of his life Goldsmith's income from literary work may have been as high as £800 the year. He never learned, however, how to control his expenditures, and as his income rose so did his debts, with the result that he was never free from financial difficulties, and at the time of his death owed not less than £2000. "Was ever poet," asked Dr. Johnson, "so trusted before?"

Much of Goldsmith's writing was ephemeral and perished with his age, yet he contrived to give lasting interest to a surprising variety of work, and is still remembered as essayist (*The Citizen of the World*, 1760–1761), as poet (*The Traveler*, 1764; *The Deserted Village*, 1770; *Retaliation*, 1774), as novelist (*The Vicar of Wakefield*, 1766), and as playwright (*The Good-Natured Man*, 1768; *She Stoops to Conquer*, 1773). Probably he took greater care with his poems than with anything else, as we know that he wrote them very slowly and spent much time in revising them. *The Vicar of Wakefield*, on the other hand, he never revised, although it was not published until several years after it was written. It was, he explained, already paid for, so that there was no need to take further trouble with it. Yet, as Scott says, "we read *The Vicar of Wakefield* in youth and in age. We return to it again and again, and bless the memory of an author who contrives so well to reconcile us to human nature." Keen observation lay always behind Goldsmith's quiet satire, to give substance to this happy reconciliation; but it is his exquisite good humor which his readers remember best and longest. "Who," asked Thackeray, "of the millions whom he has amused, does not love him? To be the most beloved of English writers, what a title that is for a man!"

THE CITIZEN OF THE WORLD[1]

OR LETTERS FROM A CHINESE PHILOSOPHER, RESIDING IN LONDON, TO HIS FRIENDS IN THE EAST

LETTER XIII

FROM LIEN CHI ALTANGI TO FUM HOAM, FIRST PRESIDENT OF THE CEREMONIAL ACADEMY AT PEKIN, IN CHINA

AN ACCOUNT OF WESTMINSTER ABBEY

I AM just returned from Westminster Abbey, the place of sepulture for the philosophers, heroes, and kings of England. What a gloom do monumental inscriptions, and all the venerable remains of deceased merit inspire! Imagine a temple marked with the hand of antiquity, solemn as religious awe, adorned with all the magnificence of barbarous profusion, dim windows, fretted pillars, long colonnades, and dark ceilings. Think, then, what were my sensations at being introduced to such a scene. I stood in the midst of the temple, and threw my eyes round on the walls, filled with the statues, the inscriptions, and the monuments of the dead.

Alas! I said to myself, how does pride attend the puny child of dust even to the grave! Even humble as I am, I possess more consequence in the present scene than the greatest hero of them all: they have toiled for an hour to gain a transient immortality, and are at length retired to the grave, where they have no attendant but the worm, none to flatter but the epitaph.

As I was indulging such reflections, a gentleman dressed in black, perceiving me to be a stranger, came up, entered into conversation, and politely offered to be my instructor and guide through the temple. "If any monument," said he, "should particularly excite your curiosity, I shall endeavor to satisfy your demands." I accepted, with thanks, the gentleman's offer, adding, that "I was come to observe the policy, the wisdom, and the justice of the English, in conferring rewards upon deceased merit. If adulation like this," continued I, "be properly conducted, as it can no ways injure those who are flattered, so it may be a glorious incentive to those who are now capable of enjoying it. It is the duty of every good government to turn this monumental pride to its own advantage; to become strong in the aggregate from the weakness of the individual. If none but the truly great have a place in this awful repository, a temple like this will give the finest lessons of morality, and be a strong incentive to true ambition. I am told that none have a place here but characters of the most distinguished merit." The man in black seemed impatient at my observations, so I discontinued my remarks, and we walked on together to take a view of every particular monument in order as it lay.

As the eye is naturally caught by the finest objects, I could not avoid being particularly curious about one monument, which appeared more beautiful than the rest: "That," said I to my guide, "I take to be the tomb of some very great man. By the peculiar excellence of the workmanship, and the magnificence of the design, this must be a trophy raised to the memory of some king who has saved his country from ruin, or lawgiver who has reduced his fellow-citizens from anarchy into just subjection."—"It is not requisite," replied my companion, smiling, "to have such qualifications in order to have a very fine monument here: more humble abilities will suffice."—"What, I suppose, then, the gaining two or three battles, or the taking half a score towns, is thought a sufficient qualification?"—"Gaining battles, or taking towns," replied the man in black, "may be of service; but a gentleman may have a very fine monument here without ever seeing a battle or a siege."—"This, then, is the monument of some poet, I presume—of one whose wit has gained him immortality?"—"No, Sir," replied my guide, "the gentleman who lies here never made verses; and as for wit, he despised it in others, because he had none himself."—"Pray tell me, then, in a word," said I, peevishly, "what is the great man who lies here particularly remarkable for?"—"Remarkable, Sir?" said my companion; "why, Sir, the gentleman that lies here is remarkable, very remarkable—

[1]These essays first appeared in a newspaper, *The Public Ledger*, in 1760–1761, and were then collected and published (with some changes and additions) in 1762. Goldsmith's device of writing over the name of an imaginary Asiatic was not of his own invention. He had before him the example of Montesquieu, of Voltaire, and of other French writers, and also, closer at hand, of Horace Walpole's very popular *Letter from Xo Ho, a Chinese Philosopher at London, to his Friend Lien-Chi, at Peking* (1757).

for a tomb in Westminster Abbey."—"But, head of my Ancestors! how has he got here? I fancy he could never bribe the guardians of the temple to give him a place: should he not be ashamed to be seen among company where even moderate merit would look like infamy?" —"I suppose," replied the man in black, "the gentleman was rich, and his friends, as is usual in such a case, told him he was great. He readily believed them; the guardians of the temple, as they got by the self-delusion, were ready to believe him too; so he paid his money for a fine monument; and the workman, as you see, has made him one of the most beautiful. Think not, however, that this gentleman is singular in his desire of being buried among the great; there are several others in the temple, who, hated and shunned by the great while alive, have come here, fully resolved to keep them company now they are dead."

As we walked along to a particular part of the temple, "There," says the gentleman, pointing with his finger, "that is the Poet's Corner; there you see the monuments of Shakespeare, and Milton, and Prior, and Drayton."—"Drayton!" I replied; "I never heard of him before; but I have been told of one Pope—is he there?"—"It is time enough," replied my guide, "these hundred years; he is not long dead; people have not done hating him yet."—"Strange," cried I; "can any be found to hate a man whose life was wholly spent in entertaining and instructing his fellow-creatures?"—"Yes," says my guide, "they hate him for that very reason. There are a set of men called answerers of books, who take upon them to watch the republic of letters, and distribute reputation by the sheet; they somewhat resemble the eunuchs in a seraglio, who are incapable of giving pleasure themselves, and hinder those that would. These answerers have no other employment but to cry out Dunce and Scribbler; to praise the dead, and revile the living; to grant a man of confessed abilities some small share of merit; to applaud twenty blockheads in order to gain the reputation of candor; and to revile the moral character of the man whose writings they cannot injure. Such wretches are kept in pay by some mercenary bookseller, or, more frequently, the bookseller himself takes this dirty work off their hands, as all that is required is to be very abusive and very dull. Every poet of any genius is sure to find such enemies; he feels, though he seems to despise their malice; they make him miserable here, and in the pursuit of empty fame, at last he gains solid anxiety."

"Has this been the case with every poet I see here?" cried I. "Yes, with every mother's son of them," replied he, "except he happened to be born a mandarin. If he has much money, he may buy reputation from your book-answerers, as well as a monument from the guardians of the temple."

"But are there not some men of distinguished taste, as in China, who are willing to patronize men of merit, and soften the rancor of malevolent dullness?"

"I own there are many," replied the man in black; "but, alas! Sir, the book-answerers crowd about them, and call themselves the writers of books; and the patron is too indolent to distinguish: thus poets are kept at a distance, while their enemies eat up all their rewards at the mandarin's table."

Leaving this part of the temple, we made up to an iron gate, through which my companion told me we were to pass, in order to see the monuments of the kings. Accordingly, I marched up without further ceremony, and was going to enter, when a person, who held the gate in his hand, told me I must pay first. I was surprised at such a demand; and asked the man, whether the people of England kept a *show*—whether the paltry sum he demanded was not a national reproach?—whether it was not more to the honor of the country to let their magnificence, or their antiquities, be openly seen, than thus meanly to tax a curiosity which tended to their own honor? "As for your questions," replied the gate-keeper, "to be sure they may be very right, because I don't understand them; but, as for that there threepence, I farm it from one—who rents it from another—who hires it from a third—who leases it from the guardians of the temple, —and we all must live." I expected, upon paying here, to see something extraordinary, since what I had seen for nothing filled me with so much surprise: but in this I was disappointed; there was little more within than black coffins, rusty armor, tattered standards, and some few slovenly figures in wax. I was sorry I had paid, but I comforted myself by considering it would be my last payment. A person attended us, who, without once blushing, told a hundred lies: he talked of a lady who died by pricking her finger;[1] of a king with a golden head,[2] and twenty such pieces of absurdity. "Look ye there, gentlemen," says he, pointing to an old oak chair, "there's a curiosity for ye; in that chair the kings of England were crowned: you see also a stone underneath, and that stone is Jacob's pillow." I could see no curiosity either in the oak chair or the stone: could I, indeed, behold one of the old kings of England seated in this, or Jacob's head laid upon the other, there might be something curious in the sight; but in the present case, there was no more reason for my surprise, than if I should pick a stone from their streets, and call it a curiosity, merely because one of the kings happened to tread upon it as he passed in a procession.

From hence our conductor led us through several dark walks and winding ways, uttering lies, talking to himself, and flourishing a wand which he held in his hand. He reminded me of the black magicians of Kobi.[3] After we had been almost fatigued with a variety of objects, he at last desired me to consider attentively a certain suit of armor, which seemed to show nothing remarkable, "This armor," said he, "belonged to General Monk."—"Very surprising that a general should wear armor!"—"And pray," added he, "observe this cap; this is General Monk's cap."—"Very strange, indeed, very strange, that a general should have a cap also! Pray, friend, what might this cap have cost originally?"—"That, Sir," says he, "I don't know; but this cap is all the wages I have for my trouble."—"A very small recompense, truly," said I. "Not so very small," replied he, "for every gentleman puts some money into it, and I spend the money." —"What—more money! still more money!" —"Every gentleman gives something, Sir."—"I'll give thee nothing," returned I; "the guardians of the temple should pay you your wages, friend, and not permit you to squeeze thus from every spectator. When we pay our money at the door to see a show, we never give more as we are going out. Sure, the guardians of the temple can never think they get enough. Show me the gate; if I stay longer I may probably meet with more of those ecclesiastical beggars."

Thus leaving the temple precipitately, I returned to my lodgings, in order to ruminate over what was great, and to despise what was mean, in the occurrences of the day.

---

[1]Lady Elizabeth Russell. Her tomb is in the chapel of St. Edmund.

[2]The head (of the figure of Henry V, chapel of St. Edward) was of silver, but it had disappeared before the close of the 16th century.

[3]Or Gobi, the desert of central Asia.

LETTER XXI

TO THE SAME

THE CHINESE GOES TO SEE A PLAY

The English are as fond of seeing plays acted as the Chinese; but there is a vast difference in the manner of conducting them. We play our pieces in the open air, the English theirs under cover; we act by daylight, they by the blaze of torches. One of our plays continues eight or ten days successively; an English piece seldom takes up above four hours in the representation.

My companion in black, with whom I am now beginning to contract an intimacy, introduced me a few nights ago to the playhouse, where we placed ourselves conveniently at the foot of the stage. As the curtain was not drawn before my arrival, I had an opportunity of observing the behavior of the spectators, and indulging those reflections which novelty generally inspires.

The rich in general were placed in the lowest seats, and the poor rose above them in degrees proportioned to their poverty. The order of precedence seemed here inverted; those who were undermost all the day, now enjoyed a temporary eminence, and became masters of the ceremonies. It was they who called for the music, indulging every noisy freedom, and testifying all the insolence of beggary in exaltation.

They who held the middle region seemed not so riotous as those above them, nor yet so tame as those below: to judge by their looks, many of them seemed strangers there as well as myself. They were chiefly employed, during this period of expectation, in eating oranges, reading the story of the play, or making assignations.

Those who sat in the lowest rows, which are called the pit, seemed to consider themselves as judges of the merit of the poet and the performers; they were assembled partly to be amused, and partly to show their taste; appearing to labor under that restraint which an affectation of superior discernment generally produces. My companion, however, informed me, that not one in a hundred of them knew even the first principles of criticism; that they assumed the right of being censors because there was none to contradict their pretensions; and that every man who now called himself a connoisseur, became such to all intents and purposes.

Those who sat in the boxes appeared in the most unhappy situation of all. The rest of the audience came merely for their own amusement; these, rather to furnish out a part of the entertainment themselves. I could not avoid considering them as acting parts in dumb show—not a courtesy or nod, that was not all the result of art; not a look nor a smile that was not designed for murder. Gentlemen and ladies ogled each other through spectacles; for, my companion observed, that blindness was of late become fashionable; all affected indifference and ease, while their hearts at the same time burned for conquest. Upon the whole, the lights, the music, the ladies in their gayest dresses, the men with cheerfulness and expectation in their looks, all conspired to make a most agreeable picture, and to fill a heart that sympathizes at human happiness with inexpressible serenity.

The expected time for the play to begin at last arrived; the curtain was drawn, and the actors came on. A woman, who personated a queen, came in curtseying to the audience, who clapped their hands upon her appearance. Clapping of hands is, it seems, the manner of applauding in England; the manner is absurd, but every country, you know, has its peculiar absurdities. I was equally surprised, however, at the submission of the actress, who should have considered herself as a queen, as at the little discernment of the audience who gave her such marks of applause before she attempted to deserve them. Preliminaries between her and the audience being thus adjusted, the dialogue was supported between her and a most hopeful youth, who acted the part of her confidant. They both appeared in extreme distress, for it seems the queen had lost a child some fifteen years before, and still kept its dear resemblance next her heart, while her kind companion bore a part in her sorrows.

Her lamentations grew loud; comfort is offered, but she detests the very sound: she bids them preach comfort to the winds. Upon this her husband comes in, who, seeing the queen so much afflicted, can himself hardly refrain from tears, or avoid partaking in the soft distress. After thus grieving through three scenes, the curtain dropped for the first act.

"Truly," said I to my companion, "these kings and queens are very much disturbed at no very great misfortune: certain I am, were people of humbler stations to act in this manner, they would be thought divested of common sense." I had scarcely finished this observation, when the curtain rose, and the king came on in a violent passion. His wife had, it seems, refused his proffered tenderness, had spurned his royal embrace, and he seemed resolved not to survive her fierce disdain. After he had thus fretted, and the queen had fretted through the second act, the curtain was let down once more.

"Now," says my companion, "you perceive the king to be a man of spirit; he feels at every pore: one of your phlegmatic sons of clay would have given the queen her own way, and let her come to herself by degrees; but the king is for immediate tenderness, or instant death: death and tenderness are leading passions of every modern buskined hero; this moment they embrace, and the next stab, mixing daggers and kisses in every period."

I was going to second his remarks, when my attention was engrossed by a new object; a man came in balancing a straw upon his nose, and the audience were clapping their hands in all the raptures of applause. "To what purpose," cried I, "does this unmeaning figure make his appearance? is he a part of the plot?"—"Unmeaning do you call him?" replied my friend in black; "this is one of the most important characters of the whole play; nothing pleases the people more than seeing a straw balanced: there is a good deal of meaning in the straw: there is something suited to every apprehension in the sight; and a fellow possessed of talents like these is sure of making his fortune."

The third act now began with an actor who came to inform us that he was the villain of the play, and intended to show strange things before all was over. He was joined by another who seemed as much disposed for mischief as he: their intrigues continued through this whole division. "If that be a villain," said I, "he must be a very stupid one to tell his secrets without being asked; such soliloquies of late are never admitted in China."

The noise of clapping interrupted me once more; a child of six years old was learning to dance on the stage, which gave the ladies and mandarins infinite satisfaction. "I am sorry," said I, "to see the pretty creature so early learning so very bad a trade; dancing being, I presume, as contemptible here as in China."—"Quite the reverse," interrupted my companion; "dancing is a very reputable and genteel employment here; men have a greater chance for encouragement from the merit of their heels than their heads. One who jumps up and flourishes his toes three times before he comes to the ground, may have three hundred a year; he who flourishes them four times, gets four hundred; but he who arrives at five is inestimable, and may demand what salary he thinks proper. The female dancers, too, are valued for this sort of jumping and crossing; and it is a cant word amongst them, that she deserves most who shows highest. But the fourth act is begun; let us be attentive."

In the fourth act the queen finds her long lost child, now grown up into a youth of smart parts and great qualifications; wherefore she wisely considers that the crown will fit his head better than that of her husband, whom she knows to be a driveler. The king discovers her design, and here comes on the deep distress: he loves the queen, and he loves the kingdom; he resolves, therefore, in order to possess both, that her son must die. The queen exclaims at his barbarity, is frantic with rage, and at length, overcome with sorrow, falls into a fit; upon which the curtain drops, and the act is concluded.

"Observe the art of the poet," cries my companion. "When the queen can say no more, she falls into a fit. While thus her eyes are shut, while she is supported in the arms of Abigail, what horrors do we not fancy! We feel it in every nerve: take my word for it, that fits are the true *aposiopesis*[1] of modern tragedy."

The fifth act began, and a busy piece it was. Scenes shifting, trumpets sounding, mobs hallooing, carpets spreading, guards bustling from one door to another; gods, demons, daggers, racks, and ratsbane. But whether the king was killed, or the queen was drowned, or the son was poisoned, I have absolutely forgotten.

When the play was over, I could not avoid observing that the persons of the drama appeared in as much distress in the first act as the last. "How is it possible," said I, "to sympathize with them through five long acts? Pity is but a short-lived passion. I hate to hear an actor mouthing trifles. Neither startings, strainings, nor attitudes, affect me, unless there be cause: after I have been once or twice deceived by those unmeaning alarms, my heart sleeps in peace, probably unaffected by the principal distress. There should be one great passion aimed at by the actor as well as the poet; all the rest should be subordinate, and only contribute to make that the greater; if the actor, therefore, exclaims upon every occasion, in the tones of despair, he attempts to move us too soon; he anticipates the blow, he ceases to affect, though he gains our applause."

I scarce perceived that the audience were almost all departed; wherefore, mixing with the crowd, my companion and I got into the street, where, essaying a hundred obstacles from coach-wheels and palanquin poles, like birds in their flight through the branches of a forest, after various turnings, we both at length got home in safety. Adieu.

LETTER XXXIII

TO THE SAME

THE MANNER OF WRITING AMONG THE CHINESE—THE EASTERN TALES OF MAGAZINES, *ETC.*, RIDICULED

I AM disgusted, O Fum Hoam, even to sickness disgusted. Is it possible to bear the presumption of those islanders, when they pretend to instruct me in the ceremonies of China! They lay it down as a maxim, that every person who comes from thence must express himself in metaphor, swear by Alla, rail against wine, and behave, and talk, and write, like a Turk or Persian. They make no distinction between our elegant manners, and the voluptuous barbarities of our Eastern

[1]Sudden breaking-off in the middle of a speech.

neighbors. Wherever I come, I raise either diffidence or astonishment: some fancy me no Chinese, because I am formed more like a man than a monster; and others wonder to find one born five thousand miles from England, endued with common sense. "Strange," say they, "that a man who has received his education at such a distance from London, should have common sense; to be born out of England, and yet have common sense! Impossible! He must be some Englishman in disguise; his very visage has nothing of the true exotic barbarity."

I yesterday received an invitation from a lady of distinction, who, it seems, had collected all her knowledge of Eastern manners from fictions every day propagated here, under the titles of Eastern Tales and Oriental Histories. She received me very politely, but seemed to wonder that I neglected bringing opium and a tobacco-box: when chairs were drawn for the rest of the company, I was assigned my place on a cushion on the floor. It was in vain that I protested the Chinese used chairs as in Europe; she understood decorums too well to entertain me with the ordinary civilities.

I had scarce been seated according to her directions, when the footman was ordered to pin a napkin under my chin: this I protested against, as being no way Chinese; however, the whole company, who, it seems, were a club of connoisseurs, gave it unanimously against me, and the napkin was pinned accordingly.

It was impossible to be angry with people, who seemed to err only from an excess of politeness, and I sat contented, expecting their importunities were now at an end; but as soon as ever dinner was served, the lady demanded, whether I was for a plate of bear's claws, or a slice of birds' nests. As these were dishes with which I was utterly unacquainted, I was desirous of eating only what I knew, and therefore begged to be helped from a piece of beef that lay on the side-table: my request at once disconcerted the whole company. A Chinese eat beef! that could never be: there was no local propriety in Chinese beef, whatever there might be in Chinese pheasant. "Sir," said my entertainer, "I think I have some reason to fancy myself a judge of these matters; in short, the Chinese never eat beef; so that I must be permitted to recommend the pilaw.[1] There was never better dressed at Pekin; the saffron and rice are well boiled, and the spices in perfection."

I had no sooner begun to eat what was laid before me, than I found the whole company as much astonished as before: it seems I made no use of my chop-sticks. A grave gentleman, whom I take to be an author, harangued very learnedly (as the company seemed to think) upon the use which was made of them in China. He entered into a long argument with himself about their first introduction, without once appealing to me, who might be supposed best capable of silencing the inquiry. As the gentleman therefore took my silence for a mark of his own superior sagacity, he was resolved to pursue the triumph: he talked of our cities, mountains, and animals, as familiarly as if he had been born in Quamsi, but as erroneously as if a native of the moon. He attempted to prove that I had nothing of the true Chinese cut in my visage; showed that my cheek-bones should have been higher, and my forehead broader. In short, he almost reasoned me out of my country, and effectually persuaded the rest of the company to be of his opinion.

I was going to expose his mistakes, when it was insisted, that I had nothing of the true Eastern manner in my delivery. "This gentleman's conversation," says one of the ladies, who was a great reader, "is like our own,—mere chit-chat and common sense: there is nothing like sense in the true Eastern style, where nothing more is required but sublimity. Oh! for a history of Aboulfaouris, the grand voyager, of genii, magicians, rocks, bags of bullets, giants, and enchanters, where all is great, obscure, magnificent, and unintelligible!"—"I have written many a sheet of Eastern tale myself," interrupts the author, "and I defy the severest critic to say but that I have stuck close to the true manner. I have compared a lady's chin to the snow upon the mountains of Bomek; a soldier's sword to the clouds that obscure the face of heaven. If riches are mentioned, I compare them to the flocks that graze the verdant Tefflis; if poverty, to the mists that veil the brow of Mount Baku. I have used *thee* and *thou* upon all occasions; I have described fallen stars, and splitting mountains, not forgetting the

[1]An oriental dish of rice with meat, spices, *etc.*

little houries, who make a pretty figure in every description. But you shall hear how I generally begin—'Eben-ben-bolo, who was the son of Ban, was born on the foggy summits of Benderabassi. His beard was whiter than the feathers which veil the breast of the penguin; his eyes were like the eyes of doves when washed by the dews of the morning; his hair, which hung like the willow weeping over the glassy stream, was so beautiful that it seemed to reflect its own brightness; and his feet were as the feet of a wild deer which fleeth to the tops of the mountains.' There, there is the true Eastern taste for you; every advance made towards sense, is only a deviation from sound. Eastern tales should always be sonorous, lofty, musical, and unmeaning."

I could not avoid smiling, to hear a native of England attempt to instruct me in the true Eastern idiom; and after he looked round some time for applause, I presumed to ask him, whether he had ever traveled into the East? to which he replied in the negative. I demanded whether he understood Chinese, or Arabic? to which also he answered as before. "Then how, Sir," said I, "can you pretend to determine upon the Eastern style, who are entirely unacquainted with the Eastern writings? Take, Sir, the word of one who is professedly a Chinese, and who is actually acquainted with the Arabian writers, that what is palmed upon you daily for an imitation of Eastern writing, no way resembles their manner, either in sentiment or diction. In the East, similes are seldom used, and metaphors almost wholly unknown; but in China particularly, the very reverse of what you allude to takes place: a cool phlegmatic method of writing prevails there. The writers of that country, ever more assiduous to instruct than to please, address rather the judgment than the fancy. Unlike many authors of Europe who have no consideration of the reader's time, they generally leave more to be understood than they express.

"Besides, Sir, you must not expect from an inhabitant of China the same ignorance, the same unlettered simplicity, that you find in a Turk, Persian, or native of Peru. The Chinese are versed in the sciences as well as you, and are masters of several arts unknown to the people of Europe. Many of them are instructed not only in their own national learning, but are perfectly well acquainted with the languages and learning of the West. If my word in such a case is not to be taken, consult your own travelers on this head, who affirm, that the scholars of Pekin and Siam sustain theological theses in Latin. 'The college of Masprend, which is but a league from Siam,' says one of your travelers, 'came in a body to salute our ambassador. Nothing gave me more sincere pleasure, than to behold a number of priests, venerable both from age and modesty, followed by a number of youths of all nations, Chinese, Japanese, Tonquinese, of Cochin China, Pegu, and Siam, all willing to pay their respects in the most polite manner imaginable. A Cochin Chinese made an excellent Latin oration upon this occasion; he was succeeded and even outdone by a student of Tonquin, who was as well skilled in the Western learning as any scholar of Paris.' Now, Sir, if youths who never stirred from home are so perfectly skilled in your laws and learning, surely more must be expected from one like me, who have traveled so many thousand miles, who have conversed familiarly for several years with the English factors established at Canton, and the missionaries sent us from every part of Europe. The unaffected of every country nearly resemble each other, and a page of our Confucius and of your Tillotson have scarce any material difference. Paltry affectation, strained allusions, and disgusting finery, are easily attained by those who choose to wear them: and they are but too frequently the badges of ignorance or of stupidity, whenever it would endeavor to please."

I was proceeding in my discourse, when, looking round, I perceived the company no way attentive to what I attempted, with so much earnestness, to enforce. One lady was whispering her that sat next, another was studying the merits of a fan, a third began to yawn, and the author himself fell fast asleep. I thought it, therefore, high time to make a retreat, nor did the company seem to show any regret at my preparations for departure: even the lady who had invited me, with the most mortifying insensibility, saw me seize my hat, and rise from my cushion; nor was I invited to repeat my visit, because it was found that I aimed at appearing rather a reasonable creature, than an outlandish idiot. Adieu.

LETTER LI

TO THE SAME

A BOOKSELLER'S VISIT TO THE CHINESE

As I was yesterday seated at breakfast over a pensive dish of tea, my meditations were interrupted by my old friend and companion, who introduced a stranger, dressed pretty much like himself. The gentleman made several apologies for his visit, begged of me to impute his intrusion to the sincerity of his respect, and the warmth of his curiosity.

As I am very suspicious of my company when I find them very civil without any apparent reason, I answered the stranger's caresses at first with reserve; which my friend perceiving, instantly let me into my visitant's trade and character, asking Mr. Fudge, whether he had lately published anything new. I now conjectured that my guest was no other than a bookseller, and his answer confirmed my suspicions.

"Excuse me, Sir," says he, "it is not the season; books have their time as well as cucumbers. I would no more bring out a new work in summer than I would sell pork in the dog days. Nothing in my way goes off in summer, except very light goods indeed. A review, a magazine, or a Sessions paper,[1] may amuse a summer reader; but all our stock of value we reserve for a spring and winter trade." "I must confess, Sir," says I, "a curiosity to know what you call a valuable stock, which can only bear a winter perusal." —"Sir," replied the bookseller, "it is not my way to cry up my own goods; but, without exaggeration, I will venture to show with any of the trade: my books at least have the peculiar advantage of being always new; and it is my way to clear off my old to the trunkmakers every season. I have ten new title-pages now about me, which only want books to be added to make them the finest things in nature. Others may pretend to direct the vulgar; but that is not my way; I always let the vulgar direct me; wherever popular clamor arises, I always echo the million. For instance, should the people in general say that such a man is a rogue, I instantly give orders to set him down in print a villain; thus every man buys the book, not to learn new sentiments, but to have the pleasure of seeing his own reflected."—"But, Sir," interrupted I, "you speak as if you yourself wrote the books you publish; may I be so bold as to ask a sight of some of those intended publications which are shortly to surprise the world?"—"As to that, Sir," replied the talkative bookseller, "I only draw out the plans myself; and though I am very cautious of communicating them to any, yet, as in the end I have a favor to ask, you shall see a few of them. Here, Sir, here they are; diamonds of the first water, I assure you. *Imprimis*, a Translation of several Medical precepts for the use of such physicians as do not understand Latin. *Item*, the Young Clergyman's art of placing patches regularly, with a Dissertation on the different manners of smiling without distorting the face. *Item*, the whole Art of Love made perfectly easy, by a broker of 'Change Alley. *Item*, the proper manner of Cutting blacklead pencils, and making crayons, by the Right Hon. the Earl of ——. *Item*, the Muster-master-general, or the review of reviews."—"Sir," cried I, interrupting him, "my curiosity, with regard to title-pages, is satisfied; I should be glad to see some longer manuscript, a history, or an epic poem."—"Bless me!" cries the man of industry, "now you speak of an epic poem, you shall see an excellent farce. Here it is; dip into it where you will, it will be found replete with true modern humor. Strokes, Sir; it is filled with strokes of wit and satire in every line."—"Do you call these dashes of the pen strokes," replied I, "for I must confess I can see no other?"—"And pray, Sir," returned he, "what do you call them? Do you see anything good now-a-days, that is not filled with strokes—and dashes?—Sir, a well placed dash makes half the wit of our writers of modern humor. I bought a piece last season that had no other merit upon earth than nine hundred and ninety-five breaks, seventy-two ha-ha's, three good things, and a garter. And yet it played off, and bounced, and cracked, and made more sport than a firework."—"I fancy, then, Sir, you were a considerable gainer?"—"It must be owned the piece did pay; but, upon the whole, I cannot much boast of last winter's success; I gained by two murders; but then I lost by an ill-timed charity sermon. I was a considerable sufferer by my Direct Road to

[1]List of cases put down for trial.

an Estate, but the Infernal Guide brought me up again. Ah, Sir, that was a piece touched off by the hand of a master; filled with good things from one end to the other. The author had nothing but the jest in view; no dull moral lurking beneath, nor ill-natured satire to sour the reader's good-humor; he wisely considered that moral and humor at the same time were quite overdoing the business."—"To what purpose was the book then published?" cried I.—"Sir, the book was published in order to be sold; and no book sold better, except the criticisms upon it, which came out soon after: of all kinds of writing, that goes off best at present; and I generally fasten a criticism upon every selling book that is published.

"I once had an author who never left the least opening for the critics: close was the word; always very right and very dull; ever on the safe side of an argument; yet, with all his qualifications, incapable of coming into favor. I soon perceived that his bent was for criticism; and, as he was good for nothing else, supplied him with pens and paper, and planted him, at the beginning of every month, as a censor on the works of others. In short, I found him a treasure; no merit could escape him; but what is most remarkable of all, he ever wrote best and bitterest when drunk." "But are there not some works," interrupted I, "that, from the very manner of their composition, must be exempt from criticism; particularly such as profess to disregard its laws?" —"There is no work whatsoever but he can criticize," replied the bookseller; "even though you wrote in Chinese, he would have a pluck at you. Suppose you should take it into your head to publish a book, let it be a volume of Chinese letters, for instance; write how you will, he shall show the world you could have written better. Should you, with the most local exactness, stick to the manners and customs of the country from whence you come; should you confine yourself to the narrow limits of Eastern knowledge, and be perfectly simple, and perfectly natural, he has then the strongest reason to exclaim. He may, with a sneer, send you back to China for readers. He may observe that after the first or second letter, the iteration of the same simplicity is insupportably tedious. But the worst of all is, the public, in such a case, will anticipate his censures, and leave you, with all your uninstructive simplicity, to be mauled at discretion."

"Yes," cried I, "but in order to avoid his indignation, and, what I should fear more, that of the public, I would, in such a case, write with all the knowledge I was master of. As I am not possessed of much learning, at least I would not suppress what little I had; nor would I appear more stupid than nature made me."—"Here, then," cries the bookseller, "we should have you entirely in our power; unnatural, un-Eastern, quite out of character, erroneously sensible, would be the whole cry. Sir, we should then hunt you down like a rat."—"Head of my father!" said I, "sure there are but two ways; the door must either be shut or it must be open. I must either be natural or unnatural."—"Be what you will, we shall criticize you," returned the bookseller, "and prove you a dunce in spite of your teeth. But, Sir, it is time that I should come to business. I have just now in the press a history of China; and if you will but put your name to it as the author, I shall repay the obligation with gratitude."—"What, Sir!" replied I, "put my name to a work which I have not written? Never, while I retain a proper respect for the public and myself." The bluntness of my reply quite abated the ardor of the bookseller's conversation; and, after about half an hour's disagreeable reserve, he, with some ceremony, took his leave, and withdrew. Adieu.

LETTER LXVII

TO THE SAME

THE FOLLY OF ATTEMPTING TO LEARN WISDOM BY BEING RECLUSE

Books, my son, while they teach us to respect the interests of others, often make us unmindful of our own; while they instruct the youthful reader to grasp at social happiness, he grows miserable in detail, and, attentive to universal harmony, often forgets that he himself has a part to sustain in the concert. I dislike, therefore, the philosopher, who describes the inconveniences of life in such pleasing colors that the pupil grows enamored of distress, longs to try the charms of poverty, meets it without dread, nor fears its inconveniences till he severely feels them.

A youth who has thus spent his life among

books, new to the world, and unacquainted with man but by philosophic information, may be considered as a being whose mind is filled with the vulgar errors of the wise; utterly unqualified for a journey through life, yet confident of his own skill in the direction, he sets out with confidence, blunders on with vanity, and finds himself at last undone.

He first has learned from books, and then lays it down as a maxim, that all mankind are virtuous or vicious in excess; and he has been long taught to detest vice, and love virtue: warm, therefore in attachments, and steadfast in enmity, he treats every creature as a friend or foe; expects from those he loves unerring integrity, and consigns his enemies to the reproach of wanting every virtue. On this principle he proceeds; and here begin his disappointments. Upon a closer inspection of human nature he perceives that he should have moderated his friendship, and softened his severity; for he often finds the excellencies of one part of mankind clouded with vice, and the faults of the other brightened with virtue; he finds no character so sanctified that has not its failings, none so infamous but has somewhat to attract our esteem; he beholds impiety in lawn,[1] and fidelity in fetters.

He now, therefore, but too late, perceives that his regards should have been more cool, and his hatred less violent; that the truly wise seldom court romantic friendships with the good, and avoid, if possible, the resentment even of the wicked: every moment gives him fresh instances that the bonds of friendship are broken if drawn too closely, and that those whom he has treated with disrespect more than retaliate the injury; at length, therefore, he is obliged to confess that he has declared war upon the vicious half of mankind, without being able to form an alliance among the virtuous to espouse his quarrel.

Our book-taught philosopher, however, is now too far advanced to recede; and though poverty be the just consequence of the many enemies his conduct has created, yet he is resolved to meet it without shrinking. Philosophers have described poverty in most charming colors, and even his vanity is touched in thinking that he shall show the world, in himself, one more example of patience, fortitude, and resignation. "Come, then, O Poverty! for what is there in thee dreadful to the WISE? Temperance, Health, and Frugality walk in thy train; Cheerfulness and Liberty are ever thy companions. Shall any be ashamed of thee, of whom Cincinnatus was not ashamed? The running brook, the herbs of the field, can amply satisfy nature; man wants but little, nor that little long.[2] Come, then, O Poverty, while kings stand by, and gaze with admiration at the true philosopher's resignation!"

The goddess appears; for Poverty ever comes at the call; but, alas! he finds her by no means the charming figure books and his warm imagination had painted. As when an Eastern bride, whom her friends and relations had long described as a model of perfection, pays her first visit, the longing bridegroom lifts the veil to see a face he had never seen before; but instead of a countenance blazing with beauty like the sun, he beholds deformity shooting icicles to his heart: such appears Poverty to her new entertainer; all the fabric of enthusiasm is at once demolished, and a thousand miseries rise up on its ruins, while Contempt, with pointing finger, is foremost in the hideous procession.

The poor man now finds that he can get no kings to look at him while he is eating; he finds that in proportion as he grows poor, the world turns its back upon him, and gives him leave to act the philosopher in all the majesty of solitude. It might be agreeable enough to play the philosopher while we are conscious that mankind are spectators; but what signifies wearing the mask of sturdy contentment, and mounting the stage of restraint, when not one creature will assist at the exhibition! Thus is he forsaken of men, while his fortitude wants the satisfaction even of self-applause: for either he does not feel his present calamities, and that is natural insensibility; or he disguises his feelings, and that is dissimulation.

Spleen now begins to take up the man: not distinguishing in his resentments, he regards all mankind with detestation, and commencing man-hater, seeks solitude to be at liberty to rail.

It has been said, that he who retires to solitude is either a beast or an angel.[3] The censure is too severe, and the praise unmerited;

[1] The sleeves of a bishop are made of lawn.

[2] Lifted from Young's *Night Thoughts*, IV, 9.

[3] See Aristotle, *Politics*, I, ii (1253a, 2–4).

the discontented being, who retires from society, is generally some good-natured man, who has begun life without experience, and knew not how to gain it in his intercourse with mankind. Adieu.

LETTER LXXXVI

TO THE SAME

THE RACES OF NEWMARKET RIDICULED. DESCRIPTION OF A CART RACE

Of all the places of amusement where gentlemen and ladies are entertained, I have not been yet to visit Newmarket. This, I am told, is a large field, where, upon certain occasions, three or four horses are brought together, then set a-running, and that horse which runs fastest wins the wager.

This is reckoned a very polite and fashionable amusement here, much more followed by the nobility than partridge fighting at Java, or paper kites in Madagascar. Several of the great here, I am told, understand as much of farriery as their grooms; and a horse, with any share of merit, can never want a patron among the nobility.

We have a description of this entertainment almost every day in some of the gazettes, as for instance: "On such a day the Give and Take Plate was run for between his Grace's Crab, his Lordship's Periwinkle, and 'Squire Smackem's Slamerkin. All rode their own horses. There was the greatest concourse of nobility that has been known here for several seasons. The odds were in favor of Crab in the beginning; but Slamerkin, after the first heat, seemed to have the match hollow: however, it was soon seen that Periwinkle improved in wind, which at last turned out accordingly; Crab was run to a standstill, Slamerkin was knocked up, and Periwinkle was brought in with universal applause." Thus, you see, Periwinkle received universal applause, and, no doubt, his lordship came in for some share of that praise which was so liberally bestowed upon Periwinkle. Sun of China! how glorious must the senator appear in his cap and leather breeches, his whip crossed in his mouth, and thus coming to the goal, amongst the shouts of grooms, jockeys, pimps, stable-bred dukes, and degraded generals!

From the description of this princely amusement, now transcribed, and from the great veneration I have for the characters of its principal promoters, I make no doubt but I shall look upon a horse-race with becoming reverence, predisposed as I am by a similar amusement, of which I have lately been a spectator; for just now I happened to have an opportunity of being present at a cart race.

Whether this contention between three carts of different parishes was promoted by a subscription among the nobility, or whether the grand jury, in council assembled, had gloriously combined to encourage plaustral[1] merit, I cannot take upon me to determine; but certain it is, the whole was conducted with the utmost regularity and decorum, and the company, which made a brilliant appearance, were universally of opinion, that the sport was high, the running fine, and the riders influenced by no bribe.

It was run on the road from London, to a village called Brentford, between a turnip-cart, a dust-cart, and a dung-cart; each of the owners condescending to mount, and be his own driver. The odds, at starting, were Dust against Dung, five to four; but, after half a mile's going, the knowing ones found themselves all on the wrong side, and it was Turnip against the field, brass to silver.

Soon, however, the contest became more doubtful; Turnip indeed kept the way, but it was perceived that Dung had better bottom. The road re-echoed with the shouts of the spectators—"Dung against Turnip! Turnip against Dung!" was now the universal cry; neck and neck; one rode lighter, but the other had more judgment. I could not but particularly observe the ardor with which the fair sex espoused the cause of the different riders on this occasion; one was charmed with the unwashed beauties of Dung; another was captivated with the patibulary[2] aspect of Turnip; while, in the meantime, unfortunate gloomy Dust, who came whipping behind, was cheered by the encouragement of some, and pity of all.

The contention now continued for some time, without a possibility of determining to whom victory designed the prize. The winning post appeared in view, and he who drove

[1] Pertaining to a cart or wagon. (The word was apparently introduced into English by Goldsmith.)

[2] Gallows-like.

the turnip-cart assured himself of success; and successful he might have been, had his horse been as ambitious as he; but, upon approaching a turn from the road, which led homewards, the horse fairly stood still, and refused to move a foot farther. The dung-cart had scarce time to enjoy this temporary triumph, when it was pitched headlong into a ditch by the way-side, and the rider left to wallow in congenial mud. Dust, in the meantime, soon came up, and not being far from the post, came in, amidst the shouts and acclamations of all the spectators, and greatly caressed by all the quality of Brentford. Fortune was kind only to one, who ought to have been favorable to all; each had peculiar merit, each labored hard to earn the prize, and each richly deserved the cart he drove.

I do not know whether this description may not have anticipated that which I intended giving of Newmarket. I am told, there is little else to be seen even there. There may be some minute differences in the dress of the spectators, but none at all in their understandings: the quality of Brentford are as remarkable for politeness and delicacy as the breeders of Newmarket. The quality of Brentford drive their own carts, and the honorable fraternity of Newmarket ride their own horses. In short, the matches in one place are as rational as those in the other; and it is more than probable that turnips, dust, and dung, are all that can be found to furnish out description in either.

Forgive me, my friend; but a person like me, bred up in a philosophic seclusion, is apt to regard perhaps with too much asperity, those occurrences which sink man below his station in nature, and diminish the intrinsic value of humanity. Adieu.

LETTER CVI

TO THE SAME

FUNERAL ELEGIES WRITTEN UPON THE GREAT RIDICULED. A SPECIMEN OF ONE

It was formerly the custom here, when men of distinction died, for their surviving acquaintance to throw each a slight present into the grave. Several things of little value were made use of for that purpose,—perfumes, relics, spices, bitter herbs, camomile, wormwood, and verses. This custom, however, is almost discontinued, and nothing but verses alone are now lavished on such occasions; an oblation which they suppose may be interred with the dead, without any injury to the living.

Upon the death of the great, therefore, the poets and undertakers are sure of employment. While one provides the long cloak, black staff, and mourning coach, the other produces the pastoral or elegy, the monody or apotheosis. The nobility need be under no apprehensions, but die as fast as they think proper; the poet and undertaker are ready to supply them; these can find metaphorical tears and family escutcheons at an hour's warning; and when the one has soberly laid the body in the grave, the other is ready to fix it figuratively among the stars.

There are several ways of being poetically sorrowful on such occasions. The bard is now some pensive youth of science, who sits deploring among the tombs; again, he is Thyrsis, complaining in a circle of harmless sheep. Now Britannia sits upon her own shore, and gives a loose to maternal tenderness; at another time, Parnassus, even the mountain Parnassus, gives way to sorrow, and is bathed in tears of distress.

But the most usual manner is this: Damon meets Menalcas, who has got a most gloomy countenance. The shepherd asks his friend, whence that look of distress? To which the other replies, that Pollio is no more. "If that be the case, then," cries Damon, "let us retire to yonder bower at some distance off, where the cypress and the jessamine add fragrance to the breeze; and let us weep alternately for Pollio, the friend of shepherds, and the patron of every muse."—"Ah!" returns his fellow shepherd, "what think you rather of that grotto by the fountain side? the murmuring stream will help to assist our complaints, and a nightingale on a neighboring tree will join her voice to the concert!" When the place is thus settled, they begin: the brook stands still to hear their lamentations; the cows forget to graze; and the very tigers start from the forest with sympathetic concern. By the tombs of our ancestors, my dear Fum, I am quite unaffected in all this distress: the whole is liquid laudanum to my spirits; and a tiger of common sensibility has twenty times more tenderness than I.

But though I could never weep with the complaining shepherd, yet I am sometimes induced to pity the poet, whose trade is thus to make demigods and heroes for a dinner. There is not in nature a more dismal figure than a man who sits down to premeditated flattery: every stanza he writes tacitly reproaches the meanness of his occupation, till, at last, his stupidity becomes more stupid, and his dullness more diminutive.

I am amazed, therefore, that none have yet found out the secret of flattering the worthless, and yet of preserving a safe conscience. I have often wished for some method, by which a man might do himself and his deceased patron justice, without being under the hateful reproach of self-conviction. After long lucubration, I have hit upon such an expedient; and send you the specimen of a poem upon the decease of a great man, in which the flattery is perfectly fine, and yet the poet perfectly innocent.

ON THE DEATH OF THE RIGHT HONORABLE——

Ye Muses, pour the pitying tear
  For Pollio snatched away;
Oh, had he lived another year!
  —*He had not died to-day.*

Oh, were he born to bless mankind,
  In virtuous times of yore,
Heroes themselves had fall'n behind!
  —*Whene'er he went before.*

How sad the groves and plains appear,
  And sympathetic sheep;
E'en pitying hills would drop a tear!
  —*If hills could learn to weep.*

His bounty in exalted strain
  Each bard may well display;
Since none implored relief in vain!
  —*That went relieved away.*

And hark! I hear the tuneful throng
  His obsequies forbid;
He still shall live, shall live as long
  —*As ever dead man did.*

STANZAS ON WOMAN[1]

When lovely woman stoops to folly,
  And finds, too late, that men betray,
What charm can soothe her melancholy,
  What art can wash her guilt away?

The only art her guilt to cover,
  To hide her shame from every eye,
To give repentance to her lover,
  And wring his bosom, is—to die.

[1]From *The Vicar of Wakefield* (1766), chap. 24.

THE DESERTED VILLAGE (1770)

TO SIR JOSHUA REYNOLDS

Dear Sir,—I can have no expectations, in an address of this kind, either to add to your reputation, or to establish my own. You can gain nothing from my admiration, as I am ignorant of that art in which you are said to excel; and I may lose much by the severity of your judgment, as few have a juster taste in poetry than you. Setting interest, therefore, aside, to which I never paid much attention, I must be indulged at present in following my affections. The only dedication I ever made was to my brother, because I loved him better than most other men. He is since dead. Permit me to inscribe this Poem to you.

How far you may be pleased with the versification and mere mechanical parts of this attempt, I don't pretend to inquire; but I know you will object (and indeed several of our best and wisest friends concur in the opinion), that the depopulation it deplores is nowhere to be seen, and the disorders it laments are only to be found in the poet's own imagination. To this I can scarce make any other answer, than that I sincerely believe what I have written; that I have taken all possible pains, in my country excursions, for these four or five years past, to be certain of what I allege; and that all my views and inquiries have led me to believe those miseries real, which I here attempt to display. But this is not the place to enter into an inquiry whether the country be depopulating or not: the discussion would take up much room, and I should prove myself, at best, an indifferent politician, to tire the reader with a long preface, when I want his unfatigued attention to a long poem.

In regretting the depopulation of the country, I inveigh against the increase of our luxuries; and here also I expect the shout of modern politicians against me. For twenty or thirty years past, it has been the fashion to consider luxury as one of the greatest national advantages; and all the wisdom of antiquity in that particular as erroneous. Still, however, I must remain a professed ancient on that head, and continue to think those luxuries prejudicial to states by which so many vices are introduced, and so many kingdoms have been undone. Indeed, so much has been poured out of late on the other side of the question, that, merely for the sake of novelty and variety, one would sometimes wish to be in the right.

I am, dear sir, your sincere friend, and ardent admirer,

OLIVER GOLDSMITH.

SWEET Auburn![1] loveliest village of the plain,
Where health and plenty cheered the laboring swain,
Where smiling Spring its earliest visit paid,
And parting Summer's lingering blooms delayed:
Dear lovely bowers of innocence and ease,
Seats of my youth, when every sport could please:
How often have I loitered o'er thy green,
Where humble happiness endeared each scene!
How often have I paused on every charm,
The sheltered cot, the cultivated farm,
The never-failing brook, the busy mill,
The decent church that topped the neighboring hill;
The hawthorn bush, with seats beneath the shade,
For talking age and whispering lovers made!
How often have I blessed the coming day,
When toil, remitting, lent its turn to play,
And all the village train, from labor free,
Led up their sports beneath the spreading tree!
While many a pastime circled in the shade,
The young contending as the old surveyed;
And many a gambol frolicked o'er the ground,
And sleights of art and feats of strength went round;
And still, as each repeated pleasure tired,
Succeeding sports the mirthful band inspired—
The dancing pair that simply[2] sought renown,
By holding out to tire each other down;
The swain mistrustless of his smutted face,
While secret laughter tittered round the place;
The bashful virgin's side-long looks of love;
The matron's glance, that would those looks reprove.
These were thy charms, sweet village! sports like these,
With sweet succession, taught e'en toil to please;
These round thy bowers their cheerful influence shed;
These were thy charms—but all these charms are fled.
Sweet smiling village, loveliest of the lawn,
Thy sports are fled, and all thy charms withdrawn;
Amidst thy bowers the tyrant's hand is seen,
And Desolation saddens all thy green:
One only master grasps the whole domain,[3]
And half a tillage stints thy smiling plain.
No more thy glassy brook reflects the day,
But, choked with sedges, works its weedy way;
Along thy glades, a solitary guest,
The hollow-sounding bittern guards its nest:
Amidst thy desert walks the lapwing flies,
And tires their echoes with unvaried cries:
Sunk are thy bowers in shapeless ruin all,
And the long grass o'ertops the moldering wall;
And, trembling, shrinking from the spoiler's hand,
Far, far away thy children leave the land.
Ill fares the land, to hastening ills a prey,
Where wealth accumulates, and men decay.
Princes and lords may flourish, or may fade;
A breath can make them, as a breath has made:
But a bold peasantry, their country's pride,
When once destroyed, can never be supplied.
A time there was, ere England's griefs began,
When every rood of ground maintained its man;
For him light Labor spread her wholesome store,
Just gave what life required, but gave no more:
His best companions, Innocence and Health;
And his best riches, ignorance of wealth.
But times are altered: Trade's unfeeling train
Usurp the land, and dispossess the swain;
Along the lawn, where scattered hamlets rose,
Unwieldy wealth and cumbrous pomp repose;
And every want to opulence allied,
And every pang that folly pays to pride.
Those gentle hours that plenty bade to bloom,
Those calm desires that asked but little room,
Those healthful sports that graced the peaceful scene,
Lived in each look, and brightened all the green—

[1] It is practically certain that Goldsmith had Lissoy in mind (which has changed its name to Auburn), though this has been disputed.

[2] In a simple way.

[3] Landlords were empowered by the Enclosure Acts (of which there were 700 between 1760 and 1774) to enclose common land, for the improvement of their estates. This often involved ejectments.

These, far departing, seek a kinder shore,
And rural mirth and manners are no more.
Sweet Auburn! parent of the blissful hour,
Thy glades forlorn confess the tyrant's power.
Here, as I take my solitary rounds,
Amidst thy tangling walks and ruined grounds,
And, many a year elapsed, return to view
Where once the cottage stood, the hawthorn grew—
Remembrance wakes with all her busy train,
Swells at my breast, and turns the past to pain.
In all my wanderings round this world of care,
In all my griefs—and God has given my share—
I still had hopes, my latest hours to crown,
Amidst these humble bowers to lay me down;
To husband out life's taper at the close,
And keep the flame from wasting by repose:
I still had hopes, for pride attends us still,
Amidst the swains to show my book-learn'd skill,
Around my fire an evening group to draw,
And tell of all I felt, and all I saw;
And, as a hare, whom hounds and horns pursue,
Pants to the place from whence at first she flew,
I still had hopes, my long vexations past,
Here to return—and die at home at last.
O blest retirement, friend to life's decline,
Retreats from care, that never must be mine,
How happy he who crowns, in shades like these,
A youth of labor with an age of ease;
Who quits a world where strong temptations try,
And, since 'tis hard to combat, learns to fly!
For him no wretches, born to work and weep,
Explore the mine, or tempt the dangerous deep;
No surly porter stands, in guilty state,
To spurn imploring famine from the gate;
But on he moves to meet his latter end,
Angels around befriending virtue's friend;
Bends to the grave with unperceived decay,
While resignation gently slopes the way;
And, all his prospects brightening to the last,
His heaven commences ere the world be past!
Sweet was the sound, when oft, at evening's close,
Up yonder hill the village murmur rose.
There, as I passed with careless[1] steps and slow,
The mingled notes came softened from below;
The swain responsive as the milkmaid sung,
The sober herd that lowed to meet their young;
The noisy geese that gabbled o'er the pool,
The playful children just let loose from school;
The watch-dog's voice that bayed the whispering wind,
And the loud laugh that spoke the vacant[2] mind;—
These all in sweet confusion sought the shade,
And filled each pause the nightingale had made.
But now the sounds of population fail,
No cheerful murmurs fluctuate in the gale,
No busy steps the grass-grown footway tread,
For all the bloomy flush of life is fled—
All but yon widowed, solitary thing,
That feebly bends beside the plashy spring;
She, wretched matron—forced, in age, for bread,
To strip the brook with mantling cresses spread,
To pick her wintry faggot from the thorn,
To seek her nightly shed, and weep till morn,—
She only left of all the harmless train,
The sad historian of the pensive plain.
Near yonder copse, where once the garden smiled,
And still where many a garden-flower grows wild,
There, where a few torn shrubs the place disclose,
The village preacher's[3] modest mansion rose.
A man he was to all the country dear,
And passing rich with forty pounds a year.
Remote from towns he ran his godly race,
Nor e'er had changed, nor wished to change, his place;
Unpracticed he to fawn, or seek for power
By doctrines fashioned to the varying hour;
Far other aims his heart had learned to prize,
More skilled to raise the wretched than to rise.
His house was known to all the vagrant train;
He chid their wanderings, but relieved their pain;
The long-remembered beggar was his guest,
Whose beard descending swept his aged breast;
The ruined spendthrift, now no longer proud,
Claimed kindred there, and had his claims allowed;
The broken soldier, kindly bade to stay,
Sat by his fire, and talked the night away;—
Wept o'er his wounds, or, tales of sorrow done,
Shouldered his crutch, and showed how fields were won.
Pleased with his guests, the good man learned to glow,
And quite forgot their vices in their woe;
Careless their merits or their faults to scan,
His pity gave ere charity began.

[1]Care-free.

[2]Untroubled, perhaps, rather than stupid.

[3]Probably Goldsmith had both his father and his brother, Henry, in mind in describing the preacher.

Thus to relieve the wretched was his pride,
And e'en his failings leaned to virtue's side;
But in his duty prompt at every call,
He watched and wept, he prayed and felt for all;
And, as a bird each fond endearment tries,
To tempt its new-fledged offspring to the skies,
He tried each art, reproved each dull delay,
Allured to brighter worlds, and led the way.

Beside the bed where parting life was laid,
And sorrow, guilt, and pain, by turns dismayed,
The reverend champion stood. At his control,
Despair and anguish fled the struggling soul;
Comfort came down the trembling wretch to raise,
And his last faltering accents whispered praise.

At church, with meek and unaffected grace,
His looks adorned the venerable place;
Truth from his lips prevailed with double sway,
And fools, who came to scoff, remained to pray.
The service past, around the pious man
With steady zeal, each honest rustic ran;
E'en children followed, with endearing wile,
And plucked his gown, to share the good man's smile;
His ready smile a parent's warmth expressed;
Their welfare pleased him, and their cares distressed:
To them his heart, his love, his griefs were given,
But all his serious thoughts had rest in heaven.
As some tall cliff that lifts its awful form,
Swells from the vale, and midway leaves the storm,
Though round its breast the rolling clouds are spread,
Eternal sunshine settles on its head.

Beside yon straggling fence that skirts the way,
With blossomed furze unprofitably gay,
There, in his noisy mansion, skilled to rule,
The village master taught his little school.
A man severe he was, and stern to view;
I knew him well, and every truant knew:
Well had the boding tremblers learned to trace
The day's disasters in his morning face;
Full well they laughed with counterfeited glee
At all his jokes, for many a joke had he;
Full well the busy whisper, circling round,
Conveyed the dismal tidings when he frowned.
Yet he was kind, or if severe in aught,
The love he bore to learning was in fault.
The village all declared how much he knew;
'Twas certain he could write, and cipher too;
Lands he could measure, terms and tides presage,
And e'en the story ran that he could gauge.
In arguing, too, the parson owned his skill,
For e'en though vanquished, he could argue still;
While words of learned length and thundering sound
Amazed the gazing rustics ranged around;
And still they gazed, and still the wonder grew,
That one small head could carry all he knew.
But past is all his fame;—the very spot
Where many a time he triumphed, is forgot.

Near yonder thorn, that lifts its head on high,
Where once the sign-post caught the passing eye,
Low lies that house where nut-brown drafts inspired,
Where gray-beard mirth and smiling toil retired,
Where village statesmen talked with looks profound,
And news much older than their ale went round.
Imagination fondly stoops to trace
The parlor splendors of that festive place;
The whitewashed wall, the nicely-sanded floor,
The varnished clock that clicked behind the door,
The chest, contrived a double debt to pay,
A bed by night, a chest of drawers by day,
The pictures placed for ornament and use,
The twelve good rules,[1] the royal game of goose,[2]
The hearth, except when winter chilled the day,
With aspen boughs, and flowers, and fennel, gay;—
While broken tea-cups, wisely kept for show,
Ranged o'er the chimney, glistened in a row.

Vain transitory splendors! could not all
Reprieve the tottering mansion from its fall?
Obscure it sinks, nor shall it more impart
An hour's importance to the poor man's heart.
Thither no more the peasant shall repair,
To sweet oblivion of his daily care;
No more the farmer's news, the barber's tale,
No more the woodman's ballad shall prevail;
No more the smith his dusky brow shall clear,
Relax his ponderous strength, and lean to hear;
The host himself no longer shall be found
Careful to see the mantling bliss go round;
Nor the coy maid, half willing to be pressed,
Shall kiss the cup to pass it to the rest.

Yes! let the rich deride, the proud disdain,
These simple blessings of the lowly train;

[1] These rules were said to have been found in the study of Charles I after his death. Printed on a card, they were hung on the wall.

[2] Played with dice on a board divided into compartments.

To me more dear, congenial to my heart,
One native charm, than all the gloss of art.
Spontaneous joys, where nature has its play,
The soul adopts, and owns their first-born sway;
Lightly they frolic o'er the vacant mind,
Unenvied, unmolested, unconfined:
But the long pomp, the midnight masquerade,
With all the freaks of wanton wealth arrayed,
In these, ere triflers half their wish obtain,
The toiling pleasure sickens into pain;
And, e'en while Fashion's brightest arts decoy,
The heart distrusting asks, if this be joy.
Ye friends to truth, ye statesmen, who survey
The rich man's joys increase, the poor's decay,
'Tis yours to judge how wide the limits stand
Between a splendid and a happy land.
Proud swells the tide with loads of freighted ore,
And shouting Folly hails them from her shore;
Hoards, e'en beyond the miser's wish, abound,
And rich men flock from all the world around.
Yet count our gains. This wealth is but a name
That leaves our useful products still the same.
Not so the loss. The man of wealth and pride
Takes up a space that many poor supplied;
Space for his lake, his park's extended bounds,
Space for his horses, equipage, and hounds;
The robe that wraps his limbs in silken sloth,
Has robbed the neighboring fields of half their growth;
His seat, where solitary sports are seen,
Indignant spurns the cottage from the green;
Around the world each needful product flies,
For all the luxuries the world supplies;
While thus the land, adorned for pleasure all,
In barren splendor feebly waits the fall.
As some fair female, unadorned and plain,
Secure to please while youth confirms her reign,
Slights every borrowed charm that dress supplies,
Nor shares with art the triumph of her eyes;
But when those charms are past, for charms are frail,
When time advances, and when lovers fail,
She then shines forth, solicitous to bless,
In all the glaring impotence of dress:
Thus fares the land by luxury betrayed;
In nature's simplest charms at first arrayed;—
But verging to decline, its splendors rise,
Its vistas strike, its palaces surprise;
While, scourged by famine, from the smiling land
The mournful peasant leads his humble band;
And while he sinks, without one arm to save,
The country blooms—a garden and a grave!
Where, then, ah! where shall poverty reside,
To 'scape the pressure of contiguous pride?
If to some common's fenceless limits strayed,
He drives his flock to pick the scanty blade,
Those fenceless fields the sons of wealth divide,
And e'en the bare-worn common is denied.
If to the city sped—what waits him there?
To see profusion that he must not share;
To see ten thousand baneful arts combined
To pamper luxury and thin mankind;
To see those joys the sons of pleasure know
Extorted from his fellow-creature's woe:
Here while the courtier glitters in brocade,
There the pale artist[1] plies the sickly trade;
Here while the proud their long-drawn pomps display,
There the black gibbet glooms beside the way:
The dome where Pleasure holds her midnight reign,
Here, richly decked, admits the gorgeous train;
Tumultuous grandeur crowds the blazing square,
The rattling chariots clash, the torches glare.
Sure scenes like these no troubles e'er annoy!
Sure these denote one universal joy!—
Are these thy serious thoughts?—ah, turn thine eyes
Where the poor houseless shivering female lies:
She once, perhaps, in village plenty blessed,
Has wept at tales of innocence distressed;
Her modest looks the cottage might adorn,
Sweet as the primrose peeps beneath the thorn:
Now lost to all, her friends, her virtue, fled,
Near her betrayer's door she lays her head,
And, pinched with cold, and shrinking from the shower,
With heavy heart deplores that luckless hour,
When idly first, ambitious of the town,
She left her wheel, and robes of country brown.
Do thine, sweet Auburn, thine, the loveliest train,
Do thy fair tribes participate her pain?
E'en now, perhaps, by cold and hunger led,
At proud men's doors they ask a little bread!
Ah, no. To distant climes, a dreary scene,
Where half the convex world intrudes between,
Through torrid tracts with fainting steps they go,
Where wild Altama[2] murmurs to their woe.
Far different there from all that charmed before,
The various terrors of that horrid shore;
Those blazing suns that dart a downward ray,
And fiercely shed intolerable day;
Those matted woods where birds forget to sing,
But silent bats in drowsy clusters cling;

[1]Craftsman.

[2]Altamaha, a river in Georgia.

Those poisonous fields, with rank luxuriance crowned,
Where the dark scorpion gathers death around;
Where at each step the stranger fears to wake
The rattling terrors of the vengeful snake;
Where crouching tigers[1] wait their hapless prey,
And savage men more murderous still than they:
While oft in whirls the mad tornado flies,
Mingling the ravaged landscape with the skies.
Far different these from every former scene,
The cooling brook, the grassy-vested green,
The breezy covert of the warbling grove,
That only sheltered thefts of harmless love.
  Good Heaven! what sorrows gloomed that parting day,
That called them from tneir native walks away;
When the poor exiles, every pleasure past,
Hung round their bowers, and fondly looked their last,
And took a long farewell, and wished in vain,
For seats like these beyond the western main;
And shuddering still to face the distant deep,
Returned and wept, and still returned to weep!
The good old sire the first prepared to go
To new-found worlds, and wept for others' woe;
But for himself, in conscious virtue brave,
He only wished for worlds beyond the grave.
His lovely daughter, lovelier in her tears,
The fond companion of his helpless years,
Silent went next, neglectful of her charms,
And left a lover's for a father's arms.
With louder plaints the mother spoke her woes,
And blessed the cot where every pleasure rose,
And kissed her thoughtless babes with many a tear,
And clasped them close, in sorrow doubly dear;
Whilst her fond husband strove to lend relief
In all the silent manliness of grief.
  O Luxury, thou cursed by Heaven's decree,
How ill exchanged are things like these for thee!
How do thy potions, with insidious joy,
Diffuse their pleasures only to destroy!
Kingdoms by thee to sickly greatness grown,
Boast of a florid vigor not their own;
At every draft more large and large they grow,
A bloated mass of rank unwieldy woe;
Till sapped their strength, and every part unsound,
Down, down they sink, and spread a ruin round.
  E'en now the devastation is begun,
And half the business of destruction done;
E'en now, methinks, as pondering here I stand,
I see the rural Virtues leave the land.
Down where yon anchoring vessel spreads the sail
That idly waiting flaps with every gale,
Downward they move, a melancholy band,
Pass from the shore, and darken all the strand;
Contented Toil, and hospitable Care,
And kind connubial Tenderness are there;
And Piety with wishes placed above,
And steady Loyalty, and faithful Love.
  And thou, sweet Poetry, thou loveliest maid,
Still first to fly where sensual joys invade!
Unfit, in these degenerate times of shame,
To catch the heart, or strike for honest fame;
Dear charming nymph, neglected and decried,
My shame in crowds, my solitary pride;
Thou source of all my bliss and all my woe,
That found'st me poor at first, and keep'st me so;
Thou guide by which the nobler arts excel,
Thou nurse of every virtue, fare thee well!
Farewell! and oh! where'er thy voice be tried,
On Torno's[2] cliffs, or Pambamarca's[3] side,
Whether where equinoctial[4] fervors glow,
Or winter wraps the polar world in snow,
Still let thy voice, prevailing over time,
Redress the rigors of th'inclement clime;
Aid slighted Truth with thy persuasive strain;
Teach erring man to spurn the rage of gain;
Teach him that states, of native strength possessed,
Though very poor, may still be very blest;
That Trade's proud empire hastes to swift decay,
As ocean sweeps the labored mole away;
While self-dependent power can time defy,
As rocks resist the billows and the sky.[5]

[1]Goldsmith had not yet become the historian of Animated Nature; but Noah Webster later called the jaguar "the American tiger."

[2]Tornea, Gulf of Bothnia, Sweden.

[3]Mountain in Ecuador.

[4]Equatorial.

[5]According to Boswell, Dr. Johnson wrote the last four lines.

EDWARD GIBBON (1737–1794)

Gibbon's remoter ancestry remains still a problem not completely solved by genealogists. He himself was little interested in it, and wrote at one time that perhaps his grandfather was "a son of earth" who "had raised himself from the work-house or the cottage." He came, however, of "a family of ancient but undistinguished standing in the county of Kent," members of which had gone "to London to further their fortunes by commerce." (D. M. Low, *Gibbon's Journal.*) The effort was successful, and Gibbon's father possessed a considerable fortune, which enabled him to play the part of an eighteenth-century gentleman. In so doing he contrived to lose much of his money, but left his eldest son (the only survivor of seven children) enough for independence and comfort. This son was born at Putney on 27 April, 1737. He was a sickly child, and his life was more than once despaired of, but in his sixteenth year his ailments suddenly vanished, not to return. Because of them, his education in childhood and youth, at a day-school in Putney, at Kingston-on-Thames, and finally at Westminster School, was much interrupted. He entered Oxford, as a gentleman-commoner of Magdalen College, on 3 April, 1752. As a consequence of much reading, on both sides of the question—what did he not read!—the young Oxonian was received into the Roman Catholic Church on 8 June, 1753. His father at once took alarm, and carried through most energetic measures to reclaim his son from a religion which, in the England of his day, entailed grave social and civil disabilities. He was instantly taken from Oxford, before the authorities had an opportunity to eject him, and by 30 June was placed in the home of a Calvinist minister at Lausanne, in Switzerland. There he remained five years, and there he laid the real foundations of his unsurpassed scholarship. He was nominally a Protestant again after a year and a half, but this was a merely transitional stage in his passage to an ironical skepticism practically inconsistent with any theistic belief. Before the close of these five years he had met and fallen in love with Suzanne Curchod, the daughter of a Swiss pastor. His love was returned, an engagement was contracted, and in 1758 Gibbon went back to England with this news for his father, who unconditionally refused his consent to his son's marriage with a girl both poor and foreign. The young man was wholly dependent on his father; after an interval for thought he "sighed as a lover but obeyed as a son." The incident has occasioned much discussion, but, while Mlle. Curchod certainly displayed more lively feeling than did Gibbon, there can be no doubt that he was sincerely attached to her, and that he broke off the engagement only when it became clear that his father's opposition was unalterable. Mlle. Curchod within a few years married Jacques Necker, later "the minister and perhaps the legislator of the French monarchy," and their only child became famous as Mme. de Staël. Gibbon and the Neckers maintained a warm friendship throughout the former's life.

In June, 1759, Gibbon accepted a commission as captain in the Hampshire militia, in which his father was a major. His regiment was embodied in May, 1760, and was not demobilized until December, 1762. His feelings concerning his military service were mixed, but that service did not wholly debar him from serious study (though he lost many a morning to sickness caused by heavy drinking), and he concluded that "the captain of the Hampshire grenadiers" had "not been useless to the historian of the Roman empire." It was during this period that he first detected signs of the malady (hernia) which, giving him no pain and causing him no trouble, he most strangely neglected until it finally caused his death. It was also during this period (in 1761) that he published, at his father's request, his first book—the *Essai sur l'Étude de la Littérature*—which he had begun to write at Lausanne and had completed in 1759. His father hoped, not unreasonably, that this evidence of his son's perfect mastery of French might lead to state employment. The hope, however, was vain. In January, 1763, Gibbon revisited the continent, going first to Paris, then to Lausanne, and thence to Italy, where he remained some thirteen months. His great historical work was seriously occupying him by 1768. Two years later his father died, and in 1772 he established himself in London. In 1774 he became a member of the Literary Club, though Dr. Johnson did not like him, and Boswell hated him. "He is an ugly, affected, disgusting fellow and poisons our literary club to me," wrote the latter to his friend Temple. Another member of the Club (from 1782), Edmond Malone, the great Shakespearian scholar, felt very differently, and wrote, after Gibbon's death: "He had an immense fund of anecdote and of erudition of various kinds, both ancient and modern; and had acquired such a facility and elegance of talk that I had always great pleasure in listening to him. The manner and voice, though they were peculiar, and I believe artificial at first, did not at all offend, for they had become so appropriate as to appear natural." And this, there is every reason to think, fairly represents the general attitude towards him.

In 1774, too, Gibbon became a member of the House of Commons, where he remained, with one interruption, a speechless but dependable voter with the Government, until 1783. He was also a Commissioner of the Board of Trade from 1779 to 1782. Meanwhile the first volume of *The History of the Decline and Fall of the Roman Empire* had been published in 1776, and the second and third volumes had followed in 1781. The Duke of Gloucester, on accepting one of these, affably exclaimed: "Another damned thick book! Always scribble, scribble, scribble! Eh, Mr. Gibbon?" The inveterate scribbler retired in 1783, with his library and his Wedgwood china, to Lausanne, where the *History* was completed. He returned to England to see Volumes IV, V, and VI through the press, and to witness their publication on his fifty-first birthday (1788). Thereafter he was again in Lausanne until the spring of 1793, when he returned to England because of the death of Lady Sheffield, the wife of his dear friend, the first Earl of Sheffield. And in London Gibbon died, on 16 January, 1794. Less than 24 hours before his death he had remarked to a caller "that he thought himself a good life for ten, twelve, or perhaps twenty years." Three days afterwards Hannah More wrote: "Heard of the death of Mr. Gibbon, the calumniator of the despised Nazarene, the derider of Christianity. Awful dispensation! He too was my acquaintance. Lord, I bless Thee, considering how much infidel acquaintance I have had, that my soul never came into their secret! How many souls have his writings polluted! Lord preserve others from their contagion!"

Gibbon deserved these strictures, but, nevertheless, "succeeding generations have concurred in assigning to *The Decline and Fall* the primacy, which it still holds, among historical works in our literature, and in esteeming its author the most brilliant example known of 'the union of the historian and the man of letters.'" Macaulay is "the one English historian whose literary genius can be drawn into comparison with" his. But Gibbon had a very real advantage in his theme—'the greatest furnished by profane history'—and he treated it completely, lucidly, and accurately. He is, moreover, "one of the great masters of English prose. His power of narrative is at least equaled by his gift of argumentative statement, and, in all parts of his work, his style is one which holds the reader spellbound by its stately dignity, relieved by a curious subtlety of *nuance*." (A. W. Ward, *Camb. Hist.*, X.) And, as no praise can well be too high for the *History*, so also Gibbon's *Autobiography* has been acclaimed by succeeding generations as "one of the most characteristic portraits ever painted by man of himself." (Leslie Stephen.) Bagehot wrote: "A wit said of Gibbon's *Autobiography*, that he did not know the difference between himself and the Roman empire. He has narrated his progressions from London to Buriton [his father's country estate], and from Buriton to London in the same monotonous, majestic periods that record the fall of states and empires." But this, though well enough for a "wit," is a verdict depending upon a singular failure in discrimination. And the world has agreed with Birkbeck Hill that in the *Autobiography* we have "an almost perfect picture of a great scholar" and one of the few books "written by man that were wished longer by their readers." This, furthermore, has been the verdict of every competent judge despite the fact that Gibbon left his *Memoirs* in a very imperfect condition. He was at work upon them at various times from 1789 until 1792, and wrote six sketches, besides several shorter fragments, which are in the nature of trial-drafts, and with all of which he remained dissatisfied. These were very skillfully pieced together after his death by his friend and literary executor, Lord Sheffield, and the *Memoirs* were first published in 1796. The sketches were not published in their integrity, just as Gibbon wrote them, until 1896.

PASSAGES FROM

MEMOIRS OF MY LIFE AND WRITINGS[1]

YOUTH

THE curiosity which had been implanted in my infant mind was still alive and active, but my reason was not sufficiently informed to understand the value, or to lament the loss, of three precious years from my entrance at Westminster to my admission at Oxford. Instead of repining at my long and frequent confinement to the chamber or the couch, I secretly rejoiced in those infirmities which delivered me from the exercises of the school and the society of my equals. As often as I was tolerably exempt from danger and pain, reading, free desultory reading, was the employment and comfort of my solitary hours. At Westminster my aunt sought only to amuse

[1]The text is based on that in *The Autobiographies of Edward Gibbon*, edited by John Murray, 1896 (2nd ed'n, 1897). I have retained, however, the general title used by Lord Sheffield in 1796.

and indulge me; in my stations at Bath and Winchester, at Buriton and Putney, a false compassion respected my sufferings, and I was allowed without control or advice to gratify the wanderings of an unripe taste. My indiscriminate appetite subsided by degrees in the historic line, and since philosophy has exploded all innate ideas and natural propensities, I must ascribe this choice to the assiduous perusal of the *Universal History* as the octavo volumes successively appeared. This unequal work and a treatise of Hearne, the *Ductor Historicus*, referred and introduced me to the Greek and Roman historians, to as many at least as were accessible to an English reader. All that I could find were greedily devoured, from Littlebury's lame *Herodotus* and Spelman's valuable *Xenophon*, to the pompous folios of Gordon's *Tacitus* and a ragged *Procopius* of the beginning of the last century. The cheap acquisition of so much knowledge confirmed my dislike to the study of languages, and I argued with Miss Porten, that were I master of Greek and Latin, I must interpret to myself in English the thoughts of the original, and that such extemporary versions must be inferior to the elaborate translations of professed scholars—a silly sophism which could not easily be confuted by a person ignorant of any other language than her own. From the ancient I leaped to the modern world. Many crude lumps of Speed, Rapin, Mézeray, Davila, Machiavel, Father Paul,[1] Bower, *etc.*, passed through me like so many novels, and I swallowed with the same voracious appetite the descriptions of India and China, of Mexico and Peru. Our family collection was decently furnished. The circulating libraries of London and Bath afforded a rich treasure. I borrowed many books and some I contrived to purchase from my scanty allowance. My father's friends who visited the boy were astonished at finding him surrounded with a heap of folios of whose titles they were ignorant and on whose contents he could pertinently discourse.

My first introduction to the historic scenes which have since engaged so many years of my life, must be ascribed to an accident. In the summer of 1751, I accompanied my father on a visit to Mr. Hoare's in Wiltshire. But I was less delighted with the beauties of Stourhead, than with discovering in the library a common book, the continuation of Echard's *Roman History*, which is indeed executed with more skill and taste than the previous work. To me the reigns of the successors of Constantine were absolutely new, and I was immersed in the passage of the Goths over the Danube, when the summons of the dinner-bell reluctantly dragged me from my intellectual feast. This transient glance served rather to irritate than to appease my curiosity, and no sooner was I returned to Bath than I procured the second and third volumes of Howell's *History of the World*, which exhibit the Byzantine period on a larger scale. Mahomet and his Saracens soon fixed my attention, and some instinct of criticism directed me to the genuine sources. Simon Ockley, an original in every sense, first opened my eyes, and I was led from one book to another till I had ranged round the circle of oriental history. Before I was sixteen, I had exhausted all that could be learned in English of the Arabs and Persians, the Tartars and Turks, and the same ardor urged me to guess at the French of d'Herbelot, and to construe the barbarous Latin of Pocock's *Abulfaragius*. Such vague and multifarious reading could not teach me to think, to write, or to act, and the only principle that darted a ray of light into the indigested chaos, was an early and rational application to the order of time and place. The maps of Cellarius and Wells imprinted in my mind the picture of ancient geography; from Strauchius I imbibed the elements of chronology; the tables of Helvicus and Anderson, the annals of Usher and Prideaux, distinguished the connection of events and I engraved the multitude of names and dates in a clear and indelible series. But in the discussion of the first ages I overleaped the bounds of modesty and use. In my childish balance I presumed to weigh the systems of Scaliger and Petavius, of Marsham and Newton, which I could seldom study in the originals; the dynasties of Assyria and Egypt were my top and cricket ball, and my sleep has been disturbed by the difficulty of reconciling the Septuagint with the Hebrew computation. I arrived at Oxford with a stock of erudition that might have puzzled a doctor, and a degree of ignorance of which a schoolboy would have been ashamed.

At the conclusion of this first period of my life, I am tempted to enter a protest against

---

[1] Father Paulo Sarpi (1552–1623).

the trite and lavish praise of the happiness of our boyish years, which is echoed with so much affectation in the world. That happiness I have never known, that time I have never regretted; and were my poor aunt still alive, she would bear testimony to the early and constant uniformity of my sentiments. It will indeed be replied, that I am not a competent judge; that pleasure is incompatible with pain; that joy is excluded from sickness, and that the felicity of a schoolboy consists in the perpetual motion of thoughtless and playful agility, in which I was never qualified to excel. My name, it is most true, could never be enrolled among the sprightly race, the idle progeny of Eton or Westminster, who delight to cleave the water with pliant arm, to urge the flying ball, and to chase the speed of the rolling circle.[1] But I would ask the warmest and most active hero of the play-field whether he can seriously compare his childish with his manly enjoyments; whether he does not feel, as the most precious attribute of his existence, the vigorous maturity of sensual and spiritual powers which nature has reserved for the age of puberty. A state of happiness arising only from the want of foresight and reflection shall never provoke my envy. Such degenerate taste would tend to sink us in the scale of beings from a man to a child, a dog, and an oyster, till we had reached the confines of brute matter which can not suffer because it can not feel. The poet may gaily describe the short hours of recreation, but he forgets the daily tedious labors of the school, which is approached each morning with anxious and reluctant steps. Degrees of misery are proportioned to the mind rather than to the object—*parva leves capiunt animos*[2]—and few men in the trials of life have experienced a more painful sensation than the poor schoolboy with an imperfect task who trembles on the eve of the black Monday. A school is the cavern of fear and sorrow. The mobility of the captive youths is chained to a book and a desk. An inflexible master commands their attention which every moment is impatient to escape. They labor, like the soldiers of Persia, under the scourge, and their education is nearly finished before they can apprehend the sense or utility of the harsh lessons which they are forced to repeat. Such blind and absolute dependence may be necessary, but can never be delightful. Freedom is the first wish of our heart, freedom is the first blessing of our nature, and unless we bind ourselves with the voluntary chains of interest or passion, we advance in freedom as we advance in years.

[1]*Cf.* Gray's *Ode on a Distant Prospect of Eton College.*

[2]Small things take possession of youthful souls. (Ovid, *Ars Amatoria*, I, 159.)

OXFORD

A TRAVELER who visits Oxford or Cambridge is surprised and edified by the apparent order and tranquillity that prevail in the seats of the English muses. In the most celebrated universities of Holland, Germany, and Italy, the students, who swarm from different countries, are loosely dispersed in private lodgings at the houses of the burghers. They dress according to their fancy and fortune, and in the intemperate quarrels of youth and wine their swords, though less frequently than of old, are sometimes stained with each other's blood. The use of arms is banished from our English universities; the uniform habit of the academics, the square cap and black gown, is adapted to the civil and even clerical profession, and from the doctor in divinity to the undergraduate, the degrees of learning and age are externally distinguished. Instead of being scattered in a town, the students of Oxford and Cambridge are united in colleges; their maintenance is provided at their own expense, or that of the founders, and the stated hours of the hall and chapel represent the discipline of a regular and, as it were, a religious community. The eyes of the traveler are attracted by the size or beauty of the public edifices, and the principal colleges appear to be so many palaces which a liberal nation has erected and endowed for the habitation of science. My own introduction to the University of Oxford forms a new era in my life, and at the distance of forty years I still remember my first emotions of surprise and satisfaction. In my fifteenth year I felt myself suddenly raised from a boy to a man. The persons, whom I respected as my superiors in age and academical rank, entertained me with every mark of attention and civility, and my vanity was flattered by the velvet cap and silk gown which discriminate a gentleman commoner from a plebeian student. A decent allowance, more money than a schoolboy had ever seen, was at my own disposal, and I might command among the tradesmen of Oxford an indefinite and dangerous latitude of credit. A key was delivered into my hands, which gave me the free use of a numerous and learned library; my apartment consisted of three elegant and well-furnished rooms in the new building, a stately pile, of Magdalen College, and the adjacent walks, had they been frequented by Plato's disciples, might have been compared to the Attic shade on the banks of the Ilissus. Such was the fair prospect of my entrance (April 3, 1752) into the University of Oxford.

A venerable prelate, whose taste and erudition must reflect honor on the society in which they were formed, has drawn a very interesting picture of his academical life. "I was educated," says Bishop Lowth,[1] "in the University of Oxford. I enjoyed all the advantages, both public and private, which that famous seat of learning so largely affords. I spent many years in that illustrious society, in a well-regulated course of useful discipline and studies, and in the agreeable and improving commerce of gentlemen and of scholars; in a society where emulation without envy, ambition without jealousy, contention without animosity, incited industry and awakened genius; where a liberal pursuit of knowledge, and a generous freedom of thought, was raised, encouraged, and pushed forward by example, by commendation, and by authority. I breathed the same atmosphere that the Hookers, the Chillingworths, and the Lockes had breathed before; whose benevolence and humanity were as extensive as their vast genius and comprehensive knowledge; who always treated their adversaries with civility and respect; who made candor, moderation, and liberal judgment as much the rule and law as the subject of their discourses. And do you reproach me with my education in this place, and with my relation to this most respectable body which I shall always esteem my greatest advantage and my highest honor?" I transcribe with pleasure this eloquent passage, without examining what benefits or what rewards were derived by Hooker, or Chillingworth, or Locke, from their academical institution; without inquiring, whether in this angry controversy the spirit of Lowth himself is purified from the intolerant zeal which Warburton had ascribed to the genius of the place. The expression of gratitude is a virtue and a pleasure. A liberal mind will delight to cherish and celebrate the memory of its parents, and the teachers of science are the parents of the mind. I applaud the filial piety which it is impossible for me to imitate, since I must not confess an imaginary debt, to assume the merit of a just or generous retribution. To the University of Oxford I acknowledge no obligation, and she will as cheerfully renounce me for a son as I am willing to disclaim her for a mother. I spent fourteen months at Magdalen College; they proved the fourteen months the most idle and unprofitable of my whole life. The reader will pronounce between the school and the scholar, but I cannot affect to believe that nature had disqualified me for all literary pursuits. The specious and ready excuse of my tender age, imperfect preparation, and hasty departure, may doubtless be alleged, nor do I wish to defraud such excuses of their proper weight. Yet in my sixteenth year I was not devoid of capacity or application. Even my childish reading had displayed an early though blind propensity for books, and the shallow flood might have been taught to flow in a deep channel and a clear stream. In the discipline of a well-constituted academy, under the guidance of skillful and vigilant professors, I should gradually have risen from translations to originals, from the Latin to the Greek classics, from dead languages to living science. My hours would have been occupied by useful and agreeable studies, the wanderings of fancy would have been restrained, and I should have escaped the temptations of idleness which finally precipitated my departure from Oxford.

Perhaps in a separate annotation I may coolly examine the fabulous and real antiquities of our sister universities, a question which has kindled such fierce and foolish disputes among their fanatic sons. In the meanwhile it will be acknowledged that these venerable bodies are sufficiently old to partake of all the prejudices and infirmities of age. The schools of Oxford and Cambridge were founded in a dark age of false and barbarous science, and they are still tainted with the vices of their origin. Their primitive discipline was adapted to the education of priests

---

[1] Robert Lowth (1710–1787), Bishop of Oxford, after 1777 Bishop of London. Gibbon quotes from a letter in which Lowth defends himself from strictures published by William Warburton (1698–1779), Bishop of Gloucester.

and monks, and the government still remains in the hands of the clergy, an order of men whose manners are remote from the present world, and whose eyes are dazzled by the light of philosophy. The legal incorporation of these societies by the charters of popes and kings had given them a monopoly of the public instruction, and the spirit of monopolists is narrow, lazy, and oppressive. Their work is more costly and less productive than that of independent artists, and the new improvements so eagerly grasped by the competition of freedom, are admitted with slow and sullen reluctance in those proud corporations, above the fear of a rival and below the confession of an error. We may scarcely hope that any reformation will be a voluntary act, and so deeply are they rooted in law and prejudice, that even the omnipotence of parliament would shrink from an inquiry into the state and abuses of the two universities.

The use of academical degrees, as old as the thirteenth century, is visibly borrowed from the mechanic corporations, in which an apprentice, after serving his time, obtains a testimonial of his skill and a license to practice his trade and mystery. It is not my design to depreciate those honors, which could never gratify or disappoint my ambition, and I should applaud the institution if the degrees of bachelor or licentiate were bestowed as the reward of manly and successful study, if the name and rank of doctor or master were strictly reserved for the professors of science who have approved their title to the public esteem. The mysterious faculty of theology must not be scanned by a profane eye. The cloak of reason sits awkwardly on our fashionable divines, and in the ecclesiastical studies of the fathers and councils their modesty will yield to the Catholic universities. Our English civilians and canonists[1] have never been famous. Their real business is confined to a small circle, and the double jurisprudence of Rome is overwhelmed by the enormous profession of common lawyers who, in the pursuit of honors and riches, disdain the mock majesty of our budge doctors.[2] We are justly proud of the skill and learning of our physicians. Their skill is acquired in the practice of the hospitals. They seek their learning in London, in Scotland, or on the continent, and few patients would trust their pulse to a medical student if he had passed the fourteen years of his novitiate at Oxford or Cambridge, whose degrees, however, are exclusively admitted in the Royal College. The arts are supposed to include the liberal knowledge of philosophy and literature, but I am informed that some tattered shreds of the old logic and metaphysics compose the exercises for a bachelor's and master's degree, and that modern improvements, instead of introducing a more rational trial, have only served to relax the forms which are now the object of general contempt.

In all the universities of Europe except our own, the languages and sciences are distributed among a numerous list of effective professors. The students according to their taste, their calling, and their diligence, apply themselves to the proper masters, and in the annual repetition of public and private lectures, these masters are assiduously employed. Our curiosity may inquire what number of professors has been instituted at Oxford?—for I shall now confine myself to my own university. By whom are they appointed, and what may be the probable chances of merit or incapacity? How many are stationed to the three faculties, and how many are left for the liberal arts? What is the form, and what the substance of their lessons? But all these questions are silenced by one short and singular answer, "that in the University of Oxford, the greater part of the public professors have for these many years given up altogether even the pretense of teaching." Incredible as the fact may appear, I must rest my belief on the positive and impartial evidence of a philosopher who had himself resided at Oxford. Dr. Adam Smith assigns as the cause of their indolence, that instead of being paid by voluntary contributions, which would urge them to increase the number and to deserve the gratitude of their pupils, the Oxford professors are secure in the enjoyment of a fixed stipend, without the necessity of labor or the apprehension of control. It has indeed been observed, nor is the observation absurd, that except in experimental sciences, which demand a costly apparatus and a dexterous hand, the many valuable treatises that have been pub-

[1]Men learned in civil law and in canon law.

[2]Doctors in furred gowns. Gibbon seems to have misunderstood Milton's use of "budge" (*Comus*, 707), to which he refers, and to have meant by it "formal," or "stiff,"—a possible meaning though not Milton's.

lished on every subject of learning may now supersede the ancient mode of oral instruction. Were this principle true in its utmost latitude, I should only infer that the offices and salaries, which are become useless, ought without delay to be abolished. But there still remains a material difference between a book and a professor. The hour of the lecture enforces attendance; attention is fixed by the presence, the voice, and the occasional questions of the teacher; the most idle will carry something away, and the more diligent will compare the instructions which they have heard in the school, with the volumes which they peruse in their chamber. The advice of a skillful professor will adapt a course of reading to every mind and every situation. His learning will remove difficulties and solve objections, his authority will discover, admonish, and at last chastise the negligence of his disciples, and his vigilant inquiries will ascertain the steps of their literary progress. Whatsoever science he professes he may illustrate in a series of discourses, composed in the leisure of his closet, pronounced on public occasions, and finally delivered to the press. I observe with pleasure, that in the University of Oxford Dr. Lowth, with equal eloquence and erudition, has executed this task in his incomparable *Prælectiones*[1] on the poetry of the Hebrews.

The college of St. Mary Magdalen (it is vulgarly pronounced Maudlin) was founded in the fifteenth century by a bishop of Winchester, and now consists of a president, forty fellows, and a number of inferior students. It is esteemed one of the largest and most wealthy of our academical corporations, which may be compared to the Benedictine abbeys of Catholic countries; and I have loosely heard that the estates belonging to Magdalen College, which are leased by those indulgent landlords at small quit-rents and occasional fines, might be raised in the hands of private avarice to an annual revenue of near thirty thousand pounds. Our colleges are supposed to be schools of science as well as of education, nor is it unreasonable to expect that a body of literary men, addicted to a life of celibacy, exempt from the care of their own subsistence, and amply provided with books, should devote their leisure to the prosecution of study, and that some effects of their studies should be manifested to the world. The shelves of their library groan under the weight of the Benedictine folios, of the editions of the Fathers, and the collections of the middle ages which have issued from the single abbey of St. Germain de Prés at Paris. A composition of genius must be the offspring of one mind; but such works of industry as may be divided among many hands and must be continued during many years are the peculiar province of a laborious community. If I inquire into the manufactures of the monks of Magdalen, if I extend the inquiry to the other colleges of Oxford and Cambridge, a silent blush or a scornful frown will be the only reply. The fellows or monks of my time were decent easy men, who supinely enjoyed the gifts of the founder. Their days were filled by a series of uniform employments—the chapel and the hall, the coffee-house and the common room—till they retired, weary and well satisfied, to a long slumber. From the toil of reading, or thinking, or writing, they had absolved their conscience, and the first shoots of learning and ingenuity withered on the ground, without yielding any fruit to the owners or the public. The only student was a young fellow (a future bishop) who was deeply immersed in the follies of the Hutchinsonian system. The only author was an half-starved chaplain—Ballard was his name—who begged subscriptions for some *Memoirs* concerning the learned ladies of Great Britain. As a gentleman commoner I was admitted to the society of the fellows, and fondly expected that some questions of literature would be the amusing and instructive topics of their discourse. Their conversation stagnated in a round of college business, Tory politics, personal stories, and private scandal; their dull and deep potations excused the brisk intemperance of youth, and their constitutional toasts were not expressive of the most lively loyalty for the House of Hanover. A general election was now approaching; the great Oxfordshire contest already blazed with all the malevolence of party zeal. Magdalen College was devoutly attached to the old interest, and the names of Wenman and Dashwood were more frequently pronounced than those of Cicero and Chrysostom. The example of the senior fellows could not inspire the undergraduates with a liberal spirit, a

[1] Lectures.

studious emulation, and I cannot describe, as I never knew, the discipline of the college. Some duties may possibly have been imposed on the poor scholars, whose ambition aspired to the peaceful honors of a fellowship (*ascribi quietis ordinibus . . . Deorum*[1]); but no independent members were admitted below the rank of a gentleman commoner, and our velvet cap was the cap of liberty. A tradition prevailed that some of our predecessors had spoken Latin declamations in the hall, but of this ancient custom no vestige remained; the obvious methods of public exercises and examinations were totally unknown, and I have never heard that either the president or the society interfered in the private economy of the tutors and their pupils.

The silence of the Oxford professors, which deprives the youth of public instruction, is imperfectly supplied by the tutors, as they are styled, of the several colleges. Instead of confining themselves to a single science, which had satisfied the ambition of Burmann or Bernoulli, they teach, or promise to teach, either history or mathematics or ancient literature or moral philosophy; and as it is possible that they may be defective in all, it is highly probable that of some they will be ignorant. They are paid, indeed, by private contributions, but their appointment depends on the head of the house. Their diligence is voluntary and will consequently be languid, while the pupils themselves and their parents are not indulged in the liberty of choice or change. The first tutor into whose hands I was resigned appears to have been one of the best of the tribe. Dr. Waldegrave was a learned and pious man, of a mild disposition, strict morals, and abstemious life, who seldom mingled in the politics or the jollity of the college. But his knowledge of the world was confined to the university; his learning was of the last, rather than the present age; his temper was indolent; his faculties, which were not of the first rate, had been relaxed by the climate, and he was satisfied, like his fellows, with the slight and superficial discharge of an important trust. As soon as my tutor had sounded the insufficiency of his disciple in school-learning, he proposed that we should read every morning from ten to eleven the comedies of Terence. The sum of my improvement in the University of Oxford is confined to three or four Latin plays; and even the study of an elegant classic, which might have been illustrated by a comparison of ancient and modern theaters, was reduced to a dry and literal interpretation of the author's text. During the first weeks I constantly attended these lessons in my tutor's room; but as they appeared equally devoid of profit and pleasure, I was once tempted to try the experiment of a formal apology. The apology was accepted with a smile. I repeated the offense with less ceremony; the excuse was admitted with the same indulgence. The slightest motive of laziness or indisposition, the most trifling avocation at home or abroad, was allowed as a worthy impediment, nor did my tutor appear conscious of my absence or neglect. Had the hour of lecture been constantly filled, a single hour was a small portion of my academic leisure. No plan of study was recommended for my use; no exercises were prescribed for his inspection, and at the most precious season of youth, whole days and weeks were suffered to elapse without labor or amusement, without advice or account. I should have listened to the voice of reason and of my tutor; his mild behavior had gained my confidence. I preferred his society to that of the younger students, and in our evening walks to the top of Heddington hill, we freely conversed on a variety of subjects. Since the days of Pocock and Hyde, oriental learning has always been the pride of Oxford, and I once expressed an inclination to study Arabic. His prudence discouraged this childish fancy, but he neglected the fair occasion of directing the ardor of a curious mind. During my absence in the summer vacation, Dr. Waldegrave accepted a college living at Washington in Sussex, and on my return I no longer found him at Oxford. From that time I have lost sight of my first tutor; but at the end of thirty years (1781) he was still alive, and the practice of exercise and temperance had entitled him to an healthy old age.

The long recess between the Trinity and Michaelmas terms empties the colleges of Oxford, as well as the courts of Westminster. I spent, at my father's house at Buriton in Hampshire, the two months of August and September, which in the year 1752 were cur-

[1]To be enrolled in the serene ranks of the gods. (Horace, *Odes*, III, iii, 35–36.)

tailed, to my great surprise, of eleven days by the alteration of the style.[1] It is whimsical enough, that as soon as I left Magdalen College my taste for books began to revive; but it was the same blind and boyish taste for the pursuit of exotic history. Unprovided with original learning, unformed in the habits of thinking, unskilled in the arts of composition, I resolved—to write a book. The title of this first essay, *The Age of Sesostris,* was perhaps suggested by Voltaire's *Age of Louis XIV*, which was new and popular; but my sole object was to investigate the probable date of the life and reign of the conqueror of Asia. I was then enamored of Sir John Marsham's *Canon Chronicus*, an elaborate work of whose merits and defects I was not yet qualified to judge. According to his specious though narrow plan, I settled my hero about the time of Solomon, in the tenth century before the Christian era. It was therefore incumbent on me, unless I would adopt Sir Isaac Newton's shorter chronology, to remove a formidable objection, and my solution, for a youth of fifteen, is not devoid of ingenuity. In his version of the Sacred Books, Manetho the high priest has identified Sethosis, or Sesostris, with the elder brother of Danaus, who landed in Greece, according to the Parian Marble, fifteen hundred and ten years before Christ. But in my supposition the high priest is guilty of a voluntary error; flattery is the prolific parent of falsehood, and falsehood, I will now add, is not incompatible with the sacerdotal character. Manetho's *History of Egypt* is dedicated to Ptolemy Philadelphus, who derived a fabulous or illegitimate pedigree from the Macedonian kings of the race of Hercules. Danaus is the ancestor of Hercules; and after the failure of the elder branch, his descendants the Ptolemies are the sole representatives of the royal family, and may claim by inheritance the kingdom which they hold by conquest. Such were my juvenile discoveries; at a riper age I no longer presume to connect the Greek, the Jewish, and the Egyptian antiquities, which are lost in a distant cloud. Nor is this the only instance in which the belief and knowledge of the child are superseded by the more rational ignorance of the man. During my stay at Buriton, my infant labor was diligently prosecuted without much interruption from company or country diversions, and I already heard the music of public applause. The discovery of my own weakness was the first symptom of taste. On my return to Oxford, the *Age of Sesostris* was wisely relinquished; but the imperfect sheets remained twenty years at the bottom of a drawer, till in a general clearance of papers (November, 1772) they were committed to the flames.

After the departure of Dr. Waldegrave, I was transferred with the rest of his live stock to a senior fellow, whose literary and moral character did not command the respect of the college. Dr. Winchester well remembered that he had a salary to receive, and only forgot that he had a duty to perform. Instead of guiding the studies and watching over the behavior of his disciple, I was never summoned to attend even the ceremony of a lecture; and except one voluntary visit to his rooms, during the eight months of his titular office the tutor and pupil lived in the same college as strangers to each other. The want of experience, of advice, and of occupation, soon betrayed me into some improprieties of conduct, ill-chosen company, late hours, and inconsiderate expense. My growing debts might be secret; but my frequent absence was visible and scandalous, and a tour to Bath, a visit into Buckinghamshire, and four excursions to London in the same winter, were costly and dangerous frolics. They were indeed without a meaning, as without an excuse. The irksomeness of a cloistered life repeatedly tempted me to wander; but my chief pleasure was that of traveling, and I was too young and bashful to enjoy, like a manly Oxonian in town, the taverns and bagnios of Covent Garden. In all these excursions I eloped from Oxford, I returned to college; in a few days I eloped again, as if I had been an independent stranger in a hired lodging, without once hearing the voice of admonition, without once feeling the hand of control. Yet my time was lost, my expenses were multiplied, my behavior abroad was unknown. Folly as well as vice should have awakened the attention of my superiors, and my tender years would have justified a more than ordinary degree of restraint and discipline.

[1] The Gregorian calendar was established by Pope Gregory XIII in 1582, but was not adopted in England until this time, when 3 September (old style) was reckoned as 14 September (new style). At the same time the year was made to begin on 1 January instead of on 25 March.

STUDIES IN SWITZERLAND

Such, from my arrival at Lausanne during the first eighteen or twenty months (July, 1753–March, 1755), were my useful studies, the foundation of all my future improvements. But in the life of every man of letters there is an era, from a level, from whence he soars with his own wings to his proper height, and the most important part of his education is that which he bestows on himself. My worthy tutor had the good sense and modesty to discern how far he could be useful. As soon as he felt that I advanced beyond his speed and measure, he wisely left me to my genius, and the hours of lesson were soon lost in the voluntary labor of the whole morning, and sometimes of the whole day. The desire of prolonging my time, gradually confirmed the salutary habit of early rising, to which I have always adhered with some regard to seasons and situations; but it is happy for my eyes and for my health, that my temperate ardor has never been seduced to trespass on the hours of the night. During the last three years of my residence at Lausanne, I may assume the merit of serious and solid application, but I am tempted to distinguish the last eight months of the year 1755, as the period of the most extraordinary diligence and rapid progress. In my French and Latin translations I adopted an excellent method, which from my own success I would recommend to the imitation of students. I chose some classic writer such as Cicero and Vertot, the most approved for purity and elegance of style. I translated, for instance, an epistle of Cicero into French; and after throwing it aside, till the words and phrases were obliterated from my memory, I re-translated my French into such Latin as I could find, and then compared each sentence of my imperfect version, with the ease, the grace, the propriety of the Roman orator. A similar experiment was made on some pages of the *Revolutions* of Vertot; I turned them into Latin, re-turned them after a sufficient interval into my own French, and again scrutinized the resemblance or dissimilitude of the copy and the original. By degrees I was less ashamed, by degrees I was more satisfied with myself; and I persevered in the practice of these double translations, which filled several books, till I had acquired the knowledge of both idioms, and the command at least of a correct style. This useful exercise of writing was accompanied and succeeded by the more pleasing occupation of reading the best authors. Dr. Middleton's *History*, which I then appreciated above its true value, naturally directed me to the writings of Cicero. The most perfect editions, that of Olivet which may adorn the shelves of the rich, that of Ernesti which should lie on the table of the learned, were not in my power. For the familiar epistles I used the text and English commentary of Bishop Ross, but my general edition was that of Verburgius, published at Amsterdam in two large volumes in folio, with an indifferent choice of various notes. I read with application and pleasure all the epistles, all the orations, and the most important treatises of rhetoric and philosophy, and as I read, I applauded the observation of Quintilian, that every student may judge of his own proficiency by the satisfaction which he receives from the Roman orator. Cicero in Latin, and Xenophon in Greek, are indeed the two ancients whom I would first propose to a liberal scholar, not only for the merit of their style and sentiments, but for the admirable lessons, which may be applied almost to every situation of public and private life. Cicero's *Epistles* may in particular afford the models of every form of correspondence, from the careless effusions of tenderness and friendship, to the well-guarded declaration of discreet and dignified resentment. After finishing this great author, a library of eloquence and reason, I formed a more extensive plan of reviewing the Latin classics under the four divisions of, 1. historians, 2. poets, 3. orators, and 4. philosophers, in a chronological series from the days of Plautus and Sallust, to the decline of the language and empire of Rome; and this plan, in the last twenty-seven months of my residence at Lausanne (January, 1756–April, 1758), I nearly accomplished. Nor was this review, however rapid, either hasty or superficial. I indulged myself in a second and even a third perusal of Terence, Virgil, Horace, Tacitus, *etc.*, and studied to imbibe the sense and spirit most congenial to my own. I never suffered a difficult or corrupt passage to escape, till I had viewed it in every light of which it was susceptible. Though often disappointed, I always consulted the most learned or ingenious commentators, Torrentius and Dacier on

Horace, Catrou and Servius on Virgil, Lipsius on Tacitus, Meziriac on Ovid, *etc.*, and in the ardor of my inquiries I embraced a large circle of historical and critical erudition. My abstracts of each book were made in the French language; my observations often branched into particular essays, and I can still read without contempt a dissertation of eight folio pages on eight lines (287–294) of the fourth *Georgic* of Virgil. M. Deyverdun, my friend whose name will be frequently repeated, had joined with equal zeal, though not with equal perseverance in the same undertaking. To him every thought, every composition, was instantly communicated; with him I enjoyed the benefits of a free conversation on the topics of our common studies.

But it is scarcely possible for a mind endowed with any active curiosity to be long conversant with the Latin classics, without aspiring to know the Greek originals whom they celebrate as their masters, and of whom they so warmly recommended the study and imitation:

Vos exemplaria Græca
Nocturna versate manu, versate diurna.[1]

It was now that I regretted the early years which had been wasted in sickness or idleness, or more idle reading; that I condemned the perverse method of our schoolmasters, who by first teaching the mother-language, might descend with so much ease and perspicuity to the origin and etymology of a derivative idiom. In the nineteenth year of my age I determined to supply this defect, and the lessons of Pavilliard again contributed to smooth the entrance of the way, the Greek alphabet, the grammar, and the pronunciation according to the French accent. As he had possessed only such a stock as was requisite for an ecclesiastic, our first book was St. John's Gospel, and I should probably have construed the whole of the New Testament, had I not represented the absurdity of adhering to the corrupt dialect of the Hellenist Jews. At my earnest request we presumed to open the *Iliad*, and I had the pleasure of beholding, though darkly and through a glass, the true image of Homer, whom I had long since admired in an English dress. After my tutor, conscious of his inability, had left me to myself, I worked my way through about half the *Iliad*, and afterwards interpreted alone a large portion of Xenophon and Herodotus. But my ardor, destitute of aid and emulation, was gradually cooled, and, from the barren task of searching words in a lexicon, I withdrew to the free and familiar conversation of Virgil and Tacitus. Yet in my residence at Lausanne I had laid a solid foundation, which enabled me in a more propitious season to prosecute the study of Grecian literature.

From a blind idea of the usefulness of such abstract science, my father had been desirous, and even pressing, that I should devote some time to the mathematics, nor could I refuse to comply with so reasonable a wish. During two winters I attended the private lectures of Monsieur de Traytorrens, who explained the elements of algebra and geometry as far as the *Conic Sections* of the Marquis de l'Hôpital, and appeared satisfied with my diligence and improvement. But as my childish propensity for numbers and calculations was totally extinct, I was content to receive the passive impression of my professor's lectures, without any active exercise of my own powers. As soon as I understood the principles, I relinquished for ever the pursuit of the mathematics, nor can I lament that I desisted before my mind was hardened by the habit of rigid demonstration, so destructive of the finer feelings of moral evidence, which must, however, determine the actions and opinions of our lives.

ITALY

I SHALL advance with rapid brevity in the narrative of my Italian tour, in which somewhat more than a year (April 1764–May 1765) was agreeably employed. Content with tracing my line of march, and slightly touching on my personal feelings, I shall waive the minute investigation of the scenes which have been viewed by thousands, and described by hundreds of our modern travelers. Rome is the great object of our pilgrimage; and (1) the journey, (2) the residence, and (3) the return, will form the most proper and perspicuous division. 1. I climbed Mount Cenis and descended into the plain of Piedmont, not on

[1]My friends, make Greece your model when you write,
And turn her volumes over day and night.
(Horace, *De Arte Poetica*, 268–269. Conington's translation.)

the back of an elephant,[1] but on a light osier seat in the hands of the dexterous and intrepid chairmen of the Alps. The architecture and government of Turin presented the same aspect of tame and tiresome uniformity; but the court was regulated with decent and splendid economy, and I was introduced to his Sardinian majesty Charles Emanuel, who after the incomparable Frederick held the second rank—*proximus longo tamen intervallo*[2] —among the kings of Europe. The size and populousness of Milan could not surprise an inhabitant of London; the dome or cathedral is an unfinished monument of Gothic superstition and wealth, but the fancy is amused by a visit to the Borromean Islands, an enchanted palace, a work of the fairies in the midst of a lake encompassed with mountains and far removed from the haunts of men. I was less amused by the marble palaces of Genoa, than by the recent memorials of her deliverance (in December 1746) from the Austrian tyranny, and I took a military survey of every scene of action within the inclosure of her double walls. My steps were detained at Parma and Modena, by the precious relics of the Farnese and Este collections; but, alas! the far greater part had been already transported, by inheritance or purchase, to Naples and Dresden. By the road of Bologna and the Apennine I at last reached Florence, where I reposed from June to September, during the heat of the summer months. In the gallery, and especially in the Tribune, I first acknowledged at the feet of the Venus of Medicis that the chisel may dispute the preeminence with the pencil, a truth in the fine arts which cannot on this side of the Alps be felt or understood. At home I had taken some lessons of Italian; on the spot I read with a learned native the classics of the Tuscan idiom. But the shortness of my time, and the use of the French language, prevented my acquiring any facility of speaking, and I was a silent spectator in the conversations of our envoy, Sir Horace Mann, whose most serious business was that of entertaining the English at his hospitable table. After leaving Florence, I compared the solitude of Pisa with the industry of Lucca and Leghorn, and continued my journey through Sienna to Rome, where I arrived in the beginning of October. 2. My temper is not very susceptible of enthusiasm, and the enthusiasm which I do not feel, I have ever scorned to affect. But, at the distance of twenty-five years, I can neither forget nor express the strong emotions which agitated my mind as I first approached and entered the eternal city. After a sleepless night, I trod with a lofty step the ruins of the Forum. Each memorable spot, where Romulus stood, or Tully spoke, or Cæsar fell, was at once present to my eye, and several days of intoxication were lost or enjoyed before I could descend to a cool and minute investigation. My guide was Mr. Byers, a Scotch antiquary of experience and taste; but in the daily labor of eighteen weeks the powers of attention were sometimes fatigued, till I was myself qualified in a last review to select and study the capital works of ancient and modern art. Six weeks were borrowed for my tour of Naples, the most populous of cities relative to its size, whose luxurious inhabitants seem to dwell on the confines of paradise and hell-fire. I was presented to the boy king by our new envoy, Sir William Hamilton, who, wisely diverting his correspondence from the secretary of state to the Royal Society and British Museum, has elucidated a country of such inestimable value to the naturalist and antiquarian. On my return, I fondly embraced for the last time the miracles of Rome; but I departed without kissing the feet of Rezzonico (Clement XIII), who neither possessed the wit of his predecessor Lambertini, nor the virtues of his successor Ganganelli. 3. In my pilgrimage from Rome to Loretto I again crossed the Apennine. From the coast of the Adriatic I traversed a fruitful and populous country, which would alone disprove the paradox of Montesquieu, that modern Italy is a desert. Without adopting the exclusive prejudice of the natives, I sincerely admired the paintings of the Bologna school. I hastened to escape from the sad solitude of Ferrara, which in the age of Cæsar was still more desolate. The spectacle of Venice afforded some hours of astonishment and some days of disgust; the University of Padua is a dying taper; but Verona still boasts her amphitheater, and his native Vicenza is adorned by the classic architecture of Palladio. The road of Lombardy and Piedmont (did Montesquieu find them without inhabitants?) led me

[1]Gibbon alludes to Hannibal's passage of the Alps.

[2]Nearest, however, from a long distance. (Altered from *Æneid*, V. 320.)

back to Milan, Turin, and the passage of Mount Cenis, where I again crossed the Alps in my way to Lyons.

The use of foreign travel has been often debated as a general question, but the conclusion must be finally applied to the character and circumstances of each individual. With the education of boys, where or how they may pass over some juvenile years with the least mischief to themselves or others, I have no concern. But after supposing the previous and indispensable requisites of age, judgment, a competent knowledge of men and books, and a freedom from domestic prejudices, I will briefly describe the qualifications which I deem most essential to a traveler. He should be endowed with an active, indefatigable vigor of mind and body, which can seize every mode of conveyance, and support with a careless smile every hardship of the road, the weather, or the inn. It must stimulate him with a restless curiosity, impatient of ease, covetous of time and fearless of danger, which drives him forth at any hour of the day or night to brave the flood, to climb the mountain, or to fathom the mine, on the most doubtful promise of entertainment or instruction. The arts of common life are not studied in the closet. With a copious stock of classical and historical learning my traveler must blend the practical knowledge of husbandry and manufactures. He should be a chemist, a botanist, and a master of mechanics. A musical ear will multiply the pleasures of his Italian tour, but a correct and exquisite eye which commands the landscape of a country, discerns the merit of a picture and measures the proportions of a building, is more closely connected with the finer feelings of the mind, and the fleeting image shall be fixed and realized by the dexterity of the pencil. I have reserved for the last a virtue which borders on a vice, the flexible temper which can assimilate itself to every tone of society from the court to the cottage, the happy flow of spirits which can amuse and be amused in every company and situation. With the advantage of an independent fortune and the ready use of national and provincial idioms, the traveler should unite the pleasing aspect and decent familiarity which makes every stranger an acquaintance, and the art of conversing with ignorance and dullness on some topic of local or professional information. The benefits of foreign travel will correspond with the degrees of these various qualifications; but, in this sketch of ideal perfection, those to whom I am known will not accuse me of framing my own panegyric. Yet the historian of the *Decline and Fall* must not regret his time or expense, since it was the view of Italy and Rome which determined the choice of the subject. In my journal the place and moment of conception are recorded, the fifteenth of October 1764, in the close of evening, as I sat musing in the church of the Zoccolanti or Franciscan friars, while they were singing vespers in the temple of Jupiter on the ruins of the Capital. But my original plan was circumscribed to the decay of the city rather than of the empire, and though my reading and reflections began to point towards that object, some years elapsed and several avocations intervened, before I was seriously engaged in the execution of that laborious work.

REFLECTIONS ON DEPENDENCE

The renewal, or perhaps the improvement, of my English life was embittered by the alteration of my own feelings. At the age of twenty-one I was, in my proper station of a youth, delivered from the yoke of education, and delighted with the comparative state of liberty and affluence. My filial obedience was natural and easy, and in the gay prospect of futurity, my ambition did not extend beyond the enjoyment of my books, my leisure, and my patrimonial estate, undisturbed by the cares of a family and the duties of a profession. But in the militia I was armed with power, in my travels I was exempt from control; and as I approached, as I gradually transcended my thirtieth year, I began to feel the desire of being master in my own house. The most gentle authority will sometimes frown without reason, the most cheerful submission will sometimes murmur without cause, and such is the law of our imperfect nature, that we must either command or obey; that our personal liberty is supported by the obsequiousness of our own dependents. While so many of my acquaintance were married or in parliament, or advancing with a rapid step in the various roads of honors and fortune, I stood alone immovable and insignificant; for after the monthly meeting of 1770, I had even withdrawn myself from the militia by the resignation of an empty and barren commission. My temper is not susceptible of envy, and the view of successful merit has always excited my warmest applause. A matrimonial alliance has ever been the object of my terror rather than of my wishes. I was not very strongly pressed by my family or my passions to propagate the name and race of the Gibbons and, if some reasonable temptations occurred in the neighborhood, the vague idea never proceeded to the length of a serious negotiation. The miseries of a vacant life were never known to a man whose hours were insufficient for the inexhaustible pleasures of study. But I lamented that at the proper age I had not embraced the lucrative pursuits of the law or of trade, the chances of civil office or India adventure, or even the fat slumbers of the church, and my repentance became more lively as the loss of time was more irretrievable. Experience showed me the use of grafting my private consequence on the importance of a great professional body; the benefits of those firm connections which are cemented by hope and interest, by gratitude and emulation, by the mutual exchange of services and favors. From the emoluments of a profession I might have derived an ample fortune, or a competent income, instead of being stinted to the same narrow allowance, to be increased only by an event which I sincerely deprecated. The progress and the knowledge of our domestic disorders aggravated my anxiety, and I began to apprehend that I might be left in my old age without the fruits either of industry or inheritance.

THE DECLINE AND FALL OF THE ROMAN EMPIRE

My conscience does not accuse me of any act of extravagance or injustice. The remnant of my estate affords an ample and honorable provision for my declining age, and my spontaneous bounty must be received with implicit gratitude by the heirs of my choice. I shall not expatiate more minutely on my economical affairs, which cannot be instructive or amusing to the reader. It is a rule of prudence, as well as of politeness, to reserve such confidence for the ear of a private friend, without exposing our situation to the envy or pity of strangers; for envy is productive of hatred, and pity borders too nearly on contempt. Yet I may believe, and even assert, that in circumstances more indigent or more wealthy, I should never have accomplished the task, or acquired the fame of an historian; that my spirit would have been broken by poverty and contempt, and that my industry might have been relaxed in the labor and luxury of a superfluous fortune. Few works of merit and importance have been executed either in a garret or a palace. A gentleman possessed of leisure and independence, of books and talents, may be encouraged to write by the distant prospect of honor and reward, but wretched is the author and wretched will be the work where daily diligence is stimulated by daily hunger.

I had now attained the solid comforts of life—a convenient well furnished house, a domestic table, half a dozen chosen servants, my own carriage, and all those decent luxuries whose value is the more sensibly felt the longer they are enjoyed. These advantages were crowned by the first of earthly blessings, independence. I was the absolute master of my hours and actions, nor was I deceived in the hope that the establishment of my library in town would allow me to divide the day between study and society. Each year the circle of my acquaintance, the number of my dead and living companions, was enlarged. To a lover of books, the shops and sales in London present irresistible temptations, and the manufacture of my history required a various and growing stock of materials. The militia, my travels, the House of Commons, the fame of an author contributed to multiply my connections. I was chosen a member of the fashionable clubs, and before I left England there were few persons of any eminence in the literary or political world to whom I was a stranger. By my own choice I passed in town the greatest part of the year; but whenever I was desirous of breathing the air of the country, I possessed an hospitable retreat at Sheffield Place in Sussex, in the family of Mr. Holroyd, a valuable friend whose character, under the name of Lord Sheffield, has since been more conspicuous to the public.

No sooner was I settled in my house and library, than I undertook the composition of the first volume of my history. At the outset all was dark and doubtful—even the title of the work, the true era of the decline and fall of the empire, the limits of the introduction, the division of the chapters, and the order of the narrative; and I was often tempted to cast away the labor of seven years. The style of an author should be the image of his mind, but the choice and command of language is the fruit of exercise. Many experiments were made before I could hit the middle tone between a dull chronicle and a rhetorical declamation. Three times did I compose the first chapter, and twice the second and third, before I was tolerably satisfied with their effect. In the remainder of the way I advanced with a more equal and easy pace; but the fifteenth and sixteenth chapters have been reduced by three successive revisals, from a large volume to their present size, and they might still be compressed, without any loss of facts or sentiments. An opposite fault may be imputed to the concise and superficial narrative of the first reigns from Commodus to Alexander—a fault of which I have never heard, except from Mr. Hume in his last journey to London. Such an oracle might have been consulted and obeyed with rational devotion, but I was soon disgusted with the modest practice of reading the manuscript to my friends. Of such friends some will praise from politeness, and some will criticize from vanity. The author himself is the best judge of his own performances. None has so deeply meditated on the subject, none is so sincerely interested in the event.

By the friendship of Mr. (now Lord) Eliot, who had married my first cousin, I was returned at the general election for the borough of Liskeard. I took my seat[1] at the beginning of the memorable contest between Great Britain and America, and supported with many a sincere and silent vote the rights, though not perhaps the interests, of the mother country. After a fleeting illusive hope, prudence condemned me to acquiesce in the humble station of a mute. I was not armed by nature or education with the intrepid energy of mind and voice,—

Vincentem strepitus, et natum rebus agendis.[2]

Timidity was fortified by pride, and even the success of my pen discouraged the trial of my voice. But I assisted at the debates of a free assembly which agitated the most important questions of peace and war, of justice and policy. I listened to the attack and defense of eloquence and reason; I had a near prospect of the characters, views, and passions of the first men of the age. The eight sessions that I sat in parliament were a school of civil prudence, the first and most essential virtue of an historian.

The volume of my history which had been somewhat delayed by the novelty and tumult of a first session, was now ready for the press. After the perilous adventure had been declined by my timid friend Mr. Elmsley, I agreed on very easy terms with Mr. Thomas Cadell, a respectable bookseller, and Mr. William Strahan, an eminent printer; and they undertook the care and risk of the publication, which derived more credit from the name of the shop than from that of the author. The last revisal of the proofs was submitted to my vigilance, and many blemishes of style which had been invisible in the manuscript, were discovered and corrected in the printed sheet. So moderate were our hopes, that the original impression had been stinted to five hundred, till the number was doubled by the prophetic taste of Mr. Strahan. During this awful interval I was neither elated by the ambition of fame, nor depressed by the apprehension of contempt. My diligence and accuracy were attested by my own conscience. History is the most popular species of writing, since it can adapt itself to the highest or the lowest capacity. I had chosen an illustrious subject. Rome is familiar to the schoolboy and the statesman, and my narrative was deduced from the last period of classical reading. I had likewise flattered myself, that an age of light and liberty would receive without scandal an inquiry into the human causes of the progress and establishment of Christianity.

I am at a loss how to describe the success of the work, without betraying the vanity of the writer. The first impression was exhausted in a few days; a second and third edition were scarcely adequate to the demand, and the bookseller's property was twice invaded by the pirates of Dublin. My book was on every table, and almost on every toilette; the historian was crowned by the taste or fashion of the day, nor was the general voice disturbed by the barking of any profane critic

[1]In the House of Commons.

[2]Fitted to triumph over the noise [of a crowd], and formed for action. (Horace, *De Arte Poetica*, 82.)

The favor of mankind is most freely bestowed on a new acquaintance of any original merit, and the mutual surprise of the public and their favorite is productive of those warm sensibilities, which at a second meeting can no longer be rekindled. If I listened to the music of praise, I was more seriously satisfied with the approbation of my judges. The candor of Dr. Robertson embraced his disciple. A letter from Mr. Hume overpaid the labor of ten years, but I have never presumed to accept a place in the triumvirate of British historians.

My second excursion to Paris was determined by the pressing invitation of M. and Mme. Necker, who had visited England in the preceding summer. On my arrival I found M. Necker director-general of the finances, in the first bloom of power and popularity. His private fortune enabled him to support a liberal establishment, and his wife, whose talents and virtues I had long admired, was admirably qualified to preside in the conversation of her table and drawing-room. As their friend, I was introduced to the best company of both sexes, to the foreign ministers of all nations, and to the first names and characters of France, who distinguished me by such marks of civility and kindness as gratitude will not suffer me to forget, and modesty will not allow me to enumerate. The fashionable suppers often broke into the morning hours; yet I occasionally consulted the Royal Library, and that of the Abbey of St. Germain, and in the free use of their books at home I had always reason to praise the liberality of those institutions. The society of men of letters I neither courted nor declined, but I was happy in the acquaintance of M. de Buffon, who united with a sublime genius the most amiable simplicity of mind and manners. At the table of my old friend, M. de Foncemagne, I was involved in a dispute with the Abbé de Mably, and his jealous, irascible spirit revenged itself on a work which he was incapable of reading in the original.

Near two years had elapsed between the publication of my first and the commencement of my second volume, and the causes must be assigned of this long delay. 1. After a short holiday, I indulged my curiosity in some studies of a very different nature, a course of anatomy which was demonstrated by Dr. Hunter, and some lessons of chemistry, which were delivered by Mr. Higgins. The principles of these sciences, and a taste for books of natural history, contributed to multiply my ideas and images, and the anatomist or chemist may sometimes track me in their own snow. 2. I dived, perhaps too deeply, into the mud of the Arian controversy, and many days of reading, thinking, and writing were consumed in the pursuit of a phantom. 3. It is difficult to arrange with order and perspicuity the various transactions of the age of Constantine, and so much was I displeased with the first essay, that I committed to the flames above fifty sheets. 4. The six months of Paris and pleasure must be deducted from the account. But when I resumed my task I felt my improvement; I was now master of my style and subject, and while the measure of my daily performance was enlarged, I discovered less reason to cancel or correct. It has always been my practice to cast a long paragraph in a single mold, to try it by my ear, to deposit it in my memory, but to suspend the action of the pen till I had given the last polish to my work. Shall I add, that I never found my mind more vigorous, or my composition more happy than in the winter hurry of society and parliament?

Had I believed that the majority of English readers were so fondly attached even to the name and shadow of Christianity; had I foreseen that the pious, the timid, and the prudent would feel or affect to feel with such exquisite sensibility, I might perhaps have softened the two invidious chapters,[1] which would create many enemies and conciliate few friends. But the shaft was shot, the alarm was sounded, and I could only rejoice, that if the voice of our priests was clamorous and bitter, their hands were disarmed of the powers of persecution. I adhered to the wise resolution of trusting myself and my writings to the candor of the public, till Mr. Davies of Oxford presumed to attack, not the faith, but the good faith of the historian. My *Vindication*, expressive of less anger than contempt, amused for a moment the busy and idle metropolis, and the most rational part of the laity, and even of the clergy, appears to have been satisfied of my innocence and accuracy. My antagonists, however, were rewarded in this world. Poor Chelsum was indeed neglected,

[1]The 15th and 16th, treating of the early spread of Christianity.

and I dare not boast the making Dr. Watson a bishop; but I enjoyed the pleasure of giving a Royal pension to Mr. Davies, and of collating Dr. Apthorpe to an archiepiscopal living. Their success encouraged the zeal of Taylor the Arian, and Milner the Methodist, with many others whom it would be difficult to remember and tedious to rehearse. The list of my adversaries was graced with the more respectable names of Dr. Priestley, Sir David Dalrymple, and Dr. White, and every polemic of either university discharged his sermon or pamphlet against the impenetrable silence of the Roman historian. Let me frankly own that I was startled at the first volleys of this ecclesiastical ordnance; but as soon as I found that this empty noise was mischievous only in the intention, my fear was converted to indignation, and every feeling of indignation or curiosity has long since subsided in pure and placid indifference. * * *

In the premature dissolution which followed this session of parliament I lost my seat. Mr. Eliot was now deeply engaged in the measures of opposition, and the electors of Liskeard are commonly of the same opinion as Mr. Eliot.

In this interval of my senatorial life, I published the second and third volumes of the *Decline and Fall*. My ecclesiastical history still breathed the same spirit of freedom, but Protestant zeal is more indifferent to the characters and controversies of the fourth and fifth centuries. My obstinate silence had damped the ardor of the polemics. Dr. Watson, the most candid of my adversaries, assured me that he had no thoughts of renewing the attack, and my impartial balance of the virtues and vices of Julian was generally praised. This truce was interrupted only by some animadversions of the Catholics of Italy, and by some angry letters from Mr. Travis, who made me personally responsible for condemning with the best critics the spurious text of the three heavenly witnesses. The bigoted advocate of popes and monks may be turned over even to the bigots of Oxford, and the wretched Travis still howls under the lash of the merciless Porson.[1] But I perceived, and without surprise, the coldness and even prejudice of the town, nor could a whisper escape my ear, that in the judgment of many readers my continuation was much inferior to the original attempt. An author who cannot ascend will always appear to sink; envy was now prepared for my reception and the zeal of my religious, was fortified by the malice of my political, enemies. I was, however, encouraged by some domestic and foreign testimonies of applause, and the second and third volumes insensibly rose in sale and reputation to a level with the first. But the public is seldom wrong, and I am inclined to believe that, especially in the beginning, they are more prolix and less entertaining than the first. My efforts had not been relaxed by success, and I had rather deviated into the opposite fault of minute and superfluous diligence. On the continent my name and writings were slowly diffused; a French translation of the first volume had disappointed the booksellers of Paris, and a passage in the third was construed as a personal reflection on the reigning monarch.

LATER YEARS AT LAUSANNE

FROM my early acquaintance with Lausanne I had always cherished a secret wish, that the school of my youth might become the retreat of my declining age. A moderate fortune would secure the blessings of ease, leisure, and independence. The country, the people, the manners, the language were congenial to my taste, and I might indulge the hope of passing some years in the domestic society of a friend. After traveling with several English, M. Deyverdun was now settled at home in a pleasant habitation, the gift of his deceased aunt. We had long been separated, we had long been silent, yet in my

[1]Richard Porson (1759–1808), a profound Greek scholar. He conclusively vindicated Gibbon, but gave the latter excellent reason to call him "merciless," writing of the historian: "His industry is indefatigable; his accuracy scrupulous; his reading, which indeed is sometimes ostentatiously displayed, immense; his attention always awake; his memory retentive; his style emphatic and expressive; his periods harmonious. His reflections are often just and profound; he pleads eloquently for the rights of mankind, and the duty of toleration; nor does his humanity ever slumber, unless when women are ravished, or the Christians persecuted. . . . I confess that I see nothing wrong in Mr. Gibbon's attack on Christianity. It proceeded, I doubt not, from the purest and most virtuous motive. We can only blame him for carrying on the attack in an insidious manner, and with improper weapons. He often makes, when he cannot readily find, an occasion to insult our religion; which he hates so cordially that he might seem to revenge some personal injury. Such is his eagerness in the cause that he stoops to the most despicable pun, or to the most awkward perversion of language, for the purpose of turning the Scripture into ribaldry, or of calling Jesus an impostor." (*Letters to Travis*, Preface.)

first letter I exposed with the most perfect confidence my situation, my sentiments, and my designs. His immediate answer was a warm and joyful acceptance; the picture of our future life provoked my impatience, and the terms of arrangement were short and simple, as he possessed the property, and I undertook the expense of our common house. Before I could break my English chain, it was incumbent on me to struggle with the feelings of my heart, the indolence of my temper, and the opinion of the world, which unanimously condemned this voluntary banishment. In the disposal of my effects, the library, a sacred deposit, was alone excepted; as my post-chaise moved over Westminster bridge I bid a long farewell to the *fumum et opes strepitumque Romæ*.[1] My journey by the direct road through France was not attended with any accident, and I arrived at Lausanne near twenty years after my second departure. Within less than three months the coalition struck on some hidden rocks; had I remained aboard, I should have perished in the general shipwreck.

Since my establishment at Lausanne, more than seven years have elapsed, and if every day has not been equally soft and serene, not a day, not a moment has occurred in which I have repented of my choice. During my absence, a long portion of human life, many changes had happened. My elder acquaintance had left the stage; virgins were ripened into matrons, and children were grown to the age of manhood. But the same manners were transmitted from one generation to another. My friend alone was an inestimable treasure; my name was not totally forgotten, and all were ambitious to welcome the arrival of a stranger and the return of a fellow-citizen. The first winter was given to a general embrace, without any nice discrimination of persons and characters. After a more regular settlement, a more accurate survey, I discovered three solid and permanent benefits of my new situation. 1. My personal freedom had been somewhat impaired by the House of Commons and the Board of Trade, but I was now delivered from the chain of duty and dependence, from the hopes and fears of political adventure. My sober mind was no longer intoxicated by the fumes of party, and I rejoiced in my escape as often as I read of the midnight debates which preceded the dissolution of parliament. 2. My English economy had been that of a solitary bachelor who might afford some occasional dinners. In Switzerland I enjoyed at every meal, at every hour, the free and pleasant conversation of the friend of my youth, and my daily table was always provided for the reception of one or two extraordinary guests. Our importance in society is less a positive than a relative weight. In London I was lost in the crowd; I ranked with the first families of Lausanne, and my style of prudent expense enabled me to maintain a fair balance of reciprocal civilities. 3. Instead of a small house between a street and a stable-yard, I began to occupy a spacious and convenient mansion, connected on the north side with the city and open on the south to a beautiful and boundless horizon. A garden of four acres had been laid out by the taste of M. Deyverdun. From the garden a rich scenery of meadows and vineyards descends to the Leman Lake, and the prospect far beyond the Lake is crowned by the stupendous mountains of Savoy. My books and my acquaintance had been first united in London, but this happy position of my library in town and country was finally reserved for Lausanne. Possessed of every comfort in this triple alliance, I could not be tempted to change my habitation with the changes of the seasons.

My friends had been kindly apprehensive that I should not be able to exist in a Swiss town at the foot of the Alps, after so long conversing with the first men of the first cities of the world. Such lofty connections may attract the curious, and gratify the vain; but I am too modest, or too proud to rate my own value by that of my associates, and whatsoever may be the fame of learning or genius, experience has shown me that the cheaper qualifications of politeness and good sense are of more useful currency in the commerce of life. By many, conversation is esteemed as a theater or a school; but after the morning has been occupied by the labors of the library, I wish to unbend rather than to exercise my mind, and in the interval between tea and supper I am far from disdaining the innocent amusement of a game at cards. Lausanne is peopled by a numerous gentry, whose companionable idleness is seldom disturbed by the

[1]Smoke and riches and noise of Rome. (Horace, *Odes*, III, xxix, 12.)

pursuits of avarice or ambition. The women, though confined to a domestic education, are endowed for the most part with more taste and knowledge than their husbands or brothers; but the decent freedom of both sexes is equally remote from the extremes of simplicity and refinement. I shall add, as a misfortune rather than a merit, that the situation and beauty of the Pays de Vaud, the long habits of the English, the medical reputation of Dr. Tissot, and the fashion of viewing the mountains and glaciers, have opened us on all sides to the incursions of foreigners. The visits of M. and Mme. Necker, of Prince Henry of Prussia, and of Mr. Fox may form some pleasing exceptions; but in general Lausanne has appeared most agreeable in my eyes, when we have been abandoned to our own society.

My transmigration from London to Lausanne could not be effected without interrupting the course of my historical labors. The hurry of my departure, the joy of my arrival, the delay of my tools, suspended their progress, and a full twelvemonth was lost before I could resume the thread of regular and daily industry. A number of books most requisite and least common had been previously selected. The academical library of Lausanne, which I could use as my own, contains at least the fathers and councils, and I have derived some occasional succor from the public collections of Berne and Geneva. The fourth volume was soon terminated by an abstract of the controversies of the incarnation, which the learned Dr. Prideaux was apprehensive of exposing to profane eyes. In the fifth and sixth volumes the revolutions of the empire and the world are most rapid, various, and instructive, and the Greek or Roman historians are checked by the hostile narratives of the barbarians of the east and west. It was not till after many designs, and many trials, that I preferred, as I still prefer the method of grouping my picture by nations, and the seeming neglect of chronological order is surely compensated by the superior merits of interest and perspicuity. The style of the first volume is in my opinion somewhat crude and elaborate, in the second and third it is ripened into ease, correctness, and numbers; but in the three last I may have been seduced by the facility of my pen, and the constant habit of speaking one language and writing another may have infused some mixture of Gallic idioms. Happily for my eyes, I have always closed my studies with the day, and commonly with the morning, and a long but temperate labor has been accomplished without fatiguing either the mind or body. But when I computed the remainder of my time and my task, it was apparent that, according to the season of publication, the delay of a month would be productive of that of a year. I was now straining for the goal, and in the last winter many evenings were borrowed from the social pleasures of Lausanne. I could now wish that a pause, an interval, had been allowed for a serious revisal.

I have presumed to mark the moment of conception; I shall now commemorate the hour of my final deliverance. It was on the day, or rather the night of the 27th of June 1787, between the hours of eleven and twelve, that I wrote the last lines of the last page, in a summer-house in my garden. After laying down my pen, I took several turns in a *berceau*, or covered walk of acacias, which commands a prospect of the country, the lake, and the mountains. The air was temperate, the sky was serene, the silver orb of the moon was reflected from the waters, and all nature was silent. I will not dissemble the first emotions of joy on the recovery of my freedom and, perhaps, the establishment of my fame. But my pride was soon humbled, and a sober melancholy was spread over my mind, by the idea that I had taken my everlasting leave of an old and agreeable companion, and that whatsoever might be the future date of my history, the life of the historian must be short and precarious. I will add two facts, which have seldom occurred in the composition of six, or at least of five, quartos. 1. My first rough manuscript, without any intermediate copy, has been sent to the press. 2. Not a sheet has been seen by any human eyes, except those of the author and the printer; the faults and the merits are exclusively my own.

After a quiet residence of four years during which I had never moved ten miles from Lausanne, it was not without some reluctance and terror that I undertook, in a journey of two hundred leagues, to cross the mountains and the sea. Yet this formidable adventure was achieved without danger or fatigue, and at the end of a fortnight I found myself in Lord Sheffield's house and library, safe, happy, and at home. The character of my friend Mr. Holroyd had recommended him to a seat in parliament for Coventry, the command of a regiment of light dragoons, and an Irish peerage. The sense and spirit of his political writings have decided the public opinion on the great questions of our commercial intercourse with America and Ireland. He fell (in 1784) with the unpopular coalition, but his merit has been acknowledged at the last general election (1790) by the honorable invitation and free choice of the city of Bristol. During the whole time of my residence in England I was entertained at Sheffield Place and in Downing street by his hospitable kindness, and the most pleasant period was that which I passed in the domestic society of the family. In the larger circle of the metropolis I observed the country and the inhabitants with the knowledge, and without the prejudices of an Englishman; but I rejoiced in the apparent increase of wealth and prosperity, which might be fairly divided between the spirit of the nation and the wisdom of the minister. All party resentment was now lost in oblivion; since I was no man's rival, no man was my enemy. I felt the dignity of independence, and as I asked no more, I was satisfied with the general civilities of the world. The house in London which I frequented with the most pleasure and assiduity was that of Lord North. After the loss of power and of sight, he was still happy in himself and his friends, and my public tribute of gratitude and esteem could no longer be suspected of any interested motive. Before my departure from England, I assisted at the august spectacle of Mr. Hastings's trial in Westminster Hall. I shall not absolve or condemn the Governor of India; but Mr. Sheridan's eloquence demanded my applause, nor could I hear without emotion the personal compliment which he paid me in the presence of the British nation.

As the publication of my three last volumes was the principal object, so it was the first care of my English journey. The previous arrangements with the bookseller and the printer were settled in my passage through London, and the proofs, which I returned more correct, were transmitted every post from the press to Sheffield Place. The length of the operation, and the leisure of the country allowed some time to review my manuscript. Several rare and useful books, the *Assises de Jérusalem*, Ramusius *De Bello Constantinopolitano*, the Greek *Acts of the Synod of Florence*, the *Statuta Urbis Romæ, etc.*, were procured, and I introduced in their proper places the supplements which they afforded. The impression of the fourth volume had consumed three months. Our common interest required that we should move with a quicker pace, and Mr. Strahan fulfilled his engagement, which few printers could sustain, of delivering every week three thousand copies of nine sheets. The day of publication was however delayed, that it might coincide with the fifty-first anniversary of my own birthday. The double festival was celebrated by a cheerful literary dinner at Cadell's house, and I seemed to blush while they read an elegant compliment from Mr. Hayley, whose poetical talent had more than once been employed in the praise of his friend. As most of the former purchasers were naturally desirous of completing their sets, the sale of the quarto edition was quick and easy, and an octavo size was printed, to satisfy at a cheaper rate the public demand. The conclusion of my work appears to have diffused a strong sensation. It was generally read, and variously judged. The style has been exposed to much academical criticism. A religious clamor was revived, and the reproach of indecency has been loudly echoed by the rigid censors of morals. Yet upon the whole, the *History of the Decline and Fall* seems to have struck a root both at home and abroad, and may perhaps an hundred years hence still continue to be abused. The French, Italian, and German translations have been executed with various success; but instead of patronizing I should willingly suppress such imperfect copies, which injure the character while they propagate the name of the author. The Irish pirates are at once my friends and my enemies. But I cannot be displeased with the two numerous and correct impressions of the English original which have been published for the use of the continent at Basel in Switzerland. The conquests of our language and literature are not confined to Europe alone, and the writer who succeeds in London is speedily read on the banks of the Delaware and the Ganges.

In the preface of the fourth volume, while I gloried in the name of an Englishman, I announced my approaching return to the neighborhood of the Lake of Lausanne. This last trial confirmed my assurance that I had wisely chosen for my own happiness, nor did I once, in a year's visit, entertain a wish of settling in my native country. Britain is the free and fortunate island; but where is the spot in which I could unite the comforts and beauties of my establishment at Lausanne? The tumult of London astonished my eyes and ears; the amusements of public places were no longer adequate to the trouble; the clubs and assemblies were filled with new faces and young men, and our best society, our long and late dinners, would soon have been prejudicial to my health. Without any share in the political wheel, I must be idle and insignificant; yet the most splendid temptations would not have enlisted me a second time in the servitude of parliament or office. At Tunbridge, some weeks after the publication of my history, I tore myself from the embraces of Lord and Lady Sheffield, and with a young Swiss friend, whom I had introduced to the English world, I pursued the road of Dover and Lausanne. My habitation was embellished in my absence, and the last division of books, which followed my steps, increased my chosen library to the number of six or seven thousand volumes. My seraglio was ample, my choice was free, my appetite was keen. After a full repast on Homer and Aristophanes, I involved myself in the philosophic maze of the writings of Plato, of which the dramatic is perhaps more interesting than the argumentative part; but I stepped aside into every path of inquiry which reading or reflection accidentally opened.

Alas! the joy of my return and my studious ardor were soon damped by the melancholy state of my friend M. Deyverdun. His health and spirits had long suffered a gradual decline, a succession of apoplectic fits announced his dissolution, and before he expired, those who loved him could not wish for the continuance of his life. The voice of reason might congratulate his deliverance, but the feelings of nature and friendship could be subdued only by time. His amiable character was still alive in my remembrance; each room, each walk, was imprinted with our common footsteps, and I should blush at my own philosophy, if a long interval of study had not preceded and followed the death of my friend. By his last will he left me the option of purchasing his house and garden, or of possessing them during my life on the payment either of a stipulated price, or of an easy retribution to his kinsman and heir. I should probably have been tempted by the demon of property, if some legal difficulties had not been started against my title. A contest would have been vexatious, doubtful, and invidious, and the heir most gratefully subscribed an agreement which rendered my life-possession more perfect, and his future condition more advantageous. The certainty of my tenure has allowed me to lay out a considerable sum in improvements and alterations. They have been executed with skill and taste, and few men of letters, perhaps, in Europe are so desirably lodged as myself. But I feel, and with the decline of years I shall more painfully feel, that I am alone in paradise. Among the circle of my acquaintance at Lausanne, I have gradually acquired the solid and tender friendship of a respectable family. The four persons of whom it is composed are all endowed with the virtues best adapted to their age and situation, and I am encouraged to love the parents as a brother, and the children as a father. Every day we seek and find the opportunities of meeting; yet even this valuable connection cannot supply the loss of domestic society.

Within the last two or three years our tranquillity has been clouded by the disorders of France. Many families of Lausanne were alarmed and affected by the terrors of an impending bankruptcy; but the revolution, or rather the dissolution of the kingdom has been heard and felt in the adjacent lands. A swarm of emigrants of both sexes, who escaped from the public ruin, has been attracted by the vicinity, the manners, and the language of Lausanne, and our narrow habitations in town and country are now occupied by the first names and titles of the departed monarchy. These noble fugitives are entitled to our pity; they may claim our esteem, but they cannot in the present state of their mind and fortune much contribute to our amusement. Instead of looking down as calm and idle spectators on the theater of Europe, our domestic harmony is somewhat embittered by the infusion of party spirit. Our ladies and gentlemen assume the character of self-taught politicians, and the sober dictates of wisdom and experience are silenced by the clamors of the triumphant *démocrates*. The fanatic missionaries of sedition have scattered the seeds of discontent in our cities and villages, which had flourished above two hundred and fifty years without fearing the approach of war, or feeling the weight of government. Many individuals and some communities appear to be infected with the French disease, the wild theories of equal and boundless freedom; but I trust that the body of the people will be faithful to their sovereign and themselves, and I am satisfied that the failure or success of a revolt would equally terminate in the ruin of the country. While the aristocracy of Berne protects the happiness, it is superfluous to inquire whether it is founded in the rights of man; the economy of the state is liberally supplied without the aid of taxes, and the magistrates must reign with prudence and equity, since they are unarmed in the midst of an armed nation. For myself (may the omen be averted) I can only declare, that the first stroke of a rebel drum would be the signal of my immediate departure.

When I contemplate the common lot of mortality, I must acknowledge that I have drawn a high prize in the lottery of life. The far greater part of the globe is overspread with barbarism or slavery. In the civilized world the most numerous class is condemned to ignorance and poverty, and the double fortune of my birth in a free and enlightened country, in an honorable and wealthy family, is the lucky chance of an unit against millions. The general probability is about three to one, that a new-born infant will not live to complete his fiftieth year. I have now passed that age, and may fairly estimate the present value of my existence in the threefold division of mind, body, and estate.

1. The first indispensable requisite of happiness is a clear conscience, unsullied by the reproach or remembrance of an unworthy action:

> *Hic murus aheneus esto,*
> *Nil conscire sibi, nulla pallescere culpa.*[1]

I am endowed with a cheerful temper, a moderate sensibility, and a natural disposition to repose rather than to action; some mischievous appetites and habits have perhaps been corrected by philosophy or time. The love of study, a passion which derives fresh vigor from enjoyment, supplies each day, each hour with a perpetual source of independent and rational pleasure, and I am not sensible of any decay of the mental faculties. The original soil has been highly improved by labor and manure, but it may be questioned, whether some flowers of fancy, some grateful errors, have not been eradicated with the weeds of prejudice. 2. Since I have escaped from the long perils of my childhood, the serious advice of a physician has seldom been requisite. "The madness of superfluous health" I have never known; but my tender constitution has been fortified by time, the play of the animal machine still continues to be easy and regular, and the inestimable gift of the sound and peaceful slumbers of infancy may be imputed both to the mind and body. About the age of forty I was first afflicted with the gout which, in the space of fourteen years, has made seven or eight different attacks. Their duration, though not their intensity, appears to increase and after each fit I rise and walk with less strength and agility than before. But the gout has hitherto been confined to my feet and knees, the pain is never intolerable; I am surrounded by all the comforts that art and attendance can bestow; my sedentary life is amused with books and company, and in each step of my convalescence I pass through a progress of agreeable sensations 3. I have already described the merits of my society and situation, but these enjoyments would be tasteless and bitter if their possession were not assured by an annual and adequate supply. By the painful method of amputation my father's debts have been completely discharged. The labor of my pen, the sale of lands, the inheritance of a maiden aunt Miss Hester Gibbon, have improved my property and it will be exonerated on some melancholy day from the payment of Mrs. Gibbon's[2] jointure. According to the scale of Switzerland I am a rich man, and I am indeed rich, since my income is superior to my expense, and my expense is equal to my wishes. My friends, more especially Lord Sheffield, kindly relieve me from the cares to which my taste and temper are most adverse. The economy of my house is settled without avarice or profusion. At

[1]Be this your wall of brass, your coat of mail,
A guileless heart, a cheek no crime turns pale.
(Horace, *Epistles*, I, i. 59–60. Conington's translation.)

[2]Gibbon's stepmother who, however, outlived him.

stated periods all my bills are regularly paid and in the course of my life I have never been reduced to appear either as plaintiff or defendant in a court of justice. Shall I add, that since the failure of my first wishes, I have never entertained any serious thoughts of a matrimonial connection?

I am disgusted with the affectation of men of letters, who complain that they have renounced a substance for a shadow, and that their fame—which sometimes is no insupportable weight—affords a poor compensation for envy, censure, and persecution. My own experience, at least, has taught me a very different lesson. Twenty happy years have been animated by the labor of my history, and its success has given me a name, a rank, a character in the world, to which I should not otherwise have been entitled. The freedom of my writings has indeed provoked an implacable tribe, but as I was safe from the stings, I was soon accustomed to the buzzing of the hornets. My nerves are not tremblingly alive, and my literary temper is so happily framed, that I am less sensible of pain than pleasure. The rational pride of an author may be offended, rather than flattered by vague indiscriminate praise; but he cannot, he should not, be indifferent to the fair testimonies of private and public esteem. Even his social sympathy may be gratified by the idea, that now in the present hour, he is imparting some degree of amusement or knowledge to his friends in a distant land; that one day his mind will be familiar to the grandchildren of those who are yet unborn. I cannot boast of the friendship or favor of princes. The patronage of English literature has long since been devolved on our booksellers, and the measure of their liberality is the least ambiguous test of our common success. Perhaps the golden mediocrity of my fortune has contributed to fortify my application.

The present is a fleeting moment, the past is no more, and our prospect of futurity is dark and doubtful. This day may possibly be my last; but the laws of probability, so true in general, so fallacious in particular, still allow me about fifteen years, and I shall soon enter into the period which, as the most agreeable of his long life, was selected by the judgment and experience of the sage Fontenelle. His choice is approved by the eloquent historian of nature, who fixes our moral happiness to the mature season in which our passions are supposed to be calmed, our duties fulfilled, our ambition satisfied, our fame and fortune established on a solid basis. I am far more inclined to embrace than to dispute this comfortable doctrine. I will not suppose any premature decay of the mind or body; but I must reluctantly observe that two causes, the abbreviation of time, and the failure of hope, will always tinge with a browner shade the evening of life. 1. The proportion of a part to the whole is the only standard by which we can measure the length of our existence. At the age of twenty, one year is a tenth, perhaps, of the time which has elapsed within our consciousness and memory; at the age of fifty it is no more than a fortieth, and this relative value continues to decrease till the last sands are shaken by the hand of death. This reasoning may seem metaphysical but on a trial it will be found satisfactory and just. 2. The warm desires, the long expectations of youth, are founded on the ignorance of themselves and of the world. They are gradually damped by time and experience, by disappointment or possession, and after the middle season the crowd must be content to remain at the foot of the mountain, while the few who have climbed the summit aspire to descend or expect to fall. In old age the consolation of hope is reserved for the tenderness of parents who commence a new life in their children, the faith of enthusiasts who sing hallelujahs above the clouds, and the vanity of authors who presume the immortality of their name and writings.

GLOSSARY

(Words are included which occur in the poems by Chaucer, in *Piers Plowman*, in the Popular Ballads, and in Book I of Spenser's *Faerie Queene*. Words unfamiliar only by reason of their spelling, whose meaning can be determined by pronunciation, are not included. Unfamiliar words not contained in any good modern dictionary, which occur in texts other than those mentioned above, are explained in foot-notes.)

abashed, astonished.
abet, to uphold.
abrayde, awoke.
abuse, injury.
abused, deceived.
abye, to pay for.
ac, but.
accident, outward appearance.
accompted, accounted.
accordaunt, according.
ac(c)orded, to be fitting, agreed.
achaat, buying.
achatours, buyers.
acorse, to curse.
acquite, release.
addrest, prepared, ready, directed.
admired, wondered at.
affermeth, establishes as true.
affray, to alarm; panic, terror.
affyle his tonge, polish his speech.
afore, before.
after, along.
again, near, toward.
agast, frightened.
agayns, when you meet.
agraste, favored.
agrief, amiss.
al, although.
al, awl.
albe, although.
alderbest, best of all.
ale-stake, a stake projecting horizontally from a house to indicate that ale could be bought there.
algate, in every case, nevertheless.
alkin, of every kind.
alle and somme, one and all.
aller cok, the cock of all of us, *i. e.*, the host called all his guests early.
almner, almoner, giver of alms.
aloft, on high.
als, also.
al-so, as.
amate, to dismay, to dishearten.
amazed, bewildered.
amblere, a pacer.
amende, to improve.
amis, hood, cape.
amorwe, on the morrow.
ancres, anchorites.
and avowe, a vow.
andvile, anvil.
an, if.
ane, one.
an elles, and otherwise.
anlas, dagger.
anon, instantly.
antiphoner, anthem-book.
ape, to put "in the mannes hood an ape," to make a fool of a man.
apyked, sharpened, trimmed.
aread, to point out, tell, make known.
ared, made known.
areeds, to declare, to command.
areste(n), to stop.
arette, to impute.
aright, wholly.
armory, armor.
arn, are.
arras, tapestry.
aryve, disembarcation of troops; alternate reading, **armee,** expedition.
ascendent, the part of the zodiac rising above the horizon.
aslake, to assuage.
aspye, spy.
assay, *pp.* **assaid,** to try, touch, assail; an attack, value.
assent, conspiracy.
assoilling, absolution.
assynd, pointed out.
assyse, courts of assize.
asterte, to escape.
astond, amazed.
atte beste, in the best fashion.
atte Bowe, at Bow.
attempree, moderate.
Augustyn, St. Augustine.
Austin, St. Augustine.
avale, to descend, fall.
avaunt, boast.
avauntour, boaster.
aventure, chance.
avision, vision.
avizd, perceived, considered.
avize, to perceive, to consider.
avouchen, to prove.
avys, opinion.
avysed, well advised.
avyseth, consider.
awayte, to watch, to wait for.
awkwarde, backhanded.

ba, ball.
bachelere, young aspirant to knighthood.
bains, banns.
baite, to feed.
baith, both.
bake mete, meat pie.
bale, injury, evil influence, fire, sorrow.
baleful, harmful.
balys, misfortunes.
bands, bonds.
barne, man.
basnites, light helmets.
batailed, battlemented.
bawdrik, belt worn over one shoulder.
baxsteres, bakers (feminine).
bayes, bathes.
bayes, laurels.
beadmen, men of prayer.
beame, shaft, gleam.
beare up, to put the helm up.
bed, command.
bedyde, dyed.
beer, bore.
beggestere, beggar-woman.
beguyld, foiled.
behest, bidding, command.
behight, entrusted; to call, name.
behot, held out hope for, promised.
beig, necklace, collar.
bekke, nod.
Belmarye, Benmarin, a district in the north of Africa.
bemeneth, means.
bemes, trumpets.
ben, are.
Beneit, St. Benedict.
bent, a field covered with coarse grass, coarse grass.
beseemed, became.
beseemes, befits.
beseene (well), good looking.
bestedd, sorely pressed, situated.
bet, beaten.
bet, better.
bet, go bet, go as quickly as possible.
betake, deliver.
bete, to relieve.
betide, happen.
bever, lower part of a helmet.
bewray, to disclose.
beye, to buy.
bicched bones, cursed dice.
bidder, beggar.
bidding his bedes, saying his prayers.
biges, necklaces.
bihove, behooves.
biknowe(n), to acknowledge.
bile, bill, beak.
bilive, swiftly, immediately.
birk, birch.
bisette, set to work.
bismotered, stained.
bisy, anxious.
bit, commands.
(a)-blakeberied, a-blackberrying.
blame, injury.
blane, stopped.
blankmanger, creamed fowl.
blaze, to proclaim.
blent, blinds, blinded, deceived.
blered, made dim.
bless, to preserve, to brandish.
blubbred, tear-stained.
bochere, butcher.
Boece, Boethius.
boist, box.
bokeler, buckler.
bonched, struck.
boot, help, remedy.
booted, availed.
bootelesse, unavailing.
boras, borax.
bord bigonne, sat at the head of the table.
borne, brook.
borrow, ransom.
bosses, projections.
bote, remedy.
boughtes, coils, folds.
bound, to lead.
bourde, jest.
bouzing can, drinking cup
bowne, to make ready, ready.
bowr, house, chamber, muscle.
boÿs, bows.
boystrous, rough.
bracer, a guard for the arm in archery.
brae, hillside.
braid letter, a long letter or one written on a broad sheet.
brand, sword.
brast, burst.
braw, fine.
brawn, muscle.
bray, to cry out.
brayd, cried out.
breech, breeches.
breem, a fresh-water fish.
bren, bulte it to the, sift it thoroughly.
brend, burned.
bretful, full to the brim.
brevet, letter of indulgence.
brewestere, female brewer.
brode, plainly.
brook, to enjoy.
brotch, brooch.
brouke, to enjoy.
bryttlynge, cutting up.
buckle, to make ready.
buegle, bugle, wild ox.
buffe, a blow.
bugelet, bugle.
bugge, to buy.
bulle, papal rescript sealed with a lump of metal called a bull.
bulte, to sift.
burdoun, bass.
buske, bush.
buske, to make ready.
buskin, high boot.
but, unless.
but-if, unless.
buxom, yielding.
buxumnesse, submission.
by, along.

by, to pay for.
by and by, immediately.
byckarte, attacked.
byddys, abides.
byde, to endure.
byears, biers.
bylive, immediately.
bylle, sword.
byre, cow-house.
bystode, hard pressed.

caityf, captive.
call, a netted head-dress.
can, did, knows.
cancred, venomous, corrupt.
canon, a book by Avicenna.
canon bitt, smooth round bit.
capouns, capons.
capull-hyde, horse-hide.
cardiacle, a pain in the heart.
carefull, full of care.
carf, carved.
carke, sorrow.
carle, fellow.
carline, carline wife, old woman.
caroyne, body.
carpe, to talk, to joke.
carpyng, discussion.
carver, tree used for carving.
cas, accident.
cast, to intend, devised.
casten, contrived, planned.
casuelly, by chance.
catapuce, spurge.
catel, property.
caytive, captive.
ceint, girdle.
celle, a subordinate convent.
centaure, centaury.
certes, certainly.
ceruce, lead ointment.
chaffare, merchandise.
channerin, fretting.
chapman, merchant.
charge, memory.
chauffed, heated, rubbed, irritated.
chaunterie, an endowment to pay for masses.
chaw, jaw; to chew.
cheare, countenance, behavior.
chearen, to become cheered up.
cheffe, chief.
cheker, exchequer.
chere, behavior, appearance.
cherl, fellow.
cheven, to achieve.
chevisaunce, arrangement.
chide, champ.
chiknes, chickens.
chivachye, military expedition.
cink, **cinq**, five.
clappeth, chatters.
clause, in a, briefly.
clepen, to call; *pret.*, **cleped.**
clergealy, in a clerkly manner.
clergeon, little school-boy.
clerk, scholar, student.
clinke, sound.
cloches, clutches.
closs, enclosure.
clout-es, cloth, *pl.* rags.
clowe, to claw, clutch.
cod, bag; sometimes applied to the stomach.
coffer, trunk, box.
cokewold, cuckold.
cold, baneful.
colerik, of a bilious temperament (term from Galenical medicine).
colers, collars.
col-fox, one with much black in its fur.
colpons, shreds.
combred, impeded.
combrous, harassing, laborious.
compeer, comrade.
compleccіouns, collections of humors.
composicioun, arrangement.
commune, the commons.
comyn-bell, town-bell.
condicioun, condition, rank.
confiture, mixture.
conne, to learn.
conneth, they know how.
conning, skill, knowledge.
conseil, a secret.
consistone, "ecclesiastical court of an archbishop, bishop, or commissary" (Skeat).
consort, accord.
constraint, distress.
contek, strife.
contenaunce, outward show.
contrarie, foe.
conynges, conies, rabbits.
cop, top, tip.
cope, priest's cloak.
copis, copes, cloaks.
coppe, cup.
corages, hearts.
cordial, heart stimulant.
corny, strong in corn or malt. Applied to ale.
corse, body.
coste, coast.
cote, small house.
couch, to set, place.
couched, placed.
coude, knew.
counterfesaunce, an imposture.
counterfete, to imitate.
countour, king's legal representative in a county.
courtepy, short upper coat.
couthe, known, knew; **as he couthe,** as best he knew how.
coverchiefs, kerchiefs.
covyne, trickery.
cracchy, **cracche**, to scratch.
craftes, handicrafts.
crafty, skillful.
crokke, earthenware pot.
crope, crept.
croslet, small cross.
crounyng, the tonsure.
crowned, capital.
cruddy, curdled.
crulle, curled.

culled, killed.
cure, a cure of souls; care.
curious, careful.
curst turne, spiteful feat.
cut, lot.

daint, choice.
dainty, daintiness.
dalliance, amorous talk or play, trifling, social entertainment.
darrayne, to prepare for battle, to prove by wager or battle.
daun, master, from Latin *dominus.*
daunce, the olde, the old game.
daunger, control, risk.
daungerous, overbearing.
daunte, to tame, subdue.
daweninge, dawn.
dayesye, daisy.
deadly, deathlike.
deadly made, mortal.
deare, injury.
debate, fight, quarrel.
debonaire, gracious.
dee, do.
deel, bit.
dees, dice.
defame, dishonor.
defaute, fault.
defeasaunce, defeat.
defenden, to forbid; *pp.* **defended.**
defye, to digest.
degree, rank.
delices, pleasures.
deliver, active.
delivere, to set free.
deliverly, quickly.
delve, to dig.
delveres, diggers.
demen, to judge.
departed, divided.
depeint, painted.
dere, injury.
derth, scarcity.
deryve, to draw away.
despight, injury.
despiteous, cruel, malicious.
despitous, scornful.
despyt, in despite of.
devoyd, empty.
devys, decision.
devyse, to relate, tell, describe.
deye, dairy-woman.
deys, dais.
dight, adorn, put on.
dighted, wiped.
digne, worthy, haughty.
dint, stroke.
disaventrous, unfortunate.
dischevele, disheveled.
dispence, expenditure; **esy of dispence,** a small spender.
dispiteous, unpitying.
disple, to subject to penance.
disport, entertainment, pleasantry.
dispredden, spread out.
disputisoun, disputation.
disseized, deprived.
dissolute, enfeebled.
distayned, stained.
distraine, to afflict.
dites, lifts.
doen, to do.
doen to, to betake, *with reflexive.*
dois, does.
dokked, cut short.
domes, judgments.
doome, decree.
doon us honge, cause us to be hanged.
dormant, table-, a side-table kept permanently filled with food.
doted, stupid.
doubtfull, fearful.
dowve, dove.
draweth cut, draw lots.
dre, endured.
drecched, troubled.
dred, dearest, loved yet feared.
drede, doubt.
dredeth, fear.
dree, can do.
dreed, object of reverence.
drenched, drowned.
drere, sadness.
dreriment, gloom, sorrow.
drery, bloody, ghastly.
dresse, set in order.
drest, prepared, disposed.
dreynt, drowned.
drie, to feel, endure.
drift, impetus, plot.
dronkelewe, drunken.
droome, a drum.
dryven forth, to pass.
dugty, doughty.
dule, grief.
dye, hazard.
dyke, make ditches.
dykers, ditchers.
dynte, stroke.

earne, to yearn.
earst, formerly.
edifyde, built.
eek, eke, also.
eek, to increase.
effraide, frightened.
eftsoones, forthwith.
eld, age.
elles, otherwise.
elyng, miserable.
embard, imprisoned.
embayd, enclosed, bathed.
embosse, to plunge.
embost, driven to extremity; encased.
embowd, arched over.
emboyled, agitated, heated.
embrew, to plunge.
embrouded, embroidered.
emmove, to move.
empeach, to hinder.
emperst, penetrated.
emprize, enterprise.
emys, uncle's.

enchace, to depict, to engrave.
encombred, involved.
endyte, write.
enfouldred, like a thunder-cloud, hurled out like thunder and lightning.
engorged, devoured.
engrave, to bury.
engyned, put on the rack for torture.
enhaunst, raised, exalted.
enlargen, to free.
enraunged, placed in a row.
ensamples, examples.
ensewen, to follow.
entente, mind.
entraile, twisted coil.
entune, to intone.
envyned, with well-stocked wine-cellar.
erbe yve, ground ivy.
erme, grieve.
erst, first.
eschewed, shunned.
ese, doon, to provide entertainment.
esloyne, to withdraw.
espye, to perceive.
essoyne, excuse, exemption.
estatly, dignified.
eugh, yew.
even cloth, smooth cloth.
evene lengthe, medium height.
everichon, everyone.
everilkon, everyone.
every-deel, in every respect.
ewghen, of yew.
excheat, gain.
expire, to breathe out.
extirpe, to extirpate.
ey, egg.
eyas, a young hawk, newly fledged.
eyne, eyes.
eyre, air.

fa', fall.
fact, deed.
facultee, profession.
fairlies, wonders.
faitor, villain, impostor.
falding, coarse cloth.
fanglenesse, showiness, the quality of being new-fashioned.
farsed, stuffed.
fashes, troubles.
faste, close, soundly; intently.
faste by, close by.
faynd, disguised.
fayteden, begged in a deceitful manner.
faytor, deceiver.
fee, wealth.
fell, befell, happened.
fell, fierce.
felly, fiercely, cruelly.
fen, chapter of a book by Avicenna; marshland.
ferd, fear.
fere, mate, comrade.
fere, on fere, together.
ferly, wonder.
ferne, distant.
ferre, further.
ferthing, small portion.
fest, fist.
fet, feeds, fetched.
fetis / **fetys,** } neat, graceful.
fetisly, elegantly.
fey, faith.
feyne, to invent.
ffaine, glad.
ffare, to go.
ffarley, strange.
ffetteled, made ready.
fille, fell.
fillet, ribbon for the head.
finch, pulle a, meaning uncertain. Perhaps to "pluck a dupe."
finde, provide for.
fit, division of a song, strain of music, emotion condition.
fithele, fiddle.
flaggy, drooping.
flee, to fly.
fleigh, flew.
fleshly, carnally.
flit, to give way, to move.
flitting, fleeting.
florin, an English coin so called because first coined at Florence.
flowen, flew.
floytinge, playing the flute.
foile, a thin sheet of metal.
foltring, faltering.
fond, foolish.
fond / **foond,** } provided for.
fone, foes.
for, against, why.
for-by, past.
fordonne, ruined, overcome.
for-dronke, very drunk.
foreby, near.
forelifting, lifting up in front.
forespent, utterly wasted.
forlete, to give up.
for-leten, to abandon.
forn-cast, foreordained.
forneys, furnace.
for-pyned, wasted away by torment.
forrayed, ravaged.
fors, do no fors of, pay no attention to; no matter.
forsake, avoid.
for-sleuthen, to waste in idleness.
forster, forester.
for-thi, therefore.
fortuned, happened.
fortunen, to forecast favorably.
forwandred, tired out with wandering.
forward, agreement.
forwasted, laid waste.
for-wearied, utterly wearied.
forwoot, knows beforehand.
forwrapped, wrapped up, concealed.
fother, load.
fou, a dry measure varying from two to six Winchester bushels. The Winchester bushel is slightly less than standard.
foulys, birds.

fourtnet, fortnight.
fraight, fraught.
francklin / **frankeleyn** } substantial farmer, freeman.
fraternitee, guild.
fray, to frighten.
frayneth, beseeches.
frend, friend, help.
freyke, freck, bold man.
froe, from.
frounce, to gather in folds.
fruytesteres, fruit-sellers (feminine).
fry, swarm.
ful, very.
fume, harmful vapor rising from stomach to brain.
fumetere, fumitory.
fumositee, fumes caused by drunkenness.
fustian, coarse cloth.
fynde, perhaps a corruption of **fyne,** meaning end, finish.

gabbe, to jest, prate.
gage, pledge.
gain, to serve.
galingale, a sort of spice.
gall, gall-bladder.
gamed, it pleased.
gamen, to play.
gan, did.
gang, to go.
gard(e), made.
gare, ready.
garget, throat.
garlande, wreath hung on the wand in shooting contests.
gars, makes.
gatis, gates.
gat-tothed, with widely spaced teeth; *but possibly* goat-toothed (lascivious).
gaude, trickery, trifle.
gauded, fitted with gauds or beads in the rosary that mark the five joys of the Virgin.
Gaufred, Geoffrey de Vinsauf, Anglo-Norman Trouvère.
gaytres beryies, berries of the buckthorn.
gede, went.
gees, geese.
gent, gentle.
gere, utensils.
german, brother.
Gernade, Granada.
gerner, garner.
gest, exploit.
gied, gave.
gin, instrument of torture; to begin; if.
gipoun, short doublet.
gipser, wallet.
girles, young people of both sexes.
g释ternes, guitars.
giusts, jousts.
glede, glowing coal, fire.
glent, glanced, darted.
glistreth, shines.
glosed, commented on, explained.
gnarre, to growl, snarl.
go, to walk.
gobbet, fragment.
golett, part covering the throat, throat.
goliardeys, buffoon.
good, knew his good, knew how to act.
gorge, throat.
gossibs, friends, relatives.
governaunce, control.
government, conduct, control.
gowe, go we.
graile, gravel.
graine, died in graine, dyed thoroughly.
gree, favor.
greetin, weeping.
grette, greeted.
greved, grew angry.
grevis, groves.
greyn, grain, corn.
griesie, gray, grizzled.
grieslie, horrible, grim.
griple, grasp; grasping, tenacious.
gris, little pigs.
grisly, horrible.
grith, peace, "charter of peace."
grope, test.
grosse, heavy.
grotes, four-penny pieces.
ground, pattern on which lace is worked.
grucche, murmur.
gruf, on his face.
gryping, grasp.
grys, gray fur.
gryte, great.
guerdon, reward.
guize, behavior, manner, custom.
gyde, be the munkis, take charge of the monk
gypon, short coat.
gyse, way.

ha, hall.
habergeoun, coat of mail.
habite, garment.
hable, powerful, able.
hagard hauke, untamed hawk.
haire, heir.
hals, neck.
halse, to beseech.
halwes, saints, shrines of saints.
halyde, hauled.
han, have; **wiste to han,** knew he should have.
handeling, usage.
hap, lot.
harbour, shelter.
hardily, certainly.
hardiment, courage.
hardly, with difficulty.
harlot, rogue.
harlotryes, ribald actions or tales.
harneised, equipped.
harre, hinge.
harrow, a cry for aid.
hasard, the game of hazard.
hasardrye, gambling.
haunt, limit, usual resort, skill.
haunteden, practiced.
hauteyn, loud, lofty.
hawe, yard.
heasts, commands.
heben, ebony.

hee, high.
hefte, raised.
heig, high.
heigh ymaginacioun, Heaven's foreknowledge.
heled, hidden.
hende, noble, gracious.
hente, obtain, seize.
herbergage, lodging.
herberwe, harbor, inn.
herde, shepherd.
here, their.
herien, to praise.
heryinge, praising.
heste, command.
heveneriche, the kingdom of heaven.
hew, shape, condition.
heyre, hair.
hight, commanded, called; **on hight,** aloud.
hight / **highte** } was called.
hii *or* **hij,** they.
hind, deer.
hinde, courteous.
hindreste, hindmost.
hire, reward.
holde, to wager.
holland, a kind of linen.
holme, evergreen oak, or perhaps holly.
holt, wood.
homicyde, murderer.
hond, hand; **out of hond,** at once.
honest, honorable.
hoomly, simply.
hoor, gray.
hord, treasure.
hore, hoary, frosty.
horrid, bristling, rough.
hors, horses.
ho-so, whoso.
hot, was called.
houped, whooped.
housbondrye, economy.
housling, sacramental.
houves, coifs.
hove, to rise.
hoved, rocked about.
howre, time.
hulles, hills.
humour, a term from Galenical medicine. The four humors of the body were blood, phlegm, bile, and black bile.
hurtlen, to rush.
husher, usher.
hussyfskap, housewifery.
hyne, servant.

ilke, same.
ilkone, each one.
imbrew, to thrust.
impe, scion, offspring.
implyes, enfolds.
improvided, unforeseen.
incontinent, at once.
infect, invalidated.
infest, to attack, to make hostile.
inspired, breathed.
intendiment, careful consideration, knowledge.
Ise, I shall.
ith, in the.

janglere, babbler; **jangelers,** babblers.
jangleth, chatters.
jape, trick.
japers, jesters.
jaw, wave.
jet, fashion.
Jewerye, Jews'-quarters.
jolitee, pleasure.
jolly, brave, gallant, handsome.
jott, least bit.
journall, daily.
jugge, to judge.
justyse, judge.

kairen, to go up and down.
keep, keepe, heed.
keeping, be at your keeping well, be on your guard.
ken, to know.
kend, known.
kepe, to protect; **kepe I be,** care I to be.
kest, to cast.
kind / **kinde** / **kynde** } nature.
kindly, natural.
kirtle, a tunic or coat.
kithe, of same country or people.
kitte, cut.
knarre, a stump of a fellow.
knave, servant-boy.
knobbes, swellings.
knowes, knees.
kynde witte, natural intelligence.
kyngriche, kingdom.
kyrk, church.

laas, cord.
lafte, to leave off.
laike, to play.
laith, loath.
lake, pit, cavity.
lap, leaped.
large, coarsely.
last, loads.
lat, permit.
latoun, an alloy similar in appearance to brass.
laude, praise.
laugte, caught.
launcht, pierced.
lauriol, spurge-laurel.
lay, lodged.
layn, lying.
lay-stall, refuse-heap.
lazar, leper.
lea, a grassy field.
leach (*pl.* **leaches**), physician.
leaned, lay (concealed).
leasing, lie.
leed, stationary cauldron placed above furnace.
leef, lief.
leet, caused, left.
leman, lover.
lemes, flames.

lere, to teach.
lesinges, lies.
lest, delight.
leste, pleased.
let, to prevent, to hinder; hindrance, obstacle.
leten, allowed, considered.
lette, to stop, to wait; hindered.
letterure, learning.
Lettow, Lithuania.
letuaries, electuaries, prescriptions.
lente, **lewte**, loyalty.
leve, to grant.
leve, permission, a permit.
leved, believed.
leven, lawn.
lever, rather.
lewed, ignorant, rude, common.
libbard, leopard.
libbyng, living.
licour, sap.
lief(e), loved one, dear.
liflode, means of life.
liggen, to lie.
light, lightly, quickly, easily.
likerous, dainty, gluttonous.
lilled, lolled, put out (the tongue).
lillie leven, lovely lawn.
limitour, one licensed to beg within certain limits.
lin, to cease (from).
list, pleased.
litarge, ointment made from protoxide of lead.
lith, limb.
lobyes, lubbers.
lodemenage, pilotage.
loe, to love.
logge, resting-place.
lopen, leapt.
lordinges, gentlemen.
lorne, lost, deserted.
losengéour, flatterer.
loset, loosed.
lough, laughed.
louted, bowed.
louting, bowing.
love-dayes, days appointed for settlement of disputes.
lovye, to love.
lowe, hill.
lowed, stooped.
Loy, St. Eligius.
luce, carp.
lust, delight, desire.
lustlesse, feeble.
Lyes, Ayas in Asiatic Turkey.
lykam, body.
lyking, pleasure, desire.
lyne, linden.
lyne, lineage.
lyng, furze, bent grass.
lyvinge, manner of life.

magger of, in spite of.
maine, force.
maistrye, for the, to take the prize in a competition.
make, mate.
making, composition, poetry.
male, wallet.
mall, club.
maner, kind of.
March-parti, Borders.
mark, money worth 13s. 4d.
Mart, Mars.
mart, trade.
mary, marrow.
mase, state of confusion, confused fancy.
masteryes, feats of skill.
mated, stupefied, overcome.
maugree, in spite of.
maun, must.
maunciple, under-servant or buyer for the Inns of Court.
Maure, St. Maur, a disciple of St. Benedict.
may, maid.
mayne, strength, force.
maynly, violently.
mealth, melteth.
meany, troop.
mede, field, reward.
meed, reward.
meet, fitting.
mell, mingle.
mene, mean.
ment, mingled, joined.
mercenarie, hireling.
merciable, merciful.
mesurable, moderate.
met, dreamt.
mete, measure.
meteles, a dream.
meten, to dream.
mette, dreamed.
mew, den.
mewe, coop.
meynee, followers.
minisht, diminished.
mirk, murky.
mirkesome, dark.
miscarie, come to harm.
mischieves, misfortunes.
misdeem'd, misjudged.
misfeigning, feigning with evil purpose.
misseeming, unseemly, false show.
mister, kind of.
mister, trade.
miteyn, glove.
mo, more.
molde, earth.
momme, mumbling.
moniments, traces, marks.
moot, men moot, one should.
mormal, a running sore.
mort, note on horn to tell of death of deer.
mortall, deadly.
mortreux, a kind of stew.
morwe, morning.
moss, bog.
moste, might.
mote, may, must.
mottelee, parti-colored costume.
mould, form, shápe.
mountance, amount.
mowe, may.

mowen, may.
moyste, new.
muchell } much.
muckle }
myd, with.
mykel, much.
myllan, Milan steel.
mylner, miller.
myneyeple, corruption of **manople,** *perhaps* a gauntlet.
mys, mice.

namely, especially.
namo, no more.
narette, do not impute.
natheles, nevertheless.
nathemore, never the more.
nayles, nails.
ne, nor.
nedely, of necessity.
needments, things needed.
neet, cattle.
nelle, will not.
nere, were not.
nice, fastidious.
nicetie, reserve.
niste, did not know.
nobles, coins worth 6s. 8d.
noder, none other.
nones, for the, for the occasion.
noot, know not.
norice, nurse.
nose-thirles, nostrils.
nosethrill, nostril.
notabilitee, notable fact.
note, know not.
not-heed, cropped head.
nould, would not.
nourse, nurse.
noursled, trained, reared.
nouthe, as, just now.
nouther, neither.
noyd, vexed, grieved.
noyous, harmful.
ny, close.
nyce, foolish, ignorant.

observe, to favor.
of, by.
oght, at all.
onis, once.
oon, alwey after, uniform in quality.
oppyned, opened.
or, ere.
origane, wild marjoram (?).
original, source, cause.
orlogge, clock.
ounces, bunches.
oures, hours of the breviary.
outrage, clamor, violence.
outragious, violent.
out-rydere, an inspector of the farms of the monastery.
over al, everywhere.
overcraw, to exult over.
overlepe, outrun, catch.
owches, gems.
ower, over.
oweth, owneth.

paire, to impair.
Palatye, Palathia in Anatolia.
paled, fenced in with pales.
palfrey, saddle-horse, especially for ladies.
paramours, lovers.
parbreake, vomit.
pardale, panther.
pardee, Fr. *par dieu,* an oath.
pardoner, one who sold indulgences.
parfourned, performed.
parisshens, parishioners.
paroschienes, parishioners.
parti, upon a, aside.
parvys, church porch, especially at St. Paul's, London.
pas, foot-pace.
passing, surpassing.
passionate, to express with feeling.
pastes, pasties.
patente, letter of privilege.
paynim, pagan.
peece, structure, fabric, fortified place.
peire, series, set (of beads).
pennes, feathers.
pent, enclosed.
peny, a penny.
perce, pierce.
perceable, penetrable.
peren, appear.
perforce, of necessity.
pers, dark shade of blue or crimson.
persant, piercing.
persoun, parson.
peyne, take trouble.
pight, placed.
piled, thin.
pilwe-beer, pillowcase.
pin, a device for raising the fastening of a door.
pinche at, to find fault with.
pinched, pleated.
pine, suffering, sorrow.
pined, exhausted by suffering.
pitaunce, charitable gift.
plaint, complaint.
plat, flat, plainly.
plat, interfolded, entwined.
platane, oriental plane-tree.
plededen, plead.
pleyen, joke.
pleyn, full.
pleyne, to complain.
plight, plait, fold.
pligted, pledged.
point (in good), in good condition; **to point,** completely, exactly; **not a point,** not a bit.
pokkes, pustules.
pomely, dappled.
poraille, poor people.
portesse, a portable breviary.
possed, pushed.
post, pillar.
potage, broth.
poudre-marchant, flavoring powder.
pouldred, powdered.

pounces, talons.
pouped, sounded their horns.
povert, poverty.
povre, poor.
poyse, force.
prancke, to fold.
preace, to strive, to press; a crowd.
predicacioun, preaching.
prees, crowd.
presse, meaning uncertain, probably a device for pressing.
pricasour, a hard rider.
pricke-wande, rod used as a mark.
prickes, rods used as marks in shooting.
pricking, riding.
priefe, experience, power.
prime, nine o'clock in the morning; spring-time.
privily, secretly.
propre, own, well-made.
propretee, peculiar quality.
provost, chief magistrate.
prow, brave; profit.
Pruce, Prussia.
prys, renown.
puddings, sausages.
puissance, might.
pulled, plucked.
purchas, pickings and stealings.
purchase, acquisition.
purchasing, conveyancing.
purchasour, conveyancer.
purfiled, fringed.
purfled, decorated with an ornamental border.
purtreye, draw.
purveyaunce, provision.
pyned, tortured.

quad, bad.
quaile, to become dismayed.
quayd, subdued.
quell, to frighten, to kill.
quick, alive.
quight, to release.
quire, choir.
quit, to release.
quited, requited.
quod, quoth, said.
quoth, said.
quyrry, the slaughtered game.

rablement, mob.
radly, quickly.
raft, struck off.
rage, to rage; romp.
ragman, papal bull with seals of bishops attached.
raile, to flow.
raine, to reign.
ramping, raging.
rape, haste.
rapt, carried off.
raskall, base, worthless.
ratones, small rats.
raught(e), reached.
raugte, obtained, reached.
ravin, plunder, booty.
ravisedest, didst draw.
rawstye by the roote, *perhaps* rusted at the end with blood.
reacheles on, heedless about.
read, counsel, advice; to advise.
reare, to raise.
reas, rouse.
reave, to take away.
rebutte, to recoil.
rebutted, drove back.
recche, direct.
recchelees, heedless.
recoyle, to retreat, to retire.
recure, to restore.
red, distinguished.
rede, to advise.
redily, quickly.
redounding, overflowing.
reed, counsel; perceive.
reele, to roll.
remes, realms.
renable, talkative.
renke, man.
renne, to run.
rente, income.
repast, refreshment.
repleccioun, repletion.
repleet, full.
reprevable, reprehensible.
repreve, shame.
repriefe, reproach.
rethor, rhetorician.
reve, steward.
revers, contrary.
reverse, to bring back.
revokt, called back.
revyled, scolded.
rew, to pity, to be sorry.
reysed, gone on a military expedition.
ribaudye, ribaldry.
riddes, dispatches.
rife, strong; strongly.
rift, a split or fissure; rent asunder.
ring, hammer of door-knocker.
ritt, runs about, rides.
rive, to split, tear.
roberdes knaves, Robertsmen, lawless robbers living at time *Piers Plowman* was written.
rode, rood; harbor.
roghte, cared.
rompe, rump.
roste, roast meat.
rote, a stringed instrument.
rouncy, farm-horse.
route, a crowd.
rouze, to shake up.
rove, to shoot with arrows.
rowd, rolled.
Ruce, Russia.
rudeliche, rudely.
rue, to pity.
ruefulnesse, pathos.
rueth, to cause to pity.
ruffin, disorderly; ruffian.
rule, taking on.
ruth, pity, grief.
ryden out, to go on expeditions.
rynd, bark, rind.

ryotour, roisterer.
ryve, pierce.

sacred, accursed.
sad, serious, sober, firm.
saffron with, to color.
sagely, wisely.
sair, sore.
sallow, variety of willow.
salue, salute.
salvage, savage.
sam, together.
sanguin, red.
sangwyn, a term from Galenical medicine—one of the four complexions. It implies jollity and generosity.
sapience, wisdom.
Satalye, Adalia in Asiatic Turkey.
sautry, psaltery.
savour, have relish for.
sawcefleem, covered with pimples.
say, a fine cloth.
sayling, used for masts of boats.
scad, scald.
scald, scab.
scalle, scab.
scalled, scabby.
Scariot, Judas Iscariot.
scarsly, economically.
scath(e), harm, injury, pity.
schrewe, a sinner.
science, knowledge.
scoleye, attend the university.
scored, inscribed.
scowre, to run, pursue.
scrip, bag.
scriveyn, scribe.
scryne, chest for keeping books and papers.
se, protect.
sead, seed.
seare, burning.
seasd, penetrated.
secree, able to keep secrets.
securly, surely.
see, save.
seely, innocent.
segges, men.
seig, saw.
seintuarie, a consecrated object.
seke, sick.
selde, seldom.
selle, barter.
selles, cells.
sely, innocent, good.
sembled, met.
semi-cope, short cloak worn by priests.
seminge, as it seems to me.
sendal, a thin silk.
sene, visible.
sent, sensation.
sentence, significance.
serjaunt, sergeant.
sermone, to preach.
servisable, willing to serve.
sete, inflicted.
sethe, boil.
sette hir aller cappe, made fools of them all.
settyng, planting.
sewed, followed.
seweth, pursue.
seye, **was to**, meant.
seynd, smoked.
shamefast, confirmed in modesty.
shamefastnesse, bashfulness.
shapen, to plan.
shaply, fit.
shaume, musical instrument similar to an oboe.
shawes, woods.
shear, several.
sheeldes, French crowns.
sheene, bright, beautiful.
shend, to disgrace, to blame.
shent, scolded.
shente, injured.
shepe, shepherd.
shete a peny, short for a penny.
sheugh, trench, furrow.
shewes, appearances, marks.
shone, shoes.
shonye, to avoid.
shoop, planned.
shope me, arrayed myself.
shopen, arrayed.
shoures, showers.
shradds, coppices.
shrewe, to curse.
shrewe, wicked person, rascal.
shroggs, wands for marks.
shroudes, garments.
shryve, to shrive.
shyars, counties.
sic, such.
sike, sick.
sikerer, surer.
sikerly, surely.
silly, simple, harmless, innocent.
sinke, deposit.
sith, afterwards, since.
sithens, since.
slade, valley.
slake, to moderate, abate.
slaked, moderated.
slawe, slain.
sleighte, craft, trick.
sleuthe, sloth.
slight, trick, device.
slon, to slay.
smale fowles, little birds; perhaps nightingales.
smerte, hurt.
snibben, to rebuke.
snubbes, snags, knobs.
softly, gently.
solempne, important.
som-del, somewhat.
somnour, summoner, an officer who cited culprits before an ecclesiastical court.
sondry, various.
soothly, truly.
sop in wyn, bread or cake broken in wine.
sort, chance, manner.
sorwe, with, *either*, bad luck to him! *or*, to his harm.
sote, sweet.
soth, truth.

sothfastnesse, truth.
souce, to strike, to swoop upon.
souded, confirmed.
soukinge, sucking.
souning, tending toward.
soust, dipped, steeped.
sovereygne, excellent.
sovereynly, chiefly.
sownd, to wield (?).
sowne, sound.
space, space of time.
sparred, shut.
spendyd, got ready.
spersed, dispersed.
spiced conscience, an overfastidious conscience.
spies, glances, thrusts.
spill, to destroy.
sporne, to kick.
sprente, sprang, spurted.
spreyned, sprinkled.
spright, spirit.
spurn, kick (?), encounter (?).
spyced conscience, overfastidious conscience.
spyrred, asked.
stadle, prop.
stage, at a, from a floor, story.
stal, stole away.
stape in age, advanced in years.
stay, support.
stayd, caused to stay.
sted, place.
stelths, thefts.
stepe, prominent, bulging.
stere, steersman.
sterlinges, silver coins.
sterne, stern (men).
sterve, die.
steven, voice.
steven (unsett steven), at an unexpected time.
stew, hot steaming place.
stewe, fish-pond.
stewes, brothels.
still, ever.
stinte, stop.
stockes, posts.
stole, mantle.
stoor, farm-stock.
storven, died.
stot, hack, cob.
stound, stunned.
stound / **stownd** } moment, time; peril, trouble.
stour, brawl, fight.
stowre, disturbance, conflict, danger.
straunge, foreign.
streightes, closes.
streit, strict, stinted.
streite, drawn.
stremes, currents.
streneth, constrains.
strete and stalle, perhaps, on the road and housed.
streyte, strictly.
streynes, estrays; "goods which a stranger leaves behind him at death, and which go to the king or lord for default of heirs" (Skeat: *Piers the Plowman,* Glossary).
strike, hank.
stroke, moved rapidly forward.
strowd, scattered.
stub, the stock of a tree.
studieth, meditate, delay.
sturre, disturbance, tumult.
stye, alley.
stye, to mount.
suar, trusty, sure.
subject, underlying.
subtilly, secretly.
suffisaunce, competence.
superfluitee, excess.
suppress, to overcome.
surcote, upper coat.
sustened, maintained.
swaid, swung.
swal, swelled.
swapte, smote with swords.
swarved, swerved.
swat, were sweating.
sway, to swing.
sweaven, dream.
swelt, swelled, raged, fainted.
swevene, dream.
sweyved, sounded.
swich, such.
swinged, singed.
swink, toil.
swinken, to work.
swonken, toiled.
swote, sweet.
swownd, swoon.
swynke, toil.
swythe, quickly.
syen, see.
syke, ditch, trench.
syne, afterwards.
sythes, times.

tabard, rough coat worn by laborers.
tackles, equipment of a ship, rigging.
taille, by, on account.
takel, archery-gear.
talaunts, claws.
talen, to tell stories.
talent, desire.
tand, tanned.
tane, taken.
tapicer, upholsterer.
tappestere, tavern-keeper.
targe, small shield.
taverners, keepers of taverns.
teade, torch.
tear, there (?).
teene, affliction, grief.
telle . . no store, set no store by.
tellen, to count over.
tempest thee, distress thyself severely.
temple, college of law.
tempred, accommodated.
terciane, tertian.
terme, in, in set phrases, verbatim.
tett, lock (of hair or mane).
that, so that, when.
the(e), so mot I, so may I thrive.
thee'ch, so, so may I thrive.
thegither, together.

then, than.
ther-as, where.
there, where.
ther-to, in addition.
thewes, manners, habits.
thi, thy.
thilke, that.
thing, make a, draw up a writ.
tho, the, those; then.
thombe of gold, the thumb of a good miller.
thral, slave.
thriftily, carefully.
thrild, pierced.
thrill, to pierce, penetrate.
thrillant, piercing.
throuch-and-thro, through and through.
throw, pang.
tide, time.
tikelnesse, instability.
tilie, to cultivate.
timely, measured.
tipet, hood.
tire, attire, dress, train, crew.
tocke, took.
toft, an exposed elevation.
tollen, take toll.
tolleres, collectors of tolls.
tombesteres, female tumblers.
tool, weapon.
toon, toes.
to-rente, tore asunder, torn asunder.
torn, turn.
tort, wrong.
to-swinke, work overmuch.
to-tere, tear asunder.
tract, trace.
traine, **trayne** } tail, trickery.
Tramissene, Tremeyen, a district in the north of Africa.
transmew, to transform.
traynes, artifices, snares.
treachour, traitor.
treen, of trees.
trenchand, sharp, piercing.
trespas, sin, wrong.
tretys, well-proportioned.
treye, three.
triacle, a sovereign remedy.
trielich, choicely.
trinall, threefold.
tristil-tre, a tree used as a meeting-place.
trowe, believe.
truncked, beheaded.
trusse, to seize and carry away.
tukked, tucked.
twaw, two.
tway, two, twain.
twinn, in, in twain, in two's.
twinne, to depart from, to separate.
twyne, band.
tyde, time.
tyne, pain, sorrow.
tyre, head-dress.

uche a, each.
unbid, unprayed for.
unbrent, unburned.
uncoupled, loose.
uncouth, strange.
undern, noon, from nine until twelve.
undight, unfastened, removed.
uneasie, uncomfortable, disturbed.
uneath, difficult; with difficulty.
unhardy, timid.
unkindely, against nature.
unlese, unloose.
unlich, unlike.
unnethe, scarcely.
unthrifty, wicked.
untill, towards, unto.
unwary, unexpected.
unweeting, unconscious, unknowing.
upright, flat on the back.
upstaring, bristling, upstarting.
usage, custom.

vache, beast.
vavasour, a sub-vassal, landholder.
veiwe, yew.
venerye, hunting.
verament, truly.
vere, to turn.
vernicle, copy of the Veronica picture of Christ.
verraily, truly.
vertu, power.
vertuous, powerful, virtuous.
veyne, vein.
viage, journey.
viewe, yew.
vigilyës, ceremonies held the evening before a festival.
vildly, vilely.
vileinye, rudeness, unfit speech.
visour, mask, disguise.
vitaille, victuals.
vouche-sauf, vouchsafe, grant.

wafereres, confectioners.
wake, to watch, wake.
wan, pale, gloomy.
wane, meaning uncertain; perhaps a vehicle for a missile; perhaps *a number,* as "one out of a number."
wanton, wild, playful.
wantown, playful.
war, aware.
ward, to guard.
wardles make, earthly mate.
wardmotes, meetings of a ward.
wardrobe, privy.
ware, to guard.
ware, wary, sharp.
ware, wore.
wareine, warren.
warely, carefully.
warente, protect.
warison, reward.
warrayd, made war upon.
warsle, wrestle.
waryce, save.
wastel-breed, fine white bread.
wastfull, barren.

watering, a brook or watering-place for horses on the road to Canterbury.
wayne, wagon, chariot.
wayted after, demanded, expected.
weal, clench hard.
webbe, weaver.
weeds, clothes.
weene, to think.
weening, thinking.
weet, to know.
welawey, alas.
weld, to wield.
wele, happiness.
welke, to fade, wane.
welked, withered.
welkin, sky.
wende, would have supposed.
wenden, to go.
wenen, think.
werre, war.
wex, to grow.
weyves, waifs.
whally, having a tinge of green, streaked.
whelkes, pustules.
whelp, puppy.
wher, whether.
whereas, where.
whiche, what sort.
whilom, whylom, formerly, ever.
whot, hot.
whyleare, erewhile, lately.
wide, wyde, away.
wif, woman.
wight, strong; man, person.
wighty, strong.
wike, week.
wilfull of my way, lost; "and of my morning tyde," which perhaps means, "don't know what time it is."
wilfully, by choice.
wimpel, covering for the head.
wimpled, laid, lay in folds.
win, to go.
wise, wize, manner.
wisly, wysly, surely.
wist, knew.
wit, bit of wisdom; genius.
with, by.
with-alle, withal, however.
withouten, besides.
withseye, oppose.
wlatsom, loathsome.
wolden, wished.
wollewebsteres, wool-weavers.
wombe, belly.
won(e), wonne, to dwell, live, abide.
wone, custom, number, plenty.
woning, dwelling.
wonnen, won.
wont, to be accustomed.
wonted, accustomed.
wood, mad.
woodnesse, madness.
woodweele, woodpecker or thrush.
worchyng, working.
worm, snake, dragon.
worship, honor.
wortes, herbs.
worthe, be.
worthy, noble, distinguished.
wot, know.
wouche, evil.
woxen, grown, become.
wrattheth, becomes angry.
wreakes, punishments, revenges.
wrighte, carpenter.
wring, to distress.
wrizled, wrinkled, shriveled.
wrocken, avenged.
wyf, woman.
wyld, deer.
wynning, profit.
wys, to make it, to make a difficult matter of it; wise.

yaf, gave.
yblent, blinded.
y-chaped, furnished with the metal point of a scabbard; *or*, mounted.
y-cladd, clad.
y-corven, cut.
ydel, in vain.
ydrad, dreaded.
yë, eyes.
yeddinges, songs.
yede, to go.
yemen, yeomen.
yere, yeris, years.
yerne, briskly.
yes, you shall (in *Twa Sisters*).
yfere, together.
ymages, images, probably either wax images of the patient or signs of the zodiac.
ympe, imp, scion, child, youth.
yod, went.
ypight, placed.
yplaste, placed.
Ypocras, Hippocrates.
y-sene, visible.
y-shrive, shriven.
ysought, sought.
yut, yet.
y-wimpled, covered with a wimple.

INDEX OF AUTHORS, TITLES, AND FIRST LINES OF POEMS

INDEX OF AUTHORS, TITLES, AND FIRST LINES OF POEMS

Names of authors are printed in CAPITALS, and titles are printed in *italics*. Titles beginning with "A," "An," or "The" are indexed under their second words. In cases where the title of a poem is identical with its first line, or with the initial portion of it, the title only is indexed.

FAVORITES.

Congreve - Way of the World
Pope - Essay on Criticism
Essay on Man
Milton - Sonnets
L'Allegro
Il Penseroso
Canterbury Tales
Bacon - of Education, Studies } Essays.
Shakespeare Plays, Sonnets }